The Heritage of American Catholicism

A TWENTY-EIGHT-VOLUME SERIES DOCUMENTING THE HISTORY
OF AMERICA'S LARGEST RELIGIOUS DENOMINATION

EDITED BY

Timothy Walch

ASSOCIATE EDITOR
U.S. Catholic Historian

A Garland Series

Urban American Catholicism

THE CULTURE AND IDENTITY OF THE AMERICAN
CATHOLIC PEOPLE

EDITED WITH AN INTRODUCTION BY
TIMOTHY J. MEAGHER

Garland Publishing, Inc.
New York & London
1988

BX
1407
.C48U7
1988

Copyright © 1988 by Timothy J. Meagher
All Rights Reserved

Library of Congress Cataloging-in-Publication Data

Urban American Catholicism : the culture and identity of the American Catholic people / edited with an introduction by Timothy J. Meagher.
  p. cm. -- (The Heritage of American Catholicism)
  Includes bibliographies.
  ISBN 0-8240-4080-5 (alk. paper)
  1. City churches--United States--History. 2. Catholic Church--United States--History. 3. United States--Church history. 4. Urbanization--United States--History. I. Meagher, Timothy J. II. Series.
BX1407.C48U7 1988
282'.73--dc19   88-25942

Design by Mary Beth Brennan

Printed on acid-free, 250-year-life paper.
Manufactured in the United States of America

Contents

INTRODUCTION

Robert D. Cross, "The Changing Image of the City Among American Catholics," *Catholic Historical Review* 48 (1962), 33–52.   **1**

John J. Bukowczyk, "Mary the Messiah: Polish Immigrant Heresy and the Malleable Ideology of the Roman Catholic Church, 1880–1930," *Journal of American Ethnic History* 4 (1985), 6–32.   **21**

Martin Towey and Margaret Lopiccolo Sullivan, "The Knights of Father Mathew: Parallel Ethnic Reform," *Missouri Historical Review* 75 (1981), 168–183.   **49**

R. Emmet Curran, "Prelude to 'Americanism': The New York Accademia and Clerical Radicalism in the Late Nineteenth Century," *Church History* 47 (1978), 48–75.   **65**

David Carrasco, "A Perspective for a Study of Religious Dimensions in Chicano Experience: *Bless Me, Ultima* as a Religious Text," *Aztlan* 13 (1982), 195–221.   **83**

Patrick Carey, "Arguments for Lay Participation in Philadelphia Catholicism, 1820–1829," *Records of the American Catholic Historical Society* 92 (1982), 43–58.   **110**

David A. Gerber, "Modernity in the Service of Tradition: Catholic Lay Trustees at Buffalo's St. Louis Church and the Transformation of European Communal Traditions, 1829–1855," *Journal of Social History* 15 (1982), 655–684.   **126**

Leslie Woodcock Tentler, "Who is the Church? Conflict in a Polish Immigrant Parish in Late Nineteenth Century Detroit," *Comparative Studies in Society and History* 25 (1983), 241–276.   **156**

Joseph G. Mannard, "The 1839 Baltimore Nunnery Riot: An Episode in Jacksonian Nativism and Social Violence," *Maryland Historian* 11 (1980), 13–27.   **192**

Joseph J. McCadden, "Bishop Hughes Versus the Pubic School Society of New York," *Catholic Historical Review* 50 (1964), 188–207. **207**

David Gerber, "Ambivalent Anti-Catholicism: Buffalo's American Protestant Elite Faces the Challenge of the Catholic Church, 1850–1860," Civil War History (1984), 120–143. **227**

Philip T. Sylvia, "The 'Flint Affair': The French Canadian Struggle for *Survivance*," *Catholic Historical Review* 65 (1979), 414–435. **251**

Timothy J. Meagher, "'Irish All the Time': Ethnic Consciousness Among the Irish in Worcester, Massachusetts, 1880–1905," *Journal of Social History* 19 (1985), 273–303. **273**

Donald Pienkos, "Politics, Religion, and Change in Polish Milwaukee, 1900–1930," *Wisconsin Magazine of History* 61 (1978), 179–209. **305**

Introduction

Few trends over the last century of America's history have been so dramatic as the mass movement of populations from the country to the city. In 1790 less than five percent of the American people lived in cities and the percentage was falling. By 1920 over fifty percent of the people in the United States lived in urban places. The definitions of a city or urban place used in such measurements have been disputed, but the trend these measurements reveal has not. By any definition, the migration from farm or village to city or metropolis has been a central phenomenon in American history since the early nineteenth century.[1]

The importance of this phenomenon to the history of American Catholicism, however, remains obscure. With only very rare exceptions, American Catholics did not move from rural areas to urban ones within the United States. The vast majority migrated from farms or villages overseas or in neighboring North American nations, such as Canada or Mexico, to cities in the United States. This fact led many Americans, particularly Yankees nativists, to ignore the rural origins of Catholic immigrants and to merge Catholics and cities into a single image opposed to a converse image identifying Protestants with the countryside. Josiah Strong, the late nineteenth-century nativist, leader was one of the most effective popularizers of this distinction, but the dichotomy lived on and perhaps grew even stronger after him. Indeed, the Al Smith campaign of 1928 produced, perhaps, the best evidence of the power and pervasiveness of the merging of Catholic and urban in American popular thought. To many American's, then, Catholics seemed to have always been city dwellers, their culture, for good or ill (most often for ill), indistinguishable from the culture of the city.[2]

Such popular images notwithstanding, the history of American Catholics is clearly as much a part of the larger story of migration from country to city as the history of any other group in America. Indeed, the history of few groups in the world, perhaps, reflects that movement so dramatically. Virtually all of the immigrants from the major Catholic ethnic groups—Irish, Italian, Polish, Lithuanian, French Canadian, and Mexican—came from rural peasant societies. Yet a majority of the immigrants of these groups, in some cases a substantial majority, settled in American cities. Over three-fifths of the Irish and Italians and nearly as large a proportion of the Poles, for example, became city dwellers immediately or soon after their arrival in the United States.[3]

It is easier to prove that Catholics moved from rural areas to urban ones, however, than to suggest what implications that fact may have for the study of American Catholic history. Is it useful or enlightening to analyze the history of American Catholics in terms of migration and adaptation to new environments? Long and rich traditions of research in anthropology, sociology, and other social sciences on the dichotomy between urban and rural cultures and the effects of migration suggest that it may be both. In its simplest terms the dichotomy describes a rural society that is homogeneous, where relationships are based on familial or long-standing communal ties, and where life is governed by traditional rituals and non-scientific beliefs. City populations, by contrast, are heterogeneous. The relations of city dwellers are contractual and self-interested and life is governed by rational norms. The migration from rural to urban thus entails more than a simple physical movement; it transforms the culture of the migrant.[4]

This theoretical distinction is, as noted, simplistic. Social scientists and historians over the last fifty years have noted that the dichotomy presents ideal types that fit almost no known societies. As Timothy Smith has pointed out, modern values had already begun to seep into rural peasant societies throughout Europe long before the mass flight to European or American urban societies. Moreover, as he details, many Central and Eastern European peasant communities were hardly homogeneous but rather divided among a variety of competing ethnic and religious groups. Rural society has proved to be more urban than the dichotomy suggests and patterns of folk culture are more enduring in cities than theorists anticipated. Ulf Hannerz points to a number of studies of recent migrants to cities in Mexico and elsewhere that reveal the hardy vitality of rural folk culture in urban environments.[5]

If less simple than first conceived, the distinctions between rural and urban culture and the effects of migration nevertheless remain important themes in the scholarship of the social sciences. Examining the American Catholic experience in terms of the adaptation of a country people and their religion to an urban environment, therefore, places American Catholic history in the context of a rich and viable scholarly tradition. It facilitates comparisons between Catholic adaptations to the American city and similar situations in other parts of the world. More important perhaps, such scholarship suggests study of adaptation in areas of American Catholic life that have previously received only cursory attention or have been neglected altogether by historians of American Catholicism. In particular, it suggests investigation of the religious beliefs and ritual practices of Catholic migrants and their descendants in the American city, their relations to the institutional church, and their concepts of ethnic and religious identities.

Few historical analyses of American Catholicism have deliberately employed the perspective of urban adaptation in their studies of American Catholics. This introduction thus suggests a broad and very speculative outline for an overview of American Catholic history using that perspective. The articles that follow, while not explicitly employing that perspective, all examine the adjustments of Catholic immigrants or their descendants to modern American life in the three aforementioned areas of experience: belief and ritual; relations to the institutional church; definitions of group identity.

It is only recently that historians and other students of American Catholic life have begun to pay attention to the beliefs and rituals that have actually structured the religious lives of average Catholics. These ideas and customs have not necessarily been identical to those proclaimed in official church teachings. Poorly educated, often illiterate, and migrating from societies that because of oppression, poverty, or indifference provided little religious training, many of the Catholic immigrants landing in America did not even know the basic principles of their faith. Priests and bishops in New York in the 1840s, for example, complained that large numbers of the so-called faithful had not even heard of the trinity. There were not only gaps in what many Catholics knew but many peasant Catholics believed in a whole range of ideas about the supernatural or practiced rituals had no relation to official church teachings. Rudolf Vecoli has pointed out that the religion of Italian immigrants was

a folk religion . . . a syncretic melding of ancient pagan beliefs, magical practices and Christian liturgy. Cult and occult fused into a magical religious world which was deeply rooted in the psyche of the people.

Among other Catholic peasant peoples, the magical folk dimension of religion was, perhaps, less visible but nonetheless present and important. S.J. Connolly, writing about the Catholic peasants of pre-famine Ireland, for example, has argued:

For a real understanding of Irish Catholics in this period it is necessary to look beyond the doctrines and rituals to another set of beliefs . . . some of them identifiable as survivals from earlier religious traditions, others examples of the type of magical or supernatural beliefs common at any time in societies below a certain threshold of economic and social development.[6]

Catholic immigrants clung stubbornly to the myths, beliefs, and rituals that made up their "magical religious worlds" even in the radically new surroundings of American industrial cities. Indeed, for some Polish peasants, folk religious myths were employed to justify the decision to migrate itself and thus ease the pain of departure. John Bukowcyk relates a legend circulating in parts of Russian Poland in 1910 that the "new world" had been "covered in mist" for centuries.

When the mist was raised all the kings and emperors of the earth came together to decide who should take the new land. Three times they drew and always the pope won. Then, the pope at the instigation of the Virgin Mary gave the land to the Polish peasants.

Once abroad and settled in the harsh environment of American cities, peasant immigrants might find the New World less paradisical, but elements of their old folk religions persisted. Jay Dolan notes a study of the Irish on Manhattan's West Side at the turn of the century that uncovered widespread belief in the supernatural powers of charms and relics and the practice of certain folk rituals associated with birth and marriage. Herbert Gutman found evidence in Patterson, New Jersey, that even the Celtic tradition of the holy well seemed to have crossed the Atlantic from Ireland to America. Irish residents in late nineteenth-century Patterson, Gutman reports, claimed a spring in the town, "the Dublin Spring," had been created by a fairy. It was, a Paterson newspaper reported, the source of dozens of legends and superstitions for the town's Irish. Italian immigrant culture was, perhaps, as thick with folk traditions of the old country as that of any of the Catholic immigrant groups. Belief in evil spirits and precautions against them were essential to the Italian immigrant tradition. As Vecoli notes: "amulets were worn, rituals performed and incantations chanted to fend off the power of witches." The most important element in the religious tradition of the Italian immigrant, however was the *festa*, the festival celebrating the feast of a patron saint. As Vecoli, and more recently Robert Orsi, have shown the Italian *festa* mixed both official and folk religious rituals and beliefs, creating an event that reflected and reinforced a wide range of the Italian immigrant community's religious values. Transplanted from the rural *mezzogiorno* to American city streets and suspected by the official hierarchy, the *festa* nonetheless flourished.[7]

Yet if Catholic immigrants clung stubbornly to many of the rituals and beliefs of the old folk religion even in the crowded streets of American industrial cities, it is less clear what value their urban born and raised descendants placed on these customs and norms. The *festa* endures even to the present, but today its character may be affected at least in part by its role as an urban tourist attraction. Rudolf Vecoli has argued that other occult beliefs and practices also persisted among later generations of Italian Americans, but even he concedes that evidence of their importance in the spiritual or moral life of the children or grandchildren of the immigrants is at best mixed.[8]

Nevertheless, it would be a mistake to infer that the modern American urban environment destroyed either a sense of the miraculous among the descendants of Catholic immigrants or reduced their appreciation of religious ritual. Catholicism has, of course, always been rich with ritual and devotions. Over the latter half of the nineteenth century, however, a devotional revolution swept the western Catholic church. The result was a popularization of older devotions and customs and the beginning of new ones. The calendar became choked with special months, days, and weeks devoted to prayers to the Sacred Heart of Jesus, St. Joseph, or other saints or manifestations of Christ or Mary, his mother. In short, while the folk religion of the immigrants disappeared among their descendants in the new modern urban environment the ritual and devotional life of the official church did not diminish but grew even more complex; it also became more not less encouraging of faith in the miraculous. Second or third generation Catholics, therefore, may have given up the specific practices and beliefs of their parent's folk religion, but they did not have to abandon the sense of mystery or appreciation of ritual that lay at the root of their parent's faith and in the devotions of the official church. Even ambitious and streetwise children of the slums like John F. Fitzgerald, grandfather of President Kennedy, were deeply affected by these rituals and devotions. Most of Fitzgerald's memories of childhood, Doris Kearns Goodwin reports, revolved around the wide array of festivities and ceremonies organized by the church in his North End neighborhood of Boston. The emotional impact of these ceremonies on Fitzgerald, Goodwin concludes, was exceptionally powerful and continued to impress him throughout his life.[9]

The pervasiveness of folk or magical customs among many Catholic immigrants in America reveals the complexity of their relationship to the institutional church both in their rural homelands and in America cities. As those folk practices suggest, many immigrants practiced much of their religion outside and even in defiance of the official church. Thus, although all of them may have readily called themselves Catholics, that hardly suggests their faithful performance of the church's most minimal requirements to attend mass or receive the sacraments. In rural southern Italy, for example, Rudolf Vecoli claims that virtually no one attended church except on important feast days. Edward Banfield's analysis of southern Italian society in the 1950s supports Vecoli's claim. Banfield reported that less than ten percent of the Italian villagers he studied attended mass regularly. Although such low rates of regular religious observance have been most common among Catholics in Mediterranean or Latin American countries, recent research suggests that they also occurred among Northern European Catholics in certain periods as well. Even in Ireland, where the fidelity of the peasants to Catholicism is legendary, rates of attendance at mass were very low before the famine. In western Ireland, as David Miller has shown, as few as one fifth to one quarter of the rural Irish went to church regularly.[10]

Often this failure to attend church was not merely a register of the Catholic peasant's indifference to the institutional church, but also showed a measure of suspicion or wariness of the church and its leaders. Priests in most peasant societies were figures of authority; though in places like Ireland and Poland Catholic clerics were not associated with an oppressive state, they still retained power, prestige, and a degree of privilege. They also made both moral and financial demands upon the peasantry. Even in such fiercely Catholic countries as Ireland, Poland, and French Canada, peasants looked upon their priests with a certain ambivalence. In societies where the church was linked to the state or to an oppressive ruling class, as in Italy or other mediterranean countries, that ambivalence tilted more often towards suspicion and even overt hostility than to affection and respect.[11]

  The process of uprooting and resettlement in America often transformed the peasants' indifference to the institutional church and wariness of its priests into open rebellion. Indeed, battles between the faithful and their priests exploded among virtually every immigrant group over the course of the nineteenth and early twentieth century. In the Diocese of Boston alone in the 1840s, Irish parishes in Worcester, Salem, Lowell, Waltham, and the North End of Boston were torn apart by factional intrigue or conflicts between parishoners and pastors. In Worcester the people dragged their pastor out of his rectory on to the street where they manhandled him, and in Boston's North End parishoners even drove the bishop from their church when he tried to intervene in their parish's factional quarrel. Italian immigrants were notoriously suspicious of the church and resentful of its claims upon them. In 1908, in Denver, Colorado, an Italian immigrant shot a priest as the cleric was distributing communion, and Italian parishes in Boston, Providence, Rhode Island, and cities around the country rocked with revolts against pastors and priests. When not angry, Italian immigrants were at best indifferent to the institutional church in America. A survey done in Chicago in 1913 estimated that Poles gave over twenty times as much money to the church as the Italians and the Irish donated over twelve times as much. Yet if the Poles were not indifferent to the church, they were certainly not passive about how it governed them. Factionalism and conflicts between priests and people were common in virtually every major Polish settlement in America in the 1880s and 1890s.[12]

  These revolts were very complicated and it would be an oversimplification to attribute them simply to the difficulties a rural peasant people experienced in adjusting to modern urban life. Not all the rebels were bewildered peasants. Anticlerical radicals and nationalists often played important roles in the Italian and Polish parish revolts. Less ideological, less strident, but no less animated middle-class community leaders also participated in these uprisings. Moreover, both these leaders and the masses of former peasants who supported them drew upon American traditions of republicanism, or even more often, upon their own homeland traditions of lay involvement in the running of parish affairs for justification of their revolts and blueprints for their outcome. Finally, these rebellions were often justified by the abuses of the clergy they attacked. In the peak years of every group's immigration the number of priests was never large enough to meet the religious needs of the migrants. Bishops desperate for help were forced to accept some men of dubious capacity or even morality to serve rapidly growing immigrant populations.[13]

Nevertheless, the complications of rural peasant adjustments to modern urban life should not be overlooked in any explanation of these revolts. It is striking, for example, how these rebellions were concentrated in the early years of each group's mass emigration to America. Immigrants who had inherited their parishes and a rich communal life in the old world could take them for granted there, but they had to build their parishes and the other institutions that provide a sense of community in the complex world of urban America. The struggles over parishes then were often struggles over how the community itself would be created in the new world. Thomas and Znaniecki have argued that "the power of the parish in Polish American life is much greater than in even the most conservative peasant communities in Poland ... the parish is, indeed, simply the old primary community reorganized and concentrated." Thomas and Znianecki may have exaggerated the importance of the parish among Polish immigrants; parishes were, however, critical elements in the communities of virtually all Catholic immigrants, and thus control of them was an important issue, sometimes *the* important issue, for the priests and people of these early immigrant communities.[14]

Once that issue was resolved, however, it did not often reappear in later generations. The revolts within parishes seem to have ended in the immigrant generation. Even the seemingly powerful combination of American republicanism and traditions of lay control in parish affairs seemed to spark or sustain few rebellions among the generations of Catholics born and raised in the American city. Indeed, clerical authority in parish and religious affairs appeared to become stronger among virtually all American Catholic ethnic groups over time.[15]

Jay Dolan cites a number of reasons for the rising power of the clergy in the American Catholic church over the late nineteenth and early twentieth centuries. Dolan, for example, points to the church's efforts to strengthen hierarchical authority. This effort was, in part, a peculiarly Catholic phenomenon, a reflection of the renewed assertion of papal authority in the church throughout the world in the nineteenth and twentieth centuries. This reemphasis on hierarchy strengthened the authority not only of the pope but of his representatives at each level of the church's structure, the bishop in the diocese, and ultimately the priest in the parish. The tightening of authority in the American church, Dolan notes, was perhaps also a reflection of important trends occurring in all American urban institutions at that time. Not only the church but modern corporations and city governments sought to control broad expansion of facilities and increasingly diverse populations by more clearly defining lines of jurisdiction and reinforcing the hierarchical structures of their organizations.[16]

If the clerical leaders of the urban American church seemed more intent on bolstering their authority, it is less clear why new generations of urban American Catholics seemed so willing to accede to this development. It clearly was not because of their religious indifference on their mass flight from the religion of their immigrant parents. Indeed, rates of attendance at mass and other measures of commitment to the institution may have gone up among the second and third generation of Catholic urban dwellers. The parish, too, remained a critical community institution for many of these later generations of Catholics. Ellen Skerret, for example, points to the importance of parishes to second and third generation Irish who moved to the Protestant dominated and often hostile suburbs of Chicago in the early twentieth century. It is possible, perhaps, that new generations of urban Catholics who had grown accustomed to well defined hierarchies and bureaucracies in industry and government were more willing than their immigrant forbears to accept the same in their church.[17]

As Catholic immigrants fought for control of their local parish and its definition of community, many of them also confronted for the first time the question of defining their larger allegiances. Most immigrants who came to America had only a vague sense of identification with entities larger than their village or immediate region. There were, of course, variations among Catholic immigrants in the strength of their identifications with a larger nation or group. Southern Italian peasants, for example, seemed to define their group loyalties very narrowly, but other immigrants such as the Irish and even the Poles also seemed to identify themselves principally in local or regional terms. Perhaps the migration process reinforced these regional or local loyalties. Many immigrants were parts of migration chains, following kin and friends and fellow villagers to America. Upon reaching American cities, they often settled near people they knew from the homeland and relied on them for critical support and services, even for finding work.[18]

Some theorists of urbanization or modernization have speculated that homeland, village, or regional loyalties of the rural migrant would dissolve in the city and the transplanted peasant would begin to think in terms of broader functional loyalties along occupational or class lines. Immigrants and their descendants *did* seem to move beyond their local and regional allegiances; but loyalties were formed to larger ethnic or religious groups, not to social classes or occupational associations. The members of these groups shared a sense of peoplehood rooted in a common past as well as common values and customs. Yet these groups were not re-creations of an older rural folk community. They were social networks and political and economic interest groups as well as discrete cultures. They were shaped, then, by the political, economic, and social competition of the plural city, as well as by the historical traditions and cultural values and customs that members of the groups had brought to America.[19]

The triumph of a broader Catholic identification over narrower ethnic ones reflects well this complex process of group formation in the American urban environment. Later generations of American Catholic ethnics identified themselves principally by their religion, rather than by their ancestral language or country. This Catholic identity was securely anchored in the long traditions of the old world past. Peasants in the old country may have thought of their allegiances largely in local terms, but they also knew they were Catholics, not Protestants, or Orthodox Christians, or Jews, or infidels. This identification, more tribal than institutional, was particularly strong among Catholics in countries where they suffered religious persecution or were locked in competitive rivalries, as in Ireland, Poland, or French Canada. Yet if Catholicism spoke to the migrants' or their descendants' past, it was also flexible enough to permit them to adapt to the American present and future. Unlike loyalty to a foreign language or the commitment to preserve foreign customs, Catholicism permitted its adherents to participate fully in American culture. Indeed, Catholic and other religious beliefs and devotions, Timothy Smith maintains, were often "powerful impulses" promoting or encouraging adaptation to the culture of the new environment. Identification with the broader religious group of Catholicism offered Catholic ethnics social and political advantages over narrower ethnic allegiances as well. The Catholic group was much larger, more diverse, and possessed greater resources than any single ethnic group. It offered greater opportunities for social contacts and marriage partners. It also provided a wider range and more complex network of institutions, associations, and clubs. Finally, Catholic ethnics banded together had more political power, exerted more "clout," than any single Catholic nationality, particularly in the broader political arenas of large cities, states, and the nation. Thus the process of acculturation combined with the ongoing social and political competition of American city life to promote a principally religious identification for most descendants of Catholic immigrants until very recent times. It is only with the collapse of Protestant-Catholic competition in the 1960s that that identification began to recede from its place of primacy among American Catholics and other definitions of identity began to take its place.[20]

The suggestion that modern urban life is antagonistic to religion, particularly a religion so suffused with a sense of the miraculous and dense with complex ritual as Catholicism, does not appear to be true, at least in the case of American urban Catholicism. Robert Cross made that point over twenty-five years ago in the insightful essay republished here. Yet the precise nature of Catholicism's adjustment to the American city is not entirely clear. I have suggested some very speculative and broad outlines of that adaption in this introduction. None of the articles that follow invokes urbanization or modernization models or constructs, but in pursuit of their own points they focus on many of the same themes discussed here.

In the first section, David Carrasco, Emmet Curran, Martin Towey and Margaret Sullivan, and John Bukowczyk address questions about the beliefs, values, and rituals of American Catholics. Emmet Curran's clerical radicals of the Accademia, for example, dreamed of a new modern church. One of the principal items on their crowded agenda of reforms was the development of a new Catholic ritual and devotional life shorn of its European and premodern superstitious practices and beliefs. As John Bukowczyk points out in his article, however, the new generations of American urban Catholics were as likely to create or cultivate devotions as to trim them.

The articles by Patrick Carey, David Gerber, and Leslie Woodcock Tentler focus on some of the difficulties of creating a parish community in the new environment. Only Tentler addresses the problems of a largely peasant people making this effort, but Carey suggests some of the American ideas informing debates about the control of parish communities and Gerber points to the complex interplay of new world ideas and old world customs in those debates.

Finally, Donald Pienkos, Philip Sylvia, Jospeh Mannard, Joseph McCadden, David Gerber, and I explore the nature of intergroup relations in the pluralistic environment of the city. Pienkos, McCadden, and I reveal the political dimension of ethno-religious group life. Mannard and Gerber shed some new light on the complexity of native stock attitudes towards their Catholic neighbors in the city.

Timothy J. Meagher

Notes

1. Howard Chudacoff, *The Evolution of American Urban Society* (Prentice Hall: Englewood Cliffs, N.J., 1975) p.29, 179.

2. Chudacoff, *Evolution*, p.117, 148; John Higham, *Strangers in the Land: Patterns of American Nativism, 1860 to 1925* (Atheneum: New York, 1970) p.39; David Burner, *The Politics of Provincialism, the Democratic Party in Transition, 1918 to 1932* (W.W. Norton and Co.: New York, 1967) pp. 179–216.

3. Chudacoff, *Evolution*, p.94; Philip Taylor, *The Distant Magnet: European Migration to the United States* (Harper and Row: New York, 1971) pp. 173–175, pp. 197–201.

4. Ulf Hannerz, *Exploring the City: Inquiries Towards an Urban Anthropology* (Columbia University Press: New York, 1980) pp. 59–118.

5. Hannerz, *Exploring*, pp.65–72; Timothy Smith, "Religion and Ethnicity in America," *American Historical Review*, Vol. 83, no.3 (December, 1978) p.1158.

6. Rudolf Vecoli, "Cult and Occult in Italian American Culture: The Persistence of a Religious Heritage," p.26 in Randal Miller and Thomas D. Marzik eds., *Immigrants and Religion in Urban America* (Temple University Press: Philadelphia, 1977); S.J. Connolly, *Priests and People in Pre-Famine Ireland: 1780–1845* (Gill and McMillan: Dublin, 1982) p. 100.

7. John Bukowczyk, *And My Children Did Not Know Me: A History of the Polish Americans* (Indiana University Press: Bloomington, 1987) p.13; Vecoli, "Cult and Occult," pp. 28–32; Herbert Gutman, *Work, Culture and Society in Industrializing America: Essays in American Working Class and Social History* (Vintage Books: N.Y., 1977) pp.43–44; Jay Dolan, *The American Catholic Experience: A History from Colonial Times to the Present* (Doubleday and Co.: Garden City, N.Y., 1985) p. 234.

8. Vecoli, "Cult and Occult," p. 41–42.

9. Ann Taves, *The Household of Faith; Roman Catholic Devotions in Mid Nineteenth Century America* (University of Notre Dame Press: Notre Dame Ind., 1986) pp. 21–46; Thomas E. Wangler, "Catholic Religious Life in Boston in the Era of Cardinal O'Connell," in James M. O'Toole and Robert E. Sullivan eds., *Catholic Boston: Studies in Religion and Community, 1870 to 1970* (Archdiocese of Boston: Boston, 1985) pp. 239–272; Doris Kearns Goodwin, *The Fitzgeralds and the Kennedys* (Simon and Schuster: New York, 1987) pp. 24–26.

10. Rudolf Vecoli, "Prelates and Peasants: Italian Immigrants and the Catholic Church," *Journal of Social History*, Vol. 2 no. 3 (Spring, 1969) pp. 223–231; David W. Miller, "Irish Catholicism and the Great Famine," *Journal of Social History*, Vol. 9 no. 1 (Fall, 1975) pp. 81–98.

11. Vecoli, "Prelates and Peasants," pp. 240–241; Connolly, *Priests and People*, pp. 52–77:

12. Robert Lord et al., *The History of the Archdiocese of Boston* (Sheed and Ward: New York, 1944) Vol. II, pp. 295–309; Vecoli, "Prelates and Peasants," pp.222-228; Bukowczyk, *And My Children*, pp.40–44; Victor Greene, "For God and Country: The Origins of Slavic Catholic Self Consciousness in America," *Church History*, Vol. 35, no.4 (December, 1966) pp. 458–459.

13. Vecoli, "Prelates and Peasants," pp. 223–240; Bukowczyk, *And My Children*, pp. 40–44; Greene, "For God and Country," pp. 458-459.

14. William I.Thomas and Florian Znaniecki, ed. by Eli Zaretsky, *Polish Peasants in Europe and America* (University of Illinois Press: Urbana, 1984) p.281; William J. Galush, "Faith and Fatherland: Dimensions of Polish American Ethnic Religion, 1875–1975," in Miller and Twardzik eds. *Immigrants and Religion*, pp.84–92.

15. Dolan, *The American Catholic Experience*, pp. 184–194.

16. Ibid. pp.189–194.

17. Harold Abramson, *Ethnic Diversity in American Catholicism* (Wiley: New York, 1973) pp. 110–115; Ellen Skerrett, "The Catholic Dimension," in Lawerence McCaffrey ed., *The Irish in Chicago* (University of Illinois Press: Urbana, 1987) pp. 22–60.

18. Josef Barton, *Peasants and Strangers: Italians, Rumanians and Slovaks in an American City* (Harvard Univ. Press: Cambridge, 1975) pp. 48–90; William DeMarco, *Ethnics and Enclaves: Boston's Italian North End* (UMI Research Press: Ann Arbor, 1981) pp.15–44; Caroline Golab, *Immigrant Destinations* (Temple University Press: Philadelphia, 1977) pp. 120–123, pp. 43-64.

19. Hannerz, *Exploring*, pp.123–147; Abner Cohen, *Urban Ethnicity* (Tavistock: London, 1974) pp. ix–xxiii, pp. 1–76; Donald L. Horowitz, *Ethnic Groups in Conflict* (University of California Press: Berkeley, 1985) pp. 3-92.

20. Will Herberg, *Protestant Catholic Jew: An Essay in Religious Sociology* (Doubleday Inc.: Garden City, N.Y., 1955) pp. 27–71; Smith, "Religion and Ethnicity," p. 1157; Milton Gordon, *Assimilation in American Life: The Role of Race, Religion and National Origins* (Oxford Univ. Press: N. Y., 1964); Nathan Glazer and Daniel Patrick Moynihan, *Beyond the Melting Pot: the Negroes, Puerto Ricans, Jews, Italians and Irish of New York City* (M.I.T. Press: Cambridge, Mass., 1970) pp. 1vi–1xx; pp.17–18.

Acknowledgments

The editor and publisher are grateful to the following for permission to reproduce copyright material in this volume. Any further reproduction is prohibited without the permission of the copyright holder: The Catholic University of America Press for material in *Catholic Historical Review*; *Journal of American Ethnic History*; *Missouri Historical Review*; the American Society of Church History for material in *Church History*; the Chicano Studies Research Center of UCLA for material in *Aztlan*; the American Catholic Historical Society for material in their *Records*; *Journal of Social History*; Cambridge University Press for material in *Comparative Studies in Society and History*, c 1983; *Maryland Historian*; Kent State University Press for material in *Civil War History*; the State Historical Society of Wisconsin for material in *Wisconsin Magazine of History*.

THE CHANGING IMAGE OF THE CITY AMONG AMERICAN CATHOLICS[1]

By
ROBERT D. CROSS

Little is known about the impact of the city over the past hundred years on American religious life. There has been a surfeit of polemic about the nature of 'The City'; more than enough deductions about the effects of that hypostatized entity on the churches; but all too infrequent studies of the observed effects of a real city (or part of it) on religious life. In recent years, social historians and sociologists, more aware of the variety of American cities, and anxious not to confuse the direct effects of urbanization with the sometimes similar effects of immigration, industrialization, and bureaucratization, have begun to give wiser answers about the urban impact. But it is not yet possible to sum up, by some historian's calculus, the long record of differing effects. It is possible to investigate opinion about the city's impact, as voiced by influential American Catholics over the past eighty years. No selection of leaders can, of course, adequately represent the range of Catholic opinion. Furthermore, their judgments, when viewed in the context of our present knowledge of the main currents of social and intellectual history, seem too straitened in perspective to serve as wholly accurate charts of the impact even of the cities they had in mind. But that these sensitive men saw the impact as they did is an important testimony to some aspects of that impact. And their failure to arrive at wholly similar conclusions is an instructive warning against too ready generalization about a remarkably multiform experience.

I

Given his early experience, it is not surprising that John Lancaster Spalding became one of the eloquent denigrators of the urban impact. Brought up on a Kentucky plantation, he readily associated its

[1] In slightly different form this paper was presented at a joint meeting of the American Catholic Historical Association and the American Historical Association in New York, December 28, 1960. Mr. Cross is associate professor of history in Columbia University.

security, freedom, friendliness, and closeness to nature with the rural life. In such an environment, he was sure, man's noblest instincts—toward God, country, and society—most readily flourished.[2] His student years in Europe no doubt strengthened a predisposition to regard the city as an unfortunate innovation. For by the mid-nineteenth century, European city-dwellers, whether bourgeois or proletarian, were drifting away from the faith. This phenomenon was soon generalized into a basic theorem of social science; in 1880 Spalding could quote from Henry Thomas Buckle that "as a body, the inhabitants of agricultural districts pay greater respect to the teachings of their clergy than the inhabitants of manufacturing districts. The growth of cities has, therefore, been a main cause of the decline of ecclesiastical power."[3] European premonitions about the city were borne out for Spalding by his four years as a parish priest in New York City during the 1870's.[4]

Three years after he left New York to become the first Bishop of Peoria, Spalding published *The Religious Mission of the Irish People*, which remains today one of the most moving as well as one of the most comprehensive Catholic estimates of the urban impact. Intent as he was on fostering western colonization, Spalding, nevertheless, did not paint a wholly black picture of urban life. He recognized that Irish settlement in American cities had not resulted in widespread schism, heresy, or infidelity. He acknowledged that the concentration of people made possible a focus for the life of intellect and art. He was confident that the interplay of diverse intellects conduced not only to sharpening the mind, but also to stimulating "the spiritual faculties." And finally, he refused to scorn the accumulation of material goods the city's division of labor made feasible; and he admitted that concentration of population produced the possibility of a political power that conceivably could help build a juster social

[2] Agnes C. Schroll, *The Social Thought of John Lancaster Spalding* (Washington, 1944), pp. 147-148.
[3] Quoted from Buckle's *History of Civilisation* in J. L. Spalding, *The Religious Mission of the Irish People and Catholic Colonization* (New York, 1880), p. 76. Subsequent references to Spalding's ideas are drawn from this book, unless otherwise noted.
[4] Henry J. Browne, *The Parish of St. Michael, 1857-1957* (New York, 1957); while a priest in New York, however, Spalding remained at least publicly opposed to colonization: James P. Shannon, *Catholic Colonization on the Western Frontier* (New Haven, 1957), p. 257.

and economic order. Yet, with his eyes fixed on the lot of the Irish in New York City in 1880, he doubted that the city would ever realize its potentialities for improving the social, cultural, and economic life of the individual there. Instead of creating, and being recreated by, cultural institutions, the poorer Irish were devoting their leisure to the saloon, while the wealthy were truckling to the most artificial whims of "society."

Bishop Spalding deplored the levels and conditions of labor—the factory worker was worse off than the plantation slave, he thought—and he did not believe that wages could ever rise above a bare subsistence level. He certainly did not foresee that the second generation of Irish-Americans would make a great leap upward in occupational status, partly because they were living in the cities, and that American labor unions, which he dismissed as hopelessly communistic, would soon begin to improve labor's lot.[5] Mourning the living conditions of urban families, he foresaw neither the improvements the Irish as a group were making in place of residence, nor the accomplishments of the progressive era in mitigating "the tenement-house problem."[6] Indeed, writing at a time when municipal and state politics were at their nadir both of honesty and imagination, and just before Irish Catholics began to graduate from precinct and ward political life, in which official morality and popular needs were in virtually hopeless opposition, to the greater opportunities of mayoralties and governorships, the Bishop of Peoria considered politics more likely to defile a saint than to provide the conditions in which sanctity, or even modal Christianity, could prevail.[7]

Bitterly as he disliked the city's effect on the individual, however, Bishop Spalding was more influenced by his halcyon vision of the alternative that life in the country offered. In the relatively quiescent

[5] Dorothy Ross, "The Irish-Catholic Immigrant, 1880-1900: a Study in Social Mobility," M.A. essay, Columbia University, 1959.

[6] On the Irish residential mobility in one kind of city, cf. W. L. Warner and Leo Srole, *The Social Systems of American Ethnic Groups* (New Haven, 1945).

[7] Spalding's views were not atypical: J. P. Walsh, "The Catholic Church in Chicago, and Problems of an Urban Society," Ph.D. dissertation, University of Chicago, 1948, p. 272. On the long delay before the Irish rose to positions of responsible power, cf. Norman Dain, "The Social Composition of the Leadership of Tammany Hall in New York City, 1855-1865," M.A. essay, Columbia University, 1957.

years between Grangerism and Populism, he was able to reassert a Jeffersonian conviction that the farmer, because he was emancipated from the wage system, was the only free man economically; because he was free economically, he was also free politically—alike from the tyranny of party bosses and from the opiates of socialist utopianism. Only sixteen years before the smashing defeat of Bryan's ruralism, Spalding could declare that the center of political power lay in the open country. Aware that life on the farm was more conducive to plain living than to high thinking, nevertheless, he clung to the romantic faith that closeness to nature made the farmer so cognizant of the immeasurable forces in life that religion came to him readily; his city cousin, in continuous contact with the works of mere man, was more likely to develop a shell of flippant superficiality that was proof against the promptings of nature.

Spalding was convinced, too, that the country brought benefits to the Church as an institution. Birth rates, he argued, were higher in the country, and the family structure stronger. But he treasured these advantages mostly as they related to the Christian nurture of the individual. "Happy is the country child," he wrote. "With bare head and bare feet he wanders through wood and field . . . and drives the cattle home at milking-time; and all his dreams of peace and love gather around his mother and the home fireside. . . . In a little while you may push him out into the open seas of life and he will not be afraid. Let his after lot be what it will, he has had at the outset twelve years of sweet liberty, and the dews of this fair dawn will keep still some freshness in his heart."[8]

It is obvious that even in this passage of unqualified nostalgia, Spalding was able to conceive of city life as viable for the adult, if not for the child. And the great achievement of the bishop's later years, the establishment of the Catholic University of America in Washington, D.C., demonstrated his conviction that some of life's highest purposes could be realized only in the concentration of persons and talents that the city made possible. Still, even though his efforts to promote Catholic settlement on the farm were not very successful, and though an ever-increasing proportion of American Catholics found their way to the city, Spalding continued to believe that the individual was better off in the country. He experienced no such

[8] *Religious Mission*, p. 95.

stalwart opposition to this belief among eastern bishops as earlier colonizationists had found in Archbishop Hughes.[9] For the hierarchy was surer than Hughes could have been that their dioceses would not be decimated by a rush to the country, and it was more appalled at the problems posed by increasingly unwieldy cities. Possessed, like Spalding, by a notion of the countryside which owed more to European theory and to an idealized past than to present realities, most bishops acquiesced in Spalding's argument that "the agricultural life more than that of the city conduces to happiness and morality, and that it harmonizes better with the Christian ideal."[10]

II

By the 1920's, over half of the American people, and an even higher percentage of Catholics, lived in cities. So it was not surprising that the urban impact upon American Catholicism continued to elicit alarm from Catholic spokesmen. If the horrors of the "industrial city"—especially the worst of its slum life—had been somewhat abated by technological progress and civic reform, many of Spalding's strictures about the effect of large city life upon the individual still seemed appropriate. Furthermore, the massive influx of Catholics was more heterogeneous than earlier. Even in the nineteenth century, when most immigrants in a city area were of the same generation, came from the same country, and spoke the same language, it had not been simple to draw them into united, harmonious support of the Church. Now that most cities included immigrants of many nationalities and tongues, along with the partly acculturated children and grandchildren of earlier immigrant groups, it was far more difficult. In some cases, the preservation of the faith seemed in jeopardy. Spalding had been able to assume that devotion to Catholicism was so imbued in the Irish character that it would flourish in any social milieu. But by the 1920's experience with the first generation of some immigrant groups—most notably the Italians—had convinced churchmen that they must provide a full panoply of Cath-

[9] This paper might well have begun with the attitude of Hughes, had not Henry J. Browne published his excellent essay, "Archbishop Hughes and Western Colonization," *Catholic Historical Review*, XXXVI (October, 1950), 257-285, which renders further comment superfluous. For the attitude of the hierarchy cf. Shannon, *Catholic Colonization*, p. 257.
[10] *Religious Mission*, p. 80.

olic institutions that were deeply harmonious with every ethnic group's cultural proclivities.[11]

Certainly this was the motive for the rapid multiplication of national parishes, a process which reached its peak in these years. National parishes had been an urban phenomenon for over a century, but while in the nineteenth century they were often formed to placate strongly incompatible but also strongly Catholic groups, in the first thirty years of the twentieth century they were often erected first and foremost to reinforce an ethnic group's Catholicism. But the national parish was at best an emergency measure. Planned obsolescence was built into its constitution because of the canonical preference for the territorial parish; and its impermanency was ratified by the residential mobility of the ethnic group, and by the likelihood that fluency in the foreign language would not survive many generations—might not even last until the tuition in Catholicism, as it was established in the United States, was complete. The importance of the national parish in fostering social and religious unity had been generally overlooked by critics of the urban impact in Spalding's generation; most of them had regarded the city as simple horror, differentiated by class lines only. To the critics of the 1920's, national parishes and, even more, the ethnic fragmentations which made them possible were tell-tale signs of the present disunity of the city, and warnings of the further demoralization that would come when people drifted away from the parish established for them.[12]

Such pessimism was certainly the dominant theme of sociological theory which by the 1920's had systematized the premonitions of the previous century about the incompatibility of urbanism and religious life into a larger theory of the disintegrating effect of the city on all aspects of moral and institutional life.[13] The investigators at the

[11] Henry J. Browne, "The 'Italian Problem' in the Catholic Church of the United States, 1880-1900," *Historical Records and Studies*, XXXV (1946), 46-72; François Houtart, *Aspects sociologiques du catholicisme américain* (Paris, 1957), pp. 58-59.

[12] For the difference in attitude between the 1920's and today compare Saul Alinsky's characterization of ethnic enclaves as "neighborhoods of change, gradual, slow and easy change" in "The Urban Immigrant," in Thomas T. McAvoy, C.S.C. (Ed.), *Roman Catholicism and the American Way of Life* (Notre Dame, 1960), p. 143, with Robert Park *et al.*, *The City* (Chicago, 1925), pp. 120-121.

[13] Georg Simmel worked out a set of influential hypotheses connecting ecology with social psychology; cf. his "The Metropolis and Mental Life,"

University of Chicago led by Robert Park drew on studies like Thomas and Znaniecki's volumes on the demoralization of the Polish peasant in America, and *The Gold Coast and the Slum*, Zorbaugh's analysis of parts of Chicago in which the only sign of Catholicism was the floundering church in a Sicilian slum area.[14] They did not hesitate to imply that what was more or less true of a recent ethnic group in "a transition zone" of a "railroad city" like Chicago was intrinsic to the urban experience everywhere.

There was no substantial Catholic urban sociology at the time to suggest to Catholic spokesmen more favorable views of the city.[15] Well aware of the human tragedies sometimes engendered by city life, Catholic leaders tended to channel most of their efforts into immediate relief of individuals rather than investigation of social processes. Even when priests and lay scholars searched for broader understanding of city life, they tended to accept the categories of inquiry set by the socialists and laissez-faire theorists whom they opposed.[16] Thus one branch of the Central Bureau of the German Roman Catholic Central Verein conceived its purview to be "Agriculture, Industry, and Sanitation."[17] John A. Ryan devoted his great talents to industrial rather than to urban questions,—to economics rather than sociology; proposing a study of "social problems" in the seminaries, he specified such topics as "just wages, just profits, a living wage for the worker versus normal profits and interest for the employer and capitalist; reducing wages to maintain dividends; ... the aims and methods of the labor union; socialism. . . ."[18] Whatever answers were found to such problems, the assumptions of the old religious sociology went unchallenged.

---

reprinted in K. H. Wolff, *The Sociology of Georg Simmel* (Glencoe, Illinois, 1950), pp. 409-424.

[14] The orientation of Park and his associates is ably discussed in Maurice Stein, *The Eclipse of Community* (Princeton, 1960). Perhaps, the most thorough-going expression of its point of view is Louis Wirth, "Urbanism as a Way of Life," a 1938 essay reprinted in Paul Hatt and A. J. Reiss (eds.), *Reader in Urban Sociology* (Glencoe, Illinois, 1951), pp. 32-49.

[15] M. J. Williams, *Catholic Social Thought* (New York, 1950), p. 325; the first systematic study of urban sociology in American Catholic universities took place in 1929-1930.

[16] On all these points cf. Aaron I. Abell, *American Catholicism and Social Action* (Garden City, New York, 1960), pp. 1-233.

[17] Mary Harrita Fox, *Peter Dietz, Labor Priest* (Notre Dame, 1953), p. 31.

[18] Ryan, *Social Justice in Action* (New York, 1941), pp. 106-107.

So, just as in the times of Bishop Spalding, prominent Catholics in the 1920's adjudged the urban impact primarily as it compared with a romanticized rural impact.[19] It was much harder now to ignore the fact that the American countryside was in anything but a flourishing condition. Edwin V. O'Hara, who was Bishop of Great Falls from 1930 to 1939 and who died in 1956 as Bishop of Kansas City, spent most of his early years in the country, and knew it well; in 1927 when he published *The Church and the Country Community* he made perfectly clear that the concerns that had led him to found the National Catholic Rural Life Conference still concerned him. Instead of questioning the greater material well being of the city dweller, he expressed the hope that the farmer might eventually catch up again. Less willing than Spalding to shrug off the benefits to the individual of technology and social institutions, he banked on the radio, the automobile, and the hard-top road to provide the farmer with as much schooling, professional assistance, fellowship, and recreation he assumed was available to the city man. His sense of the problems of rural life was too mordant for him to support any "back to the farm" movement.[20] In explicit contrast to the faith and program of Spalding, O'Hara flatly declared that only those who had been raised on the land could hope to prosper on the land.

And yet Father O'Hara continued to regard rural life as normative, not only for the moral effects which, he agreed with Spalding, a life close to nature would have on the individual, but also for the institutional advantages accruing to any church which had a healthy rural component. Most states had begun to compile accurate birth and death statistics in the early twentieth century; they demonstrated beyond doubt that the spectacular growth in urban population—far from being the result of high fertility in the cities—masked the fact that, comparing all cities with all rural areas, the country birth rate was nearly twice as high; in 1920, there were 2,500,000 more children under ten years of age living in the country than in the cities.[21] The characteristically large families of first-generation im-

---

[19] The compelling nature of the pastoral vision is emphasized by the disposition of even John A. Ryan to succumb to its genial dualisms; cf. the account of his childhood in *Social Justice in Action,* and his preface to Edwin V. O'Hara, *The Church and the Country Community* (New York, 1927).

[20] R. P. Witte, *Twenty-Five Years of Crusading* (Des Moines, 1948), pp. 48-49.

[21] O'Hara, *Church and Country Community,* p. 25.

migrants were the exception rather than the rule. Had it not been for them, and for the advantage city children temporarily enjoyed in medical care, the disparity in family size between city and country would have been even more marked. Neither O'Hara nor the many other Catholic leaders who compared city and country failed to observe the peculiar danger of this situation for the Catholic Church, whose membership was largely urban, and who by the 1920's could no longer hope for substantial reinforcements from immigration. "The future will be with the Church that ministers to the rural population," O'Hara concluded somberly.[22]

Most observers did not doubt that Catholics were among those succumbing to the physical pressures and psychological temptations for which city life was responsible and restricting family size. To acquire some measure of the damage done to the Christian family by this practice, Edgar Schmiedeler, O.S.B., conducted a sociological survey of a mid-western city of half a million people, a nearby county seat, and the intervening countryside. His results, published in 1927 as *The Industrial Revolution and the Home*, buttressed the widely-held hypothesis that the family played a much less central role in the economy and recreation of people in the city than in the country. On the other hand, he found to his surprise that by most criteria of family disorganization the city was no worse off than the country, while the town, which in this area constituted a kind of transition zone, was in worse shape than either. Torn between ideology and evidence, Schmiedeler stoutly maintained his conviction that *other* cities would show far greater home disorganization.[23]

Father Schmiedeler's evidence bore out a related hypothesis: that habits of religious observance in the city were different from those in the country, for example, since the family was less often together, family prayer occurred less frequently. But his statistics also showed that urban Catholics received the sacraments somewhat more often than did the rural faithful. Because he was primarily concerned with the family, Schmiedeler did not pursue this line of inquiry into comparative religious observance. Such a study would almost certainly have yielded results in some respects invidious to the country life

---

[22] Quoted in Witte, *op. cit.*, p. 50.
[23] Some modern students would also regard Father Schmiedeler's city as not typically urban because of its high percentage of single-family houses, e.g., Eshref Shevky and Wendell Bell, *Social Area Analysis* (Stanford, 1955).

that was so generally admired. For, with the growing emphasis on liturgy and public devotion, rural Catholics were at a growing disadvantage. In 1851 Father John O'Hanlon, encouraging Catholics to settle in the countryside, had suggested merely that they try to find homes near enough to other Catholics that "an occasional visit from a Priest can be generally procured," especially in times of sickness and accident.[24] Bishop Spalding spoke in a very similar spirit, apparently willing to rely in great part on individual and family worship. But as the Church came to expect more and more corporate devotion, the most heroic efforts of the Catholic Church Extension Society and the National Catholic Rural Life Conference could not help the country Catholic to comply as easily as could the city man; daily communion and the practice of nocturnal adoration were almost necessarily urban prerogatives.[25]

It was still possible, however, for critics to compare the level of religious observance in the city of people just off the farm with that of people whose parents or grandparents had been born in the city. A notable example of this type of enterprise was the work of Father Michael V. Kelly, C.S.B., whose memories of a rural parish remained green long after he had been assigned to a parish in the city of Toronto. Kelly's conclusions were simple: alcoholism, socialism, divorce, mixed marriage, and race suicide were the inevitable consequences of a move to the city. He was convinced that there were "no city Catholics,"—that "a population of city Catholics left for three for four generations, without any recruits whatever from the country districts, would certainly be in the last stages of irreligion and indifference." By every important criterion, people recently from the country were better Catholics than people who had lived longer in the cities; it was axiomatic that "the faith and piety of a Catholic residing in or brought up in a large city are in proportion to the

[24] E. J. Maguire, "John J. O'Hanlon's *Irish Emigrant's Guide for the United States*," Ph.D. dissertation, St. Louis University, 1951, pp. 159, 185-186; for a similar opinion of Bishop Loras, cf. Browne, "Archbishop Hughes and Western Colonization," *loc. cit.*

[25] On the other hand, it is also true that certain services characteristic of village, if not country, life were seldom held in cities, whether in Europe or America; notable casualties were vespers, rosary, and benediction: Joseph H. Fichter, "The Americanization of Catholicism," in McAvoy, *Roman Catholicism*, p. 122; John K. Sharp, *History of the Diocese of Brooklyn, 1853-1953* (New York, 1954), II, 260.

degree in which *the country spirit* has been operative in the home in which he was reared."[26] Kelly thus helped revive, in terms of the urban impact, the fear of losses that had embittered the century-old debate over immigration and Americanization.

Confronted with the almost limitless demand for parish work and for the parochial schools, and with a lessening influx of clerics and sisters from abroad, many Catholic leaders in the 1920's came to the sad conclusion that urban life, responsible for so many afflictions, also inhibited the development of religious vocations.[27] To Father O'Hara it seemed eminently reasonable that rural life, which brought youth into contact with "nature," and which presented few "distractions" or "commercial amusements," would prove more conducive to the development of vocations.[28] Father Kelly tried to demonstrate that dioceses with many urban parishes were far shorter of priests than predominantly rural dioceses.[29] Characteristically, he believed that the country spirit might be effective only in the city's first generation. "Do I know one priest whose father and mother were born and reared in a large city?" he asked. "We think there must be such, but after ten years' inquiry into every quarter we have never heard of one."[30]

It is easy enough to suspect that Father Kelly did not look very sedulously. But what gives the special precariousness to the findings of these students of the urban impact during the 1920's is their failure to recognize clearly that the city was not a homogeneous phenomenon, and that different generations of different ethnic groups in different parts of different kinds of cities in different eras of American history almost certainly lived very different types of religious life. In their indiscriminate admiration for the countryside, they neglected to

[26] Kelly, *Some of the Pastor's Problems* (Toronto, n.d.), pp. 167-168, my italics.

[27] For an early statement cf. L. H. Bugg, *The People of Our Parish* (Boston, 1900), pp. 155-164.

[28] *Church and the Country Community*, p. 60.

[29] E.g., he calculated that Brooklyn with two urban parishes for every rural one could provide only one diocesan priest for every 1,450 laymen; Des Moines with almost four rural parishes for every urban one provided one priest for every 480 laymen: *Pastor's Problems*, pp. 195-199.

[30] Quoted in Witte, *op. cit.*, p. 21. That the second generation of Irish Catholics contributed a smaller percentage of their number to the clergy than the first is borne out by the calculations of Ross, *op cit.*, p. 57, and by E. P. Hutchinson, *Immigrants and their Children* (New York, 1956).

discriminate among the many urban impacts. Father Schmiedeler recognized that the city he studied closely did not fit his preconception of a city; Father Kelly sometimes pointed out that the real villain was the "large" city of over 50,000 people; and Father O'Hara on one occasion limited his censures to the assertion that losses would occur in the fifth generation of city dwellers.[31] But in general their philippics were less careful. They performed a valuable function in reminding contemporaries that there were still social maladjustments in the city, and in calling attention to such institutional considerations as birth rate, frequency of religious observance, losses from the faith, and religious vocations. It remained, however, for later students, with a less preconceived notion of the city, more prepared for its startling diversity, to develop a more profitable approach to such institutional questions.

III

Fundamental to the climate of opinion in the years since World War II has been a growing disinclination to regard the rural scene with the old nostalgia; no Catholic criticism of tenements or of urban industrial life in recent years has been as unsparing as the attacks of the National Catholic Rural Life Conference on the treatment of migrant labor in the countryside.[32] On the other hand, among rural people enjoying higher standards of living, birth rates have begun to fall, not yet reaching average urban levels, but contributing far less to the growth of potential church population than had been anticipated.[33] Finally, though studies of rural religious observance in the United States have been relatively rare, European religious sociology has made clear that the countryside is by no means automatically a scene of devotion.[34] And one study of the religious folk-

[31] *Pastor's Problems*, pp. 168-170; *Church and the Country Community* p. 49.
[32] New York *Times*, June 13, 1958; September 8 and 12, 1959; November 24, 1959.
[33] Dennis Clark, *Cities in Crisis: the Christian Response* (New York, 1960), pp. 64-65.
[34] European studies are summarized in Joseph Folliet, "The Effect of City Life upon Spiritual Life," in R. M. Fisher (ed.), *The Metropolis in Modern Life* (New York, 1955), pp. 319-322; on the young but growing American Catholic interest in such questions cf. Eva J. Ross, "La sociologie religieuse aux États-Unis," in *Conférence internationale de sociologie religieuse*, IV (Paris, 1955), pp. 130-149.

ways of an ethnic group in the European countryside and in an American city supports the hypothesis that though the city may be responsible for the erosion of some genuine piety, it also helps carry away the rural superstition which sometimes muddied pure faith with prayers to the full moon and spells to frustrate evil spirits.[35]

Equally important to the symbolic importance of the countryside has been the development of a third alternative. The Bureau of the Census has modified its rural-urban disjunction, and reports some individuals as "rural non-farm." Since 1920, the "metropolitan ring" of suburbs (a far cry from the old "industrial suburbs," which were hardly distinguishable from center-city) have grown faster than the center-cities themselves, while the countryside has barely kept its population from declining.[36] And Catholics, even less than in the 1920's, are not now concentrated in some chamber-of-horrors "transition zone," but diffused into every part of the urban area.[37]

Meanwhile, contemporary sociology has reacted strongly against the categorical condemnations of the city advanced so forthrightly by the Chicago school led first by Robert Park, later by Louis Wirth. Not only do modern students reject the old urban typology in favor of a rural-urban continuum—a whole range of life-styles; they also develop indices of urbanization to distinguish differences of degree rather than of kind.[38] They have shown clearly that individuals and institutions are far less demoralized by urban life than had previously been postulated. They have noted, e.g., that both birth and marriage rates have grown faster since the mid-1940's in the cities, taken as a whole, than in the country. And a whole battery of careful studies proves that there is a great deal of the "social participation" indicative of real community in all sections of the city.[39]

[35] C. P. Sirvaitis, *Religious Folkways in Lithuania and their Conservation among the Lithuanian Immigrants in the United States*, [Catholic University of America Studies in Sociology, Abstract Series #3] (1952).

[36] D. J. Bogue, "Urbanism in the United States, 1950," *American Journal of Sociology*, LX (March 1955), 471-486.

[37] This point is saliently illustrated by the maps of Catholic population in the Chicago area printed in Houtart, *Aspects*.

[38] E.g., Scott Grier, "Urbanism Reconsidered," *American Sociological Review*, XXI (February 1956), 19-25, and Richard Dewey, "The Rural-Urban Continuum: Real but Relatively Unimportant," *American Journal of Sociology*, LXVI (July 1960), 60-66.

[39] E.g., Theodore Caplow and Robert Forman, "Neighborhood Interaction in a Homogeneous Community," *American Sociological Review*, XV (June, 1950),

In recent years, Catholics have reacted variously to the new urban situation. For those still living in physically run down, ethnically heterogeneous quarters, there are today Catholic leaders like Father Clement Kern in Detroit and the several Catholic Interracial Councils ready not only to assuage suffering with the old charity, but to forestall recurrent problems with the new sociology. Careful studies by Brother Gerald Schnepp, Fathers Joseph Fichter, François Houtart, and Joseph Schuyler—like the scholarly parish histories written by Father Henry Browne and others—notably start from no doctrinaire hypotheses about the city; their conclusions respect the uniqueness in time and place and ethnic make-up of the parishes they have come to know so well.[40] By contrast, Dennis Clark in his recent *Cities in Crisis* boldly generalizes about the impact of the contemporary city on religious life. The author's service in fostering brotherhood in areas of ethnic tension in Philadelphia lends authenticity to his eloquently expressed dismay. But when considered in the context of modern parish work and modern parish studies (with which he is certainly familiar), his pessimism does not seem wholly warranted.

With a love of rural simplicity and a distaste for urban heterogeneity much like Spalding's, Clark not only concludes that the city has been responsible for "great attrition in terms of human personalities"; he goes so far as to describe city dwellers as "anomic."[41] Such a diagnosis hardly comports with the evidences of urban religious life the sociologists have delineated. Their reports, it is true, make painfully clear that many city folk born to the Catholic faith do not live as Catholics are supposed to; and Father Fichter has even developed a persuasive model of the way "marginal" Catholics are swayed by alien ideas and individuals inevitably encountered in

---

365-366 ff; and Morris Axelrod, "Urban Structure and Urban Participation," *ibid.*, XXI (February, 1956), 13-18.

[40] Typical of the informative sociological studies are: Gerald J. Schnepp, S.M., *Leakage from a Catholic Parish* (Washington, 1942); Joseph H. Fichter, S.J., *Dynamics of a City Church*, Volume I of *Southern Parish* (Chicago, 1951); Fichter, *Social Relations in the Urban Parish* (Chicago, 1954); Houtart, *Aspects*; J. B. Schuyler, S.J., *Northern Parish* (Chicago, 1960); George A. Kelly, *Catholics and the Practice of the Faith* (Washington, 1946).

[41] Clark, *Cities in Crisis*, p. 35; cf. also Thomas F. O'Dea and Renato Poblete, "*Anomie* and the 'Quest for Community': the formation of sects among the Puerto Ricans of New York," *American Catholic Sociological Review*, XXI (Spring 1960), 18-36.

the city.[42] But these students have scrupulously avoided blaming the city for all the deviations from normative Catholic life that take place in the city. Father Schuyler has shown, for example, that in a Bronx parish the level of religious observance of the first generation of some ethnic groups is well below the parish average, but also that the record improves for later generations.[43] And his research would buttress the supposition that though the second generation of Irish are less religiously observant than the first, subsequent generations maintain a high level, instead of sinking slowly into indifference, as the 1920's critics predicted.[44] When Father Fichter investigated the effect on religious observance of the residential mobility so characteristic of modern city life, he found little evidence of deterioration.[45]

Several studies have shown that among city dwellers there is a higher level of religious observance with higher amounts of education, even where that education is received in the very public schools which exemplify the impact on the individual of secularist or religiously indifferentist ideas.[46] Mixed marriages, the almost inevitable result of urban heterogeneity, do not, Father George Kelly found in a study of a Florida diocese, correlate very positively with an immediate decline in religious observance; the religious observance of the children of mixed marriages, however, does probably slacken.[47]

[42] Fichter, "The Marginal Catholic," *Social Forces* (December, 1953), 167-173.

[43] *Northern Parish*, figure 24, opposite p. 202.

[44] The hypothesis that the third generation "returns to religion" is persuasively argued in Will Herberg, *Protestant-Catholic-Jew* (New York, 1956).

[45] *Social Relations*, pp. 94-106; it should be noted that Fichter's conclusion applies primarily to those moving from place to place within the parish; his evidence is not conclusive on those making more extensive moves.

[46] Kelly, *Practice of the Faith*, pp. 120-121; Schuyler, *Northern Parish*, figure 23, opposite p. 202.

[47] *Practice of the Faith*, p. 167; Schnepp, *Leakage*, pp. 85-92, and Augustine McCaffrey, *Youth in a Catholic Parish* (Washington, 1941), pp. 121-125, point to the religious laxness of children of mixed marriages. Most Catholic observers agree that mixed marriages are inevitable in religiously heterogeneous areas, i.e., they are skeptical of the theory of a "Triple Melting-Pot" developed by R. J. Kennedy in "Intermarriage in New Haven, 1870-1940," *American Journal of Sociology*, XLIX (January 1944), 329-339, and given its most general application in Herberg, *Protestant-Catholic-Jew;* for an effective criticism cf. John L. Thomas, S.J., "Out-Group Marriage Patterns of Some Selected Ethnic Groups," *American Catholic Sociological Review*, XV (March 1954), 6-18.

Finally, Father Michael Kelly's certainty that urban life created individuals too skeptical or materialist to heed a religious vocation has been, if not completely destroyed, at least weakened by the experience of important urban dioceses. Not that there ever seem to be enough priests; but there is less ground today for concern about the inhibiting effect of the city.[48]

The urban impact on the structure of the Church and on the roles of priest and laymen has provoked especially lively discussion in recent years. Dennis Clark, e.g., argues that the urban parish has usually been too new, too big, and too heterogeneous to become "the whole church in miniature" it has sometimes been called.[49] As Catholics have spread out through the metropolitan area, there have always been parishes that are awkwardly new; and parishes like St. Patrick's in New Orleans or St. Ann's in New York, though long established, have had to be born again to meet the changing sociology of the downtown church.[50] Though the willingness of the hierarchy to create new parishes, and its unwillingness to abandon old ones, have worked to reduce the average size of urban parishes, some still are charged with the care of an inordinate number of souls. And the break-up of the older immigrant quarters coupled with the inability of newer

[48] Sharp, *Brooklyn*, II, 327; Michael J. Hynes,, *History of the Diocese of Cleveland* (Cleveland, 1953), p. 339. Houtart has shown that the number of priestly vocations in Chicago rose more rapidly than the number of Catholics since 1930; the rate declined between 1945 and 1955, but it began to increase thereafter: *Aspects*, pp. 41, 147-148, 157-159, 292. Gustave Weigel, S.J., says flatly that there is "no dearth of vocations" in contemporary America: "An Introduction to American Catholicism" in Louis Putz (ed.), *The Catholic Church, U.S.A.* (Chicago, 1956), pp. 10, 14.

[49] The expression is that of Richard Cardinal Cushing: John D. Donovan, "The Social Structure of the Parish," in C. Joseph Nuesse and Thomas J. Harte, C.SS.R. (eds.), *The Sociology of the Parish* (Milwaukee, 1951). For earlier concern about the structure and role of the parish, cf. Edward F. Garesché, S.J., *Modern Parish Problems* (New York, 1928), p. 120.

[50] Among the many studies of parishes which had to change into 'downtown churches' are: C. L. Dufour, *St. Patrick's of New Orleans* (New Orleans, 1958); Browne, *St. Ann's on East Twelfth Street, 1852-1952* (New York, 1925); Houtart, *Aspects*, on Holy Rosary parish of Chicago; M. Martina Abbott, *A City Parish Grows and Changes* (Washington, 1953) on a Pittsburgh parish; and D. H. Fosselman, *Transitions in the Development of a Downtown Parish*, [Catholic University of America Studies in Sociology, Abstract Series #6 (1952)] on St. Patrick's in Washington, D.C.

groups like the Puerto Ricans to concentrate their residence have increased the ethnic heterogeneity of many urban parishes.[51]

But American students have been less inclined than their European counterparts to despair of the parish.[52] They have placed greater reliance on the redemptive influence of the myriad voluntary associations which have flourished in American city parishes. Critics like Father Fichter certainly do not idealize the many conventional organizations with their largely nominal membership lists and their perfunctory activities.[53] But they see in such disparate developments as the parochial grammar school, with its demands for lay support and its possibilities for lay leadership, and the liturgical revival, with its emphasis on lay participation in many corporate acts of worship, hopeful signs of a social and spiritual integration of the parish.[54] They have also admired the vitality of sub-parochial organizations—like the "little parishes"—and of the many super-parochial groups which promote both good works and the closer communion of their members.[55]

Central to the contemporary estimate of the urban impact has been the concern that the parish priest does not become in the city the central figure, the *alter Christus,* necessary to genuine Catholic life. In many urban parishes the pastor, and even more his curates, whose assignments are often very brief, cannot be so well known to their flock, which is itself often highly transient, as to be real shepherds. In the city parishes where it is necessary to exhort the laity to introduce themselves to their priests—where one of the arguments for a parish census is that it provides an opportunity for the priest to meet one member of each family at least once a year—spiritual

[51] G. A. Carroll, "The Latin-American Catholic Immigrant," in McAvoy, *Roman Catholicism,* pp. 164-170.

[52] The European despair is well summed up in Fichter, "The Marginal Catholic," *Social Forces* (December, 1953), 431-432; for a typically stringent view, cf. André Brien, "Les petits communautés, soutenance de la Foi," *Études,* 279 (November, 1953), 168-186.

[53] *Social Relations,* pp. 51, 154-164; F. S. Engel, "Parish Societies," in Nuesse and Harte, *Sociology,* pp. 178-205.

[54] Fichter, *Parochial School* (Notre Dame, 1958), pp. 433-434.

[55] On the "little parishes" cf. "St. Richard's," *Jubilee,* VI (August, 1958), 26-41; on super-parochial organizations, cf. Leo Ward, C.S.C., *Catholic Life, U.S.A.* (St. Louis, 1959).

paternalism seems problematical.[56] Yet Father Schuyler's study showed that a surprising number of laymen knew the names of all six priests in "Northern Parish"; in "Yankee City" the pastor knew almost all the 4,000 parishioners by their first names.[57] Patently, more intimacy exists between shepherd and flock than has often been thought.

Urbanism has also been accused of segmentalizing the status of the priest, making him into a bureaucrat with a specific competence, a specific task, and a specific means of action—on a par with the lawyer, the doctor, the teacher, the business expert, the alderman.[58] The ubiquity of such other professionals in the urban parish undoubtedly precludes the priest from enjoying the unlimited status claimed by a western priest of a generation ago, who, the late Monsignor William J. Kerby reported, amiably contended that on *all* matters of importance he was the "best-posted and ablest man in his county."[59] The growing need of twentieth-century urban dioceses for priests able to specialize in administrative or welfare work, and the tendency to divide up the staggering load of parish work according to objective criteria of competence and the rational use of labor have necessarily jeopardized the ideal comprehensive relationship of priest and people. Yet a number of studies, both theoretical and empirical, have made it clear that the urban priest, however deprecatingly he sometimes views himself, has not come to seem a specialized functionary to the laity, who instead persist in according him the "total status" of the father—of the *alter Christus*.[60] Ironically enough, there

---

[56] Thomas F. Coakley, "Some Revelations of a Recent Parish Census," *Ecclesiastical Review*, LXXXII (March, 1930), 312-314; Coakley later wrote that in many city parishes "it is the undertaker who introduces the pastor to the corpse": "Catholic Leakage: A Factual Study," *Catholic World*, CLIV (January, 1942), 419. And a Puerto Rican member of a store-front church explained that "I used to go to the Catholic Church, there nobody knew me. . . . Now in my church they call me sister".: O'Dea and Poblete, *loc. cit.*, 32.

[57] *Northern Parish*, p. 171; Warner and Srole, *Social Systems*, pp. 173-176.

[58] A. M. Carr-Saunders, "Metropolitan Conditions and Traditional Professional Relationships," in Fisher (ed.), *Metropolis in Modern Life*, pp. 279-288.

[59] William J. Kerby, *Prophets of the Better Hope* (Philadelphia, 1937), pp. 8-9.

[60] John D. Donovan, "The Catholic Priest: a Study in the Sociology of the Professions," Ph.D. dissertation, Harvard University, 1951, pp. 203-206; J. M. Jammes, "The Social Role of the Priest," *American Catholic Sociological Review*, XVI (January 1955), pp. 94-103; Schuyler, *Northern Parish*, p. 152.

would seem to be more substance to the quite antithetical concern that in many urban parishes the priests exercise too much authority, and the laity shows too much deference, for the parish as a whole to make what Dennis Clark might call a successful Christian response to the urban impact.[61]

IV

Three sets of opinions, selectively annotated, do not constitute an adequate summary of a hundred years of Catholic experience. Yet it is hard not to conclude that the persistently pessimistic note struck by most Catholic critics does less than justice to the resilience and adaptability of American Catholics in responding to the protean challenges of the varieties of urban life. No one can reasonably dispute Spalding's argument that city living, especially in the first years of the cities and the first years of a Catholic settlement in them, was a formidable problem for the individual; or O'Hara's sense that the Church, in a period when many of its members were living in a transitional phase between country and city experience, faced grave institutional difficulties; or Clark's that the shepherd whose people are scattered through a few blocks of five-floor walk-ups—or, for that matter, through a suburban development—can hardly employ the pastoral methods hallowed by years of successful countryside use. At the time each of these men was writing, however, evidence was available that their indictments were too sweeping. Imbued with respect for the past, nostalgic for a life close to nature, and bemused—until recently—by an urban sociology that clothed similar sentiments in a majestic scientific terminology, they yielded too readily to impulses of dismay.

It would be rash to conclude that defeatism toward city life has proved a major deterrent to the realization of the promise of American Catholicism. But it does help account for the tendency of Catholic churchmen to concentrate upon resisting the city's impact on the

---

[61] It can be argued that the absence in the city of a "natural community" with "natural leaders" prompted the clergy to act more forcefully than if their authority were bulwarked by an easy superiority in a parish of simple farmers. For a somewhat similar contention, cf. Archbishop Hughes' belief that a city diocese required much more forceful leadership than a rural one: Henry J. Browne, "A Memoir of Archbishop Hughes," *Historical Records and Studies*, XXXIX-XL (1951), 183.

Church, instead of upon developing the Church's impact on the city. Trying to secure decent physical and moral conditions for their flocks, they scanted the task (incumbent on all who live in a heterogeneous city) of developing procedures for working equably with non-Catholic groups, either in voluntary associations or through the state, to promote the general urban welfare. As government has taken on more and more "welfare" activities, individual Catholic churchmen have exercised considerable influence, but their modes of action have not been wholly satisfactory either to non-Catholics or to all other Catholics.[62] Little attention, furthermore, has been devoted to developing a constructive approach to the religious pluralism of the cities. Most Catholic leaders have been preoccupied with the effect on newly-arrived Catholics of their Protestant and free-thinker neighbors; what time they could spare to dispelling religious ignorance they tended to devote to the countryside, despite mounting evidence that the country, rather than the city, is the center of the most virulent anti-Catholicism. Now that urban Catholicism is part of the Establishment, a more active, confident role would seem plausible; now that the cities are being invaded by largely non-Catholic migrants, Catholic churchmen have an especial incentive to abandon a defensive tradition toward the urban impact on religious life.

Columbia University

[62] For illustrations of this general truth, cf. Robert D. Cross, "The Changing Image of Catholicism in America," *Yale Review*, XLVIII (Summer, 1959), 567, 576; cf. also K. W. Underwood, *Protestant and Catholic* (Boston, 1957).

Mary the Messiah: Polish Immigrant Heresy and the Malleable Ideology of the Roman Catholic Church, 1880-1930

JOHN J. BUKOWCZYK

"IN RELIGION the Poles are predominantly Roman Catholic," Presbyterian minister Paul Fox observed in 1922. And although Rev. Fox lamented that theirs was "a religion of external rites, symbolic forms, servile fear, and magical personal salvation," he nonetheless praised them as "a church-going people." Group writers would not endorse Fox's condescending nativist view, but have nonetheless concurred with his central point, "the earliest and most important institution among Polish immigrants was the church."[1] Immigration historians, too, have accepted this conclusion about Polish immigrant religiosity. Roman Catholicism formed a ponderous proportion of the "cultural baggage" that Poles carried with them when they journeyed to America; they held on to this attachment tightly even after they settled here.[2]

When the social history of immigrant religion is examined however, we find that the Poles' faith did not fall into place quite so automatically as this broad concord of opinion might suggest. In Poland and in the immigrant districts of America, popular belief often diverged from religious orthodoxy, incorporating an assortment of beliefs and practices with magical or pagan connections.[3] In America, dispersal of the Roman Catholic immigrant population and assimilation eroded belief, while assorted radical ideologies spawned in reaction to industrial capitalism became an attractive alternative to the doleful submissiveness counselled by the church.[4]

To be sure, the erosion in traditional religious practice was not the result of immigration alone. Polish sociologists, for example, have observed that marked secularization later in Poland itself was associated with industrialization, urbanization, and the rationalization of agriculture.[5] Yet immigrant and native-born clerics alike often identified loss of faith principally as an immigrant problem. Rev. Wenceslaus Kruszka, Polish America's authoritative early historian, estimated the Poles' resulting "leakage" from the church at the staggering rate of one-third.[6]

Though Kruszka's figure was dubiously high, by 1920 denominational statistics did show a total of thirty-one Polish Protestant churches and missions in the United States with nearly four thousand adherents.[7] Other Polish defectors remained apostate or succumbed to the appeal of secular ideologies like socialism, anarchism, syndicalism, positivism, and secular variants of Polish nationalism. Of these, Polish socialists alone numbered up to a few thousand.[8] Clearly, immigration, urbanization, and industrialization were taking their toll, and Roman Catholicism consequently enjoyed far weaker ties to its immigrant parishioners than stereotypes have depicted.

Churchmen and their lay allies could not agree on what strategy would best counter the growing threat posed by popular religious deviations, secularism, disobedience, and heresy. Marching in lock step with the progressive encyclical, *Rerum Novarum* ("On the Condition of Labor"), which Pope Leo XIII issued in 1891, church liberals argued that they could win over those who strayed by becoming more responsive to the needs of their urban industrial flock.[9] As a whole, the American church lay closer to the liberal position, so much so that church liberalism would come to be called "Americanism."[10] But because conservatives led so many heavily immigrant dioceses and archdioceses—e.g., New York, Brooklyn, Cleveland, Philadelphia, Rochester, and Milwaukee, working-class immigrants like the Poles more often encountered conservative strategies to keep them in the church. If the Poles' reputation for religiosity survived, it was thus not the persistence of premigration rural culture alone, but the success of those conservative strategies which reinforced—imposed and extended—habits of religious devotion among them.

Of the strategies that conservative bishops employed in order to retain immigrants within the fold, none was more important than their reliance upon national, i.e., ethnic, parishes.[11] By 1912, six years before a revision in Canon Law froze the number of ethnic parishes in the United States, the *Official Catholic Directory* listed nearly 1600 national parishes in the United States, including 214 Italian, 346 German, and 336 Polish.[12] That figure, however, was vastly undercounted, for by 1900 Polish Roman Catholic parishes alone already had numbered 517.[13]

This multiplication of national parishes gave a distinctive stamp to the church's campaign against unbelief and decisively influenced the shape of American Catholicism during the period. First, by using immigrant priests to serve the foreign-born flock, bishops sacrificed religious uniformity in the interest of more effectively reaching their linguistically and culturally diverse communicants. Sanctioning the creation of national parishes institutionalized the growing ethnic divisions that fractured the American church, but it also insured that Roman Catholicism would remain a powerful force in immigrant life. Secondly, the endorsement of national parishes helped to decentralize power and authority within the American church. While immigrant priests still failed to gain access to positions in the church hierarchy, within their own ethnic parishes they acquired wide de facto autonomy in preserving and defending immigrant faith.[14] In 1871 in Chicago, for example, the Polish missionary Congregation of the Resurrection of Our Lord Jesus Christ negotiated a jurisdictional arrangement with Bishop Thomas Foley under which the Resurrectionists won the right to administer all non-diocesan Polish parishes in the Chicago diocese for ninety-nine years.[15] Yet if Chicago's Resurrectionist Fathers were at all atypical, it was not in kind, but only in degree. Other Polish pastors like Buffalo's Jan Pitass and Connecticut's Lucyan Bójnowski also enjoyed huge power, while scores of lesser Polish clerics wielded more modest though still extensive authority in their own parishes.[16] Many of them were Polish born. But after 1884, Polish born and trained priests' monopoly over Polish-American parishes began slowly to crack. In that year, Bishop Caspar Borgess approved Rev. Joseph Dąbrowski's request to establish a Polish seminary in Detroit, the first in the United States.[17]

The creation of national parishes meant that, henceforth, the day-to-day battle against Polish unbelief would be fought and led by Polish priests. Indeed, the Polish-American clergy pressed its own two-pronged offensive against secularism, apostasy, and deviations from orthodox belief. In the campaign to counter superstition and nagging vestiges of paganism, Polish priests selected a tactic of sapping and strategic retreat. In time-honored ways, they seemed largely to have coexisted with magic, superstition, and the occult—criticizing them when they undercut priestly authority, hoping they would eventually fade, and meanwhile co-opting them through the quasi-magical "theater" of the mass.[18] The fight against secularism was, however, a different matter. Such a direct challenge to religion, the church, and their own pastorates impelled Polish priests to confront irreligion head on. The staunch efforts made by priests like New Britain's Rev. Bójnowski are by now quite familiar, but the campaign these few celebrated Polish pastors waged was hardly unique.[19] Ordinary immigrant priests like Brooklyn's Rev. Leon Wysiecki and Rev. Joseph Lenarkiewicz of Shenandoah, Pennsylvania, pursued their own local efforts against "the socialists" in the 1890s.[20] Of course, it remains difficult to gauge the effect of the Polish clergy's campaign, but at least some priests thought it was working. In 1897, for example, Brooklyn's Rev. Wysiecki proudly informed his bishop that even the socialists had started coming to confession.[21]

However doggedly and successfully immigrant clerics fought against unbelief, their efforts remained largely a holding action. The real locus of the battle to uphold the faith lay not among the adult immigrants, but among their innocent, vulnerable children. In November of 1884, the Third Plenary Council of Roman Catholic prelates in America had met in Baltimore and ordered that all American Catholics—native-born and immigrant alike—should educate their children in parochial schools in order to protect them from Protestant and secular influences.[22] In the next three decades, Polish pastors rose to the challenge, judging by Polish-American education statistics. Between 1887 and 1914, the number of Polish parochial schools rose from fifty to nearly four hundred, while enrollments climbed from 14,150 to 128,540 during the same period. These figures become more impressive when set in context. Before World War One, the ratio of Polish parochial schools to Polish parishes stood at roughly two to three.[23]

In the 1920s, this extensive parochial education system taught approximately two-thirds of the Polish children in the United States;[24] clearly, immigrant parents accepted church-sponsored education as an obligation, in part out of obedience to their clergy, in part as a means to inhibit deculturation of the second generation. But church strategy to educate Catholic youth in parochial schools depended on more than just the compliance of immigrant parents. It also required a corps of religiously reliable teachers to staff the church-run institutions. The centerpiece of that strategy therefore became the burgeoning female religious congregations of teaching nuns, with which the Poles were especially well endowed by the second half of the nineteenth century.

Socially active sisterhoods began to multiply in Poland between the 1850s and 1880s with the formation of congregations like the Sisters of Saint Felix (Felicians) and the Sisters of the Holy Family of Nazareth. During this period of religious renewal, Polish nationalist passions, repeatedly thwarted in a series of failed insurrections, sought a new outlet in religious mysticism, while a growing Polish economy for the first time afforded the daughters of Poland's propertied classes the leisure to translate spiritual piety into a new way of life. The sisterhoods, moreover, grew up at a time when the dislocations of urbanization and industrialization called educated men and women on both sides of the Atlantic into careers of social service and reform. Finally, the female congregations also gave young Polish women an opportunity for achievement largely absent in male-dominated secular society.[25]

Poland's female religious congregations checked dangerous social ferment by counseling that classes should exist in Christian harmony. The Felicians revitalized religious zeal among "the laiety of all classes," for example, by "bringing together humble servants and seamstresses,... teachers, public officials, and even women from the aristocracy." They also labored for religious and social reform in the Polish countryside. After the Polish Agricultural Society, an association founded by Count Zamoyski, asked the Felician congregation to perform social service work among the Polish peasantry, the Felicians staffed twenty-seven rural social centers (*ochrony*) in the Polish Congress Kingdom (central and eastern Poland) between 1859 and 1863. When members of the Agricultural Society inspected the centers a year after their opening, according to a Felician historian, "They were astounded by the manifest improvement in morals and in mutual relations between the peasants and their lords."[26] Thus Roman Catholic prelates were able to harness the nuns' religious zeal and keep it as a capable defender of the social status quo, the church's spiritual affairs, and the temporal interests of Poland's propertied classes.

As Polish immigration mounted, it was not long before Polish pastors in the United States also discovered similar uses for the new Polish sisters and invited successive Polish congregations to establish convent houses and take up teaching duties in America. So successful were these efforts that, already before the war, 2180 teaching sisters served the Polish parochial education system in the United States.[27] The addition of nuns to the staff of the urban parish provided the fortunate pastor with a trained corps of assistants who could aid in the administration of religious and temporal affairs in the parish. Sisters performed services for the various parish societies, cared for the altars and decorated the church, drilled the altar boys and looked after their vestments, enlisted immigrant children for service to the parish, and organized "vocation days" to recruit new nuns and priests.[28] Yet the Polish nuns exerted a broader influence on the immigrants' popular religious culture. Teaching in the parochial schools, where they disseminated the articles of faith, the sisters espoused innovative church doctrine: the mystical adoration of the Blessed Virgin Mary.

Of itself, Marianism was not a new idea. In the Middle Ages, mysticism—direct, personal, intuitive relations with the Divine—and Marianism—cultic devotions to the Blessed Virgin Mary—became touchstones of the Roman Catholic faith.[29] Later, during the Counter Reformation, Marian mysticism developed as an especially pervasive feature of *Polish* belief and would remain so into the modern period.[30] Marian influences were thus a commonplace in Poland's Roman Catholic church and in the immigrant districts of America where Poles often encountered Resurrectionist Fathers and other priests who were steeped in Marian piety.[31] What made the Polish nuns a unique fount of Marian mysticism, however, was the lengths to which they carried their devotion to the Blessed Virgin and the way they personalized their relationship to her and to Christ. Polish sisters singlemindedly embraced Marian mysticism as the rule for their spiritual lives and as the moral dimension of their social activities— teaching, charity, and social work.

Each Polish female congregation highlighted a different aspect of the Marian cult, from which it derived its own distinctive character. Under Felician rule, for example, female religious practiced humility, poverty, "seraphic love," constant expiation, and, most characteristically, continual self-abnegation in order to atone for the sins of the world. Each Felician nun was "a Bride of a thorn-crowned Spouse," offering each year a waxen image of a pierced heart on the Feast of the Immaculate Heart in order to symbolize "total consecration."[32] The Sisters of the Holy Family of Nazareth shared the Felicians' main purpose, "total self-immolation through prayer, work and suffering offered for the intentions of the Vicar of Christ [the Pope] and the Church," but eliminated many of the austerities practiced by the older sisterhoods. Instead, they sought to create a Marian "family atmosphere" within their convents.[33] Sisters of the Holy Family were encouraged to develop "a sound appreciation of Mary's role in the mystery of the Redemption and . . . a filial confidence in her patronage," and alternatively told to become "a little Mary," "a true daughter of the immaculate Virgin Mary," "Mary-like," "a slave of Mary."[34] Still, like the Felicians, Nazarethan Sisters also embraced "the mysticism of reparation" in order to help souls to salvation. In the final profession ceremonies of the congregation, Sisters of the Holy Family of Nazareth therefore received rings to signify them as "spouses of Christ" as each solemnly pledged, "I renew and confirm it, and again renounce forever the devil, the world, and myself, in order to live only for Jesus Christ Our Lord."[35]

This Marian mysticism which the Polish nuns catechized in the parochial schools represented a new development in the religion of rural Polish immigrants. Though sparse elementary education had sometimes been provided by village priests in Polish country districts, more usually it was conducted by literate farmers or male or female lay teachers, not by teaching sisters.[36] The cult of the Blessed Virgin Mary had been introduced into the Polish countryside by the higher classes, and Polish peasants had adopted Mary as a character in hundreds of parables and stories in the popular religious folklore.[37] But even though Mary had penetrated into local lore, Polish peasants still had not adopted any of the elements that composed Marian *mystical* belief. Religion—like magic—remained a mechanical means to influence practical affairs. Polish peasants saw themselves related to the Roman Catholic God only through the Roman Catholic church.[38] This changed in America. Teaching in the parochial schools, the Polish Roman Catholic sisters now systematically indoctrinated immigrant youth in Marian mysticism—an individual spiritual connection to an esoteric Divinity aided by the intercession of the meek, mild, long-suffering Blessed Virgin.

At a time when churchmen increasingly were relying upon a mystical Mary to counter the rationalist influences of a secular age, obedient Polish female religious who instilled Marian mystical ideals in immigrant youth marched in the church's vanguard to proselytize and defend the faith.[39] But disseminating mystical belief could only counter the rationalist secular threat. Alone it could do little to prevent another problem that confronted the clergy during these years, namely, disobedience *within* the church. Moreover, in some cases, the supposed personal, intuitive link with the Divine that lay at the core of mystical belief itself could become an alternative source of religious legitimacy which could undercut the authority of the clergy. In the 1880s and 1890s, this would create a new and far more subtle problem for the shepherds of the church.

Disobedience to clerical authority issued from several sources during the mass migration years. On the local level, immigrant parishioners reacting against the trend toward greater centralization in ecclesiastical administration often challenged pastoral control over parish finances and management.[40] Frequently, these advocates of lay trusteeism and parishioner democracy were themselves devout yet ambitious members of the rising immigrant middle-class.[41] More serious still, secular Polish nationalists, without disavowing the faith, often objected to clerical domination over immigrant politics. In fact, the Polish National Alliance, the immigrants' most important fraternal benevolent organization, typified this position, to the consternation of the immigrant clergy.[42] Finally, the nuns who worked in the parishes also sometimes collided with pastoral authority over, for example, congregation jurisdictional issues.[43] Not so easily dismissed as outlaws, such assorted internal critics of ecclesiastical policy and practice confounded the church.

Yet immigrant churchmen, however confounded, repeatedly rose to counter disobedience within the flock. Against secular organizations like the Polish National Alliance, Polish priests formed their own organizations, like the Polish Roman Catholic Union, a large religious fraternal which competed for immigrant working-class loyalties in the late nineteenth century.[44] More routinely, they relied upon the sacerdotal traditions of Roman Catholicism to bolster their priestly authority and at once undercut the religious legitimacy of opponents who, as laymen, could not consecrate the Eucharist in the holy sacrifice of the mass. It therefore represented a severe turn of events when disobedient laymen joined with dissident clerics or when renegade priests themselves challenged pastoral or episcopal authority—viz., Rev. Anthony Kozłowski, Rev. Stefan Kamiński, Rev. Dominik Kolasiński, Rev. Francis Kolaszewski [Rademacher], and Rev. Anthony Klawiter.[45] Priestly opposition threatened to sidestep the obstacle of sacerdotalism and create a parallel religious hierarchy, seemingly as legitimate as the pastors it criticized. But the church could still up the ante and did so, disciplining insurgent priests or excommunicating them and thereby nullifying their priestly functions. Discipline and excommunication worked, of course, because all parties in these disputes—pastors and parishioners, bishops and priestly renegades—all operated *within* the same religious system. As historians have recently used the term, that system was "hegemonic" because its symbols and meanings always belonged to Rome, the apex of the hierarchy.[46] But Rome, too, sometimes could be circumvented. In fact, a more dangerous threat to church authority would arise if sacerdotally valid insurgents would intentionally break with the symbols of the church and create an alternative religion which could challenge the authority of the Pope in Rome. In the nineteenth and early twentieth centuries, as Poles on both sides of the Atlantic chose this course of action, in the eyes of the church they opted for heresy and schism.

Two major heresies fractured the unity of Polish Roman Catholicism during the period of the partitions. The first grew up in the 1830s as Polish nationalists came to blows with the Roman Catholic hierarchy over the thorny "Polish question." During that time, Rome's recognition of the Polish partitions inspired nationalist partisans like Poland's great Romantic poet, Adam Mickiewicz, to create a Romantic, radical Polish nationalist tradition, still distinctly Christian but, after the fashion of French liberal Catholic Hugues-Felicité-Robert de Lamennais (1782-1854), decidedly anti-clerical.[47] Called Polish messianism, Mickiewicz's heretical religious nationalism endowed the Polish nation with the mission of a chosen people whose tribulations and sufferings would redeem

Poland and earn its resurrection.[48] The resurrected Poland would herald the moral regeneration of the Universe and thus become the "Christ of Nations."[49]

Polish messianism passed out of vogue between the positivist 1860s and 1880s, but was revived by nationalist publicists late in the century. In an atmosphere of renewed nationalist ferment, it comes as no surprise that Polish messianic writings found a receptive audience among Poles who migrated to the United States during this period. Polish immigrants voraciously read Mickiewicz, Julius Słowacki, and other messianic poets whose works appeared excerpted on fraternal benevolent association calendars and almanacs and filled Polish language libraries. Polish messianism raised the nationalist ardor of working-class immigrants, but parenthetically also offered them a compelling alternative to the ideology of orthodox Roman Catholicism and to the domination of the clergy. Positing a mystical, visionary link between Poles and their God, Polish messianism resembled the Marian mysticism espoused by the Polish sisterhoods. Indeed, Mary held a prominent place in the Polish messianists' devotions.[50] But because Mary so much symbolized long suffering, docility, patience, humility, and above all obedience to the church, the message of Marian mysticism was other-worldly, passive, and escapist—in short, hardly a suitable inspiration for a broader religious or political activism.[51] The Polish messianists' mysticism therefore highlighted Jesus Christ, the Redeemer. Crucified or resurrected, Christ symbolized a religious involvement that was politicized and active. Polish messianism thus added a terrestrial purpose to orthodox Roman Catholic mysticism: Polish national liberation.

Between the 1850s and the 1880s, the church in Poland increasingly had absorbed some of the messianists' concerns—e.g., opposition to the partitions—while some Polish clerics, principally from the Galician lower clergy, began to echo the messianists' calls for social justice.[52] Doctrinally, however, Poland's church remained very conservative and, as noted, developed a pronounced Marian devotionalism—derisively termed "Mariolatry"—which became a dual prop of the first and second estates—the clergy and the aristocracy.[53] Polish churchmen remained thus preoccupied when the Western European church—in such varied countries as France, England, Italy, Germany, and Austria—was subsequently gripped by the diverse and eclectic movement for reform which came to be known as modernism. Peaking around 1900, church modernists challenged ecclesiastical authority as centered in Rome, stressed the importance of revelation over dogma, sympathized with efforts at social reform, supported scientific research free from dogmatic constraints, and sought to have the church come to grips with the undeniable facts of the modern rational world.[54] Deeply absorbed in their own national religious affairs, Poles seem to have escaped these modernist influences during this period.[55] Yet despite the country's reputed theological retardation, it seems likely that some Polish clerics had to have been familiar with modernist ideas, given Poland's intellectual proximity to France and its geographical proximity to Germany.[56] Immigrant priests might have been similarly exposed because of the English influences on Christianity in America.[57] Meanwhile, social and economic change in Poland became an independent source for modernist-sounding thought.

Though difficult to characterize, the period's second major Polish heresy, the Mariavite movement, blended together conservative Marian devotional themes with reformist tendencies which in the West might have been termed modernist. At the outset, the religious revival that coalesced into the Mariavite movement differed little from other outcroppings of Marianism in nineteenth-century Poland. In 1888, a pious young Pole named Feliksa Kozłowska founded a small religious community, not unlike other female religious congregations which were spawned in post-insurrectionary Poland. By 1893, however, Kozłowska claimed to have had a series of relevations in which God showed her "the universal corruption of the world . . . [and] the laxity of morals among the clergy and the sins committed by priests." The doomed world's last chance for rescue was "in the Veneration of the Most Holy Sacrament and in Mary's help." To spread this doctrine God reportedly directed Kozłowska to help organize a congregation of priests aptly called the "Mariavites" after their Marian devotionalism. God allegedly made Kozłowska the "mistress and mother" of the Mariavite congregation. In good Marian fashion—viz., the Annunciation (Luke 1:26–38)—she replied, "Behold! the handmaid of the Lord; be it unto me according to thy word."[58]

The sect that Feliksa Kozłowska and Rev. Jan Maria Michał Kowalski, her later collaborator, founded was piously Marian, but it also explored themes that paralleled some of the modernists' concerns. Responding to contemporary social issues, the Mariavites challenged the authority of Rome, questioned the doctrine of papal infallibility, and criticized the clergy. They advocated a kind of religious democracy, replaced Latin with Polish in the liturgy, and—as they watched Poland changing around them—promoted new social service functions for a changing church that would cushion ordinary people from the shocks of Poland's social and economic transformation, e.g., mutual aid and savings associations, schools, commercial and agricultural cooperatives.[59] Finally, they espoused a personal revelatory mysticism that shook dogmatic certitude. Whereas some modernists had reasoned that revelation was a more immediate, direct religious experience than dogma or other intellectual formulations of the faith, the Mariavites practiced what they preached and lived the living faith.[60] Because of the Mariavites' disobedience to episcopal authority and their mystical tendencies (but probably also because of their alleged sexual aberrations) Kozłowska and the Mariavite priests were excommunicated in 1906. Thereupon they opted for schism. At their peak, around 1911, the Mariavites gathered in as many as two hundred thousand adherents. If they were not clearly "modernist" in orientation, in some ways they certainly could claim to be "modern." More a popular movement than an intellectual heresy as was Western European modernism, the socially active Mariavites showed particular strength in industrial centers of Poland like the coal-mining region of Silesia and the textiles city of Łódź, the "Polish Manchester."[61]

No record of direct Mariavite involvement in the United States has surfaced; perhaps there was none. Yet a third heresy did arise among the Polish immigrants in the United States which shared a number of elements in common with the Mariavites, the modernists, and the Polish messianists. That heresy, the Polish National Catholic movement, emerged during the 1890s and early 1900s in the heavily Polish anthracite region of eastern Pennsylvania to produce the only major schism ever to split the Roman Catholic church in the United States.

The roots of schism in eastern Pennsylvania ran as deeply as the region's coal veins. Throughout the 1880s and 1890s, Polish demands for control of parish property and Polish-speaking priests had sparked intermittent local conflicts with Roman Catholic pastors and bishops throughout America, but because so many conservative urban bishops favored an accommodation with the immigrant Catholics, most of these early fights did not result in the formation of schismatic churches, but in the founding of new Roman Catholic parishes led by the dissidents.[62] In 1896, however, Poles in Scranton, Pennsylvania, who sought parishioner representation in the management of parish affairs were sharply rebuked by their pastor and reprimanded by the local Irish bishop. With tensions mounting, dissidents asked Rev. Francis Hodur, pastor of a nearby Polish parish, for aid, and he advised them to build their own church. When the bishop refused to consecrate the new church unless they turned over the deed to the property, the insurgent Poles invited Hodur to defy episcopal authority and establish a dissenting parish.[63] Therewith Scranton's working-class Polish immigrants passed the point of no return. In 1904, the conflict finally climaxed when what had formerly been an "independent" or "people's" church consolidated the evergrowing number of breakaway parishes in the region into the Polish National Catholic church, with Hodur himself eventually serving as bishop.[64]

If Polish National Catholicism articulated working-class immigrant concerns, its success or failure ultimately would depend upon other more practical matters. The Polish National Catholics' insurgency was able to take root and spread because it circumvented the single greatest obstacle that often had thwarted Polish religious dissent, the Poles' religious tradition of sacerdotalism. The defection of legally ordained Polish Roman Catholic priests to the Polish National Catholic church and, more importantly, the legal consecration of Hodur as an Old Cathlic bishop (which thus made him a part of the apostolic succession and empowered him to ordain new priests) now enabled excommunicated schismatics to acquire sacramental mediators who were religiously as valid as Roman Catholic clerics. The structure of the schismatic Polish National Catholic church thus fortuitously accommodated Polish religious tradition and produced a system of authority that conformed to the Poles' religious expectations. As for the underlying religious ideology that could legitimize the antecedent act of schism, Bishop Hodur sought a doctrine which would connect schismatic clerics directly to God, sidestep their episcopal or papal superiors, and command wide popular appeal. In fact, a suitable ideology was not hard to find, for only one such tradition of extra-institutional religious dissent had made a serious mark on nineteenth-century Poland and Polish America—Polish Messianism. As a young seminarian in Cracow, Hodur had read all of Adam Mickiewicz's mystical poetry. With the founding of the schismatic church, he now built an institutional home for the heresy of Polish messianism.[65]

Three major messianic themes formed the centerpiece of Polish National Catholic doctrine. The first theme was a pointed anticlericalism. "The Roman bishops," Hodur wrote in 1928, "greedy for power and domination over the whole world, withdrew from the people and ceased working the way the Apostles worked." In the Polish National Catholic church, Hodur believed, "Our measure of religion is our personal relationship to Jesus Christ, to the Holy Teacher." "The duty of every priest of the national church" is not self-aggrandisement, but "to aspire to a surplus of justice" for the people.[66] The Polish National Catholic priest still retained special authority in the spiritual and moral affairs of the parish and, accordingly, significant influence in its temporal affairs as well. But given the fact that intense struggle between parishioners and their priests had helped spark the schism, that temporal influence was deliberately curtailed. Management and administration of Polish National Catholic parishes passed largely into the hands of laymen, who also had a voice in clergy assignments.[67] Church procedure abolished pew collections and required clerics to perform all sacramental services free of charge "according to Jesus' injunction," unlike their Roman Catholic counterparts. Adult parishioners also were freed from the symbolically submissive act of individual confessions to particular priests, but instead could publicly confess their sins in a group at mass. Finally, the Polish National Catholic church denounced the Roman Catholic dogma of papal infallibility and instead expounded religious law at meetings of the General Synod of the church.[68]

The schismatics' belief that the Roman Catholic clergy oppressed Polish working people revealed a second Polish messianic theme carried over into Polish National Catholic doctrine: progressive social politics. Hodur's political consciousness had been influenced by 1890s Galician populism, a radical agrarian movement which had inherited democratic traditions popularized by Polish Romantic nationalists in the 1830s. During the schismatic ferment in eastern Pennsylvania, the Polish National Catholic church shaped these progressive social concerns around the needs of Polish anthracite miners and incorporated them into church doctrine. Polish National Catholicism sought to become a working-class religion, to provide an active social ministry to Polish laboring people, and "to defend the interests of the oppressed and down-trodden."[69] Church doctrine thus embraced egalitarianism. In it, Christ was "the leader, teacher and friend of the poor, spurned, disinherited . . . masses of the nation." Indeed, the poor formed an integral part of the religion.[70] The Polish National Catholic church's liturgical calendar featured a Feast of the Poor Shepherds, which "signifies, through the visit of the shepherds to the infant Christ, the part played by poor and homeless people . . . in helping to make known God's love to mankind."[71] Not surprisingly, the church also promoted the interests of the downtrodden through temporal activities. For example, unlike the local Roman Catholic parishes, the church sided with Polish working people after the 1897 Lattimer Massacre and during the 1900 and 1902 anthracite strikes.[72]

However central anti-clericalism and social progressivism were in Polish National Catholic ideology, a third theme became the wellspring of legitimacy for the schismatic religion. That theme was messianic Polish nationalism. Like its messianic forbears, the Polish National Catholic movement inverted Roman Catholic symbolism. It shifted symbolic focus away from the crucified Christ or the merciful Mary, with their passive, long-suffering connotations; and it discarded religious devices like pilgrimages, indulgences, relics, and Marian scapular medals which the Roman Catholic church had used to control the faithful.[73] Instead, Polish National Catholics emphasized Christ resurrected and ascendant. By further shifting emphasis to Christ's glorious Second Coming, the apocalyptic Millennium contained in the Book of Revelation, the Polish National Catholic church transformed the text that Roman Catholic theologians had used to promote belief in the Immaculate Conception of Mary into a tract with revolutionary political implications for the Christian person and the Polish people.[74] Drawing on the religious legacy of Roman Catholic mysticism, the Polish National Catholic church envisioned that spiritually reawakened individuals would come "nearer to God" in a personal, direct, unmediated way.[75] But by focusing on Jesus the Messiah, the risen Christ, the Polish National Catholic church, unlike its Roman Catholic counterpart, counseled not passivity, but action; not obedience, but initiative; not denial, but affirmation.

The resurrection allegory and apocalyptic promise contained in Polish National Catholic ideology pointedly applied to Poland, for Polish National Catholicism tried to become the messianic religion of the oppressed Polish nation.[76] Practice throughout the church stressed Polish nationalism. One of Hodur's first acts when he broke completely with Rome in 1900 was to replace Latin with Polish as the language of the mass. In 1904, the church opened a seminary which it named Bartosz Głowacki House, in honor of the Polish peasant hero who fought under Kościuszko at the celebrated Battle of Racławice.[77] In 1914, the Polish National Catholic church synod added a feast to the liturgy, the Feast of the Polish Homeland. Among the Polish national heroes that church holidays honored were the three Polish messianists—Zygmunt Krasinski, Julius Słowacki, and Adam Mickiewicz—and the Polish Romantic nationalist poet, Marja Konopnicka.[78]

Though the Polish National Catholics adopted a religious organization that had a distinctly congregational look, it seems that contact with American Protestantism and exposure to American political institutions exerted little if any influence on this Polish religious and social movement.[79] To the contrary, Polish National Catholicism arose from the circumstances and conditions Polish immigrants faced in industrial America and drew upon intellectual and ideological traditions indigenous to the Polish group. The Polish National Catholics' ties to Polish messianism are palpable. Hodur's theology, however, also evoked some of the concerns of the Roman Catholic modernists—viz., opposition to the doctrine of papal infallibility, commitment to social reform, criticism of the clergy. Moreover, some of the intellectual antecedents of both movements were similar. Both were linked to the French reformer Lamennais, modernism indirectly through liberal Catholicism, Polish National Catholicism directly through the Polish messianists.[80] Also, Hodur had formal ties and the modernists informal connections with the anti-papal Old Catholic church.[81] Still, despite these points of concourse with modernism, Polish National Catholicism in the United States shared more in common with Poland's Mariavite movement. Reflecting late nineteenth-century social change, both movements democratized religious practice, attacked papal authority and Roman Catholic dogma, invoked Polish messianic symbols, promoted social service, and drew their strength in industrial areas.[82] Perhaps it comes as no surprise, then, that the Polish National Catholics and the Mariavites developed some institutional links, however transitory. The Mariavites briefly cooperated with the Polish National Catholics, until a quarrel between Mariavite leader Jan Michał Kowalski and Hodur drove them apart. One Mariavite priest, Szczepan Żebrowski, broke with the sect and emigrated to the United States where he was consecrated as a Polish National Catholic bishop. Finally, it should be recalled, both Hodur and Kowalski themselves were consecrated bishops by Old Catholic bishops in Utrecht.[83]

It is impossible to gauge how quickly—or deeply—adherents to the new church embraced these doctrinal innovations. In terms of sheer numbers, however, the church's partisan stance paid off during the World War period, when Poland was "resurrected." The rising tide of left-wing Polish nationalism boosted church membership in the United States to between sixty thousand and eighty-five thousand members by 1925-26.[84] Even so, the success of Polish National Catholicism fell far short of the leaders' more sanguine expectations, for it never became the official church of Poland nor the majority religion in Polish America. In part this resulted from the church's own institutional limitations. In part, however, it also resulted from popular religious conservatism. Tradition dies hard, and given the nature of Polish peasant religiosity—the centrality of magic, sensualism, and ritual in Polish rural religious practice and the longstanding association between Roman Catholicism and Polish national identity—there are reasons why the Polish National Catholic church might have had only modest appeal despite its attempts to attract working-class communicants.[85]

But Polish National Catholicism also found that it had to reckon with a determined Roman Catholic opposition which likened the heretical Polish nationalist challenge to assorted secular threats it had faced and took decisive steps to outmaneuver it during those turbulent years. Polish Roman Catholic priests branded the nationalist schismatics "pagans," "heathens," "atheists," "revolutionaries," "lawbreakers," and "heretics."[86] Moreover, given the nature of patronage and clientage networks in immigrant settlements, National Catholic dissenters also faced economic and social sanctions because of their religious secession. But Polish National Catholicism threatened the Roman Catholic church, it should be noted, *because* it made a persuasive and compelling ideological argument. The Roman Catholic church therefore also met the schismatics' thrust with an artful ideological parry.

Though Polish National Catholicism attacked the authority of the entire American church hierarchy, it fell to Polish-American priests, who held day-to-day responsibility for Polish immigrant religious affairs, to counter the schismatic insurgency touched off by their immigrant conationals. Many Polish priests themselves had participated in Polish nationalist politics. Shunning heresy but nonetheless attempting to bend Roman Catholic orthodoxy to fit Polish political requirements, they succeeded in fashioning an ideology with such wide appeal in Polish America that it stole the schismatics' rhetorical thunder. Cleverly merging formerly incompatible iconographies, they took the messianic elements of the Polish Romantic nationalist tradition and harnessed them to the Roman Catholic church's hegemonic symbol system, Marianism.[87] The resulting fusion might be called "Marian messianism."

In the history of the church, there was another side to the docile, long-suffering Mary. Mary was a splendidly malleable symbol who elicited submission to the church, but also invoked resistance against its foes. Nowhere was Mary's dual nature more pronounced than in Poland. During the MIddle Ages, Polish knights sang a hymn to the Blessed Virgin Mary before battle, and Mary's miraculous martial role recurred frequently thereafter. Poles defending the monastery at *Jasna Góra* against an invading Swedish Protestant Army in 1655 raised the icon-like image of Our Lady of Częstochowa before the enemy force and, it was claimed, saw the seige miraculously lifted.[88] After that victory, Poland's King John Casimir named the Blessed Virgin Mary as Queen of the Polish Crown. Henceforth, too, the Galician town of Częstochowa became a popular pilgrimage site and patriotic Poles forevermore would associate a feminine Poland with her patroness, the Blessed Mother. Marian martial usages thus continued. At the Polish relief of Vienna in 1683, the battle cry of Jan Sobieski's forces as they charged the Turkish host was Marian, "In the name of Mary, help us, Lord God!"[89] A century later Poles who joined Kościuszko's insurrectionary army to fight for Polish freedom in the 1790s reputedly wore Marian scapular medals, given to them by wives, sisters, and mothers.[90] By the period of the partitions, Mary clearly had become Poland's foremost nationalist emblem.

In all of these instances, perhaps Mary merely functioned as any mother would, protecting her imperilled children. But the Cult of Mary contained elements that went beyond the Blessed Mother's traditional protective, maternal, nurturing role. It contained elements that imputed *redemptive* attributes directly to her. This occurred as early as the Middle Ages when Mary was identified with Jesus through such devices as the doctrine of Mary's compassionate martyrdom and the "cult of sorrows" to which it gave rise. In it, Mary was believed to have felt all the suffering from the tortures that Jesus was to experience.[91] The image of Mary promulgated by the "cult of sorrows" it spawned thus featured many of the same elements attributed to Christ's martyrdom—pierced heart, bloody tears, crown of thorns—and Mary became a redemptive figure in her own right.

The Blessed Virgin Mary's "cooperation with Jesus in redeeming mankind" came to be known as the doctrine of "coredemption." In it, Mary became a coredeemer, wholly dependent upon Christ, but in perfect spiritual union with him. "By her compassion," Roman Catholic theologians granted, "Mary comerited for man all that Christ merited by His Passion."[92] The Polish Resurrectionist Fathers, who dominated immigrant religious affairs in Chicago, embraced the mystery of coredemption in the devotional life of their congregation.[93] Poland's Mariavite sect also celebrated the doctrine of coredemption but carried it to the point of heresy, when the sect's foundress, Feliksa Kozłowska, lost herself in revelatory mysticism, when her followers styled her a second Virgin Mary or Mary reincarnate, and when the Mariavites defied the authority of the Roman pontiff.[94]

Significantly, when Roman Catholic churchmen and their lay partisans plunged into Polish nationalist politics in the late nineteenth century, they too drew upon the doctrine of coredemption and the symbolism of the Cult of Sorrows: a Mary-like Poland compassionately suffered a Christ-like martyrdom. A long address delivered at a Chicago Polish nationalist demonstration in 1895 typified this new ideological genre. Poland, one speaker intoned, is "nailed to a cross"; "its hands and feet tied," it "cannot shed its fetters."

> You, our beloved mother, be glorified the more through your poverty, martyrdom and defamation, for all these will help make a crown [viz., of thorns] for your glorious head.[95]

The Chicago speech once again made it abundantly clear that Marianism could be readily changed from a submissive doctrine into an ideological weapon. Marianism thus became messianic, as Mary shed part of her meekness and acquired active, mystical redemptive powers, similar to Christ's but virtually independent of his. Like the Marianism of the Mariavites, this bordered on heresy. But like the Marianism of the Resurrectionists and the various Polish sisterhoods—that is to say, like orthodox Marianism—it stayed safely on this side of the invisible, indelible line that defined the bounds of acceptable religious belief and practice. Marian messianism, however mystical, did not challenge the authority of the Pope or his bishops, did not undercut the institutional church. To the contrary, Mary the Messiah enabled the church to bridge the gap between piety and modernity. A political redeemer but not a religious one, she allowed the church to extend its ideological influence into the relatively alien sphere of aggressive Polish nationalist politics.

As this turn widened the secular political influence of Polish Roman Catholic churchmen, it also placed them on a collision course with the schismatic Polish National Catholics. With war impending in Europe, in December 1912, Polish immigrant factions patriotically resolved to close ranks in a Committee for National Defense (*Komitet Obrony Narodowej*, abbreviated K.O.N.).[96] While the Polish Roman Catholic clerical leadership pushed to give this body a Roman Catholic cast, Polish National Catholic leaders insisted on an equal role, for not to have done so would have belied the purpose of their schismatic movement.[97] Clearly, K.O.N. could not contain two Polish churches with equal ambitions yet diametrically opposed claims to legitimacy and political programs. When a vote for seating the schismatic Polish National Catholics split evenly, the resolution was moved that representatives of the Roman Catholic Alliance of Polish Priests also be excluded.[98] Incensed, the Roman Catholic clerical faction bolted from the meeting and formed its own organization, the Polish National Council (*Polska Rada Narodowa*).[99] Thus engaged, Polish Roman Catholic prelates and their proclericalist partisans also raised the tempo of ideological warfare against their leftist and schismatic opponents. At their disposal was the entire Marian messianic symbology.

During the next ten years, a messianic Mary became the central ideological symbol of Polish Roman Catholics involved at home and abroad in Polish nationalist politics. A Polish political poster published for a Polish-American convention in Buffalo, New York, in 1914 solidified the image of the 1895 Chicago speech by depicting a seated woman, chained and crowned with thorns, who represented the shackled, martyred, Mary-like Poland.[100] In the Polish Army's training camp at Niagara-on-the-Lake, Canada, at the start of World War One, Polish immigrant troops sang the Polish anthem, *"Boże Coś Polskę"* (God Who Helped Poland), beneath a flag that bore an image of the Blessed Virgin Mary.[101] Donors to the campaign to raise money for the Polish Army in France, a fund drive conducted by the immigrants' proclerical, conservative leadership, received prints of Ladislaus Benda's painting in which the Blessed Virgin of Częstochowa united the three Polish partitions—redeemed them—and blessed Polish-American troops speeding to battle.[102]

In Poland, too, messianic Marian symbols filled Polish Roman Catholics' ideological arsenal. A huge nationalist demonstration in Cracow in 1910, commemorating the five-hundredth anniversary of the victory over the Teutonic Knights at the Battle of Grünwald, featured the mass singing of the medieval hymn to the Blessed Virgin Mary, *"Bogu Rodzica"* (Mother of God).[103] But the best example occurred ten years later when General Joseph Piłsudski, an anticlericalist and moderate socialist, defeated an invading Bolshevik army on the outskirts of Warsaw on the banks of the Vistula River. The battle took place on 15 August 1920, the Roman Catholic Feast of the Assumption of the Blessed Virgin Mary; to counter Bolshevik antireligious propaganda and to neutralize Piłsudski's political gain from the victory, Polish rightists, noting the date, ascribed victory to Mary's miraculous intervention and dubbed the triumph *"Cud Wisły,"* "the miracle on the Vistula."[104] The Pope soon followed suit. By designating May 3 as the Feast of the Queen of Poland, the Pope shrewdly turned the anniversary of Poland's revolutionary Constitution of the Third of May (1791) into a Polish national holiday to honor Mary, Poland's Saviour.[105]

Thereafter, Roman Catholic churchmen—both immigrant and American-born—alternated Marian themes according to circumstances and situation. As the political excitement of the early twenties subsided, Marian messianism easily yielded to the Roman Catholic church's time-honored ideological mainstay, Marian mysticism, which continued to serve a hegemonic function. Here, the highlights of devotional life in one Roman Catholic parish in New York are instructive. In the early 1920s, the Vincentian Fathers, a missionary order devoted to Marian mystical doctrine, assumed control of Brooklyn's Saint Stanislaus Kostka parish. In 1926, the new pastor returned from a visit to Rome with a relic of Saint Theresa of the Infant Jesus, a recently canonized nun, and instituted regular devotions to this Marian figure. With the outbreak of the Depression and amidst the rising tide of Marianism, in autumn of 1930 the parish celebrated the hundredth anniversary of the apparitions of Our Lady of the Miraculous Medal to Catherine Labouré, a Daughter of Charity, while in the same year a Saint Theresa Society was formed there. In 1934, as the Depression deepened, Marian mystical devotions reached a new height when the parish received a gift painting of the popular Saint Theresa from artist Tadeusz Styka.[106] Needless to say, Marianism was not confined to this one parish during the period. Since 1927, New York Poles also encountered Marian radio broadcasts, as Father Justin Figas of Buffalo, New York, began his syndicated "Rosary Hour."[107]

As Marian mysticism helped contain popular ferment in the 1920s and 1930s, Marian messianism once again helped mobilize Polish Roman Catholics during the following decade. In September 1939, over four decades after the female image of a martyred Poland had gained ideological currency in the United States during the Polish nationalist agitation in the 1890s, Poland once again endured an hour of national crisis. As Nazi and Soviet armies overran their homeland, Poles in America rallied anew behind familiar ideological banners—messianic and implicitly Marian. In one newspaper advertisement printed in November 1939, a thorn-crowned, shackled woman, dressed in royal robes bearing the Polish coat-of-arms, sat beside a thorn-framed visionary panorama depicting the devastated Polish countryside.[108] A political cartoon of similar vintage was even more striking. The cartoon showed a blood-stained sword bearing swastika and hammer-and-sickle markings, plunged into a Polish city's smoking ruins. A peasant woman, labelled "Poland," hung from the hilt of the sword: the woman was crucified.[109]

In the nineteenth and early twentieth centuries, Roman Catholic churchmen had tried a variety of approaches to hold on to communicants whose faith they could no longer take for granted. Lacking the support of a devout landed gentry that had sustained it in Europe, the Roman Catholic church still had to seek for new secular allies that would bolster it against the strains of a modern American society locked in the throes of industrial growth and urban change during the period. At the diocesan level, native-born bishops made overtures to industrialists and they in turn reciprocated, recognizing, as William Howard Taft remarked, that the church formed "one of the bulwarks against socialism and anarchy in this country."[110] At the parochial level, meanwhile, immigrant pastors courted local factory managers and eventually worked out a *modus operandi* with middle-class parishioners who became pillars of their communities and mainstays of the ethnic parishes.[111]

But despite these secular props, in American factory districts religious practice simply could no longer be coerced as it could in manorial Europe. To be sure, religion could still serve a powerful function in working-class lives, but in order to do so that religion necessarily had to change to accommodate the needs of men and women who had entered the urban, industrial world. Meanwhile, changing pastoral and clerical style also tried to conform to the changing sensitivities and identities of working-class parishioners.[112] The changing composition of the clergy also fitted working-class parishes more closely, as peasant, working-class, and lower middle-class sons began to enter the priesthood on both sides of the Atlantic.[113] Yet perhaps most important were the political moves that churchmen undertook to keep the allegiance of working-class immigrants. The malleable Marian symbols which they used fired immigrant hearts, excited their minds, and preserved their souls in the bargain. Marian ideology operated as a mechanism of control. But it also worked as a militant engine. In both roles, it powerfully countered erosive secular ideologies and dangerous heresies wielded by anticlericalists of all political persuasions.

NOTES

Versions of this article were presented at the 1980 meeting of the Organization of American Historians in San Francisco and the History Workshop on Religion and Society, held during July 1983, in London. I wish to thank Ronald Bayor, Stanley Blejwas, Christa Walck, Christopher Clark, Stephan Thernstrom, Mark Stolarik, Victor Greene, Christopher Johnson, Daniel Buczek, and the members of the conference panels for their helpful discussion, suggestions, and comments at various stages in its preparation.

1. Paul Fox, *The Poles in America* (New York, 1922), pp. 107, 109, 110; Sr. M. Liguori, "Parish Records as Source Material for a History of American Poles," *Polish American Studies*, 1 (1944): 15–16, quoted in Theresita Polzin, *The Polish Americans: Whence and Whither* (Pulaski, Wis., 1973), p. 88.
2. See, for example, Leonard Dinnerstein, Roger L. Nichols, and David M. Reimers, *Natives and Strangers: Ethnic Groups and the Building of America* (New York, 1979), p. 168.
3. On popular religion in rural Poland, see William I. Thomas and Florian Znaniecki, *The Polish Peasant in Europe and America*, 2 vols. (New York, 1927), 1: 205–288; Sula Benet, *Songs, Dance, and Customs of Peasant Poland* (New York, 1951); Jan Stanisław Bystrob, *Kultura Ludowa*, 2d. ed. (Warsaw, 1947). Examples of immigrant popular belief that departed from religious orthodoxy are plentiful. See, for example, Mary Adele Dąbrowska, "A History and Survey of the Polish Community in Brooklyn" (M.A. thesis, Fordham University, 1946), pp. 120–121; Arthur Evans Wood, *Hamtramck, Then and*

Now: A Sociological Study of a Polish American Community (New York, 1955), pp. 40–42; Murray Godwin, "Motor City Witchcraft," *North American Review*, 233 (June 1932): 530; Jan L. Perkowski, *Vampires, Dwarves, and Witches Among the Ontario Kashubs*, Canadian Centre for Folk Culture Studies, Paper No. 1 (Ottawa, 1980). For an Italian immigrant comparison, cf. Rulolph J. Vecoli, "Cult and Occult in Italian-American Culture: The Persistence of a Religious Heritage," in *Immigrants and Religion in Urban America*, eds. Randall M. Miller and Thomas D. Marzik (Philadelphia, 1977), pp. 25–47.

4. See Richard M. Linkh, *American Catholicism and European Immigrants (1900–1924)* (Staten Island, N.Y., 1975), pp. 35–48; and for the larger European context, Lillian Parker Wallace, *Leo XIII and the Rise of Socialism* (n.p., 1966). On radicalism *within* the American church, cf. Mel Piehl, *Breaking Bread: The Catholic Worker and the Origin of Catholic Radicalism in America* (Philadelphia, 1982).

5. See Władysław Piwowarski, *Religijność Wiejska w Warunkach Urbanizacji: Studium Socjologiczne* (Warsaw, 1971), 31ff.; idem, "La Pratique Religieuse dan les Villes Polonaises au Cours des Vingt Dernieres Annees," Social Compass: International Review of Socio-Religious Studies, 15 (1968): 277–284; idem, "L'influence de l'industrialisation sur la religiosité populaire en Pologne," *Changement Sociale et Religion, Conference Internationale de Sociologie Religieuse, Actes de la 13e Conference, Lloret de Mar, Espagne, 31 Aout–4 Septembre 1975* (Lille, France, n.d.), pp. 425–431.

6. This estimate was probably too high, as Kruszka presented the threat of high and increasing Polish "leakage" from the faith as an argument for the appointment of a Polish bishop in America. See Fox, *Poles in America*, p. 112. I have been unable to locate Fox's source for Kruszka's estimate; none is given in the text.

7. Fox, *Poles in America*, pp. 114–116. Cf. Barbara Leś, *Kościół w Procesie Asymilacji Polonii Amerikańskiej: Przemiany Funkcji Polonijnych Instytucji i Organizacji Religijnych w Środowisku Polonii Chicagoski*, Biblioteka Polonijna, no. 9 (Wrocław, 1981), pp. 243–266.

8. Victor Greene, "Poles," in *Harvard Encyclopedia of American Ethnic Groups*, ed. Stephan Thernstrom (Cambridge, Mass., 1980), p. 795. Also see Wiktor Tylewski, "Materiały do Dziejów Polskiego Socjalizmu w Stanach Zjednoczonych," *Problemy Polonii Zagranicznej*, 2 (1961): 210–216.

9. Robert D. Cross, *The Emergence of Liberal Catholicism in America* (Cambridge, Mass., 1967), pp. 23, 38, 47, 109–110, 113. For a representative example of Church liberalism, see Bishop J.L. Spalding, *Socialism and Labor, and other arguments social, political, and patriotic* (Chicago, 1902).

10. See Thomas T. McAvoy, *The Great Crisis in American Catholic History, 1895–1900* (Chicago, 1957).

11. See Joseph E. Ciesluk, *National Parishes in the United States* (Washington, D.C., 1947).

12. Linkh, *American Catholicism and European Immigrants*, p. 108. These figures were obtained by counting the parishes identified in the 1912 *Directory*. See *The Official Catholic Directory and Clergy List... 1912* (New York, 1912), p. 16–763.

13. Wacław Kruszka, *Historya Polska w Ameryce*, 13 vols. (Milwaukee, 1905–1908), 1: 90–139, 2: 6–10. The *Directory*, for example, fails to identify the largest Polish parish in the United States, Chicago's Saint Stanislaus Kostka, as Polish. See *Official Catholic Directory... 1912*, p. 60.

14. On the fight for Polish representation in the church hierarchy, see Victor Greene, *For God and Country: The Rise of Polish and Lithuanian Ethnic Consciousness in America, 1860–1910* (Madison Wis., 1975); Anthony J. Kuzniewski, *Faith and Fatherland: The Polish Church War in Wisconsin, 1896–1918*, Notre Dame Studies in American Catholicism, no. 3 (Notre Dame, Ind., 1980); Wacław Kruszka, *Siedm Siedmioleci czyli*

Pół Wieku Życia: Pamiętniki i Przyczynek do Historji Polskiej w Ameryce, 2 vols. (Milwaukee, 1924), 1: 389–397. On the broader issue of immigrant representation in the hierarchy, also cf. Colman J. Barry, O.S.B., *The Catholic Church and the German Americans* (Milwaukee, 1953); John Meng, "Cahenslyism: The First Stage, 1883–1891," *Catholic Historical Review,* 31 (January 1946): 389–413; idem "Cahenslyism: The Second Chapter, 1891–1910," *Catholic Historical Review,* 32 (October 1946): 302–340.

15. Joseph John Parot, *Polish Catholics in Chicago, 1850–1920* (DeKalb, Ill., 1981), pp. 49–51, 227–228.

16. There is still no satisfactory study of Buffalo Polonia or of Rev. Jan Pitass, but one may consult M. Donata Slominska, "Rev. John Pitass, Pioneer Priest of Buffalo," *Polish American Studies,* 17 (1960): 28–41. For treatments of Rev. Lucyan Bójnowski, see Daniel S. Buczek, *Immigrant Pastor: The Life of Right Reverend Monsignor Lucyan Bójnowski of New Britain, Connecticut* (Waterbury, Conn., 1974); Stanislaus A. Blejwas, "A Polish Community in Transition: The Origins of Holy Cross Parish, New Britain, Connecticut," *Polish American Studies,* 34 (Spring, 1977): 26–69.

17. See Joseph Swastek, "The Formative Years of the Polish Seminary in the United States," *Sacrum Poloniae Millennium,* 13 vols. (Rome, 1959), 6: 39–150; Lawrence D. Orton, *Polish Detroit and the Kolasiński Affair* (Detroit, Mich., 1981), p. 57.

18. Fragments describing early Polish immigrant religious practices can be found in parish commemorative journals, masters theses, folklore and oral history interviews, and fileopietistic accounts. See, for example, *St. Stanislaus Kostka, Brooklyn/Greenpoint-New York, 1896–1971* (South Hackensack, N.J., 1972), pp. 42–44; Dąbrowska, "Polish Community in Brooklyn"; Polish and Polish American Folklore Collections, 1953 (42), 1959 (12), 1964 (99), 1967 (102), Wayne State University Folklore Archive, Detroit, Michigan; Joseph A. Wytrwal, *Behold! The Polish-Americans* (Detroit, 1977), pp. 288–301. Also cf. E.P. Thompson, "Patrician Society, Plebian Culture," *Journal of Social History,* 7 (Summer 1974): 382–405; James Obelkevich, *Religion and Rural Society: South Lindsey, 1825–1875* (Oxford, 1976).

19. Buczek, *Immigrant Pastor,* pp. 39, 55–56, 75, 91; Blejwas, "Polish Community in Transition," p. 34. See *Przewodnik Katolicki* (New Britain, Conn.), 14 January, 15 April 1921, for examples of Bójnowski's approach.

20. Rev. Leon Wysiecki to Bishop Charles E. McDonnell, 30 April 1897, Chancery Archives, Roman Catholic Diocese of Brooklyn, N.Y.; Victor R. Greene, *The Slavic Community on Strike: Immigrant Labor in Pennsylvania Anthracite* (Notre Dame, Ind., 1968), p. 248.

21. Rev. Leon Wysiecki to Bishop Charles E. McDonnell, 1 February 1897, Chancery Archives, Roman Catholic Diocese of Brooklyn, Brooklyn, N.Y.

22. John Tracy Ellis, *American Catholicism,* 2d. ed. rev. (Chicago, 1969), p. 104. Also see Peter Guilday, *A History of the Councils of Baltimore* (New York, 1932), pp. 221–249; Rev. James A. Burns, *The Growth and Development of the Catholic School System in the United States* (New York, 1912).

23. Józef Miąso, *The History of the Education of Polish Immigrants in the United States,* trans. Ludwik Krzyżanowski, Library of Polish Studies, vol. 6 (New York, 1977), pp. 47, 103, 117.

24. Ibid., p. 230.

25. Sr. M. DeChantal, *Out of Nazareth: A Centenary of the Holy Family of Nazareth in the Service of the Church* (New York, 1974), p. ix; Sr. Mary Tullia Doman, *Mother Mary Angela Truszkowska, Foundress of the Felician Sisters* (Livonia, Mich., 1954), p. 14; Marina Warner, *Alone of All Her Sex: The Myth and the Cult of the Virgin Mary* (New York, 1976), p. 185; Thaddeus C. Radzialowski, "Reflections on the History of the Felicians in America," *Polish American Studies,* 32 (Spring 1975): 19–28. On religious revi-

val and renewal in the United States during the same period, see Jay P. Dolan, *Catholic Revivalism: The American Experience, 1830–1900* (Notre Dame, Ind., 1978).

26. Doman, *Mother Mary Angela Truszkowska*, pp. 16–17.

27. Kuzniewski, "The Catholic Church in the Life of the Polish Americans," p. 411. Also see Sr. Mary Tullia, C.S.S.F., "Polish American Sisterhoods and their Contribution to the Catholic Church in the United States," *Sacrum Poloniae Millennium* 13 vols. (Rome, 1959), 6: 371–612.

28. *Saint Stanislaus Kostka Parish Golden Jubilee, 1896–1946* (Brooklyn, n.d.), pp. 54, 81; *St. Stanislaus Kostka . . . 1896–1971*, pp. 119–120.

29. See Warner, *Alone of All Her Sex*, pp. 147, 214, 218, 247, 301, 306–308, 328, 390–391.

30. See Marian Helm-Pirgo, *Virgin Mary Queen of Poland (Historical Essay)* (New York, 1966); Maria Winowska, "Le Culte Marial en Pologne," in *Maria: Etudes sur la Sainte Vierge*, ed. Hubert du Manoir, 7 vols. (Paris, 1956), 4: 683–710.

31. On the history of the Resurrectionists in America, see Rev. John Iwicki, *The First One Hundred Years: A Study of the Congregation of the Resurrection in the United States, 1866–1966* (Rome, 1966).

32. Doman, *Mother Mary Angela Truszkowska*, pp. 9, 13; *Magnificat: A Centennial Record of the Congregation of the Sisters of Saint Felix (The Felician Sisters), 1855 Nov. - 1955* (n.p., n.d.), pp. 16, 47–49.

33. DeChantal, *Out of Nazareth*, pp. 26, 39; Rev. Francis A. Cegielka, *"Nazareth" Spirituality*, trans. Sr. M. Theophame [sic] and Mother M. Laurence (Milwaukee, Wis., 1966), p. 65.

34. DeChantal, *Out of Nazareth*, pp. 14, 22–23, 41; Rev. Francis A. Cegielka, *Reparatory Mysticism of "Nazareth"*, trans. A Sister of the Holy Family of Nazareth (Philadelphia, 1951), pp. 100–102.

35. Cegielka, *Reparatory Mysticism*, pp. xvi, 8, 12, 13, 19; DeChantal, *Out of Nazareth*, p. 52.

36. Louis E. Van Norman, *Poland: The Knight Among Nations* (New York, 1907), pp. 243–244; Jan Słomka, *From Serfdom to Self-Government: Memoirs of a Polish Village Mayor, 1842–1927*, trans. William John Rose, shortened Engl. ed. (London, 1941), pp. 5, 167–168.

37. Thomas and Znaniecki, *Polish Peasant*, 1: 286–287; Van Norman, *Poland*, pp. 245–246.

38. Thomas and Znaniecki, *Polish Peasant*, 1: 286–287.

39. On 8 December 1854, Pope Pius IX proclaimed the Immaculate Conception of the Blessed Virgin Mary—her freedom from original sin—and four years later the Virgin reportedly appeared to a local shepherdess at Lourdes. These events set the stage for what was to follow. In an 1883 encyclical, Pope Leo XIII urged daily recitation of the rosary and the Litany of the Blessed Virgin in all churches during the month of October and, in particular, stressed the efficacy of the former in combatting modern evils. Two years later, the Pope fixed March as the month to honor St. Joseph, the foster father of Christ. The Pope commended Mary's husband as "a model of all laboring classes and of the poor," presumably for his role as the good, humble, and faithful worker. In 1919, the crescendo of Marian mysticism culminated in the visions at Fatima, Portugal. See Warner, *Alone of All Her Sex*, pp. 52, 236, 259; DeChantal, *Out of Nazareth*, pp. 30, 81, 153.

40. On the early history of trusteeism, see Msgr. Peter Keenan Guilday, *Trusteeism (1814–1821)* (New York, 1928). Also see David Gerber, "Trusteeism and the Survival of European Communal Traditions?—The Case for a New Perspective: Notes Based on the Experience of Buffalo's St. Louis Church, 1829–1856," *American Catholic Studies Newsletter*, 6 (Spring 1980); Patrick Carey, "Two Episcopal Views of Lay-Clerical Conflicts: 1785–1860," *Records of the American Catholic Historical Society*, 87 (March-

December, 1976): 85–98; idem, "The Laity's Understanding of the Trustee System, 1785–1855," *Catholic Historical Review*, 64 (July 1978): 357–376; idem, *A National Church: Catholic Search for Identity, 1820–1829*, Center for the Study of American Catholicism, Working Paper Series, no. 3 (Fall 1977); idem, "Trusteeism: American Catholic Search for Identity, 1785–1860," *American Catholic Studies Newsletter*, 3 (Fall 1977).

41. See John J. Bukowczyk, "The Immigrant 'Community' Re-examined: Political and Economic Tensions in a Brooklyn Polish Settlement, 1888–1894," *Polish American Studies*, 37 (Autumn 1980): 5–16.

42. See Stanisław Osada, *Historya Związku Narodowego Polskiego i Rozwój Ruchu Narodowego Polskiego w Ameryce Północnej* (Chicago, 1905); Victor Greene, *For God and Country*; Joseph A. Wytrwal, *America's Polish Heritage: A Social History of the Poles in America* (Detroit, 1961), ch. 9.

43. John J. Bukowczyk, "Steeples and Smokestacks: Class, Religion, and Ideology in the Polish Immigrant Settlements in Greenpoint and Williamsburg, Brooklyn, 1880–1929" (Ph.D. diss., Harvard University, 1980), pp.205–206.

44. For a history of the P.R.C.U., see Mieczysław Haiman, *Zjednoczenie Polskie Rzymsko-Katolickie w Ameryce, 1873–1948* (Chicago, 1948).

45. See John J. Bukowczyk, "Factionalism and the Composition of the Polish Immigrant Clergy," p. 41; Orton, *Polish Detroit*; Greene, *For God and Country*, pp. 102, 111.

46. See Alan Dawley, "E.P. Thompson and the Peculiarities of the Americans," *Radical History Review*, 19 (Winter 1978–79): 43.

47. DeChantal, *Out of Nazareth*, pp. 6, 9; Peter Brock, "The Socialists of the Polish 'Great Emigration,'" in *Essays in Labour History in Memory of G.D.H. Cole 25 September 1889–14 January 1959*, eds. Asa Briggs and John Saville (New York and London, 1960), p. 148.

48. Nikolai Onufrievich Losskii, *Three Chapters from the History of Polish Messianism*, International Philosophical Library Periodical Publication, vol. 2, no. 9 (Prague, 1936), pp. 20–21.

49. Monica Gardner, "The Great Emigration and Polish Romanticism," in *The Cambridge History of Poland*, eds. William F. Reddaway et. al., 2 vols. (New York and London, 1941), 2: 326; Brock, "Socialists," p. 157.

50. Jerzy Peterkiewicz, *The Third Adam* (London, 1975), pp. 64–65.

51. Cf. Guenter Lewy, *Religion and Revolution* (New York, 1974), pp. 253–254.

52. Piotr S. Wandycz, *The Lands of Partitioned Poland, 1795–1918* (Seattle, Wash., 1974), pp. 136, 196, 226, 234.

53. See Winowska, "Le Culte Marial en Pologne," passim.

54. On modernism in the church, see J.J. Heaney, "Modernism," *New Catholic Encyclopedia*, 17 vols. (New York, 1967), 9: 991–995; Roger Aubert, *The Church in a Secularised Society*, trans. Janet Sondheimer (New York, 1978), pp. 186–203; Alec R. Vidler, *The Modernist Movement in the Roman Church: Its Origins & Outcome* (Cambridge, 1934); Bernard M.G. Reardon, ed., *Roman Catholic Modernism* (Stanford, Calif., 1970), pp. 9–67.

55. Vidler, *The Modernist Movement in the Roman Church*, p. 213.

56. Wilfried Daim, *The Vatican and Eastern Europe*, trans. Alexander Gode (New York, 1970), p. 81.

57. Of course, George Tyrrell, Irish by birth and English by upbringing, was a chief exponent of religious modernism within the church. See Vidler, *The Modernist Movement in the Roman Church*, pp. 143–181. On other English modernists, cf. Alec R. Vidler, *A Variety of Catholic Modernists* (Cambridge, 1970), pp. 109–133.

58. Peterkiewicz, *The Third Adam*, pp. 10ff. On the development of the Mariavite sect, also see Émile Appolis, "Une Église des Derniers Temps: L'Église Mariavite," *Archives*

de Sociologie des Religion, 10 (1965): 51–67; B. Stasiewski, "Mariavites," *New Catholic Encyclopedia*, 9: 217–218.
    59. Peterkiewicz, *The Third Adam*, pp. 36–37, 61, 119; Appolis, "Une Énglise des Derniers Temps," p. 53.
    60. Peterkiewicz, *The Third Adam*, pp. 12–13. Cf. Aubert, *The Church in a Secularised Society*, p. 193; Michele Ranchetti, *The Catholic Modernists: A Study of the Religious Reform Movement, 1864–1907*, trans. Isabel Quigly (London, 1969), pp. 157–158; Vidler, *The Modernist Movement in the Roman Church*, p. 142.
    61. Stasiewski, "Mariavites," p. 217–218; Peterkiewicz, *The Third Adam*, pp. 35, 119.
    62. In New York City, for example, cf. Theodore F. Abel, "The Poles in New York: A Study of the Polish Communities in Greater New York" (M.A. thesis, Columbia University, 1924), p. 19.
    63. Theodore Andrews, *The Polish National Catholic Church in America and Poland* (London, 1953), pp. 17–19, 26–29; Rev. Stephen Wlodarski, *The Origin and Growth of the Polish National Catholic Church* (Scranton, Pa., 1974), pp. 21–23, 25; Greene, *For God and Country*, p. 113.
    64. Andrews, *Polish National Catholic Church*, pp. 19–20, 31; Wlodarski, *Origin and Growth*, p. 181; Greene, *For God and Country*, pp. 98, 113; Paul Fox, *The Polish National Catholic Church* (Scranton, Pa., 1961), p. 28.
    65. Wlodarski, *Origin and Growth*, p. 39.
    66. Francis Hodur, "Doctrines of Faith of the National Church," (lecture given at the Warsaw Synod, 1928), typewritten translation, ms. pp. 3–4.
    67. Fox, *Polish National Catholic Church*, pp. 24, 117; Andrews, *Polish National Catholic Church*, pp. 39, 69–70.
    68. Wlodarski, *Origin and Growth*, pp. 109, 177, 188; Fox, *Polish National Catholic Church*, p. 82; Andrews, *Polish National Catholic Church*, pp. 42, 48.
    69. Wlodarski, *Origin and Growth*, pp. 40–41; 50.
    70. Franciszek Hodur, *Our Faith*, trans. Theodore L. Zawistowski and Joseph C. Zawistowski, mimeographed (n.p., 1966), [p. 13].
    71. Andrews, *Polish National Catholic Church*, p. 60.
    72. Greene, *Slavic Community on Strike*, pp. 141, 155, 183; Buczek, *Immigrant Pastor*, p. 154. On Hodur's socialist connections, see Joseph W. Wieczerzak, "Bishop Francis Hodur and the Socialists: Associations and Disassociations," *Polish American Studies*, 40 (Autumn, 1983): 5–35.
    73. Wlodarski, *Origin and Growth*, pp. 187–188; Fox, *Polish National Catholic Church*, p. 49.
    74. Cf. Lewy, *Religion and Revolution*, pp. 39–41; Rev. 12:1.
    75. Hodur, *Our Faith*, [pp. 7–9].
    76. Fox, *Polish National Catholic Church*, p. 90; Hodur, *Our Faith*", [p. 13].
    77. Wlodarski, *Origin and Growth*, pp. 71–72, 90. In the Battle of Racławice in 1794, a small Polish force defeated an invading Russian army. The victory marked the highpoint of Polish resistance to the Second Partition.
    78. Wlodarski, *Origin and Growth*, p. 103; Andrews, *Polish National Catholic Church*, pp. 60, 74.
    79. See Timothy L. Smith, "Lay Initiative in the Religious Life of American Immigrants, 1880–1950," in *Anonymous Americans*, ed. Tamara Hareven (Englewood Cliffs, N.J., 1971), pp. 214–249.
    80. Vidler, *The Modernist Movement in the Roman Church*, pp. 22–23. Also see Oskar Schroeder, *Aufbruch und Misverständnis: Zur Geschichte der Reformkatolischen Bewegung* (Vienna, 1969), pp. 13–46.
    81. Vidler, *The Modernist Movement in the Roman Church*, pp. 235–236.

82. On the messianism of the Mariavites, see Appolis, "Une Église des Derniers Temps," p. 58.
83. Peterkiewicz, *The Third Adam,* pp. 39, 44–45, 164n; Appolis, "Une Église des Derniers Temps," pp. 53, 59; Greene, *For God and Country,* p. 113.
84. Wlodarski, *Origin and Growth,* p. 117; Fox, *Polish National Catholic Church,* pp. 62–63; Hieronim Kubiak, *Polski Narodowy Kościół Katolicki w Stanach Zjednoczonych Ameryki w Latach 1897–1965: Jego Społeczne Uwarunkowania i Społeczne Funkcje* (Kraków, 1970), p. 134.
85. Cf. the interesting discussion of religious decline, persistence, and change under more recent conditions of urbanization in Władysław Piwowarski, *Religijność Wiejska w Warunkach Urbanizacji,* passim.
86. *Nowy Świat* (New York), 21 September 1922, 19 October 1922.
87. See above, pp. 10, 35.
88. Helen Laura Bilda, "The Influence of Częstochowa on Polish Nationalism" (M.A. thesis, St. John's University, 1948), pp. 17–18, 20, 22–23, 25–26, 123–124; Walter J. Slowiak, "A Comparative Study of the Social Organization of the Family in Poland and the Polish Immigrant Family in Chicago" (M.A. thesis, Loyola University, 1950), p. 63; Helm-Pirgo, *Virgin Mary Queen of Poland,* p. 27; Stanley Bruno Stefan, "The Preparation of the American Poles for Polish Independence, 1880–1918" (M.A. thesis, University of Detroit, 1939), pp. 100–101; Dąbrowska, "Polish Community in Brooklyn," p. 129.
89. Winowska, "Le Culte Marial en Pologne," p. 696.
90. Bilda, "Influence of Częstochowa," p. 58; *Dziennik Chicagoski* (Chicago), 4 April 1894, Reel 56, IIIB3a, IIH, IG, Chicago Foreign Language Press Survey.
91. Warner, *Alone of All Her Sex,* p. 218.
92. See M.J. Horak, "Coredemption," *New Catholic Encyclopedia,* 4: 323–324.
93. Winowska, "Le Culte Marial en Pologne," p. 704.
94. Appolis, "Une Église des Derniers Temps," pp. 57, 59.
95. *Dziennik Chicagoski,* 2 December 1895, Reel 56, IIIB3a, Chicago Foreign Language Press Survey.
96. Stefan, "Preparation," pp. 58, 100; Buczek, *Immigrant Pastor,* p. 48; Frank Renkiewicz, *The Poles in America, 1608–1972: A Chronology and Fact Book* (Dobbs Ferry, N.Y., 1973), p. 16.
97. William Galush, "American Poles and the New Poland: An Example of Change in Ethnic Orientation," *Ethnicity,* 1 (October 1974): 211.
98. Ibid.; Stefan, "Preparation," pp. 63–64.
99. Stanley R. Pliska, "Polish Independence and the Polish Americans" (Ed.D. diss., Columbia University, 1955), p. 82; Galush, "American Poles," pp. 211–212; Stefan, "Preparation," p. 63; Buczek, *Immigrant Pastor,* p. 48; idem, "Polish-Americans and the Roman Catholic Church," *Polish Review,* 21 (1976): 55.
100. Arthur L. Waldo, *Sokolstwo, Przednia Straż Narodu: Dzieje Idei i Organizacji w Ameryce,* 4 vols. (Pittsburgh, 1953, 1956, 1972, 1974), 4: 184.
101. Stefan, "Preparation," pp. 138–139. The flag that flew over the troops, which were trained by the Polish Falcons, a paramilitary nationalist fraternal, might have been a Falcon Banner. The standard of the Lwów Falcon Nest, for example, depicted the Queen of the Polish Crown, Our Lady of Częstochowa. See Waldo, *Sokolstwo,* 1: 187.
102. Pliska, "Polish Independence," p. 248.
103. Stefan, "Preparation," pp. 100–101.
104. Piotr S. Wandycz, *Soviet-Polish Relations, 1917–1921* (Cambridge, Mass., 1969), p. 241.
105. Bilda, "Influence of Częstochowa," pp. 58, 131.
106. *Saint Stanislaus Kostka, 1896–1971,* p. 42–43, 84.

107. Buczek, *Immigrant Pastor*, p. 111; Justyn [M. Figas], *Mowy Radiowe, 1931–1934–1944–1946*, 8 vols. (Milwaukee, Wis., 1934–1947).
108. *Czas* (Brooklyn), 24 November 1939.
109. Waldo, *Sokolstwo*, 1: 242. I would like to extend warmest thanks to Arthur Waldo for his long and thorough reply to my query about dating the illustration.
110. Cross, *Emergence of Liberal Catholicism*, pp. 34–35.
111. This is discussed at length in Bukowczyk, "Steeples and Smokestacks," pp. 239–256, 270–277.
112. Consideration of these changes is beyond the scope of this article, but the reader may wish to consult Daniel S. Buczek, "Three Generations of the Polish Immigrant Church: Changing Styles of Pastoral Leadership," in *Pastor of the Poles: Polish American Essays*, eds. S. Blejwas and M. Biskupski, Polish Studies Program Monographs, no. 1 (New Britain, Conn., 1982), pp. 20–36.
113. Bukowczyk, "Factionalism and the Composition of the Polish Immigrant Clergy," pp. 45–46; Edward Ciupak, *Kult Religijny i Jego Społeczne Podłoże: Studia nad Katolicyzmem Polskim* (Warsaw, 1965), p. 401.

Father Theobold Mathew

The Knights of Father Mathew: Parallel Ethnic Reform

BY MARTIN G. TOWEY AND MARGARET LOPICCOLO SULLIVAN*

For years reformers and historians have considered immigrants and their children a major stumbling block in the perfection of society. Articulate middle-class progressives saw the slums and their foreign inhabitants as the bedrock of boss rule and corruption in urban politics. Prohibitionists viewed the same slum dwellers as both the chief opponents and major beneficiaries of dry legislation.

---

*Martin G. Towey is associate professor of History and American Studies at Saint Louis University, where he received a doctorate in History. He also serves as director of the Gasconade County Historic Survey Project for the Missouri Department of Natural Resources and the National Trust for Historic Preservation.

Margaret LoPiccolo Sullivan is adjunct assistant professor of History at Saint Louis University and on the faculty of the Parkway School District. She holds a doctorate in History from Saint Louis University.

More recently, historians have begun to recognize immigrant contributions to reform, particularly during the first half of the twentieth century. Joseph Huthmacher credits the urban poor and their political representatives for formulating much of the reform legislation during the progressive period and a contribution positively to the idealism of the New Deal. Thomas Brown stressed urban Irish support for Henry George in the late nineteenth century; and Humbert Nelli finds Italian support for at least one Chicago reformer.[1]

Such works indicate an entrance into the mainstream of American politics, that immigrants contributed in some positive way to the reforms favored by the host society. However, in another kind of reform, called "parallel reform", ethnic group members drew heavily upon their own traditions in meeting the problems they found in America. In the *Conservative Reformer,* Philip Gleason writes of the unique German-American Catholic response to the inequalities and evils in American society.[2] The Knights of Father Mathew represent such a movement, a response by Irish-Americans to the problem of alcohol but one that came out of their own tradition and remained almost completely aloof from the Anglo-American prohibitionist crusade.

The Knights of Father Mathew proved something more than a reform movement. It also provided a vehicle of upward mobility for second generation Irish-Americans grappling with the problems of acculturation, assimilation and the maintenance of an intergenerational ethnic tradition. While distinctly Irish in membership and ideology, the Knights of Father Mathew exhibited signs of structural assimilation supportive of Milton Gordon's triple melting pot thesis.[3]

The ideological impetus for the Knights of Father Mathew came from the mid-nineteenth-century Apostle of Irish temperance, Father Theobold Mathew. Born of a middle-class family in Thomastown, County Tipperary, Ireland, he became a Capuchine monk and worked for some twenty years among the poor in the city of Cork. In 1838 he joined the Cork Total Abstinence Society by

---

[1] Joseph Huthmacher, "Urban Liberalism and the Age of Reform," *Mississippi Valley Historical Review*, XLIX (September, 1962), 231-241; Thomas N. Brown, *Irish-American Nationalism, 1870-1890* (New York, 1966); and Humbert S. Nelli, "John Powers and the Italians: Politics in a Chicago Ward, 1896-1921," *Journal of American History*, LVII (June, 1970), 67-84.

[2] Philip Gleason, *Conservative Reformers: German American Catholics and the Social Order* (South Bend, Ind., 1968).

[3] Milton M. Gordon, *Assimilation in American Life: The Role of Race, Religion and National Origins* (New York, 1964).

taking "the pledge" to ". . . abstain from all intoxicating drinks, except used medicinally and by order of a medical man, and to discountenance the cause and practice of intemperance." Buoyed by his leadership and charismatic personality, the faltering Irish temperance movement began attracting large numbers who "took the pledge" at Father Mathew's feet. By 1845 the movement peaked with five million Irishmen enrolled in its ranks.[4]

Father Mathew extended his mission to the United States, preaching his message of total abstinence as the only way to combat the "Irish curse" and enrolling hundreds of thousands. Between December 1849 and November 1851, he toured much of the eastern half of the nation. Beginning in New York, he made a swing through New England, particularly Boston with its large Irish population, returned to the middle-Atlantic states and then visited the South. He spent much of his tour in New Orleans feeling comfortable because of its cosmopolitan and Catholic atmosphere. His reception appeared very warm and enthusiastic with the exception of New England. There he found confronting him the fact that abstinence was associated with abolition. William Lloyd Garrison and his association expected Father Mathew

---

[4] Sister Mary Francis Clare, *The Life of Father Mathew* (New York, 1872).

Father Mathew Addressing a Temperance Meeting

to speak out against slavery as well as alcoholism, but he refused to do so.

Father Mathew found St. Louis a fertile field for his endeavors. The major transshipment point for goods going north and south along the Mississippi and east and west along the Missouri and Ohio rivers, the booming river town had recently experienced a period of rapid growth. A village of little more than 2,000 in 1820, St. Louis had 5,852 inhabitants in 1830, 16,469 in 1840 and 77,860 in 1850. St. Louis's growth drew heavily on mid-nineteenth-century immigration. By 1850 almost half of the city's inhabitants were born outside the United States and by 1860, with nearly 60 percent of its residents coming from abroad, it had become the most heavily foreign-born city in the nation.[5]

Although Germans predominated in the mid-century migrations, outnumbering the native-born Missourians 22,571 to 20,321 in 1850, the Irish had a long history in St. Louis. Shortly after 1800, when St. Louis was still a French speaking village, about one hundred Irish business and professional men settled in the enclave. They contributed the town's first sheriff, newspaper editor and millionaire as well as a goodly number of merchants and lawyers. Well educated, prosperous and often French speaking, this group fit well into the village's existing social, economic, religious and political life.

The Irish who came at mid-century constituted a different lot. Refugees from famine, they settled in the poorest parts of the city, had few skills and strained the town's existing charitable resources. Numbering about 10,000, they were outnumbered by the German immigrants by three to one, a ratio that persisted throughout the remainder of the nineteenth century. Compared to the largely middle-class mid-century Germans, the Irish had a strong upper class (the residue of the earlier migrants who had merged with the French) an extremely weak middle class and very large lower class.[6]

To this poverty-striken, poorly organized Irish community in St. Louis, Father Mathew came in 1850. Exhausted by his numer-

---
[5] U.S. Department of Interior, *Population of the United States in 1860* . . . (Washington, D.C., 1864), 300, 614.
[6] Sister Mary Hayes, "Politics and Government in Colonial St. Louis: A Study on the Growth of Political Awareness" (unpublished Ph.D. dissertation, Saint Louis University, 1972); Frederick Hodes, "The Urbanization of St. Louis: A Study in Urban Residential Patterns in the Nineteenth Century" (unpublished Ph.D. dissertation, Saint Louis University, 1973); Sister Marie Felicite Hanratty, "A Study of Early Irish Contributions to the Growth of St. Louis, 1804-1840" (unpublished Master's thesis, Saint Louis University, 1933).

ous speeches and suffering from severe laryngitis, he was unable to give any sermons or to speak in public. However, this made little difference, his fame proved so widespread and his audience so receptive that he administered the pledge to over nine thousand in one public appearance. In a letter to a friend in Ireland discussing his success in St. Louis, Father Mathew wrote:

> The success that has attended my exertions in the City of St. Louis has exceeded my most sanguine expectations. Nine thousand persons have taken the total abstinence pledge, and when you are informed that I have not been able to lecture in the temperance halls from infirmity, you must deem it a very considerable number.[7]

The seeds planted by Father Mathew led to the formation in St. Louis of the Catholic Young Men's Total Abstinence Society two decades later. This social and semimilitary organization quickly became known for its handsome uniforms, precision drills and participation in civic events, as well as its dedication to sobriety. Reorganized as the Knights of Father Mathew in 1881, it retained its total abstinence function, added insurance benefits and relegated its military activities to a subsidiary organization known as the Uniformed Rank of the Knights of Father Mathew. In that year, the Knights also joined the Catholic Total Abstinence Union, founded in Hartford, Connecticut, in 1870 as a federation of Irish-Catholic temperance organizations.[8]

The St. Louis based Knights grew to 3,000 members in 1898, declined to approximately 1,200 members in 1901 and rose to 2,500 members in 1903. In the same year the organization initiated a membership drive hoping to raise its membership to better than 3,000 before the Catholic Total Abstinence Union held its annual convention in St. Louis in October 1904. The results were astonishing. The Knights had over 5,000 members by mid-summer and over 6,000 members by October, making it the largest single member of the Catholic Total Abstinence Union.[9]

Who belonged to the Knights of Father Mathew in 1904? A majority, but not all the 6,000 members were St. Louisans.

---

[7] Katharine Tynan, *Father Mathew* (Chicago, 1908), 163.

[8] For the history of temperance in St. Louis see Katherine Teasdale Condie, "The Temperance Movement in Missouri, 1869-1887" (unpublished Master's thesis, Washington University, St. Louis, 1937); Laura Louise Martin, "The Temperance Movement in Missouri 1846-1869" (unpublished Master's thesis, Washington University, St. Louis, 1935). There are no existing records of the Knights of Father Mathew or its councils in St. Louis.

[9] *St. Louis Globe-Democrat*, November 9, 1902; St. Louis *Western Watchman*, February 4, May 26, August 4, 11, and September 1, 1904. The *Western Watchman* was the Catholic newspaper in St. Louis during this period.

54

The Father Mathew Temperance Medal, front and back, appears above left. Father Mathew speaks on temperance, above right.

Twenty-five of the organization's 37 parish councils were in St. Louis. By 1906, councils existed in Kansas City, St. Joseph, Moberly, Hannibal, St. Charles, Lexington, Monett, Chillicothe, Sedalia, DeSoto and Springfield in Missouri; Alton, Rock Island, Joliet, Decatur, Chicago and East St. Louis in Illinois; DesMoines and Dubuque in Iowa; and Rosedale, Kansas. The Supreme Council, which met semiannually in St. Louis, reflected the city's dominance of the organization. Typically, in 1904 the Reverend James T. Coffey of St. Louis became Supreme Spiritual Director. Other officers included William H. O'Brien of St. Louis, Chief Sir Knight; Frank J. O'Loughlin of Kansas City, Supreme Deputy Sir Knight; Thomas S. Bowdern of St. Louis, Chief Recorder; Forlance J. Curran of St. Louis, Chief Banker; and Dr. J. J. McLoughlin of Chicago, John Caples of Kansas City and Patrick Mulcahy of St. Louis, Supreme Trustees.[10]

Members also appeared relatively young and usually Irish. In September 1904, the Supreme Recorder announced that during the recent membership drive, the average age of Knights dropped from 35 to 28. In an era of a rapidly aging Irish-born population and its steady decline in both the percentage of general population and Irish-American population, this also indicated a preponderance of second generation members. All St. Louis councils were in English speaking parishes with large Irish-American congregations. Eighteen parishes served the heavily Irish areas of the city, and two were located on its northern fringes with the other five scattered throughout South St. Louis. A sampling of 295 names taken at random from officers and committee members confirmed the preponderance of Irish-Americans, indicating 212, or 72 percent clearly of Irish derivation.[11]

Evidence also exists that the Knights of Father Mathew were upwardly mobile. This becomes obvious in comparing a random sample of Knights officers and active members, between 1900 and 1920, with a similar sample from the Ancient Order of Hibernians, another large Irish-American fraternal organization in the city. Occupational figures for the Irish born and those of Irish parentage exist only for 1900 but provide some basis for a rough comparison. Only 8.6 percent of the Irish-American community in 1900 could be classified as business executives, including owners of small firms, or professional men. Such occupations represented 15 percent of the active Hibernians and 49 percent of the Knights. The Hibernians included a greater preponderance of white collar workers, 47.5 percent (compared to 14.1 percent for the Irish-American community in 1900). They made up only 25 percent of the membership in the Knights. The remaining members of both organizations fell almost unanimously into the ranks of skilled or supervisory labor.[12]

An offshoot of the Knights of Father Mathew, the Irish-American Society, sheds additional light on the character of the parent organization. This Society, founded in 1900 to celebrate

---

[10] The parishes are listed in the St. Louis *Western Watchman*, December 1, 1904 and the officers in *ibid.*, January 21, 1904.

[11] The sample was taken from names appearing in the St. Louis *Western Watchman*, 1900-1920. See also Margaret LoPiccolo Sullivan, "St. Louis' Ethnic Neighborhoods, An Overview," *Missouri Historical Society Bulletin*, XXXIV (January, 1977), 64-76.

[12] Samples were compiled from notices in St. Louis newspapers and checked in Gould's, *St. Louis Directories*, 1900-1920, and U.S. 12th Census.

St. Patrick's Day in a befitting, nonalcoholic manner, was the first in the city specifically founded for the American-born. It rivalled the old line Knights of St. Patrick, founded in 1870, by the city's Irish-American elite.[13]

The Knights of Father Mathew, although largely second generation and upwardly mobile, retained a distinctly Irish approach to the problems of alcohol. It remained philosophically true to Father Theobold Mathew. The personal approach of total abstinence remained the bedrock of the organization. "Taking the pledge" appeared an important event in the life of a Knight and the central focus of the initiating of new members. The ceremony evidently had a tremendous impact on new members. One former member interviewed some fifty-two years after his initiation still recalled the specific questions asked during the religious examination portion of the initiation. He claimed that he drank only slightly because the pledge still had some influence on his conscience.[14] During the membership drive of 1904, one thousand new Knights swore to personal abstinence in what the *Western Watchman* called the greatest temperance demonstration the city had ever seen.[15]

Their Spiritual Director, Father Coffey, exhorted members to show Protestants that Catholics had a high sense of civic morality by fighting the liquor interests. Nevertheless, the Knights generally eschewed the Anglo-American approach of reforming society through legislation. In fact, between 1900 and 1920, they entered the public arena only twice. Once, they worked with the Redemptorist Fathers to stop the issuance of a liquor license to a saloon at Grand and Finney, across the street from St. Alphonsus (Rock) Church. In the other instance, they joined the Woman's Christian Temperance Union and the Home Protective Association in protesting the sale of liquor at the Cottage, a food and beverage concession in Forest Park. On the whole, they followed the advice of St. Louis's archbishop to avoid the fanaticism of other groups who exalted abstinence as the indispensable virtue to be foisted upon all society.[16]

Drawing on their Irish heritage and the needs of an ethnic

---

[13] St. Louis *Republic*, March 5, 18, 1900; *St. Louis Post-Dispatch*, March 17, 1907.
[14] Interview with Thomas Finan, former member of the Knights of Father Mathew, on April 22, 1979, on file at St. Louis University Archives and Oral History Center.
[15] St. Louis *Western Watchman*, August 11, 1904.
[16] St. Louis *Times*, October 12, 1908; St. Louis *Western Watchman*, March 3, August 18, February 18, April 21, 1904.

Rev. James T. Coffey, Supreme Spiritual Director

group in American society, the Knights also differed from native American temperance organizations in creating a complete social atmosphere for members and their families. Within its ranks, the Knights provided not only a solution for the liquor problem, but insurance benefits and a social life catering to a variety of life styles and interests. In responding to the needs of its members, the Knights spawned a number of subsidiary organizations whose diversified functions strengthened the parent organization.

Insurance, both death and sick benefits, continued to be a vital function of the Knights of Father Mathew. During the 1904 recruiting drive, the Knights advertised that they not only stood for sobriety but had "the cheapest insurance to be had" in amounts ranging from $250 to $2,000. By 1910, officers claimed that the Knights had paid over $1,000,000 to widows and orphans and had maintained their own insurance program without the benefit of state supervision or aid of outside companies.[17]

The Junior Knights of Father Mathew provided an initial link in the chain of Knights' organization welding the family together. It attracted boys before they turned to alcohol and provided activities for members' sons. In 1900, this division included 1,200

---

[17] *Ibid.*, March 10, 1910, March 31, 1904, November 30, 1911, and October 22, 1914.

boys between the ages of 10 and 20 in six parishes; later the minimum age rose to 16 and then lowered again in 1913 to 12 years of age.[18] The organization provided the Junior Knights with an extensive range of athletic and social activities, including tennis, basketball and soccer. One highlight of the social activities was the dances held monthly in the large hall of the Knights' building at Cook and Sarah avenues.[19]

The Knights organized a Ladies Auxiliary in 1902, "because only a mother could deliver her sons to the Knights at such an early age and convince their daughters to shun young men who drank." Like the male organization, it had parish councils, a Supreme Council and an Auxiliary of the Uniformed Rank. Much of the ladies leadership, that is most of the officers, came from Kansas City, with Miss Katherine Kelly of that city acting as its perennial president. In 1914, the Knights voted to admit women on the same basis and with the same privileges as male members. It changed the organization's name to the Knights and Ladies of Father Mathew on January 1, 1915. Thus when the Knights gave a grand rally and open meeting in late December 1914, they advised their members that it would be the last stag Knights' function they could attend.[20]

---

[18] *Ibid.*, July 10, 1913; *St. Louis Post-Dispatch*, June 16, 1901.
[19] Finan interview.
[20] *St. Louis Globe-Democrat*, October 17, 1914; *St. Louis Western Watchman*, October 22, 1914, and November 17, 1904.

Uniformed Rank on Parade, 1890s

Archives & Oral History Center St. Louis Univ.

The Uniformed Rank maintained an independent and highly visible existence throughout the period. It drew members from the Knights ranks and consequently appealed for financial assistance to pay for its elaborate uniforms and equestrian mounts from the parent organization. The Knights supported the Uniformed Rank because of its historic ties to the organization and the links it provided to the greater community. The Uniformed Rank took part in such civic events as a 1900 parade honoring Admiral George Dewey's visit to St. Louis and the 1904 dedication of the World's Fairgrounds.[21]

The already mentioned Irish-American Society continued to cater to the more affluent and ambitious Knights. Its sumptuous St. Patrick's Day banquets at the city's finest hotels provided an annual event for its approximately three hundred members. In 1907, a splinter group organized the more exclusive American Sons of Erin, which restricted membership to one hundred business and professional men. By 1915, the split was healed and the renamed Irish-American Sons of Erin boasted a membership of nearly one thousand. Perhaps due to the stresses of the oncoming war and the problems of neutrality, the American Sons of Erin strayed from the Knights fold in 1916 and began serving alcoholic beverages.[22]

The St. Louis Officer's Association of the Knights of Father Mathew, composed of representatives of the city's parish councils, met monthly to direct and coordinate local events. It supervised various recruiting drives, organized mass initiations and gave a yearly grand picnic with speeches, dancing and a host of athletic competitions. It also sponsored an annual communion breakfast, usually held simultaneously at a north and a south side church.[23]

The Officer's Association took temporary charge of another activity—sports—and created an additional organization to permanently direct efforts in that area. Interest in sporting competitions was hardly new with the Knights. Over the years various parish councils had fielded baseball and basketball teams and formed semiofficial leagues. In 1911, the Officer's Association established

---

[21] St. Louis *Times,* January 4, 1908; St. Louis *Western Watchman,* October 25, January 18, 1906, September 7, 1911, and December 1, 1904.

[22] *St. Louis Post-Dispatch,* March 18, 1904, January 20, 1916; *St. Louis Globe-Democrat,* January 3, 1902, December 8, 1907, November 8, 9, 1911, March 15, 1914; St. Louis *Times,* March 18, 1908; St. Louis *Western Watchman,* January 21, 1909, and December 3, 1908.

[23] *Ibid.,* April 30, 1914, August 18, 1910, August 3, 1911, and August 10, 1910.

an Athletic Association. As an independent organization recruited from individual Knights' councils, the Athletic Association, not only purposed to provide athletic competition but also to secure a gymnasium and other athletic facilities. Within a short time, the Knights' Supreme Council purchased a building at Cook and Sarah avenues to serve as a meeting hall for various Knights' groups, an athletic facility for the five hundred members of the Athletic Association and a library. Three years later, however, the Knights and Ladies Auxiliary were still raising money for a modern gymnasium, a swimming pool, bowling alleys and tennis courts.[24]

The Officer's Association became only one of the coterie of Knights' organizations to offer entertainments. The Uniformed Rank held an annual ball with admission by invitation only. They also sponsored an annual festive day-long railroad excursion and held Memorial Day services at Calvary and Saints Peter and Paul cemeteries. Local councils and ladies auxiliaries gave a plethora of events, an endless array of dances, card parties, plays, debates, lectures, musical programs and picnics to suit every taste and interest. Council entertainments ranged from grand lawn parties at Sportsman Park, St. Louis's baseball stadium, to a lecture by Brother Thomas J. Moynihan "On plumbing from a sanitary and scientific standpoint."[25] Presumably, a young man could join the Knights at the age of 12, gain a small measure of financial security, engage in athletic competitions, attend its dances and entertainments and meet suitable young ladies all within the organization's sheltering ranks and without the threat of alcohol.

While the Knights of Father Mathew appeared undoubtedly Irish in origin, ideology and membership, it moved away from a strictly Irish identity and showed definite signs of structural assimilation. Catholicity, not Irish ancestry, became a prime condition of membership. The trappings of Irish ethnicity often were present—flags, shamrocks, hornpipes and jigs, and Irish melodies. But one thing proved conspicuously absent. The Knights were the only Irish-American organization in the city that did not take any political stands during these volatile years in Irish politics. In fact, they did not even take a public stand for Irish freedom as did the city's Irish-American nationalistic organiza-

---

[24] For examples of activities, see *ibid.*, May 12, 1904, April 7, 1910, and August 10, 1911.
[25] *Ibid.*, November 17 and July 12, 1904.

Records in both St. Louis Parishes, St. Bridget, left, and St. Teresa, above, contain many Irish surnames.

tions, cultural organizations, the Ancient Order of Hibernians, the *Western Watchman*, several prominent pastors and the archbishop.[26]

Perhaps the Knights partially avoided pronouncements on Ireland to attract and hold non-Irish members. While the Knights never made any inroads into foreign language parishes, the English speaking parishes became increasingly multi-ethnic. Although the

---

[26] Margaret LoPiccolo Sullivan, "Constitution, Revolution and Culture, Irish-American Nationalism in St. Louis, 1902-1914," *Missouri Historical Society Bulletin*, XXVIII (July, 1972), 234-245, and "Fighting for Irish Freedom: St. Louis Irish-Americans, 1918-1922," MISSOURI HISTORICAL REVIEW, LXV (January, 1971), 184-206.

first generation Germans and others might cling to the foreign language parishes, the second generation moved out of the old neighborhood and into English-speaking parishes. A study of baptismal records in five parishes in 1900, 1910 and 1920 indicates a growing multiethnicity as the Irish moved westward. In 1900, Irish surnames ranged from 48 percent at St. Bridget in downtown St. Louis to 61 percent at St. Teresa Parish on Grand Boulevard in the central city, and less than 50 percent at St. Mathew and St. Mark parishes in the west end. By 1920 the study reveals only 23 percent of such names at St. Bridget, 46 percent at St. Teresa, and still slightly under 50 percent at Sts. Mathew and Mark. Not surprisingly, by 1910 the names of Council Recorders included Benjamin Savignac, George Klosterman and R. L. Odenwalder.[27]

The 1904 recruiting drive became a high point in the history of the Knights of Father Mathew. Other recruiting drives in 1911 and 1914 did not match the success of the 1904 effort. At the beginning of the century's second decade, the *Western Watchman* consistently noted representatives of twenty parish councils attending the St. Louis Officer's Association meetings. Additional notices in the newspaper leave no doubt that these twenty councils remained very active, at least socially. In 1920, the organization sold its property at Cook and Sarah avenues and purchased even more lavish quarters at 4053 Lindell Boulevard, remodeling it with the necessary athletic equipment and game rooms.[28]

In the early 1920s, however, notices of Knights' activities began to decline. Although the Knights remained a viable organization throughout the early part of the decade, membership declined drastically as the 1930s approached. In 1931, the Knights sold their property on Lindell and distributed the proceeds to all members of record at the time of the sale, effectively disbanding the society. Thereafter, a handful of older members met weekly to play cards until their deaths in the 1950s.[29]

As to the causes of the Knights' decline, a number of interesting options present themselves. Prohibition, the seeming success of the Anglo-American approach to the liquor problem, undoubtedly made further struggles in the battle for total abstinence seem

---

[27] Based on *Baptismal Records*, 1900, 1910 and 1920 and *Marriage Records*, 1900-1901, 1910-1911 and 1920-1921 at St. Bridget, St. Leo, St. Teresa, St. Mark and St. Mathew Catholic Churches, St. Louis, Missouri.
[28] St. Louis *Western Watchman*, October 26, 1911, and January 22, 1914.
[29] Based on notices of club events in *ibid.*, 1920-1930 and City of St. Louis, Recorder of Deeds, *Deed Book*, Number 5167 (September 25, 1931), 517. See also Finan interview.

unnecessary. Then, with rapid disregard for the legislation in St. Louis, as in most major cities, the whole prohibition movement seemed a dismal, silly failure, hardly an encouraging atmosphere for the Knights' total abstinence crusade. One former member thought that prohibition subverted the total abstinence movement. Irishmen, willing to accept total abstinence when it appeared voluntary, refused to accept the same prohibition against alcohol when forced upon them.[30]

Another problem centered around the Knights' insurance program. According to the rate structure, premiums increased as the individual aged. As a result, the premium costs tended to drive older members out of the organization and discourage younger men and women from joining their society. One individual recalled his father paying $36.52 per month for a $2,000 life insurance policy.[31]

Thirdly, in the 1920s when all ethnic organizations seemed to decline, the rise of mass entertainment undoubtedly weakened the Knights' social function. During this period, ethnic organizations that sponsored amateur entertainment met formidable competition from the phonograph and the radio. The spread of motion picture theaters into residential neighborhoods as well as downtown and mid-town added even more opportunities for amusement. Young men and women in search of entertainment surely would have found Rudolph Valentino and Theta Bara more appealing than amateur plays and Brother Moynihan's paper on plumbing.

To further the decline, another organization coopted the upwardly mobile, Catholic middle-class position. As news of the Knights of Father Mathew dwindled in the columns of the *Western Watchman*, notices of Knights of Columbus meetings rapidly increased. Founded in New Haven, Connecticut, in 1882, for Catholics "regardless of race", the organization grew rapidly in early twentieth-century St. Louis. With thirteen local councils by 1905, it had an impressive new headquarters on Olive Boulevard, just west of Grand, three years later. A sample indicated that about half of all officers and active members had Irish surnames and a clearly middle-class orientation, with 46 percent business or professional men and 49 percent white collar workers. The Knights

---
[30] *Ibid.*
[31] *Ibid.*

of Columbus obviously appealed to the same group as did the Knights of Father Mathew.[32]

Whatever the causes of its decline, the Knights of Father Mathew served its purpose of successfully providing second generation Irish-Americans with a link between the ethnic past and the present. Starting as an Irish total abstinence society, it also provided some financial and social security. It forged a position midway between Irish-American and Catholic-Americanism aiding and abetting both acculturation and assimilation.

[32] Sample based on 250 names of officials and active members taken from the St. Louis *Western Watchman*. Also *ibid.*, October 8, 1914; John J. Glennon Council, *Golden Jubilee Booklet* (St. Louis, 1953), and Knights of Columbus, *National Convention Souvenir Program* (St. Louis, 1908).

Prelude To "Americanism": The New York Accademia and Clerical Radicalism in the Late Nineteenth Century

Robert Emmett Curran

The Americanist crisis in the last decade of the nineteenth century climaxed the attempt of a group of liberal prelates and their associates to adapt Roman Catholicism to democratic institutions and values. Almost twenty years ago Robert Cross put this complex movement within the context of a growing American Catholic liberalism in the postbellum period.[1] The full dimensions of that liberalism are still coming into focus as archival materials and unpublished sources become more available to the historian. The recent discovery of a remarkable association of New York priests shows another facet of the Americanist controversy that better enables us to appreciate the peculiar lines that the episcopal struggle assumed. It makes clear that as early as the 1860s certain American priests were adumbrating the key issues that would constitute Americanism and that these clerics had an important influence upon the conflict that tore apart the hierarchy in the 1890s.

By 1860 the American priest found himself a prime victim of the power struggle that the episcopacy had waged with the laity during the peak of trusteeism. Autocratic episcopal government might have been an effective means for preventing the schism of various ethnic groups and for consolidating the rapid expansion of the church, but for the American priest it meant chiefly an erosion of his own authority and independence.[2] Groups of priests across the country began pressing for their full rights under canon law. One such group in the Cleveland diocese began to gather for monthly meetings in 1862 to discuss issues related to dogma, scripture, and moral theology, in addition to those regarding canon law. On the eve of the Vatican council its leader Eugene O'Callaghan wrote series of articles written under the *nom de plume "Jus"* for the New York *Freeman's Journal and Catholic Register* which called for

---

1. *The Emergence of Liberal Catholicism in America* (Cambridge, 1958).
2. For an analysis of this development, see Jay P. Dolan, *The Immigrant Church: New York's Irish and German Catholics, 1815–1865* (Baltimore, 1975), pp 163–166. Dolan considers nineteenth-century Catholic theology with its model of monarchial authority to have provided the rationale for the new style of episcopal government and urbanization to have fostered its implementation in America.

Mr. Curran is assistant professor of history in Georgetown University, Washington, D.C.

an ecclesiastical juridical process based upon canon law to replace the existing arbitrary system, in which bishops had the right to transfer or even dismiss priests at will. A thousand clerics responded to the *Journal* in support of *"Jus"*.[3]

Elsewhere canonists such as Sebastian Smith of Newark took the bishops to task for failing to observe not only the provisions of canon law but the hierarchy's own conciliar directives as well.[4] Smith's *Notes on the Second Plenary Council*, published in 1874, became a rallying point for reformers, as had the *"Jus"* letters five years earlier. Smith was part of a loosely associated Newark clerical clique that pressured both James Roosevelt Bayley and his successor, Michael Augustine Corrigan, to change their arbitrary administrative practices as ordinaries of that diocese.

The most notorious of these groups of clerical dissidents was one based in New York City and known, at least in chancery circles, as the Accademia. The focal point of conservative suspicions for over twenty years, the Accademia came to be regarded as the epitome of the unrest fomenting against the established order of American Catholicism, a cabal of liberalism in which the question of priests' rights was only the tip of an ideological iceberg that threatened the faith and polity of the church. Although there was little or no contact among the Accademia and other groups of priests, conservative leaders like Corrigan and Bishop Bernard McQuaid of Rochester became convinced that these groups were deviously promoting what amounted to a national conspiracy against episcopal authority.

The Accademia began in 1865 as an approved theological society of the Archdiocese of New York after the model of a society begun in London by Cardinal Manning. Under the initiative of Jeremiah Cummings, the first American graduate of the Urban College of the Sacred Congregation for the Propagation of the Faith (Propaganda), and of Henry Brann, who had studied at the same college, the society was originally intended as a forum for the continuing theological education of the former Roman students in the area. From the outset, however, the so-

---

3. For a short account, see Nelson Callaghan, *A Case For Due Process in the Church: Father Eugene O'Callaghan, American Pioneer of Dissent* (New York, 1971).

4. Both priests and bishops used the law when it suited their interests and ignored it when it did not. That, at least, was the conclusion of George Conroy, the Irish bishop who was sent on a fact finding mission to the United States in 1878 after Vatican officials decided they needed some better information to settle the numerous appeals they were getting from American priests against their ordinaries. Conroy found that few wished to abide by the body of laws set down by the old canon law or the Councils of Baltimore. For an excellent survey of this whole question of the relationship between episcopal and clerical rights, cf. Robert Trisco, "Bishops and Their Priests in the United States," in John Tracy Ellis, ed. *The Catholic Priest in the United States: Historical Investigations* (Collegeville, Minn., 1971), pp. 111-292.

ciety's meetings for the reading and discussion of original papers were open to all members of the clergy. After less than a year's existence, the society voted to disband because many New York priests, according to one member, Richard Burtsell, found it dominated by abolitionists and those trained in Rome. At their last meeting the members appointed a committee to obtain Archbishop John McCloskey's approval for a new society, one presumably more representative and less dominated by Progagandists, those who had studied at the Urban College.[5]

By the fall of 1866 Archbishop McCloskey had not yet taken any initiative toward setting up a new society and Thomas Farrell, the pastor of St. Joseph's Church on Sixth Avenue, was privately threatening to set up his own theogical group if the archbishop did not establish a similar institution for his clergy when he returned from the Second Plenary Council being held that fall.[6] Shortly thereafter Farrell began hosting almost weekly meetings at his rectory. The regular attendants were Farrell, Patrick McSweeny, Sylvester Malone, James Nilan, Thomas McLoughlin, Richard Burtsell, and Edward McGlynn, who would eventually become its most famous member with his controversial support of Henry George in 1886. On the periphery of the group were several Paulists, including the noted converts Isaac Hecker and Augustine L. Hewit, as well as John Moore, a Propagandist who was doing pastoral work in Florida and would later become bishop of St. Augustine. Most of them were young (Burtsell, McSweeny, Nilan, McGlynn, and Moore were in their twenties) and most had been trained in Rome.

We know all too little of their ideology during these years. Outside of Hecker, who was not a regular member, they published virtually nothing. A major source for our knowledge of their thought is the diary which Burtsell kept at the time. We do know that the regular members prided themselves on their radical views. They supported Radical Reconstruction in the South and Fenianism in the North. They defended the public school as a legitimate educational environment for Catholic

5. Archives of the Archdiocese of New York (hereafter AANY), Burtsell Diary (hereafter Diary), 2, April 17, 1866. Propagandists had two special privileges which tended to set them apart from their fellow clergy. They had the right of appeal to the pope upon being removed or disciplined by their ordinary. Second, their letters to Propaganda would not be returned to their ordinaries, as was the standard procedure. In fact they had the obligation of making annual reports to the Sacred Congregation, a tradition that many American bishops considered an undermining of their own authority.

A different version of the official Accademia's demise is given in an unsigned typed manuscript housed in the Archdiocesan Archives of New York and entitled "Private Record of the Case of Rev. Edward J. McGlynn." According to this 1901 account McGlynn himself led the move to dissolve the society. Thereafter—in the "Private Record's" version—the Accademia, now limited to the McGlynn circle, drifted into heterodoxy (AANY 50-3, pp. 517–525).

6. AANY, Diary, 2, September 17, 1866.

children. They were opposed to the temporal power of the pope and had open minds about the inspiration and inerrancy of the scriptures, infallibility, celibacy, and many other topics that were considered beyond discussion in higher circles of the archdiocese.

Monsignor Thomas Preston, Burtsell's pastor during these years, later claimed that the aim of Farrell's Accademia was "to establish an American school of theology with liberal ideas" by minimizing the authority of the Holy See and adapting Catholicism to democratic forms and institutions.[7] Burtsell himself confessed to James Nilan in January 1867, about the time Farrell's group was forming, that "a revision of the fundamental principles of theology" was badly needed and that he considered his theological studies to be commencing "*ab ovo.*"[8] The genesis of Burtsell's radical approach to theology, as well as that of the other young priests in the group, apparently did not go back to any Roman education. Although they chafed under the authoritarianism of the Urban College and the aristocratic prejudice of the Roman clergy, especially the Jesuits, both Burtsell and McGlynn, by Burtsell's admission, had been staunchly conservative seminarians with very orthodox ideas.[9] The trauma of the Civil War was evidently the catalyst that radically committed them to American democracy and all its implications for the form that Catholicism should take in America.

As Michael Gannon suggests, the Civil War was "a watershed in the maturation of the American Church," forcing bishops and priests to enter "national politics on an issue not directly affecting Catholicism as such."[10] This seems especially true of clerics like Burtsell, Malone and McGlynn. When Henry Brann in 1865 excoriated the Protestant ministers, north and south, for having brought on the war, and praised Catholics for having "kept aloof altogether" from the sectional controversy that had dominated the Fifties, Burtsell's comment was that Catholics had done so "through cowardice, because we ought to have spoken in favor of the Union and the abolition of slavery."[11] Burtsell had returned to America in the bitterest year of the war—1862—and apparently was disconcerted by the Church's continuing failure to support emancipation as a war goal.

Sylvester Malone was a staunch and outspoken unionist in his Brooklyn parish, which was sharply divided about the war. After Appomatox a tour of the South committed Malone all the more to securing full justice for the freedman. Edward McGlynn had returned on the eve

---

7. AANY 50-3, "Private Record," 521.
8. AANY, Diary, 3, January 25, 1867.
9. AANY, Diary, 2, September 10, 1866.
10. "Before and After Modernism: The Intellectual Isolation of the American Priest," in Ellis, *Catholic Priest*, pp. 311-312.
11. AANY, Diary, 1, May 31, 1865.

of the war in 1860. Before it was over he had charge of a floating parish in Central Park made up largely of Irish squatters and a hospital for Federal soldiers. He was there in July 1863 when the New York Irish began rioting and hanging blacks in protest of the draft laws. It was the perfect setting for some inescapable reflections on the meaning of the war.

Their war experiences evidently made them aware that their fellow Irish were still below the middle class status that the families of the Accademia had attained. Moreover, these priests seemed to sense that the "new freedom" which northern intellectuals saw coming to birth in the fields of Antietam, Gettysburg and Cold Harbor raised new hopes for Irish nationalism as well. Supporting the cause of the Fenians in abolishing English oppression was a natural commitment for one embracing the Radical Republican ideology.

When Brann expressed shock at Burtsell's mercurial change from his Roman conservatism to the radicalism he was exhibiting by the late Sixties, Burtsell told him: "I once thought rulers ought to take care of the people: in America I have learned that the people knows how to take care of itself."[12] For Burtsell and his fellow reformers learned from the war experience of democracy in action, and drew conclusions for American Catholicism. The country had survived because of the basic wisdom and courage of the people themselves, and the structure and principles of the church in America should be determined with the participation of its members. As with another generation of American Catholics a century later, political radicalism fostered religious radicalism.

The inspiration of scripture and the infallibility of the pope were two doctrinal questions the members of the Accademia most frequently discussed. Regarding the former there was a range of opinions. For James Nilan to call the scriptures inspired meant no more than calling Dante's Divine Comedy "inspired."[13] Burtsell, on the other hand, thought that the old and new testaments were uniquely inspired and free of error insofar as they dealt with matters of faith and morals defined by the Church. All its members doubted the authenticity of the Genesis account of the fall of the first parents; indeed they held that there were probably more than one set of such parents, although they did not venture to consider evolution as an hypothesis.[14]

12. AANY, Diary, 2, September 10, 1866.
13. AANY, Diary, 3, January 25, 1867.
14. "We doubted the inspiration of the history of our first parents' fall," Burtsell recorded, "and thought that many Adams may have been created, as long as the whole human race fell from original justice. The reasoning [of] Rom[ans]. 5 about sin entering by one man, is not of faith.... St. Paul's reasoning there is very illogical" (AANY, Diary, 3, February 27, 1867). Strangely there is no mention of the theory of evolution al-

With Pius IX's definition of the dogma of the Immaculate Conception hardly more than a decade old, infallibility was a live topic. The Accademians found that neither dogma was sufficient to prove the other. Conversely they interpreted history to prove that the Church had earlier held that the pope could err in matters of faith. With their democratic convictions they preferred to profess the infallibility of the Church as opposed to that of the pope. They were uneasy with the definition of the Immaculate Conception precisely because it seemed to rest on the pope's unique infallibility. The latter claim was particularly unacceptable to Burtsell because he interpreted it to include the pope's indirect power to depose sovereigns.[15]

Many of the practices of the Church they found exceedingly legalistic. Convinced that the material integrity of confession (the exact recitation of one's sins) had not been a prime concern for the Apostolic Church, they felt that their large congregations warranted the use of general absolution. It was absurd, Burtsell and McGlynn concluded, for a priest to waste five hours listening to "the tomfooleries of servant girls!"[16] Other practices such as the wearing of vestments and Latin Masses they dismissed as medieval vestiges which had come to be considered peculiarly sacred. They were promoting the adoption of English in the popular devotions as the first step toward making the vernacular the normal language for the liturgy.

Most of the Accademians opposed mandatory celibacy since it retarded emotional growth and tended to produce too many selfish and lonely priests. Eliminating this requirement, they reasoned, would attract more talented and attractive men to the priesthood. In the present dispensation the influence of the celibate clergy stemmed from "a superstitious reverence" on the part of the laity for a clerical mystique created by the priest's separation from the laity.[17] Religious orders they likewise found outmoded, stifled by their traditions and dominated by small minded men whose vision was fixed on the past. Burtsell remarked in

---

though Hecker's *Catholic World* was taking up the issue during these years. This of course was before the publication of *The Descent of Man* in which Darwin explicitly included man within his theory.

15. AANY, Diary, 3, May 19, 1867. The theory of the pope's indirect temporal power asserted that while Church and State are independent societies, the pope has the right to intervene in temporal affairs, even to the point of deposing heretical rulers, when the faith and morals of the people are endangered.
16. "If anyone wishes special advice," Burtsell suggested, "let him confess that special sin privately" (AANY, Diary, 3, January 23, 1867).
17. Nilan, McSweeny, and Burtsell agreed that "celibacy never allows priests to become men, marriage sobers men at once: Celibacy brings lonesome hours to the priest: marriage would give him a perpetual object to be loved; Celibacy makes priests selfish; marriage would make him more social.... So few choose celibacy, that few smart and good men become priests. The Protestant clergy has more social influence than the Catholic" (AANY, Diary, 2, July 21, 1866).

1865 that he had once looked to the Jesuits as the leaders of the age; in the light of his subsequent experience he now saw them trying to "fossilize" Americans "with the habits of the Middle Ages." Hecker especially condemned the Jesuits' insistence upon making all the decisions in their direction of others, thus stripping people of their responsibility in making moral judgments.[18]

The Accademians expected authority in the Church to be exercised in a manner suiting mature men. "A diocese or the Universal Church is not to be governed as a large friary or college," Burtsell observed in a discussion with Patrick McSweeny in 1865.[19] Burtsell himself had nearly left the Urban College because of its authoritarian regimen. In democratic America the "boss rule" of a John Hughes appalled Burtsell and his colleagues all the more.[20] What especially irritated them was the growing efforts of the episcopacy to make laws governing the whole lifestyle of the clergy, from the prohibition of beards to the wearing of the Roman collar. This they saw as a further removal of the priest from the general life of the people to be confined to a more cloistered range of activities closely monitored by his bishop. The contemporary style of authority, they were convinced, induced priests to look on bishops as demigods; the laity, in turn, had the same attitude toward priests. It was an enervating situation that impelled the Accademians to seek root changes that would revitalize the Church.

In brief, the Accademians believed that in America the Church had to be radically different from what it had been in the Old World. It had to be open to the uniqueness of its new milieu and reflect that milieu. If only the American Church could break out of its feudal patterns, there was no limit to its possible effect upon the country.[21] American Catholicism had to abandon its tradition of prudent silence on social questions and begin taking the lead in the reform movement. It had to cease its isolation from Protestants and its condemnations of American groups like the Masons, simply on the basis of the reputations of their European counterparts.

By 1867 McGlynn was already preaching this "American Idea" from the secular pulpits that would make him a national figure over the next thirty years. Speaking in Cooper Union McGlynn alluded to the destiny

18. AANY, Diary, 3, December 31, 1866.
19. AANY, Diary, 1, June 20, 1865.
20. When some New York priests had approached Hughes about their rights under canon law, the prelate told them "that he would teach them [County] Monaghan canon law; he would send them back to the bogs whence they came" (AANY, Diary, 1, July 26, 1865).
21. "We agreed," Burtsell wrote of a conversation he had with McGlynn in 1865, "that a different spirit is to be brought into the church's legislation. We have the country whence a new activity may spread throughout the whole Christian world. A little more democracy would be of use" (AANY, Diary, 1, March 30, 1865).

RADICALISM IN THE LATE NINETEENTH CENTURY

God had given America by creating this continent on such a vast scale, preparing it for a "gigantic race of men not in physical but moral stature of enterprise, intelligence and virtue." To fulfill its destiny America had to become Catholic, McGlynn asserted, because Catholicism, unlike Protestantism, denied the total depravity of human nature, a doctrine that would ever impede human progress.[22] As Isaac Hecker wrote in the *Catholic World* that same year (and likely a chief source for McGlynn's remarks):

> There is no ground [in Protestantism] on which to assert the natural rights of man, for the fall has deprived man of all his natural rights; and for republican equality the reformation [sic] founds at best the aristocracy of grace, of the elect, as was . . . attempted to be realized . . . by the Puritans in New England, who confined the elective franchise and eligibility to the saints, which is repugnant to both civil and religious liberty for all men.[23]

The vision of Hecker and McGlynn was that only under Catholicism could the country achieve its potential and realize true unity. To make this possible, the Church had to Americanize. "It will be [American] in spite of us," McGlynn warned.[24]

With these convictions it was inevitable that conflicts should have early arisen between members of the Accademia and the chancery. Burtsell and McGlynn became archdiocesan gadflies to spur the archbishop to more vigorous measures to serve the pressing spiritual needs of a growing immigrant population among which were many Irish Catholics with little or no contact with the Church. The two priests continually pointed out the lack of churches and accused the chancery of underestimating the number of Catholics in the metropolitan area in order to justify the archdiocese's standpat policies.[25] In his presence they charged the archbishop with being too remote from his people and allowing his clergy to live too luxuriously while spiritual necessities were going unheeded. They attacked the helter-skelter administration of the archdiocesan charitable institutions and the practice of charging fees for dispensations from the laws of the Church. If such fees had to be charged, they insisted that the revenue at least go toward building new churches and training additional priests. Sharing the misgivings of other

---

22. AANY, Diary, 3, April 28, 1867.
23. "The Church and Monarchy," *Catholic World* 4, no. 23 (February 1867): 638.
24. AANY, Diary, 3, April 28, 1867.
25. Burtsell and McGlynn were arguing that the Catholic population of New York was at least 500,000 whereas the archbishop contended it was not above 300,000 (AANY, Diary, 1, May 25, 1865). Donna Merwick in her study of the Boston Archdiocese during this period finds a similar pattern of polarization between a rising group of Irish-American clerics and a native-born archbishop (John Williams) hesitant to endanger the Church's standing with the Yankee community by responding in a vigorous fashion to the challenges that a rapidly growing immigrant population was raising for the structures of the Church and the larger society *Boston Priests, 1848–1910: A Study of Social and Intellectual Change* [Cambridge, 1973], pp. 61–93.

New York Catholics about the prodigious growth of the parochial school system, Burtsell and McGlynn argued that the Church in New York was consuming too much money and energy in building and running schools at the expense of neglecting the religious ignorance of the vast numbers of poor immigrant Catholics in the city. Secular education, they contended, was the proper realm of the State, not the Church.[26]

Burtsell, McGlynn, and Nilan clashed with McCloskey over the latter's policy of denying the sacraments to the Fenian Brotherhood, the Irish-American organization dedicated to securing independence for Ireland. The three priests not only challenged the hierarchy's right to dictate politics to the Irish but Burtsell and Nilon wrote a pamphlet setting forth the philosophical and theological justification for the Fenians' position.[27] Furthermore, the Accademians defended the Masons in the United States as a legitimate organization that should not fall under the Church's ban inasmuch as it did not seek the overthrow of religion or the civil government, the reason for the Church's condemnation of the Masons in Europe. McGlynn and his colleagues also deepened the suspicions of conservatives by taking part in ecumenical affairs with Protestant clergymen, such as the Christian United Association. Cooperating with non-Catholics in charitable work was a measure that even as intransigent a convert as Thomas Preston could and did conscientiously support. Joining with Protestants, often in liturgical settings, in pursuit of common traditions and values, was something quite different.[28]

With the pope's dominions in central Italy reduced to the environs of Rome, the temporal power of the pontiff was an especially sensitive issue. When Thomas Farrell publicly questioned certain papal prerogatives, including the temporal power, a special diocesan committee appointed to consider possible disciplinary action against Farrell voted unanimously for his removal from St. Joseph's, but the recommendation was stayed by McCloskey's perennial desire for peace.[29] Burtsell published a series of letters in the *Catholic Standard* of Philadelphia

---

26. AANY, Diary, 1, May 25, 1865. In that year seventy-five percent of the New York parishes had schools with a total student population of 16,000. This was an estimated one-third of the Catholic children (Dolan, *Immigrant Church*, pp. 105–108).
27. When Burtsell and Nilan visited Fenian headquarters in Union Square, the officers there were surprised to encounter two sympathetic priests (AANY, Diary, 1, November 29, 1865). Rome subsequently condemned the Fenians as a secret society in January 1870.
28. Burtsell was appalled when Archbishop McCloskey refused to take part in an ecumenical service for Lincoln in April 1865 on the grounds that "it would not look well for him to be praying where Prot[estant] clergymen were present! Oh bright theology!" Burtsell commented, "Oh cowardice! Does the Catholic Church forbid us to bless our countrymen!" (AANY, Diary, 1, April 15, 1865)
29. AANY, 50-3, "Private Record," pp. 522–523.

under the pseudonym "*Excelsius*" in which he attacked the attempt of the Papal States to preserve the temporal power of the pope by raising a loan in the United States. When McCloskey learned that Burtsell was *Excelsius* he summoned him to express his objection to Burtsell's apparent direction, and warned him against any future repetitions.[30]

By May of 1867 the members of the Accademia learned that the archbishop was decrying "a class of young priests" who "pretended to know more than the Church" knows.[31] Five months later he told the pastors of the archdiocese that opinion prevailing outside of New York held that some of his clergy were holding opinions condemned by the Holy See.[32] That same fall the Accademians considered abolishing their society since imprudent members were leaking reports of their freewheeling discussions and the group was widely regarded as systematically opposed to ecclesiastical authority.[33]

It is unclear how long Farrell's theological society lasted. In the wake of the ultramontane victory at Vatican I the intellectual and social ferment of the late sixties ebbed, and the ebullient radicalism of most of the Accademians cooled with advancing age and vested interests within the archdiocesan bureaucracy. Burtsell, for instance, whom even McGlynn in 1866 had accused of being too imprudent in the expression of his radical ideas, had learned the lesson of discretion from his *Excelsius* experience and thereafter was very cautious not to lose his influence within the archdiocese by provocative remarks. In time Archbishop McCloskey's suspicions were overcome and promotions for the Accademia members began to follow. McGlynn was even chosen for the prestigious role of archpriest at the mass in New York celebrating McCloskey's elevation to the cardinalate in 1875.

Nevertheless, stories of the unreconstructed views of Farrell's circle continued. In 1874 Alessandro Cardinal Barnabò, the prefect of Propaganda, instructed McCloskey to warn Burtsell and McGlynn about "the ultra liberal ideas they were indulging in."[34] James Nilan, who had begun a controversial school plan at his parish in Poughkeepsie under which the town government exercised certain controls over the school in return for certain subsidies, heard in 1883 that diocesan authorities were disturbed about bimonthly meetings that Nilan was sponsoring for his fellow priests in the area. Nilan felt constrained to explain that these meetings were not intended to rival the diocesan conferences that had finally been reinstituted but were merely designed to afford entertain-

30. AANY, Diary, 3, February 18, 1867.
31. Ibid., May 15, 1867.
32. Ibid., October 8, 1867.
33. Ibid., September 10, 1867.
34. AANY, unclassified, cited in a letter from Archbishop Corrigan to Giovanni Cardinal Simeoni, October 12, 1888, draft.

ment and stimulation of the mind.[35] Such assurances did little to assuage chancery suspicions that Nilan was beginning an upstate branch of the Accademia.

By 1883 Edward McGlynn had publicly cast his lot with the radical Irish nationalists who had discovered Henry George as the messiah who would return the land to the people through his single tax panacea. McGlynn played a key role in persuading Irish-Americans that George's land doctrine was "good gospel, not only for Ireland, but for England, Scotland, and for America, too."[36] Whether through Michael Corrigan, who had become McCloskey's coadjutor in 1880, or Ella Edes, the American journalist in Rome who had close ties with both Propaganda and the New York chancery, Giovanni Simeoni, the cardinal prefect of Propaganda, received clippings of McGlynn's speech. The Vatican was then in the delicate process of trying to reestablish diplomatic relations with England. Having priests involved in the Irish question would certainly impede any rapprochement. Simeoni informed Corrigan that certain statements attributed to McGlynn regarding the ownership of land contained propositions opposed to the Church's teaching and advised that the clergy abstain from political disputes.[37] Shortly afterwards a second epistle arrived from Propaganda communicating the pope's order to suspend McGlynn from his ministry unless McCloskey judged otherwise. Other prelates such as Silas Chatard of Vincennes and William Henry Elder of Cincinnati were urging McCloskey to take action against McGlynn. McCloskey did drop McGlynn without explanation from a key diocesan committee but declined to impose any further sanctions upon him after McGlynn promised to abstain from future political gatherings.[38]

When McCloskey died in 1885, Corrigan as his successor came to be

35. AANY C-10, Nilan to Corrigan, Poughkeepsie, September 20, 1883.
36. Stephen Bell, *Rebel, Priest and Prophet: A Biography of Dr. Edward McGlynn* (New York, 1937), pp. 26-27. By a fortuitous coincidence, Henry George's *Progress and Poverty* was published in the very year that the Land League was formed. The Land League was the result of the movement known as the "New Departure" that brought together the Home Rule forces of Charles Stewart Parnell, the Irish proponents of social reform led by Michael Davitt, and the American Fenians under John Devoy. George's indictment of the land monopoly as the primary source of economic inequity had an enormous impact upon Irish-American reformers both here and in Ireland (Cf. Thomas N. Brown, *Irish-American Nationalism, 1870-1890* [Philadelphia & New York, 1966]).
37. AANY I-41, Simeoni to Corrigan, Rome, August 9, 1882, Italian. Propaganda was sending similar directives concerning clergy political abstinence to the Irish hierarchy during this summer.
38. McGlynn later claimed that he had voluntarily promised to refrain from making Land League speeches "not because I acknowledge the right of any one to forbid me, but because I knew too well the power of my ecclesiastical superiors to impair and almost destroy my usefulness in the ministry of Christ's Church . . ." (New York *Daily Tribune*, February 4, 1887).

very much under the influence of those who were continuing to smell heterodoxy in the actions and motivations of McGlynn and his clerical associates. Corrigan's vicars general, Thomas Preston and Arthur Donnelly, and the former president of the first Accademia, Henry Brann, were three hard liners who most shaped Corrigan's response to McGlynn's support of Henry George during the mayoralty campaign of 1886 and the sequence of events that extended the controversy for the next eight years. The memories of the radicalism associated with the Accademia continued to color the interpretations that the archbishop and his advisors put upon the position of the clerical dissidents during the controversy. Corrigan, for instance, informed Cardinal Simeoni in November 1886 that McGlynn was persisting in preaching doctrines that were against Catholic teaching. He accused him of denigrating the pope and expounding the heresy that ministry "is not from the bishop but derives its power from the laity," an impudent attempt, Corrigan thought, to democratize "sacred cult in the church," and to substitute George for Leo XIII as the "pontiff of a democratic church without dominion or tiara."[39] In another letter to Simeoni he claimed that McGlynn was denying the principle of *ex opere operato* in contending that the sacraments were valueless without the presence of love.[40]

When McGlynn issued a public statement denouncing the right of "Bishop, Propaganda, or Pope" to prevent him from exercising his civil rights as an American citizen, Corrigan concluded that "the poison of anti-Catholic opinions," which McGlynn had long cultivated in private, was now being spread openly.[41] In McGlynn's refusal to respond to the pope's summons to come to Rome in the spring of 1887 Corrigan found the heresy of denying the primacy of the pope in matters that pertain not only to faith and morals but also to the discipline and government of the Church throughout the world. Significantly, the archbishop on his visitations throughout the archdiocese that spring, instructed congregations on this article of faith that Vatican I had declared.[42]

39. AANY, unclassified, [Corrigan] to [Simeoni], New York, November 24, 1886, draft.
40. AANY, unclassified, Corrigan to Simeoni, March 18, 1887, draft. The basis of Corrigan's charge was a letter which McGlynn had written to a Protestant minister at the time of Henry Ward Beecher's death. In his letter McGlynn had stated: "I am glad ... that the theology of the old church agrees with his [Beecher's] in this, that the essence of religion is in communion with God through the love of Him for His own sake, and in loving all men for God's sake with the best love with which we love ourselves; and that while sacrifice and sacrament, creed and ritual prayer and sermon and song, may be and are powerful helps and necessary manipulations of this religion, which is love; without it they are a mockery, a sacrilege and a blasphemy..." (New York *Daily Tribune*, March 14, 1887).
41. AANY, unclassified, Corrigan to Preston, Nassau, February 11, 1887.
42. The definition of the Vatican Council that the archbishop was citing against McGlynn read in part: "If anyone therefore says that the Roman Pontiff has only the office of inspection or direction, but not the full and supreme power of jurisdiction over the

The excommunication of McGlynn in July 1887 for his failure to heed the pope's order only seemed to increase the threat of schism and made it all the more imperative to discipline the clerical friends of McGlynn who were maintaining contact with him and absolving Catholics who attended the weekly meetings of his Anti-Poverty society to listen to McGlynn's diatribes against "the ecclesiastical machine." In early 1888 Corrigan obtained instructions from Propaganda to impose silence upon McGlynn's clerical colleagues, forbidding them to advocate or discuss the theories of George or take part in the Anti-Poverty meetings. None of the other former members of the Accademia were promoting Georgian theories but they persisted in asserting that McGlynn had been condemned without the due process guaranteed by canon law for economic doctrines on which the Church had made no pronouncement.

The chancery pressured the clerical friends of McGlynn in various ways, one of which was to threaten to examine the finances of their parishes. As early as October 1887 Corrigan had instructed his fiscal procurator to call Burtsell and Nilan to his court, presumably to examine their account books, "unless they can explain away their objectionable utterances on the Land Theory."[43] Another tactic was to eliminate them from key diocesan positions. Thus in November 1889 Burtsell was dropped as a synodal examiner, Nilan was removed from the school board, and McSweeny was discontinued as a diocesan consultor. Transferral of priests to upstate parishes ("The brains of the diocese are

---

whole Church, not only in matters that pertain to faith and morals, but also in matters that pertain to the discipline and government of the Church throughout the whole world ... or if anyone says that this power is not ordinary and immediate either over each and every church or over each and every shepherd and faithful member, let him be anathema" (Constitutio de Ecclesia Christi, Sessio 4, Conc. Vaticanum 1869–1870, in Henricus Denziger, *Enchiridion Symbolorum Definitinum et Declarationum, De Rebus Fidei et Morum* [Karl Rahner, ed., Freiburg, 1955], p. 505.

43. Archives of the Diocese of Rochester (hereafter ADR), Corrigan to Bernard McQuaid, New York, October 4, 1888. For some reason this instruction was not carried out but another McGlynn supporter, Thomas Ducey, the pastor of St. Leo's on Twenty-Eighth Street, was subsequently ordered to turn over his books for examination. When the examination revealed a deficit of some forty thousand dollars a year, the diocesan consultors began to consider several options, including the removal of Ducey from St. Leo's and/or the closing of the parish. That the concern was not merely financial, however, is clearly evident in the minutes of the diocesan consultors for November 5, 1890, when they decided to defer action until they could study Ducey's next sermon (AANY C-18, Corrigan to Ducey, New York, January 31, 1888; ibid., same to same, New York, April 5, 1889, copy; AANY, unclassified, Minutes of Meeting of Diocesan Consultors, Wednesday, November 5, 1890.

The financial condition of St. Stephen's was also one of the reasons given by Corrigan to Propaganda for removing McGlynn as pastor in January 1887. In 1886 St. Stephen's showed an indebtedness of $154,464.54. Even McGlynn's friends admitted he was a poor administrator but he had reduced his church's debt by more than $142,000 during his last four years as pastor (AANY, Financial Report of St. Stephen's Church, 1886).

up the Hudson" became a common saying during the period), as well as a refusal to promote any priests who were sympathetic to McGlynn, were other sanctions that the chancery exercised.[44]

Since none of these measures successfully stifled the McGlynn controversy, Richard Burtsell drew increasing attention from archdiocesan officials as the major cause of the continuing dissent among the clergy. Burtsell was no McGlynn. He did not support the land theories of George or the Anti-Poverty Society. He was not going to take to the hustings to harangue "the ecclesiastical machine" nor was he about to lead a schism. The lesson of the *Excelsius* experience was not second nature to him. But he was deeply respected at home and in Rome for his understanding of Church law and, in a way, this made him a special menace to episcopal authority. Burtsell was continually a goad as a canonist much in demand to defend priests in their contests with ordinaries across the country. His advocacy of priests' rights was making him a threat to episcopal authority far beyond New York. His book on *The Canonical Status of Priests* published in December 1887 had enhanced his influence.[45] Two months later he was a key witness in a suit brought against the trustees of Calvary Cemetery for refusing burial to a man who had died suddenly at an Anti-Poverty meeting, and contended that since the archbishop had issued no regulation forbidding Catholics from attending the meetings, he could hardly deny Christian burial to someone who in good faith had gone to hear McGlynn. The Church recognized, Burtsell maintained under questioning, that people could disobey out of good conscience.[46]

Chancery officials were sure that to allow Burtsell and his fellows to continue to preach about the rights of conscience of Anti-Poverty people

---

44. From the available evidence it is clear that at least six assistants were moved for their support of McGlynn. Chancery officials obviously regarded three parishes as strategic centers of McGlynnites among the clergy: St. Stephen's, Epiphany (Burtsell's church) and St. Leo's. Thus James Curran, John Barry, Thomas McLoughlin, and P. F. Maughan were transferred from St. Stephen's, John Power from the Epiphany, and Daniel Burke from St. Leo's.
45. "The whole tendency of the book is ... calculated to do harm," Corrigan wrote his secretary, Charles McDonnell. What especially bothered the archbishop was a note inside the cover requesting recipients to send one dollar to a New York address for the creation of a fund which would be employed "for the defense of priests unjustly deprived of their ecclesiastical positions." The archbishop ordered Burtsell to withdraw it from publication since he had not gotten his approval, but Burtsell claimed that he had not suspected that Corrigan would impose the normal regulations on a pamphlet that had already appeared in a Catholic newspaper (as a series of articles in the New York *Tablet* in the spring of 1887), had been privately printed, and was not for public sale (AANY C-18, Corrigan to McDonnell, New York, December 15, 1887, copy; ibid., Corrigan to Burtsell, New York, December 14, 1887, copy; AANY, Diary, VI, December 16, 1887).
46. AANY, unclassified, Court Record, Philip McGuire vs. Trustees of St. Patrick's Cathedral, November 15, 1888, copy.

would destroy ecclesiastical government in New York. When the archbishop subsequently made attendance at the meetings a case which priests had to refer to the chancery, Burtsell was finally forced to take a stand in the matter. In October 1889 he buried with full honors of the Church a woman parishioner who had been a regular attendant at the Anti-Poverty meetings.

Corrigan, convinced by now that Burtsell was "the backbone of the rebellion," transferred him to a parish in upstate New York[47] and Burtsell thereupon appealed to Propaganda, as was his right as an alumnus.[48] Corrigan defended the necessity for removing Burtsell in an extrajudicial manner rather than going through the normal channels of censuring him for his disobedience. The experience of the McGlynn case was evidence enough for the archbishop that any outright attempt to suspend Burtsell would have renewed the turmoil and mass protest that McGlynn's suspension and removal had first ignited.[49]

Thomas Preston was confident that Rome would sustain Corrigan once more but he was taking no chances. In early January 1890 he laid out to a Vatican official what was at stake in the Burtsell case. It was a question, he said

> of a few priests who are really disloyal to the Holy See. They minimize all the declarations of His Holiness. They were opposed to the Infallibility until its definition, and now are disposed to make it as little as possible consistent with a profession of faith. They are opposed to parochial schools. . . . They have spoken in favor of saying Mass in the English language, of doing away with the vestments and ceremonies prescribed by the church, of getting rid of what they call medieval customs and obsolete practices, and of Americanizing the Catholic Church here, and adapting it to our liberal and republican institutions.[50]

Burtsell was unable to prevent his own transfer but Francisco Satolli, the apostolic delegate sent to America by Leo XIII in the fall of 1892, re-

---

47. AANY C-18, Corrigan to Ella Edes, New York, Oct. 29, 1889, copy.
48. In his *Canonical Status of Priests in the United States* Burtsell admitted that ordinary rectors like himself were removable at the will of the bishop but "natural equity and the Plenary Councils and the Propaganda," he argued, "have interpreted that this 'will' must be determined by serious motives and be guided by anxious care to save the good name of any one affected by the removal." Since his removal as rector of the Epiphany would inevitably be interpreted as a punishment for some "serious wrongdoing," Burtsell contended that he had the right to a trial to preserve his reputation. Corrigan took shelter in the March 1887 declaration of Propaganda that American bishops were not bound to follow the canonical procedure, so long as there was "serious reason for such action, and full account taken of the past merits . . ." (*Canonical Status*, 46, 101; AANY C-18, Burtsell to Corrigan, New York, December 16th, 1889; ADR, Simeoni to Gibbons, Rome, May 20, 1887, Latin, printed copy; AANY C-18, Corrigan to Burtsell, New York, Dec. 17, 1889; ibid., same to same, New York, December 21, 1889, copy).
49. AANY, unclassified, *Relatio Translationis Statutae Quidem, Sed Nondum Peractae, Doctoris Richardi L. Burtsell, Rectoris Amovibilis Ad Nutum Ab Ecclesia Epiphaniae Ad Ecclesiam Sanctae Mariae, Et Ejusdem Doctoris Recursus ad Superiorem* (1890).
50. AANY S-1, Preston to Archbishop Domenico Jacobini, New York, Jan. 2, 1890, copy.

vived the hopes of the old radicals for the Americanization of the Church, especially when clerical dissidents, including McGlynn, found him an effective court of appeal against their ordinaries. When Satolli lifted the excommunication against McGlynn shortly before Christmas of 1892 the New York *Tribune* found that it meant that American Catholicism was finally "adjusting to the free institutions of the country." Hereafter, it predicted, "the priests of the Church will enjoy a freedom of utterance and action that in many cases has heretofore been denied them, and the whole Church will grow into closer touch with American life and institutions. The ultra-montane type of Churchmanship in this country has received a serious blow from which it may never recover."[51]

It was poor prophecy, for the McGlynn restoration was to be the highwater mark for the dissidents in New York and elsewhere. Archbishop Corrigan's exploitation of divisions within the Roman curia was to be instrumental in ending the alliance between the American liberals and the apostolic delegate.[52] Richard Burtsell experienced at firsthand the changing climate in Rome toward the American liberals in the fall and winter of 1893-1894. After being kept waiting for nearly eight months while trying to obtain a hearing for himself and a parish for McGlynn, he came away with nothing more than some advice from a Vatican official that Americans like himself were wasting their time in trying to "bring Republicanism into the Church."[53]

By the 1890s Burtsell, McGlynn, and Hecker had come to be largely pawns of a new movement toward liberalism which derived its leadership from the hierarchy itself, notably Archbishop John Ireland of St. Paul and Bishop John Keane of the Catholic University of America. Ireland and Keane's attempt to intervene with Vatican officials regarding the McGlynn case in 1886 had been one of the first skirmishes in the ideological struggle that was dividing the American hierarchy into liberal and conservative camps in the last decade of the century. Already in 1890 Corrigan was warning Rome of the "ultra-Americanism" of the liberal party that he saw Ireland and other prelates forming. To Corrigan, Preston, and their conservative allies, the Americanist movement of Ireland and the liberal prelates was the natural outgrowth of the clerical radicalism that had first manifested itself in the sixties.

The relationship of the Accademians to the Americanists is an intriguing one. Sylvester Malone was a close friend of John Ireland, although how much the latter knew of the Accademia is uncertain. Beginning in 1887 Richard Burtsell had regular contact with the Americanist prelates.

---

51. *Tribune*, December 25, 1892.
52. For an analysis of this strategy see R. Emmett Curran, S. J., *Michael Augustine Corrigan and the Shaping of Conservative Catholicism in America, 1878-1902* (diss., New York, 1978), pp. 422-427.
53. AANY, Diary, 9, May 5, 1894.

The two groups took basically similar stands regarding secret societies, the rapid Americanization of immigrants, and parochial schools. It is significant that John Ireland adopted James Nilan's Poughkeepsie Plan as the model for his own controversial school arrangements in Minnesota in 1891. Both groups tended to downgrade the relevance of religious orders in a democratic society. They both were pressing for some form of democratization in the church, to enable it to internalize the values of individual initative and freedom that they saw as the hallmarks of American life. While the Americanists restricted their reform aims largely to church polity, the Accademians were raising some basic doctrinal questions that foreshadowed the Modernist crisis in Europe a few years after the Americanist controversy. Changes in the discipline and liturgical life of the Church were also questions that went beyond the concerns of most Americanists although Denis O'Connell's proposal of substituting the common law as a much more appropriate basis than Roman law for the law of the Church had implications for the reform of ecclesiastical discipline that would have been much more radical than the demand of the Accademians for the full institution of canon law in this country.[54]

Both groups favored the Republican Party but by the 1890s the GOP had shed any radical idealism that had attracted the Accademians. It now stood unequivocally for the new capitalism that Ireland thought to be the foundation for the success of American democracy.

Both the Accademians and the Americanists accepted the separation of Church and State as the ideal environment in which the Church could grow in America. An inference of the liberal program as developed by Ireland was that the American Church under liberal leadership would obtain a favored position because of the liberals' ties with the Republicans, and Americanists successfully used this theme in certain Vatican circles in the early nineties to win papal support for their claims to serve as brokers between Washington and Rome. Such posturing was alien to the concept of Church and State that the Accademians were developing in the 1860s. The Americanists, moreover, went much further than the Accademians in touting the American experience as a paradigm for the rest of the world including the Church universal. Just as the American triumph over Spain in 1898 signaled to Americanists like O'Connell that the axis of civilization was providentially passing from Europe to America, so too were they confident that the American Church was to be the fulcrum for the Roman Catholicism of the twentieth century. The Americanists unmistakably manifest a cultural imperialism that makes

---

54. Cf. Gerald P. Fogarty, S. J., *The Vatican and the Americanist Crisis: Denis J. O'Connell, American Agent in Rome, 1885–1903* (Rome, 1973), pp. 263–265.

Testem Benevolentiae, Leo XIII's encyclical condemning Americanism in 1899, seem a mixed blessing.

No doubt the euphoria of the Spanish-American War accounts for some of the jingoism of O'Connell and Keane in the late nineties but they seem never to have ingested Isaac Hecker's more Christian vision of cultural pluralism. Hecker wrote in 1867:

> The mistake is that people are too ready to make a religion of their politics, and to seek to make the system of government they happen to be enamored of . . . a universal system, and to look upon all nations that do not accept it, or are not blessed with it, as deprived of the advantages of civil society. They make their system the standard by which all institutions, all men and nations, are to be tried. . . . Our government is best for us, but that does not prove that in political matters we are wiser or better than other civilized nations, or that we have the right to set ourselves up as the model nation of the world.[55]

With *Testem Benevolentiae* the liberal prelates got the same message that Burtsell had received in Rome in 1894, and they quietly abandoned their movement. Despite this setback the first years of the new century saw an intellectual fermentation in the Catholic University and several seminaries that promised to renew the spirit of theological openness and investigation that had marked the Accademia. The outstanding forum for this renewal was appropriately enough the *New York Review* which began in 1905 at St. Joseph's Seminary in Yonkers under the spirited sponsorship of Archbishop John Farley, Corrigan's successor. But the suspicion that set in after the condemnation of Modernism in 1907 ended the *Review* and ensured another fifty years of ideological sediment. When the juices finally came to a boil in the 1960s, one could often get the distinct aroma of a century old brew.

55. Hecker, "Church and Monarchy," 639.

A Perspective for a Study of Religious Dimensions in Chicano Experience: *Bless Me, Ultima* as a Religious Text

David Carrasco

> "There are many gods," Cico whispered, "gods of beauty and magic, gods of the garden, gods of our own backyards,—but we go off to foreign countries to find new ones, we reach to the stars to find new ones."[1]

This research is intended to encourage Chicano students and scholars to study and interpret the religious meanings and structures of Chicano life. First, I must describe the general orientation in which I work, an orientation known in the United States as the History of Religions.[2] More specifically, I will outline several hermeneutical principles articulated by the Chicago School of the History of Religions, present part of the approach I take toward religious experiences and expressions and show this approach in action by focusing on passages depicted in the Chicano classic, *Bless Me, Ultima.*[3]

David Carrasco is Professor in the Department of Religious Studies, University of Colorado, Boulder. This paper was presented to the Chicano Studies Colloquium at the University of California, Santa Barbara, April 1979. Research for the paper was supported by a postdoctoral grant from the National Chicano Council on Higher Education.

© 1982 by David Carrasco

Passages from *Bless Me, Ultima* represent a few religious dimensions characteristic of and perhaps fundamental to Chicano experience. As a historian of religion, fascinated by the way in which human beings experience and express their sense of the sacred powers in their lives, I will discuss two religious dimensions of Chicano life reflected in the novel: (a) the dimension of the *sacred landscape,* and (b) the dimension of the *sacred human being.* In the first case I will pay special attention to powerful parts of the novel's natural landscape such as: the "presence of the river"; the golden carp who is described as a god; and the energies embedded in the hero's name, Antonio Luna y Márez. In discussing the sacred human, the focus is on Ultima's powers for dealing with supernatural forces and the dynamic relationship she has with Antonio. This relationship results in Antonio's initiation into the world of sacrality known to Ultima and his discovery that "the tragic consequences of life can be overcome by the magical strength that resides in the human heart." This study will illustrate the pattern of spiritual transformation that Antonio experiences under Ultima's guidance and in his dreams. Within this transformation, Antonio discovers magical strength within himself.

Christian Theology as a Limiting Discipline

My approach to the Chicano experience and *Bless Me, Ultima* is not as a Christian theologian. The theological approach, whether articulated by a theologian or a social scientist influenced by Judeo-Christian concepts and categories, tends to view the tremendous variety of religious phenomena in human experience, or even with Mexican and Chicano experience, by explicitly or implicitly measuring them against the beliefs, doctrines, teachings, and values of the Christian religion, usually judging them as inferior or degraded religious elements. This approach uses Christian categories of spirituality, value, morality, and truth as a powerful NORM, to establish the acceptability and even superiority of Christianity while marking other religions as inferior and sometimes evil. For the student attempting to understand, not just the Christian view of God, but the human experience of divine powers and beings, such an approach can limit and distort his understanding of the spiritual universe(s) within the Chicano community. Such an approach also inhibits our rigorous intellectual and emotional understanding of its many dimensions and richness. The Christian-centric orientation of most Chicano studies is a serious problem. Although the intellectual opportunities of Chicano students have been expanded, they are still shy and defensive about examining the religious realities (Euro-American and Indigenous) of Chicano history and culture. A more humane and humanistic approach is necessary but difficult to cultivate.

85

Let me illustrate how the Christian-centric approach has limited our understanding of our Indian ancestors as creative human beings. When the Spanish conquistadores arrived in Anahuac, they were impressed by the crosses present in different parts of Indian society, and immediately thought that some Christian contact had preceded them. They were even more impressed by stories they heard in various places about an ancient Indian lord named Quetzalcoatl, the Feathered Serpent, also called Topiltzin Quetzalcoatl, Our Young Prince, the Feathered Serpent, who had been a great religious and political leader centuries earlier. The indigenous tradition told how this man-god preached with great authority, invented new rituals of sacrifice, possessed the power to go into ecstasy and visit heaven, and built the magnificent city of Tollan. In response, a debate broke out among Spanish authorities and mendicants. They played great intellectual and theological games with this tradition and tried to fit it within the Christian view of the world. One group argued that this story was evidence of pre-Hispanic demonic influences in New Spain, and these influences had misled the Indians into their terrible idolatry; this justified the conquest and missionization of the Indians. But another group saw this tradition as evidence of pre-Hispanic redeeming contact from the Christian religion suggesting that God had prepared the way for their great conquest and conversion. Some theologians claimed that Moses, or perhaps Jesus, and certainly

Saint Thomas had visited the Indians centuries before, spreading the truths of the Old and New Testament, and that Quetzalcoatl was not really an Indian genius or hero but a foreign missionary. That is, he was like the Spaniards! The application of the Christian theological view of history allows no room for the consideration of Indian creativity, Indian genius, Indian imagination or spirituality. My point is not that these Christians were bad people, for surely there were good and bad people among them. My point is that the aggressive use of a particular religious world view to define the nature and value of another religious tradition does damage to an understanding of the "objects" of this exercise, in this case the Indians.

Chicano Studies has generally obscured the significance of religious dimensions of Chicano life through its captivity by the Christian world view or its inability to appreciate the intertwining of religious meanings with all of Chicano history. Consider the lack of interest in religious structures expressed in, for example, *El Plan de Santa Barbara* or even in the recent Chicano newsletter, *La Red*. These two different statements of present day Chicano scholarship reflect the fact that not just the "faithful" but even Chicanos who consider themselves "not religious" lack a methodology to investigate, criticize, and understand Catholic traditions and folk religious practices. (The reasons for this lacuna in academic programs would be a fascinating study in itself.)

The historian of religions aligns himself more closely to the position developed in an illuminating debate between the novel's hero Antonio and his friend Florence. The debate concerns the existence and cruelty of God in their lives. Antonio hears Florence challenge him:

> "My mother died when I was three, my old man drank himself to death, and" he paused and looked toward the church which already loomed ahead of us. His inquiring, angelic face smiled. "And my sisters are whores, working at Rosie's place . . . So I ask myself," he continued, "how can God let this happen to a kid. I never asked to be born.

> But he gives me birth, a soul, and puts me here to punish me. Why? What did I ever do to Him to deserve this, huh?" ...

Antonio's mind is pushed by his friend's blunt questions to consider the absence of God, and he begins to see a new possibility about the nature of divine beings as he responds:

> "My father says the weather comes in cycles," I said instead, "there are years of good weather, and there are years of bad weather—"
> "I don't understand?" Florence said.
> Perhaps I didn't either, but my mind was seeking answers to Florence's questions,
> "Maybe God comes in cycles, like the weather,'' I answered. "Maybe there are times when God is with us, and times when he is not. Maybe it is like that now, God is hidden. He will be gone for many years, maybe centuries."
> I talked rapidly, excited about the possibilities my mind seemed to be reaching.
> "But we cannot change the weather," Florence said, "and we cannot ask God to return."
> "No," I nodded, "but what if there were different gods to rule in his absence?" Florence could not have been more surprised by what I said than I. I grabbed him by the collar and shouted. "What if the Virgin Mary or the Golden Carp ruled instead of ... (pp.188-90).

Understanding Homo Religiosus

The History of Religions as a discipline works from the conviction that religious experiences and the religions which form around them can be understood if they are approached as an (a) area for scientific inquiry and (b) in relation to the endless variety of human expressions which appear to have a religious nature. The historian of religions examines many accounts of human encounters with God and he attempts to understand the distinctiveness of these experiences and the common underlying patterns.[4] These patterns reveal a human desire and quest to transcend human limits and to participate in sacred realities and structures. Alan McGlashan has noted, "There is strong archaeological evidence to show that with the birth of human consciousness there was born, like a twin, the impulse to transcend it."[5] That is, religion is a part of human nature.

This research does not presuppose the God-human relationship but examines the endless claims and accounts of humans who tell how their lives have been interrupted, impressed, blessed, cursed, and determined by manifestations of a sacred nature and quality. This work begins with the accounts of how humans see, feel, hear, smell, think about the divine forces in their lives and attempts to see what these accounts tell about the human mode of being. Perhaps the reality of God is witnessed in these accounts. But our primary concern is understanding the human being and not believing or disbelieving in his god.

To illustrate a partial curriculum developed under this approach, listed here are some areas of inquiry into religious traditions where I have done research. I have studied the various types of sacred kingship in Burmese Buddhism;[6] primitive religious structures such as the Trickster;[7] the Master of the Animals;[8] the ecstasy of the Shaman;[9] and the role of religious symbols in the rise of man's great invention —the city,[10] with special focus on the coincidence of city and symbol in pre-Columbian Mexico.[11] I have spent time analyzing the dynamics of religious movements such as cargo cults and crisis cults,[12] and the methodological problems involved in studying all these areas.[13] From this journey through the religious worlds of other men, I have developed a perspective that leads me, when I came upon *Bless Me, Ultima* and other Chicano texts, to be *as* impressed by the presence of an "archaic consciousness" in Mexican and Chicano life, as I am by the presence of Catholic or Protestant consciousness. And Chicanos are basically Catholic! Neither the Western nor the indigenous religious traditions within Chicano life have been seriously looked at by Chicanos from the history of religion view point.

These intellectual experiences and journeys into the spiritual universes of significant others produced in me an awakening that human beings, popularly referred to as homo sapiens (in the context of certain Chicano scholars, it is homo chicano) need to be understood as *homo religiosus*. That is, human beings appear to be "wired" for religion. It is almost as though in the makeup of human life there is a religiogram, a program which insures that human beings will develop religious movements and traditions, texts, and rituals. This persistence for religion is reflected in the novel when Antonio is driven to great confusion about his communion experience ("only emptiness"), and asks his father, "Papa, can a new religion be made?" Certainly, new religions are made every-day somewhere on this planet.

Respecting Powerful Data

Religion in Essence and Manifestation by the Dutch phenomenologist of religion, Gerardus Van der Leeuw, gives this definition of religion:

> Religious experience, in other terms, is concerned with a "Somewhat." But this assertion often means no more than that this "Somewhat" is merely a vague "something"; and in order that man may be able to make more significant statements about this "Somewhat," it must force itself upon him, must oppose itself to him as being Something Other. Thus the first affirmation we can make about the Object of Religion is that it is a highly exceptional and extremely impressive "Other."[14]

This simple but strange statement is a helpful place to begin our approach to the religious dimensions of *Bless Me, Ultima,* because it reflects one part of the methodological position taken by historians of religion. In short, it states that religions begin or are characterized by manifestations, epiphanies, apparitions, revelations of strange forces which humans perceived as "highly exceptional and extremely impressive" Otherness. These experiences are familiar, for example: Moses at the Burning Bush, Saul on the Road to Damascus, Juan Diego passing by Tepeyac, or Reíes López Tijerina's prophetic dreams. The methodological position states that religious expressions must be respected and appreciated for their peculiar intentionality if they are to be understood. Van der Leeuw has demonstrated that religious representations, myths, dreams, apparitions, and rituals will not be adequately understood if they are reduced to social, psychological, or rational functions. Scholars who follow this approach explain religion by saying that it is really not religion, but something else like a system of social cohesion, an expression of infantile trauma, a mask for oppression. Religions may involve all these things. But they are something more, and the history of religions seeks to illuminate the inner structures and meanings of religious phenomena.

This approach of respecting the intended and often obscure meaning of religious data has been expanded by Mircea Eliade who summarizes our task through a comparison of religion with works of art.

> Works of art, like "religious data," have a mode of being that is peculiar to themselves; *they exist on their own plane of reference,* in their particular universe. The fact that this universe is not the physical universe of immediate experience does not imply their nonreality. . . . A work of art reveals the meaning, only insofar as it is regarded as an autonomous creation: that is, insofar as we accept its mode of being—that of an artistic creation—and do not reduce it to one of its constituent elements (in the case of a poem, sound, vocabulary, linguistic structure, etc.) or in to one of its subsequent uses (a poem which carries a political message or which can serve as a document for sociology, ethnography, etc.).
>
> In the same way, it seems to us that a religious datum reveals its deeper meaning when it is considered on its plane of reference, and not when it is reduced to one of its secondary aspects or its contexts.

And, Eliade continues, the history of religion must work "to bring out the autonomous value—the value as spiritual creation—" of all religious movements and expressions.[15]

To make this method more relevant, when Antonio and Cico beheld the golden carp as a miraculous being, some insight can be gained by approaching it as a religious manifestation, an extremely impressive "other," rather than by quickly insisting that the fish is not a miraculous being, but an object of fantasy that functioned to create social cohesion among bored children. Like most religions, the golden carp does have a social function and it may be a psychological projection, much of religion does invoke projection, but the golden carp, the owl of Ultima, the Juniper tree, the presence of the river will be better understood and point more directly to a Chicano mode of being in the world if approached as manifestations of power in Antonio's life, as expressions of the sacred, by which I mean the powerful, the valuable, the wonderful, and the terrifying.[16]

Hierophany and the Sacred Landscape

To clarify what I mean by "experiencing the sacred," let us turn to a term which has been utilized by Mircea Eliade, Hierophany. This word means simply "manifestation of the sacred." In Eliade's view, all religions are based on hierophanies or dramatic encounters which human beings have with what they consider to be supernatural forces manifesting themselves in natural objects. These manifestations transform those objects into power spots, power objects, wonderful trees, terrifying bends in the river, sacred animals. The stones, trees, animals, or humans through which a hierophany takes place are considered valuable, full of mana, things to be respected and revered. Human beings who feel these transformations in their landscape believe that a power from another plane of reality has interrupted their lives. Usually, they respond with a combination of great attraction and great fear. Their lives are deeply changed as a result of this encounter with *numinous places*.[17] The three following examples of hierophany illustrate this important notion. One is from Sioux religion, one is from a high religion, Islam, and the third relates to the origins of Chicano culture, the conquest of Mexico.

In Joseph Epes Brown's *The Sacred Pipe*, White Buffalo Cow Woman gives the sacred pipe to the Oglala Sioux. According to their mythic traditions, many winters ago two Lakota braves were out hunting when "they saw in the distance something coming towards them in a very strange and wonderful manner." The strange and wonderful "something" (to emphasize Van der Leeuw's phrase) turned out to be a very beautiful woman bringing them the sacred pipe. When she arrived at the tribal village and met the chief and the elders, she presented her gift, exorting "Behold this and always love it." She produced the pipe miraculously and told how each intricate part of its structure and decoration represented some part of the cosmos where the Sioux dwelled. She announced that this object of stone and wood is a sacred force that will insure the continuity of tribal existence. The visitation ended when the sacred woman stated:

> Behold what you see. Behold this pipe. Always remember how sacred it is, and treat it as such, for it will take you to the end. Remember, in me there are four ages. I am leaving now, but I shall look back upon your people in every age and at the end I shall return.

The "wakan" or sacred woman walks away, turning three times into a buffalo of different colors.[18]

This story initiates the account of the seven rites of the Sioux and is a brilliant example of hierophany. All of the sacred rites revolve around the sacred pipe which *appeared* to the tribe through the coming of the sacred woman who showed them their destiny. She repeatedly orders them, "Behold, Behold," alerting them to this hierophany, this gift from a sacred being.

A similar revelation gave birth to the religion of Islam. W. Montgomery Watt's chapter, "The Call of Prophethood" describes the events surrounding the origins of this great religion. He also notes that Muhammad, the founder of Islam, was previously a caravan agent who experienced periods of doubt and despair.

> On one of the barren rocky hills in the neighborhood there was a cave where he sometimes went for several nights at a time to be alone and to pray and meditate. During these solitary vigils he began to have strange experiences. First of all there were vivid dreams or visions. Two in particular stood out as being of special significance. In the first visitation there appeared to him a glorious Being standing erect high up in the sky near the horizon; then this strong and mighty One moved down towards him until he was only two bow-shots or less from him, and communicated to him a revelation, that is, some passage of the Quran.

This mighty being interrupts Muhammad in his moments of meditation and commands him to become his spokesman. The relevant passage reads:

> Recite
> In the Name of thy Lord, who created—
> Created man from a blood clot.[19]

One tradition tells that Muhammad resisted this strange appearance, protesting his inability to change his life, and the Being began to choke him to death in order to impress him with the reality of his situation. Again, we have an example of a powerful manifestation of a sacred reality to a human being who is impressed, opposed to and eventually overcome by the other reality. In the Sioux example, the gift of the sacred pipe embodied the reality. In the Muslim case, the gift of the sacred book, the Qur'an, and the prophethood of Muhammad contained the reality.

The hierophany of the Virgin of Guadalupe caused one of the turning points of Mexican history. According to Mexican traditions, in 1531 a Christianized Indian was walking near the hill of Tepeyac, which had been the site of the Aztec shrine to the mother goddess, when he heard beautiful music.[20] As he sought out the source of this melody, a lovely lady speaking in Nahautl appeared to him. Astounded by this glimmering figure, he listened as she commanded him to visit the palace of the archbishop of Mexico at Tlatelolco and tell him that the Virgin Mary, "Mother of the true God through whom one lives," wishes a sacred shrine to be built at the site of the apparition so she "can show and give forth all my love, compassion, help, and defense to all the inhabitants of this land . . . to hear their lamentation, and remedy their miseries, pain and sufferings." The archbishop was not persuaded by this story from an Indian commoner. Then the Virgin displayed her powers and intentions more directly. She led Juan Diego to a site where roses were blooming out of season and commanded him to arrange them in a cloak. As Juan Diego unfolded his cloak in the presence of the archbishop, the roses fell to the ground and the image of the Virgin appeared on the cloak. The Mexican people came to life through this event and the site became the new spiritual center of colonial Mexico.[21]

In each of these three examples human beings claim that some sacred being came into their lives and manifested "highly exceptional and extremely impressive Otherness," bestowing on their lives sacred values, meanings, and blessings. And the objects through which the manifestations took place became "numinous centers" in their new world. Eliade has written extensively about the "axis mundi." By axis mundi, he means a point in the environment that becomes the "center" of the verticle and horizontal cosmos as a result of a hierophany. The place or object is appreciated as the point of communication between the human community and the world of the gods.

The Sacred Human

In the history of religions we find endless accounts of sacred specialists. These are individuals who have developed a profound knowledge of the sacred realities which guide their particular communities. They have also acquired sophisticated and ecstatic techniques that enable them to confront, utilize and even evoke spiritual forces. This knowledge is usually transmitted to them by older sacred specialists, religious *virtuosos*, who were their teachers during a period of suffering and growth. Such a pattern of transmission is referred to in the case of Ultima who tells Antonio on her deathbed:

> "I was taught my life's work by a wise old man, a good man (referred to elsewhere as "el hombre volador"). He gave me the owl and said the owl was my spirit, bond to the time and the harmony of the universe. . . . My work was to do good . . . I was to heal the sick and show them the path of goodness. But I was not to interfere with the destiny of any man" (p. 247).

The most archaic sacred specialists we know were shamans. I am suggesting here, not that Ultima and Antonio are shamans, but that their relationship reflects some characteristics of the initiation scenario typical of shamanic ecstasy. In this regard we are witnessing in Anaya's novel a Chicano variation of an archaic pattern of spiritual creativity; what I would call the lyrics of Chicano spirituality.

The pattern of shamanic ecstasy includes (a) sensitive and troubled individuals who (b) receive sacred knowledge through fantastic dreams and visions plus formal instructions under the (c) guidance of a great shaman (la Grande) during which the initiate (d) forms relationships with helping spirits, usually in the form of animals, which enable the seeker to (e) grasp a deep truth and techniques that enable him to renew contact with that wisdom and (f) obtain the powers to heal varieties of sickness and attack and kill enemies.

This pattern of initiation usually involves a great ordeal, sometimes experienced during a sickness which takes the novice close to death, and introduces him to the terrors of finitude and spiritual forces. During this ordeal, which often includes ecstatic dreams, the hero is tested. He is symbolically killed and reborn into the vocation of singer, healer, and poet. This ordeal involves face to face encounters with terrible monsters, scenarios of chaos that may include visualizing the dismemberment and destruction of one's own body, community and cosmos. For instance, in some shamanic ecstasies, the would-be sorcerer is confronted with his own skeleton, completely stripped of skin and hair and organs.[22] This total crisis emerges into a new integration of the self and the acquisition of sacred knowledge which is to be used to benefit the community. This is the meaning and purpose of much religious ecstasy. The novel reflects some of these characteristics.

Antonio's Sacred Landscape

The setting for Antonio's growth is a magical landscape overflowing with manifestations of religious power. In the hero's name and the qualities attributed to his name are reflected the Chicano respect for powerful earthly and heavenly places. He is Luna y Márez, moon and sea. Anaya's portrayal of these names show that the Chicanos in the story do not regard them as simple, natural objects but as powers that influence the boy's life from birth. From one side he descends from the people of the "earthly sea," "people who hold the wind as brother," and his character is full of the spirits of this sea. From the other side he carries the blood and the spirits of the people of El Puerto who are "steady, settled," and "hold the earth as brother." The influence of these realities is vividly portrayed in his first dream where he flies (like a shaman) back to the place and time of his birth. There he witnesses a struggle almost to the death of relatives from both sides of his family who wish to take the afterbirth and bury it in the llano or in the valley. A vigorous argument develops, and at the critical moment when death is about to appear, Ultima cries, "Cease . . . I pulled this baby into the light of life, so I will bury the afterbirth and cord that once linked him to eternity. Only I will know his destiny" (p. 6).

Throughout the novel this conflict charges the boy's waking and dreaming life while the secret of his destiny obsesses him. Ultima, in another dream, hints to him the solution to his agony, caused by the struggle of these forces. He dreams of another argument, this time between his mother, who descends to a lake on the glowing moon, and his father, who stands on a corpse strewn shore. They argue about his nature and destiny causing an excruciating pain to sear through his body while he sees the forces of doom descend upon him. Again, Ultima appears and cries:

> Cease . . . the sweet water of the moon which falls as rain is the same water that gathers into rivers and flows to fill the seas. Without the waters of the moon to replenish the oceans there would be no oceans. And the same salt waters of the oceans are drawn by the sun to the heavens, and in turn becomes again the waters of the moon. . . . The waters are one, You (Antonio) have been seeing only parts.

97

This stunning dream scenario shows the antagonistic relationship of the powers in his life and hints at the great message of his initiation.

Sacred space appears again in the scenes near the river. The river flowing through Antonio's world is not just a water source, but a presence, a manifestation of some "other" power. In his dreams a "goddess," la llorona, guards the river. On one occasion the "great presence of the river" evokes his curiosity about his destiny. Ultima and Antonio are walking by the river which was

> silent and brooding. The presence was watching over us. . . . "Ultima," I asked, "why are they (the Lunas) so strange and quiet? And why are my father's people so loud and wild?" She answered, "It is the blood of the Lunas to be quiet, for only a quiet man can learn the secrets of the earth that are necessary for planting . . . they are quiet like the moon—And it is the blood of the Márez to be wild, like the ocean from which they take their name, and the spaces of the llano that have become their home."

They sat in silence, pondering these relationships, and the river manifested itself to them:

The silence spoke, not with harsh sounds, but softly to the rhythm of our blood. "What is it?" I asked, for I was still afraid. "It is the presence of the river" Ultima answered. I held my breath and looked at the giant, gnarled cottonwood trees that surrounded us. Somewhere a bird cried, and up on the hill the tinkling sound of a cowbell rang. The presence was immense, lifeless, yet throbbing with its secret message. "Can it speak" I asked and drew closer to Ultima, "If you listen carefully" she whispered. . . . (p. 38).

There are many similar power spots in Antonio's world; the bend in the river is an evil place, the Juniper tree which is the scene of a murder, and a forked Juniper under which Ultima's owl is buried. During the curing of the Tellez house, Ultima tells the adults to let Antonio go and gather branches from a Juniper tree "Let Tony cut it, he understands the power in the tree." And, of course, Ultima's owl, which is her spirit, is a classic spiritual helper found throughout the shamanic life style. But, our attention is drawn to the amazing figure of the Golden Carp. Antonio's companion Cico takes him to the secret spot where the Golden Carp appears. The scene exudes the quality of mystery and sacrality that appear in the form of this amazing animal. The text bustles with power.

> We sat for a long time, waiting for the golden carp. It was very pleasant to sit in the warm sunshine and watch the pure waters drift by. . . . Then the golden carp came. Cico pointed and I turned to where the stream came out of the dark grotto of overhanging tree branches. At first I thought I must be dreaming. I had expected to see a carp the size of a river carp. . . . I rubbed my eyes and watched in astonishment.
> "Behold the golden carp, Lord of the waters—" I turned and saw Cico standing; his spear held across his chest as if in acknowledgement of the presence of a ruler.
> The huge, beautiful form glided through the blue waters. I could not believe its size. It was bigger than me! And bright orange! The sunlight glistened off his golden scales.

> He glided down the creek with a couple of smaller carp following.
> "The golden carp," I whispered in awe. I could not have been more entranced if I had seen the Virgin, or God Himself. The golden carp had seen me.... I could have reached out into the water and touched the holy fish.... I felt my body trembling as I saw the bright golden form disappear. I know I had witnessed a miraculous thing, the appearance of a pagan god, a thing as miraculous as the curing of my uncle Lucas. And I thought the power of God failed where Ultima's worked. And then a sudden illumination of beauty and understanding flashed through my mind. This is what I had expected God to do at my first holy communion. If God was witness to my beholding of the golden carp then I had sinned. I clasped my hands and was about to pray to the heavens when the waters of the pond exploded (pp. 104-105).

In a sense this episode says it all. The boys are awestruck by the appearance of a "holy fish" whose coming is announced as was the buffalo woman announced to the Sioux—"Behold, the golden carp." The impact is deep, reverent and frightening; both attracting and repulsing the young Antonio. His picture of heavenly beings is garbled and intensified by the appearance of a "miraculous thing." Sacrality has appeared to him in his blood, in the river that flows by his town, and in the golden carp that is lord of the waters.

Initiation into Sacred Knowledge: Death and Rebirth

To restate my description of the sacred human, power manifests itself to a human being who acquires insight into and techniques to deal with the sacred. This individual, touched deeply by sacred forces, passes through an initiatory process under the guidance of a religious virtuoso. He may participate so directly in the world of the sacred that he comes to represent a living hierophany. The shamanic paradigm outlined earlier illustrates the religious paradigm for the Chicano experience.

Ultima appears, as her name suggests, to be completely in touch with the ultimate powers of the universe. She can heal and apparently kill through the use of her magical force. A dynamic relationship exists between the curandera and Antonio and the initiatory process, which runs throughout Antonio's life. In the initiation process Antonio becomes a new person; he acquires new and special knowledge of not only Ultima and the forces of his world, but of himself. This new knowledge (superior to the knowledge of his family's members) emerges through powerful personal experiences highlighted by religious ecstasies. As in shamanic or archaic mystical initiations, Antonio is taught wisdom through (a) transmission of information about herbs, geneology, and myths, (b) dream messages which reveal the world of spirits and cosmic forces that dismember and reintegrate him and his world, and (c) direct encounters with spirits while working as Ultima's helper and apprentice. In the last two types of instruction, a valuable lesson is forced into his consciousness. This lesson, which reflects the pattern of spiritual death and rebirth, is revealed in magnificent dream and waking scenarios of lyric and ecstatic quality.

The novel begins with Ultima's appearance in Antonio's life. Her arrival at the Márez home is not just another important event in his life, but a new beginning, a birth of awareness. The text reads,

> When she came the beauty of the llano unfolds before my eyes, and the gurgling waters of the river sang to the hum of the turning earth. The magical time of childhood stood still, and the pulse of the living earth pressed its mystery into my living blood. She took my hand and the silent magic powers she possessed made beauty from the raw, sun baked llano, the green river valley, and the blue bowl which was the white sun's home. My bare feet felt the throbbing earth and my body trembled with excitement. Time stood still, and it shared with me all that had been, and all that was to come. . . .
> Let me begin at the beginning. I do not mean the beginning that was in my dreams and the stories they whispered

to me about my birth, and the people of my father and mother, and my three brothers,—but the beginning that came with Ultima (p. 7).

Ultima's arrival opened up the magical powers of his environment, the beauty of the land, the songs of the river, the mystery of the earth, and the magical force within a human being. His life trembles at her presence and he is reborn. The trembling is a physical reaction to Ultima's presence; this is seen in the first encounter between the two.

> I looked up into her clear brown eyes and shivered. Her face was old and wrinkled, but her eyes were clear and sparkling, like the eyes of a young child.
> "Antonio" she smiled. She took my hand and I felt the power of a whirlwind sweep around me. Her eyes swept the surrounding hills and through them I saw for the first time the wild beauty of our hills and the magic of the green river. My nostrils quivered as I felt the song of the mockingbirds and the drone of the grasshoppers mingle with the pulse of the earth. The four directions of the llano met in me and the white sun shone on my soul. The granules of sand at my feet and the sun and sky above me seemed to dissolve into one strange, complete being (p. 11).

The boy experiences himself as a trembling center of some new power. The four winds meet in him, the sounds of the world fill his being, and his depths are warmed by the sun. The intimation that Ultima is related to his whole being is communicated to him in his first dream, already discussed, where Ultima announces her secret knowledge of his destiny.

Antonio is allowed to address her by her name, "Ultima," while the others are symbolically separated from her by the use of "Grande." Ultima reciprocates this familiarity when she announces, "I knew there would be something between us." Indeed, it is a "powerful something" which quickly takes on the form of instruction and a secret alliance between the two. As the story progresses, Ultima manifests her powers and knowledge to him in nocturnal and daylight encounters.

Soon after her arrival, Antonio witnesses the midnight killing of Lupito by the river, and he rushes home in terror ("the horror of darkness"), cutting and bruising himself along the way. Heartened by the watchful presence of Ultima's owl, the boy arrives home to find Ultima waiting for him and knowing what he has witnessed. She gives him her potion which miraculously heals his wounds during the night and makes him realize, "There was a strange power in Ultima's medicine." As time passes, Antonio becomes aware that these "strange powers" penetrate deeper than his cuts and bruises and that he is "growing up and changing" through the magic of Ultima. This change and growth intensifies through the teachings of Ultima. The great curandera takes Antonio on her hunts for herbs and transmits her knowledge to him, carefully and systematically. He learns the details of the medicinal plants, to imitate her walk, to acknowledge the spirits that inhabit the plants. He feels that "my soul grew under her careful guidance."

> Ultima and I continued to search for plants and roots in the hills. I felt more attached to Ultima than to my own mother. Ultima told me the stories and legends of my ancestors. From her I learned the glory and the tragedy of the history of my people, and I came to understand how that history stirred in my blood.
> I spent most of the long summer evenings in her room. We talked, stored the dry herbs, or played cards (p. 115).

Ultima shows him the twisted dolls on her shelf, which represent her magical combat with the Trementina family, and he begins to realize the dangers involved in her way of life. She gives him her scapular full of "helpful herbs," something she has carried since childhood. Now, he has become part of the terrible combat of spiritual forces. Later, this sacred object protects him from Tenorio's attempt to kill him.

Antonio's initiation into the world of magical regeneration develops dramatically in two episodes: the curing of his uncle Lucas and the magnificent dream of the apocalypse of the world. Although this initiation has numerous other stages, these two events are outstanding. In the first event, Antonio is put through a cycle of sickness and healing as he assists Ultima with a cure. In the second, he witnesses the decay, destruction and regeneration of the earth in his dream. Both give him messages about the ultimate meaning of life.

During the healing of Lucas, a three day ordeal, Antonio acts as a spiritual conduit. Earlier, when Ultima accepted the challenge to cure Antonio's uncle, Ultima announces that she needs a helper and that it is "necessary" for Antonio to face the ordeal ahead with her. He accepts without fear for his life or reputation. Ultima states that she will have to "work the magic beyond evil, the magic that endures forever," for "forty dollars to cheat la muerte." Next, the two spiritual warriors prepare the room where this cure will take place. Outside, Ultima's owl guards them by attacking the barking hungry coyotes, spiritual helpers of the Trementina sisters. As the curing proceeds, Antonio, exhausted, falls into a trance and becomes a double of his bewitched uncle. Captured in a "deep stupor," he is unable to take his eyes off his uncle.

> I was aware of what happened in the room but my senses did not seem to respond to commands. Instead I remained in that waking dream. I saw Ultima make some medicine for my uncle, and when she forced it down his throat and his face showed pain, my body too felt pain. I could almost taste the oily hot liquid. I saw his convulsion and my body too was seized with aching cramps. I felt my body wet with sweat. I tried to call to Ultima but there was no voice, I tried to move but there was no movement. I suffered the spasm of pain my uncle suffered and these alternated with feelings of elation and power. . . . I felt that somehow we were going through the same cure . . . He was across the room from me, but our bodies did not seem separated by the distance. We dissolved into each other, and we shared a common struggle against the evil within, which fought to repulse Ultima's magic (pp. 92-93).

This merging of identities marks his full participation in the magical combat. The combat culminates when Antonio drinks the sacred blue atole and vomits up a poisonous green bile. Almost immediately, Lucas emits a horrible series of screams, and through a contorted face, he vomits the evil green bile and a huge ball of hair, "hot and steaming and wiggling like live snakes." Antonio has experienced a terrible familiarity with death and a swooning reprieve. But afterward, he is still only partially aware of the meaning of this overwhelming event. Much later in a dream, the Trementina sisters tell him what his role was. In a scene of diabolic hullabaloo, the sisters dance around him and cry, "Hie, Hie, through your body went the spell that cured Lucas, and your name lent strength to the curse that took one of us from the service of our Master. We will have our vengeance on you" (p. 166).

In this dream the religious pattern of decay, destruction, dismemberment and regeneration is most vividly communicated to Antonio. The dream overflows with images of cosmic forces, human monsters, murder, and rebirth. It is like a Hieronymus Bosch painting turned into sound and motion. I cannot begin to interpret the entire dream but will merely comment on four phases which may represent stages in the ecstatic acquisition of knowledge.

(1) After Antonio witnesses the murder of Narciso under the Juniper tree, he feels himself drowning in the "awful power" of his "ocean of pesadilla." The nightmare's first sequence represents his spiritual crises. He enters into a pleading, screaming argument with God about forgiveness for his brother and Narciso, and punishment for Tenorio. He is told by a "roaring" God that God's power cannot be reduced to his "personal whims" and that God will forgive even Tenorio, though he is a murderer. Antonio feels utterly lost and sinful.

(2) In his nightmare, Antonio encounters the Trementina sisters, who have cast an evil spell on the world. Following this Antonio sees himself "withering away." "A long, dark night came upon me in which I sought the face of God, but I

could not find Him . . . In front of the dark doors of Purgatory, *my bleached bones were laid to rest.*" This image of reduction to his bones represents, in religious terms, the disintegration of one's being.

(3) Next, his home is set afire and his family burned to death. His cosmos is disintegrating. Ultima's owl is killed, and the curandera, now powerless, is beheaded by a mob who drinks and bathes in her blood before driving a stake through her heart and burning her. The golden carp is cooked in the fires of Ultima's ashes and eaten. Then the entire earth crumbles.

> There was a thundering of the earth and a great rift opened. The church building crumbled, and the school collapsed into dust and the whole town disappeared in the chasm. A great cry went up from the people as they saw crashing tumultous waters fill the dark hole.

The disintegration of life continues as

> the people looked upon each other and they saw their skin rot and fall off. Shrieks of pain and agony filled the air . . . the walking dead buried the sleeping dead . . . disease and filth throughout. In the end no one was left.

Here we have a Chicano apocalypse in which the hero is reduced to bones, the curandera of goodness ripped apart and cremated, the divine fish skinned and eaten, and the earth transformed into a black hole! It is the ultimate "melt down"! It is a return to the cosmic womb of nothingness.

(4) But nothingness in religious terms is also the potential source of new life. Out of nothingness comes regenerative powers. And in the shamanic imagination, new life cannot emerge unless there has been a death. And so the dream continues to carry us into the completeness of Ultima's teachings and religious wisdom.

> Evening settled over the land and the waters. The stars came out and glittered in the dark sky. In the lake, the

golden carp appeared. His beautiful body glittered in the moonlight. He had been witness to everything that happened, and he decided that everyone should survive, but in a new form. He opened his huge mouth and swallowed everything, everything there was, good and evil. Then he swam into the blue velvet of the night, glittering as he rose towards the stars. The moon smiled on him and guided him, and his golden body burned with such beautiful brilliance that he became a new sun in the heavens. A new sun to shine its good light upon a new earth (p. 116-67)

This dramatic nightmare carries, at the dream ecstasy level, a heightened sense of the message that comes to Antonio toward the end when he is working in El Puerto. He has seen more of Ultima's curing power, experienced the failure of holy communion, witnessed the death of his companion, Florence. The secret message of Ultima's teachings and his dreams comes to the consciousness level. The message states plainly and directly the pattern of death and rebirth, decay and regeneration. During a memorable conversation with his father he thinks,

> Take the llano and the river valley, the moon and the sea God and the golden carp—and make something new, I said to myself. That is what Ultima meant by building strength from life. "Papa," I asked, "can a new religion be made?" And then later,

> The rest of the summer was good for me, good in the sense that I was filled with its richness and I made strength from everything that had happened to me, so that in the end, the final tragedy could not defeat me. And that is what Ultima tried to teach me, that the tragic consequences of life can be overcome by the magical strength that resides in the human heart (p. 237).

Antonio articulates, at the level of his waking life, the knowledge that the integration of his diverse and conflicting elements and the cultivation of sacred forces within a human being can lead to a life full of blessings. This was the gift of Ultima and it is a form of religious wisdom.

In this research I have demonstrated how the Chicano classic, *Bless Me, Ultima*, contains two general religious patterns which are important in the understanding of Chicano Experience. These patterns are the sacrality of the landscape and the shamanic relationship between Antonio and Ultima. My approach as an historian of religions led me to place this discussion within the scope of the methods and discoveries of the comparative study of religions. This leads us away from viewing Chicano life from within the norms of Christian ethics and experience. It allows us to consider the specific character of Chicano experience and imagination within a general understanding of religious creativity. This creativity is similar to what Mircea Eliade calls an "archaic consciousness," a consciousness which is concerned with the reintegration of primordial forces of the land and the magic of human consciousness. I hope this approach to the novel can enrich our perspective for the study of religious dimensions in Chicano culture.

Notes

1. Rudolfo A. Anaya, *Bless Me, Ultima* (Berkeley, California: Quinto Sol Publications, 1972). This and subsequent quotations from *Bless Me, Ultima* are from this edition.
2. History of Religions is an outgrowth of the attempts to establish a *Religionswissenschaft* or science of religion in a number of European universities in the nineteenth century. For a short history of this movement and the present state of the art, see Charles H. Long, "The History of the History of Religions," *A Reader's Guide to the Great Religions*, ed. Charles J. Adams. As Joachim Wach noted concerning this discipline, "The Term 'science of religion' (Religionswissenschaft) was used to denote the emancipation of the new discipline from philosophy of religion and especially theology." See *The Comparative Study of Religions* (New York: Columbia University Press, 1958), p. 3.
3. This essay is intended as an introduction of a complex approach to understanding human culture. Therefore, I am not presenting a full picture of the methods utilized by the historian of religions. The emphasis here is placed on the phenomenological approach to religious data, as articulated

by Gerardus Van der Leeuw and Mircea Eliade. Most historians of religions are also concerned with the history of religious manifestations and elements; the context in which religions appear, the uses made by elites and folk communities, the development and degradation of religious symbols and myths, the interaction between the sacred and all other dimensions of a society. Long articulates the underlying methodological concern that I have attempted to reflect. Long writes in his article, "Primitive Religion," *A Reader's Guide to the Great Religions*, ed. Charles J. Adams,

> Though Van der Leeuw's work is permeated by a general theory of "religious dynamism," he does relate every mode of the religious consciousness and behavior to an objective form of the world, whether this form be a structure of nature or of human community. This kind of transition is completed in the work of Mircea Eliade. In a certain sense Eliade moves towards the objectivity and neo-positivism of Levi-Strauss, but instead of understanding the human consciousness as a purely intellectual structure, Eliade tends to see human consciousness as a locus for the intellectual and imaginative ordering of the world (p. 11).

4. A succinct statement of this approach appears in Joseph M. Kitagawa's Centennial article where he notes, ". . . I am conscious of the two important foci of the discipline of History of Religions, namely, the unity and continuity of the religious experience of man on the one hand, and the integrity and autonomous character of particular religious traditions, on the other," in "One Hundredth Anniversary Celebration," *The Criterion* (Fall 1969), p. 14.

5. Loren Eiseley, *The Unexpected Universe* (New York: Harcourt Brace Jovanovich, Inc., 1969), p. 172.

6. See such important works concerning this problem as Emanuel Sarkisyanz, *Buddhist Backgrounds of the Burmese Revolution* (The Hague: Martinus Nijhoff, 1965); Michael Mendelson, *Samgha and State* (Ithaca: Cornell University Press, 1975); and Htin Aung, trans., *Burmese Monk's Tales* (New York: Columbia University Press, 1966).

7. Paul Radin, *The Trickster, A Study in American Indian Mythology* (New York: Schocken Press, 1973).

8. A. E. Jensen, *Myth and Cult Among Primitive Peoples* (Chicago: University of Chicago Press, 1963).

9. Mircea Eliade, *Shamanism, Archaic Techniques in Ecstasy* (Bollingen Foundation, 1964).

10. Mircea Eliade, *The Myth of the Eternal Return* (New York: Pantheon Books, 1959); and the outstanding comparative work by Paul Wheatley, *The Pivot of the Four Quarters, A Preliminary Enquiry Into the Origins and Character of the Ancient Chinese City* (Chicago: Aldine Press, 1971).

11. Walter Krickeberg, *Las Antiguas Culturas Mexicanas* (México: Fondo de Cultura Económica, 1964).

12. Kenelm Burridge, *Mambu* (New York: Harper and Row, 1970); and Peter Worsley, *The Trumpet Shall Sound* (New York: Schocken Books, 1970).

13. Mircea Eliade, *The Quest* (Chicago: University of Chicago Press, 1969).

14. Gerardus Van der Leeuw, *Religion in Essence and Manifestation* (New York: Harper and Row, 1963), p. 23.

15. Eliade, *The Quest*, p. 7.

16. Eliade's description of SACRED is as follows: "... the sacred is equivalent to a power, and, in the last analysis, to reality. The sacred is saturated with *being*. Sacred power means reality and at the same time enduringness and efficacy." *The Sacred and Profane* (New York: Harcourt, Brace, and World, 1959).

17. For an exhausting analysis of sacred places see Mircea Eliade, *Patterns in Comparative Religions* (New York: Meridian Books, 1972).

18. Joseph Epes Brown, *The Sacred Pipe* (New York: Penguin Books, 1977). Concerning the term "wakan," Joseph Brown writes, "Throughout this work I shall translate the Lakota word wakan as 'holy' or 'sacred' rather than as 'power' or 'powerful' as used by some ethnologists. The latter term may be a true translation, yet it is not really complete, for with the Sioux, and with all traditional peoples in general, the 'power' (really the sacredness) of a being or a thing is in proportion to its nearness to its prototype; or better, it is in proportion to the ability of the object or act to reflect most directly the principle or principles which are in Wakan-Tanka, the Great Spirit, who is One" (pp. 3-4).

19. W. Montgomery Watt, *Muhammad, Prophet and Statesman* (New York: Oxford University Press, 1976), p. 19.

20. I am utilizing the account of Father Virgilio Elizondo, "Our Lady of Guadalupe as a Cultural Symbol: The Power of the Powerless," in *Concilium*, 1977.

21. For a brilliant account of the impact of this tradition on Mexican National consciousness, see Jacques La Faye, *Quetzalcoatl and Guadalupe: The Origin of Mexican National Consciousness* (Chicago: University of Chicago Press, 1975).

The persistence of this tradition was made vividly clear to me one day in the summer of 1973 in Pilsen, the largest Chicano barrio in Chicago, where I saw a sign painter with a tattoo of the Virgin covering his *entire back*.

22. For accounts of this kind of ecstasy experienced in many cultures, see especially the chapter "Initiatory Sicknesses and Dreams," in Eliade's *Shamanism*, pp. 33-66.

Arguments for Lay Participation in Philadelphia Catholicism, 1820-1829

By Patrick Carey*

A history of American Catholicism that incorporates the role of the laity in its formation has yet to be written. When such a history is written the complicated troubles of trusteeism will have to be included and the analysis will have to proceed from the lay as well as the clerical perspectives. When the historian considers trusteeism, moreover, he or she will have to examine the dissensions between the laity and the clergy of St. Mary's congregation in Philadelphia between 1820 and 1829. The Philadelphia conflicts are important because the participants on both sides of the debates saw themselves as national spokesmen for competing definitions of American Catholicism: furthermore, the ideological issues are more clearly articulated here than in any other urban conflict.

When viewed from St. Mary's trustees' perspectives, this paper argues, trusteeism must be interpreted as an attempt to create an American national church—one identified with American republicanism, incorporating lay and clerical participation in local and national ecclesiastical administration, thereby establishing a constitutional balance of powers within church government. Yet, this proposed national church would be loyal to the Roman papacy in matters of doctrine and ecclesiastical communion. Such a plan to uncover the republican side of Catholicism corresponded to numerous contemporaneous American Protestant and Catholic attempts to reconcile religious with republican ideologies and institutions.[1]

This study focuses upon the trustees' side of the debates, describing their plan for a national Catholic Church as they delineated it in pamphlets, letters and newspaper articles. Historians of American Catholicism have rarely analyzed the reasoning behind the lay and clerical trustees' proposal.[2] To fill in this historical gap is the object of the present examination. To accomplish this task, the paper outlines, first, the trustees' views of adaptation; second, their attempt to implement their views by negotiating a concordat with Rome; and, third, their method for accommodating the European Catholic Church to American republicanism by having the concordat acknowledge the laity's right of patronage.

ADAPTATION

American Catholics, in the trustees' opinion, lived in a new age which demanded a new style of life and government in the church as in the state.

---

*Theology Department, Marquette University, Milwaukee, Wisconsin.

The trustees saw the essential issue between the clergy and themselves as a question of conflicting perceptions of the right mode for adapting European Catholicism to American republican ways. The trustees argued that the ecclesiastical government and discipline of the European Catholic Church had to be reformed to meet the demands and consciousness of the new political age of republicanism and voluntaryism. The anti-trustees countered that to do so would be tantamount to a destruction of Catholic identity. The trustees admitted that they were not competent to understand the subtleties of ecclesiastical law, but they insisted that in matters of discipline and government the "wisdom of the church has always varied to suit the times and circumstances, and which we have every right to insist upon being adapted to our peculiar situation; for this is the real question at issue."[3]

Within the context of the essential issue of adaptation, two problems, in particular, disturbed the trustees: the European clerics' understanding and exercise of ecclesiastical authority and their perception of lay and clerical participation in the life and government of the church. The European clergy had not adapted themselves, in the trustees' view, to American sensitivities in both these regards. This failure produced the conflicts. The trustees believed, in the words of one of their supporters, Mathew Carey, that bishops who had just arrived from Ireland and Europe exercised an "extravagantly high-handed authority" over their people and their people suffered from their own "servile submission." He maintained that American Catholics "will never submit to the regime in civil or ecclesiastical affairs that prevails in Europe."[4] Americans, nonetheless, respected authority, but only reasonable authority. William Hogan, a clerical trustee, outlined this concept of authority for Bishop John England of Charleston:

> learn that laymen are not your inferiors in society, nor perhaps in the order of christianity, although not considered so in the Hierarchy—learn that talents and elevated stations, unless supported by virtue and a strict regard for the rights of others, so far from conferring honour on him who possesses them, only render him an object of contempt.[5]

Two opposing conceptions of participation in the life and government of the American church also contributed to the hostilities. The trustees saw themselves as administrators of the temporal life of the church; that included not only the management of temporalities, but also a participation in the selection of their pastors and bishops. The anti-Trustees viewed the hierarchy as the principal managers of the temporalities and denied that the laity had any right to nominate their priests or bishops.

As a result of the clerics' failures to understand or even sympathize with the American way of life, the trustees protested, neither the French bishops nor the newly-arrived Irish bishops could direct a proper accommodation of

Catholicism to the democratic age. This also meant that episcopal reports to Rome could not adequately represent the state of the church in the nation.[6] Thus, the trustees asserted that they needed a "second Carroll" who as a native of the land not only knew but loved and respected the institutions of the country.[7] The bishops in the United States were acquainted with the Catholic Church in Europe, England or Ireland, but, as Mathew Carey put it, the circumstances of Catholicism in those countries "does not exactly quadrate with the practice in this country." On the Continent, he continued, civil authority supported ecclesiastical; in England and Ireland, "The horrible oppression and tyranny which the Catholics have groaned [sic] for ages, have produced a subservience of the laity to the clergy, which operates as effectively as the dread of the civil authority does on the continent." This was not the condition of Catholicism in the United States.

> A different order of things prevails in this country . . . I merely state the fact of the extreme difference. The hierarchy here has no such resources. The extreme freedom of our civil institutions has produced a corresponding independent spirit respecting our church affairs, to which sound sense will never fail to pay attention, and which it would be a manifest impropriety to dispise or attempt to control by harsh or violent measures. The opinions and wishes of the people require to be consulted to a degree unknown in Europe.[8]

The new spirit in the United States did not mean that ecclesiastical authority was destroyed. It meant, however, that all authority must be exercised under an acknowledged law. The experience of more than one hundred years in America showed, Carey asserted, that freedom-loving citizens have respected and esteemed clerical authority when it had been properly exercised.[89]

For Carey, as for the Philadelphia trustees, the "different order of things" demanded a respect for individual rights and a consultation with the will of the people in the exercise of ecclesiastical government. Thadeus O'Meally, another of the clerical trustees, coached the bishops of the United States to be more sensitive to the political maxims of the country. One of the most cherished of those maxims "the voice of the people is the voice of God" must be respected even in ecclesiastical affairs. "Is it wise," he asked, "is it prudent, that those whose voice is *law* in everything else, should be made to feel, that *in that very thing*, in which they are most deeply interested, they have *no voice at all*."[10]

According to the trustees, the European Catholic Church could adopt American ways and still remain Catholic. The Catholic Church could, for example, do as the Protestant Episcopal Church had done in organizing itself in this new country. While accommodating its form of government to the republican forms of government, it had "maintained a fraternal, but not a filial relation to the Church of England." It made some alterations in non-essentials, but retained all the essentials of communion. The Episcopalians, for example, held conventions of clergy and laity in governing their church here. In England, the church held convocations for the clergy only.[11] The American Catholic Church could do something analogous in adapting itself to the sensitivities and institutions here.

The Philadelphia trustees saw themselves as leaders of the American Catholic communities in applying political experiences to ecclesiastical affairs. They believed they were in the forefront of a movement to create an American church that was republican as well as Catholic. Philadelphia was the scene of political independence; they also wanted to see it become the showplace of Catholic freedoms.

> Philadelphia has been the theatre of those sublime moral movements which have made you, as *Americans*, independent. Let it also originate those movements whose result will be to make you independent as *Catholics*. I do not ask you, nor do I wish you to disclaim or discard the spiritual supremacy of the Apostolic See-retain it by all means—but retain it as the bond of a federal union, not as the yoke of a servile dependency.[12]

While calling for a change in the mode of exercising ecclesiastical authority and an incorporation of lay participation in church government, the trustees were aware that they were advocating a new type of Catholic Church for the United States. They did not consider themselves innovators, however. They believed their proposals were in conformity with ancient Catholic traditions. They protested that "their only object is, and ever has been, to preserve the doctrine of that Church in its primitive purity, and to sustain their rights as citizens of this country, against the increasing pretensions and despotism of a few foreigners."[13] They wanted to be viewed as loyal Catholics; but they also wanted to be perceived as democrats in their ecclesiastical as well as political affairs.

The trustees also knew that in calling for the creation of a national church they were rejecting the status-quo designation of the American church as a "missionary church."[14] They vehemently opposed the implications of this terminology and their subjection to the authority of Roman Congregation of Propaganda Fide. That Roman congregation, they aserted, was originally established for the "propagation of the catholic religion in those countries where the gospels were unknown." They were insulted by the implications of such a purpose in the United States.

> We are, therefore, viewed in the same light as the nation of Cherokees or Choctaws, or the natives of the coast of Africa—our

country is termed a missionary colony, and for want of a proper understanding with our Holy Father, we are subjected to receive foreigners of every class and description, to direct and command us, as if we were incapable of understanding our religion, or protecting our own property.[15]

Propaganda, they maintained, did not adequately understand the American way of life and therefore could not govern the American church with wisdom.[16] This judgment was supported, they believed, by Propaganda's most recent "ill-advised" appointments to the American episcopacy (referring, in particular, to their bishop Henry Conwell). Thus, the need for a national church was based upon the ancient Christian practices of accommodation in new countries, the current necessity of relating Catholicism and American republicanism, and the past and present failures of Propaganda to govern the American church with wise appointments to the episcopacy.

A Concordat

The one great need in the American Catholic Church was for some king of constitutionally defined system that would respect the rights and duties of all in the Catholic Community. In 1821, the Philadelphia trustees, therefore, called upon American Catholics

to adapt some measures, by which a uniform system may be established for the future regulation of our churches; the propagation of our Holy faith, by the nomination and selection of proper pastors from our own citizens; from whom alone ought to be chosen our bishops, without our being compelled to depend on persons sent to us from abroad, who have uniformly shown themselves hostile to our institutions, and completely ignorant of our country; in fine, for the adoption of such measures as will fix the respective rights of the clergy and the congregation.[17]

To implement the plan for a national church, the trustees suggested, among other things, that American Catholics send a representative, "a person of respectability and literary acquirements,"[18] to the papacy to establish a concordat with the Roman Church. Many of the trustees' pamphlets favored the proposal.[19] Some trustees suggested that a general convention of American Catholics be convoked to elect a representative and to outline the details of an agreement between the papacy and American Catholics.[20] Thadeus O'Meally proposed, moreover, that John England, Bishop of Charleston, S.C., be elected to negotiate the concordat.[21]

The trustees wanted some kind of constitutional government in the American church and they saw the concordat as a way to accomplish the goal. They suggested that the agreement provide for the election of priests and bishops, annual convocations of provincial councils and diocesan synods, an ecclesiastical juridical system that would allow no person to be condemned or removed from office in the church without a fair trial, a system of legal appeals to higher ecclesiastical courts, and that all of these provisions would be spelled out in a written concordat.[22] These propositions were certainly an attempt to create a republican system of government in the Catholic Church, with a carefully worked out constitutional balance of powers, a system of accountability, and a respect for authority and individual rights within the church. In the trustees' opinion, the proposal in no way lessened respect for papal authority. In fact, they suggested that the concordat begin with an acknowledgement of the pope's authority "as our spiritual father."[23]

RIGHT OF PATRONAGE

The primary objective of the concordat was to get Rome to acknowledge the laity's right of patronage.[24] The trustees understood patronage as a right they possessed because they owned the ecclesiastical property and voluntarily supported the church and the pastors; as patrons, they believed they were entitled to select duly-ordained priests for their congregations. Many also believed this right should be extended to the selection of bishops for their dioceses.

The troubles between the clergy and the laity one trustee argued, "gave rise to a spirit of inquiry on the part of the people, into the various relative rights and duties of the clergy, to which, in a great measure, the present conflict of opinions between them and the laity is to be attributed."[25] The trustees searched the sources of the Christian tradition in order to find a rationale for settling their disputes and to discover what rights the laity had for participating in the life and government of the church. Their investigation produced a number of sources upon which they based their claims for patronage: historical precedent, interpretations of canon law, decrees of the Council of Trent, current Catholic practices in Europe and South America, principles found in a contemporary papal letter, and Propaganda Fide's recent acknowledgement of the right in the United States. They also argued that the right had to be adapted to the American practice of voluntaryism; therefore, in some respects it had to differ from the European practice.

The trustees saw the law of patronage as a matter of discipline not doctrine; therefore, they felt that they had every right to have it acknowledged by a concordat. They did not consider the right to be an interference in the spiritual jurisdiction of the hierarchy, as some of their opponents claimed,[26] but simply a matter of temporal administration in which the laity had every right to participate.[27] The trustees appealed to historical experience to support this claim.

> Had the church ever considered the appointment of pastors to livings or benefices an article of faith, the right would not, or

Could not have been conceded to lay patrons in all Catholic countries.[28]

They maintained that originally the right was granted to laymen to encourage them to build or endow churches. When the laymen fulfilled their part of the agreement, the hierarchy granted them the responsibility of nominating their own pastors.

> When, therefore, the layman filled his part of the conditional contract, he acquired a *de jure* right of presentation; and the hierarchy, on their part, were bound by their promise to make it a *de facto* one by giving their juridical sanction, and thus make the contract perfect.[29]

This practice, they believed, had a long tradition in the Catholic Church; the exact origins of the tradition, however, remained obscure.

According to the trustees, the practice of granting the laity the right of nominating pastors for the churches they built or endowed could be found in the early stages of church history.[30] It was most certainly evident in England prior to the Reformation. Numerous English laws supported the practice.[31] The trustees quoted, as an example, a 1222 law of the Archbishop of Canterbury, Stephen Langton (d. 1228), which they thought confirmed their own claims.

> We excommunicate all those who, upon the vacancy of a church, maliciously oppose, or cause to be opposed, the *right of patronage*, in order to defeat the true patron of the Collation, that is, as the law interprets it; the bestowing of a benefice.[32]

The trustees also discovered justification for their claims in the current collection of ecclesiastical laws, the *Codex Juris Canonici*. Mathew Carey, for example, was astonished to find in the *Codex* a number of statements regarding the election of bishops which he felt American Catholics should definitely know.

> By this code it is most expressly declared, that no Bishop shall be appointed for a people unwilling to receive him—and even that those are not to be regarded as Bishops, who are not chosen by the clergy—or desired by the people.[33]

According to Thadeus O'Meally, even the Council of Trent, which attempted to limit the practice of patronage, upheld the right when it stated:

> In order, therefore, that an even balance be held, the sacred council decrees, that the title of right of patronage shall be and is acquired by the founding or by the endowing of a church; which title is to be proven by an authentic document, clothed with the requisite formalities of law.[34]

In addition to evidence from the *Codex* and the Council of Trent, the trustees found French canonists who corroborated their arguments. Richard W. Meade, a trustee, quoted from DuMassais' work on the liberties of the Gallican Church to substantiate the trustees' claims.

> The right of patronage is the right of presenting to the Collator a clerk for a vacant benefice, and the Collator is *obliged* to confer the benefice on him presented by the patron. The *lay* patron is he whose predecessors have *founded* or *endowed a church*; it is he who has the right of presenting to benefices *which his ancestors or he have founded*.[35]

The French lawyer was even more forceful when he spoke of "the temporal sovereignty of the revenues of the church." In typical Gallican fashion, he interpreted the rights of the laity in such a way as to exclude any papal interference in the right. In regard to church revenues, therefore, he wrote:

> *no regard must be paid to the provisions of the Court of Rome, if they be contrary to the rights of the lay patron*; thus the lay patron cannot be disturbed by the Sovereign Pontiff or his legate; and everything that concerns the rights of the lay patrons and possession of benefices, is treated of before the royal judge.[36]

Meade also quoted from numerous concordats between Spain and the papacy to show the extensive use of the right in Europe.[37]

Current practices in the European church also aided the trustees' arguments. Many European monarchs possessed the right of patronage for their national churches; they had obtained the right by a concordat with the papacy. The trustees used this present experience to argue their own case. They believed that what was formerly granted (i.e., patronage) to Sovereigns in Europe, should now be granted to the Catholic people in the United States since here the people are sovereign.

> in our happier day, and in this new world, the majesty of kings is supplanted by the more legitimate majesty of the people, and it remains therefore for the latter, to insist on retaining *at the least* the *same* privileges as the former.[38]

In the United States, the Catholic people should now be responsible for appointing pastors and bishops, just as the monarchs in Europe had formerly nominated them.[39] In most Catholic countries, the trustees asserted, the government, not the See of Rome, selected the clergy. While the hierarchy ordained and consecrated, the European governments and the people appointed the clergy to their livings. "To every man who has resided in those countries," the immigrant trustees claimed, this experience has been viewed as beneficial both for the laity and the clergy: for the laity, because they have some say in the selection of their clergy and are therefore not despotically controlled by them; for the clergy, because they are appointed for life and once a pastor is appointed "he cannot be deprived of it [his office] any more than one of the judges of the supreme court of the United States, who hold [sic] their [sic] offices on the tenor [sic] of their [sic] good behavior and can only be suspended when regularly impeached and tried."[40] Thus, according to the trustees, the right of patronage would provide for lay participation, accountability, stability, and permanence in the American Church. Furthermore, it would be consistent with American principles of government and justice.

Even in the year 1824, the governments of Caracas, Venezuela, and Bogota, Columbia, had formed concordats with the Holy See and those agreements provided for the right of patronage in those South American countries. Those concordats gave the governments, in the words of the trustees, some control over the clergy in the country and did not subject the church in those countries to undue foreign interference. After reviewing these recent concordats, Thadeus O'Meally called upon the Catholics of North America "to take a lesson from the catholics of the south."[41] Patronage, he thought, could establish legitimate boundaries on the power of the clergy and "remedy all existing abuses."[42]

The writings of recent popes also verified the principles and claims of the trustees. They quoted, for example, Pope Pius VII's February 1, 1816, letter to the Irish Bishops in which he tried to justify the church's right to establish concordats with governments, even with a Protestant government like that of Great Britain, for the benefit of religion. In this letter, he argued for the British government's right to obtain a veto over nominations to Irish Sees. He quoted from Pope Leo I to support his claim that only bishops favorable to state governments should be appointed to dioceses because "none [should] be ordained Bishops without the consent and postulation of the flock, lest an unwelcome intruder incur its contempt or hatred." Since a British veto over nominations to Irish Sees would have entailed a change in Irish ecclesiastical discipline, the pope again used Pope Leo to substantiate his own call for an alteration in the nominating policy in the Irish Church: "As there are certain things which can on no account be altered, so are there many which, from a due consideration of times or from the necessity of things it may be right to modify." Pope Innocent III had also recognized this principle when he advocated a change in discipline: "It is not to be considered blameable if, in the consequence of a change of times, a change of human laws also be effected, especially when an urgent necessity or an evident utility calls for such a change."[43] The Philadelphia trustees enthusiastically accepted the principles, though not the purpose, of this letter and used the papal declaration to aid their own vastly different cause in the United States.[44]

Not only the popes, but other "living authorities of the church" had recently validated the American trustees' claim. On September 20, 1817,

Cardinal Litta, prefect of Propaganda, wrote to one of the Norfolk, Virginia trustees, Dr. John F. O. Fernandez, acknowledging the possibility of the right of patronage in the United States. The cardinal admitted that those who built the churches or provided for them "could not be denied the right of patronage."[45] The Philadelphia trustees frequently quoted this recent Roman statement to show that Rome was not adverse to the practice in the United States.[46]

All of the above agruments were not used simultaneously to support the trustees' attempts to gain the right of patronage, but they were all used at one time or another between 1820 and 1829. They reveal the mind of the trustees in their attempts to accommodate European Catholic practices and laws to American circumstances. They also show that the trustees were well acquainted with European Catholic experiences, and that their claims had some countenance in traditional and current European ecclesiastical practices, canon law, and in contemporary Roman authorities.

The trustees' claims, however, were vigorously opposed by a majority of the American hierarchy,[47] some articulate priests, and a few laymen. The bulk of the opposition came from the hierarchy and was based upon the fact that the granting of patronage demanded "a fixed, permanent and inalienable"[48] fund or benefice for the support of the clergy. American Catholics could secure none of these provisions which were required by the church's law of patronage. This was certainly true and the trustees did not deny it. They were not advocating, however, that the church's law of patronage be simply transported across the ocean without any transformation. Because the political and religious situation in the United States differed from that of Europe, so also must the law of patronage. Patronage had to be changed to meet the needs of American laws and the practice of voluntaryism. Because of American laws, the trustees could not surrender church property to the hierarchy, thus providing an endowment or a benefice. The situation of voluntaryism in America and especially its long practice among the Irish immigrants, however, would provide an even more fixed, permanent, and inalienable source of income for the church and its pastors than had the old patronage practice in Europe.

> They [trustees] can and are pledged to give to the pastor whom they present *a fixed salary for life*, and the difference between *his* living and that of a beneficed rector of the old world, is strikingly in his favour. Unencumbered with the *unprofitable dominion* of the church revenues, he enjoys the fruits without the drudgery of gathering them . . . It is enhanced with all the benefits of the tithe system, without its odium to the priest or its burden to the people. It is . . . the free offering of a free people, given him for his merits by the representatives of the givers; and not like that of the

beneficed sinecurist of the 'old country', the reluctant contribution of begrudging parishioners.[49]

The situation of voluntaryism, therefore, necessarily made the American right of patronage different from the European; and, in the opinion of the trustees, it made it a better relationship between priests and people.

An American patronage system, with voluntary contributions as the guarantee of income, would make a pastor "dependently independent." The pastor had to rely upon the liberty of the trustees for his material well being, but he was also freed from the temporal cares of the church—giving him more time for his spiritual ministry. At the same time, patronage gave the pastor complete independence from the trustees in his priestly and sacramental functions. Thus, by granting patronage

> you not only considerably *lessen* those powers [of the trustees] but you so accurately define them; for, be it remembered, the law of patronage is thrice armed; it equally protects and defines the rights of the bishop, the rights of the pastor, and the rights of the people.[50]

In addition to the other benefits, patronage would establish a constitutional balance of powers in the church. Without it, the powers of the trustees would remain " 'unbounded' and consequently anarchical."[51] With it, the powers of the clergy as well as the laity would be limited. The right of patronage would not allow the trustees to interfere with "the free exercise of the Episcopal office; their right when acknowledged, will only place a barrier, and in my mind a very happy one, to the abuses of episcopal power."[52]

Thus, patronage, adapted to the American situation, would provide for lay participation in the selection of priests and bishops, establish a permanent source of income for the pastors and churches without burdening the clergy with excessive concern for temporal and financial affairs, "prevent feuds and discords,"[53] regulate future differences in the congregations, restore peace, and constitutionally define and limit the various functions in the church—providing for a balance of powers and an orderly and symmetrical system of government in the American church. Finally, of course, all these benefits would show how closely the government and administration of the American Catholic Church corresponded to the American system of government. Thus, the trustees could say, in the words of Richard Meade,

> Every person who opposes this principle, is not only an enemy of the Catholic religion but of every institution of this free and happy country.[54]

The entire trustee movement, as articulated clearly by the Philadelphia trustees, tried to erect an American National Church. The proposal for establishing a concordat and the arguments favoring patronage were expressions of that purpose. They envisioned a national church that was independently-dependent upon the Roman Church. In matters of discipline, temporal administration, and other non-doctrinal areas of ecclesiastical life, they sought independence from European control and identification with the ways of American republicanism. Even in this, however, they would only alter European Catholic practices to meet the needs of American laws and practices. In matters of doctrine and fraternal communion, they professed their dependence upon the papacy and acknowledged the supremacy of the pope in the "spiritual" government of the universal church.

The trustees' campaign to Americanize the European church failed to accomplish its intended goals. They did not obtain a concordat, nor did they advance the cause of lay and clerical participation in the administration of the church. Their movement, however, did influence the formation of the American church, even though, from their perspective, it was a negative contribution.

For a number of reasons, the trustees could not move the church in the direction of Americanization as much as they desired. First of all, their plans, arising amidst the hostile lay-clerical tensions of the day, were filled with the bitterness of internecine controversy. The trustees eventually tired of the tensions and desired peace over their former principles and programs. Moreover, they did not institutionalize their movement either locally or nationally to promote their programs. That failure made their campaign appear to be a minority movement, thus suffering the consequence of most unorganized minority causes—extinction. From 1822 onward, furthermore, Roman officials opposed many of their efforts. In addition, the American bishops in the Baltimore Council of 1829 finally organized their opposition to the trustees' cause and legislated against a number of their proposals. Also, increased Protestant opposition to Catholicism, partly caused by Catholic intramural warfare, forced the Philadelphia trustees to unite with their former Catholic opponents in the struggle against the "Protestant Crusade."[55] The rapid increase of Catholic immigrants from the less educated and articulate members of the European Catholic communities also made the trustee movement impractical. That campaign demanded articulate leaders and men acquainted with democratic ways and American laws; the newer immigrants did not possess these talents. Likewise, after the 1830's, the newer immigrants, for the most part, found themselves incorporated into a church embattled against the Protestant majority. Cultural and religious identity forced most groups within the Catholic community to minimize their former differences. Opposition from outside the church forged a less self-critical Catholic unity; in such circumstances, the former trustee issues faded into the background[56] and the movement lost its vigor and urgency.

The trustee campaign represented one side of the American Catholic search for identity at a time when the new age of republicanism made that identity unclear. As a force in the new world, trusteeism did influence the formation of the American Catholic Church. Because of the trustees' lack of organization, the leadership in defining American Catholic identity eventually passed from the hands of the trustees to those of the bishops. The trustees unwittingly strengthened the episcopal structures in this country. In response to the hostilities of trusteeism, the American bishops through the provincial councils of Baltimore began to define their own view of American Catholic identity. That identity, of course, was described in opposition to the trustees' attempted definition, but it did incorporate some of the trustees' objectives. Through the councils, the bishops defined and limited the powers of various functions within the church. Thus, it fulfilled the trustees' desire for an organized institution on the national and local levels. But these accomplishments were gained at a price. The episcopacy strengthened its own offices in the church and severely limited, almost annihilated, lay and clerical powers. Thus, the trustee movement indirectly contributed to the formation of a strong episcopacy in the American church and almost destroyed any significant lay and clerical participation in decision-making processes.

While the trustee movement failed to accomplish its intended goals, it did succeed in underlining the inherent conflicts of accommodating Catholicism to the new age of democracy without reforming some of the European Catholic practices. The trustees, at least, sensed the necessity of changing Catholic discipline and structures long before it became popular in the American Catholic Church. Some of their principles and programs are still being debted today.

FOOTNOTES

1. On the widespread religious appeals to republicanism, see, e.g., William Gribbin, "Republican Religion and the American Churches in the Early National Period," *The Historian* XXXV (Nov., 1972), 61-74; Belden C. Lane, "Presbyterian Repupblicanism: Miller and the Eldership as an Answer to Lay-Clerical Tensions," *The Journal of Presbyterian History*, LVI (Winter, 1978), 311-324; Charles Franklin Kilgore, *The James O'Kelly Schism in the Methodist Episcopal Church* (Mexico: Casa Unida de Publicaciones, 1963).

2. For General histories of lay-clerical disputes in the United States, see Peter Guilday, "Trusteeism," *Historical Records and Studies*, XVIII (1928), 14-73; Patrick J. Dignan, *A History of the legal Incorporation of Catholic Church Property in the United States (1784-1932)*, (New York: P.J. Kenedy & Sons, 1935); Robert F. McNamara, "Trusteeism in the Atlantic States, 1785-1855," *Catholic Historical Review*, LXIV (July, 1978), 357-376. Other than these articles no comprehensive history of the subject has yet been written. For histories of trustee troubles in Philadelphia before 1820, see Joseph L.J. Kirlin, *Catholicity in Philadelphia from the Earliest Missionaries down to the Present Times* (Philadelphia: John McVey, 1909); James F. connelly (ed.), *The History of the Archdiocese of Philadelphia* (Philadelphia: Archdiocese of Philadelphia, 1976); V.J. Fecher, S.V.D., *A study of the movement for German National Parishes in Philadelphia and Baltimore (1787-1802)*, Vol. LXXVII Series Facultatis Historiae Ecclesiasticae (Rome: Gregorian University, 1955). For histories f the battles in Philadelphia between 1820 and 1829, see Marttin I.J. Griffin, "The

Life of Bishop Conwell," *Records of the American Catholic Historical Society* (thereafter *RACHS*), XXIV (1913), 16-42, 162-178, 217-250, 348-361; XXV (1914), 52-67, 146-178, 217-248, 296-341; XXVI (1915), 64-77, 131-165, 227-249; XXVII (1916), 74-87, 145-160, 275-283, 359-378; XXVIII (1917), 64-84, 150-183, 244-265, 310-347; XXIX (1918), 170-182, 250-261, 260-384; Francis E. Tourscher, *The Hogan Schism and Trustee Troubles in St. Mary's Church, Philadelphia, 1820-1829* (Philadelphia: The Peter Reilly Co., 1930); Peter Guilday, *The Life and Times of John England* (2 vols.; New York: The America Press, 1927), I, 380-425.

3. *Address of the Lay Trustees to the Congregation of St. Mary's Church on the Subject of the Approaching Election* (Philadelphia: Robert Desilver, 1822), p. 24; cf. also *Address of the Committee of St. Mary's Church of Philadelphia, To Their Brethren of the Roman Catholic Faith Throughout the United States of America, on the Subject of a Reform of Sundry Abuses in the Administration of Our Church Discipline* (New York: J. Kingsland & Co., 1821), p. 3.

4. Mathew Carey, *Address to the Right Rev. Bishop Conwell and the Members of St. Mary's Congregation* (Philadelphia, 1821), p. 4. Carey characterized the European type of ecclesiastical authority with the adage: "Sic volo, sic jubeo: stat pro ratione voluntas"; see Carey's *Address to the Right Reverend the Bishop of Pennsylvania, the Catholic Clergy of Philadelphia, and the Congregation of St. Mary's in this city* (Philadelphia: H. C. Caey & I. Lea, 1822), p. 19; cf. also *An Inquiry into the Causes Which Led to the Dissentions [sic.] Actually Existing in the Congregation of St. Mary's* (1821), p. 9.

5. William Hogan, *An Answer to a Paragraph Contained in the United States Catholic Miscellany* (Philadelphia, 1822), p. 33. Cf. also idem, *A Brief Reply to a Ludicrous Pamphlet compiled from the affidavits, Letters and Assertions of a number of Theologians, with the Signature of Henry, Bishop, and entitled Sundry Documents, Addressed to St. Mary's Congregation* [Philadelphia], 1821, p. 25.

6. *A Republication of Two Addresses, Lately Published in Philadelphia, the First by a Committee of St. Mary's Church on Reform of Church Discipline, the Second by a Layman of St. Mary's Congregation in Reply to the Same with Introductory Remarks by a Layman of New York* (New York: William Grattan, 1821), p. 9.

7. *Address . . . on the Subject of a Reform*, p.4.

8. [Mathew Carey], *Address to the Right Rev. the Bishop of Pennsylvania and the Members of St. Mary's Congregation* (Philadelphia, 1820), p. 3; cf. also Hogan, *A Brief Reply*, pp. 44-45; *Address . . . on the Subject of a Reform*, p. 14; *An Answer to an "Address by a Catholic Layman to the Roman Catholics of the United States."* (Philadelphia, 1821), pp. 20-21.

9. Mathew Carey, *Address to the Right Rev. the Bishop of Pennsylvania and the Members of St. Mary's Congregation* (Philadelphia, Dec. 21, 1810), p. 3.

10. Thadeus O'Meally, *An Address Explanatory and Vindicatory to Both Parties of the Congregation of St. Mary's* (Philadlephia: Wm. Brown, 1824), p. 64.

11. *A Letter to the Roman Catholics of Philadelphia and the United States. By a Friend to the Civil and Religious Liberties of Man* (Philadelphia: Robert Desilver, 1822), p. 33.

12. Thadeus O'Meally, *A Series of Letters Relating to the Late Attempt at a Reconciliation Between the Members of the Congregation of St. Mary's and St. Joseph's with a brief Notice of the Present State of the Controversy Between Them* (Philadelphia: William Brown, 1825), p. 35.

13. *Address of the Trustees of St. Mary's Church to their Fellow Citizens . . . on a Late Attempt at a Reconciliation Between the Contending Parties of the Congregation of Said Church* (Philadelphia: Lydia R. Bailey, 1823), p. 4.

14. *A Republication*, p. 8.

15. *Address . . . on the Subject of a Reform*, p. 9.

16. *A Republication*, p. 5; *An Answer to an Address*, p. 4.

17. *Address . . . on the Subject of a Reform*, p. 3.

18. Ibid., p. 9.

19. E.g., O'Meally, *A Series of Letters*, p. 33; *An Answer to an Address*, p. 8.

20. Carey, *Address . . . in this city*, p. 30; O'Meally, *A Series of Letters*, p. 35.

21. O'Meally, *A Series of Letters*, p. 35.

22. *A Letter to the Rev. William Vincent Harold on Reading his Late Reply to a "Catholic Layman." By an Admirer of Fenelon* (Philadelphia: Robert Desilver, 1822), pp. 26-30; cf. also *Address . . . on the Subject of a Reform*, pp. 9-10.

23. *Address . . . on the Subject of a Reform*, p. 10.

24. On the history of the right of patronage, see John A. Godfrey, *The Right of Patronage According to the Code of Canon Law* (Washington, D.C.: The Catholic University of America,

1924); John J. Coady, *The Appointment of Pastors*, No. LII, *The Catholic University of America Canon Law Studies* (Washington, D.C.: The Catholic University of America, 1929).
25. *Reflections on the Dissension Actually Existing in St. Mary's Congregation . . . By a Roman Catholic* (Philadelphia: Lydia R. Bailey, 1824), p. 3.
26. Bishop Henry Conwell and other opponents of the claim asserted: "We hold it as an article of faith, that the government of the church, the mission and appointment of its pastors, and the right to judge in cases spiritual and ecclesiastical, appertain exclusively to the hierarchy; and that these powers cannot, consistently with Catholic principles be claimed or exercised by lay persons." See, *Address of the Trustees . . . of Said Church*, p. 12.
27. Richard W. Meade, *An Address to the Roman Catholics of the City of Philadelphia in Reply to Mr. Harold's Address* (Philadelphia, 1823), p. 6.
28. *Address of the Trustees . . . of Said Church*, p. 6.
29. O'Meally, *an Address Explanatory*, p. 17.
30. *A Letter . . . Religious Liberties of Man*, p. 21.
31. *Ibid.*, pp. 38-42.
32. *ibid.*, p. 72.
33. Carey, *Address . . . in this city*, p. 30, quoting from the *Codex Juris Canonici*, I, 82: "Nullus invitis detur episcopus, Cleri, plebis, et ordinis consensus et desiderium requiratur."
34. O'Meally, *An Address Explanatory*, pp. 60-61, quoting from Trent, Sess, XXV, *de ref.* c. 9; cf. also Sess Vii, *de ref.* c. 13; Sess, XIV, *de ref.* cc. 12-13. Both trustees and anti-trustees used the *Codex* and Trent to support their opposing positions regarding the claims of patronage. Like the trustees and anti-trustees, canon lawyers and historians of the day disagreed on the precise meaning and application of the law of patronage. On this, see Godfrey, *Patronage*, pp. 9, 19, 21, 31. Before the 1829 Baltimore Council, there was no legislation against the right in the United States; therefore, the possibility of establishing such here was an open question. Even after the 1829 decrees against patronage, the legal possibility for such still remained. On this, see my "John England and Irish American Catholicism 1815-1842: A study of Conflict," (unpublished Ph.D. dissertation, Fordham University, 1975), p. 187, n. 81.
35. Meade, *An Address . . . in Reply to Harold*, p. 11; Meade refers to Du Massais' work, but does not cite the source. Perhaps he is referring to Cesar Chesneau Du Marsais' (1676-1756) *Exposition de la doctrine de l'Eglise gallicane par rapport aux pretentions de la cour de Rome* (Paris, 1758); cf. *Reflections*, p. 21.
36. Meade, *An Address . . . in Reply to Harold*, p. 12.
37. *Ibid.*, pp. 13-14.
38. O'Meally, *A Series of Letters*, p. 33; cf. *Reflections*, p. 10.
39. *A Republication*, p. 6.
40. *Address . . . on the Subject of a Reform*, p. 6
41. O'Meally, *A Series of letters*, p. 32
42. *Ibid.*, p. 33
43. The entire papal letter is published in the *Dublin Evening Post*, July 7, 1818.
44. *Reflections*, pp. 13-14.
45. Letter in Peter Guilday, *The Catholic Church in Virginia (1815-1822)*, Series VIII, United States Catholic Historical Society Monograph (New York: The United States Catholic Historical Society, 1924), pp. 72-73. The trustees never mentioned the conditions attached to the right when they cited the letter, though the letter made these conditions clear. On this, see my "John England," p. 189, n. 85.
46. O'Meally, *An Address Explanatory*, p. 62; Meade, *An Address . . . in Reply to Harold* p. 6; *O'Meally to Henry Conwell, December 23, 1823*, photo copy of letter in New York Archdiocesan Archives at Dunwoodie, New York.
47. On this, see my "Two Episcopal Views of the Lay-Clerical Conflicts, 1785-1860," *RACHS*, LXXXVII (March-December, 1976), 85-98.
48. E.g., H. Conwell to R. W. Meade, J. Leamy and J. Ashley, July 17, 1823; letter in Griffin, "Conwell," *RACHS*, XXVI (1915), 154.
49. O'Meally, *An Address Explanatory*, pp. 33-34.
50. *Ibid.* p. 63.
51. *Ibid.*, p. 63.
52. *Ibid.*, p. 12.
53. Carey, *Address . . . in this city*, p. 31.
54. Richard Meade, *Continuation of An Address to the Roman Catholics . . . Containing the Documents of the Reverend A. Inglesi*, (Philadelphia, 1823) p. 36; cf. O'Meally, *An Address Explanatory*, pp. 66-67; O'Meally suggested that by adapting patronage American Catholics would have "as beautiful a subordination in your ecclesiastical as in your civil government."

55. On October 31, 1826, the two different factions at St. Mary's joined forces to resist Protestant attacks on their religion. They formed the "Society for the Defense of the Catholic Religion from Calumny and Abuse." William Harold, who had supported the episcopal side of the controversies, was elected president of the group and Mathew Carey, who had supported the trustees, was elected vice president.

56. The issues of the 1820's did not entirely disappear, as the Catholic experience of the 1840's and 1850's in New Orleans, New York State, and other places reveal; but, much of the trustee effort in other places was local in nature and did not appeal to the national Catholic consciousness as much as the Philadelphia events did.

MODERNITY IN THE SERVICE OF TRADITION: CATHOLIC LAY TRUSTEES AT BUFFALO'S ST. LOUIS CHURCH AND THE TRANSFORMATION OF EUROPEAN COMMUNAL TRADITIONS, 1829-1855

In 1852, a substantial majority of the male parishioners of Buffalo's immigrant St. Louis Church petitioned Pope Pius IX for support in pressing grievances against diocesan bishop, Rev. John Timon.[1] This 414-signature petition was a consequence of over a decade of efforts by the parish's predominantly German and Alsatian laymen and their elected trustees to achieve control over the parish's property and the hiring of its secular employees.[2] At the time of the petition, St. Louis Church had been without a priest for 15 months because of the parish's refusal to allow Timon to disband an uncooperative trustee board and replace it with one of his own choosing. The bases of the parish's claim to these prerogatives were complex, involving legalities and customs which spanned old and new worlds. But whatever those bases were, such lay power was not, in the minds of the nation's Catholic hierarchy, supported by Catholic tradition. Increasingly after the 1829 Baltimore Council, the American hierarchy demanded that diocesan property be held in the name of and subject to direct control by the diocesan bishop.[3] (Many bishops remained willing, as a practical matter, to allow for daily self-management.)

Other parishes had fought with their bishops about such matters, but the St. Louis affair was unique in one important way: it reached a climax in the 1850s, during an era of intense anti-Catholicism. It received ample coverage not only in the daily newspapers, but also in the nativist press, which saw it as a struggle between republican ideals and Papal despotism. In consequence, the Pope gave serious attention to the petition, for he was conscious that the public controversy born of the parish's struggle not only threatened the internal unity of the American Church, but bolstered the forces which jeopardized its very existence. He sent a personal emissary, Archbishop Gaetano Bedini, to America in 1853 to mediate.[4] But neither Bedini's emphatic judgment that the parish must obey Timon, nor the excommunication of the trustees because of their refusal to accept that judgment, nor the continuing of the interdict denying the parish a priest, led the laymen to surrender. Indeed, the lengths the trustees and their lay supporters soon went in carrying their fight beyond the Church probably are unique in the annals of American Catholicism. Through petitioning and lobbying, they won the cooperation of anti-Catholic, New York State legislators in obtaining passage of a law making legal ownership and inheritance of church property by members of an episcopal hierarchy impossible.[5] Yet but a few months after the passage of the Putnam Law,[6] the parish accepted a compromise, which though preserving some unique law powers, gave its bishop substantial oversight of parish affairs.

This essay analyses the social and ideological forces and the aspirations and fears which led St. Louis parish's laymen first to a strikingly bitter opposition to their Church, and then to an equally striking, sudden reconciliation with it.

The St. Louis conflict is an example of "trusteeism" — the struggle between the American Catholic episcopacy and laity, as represented by democratically elected parish trustees, over control of ecclesiastical properties and/or investitures. (The latter was not at issue in Buffalo, and will not be discussed here.) In the early nineteenth century, elected trustees exercising various powers over properties and employees were quite common. Trustees had existed at St. Louis from the time of its founding in 1829. Legal incorporation of trustee bodies, which had existed since 1838 at St. Louis and provided the legal basis for its claims, was less common, though easily accomplished under New York State Law. Even in New York, however, incorporated trusteeship was not necessarily coterminous with legal ownership; as at St. Louis, trustees often had their property titles state that property was being held in trust for the diocesan bishop. In still other parishes, a number of *ad hoc* arrangements governed both property ownership and management.[7] The diversity of early nineteenth-century arrangements was a consequence of two factors. First, Catholic population grew rapidly and spread over a vast territory, while the expansion of episcopal authority, in the form of new dioceses, was much slower to occur and to spread beyond the eastern seaboard. Second, and relatedly, the ever-present Protestant pattern of church governance surrounded, and suggested models for, American Catholics establishing their parishes in this episcopal vacuum.[8] But all arrangements, *ad hoc* or formal, depended on the willingness of both clergy and laity to cooperate in the creation and maintenance of well-defined principles of lay management and clerical oversight. When such cooperation broke down, as at St. Louis Church and a significant number of other parishes at the time, the result was often intense controversy.

One of the most abiding concerns of American Catholic historiography, trusteeism has had two explanations. Dating from the nineteenth century, the first may be associated largely with the clergymen and small group of eminent Catholic laymen, most notably John Gilmary Shea, who were Catholic America's pioneer historians. Their position was hardly different from that of the episcopal participants in these conflicts, who were their contemporaries. They were horrified by the disunity and well-publicized quarreling, both to the satisfaction of Catholicism's many enemies, which lay assertiveness always seemed to bring with it. Moreover, they found little value in the usual justifications for lay assertiveness, such as ethnic rivalries and mistrust between Irish and continental Catholic immigrants. Instead, they returned always to the belief that laymen had the unquestionable duty to obey priestly authority in church matters. All else was insubordination.[9] Bent on condemnation, and utilizing sources of reflecting the hierarchy's view, this episcopal perspective was unable to conceive of trusteeism as an historical phenomenon, with complex antecedents and contemporary influences, let alone take lay trustees on their own terms, examining their motives and goals as the laymen themselves articulated them. Nor could it explain why such wayward Catholics fought so singlehandedly for prerogatives within a Church they might easily have left.

Recently a new perspective, with faint echoes of the antebellum nativist interpretation, has emerged in the work of Patrick Carey.[10] While acknowledging that trusteeism correlates with class and particularly with ethnic divisions among Catholics, Carey has located the roots of trusteeism in ideology. He contends that trusteeism developed out of the gradual absorption by American and immigrant Catholics of the native republican tradition (with its emphasis on citizens rights, individual conscience, anti-elitism, restriction of the secular power of organized religion, and local self-government) and the subsequent, conscious struggle of laymen to change European-fashioned, hierarchical, and bureaucratic, formal church practice as defended by intransigent bishops, to meet American ideological requirements.[11]

This challenging view demands close inspection on a number of fronts. Its assertion of the centrality of republicanism leads us to ask for a deeper exploration of this secular political ideology than Carey provides. After all, republicanism was hardly a monolithic ideology in ante-bellum America: Whig, Democrat, and Republican; northerner and southerner; abolitionist and slaveowner — all paid obeisance to republican values in their diverse, contradictory, and at times deeply ambivalent, ways. So, too, did anti-Catholic nativists.[12] And so, too, did the nineteenth-century hierarchy in frequent efforts to demonstrate the Americanness of Catholicism in order to counteract nativist claims to the contrary.[13] The point is not the irrelevance of republicanism, but rather its complexity as revealed in its many formulations, and the consequent difficulties involved in using this ideological tradition as a general causality. If there was no single republican tradition in America, we must ask ourselves which one rebellious Catholic laymen appropriated? Or did they formulate their own? As we shall see, the St. Louis laymen were deeply but ambivalently engaged by republican values, and their ambivalence will ultimately tell us more about them and their conflict with the Church than their republicanism.

Furthermore, the new perspective on trusteeism may well claim an explanatory universality it cannot sustain. Much of Carey's work up to this time has been on the formative period of American Catholicism — from the ascendence of Bishop Carroll in 1780 to the Baltimore Council of 1829. Perhaps this is the reason his views do not seem applicable to the St. Louis parish conflict. The controversies he examined almost entirely involved Catholic laymen who were native-born Anglo-Americans or, in a minority of cases, relatively assimilated, pre-Famine Irish-Americans. For these groups, the ideological influences posited may well have been at work. Both groups were in a position to be directly engaged by American political and social values. Though of recent immigration, the Irish had been prepared (perhaps uniquely so in American immigration history) to assimilate native republicanism through development in the Old World of vital, popular traditions of both prepolitical and political opposition to British colonialism. Yet this very colonial subjugation, the brutalities of which reached a zenith in the mid-nineteenth century, thrust the Church and clergy into the forefront of the Irish struggle for national survival. Both Church and clergy gained in authority because they provided bastions of stability, continuity, and cultural coherence in a society of improverished near-powerless peasants who lived amidst increasingly desperate circumstances.[14] We should not be surprised tha, outside of a few, isolated examples, nineteenth-century Irish-American laymen were rarely (and, at that, decreasingly) involved in conflict with their Church.[15]

The lay trustee conflicts of the four decades before the Civil War, however, often involved recent, continental immigrants, particularly German-speakers of various regional and national backgrounds.[16] At the center of the St. Louis struggle, for example, were Alsatians and Germans, principally Rhinelanders. At a time when social historians have frequently pointed out the resilience of European folk and communal traditions in American ethnic cultures, one may question a view of trusteeism which asks us to see recently arrived German immigrants as self-conscious forwarders of American republican ideology. Political history invites the same conclusion. The large majority of ante-bellum German-speaking immigrants, who came from Bavaria and the Rhine Valley states, lacked experience with democratic politics based on popular participation.

Self-evident in the case of the peasants, this is also true of the substantial number of town dwellers among the immigrants. With their cooptive offices and strong deference to (and functional reinforcement of) traditional status hierarchies, town governments of Bavaria and Rhenish Bavaria, Baden, Rhenish Prussia, and Würtemburg hardly prepared their residents to step easily into the role of American republican.[17] The St. Louis conflict establishes good reason to take seriously the importance of both tradition and customary status hierarchies in immigrant political life. For, as we shall also see, even though a frequent, public theme of the parish's dissent was its legal right under state law, by virtue of incorporation, the laymen also spoke of wishing to continue to enjoy prerogatives in chruch governance known in Europe.[18] Their dissent expressed alongside their concern with democratic rights and republican freedom from coercive control, a preoccupation with obedience to legitimate authority, suggesting they had not broken with the deeper political concerns of the Catholic tradition. Finally, their own, formally democratic parish government was informally structured to give functional support to emergent ethnic status hierarchies within their parish.

It is hardly desirable, however, to deny that republican ideology had any role to play in influencing rebellious Catholic laymen. What is doubtful is not the salience of ideological conflict, but rather an interpretation of such conflict lacking a firm foundation in a theory of immigrant adjustment. If we are to understand the origins and social meanings of trusteeism among ante-bellum continental immigrants, we must have a view of cultural change among immigrants which departs from a notion of lock-step, unilinear movement. Instead we must have a perspective which allows for an interplay of communal and folk tradition, modernity and democracy as experienced in America, and practical responses to the exigencies daily presented by resettlement in another society.[19]

Proceeding from these remarks, and based on the admittedly limited, single case of St. Louis parish, the present analysis will advance this framework for interpreting trusteeism among ante-bellum continental immigrants:

(1) The impetus to lay assertiveness originated in the desire to preserve European communal traditions of lay management of parish temporal affairs. Over time, in America, these traditions were consciously and unconsciously altered, as immigrants met the challenges of resettlement and absorbed a new culture.

(2) The desire to preserve such traditions was based upon the felt-necessity of maintaining group identity and cultural coherence admist the potentially disorganizing circumstances of resettlement. The defense of old, though altered forms of lay involvement may have appropriated American republican ideas and such modern republican civil procedures as church incorporation. But republicanism was less the inspiration for lay assertiveness than one of its subsequent justifications. Though this justification would itself come to have a life of its own in the consciousness of the laymen, its formulation in the context of the immigrant's commitment to an Old World, Catholic ethnoreligious tradition always sharply limited its ability to emerge as an ideology comfortable with modern conceptions of liberty.

(3) Interethnic mistrust, cultural misunderstanding, and rivalries for resources and power within the American Catholic Church, which took their most acute form at the time in Irish-German relations, did not determine the direction of trusteeism, but rather exacerbated it by reinforcing ideological and cultural conflict with objective social divisions.

This perspective sees lay Catholic assertiveness not as a battle between the modern (i.e., republican trustees) and the traditional (i.e., unyielding bishops) but as a conflict of two traditions, both responding to and appropriating American influences during a formative period of ethnic and institutional assimilation.

Indeed, at St. Louis parish, it was the modern, in the form of republican ideas and republican politics and government, which served the traditional, as represented by communal customs of lay governance.

In the next section this essay will establish the social bases of trusteeism in Buffalo by analyzing structural patterns of authority and power among the various social groups comprising Catholicism in the city and in St. Louis parish. Then we will proceed to an analysis of the ideological and cultural foundations of lay assertiveness, examining both European and American political and religious attitudes and practices. Here we will discover that the Alsatian and German immigrants who were the parish's most influential members had brought with them from Europe a centuries-old tradition of lay management of parish temporal affairs. This tradition, which was itself being transformed by contact with American institutions and ideologies, was at the heart of the conflict between parish and hierarchy.

Founded in 1829, St. Louis was Buffalo's first parish. It was created in response to the religious needs of a rapidly growing Catholic population, much of which was very recently settled in the strategically located boom-town at the terminus of the Erie Canal. At its inception, the parish was totally ethnic, and at that heterogeneous, in a pattern which increasingly reflected the sociology of Catholicism in the North. However, German-speakers were dominant in the parish, outnumbering the Irish and few Canadian and continental French-speakers approximately three to one in the first years. The German-speakers were a mixed lot, composed of a few Swiss (soon to travel further West as a group), many more Bavarians, and still a larger number of Alsatian and German Rhinelanders. Sacramental records, various printed sources, and oral tradition indicate that Alsatians were the most numerous of the German-speakers, though not necessarily a majority. The impression of Alsatian numerical predominance is reinforced by the Alsatian origin of a number of early trustees and the Alsatian or Lorrainian birth of the parish's first several priests. Alsatian *social* predominance was enhanced by the fact that the parish's beloved benefactor, Louis LeCouteulx, who donated land on which the church was built, looked upon them with favor as fellow countrymen. Under any circumstance, Rhinelanders, principally French-born, but also German, would dominate the parish population and provide leadership throughout the ante-bellum period. This leadership carried considerable prestige: throughout the ante-bellum years, St. Louis was Buffalo's largest church and its most populous and affluent parish.[20]

During the '30s and '40s a number of social processes changed the parish's ethnic and class composition, and consequently influenced its attitudes and behavior in the conflict with its bishops. First, until 1843 when a larger structure was completed, the church's physical space proved more and more inadequate to accommodate a Catholic population constantly supplemented through immigration.[21] Second, ethnocultural differences of language, identity, and traditions of worship, which were doubltess exacerbated by pressures on physical space, began to become sources of division. Furthermore, the emergence of such ethnocultural divisions was hastened by differing orientations within the parish on the trustee conflict.[22] Third, the emergence of new neighborhoods, far from St. Louis Church, necessitated the building of new churches. These new residential areas were the product of the settling in Buffalo of growing numbers of recently arrived, poor Irish and German immigrants, who carved out neighborhoods on land which was, relative to that adjacent to St. Louis Church, more low-lying and unhealthy and less valuable. Moreover, the new working class neighborhoods, which were located east and south of the central business district, were within short walking distance of the location of many of the industrial, commercial, and transport jobs held by the recent immigrants. By contrast, St. Louis parish lay on high ground, considerably north of the central business district, in an area which became one of Buffalo's more affluent residential neighborhoods.[23]

The net result of the simultaneous evolution of these segmenting processes was the creation of new parishes. The movement of the Irish out of St. Louis Church began in 1837, when, charging harrassment by the German-speakers, a few Irish withdrew to worship in rented rooms. The remaining Irish left over the next decade, particularly because of their opposition to the disobedience of the German-speakers to hierarchical (and it must be noted, *Irish*) authority in the persons of the second and third bishops, John Hughes and Timon.[24] The refusal of St. Louis trustees in 1848 to allow just-appointed Bishop Timon, the first bishop of the new Buffalo diocese, to make the church his cathedral surely must have led the last Irish to leave.[25] A similar process of detachment, marked by intercultural misunderstanding and charges of harassment, led to the bitter exodus of the small French-speaking population from St. Louis parish in the late '40s.[26] Finally, beginning in the late '40s with the creation of St. Mary's, which the more affluent congregants of St. Louis Church derisively called "the woodchoppers' church" because so many poor sawyers and wood haulers worshipped here, there was the rise of a number of working-class German parishes in the city's expanding, "Deutschen Dörfchen" on the east side.[27] Contentions over trusteeism also influenced the development of German parishes. The city's second-largest German-speaking parish, St. Michael's, was founded in 1851 by German Jesuits in an only partly successful effort to break the solidarity of St. Louis's ranks.[28]

Just as St. Louis's affluence gave it a singular position among local parishes, so did its ethnic composition. No doubt it appeared to Buffalonians by 1850 that the parish was exclusively German — which was certainly true in regard to *language*. But the parish also contained the overwhelming majority of the city's nearly 700 Alsatian Catholics,[29] whose national origin was French and whose ethnic identity was the product of a unique history.

Though Alsatians played a crucial role in the parish's governance, and hence in its conflict with the hierarchy, there is little evidence that they were ever recognized as a distinct people, neither French nor German, by the bishops who dealt with them. This lack of intercultural awareness was only in part a result of the lamentable lack of practical knowledge of the parish held by its various bishops. It is also true that Alsatian immigrants were not readily identifiable, and were easily lost among other German-speaking immigrants. In contrast to the approximately two million Germans migrating here between 1820-1860, only some 20,000 Alsatians came, and while German immigration continued after the Civil War, Alsatian immigration declined rapidly after the late '40s. Moreover, typically the Alsatian immigrants, who were largely from Catholic Upper Alsace, migrated up the Rhine to Rotterdam and across the Atlantic accompanied by much large numbers of Bavarians, Swiss, and German Rhinelanders, among whom Alsatians often settled in America, and from whom they appeared indistinguishable to outsiders.[30]

Alsatian immigrants were culturally as well as physically elusive. Toward the close of the ante-bellum Alsatian migrations to America, almost two centuries had passed since the conquest of 1648, which had resulted in Alsace's annexation by France. Yet there had still been no conclusive resolution of the province's cultural identity. Though politically integrated into France, Alsace had always rejected French language, education, and high culture, and, due in large part to the province's territorial isolation, little French-Alsatian intermarriage had taken place. Under Louis Philippe (1830-1848) determined efforts were made to draw Alsatians to French culture through education and propagation of the French language. But this effort failed. Alsatians clung tenaciously to their folk traditions and their singular German dialect (in Upper Alsace, a Franconian speech, like Palatine German across the Rhine), and continued to send their children to German-language schools. Because German remained the language of almost all daily business and social relations, few vital inducements existed to change languages. But at the same time a more self-conscious, ethnic rejection of French was taking shape, and it was rejuvenating Alsatian identity. In response to French assimilationist policies, cultural nationalism swept the province, manifesting itself, for example, in increased identification with German and Alsatian art, music, and literature.[31] St. Louis Church's Alsatian immigrant parishioners were the legates of this cultural nationalism, and it is not difficult to imagine that, however invisible as a people they might have been to those around them, they came to America with a heightened sense of their cultural identity.

Yet distinctive as Alsatian identity was, ample bases existed for communal feeling and collective action among the parish's Alsatians and Germans. The differences among all the German dialects present in the parish were hardly great enough to inhibit communication among Alsatians, Swiss, Swabians, and Rhinelanders.[32] There are other indications as well of the Germanness of the Alsatians. Alsatians with European schooling (and the signatures themselves on the 1853 petition suggest most of the Alsatians, and other parishioners, too, had some schooling) had received a German educaton, probably in parish schools. The likelihood of a German education, if any at all, among the Alsatians was testified to by the fact that the trustees of the '50s, the large majority of whom were Alsatian, seem not to have been able to write in French. (It is possible, of course, that they refused to.) They never communicated parish business, even with the Vatican, in French, which was, along with Latin, the language of Church diplomacy. In fact, they were represented in dealings with the Vatican by a French ethnic parishioner. Further testimony to the German education of the Alsatians was their frequent recording of their signatures in the same old-style German handwriting used by their co-parishioners from across the Rhine.[33] Above all else perhaps, Alsatians and Germans in the parish shared a particularly devout Catholicism. All came from the region of western Europe where, as Michael Fogarty has observed, the results of the Reformation remained indeterminate. In an arc descending from Holland in the northwest to northern Italy in the southeast, the numbers of Protestants and Catholics were more likely to be approximately equal then elsewhere in western Europe, a situation which lent itself to intense religious competition, and, Fogarty argues, to greater religious concern and observance.[34] Such intense concern, when fused with a tradition of lay management of temporal affairs shared, as we shall see in the next section, among many parishioners, across national lines, was at the heart of the conflict between parish and hierarchy.

St. Louis parish Alsatians and Germans also shared many common elements of an American way of life, which formed the vessel in which their common cultural background was contained. St. Louis parish had a singular social structure which contrasted markedly with other local German-speaking parishes. But within St. Louis parish, social differences between Alsatians and non-Alsatians and between residential persisters and more recently settled parishioners were also pronounced. These differences help greatly to account for patterns of authority and power both in parish government and in the trustee controversy.

We may more fully grasp social patterns within and among parishes by analyzing the social bases of German-speaking Catholicism in Buffalo in the early '50s. From population samples drawn from sacramental records (and, for St. Louis parish, from the 1852 petition), we may begin by comparing the church-going populations of St. Louis and St. Michael's.[35] The latter provides the best comparison not only because it was then the city's second-largest German-speaking parish, but also because it was established for the purpose of attracting St. Louis parishioners loyal to Bishop Timon. Consequently, a comparison of the two may also provide insight into the social bases of trusteeism itself.

In point of fact, the early character of St. Michael's appears not to have been determined by the exodus of St. Louis Catholics, though some 19 families left the older parish in protest against its trustees.[36] Instead St. Michael's in the early '50s was shaped largely by the recency of arrival in Buffalo (and most probably in America) of the majority of its parishioners, whose collective portrait, as revealed in the samples, suggests a typical immigrant social demography. Thus (Table I) relative to St. Louis, the newer parish had many more males who were under age 40; who had more recently arrived in Buffalo; and who were not naturalized citizens. Furthermore, sacramental records reveal that, in proportion to its total population, St. Michael's had fewer burials of adults than St. Louis.[37] These patterns are easily explained: located in a neighborhood convenient to Buffalo's less affluent eastern sector, where the large majority of recent German immigrants were settling, the newer parish attracted larger numbers of recent arrivals than the less convenient St. Louis. (Reinforcing this choice of parish was the interdict which closed St. Louis between mid-1851 and mid-1855, and made access of its parishioners to the sacraments unsure.)[38] One consequence of relative youthfulness and recency of arrival was that St. Michael's parishioners, in comparison with those at St. Louis, were lower in factors making for civic influence — age, citizenship, and significant length of residence. Another consequence was that (Table I) St. Michael's parishioners had lower socio-economic status: relative to St. Louis, there were fewer owners of land among them; fewer of them were in white collar occupations (business ownership, professions, management); fewer lived in residences with high value; and more lived in Buffalo's poorer residential wards. Reflecting the fact that the city's German-speakers either dominated or were overrepresented in many crafts,[39] both parishes had large, similar percentages of men employed in craft occupations (58% St. Louis; 50% St. Michael's). But the newer parish had a much greater percentage in lower status occupations (unskilled labor/domestic service/teamsters) — 20% for St. Louis and 37% for St. Michael's.

St. Louis parishioners themselves did not show uniformity in the same civil and socio-economic attributes. The parish's probable "charter group," the Alsatians (42% of the St. Louis sample, while but 10% of the St. Michael's), registered higher than others in a considerable number of them. In contrast to the non-French-born (Table II), they were much more likely to be American citizens and to have spent over a decade in Buffalo. Alsatians were also more likely to be among the oldest men in the parish, a reflection perhaps of the slowing down of Alsatian immigration to the U.S. after the late '40s. While some of the differences in socio-economic position (ownership of property; presence in lower status

MODERNITY IN THE SERVICE OF TRADITION

TABLE I
INTERPARISH SOCIAL PATTERNS:
ST. LOUIS AND ST. MICHAEL'S

		St. Louis[1] % of sample	N	St. Michael's[2] % of sample	N
Age	(40+)	43%	(55)	13%	(11)
Years in Buffalo (as of 1855)	0-15	17%	(20)	48%	(27)
	6-10	25%	(29)	27%	(15)
	11-	58%	(65)	25%	(14)
Citizenship	Alien	24%	(26)	59%	(30)
	Naturalized	74% >77%	(81)	39% >41%	(20)
	Native	3%	(4)	2%	(1)
Occupation[3]	Unskilled	12%	(23)	18%	(14)
	Craft	62%	(116)	63%	(44)
	Owns Business	16% >19%	(30)	6% >10%	(5)
	Managerial-Professional	3%	(5)	4%	(3)
	Domestic/Service	2%	(3)	1%	(1)
	Transportation	2%	(4)[A]	5%	(4)
	Miscellaneous	1%	(2)	2%	(2)
	No occupation	3%	(5)[B]	0%	(0)
"Owns Land"[4]		39%	(47)	20%	(12)
Values of Residential Property[C]	0$999	37%	(44)	61%	(34)
	$1000-2999	47% >63%	(56)	32% >39%	(18)
	3000-	16%	(20)	7%	(4)
Residence in Higher Valued, Primarily Residential Wards[5]		62%	(204)	56%	(80)

SOURCES AND NOTES

[1,2] Samples based on: 1852 parish petition (St. Louis); sacramental records of baptism, marriage, and death (St. Michael's); *Buffalo City Directory* (1852-1855); 1855 New York State Census (alphabetized, coded, compiled by Laurence Glasco).

[3] Occupational classification based (with some modifications) on Laurence Glasco, "Ethnicity and Social Structure: Irish, Germans, and Native-Born in Buffalo, New York, 1850-1860" (unpublished Ph.D. dissertation, SUNY/Buffalo, 1973).

[4] Category used by 1855 New York State Census.

[5] Based valuations in Buffalo *Commercial-Advertiser*, 9/2/1855, 2/2/1856.

[A] All teamsters.
[B] All but one of five, over 65 yrs. of age and presumed retired.
[C] No boarders or lodgers in samples.

TABLE II
INTRAPARISH SOCIAL PATTERNS: ST. LOUIS CHURCH BY NATIVITY[1]

		French-born[2] % of sample	N	Others[3] % of sample	N
Age 40+	40-49	40%	(8)	37%	(13)
Years in Buffalo (as of 1855)	0-15	11%	(5)	22%	(15)
	6-10	21%	(10)	27%	(19)
	11-	68%	(30)	51%	(35)
Citizenship	Alien	15%	(6)	69%	(45)
	Naturalized	85%	(34)	29%	(20)
		>85%		>33%	
	Native	0%	(0)	4%	(3)
Occupation[3]	Unskilled	14%	(7)	15%	(10)
	Craft	45%	(23)	57%	(38)
	Owns Business	20%	(10)	14%	(9)
		>24%		>17%	
	Managerial-Professional	4%	(2)	3%	(2)
	Domestic/Service	2%	(1)	6%	(4)
	Transportation	4%	(2)[4]	3%	(2)
	Miscellaneous	2%	(2)	1%	(1)
	No occupation	9%	(5)[5]	1%	(1)
"Owns Land"[4]		40%	(17)	37%	(30)
Values of Residential Property[6]	0$999	29%	(12)	42%	(31)
	$1000-2999	46%	(21)	47%	(35)
		>71%		>58%	
	3000-	25%	(11)	11%	(8)
Residence in Higher Valuated, Primarily Residential Wards		80%	(31)	63%	(46)

SOURCES AND NOTES

[1] Sources for this table are the same as for Table I. However sizes for ward and occupation are smaller than for I, because city directories, which do not provide nativity data, could be used to identify individuals for I, but not II.

[2] "French-born" is the closest category to "Alsatian" the census will allow us; the German names of the "French-born," in every case but one of the petition signers, combine with other impressionistic evidence, to establish that the overwhelmingly majority (c.98%) were Alsatians. The total sample of French-born=55. Data could not always be found for every category for each of 55, so sample sizes for individual categories of information differ.

[3] Others: total sample=74 (63/Germany; 4/USA; 7/Etc.), but data not always found for every category for each of 74.

[4] All teamsters.

[5] All but one of five over 65, and presumed retired.

[6] No boarders or lodgers in samples.

occupations) are not large, and while there were actually fewer Alsatians in craft occupations, Alsatians were significantly more likely to be in white collar employment; to be able to retire at an advanced age in an era when few could afford to do so; to have the most valuable residences; and to live in the more affluent wards.

Because, as we shall see soon, Alsatians were, relative to their numbers in the parish population, overrepresented — indeed always a majority — on trustee boards in the '50s, we must keep these sources of their influence in mind. But it is also necessary to find other perspectives on intraparish stratification. The most important reason for doing so is that Alsatians were a minority, if sizeable, in the parish in the '50s, and could not have exercised dominance in a democratic polity unless able to forge alliances and share power with those having the same vision of parish governance. Length of residence in Buffalo provides an important foundation for such a process of cohesion, and hence it provides another perspective from which to view intraparish stratification. (If projected back far enough into the past, length of residence also is a measure of years of attendance at St. Louis; there were no alternatives for German-speakers until the mid-'40s). Other parishioners likely to share the Alsatians' views would have demonstrated their agreement in no better way than by remaining loyal to the church from its earliest years, through such critical decisions as the adoption of the trustee format and of incorporation, and through the parish's various crises. Moreover, to the extent that length of residence correlates with the attainment of other attributes of civil influence and socio-economic status, there would be a yet broader basis for intergroup cohesion.

Specifically we may compare the relative position in regard to these civil and socio-economic attributes of those parishioners who in 1855, the climax of the crisis, had lived in Buffalo 18 or more, or less than 18, years. Eighteen years has been chosen because it represents the median number of years spent in Buffalo of the French-born sample of signers of the 1852 petition. Coincidentally, this takes us back to the years just prior to the parish's incorporation, and thus draws in those who participated in that decision and remained to defend it.

Table III contains data on St. Louis parishioners by length of residence. It establishes a very pronounced, comparative residential persistence for the group of 49 parishioners (59% Alsatian; 39% German; 2% other) who had been in the city 18 or more years. This is clear when we contrast the 23.5 years median of the 49 not only with the median years residence (13) of the remaining 70 parishioners in the sample, but with all Buffalo's male household heads (8.8) and with Buffalo's oldest males (35-44 years, 9.2; 45-54, 11.4; and 55 and over, 13.4). The 49 were unusual both for a parish with high persistence even for its *less* persistent members and for the city-at-large. These findings point to the opportunities the 49 parishioners had to gain influence simply by having become rooted in a nineteenth-century American community with characteristically high population turnover.[40] This civic influence was increased by the greater likelihood that these laymen were of mature age and were naturalized American citizens. Moreover their persistence also interlocked with attributes of high socio-economic status, providing additional bases for influence: more white collar and less low status employment; residence in more affluent wards; and greater likelihood of living in higher valued residences. Of course, these attributes were sources of cohesion as well as influence, and cohesion was itself increased by the presence of family relations among the 49. On the basis of comparison of names, ages, length of residence, and birthplace, as well as the contiguity of signatures on the 1852 petition, it appears that at least 27% (13) were related.

TABLE III
INTRAPARISH SOCIAL PATTERNS:
ST. LOUIS, BY LENGTH OF RESIDENCE[1]

		18 or more years residence % of sample	N	less than 18 years residence % of sample	N
Nativity	France	59%	(29)	33%	(26)
	German Rhineland[2]	18%	(9)	18%	(14)
	"Germany" unspecified	17%	(7)	13%	(10)
	Bavaria	6%	(3)	26%	(21)
	Etc.	2%	(1)	10%	(8)
Age	(40-)	61%	(30)	32%	(25)
Years in Buffalo (as of 1855)	Average	23.5	(N=49)	13	(N=79)
	Median	22.5	(N=49)	6	(N=79)
Citizenship	Alien	2%	(1)	33%	(22)
	Naturalized	91% >98%	(30)	64% >67%	(43)
	Native	7%	(3)	3%	(2)
Occupation[3]	Unskilled	4%	(2)	16%	(10)
	Craft	56%	(27)	60%	(39)
	Owns Business	21% >23%	(10)	12% >15%	(9)
	Managerial-Professional	2%	(2)	16%	(10)
	Domestic/Service	2%	(1)	4%	(3)
	Transportation	4%	(2)[3]	3%	(2)
	Miscellaneous	0%	(0)	1%	(1)
	No occupation	10%	(4)[4]	1%	(1)
"Owns Land"[4]		38%	(18)	40%	(29)
Values of Residential Property[5]	0-$999	31%	(15)	42%	(29)
	$1000-2999	51% >69%	(25)	41% >17%	(28)
	$3000+	18%	(9)	17%	(12)
Residence in Higher Valuated, Primarily Residential Wards		86%	(42)	55%	(39)

SOURCES AND NOTES

[1] Same sources as Table I, with some limitations upon the use of city directories because of need to identify nativity.
[2] Rhenish Prussia, Baden, Würtemberg
[3] All teamsters.
[4] All but one over 65 years and presumed retired.
[5] No boarders or lodgers in samples.

There are two significant implications of these patterns — one, having to do with authority and power within the parish; the other, concerning the nature of cultural change among St. Louis's immigrant parishioners. Examining the first, we are now able to understand the nature of political relations among the parishioners. Authority flowed outward into the general population of parishioners from a small, higher status group, members of which had been rooted in the city and probably the parish for many years. Within this group was an Alsatian majority. The numerical prominence of the Alsatians within this minority, combined with their position as the parish's largest individual ethnic group in its early years and their favored relationship with the parish's founder, explain how it was that they continued to play a considerable role in church governance in spite of declining numbers (as revealed in the data on the origin of those living in Buffalo less than 18 years). Furthermore, within the group of the most residentially persistent, we can see the possibility of an especially strong, though not necessarily exclusive, community of feeling between Alsatian and German Rhinelanders (at least 18% of those with 18 or more years residence). In contrast to Bavarians, the other large group of the parish's Germans, the Rhinelanders were more likely to have been in Buffalo many years; and their homeland was close to Alsace, their dialect much like Upper Alsatian.

The key political manifestation of these patterns of authority and cohesion lay in their translation into power in the composition of the annually elected boards of trustees. Trustee boards of 1850, '51, '52, and '54 have been analyzed in Table IV.[41] In each of these years, seven men were elected to serve as trustees. (Since nine of them were elected two or three times, there is need only to discover information about 19 of them; of this number, data of at least some sort were found for 16.) The majority of the sixteen trustees show high socio-economic status and rank high in attributes of civic influence. Moreover, the majority, and hence successive trustee boards of the crucial '50s, were French-born: at least 5 of 7 of two boards and fully 4 of 7 of the other two were French-born. The non-French-born were in three cases Rhinelanders (all from Baden); in two other cases, Bavarians; and in the two remaining, were said by the census to be from "Germany, unspecified."* Though ages varied (while usually over 40), the trustees showed a pronounced residential persistence: the median years resident in the city for the 1850 board was 18; the 1851 board, 21; the 1852 board, 19; and the 1854 board, 20. Apparently the approximately 400 adult males in the parish in the '50s were of one mind on the requirements for membership on trustee boards: Members had to share a common commitment to lay control of church temporal affairs; nothing seemed more likely to ensure this commitment, in the minds of parish voters, than being born in France or the German Rhineland, and having roots in the parish from it earliest years.

---

*Whether the census category "Germany, unspecified" was a consequence of a general answer individuals gave to the question of their origin, or of the censustakers's inability to understand more precise answers, it is likely that the actual origin of those in this category reflected the proportions of the specific German subgroups around them. Thus, given the origins of the non-French German-speakers revealed in Table III, it is probable that those here described as "Germany, unspecified" were also Rhinelanders, with some, but less likelihood of their being Bavarian. The census category "Bavarian" probably applied to both Bavarians and residents of the small Rhenish Bavarian province. I believe our knowledge of German immigration allows us to assume, as I have done here, that a very large majority of those in this category were from Bavaria itself.

TABLE IV
SOCIAL CHARACTERISTICS: ST. LOUIS CHURCH TRUSTEES
1850, 1851, 1852, 1854.[1]

Nativity	French-born	56%	(9)
	German Rhineland	5%	(3)
	Bavaria	12.5%	(2)
	"Germany" (unspecified)	12.5%	(2)
Age	40 or over =	58%	(7)
	Median = 49 years		N=12)
Years in Buffalo (as of 1855)[2]	Average = 21.5 years		(N=14)
	Median = 23 years		(N=14)
Citizenship	Alien	0%	(0)
	Naturalized	100%	(10)
	Native	0%	(0)
Occupation	Craft	23%	(3)
	Owns business	61%	(8)
	Miscellaneous	8%	(1)
	No occupation	8%	(1)
	Unskilled, domestic/ service; transportation; managerial/professional	0%	(0)
"Owns Land"		61%	(8)
Values of residential property[3]	$0-999	9%	(1)
	$1000-2999	36%	(4)
	$3000-	55%	(6)
	Median = $3000		
Residence in higher primarily residential ward		75%	(9)

[1] Same sources as Tables I and III, with same limitations.
[2] All were still residents in 1855.
[3] No boarders or lodgers in sample.

Trustees with this commitment were not new at St. Louis. In 1843, for example, during the parish's first confrontation with the hierarchy (Bishop Hughes), 292 adult males cast ballots for two contested seats on the board. Of the three candidates, the one against lay control got four votes; the other two split the remaining 288.[42] But the 1843 election was held when the parish was still young, and a relatively few years separated established parishioners from newcomers. By the 1850s, however, the gap could be decades, not years. In fact, of the 79 parishioners in the sample with less than 18 years residence, 22 (28%) had been in the city five years or less in 1855. This group of pro-trustee newcomers poses, in sharp relief, the problem of the political relations between trustee and voter. We must assume that a continual pattern of election of the same sort of individual, and a backing — even by the most recent newcomers — of the struggle waged by those individuals, suggests the existence within the parish of well-rooted deference relations, not merely of simple collective agreement. This, in turn, suggests strongly that in St. Louis parish the formal mechanisms of democracy and formal principles of republican self-government masked communal loyalties and commitment to emergent status hierarchies.[43] Thus, St. Louis parish was busy creating its own traditions of governance and leadership, which may only superficially be described as "republican." Then, too, the backing of newcomers for trustees standing for lay control may also suggest the extent to which lay control was part of the cultural baggage of many of the immigrants. In fact, as the next section will demonstrate, the notion of lay control of church temporalities did have roots in the Old World, so that the issues in the American parish were translatable into terms which even most of the most recently immigrated parishioners could understand.

The second implication of the findings derived from the parish sample is more far-reaching. On the face of it, the notion advanced by this essay — that European communal tradition in an emergent American form (i.e., parish trusteeism) played a role in the defiance of the hierarchy — is puzzling in light of the social profile of the petition signers. According to several common civil and socioeconomic indicators of assimilation, the parishioners and trustees registered high for Buffalo's German Catholics, and thus would appear to be in lock-step movement toward becoming "American." Such a conclusion, however, would not help us understand the ethnic culture of the parish. Whatever theorems might have been developed at a later day to dichotomize "old" and "new" in the lives of immigrants, St. Louis parishioners were creating a more complex reality, combining effectiveness in coming to terms with the American social and economic systems with a desire to uphold those European traditions they continued to believe culturally significant. Yet they did not defend tradition without ambivalence and even confusion, for inevitably, while engaged in the defense of tradition, they acted in the changed circumstances of American life in a manner which transformed tradition. In order to understand this situation, we must now investigate the parish's defense of its position, analyzing the European roots of St. Louis's belief in lay prerogatives, and exploring the limits of the parish's dissent inherent in its complex relation to tradition.

Over approximately a dozen years of conflict, the defense of trustee prerogatives at St. Louis Church involved two distinct arguments. As stated, for example, in the 1852 petition and in the parish's memorial to Bedini during his 1853 mediation, the first held that through its articles of incorporation the parish had obtained rights to the management and control of its property. In addition, the parish had incurred a legal obligation to abide by the terms of its incorporation — in other words, through their trustees, the laymen had no legal choice but to exercise the powers legally granted them.[44] Both aspects of the first argument held that the law mandated implicitly that the Catholic clergy must play only a secondary role, largely consultative, in managing such property. The second argument, also stated in the petition, held that the parish's first church-goers and its subsequent members had enjoyed privileges of lay management of church property in their European villages, and simply wished to exercise the same prerogatives, in partnership with the clergy, in their new, American homes. It was the obstinacy of its bishops alone which forced the parish into conflict with the Church.[45]

These arguments appear quite different. The first is based on political and ideological concerns arising from life in a modernizing republican polity, in which citizens wished to rule themselves, and in which there was widespread desire to limit the political power and secular activity of organized religion. The second harkens back to European communal traditions. The first would lead us to see lay assertiveness as a hopeful reaching out for self-government and new, American liberties, a natural course of events for citizens eagerly assimilating into republican society. The second, however, would lead us to see lay assertiveness as based upon a desire to reestablish Old World tradition without particular regard for, or perhaps in spite of, New World ideals and realities.

Yet, while distinctive, these arguments are not mutually exclusive. The key to resolving this paradox lies in the parish's decision in 1838 to incorporate — a voluntary, and for Catholic parishes not common, step taken under a state law which did not force religious institutions to take advantage of its provisions.[46] Analyzed in the context of the parish's previous and subsequent history, incorporation emerges as an act undertaken to safeguard an Old World tradition of lay management which had become institutionalized in 1829, at the time of the parish's establishment, but was perceived a decade later to be threatened. The situation was not static, however, for the act of incorporation set the parish's laymen on the path of a civil acculturation which they did not intend and which created contradictory impulses in their relationship to their church and its leadership.

Unfortunately, this "key" is not as easily grasped as one searching for neat explanations would prefer. There is a gnawing evidentiary gap in reconstructing the history of the parish prior to the point in the early '40s when the laity clashed with Bishop Hughes, and generated a large number of printed documents in defense of its position. Much has to be inferred from the sparse record of the parish's earliest years, or read backward from statements made in the heat of later events.

A further problem is the "voice" with which the parish spoke. Much of the parish's defense, in print and in interviews before the Catholic hierarchy, was put forward by its most prominent laymen, William LeCouteulx, the elderly, intellectual son of the church's founder. (He also had the virtue of being able to address the Vatican in decorous French.) His father, Louis, the scion of a titled Norman family who had come to America during the Terror and accumulated considerable wealth speculating in western New York land, had donated the property on which St. Louis Church and its school and cemetery were established. The 1852 petition bears the mark of William LeCouteulx's influence. It repeats his careful, considered arguments, and was written in his hand. Since we often must depend on his view of the parish's early years, it is necessary to sort out the problem that his advocacy poses in reconstructing events.[47]

The problem lies in the fact that he often wrote about the early years of the parish as if the majority of its members were, in his words, "French," as were he and his father.[48] Though perhaps natural for a French ethnic used to thinking of the homeland as homogeneous, his use of "French" obscured both the distinct nature of Alsatian identity and the very great probability that, even though the largest ethnic group was probably Alsatian, the majority of the parish was composed of Germans from the various states of the south and west. This description of the parish's early population, which he sometimes extended into its present, must have created confusion in the minds of the parish's chief antagonists, its second and third bishops, the Irishmen Hughes and Timon. After all, their tenures post-dated St. Louis parish's early years, so they were not intimately aware of its history. Moreover, *their* descriptions of the parish as "German,"[49] in both its past and present, suggest that they did not understand the nice distinctions between "Alsatian" and "German," just as LeCouteulx neglected the difference between "French" and "Alsatian." In consequence, the two bishops were never prepared to entertain seriously LeCouteulx's claim that the *French* laymen of the parish, with his father's consent, were instrumental in its incorporation, desirous as they then were said to be to protect their customary privileges in managing the church temporalities. At other times, the claim simply infuriated the bishops, for when they bothered at all to take it on its own terms, they were quick to point out that nothing in the French Catholic tradition allowed for the veritable and legalized control they believed the laymen demanded, let alone the insubordination they displayed. On both counts the clerical position was the stronger,[50] but, as we shall now see, the chaotic situation of ethnic Catholicism in the mid-nineteenth century, which is suggested by the jumble of misconstrued ethnicities complicating the parish's relations with its bishops, led an accepted Old World religious tradition to become the circumstance for New World disobedience.

While the legally sanctioned control the trustees sought bore little resemblance to the episcopally controlled parish governance of Alsace or of France, a tradition of lay management was well-entrenched in both places from the early Middle Ages[51] to the very eve of the era of mass migration, and over long centuries had weathered and indeed been strengthened by the vicissitudes of history. The Reformation and Counter Reformation brought no change, and indeed actually reinforced, communal traditions of lay management. The Council of Trent specifically approved of such parish arrangements, because, in its enhanced concern for the spiritual welfare and religious involvement of the laity, it wished to reorient Catholicism so that the Church might become more parish-centered.[52] Moreover, reinforcement also came from the new rivalry between Protestant and Catholic, which strengthened the two faiths in contested areas like Alsace by increasing individual religious involvement.[53] Nor for Alsatians was the situation changed in the 17th century by annexation into France, for Alsatians carried their own parish traditions into the new episcopal structure whose traditions, in this regard, were complementary. While the repression suffered by institutional Catholicism during the French Revolution did briefly lead to a degeneration of lay management traditions, they were reinstitutionalized, with guarantees added in the civil law, at the time in 1801 of the restoration of episcopal structure and authority under Napoleon.[54]

In France and in Alsace there were parish management bodies (called "fabrique"*) on which sat both lay trustees (called "marguilliers"), who were appointed from among prominent parishioners by the Bishop and the parish priest. Toward the modern era, secular influences entered into the appointment of the *fabrique,* so that one finds the civil authority now appointing a minority of its members and itself represented in the person of the mayor. The criteria for appointment usually were the exercise of religious obligations; residence convenient to the church; and freedom from indebtedness.[55] Canon law defined little of the daily responsibilities of the *fabrique*. In the individual diocese, these were usually established by the bishop, though over many centuries countless local customs initiated by the laity came to supplement episcopal principles. The duties of the *fabrique* usually included not only providing for maintenance of parish buildings and religious objects and art, but also paying parish employees. Once a year, the financial records of the parish were opened to the bishop, who visited the *marguilliers* at their church, examining the books and the maintenance of the church. Bishops found, and routinely complained over many centuries, that the *marguilliers* were squandering funds, complaints reappearing many centuries later in the judgments of American bishops about trustee bodies in their dioceses. But, as in many American dioceses, Old World episcopal authorities had little choice but to accept the system of lay management with clerical oversight. The alternatives were impossible: total control by an already overworked priest, or the

---

*Alsatians used this French term; see below.

centralization of all parish finances, down to the pettiest expenditures, in the hands of a distant bishop. After centuries, too, it would have been very difficult to end the system, for what bishops might regard as an unfortunate expedient, parishioners doubtless had come to regard as a legitimate prerogative. So the system lumbered on from century to century, with the *fabrique* alternately entreated to do better and threatened when it failed, but largely undisturbed in its role.[56]

The tradition of *fabrique* and *marguillier* took root in French North American communities (Quebec,[57] Detroit[58] and Louisiana[59]) and then began its own local processes of evolution, adding, for example, trustee election to replace episcopal nomination. In these French areas, the legitimacy of trusteeship, even when combined with such a democratic apparatus as election, is attested to in each case by the fact that it was established under conditions of episcopal oversight.[60] In contrast, late 18th- and 19th-century Anglo-American or (in many fewer instances) Irish-American trusteeship lacked such legitimacy: it was without the sanction of custom, and had taken root in an episcopal vacuum, in which Catholicism was influenced by the Protestant practice which surrounded it. And, as we have noted, historical circumstances unique to 19th-century Ireland rendered the possibility of conflict between Irish immigrant laymen in America and the Church increasingly unlikely.

These ethnic differences in religious tradition suggest the difficulties St. Louis parish's Alsatians, in contrast to their French countrymen elsewhere in North America, were likely to experience preserving their customary mehtods of conducting parish affairs.[61] At first, the Alsatians were numerically significant, and influenced perhaps by the intensification of cultural nationalism in their homeland at the time of their emigration, firmly committed to preserving their customs. Moreover, their influence was enhanced by the favor accorded them by the parish's French benefactor. For his part, too, the elder LeCouteulx approved of lay management, and may also have approved of incorporation, though the point was hotly contested for many years.[62] Moreover, because of his own French background and the problems the aging, increasingly ineffectual prelate had administering a diocese then as large as New York State, their first bishop, Jean DuBois, had accepted trustees as a necessary evil. He had even consented both to their election, which was certainly easier for him than appointing them from 360 miles away, and apparently to the parish's incorporation, though here too the matter was contested.[63] But after DuBois came Hughes and Timon, both of whom had little personal experience with or cultural heritage of lay management, and seemed confused about the very identity of the Alsatians. They were unlikely either to understand the Alsatians' cultural imperatives or to see the prerogatives St. Louis laymen sought as anything but evil. The consequences were predictable, and went beyond the fact that it was difficult for either bishop to give the parish a sympathetic hearing. As important, there was no common frame of reference through which the parish and its bishops could work out the carefully defined division of lay and clerical duties on which the *fabrique* in Alsace had depended for the maintenance of its moral integrity within the Church.

Once we consider that the defense of trustee prerogatives may well have involved the defense of an Old World tradition, crucial, but at the time inadequately explained, aspects of the struggle became clear. First, the 1838 decision to incorporate may be seen as a defensive reaction. On the one hand, the parish may have been responding to the decision of the 1829 Baltimore Council to curb trustee power in American parishes,[64] and even more immediately to the prospect of a local implementation of the decision. Earlier in 1838 tough-minded

John Hughes became bishop of the diocese of New York. As DuBois' coadjutor, he had recently established a reputation for opposing lay trustees at the New York City cathedral and was almost certain, as Bishop, to be more insistent on the universal application of the council's resolve than DuBois had been. Hughes soon proved these likely fears correct, promulgating an anti-trustee *Pastoral Letter* and acting to discipline the trustees of New York City parishes, before eventually, in 1843, turning his attention to Buffalo.[65]

On the other hand, within a pluralistic institution like the parish, ethnic diversity itself might have been perceived to be as great a threat to one group's tradition as the Irish hierarchy. There may well have been a feeling among the Alsatians of a need to consolidate or freeze their influence through incorporation, because of the threat beginning to be posed by the growing number of newly immigrated Catholics in Buffalo. Recall that at the time of incorporation St. Louis was still the city's only Catholic Church. Though one year before a small number of Irish had left St. Louis, claiming they had been, in the words of the diocesan historian, "forced out"[66] they did not have their own church until 1841. The increasing pressure they felt to leave St. Louis may well point to new anxieties among the St. Louis Alsatians.

Amidst perceived threats to Alsatian predominance, it was probably at this point in the parish's history that a less conscious process of development than the public act of incorporation took shape: a hardening of lines of cooperation, influence, and authority. The parish was increasingly not Alsatian. But its leadership, both informal and trustee, was probably composed of residentially persistent, mature (if not in some cases already aging) Alsatian men, who enjoyed power under minority circumstances, but felt threatened in its future exercise. An outstanding fact of the struggle in the parish is that this minority convinced others, non-Alsatian German-speakers, to follow its lead — German Rhinelanders particularly, who also had a tradition of lay management among the cultural baggage they brought to America. It is known that the institution of *kirchenraten* (church councils), which functioned like *fabrique*, existed in the Rhineland.[67] No doubt both the Alsatian *fabrique* and the Rhineland *kirchenrat* had a common origin in a distant, prenational past, though after the French conquest of Alsace, customs of lay management of church temporalities on each side of the Rhine had ceased their simultaneous development.[68]

Of course, self-conscious disobedience to clerical authority, even in temporal affairs, was not an accepted tradition west or east of the Rhine. There can be little doubt that the parishioners felt the weight of the burden they had created for themselves in struggling, against their own priests, to organize their communities in familiar ways. The laymen's dilemma is constantly highlighted by the complex rhetoric they marshaled when explaining their position. There is, for example, the elaborately deferential language employed when addressing the hierarchy, particularly Archbishop Bedini, even after he abruptly set aside their claims.[69] But even more, their division against themselves is revealed in a defense which shifts in ways revealing ambivalence about disobedience in the name of reaching out after new freedoms. Thus, though they do speak increasingly of "rights" and "freedoms" which are theirs as citizens and by virtue of incorporation,[70] they also speak to Bedini of their obligation to the legitimate authority of the law under which they incorporated.[71] Furthermore, they promise at times that if their claims are recognized they can better obey their priests;[72] and they announce, too, that they are loyal Catholics and that their disobedience is reluctant, a consequence of unfortunate circumstance or of their bishop's misuse of power (thus disavowing any intention to break with the bishop over his *legitimate* powers).[73] They did not seem able to convince themselves that rights were the sole or best basis for establishing a view of what was good or moral. This ambivalence suggests both an inability to break with the abiding concern of the Catholic tradition for obedience to legitimate authority, and a refusal to embrace comfortably the individualistic and democratic-republican formulations of American political ideology. Critics like Bedini, who saw as wholly disingenuous insistence upon obedience to a law one need not have chosen to obey in the first place, failed to see the terrible choice the parish embraced in incorporating. It had to balance off the demands of two legitimate, competing authorities, *both* with compelling claims to its obedience: the Church, which exacted obedience as the price of salvation; and the State, which exacted self-government as the price of liberty.

Certainly St. Louis parish's situation may have been more complex than most cases of trusteeism, particularly because of its incorporation. But the parish's larger dilemma, the battle of the claims of two respected traditions — a communal form and a religious doctrine of obedience — between which the state might be asked to interpose itself, may well have been a problem more common to Catholic laymen than has previously been recognized. Other parishes may not have been as articulate in stating the Old World roots of trusteeism, assuming perhaps that what seemed so natural needed no historical justification. In St. Louis's case, it took William LeCouteulx, as an engaged intellectual, to make explicit what others around him saw as self-evident.

But the dilemma remained, and with their church closed by an interdict and their trustees excommunicated, the parish had to choose.

In the end, it opted for the Church. Nothing proves its commitment to tradition more than the way in which the conflict ended. Within a mere two months after seeking the eager embrace of nativist politicians and hence successfully obtaining legislation to make Timon's claims on their property and polity impossible,[74] the parish's resistance completely collapsed. It accepted the mediation of the eminent Jesuit missionary, Father F.X. Weninger. He achieved a compromise which allowed the parish some autonomy, but gave Timon a good deal of power in its affairs. Thus, while not allowed to hand-pick the slate of nominees for trustee, as he had wished, Timon was now able to examine the parish's books and consult with it on all major expenditures and the hiring of church employees; for its part, the parish was granted the right to remain incorporated, and generally henceforth to enjoy a greater degree of practical self-government, through its trustees, than any other Buffalo parish.[75] The most telling aspect of the process of conciliation was the underlying reason why the trustees consented, in the first place, to Weninger's mediation. Simply stated: the parish hungered for its religion, for the ritual and sacraments of the Church. The signs had been present for some time. Their church closed by an interdict (and thus all parishioners' access to the sacraments unsure to the extent they must now be accepted at another church), and their trustees, in June, 1854, excommunicated, the parishioners worried about the fate of their souls. Since 1852, there had been a steady barrage of complaints that the interdict "deprived [them] of religious succor;" that they suffered "spiritual deprivations," and "the greatest spiritual privations;" and they wrote the Pope in 1852 of their "spiritual suffering."[76] The exact nature of this suffering is unclear, for there is no evidence that rank-and-file St. Louis loyalists were denied the sacraments when they presented themselves at other churches.[77] The situation of the trustees (prior to excommunication) many well, of course, have been different, though the evidence even here is not substantial.

It is not clear how common was the situation implied by the marriage of a trustee's son and the daughter of a long-time, pro-trustee parishioner, which had to be solemnized by a Protestant minister for want of an obliging priest.[78] Perhaps more powerful than anything else was the intense anxiety bred of the *possibility* (and eventually, for the trustees, the certainty) of being denied the sacraments, particularly the last rites — which may well have been on the minds of the approximately one-quarter of the parish over 50.[79]

By September, 1854, the signs of a spiritual crisis were manifest. At that time, with Timon's permission, the interdict and excommunication were temporarily lifted, and Father Weninger gave a "mission" (i.e., revival), which a number of parishioners attended. But the trustees appear to have stayed away. Moreover, they and the parish's male voters unanimously rejected the efforts toward mediation of the conflict which Timon proposed at that time. A year later, not long after the passage of the Putnam Law, Timon again temporarily lifted the interdict and the excommunication to enable Weninger to conduct a mission. The event was a huge success. Perhaps having risked so much in allying with the Church's enemies, the parishioners' spiritual anxieties had reached intolerable proportions. Three of the trustees, said Timon, were "converted" on the spot. It is unclear whether Timon used "converted" here in a spiritual or political sense. It is clear, however, that Weninger's mediation, a political act with immediate spiritual consequences, came very soon after the mission. And after the drafting of an agreement, the church was reopened.[80]

In the charged religious atmosphere of the mid-'50s, the collapse of St. Louis's resistance was a great disappointment to Buffalo's Protestant politicians and opinion leaders. In encouraging the parish over the years, they had apparently looked to the controversy to check Timon's power and to provide a local vindication of the Reformation.[81] Perhaps they hoped that, like Buffalo's small, German "Free Catholic" congregation, which had broken with institutional Catholicism,[82] St. Louis would leave the Church. (This hope was probably strengthened in 1851 when the parish briefly held services without a priest, and in 1855 when it publicly allied with nativists.) But there is no record of any individual St. Louis parishioner, including the excommunicated trustees, leaving the Church. Indeed, the excommunication was soon lifted, and the trustees reentered the fold.[83] So did William LeCouteulx, who, it was well-known in Buffalo, called for and received the last rites from Timon himself when mortally ill in 1859.[84] Doubtless the parishioners were changed by the conflict, at the end perhaps more deeply involved with American ideology, and thus more self-consciously "American" in their conception of themselves. But their ambivalence remained. In the end they settled for the prerogatives (to some extent themselves transformed, it was true) they and their ancestors had enjoyed in the European Church, and they eschewed any antagonistic relation to Catholicism based on new rights and liberties.

But while St. Louis parish failed to fulfill the hopes of many Buffalo Protestants, the Catholic Church failed to fulfill their worst fears — and this perhaps helps to explain why political, as opposed to cultural, anti-Catholicism collapsed in Buffalo in the mid-'50s. To be sure, locally as nationally the issue of the expansion of slavery overwhelmed fears of Papal subversion. As elsewhere, the Republican Party drew the votes of the large majority of Buffalo Protestants who had once backed the nativist American Party.[85] But it was also true that even while marshaling local Protestants against Catholicism and encouraging the St. Louis laity, local Protestant opinion leaders, such as the editor of the prestigious

Commercial Advertiser, had been forced to acknowledge that the Church was proving itself a socially stabilizing force. Publicly this was granted because of the charitable, educational, and hospital work of the diocese among impoverished or working class German and particularly Irish immigrants.[86]

But less evident to the public eye, as the St. Louis struggle established and as many thoughtful Protestants may have sensed, the Church was proving a fortress of moral order in the midst of the fragmenting, custom-smashing forces unleashed by democracy and capitalism. However great remained Protestant doubts about Catholic ritual and doctrine, the social meaning of the St. Louis conflict for them may well have been that the Church had the authority to make men question liberating but potentially disorganizing actions taken in response to the social opportunities presented in a liberal and democratic republic. In the battle within ante-bellum American Protestantism between the imperatives of moral freedom and those of moral order, between conservative evangelical reformers bent on the perfection of the individual and radical evangelical liberationists bent on the perfection of society, most higher status Buffalo Protestants had chosen order. They had crusaded against liquor and the desecration of the Sabbath; proposed the development of custodial, penal, and educational institutions; and opposed abolitionism. So also had the majority of middle class American Protestants elsewhere, all responding to the frightening pace of seemingly inchoate social change around them.[87] In opting for order, they found the Catholic Church and socially respectable Catholics like the St. Louis laymen logical, it not entirely acceptable, allies.

SUNY/Buffalo David A. Gerber

FOOTNOTES

The author gratefully acknowledges the assistance of the American Philosophical Society, the Center for the Study of American Catholicism and the Research Foundation of the State University of New York in providing funds for the support of research.

1. "A Notre Saint Père, le Pape Pie IX . . .," (petition dated) Sept. 1, 1852, folio 176, *Scritture Riferite nei Congressi: America Centrale* (hereafter as, *Scritture*), Congregation of Propaganda Fide (hereafter as, CPF), Rome, microfilms at Archives of the University of Notre Dame (hereafter as, AUND).

2. A summary of the conflict can be found in Rev. Thomas Donahue, D.D., *History of The Catholic Church in Western New York* (Buffalo, 1904), pp. 141-189. Also, see, [author unknown] *Belege und Berichte über Angelegenheiten der St. Louis Kirche* (Buffalo, 1852), Canisius College Archives, Buffalo (hereafter as, CCA).

3. Rev. Peter Guilday, *A History of the Councils of Baltimore, 1791-1884* (New York, 1932), pp. 87, 90-91; R.F. McNamara, "Trusteeism in The Atlantic States, 1785-1863," *Catholic Historical Review* XXX (1944): 146-147.

4. Rev. James F. Connelly, *The Visit of Archbishop Gaetano Bedini to The United States of America (June, 1853-February, 1854)* (Rome, 1960), pp. 3, 13, 50, 73. New York *Journal of Commerce,* Sept. 17, Oct. 22, Nov. 19, 1842; Boston *Congregationalist,* Apr. 2, 1852, July 22, 1853, New York *Observer,* June 30, 1853; Cincinnati *Gazette,* Nov. 9, 1853.

5. Other parishes, in Philadelphia (1812, 1821) and New Orleans (1828, 1838), had gone to state legislatures in battles against their bishops, but none of these had allied with anti-Catholic politicians nor sought legislation putting general constraints upon the Church. See, John Gilmary Shea, *The History of The Catholic Church in The United States*, 4 vol. (New York, 1886-1892), III, pp. 215, 242, 403, 672-679.

6. On St. Louis parish's brief alliance with nativist politicians and the drafting and passage of the Putnam Law, see, Donohue, *History of The Catholic Church in Western New York*, p. 179; W.S. Tisdale, ed., *The Controversy between Senator Brooks and John, Archbishop of New York . . . .* (New York, 1855); Rev. Joseph P. Murphy, *The laws of The State of New York Affecting Church Property* (Washington, D.C., 1957), pp. 46-49; John, Cardinal Farley, *The Life of John, Cardinal McCloskey: First Prince of The Church in America, 1810-1885* (New York, 1918), pp. 184-194. Richard Shaw, *Dagger John: The Unquiet Life and Times of Archbishop John Hughes of New York* (New York, 1977), pp. 294-297.

7. On the related problems of church property ownership, incorporation, and church governance, see, Patrick J. Dignan, *A History of the Legal Incorporation of Church Property in The United States, 1784-1932* (Washington, D.C., 1933); Martin Joseph Becker, *A History of Catholic Life in The Diocese of Albany, 1609-1864* (New York, 1975), pp. 116-119, 122-130, 132-162, 169-202; Rev. Joseph P. Murphy, *The Laws of New York Affecting Church Property*. For other relevant citations of a more specific and empirical nature, see, notes 9 and 10, *infra*.

8. Rev. Thomas T. McAvoy, *A History of the Catholic Church in The United States* (Notre Dame, 1969), pp. 93-94.

9. E.g.: Shea, *History of the Catholic Church . . . .*, III, pp. 214-216, 229-251, 399-400, 495-496, 672-680; McNamara, "Trusteeism in the Atlantic States . . . ."; Rev. Gerald C. Tracey, "Evils of Trusteeism," *Historical Studies and Records* VIII (1915): 137; Donohue, *History of the Catholic Church in Western New York*, pp. 141-142; C.J. Nuesse, *The Social Thought of American Catholics, 1634-1829* (Westminster, Md., 1945), pp. 175-178; Rev. Peter Guilday, "Trusteeism," *Catholic Historical Records and Studies* (XVIII (1928): 7-13. Written in this vein, to the extent it continues to see trusteeism as a "problem" not a phenomenon to be analyzed, but considerably more dispassionate and subtle, is Rev. John Tracey Ellis, *Catholics in Colonial America* (Baltimore, 1965), pp. 443-445.

10. Patrick Carey, "Two Episcopal Views of Lay-Clerical Conflicts: 1785-1860," *Records of the American Catholic Historical Society* LLXXXVII (1976): 85-114; *A National Church: Catholic Search for Identity, 1820-1829*, Center for The Study of American Catholicism, Working Paper Series, No. 3 (Fall, 1977); "The Laity's Understanding of The Trustee System, 1785-1855," *Catholic Historical Review* LXIV (July, 1978): 357-376; and "Trusteeism: American Catholic Search for Identity, 1785-1860" (a research note) *American Catholic Studies Newsletter* III (Fall, 1977): 4-6.

11. Carey's interpretation leads him to conclusions with which the more thoughtful, less phobic nativists might not have been ill at ease. He contends that the almost total failure of the American hierarchy to respond creatively and flexibly to republican culture has added significantly to American Catholicism's problems. By refusing to make peace with a new world of democratic ideas and republican political practice through, for example, compromise with trustee demands for greater parish self-government, Carey believes that an uncompromising hierarchy exiled American Catholicism to the margins of a liberal, pluralist society. See Carey, *A National Church . . . .*, pp. 21-24; and "The Laity's Understanding . . . .," 373-376.

12. For an extensive and brilliant exposition of the various formulations of ante-bellum republicanism, see, Michael F. Holt, *The Political Crisis of the 1850s* (New York, 1978). Also, Rush Welter, *The Mind of America, 1820-1860* (New York, 1975).

13. Nuesse, *The Social Thought of American Catholics* . . . ., pp. 179-180, 281-286.

14. Emmet Larkin, "The Devotional Revolution in Ireland, 1850-1875," *American Historical Review* 77 (1962): 625-652; David W. Miller, "Irish Catholicism and The Great Famine," *Journal of Social History* IX (Fall, 1975-6): 81-98. William V. Shannon, *The American Irish: A Political and Social Portrait* (New York, 1963), pp. 15-19; Edward M. Levine, *The Irish and Irish Politicians* (Notre Dame, 1966), pp. 31-51. Thomas N. Brown, "The Origins and Character of Irish-American Nationalism," *Review of Politics* XVIII (1956): 346-348.

15. Indeed, as is very well known, Irish-Americans were not only for many decades the Church's principal defender against various varieties of nativism but came early in the nation's history to control its episcopacy. Conflicts between Irish priests and laymen and the hierarchy seem limited exclusively to a brief period in the early nineteenth century when the Irish and French battled for prominence within the Church; see, John Tracey Ellis, *American Catholicism* (Chicago, 1969), pp. 47-50; McAvoy, *A History of the American Catholic Church* . . . ., Chapters 4, 5, 6, 7, 8, passim.

16. Alfred G. Stritch, "Trusteeism in The Old Northwest," *Catholic Historical Review* XXX (July, 1944): 156-164; McNamara, "Trusteeism in The Atlantic States," 144-149; Becker, *A History of Catholic Life in The Diocese of Albany* . . . .," pp. 169-202 passim; Jay Dolan, *The Immigrant Church: New York's Irish and German Catholics, 1815-1865* (Baltimore, 1975), pp. 89-91; Rev. Emmet H. Rothan, *The German Catholic Immigrant in The United States (1830-1860)* (Washington, D.C., 1946), p. 59; Bishop John Timon to Bishop Peter Paul Lefevere, September 7, 1851, Collection: Detroit Diocese, 1843-1852, III-2-h, AUND.

17. Mack Walker, *German Hometowns: Community, State, and General Estate, 1648-1871* (Ithaca, 1971), Chapters 2, 4, 5, 7, 8, and 10 passim.

18. Both Ellis, *Catholics in Colonial America*, pp. 443-444 (regarding the Old World origins of the trustees invoking *jus patronatus*), and Carey, "The Laity's Understanding of the Trustee System," 368-376 (in ways at odds, I believe, with his larger thesis on republican origins of trustee conflict) have suggested the possible relevance of European roots of trusteeism. But only Rev. V.J. Fecher, *A Study of The Movement for German National Parishes in Philadelphia and Baltimore, 1787-1802* (Rome, 1955), pp. 254-279 has sought seriously to uncover those roots and discuss their significance and meanings. This essay, which develops the relevance of those European roots, is greatly indebted to Rev. Fecher, though he was less concerned with trusteeism as such than with ethnic rivalries and conflicts wihtin Catholicism.

19. A conceptualization of immigrant experience derives from Herbert Gutman's now class, "Work, Culture, and Society in Industrializing America, 1815-1919," *American Historical Review* 78 (1973): 531-588, and is suggested in his *The Black Family in Slavery and Freedom, 1750-1920* (New York, 1976), Chapter I and passim. Also, see, Timothy L. Smith, "Religious Denominations as Ethnic Communities: A Regional Case Study," *Church History* 35 (1966): 207-226, and "Religion and Ethnicity in America," *American Historical Review*, 83 (1978): 1155-1185.

20. Buffalo, *Die Weltbürger*, January 29, 1839; Rev. Joseph Salzbacher, *Meine Reise nach Nord-Amerika* (Vienna, 1845), p. 260; Donohue, *History of the Catholic Church in Western New York*, pp. 114-127, 253-254; Anita Louise Beaudette, *A Man and A Church Named Louis* (undated typescript at St. Louis Church, Buffalo), pp. 2, 15-16, 25, 28-29; Paul Batt, "The Enduring Spirit of St. Louis Church," *Buffalo News Magazine*, Nov. 19, 1978, 6-9; Martha J.F. Murray, "Memoir of Stephen Louis Le Couteulx de Caumont," *Publications of The Buffalo Historical Society*, IX (1906), 449; St. Louis Church, *Matrimonial Register, 1829-1836*, and *Baptismorum Registrum, 1829-1836*, at St. Louis Church, Buffalo. (One can get little more from sacramental records than impressions of nationality revealed by names; only occasionally is place of birth recorded. For these early years, it is also very difficult to find

other sources for the sake of crosschecking the names recorded.) Employing François Houtart's "Sacramental index" (see his *Aspects Sociologiques du Catholicisme Américain* [Paris, 1957], pp. 227 ff.), St. Louis, before 1860, registers much higher than other, comparably sized German-speaking parishes (St. Ann's and St. Michael's) in number of congregants. No non-German parish was anywhere near to equal in size to these three before 1860.

21. Rev. Robert T. Bapst, "A Brief History of St. Louis Church," in Bapst, ed., *125th Anniversary, 1829-1954, St. Louis Church, Buffalo* (Buffalo, 1954), 13-14.

22. Rev. John Timon, *Missions in Western New York and Church History of the Diocese of Buffalo* (Buffalo, 1862), pp. 215-216, CCA; Donohue, *History of The Catholic Church in Western New York*, pp. 229-257 passim.

23. Buffalo *Commercial Advertiser*, February 10, 1854, February 2, 1856; [no author], "The Health of The City of Buffalo: Past, Present, and Prospective," *Buffalo Medical Journal*, X (1854-1855), 373-381; *Buffalo Medical Journal*, IXX (1852-1853), 333 [cholera statistics]; Laurence Glascoe, "Ethnicity and Social Structure: Irish, Germans, and Native-Born in Buffalo, New York, 1850-1860" (unpublished Ph.D. dissertation, SUNY/Buffalo, 1973), pp. 5, 9-10, 13, 16-17, and Chapters 2 and 3, *passim*.

24. Timon, *Missions in Western New York* . . . ., p. 216; Donohue, *History of The Catholic Church in Western New York*, pp. 245-246, 250-251, 258-260; Buffalo *Commercial Advertiser*, February 10, 1854. St. Louis Church, *Matrimonial Register, 1829-1836, Baptismorum Registrum, 1829-1836*, and *Liber Defunctorium*, at St. Louis Church, Buffalo, all trace the gradual decline of Irish names in the parish.

25. Charles G. Deuther, *The Life and Times of Right Rev. John Timon, D.D., First Roman Catholic Bishop of The Diocese of Buffalo* (Buffalo, 1870), p. 113.

26. Donohue, *History of The Catholic Church in Western New York*, pp. 260-261; Pierre Alphonse Le Couteulx [draft, legal documents about property gift to French who who left St. Louis], July 26, 1851, at Our Lady of Lourdes Church, Buffalo; Rev. N.J. Perche to Rev. S. Rousselon, October 6, 1850, Collection: New Orleans, 1850, V-5-n, AUND.

27. H. Perry Smith, *History of The City of Buffalo and Erie County*, 2 vol. (Syracuse, 1884), II, pp. 150-154; Deutsch-Amerikanische Historische und Biographische Gesellschaft, *Buffalo und Sein Deutschtum* (Buffalo, 1912), pp. 51-52; Donohue, *The History of The Catholic Church in Western New York*, pp. 242-245, 254-257, 261-262; [no author], *The Centenary of St. Mary's Church, 1844-1944* (Buffalo, 1944), p. 17; [no author], Die Geschichte der St. Anna Gemeinde, 1858-1908," *St. Anna Bote* Buffalo, 1908), pp. 101-103.

28. Donohue, *History of The Catholic Church in Western New York*, pp. 256-257; *St. Michael's Bazar* [sic] *Papers, July 22-August 14, 1889* (typescript, no pagination, at St. Michael's Church, Buffalo).

29. Estimate based on figures on French and French Canadians found in Glascoe, "Ethnicity and Social Structure . . . .," p. 21; Shea, *History of the Catholic Church* . . . ., IV, p. 121; St. Peter's Church, *Sepulturae, 1851-1858, Liber Mortuorim*, and *Marriages, 1850-1858, a L'eglise francaise St. Pierre*, at Our Lady of Lourdes Church, Buffalo. There does not appear to have been a community of German-speaking Lorrainians in Buffalo, so I have adopted the premise that all German-speaking French were Alsatian.

30. P. Leuilliot, "L'Émigration Alsacienne sous L'Empire et au Début de la Restauration," *Revue Historique* CLXV (1930): 254-279, and *L'Alsace au Début du XIXe Siècle: Essais d'Historie politique, économique, et religieuse, 1815-1830* (Paris, 1959), II, pp. 32-40; L. Chevalier, "L'Emigration française au XIXe Siecle," *Etudes d'Histoire moderne et contemporaine* I (1947): 130-132, 143-148, 150, 156-158, 160-162; Heinrich Neu, "Elsasser

und Lothringer als Anseidler in Nordamerika," *Elsass-Lothringische Wissenshaftliche Gesellschaft für Strassberg,* III (1930): 98-129. Like the German immigration at the time, the Alsatian was a consequence of the socio-economic dislocations which, beginning in the 1820s, accompanied industrialization and the commercialization of agriculture. France's 1847 annexation of Algeria, however, ended the convergence of these two streams of mass migration, for many Alsatians bent on migrating were quickly diverted by the lure of French North Africa; Chevalier, *"L'Emigration française...,"* 160-161.

31. Leuilliot, *L'Alsace au Début du XIXe Siècle,* III, pp. 318-329; Buffalo, *Die Weltbürger,* Jan. 26, 1839; Franklin Ford, *Strasbourg in Transition, 1648-1789* (Cambridge, 1958), pp. 170-173, 190 (suggesting Strasbourg was an exception to certain of the generalizations here, but confirming others); Frederick C. Luebke, "Alsatians," *Harvard Encyclopedia of American Ethnic Groups* (Cambridge, 1980), pp. 30. In 1839, an Alsatian correspondent of the German press remarked, with evident surprise, "how powerfully and determinedly the German type and nature continues to make itself valuable in Alsace," after so many years of French rule. Quoted in Buffalo, *Wie Weltbürger,* Jan. 26, 1839.

32. I wish to thank Professor Wilma Iggers of the German Department, Canisius College, for clarifying this linguistic situation for me.

33. Although the French-born did so less often than the German-born, an appreciable 43% (23) of them (in contrast to 69%, or 247 of the latter) used the old Germanic-style handwriting in signing the petition.

34. Michael P. Fogarty, *Christian Democracy in Western Europe, 1820-1953* (London, 1957), p. 7. Also, see, David Martin, *A General Theory of Secularization* (New York, 1978), pp. 19, 79, 142.

35. Supplementing parish records were city directories and the Buffalo manuscripts of the 1855 New York State Census. An alphabetized print-out derived from the 1855 New York State Census for Buffalo is located at the University Archives, SUNY at Buffalo. The St. Michael's sample was generated from names of males appearing in the years 1851-1855 in: *Burials from 1851-1868; Part I Marriages, from 1851-1873;* and *Baptisms from 1851 to 1882,* at St. Michael's Church, Buffalo.

36. *Supra,* note 28.

37. Based on the ratio of adults (age 16 and over) buried to the total of parishioners buried, as revealed in the parish's sacramental index (See, *supra,* note 20) for both parishes: St. Michael's (1854 = .037; 1855 = .008; 1856 = .019); St. Louis (1850 = .021; 1855 = .020; 1856 = .024). When children's burials are included, the ratios are usually the inverse, again suggesting a younger age structure at St. Michael's: St. Michael's (1851 = .150; 1852 = .397; 1858 = .100); St. Louis (1851 = .047; 1856 = .165; 1858 = .124). Unfortunately, it wasn't possible consistently to compare the same years.

38. Donohue, *History of The Catholic Church in Western New York,* pp. 156-189.

39. Glascoe, "Ethnicity and Social Structure . . . .," Chapter II.

40. Michael Katz, Michael Doucet, and Mark Stern, "Migration and The Social Order in Erie County, New York: 1855," *Journal of Interdisciplinary History* (1978): 679-682.

41. Lists of the names of those comprising the four boards came from: [no author] *Documents and History of The Affairs of St. Louis Church* (n.p., n.d.), p. 4, CCA; [no author], *Belege und Berichte* . . . ., p. 16, CCA; "A Notre Saint Père . . . ." (petition, 1852); Buffalo *Commercial Advertiser,* June 27, 1854.

42. Buffalo *Daily Gazette*, Oct. 19, 1843. This board also had an Alsatian majority: of its 7 members, 4 could be traced; all 4 were born in France; Buffalo *Commercial Advertiser*, Aug. 10, 1844.

43. Cf., Kenneth A. Lockridge, *A New England Town: The First Hundred Years* (New York, 1970), pp. 37-56; Kenneth A. Lockridge and Alan Kreider, "The Evolution of Massachusetts Town Government, 1640 to 1740," *William and Mary Quarterly*, XXIII (1966), 549-574.

44. "A Notre Saint Père . . . ." (petition, 1852); [no author], *Affairs of St. Louis Church* (Buffalo, 1853), pp. 3-11 (memorial to Bedini); W.B. Le Couteulx (public letter), Buffalo *Morning Express*, June 28, 1851.

45. "A Notre Saint Père . . . ." (petition, 1852). Also, W.B. LeCouteulx, "To the Right Reverence John Hughes . . . . 31 March, A.D., 1852" (Buffalo, 1852), in folios 73 and 74, *Scritture*, CPF, Rome, AUND; and W.B. LeCouteulx to CPF, Feb. 2, 1853, folios 503 and 504, *Scritture*, CPF, Rome, AUND; and Buffalo *Morning Express*, June 28, 1851.

46. Church incorporation legislation passed in New York State in 1784 and, superseding the former, in 1813. On these laws, see, John Webb Pratt, *Religion, Politics, and Diversity: The Church-State Theme in New York History* (Ithaca, 1967), pp. 100-101; Dignan, *A History of Legal Incorporation* . . . ., pp. 52-54, 64-67.

47. Murray, "Memoir of Stephen Louis LeCouteulx de Caumont," 431-483; "Le Couteulx, Rouen, Juillet 1764 . . . . Lettres de leur Annoblissement," Bibliotheque Nationale, Paris. In addition to frequent letter writing, William LeCouteulx journeyed to Rome late in 1852 and again in 1853 to present the parish's case before the Congregation of the Propaganda Fide; Buffalo *Courier*, Oct. 8, 1852; Sept. 22, 1853. As Bishop Timon frequently complained (e.g., Timon to Archbishop Kenrick, Sept. 27, 1853, Kenrick Papers, Archives of the Archdiocese of Balitmore — hereafter, AAB), William LeCouteulx had "friends in power" within the Church in Europe, probably as a consequence of ties created through branches of the family remaining in France. It is clear, for example, that he knew Cardinal Fornari of Paris, and influenced him to intervene on the parish's behalf during a dispute with Bishop Hughes in the early '40s; see, Donohue, *History of the Catholic Church in Western New York*, p. 181. He also knew Count A. de Reyneval, French Ambassador to the Holy See, who wrote a letter of introduction for him in 1853; see, de Reyneval to CPF, Jan. 27, 1853, folio 598, *Scritture*, CPF, Rome, AUND. The traditional explanation of William LeCouteulx's involvement (Donohue, *The History of the Catholic Church in Western New York*, p. 153) is that he wished through the trustees to get back valuable property his father had deeded to the parish. There is no evidence, however, to sustain such a view, and the great wealth of the family rather firmly militates against it.

48. See citations, *supra*, note 45, for example.

49. E.g., Timon, *Missions in Western New York* . . . ., pp. 214-215, 224-226; Bishop Timon to Bishop Peter Lefevre, September 7, 1851, Collection: Detroit, 1843-1852, III-2-n, AUND; Archbishop John Huges to W.B. LeCouteulx, no date, in Boston *Pilot*, Apr. 21, 1855. Under the circumstances, it was to be expected that authorities in Rome would come to see the parish the same way; see, "Instructions for Mon. Bedini . . . . Special Envoy of the Holy Father in the U.S.A.," Apr. 4, 1853, folios 315-317, *Lettere e Decreti della S. Congregazione*, CPF, Rome AUND, which proves that the Vatican saw St. Louis parish in the same manner.

50. Both Hughes and Timon (and their supporters) proved adept at pointing out the gap between French law and practice and the prerogatives St. Louis parish claimed for itself; see, [no author], *Belege und Berichte* . . . ., pp. 20-21; CCA; Donohue, *The History of the Catholic Church in Western New York*, pp. 184-188.

51. L. Pfleger, "Untersuchungen zur Geschicte des Pfarrei-Institute in Elsass," 3 parts, "Die Einkommensquellen, i. Das Kirchenvermögen," part 3, *Archiv für Elsassiche Kirchengeschicte* VIII (1932): 14; Andre Schaer, "Le Chapitre Rural Ultra Colles Ottinis en Haute-Alsac, Après La Guerre de Trente Ans Jusque à La Révolution. La Vie Paroissale dans Un Doyen Alsacien D'Ancien Régime (1648-1789)," *Archiv de L'Eglise D'Alsace,* XVI (new series) (1967-68): 200.

52. Rev. H.J. Schroeder, *Canons and Decrees of the Council of Trent* (St. Louis, 1941), pp. 157, 429; John Bossy, "The Counter-Reformation and The Catholic People of Europe," *Past and Present* (1970): 51-70.

53. Fogarty, *Christian Democracy in Western Europe* . . . ., p. 7.

54. Schaer, "Le Chapitre Rural Ultra Colles Ottinis . . . .," Part 1, 168, 197, 299-205; Georg Fritz, "Zur Kirchengeschicte der Jahre, 1790-1810," *Archiv für elsassischen Kirchengeschicte,* XVI (1943), 384-387; Leuilliot, *L'Alsace au Début du XIXe Siecle* . . . ., III, pp. 1-17; "Fabrique," *Le Grand Larousse Encyclopédie,* IV, 875-876.

55. Pierre Basile Mignault, *Le Droit Paroissial - Etant Une Étude Historique et Légale de La Paroisse Catholique, de Sa Création, de Son Gouvernment, et de Ses Biens* (Montreal, 1893), pp. 210-215. "Fabrique" is descended from the Latin "Fabrica," which, in its meaning in canon law, referred to both the church as a physical structure and the maintenance of local churches by their congregants through diverse arrangements; see Schaer, "Le Chapitre Rural Ultra Colles Ottinis . . . .," Part 1, 200.

56. Schaer, "Le Chapitre Rural Ultra Colles Ottinis . . . .," Part 1, 200-206, and Part 3 in *Archiv de L'Eglise D'Alsace* XVIII (1970): 174-175.

57. Mignault, *Le Droit Paroissial* . . . ., pp. vi-viii, 44, 214,-225, 234-246, 260-264, 272-273, 308-311.

58. George Pare, *The Catholic Church in Detroit, 1701-1888* (Detroit, 1951), pp. 199-200, 339-340, 443-444.

59. Roger Baudier, *The Catholic Church in Louisiana* (New Orleans, 1939), pp. 91, 121, 158, 255-258, 335, 344-348.

60. *Ibid.*; the Louisiana situation is complicated by the fact that the *fabrique* existed before the diocese was created (when the Church was administered from metropolitan France), and then during the first years of the diocese from 1793 to 1801 with no apparent problems between the *marguilliers* and the episcopacy. Between 1801-1815, however, the diocese had no bishop and the delicate balance on which the system of lay management depended broke down, particularly at the New Orleans cathedral where there were consequently years of struggle. Under more stable parish circumstances, however, the *fabrique* system worked well — from the French hierarchy's point of view. The latter would, therefore, have agreed with Pare's assessment of the contrast between Anglo-American and French trusteeship. In evaluating the *fabriques* of Detroit, Pare said, "[This] parish organization is not to be compared with the lawless trustee system that disgraced the beginnings of the Church in the United States. In the French system there was never any doubt concerning the scope of the bishop's or the pastor's authority and the rights and the extent of the laity's participation were minutely regulated." Pare, *The Catholic Church in Detroit* . . . ., p. 199, note 54.

61. The same difficulties, in fact, befell Alsatian Catholics in a rural parish, just outside Buffalo, in the 1840s; they clashed with German priests, assigned to their church, over trustee prerogatives. See, Glenn R. Atwell and Ronald E. Batt, *The Chapel: A Comprehensive History of the Chapel and Pilgrimmage of Our Lady Help of Cheektowaga, New York and of the Alsatian Immigrant Community at Williamsville, New York* (Buffalo, 1979), pp. 1-7. And *French*

Catholics at Buffalo briefly clashed with Bishop Timon over the same issues; see, Buffalo *Commercial Advertiser,* Aug. 6, 8, 1855.

62. His sons, William and Pierre (who sided with the bishops) disagreed for many years about their father's wishes regarding incorporation, and hence established the lines of argument for all those wishing to claim the deceased, elder LeCouteulx's authority for their views. See, P.A. LeCouteulx to Bishop Timon, August , 1851, in Donohue, *The History of the Catholic Church in Western New York,* pp. 175-176; William LeCouteulx, "Exposition of The Deplorable Conditions . . . . of the Buffalo Church of St. Louis," Feb. 2, 1853, folios 503-504, *Scritture,* CPF, Rome, AUND.

63. Shaw, *Dagger John . . . .,* pp. 115-137; William LeCouteulx, "Exposition of The Deplorable Conditions . . . .;" N. Ottenot to Archbishop Bedini, October 23, 1853, folio 742, *Scritturi,* CPF, Rome, AUND. Such consent would certainly have had precedent in 1838. See Dignan, *A History of Legal Incorporation . . . .,* pp. 91, 129-132, 148.

64. Guilday, *A History of The Councils of Baltimore,* pp. 87, 90-91.

65. Bishop John Hughes, "In Regard to . . . . Church Property," (*Pastoral Letter,* Sept. 8, 1842) in Lawrence Kehoe, ed., *Complete Works of The Most Reverend John Hughes . . . .,* 2 vol. (New York, 1864), I, pp. 314-327 and III, pp. 555-559; Shaw, *Dagger John . . . .,* pp. 129-132, 177, 181; Dolan, *The Immigrant Church,* pp. 47-48, 90-91. For the best summary of the brief (1843-1844) but bitter controversy, which ended in indecisive compromise, between Hughes and St. Louis parish, see, Donohue, *History of The Catholic Church in Western New York,* pp. 144-155.

66. Donohue, *A History of The Catholic Church in Western New York,* p. 250.

67. Fecher, *A Study of The Movement for German National Parishes . . . .,* pp. 254-279; R.F. McNamara, "Trusteeism," *New Catholic Encylcopedia,* v. XIV, p. 324.

68. Pfleger, "Untersuchungen zur Geschicte . . . .," 13.

69. [No author], *Belege und Berichte . . . .,* pp. 10-16; CCA; [no author], *Affairs of St. Louis Church,* p. 12; "A Notre Saint Père . . . ." (petition, 1852).

70. William LeCouteulx, "To The Right Rev. John Hughes . . . .," folios 73-74; [letter] to CPF, Apr. 20, 1853, folio 573; [letter] to CPF, Dec. 18, 1853, folios 860-861, *Scritture,* CPF, Rome, AUND; and Buffalo *Courier,* Aug. 27, 1853; Buffalo *Commercial Advertiser,* Jan. 11, Apr. 5, 16, 1855.

71. [No author], *Affairs of St. Louis Church,* p. 8. Also, see [public letter] signed, "A Layman," Buffalo *Commercial Advertiser,* June 29, 1854.

72. [No author], *Belege und Berichte . . . .,* p. 4; CCAA; Buffalo *Commercial Advertiser,* June 19, 1854, Apr. 5, 1855.

73. [No author], *Belege und Berichte . . . .,* p. 16; CCA; Buffalo *Commercial Advertiser,* July 12, 1854, Apr. 13, 1855.

74. From the start, however, the Putnam Law was neither utilized by parishes against their bishops nor enforced by state authorities, justifying the contention made at the time of its passage that its purpose was more symbolic (to appease anti-Catholic prejudice) than practical. It was repealed in 1863, and replaced by a statute accommodating Catholic practice. See, note 6, *supra.*

75. Buffalo *Commercial Advertiser,* June 23, 27, 29, 1855. Trustees retained major powers at St. Louis, alone among Buffalo parishes, until 1979 when these were surrendered to the diocese by the trustees; Buffalo *Evening News,* Oct. 2, 3, 1979.

76. "A Notre Saint Père . . . ." (petition, 1852); Buffalo *Courier,* Aug. 27, 1853; Buffalo *Commercial Advertiser,* June 24, 1854, June 23, 1855; W.P. LeCouteulx to CPF, Mar. 31, 1852, folios 73-74, W.B. LeCouteulx, "To The Right Reverend John Hughes . . . . 1852," foliors 73-74, W.B. LeCouteulx to CPF, Feb. 2, 1853, folios 489-490, *Scritture,* CPF, Rome, AUND.

77. Bishop Timon to Archbishop Francis Kenrick, July 10, 1852, Kenrich Papers, AAB; Archbishop Bedini to CPF, Apr. 2, 1854, folios 967-972, *Scritture,* CPF, Rome, AUND.

78. William LeCouteulx to Congregation of the Propaganda Fide, September 20, 1854, folios 1119-1126, *Scritture,* CPF, Rome, AUND.

79. No one feared more that the prospect of death outside the Church would exert pressure to compromise than Protestant nativist politicians who publicly aligned with the trustees. Wrote George R. Babcock, an American Party State Senator and a cosponsor of the Putnam Law, in a letter to nativist politician James W. Beekman, "The St. Louis Trustees still hold out against Bishop Timon. I fear they will not always be sustained by their congregation. In the process of time, unless there is a revolution in the Church they must be undermined by the gradual falling off of those who dare not die under the curses of the Vatican." (July 10, 1855 in Box 2, Beekman Papers, New York Historical Society.)

80. Deuther, *The Life and Times of Rt. Rev. John Timon . . . . ,* pp. 208-212; Bishop Timon to CPF, July 5, 1855, folios 366-367, *Scritturi,* CPF, Rome, AUND; "Proclamation, John, Bishop of Buffalo," Sept. 28, 1854, at St. Michael's Church, Buffalo; Buffalo *Commercial Advertiser,* Sept. 12, 1854, June 23, 1855.

81. Buffalo, *Morning Express,* June 21, 1851; Buffalo *Courier,* Feb. 23, Oct. 8, 1852, June 30, Sept. 14, Oct. 31, Nov. 19, 1853; Buffalo Christian *Advocate,* July 6, 20, 1853; Buffalo *Commercial Advertiser,* June 27, 30, July 5, 12, Aug. 28, Sept. 12, Oct. 3, 1843, Feb. 2, Mar. 5, May 24, 29, June 23, 1855. For expressions of Protestant support from the press outside Buffalo, see Boston *Congregationalist,* Apr. 2, 1852, July 22, 1853, Apr. 27, 1855; Cincinnati *Gazette,* Nov. 9, 1853; *American and Foreign Christian Union,* V (June, 1854), 9-16.

82. [No author], "Missionary Intelligence: The Mission among The German Catholics at Buffalo," *The American Protestant,* V (1849): 49-50; [no author], "Free German Catholics at Buffalo," *Ibid.,* V (1849): 172-173.

83. Deuther, *The Life and Times of Rt. Rev. John Timon . . . . ,* p. 210.

84. Donohue, *A History of The Catholic Church in Western New York,* p. 189.

85. Glascoe, "Ethnicity and Social Structure . . . .," Chapter IV, passim.

86. Buffalo *Commercial Advertiser,* e.g., Nov. 23, 28, 1853; June 7, Dec. 30, 1854, Aug. 23, 1855. Also, see, e.g., Buffalo *Courier,* Jan. 4, Apr. 28, Aug. 22, 1851, Jan. 30, 1852. This praise grew more frequent and fullsome in the later '50s, though it remained balanced by criticism of Catholic ritual; see, *Ibid.,* e.g., Jan. 22, 30, Mar. 19, 26, June 7, Sept. 21 1858.

87. Clifford S. Griffen, *Their Brother's Keepers: Moral Stewardship in the United States, 1800-1865* (New Brunswick, 1960); William G. McLoughlin, "Pietism and The American Character," *American Quarterly* XIII (1965): 163-186; David J. Rothman, *The Discovery of The Asylum* (Boston, 1971); Anthony F.C. Wallace, *Rockdale* (New York, 1978), pp. 243-474.

Who Is the Church? Conflict in a Polish Immigrant Parish in Late Nineteenth-Century Detroit

LESLIE WOODCOCK TENTLER

University of Michigan—Dearborn

Early on the cold morning of Wednesday, December 2, 1885, a crowd began to gather in the forecourt of a handsome brick church on the outskirts of Detroit. The church, only recently blessed, was the Polish Roman Catholic church of Saint Albertus; the crowd, eventually numbering perhaps eight hundred, were Polish immigrants. Most of them were women. Shortly after 6:00, seven policemen marched into the convent opposite the church and soon emerged escorting two Polish priests. The group moved toward the church, but at the church steps the crowd—"the women," according to witnesses—began to jeer at and jostle the priests, and even pelted them with gravel. The police responded vigorously, but they and the priests were pushed from the door several times before they were finally able to enter.[1]

There were too few officers to bar the crowd from the church; the pews filled rapidly with agitated parishioners. And when a priest vested for mass appeared at the altar, the sanctuary rang with cries of anger and denunciation. The mass proceeded, but as the police began to remove the loudest protestors, the din intensified. Women clung to the pews and to each other and even struck policemen in their efforts to remain in the church. The service was hurried to its conclusion, at which most of the crowd left to mill outside. Then at 7:30, the two priests reappeared at the altar to say a second scheduled mass.

The police, by now well reinforced, tried to limit the number entering the church, but women already inside unlocked a side door and a large crowd swarmed into the sanctuary. Several women surged toward the altar. They

---

I wish to acknowledge, with thanks, the assistance of my colleagues Peter Amann, Jonathan Marwil, Thomas Tentler, and Olivier Zunz, of Father Leonard Blair of the Archives of the Archdiocese of Detroit, and of Father Bohdan Kosicki, until recently the pastor of Sweetest Heart of Mary parish in Detroit. A University of Michigan–Dearborn summer stipend in 1979 helped to support my research.

[1] The narrative here and in the next three paragraphs is drawn from *Detroit Evening News*, 2 December 1885, 1:4–5; *Detroit Evening Journal*, 2 December 1885, 1:1–2; *Detroit Free Press*, 3 December 1885, 5:2–3; *Detroit Tribune*, 3 December 1885, 1:2–3.

0010-4175/83/2186-0426 $2.50 © 1983 Society for Comparative Study of Society and History

were restrained by the police, but soon "an excited crowd was leaning over the communion rail, yelling and brandishing fists." The assisting priest moved forward to reason with the crowd, but could not be heard. As he reached the communion rail, "a dozen hands grabbed his habit and tore it nearly off."[2]

Evidently the priests abandoned the service soon after, but before they had left the sanctuary a woman ascended the altar steps, raised her arms and called for prayer—not for forgiveness but for redress. The protestors responded, falling to their knees. The peace was short-lived. As the two priests, surrounded by a large crowd of police, moved through the churchyard toward the convent, the angry crowd from the church showered them with clods of frozen mud.

Detroit newspapermen were present to record these events—in what was ordinarily a little-visited quarter of the city—because the violence of December 2 was not the first evidence of trouble at Saint Albertus. Only the day before, a large crowd, again mainly women, had forcibly ejected a priest from the church as he tried to say early mass. Nor did the violence of December 2 end discord in the parish. On six occasions during the next eighteen months, parishioners battled with police or each other. Many were injured and one man was killed. And on each of these occasions women were prominently involved.[3]

The violence, which caused the Bishop of Detroit to place Saint Albertus church under interdict for nineteen months, bitterly divided the local Polish community. The angriest dissidents eventually seceded from the parish and, notwithstanding their poverty, built a church even grander than Saint Albertus and only two blocks away. To those who remained loyal to Saint Albertus these dissidents were schismatics: they had cut themselves off from the Roman Catholic Church and from salvation. The dissidents, however, always insisted that despite their acknowledged defiance of the Bishop of Detroit, they remained good Roman Catholics. In February 1894, nine years after the troubles began, their confidence was rewarded: by order of the Apostolic Delegate in Washington, the rebellious parish and its priest were formally reconciled with the local bishop.

* * *

Do these curious events, exceptional even in immigrant parishes, contribute significantly to our understanding of the history of American Catholicism? I think they do. The American Church in the nineteenth century became at once more authoritarian and more heterogeneous; this peculiar pattern of develop-

---

[2] *Detroit Evening News*, 2 December 1885, 1:4-5.
[3] *Detroit Evening News*, 1 December 1885, 4:1; *Detroit Evening Journal*, 1 December 1885, 1:3; *Detroit Free Press*, 2 December 1885, 5:2-3; *Detroit Tribune*, 2 December 1885, 2:5.

ment caused serious tensions and a fair degree of conflict between bishops and the laity, bishops and priests, and priests and their congregations. One can surely argue, as many historians do, that the success of the American Church in integrating vast heterogeneous populations into what became a remarkably uniform community was an immense triumph of social control. But the eventual triumph should not blind us to the conflict that troubled the nineteenth-century Church or to the many parishes besides Saint Albertus where dissent erupted into violence.

The emphasis on disciplined conformity in many Church histories usually reflects an excessive preoccupation with the ideas and behavior of the clergy, particularly the bishops. The laity in the parish, difficult to study, are correspondingly slighted. But a focus on the clergy means a limited and often misleading view of the Church. Indeed, Timothy Smith has suggested that a fuller understanding of ethnic Catholicism in the parish may lead to a dramatic revision of the history of the American Church, to a history that "will resemble much more closely that of Protestantism." The important work of Jay Dolan and William Galush amply supports him.[4]

But if a focus on parishioners is a necessary corrective to the clerical bias of much Church history, greater attention to the parish in conflict is necessary to temper the tendency to describe American Church history as an inexorable process of discipline, homogenization, and consolidation. We are most of us too prone to see in the Catholic Church an institution peerlessly capable of inducing conformity within its ranks. The quarrel at Saint Albertus church in late nineteenth-century Detroit challenges our assumptions, and shows us a largely uneducated laity in serious dispute about the nature of Church authority. Their dispute is evidence important to a full understanding of American Church history. And the events in their parish suggest that a revised history of the American Church will include a reassessment of the place of women in this formally patriarchal institution. Recent parish studies have not explored the ways in which lay women understood Church authority and exerted their own authority in the parish.

Poles were not the only Catholics in the nineteenth century to quarrel with Church authority. There were disputes of varying severity between local bishops and congregations with Irish, German, Italian, Slavic, and French

---

[4] Timothy L. Smith, "Religious Denominations as Ethnic Communities: A Regional Case Study," *Church History*, 35:2 (June 1966), 226; Jay P. Dolan, *The Immigrant Church: New York's Irish and German Catholics, 1815–1865* (Baltimore: The Johns Hopkins University Press, 1975); William Galush, "Faith and Fatherland: Dimensions of Polish-American Ethnoreligion, 1875–1925," in *Immigrants and Religion in Urban America*, Randall Miller and Thomas Marzik, eds. (Philadelphia: Temple University Press, 1977); idem, "Forming Polonia: A Study of Four Polish-American Communities, 1890–1914" (Ph.D. diss., University of Minnesota, 1975). See also Timothy L. Smith, "Lay Initiative in the Religious Life of American Immigrants, 1880–1950," in *Anonymous Americans*, Tamara Hareven, ed. (Englewood Cliffs, N.J.: Prentice-Hall, 1971).

Canadian majorities.[5] But Polish parishes in the late nineteenth century were more prone than others to serious conflict and their conflict more likely to erupt into violence. Most major centers of Polish settlement experienced at least one disruptive parish dispute in the 1880s and 1890s. Buffalo, Cleveland, and Chicago, like Detroit, witnessed the violent birth of secessionist Polish parishes. And in many smaller communities, parish factionalism among Poles led to destruction of property, arrests, injury, and even death.[6] The Detroit papers, alert to the phenomenon in the wake of the troubles at Saint Albertus, reported between 1886 and 1898 violent disputes in Milwaukee, Toledo, Manistee (Michigan), Bay City (Michigan), Posen (Michigan), Plymouth (Pennsylvania), Mill Creek (Pennsylvania), and Depew (New York). In a number of these conflicts women were reported to have been remarkably violent participants.[7]

---

[5] Patrick Carey, "The Laity's Understanding of the Trustee System, 1785-1855," *The Catholic Historical Review,* 64:3 (July 1978), 357-76; Dolan, *Immigrant Church,* 87-98; Galush, "Forming Polonia," 58-59; James Hennesey, S. J., *American Catholics: A History of the Roman Catholic Community in the United States* (New York: Oxford University Press, 1981), 93-100; Richard M. Linkh, *American Catholicism and European Immigrants, 1900-1924* (Staten Island: Center for Migration Studies, 1976), 106-7; Thomas T. McAvoy, *A History of the Catholic Church in the United States* (Notre Dame: University of Notre Dame Press, 1969), 92-125; Robert F. McNamara, "Trusteeism in the Atlantic States, 1785-1863," *Catholic Historical Review,* 30 (July 1944), 135-54; Alfred G. Stritch, "Trusteeism in the Old Northwest, 1800-1850," *Catholic Historical Review,* 30 (July 1944), 155-164; Silvano M. Tomasi, *Piety and Power: The Role of the Italian Parishes in the New York Metropolitan Area, 1880-1930* (Staten Island: Center for Migration Studies, 1975), 148-53. For late nineteenth-century conflicts in a German and in a French-Canadian parish in Detroit, see *Detroit Evening News,* 10 December 1885, 1:1; *Detroit Sunday News,* 17 April 1892, 3:3; *Detroit Evening News,* 21 April 1892, 5:3-4; 29 October 1892, 7:3; 16 January 1893, 4:4; 18 January 1893, 5:3; 24 July 1893, 4:6; *Detroit Free Press,* 11 December 1885, 5:4.

[6] Daniel S. Buczek, "Polish-Americans and the Roman Catholic Church," *The Polish Review,* 21:3 (1976), 47-49; Galush, "Faith and Fatherland," 90; Victor R. Greene, *For God and Country: The Rise of Polish and Lithuanian Ethnic Consciousness in America* (Madison: State Historical Society of Wisconsin, 1975), 100-121; Edward R. Kantowicz, "Polish Chicago: Survival through Solidarity," in *The Ethnic Frontier,* Melvin G. Holli and Peter d'A Jones, eds. (Grand Rapids, Michigan: William B. Eerdmans Publishing Company, 1977), 194-95; Laurence Orzell, "A Minority within a Minority: The Polish National Catholic Church, 1896-1907," *Polish-American Studies,* 36:1 (Spring 1979), 9-15; Edward Adam Skendzel, *The Kolasinski Story* (Grand Rapids, Michigan: Littleshield Press, 1979), 41-42; W. I. Thomas and Florian Znaniecki, *The Polish Peasant in Europe and America* (New York: Dover Publications, 1958), II, 1528-30, 1551-53. See also *Detroit Sunday News,* 26 January 1890, 1:6; *Detroit Evening News,* 3 February 1890, 2:3; 15 June 1892, 2:3; *Detroit Sunday News,* 19 June 1892, 2:6; *Detroit Evening News,* 22 June 1894, 3:1; 20 August 1894, 3:1.

[7] *Detroit Evening News,* 11 January 1886, 3:5; 4 May 1889, 1:4; 6 May 1889, 1:1; 13 May 1889, 1:5; 23 October 1889, 1:3; 25 March 1890, 2:3; *Detroit Sunday News-Tribune,* 4 October 1896, 8:4; *Detroit Evening News,* 24 November 1896, 4:1; 25 November 1896, 4:3; 4 January 1897, 4:3; 5 January 1897, 6:5; 8 January 1897, 4:4; 9 January 1897, 4:4; *Detroit Sunday News-Tribune,* 10 January 1897, 8:3; *Detroit Evening News,* 11 January 1897, 4:8; *Detroit Sunday News-Tribune,* 17 January 1897, 8:4; *Detroit Evening News,* 20 January 1897, 3:3; 21 January 1897, 4:2; 22 January 1897, 4:3; 25 January 1897, 4:1; 2 February 1897, 4:5; *Detroit Sunday News-Tribune,* 7 February 1897, 8:3; *Detroit Evening News,* 8 February 1897, 4:2; *Detroit*

The Poles, moreover, were the only Catholic group in the United States to generate a large and enduring schismatic church: the Polish National Catholic Chur h. identifiably Roman Catholic in much of its theology but independent of Ron. , was formally organized in 1898. By 1914 it had at least twenty-five parishes, and it enjoyed a healthy growth in the 1920s, a period of concerted assimilationist pressure on immigrant parishes by the American hierarchy. The apparent decline in the twentieth century in the violence generated by Polish parish disputes is at least partly due to the alternative that the Polish National Catholic Church offered to the most bitterly disaffected of the Polish laity. Even so, bitter quarrels within Polish parishes that remained Roman Catholic continued into the twenti_th century.[8]

In nearly all Polish parish disputes, principal grievances concerned the desire of the congregation to control parish finances or even hold title to parish property, and to determine or help determine who the pastor would be.[9] One could say, as their clerical critics did, that Polish dissidents insisted on a Protestant model of the church, with congregations functioning virtually autonomously, acknowledging the hierarchy as authority only in matters of doctrine. The most recalcitrant Polish layperson, however, would not have recognized his desires as "Protestant." A Protestant identity was culturally alien to him. And his unwavering commitment to a sacramental theology meant that his dissenting vision of the Church differed in important ways from the understanding common to most Protestant denominations, as we shall see.

Ironically, the group that earlier in the century had caused the most difficulty for their bishops were the Irish, and their difficulties had turned on just those issues that informed later disputes in Polish parishes.[10] The average Irish Catholic was no more disposed than his Polish counterpart to consider himself a covert Protestant, or to join a Protestant church in pursuit of his desire for congregational autonomy. Indeed, considering the degree of support for Catholic institutions and the infrequency of conversion to Protestantism, no ethnic groups were more intensely Catholic than the Poles and the Irish. And yet these groups generated, each in turn, more pressure than any others for a degree of parish autonomy and lay participation in church government always unacceptable to the hierarchy.

It does not appear that either the Poles or the Irish were accustomed in their

---

Sunday News-Tribune, 21 February 1897, 8:4; *Detroit Evening News,* 22 February 1897, 4:1; 2 March 1897, 4:1; 3 March 1897, 4:5; 29 March 1897, 6:4; 3 April 1897, 4:3; 12 April 1897, 8:1; 7 January 1898, 6:2; 21 February 1898, 4:1.

[8] Galush, "Forming Polonia," 65-68; Orzell, "Minority within a Minority," 5-32.

[9] Galush, "Faith and Fatherland," 90-91; Greene, *For God and Country,* 100-101; Kantowicz, "Polish Chicago," 192-95.

[10] Thomas J. Curran, "The Immigrant Influence on the Roman Catholic Church: New York, a Test Case," in *An American Church: Essays on the Americanization of the Catholic Church,* David J. Alvarez, ed. (Moraga, Calif.: St. Mary's College of California, 1979), 125-128; Dolan, *Immigrant Church,* 89, 92-93; Hennesey, *American Catholics,* 97-100.

homelands to challenge episcopal authority as they did in the United States.[11] There was no strong anticlerical tradition in the popular religion of either nation. Rather, a loyalty to one's priests and bishop was often a defiant statement of support for one's culture and national identity, because in Ireland and in parts of partitioned Poland, Catholicism had been a persecuted religion and a source of resistance to foreign domination. A powerful fusion of national and religious identity inclined Polish and Irish immigrants in the United States to a particularly tenacious defense of traditional religious life against control by outsiders. And like all Catholic immigrants, the Poles and the Irish could be disposed to congregational assertiveness by the heady American experience of parish founding and church building.

It was not without cause, moreover, that many immigrant Catholics felt vulnerable to potentially unsympathetic episcopal authority. As the American hierarchy in the nineteenth century expanded, became more confident and more able effectively to exert authority, parish life was brought increasingly under centralized diocesan control. This control was necessarily administered by a bishop and advisors who were "foreigners" in the eyes of many immigrant Catholics, and who were likely to be proponents of uniformity in the American Church and of swift assimilation for its communicants. Not surprisingly, the pattern of ethnic conflict in the nineteenth-century Church was largely determined by how and when strong episcopal authority was established in the various American dioceses.

The move toward greatly strengthened episcopal authority began in the East. It was here that the growing number of bishops, presiding over dioceses that were increasingly of manageable size, moved decisively during and after the 1820s to secure, in fact as well as in law, episcopal control over parish property, parish financial affairs, and appointment of the clergy. And they met resistance: before the Civil War, the largest number and the bitterest of disputes between individual parishes and the various bishops occurred in the East. By the later nineteenth century, however, the bishops' battle in the East was largely won, with the Irish neatly compensated for their loss of parish autonomy by Irish domination of the hierarchy.[12]

The Church in the Midwest during the antebellum period was not seriously afflicted with struggles over parish rights, and the disputes that did occur there were notably less prolonged and bitter than many in the East. Many midwestern parishes had been founded and were at least partially governed by

[11] William Galush has worked in Polish archives with an eye to locating parish disputes in Poland similar to those which occurred in Polish parishes in the United States. The single example he reports, in Galicia in 1914, was in some important respects different from the typical parish quarrel in the American setting. He does find in Galicia, where the clergy were closely allied with the state, the beginnings of an anticlericalism among elements of the peasantry that sometimes led to demands for greater lay control of parish life. Galush, "Forming Polonia," 27, 43.

[12] McNamara, "Trusteeism," 135-54.

strong boards of trustees, and the relative weakness of the region's bishops, caused by the vastness of their territories and the dispersed Catholic population, meant that the trustees' authority was often not directly challenged.[13]

By the later nineteenth century, however, burgeoning midwestern parishes were increasingly subject to strict diocesan discipline. In Detroit, for example, lenient episcopal administration had until 1870 allowed parishes to grow and build with few external controls. But the arrival in the city of Bishop Caspar Borgess in 1870 signaled the beginning of a more centralized, authoritarian administration. Borgess quickly asserted his right to make independent decisions about the founding of new parishes and the expansion of existing ones, to regulate parish fund raising and expenditure, and to appoint and remove priests without congregational interference. He was a bishop with the bureaucratic background common in the hierarchy of the modern Church; his career had been spent largely in the Chancery at Cincinnati. His predecessor, by contrast, had come to the episcopate from a mission pastorate.[14]

The consolidation of episcopal authority before the Civil War seems to have threatened the Irish more immediately than any other group, although German parishes too offered resistance to the bishops. In the later nineteenth century, and particularly in the Midwest, consolidation of episcopal authority most directly threatened the Poles, by then one of the largest and perhaps the most psychologically vulnerable of immigrant Catholic populations. Probably the majority of Poles settled in dioceses whose bishops were in the late nineteenth century only then establishing direct control over parish affairs; these bishops may have been unusually sensitive to challenges to episcopal authority and often liable to deal less than tactfully with troublesome immigrant congregations. But the fears of Polish newcomers often made them hostile to episcopal authority even in old established dioceses. The spread of strong diocesan administration throughout most of the country by the end of the nineteenth century meant simply that sensitive minorities had fewer and fewer opportunities to develop their parishes under mostly nominal outside control. That is why immigrants continued to cause conflict in the Church.

The violence at Saint Albertus, then, exemplifies tensions that affected many Catholic parishes. At issue in this dispute and others like it were two conflicting visions of the Church and Church authority. The clerical vision, forcefully argued in this case by Bishop Borgess and his more tactful but equally resolute successor Bishop John Foley, demanded of the faithful obedience to the clergy not only in matters of faith and morals, but in all aspects of Church life. The American Church might grow and thrive in a democracy,

---

[13] Stritch, "Trusteeism," 155–64.
[14] George Pare, *The Catholic Church in Detroit, 1701–1888* (Detroit: Gabriel Richard Press, 1951), 527–61; Joseph Swastek, *Detroit's Oldest Polish Parish: St. Albertus, Detroit, Michigan, 1872–1972* (n.p., n.p., n.d.), 41–44; *Detroit Evening News*, 3 May 1887, 4:1–3; 30 April 1890, 7:1, 8:2; *Detroit Free Press*, 3 May 1887, 1:5–7.

but it could not be a democratic institution. The Church was of God, and an ordained clergy, as His representatives, necessarily possessed immense authority. Priests were under an imperative obligation to serve the laity selflessly. But they might not, according to Church law and the logic of most Catholic theology, permit the laity a significant share of decision-making power in Church life.

Most clergy and many lay Catholics readily assented to this vision of the Church, although in parishes relatively free of conflict most laypersons probably worried little about the nature of Church authority. But situations of sustained conflict, like that at Saint Albertus, permit us to see, primarily in the behavior of a portion of the laity, the existence of an alternative vision of Church authority, one that is obviously more democratic. Those laypersons at Saint Albertus who resisted the counsels of their priests and their bishops believed firmly that their behavior was justified and that they never ceased to be full communicants of the Roman Catholic Church. If we can understand what notion of right informed their behavior and sustained them as a rebellious congregation, we can understand their vision of the Church and of the authority that governs it.

It is necessary, in this endeavor, to infer a good deal from people's reported behavior. The dissident parishioners from Saint Albertus bequeathed to posterity no disquisitions on the nature of Church authority. But their behavior and the justifications their leaders offered in statements to the local press give evidence of a surprisingly sophisticated vision. While they willingly granted recognition and honor to hierarchical authority, the dissidents reserved to the immediate community an important degree of autonomy. While they embraced a sacramental theology and an ordained priesthood, they identified the Church with the entire worshipping community. And while they sanctioned exclusively male hierarchical authority and male leadership in the parish, they recognized the legitimacy of women's active defense of parish rights.[15]

---

[15] Aside from occasional single editions, no copies of Detroit's Polish-language newspapers survive from the nineteenth century. There is, therefore, no adequate substitute, as a principal source of my narrative, for local English-language newspapers, though I am aware of the weaknesses of such sources. Fortunately, there were in the late 1880s and 1890s four English-language dailies in Detroit, and each covered the dispute at Saint Albertus and its lengthy aftermath attentively. For nearly all important public events in the history of the long dispute there were, then, at least four eyewitnesses who recorded their perceptions, and if they were individually not wholly satisfactory witnesses, each testimony can be checked against that of the others to good effect. I have not reported incidents that were not attested to by at least two newspaper sources, and usually more than two. Fortunately too, the English-language dailies were used by leaders on both sides of the dispute to present their positions to a larger city audience.

Lawrence D. Orton's recent study, *Polish Detroit and the Kolasinski Affair* (Detroit: Wayne State University Press, 1981), provides a narrative of Kolasinski's career between 1882 and 1898. Orton's concerns in his book are substantially different from mine here, and our conclusions differ as well. "The Kolasinski affair," he writes, "was essentially the story of one man's struggle to vindicate himself and triumph at all costs. Although there can be no doubt that Kolasinski cared deeply for the welfare of his congregation, circumstances made them pawns in

The immediate cause of the violence at Saint Albertus in December 1885 was the dismissal of the pastor, Father Dominic Kolasinski, by the Bishop of Detroit. The Galician-born Kolasinski had come to Saint Albertus in March 1882 from Cracow when he was forty-three years old, a robust, floridly handsome man. Described by contemporaries as an eloquent preacher and charismatic leader, he had successfully exhorted his immigrant flock to replace their modest wooden church with a stately brick one, elaborately decorated and seating 2,500. At its completion in the summer of 1885, the new Saint Albertus was the largest Catholic church in the city.[16]

Kolasinski was a popular priest, but he had influential opponents in his congregation, particularly among the parish trustees, who had in February 1883 petitioned the bishop to overrule their pastor's decisions on the location and cost of the new church. Bishop Borgess, wary of lay assertiveness, upheld Father Kolasinski. His ruling did not, however, quell the tensions between the priest and certain trustees, and in November 1885 complaints against Kolasinski were again lodged with the bishop by certain trustees. This time they accused the priest of financial mismanagement, of charging arbitrary and sometimes excessive fees for services to parishioners, and of sexual immorality. The bishop demanded from Kolasinski the immediate surrender of all parish financial records, which the priest refused, requesting time to make additional entries and corrections. On November 28, without an ecclesiastical hearing, the bishop dismissed him from his pastorate.[17]

the struggle between their stubborn pastor and two strong-willed bishops'' (p. 157). I find the parishioners considerably more important as independent actors in the Kolasinski drama than Orton does.

For the history of the initial dispute and subsequent formation of an ''independent'' parish from the point of view of the children and grandchildren of the disputants, see ''50cio Letnia Rocznica Parafii Najsłodszego Serca Marii Panny, 1890-1940'' (Detroit: n.p., ca. 1940); ''Pamiętnik Diamentowego Jubileuszu Parafji Najsłodszego Serca Marji, Detroit, Michigan, 1890-1965'' (Detroit: n.p., ca. 1965).

[16] Skendzel, *Kolasinski Story*, 4-6; Swastek, *Detroit's Oldest Polish Parish*, 65, 67; *Detroit Evening News*, 4 July 1885, 1:8; *Detroit Free Press*, 5 July 1885, 5:4.

[17] Father Kolasinski's guilt or innocence is, happily, not an issue that requires resolution here. Needless to say, the question sparked passionate debate in Detroit's Polish community for many decades after the actual events. Much, though not all, of the correspondence that passed between Bishop Borgess and Kolasinski and Kolasinski's accusers and his defenders can be found in the archives of the Archdiocese of Detroit. One could not, I think, prove the case for or against the priest based on the evidence there, but it is clear that both his accusers and his supporters believed fervently that their version of events was the correct one.

The accusations of sexual misconduct, never proved and disbelieved even by some of Kolasinski's foes, probably largely explain the inflexibility of Bishop Borgess and his successor with regard to Kolasinski. Bishop Borgess, who had few sources of information within the Polish community and who relied principally on Father Joseph Dombrowski, a local Kolasinski rival, for guidance in the Kolasinski matter, evidently believed that the priest was guilty of a series of sexual affairs with women and girls in his congregation. He detailed his suspicions in a letter to Archbishop William Henry Elder in Cincinnati. (Bishop Caspar Borgess to Archbishop William Henry Elder, 21 March 1886, Bishop Foley papers, Correspondence, Rev. Kolasinski, ''Exhib-

Kolasinski said a farewell mass at Saint Albertus on Sunday, November 29. He preached an emotional sermon, denying all charges, denouncing his accusers, and appealing to the congregation to attend a meeting in his defense to be held after vespers. The late afternoon meeting, which many women attended, was tense. Supporters and opponents of the priest argued hotly, and someone fearing violence called in the police. Many of those present signed, or had signed for them, a petition addressed to Bishop Borgess expressing confidence in Father Kolasinski; it was the first of several pro-Kolasinski petitions sent to the bishop, all of them apparently widely supported. Notwithstanding, Bishop Borgess on November 30 assigned temporary charge of the parish to Father Joseph Dombrowski; the Polish-born chaplain of the nearby convent of the Felician Sisters. Father Kolasinski, however, refused to vacate the Saint Albertus rectory.[18]

It was Father Dombrowski's attempt to function as head of the parish that sparked the violence of December 1 and 2. The crowds of angry women who disrupted mass were determined to uphold Father Kolasinski's claims to his pastorate. On December 3, the assembled women forced the closing of the parish school. And on December 4, in response to the violence, Bishop Borgess ordered Saint Albertus church closed for an indefinite period. Father Dombrowski, however, continued to say mass for an apparently small number of parishioners in the chapel of the Felician convent until he left Detroit some sixteen months later.[19]

its," Archives of the Archdiocese of Detroit (hereafter cited as AAD).) Shortly thereafter, Father Dombrowski attested to Kolasinski's immorality in a report to the Congregation of the Propaganda in Rome. ("Report of the Rev. Joseph Dombrowski to the Propaganda in July, 1886," Bishop Borgess papers, Box 3, File 4, AAD.) When the Detroit Chancery late in 1893 forwarded charges against Kolasinski to Rome at the request of the Propaganda, those charges included the same bill of sexual particulars that Bishop Borgess had sent to Archbishop Elder in 1886. ("In Materia Applicationis Reverendi D. Kolasinski in Quantam ad Nos Aliquo Modo Pertineat," Bishop Foley papers, Correspondence, Rev. Kolasinski, undated, 1892–1893, AAD.) Probably the extravagance of the original accusations of immorality and the embarrassing publicity that attended them caused not only Bishop Borgess but his successor to insist—and to believe—that the accusations were true. And it is likely that the 1885 decision to dismiss Kolasinski without a hearing was precipitated by Bishop Borgess's angry conviction that Kolasinski was an immoral man. The abrupt dismissal led to a series of violent events, each of which increased for Bishop Borgess the need to believe that he had judged Kolasinski rightly. (Bishop Caspar Borgess to Archbishop William Henry Elder, 1 April 1886, Bishop Foley papers, Correspondence, Rev. Kolasinski, "Exhibits," AAD.) Bishop Foley in turn inherited the burden.

See also Skendzel, *Kolasinski Story*, 6–7, 104B–104G; Swaktek, *Detroit's Oldest Polish Parish*, 66–67, 72–73; *Detroit Evening News*, 24 November 1885, 4:1; *Detroit Evening Journal*, 27 November 1885, 1:3.

[18] Skendzel, *Kolasinski Story*, 7; Swastek, *Detroit's Oldest Polish Parish*, 73; *Detroit Evening News*, 30 November 1885, 4:3; *Detroit Evening Journal*, 30 November 1885, 1:1; *Detroit Free Press*, 1 December 1885, 3:3; *Detroit Tribune*, 1 December 1885, 2:5.

[19] Skendzel, *Kolasinski Story*, 7; *Detroit Evening News*, 1 December 1885, 4:1; 3 December 1885, 3:3; *Detroit Sunday News*, 6 December 1885, 4:1; *Detroit Evening Journal*, 1 December 1885, 1:3; 3 December 1885, 4:1; *Detroit Free Press*, 2 December 1885, 5:2–3; 4 December 1885, 3:4–5; 5 December 1885, 4:6; *Detroit Tribune*, 2 December 1885, 2:5; 4 December 1885, 2:6.

WHO IS THE CHURCH? CONFLICT IN A POLISH PARISH   251

The steps of the locked church were the site in early December of several prayer vigils by Father Kolasinski's female supporters. But the intensity of the anger generated by Kolasinski's dismissal and the closing of the church were not again publicly evident until Christmas Day. Early Christmas morning, a large crowd estimated variously at 3,000 to 5,000 persons marched some two miles to the bishop's residence to request the opening of Saint Albertus church for Christmas services. Men, women, and children, dressed in traditional holiday costumes, kept a chilly vigil in the street before the residence for more than two hours, while a six-man delegation tried in vain to see the bishop.[20]

Disappointed, the parishioners vented their frustrations in their own neighborhood. A particular target of verbal abuse throughout the rest of Christmas Day was the shuttered store and house of John Lemke, a leader of the anti-Kolasinski trustees. In the late afternoon, someone fired shots from within the store into an apparently threatening crowd outside, and a young man fell dead. The shooting outraged Kolasinski's supporters, and on December 26 a crowd stoned the store of Thomas Zoltowski, another of Kolasinski's chief opponents. Kolasinski himself still remained in the Saint Albertus rectory, guarded by an armed contingent from the Kosciusko Guard, a military company composed of parish youths.[21]

A heavy police presence enforced an uneasy calm on December 27, and there were no further outbreaks of serious violence until August 16, 1886, some four months after Kolasinski had left Detroit. On that day a large crowd, again primarily women, threw stones at a priest as he left the convent and attacked a second priest when he went to visit a dying parishioner. On August 17 a group of women hired by the diocese to clean the long-empty church were driven from the doors by a largely female crowd whose members "all had either brickbats or lumps of mud in their hands." In the evening the crowd, now reinforced by husbands and sons, threw stones at the police and at the convent. These disturbances were evidently occasioned by rumors that the church would soon be reopened for worship. Kolasinski's followers were determined that no other priest should hold his pastorate.[22]

The same determination sparked conflict with the police seven months later. On March 20, 1887, rumors of the imminent reopening of Saint Albertus caused a crowd to gather at the church for a day-long vigil, and in the

---

[20] *Detroit Sunday News,* 6 December 1885, 4:1; *Detroit Evening News,* 7 December 1885, 2:1; 25 December 1885, 1:1–2; *Detroit Evening Journal,* 25 December 1885, 1:1–2; *Detroit Free Press,* 26 December 1885, 1:5–6; *Detroit Tribune,* 26 December 1885, 1:5.

[21] *Detroit Evening News,* 26 December 1885, 1:1–4; *Detroit Sunday News,* 27 December 1885, 1:1–4; *Detroit Evening Journal,* 26 December 1885, 1:1–3; *Detroit Free Press,* 26 December 1885, 1:5–6; 28 December 1885, 3:1–4; *Detroit Tribune,* 26 December 1885, 1:5; 27 December 1885, 2:1.

[22] *Detroit Evening News,* 28 December 1885, 4:2–3; 17 August 1886, 4:2; *Detroit Evening Journal,* 28 December 1885, 4:1; 17 August 1886, 4:3; *Detroit Free Press,* 18 August 1886, 5:5; *Detroit Tribune,* 28 December 1885, 4:1–2; 17 August 1886, 4:4; 18 August 1886, 2:5.

evening Kolasinski's supporters attacked the police as they tried to clear the street. Twenty were arrested. And on May 19, 1887—Ascension Day—Kolasinski's supporters tried to take possession of the parish rectory. They were thwarted by the police, who were joined by a sizeable contingent of Saint Albertans who hoped for the reopening of their church and were most anxious that violence not jeopardize this. No further crowd violence disturbed the neighborhood, although the community remained bitterly divided even after Father Kolasinski's eventual reconciliation with the bishop.[23]

But what determined which members of the parish, which numbered at least 7,000 in 1885, were willing to defend Kolasinski with force? Only a minority was prepared to do so: the angry crowds of early December were generally estimated at about 1,000 persons, though we can assume that many of the women spoke for aggrieved family members as well as for themselves. Opponents of Father Kolasinski claimed that most of his ardent supporters were recently arrived Galicians, blindly loyal to their countryman and too ignorant of American customs to understand that one should not slavishly venerate one's priest. The most influential of Kolasinski's opponents were Prussian Poles, who had lived in Detroit for many years. The parish quarrel, they argued, was simply a reflection of ancient regional antagonisms, exacerbated by the unfamiliarity of the new immigrants with their adopted country.[24]

Regional rivalries, however, could not have been a principal cause of the conflict, for both supporters and opponents of Father Kolasinski were mostly of German birth. The records of the secessionist parish that emerged from the dispute—the parish of the Sweetest Heart of Mary—do not provide information on the birthplace of parishioners. But county marriage records for 1889 and 1890, the first two years of Kolasinski's pastorate at the dissident congregation, show that about 87 percent of those marrying at Saint Albertus were born in Germany or Prussia, compared to about 82 percent of those married by Father Kolasinski. An Austrian-born minority existed in Kolasinski's congregation: 8.5 percent of those marrying there in 1889 and 1890 were of Austrian birth, while fewer than 1 percent of the persons married at Saint Albertus were from Austria. We can assume, then, that the small minority of Austrian-born Poles living in the local Polish community in the mid-1880s were largely loyal to Father Kolasinski, perhaps simply because he too was of Austrian birth. But Kolasinski's compelling personality transcended regional loyalties in its appeal, and many in his congregation

[23] *Detroit Evening News*, 21 March 1887, 4:1-2; 20 May 1887, 4:1; *Detroit Evening Journal*, 21 March 1887, 4:3; 20 May 1887, 4:3; *Detroit Free Press*, 21 March 1887, 1:6-7; 20 May 1887, 4:7.
[24] Swastek, *Detroit's Oldest Polish Parish*, 73, 75, 83-84. *Detroit Evening News*, 10 December 1885, 2:3; 5 April 1886, 4:2; *Detroit Free Press*, 4 December 1885, 3:4-5.

were evidently able to understand themselves as Poles, members of a larger community than the region of Poland in which they had been born.[25]

It is possible, even likely, that the anti-Kolasinski leaders hoped to discredit the movement in support of the priest by identifying it with the poor, low-status Galician minority in the community. Certainly the anti-Kolasinski leaders were visibly wealthier and of higher status than their opponents. Kolasinski's most prominent supporters were, by the standards of the community, relatively well-to-do, but they were mostly skilled workers, not entrepreneurs, and their prosperity was more tenuous than that of their leading opponents, who included a contractor, a wealthy grocer, and several saloonkeepers. Few of Kolasinski's leading defenders had previously been trustees at Saint Albertus. Most of them probably found in his cause a welcome first opportunity to exercise church leadership.[26]

Perhaps, then, the dispute at Saint Albertus was fueled essentially by the accumulated grievances of the poorer parishioners against the parish—and community—elite. There is evidence to suggest this. The Saint Albertus loyalists were probably a wealthier group than the pro-Kolasinski dissidents. Again, county marriage records for 1889 and 1890 allow us to compare certain members of the two congregations, although the occupations of young men in their twenties, as most of the bridegrooms were, may not represent the diversity of occupation in a parish as accurately as would a sample of men in their thirties and forties. Still, we could expect that relatively secure fathers would often try to establish marriageable sons as something other than unskilled laborers.

Laborers, however, were far and away the most populous occupational group in both parishes: 51 percent of the bridegrooms at Saint Albertus and 60 percent of those at Sweetest Heart of Mary worked as laborers. Skilled workers were a distinct minority: about 21 percent of the Saint Albertus bridegrooms were skilled or craft workers, compared to 12.5 percent of those at Sweetest Heart of Mary. And entrepreneurs were few: 5.5 percent (nine) of the men at Saint Albertus, less than 1.5 percent (two) at Sweetest Heart of Mary. Both parishes, then, had poor, working-class majorities, but Kolasinski's congregation probably had a larger representation of unskilled workers and fewer members who could claim high status in the community because of wealth or business achievement. Young women's work patterns also support this hypothesis. About 26 percent of the brides at Saint Albertus in 1889 and 1890 reported being employed, mainly as servants and factory workers, but nearly 50 percent of the brides from Kolasinski's congregation

---

[25] Register of Marriages, Wayne County, Michigan, 1889–90. See also Peter A. Ostafin, "The Polish Peasant in Transition: A Study of Group Interaction as a Function of Symbiosis and Common Definition" (Ph.D. diss., University of Michigan, 1948), 251.

[26] Polk's *Directory of Detroit*, 1886, 1887, 1888.

claimed to be working for wages. In this parochial and isolated community, the working daughter was often a sign of family poverty. Greater prosperity, at least in these years, meant that women could stay properly at home.[27]

The Kolasinski dispute, then, was not simply a revolt of the poor against the secure. Too many loyal members of Saint Albertus parish lived in poverty. But the evidently greater prosperity of those antagonistic to Kolasinski suggests that the choice for or against the priest did have a dimension related to economics and social standing. Perhaps the dispute was nourished by conflicting world views that both reflected and affected economic status. Those who supported Kolasinski may have identified with him strongly because his vulnerability to outside attack underscored the tenuous nature of immigrant success in America. Their own hard lives and fear of the future helped to make Kolasinski for them an evocative figure. Those who opposed the priest, or refused to defy the bishop on his behalf, may have been generally less anxious about their vulnerability as mostly poor immigrants in a strange country. They chose to respect the authority of long-established community leadership, and evidently did not see in Bishop Borgess a potent threat to the integrity of the Polish community.

That Kolasinski's supporters were unusually apprehensive of the world beyond the community is well illustrated by their attitudes toward Father Dombrowski, Kolasinski's successor at Saint Albertus and a target of the December 1885 disturbances. Father Dombrowski, as founder of the Polish Seminary in Detroit, was an ardent proponent of a distinctively Polish Roman Catholicism. He was also a rival to Father Kolasinski for leadership in the local community. But Kolasinski's supporters saw in Father Dombrowski more than a successful rival to their deposed priest; he was for them a man uncritically, even dangerously, loyal to a hostile bishop. Despite his demonstrated commitment to preserving Polish culture in the United States, many Kolasinski adherents believed that Dombrowski had betrayed the ethnic group to serve personal ambition. Their fears, and to some extent their support of Father Kolasinski, were probably rooted in a sharp sense of economic and cultural vulnerability, and a concomitant dread of change.

Nothing in this discussion begins to explain the prominent role of women in the demonstrations unless it be that employed women are more likely to be assertive than those who stay at home. The most aggressive of Kolasinski's

---

[27] Register of Marriages, Wayne County, Michigan, 1889-90. On the economic status of Poles in late nineteenth-century Detroit, see also Sister Mary Remigia Napolska, "The Polish Immigrant in Detroit to 1914," *Annals of the Polish Roman Catholic Union Archives and Museum*, 10 (1946), Chicago, 34-36; Ostafin, "Polish Peasant in Transition," 371-72; Olivier Zunz, "Detroit's Ethnic Neighborhoods at the End of the Nineteenth Century," Center for Research on Social Organization, Working Paper no. 161 (Ann Arbor: University of Michigan, February 1978), 70.

female supporters, however, were long-married and mothers of many children, women unlikely to work outside the home. Their prominence as Kolasinski supporters was, at least initially, a matter of circumstance. Most of the early demonstrations occurred at short notice on weekday mornings. With husbands and sons at work for long hours away from the neighborhood, homebound women were necessarily the first line of Kolasinski's defense at what they deemed critical moments in the campaign.

But these women evidently believed, or quickly came to believe, that violent behavior on their part was justified by something more than necessity; even in battles where many men were present, women were still aggressive participants. Evidently, too, their husbands and children endorsed this clearly unconventional female behavior, although the willingness of the women to confront the police made them de facto the principal strategists of the campaign to retain Kolasinski. And those who petitioned the bishop on Christmas Day to open Saint Albertus Church—not all of them ardent supporters of Kolasinski—did not find the behavior of the women in early December so unjustifiable as to warrant an interdict.[28]

There was, then, considerable support among the dissidents and even their less committed sympathizers for women who actively sought to affect clerical decision making. But in the meetings of the dissident group and in the eventual organization of a secessionist parish, men alone assumed leadership. The extent to which and the ways in which the dissident community permitted women to excercize authority will be discussed more fully later. It can be said here that the community was evidently not troubled by what might appear to be inconsistencies in its expectations of women.

* * *

Whatever the wellsprings of rebellion, support for Father Kolasinski was initially understood by the dissidents purely in terms of personal loyalty. The first wave of resistance to the bishop was not, to all appearances, occasioned by commitment to any theory of congregational rights. But the extremity of their behavior in defense of the priest soon required of Kolasinski's adherents a more disinterested justification of their resistance to episcopal authority. So did their increasing isolation. Kolasinski left Detroit in April 1886; during his thirty-two month absence his supporters functioned as a congregation without a priest. In April 1887 Bishop Borgess, angered by the recurrent violence which prevented the reopening of Saint Albertus for worship, issued a decree

---

[28] *Detroit Evening News*, 19 March 1887, 1:3; 21 March 1887, 4:1-2; 20 May 1887, 4:1; 7 December 1888, 4:1; *Detroit Evening Journal*, 25 December 1885, 1:1-2; 26 December 1885, 1:1-3; 28 December 1885, 4:1; 17 August 1886, 4:3; 21 March 1887, 4:3; *Detroit Free Press*, 28 December 1885, 3:1-4; 21 March 1887, 1:6-7; 27 June 1887, 2:2; *Detroit Tribune*, 17 August 1886, 4:4; 18 August 1886, 2:5.

of excommunication against those active on Kolasinski's behalf.[29] In June 1887 the interdict on Saint Albertus was finally lifted, and that parish resumed its normal, vigorous life. Many who initially protested Bishop Borgess's abrupt removal of Kolasinski by signing petitions or by refusing to attend Father Dombrowski's convent masses returned to Saint Albertus under the ministrations of a new priest, Father Vincent Bronikowski. In such demoralizing circumstances, those still loyal to Kolasinski needed more than their loyalty to him to justify and sustain themselves as a dissident community.

Lay leaders of the Kolasinski faction early in the dispute articulated a principled defense of their defiance of episcopal authority. The bishop, they argued, had dismissed Father Kolasinski without a hearing, thus denying the priest's right to due process. Although Kolasinski's rights were unclear under the canon law governing the American Church in 1885, Kolasinski's supporters insisted that both the claim to due process and lay defense of this claim were legitimate. Here, clearly, they departed from the vision of the Church found in canon law. A priest's right to trial before removal for cause by his bishop was in fact established for the American Church by the Congregation of the Propaganda in 1887, and an eminent Michigan canonist argued in 1893 that Kolasinski's removal had been arbitrary. But no canonist or bishop was prepared to recognize the laity as legitimate definers and defenders of clerical rights.[30]

Kolasinski's supporters also raised in their defense an American interpretation of the ancient right of patronage. In many European communities, and certainly in Poland, wealthy individuals or families held the right to nominate the parish priest, because the patron or his forebears had given the money to build the church. But in the United States, donors to the church fund might

---

[29] *Detroit Evening News*, 3 May 1887, 4:1–3; *Detroit Free Press*, 3 May 1887 1:5–7. Such a decree of excommunication would certainly be questionable in the eyes of many canon lawyers. Bishop Foley, successor to Bishop Borgess, obliquely acknowledged the considerable difficulties of excommunication in these circumstances when he declared in January 1889 that all who participated in services at which Father Kolasinski officiated would incur automatic excommunication. See *Detroit Evening News*, 25 January 1889, 1:4; *Detroit Tribune*, 26 January 1889, 5:2.

[30] *The Catholic Encyclopedia* (New York: Robert Appleton Company, 1911), XI, 502, 538; *Detroit Evening News*, 4 December 1885, 4:1; 6 December 1885, 4:1; *Detroit Sunday News*, 27 December 1885, 1:1–4; *Detroit Evening News*, 30 December 1893, 5:4–5; *Detroit Evening Journal*, 7 December 1888, 1:1; *Detroit Free Press*, 2 December 1885, 5:2–3; 3 December 1885, 5:2–3; 28 December 1885, 3:1–4; 8 June 1888, 8:5.

In 1890, the trustees of Sweetest Heart of Mary issued a statement in which they compared Kolasinski's situation to that of Father Edward McGlynn, who was suspended as a priest in the diocese of New York and eventually excommunicated for his refusal to cease speaking on behalf of Henry George and the single tax movement. McGlynn was eventually reinstated, but not until December 1892. That Kolasinski's trustees were aware of the McGlynn case and able in 1890 to consider him still a priest because his superiors had dealt with him unjustly demonstrates that their defense of themselves was broad and principled. They could endorse a priest of another nationality, in a distant city, whose disobedience had occurred in a very different context from that of Father Kolasinski. See *Detroit Sunday News*, 28 September 1890, 2:1.

include most of the congregation. This was usually true in Polish immigrant parishes. As builders of the church, argued Kolasinski's aggrieved supporters, they possessed the right to name the pastor. The staunchly anti-Kolasinski congregation at Saint Albertus made the same argument in 1891 when they withheld their annual pew rents to force the bishop to remove a priest who they claimed spoke inadequate Polish.[31]

The conviction that generous support of the parish entitled a congregation to certain decision-making rights informed most disputes over parish rights between ethnic Catholics and their American bishops. And new immigrant congregations, not surprisingly, were the most likely to assert their purported rights as patrons. Not only did they make considerable sacrifices to support the parish, but their contributions produced schools, churches, convents—all the result of congregational effort and powerful stimuli to strong feelings of ownership. It was the immigrant generation, moreover, who as parish founders were forced to cede title to parish property to the bishop, a requirement which made more than usually evident authority relations in the Church and which occasionally provoked outright resistance. It was the immigrant generation that needed priests who spoke their language and upheld group traditions; their children and grandchildren generally had fewer reasons to fear the independent selection of pastors by a bishop. And the immigrant generation, especially among the Poles, normally found in the parish a primary focus of social, cultural, and emotional life. For their children and grandchildren, the parish was more likely to be one focus among many.[32]

Thus the experiences and needs of the immigrant laity sustained them in their arguments for parish autonomy, and in disputes over parish rights the invocation of Church law by the bishop was rarely persuasive. The First Provisional Synod of the American Church had in 1829 expressly prohibited the right of patronage in the United States, and the American hierarchy, with full papal support, steadfastly denied that congregations or boards of trustees were empowered to make independent decisions about church finances or the parish priest. The Third Plenary Council, meeting in Baltimore in 1884, ruled that trustees were the creatures of the bishop, and that their selection, should they exist at all, was to be by nomination of the pastor to the bishop, who might remove them at his pleasure. That many immigrant congregations continued, often until World War I, to elect their trustees indicates that many

[31] Galush, "Faith and Fatherland," 85–86; idem, "Forming Polonia," 27, 58–59; Swastek, *Detroit's Oldest Polish Parish*, 54, 83; *Detroit Evening News*, 17 August 1886, 4:2; 21 March 1887, 4:1–2; 7 December 1888, 4:1; 10 December 1888, 2:3; *Detroit Sunday News*, 28 September 1890, 2:1; *Detroit Evening News*, 11 June 1891, 1:3; 12 June 1891, 1:5; 13 June 1891, 1:3; 15 June 1891, 1:2; 16 June 1891, 1:2, 2:3; 17 June 1891, 1:4; 18 June 1891, 1:3; 20 June 1891, 1:1; *Detroit Sunday News*, 21 June 1891, 2:8; *Detroit Evening News*, 26 June 1891, 1:5; 13 July 1891, 1:1; 16 July 1891, 5:1 *Detroit Sunday News*, 19 July 1891, 2:5; *Detroit Free Press*, 5 April 1886, 4:4; 14 June 1891, 18:3; *Detroit Tribune*, 10 December 1888, 4:4; 10 June 1889, 4:3.

[32] Galush, "Faith and Fatherland," 89; Linkh, *American Catholicism*, 106; Thomas and Znaniecki, *Polish Peasant*, 1523–28, 1545–47.

laypersons postulated a very different model of church authority from that embodied in canon law.[33]

What the laity proposed when they claimed the right, as patrons, to choose the pastor was a contractual relationship between priest and people. They recognized their obligation to support the pastor, but believed that that support obliged the pastor to serve the congregation to its own satisfaction. Those who called a priest might dismiss him, or they might, as Kolasinski's congregation eventually did, alter the terms of his service or compensation. Such contractual notions could imply an assumption that priest and people are social equals, but Kolasinski's parishioners, and many other immigrant Catholics, did not behave as though they believed that this was true. Kolasinski's congregation supported him generously; he lived comfortably, dressed fashionably, and kept an expensive carriage and team—a gift from his parishioners.

Certainly many in the parish were pleased to subsidize a priest who represented them so handsomely in a city where Poles were often regarded with contempt. But they also believed that the pastor, by virtue of his ordination to a sacramental priesthood, stood apart from the people spiritually as well as socially. Kolasinski's supporters thus acted on an understanding of the relationship between clergy and laity that incorporated both democratic and hierarchic ideas, recognizing the uniqueness and sacredness of the priesthood but demanding that the priest respond to congregational wishes in his administration of the parish. Church law, of course, posited a very different relationship between priest and people: congregations were obliged to support their priests, but priests were to remain independent of congregational control. The priest's obligation to his flock was defined solely by his pastoral commission.[34]

Finally, Kolasinski's defenders invoked the specter of a contractual relationship between the laity and the bishop by arguing that Bishop Borgess had forfeited his right to their obedience. Not only had he dealt unjustly with Father Kolasinski, he had failed in his pastoral obligation: when he gave Father Dombrowski, a prominent rival to Kolasinski, the pastorate at Saint Albertus, argued the dissidents, the bishop had made it emotionally impossible for them to baptize their children, marry the young, comfort the dying, and properly bury the dead. Subsequently, the bishop had—unjustly, in their view—formally barred them from the sacraments. To what extent Kolasinski's adherents actually did without the sacraments is impossible to determine; certainly there were priests near the area of Polish settlement who ministered

---

[33] *Catholic Encyclopedia*, XV, 71; Galush, "Forming Polonia," 87, 92-93, 218-20, 258-61; McNamara, "Trusteeism," 146; *Detroit Sunday News*, 19 July 1891, 2:5.

[34] Edward A. Chmielewski, "Minneapolis' Polish Priests, 1886-1914," *Polish-American Studies*, 19:1 (January-June 1962), 31-32; Galush, "Forming Polonia," 221; *Detroit Sunday News*, 9 June 1889, 2:4; *Detroit Evening News*, 8 July 1889, 3:3; 4 January 1898, 1:5, 6:5; *Detroit Free Press*, 31 October 1889, 5:1.

to them in his absence. And the bishop might properly have responded that a priest's personality was not sufficient cause for a Catholic to abstain from the sacraments.[35]

But Kolasinski's advocates believed firmly that they had been unjustifiably denied pastoral care, and this was evidently an important theme in the appeals lodged by Kolasinski and his leading lay supporters with Archbishop William Henry Elder at Cincinnati, with Bishop-designate Foley, with the Apostolic Delegate at Washington, and with the Congregation of the Propaganda at Rome. A higher authority, Kolasinski's spokesmen asserted throughout the life of the rebellious parish, would eventually uphold their actions, and this certainty permitted them to consider themselves good Roman Catholics. Again, a dissident laity finds persuasive a view of church authority that includes elements both of democratic and hierarchical theory. An appeal to the Vatican will surely force the local bishop to respond to the desires of his constituents. Happily, Kolasinski's congregation was never confronted with a definitive denial of redress from Rome.[36]

The lay leaders of Kolasinski's rebellious parish were understandably anxious to justify what many of their neighbors saw as apostasy. But did the ordinary parishioner—a recent immigrant, possibly illiterate, living in poverty—really concern himself with the legitimacy of his priest? Perhaps he was attracted to the parish by Father Kolasinski's eloquent preaching. Perhaps he came to the parish because his kin had chosen to do so.

Most parishioners, however, would have known that the choice was not risk-free. Both Bishops Borgess and Foley had it widely announced in the Polish community that Kolasinski's adherents had excommunicated themselves. The local Polish-language weekly, fiercely anti-Kolasinski, constantly reminded the community that the priest's supporters had cut themselves off from the Church. There was, therefore, considerable incentive for even the most casual member of the rebellious parish to find grounds on which the bishops' pronouncements might be disallowed. And throughout the history of the rebellious parish a preoccupation with legitimacy was continuous and apparently widely held. Kolasinski's sermons dealt with the issue, as did his statements to the press; defectors trying to promote disaffection among his followers argued on the grounds of Kolasinski's illegitimacy as a priest in rebellion; the congregation was adamant that a bishop must bless the cornerstone of their new church because an episcopal blessing was the norm for

---

[35] *Detroit Sunday News,* 25 November 1888, 8:1; *Detroit Evening News,* 5 July 1890, 4:3; *Detroit Sunday News,* 28 September 1890, 2:1; *Detroit Evening News,* 16 October 1893, 5:3-7; *Detroit Tribune,* 10 June 1889, 4:3.
[36] *Detroit Evening News,* 21 March 1887, 4:1-2; *Detroit Sunday News,* 25 November 1888, 8:1; *Detroit Evening News,* 26 January 1889, 1:5; *Detroit Sunday News,* 29 September 1889, 13:1; *Detroit Evening News,* 24 September 1890, 1:1; 20 July 1891, 5:3; 2 December 1893, 6:3; *Detroit Evening Journal,* 26 January 1889, 1:3; *Detroit Free Press,* 1 December 1888, 8:3; *Michigan Catholic,* 3 October 1889, 4:4-5.

such ceremonies and would give the community an assurance of regularity. The spiritual and social consequences of apostasy in a Polish immigrant community were likely sufficient to make a political philosopher of the most untutored member of a rebellious parish.[37]

* * *

Kolasinski finally surrendered the Saint Albertus rectory and left Detroit in April 1886. Soon after his departure he was granted an exeat by Bishop Borgess, evidently on the intercession of the Archbishop at Cincinnati. He then proceeded to a small Polish settlement in the Dakota Territory, where he remained as pastor until December 1888. In Detroit, news of Kolasinski's new pastorate angered his supporters, who saw in it a tacit acknowledgment by Bishop Borgess that the priest had been innocent of serious wrongdoing. And the news also gave rise to expectations that the priest might soon return as pastor to those who remained loyal in his absence. "We wait each Sunday for our pastoral Father," wrote a fervent Detroit supporter to the initially pro-Kolasinski *Wiarus* in Winona, Minnesota, and look forward to the day when "the Heavenly Father returns him to us as He returned the crucified Jesus to the Sorrowing Mother of God."[38]

In this intoxicating climate of indignation and expectation, an undetermined number of Kolasinski's supporters in his absence organized themselves as a congregation. They also established a school, which was under the direction of Anton Dlugi, a recent immigrant who may have been a blacksmith in Poland but who became schoolmaster and principal lay leader of the new congregation. The earliest extant mention of the new school is a letter from Dlugi to the *Wiarus* in August 1886; he had, he wrote, about two hundred pupils. The school had certainly been organized by the time the letter was written; later testimony, not unimpeachable, claimed that the school was founded in March of that year. No records survive from this period in the history of the new parish, but it is certain that the new school continued under Dlugi's control, meeting in a large frame house near Saint Albertus church, until Kolasinski returned in December 1888. Dlugi left the congregation shortly thereafter, but the school survived and by June 1889 was housed in considerably more substantial quarters.[39]

[37] *Detroit Evening News*, 2 June 1890, 1:3; 10 June 1890, 1:1-2; 2 July 1890, 1:1; 4 July 1890, 1:1; 24 July 1890, 1:2; 24 September 1890, 1:1; 25 September 1890, 1:3; 29 September 1890, 1:1-2; 16 June 1891, 1:1-2; 16 July 1891, 5:1; 25 July 1891, 1:2; 3 September 1891, 2:1; *Detroit Sunday News*, 5 June 1892, 1:8; *Detroit Evening News*, 2 December 1893, 6:3; *Detroit Sunday News-Tribune*, 24 December 1893, 1:2-3; *Detroit Free Press*, 6 June 1892, 5:2-3; 25 December 1893, 1:6-7; *Detroit Tribune*, 6 June 1892, 5:2-4.

[38] *Wiarus*, 20 May 1886, 3:2; 27 May 1886, 1:6. Bishop Caspar H. Borgess to Rt. Rev. Dr. Marty, 3 April 1886 (appended to Chancery brief, "To the Congregation De Propaganda Fide, in re Diocese of Detroit vs. Rev. Dominic Kolasinski," undated, but late 1893), Bishop Foley papers, Rev. Kolasinski, transcripts, folder 2, AAD.

[39] *Wiarus*, 19 August 1886, 2:4; *Detroit Evening News*, 30 November 1888, 1:3; 12 May 1889, 2:1; *Detroit Evening Journal*, 3 January 1889, 1:5; *Detroit Tribune*, 8 June 1888, 5:5-6.

The frame schoolhouse also served the congregation as a meeting house and place of worship during Kolasinski's absence. Regular Sunday services were held there. Mass could not be celebrated, but evidently the group sang hymns, prayed, and recited the rosary. "There was singing and prayer," noted one observer, "and a sort of exercise in which responsive murmurs were made by the people to their leader's intonations." Polish Catholics brought to the United States a rich liturgical tradition; the mass might provide the most intense spiritual experience for most, but they were familiar with a number of nonsacramental devotions. In this sense immigrant Catholics were rather better prepared than Catholics today to sustain a congregation without a priest.[40]

A priest was necessary, however, if parishioners were to fulfill their minimum obligations as Catholics to confess and receive communion during the Easter season, if they were to contract canonically valid marriages, if they were to have the comfort of absolution and anointment at the point of death. In emergencies, laypersons might baptize, but the scrupulous among Kolasinski's supporters might have worried that their situation was not the sort of emergency that, according to Catholic teaching, justified lay baptism. What, then, did the Kolasinski loyalists do? Their leaders claimed that most of the congregation had no access to the sacraments, that as many as eight hundred infants were unbaptized at the time of Kolasinski's return, that the young had been unable to marry in the Church, that the dead had been denied Christian burial—although it was not said that any died unconfessed. If these assertions are true, then perhaps in their priestless years Kolasinski's supporters began to develop an understanding of their religion that was largely nonsacramental. This would represent a major theological reorientation, developing without anyone's intent from defiance of a particular act of ecclesiastical authority.[41]

Extant evidence, however, belies most of the leaders' claims. Perhaps they made extravagant charges to pressure diocesan authorities into allowing Father Kolasinski to return to Detroit. Perhaps their claims expressed anger and anguish at having to receive the sacraments in parishes that were not their own, and sometimes only at the cost of concealing their identities as Kolasinski loyalists. Perhaps they wished to justify their own irregularity by

---

[40] *Detroit Evening News,* 10 December 1888, 2:3; *Detroit Evening Journal,* 8 December 1888, 5:1; 10 December 1888, 4:3; 12 December 1888, 1:2; *Detroit Free Press,* 10 December 1888, 4:2; *Detroit Tribune,* 8 June 1888, 5:5–6; 9 June 1888, 5:3; 10 December 1888, 4:4.

[41] *Detroit Sunday News,* 18 November 1888, 2:1; *Detroit Evening News,* 7 December 1888, 4:1; 20 February 1889, 1:4; *Detroit Sunday News,* 28 September 1890, 2:1; *Detroit Evening News,* 16 October 1893, 5:3–7; 30 December 1893, 5:4–5. Kolasinski himself variously claimed to have baptized 680 children within three months of his return, and also "more than a thousand." (Fr. Dominic Kolasinski to Fr. Peter, 30 May 1890, Bishop Foley papers, Correspondence, Rev. Kolasinski, undated, 1889–1892, AAD; Petition, Rev. Dominic Kolasinski to Archbishop Satolli, 19 January 1893, Bishop Foley papers, Correspondence, Rev. Kolasinski, 1893–1894, folder 2, AAD.) And he claimed as well that, on his return, "very many were living in marriages [considered] illicit by the Church" (*ibid.*).

reminding the world yet again that Bishop Borgess had failed them in his pastoral ministry. But whatever their leaders' motives, it is not the case that most members of the dissident congregation were denied the sacraments in Kolasinski's absence. This is especially clear with regard to marriage and baptism.

The surviving marriage register at Sweetest Heart of Mary church dates from February 1890 and provides no information about the number of marriages previously performed in the parish. But county marriage records show that Father Kolasinski married thirty-one couples in early 1889. This is an unusually large number for a period of less than two and a half months, but not large enough to suggest a three-year moratorium on weddings in the congregation. Kolasinski married an additional thirty-one couples during the remainder of 1889 and seventy-two couples in 1890. Perhaps a few couples had indeed waited through the long uncertain months of Kolasinski's absence for their weddings. But more probably the majority of those marrying in early 1889 were taking advantage of the interval between Advent and Lent—seasons when marriages were not normally performed in Polish parishes—and making January and February normally busy for their pastor. (Kolasinski married twenty-one couples in January and February of 1890.) Possibly too some couples postponed November weddings in 1888 in anticipation of Kolasinski's rumored return. And perhaps the euphoria that marked his return even prompted a few hesitant courting pairs to marry.[42]

How, then, did members of the dissident congregation marry in their priest's absence? Did they resort to civil ceremonies? There would naturally be great reluctance among persons who considered themselves Catholics to sanction marriages which the Church did not regard as valid. And in fact county marriage records show that very few, if any, of Kolasinski's supporters were married by civil authorities. There were twenty-three civil marriages in Detroit between persons of German, Prussian, Austrian, Russian, or Polish birth in 1888, compared to fifteen such marriages in 1889 and seventeen in 1890. (These figures do not include couples with identifiably Jewish names.) Possibly the larger 1888 total included couples from Kolasinski's parish. But none of those 1888 couples who might plausibly have been from his congregation, given certain information about occupation and residence, appears subsequently as parents in the parish baptismal register. We must conclude that most if not all marriages that took place among Kolasinski's supporters were performed by priests.[43]

Just which priests were willing to marry persons who were by many considered excommunicate cannot be fully determined. Betrothed couples probably turned to priests at neighboring German parishes. They may sometimes have

[42] Register of Marriages, Wayne County, Michigan, 1888, 1889, 1890.
[43] Ibid.

concealed their ties to the dissident congregation and claimed membership in the priest's parish as fellow German-speakers, for many of the German-born Poles spoke some German, and some were fluent in the language. But probably some local priests, reluctant to drive young Kolasinski supporters further into error, married them knowing full well who they were. Father Charles Reilly, the liberal pastor of the Irish-American Saint Patrick parish, in February 1888 married a couple who appeared in 1890 as parents in the Sweetest Heart of Mary baptismal register. Other priests may have believed with Father Reilly that pastoral concern must sometimes mitigate Church discipline. A church survives and grows because it accommodates, even encourages, this kind of flexibility.[44]

Baptism by a priest was certainly deferred in Kolasinski's absence by a number of parents among his supporters. The parish baptismal register records seventy-eight obviously late baptisms in January and February of 1889; eleven more were recorded by August 31 of that year. Kolasinski was, moreover, a notoriously poor recordkeeper, and there may well have been more baptisms of children well beyond early infancy. But it seems most unlikely that hundreds of unbaptized children awaited Kolasinski's return, and it may be that those who were waiting had already been baptized by laymembers of the parish. Catholic theology clearly taught that unbaptized infants had no hope of heaven. The infant death rate in Detroit's Polish community was tragically high: of 233 deaths recorded in the Sweetest Heart of Mary register between April 3, 1898, and November 6, 1899—the earliest surviving death records—113 were those of children under the age of one year, and a further 34 were those of children aged one to five. If most parents in Kolasinski's absence contrived to have their children baptized by a priest, their concern indicated not a lack of loyalty to him but the seriousness with which they regarded the sacrament.[45]

It is probable that many from the dissident congregation regularly attended Sunday mass at various local churches. In April 1888 one Kolasinski loyalist admitted as much to a reporter. By that time, indeed, members of the congregation had on at least two occasions assembled in force during Saturday masses at highly visible downtown churches. Their presence—inspired perhaps in part by the apparent diffusion of diocesan authority after the resignation of Bishop Borgess in April 1887—asserted their stubborn conviction that nothing had occurred which might legitimately exclude them from the worshipping community.[46]

---

[44] Register of Marriages, Wayne County, Michigan, 1888; Baptismal Register, Sweetest Heart of Mary Church, Detroit.
[45] Baptismal Register, Sweetest Heart of Mary Church, Detroit; Death Register, Sweetest Heart of Mary Church, Detroit.
[46] *Detroit Evening News*, 14 April 1888, 4:3.

Whether Kolasinski's adherents in his absence received communion and were confessed at local churches is less clear. But there were opportunities for many of them to do so. Before the reopening of Saint Albertus church in June 1887 other local churches were apparently expected to serve those parishioners loyal to the bishop. Their priests would hardly know who among the Poles approaching the communion rail was loyal to Kolasinski, and the confessional assured anonymity. Kolasinski's leading defenders also acknowledged that Father Reilly at Saint Patrick church permitted at least some of their number to receive the sacraments there. And in November 1888 a reporter spoke to a young girl who claimed that, while she attended Dlugi's school, her mother still went to mass and confession at Saint Albertus, although the mother was a supporter of Kolasinski. The Saint Albertus congregation was very large, and perhaps its overworked priests did not know by sight all who had ties to the dissident community. The Polish faithful, moreover, although regular church-goers, apparently received communion infrequently, which limited the ability of priests to discipline through exclusion from the sacrament.[47]

The period during which the rebellious congregation was priestless, though not leaderless, illustrates again the subtle combination of democratic values and respect for hierarchy that informed the parishioners' understanding of the Church. On the one hand, they were as capable as the most radical Protestant sect of sustaining themselves as a community of worshippers under lay leadership. But at the same time, they understood the sacraments, administered by an ordained priesthood, as necessary to their salvation, and many of them evidently had at least occasional recourse to local priests in order to receive them. Despite their anomalous situation as a congregation without a priest, Kolasinski's supporters obviously considered themselves Catholics in good standing, able to participate in the sacraments. Indeed, the months of conflict with the bishop may have intensified for these immigrant men and women a sense that their identity as Catholics was centered in the sacraments rather than in a particular set of authority relations.

The congregation lived without a priest of its own until December 1888, when Kolasinski returned permanently to Detroit. (He had, the previous summer, paid a three-day visit to the city.) Kolasinski's December return was prompted both by optimism and by apprehension. The appointment in November 1888 of Bishop John Foley to the long-vacant see at Detroit raised hopes in the dissident community—and the hopes of Father Kolasinski—that he would soon be reinstated as a priest in Detroit. Several delegations from the congregation met with the new bishop to plead his case. But Bishop Foley was unyielding; he was determined to end the dispute, but on terms he himself

[47] *Detroit Evening News,* 7 December 1885, 2:1; 29 November 1886, 1:1; 16 October 1893, 5:3-7; 16 December 1893, 8:2-3; *Detroit Evening Journal,* 27 June 1887, 4:3; *Detroit Free Press,* 1 December 1888, 8:3.

found acceptable. His near success in doing so brought Father Kolasinski to Detroit in December.[48]

Bishop Foley evidently hoped to end the dispute by appealing personally, and sympathetically, to individual dissidents. In late November and early December he paid two visits to the east-side Polish community, accompanied by Father Dombrowski as interpreter, and called on a number of Kolasinski's followers. He reaffirmed to them Kolasinski's permanent dismissal from the diocese, urged their return to Saint Albertus, but offered himself to baptize any unbaptized children from the dissident community. Despite his unwitting error in appearing with Father Dombrowski, Kolasinski's supporters greeted the bishop emotionally: they knelt for his blessing, kissed his ring, and many apparently promised obedience. But they did not subsequently bring their unbaptized children to him. One local paper mentioned the bishop's baptizing a two-year-old from the dissident congregation in early December, but there are no records of any such baptisms in the bishop's private sacramental records, at Saint Albertus or at the church attached to the Chancery.[49]

Had Father Kolasinski not sent word at this point of his imminent return, it is possible that his Detroit congregation would have lost critically large numbers. Kolasinski's supporters were clearly moved by the bishop's willingness to come to them as a pastor, and his pastoral concern strengthened, in their eyes, his claims to their obedience. They responded as well to the power of his office. Despite their efforts to limit episcopal control of parish life, the Kolasinski loyalists had never challenged the legitimacy of episcopal authority. But Kolasinski's arrival in Detroit on December 8 revived the issue of congregational rights, and forced the wavering parishioners to choose sides. They did not hesitate. Insisting that they remained loyal to a hierarchical church, they argued again that a bishop who violated their rights as laypersons forfeited his claims to their obedience. Bishop Foley further justified them in this course, they believed, by refusing a personal appeal from Father Kolasinski for his own reinstatement.[50]

---

[48] *Detroit Evening News*, 7 June 1888, 1:5; 11 June 1888, 4:2; *Detroit Sunday News*, 18 November 1888, 2:1; 25 November 1888, 8:1; *Detroit Evening News*, 30 November 1888, 1:3; 7 December 1888, 4:1; *Detroit Sunday News*, 9 December 1888, 2:1; *Detroit Evening Journal*, 1 December 1888, 5:1; 10 December 1888, 4:3; *Detroit Free Press*, 8 June 1888, 8:5; 11 June 1888, 2:5; 8 December 1888, 8:2; 9 December 1888, 19:5; *Detroit Tribune*, 8 June 1888, 5:5 6; 9 June 1888, 5:3; 10 June 1888, 5:1; 6 December 1888, 5:5; 7 December 1888, 4:5; 9 December 1888, 5:3.

[49] *Detroit Evening News*, 1 December 1888, 1:3; *Detroit Sunday News*, 2 December 1888, 2:7; *Detroit Evening Journal*, 29 November 1888, 1:5; 3 December 1888, 2:4; *Detroit Free Press*, 1 December 1888, 8:3; 2 December 1888, 18:3; *Detroit Tribune*, 8 December 1888, 5:1; Baptismal Register, St. Albertus Church, Detroit, Michigan (entries for November and December, 1888); Baptismal Register, St. Aloysius Church, Detroit, Michigan (entries for November and December, 1888); Bishops' Private Sacramental Records, AAD.

[50] *Detroit Sunday News*, 9 December 1888, 2:1; *Detroit Evening News*, 10 December 1888, 2:3; *Detroit Sunday News*, 16 December 1888, 1:4; *Detroit Evening Journal*, 10 December 1888, 4:3; 17 December 1888, 2:3; *Detroit Free Press*, 9 December 1888, 19:5; 10 December 1888, 4:2; *Detroit Tribune*, 10 December 1888, 4:4; 18 December 1888, 5:4.

Kolasinski appears to have been reluctant, even after this rebuff, to defy the bishop openly; he did not say mass publicly until January 23. But already in mid-December a committee from his congregation was negotiating to buy a large plot of land two blocks west of Saint Albertus. The first installment was paid on December 28, and in late January plans were announced for a schoolhouse and for the eventual construction of an enormous church, the cost of which was placed at $100,000. A parish spokesman explained that the construction would be financed by a $50 gift from each of the congregation's 2,000 families. Doubtless he exaggerated—the congregation was mostly poor and its numbers probably fewer than claimed. He spoke in the hyperbolic mode of nineteenth-century parish rivalry, and expressed as well the emotions that sustained the group in the face of the new bishop's opposition.[51]

A lay committee of eighteen men drew up formal articles of association for the new parish in early February 1889, stipulating a largely lay-controlled mode of parish government. The three years of conflict—and experience as a priestless congregation—bore fruit in this clear statement of congregational prerogatives. Seven male trustees, at least twenty-one years of age, were to manage the "temporal affairs" of the parish. The trustees were to be elected annually by the congregation—presumably its adult male members, although the articles of association mention no age or sex requirements for voter eligibility. The pastor was to be an ex-officio member of the board of trustees, party to the deliberations of the board, but without a vote of his own. And the pastor—to whom the "spiritual affairs" of the parish were "left entirely"—was to be chosen by the trustees, who might elect a candidate "for one or more years in their discretion." (Father Kolasinski was apparently elected pastor for the full thirty-year legal life of the corporation, granted the status and security his people believed was his due but within the context of explicitly defined congregational rights.) Few founding documents can have been further from the letter and spirit of the canon law governing American parishes in the nineteenth century, but the signators were secure in their Roman Catholic identity: "every person who believes in the Roman Catholic faith and performs their Easter duties shall be eligible for membership in said corporation."[52]

---

[51] *Detroit Evening News*, 24 January 1889, 1:2; 26 January 1889, 1:5; *Detroit Evening Journal*, 15 December 1888, 5:3; 29 December 1888, 8:2; 23 January 1889, 1:3; 24 January 1889, 1:2; *Detroit Tribune*, 27 January 1889, 5:4. Sweetest Heart of Mary parish claimed 2,000 families in 1898, the first year for which the Diocese of Detroit recorded annual statistics for this parish. There is good evidence that parish membership grew considerably between 1889 and 1898. (Account Book 15: Parish Statistics and Accounts, 1894-1916, p. 11, AAD.) Late in 1893, however, Father Baart of Marshall, Michigan, a sympathetic but relatively dispassionate observer of the Kolasinski affair, argued that "Polish priests who have charge of other parishes, not friendly to him, state he has from 1800 to 3000 families, ie. from 9000 to 15000 souls, who recognize his pastorate over them." (Rev. P. A. Baart to Rev. Charles P. Grannan, 4 November 1893, Bishop Foley papers, Correspondence, Rev. Kolasinski, folder 2, AAD.)

[52] Articles of Association of the Roman Catholic Parish of the Sacred Heart of St. Mary of the

That the congregation so established was large and dedicated is demonstrated by the rapid completion of the parish school, which was blessed in June 1889. Said to have cost some $20,000, the school was a three-story brick building, with classrooms and the priest's quarters on the upper stories and a church that could seat nearly 1,000 on the ground floor. The spirit and size of the parish were evident at the building's dedication: two bands led a procession of 3,000 persons, including members of the Kosciusko Guard and four parish fraternities. Father Kolasinski, assisted by eighteen acolytes, blessed the exterior of the building and the interior of the church. Massive crowds—parishioners and the curious—flooded the church grounds. While high mass was sung, from noon until 2:00 o'clock, "the thousands on the outside were seen to kneel, some in the mud and others on pieces of stone, slate and boards. A lively little shower came down about 12:30 o'clock, but the rain had no terror for those outside as they devoutly knelt with bared heads." An hour after the conclusion of the mass, a large crowd attended vespers.[53]

The fervor of the worshippers, marvelous to middle-class witnesses on this and other occasions, merits a brief discussion here. Particularly for cohesive ethnic groups, worship is an important source of communal emotion and identity, and a key to understanding how individuals view themselves, their place in the worshipping community, and their relationship to the larger society. It is not possible here to consider the ways in which liturgy and communal identity were linked for Polish immigrants. But we can consider how the experience of the liturgy affected immigrant perceptions of Church authority in the American setting.

It is evident that participation in the liturgy was an intensely emotional experience for many of the immigrant faithful at the Sweetest Heart of Mary church, and at other Polish churches in Detroit. In part this was because the traditional liturgy evoked strong memories of Poland. More important, the traditional Polish liturgy invited the congregation to participate fully, drawing individuals into the drama of the service in active affirmation of their culture and their faith. The mass, of course, was said in Latin, and the essentials of the rite were priest-centered. But the congregation sang and chanted responses, and were a responsive audience for the long, emotional sermon. Father Kolasinski could move his hearers to tears and exclamations as effectively as a revivalist preacher, and his gifts were widely admired in the Polish community. Vespers, popular in his and other Polish parishes, were genuinely

City of Detroit of the State of Michigan, 9 February 1889. (Bishop Borgess papers, Box 3, file 4, AAD.) The name of the new parish, for many years mistranslated into English as the Sacred Heart of Mary, is readily identifiable as Roman Catholic. This may well have been a factor in the choice. And the Virgin may have represented for many in the parish the accepting, nurturant aspects of their faith as opposed to the harsh discipline they had come to associate with the local Chancery.

[53] *Detroit Evening News,* 9 June 1889, 2:4; 10 June 1889, 4:1; 5 September 1891, 1:1-2; *Detroit Free Press,* 10 June 1889, 4:3; *Detroit Tribune,* 10 June 1889, 4:3.

congregational worship. Parishioners usually sang hymns and psalms in Polish, then knelt for the Benediction of the Blessed Sacrament.[54]

The liturgical year in the Polish Church, moreover, was marked by celebrations that embraced the whole community. Public processions, at Corpus Christi and the Marian devotions in May and often on other occasions as well, were dramatic affirmations of community solidarity and religious faith. A distinctively Polish liturgy at major feasts accomplished the powerful fusion of cultural identity and religious belief. Certain ceremonies, such as the initialing of the doors of the home at Epiphany, the blessing of the candles on the feast of Candlemas, the blessing of the Easter food on Holy Saturday, dignified the family as a worshipping group. The traditional liturgy, in short, engaged the individual as a member of the congregation, of the community, and of the family, and gave him the means to respond actively in each of these roles.[55]

But the vitality of congregational worship among Poles and other Catholic groups was in the United States relatively short-lived. With assimilation, traditional liturgies fell increasingly into disuse among all ethnic groups, and by the time of the Second Vatican Council the nonparticipation of the congregation in the liturgy was considered by many Catholics an aspect of church life in serious need of reform. We know already that assimilation also meant that Catholics were increasingly unlikely to claim patronage rights in the parish. What is the relationship between these two phenomena?

The passing of traditional liturgies did not in itself cause a waning sense of congregational patronage, nor can the reverse be true. But since participation in a traditional liturgy strengthens communal identity, it makes the worshipper in a multiethnic society sharply aware of the cultural divisions which can permeate a church that is uniform in terms of theology and law. The impulse to identify "church" with "congregation" is strengthened, as is the tendency to see church authority beyond the parish as unsympathetic or even hostile. Beyond questions of ethnic identity, and more fundamental, full participation in the liturgy enables individuals to understand the church as a worshipping community to which the people are no less essential than the priest or leader.

Thus, in the right circumstances, as for example where the congregation are the builders of the church and fear that ecclesiastical authority threatens their

---

[54] Swastek, *Detroit's Oldest Polish Parish*, 114, 154; *Detroit Evening News*, 4 July 1890, 1:1; 29 September 1890, 1:1-2; 23 December 1893, 1:1-2; *Detroit Free Press*, 25 June 1887, 5:2; 10 June 1889, 4:3; 6 June 1892, 5:2-3; 19 February 1894, 1:5-6, 3:4-5; *Detroit Tribune*, 19 February 1894, 1:2-3, 3:6-7; 9 July 1894, 5:6; *Michigan Catholic*, 31 January 1889, 8:4. On preaching in nineteenth-century American Catholicism, see Jay Dolan, *Catholic Revivalism: the American Experience, 1830-1900* (Notre Dame: University of Notre Dame Press, 1978).

[55] Galush, "Forming Polonia," 156; Napolska, "Polish Immigrant in Detroit," 64-66; Swastek, *Detroit's Oldest Polish Parish*, 114; Peter Roberts, *Anthracite Coal Communities* (New York: Macmillan Company, 1904), 215; *Detroit Evening News*, 25 December 1897, 5:3-4; *Detroit Free Press*, 25 June 1887, 5:2.

cultural integrity, the liturgy may provide important support for an emerging ethic of lay participation in church government. And when a people surrenders its traditions of congregational worship, one element of support for lay activism disappears. Significantly, the reforms of the 1960s revived for the American Church not only a more genuinely congregational liturgy but active lay involvement in parish government.

* * *

Kolasinski's congregation continued to grow during the early 1890s, although another Polish church was opened in 1890 just five blocks west of the Sweetest Heart of Mary. Most of the new members of Kolasinski's parish were probably immigrants recently arrived in Detroit. Some of them may not have been fully aware of Kolasinski's irregular status: the newcomers had not experienced the initial troubles, the liturgy and social life of the parish were conventional, and Kolasinski himself frequently assured his flock that they were good Roman Catholics. Bitter jealousy, moreover, characterized relations between some Polish priests in the United States, and some new parishioners might have assumed that accusations against Father Kolasinski were merely spiteful propaganda. There would then be no need to think about what defined legitimacy in the Church.[56]

Nonetheless, some members of the congregation were sufficiently anxious about the status of the parish to insist that a bishop bless the cornerstone of the proposed church, and their numbers were sufficiently large that their unease delayed for a time the collection of funds and excavation of the site, the latter task done principally by the men in the congregation. Ground was finally broken in July 1890 but the cornerstone was not blessed until June 1892. The June ceremonies were even more elaborate than those which marked the blessing of the schoolhouse, and the congregation now supported eight societies in addition to the Kosciusko Guard. The bishop imported for the occasion was identified only as a visitor from Russian Poland; he was evidently an irregular Polish priest who had lived for some time in the United States. The ruse was effective, however, in stilling most congregational doubt, and the church was substantially completed by December 1893. It was blessed on December 24, the officiating bishop a Frenchman who claimed to have been consecrated by the Old Catholics in Utrecht and hence in the apostolic succession.[57]

[56] *Detroit Evening News*, 14 September 1891, 1:5; 7 January 1892, 5:4; 23 January 1893, 1:1.
[57] *Detroit Evening News*, 27 May 1890, 2:3; 26 July 1890, 1:5; 26 September 1890, 1:5; *Detroit Sunday News*, 14 December 1890, 1:7–8; *Detroit Evening News*, 16 July 1891, 5:1; 20 July 1891, 5:3; 3 September 1891, 2:1; 5 September 1891, 1:1; *Detroit Sunday News*, 5 June 1892, 1:8; *Detroit Evening News*, 6 June 1892, 4:4–5; 4 July 1892, 1:1–2; 23 December 1893, 1:1–2; 25 December 1893, 1:1–6, 6:3; 26 December 1893, 5:4–5; *Detroit Free Press*, 6 June 1892, 5:2–3; 25 December 1893, 1:6–7; *Detroit Tribune*, 6 June 1892, 5:2–4; 25 December 1893, 1:2–3. (Continued on next page.)

The new church, seating 2,500 and larger than Saint Albertus, was an awesome building, at least in its setting of modest frame cottages and dusty streets. Its two massive bell towers soared 226 feet, dominating the eastside skyline, and the interior was elaborate, with high Gothic arches, a star-studded vault, and carved altars. The transept was lit by enormous stained-glass windows. The church was said to have cost in excess of $120,000, and, while this figure may have been inflated for public consumption, there is no doubt that this church was immensely expensive. The money came almost exclusively from parishioners; sixteen families were said to have mortgaged their homes to make long-term loans to the church fund. The parish was deeply in debt by December 1893, and a gathering depression was already evident in Detroit. But December 24 was a day of triumph and hope. Twelve church societies, two parish military companies, and thousands of gaily dressed spectators provided vivid testimony to the spiritual health of the young parish.[58]

The great and growing number in Kolasinski's congregation, variously estimated at 10,000 to 15,000, provided compelling reason for the Apostolic Delegate in Washington to seek to effect a reconciliation between the priest and his bishop. Kolasinski himself was anxious for reconciliation, although only on certain terms, and his case was strengthened by a recent liberalization of procedures governing the dismissal of priests in the American Church, procedures which, although not in effect in 1885, lent a certain support to Kolasinski's claims that his own dismissal without a hearing had been excessively arbitrary. The Apostolic Delegate, moreover, had arrived in Washington in 1892 expressly to impose discipline and uniform procedures on bishops too often in conflict with one another and their priests. Kolasinski's reinstatement was first discussed not long after the Delegate reinstated Father Edward McGlynn, who had been suspended for his political activities by New York's conservative Archbishop Michael Corrigan. Negotiations in the Kolasinski case lasted for more than a year, and eventually involved the Congregation of the Propaganda at Rome. Bishop Foley was most reluctant to have Kolasinski as a priest in his diocese, while Kolasinski refused to be

---

Descriptions of the event and speculation about the identity of Kolasinski's imported "bishop" can also be found in the reports of a Detroit detective agency, hired by diocesan authorities to infiltrate the crowds around the church and to send confidential reports directly to Bishop Foley. The reports cover the activities around the church during December 23-26, 1893. Only one agency operative spoke Polish, however, and two hapless agents were arrested on December 24 for suspicious loitering. They spent most of the day at the local police station. Given the circumstances, the confidential reports offered the Bishop little he could not have read in the local papers. See Bishop Foley papers, Correspondence, Rev. Kolasinski, 1893-1894, folders 5 and 6, AAD.

[58] *Detroit Evening News*, 26 July 1890, 1:5; 16 October 1893, 5:3-7; 23 December 1893, 1:1-2; *Detroit Sunday News-Tribune*, 24 December 1893, 1:2-3; *Detroit Free Press*, 25 December 1893, 1:6-7; *Detroit Tribune*, 25 December 1893, 1:2-3.

moved from his pastorate. There was also bitter opposition among many Detroit priests to a reconciliation.[59]

Eventually, however, agreement was achieved and on February 18, 1894, an immense crowd filled Sweetest Heart of Mary church to witness Father Kolasinski's reconciliation with his superiors. The priest was allowed to preach before having to read—in English, German, and Polish—a prescribed retraction of his acts and statements in defiance of episcopal authority. Evidently his sermon was masterful; his rich voice filled the church and he moved many in the vast crowd to tears. His theme was the sufferings of his congregation in exile. But when, at the close of the sermon, he began to read his confession, his voice dropped to a whisper. In vain, Monsignor Donato Sbarretti, the representative of the Apostolic Delegate, ordered him to speak more loudly. Few in the congregation heard the retraction, and observers believed that most in the parish thought that Father Kolasinski had never been in error. He was simply being granted, by a benevolent higher authority, the recognition unfairly denied him by the bishop.[60]

The conditions of Kolasinski's readmission to the Church were not ungenerous. Besides the public retraction and a public profession of faith, he had been required to spend a week of penitent meditation in a Chicago monastery. The church itself was blessed by Monsignor Sbarretti, the earlier blessing thus publicly declared invalid. Kolasinski was not made the permanent rector of his church, and he was to dismiss his assistant priests, with future assistants to be appointed by the bishop. But he was to remain the pastor of his congregation, and that congregation was to hold title to its property until it was free of debt. This latter provision, almost certainly stemming from the bishop's fear that the congregation could not meet its debts, was seen as a victory in the parish. The negotiations, from the pa-

---

[59] McAvoy, *History*, 277, 303-4, 309; *Detroit Evening News*, 12 August 1891, 5:5; 5 September 1891, 1:1; 23 January 1893, 1:1; 24 January 1893, 1:1; 26 January 1893, 1:3; 28 January 1893, 5:2; 16 October 1893, 5:3-7; 2 December 1893, 6:3; 16 December 1893, 8:2-3; 22 December 1893 1:1; 23 December 1893, 1:1-2; 30 December 1893, 5:4-5; 5 January 1894, 1:5, 4:6-7; 10 January 1894, 1:1, 6:3-4; 12 January 1894, 1:5; 7 February 1894, 5:3. *Detroit Sunday News-Tribune*, 11 February 1894, 1:8; *Detroit Evening News*, 12 February 1894, 6:4; *Detroit Sunday News-Tribune*, 18 February 1894, 8:3; *Detroit Free Press*, 7 February 1894, 4:5; 12 February 1894, 5:4; *Michigan Catholic*, 15 February 1894, 4:2. Extensive correspondence concerning the negotiations involving Archbishop Satolli, Bishop Foley, and Father Kolasinski can be found in the Bishop Foley papers for the years 1893 and 1894. The Foley papers also include six petitions from priests in the diocese objecting to Kolasinski's reinstatement (Correspondence, Rev. Kolasinski, 1893-1894, folder 1, AAD).

[60] *Detroit Evening News*, 19 February 1894, 5:2-4; *Detroit Free Press*, 19 February 1894, 1:5-6, 3:4-5; *Detroit Tribune*, 19 February 1894, 1:2-3, 3:6-7; *Michigan Catholic*, 22 February 1894, 4:2. See also "Draft of Agreement between Bishop John Foley and Rev. Dominic Kolasinski," Bishop Foley papers, Correspondence, Rev. Kolasinski, 1893-1894, folder 3, AAD; "Form of Retraction to be Read in Public by Rev. Dominic Kolasinski on the Occasion of his Reconciliation with the Church," Bishop Foley papers, Correspondence, Rev. Kolasinski, 1893-1894, folder 3, AAD. Both the agreement and the form of retraction were reported accurately in the newspaper accounts.

rishioners' point of view, had granted them the rights their rebellion had defended. They had chosen their pastor and they alone would make decisions about parish finances.⁶¹

Those decisions proved over the next few years to be difficult ones. The depression of the mid-1890s seriously affected Detroit's Poles, dependent as they were on unskilled factory work and day labor. It was evident by late 1894 that the parish could not meet all of its considerable debts, and on February 1, 1897, the church property was placed at auction by order of a city court. The property was sold in early March, to the grief and anger of the congregation. Without the protection of ownership, one parishioner told a reporter, the parish would be completely under control of the bishop, "our stepfather." Unlike Kolasinski, "our real father," he explained, the bishop cared not for the needs of the parishioners but only for their money. He gave voice to the anxieties that seem to a latter-day observer so important a source of the "Kolasinski crisis."⁶²

In mid-April, however, the congregation, through its board of trustees, secured a loan from a Canadian bank which enabled them to repurchase the church property. But the financial situation remained precarious, and eventually occasioned Father Kolasinski's only serious defeat in parish politics. Although he had to work with his board of trustees, who were elected annually by the congregation, Kolasinski evidently exerted considerable leverage on financial decision making and accounted only vaguely for the many fees he received above his $700 yearly salary. The trustees, however, were determined to enforce strict economies in parish administration despite Kolasinski's extravagant style, and by December 1897 the priest and trustees were in open conflict. Kolasinski publicly urged the congregation to repudiate the board at its next election. But on January 3, 1898, the annual parish meeting not only reelected the trustees, but stripped the priest of all authority in financial matters and regulated the amounts of the fees he was entitled to receive.⁶³

Kolasinski died only four months later, on April 11, 1898. The frenzied scenes of grief at the bier and at the funeral, which an estimated 20,000 attended, caused observers to muse on the extraordinary power this charismat-

⁶¹ *Detroit Evening News*, 5 September 1891, 1:1; 7 February 1894, 5:3; 11 February 1894, 1:8; 17 February 1894, 1:5; *Detroit Free Press*, 19 February 1894, 1:5-6, 3:4-5; *Detroit Tribune*, 19 February 1894, 1:2-3, 3:6-7.

⁶² *Detroit Evening News*, 10 August 1893, 4:5; *Detroit Sunday News-Tribune*, 18 November 1894, 8:2; 2 December 1894, 8:2; *Detroit Evening News*, 1 February 1897, 6:2; 2 February 1897, 6:2; 4 March 1897, 5:2; 5 March 1897, 5:3-5; 17 March 1897, 5:6; *Detroit Free Press*, 2 February 1897, 7:3; 3 February 1897, 5:5; 5 March 1897, 5:4; 6 March 1897, 10:2.

⁶³ *Detroit Evening News*, 20 April 1897, 1:5; 13 December 1897, 1:1; 4 January 1898, 1:5, 6:5; 5 January 1898, 6:4; 10 January 1898, 6:1; 15 January 1898, 1:6; *Detroit Free Press*, 21 April 1897, 3:5; 5 January 1898, 7:1; *Detroit Tribune*, 4 January 1898, 5:3; 5 January 1898, 8:4; 6 January 1898, 8:4; 7 January 1898, 8:3.

ic priest had exercized over his people. But the largely forgotten parish meeting in January indicates a more complex relationship. Kolasinski was passionately loved and revered by many in his congregation, and nearly all seemed willing to support him handsomely. But despite his honored and privileged status, he was not above congregational control in matters of parish administration. Authority in the Church, his parishioners' behavior said, could legitimately command deference and loyalty beyond that appropriate to secular authority. But it was not beyond a measure of popular control.[64]

* * *

The events discussed in this article were unusual, even in Polish-American parishes at the end of the nineteenth century. They were not, however, so rare that historians can afford to ignore them. They are events which broaden our understanding of the history of the Catholic Church in the United States. The view from the pew is not the view from the pulpit, which in turn differs from the view from the episcopal residence. All three perspectives are necessary for an adequate understanding of Church history. These events should also prompt us to examine the parish in times of conflict as well as times of peace. For it is in times of conflict that individuals are forced to ask themselves difficult questions about what the Church is and what authorities legitimately govern it. And in times of conflict we can see, in peoples' statements and behavior, how they choose to answer these questions.

The particular conflict discussed in these pages cannot be evidence for conclusions about the whole of the American Church in the late nineteenth century. But this single parish narrative does suggest that historians of American Catholicism should in their studies consider the following hypotheses. First, the history of Catholicism in the United States includes a good deal more lay initiative at the parish level than has generally been reported. Many immigrant parishes in particular were in their early years as substantially lay controlled as many Protestant congregations. And second, the defense of lay authority, when it was challenged, included important democratic elements. Many Catholics, it seems, even without the benefit of liberal education, could not accept without significant modification the extreme hierarchicalism of nineteenth- and early-twentieth-century Catholic teaching. Still, as we have seen, popular Catholic understanding of Church authority differed from that held by many Protestants, for most Catholics did not fundamentally challenge the legitimacy of hierarchical authority. They did not both for theological reasons and because the reality of a strong hierarchy was an effective limitation on the scope of debate within the Church.

---

[64] *Detroit Evening News*, 11 April 1898, 5:1–3; 12 April 1898, 8:1; 13 April 1898, 6:1–2; *Detroit Free Press*, 12 April 1898, 10:6; 14 April 1898, 10:2; *Detroit Tribune*, 12 April 1898, 5:2–3; 13 April 1898, 8:2; 14 April 1898, 5:5–6.

In their years of conflict with their bishops, Kolasinski's parishioners articulated a view of the Church and its authority that, ironically, anticipated several significant reforms of the Second Vatican Council. Their arguments were predicated on an understanding of the Church as the community of all the faithful. They understood their parish to have been born in the years of Kolasinski's absence, when they constituted a community of faith and worship but were without a priest. The Constitution on the Church of the Second Vatican Council affirms the understanding of Church as community, though it does not justify defiance of episcopal authority. Kolasinski's parishioners argued for a measure of congregational autonomy in order to preserve ethnic traditions within a universal Church. The Second Vatican Council encouraged the support of cultural diversity within the Roman Church, gently repudiating an older policy of absolute conformity to certain European traditions. And Kolasinski's congregation achieved he vital parish life regarded as essential to Church renewal by progressives and moderates at Vatican II. A vital parish life cannot flourish if the laity are not given broad opportunities to participate in parish government as well as congregational worship, as these same Council delegates recognized.[65]

Like the reformers of Vatican II, however, Kolasinski's parishioners articulated a view of the Church that contained important ambiguities. Both groups endorsed a greater role for the laity in Church affairs, but both invested a hierarchy of ordained priests with immense powers over the spiritual and temporal life of the Church. Clearly, there are many occasions on which lay initiative and clerical authority will conflict. For Kolasinski's parishioners, and for Kolasinski himself, a definitive declaration from Rome that they were schismatics would have created an agonizing crisis, one resolved by some American Poles by joining the Polish National Catholic Church, which guaranteed considerable autonomy to its congregations. But since trained theologians have not succeeded in articulating a consistent theory that enables the Church to be both democratic and hierarchical, we can hardly fault the Kolasinskians for their failure.

The roles which women might legitimately play in parish decision making were also defined by Kolasinski's parishioners in a manner delicately poised between democratic norms and patriarchal tradition. Women, the parishioners' behavior says, might defend basic parish rights but they were not formally to govern the parish. They could make and enforce decisions as members of demonstrations, but not as parish trustees. The former role, for all its aggressiveness, was a defensive role as well as an informal one, and in their unconventional incarnation as street combatants, women were fighting

---

[65] Austin P. Flannery, ed., *Documents of Vatican II* (Grand Rapids, Mich.: William P. Eerdmans Company, 1975), esp. "The Constitution on the Sacred Liturgy," "Decree on the Catholic Eastern Churches," "Decree on the Apostolate of Lay People," "Lumen Gentium," "Gaudium et Spes."

to maintain the community's traditions. The position of trustee, on the other hand, formally conferred power to control and even change the community; it was an assertive and not simply a reactive role, and thus appropriate only to men. And while the women of the parish were remarkably aggressive in street battles, as women were reported to be in other, similar conflicts, there is no evidence that they regarded their exclusion from parish leadership positions as wrong. Indeed, the day-to-day organizational life of the parish was largely segregated according to sex.

The women of the parish had, in fact, a considerable stake in the maintenance of traditional ways, and this helps to explain their militancy as defenders of Kolasinski's cause. Their lives were much more circumscribed than those of their husbands and sons. Wives in Detroit's Polish community rarely worked outside the home, many could speak no English, and many were illiterate or semiliterate. A high birth rate meant that their lives were centered on the family and on the oppressively crowded house. A high infant death rate infused the weariness of daily life with periodic sorrow.[66] For these women, traditional religious observances gave color and meaning to life, and it was their good fortune to inherit a rich celebratory tradition. Traditional Polish Catholicism, moreover, emphasized the importance of home and family against the attractions of the outside world, and enhanced the status of women as keepers of the home and guardians of traditional culture. When Kolasinski's female supporters took to the streets, they were defending not only a revered priest but a closed and traditional community against the interference of critical outsiders.

It is also clear that women regarded themselves as patrons of the parish, and thus entitled to a voice in its affairs. Women did not work outside the home, but their labor in the home was essential to family survival, and their gardening and fuel gathering were wealth-producing activities. Any contributions to the church were obviously the result of family labor and not simply the work of men. Thus, there was ample reason for women as well as men to say that "we built the church." But their commitment to tradition was sufficiently strong that a sense of patronage did not translate into a demand to share parish government with men.

One wonders, certainly, whether women who had literally fought for their parish were not changed by the experience, whether they did not regard authority in the parish—of male clergy and male trustees—with the critical eyes of idled veterans. And this may be true. But the typical Polish parish was so rich in sex-segregated voluntary groups—Sweetest Heart of Mary had fourteen associations and three military companies by 1898—that the energies of the most ambitious lay men and women could probably find adequate channels. These groups played important roles in the devotional life of the

[66] Zunz, "Detroit's Ethnic Neighborhoods", 54, 57, 63-64, 67-68.

parish and in its day-to-day administration; in the large parish, particularly, and in certain areas of parish life, lay associations might come to rival the authority of the clergy and the trustees. A woman who accepted her formally subordinate role in the parish could if she wished find socially legitimate ways of asserting herself, and in this sense the sexual politics of the parish mirrored the sexual politics of the family. In both institutions, patriarchal values were at once accepted and subtly undermined by very traditional women.

A discussion of nineteenth-century immigrant Catholicism that draws parallels to the Second Vatican Council can appropriately conclude with a word about the recent history of the American Church. That recent history must also be examined from the perspective of the congregation as well as the hierarchy. In some respects, this is comparatively easy to do. A well-educated laity now voice opinions in print on a wide variety of church-related issues. The contemporary clergy is unprecedentedly supportive of discussions of the nature of the Church and ecclesiastical authority.

But in one important respect the historian of the recent Church faces a more difficult task than the historian of immigrant Catholicism: the issues that are today most likely to prompt Catholics to reflection on the nature of Church authority are not the ownership of parish property or the selection of the priest, but issues of sexual morality, specifically birth control, divorce, and abortion. Issues relating to parish rights are public and generally defended collectively. Issues of sexual morality are private and resolved individually. Catholics who practice birth control do not issue public statements in their own defense. And yet, because many who call themselves Catholics do practice birth control, we must assume that their vision of the Church and its authority encompasses this apparent contradiction. I suspect that for these Catholics, as for Kolasinski's parishioners, Catholicism is most importantly both a valued cultural inheritance and a body of sacrament and liturgy that gives meaning to life. It is much less essentially a matter of strict obedience to hierarchical authority.

THE 1839 BALTIMORE NUNNERY RIOT: AN EPISODE IN JACKSONIAN NATIVISM AND SOCIAL VIOLENCE

Nativism in antebellum America offers an easy target for historical moralizing.[1] Historians have often condemned nativists as bigoted, irrational, and paranoid aberrants in American life. The psychoanalysis of Jacksonian nativists began in the early 1960s with articles by David Brion Davis. Elaborating on Davis' interpretation, Richard Hofstadter placed nativism in the "paranoid style" that he believed had developed as the dark side of the American political tradition. More recently, sociologists Seymour Lipset and Earl Raab have written about how nativists practiced the "politics of unreason".[2]

Such views contain some truth but rely more on historical imagination than historical verification. The basic weakness of these interpretations stems from their heavy reliance on the writings and speeches of nativist authors and political leaders, and the assumption that these sources accurately reflected nativist ideology as a whole. From reading Samuel F.B. Morse's *Foreign Conspiracy against the Liberties of the United States* (1835) or Reverend Edward Beecher's *Papal Conspiracy Exposed* (1855), one would have to agree that nativists feared imaginary foes. Such anti-Catholic writings, however, represented only one, and often the most extreme, aspect of nativism. Another method for determining nativist attitudes is to analyze events that might provide insight into the thinking of rank-and-file nativists. An opportunity presents itself in nativist reaction to Roman Catholic convents.

In antebellum America the convent served as a major focal point for nativist fears and hatreds. From 1830 to 1860 the country witnessed a flood of anti-convent literature, numerous attempts to investigate and legislate against nunneries, and several assaults upon these institutions.[3] The burning of the Ursuline Convent in Charlestown, Massachusetts, in August 1834, constitutes the most notorious example of this phenomenon. Historians of nativism have little noted other similar violent occurrences and have ventured even fewer opinions as to their possible significance. Convent riots, if mentioned at all, have been cited as evidence of the "irrational" basis of nativism.

This paper examines one such incident, a disturbance in Baltimore in August 1839 which lasted for three days. On first consideration, the action of a mob storming a convent of defenseless nuns appears to rank among the most cowardly and reprehensible acts in American history. According to Archbishop Samuel Eccleston of Baltimore, that such a tragedy nearly happened in the city whose "very name . . . reminds us of the Catholic founder of Maryland, one of the earliest and truest friends of civil and religious liberty," only added to the outrage.[4] Upon closer investigation, however, the Baltimore riot reveals complex motivations and behavior. The incident can be assessed not only for its implications about nativist thought and action but also for how the riot itself fits into the broader framework of Jacksonian social violence and "crowd" behavior.[5]

* * *

On Sunday morning, August 18, 1839, several Baltimore citizens witnessed the "escape" of a nun from a convent near the center of town.[6] The woman, Sister Isabella Neale, scurried from house to house in search of sanctuary. She finally succeeded in gaining asylum in the home of Mr. Wilcox, the town jailer. Sister Isabella, who later was found to be mentally unstable, explained to him that she had fled from the nearby Carmelite Convent on Aisquith Street. News of her story agitated a crowd of spectators that had begun to block the street in front of the convent. The arrival of Mayor Sheppard C. Leakin helped momentarily to reduce the excitement. He attempted to alleviate the concern for the safety of the nun by promising to protect her. At the crowd's insistence Leakin transported Sister Isabella to Washington College in Baltimore for observation by its faculty of physicians.

The escape of the nun triggered three nights of rioting in the city. The crowd's formation appears to have been spontaneous, an immediate response to an unusual and unexpected event. Some individuals in the crowd obviously reacted to the flight out of latent anti-Catholicism or nativism. At the same time, the rioters' justification for attack was one of sympathy for the presumed suffering of an unfortunate woman. Rioting out of moral concern continued later that afternoon when the crowd, by then numbering in the thousands, expressed the intention to tear down the nunnery and release the other females "imprisoned" there.[7]

In 1834, almost five years to the day earlier, a mob under similar guise had destroyed the Ursuline Convent in Charlestown, Massachusetts. Seeking to avert such a tragedy in Baltimore, the mayor immediately called out the City Guards to reinforce the local constables in protecting the Carmelite institution. The defense of the convent gained bipartisan support from town officials. Mayor Leakin, a Whig, Councilman John B. Seidenstricker, a Democrat, and Judge William G.D. Worthington individually addressed the hostile gathering in front of the convent. They stalled the mob until relief columns arrived. The City Guards, under the command of General Columbus O'Donnell, arranged themselves into a formidable defensive bulwark of approximately six hundred men.[8]

At the request of the convent supervisor, Father Gildea, a committee of Leakin, Worthington, and Henry Myers, a respected merchant, inspected the entire building. The group also questioned individual nuns regarding conditions in the nunnery. All of the Sisters affirmed that they had suffered no ill treatment and wished to remain in the institution. The committee reported its findings to the mob, but the rioters remained suspicious and unwilling to disperse. As a result, the threat of violence hung in the air until late into the night.

The following morning, Monday, August 19, the mayor issued a proclamation in an effort to thwart further disturbances.[9] It warned the townspeople to keep off the streets in the vicinity of the convent in order to prevent harm to themselves and others. Much of the populace ignored this command, for a mob collected again on Monday night. Nevertheless, Leakin wisely employed restraint in attempting to restore order.

The crowd had been influenced by rumors and an erroneous article that had appeared in Monday evening's Baltimore *Post*. The newspaper mistakenly reported that "it was the opinion of the Faculty of the Washington College that Miss Isabella Neale was sane."[10] Its moral indignation thus aroused, the mob ignored an order to disperse and began to hurl rocks at the regiment of City Guards protecting the convent. Several of the defenders sustained injuries in the barrage. One young guardman nearly lost his life when the mob caught him outside his lines. The Guards refrained from firing because of the danger to nearby residents. Instead, the regiment fixed bayonets and frightened the rioters from the street without further bloodshed.[11]

By Tuesday, August 20, the third night of rioting, the situation had lessened in seriousness. A mob formed again, and several arrests occurred, but the immediate peril to the nunnery had passed. Sensing a change in the crowd's attitude, the police released those individuals against whom no proof of overt acts of violence existed, provided the latter promised to keep the peace for six months.[12]

On Wednesday morning, August 21, the local press published separate statements by two physicians on the condition of Sister Isabella. Dr. P. Chatard, Sister Isabella's personal physician, judged the nun to be suffering from an affliction known as "monomania." Dr. J.H. Miller, president of the faculty at Washington College, agreed, declaring Sister Isabella to be a "perfect maniac."[13] This news convinced most of the townspeople of the propriety of the convent and facilitated the return of peace and order to the city. A reporter for the *National Intelligencer*, in Baltimore on special assignment, concluded that the certificates "have had a tranquilizing effect upon the public mind. . . . [M]any intelligent persons today expressed the opinion that the unhappy fugitive was certainly deranged, who but yesterday thought and spoke quite differently on the subject." No crowd gathered that evening.[14] Force had prevented serious damage on the nights of the rioting, but a sense of fair, scientific resolution of the immediate cause had quelled the riotous spirit.

The riot reflected the extent to which nativist propaganda had succeeded in creating anti-convent sentiment. The decade of the 1830s, besides marking the first convent burning, also witnessed the flowering of a new genre in popular American literature, the convent "exposé" and novel. Two books, Rebecca Reed's *Six Months in a Convent* (1835) and Maria Monk's *Awful Disclosures of the Hotel Dieu Nunnery of Montreal* (1836), emerged as prototypes of this theme. These often lurid works purported to be the true revelations of escaped nuns. Maria Monk's tale became the best selling volume of the year and eventually sold over 300,000 copies.[15] The book proved as successful in Baltimore as elsewhere. "Everybody seems to have heard or read something about it," gushed one reviewer. "Thousands upon thousands of copies of it have been published, and sold, and read."[16] As a result of contact with these works and their countless imitations, many Americans pictured the convent as a den of sex, secrecy, and sedition, a concrete symbol of the decadence of Popery.[17]

During the Jacksonian era, with its faith in equality and laissez-faire democracy, the convent appeared particularly "un-American" in its authoritarian restrictions and its alleged denial of freedom of choice for the individual. In addition, the emerging industrial society was redefining the role of woman into the domestic stereotype of the "cult of true womanhood."[18] "In the United States," observed Alexis de Tocqueville in the 1830s, "the inexorable opinion of the public carefully circumscribes woman within the narrow circle of domestic interests and duties and forbids her to step beyond it."[19] The nunnery appeared to oppose the virtues of marriage and motherhood. Furthermore, it offered a disturbingly different lifestyle that served as a role model for impressionable girls in its convent schools.[20]

Some Protestants in the Monumental City encouraged this hostile portrayal of convents. In January 1835, two Presbyterian ministers, Reverend Robert J. Breckinridge and Reverend Andrew B. Cross, published the first issue of the *Baltimore Literary and Religious Magazine*.[21] This journal printed some of the most vitriolic anti-Catholic propaganda found anywhere in the nation. The subject of nunneries held particular interest for the two editors. From the start they railed against the convent system in general and the Carmelite institution on Aisquith Street in particular.[22] In 1831, Breckinridge had toured this building upon its opening and found nothing of an incriminating nature. He, nonetheless, remained unshakeable in his belief that he had been prohibited from visiting the cellar because it contained the various torture devices of the Inquisition.[23]

A few months after the magazine's founding, it published a lead article with the provocative title "Carmelite Convent in Baltimore—An Outrage Which Was Probably Committed Therein." The story contained the sworn statement of five women and one man who were members of the Methodist Protestant Church located a few streets south of the nunnery. They testified that one evening, upon returning home from a church meeting, they had heard three cries for help coming from the fourth floor of the Carmelite Convent. Using this testimony, Breckinridge charged that within the institution Father Gildea held young women against their will and tortured those who attempted to flee. The escape of a nun, noted Breckinridge, had "led to the burning of the 'cage of unclean birds'—last summer," an ominous reference to the destruction of the Ursuline Convent in Massachusetts. "We have changed our opinion about poor Carmelites," Breckinridge continued, "in so far, that whereas we once thought they were willing victims we are now convinced, they are not." He then challenged Archbishop Samuel Eccleston to explain the screams heard emanating from the Carmelite Convent.[24] It was this idea—that the nuns were prisoners—that four years later encouraged mob response to Sister Isabella's deranged actions.

In another issue Breckinridge warned against the Trojan Horse of Catholic education. On October 1, 1832, the Academy of the Carmelite Sisters in Baltimore had opened its doors. The nuns welcomed children of all denominations, promising no interference in their pupils' religious beliefs.[25] According to Breckinridge, this pledge revealed the extent of papist treachery. "Immured within . . . [those] walls," he admonished Protestant parents, "our daughters are to learn the intolerant dogmas and practice the superstitions and idolatrous ceremonies of the Church of Rome."[26]

The editors also listed a set of demands for the reform of convents in the United States, a proposal for which Reverend Cross, in particular, launched a righteous crusade. They called on legislators to pass laws to suppress convents. Failing that, the civil authorities should investigate and regulate the institutions.

If elected officials refused to act, it remained for the concerned citizens of the community to arouse sentiment against nunneries. Still, the editors refrained from advocacy of extra-legal means. "Let no man violate any law, even bad ones," they cautioned. "Let the persons, property, and rights of all be held sacred."[27]

Their jeremiads against nunneries perhaps produced a more abrupt and riotous result than the editors had expected. During the Baltimore Bank Riot of August 1835, at least some members of the mob considered sacking the Carmelite Convent.[28] Fearing that the rioters would desecrate the remains of the deceased sisters, Father Gildea removed the bones to St. James Chapel.[29] During the Maryland General Assembly investigation of the Bank Riot, William George Read, a Catholic lawyer, gave testimony that blamed inflammatory articles in the *Baltimore Literary and Religious Magazine* for having "pointed the fury of the populace against the convent."[30] The editors denied any responsibility for either the thoughts or actions of the Bank mob. They expressed no surprise, however, that some Baltimoreans had shown animosity toward the nunnery. Breckinridge and Cross defended themselves on the ground that their readership extended, so far as they knew, only to "worthy and respectable men . . . strange persons indeed to engage in riot and plunder."[31] Strange perhaps, but the participation of "gentlemen of property and standing" in Jacksonian riots had numerous precedents in the anti-abolitionist mobs of the decade.[32]

While people of high status made up the bulk of the subscribers to the journal, the middle and lower levels of society also had the opportunity to familiarize themselves with its arguments against nunneries and other reputed abuses of the Catholic Church. Pamphlet reprints of selected articles permitted the editors to disseminate their propaganda to a far greater number of readers than through the magazine alone.[33] Besides the article directed against the Carmelite Convent, other titles included, "The Papal Controversy and Papal Influence in Baltimore" and "A Plea For the Restoration of the Scripture to the Schools."[34] No doubt many people never read anything about convents, but they may have known of these stories by hearsay. Clearly, then, the anti-Catholicism found in the *Baltimore Literary and Religious Magazine* helped to create a setting in which the escape of Sister Isabella could elicit a strong reaction from certain members of the community. Spontaneous in its immediate cause, the Nunnery Riot actually reflected a long simmering antagonism that required the catalyst of a Sister Isabella to boil over in righteous fury.

Nonetheless, the Carmelite Riot revealed more spontaneity than the earlier Ursuline Riot in that it exhibited no sign of preplanning.[35] It had no recognized leaders, at least no contemporary accounts mentioned any. One newspaper, in an allusion to Breckinridge and Cross, blamed the riot on intolerant propagandists who, having raised their audience to a feverish state, stood aloof from their followers' excesses.[36] No evidence exists, however, that either minister directly encouraged or sanctioned the mob's actions.

The most striking fact about the mob was the limited nature of its response. Selectivity and restraint remained its hallmark, though this owed something to the armed force that checked any easy destructive action. The mob focused on the Carmelite Convent and threatened neither individual Catholics nor their churches nor any other religious buildings.[37] Unlike Breckinridge and Cross, the rioters refrained from a wholesale condemnation of the Catholic Church and its convent system. Rather, they sought to correct what appeared to them to be a particularly flagrant example of convent abuse without necessarily passing judgment on any other similar institutions.[38] This remarkable illustration of emotional fervor, mixed with rational, or at least moderate, behavior typified many of the mobs of the Jacksonian period.

During each night of the riot, the police arrested approximately twenty people. If the identifiable individuals were typical, then the members of the mob belonged to the lower-middle to middle levels of society, worked at skilled or semi-skilled jobs, and owned property within the neighborhood of the convent. Except for Sunday afternoon, August 18th, the rioters gathered only in the evenings, suggesting that during the weekdays they were at their jobs. One individual, James Williamson, was an apothecary. Another, John Fishback, was employed at a lottery and exchange office. The other men labored as manufacturers and tradesmen: two bricklayers, two coachmakers, a carriage maker, a segar (cigar) manufacturer, a shoemaker, a rope maker, a comb maker, a blacksmith, a slater, a cord-wainer, and a turner.[39] This occupational breakdown was characteristic of antebellum mobs.

The age of the rioters has significance. Jacksonian rioters tended to be young, often in their late teens or twenties.[40] Editorials of the day reflected concern over the "rowdyism" of the younger generation. On the way to joining Sunday's mob, four young men, John Cramer, John Wise, Barney Toner, and Francis Steever, destroyed some steps on North Street, a half-mile due west of Aisquith.[41] Their vandalism was probably not gratuitous but an attempt to produce ammunition for storming the nunnery. Many Baltimore youths undoubtedly joined the nunnery mob in quest of excitement on a summer night. Some of the rioters whose names could not be identified by reference to the city directory may have been youths living at home.

Cramer and his friends attempted to rally the rest of the crowd with the cry: "[D]own with the nunnery and up with the railroads."[42] This slogan perhaps showed how a few members of the mob manipulated the hostility toward the nunnery to their own self-interest. The mention of railroads referred to the extension of the Baltimore and Susquehanna Line then in progress. Some of the rioters may have believed that the destruction of the nunnery would open the way for running the railroad down Aisquith Street.[43]

The contributing influence to the riot of any more general economic unrest in the period remains impossible to locate. As was normal for August, business was slack in Baltimore.[44] The city attempted to cope with the depression which had gripped the nation for two years. Overall, however, the Baltimore economy was not affected as badly as that of other parts of the country. In general, workers experienced better times in the deflationary period of the later 1830s than during the inflationary upswing of the first half of the decade. In 1839, unemployment was no worse than it had been in the pre-depression period; real wages of factory workers were, in fact, rising.[45] Nevertheless, this trend was not necessarily true for all occupations. Indeed, the success of factories might have hurt skilled craftsmen of the type arrested during the riot. Whatever economic tensions some participants may have released by rioting, however, opposition to the nunnery itself remained the mob's overriding concern and the release of the nuns its principal goal.

Although none mentioned economics, several contemporary reports cited curiosity as a major element in the formation of the crowd.[46] The curious probably composed the largest segment of those who gathered outside the walls of the nunnery. Moreover, the convent offered an especially tantalizing lure to certain people. Many Americans itched to know about the inner sanctums of the cloister. The interest derived in part from the influence of European romantic tales as well as the impact of anti-convent literature.[47] In an era of increasing Victorian prudery anti-convent writings also served as "respectable" pornography which nativists could enjoy without guilt.[48] The Catholic Church viewed the misconceptions about the mysteries of the convent as a serious problem and sought to refute them with its own publications.[49] Probably most people gave little credence to immoral tales of clandestine convent activities; nevertheless, the impulse to see for oneself must have entered many minds once the opportunity arrived.

Even more than convent stories the presence of an institution enclosed behind walls or high fences barring their entry aroused the inquisitiveness as well as the ire of many people. To some Americans the secrecy of the convent proved its intriguing, if not iniquitous, activities.[50] Frederick Marryat, a renowned foreign commentator on Jacksonian society, was told that curiosity had chiefly motivated the mob that destroyed the Ursuline Convent. Marryat doubted this explanation, but agreed that Americans, "especially the mob, cannot bear anything like a secret—that's *unconstitutional*."[51]

Whatever contemporaries believed caused the riot, they generally agreed on why it failed. The hero of the week's events, by unanimous acclamation of the press and the pulpit, was Mayor Sheppard C. Leakin. In a personal letter to Leakin, Archbishop Eccleston gratefully acknowledged that his "promptness and energy" had rescued the nunnery. Even Breckinridge grudgingly admitted that the mayor had upheld the duties of his office in preventing an attack on the convent.[52] Praise came from as far away as New York. Newspaper articles with titles like "How to Deal with Mobs" reflected a growing disenchantment with the seeming anarchy of Jacksonian society.[53]

The mayor garnered the lion's share of the credit for saving the nunnery. A veteran of the bombardment of Fort McHenry in 1814, Leakin remained cool and decisive throughout the riot. Still, his efforts needed the active and immediate support of most of the community. From the outset the secular newspapers of the city condemned the riot as an outrage upon womanhood and a frightening attack on the sanctity of private property.[54] An implicit sensitivity to Baltimore's reputation as "Mobtown" also filtered through the various editorials.[55] The press displayed a conscious determination to avoid a tragedy similar to the Charlestown Riot. On Monday, August 19th, the Baltimore *Sun* reassured its readers of the civil authorities' resolve to act swiftly "should there be any ruffians found in this community dastards enough to imitate the Boston mob and attack a household of weak females."[56]

Ironically, both the attackers and the defenders believed that they were saving the women in the convent. The mob directed its rage not at the nuns but at the priests and institution which supposedly exploited them. It saw itself as a harbinger of justice. In their endeavors the rioters had expected the support, or at least the tacit approval, of the community.[57] The crowd must have been both bewildered and dismayed when the politicians, police, and press rose in opposition to it.

Beyond the labors of the mayor and the support of the press, it required the firm stand of volunteers from the community to ensure the preservation of the Carmelite Convent. Even before the City Guards responded, several private citizens enlisted in the ranks of the defenders. The existence of two indemnity laws that had been passed by the state legislature in 1836 provided citizens with an added incentive to fulfill their civic duties.[58] The tolerance of extra-legal violence that the authorities had displayed during some stages of the Bank Riot of 1835 could not occur in 1839 when the burden of reimbursement would fall upon the city's taxpayers.

The City Guards, a voluntary body, had been organized following the Bank Riot as a deterrent to future social violence. They faithfully performed their assignment even though most of the force of six hundred men were Protestant. One member of the Guards recalled that he and another Protestant friend had instantly answered the summons to aid the nunnery. He recollected that at his side "stood good old Mr. Peter Fenley with musket in hand . . . as staunch an old Presbyterian as ever lived. The Presbyterians are always on the side of law and order."[59]

The riot also provided an ironic twist to traditional political ties. Mayor Leakin attempted to show the city's gratitude to the Guards by requesting five hundred dollars in funds from the Council for an appreciation dinner. Councilman Seidenstricker, a Democrat, voted against the proposal. The Whigs, normally the more nativistic party, tried to imply that Seidenstricker, although he had been a convent defender, had voted against the appropriation out of anti-Catholic motives.[60]

Partisan attempts at using the riot foundered because of the city's inclination to forget about the disturbance. Common to other riots of the Jacksonian era, an odd communal amnesia descended on Baltimore soon after the disturbance.[61] On Monday, August 19, at the height of the furor, a resolution calling for an investigation into the causes of the riot had come before the City Council. The resolution advocated establishment of a joint committee of the Council's two branches to conduct the proceedings. Once the excitement subsided, interest in such a committee dissolved.[62]

Newspapers reflected a similar change in attitude. The press had covered the riot closely and had commented extensively for a few days afterwards. Soon, attention returned completely to the normal political events of the time. Except for the *Niles' Register*, which circulated nationally, the local newspapers made no serious attempts to follow up any aspect of the disturbance. Among Baltimore's residents there seemed to exist a tacit agreement to refrain from dredging up something that reflected unflatteringly on the Monumental City.

The desire to forget the embarrassing incident created indifference toward the trials of the rioters. On October 16, 1839, the Baltimore City Court convicted John Cramer, Francis Steever, Barney Toner, and John Wise of "riotous conduct and tearing up steps." For this breach of social etiquette the penalties were light. Each man paid a fine of five dollars plus court costs. The court dismissed the charges of "riotous conduct" against the remaining thirteen defendants.[63] In reporting on the cases, the Baltimore *Sun* noted only that the four convicted men had paid fines "for disorderly conduct in the street on a Sunday night."[64]

Local inhabitants succeeded in turning their thoughts from the riot in spite of the continued entreaties of Breckinridge and Cross. The initial reaction of Baltimore's two most prominent nativists to the Carmelite Riot comprised a masterful exercise in ambiguity. Word of Sister Isabella's escape and its repercussions reached them just as the September issue of their journal was about to go to press. In that issue they acclaimed her flight as verification of their previous warnings about the convent. Stung by the barbs of "pestilent slanderers," Breckinridge felt obliged to explain his own part in the events. As he had done following the Bank Riot of 1835, he disassociated himself from the projected excesses of the mob to which his own writings had contributed greatly. Yet, although Breckinridge claimed to reject violence, the tone of his arguments against nunneries had a moralistic appeal to "higher law" about them which his readers might easily have interpreted as justifying extra-legal action. "If there remains no other mode of redress against intolerable evils," wrote Breckinridge about convents while the riot was in progress, "society *en masse* is divinely commissioned to rise and correct them. The right of revolution is a sacred and inalienable right."[65]

In subsequent months Breckinridge and Cross resumed the offensive in earnest. They vigorously defended the sanity of Sister Isabella by assailing the reputations of the physicians who had examined her. They hinted darkly that papists had liquidated the unfortunate nun for fear that she would write an exposé. Increasingly, political remarks began to creep into their tirades against Popery. The editors accused the mayor of angling for the Catholic vote. They also called for the establishment of a nativist daily newspaper to offset the influence of the local Catholic hierarchy on the secular press.

Some of Breckinridge's statements following the riot suggest that he began to associate his anti-Catholicism more closely with a fear of immigrants. He asserted that during the riot "an armed conspiracy had been formed in the city, composed chiefly of foreign ruffians, to defend at all hazards, these prisons for women." Two thousand immigrants, he believed, had awaited only the signal of the cathedral bell to attack American persons and property. Still, his opposition to foreigners remained directed less at the immigrants themselves than at the foreign priests who supposedly controlled them.[66]

Except for the irrepressible Breckinridge and Cross, the riot seemingly had little impact toward solidifying local nativist attitudes. On Monday, August 19, handbills had announced the prospectus of a new nativist weekly, *The Standard and Protestant Banner*, probably an effort to fuel and to exploit the riotous spirit.[67] The venture proved unsuccessful, as apparently no issue of the proposed periodical ever appeared. This failure pointed to the lack of communication and organization among nativists in Baltimore. The local problem illustrated a nation-wide weakness—the inability of all nativists to agree on a common enemy. Some xenophobes held both anti-Catholic and anti-immigrant views. Others felt threatened by immigrants but not the Catholic faith which most of the latter practiced. Still others hated Catholicism but welcomed immigrants as workers and as prospective converts to Protestantism.

The extent of the role that anti-immigrant sentiment played in precipitating and maintaining the riot remains unclear.[68] The number of Irish-sounding names among the rioters (Timothy O'Mara, James McGrath, Peter Kelly, Joseph Miskelly, Andrew McClellan, Henry Hagerty) presents an enigma.[69] If these men were Irish, why would they riot against a Catholic convent? Presumably, they must have been Orangemen, that is, Protestant Irish. Orange Irish bricklayers had figured prominently in the mob during the Charlestown Riot, and it is plausible that traditional hatred between Protestant and Catholic Irish acted as a factor in the Carmelite Riot as well.

In contrast to the Ursuline Riot, the Carmelite Riot showed little direct connection to native Americans' fear of immigrants. For example, the Washington *Native American* joined the chorus in denouncing the assault on the convent as a disgraceful illustration of "Mobocracy." The paper served as the news organ of the Native American Association, a group that had formed in 1837 to advocate its own brand of anti-foreign nativism. Surprisingly, Henry J. Brent, a Roman Catholic, figured prominently in the founding of the association. Also listed within its ranks were "the names of many highly respectable members of the Catholic Church."[70] The society particularly resented British influence in America and the influx of Irish paupers to its shores. Article Five of its constitution renounced all connections with particular religious faiths and promised to tolerate all creeds. The organization's stated interests included the establishment of a national character, the preservation of national institutions, and the repeal of naturalization laws.[71] These political goals related only indirectly to the principally theological purpose of the *Baltimore Literary and Religious Magazine*.

A closer alliance of political and religious nativism occurred in 1844 with the establishment of the American Republican Party, the first national nativist party. On November 5, 1844, the Baltimore *Clipper* signalled the strength of nativism in the city when it announced its affiliation with the new party and changed its name to the *American Republican*.[72] The true heyday of nativism in Baltimore awaited the Know-Nothing era of the 1850s. At that time the convent issue resurfaced in Maryland. During an 1856 session of the Maryland legislature, Reverend Andrew Cross presented a petition proposing an investigation of nunneries in the state. The bill foundered when the legislative committee decided that the existence of *habeas corpus* provided a sufficient guarantee of the rights of nuns not to be detained in a convent against their will.[73] Undaunted, Cross chased his chimera again in 1858. This time he camouflaged his proposal by requesting "the suppression of abuses and protection of persons confined in prisons, convents and madhouses."[74] The failure of this watered-down version effectively marked the end of two decades of anti-convent agitation in Maryland.

In the 1850s, the convent issue also reappeared in other states. Nativist legislators introduced bills to investigate convents in Massachusetts, Michigan, and Pennsylvania. Nativist mobs attacked nunneries in the cities of New Orleans, Galveston, Charleston, and Providence.[75] Investigation of these incidents would provide further understanding of nativist thought and behavior. A comparative study of the Carmelite Riot to its sister disturbances might uncover a pattern of basic attitudes, goals, or grievances that would offer much more definitive results than this single study.

Analysis of the Carmelite Riot tends to reinforce previous findings on antebellum collective violence. The selectivity and restraint of the mob made the riot characteristic of most other social disturbances of Jacksonian America. The social and economic status and age of the rioters were also typical. The prompt reaction of city officials and townspeople in defense of the nunnery, however, marked a distinct departure from the frequent toleration of extra-legal violence earlier in the decade. Civic concerns over restitution costs and genuine fears for the safety of defenseless nuns combined to secure the preservation of the convent. Exhibiting a better understanding of crowd control, the authorities averted a tragedy and showed that Baltimore, at least on this occasion, was better named the Monumental City than "Mobtown."

In a larger sense, the Carmelite Riot underscores the difficulties involved in generalizing about nativism, particularly regarding the linkage between nativist thought and action. Although the incident had its origins in anti-Catholic propaganda, it also reflected broader societal notions concerning the right to individual freedom, dislike of authoritarianism, suspicion of secrecy, the obligation to protect women, and the importance of restricting them to their proper sphere. More importantly, the irrational content of anti-Catholic polemics found only limited expression in the basically moderate behavior of the mob. The events of the Carmelite Riot indicate that the degree of popular response to xenophobic rhetoric depended upon particular social conditions present at a given time and setting.

Joseph G. Mannard
University of Maryland, College Park

NOTES

The author wishes to acknowledge the patient guidance of Professor David A. Grimsted in the preparation of this paper.

[1] The best definition of nativism is offered by John Higham—"intense opposition to an internal minority on the ground of its foreign (i.e., ûn-American') connection." He cites three types of nativism: 1) anti-Catholicism, 2) anti-foreign radicalism, 3) Anglo-Saxon racism. Prior to the Civil War anti-Catholicism was the principal form of nativism. See his *Strangers in the Land: Patterns of American Nativism, 1860-1925* (New Brunswick,N.J.: Rutgers University Press, 1955), pp. 4-10.

[2] David Brion Davis, "Some Themes of Counter-Subversion: An Analysis of Anti-Masonic, Anti-Catholic, and Anti-Mormon Literature," *Mississippi Valley Historical Review* 47 (September 1960): 205-224; Richard Hofstadter, *The Paranoid Style in American Politics and Other Essays* (New York: Alfred A. Knopf, 1965); Seymour Lipset and Earl Raab, *The Politics of Unreason: Right Wing Extremism in America, 1790-1970* (New York: Harper and Row, 1970).

[3] Ray A. Billington, *The Protestant Crusade, 1800-1860: A Study of the Origins of Nativism* (New York: The Macmillan Company, 1938; reprint edition, Gloucester, Mass.: Peter Smith, 1963), pp. 53-84, 345-379, 407-436.

[4] Samuel Eccleston to Sheppard C. Leakin, August 31, 1839, printed in *Niles' National Register* 56 (September 21, 1839): 56.

[5] David Grimsted defines riot as "those incidents where a number of people group together to enforce their will immediately, by threatening or perpetrating injury to people or property outside of legal procedures but without intending to challenge the general structure of society." David Grimsted, "Rioting in its Jacksonian Setting," *American Historical Review* 77 (April 1972): 365. In keeping with this definition, I would define mob as a riotous crowd. The terms "mob" and "crowd" are used interchangeably in this paper.

[6] This account of the riot is derived from J. Thomas Scharf, *History of Baltimore City and County* (Baltimore: Regional Publishing Company, 1971), originally published 1881, p. 786; the following newspapers for the period August 19 through August 24, 1839: Baltimore *Sun*, Baltimore *American and Commercial Daily Advertiser*, *National Intelligencer*, *Niles' Register*; and articles in these papers reprinted from the Baltimore *Post*, Baltimore *Patriot*, and the Baltimore *Chronicle*.

[7] Crowd estimate is taken from the *Baltimore Literary and Religious Magazine* 5 (September 1839): 429. Hereafter cited as *BLRM*.

[8] The estimates of the number of defenders are found in the Baltimore *Sun*, August 20, 1839, and the *National Intelligencer*, August 21, 1839.

[9] The proclamation was posted throughout the city and was printed in the Baltimore *Patriot*, August 19, 1839; the Baltimore *Sun*, August 20, 1839; the Baltimore *American*, August 20, 1839; and reprinted in the *National Intelligencer*, August 21, 1839.

[10] A letter of denial by Dr. J. H. Miller, president of the faculty of Washington College, was not published until Wednesday. Baltimore *American*, August 21, 1839.

[11] This account of Monday's rioting comes from the reminiscences of an anonymous former member of the City Guards. It was printed in the Baltimore *American*, October 17, 1882.

[12] Baltimore *Sun*, August 24, 1839.

[13] Baltimore *American*, August 21, 1839; Baltimore *Chronicle*, August 21, 1839. On August 21, the official faculty report on the condition of Sister Isabella also appeared. It stated, "...[W]e are unanimous in the belief that she is a monomaniac. We also feel it an act of justice to state that she made no complaint of her treatment while in the convent, other than having been compelled to take food and medicine." The certificate was reprinted in the Baltimore *Sun*, August 23, 1839; and the Baltimore *American*, August 23, 1839. Sister Isabella lived under the care of the Sisters of Charity at Mount Hope until her death in 1867. Baltimore *American*, October 14, 1882.

[14] *National Intelligencer*, August 22, 1839.

[15] Billington, *The Protestant Crusade*, p. 108.

[16] *BLRM* 2 (September 1836): 355.

[17] For a more thorough discussion of anti-convent literature, see Joseph G. Mannard, "Veiled Threats to American Institutions: The Image of the Convent in Anti-Catholic Literature" (M.A. Thesis, University of South Florida, 1979), pp. 31-91 *passim*.

[18] Barbara Welter, "The Cult of True Womanhood: 1820-1860," *American Quarterly* 18 (Summer 1966): 151-174.

[19] Alexis de Tocqueville, *Democracy in America*, 2 vols, vol. 2, ed. Phillips Bradley, trans. Henry Reeve (reprint edition, New York: Vintage Books, 1945), p. 212.

[20] Both Protestant and Catholic girls were enrolled in convent academies which served as finishing schools. Mannard, "Veiled Threats to American Institutions," pp. 45-47.

[21] Since Breckinridge was the senior editor and personally wrote more than half of the material found in the journal, I will normally refer only to him as its editor. See *Spirit of the XIXth Century* 2 (December 1843): 662.

[22] *BLRM* 1 (May 1835): 129-132; (August 1835): 242-246; (September 1835): 280-283; (November 1835): 341-342, 348-351; (December 1835): 377-380; 2 (March 1836): 120; (July 1836): 277-279; (September 1836): 355-360.

[23] In 1840, Breckinridge recalled this event of nine years earlier. *BLRM* 6 (January 1840): 1.

[24] Ibid. 1 (May 1835): 130.

[25] Charles Warren Currier, *Carmel in America: A Centennial History of the Discalced Carmelites in the United States* (Baltimore: John Murphy and Co., 1890), pp. 196-197.

[26] *BLRM* 1 (December 1835): 377-379.

[27] Ibid. 1 (May 1835): 133; see also 3 (March 1837): 102.

[28] The Bank Riot was a popular protest resulting from the continued failure of the trustees of the defunct Bank of Maryland to settle accounts almost a year and a half after its closing. Grimsted, "Rioting in its Jacksonian Setting," p. 376.

[29] Currier, *Carmel in America*, p. 202.

[30] Testimony of William George Read before the Committee of the Legislature in Annapolis (August 1836); quoted in *BLRM* 3 (March 1837): 97-98.

[31] *BLRM* 3 (March 1837): 101.

[32] Leonard L. Richards, *"Gentlemen of Property and Standing": Anti-Abolition Mobs in Jacksonian America* (New York: Oxford University Press, 1970), p. 5.

[33] According to the editors, one quarter of their subscribers were ministers, "while by far the larger part of the rest occupy such positions in society that there is scarcely one who might not aid us materially with very little inconvenience to themselves." Approximately 150 subscribers lived in Maryland at the time of the riot. *BLRM* 5 (September 1839): 432. At the end of 1843, the *Spirit of the XIXth Century* (the *BLRM* had adopted this new name in January 1842) closed its presses and announced figures on its nine year existence. The average number of subscriptions had been 800 per year, reaching one thousand at its peak. However, over 100,000 pamphlets, some 4-5 million pages, had also been distributed. There seems little reason to doubt these estimates, as they simply reflected business matters. *Spirit of the XIXth Century* 2 (December 1843): 663.

[34] Robert J. Breckinridge, *The Papal Controversy and Papal Influence* (Baltimore: n. p., 1835), and *A Plea for the Restoration of the Scriptures to the Schools* (Baltimore: Matchett and Neilson, 1839).

[35] On the Charlestown Riot see Billington, *The Protestant Crusade*, pp. 53-84.

[36] Baltimore *Sun*, August 21, 1839.

[37] Currier, a Catholic priest, avers that the cathedral was also endangered. No contemporary reports corroborate his assertion, however. Currier's book, though a very helpful chronicle, is highly biased and contains some factual inaccuracies. For example, he mistakenly dates the testimony of William George Read as following the 1839 Nunnery Riot rather than the 1835 Bank Riot. Currier, *Carmel in America*, pp. 215, 224.

[38] At the time of the 1839 riot, Baltimore had at least three other communities of nuns: the Convent of the Visitation, the (Negro) Oblate Sisters of Providence, and the Sisters of Charity. Scharf, *History of Baltimore City and County*, p. 598.

[39] Job identifications were made by reference to *Matchett's City Director* for the years 1837-38, 1840-41, and 1842. In the case of duplicate names, place of residence seems to be a good indicator of who was in the mob. The convent was in the third ward. Most of the rioters came from the third and adjacent fourth wards. On the ward pattern in Baltimore in 1839 see William Lefurgy, "Baltimore's Wards, 1797-1979: A Guide," *Maryland Historical Magazine* 75 (June 1980): 145-153. The obvious question is whether those arrested were necessarily the most active rioters, the "heart of the mob." No definitive answer can be given. Yet, any conclusions about the nature of the mob and the attitudes of its members must rely principally on these findings. This methodology was pioneered by George Rudé in the 1950s and has proven its value time after time in subsequent studies. See for example his *The Crowd in History: A Study of Popular Disturbances in France and England, 1730-1848* (New York: Wiley, 1964).

[40] On emotional, occupational, and age characteristics see Grimsted, "Rioting in its Jacksonian Setting," pp. 378-386. See also Richards, "*Gentlemen of Property and Standing*," pp. 82-130, and Michael Feldberg, *The Philadelphia Riots of 1844: A Study of Ethnic Conflict* (Westport, Conn.: Greenwood Press, 1975), pp. 58, 105, 107, 113, and Michael Feldberg, "The Crowd in Philadelphia History: A Comparative Perspective," *Labor History* 15 (Summer 1974): 323-336.

[41] Baltimore *Sun*, August 24, 1839.

[42] Baltimore *Clipper*, October 17, 1839.

[43] In 1838 a petition was sent to Mayor Samuel Smith requesting that the proposed railroad extension be changed from the narrow and curving route down North and High Streets to a wider, less hazardous path down Monument and Canal Streets. This became the actual route. John Steever, father of Francis and himself in the 1839 mob, had signed the document. The petition can be found in the Baltimore City Archives, Mayor's Records, R.G. 9, Series 2, Box 19, 1838, No. 1213.

[44] *National Intelligencer*, August 23, 1839.

[45] Gary Lawson Browne, "Baltimore in the Nation, 1789-1861: A Social Economy in Industrial Revolution" (Unpublished Ph.D. dissertation, Wayne State University, 1973), pp. 276-279. Browne's emphasis is on business rather than on labor. His evidence for workers is therefore sketchy and highly impressionistic. A thorough study of the Baltimore working class in the antebellum period is still needed.

[46] Baltimore *Sun*, August 19 and 20, 1839; Baltimore *American*, August 20 and 22, 1839; Baltimore *Patriot*, August 20, 1839, reprinted in *National Intelligencer*, August 22, 1839.

[47]*National Intelligencer*, August 26, 1839; September 3, 1839. See also Mannard, "Veiled Threats to American Institutions," pp. 53-57.

[48]Davis, "Some Themes of Counter Subversion," pp. 217-223.

[49]Billington, *The Protestant Crusade*, p. 102.

[50]Mannard, "Veiled Threats to American Institutions," p. 56. Secrecy among the Masons had led to the formation of the Anti-Masonic Party. In 1831, the party held its convention in Baltimore and nominated William Wirt of Baltimore for President. Scharf, *History of Baltimore City and County*, pp. 120, 644.

[51]Frederick Marryat, *A Diary in America: With Remarks on its Institutions*, ed. by Sidney Jackson (New York: Alfred A. Knopf, 1962), pp. 50-51.

[52]Eccleston to Leakin, August 31, 1839, printed in *Niles' Register* 56 (September 21, 1839): 56; *BLRM* 5 (November 1839): 485; Baltimore *Sun*, August 21, 1839; Baltimore *American*, August 22, 1839; *National Intelligencer*, August 26, 1839; Baltimore *Patriot*, August 19, 1839 and Baltimore *Chronicle*, August 20, 1839, both reprinted in *National Intelligencer*, August 21, 1839.

[53]New York *Post*, reprinted in the *National Intelligencer*, August 30, 1839.

[54]Baltimore *Sun*, August 19, 20, 21, 1839; Baltimore *American*, August 22, 1839; *Niles' Register*, 56 (August 24, 1839); *National Intelligencer*, August 20, 1839; both the Baltimore *Patriot*, August 19, 1839, and Baltimore *Chronicle*, August 20, 1839, reprinted in the *National Intelligencer*, August 21, 1839.

[55]Baltimore received the name "Mobtown" after the 1812 riot in the city. Scharf, *History of Baltimore City and County*, p. 784. The "Mobtown" idea finds expression in Francis F. Beirne, *The Amiable Baltimoreans* (New York: E.P. Dutton, 1951). Belying his title, Beirne refers to the Nunnery Riot as "a striking example of Baltimore's virtually psychopathic urge to mob violence...."

[56]Baltimore *Sun*, August 19, 1839.

[57]On communal tolerance and support see Grimsted, "Rioting in its Jacksonian Setting," p. 389.

[58]One law required local communities to pay their own bills resulting from rioting; the other demanded restitution be made to victims. Grimsted, "Rioting in its Jacksonian Setting," p. 389.

[59]Baltimore *American*, October 17, 1882. On the bireligious nature of the defenders see Eccleston to Leakin, August 31, 1839, published in *Niles' Register* 56 (September 21, 1839): 56; *BLRM* 5 (October 1839): 441.

[60]Baltimore *Republican*, August 27, 1839.

[61]On communal amnesia see Grimsted, "Rioting in its Jacksonian Setting," p. 364.

[62]The resolution can be found in Baltimore City Archives, City Council Records, R.G. 16, Series 1, 1839, No. 1217.

[63]Baltimore City Court (Docket and Minutes) 1839, October term, Nos. 75-86.

[64]Baltimore *Sun*, October 17, 1839.

[65]*BLRM* 5 (September 1839): 429-431.

[66]Ibid. 5 (October 1839): 441, 443, 445; (November 1839): 485, 496; 6 (January 1840): 3; (August 1840): 364.

[67]*National Intelligencer*, August 24, 1839; and Baltimore *Sun*, August 22, 1839.

[68]W. Darrell Overdyke, *The Know-Nothing Party in the South* (New York: Peter Smith, 1950), pp. 2, 13. Overdyke contends that the Baltimore *Native American* was an anti-foreign nativist weekly paper which published from 1837 to 1840. My research has convinced me that no Baltimore *Native American* has ever existed, but that Overdyke confused it with the Washington *Native American*. To compare the stories and quotes which he attributes to the Baltimore paper with those appearing on the same dates in the Washington paper see Overdyke, pp. 4-7 and the Washington *Native American*, December 9, 1837; December 16, 1837; September 5, 1840; November 7, 1840.

[69]Baltimore City Jail (Criminal Dockets) 1839, Nos. 605, 614, 617. Baltimore City Court (Docket and Minutes) 1839 June term, Nos. 1067, 1068, 1080.

[70]Quoted in George W. Potter, *To the Golden Door: The Story of the Irish in Ireland and America* (Boston: Little, Brown, and Co., 1960), p. 266.

[71] Washington *Native American*, March 17, 1838; August 24, 1839.

[72] Benjamin Tuska, "Know-Nothingism in Baltimore, 1854-1860," *Catholic Historical Review* 12 (July 1925): 218; Scharf, *History of Baltimore City and County*, p. 624.

[73] Sister Mary McConville, *Political Nativism in the State of Maryland, 1830-1860* (Washington, D.C.: Catholic University Press, 1928), pp. 108-111. Jean H. Baker, *Ambivalent Americans: The Know-Nothing Party in Maryland* (Baltimore: Johns Hopkins University Press, 1977), pp. 88-99.

[74] *Journal of the Proceedings of the House of Delegates of the State of Maryland* (Annapolis: Requa and Wilson, 1858), p. 281, quoted in Baker, *Ambivalent Americans*, p. 100.

[75] Billington, *The Protestant Crusade*, pp. 311, 413-416.

BISHOP HUGHES VERSUS THE PUBLIC SCHOOL SOCIETY OF NEW YORK

By

Joseph J. McCadden*

The Archdiocese of New York recently marked the centenary of the death (January 3, 1864) of its first archbishop, the Most Reverend John Joseph Hughes. Paradoxically, this notable prelate's vigorous but unsuccessful activities toward state aid for parochial schools triggered the establishment, along secular lines, of New York City's present-day public school system.

When Hughes came to New York as coadjutor bishop in 1838, the diocese, covering all of New York State and eastern New Jersey, was a sprawling mission dependent on Europe for money and personnel. It suffered from a shortage of churches, priests, and qualified teachers; from hostility of the Protestant majority; and from dissension within its own ranks. A problem existed in that the state law—in the spirit of the young republic, but in violation of traditional Catholic discipline —favored control of parish policies by elected trustees.

There were also problems in regard to education. In New York City, eight makeshift parochial schools, meeting in church basements or rented halls, had on register about 5,000 Catholic children. An additional 7,000 either lacked accommodation or made no effort to go to school. Public aid to church-related schools, granted regularly during the first quarter of the century, had been suspended since 1825. Catholics in the metropolis, most of them refugees from European persecution and poverty, could not finance the education of their own numerous offspring.

There were no city-operated schools in New York at this time. The privately incorporated Public School Society of the City of New York, which ran the so-called 'public' schools, was a Quaker-oriented philanthropy designed originally "for the establishment of a free school for the education of poor children who do not belong to, or are not provided for by, any religious society."[1] Financed by state aid and

---

* Dr. McCadden has recently retired after long service with the Department of Education at Hunter College of the City University of New York.

[1] William Oland Bourne, *History of the Public School Society of the City of New York* (New York, 1873), pp. 4-5. The Society was originally incor-

city taxation, this Society had gradually expanded its operations to offer instruction, in a network of schools, for children of all faiths and economic conditions. Professedly non-denominational, the Public School Society and its institutions leaned heavily toward evangelistic Protestantism.

After cutting other religious institutions off from the common school fund, which it virtually monopolized, the Public School Society had absorbed the schools of several Protestant congregations. But Catholics, who could least afford to operate without government help, had continued their over-crowded parish schools, declaring that they would rather let their children run illiterate than enroll them in the Protestant 'public' schools. The School Society trustees, proponents of the white-Protestant-Anglo-Saxon concept of Americanism, tried several methods of inveigling youngsters into their sphere of influence. Committees of benevolent ladies, and later a paid agent, Samuel Waddington Seton—half-brother to the husband of Elizabeth Bayley Seton—canvassed the poorer neighborhoods and ferreted out uninstructed lads. When gentler pressures failed, the School Society pushed through the common council a resolution denying relief to welfare clients who failed to send their children to school. The organization further proposed a law "making it an offence in a minor to be found idle and uninstructed, and subject to commitment [in a manual labor farm school] if reformation did not take place."[2] But these threats, instead of bringing Catholic children into the schools, only made parents more suspicious of the Society and its works.

Bishop John Dubois, Hughes' scholarly predecessor, shared futilely the concern of the Public School Society over the untutored thousands of school-age youngsters. His priests, garnered from many foreign parts, were restive. His immigrant congregation walked out on his French-accented sermons.[3] The lay trustees of St. Patrick's Cathedral blocked his efforts to establish an academy with teaching brothers

---

porated as the New York Free School Society, by an act of the legislature passed on April 9, 1805. Over seventy of its record books and reports, including the manuscript minutes, are in the New York Historical Society, bequeathed by the School Society at its dissolution in 1853.

[2] Bourne, p. 175.

[3] John Power, Vicar-General, to Henry Conwell, Bishop of Philadelphia [then in Rome], New York, January 30, 1829; photostat in the collection of the Reverend Henry J. Browne, Archives of the Archdiocese of New York, St. Joseph's Seminary, Yonkers, New York (hereafter cited as AANY).

imported from Ireland; they even appointed Father Thomas Levins—whom he had suspended—to superintend the cathedral school. In 1834 fire destroyed the School of the Sisters of Charity on Mulberry Street; and Bishop Dubois, rather than turn to his own people for help, sounded out the Public School Society for possible collaboration. The Society's Public School Number 5, just across from the cathedral, was half-empty. Dubois, in return for certain supervisory privileges over teachers and textbooks, offered to help the public schools gain "the confidence of Catholic parents, and remove the false excuses of those who cover their neglect under the false pretext of religion which they do not practise."

In reply, the Public School Society informed Dubois that "religious and moral instruction is given in the schools entirely free from sectarianism," and that to accede to the bishop's proposals would be "unconstitutional." It did, however, invite Catholic laymen to join its board, which contained a preponderance of Quakers and several Presbyterian and Baptist ministers. In further conciliation, the group proposed: "If there be in the system of the schools, or in the books used in them, any matter which can reasonably be objected to by any denomination, they would gladly remove the same."[4] Bedeviled by diocesan unrest, the aged prelate let slip this opportunity to modify the climate of the Society's schools;[5] and so he bequeathed the problem to his successor.

Unlike the harried Dubois, Bishop Hughes, who became administrator of the See in 1839, was young, energetic, penetrating, and masterful—an Irish-born prelate whose background made him seem a highly suitable leader for the new Americans from Erin. He was already a seasoned campaigner against insubordinate laymen within the Church and against Protestant challengers in the community at large. As a parish priest in Philadelphia, he had bested the Hogan rebels of strife-torn St. Mary's Cathedral and built a new, trusteeless church whose deed was in the pastor's own name. He had likewise founded the Catholic Tract Society, engaged eminent ministers

[4] For the letter of Dubois and the resolutions and reply of the Public School Society cf. Bourne, pp. 160-163.

[5] Bishop Dubois' troubles with the trustees and his hampered efforts to further diocesan education are related in "The Rt. Rev. John Dubois, D.D., Third Bishop of New York," by Charles G. Herbermann, *Historical Records and Studies*, I (1899-1900), 278-385.

in rough-and-tumble public controversy, and played a humiliating hoax on the militant editors of *The Protestant*.[6]

Removed now to New York, Hughes in a single well-planned and forceful maneuver in February, 1839, destroyed the power of the troublesome lay board of St. Patrick's Cathedral, an action which helped to establish for the Catholic Church in the United States the principle that—civil statutes notwithstanding—the clergy who minister to the people must have control of ecclesiastical activities and of the parish purse. Then he sailed for Europe on a fund-raising tour. He entrusted matters in his absence to two vicars-general: Father Félix Varela, philosopher and political refugee from Spanish Cuba, and the Very Reverend John Power, pastor of St. Peter's in Barclay Street who had been the people's choice for the office of bishop when Dubois and Hughes were selected.

The question of public aid to religious education was quiescent when Hughes left New York; but it did not long remain so. In his annual address to the legislature, in January, 1840, the Protestant, Whig governor, William Henry Seward, sparked an explosion on the subject. Seward, chronic battler for the underdog, espoused the cause of the immigrants whom 'native' Americans despised, exploited, and feared. He had learned that thousands of children (his advisers said 25,000) were receiving no education whatever, and that in New York City those most in need of instruction would not, for conscience sake, avail themselves of the services of the Public School Society. The governor consulted with two eminent divines—the venerable Eliphalet Nott, long-time Presbyterian president of Union College and counsellor to statesmen, and the Methodist preacher, teacher, and editor, Dr. Samuel Luckey; and they advised that education, essential to American citizenship, be made so inviting as to become universal. If necessary, said Seward in his address, children of foreigners might receive instruction from teachers professing the faith of their fathers and speaking their native language.

There would be no inequality in such a measure, since it happens from the force of circumstances, if not from choice, that the responsibilities of education are in most instances confided by us to native citizens,

---

[6] Hughes' activities in Philadelphia are detailed in John R. G. Hassard, *Life of the Most Reverend John Hughes, D.D., First Archbishop of New York. With extracts from his private correspondence* (New York, 1865), pp. 49-183.

and occasions seldom offer for a trial of our magnanimity by committing that trust to persons differing from ourselves in language or religion. Since we have opened our country and all its fullness to the oppressed of every nation, we should evince wisdom equal to such generosity by qualifying their children for the high responsibilities of citizenship.[7]

Nativist Whigs who had put Seward in office were incensed at his proposals, and they hinted that he had sold his birthright for a mess of immigrant votes. Democrats accused him of trying to undercut them as poll-patrons of the Irish. Advocates of speedy reshaping of newcomers to the nativist pattern scoffed particularly at the separate schools idea. Said the Albany *Argus:*

> For ourselves, we had supposed that it was desirable that the children of all foreigners who take up their abode among us, should be taught at the same schools with the children of native citizens, and that all distinctions between them should be done away with, by instruction at the same school and by the friendly assistance of childhood. In this way only can the rising generation be made 'one people.'[8]

Among Catholics, reaction to the governor's speech was mixed. Some jumped to the hope that with proper pressures state aid to church-affiliated schools, suspended since 1825, might now be resumed although Seward had omitted direct mention of such schools.[9] Others, like George Pardow—Jacksonian Democrat, trustee of the Public School Society, and co-editor of the diocesan organ, the *Truth-Teller* —ridiculed Seward's recommendations and argued that children could get all the religion they needed after regular sessions at the Society's schools.[10]

John Power, noted for accomplishment during his successive terms as vicar-general, saw the time ripe for action. He summoned the trustees of the metropolitan parishes to a secret meeting at St. Peter's, which directed a petition to the common council for funds, and they

[7] George E. Baker (Ed.), *Life of William Henry Seward, with Selections from His Works* (New York, 1855), p. 212.

[8] Albany *Argus Extra*, January, 1840, "Seward's Message. Its Misrepresentations and Perversions Exposed," which was a twenty-page attack; pp. 1-3.

[9] This hope was fostered by the Reverend Joseph A. Schneller, pastor of St. Mary's Church, Albany, in a letter to Vicar-General John Power. Cf. *The Life of Archbishop Hughes, with a full account of his funeral . . .* (New York, 1864), p. 41.

[10] *Truth-Teller*, February 15, 1840.

voted Power $100 to go lobbying in Albany. The Catholics argued that they paid taxes like other citizens and, therefore, they should have an equal share of benefits. *The Truth-Teller,* although it denounced the governor's proposals, endorsed the petition.

In a remonstrance, the trustees of the Public School Society, overlooking the religious character of their own state-financed schools, protested that aid to Catholic institutions would violate the basic law of the land. They claimed, moreover, that one publicly subsidized school system (their own) would be more economical than multiple systems. The trustees disclaimed a lack of sympathy with distressed refugees in these words:

> On the contrary, they act under a firm conviction that the sooner such persons abandon any unfavorable prejudices with which they may arrive among us, and become familiar with our language and reconciled to our institutions and habits, the better it will be for them, and for the country of their adoption.[11]

While the appeal for Catholic school aid was pending before the council, Father Power's colleague, Father Félix Varela, tackled the problem from a different angle. He obtained a set of textbooks from the Society with a view to determining whether they contained objectionable passages. He found the trustees eager to conciliate. "Any suggestion or remarks which the Rev. Mr. Varela may deem it right to make, on his own behalf and that of his associates, after said books have been examined, shall receive the most serious and respectful consideration of this board."[12] Varela, an earnest and intellectual priest, read the texts and noted several slighting references to Catholicism in them. The Public School Society, for its part, appointed a committee to examine all its books, including those in the circulating libraries, and to expurgate sections which might give offense to any religious group.

Father Varela constituted at this time a link between the absent Bishop Hughes and the laymen acting under Vicar-General Power. His *Catholic Register,* initiated in September, 1839, kept the bishop in touch with developments, and Hughes, by return letter, sanctioned the proceedings in the school matter. In his weekly Varela laid down the line which Hughes later found advisable to follow: that the tax-

[11] For the text of the Society's remonstrances against the Catholic petition, cf. Bourne, pp. 180-186.
[12] *Ibid.,* p. 325.

supported schools of the Public School Society were really Protestant schools, and that Catholics could not get back their share of the tax money by patronizing the Society's schools, since their children's faith would thereby be endangered.[13]

The Catholic petition for school aid was foredoomed to failure, for there was an interlocking directorate among the commissioners of the school fund, the common council, and the board of the Public School Society. The city fathers made the rejection official on April 27, 1840, on the pretext of constitutionality.[14] After this victory, the Society's trustees renewed their efforts to gain the confidence of the vanquished. They called on Power, gave him a set of their books, and solicited his aid in making their schools acceptable to all. Then they waited two months for word from him.

John Power's superior, Bishop Hughes, was meanwhile en route to New York aboard the *British Queen*. Hughes did not fancy priests who truckled with the opposition; "Protestant priests," he called them. On July 4, 1840, Power set up a new weekly, the *Freeman's Journal*, with lawyer James W. White as editor, to supplant as diocesan organ the unco-operative *Truth-Teller*. The stated purpose of the *Journal* was to gain participation in the public school fund for Catholic children.[15] In the new weekly's second number Power published his reply to the Public School Society in the form of an open letter to the editor. It constituted a declaration of war on the Society. "I am decidedly opposed," wrote the vicar-general, "to the education which is now given in our 'public schools.' It is not based, as in a Christian community it ought to be, on the Christian religion. Its tendency is to make deists." Having accused the Society's schools of being unreligious, Power went on to bestow an opposite label.

> My second exception is founded on the *sectarian* character of the public schools. The Holy Scriptures are read every day, with the restriction that no specific tenets are to be inculcated. Here, sir, we find the great demarcating principle between the Catholic Church and the

---

[13] Varela's varied activities are discussed in the present writer's article, "The New York-to-Cuba Axis of Father Varela," *The Americas*, XX (April, 1964), 376-392.

[14] New York *Observer*, May 2, 1840; cf. Ray Allen Billington, *The Protestant Crusade, 1800-1860* (New York, 1938), p. 160. The *Observer* was a vigorous Protestant organ of the day.

[15] *New York Freeman's Journal*, July 4, 1840.

sectaries introduced *silently*. The Catholic Church tells her children that they must be taught their religion by AUTHORITY. The sects say, Read the Bible; the children are allowed to judge for themselves. The Protestant principle is therefore acted upon, silently inculcated, and the schools are sectarian.[16]

Bishop Hughes later adopted both Power's belligerency and his contradictory accusations in his orations against the Public School Society.

The bishop returned to New York on July 18, 1840, six months after Seward's provocative address. He found his people arrayed against the common council, the Native Americans, and the Public School Society in a demand for aid to Catholic schools. Heading the movement were his vicars-general, the lay Catholic Association, and the *Freeman's Journal*. Here was a situation which the bishop must control, or face disaster: the laymen, so recently subdued, must not get out of hand again. Two days later, Hughes took the chair at a meeting of the Catholic Association in St. Patrick's School. He promised that he would carry on the fight, in such a manner as to rally all Catholics, regardless of politics. Father Power left the city for his health shortly after this meeting, and Father Varela's *Catholic Register* was within a few months absorbed by the *Freeman's Journal*.[17]

From the beginning Hughes had not been unduly optimistic about his chances of cutting into the common school fund. He shrewdly anticipated that the effort could be used to unite his flock while publicizing the need for Catholic education. In late August, he wrote to a fellow bishop of:

> . . . an effort which I find it my duty to make to detach the children of our Holy Faith from the dangerous connexion and influence of the Public Schools. . . Whether we shall succeed or not in getting our proportion of the public money or not, at all events the effort will cause an entire separation of our children from those schools—and excite greater zeal on the part of our people for Catholic education.[18]

---

[16] *Ibid.*, July 11, 1840. The letter was dated July 9 and signed by John Power as vicar-general of the Diocese of New York.

[17] For the text of a letter by Hughes commending this union, cf. the *New York Freeman's Journal and Catholic Register*, January 9, 1841, p. 220.

[18] Hughes to unnamed bishop, New York, August 27, 1840; photostat in the Browne collection, AANY.

His lay trustees, he added, were causing him no further trouble.

The conflict to which Hughes committed himself was from the first an unequal one. In the United States there were at that time thirteen non-Catholics to one Catholic, forty-two ministers to one priest, fifty Protestant congregations to one Roman Catholic.[19] Moreover, even in proportion to their numbers the Catholics, being poor and torn by racial and political animosities, carried little weight in the community. This was particularly true in the immigrant port of New York, from which emanated much of the organized hatred of Catholicism then spreading throughout the country.

Hughes' opponents in the Public School Society were formidable, although the description he applied to them—"that wicked monopoly which claimed to take charge of the minds and hearts of Catholic children"—was hardly accurate.[20] The trustees were solid citizens, conservative, successful, and generally esteemed, giving of their time and substance to the benevolent cause of public enlightenment. President of the Society was Robert C. Cornell, who had retired from business in early manhood to devote himself to good works. Anthony P. Halsey, cashier for the Bank of New York in Wall Street, was secretary, and Lindley Murray, druggist—of the same Quaker family as the famous grammarian—was vice-president, while the treasurer from 1830 to 1843 was Samuel F. Mott, president of two Wall Street insurance companies; the name of Mott was also prominent in Quaker annals.

These men were less outspokenly bigoted than many of their contemporaries and they did not subscribe exclusively to any one creed; but they certainly did not exclude religion from education. Scripture lessons and a non-sectarian catechism had an accepted place in their curriculum. The Society had lately appointed a committee to report, it was said:

> upon the expediency of introducing into all the schools suitable books setting forth in concise terms the fundamental truths of the Christian religion free from sectarian bias; also special articles on the moral

---

[19] *Catholic Expositor*, III, 245; quoted in Herbermann, p. 330.
[20] Cf. Henry J. Browne (Ed.), "The Archdiocese of New York a Century Ago; a Memoir of Archbishop Hughes, 1838-1858," *Historical Records and Studies*, XXXIX-XL (1952), 149-151. For a twentieth-century appraisal of the Society, cf. J. T. McManis, "The Public School Society of New York City," *Educational Review*, XXIX (January-May, 1905), 301-311.

code upon which the good order and welfare of society are based, the substance of which shall be committed to memory by the pupils.[21]

Serving on this committee were Joseph B. Collins, banker and insurance man of Quaker background, and journalist William L. Stone, whose father, a Congregationalist minister, had carried in his knapsack throughout his three years of service in the Revolutionary War, a Hebrew Bible and the works of Josephus.[22] Stone, although anti-Catholic at heart, had yet been fair enough to publish a personally researched refutation[23] of *The Awful Disclosures of Maria Monk*.

In his declared war on the Public School Society, Bishop Hughes paid his opponents the compliment of imitation. Rallies, organizations, special committees, broadsides to the public, petitions to the city fathers, memorials to the legislature, propaganda in the press, lobbying among lawmakers—he employed them all, as had the Society in building up its monopoly of the school fund. Early in the struggle, Hughes sought alliance with William Seward. On August 29, 1840, he forwarded to the governor, along with an ingratiating letter, a copy of the *Address of the Roman Catholics to Their Fellow-Citizens, of the City and State of New York*.[24] This vigorous document from the pen of Hughes, adopted by acclamation in the Catholic Association's general meeting of August 10, 1840, and duplicated in 5,000 copies for wide distribution, contained a scathing attack on the Public School Society for its godless, anti-Catholic schools and on the common council for misusing the shibboleth of constitutionality and favoring the new sectarianism of infidelity.

Seward, at whose elbow hovered the political genius of Thurlow Weed, replied circumspectly to this overture by the bishop, inviting

[21] Thomas Boesé (Clerk of the Board), *Public Education in the City of New York; Its History, Condition and Statistics* (New York, 1869), p. 110. Cf. also the section, "Moral and Religious Instruction," Bourne, pp. 636-644.
[22] *Dictionary of American Biography*, XVIII, 89.
[23] Bishop Hughes acknowledged this act of fairmindedness by a Protestant in his speech of Monday, June 21, 1841, at Carroll Hall. Cf. Bourne, p. 478. Lawrence Kehoe (Ed.), *Complete Works of the Most Rev. John Hughes, D.D., Archbishop of New York* . . . (2nd edition, revised and corrected, 2 volumes; New York, 1864-1865), has commentaries and texts of Hughes' addresses and writings.
[24] It was a fourteen-page document printed by Hugh Cassidy of New York. The *Address* also appeared in the *Freeman's Journal*, August 13, 1840. Cf. Henry J. Browne, "Public Support of Catholic Education in New York, 1825-1842; Some New Aspects," *Historical Records and Studies*, XLI (1953), 14-41.

him to visit Albany, sympathizing with Hughes' ultimate objective of bringing education to all children, and promising his support in measures calculated to advance that object.[25] Seward did not say, then or on other occasions, that he favored outright grants to church-controlled schools. But he was flattering and cordial, and he seemed to be on the bishop's side.[26] For his part, Hughes promised to declare what he termed a "holy war" on the uncompromisingly anti-Seward *Truth-Teller.*

Having the prospect of support in Albany, Hughes renewed the petition for aid from the city corporation. The Public School Society had sought to forestall further conflict, answering the challenging *Address of the Roman Catholics* with a conciliatory public *Reply,* waiting on Hughes with another set of the controversial textbooks, and stating bravely:

> A hope still lingers that every obstacle may be removed, and that their fellow-citizens of the Roman Catholic Church may be induced to permit their children to participate in the advantages which the public schools undeniably afford. For the attainment of this desirable end, the trustees will make every sacrifice compatible with justice and propriety. They remain ready and anxious to join with the Roman Catholics in efforts so to model the books and studies in the public schools as to obviate existing difficulties. They think that it may be done.[27]

The trustees would go to any extreme, they added, short of obtaining sanction from the pope. And when Hughes made it clear that he wanted the textbooks for ammunition rather than for expurgation, the trustees of the School Society knew that a battle was on. This was no tired Bishop Dubois nor scholarly Father Varela, but a subtle and vigorous opponent. Instead of striking back, they tried to remove Hughes' grounds for complaint. On their own initiative, they proceeded with

---

[25] Seward to Hughes, Albany, September 1, 1840; photostat in the Browne collection, AANY.

[26] From this interchange of letters between Hughes and Seward, there developed a political friendship which, during the Civil War, when Seward was Secretary of State, involved Hughes in an important mission for the federal government. His alliance with the Catholics is said to have cost the Whig politician a chance at the presidency of the United States in 1860.

[27] Bourne, p. 343. *The Reply of the Trustees of the Public School Society to the Address of the Roman Catholics,* dated New York, August 27, 1840, was published that year in New York as a seven-page quarto pamphlet. Bourne reproduces it in full, pp. 338-344.

the task of eliminating tactless volumes from their libraries and expunging from school books passages and entire pages which reflected the specifically Protestant interpretation of history. They even submitted, in their *Scripture Lessons,* to the erasure from the title page of the beloved phrase, "without note or comment."[28]

It was a herculean labor, excising individually, with scissors, paste, and ink blocks, the books for the thousands of children in the Society's many schools. "This course, however, on the part of the trustees," comments the historian of the Society sadly, "was not satisfactory, and did not in the least abate the demands of the applicants for a separate provision to be made for their schools from the school fund, and the controversy subsequently became more animated than ever before."[29]

The school-aid conflict now developed into a verbal and emotional donnybrook which captured national headlines and influenced the direction of education into the present day.[30]

In their renewed petition to the city corporation the Catholics, led by Hughes, attacked the Public School Society as a "large, wealthy, and concentrated influence" which, they said, had secured "the monopoly of the public education of children in the City of New York, and of the funds provided for that purpose, at the expense of the State." By admitting the need of expurgating its books, the Society, it was charged, had convicted itself of incompetence. The Catholics

---

[28] Bourne, p. 348. The use of the phrase was by no means confined to the Society. S. S. Randall, Acting State Superintendent of Common Schools during early 1842, later praised the 1838 Annual Report of Superintendent General John Adams Dix, for "its very valuable and pertinent remarks in reference to the vital importance of moral and religious instruction in the common schools free from all taint of sectarianism, and based exclusively on the teachings of the BIBLE, without note or comment." Randall, *History of the State of New York* . . . (New York, 1870), p. 241.

[29] Bourne, pp. 348-349.

[30] For a word-by-word account of the struggle cf. Bourne, pp. 178-525. For a detailed analysis of Hughes' part in it, cf. Sister Marie Léonore Fell, S.C., unpublished Master's dissertation, "Bishop Hughes and the Common School Controversy," Catholic University of America (June, 1936). Cf. also Henry J. Browne, "Public Support of Catholic Education in New York," and Edward M. Connors, *Church-State Relationships in the State of New York* (Washington, 1951).

A scholarly non-Catholic's interpretation is given in Billington, *op. cit.,* Chapter VI, "Saving the Children for Protestantism, 1840-44," pp. 142 ff.

offered to exclude all religious instruction from their parish schools during regular school hours, and to submit to supervision by city appointees, even by the Society, if only they were granted a share of the public funds. Their petition drew a defensive remonstrance from the Public School Society and an aggressive statement from the Methodist Episcopal Church. The Methodist alleged that the Church of Rome had a centuries-long history of intolerance and exclusiveness and sanctioned the murder of heretics, as in "the revocation of the Edict of Nantes, the massacre of St. Bartholomew's Day, the fires of Smithfield, or the crusade against the Waldenses."[31] This open attack on the Church demonstrated that the school issue had now struck the already throbbing nerve of religious bigotry. In frequent meetings of the Catholic Association, to the accompaniment of applause and hat-slinging, Hughes thundered against the School Society and incited his people to united action. Agents of the Society shot back that it was undignified for so high a churchman to play for the cheers of the multitude.

The airing of the Catholic claims before the Board of Aldermen was set for October 29. There were several laymen eager and competent to represent their Church's position, men with long experience in public life, acquainted with the needs of their coreligionists and sympathetic with the stand of their bishop: the journalist and Irish exile of 1798, Thomas O'Connor; Francis Cooper and James W. McKeon, legislators; Gregory Dillon, head of the Irish Emigrant Society; and the lawyer-publicist James W. White. But Hughes, perhaps still fearing the self-assertiveness of the laity in republican America, being temperamentally unable to yield to another, and wishing, as he said, to keep the argument consistent, took the rostrum alone for four hours on two successive days. When Dr. Hugh Sweeney, chairman of the lay trustees' committee, was offered an opportunity to speak, he deferred to Bishop Hughes.

In the course of those two days, in arguments which reverberated throughout the United States, Hughes pleaded for aid to Catholic schools in the name of freedom of conscience. He lampooned the School Society trustees as good men whose objections to the Catholic petition were full of misconceptions and misrepresentations. At charges of past persecution under the Catholic Church, he launched into a history of the sufferings of Ireland and the bigotry of colonial America.

[31] Bourne, p. 201.

Again and again, he averred that he wanted public money not to foster his own religion but to give bias-free instruction to Catholic children, such as the Public School Society did not and could not provide.[32]

Opposing his plea were two able lawyers for the School Society and a succession of ministers marshalled by the Reverend William Craig Brownlee, champion of militant Protestantism in press, pulpit, and lecture hall. One of the Society's men, Theodore Sedgwick, argued for moral education based soundly on Christian ethics but separated from divisive dogmas. "Mankind has never disagreed," he said, "as to the propriety of robbing, or cheating, or bearing false witness." In regard to the Scriptures, the main source of contention, Sedgwick proposed:

> If the whole Bible cannot be used, cannot such extracts from it be compiled as will satisfy all parties? . . . On one point surely we of the Protestant faith cannot claim any superiority. In the *moral teaching* of the two versions, there is no considerable difference. . . The great moral precepts (I speak now of the teaching of Our Saviour) are the same. How can it be otherwise? We are all Christians; either Bible is the code of Christ.[33]

However, in the general clashing of lances, Sedgwick's temperate words went unheeded.

When the dust of battle settled, several facts stood out. Catholics, a despised minority sect, mistrusted the dominant caste and were determined to educate their own children, preferably with government aid. Protestant divines feared the growing power of the Church of Rome in the United States to the extent that they would sacrifice religious education in their own creeds to keep her out of the public till; having control of civic life, they could rest assured there would be nothing damaging to Protestantism in public education.

Recalling the occasion in a letter to Propaganda eighteen years later, Hughes declared that he had the best of the argument but the aldermen turned him down.[34] The vote, taken after an ineffectual show at arbitration, was fifteen to one against aid to Catholic schools. A major consideration in their decision, the aldermen intimated, was

---

[32] Kehoe, I, 126-183.
[33] Bourne, p. 236.
[34] Browne, "The Archdiocese of New York a Century Ago," p. 151. This "Memoir" is Hughes' report to Propaganda.

the threat of violence and bloodshed if Catholics should receive any favors.[35]

Bishop Hughes was now the special object of obloquy in the non-Catholic community. A foreigner out of Ireland via Baltimore and Philadelphia; a mitred bishop who sought to invade the public treasury and to run the city "with a wave of his crosier"; a papist emissary who had bested their champions in eloquence and reduced his own people to salaaming yes-men—in Protestant eyes, he was such a one as Samuel F. B. Morse's *Foreign Conspiracy* had warned against. Particularly alarming was the bishop's attack on the schools' use of the King James Bible "without note or comment"—the bedrock of Protestantism, on which rested the theory of individual interpretation.

Rebuffed by the Board of Aldermen, Hughes continued his assault on the School Society. Hours-long, in the basement of St. James Church and later in more commodious halls, he harangued his people on the evils of the "public" schools. The bishop likened his antagonist to the Kildare Place Society, that Quaker philanthropy in Ireland which dispensed Protestantism along with the rudiments of learning.[36] The New York and the Irish organization, it was true, were both offshoots of London's British and Foreign School Society, and both followed the educational principles of the Friend from Southwark, Joseph Lancaster. The New York Society, insisted Hughes, wished to get hold of Catholic children so as to mold them according to its own discretion, to nip the tender bud of their faith. But, he proclaimed, the plot would not succeed; Catholics would rather pay double than send their children where they would be made ashamed of their parents, their religion, their glorious heritage. "The Union," he cried to loud applause, "is repealed." The Church would make no compromise with the existing schools.

Meanwhile, John Hughes, who persistently disavowed political interference, cemented his unpublished alliance with Governor Seward. He took pains to send the governor copies of his speeches on the school question. The two men met on a railway train in western New York; and they continued to correspond with much show of mutual encouragement and understanding. Seward, in his 1841 an-

---

[35] Bourne, p. 319.
[36] Hughes to John McCaffrey, President of Mount St. Mary's College (Emmitsburg, Maryland), 1841; photostat in the Browne collection, AANY.

nual address to the legislature, echoed the bishop's complaints against the Society, charging that its schools had failed to reach children who needed them most. He did not, however, repeat his much-derided recommendation for schools conducted in immigrant tongues.[37]

New York City's Catholics now centered their hopes on Albany. They prepared a petition with 7,000 signatures, belaboring the School Society and asking "that every school established by the taxable inhabitants of the city may be entitled to a distributive share of the public school moneys; and that the persons to control and administer the system of public instruction in the city may be appointed by the electors and taxable inhabitants."[38] To cover their religious identity, the sponsors of this petition, on advice from Albany lobbyists, termed themselves a Citizens' Committee.

Seward's Secretary of State and ex-officio Superintendent of Schools, John C. Spencer, who had spent years in the codifying of state statutes and the study of educational problems, was sympathetic to the request. His 1841 report as Superintendent of Schools stated clearly the need in the United States for a variety of schools, so that parents might exercise their right to choose one that accorded with their consciences. He praised the Public School Society for its achievements but scolded it for conceiving of itself as the only deserving educational organization in the metropolis. Both Bishop Hughes and the School Society had tried to straddle the religious issue, claiming in one breath that their instruction was not sectarian and disclaiming in the next any tolerance for godless teaching. Spencer set the record straight on this point. In a country like the United States, founded on Christian tradition, education without religion would, he declared, be unthinkable.

> It is believed that, in a country where the great body of our fellow-citizens recognize the fundamental truths of Christianity, public sentiment would be shocked by the attempt to exclude all instruction of a religious nature from the public schools; and that any plan or scheme of education, in which no reference whatever was had to moral prin-

---

[37] George E. Baker, *The Works of William H. Seward* (5 vols.; Boston, 1844), II, 256 ff.

[38] Quotation taken from paraphrase of memorial in the "Report" of Secretary of State Spencer to the Senate, April 26, 1841, "upon Memorials from the City of New York, respecting the Distribution of the Common School Moneys in that City, referred to him by the Senate," Bourne, pp. 356-373; pp. 356-357.

ciples founded on these truths, would be abandoned by all. . . . Viewing the subject, then practically, it may be regarded as a settled axiom in all schemes of education intended for the youth of this country, that there must be, of necessity, a very considerable amount of religious instruction.

In Spencer's report full cognizance was taken of the no-establishment clause in the federal Constitution and the New York State clause guaranteeing "the free exercise and enjoyment of religious profession and worship." He interpreted these to mean "absolute nonintervention" by the government in the matter of religious instruction, so that the people themselves in each locality should have wide discretion in school policies. To secularize all public education, Spencer declared, would indeed be unconstitutional.

> It is believed to be an error to suppose that the absence of all religious instruction, if it were practicable, is a mode of avoiding sectarianism. On the contrary, it would be in itself sectarian, because it would be consonant to the views of a particular class, and opposed to the views of other classes.[39]

Spencer's bill envisioned the harmonious co-existence, under public subsidy, of both state-sponsored and church-related schools. Such an arrangement already existed in Ireland.

The Public School Society, at the prospect of being cut down to size, threw all its influence into an assault on Spencer's proposals. Casting aside the usual gentlemanly restraint, a Society agent placed on each senator's desk, on the day for consideration of the bill, a slanderously anti-Catholic article from the New York *Journal of Commerce;* and one of the Society's advocates hinted darkly that "it would be a serious error to suppose that Catholic citizens would be permitted to enjoy the benefits of this bill without opposition."[40] The heat engendered by the school conflict proved too much for the Senate, which postponed consideration of the Spencer plan until the following January. The decision now rested with the voters in the November, 1841, elections.

Bishop Hughes, with whom Seward and his Secretary of State had conferred while in the metropolis, kept the issue before his flock

[39] *Ibid.*
[40] *Ibid.*, p. 421; for the "Memorial and Remonstrance of the Public School Society of the City of New York," addressed to the Senate, May 21, 1841, cf. pp. 403-425.

in successive meetings at Carroll Hall on June 16, 17, and 21. Many Protestants, including Lieutenant-Governor Bradish and several state senators, were in the audience. Hughes' three-day speech was subsequently printed in pamphlet form for general distribution.[41] Four days before the November election, the Friends of Education held a massive rally in Carroll Hall. Hughes dined that evening with Thurlow Weed, who slipped into the hall incognito.[42] At the rally Hughes announced that a Catholic Party (a radical innovation in American politics) would enter an independent ticket. His slate contained the names of regular party candidates favorable to the Spencer bill (all of them Democrats) and of several others nominated specifically by the Catholic Party. After whipping his hearers up to a frenzy of enthusiasm, the bishop made them pledge to support the names put in their hands.[43]

Next day the Tammany Democrats held a meeting, with a clutch of Irish and German-Catholic party faithfuls on the platform, to "rebuke, censure, and denounce" the bishop's meddling in politics.[44] Nativists were even more violent in their condemnation of the prelate's interference in American affairs of state. The *Morning Herald,* for example, accused "the Romish bishop" of fraud and dishonesty, attacked "his impudent and atrocious attempt to convert his Church into a political faction," and extolled "the majesty of pure American sentiment when set against the worn-out impudence of priestcraft imported from Rome."[45]

The Catholic Party did not win the election. The independent names on its slate scored 2,200 votes. Only one-third of registered Catholics went along with the bishop; the rest adhered to their Tammany-Democrat allegiance. But the Catholic Party did demonstrate that

[41] *The Speech of the Right Reverend Dr. Hughes on the subject of common school education,* recorded by special reporter Dr. J. A. Houston, printed by the *Freeman's Journal,* 1841; also in Kehoe, I, 183-227. Cf. also the *Freeman's Journal,* June 24, 1841.

[42] Frederic Bancroft, *Life of William H. Seward* (2 vols.; New York, 1900), I, 99.

[43] For a melodramatic account of Hughes' speech and its tumultuous reception, cf. Hassard, pp. 244 f., also Bourne, p. 480. Both of these men are indebted to the *New York Freeman's Journal,* October 20, 1841.

[44] George Potter, *To the Golden Door: the Story of the Irish in Ireland and America* (Boston, 1960), pp. 414-415. The Boston *Pilot* printed the names of these defectors in a black-bordered box.

[45] New York *Morning Herald,* November 2, 1841.

it held the balance of power. The regular Democrats it had endorsed were elected; those whom it had scratched lost out to their Whig opponents. The election began a new era in New York City politics.

"This demonstration at the ballot box of a religious body, under the leadership of its most popular and prominent dignitary, occupying the chair of bishop of the diocese, was universally regarded by the people at large, and especially by members of other communions, as highly offensive and dangerous as a precedent, and antagonistic to the spirit of our republican institutions." Thus did the historian of the Public School Society describe the reaction to Bishop Hughes' excursion into American politics.[46]

When the 1842 Legislature convened, it appeared that the bishop's strategy at the election might pay off. Both Governor Seward and William Maclay, chairman of the House Committee on Schools, renewed the attack on the Public School Society as a private monopoly incapable of accomplishing the tremendous self-assumed task of public education. Maclay, son of a popular Baptist minister in the metropolis, introduced a bill similar to Spencer's and he guided it to easy victory in the Assembly. The battle now loomed in the Senate. Here the forces of the Public School Society, the militant Protestants, and the Nativists made their united stand. A monster mass meeting near New York's city hall, attended by 20,000 persons, had dispatched delegates to Albany to exert necessary pressures. Catholics meanwhile assembled a gargantuan petition in favor of the Maclay bill, bearing 13,000 signatures and requiring several men to carry it onto the platform of the Senate chamber. In the city, the Catholic Party again entered its own slate, this time in the April municipal election.

All four state senators from the New York City area were friends of the Public School Society; and it was darkly hinted that, if the assembly bill passed the Senate, the streets of the metropolis would be "drenched with blood." Of these senators, the two Democrats met with Maclay and the Senate Committee on Education in a secret session and agreed on an amended bill. The Maclay Act, as it became law in April, 1842, gave New York City its first elected Board of Education, with control over all school monies and power to build genuinely public schools where needed. The commissioners were also to allot funds to, and have general jurisdiction over, the schools of the School Society, the orphan and half-orphan asylums, the Me-

[46] Bourne, p. 481.

chanics' School, and other stated institutions. The eight schools of the Roman Catholic parishes were not on the list.

The section added in committee had doomed Catholic prospects of obtaining school aid:

> SEC. 14. No school above mentioned, or which shall be organized under this act, in which any religious sectarian doctrine or tenet shall be taught, inculcated, or practised, shall receive any portion of the school moneys to be distributed by this act, as hereinafter provided; and it shall be the duty of the trustees, inspectors, and commissioners of schools in each ward, and of the deputy Superintendent of Schools, from time to time, and as frequently as need be, to examine and ascertain and report to the said Board of Education whether any religious sectarian doctrine or tenet shall have been taught, inculcated, or practised in any of the schools in their respective wards. . . .[47]

This proviso, which has remained substantially in effect to the present day, was aimed specifically at Catholic schools. But Catholics and, latterly, atheists have since induced its application also against the Protestant hymns, prayers, and Bible reading long traditional in the State's common schools.

When passage of the Maclay Act was announced in the city, angry citizens shattered the windows of St. Patrick's Cathedral. They also stoned the Mulberry Street residence of Bishop Hughes, who was out of town. For bringing about the law which displaced the Public School Society with an elected Board of Education, they held the Catholic Bishop of New York as culpably responsible. However, those among them—and their number was at that time minimal—who wished a complete hands-off policy as between Church and State need not have been dismayed. The school law which the Right Reverend John Hughes had endorsed not only ensured that parochial schools must thenceforth be separate and self-supporting; it also opened the way toward a completely secular system of public schools.

---

[47] The full text of the School Law of 1842 may be found in the *Laws of New York*, 1842 (Albany, 1843), Chapter 110; cf. also Bourne, pp. 521-525.

AMBIVALENT ANTI-CATHOLICISM: BUFFALO'S AMERICAN PROTESTANT ELITE FACES THE CHALLENGE OF THE CATHOLIC CHURCH, 1850-1860

David A. Gerber

TWO WELL-KNOWN WORKS in American history—Barbara Miller Solomon's *Ancestors and Immigrants: A Changing New England Tradition* (1956) and Jackson Lears's *No Place of Grace: Antimodernism and the Transformation of American Culture, 1880-1920* (1981)—have briefly called attention to a surprising complexity of attitudes toward Catholicism found among higher status American Protestants in the late nineteenth and early twentieth centuries. These Americans are portrayed as hardly the bigoted nativists we might have anticipated, and they are found to be deeply ambivalent toward the Catholic Church— at once attracted to and repelled by various aspects of Catholic dogma, culture, and polity. Neither book unfortunately attempts to develop systematically an analysis of this ambivalent combination of attraction and repulsion, and thus far, to the best of this author's knowledge, no one else has attempted such an extended analysis.[1]

I have discovered that the same ambivalence was given public expression much earlier, in the 1850s. That we lack such an extended analysis of the complexity of attitudes toward Catholicism and the Catholic church in the critical 1850s is especially unfortunate, for it was during that decade that for the first, and last, time a mass movement with a national political party of its own existed among American Protestants of all classes to challenge the very presence of the Church in the United States. The historical literature we do have is excellent, to be sure, but limited in this and in other respects. Ray Allen Billington's pathbreaking *The Protestant Crusade* (1938) laid out a basic narrative structure for the history of antebellum nativism which is still useful today. But the book is greatly in need of reconsideration in light of new

[1] Barbara Miller Solomon, *Ancestors and Immigrants: A Changing New England Tradition* (Cambridge, Mass.: Harvard Univ. Press, 1956), pp. 6, 10, 12, 48-49, 53, 91, 97, 124-25, 132, 144, 174, 184-85, 205-7, 232; Jackson Lears, *No Place of Grace: Antimodernism and the Transformation of American Culture* (New York: Pantheon, 1981), pp. 147, 151-52, 159-62, 184-216, 241-42, 251.

understandings achieved by historians in the last two decades, of class, ethnicity, ethnocultural conflict, and the social functions of prejudice.² For example, David Brion Davis and Michael Holt have seen anti-Catholicism as a symptomatic of a fear, particularly among affluent, educated antebellum Protestants, of sinister sectional and sectarian conspiracies against republican institutions. To varying degrees, both Holt and Davis have tied this fear to deeper anxieties concerning the capacity of later generations to safeguard the republican experiment of the Founding Fathers amidst the social and political crises of the antebellum decades. These suggestive insights take us much beyond Billington, to be sure, but they themselves do not consider the ambiguity present in the body of public pronouncements which express both positive and negative assessments of the Church and its organization, works, and beliefs. Moreover, like other political historians, Holt views nativism less as a cultural phenomenon than as a political one. In this guise nativism logically presents itself as a transitory, partisan affiliation, which in effect fulfilled its brief historical mission by providing former Whigs of American Protestant background, whose party lay in ruins in the mid-1850s, with a conservative, nationalist political identity while they were on their way to eventual incorporation in the new Republican party.

This perspective carries with it a significant conceptual difficulty: it judges an aspect of the past (nativism) too heavily by the outcomes of separate, if indirectly, related developments (i.e., sectional conflict, partisan realignment, and electoral shifts). Moreover, it obscures the abundance of anti-Catholicism in Protestant historical tradition and the vast realm of daily Catholic-Protestant social relations, both of which give attitudes toward the Church a profound reality beyond partisan politics. Under any circumstances, the intense, organized, political anti-Catholicism of the 1850s may well have had a brief public life not because it served transitory political functions, but instead because large and important segments of Protestant opinion remained divided against themselves on the utility of the Church and the worthiness of Roman Catholicism.[3]

---

[2] Ray Allen Billington, *The Protestant Crusade: 1880-1860: A Study of the Origins of American Nativism* (New York: Quadrangle, 1938). The other recognized classic study of nativism focuses on a later period of time and, in contrast to Lears, for example, does not explore the possibility of ambivalence in Protestant attitudes toward Catholicism and the Catholic church; see John Higham, *Strangers in the Land: Patterns of American Nativism, 1860-1925* (New York: Atheneum, 1965). A tantalizing suggestion of that very phenomenon does, however, appear very briefly in Higham's essay, "Another Look at Nativism," in *Send These to Me: Jews and Other Immigrants in Urban American* (New York: Atheneum, 1975), p. 112, in which the author discusses the attraction of Catholic parochial schools to Protestant parents in the nineteenth century.

[3] Michael F. Holt, *The Political Crisis of the 1850s* (New York: John Wiley and Sons, 1978). Holt, however, is not unaware that voters could also express anti-Catholic sentiments by voting Republican, because Republicans were deemed more anti-Catholic than

This essay is a speculative reconsideration of elite anti-Catholicism. The principal observations are based on the experience of antebellum Buffalo, New York, which by the inception of a mass nativist movement in the mid-1850s was a metropolis of fifty thousand, a majority of whom were German and Irish Catholic immigrants.[4] The experience of one city would be less than illustratively representative if that city's history were unique. But it is precisely the typicality of the daily public conflicts and underlying social tensions which were faced by the Buffalo American Protestant elite, and which led directly to the formation of complex and apparently contradictory attitudes toward Catholicism and the Church, that makes Buffalo's experience worthy of our attention.[5] Furthermore, this analysis will be brought yet closer to the typical interactions of daily life in the mid-nineteenth century northern city because, unlike the works of Lears and Solomon, it is not concerned with a small number of self-conscious literary or political intellectuals possessing a cosmopolitan viewpoint. The views analyzed here are those of local opinion leaders, in particular the editors of the evangelical Protestant press and regular, daily press. The two papers most extensively utilized are the *Buffalo Commercial Advertiser*, a prestigious and articulate Whig, and then nativistic, American party paper, and the *Buffalo Christian Advocate*, a nonpartisan, but evangelical weekly, which frequently expressed distrust for the Catholic clergy and questioned Catholic doctrine. Both had extensive circulation among, and hence must have tended to reflect the views of, many of the city's practical men of affairs. In fact, both papers were widely perceived to speak for the men of substance—professionals, merchants, and manufacturers, of American Protestant background, who constituted the city's economic and political elite.[6]

Democrats; see Holt, p. 276. There is controversy on this point, however; see for example, Eric Foner, *Free Soil, Free Labor, Free Men: The Ideology of the Republican Party Before the Civil War* (New York: Oxford Univ. Press, 1970), pp. 253-60, and also, David Brion Davis, "Some Themes of Counter-Subversion: An Analysis of Anti-Masonic, Anti-Catholic, and Anti-Mormon Literature," *Mississippi Valley Historical Review* 47 (September 1960): 205-24; idem, *The Slave Power Conspiracy and the Paranoid Style* (Baton Rouge: Louisiana State Univ. Press, 1969), pp. 62-98.

[4] The structure of the Buffalo population at the time is elaborately analyzed in Laurence A. Glasco, *Ethnicity and Social Structure: Irish, Germans, and Native Born of Buffalo, New York, 1850-1860* (New York: Arno Press, 1980).

[5] The argument for the representativeness of Buffalo in regard to broad lines of socioeconomic, political, and cultural development is made in somewhat more extended fashion in David A. Gerber, "Cutting Out Shylock: Elite Anti-Semitism and the Quest for Moral Order in the Mid-Nineteenth Century Market Place," *Journal of American History* 69 (December 1982): 615-37.

[6] While difficult to document, this perception of both papers is clear in the serious analysis given to them continually, over the course of many years, by the city's ethnic press *(Die Buffalo Weltbürger, The American Celt and Catholic Citizen, The Buffalo Catholic Sentinel,* and *Die Aurora und Christliche Woche),* which paid careful attention to both their editorial positions and treatment of news in the effort to discern elite Prot-

My purpose, however, is not merely to lay out evidence of an ambivalent or unrationalized social view in these newspapers. Though there is doubtless reason to believe that, like other social attitudes, anti-Catholic nativism was neither morally nor logically consistent, if the matter were left at that, it would be impossible to explain why elite attitudes, whether positive or negative, clustered in certain distinguishable and predictable patterns. Failing that, it would be impossible to proceed to tie those patterns, which at bottom point to fundamental internal divisions in the worldview of many educated and affluent American Protestants, to the central cultural conflicts such people confronted in the troubled years before the Civil War. What is intended here, therefore, is both an elaboration of attitudes and the exploration of a conceptual scheme, which is derived from both existing historical literature and my own research on antebellum Buffalo, for understanding the social evolution and intellectual structuring of attitudes toward the Church and Catholicism. This scheme will be analyzed through presentation of two sets of conflicts within elite Protestant culture. The first of the two is that between republican and democratic values, and it has its deepest significance for this essay in relation to social order and disorder. Though elite Protestants possessed different formulations of technical qualifications for voting, they had a democratic commitment to universal, white male suffrage. But they were also committed to a republican conception of government, which saw the responsibility of government to be the protection of the liberty of the ordinary citizen from the machinations of conspirators and corruptionists. They feared that presumably disorderly moral and social conditions in the daily lives of the immigrant lower classes would provide demagogues with the opportunity to excite majoritarian passions through the mechanisms of mass, democratic politics, and thus to destroy republican institutions. They believed that ultimately only a social order fashioned after their own moral culture could insure the preservation of republican government. How an elite with a basic democratic commitment, living in a society with substantial democratic features, could impose its moral culture on an unwilling, increasingly foreign and enfranchised population was an essential problem for higher status Protestants.[7] The

estant opinion. Moreover, the *Commercial Advertiser* was the organ of the powerful Fillmore or "Silver Grey" conservative wing of the New York State Whig Party as well as of local manufacturers and merchants, as is evident from the fact that it had much more extensive economic coverage than any other city paper. Its multipage, yearly review of local commerce, banking, and industry was unique in local journalism.

[7] Isaac Kramnick, "Republican Revisionism Revisited," *American Historical Review* 77 (June 1982): 629-64; Robert E. Shalhope, "Toward A Republican Synthesis: The Emergence of An Understanding of Republicanism in American Historiography," *William and Mary Quarterly*, 3d ser. 31 (1974): 48-65; Bernard Bailyn, "Origins of American Politics," *Perspectives* 1 (1967): 120; Marvin Myers, *The Jacksonian Persuasion: Politics and Belief* (Stanford: Stanford Univ. Press, 1957), pp. 162-64; Davis, "Some Themes of Counter-Subversion," 209-11, 214-17.

second set of conflicts is that between, on the one hand, the daily claims of the moral and practical economy of modernizing capitalism, founded upon a materialistic ideology and structured around the cash nexus, and on the other, a quasi-religious striving for spirituality, transcendence, and aesthetic values, which, as we shall see, both capitalism and the more theologically liberal variants of evangelical Protestantism seemed unable to fulfill.[8]

The conflict between order and republican liberty and disorder and democracy may be illustrated by juxtaposing two apparently contradictory images of the Catholic clergy which appeared in editorials in the *Commercial Advertiser* in 1858. The first editorial, and doubtless the more familiar in its message, is titled "The Bible—The Common Schools." It states that the reading of the Bible (King James version) and the daily invocation of the Lord's Prayer have been banned from the public schools of New York's fourth and eighteenth wards. The paper laments that with the nativist American party in electoral decline forces inimical to "the progress of the foreign element" to complete Americanization are again on the rise. The editorial writer had no doubt about the identity of those forces. The situation was blamed on both "Jesuitism and radical anarchism-atheism," but particularly on the former, since the school officers of the two wards were, "as may be seen by their names" (which were doubtless Irish), "the slime of the Order of Jesuits." Whether this was intended to mean that Jesuits, perhaps in disguise, actually were school board members is not clear. The implications, however, were probably obvious to the paper's readers: in order to keep its immigrant adherents' minds under control and smother the stirrings of American liberty within them, the Catholic clergy was interfering in the public schools. No more potent symbol of this behavior existed for Protestants than the effort to ban from the school curriculum the Bible, which the Protestant Reformation was thought to have freed of clerical domination. Like the historical model of the Reformation itself, the Bible, especially in its Protestant version, was seen as one of the sources of those ideas of republican liberty which had informed the Founding Fathers. Thus, barring the Bible directly imperiled the usefulness of one of the principal institutions which safeguarded republican liberty.[9]

There is nothing surprising here. The editorial is the basic stuff of nativist social analysis, as Billington and others have presented it to us.

---

[8] This tension, analyzed extensively in the light of the broad forces which shaped nineteenth-century American society and culture, is finely described in Lears, *No Place of Grace*, pp. xiii-xviii, 4-58.

[9] *Buffalo Commercial Advertiser*, April 27, 1858. On the significance of the symbols of the Bible and of the Refomation in Protestant-Catholic contentions, see Billington, *The Protestant Crusade*, pp. 42-43, 142-57, 172-73, 221-22, 292-95; Davis, *The Slave Power Conspiracy*, pp. 75-76; *Buffalo Christian Advocate*, December 20, 1853.

But compare it with another editorial, "Sisters of Charity, Monks, and Nuns," which appeared in that newspaper three months previously.[10] Whether it was written by the same individual, there is no way to determine. But so different is much of the tone and content, the very fact of publication in the same newspaper is in itself noteworthy. The writer chastised the fallacious view of "monks and nuns" then widespread in popular novels and nativist polemical literature. In the conventional view, he said, "Monks are presented as deep, dark, and mysterious, and the nuns—but everyone knows how they are represented—forced into a convent by some cruel father or guardian, and ready to elope by means of a convenient rope ladder, scale the garden wall, and then all trembling, fall into the arms of a gallant lover."

The reality was said to be greatly different from either of these romantic or sinister caricatures—and not only different, but much better, if still somewhat fancifully conceived. Monks were "jolly fellows," according to the writer. The Dominicans and Benedictines, two of the teaching orders the first diocesan bishop, John Timon, had invited to Buffalo after the creation of the diocese in 1847, were said to contain "some of the most accomplished gentlemen [I] have ever known." Of several Sisters of Charity encountered recently in their habits on a Buffalo street, the writer added, they were "young, fresh, and fair," while, based on observations made during a recent trip abroad, he said of European nuns, who made up the large majority of those then at work in northern cities, a "fairer set of ladies we have rarely looked upon, or more graceful in their manner. That they at times had longings for the great world they had left, can hardly be doubted, but they seemed happy."

But even more noteworthy for our purposes than this sympathetic evaluation, one based on personal encounters and not, as was often the case, on popular mythology, was the simultaneous praise for the activities of the Sisters of Charity *and* the nativistic cautions which the editorial posed in closing. There was, the author stated, "something very beautiful and touching" in the devotion to the sick and dying of the Sisters, who had for a decade operated the city's only hospital, public or private, an institution which served people of all faiths, classes, and ethnicities. Their admirable selflessness and lack of fear of death in the face of the cholera epidemics of the early 1850s, for which they had won the praise of Buffalo's most prestigious doctors (all of them American Protestants), were to be attributed to their understanding of the doctrine of the Church. In explaining, the editorial writer offered a comparison between the religious and social worlds of the Sisters and those of individuals, such as Protestant men of affairs, who lived for the rewards of this world and were sustained in their temporal preoccu-

[10] *Buffalo Commercial Advertiser*, January 22, 1858.

pation by their religion, and whose condition seemed filled with pathos:

How poor and insignificant must appear the fleeting strifes, competitions, and honors of this world to those animated by the firm belief of the certainty of enjoying eternal bliss. It is this, more than anything else, that is the secret of the enduring power of the Roman Catholic faith. The Roman church offers not a mere life assurance, but an eternal one. The Protestants can do no such thing. Their teaching is "work out your own salvation with fear and trembling," and we are often compelled to fear with Paul that we may be castaways.

But having implored readers to reject simplistic, ungenerous views of the Catholic clergy, the writer nonetheless closed with a grim warning. It was not Catholic religious dogma nor the daily, public activities of the Catholic clergy that the Protestant public had "to fear and guard against," but rather "the political enginery of the Romish Church—the most subtle, potent, and widespreading ever devised by the wit of man. It may also be said to be omniscient and omnipresent." But no particularly compelling examples were given to illustrate this contention. It was simply said, somewhat anticlimactically, that the writer had met two priests, one in Italy and the other in South America, who knew of Bishop Timon and his work in the Buffalo Diocese. Since nothing else is said of the encounter with these priests beyond the fact that they possessed this knowledge, we have to infer that possession of such information was seen as proof of the "political enginery" the writer feared.

These two editorials are representative of a central tension, a dissonance within nativist thought, which repeatedly appeared in the fifties, and which helps to explain the ambivalence toward the Church we have noted. Simply put: when the Church is seen as threatening republican liberty, it is hateful; but when, in vastly varied ways, by example or practical activity, it supports order against social disorganization or upheaval emanating from poor and working class immigrants, it is to be praised and encouraged.

Examples of the perceived Catholic threat to republican liberty are not difficult to find in the extant sources. Many monographs have been written illustrating how the Church's public activities, and indirectly its doctrines, were perceived by American Protestants to threaten the central tenets of republican society: that government must be restrained by law; and that the purpose of government must be the protection of the liberty and equality before the law of individual citizens from assault by any source of aristocratic privilege, corruption, or arbitrary power. Jesuits were frequently seen as the vanguard of this subversion, but by no means were the general ranks of the Catholic clergy, male and female alike, exempted from suspicion. Several relevant areas of Protestant-Catholic conflict stand out in the historical literature. Perhaps the most emotionally charged arena of contention was the public schools, in which Catholics objected to the Protestant-influenced curriculum and sought to have Catholicism represented in the curriculum of those schools in which most students were Catholic. If they could afford it, Catholics might send their children to parochial schools rather than fight for equality of creeds in public schools, but they would still continue to have to pay taxes toward the support of public education and this, too, was a source of conflict. Closely related to these instances of sectarian friction were conflicts over such public institutions as poorhouses, prisons, orphanages, and hospitals, in which Catholic clergy were regularly denied equality with Protestants in the right to administer the spiritual needs of inmates and residents. Fearing that coreligionists would be subjected to the pressures to convert, Catholics protested. protested against this discrimination.[11] Also, there were frequent charges that the Catholic clergy worked, whether secretly or openly, to influence Catholic voters in partisan (almost always Democratic) direction at elections.[12] Finally, another source of friction lay in the efforts of the Catholic hierarchy to undermine and destroy lay control of parish properties, such as churches and cemeteries, and to place control firmly in the hands of parish clergy responsible only to the diocesan bishop. Though this last issue was fought inside the Church, with the exception of an occasional resort to civil courts, Protestants adamantly defended and encouraged lay Catholics in the daily and religious press.[13] Such was the case at Buffalo during the 1840s and 1850s, when Protestants sided with lay trustees of St. Louis Church in their bitter struggle to retain control of parish property.[14]

[11] Billington, *The Protestant Crusade*, pp. 142-65, 220-23; Vincent P. Lannie, "Alienation in America: The Immigrant Catholic and Public Education in Pre-Civil War America," *Review of Politics* 1970, no. 4: 503-21, and *Public Money and Parochial Education: Bishop Hughes, Governor Seward, and the New York School Controversy* (Cleveland: Case Western Reserve Univ. Press, 1968); David Tyack, "Onward Christian Soldiers: Religion in the American Common School," in *History & Education: The Educational Uses of the Past*, ed. Paul Nash (New York: Random House, 1970), pp. 212-55; Charles G. Deuther, *The Life and Times of Right Reverend John Timon, D. D., First Roman Catholic Bishop of the Diocese of Buffalo* (Buffalo, 1870), pp. 257-62, 271, 276; John T. Horton et al., *History of Northwestern New York: Erie, Niagara, Wyoming, Genesee, and Orleans Counties*, 3 vols. (New York: Lewis Historical Publishing Company, 1947), 1: 154-55; *Buffalo Commercial Advertiser*, December 27-30, 1856; *Buffalo Courier*, July 20, 28, September 17, 20, 22, 1852; December 29, 1856.

[12] Billington, *The Protestant Crusade*, passim, esp. pp. 198-211, 325-27. *Buffalo Commercial Advertiser*, October 30, November 19, 1855; November 24, 1856; April 25, 1857.

[13] Billington, *The Protestant Crusade*, pp. 38-41, 295-300; Patrick J. Dignan, *A History of the Legal Incorporation of Church Property in the United States, 1784-1932* (Washington, D.C.: Catholic Univ. Press, 1933); Patrick Carey, "The Laity's Understanding of the Trustee System, 1785-1855," *Catholic Historical Review* 64 (July 1978): 357-76, and "A National Church: Catholic Search for Identity, 1820-1829," Center for the Study of American Catholicism, University of Notre Dame, Working Paper Series, no. 3 (Notre Dame, 1977).

[14] David A. Gerber, "Modernity in the Service of Tradition: Ante-Bellum Catholic Laymen at Buffalo's St. Louis Church, 1829-1854," *Journal of Social History* 15 (June 1982): 655-84.

For a variety of reasons, the activism of the Catholic clergy in such matters was interpreted as threatening liberty. Many Protestants saw Catholic "interference" in the public schools as an effort to subvert the one public agency which prepared the young for civic responsibility and participation in a self-governing republic. Along with the efforts to gain entrance into public institutions and influence voting behavior, such activities also threatened much valued traditions of separation of church and state, which themselves protected republican institutions from another direction. The success of the hierarchy in gradually wresting control of parish properties placed vast sums of money in its control in perpetuity. It was feared that these assets would be employed to provide a material foundation for papal subversion.[15]

Looking from outside the Church at these activities, which were presumed to be connected, and possessing both a heritage of anti-Catholic attitudes and a tendency (which Davis and Richard Hofstadter, among others, have explained)[16] to see history in conspiratorial terms, Protestants reached fantastic conclusions about the plans the Vatican had for republican America. Yet the activities of the Catholic clergy and hierarchy and the laymen standing with them were undertaken in the light of their own, culturally pluralistic, understanding of American liberty: fairness and equality for all creeds before the law and in affairs of government. They challenged what they believed to be a fundamentally *unrepublican* idea: that America was a Protestant country, an assumption, there can be little doubt, which most American Protestants shared. This belief was continally demonstrated in the explicit defense of Protestants of their special role in the public schools and other public institutions, and yet more fundamentally, in their semiconscious equation of "Protestant," "American," and "public." In effect, they often honored only in the breach the doctrine of separation of church and state which they claimed to revere.[17]

But if the Protestant nativist tendency to view matters of competing and conflicting ideologies and interests according to a devil theory of papal subversion missed the point, the Catholic clergy was not without a good deal of responsibility for Protestant misperceptions. The Amer-

[15] Billington, *The Protestant Crusade*, passim, esp. pp. 32-53, 142-65, 193-220, 345-406; Davis, "Some Themes of Counter-Subversion," 208-12, 214-17.

[16] Davis, *The Slave Power Conspiracy*; Richard Hofstadter, *The Paranoid Style in American Politics and Other Essays* (New York: Alfred Knopf, 1965).

[17] Lannie, *Public Money and Parochial Education*, and "Alienation in America," 502-21; Timothy L. Smith, "Protestant Schooling and American Nationality, 1800-1850," *Journal of American History* 63 (March 1967): 679-95; John Tracy Ellis, *American Catholicism* (Chicago: Univ. of Chicago Press, 1956), pp. 61-83, passim. When Catholics protested that their priests were not allowed to visit Catholic inmates of the public poorhouse, the *Christian Advocate* hardly allayed their fears about religious liberties in public institutions when it stated, regarding the poor house, "Our Protestant institutions never oppressed a Catholic or invaded his rights since the Republic was born and never will will. . . ," ibid., September 23, 1852.

ican clergy was heavily Irish in origin, and theirs was no self-effacing, irresolute mentality when it came to the interests of what they regarded as the one true Christian faith. Possessing a rich heritage of resistance to Britain's seventeenth and eighteenth century anti-Catholic penal laws, and a positive model of Catholic assertion in behalf of civil rights in the early nineteenth-century campaign for Catholic emancipation in Ireland, the Irish exhibited an especially aggressive, unapologetic style of Catholic leadership. They were just as prone to see ideological conflicts in black-and-white terms, as simple matters of right against wrong, as were Protestant nativists. Moreover, their active embrace of the right and duty to seek converts among Protestants and their sometimes publicly argued belief in the superiority of Catholicism, were unlikely to win over the hearts of even those Protestants apathetic about the condition of republican liberty and inclined to tolerance in matters of creed.[18]

Animosity of this sort was not by any means the only face of Protestant-Catholic relations, however, for it was a measure of their ambivalence toward the Church that Protestants were completely willing to enlist the active support of Catholic clergy and laity in the struggle for social order in the rapidly growing city and moral control of the immigrant masses. It is not clear if this tendency to ally informally in behalf of social order and moral control counterbalanced deep Protestant suspicion of the Church. Nor was this informal, unspoken understanding without its own conflicting areas: the Church's doctrinally-based support for the Continental Sunday, which led it to give sanction—to the outrage of many pious, order-conscious Protestants—to public religious processions with musical bands on the Lord's Day, and its refusal to espouse prohibition or other coercive temperance measures, both were continuing sources of friction.[19]

What is clear, however, is that even in the bitter 1850s certain public activities of the Church were applauded because they contributed to social order and to peace between classes and ethnic groups. Thus the *Commercial Advertiser* and *Christian Advocate* had words of praise for Catholic temperance crusader Father Matthew when he visited Buffalo in 1851 and administered "the pledge" to hundreds of Irish

---

[18] John Higham, "Les Deux Irlandes en Amerique," *Critique* (June-July 1982): 615; Billington, *The Protestant Crusade*, pp. 289-21; Lannie, "Alienation in America," pp. 507-8. Nowhere is this style more vividly expressed than the career of Archbishop John Hughes of New York; see Richard Shaw, *Dagger John: The Life and Unquiet Times of Archbishop John Hughes of New York* (New York: Paulist Press, 1977).

[19] *Buffalo Christian Advocate*, January 30, 1851, April 8, 1952, April 27, 1854; November 15, 1855; July 14, 1859. The Catholic church's position on liquor was, in fact ambivalent, lent, for it blessed the work of total abstinence societies and exponents like Father Matthew, while recognizing the utility of moderate use of alcohol; see Richard Stivers, *A Hair of the Dog: Irish Drinking and American Stereotype* (University Park: Pennsylvania State Univ. Press, 1976), pp. 95-98.

working men;[20] and both papers applauded the Church's local charities—its hospitals, orphanages, and during the depression of the late fifties, its soup kitchens.[21] It should be noted, too, that such approval was forthcoming in spite of the fact that Catholic hospitals and orphanages in Buffalo, and elsewhere in New York State, received public monies under state legislation, which subsidized both the charitable work of private hospitals in providing care to indigent patients and the educational work done in private orphanage schools. State grants to the first Sisters of Charity Hospital (a second, for maternity patients, opened in 1854) created some controversy when initially obtained in the late 1840s. But with the cholera epidemics of the following years, and the subsequent testimony of Buffalo's most respected, Protestant doctors, the majority of whom were on the hospital's staff, that the hospital was necessary for the maintenance of public health and of order during epidemics, and for the training of local physicians, these complaints disappeared from public discourse. They did not even resurface during the climax of political nativism in the mid-1850s.[22] Moreover, elite Protestants and their families themselves were not immune to the diseases which swept the city, and they also relied on the Sisters' services. When Judge Nathan K. Hall, Millard Fillmore's friend, cabinet member, and close political confidant, who followed Fillmore into the American party in 1856, concluded that his ailing son could not be treated at home, Hall was quite willing to send him to Sisters of Charity Hospital for care.[23] Thus, this unmistakable breach of the doctrine of separation of church and state, one which fed money into the coffers of the Catholic clergy, was not simply tolerated but endorsed by Protestants. Finally, also in the name of order, in spite of their distrust of Timon,

---

[20] *Buffalo Christian Advocate*, August 28, 1851; *Buffalo Commercial Advertiser*, August 26, September 1, 1851.

[21] E.g., *Buffalo Christian Advocate*, August 23, 1860; *Buffalo Commercial Advertiser*, June 7, 1854; August 23, 1855; January 18, 1856; August 6, 1860. Timon has been considered one of the leading early forces in the development of American Catholic welfare and charities. It is not difficult to understand why. When he became bishop in 1847, there were no diocesan institutions of Catholic charity or welfare. When he died in 1867, the diocese contained two Catholic orphan asylums, an infants' home, a widows' home, a hospital, an institution for the deaf, and an industrial school, almost all of them at Buffalo. See John O'Grady, *Catholic Charities in the United States: History and Problems*, (Washington, D.C.: Catholic Univ. Press, 1930), pp. 72-88, 110-28, 129-31.

[22] *Discussions Relative to the Buffalo Hospital of the Sisters of Charity*, (Buffalo: *Buffalo Republic*, 1850); Buffalo Medical Society, *Buffalo Medical Journal* 4 (1848-49): 326, 659-61, 775-76; 5 (1849-50): 319, 362, 433-34; 6 (1850-51): 574; 8 (1852-53): 255; *Buffalo Courier*, January 30, 1852; *Buffalo Commercial Advertiser*, August 23, 1855. The organ of the overwhelmingly Protestant medical establishment, the *Buffalo Medical Journal*, in 1850 dismissed opposition to Sisters' Hospital as "prejudice," which was "excited by denominational feeling alone"; ibid, 5 (1849-50): 373.

[23] Nathan K. Hall to Millard Fillmore, August 12, 1854, Roll #41, Millard Fillmore Papers, Archives, Buffalo and Erie County Historical Society, Buffalo, New York (hereafter BECHS).

Protestant opinion leaders applauded the bishop's annual pleas for peace at the polls and his campaign for dignity and quiet at the boisterous processions and wakes which accompanied Irish funerals.[24]

To be sure, there is ample reason to see this Protestant support for the activities of the Catholic clergy as little more than a grudging, perhaps desperate, expedient for dealing with concrete social problems particularly common to the immigrant Catholic flock. These activities did indeed fill a vacuum which Protestants themselves did not seek to, or simply could not, fill. Local experience demonstrated repeatedly that the Protestant elite was either ideologically and practically incapable, or at best merely painfully slow, to mount similar, organized responses to the social problems of the immigrant majority. The organized, private Protestant response to poverty was bedeviled continually by difficulties raising funds and, perhaps even more, by the impossible effort, through home visitations of relief applicants, to separate the "worthy" from the "unworthy" poor. The passions for rooting out the latter impaired the ability of the Protestant-organized Buffalo Association for the Relief of the Poor, which was the most active and well-organized of all antebellum, Protestant relief organizations, to reach people too proud to have the middle-class American investigators snooping about their homes and into their lives.[25] When angry groups of the unemployed, led by Irish workers and ward politicians, gathered in the depths of the 1857 to 1859 depression to demand "work or bread" from municipal officials, Protestants had special reason to be grateful that the Sisters of Charity were giving out food to everyone, "worthy" or not, at their soup kitchens.[26]

Protestants did show a desire to institutionalize some public welfare activities, but like their experience with systematic, private relief, their efforts were either too slow to gather force, or simply ineffective. Protestants superintended the creation and administration of the county

---

[24] *Buffalo Christian Advocate*, October 30, 1956; *Buffalo Commercial Advertiser*, May 3, 13, 1859; November 3, 1860.

[25] Founded amidst great fanfare in 1853 as the cure for street begging and other forms of parasitism, the Buffalo Association for the Relief of the Poor was directed by affluent and prestigious merchants and professionals. By January 1856, however, there were reports that contributions were inadequate, and during the 1857 to 1859 depression, complaints about a lack of contributions increased, suggesting the usefulness of the association was at an end. *Buffalo Commercial Advertiser*, January 10, April 18, December 18, 1853; January 8, June 20, 1855; January 24, 28, February 16, April 23, 1856; January 17, 1857; February 17, 1858; February 14, March 2, 1859. Poor relief by individual congre-congregations tended to be limited to neighborhood Protestants; see *Buffalo Christian Advocate*, March 4, 1858.

[26] *Buffalo Commercial Advertiser*, November 7, 1857; January 29, February 6, 9, 17, April 3, June 14-17, October 10, December 24, 1859; *Buffalo Christian Advocate*, June 17, 1858; January 20, 1859; Timon to "Conseil," February 20, 1859, Société de La Propaganda de La Foi de Paris et Lyon Collection, Archives, University of Notre Dame, Notre Dame, Indiana (hereafter UND).

poorhouse, which was the subject of constant criticism by priests and other spokesmen for the immigrant poor, who reportedly received cruel treatment there. Major figures in the Protestant medical establishment complained about the very high mortality rate for the sick poor at the poorhouse relative to that at the Sisters' hospital. During a period of intense controversy about the former institution's routine brutalities, it was completely destroyed by a fire of mysterious origins.[27] A public dispensary, providing free medicine to the sick poor upon referral of a subscribing doctor, was also in existence for many years, but few knew of its existence, and the use of the facility posed great inconvenience to the sick, who were required to get their prescriptions and medicine at different locations.[28] It took many years and a number of false starts before the private Buffalo General Hospital was opened in 1858, while the Buffalo Protestant Orphanage, opened in 1839, semipublic and limited to Protestant orphans of American parents, appears to have had an episodic existence. Protestants did create an industrial school to teach poor girls and women to make their own clothing, but it aided mostly church-affiliated, American Protestants.[29] It is certainly not the case that all these efforts were meaningless, but it is true that somehow they were either impaired or did not reach the immigrant poor, who made up the vast majority of those truly needing help. Thus, for practical reasons alone, Catholic charities needed to be supported, if only morally supported. The alternative was chaos.

Yet if we seek a deeper level of social understanding, we find that support for the charitable and welfare activities of the Catholic clergy was not always merely given expediently. To an extent, too, it flowed directly, if implicitly, from larger concerns about the relationship between moral order and individual character. Perhaps more in keeping with elite Protestant culture than organized charities and institutionalized public welfare were efforts in behalf of internal moral reform, which was believed to be best achieved less through what was done for individuals than what they purposefully did for themselves. (Indeed what was done for them, in the form of charity, was widely believed to create dependence and sap initiative.) Of course, public school and

---

[27] *Buffalo Courier*, November 19, 26, 1849; July 28, September 17, 20, 22, 24, October 16, November 2, 1852; *Buffalo Commercial Advertiser*, July 21, 1854; *Buffalo Medical Journal*, 4 (1848–49): 446–54, and 5 (1849–50): 424–28 (untitled commentaries on the mortality rates at the poorhouse); *Buffalo Christian Advocate*, September 23, 1852.

[28] *Buffalo Commercial Advertiser*, November 23, 1853; February 3, 1857; *Buffalo Courier*, August 6, 1852.

[29] *Buffalo Commercial Advertiser*, February 1, June 12, September 26, 1854; March 19, 1858; March 1, 1860; *Buffalo Christian Advocate*, December 2, 1858; December 8, 1859; October 11, November 15, 1860; Evelyn Hawes, *Proud Vision: A History of Buffalo General Hospital* (New York, 1964), pp. 1–13; no author, *Semi-Centennial Celebration, The Buffalo Orphan Asylum, April 26, 1887*, (Buffalo, 1887), pp. 1, 22, 38–39. Fundraising for the hospital was actually abandoned in 1854 because of a lack of interest; it was begun again, however, a year later.

church were seen as necessary to the proper socialization of the young and to the spiritual and moral life of the adult. Sabbath and temperance, and particularly in the fifties, prohibition laws might be needed to aid in the achievement of self-control and piety. But American Protestant opinion leaders did not fully trust arrangements which suggested that the laws and institutions of society might provide for individuals what their own characters lacked. And this was perhaps, in part, the ultimate meaning of these faulty and perfunctory efforts at charity organization, and certainly of the occasional expressions of contempt for those among the poor observed begging, taking charity, or protesting for "work or bread." After all, Protestantism was the religion of "work out your own salvation with fear and trembling," a religion of individual struggle unmediated by an apostolic church and its clergy. It is not surprising that Protestants saw the internalization of the necessary bourgeois values (self-help, self-control, deferred gratification, sacrifice for family, and obedience to legitimate authority) as likely to be the consequence of having familar, individual models of such behavior around one in family, teachers, ministers, and public men and women, and of a lifelong, internal struggle to follow those models and to stay on a personal straight-and-narrow path. Upon these individual foundations self-government, liberty, and urban and political order were thought ultimately to depend. For only by denying in some part the egoistic self, now increasingly set apart from society by an ideology of laissez-faire individualism, could a sense of the good of the whole be attained and an American nation be forged out of its diverse parts, a matter of special responsibility for descendents of the country's charter group.[30]

[30] Citations could be marshalled from almost every issue of the *Christian Advocate* to illustrate this ideology, with its explicit understanding of the supportive relations, in forging individual character, of temperance, religion, Sabbath observation, family role models, and the struggle for personal discipline and self-control; see, e.g., ibid., January 10, March 14, April 11, May 9, 1850; February 18, 1851; April 15, September 23, November 18, 1852; October 29, 1857; April 29, 1858. Theoretical, conceptual, and interpretive approaches to this ideology are to be found in, among others, Lois Banner, "Religious Benevolence as Social Control: A Critique of An Interpretation," *Journal of American History* 50 (June 1973): 23-41; Paul Boyer, *Urban Masses and Moral Order in America, 1820-1920* (Cambridge, Mass.: Harvard Univ. Press, 1978), pp. viii-ix, 5, 12, 30, 45-46, 55, 64, 90; Michael Katz, *The Irony of Early School Reform: Educational Innovation in Mid-Nineteenth Century Massachusetts* (Cambridge, Mass.: Harvard Univ. Press, 1968); Paul Johnson, *A Shopkeepers Millenium: Society and Revivals in Rochester, New York, 1815-1837* (New York: Hill and Wang, 1978), esp. pp. 79-141; David J. Rothman, *The Discovery of the Asylum: Social Order and Disorder in the New Republic* (Boston: Little, Brown, and Company, 1971), pp. 57-78, 161-79; Mary Ryan, *Cradle of the Middle Class: The Family in Oneida County, New York, 1790-1865* (New York: Cambridge Univ. Press, 1981), pp. 145-85 passim, 230-42; Ian R. Tyrell, *Sobering Up: From Temperance to Prohibition in Ante-Bellfum America, 1800-1860*, (Westport, Ct.: Greenwood Press, 1979). For expressions of contempt for the poor, particularly those begging, accepting charity, residing at the poorhouse, or engaging in "work or bread" demonstrations, see *Buffalo Commercial Advertiser*, June 15, 1858; August 22, 1859; January 27, 29, February 15, 1860.

Holding such views of the origins of moral order in society, American Protestant elites in cities like Buffalo could hardly be optimistic about their ability to influence, by example or institutionalized coercion, a constantly expanding immigrant population upon whose behavior the stability of society now depended. Tens of thousands of uprooted peasants with traditional, prebourgeois habits and values attended foreign churches, and often sent their children to Catholic and Lutheran parochial schools in order to protect them from the very cultural influences which Americans wished them to assimilate. The foreigners routinely violated temperance and Sabbath laws. But they voted in such large numbers, motivated to a considerable degree by a desire to safeguard their own traditions through the exercise of political power, that they were allowed to break the law with near impunity. The city's mayors, American Protestants usually willing to compromise the standards of their class and ethnic group to obtain votes, chose the police with partisan rather than law enforcement criteria in mind. The police, who were usually naturalized foreigners in Buffalo's immigrant neighborhoods, had little desire to enforce laws they, too, probably felt were as unneeded as they were repressive. American Protestants, especially more affluent ones, did not live among immigrants. (Indeed, Buffalo had one of the more pronounced tendencies toward ethnic segregation between native and foreigner among the sizable cities of the North.) An occasional American Tract Society colporteur aside, few Protestants had the audacity to venture forth among the immigrants to preach about proper belief and behavior. Along with denominational divisions, this reticence provides an explanation of the meager results of Protestant efforts at converting immigrant Catholics in antebellum Buffalo.[31] Under these circumstances of veritable cultural impotence, pessimists could be excused for their nightmare vision of the republican experiment bequeathed by the Founding Fathers degenerating into a majoritarian tyranny, in which the votes of uneducated foreigners were swayed by the emotional rhetoric of conspiring demagogues.

---

[31] On politics, the police, and Sabbath and temperance laws, see *Buffalo Christian Advocate*, August 15, November 14, December 19, 1850; April 3, May 22, 29, November 27, 1851; July 19, 1854; June 12, 1856; June 4, 1857; *Buffalo Courier*, March 18, April 10, August 23, 1850; *Buffalo Commercial Advertiser*, April 18, 1859. There was a flurry of interest in evangelizing Catholic immigrants in the late 1840s, but by August 1850 it was already maintained that too little was being done, and after that the subject completely disappears from public discussion; see, no author, "Missionary Intelligence," and "Mission Among the Roman Catholic Germans at Buffalo," *The American Protestant*, 5 July 1849): 44-50, and 5 (October, 1849): 145. On ethnic segregation, see Glasco, *Ethnicity and Social Structure*, pp. 65-66, and compare with Sam Bass Warner, Jr., "If All the World Were Philadelphia: A Scaffolding for Urban History, 1774-1930," *American Historical Review*, 73 (February 1968): 35-38. On working class traditionalism, see Herbert Gutman, "Work, Culture, and Society in Industrializing America, 1815-1919," *American Historical Review*, 78 (June 1973): 531-88.

Such a vision was, in fact, central to the message of nativist politicians everywhere in the North.[32]

This very inability to transform political and economic power into cultural authority over the immigrant majority led to a deeper appreciation of Catholic charity, the Catholic clergy, and the Church itself. As the editorial writer previously quoted said of the Sisters of Charity, the Catholic clergy were models of compassionate charity, self-sacrifice, discipline, and, under the rule of the ascetic Timon, not simply thrift, but penury—a penury which, Timon demanded, had to be uncomplaining.[33] Even at the height of nativist agitation, no editorial in either paper ever questioned the personal habits of the Catholic clergy as opposed to its presumed political activities, or made allusion to the lurid gossip about the sex lives of nuns and priests which circulated in nativist circles. A religion which could exact such disciplined behavior in behalf of order and benevolence from its clergy could do so, too, from its lay adherents; and while such secular influence may have been criticized when it came to partisan politics, when the matter was ultimately influencing the development of the type of moral character that kept people orderly and out of the poorhouse, it was deemed laudable. By contrast, Protestantism seemed, in this context at least, flaccid and unsure of itself.

These themes were examined in an editorial, "Matins," in the *Commercial Advertiser* early in 1858; the essay was, that very same day, reprinted in the *Christian Advocate*. The writer reflected on the bells of St. Louis Church sounding early in the morning to summon Catholics to mass, and he conjured up the vision of "the vast, cold church and its kneeling worshippers" attending to their devotions in the semidarkness of a winter dawn. He marveled that the Catholic immigrant worker in the city's factories, "the man whom we see going to his work before the steam-whistle sounds seven o'clock," had probably already been to his prayers at St. Louis or another church. Such rigor and discipline, it was said, "must have a wide influence in shaping the character of our foreign population." Not only were Protestants unable to exert such influ-

---

[32] Billington, *The Protestant Crusade*, pp. 32-84, 322-406; *Buffalo Christian Advocate*, January 1, 1852; *Buffalo Commercial Advertiser*, July 24, 1854; Davis, "Some Themes of Counter-Subversion," pp. 205-24.

[33] Timon to Bishop Kenrick, May 21, 1860, Kenrick Papers, Archives of the Archdiocese of Baltimore, Baltimore, Maryland (hereafter AB); Rev. Thomas Donahue, *History of the Catholic Church in Western New York* (Buffalo: Buffalo Catholic Historical Publishing Co., 1904), pp. 205-6; Deuther, *The Life and Times of the Right Reverend John Timon*, pp. 294, 312-18. As both Donahue and Deuther record, Timon's related insistence on clerical poverty and discipline led to not infrequent conflicts with his priests. Toward the end of Timon's life, in 1864, these conflicts became public when a number of priests published an unsigned pamphlet accusing Timon of greed and persecution of his clergy; see, no author, *To The Right Reverent Bishop Timon* (Buffalo, 1864), Hartford Diocese Collection (1862-1866, I-1-b), UND.

ence upon immigrants, but Protestantism itself, in comparison to Catholicism, seemed lacking in the strictness which formed moral character. Thus, the writer continued, the early morning scene of cold, kneeling worshippers could "never occur in a Protestant Church," for Protestantism was "less exacting of time and physical comfort." A tone not merely of grudging respect, but, it may well be argued, of semiconscious longing for the certainties and discipline of Catholicism, was revealed in closing: the very sound of these bells in the dawn "is sufficient to remind the Protestant of the existence of the religious sentiment within him."[34]

It was perhaps with such thoughts in mind that both papers were pleased by the success of Catholic churches in attracting unusually large crowds of worshippers during that year's Lenten season, and also that the *Christian Advocate* felt encouraged by the "good work" done by Vincentian Fathers when they held a well-attended mission (a Catholic revival) at the cathedral. That at both times these occasions coincided with Protestant revivals or with a general increase in Protestant church attendance may well have further impressed the evangelical paper with the possibility that the parallel activities of both faiths could yield similar, positive results—increased piety, and hence public order and morality.[35] At that particular point, Protestantism and Catholicism could be conceived as having a great deal in common.

Of course, from the point of view of many thoughtful American Protestants, the situation was still far from perfect. Especially to the extent that leaders of Protestant opinion continued to have fears about the political activity of the Catholic clergy, distrust would balance off both admiration and occasional perceptions of common interests. The *Christian Advocate* continued to print letters which called Timon "the enemy" and "anti-Christ" at the very time that it seemed to draw hope from the spread of Catholic religiosity.[36] Both perspectives expressed the divided, ambivalent consciousness Protestants brought to their confrontation with Roman Catholicism.

The two editorials quoted extensively thus far have expressed in diverse ways ambivalence about Catholicism. But if we adjust our angle of vision somewhat, we find another current of ambivalence in them—toward Protestantism and its culture in America. In both editorials, we begin to sense a rueful longing for religious certaintly and for a surrender to faith, both of which might offer resistance to the creeping rationalism and the analytical cast of mind which were eventually, in the late

---

[34] *Buffalo Commercial Advertiser*, January 12, 1858; *Buffalo Christian Advocate*, January 12, 1858.

[35] *Buffalo Commercial Advertiser*, March 18, 1858; *Buffalo Christian Advocate*, March 18, 1858; February 1, 7, 1861.

[36] "Mellen," "Bishop Timon and His Indulgence," letter in *Buffalo Christian Advocate*, October 11, 1860.

nineteenth and early twentieth centuries, to overtake the more theologically liberal sectors of American Protestantism. For many educated, higher status Protestants, as Christopher Lasch pointed out in his striking essay on Jane Addams, religion would gradually be transformed from a set of fixed beliefs based on faith to a code of right conduct based on a loosely conceived religious ethic.[77] Thus, under the influence of much prized, Protestant-inspirited secular values of optimism, individualism, and liberty, liberal Protestantism was being deprived of Christian mystery and religious certainty. While Protestant culture nourished civil society, many of its more liberal adherents were increasingly soul-starved in the realm of faith. A foreshadowing of the resistance to this evolutionary process is clearly visible in the second set of conflicts within elite Protestant culture which influenced the ambivalent response to Catholicism. This was the conflict between the claims of the moral and practical economy of rapidly modernizing American capitalism, with its emphasis on rationalism, materialism, and functionalism, and a quasi-religious striving for spirituality, transcendence of the workaday world, and aesthetic values. This striving created the basis for a hesitant, occasional flirtation, considerably short of religious conversion, with aspects of Catholic culture. To grasp the dynamics of this conflict we must first seek to understand the evolution of Buffalo as a type of new American community and of its American Protestant elite as an aspiring civil leadership group.

In few American cities were the functional relationships between location and commerce which normally provided the raison d'etre for the nation's new, post-1815 cities more apparent than in Buffalo. The city owed its existence and subsequent prosperity and dynamism to its position at the furthest eastern point of continuous navigation of the Great Lakes which had made it the logical choice in 1823 for the location of the terminus of the Erie Canal. Commercial life and the sorting out of social and economic relations across space quickly thereafter came to center around the congested docks of the lake-canal complex, the central point of transshipment for the enormous east-west trade which integrated the economies of most of the antebellum northern states.[78]

In proportion to the local preoccupation with commerce, Buffalo re-

[77] Christopher Lasch, "Jane Addams: The College Woman and the Family Claim," in *The New Radicalism in America, 1889-1963* (New York: Vintage, 1965), pp. 3-37, esp. pp. 3-12; Paul A. Carter, *The Spiritual Crisis of the Gilded Age* (Dekalb: Northern Illinois Univ. Press, 1972); Kenneth Cauthen, *The Impact of American Religious Liberalism* (New York: Harper and Row, Publishers, 1962).

[78] Arthur A. Markowitz, "Joseph Dart and The Emergence of Buffalo as a Grain Port, 1820-1860," *Inland Seas* 25 (Fall 1969): 179-97; Marvin A. Rapp, "The Port of Buffalo, 1825-1860," (unpublished Ph. D. diss., Duke University, 1948), 16-43, 45-99; John G. Clark, *The Grain Trade of the Old Northwest* (Urbana: Univ. of Illinois Press, 1969), pp. 102-23.

mained a rough-hewn city, lacking beauty and civic amenities. As early as the 1830s, the city already looked, as such visitors as Francis Trollope and Harriet Martineau noted, aged, seamy, and shabby—much less because of the passage of time than because of ill-use and inattention to improvement and aesthetics. The streets of the central business district were unpaved and frequently littered, particularly in the crowded area surrounding the docks. Furthermore, like the residential buildings to be found not far away in Buffalo's vast working-class neighborhoods, the commercial structures of the central business district had an ugly, ramshackle uniformity suggesting at once decrepitude, impermanence, and functionalism. Few distinctive buildings gave dignity to the scene observed daily by the city's elite retail and commission merchants, professionals, and manufacturers. Public space in the business district was undeveloped, used, abused, and left to the ravages of neglect. As the city entered the troubled 1850s, few parks or planted squares provided opportunity for quiet repose. For those seeking beauty or culture this was hardly an inspired or inspiring landscape.[30]

As the city's American Protestant elite matured as a social class, and especially after the sobering experience of the 1837 to 1843 depression, it sought increasingly to strike a socially responsible balance between economic stewardship and the pursuit of individual gain, and the exertion of leadership in behalf of civic beautification and improvement. But, like elite welfare activities, these efforts fell short of the mark. American Protestants disagreed among themselves on the exact goals, and especially on the rates, of municipal taxation, and those particularly adamant against taxation for all but the most essential civic needs, such as law enforcement and street paving, found allies in the large population of German cottage owners, who were notably parsimonious. Thus, ambitious plans for public fountains and parks, municipal markets, etc., while not always blocked, were often subject to lengthy, acrimonious, and divisive debate, and at times such plans ultimately were vastly scaled down. Pressure toward the same constraining end in the 1850s came from the decade's two downturns in the business cycle.

[30] Francis Trollope, *Domestic Manners of The Americans* (London: Routledge, 1832), 2: 270-73; Harriet Martineau, *Retrospect of Western Travel* (London: Saunders and Otley, 1838), 1: 90-91; *Buffalo Commercial Advertiser*, March 27, 1854; April 8, 11, 1856; October 31, 1860; Quackenboss and Kennedy, Directors, *Map of The City of Buffalo, New York, Surveyed under The Direction of Quackenboss and Kennedy, Insurance Agents* (New York: Quackenboss and Kennedy, 1854), BECHS; D. A. Sanborn, *Insurance Map of Buffalo, New York, 1868* (New York: Sanborn, 1868), BECHS. Also see Edward Hildebrandt's painting, "Street in Buffalo, New York, 1844" reproduced in Hugh Honor, *The New Golden Land: European Images of America from The Discoveries to The Present Time* (New York: Pantheon, 1975), p. 202. I have identified the scene Hildebrandt painted as a section of lower Main Street in the heart of the central business district. Hildebrandt's depiction of the setting captures its shabbiness, litter and architectural squalor. Honor, p. 203, aptly comments that the city looks "blasted ere her prime" in the painting. The original is in the National-Galerie, Staatliche Museen, East Berlin, German Democratic Republic.

Moreover, by the mid-50s, in both passenger and commodity traffic effective railroad competition with the Erie Canal had created widespread pessimism about Buffalo's future, and necessitated a redevelopment strategy which sought to divert private capital from commerce to manufacturing. Amidst these life and death concerns, civic amenities seemed a luxury. In the last analysis, the compulsions of money-making and demands of economic stewardship always seemed to win out over realization of a civic vision of quality urban life.[40]

Such compulsions and demands also limited the American Protestant elite's own cultural life. Largely in reaction to the growing ethnocultural diversity around them, Americans began in the 1850s to develop ethnic consciousness in the form of concern for the study of local history and for the creation of a local pioneer legend. Even these efforts were impeded by the requirements of commerce. In mid-December 1854, weeks after the brief but intense panic on the New York Stock Exchange, the newly established Pilgrim's Day banquet had to be cancelled by the New England Society because of "the unusual absorption of the community in business." The New England Society itself ceased to exist in the late 1850s, and it wasn't until 1862 that the long-standing desire for local history led to the founding of the Buffalo Historical Society.[41] It is not surprising that in comparison with the Germans and Irish the ethnic communal life of Americans seems, in retrospect, feeble. The *Commercial Advertiser* regularly admitted that the American businessmen and professionals were too engrossed in commerce to organize the picnics, excursions, musical entertainments, and gymnastic demonstrations which were a regular part of German life in Buffalo, but which Americans frequently attended.[42]

The Catholic church came to play a role in local high culture like that

---

[40] Roger Whitman, *Queen's Epic: Benjamin Rathbun and His Times* (unpublished typescript, 1942), pp. 104-87, BECHS; Frank H. Severence, "Historical Sketch of the Board of Trade, the Merchant's Exchange, and the Chamber of Commerce, Buffalo," *Buffalo Historical Society Publications*, 8 (1909); 241-45; John Horton et al., *History of Northwestern New York*, 1: 120-27, 143-72; Sanford B. Hunt, "Buffalo: A Glance at Its Progress down to the Present Time", in no author, *The Manufacturing Interests in the City of Buffalo* (Buffalo, 1866), pp. 13-17; Peter Heller, "Trade and Development in Buffalo from 1815 to 1863" (unpublished typescript, 1968), pp. 51-77, BECHS; *Buffalo Commercial Advertiser*, February 4, 15, 1860.

[41] The most evident manifestation of this "absorption" was that no one had gotten around to commissioning an orator for the occasion; see *Buffalo Commercial Advertiser*, December 19, 1854. A New England Society, the first evidence of more or less explicit ethnic consciousness among Americans, had been founded the year before; ibid., December 22, 1853. Also, ibid., December 4, 14, 1858; and December 31, 1859. N.a., *Seventy-Fifth Anniversary of The Founding of the Buffalo Historical Society* (Buffalo: Buffalo Historical Society, 1937).

[42] *Buffalo Commercial Advertiser*, January 31, June 8, October 14, 1854; November 14, 1856; January 22, March 13, 31, April 6, 1857; January 7, March 10, November 24, 1858; June 14, 15, 21, July 22, August 29, November 8, 1859; May 8, 10, June 28, July 21-26, October 29, 1860; *Buffalo Christian Advocate*, November 17, 1859; July 26, 1860.

played by the Germans in enhancing the quality of life in other cultural contexts. In so doing, the Church helped to foster for many elite American Protestants suffering from cultural anomie the feeling of Buffalo as something more than merely a utilitarian transshipment point, an arena of battles for wealth and power, and an inchoate agglomeration of shabby ethnic neighborhoods besieged by social problems. Through the Church, the city seemed instead a community with roots in a continuous past, and hence in an ancient, Christian tradition within Western civilization. This feeling allowed the city's American Protestant elite to transcend its habitual, daily immersion in one-dimensional, functional and material values and activities, to anchor itself in a past beyond its own existence, and to pay heed to aesthetic values. Of course, Protestantism and the cultural myths of the Founding Fathers and of the Yankee and Yorker pioneers in frontier western New York played similar roles. But evangelical Protestantism was too austere to explore either art or the aesthetic dimensions of religion, both of which were more the domain of Catholicism; and these secular, partriotic myths were too new and unformed to supply a feeling of continuity and rootedness.

These impulses may best be understood in connection with the complex relationship of American Protestant opinion leaders to St. Joseph's Cathedral, the seat of the Buffalo diocese, which Timon struggled for almost a decade to raise sufficient funds—in Mexico, Europe, and America—to build. When completed in 1855, the cathedral, which dwarfed nearby St. John's Episcopal Church and was considerably more ornate, was clearly the most impressive and artistically appealing structure in Buffalo. It was powerful material evidence, as Timon himself understood, of the cultural authority and permanence of Roman Catholicism, and it was positioned intentionally close enough to the docks and railroad stations to be seen by tens of thousands of travelers and immigrants every year. In soliciting funds, visibility had been one of Timon's main arguments: this was to be not just any cathedral, but one symbolizing Catholicism for the many travelers passing through the leading transportation center of the nation's northern heartland.[43]

There was a good deal of Protestant criticism of the costs of the construction and decoration of the cathedral and other Catholic churches. Both the nativistic *Express* and the *Christian Advocate* argued that the

---

[43] Donahue, *History of the Catholic Church in Western New York*, pp. 139-40; Timon to Cardinal Barnabo, June 5, 1862, Scritturi, Congregation of the Propaganda Fide Collection, and Timon to Archbishop Bedini, August 28, 1856, Udienzi, Congregation of the Propaganda Fide Collection, UND; Timon to Archbishop Kenrick, December 9, 1852, Kenrick Papers, AB; Timon to M. les Directeurs, December 28, 1849, Société de La Propaganda de La Foi de Paris et Lyon Collection, UND. Cincinnati's Bishop Purcell also used strategically placed, decorative and large churches to impress non-Catholics; Joseph White, "Religion and Community: Cincinnati Germans, 1814-1870" (unpublished Ph.D. diss., University of Notre Dame, 1980), 173, 184-185.

Church would better serve Christ and society by relieving the growing number of immigrant, Catholic poor. The evangelical paper also maintained that such ostentatious cathedrals were merely ideal sites for "the egregiously nonsensical and pompous" Catholic ceremonies and "proud aristocracy and emblazoned buffonery" which it said characterized the Church. It charged, too, that the outdoor processions and ceremonies, accompanied by loud music, which were part of church dedications, were too often held on the Sabbath.[44] For its part, the *Commercial Advertiser*, which understood that the money for the construction of the cathedral and other churches was often raised outside the city, objected to the notion of the diocesan weekly, the *Sentinel*, that the new structures were evidence of local Catholic prosperity. The *Advertiser* worried about what presumably malevolent forces were really paying the bills.[45]

But the fact remained that many Protestants of the upper classes were also drawn to the cathedral, both in its blueprint and finished stages. Some may simply have recognized that it would bring tourists to Buffalo,[46] but for others the attractions of the cathedral seem to have sprung from much deeper sources. Millard Fillmore and a number of other Protestant leaders contributed to the construction fund.[47] In the case of Fillmore, a Unitarian, we sense a furtive flirtation with the ceremony, decoration, and history of Catholicism, which he and a small group of wealthy Buffalonians were also absorbing during trips to Europe to seek cultivation in the 1850s.[48] The fact that Fillmore had been secretly inducted into a local Know-Nothing lodge early in 1855 (amidst a different pomp and ceremony) did not stop him from seeking an audience with the Pope during a European tour ten months later; and several months after that cordial audience Fillmore accepted the American party nomination for president![49] The *Commercial Advertiser* found the cathedral's artwork, much of which Timon had brought from Europe, "beautiful" and the ceremonies accompanying the var-

[44] *Buffalo Christian Advocate*, February 13, 1851; December 25, 1856; November 26, 1857; *Buffalo Courier*, November 24, 1857 (in which an unsigned letter states, in order to refute, the opinion of the *Express*).

[45] *Buffalo Commercial Advertiser*, June 7, 1858.

[46] *Buffalo Courier*, November 24, 1857.

[47] Donahue, *History of the Catholic Church in Western New York*, pp. 202-4; Robert J. Rayback, *Millard Fillmore: Biography of A President* (Buffalo: Buffalo Historical Society, 1959), p. 407.

[48] On elite travel to Europe, *Buffalo Commercial Advertiser*, June 4, 1857; no author, *Fifth Annual Festival of the Old Settlers of Buffalo* (Buffalo: Old Settlers of Buffalo, 1868), p. 13.

[49] Rayback, *Millard Fillmore*, pp. 396-407; Elbridge Spaulding to William Henry Seward, August 2, 1856, Seward-Weed Papers, Archives, University of Rochester, Rochester, New York; Millard Fillmore to Solomon G. Haven, January 22, 1856, in *The Papers of Millard Fillmore, Publications of the Buffalo Historical Society*, ed. Frank Severance (Buffalo: Buffalo Historical Society, 1907), 2: 354-57.

ious dedications, like the consecration of the chimes in 1857, "very imposing."[50] Some Protestants regularly attended lectures by Timon and other priests (even when the subject was religion) at the cathedral and other Catholic churches, while an even larger number were present at concerts for Catholic charities, such as the 1857 and 1859 performances at the cathedral of Handel's Messiah.[51] It is difficult not to accept Jackson Lears's evaluation of this attraction: that the Catholic cathedral, in Buffalo and elsewhere, created a cultured counterworld within the city, outside the utilitarian, commercial environment, and offered therapeutic repose.[52]

Similar strivings for high culture and identification with a continuous cultural tradition motivated Protestant patronage of the expensive boarding and day schools, which European teaching orders, invited to Buffalo by Timon, established in the early 1850s. Sisters of the Sacred Heart, who were said by a correspondent of the *Commercial Advertiser* to have the advantage of being "of high birth, great merit, and . . . French," conducted, according to the same correspondent, "the best female school in the city." In order to attract Protestant students, who were, practically speaking, the only ones likely to be able to pay the tuition, these schools promised that no theology or religion would be taught and that the curriculum would not depart from the formal academic model of the day (classical and modern languages, the arts, and the history of Western civilization), which was perhaps risky enough. This was the promise contained, for example, in the "Prospectus" of St. Joseph's College, a high school opened in 1851 by the French Oblates of St. Mary.[53]

But here again, Protestant ambivalence is in evidence. Neither of these efforts appears to have been able to survive the deepening of sectarian hostilities, and it is not clear the extent to which the small, nondiocesan day school begun by several teaching orders in the later 1850s succeeded in attracting Protestants.[54] Doubtless many affluent Protestant parents had begun to fear clerical influence over their children, perhaps at the very same time they were recognizing the important role

---

[50] *Buffalo Commercial Advertiser*, May 17, 1856; August 3, 1857. The paper had similar comments about other Catholic church dedications; ibid., August 23, 25, 1856; February 23, 1857; March 26, 1858. At the dedication of the Church of the Immaculate Conception in August 1856, the paper described what it called "a fine scene," but added, perhaps displaying some ambivalence, how far America had come from "the primitive simplicity of Plymouth Rock."

[51] *Buffalo Courier*, January 30, 1858; *Buffalo Commercial Advertiser*, January 30, 1858; April 13, 1858; June 29, 1859.

[52] Lears, *No Place of Grace*, p. 194.

[53] Donahue, *History of the Catholic Church in Western New York*, pp. 200-1, 319-24; *Buffalo Courier*, January 4, April 28, 1851; *Buffalo Commercial Advertiser*, November 28, 1853. Fillmore sent his own daughter to the Academy of the Sacred Heart; Rayback, *Millard Fillmore*, p. 407.

[54] Donahue, *History of the Catholic Church in Western New York*, pp. 201, 319-24.

the Catholic clergy was carving out for itself through its charitable and public health activities, or they were contributing money toward the construction of the cathedral. We should not allow such contradictory behavior merely to suggest confusion or hypocrisy. In its historical context, it may instead be seen as evidence of a process, only then just beginning and as yet unrationalized, of accommodation and ultimately social conciliation between affluent Protestants and the Catholic church. Though certainly not without its sore points, this process would grow in intensity during the next century. It would be furthered considerably in the midst of yet more massive immigration during the period from 1870 to 1920 by a continuing consensus on the necessity of determined efforts to create the individual and institutional foundations of moral order in a pluralistic, increasingly urbanized society. Furthermore, in the concurrent age of industrialization, this process would be strongly reinforced by a mutual antagonism to labor radicalism and socialism, and separate, though similar, searches for a social gospel through which to confront the severe social dislocations and suffering accompanying the rise of the modern factory.[35] But, as Lears had demonstrated in examining these later transitional decades, this process would also be aided by the curious psychological and cultural attraction a faith with deep and abiding premodern roots held for some members of the class and ethnic group which produced America's most determined modernizers.

[35] Henry May, *Protestant Churches and Industrial America* (New York: Harper and Row, Publishers, 1949); Aaron I. Abell, *American Catholicism and Social Action: A Search for Social Justice, 1865-1950* (Garden City: Doubleday and Co., 1960); Henry J. Browne, *The Catholic Church and the Knights of Labor* (Washington, D.C.: Catholic Univ. Press, 1949).

THE "FLINT AFFAIR":
FRENCH-CANADIAN STRUGGLE FOR *SURVIVANCE*

BY

PHILIP T. SILVIA, JR.*

Fall River, situated at the southeastern corner of Massachusetts, fifty miles south of Boston, was the largest city in Bristol County during its halcyon years. More importantly, in the generation following the Civil War it became the foremost center of cotton textile manufacturing in the Western Hemisphere. At the outbreak of the Civil War the conversion process from a slumbering early nineteenth-century agrarian village into a thriving manufacturing community had been partially effected. By then local Yankee investors had constructed eight textile mills along the Quequechan stream whose course flowed through the heart of the city. But it was in the postwar era, when the introduction of steam power lessened dependence upon a water source, that Fall River enjoyed its most impressive industrial growth. Cotton reigned as king by the 1880's, for this one-industry community boasted fifty-two cotton mills which produced three-fifths of the nation's medium-grade print cloth.[1]

This industrial acceleration fed at first upon a local, native-American labor supply. An insatiable demand for mill hands was then supplied by successive waves of people from England, Ireland, and Quebec which converted Fall River into a city of immigrants. The magnetic attraction was the nearly guaranteed mill employment, even for the unskilled. As a result, Fall River's population swelled beyond 56,000 by 1885, more than triple the figure of twenty years prior. The impact of the foreign-born was obvious, for as early as 1875 they comprised more than one-half of the population. A disproportionate percentage of these newcomers sought mill employment; by the late 1870's three-quarters of the operatives had been

* Mr. Silvia is an associate professor of history in Bridgewater State College, Massachusetts.

[1] Victor S. Clark, *History of Manufactures in the United States* (New York, 1929), II, 394; Massachusetts Bureau of Statistics of Labor, *Thirteenth Annual Report* (1882), pp. 220, 228-229.

born outside the United States.[2]

Of all the newcomers, the French Canadians generated the most controversy. Their timing was poor. Thousands of them poured into the city during the turbulent 1870's, a decade marred by labor discord.[3] A portion of immigrants from the British Isles already settled in Fall River by that time had brought with them the textile training and special skills necessary for mill expansion. Ever since the 1840's, however, their aggressive trade unionism had been a source of exasperation for the Yankee hierarchy who controlled the factories. By the 1870's the owners were determined to crush the organized workers. The Canadians were useful pawns in the struggle; escaping farmland poverty, they wanted work for sustenance only, without conflict. Although careful to preserve a social barrier, management for selfish reasons welcomed the French Canadians as correctives offsetting the Lancashire "agitator" segment of their mill force. The reaction of the skilled unionists, especially among the mule spinners, was understandably different when the French refused to support Irish and English workers who walked off their jobs three times between 1870 and 1879 in valiant but futile efforts to prevent severe wage cutbacks. Canadian submissiveness in the economic realm of affairs was incomprehensible to the skilled craftsmen, who contemptuously agreed with the statement, hardly a compliment in its day, that these French were "the Chinese of the Eastern States."[4]

From the moment of their arrival, then, these French Canadians were bewildered cultural strangers in an English-language society which was, at best, indifferent to them. Driven to a sense of ethnic survival, they sought to cling tenaciously to their religion which

---

[2] Commonwealth of Massachusetts, Bureau of Statistics of Labor, *Census of Massachusetts: 1885. Population and Social Statistics*, I, pt. 1, lxxiv, 66-67; Massachusetts Bureau of Statistics of Labor, *Thirteenth Annual Report* (1882), p. 204.

[3] Despite a noticeable tendency toward out-migration by Canadians returning to Quebec, which gave them a reputation as "rolling stones," their net gain in Fall River was remarkable between 1870 and 1888—from 1,129 to 15,551. U.S., Bureau of the Census, *Ninth Census of the United States: 1870. Population*, I, 386; *Le Guide Canadien-Français de Fall River et Notes Historiques sur les Canadiens de Fall River*, ed. Edmond F. Lamoureux (Fall River, 1888), p. 256.

[4] Massachusetts Bureau of Statistics of Labor, *Twelfth Annual Report* (1881), p. 470; *Thirteenth Annual Report* (1882), p. 3. A section of the 1882 publication contains a wealth of recorded testimony given by prominent French-Canadian spokesmen who stressed the positive contributions being made within various New England communities by their ethnic group. They managed to contradict effectively charges of racial inferiority which had been leveled against their people in the previous report.

would additionally help to preserve their language and culture. At first they were frustrated because they usually lived without the spiritual solace of their own priests. Despite the appeals by Archbishop John J. Williams of Boston and Bishop Louis de Goësbriand of Burlington, Vermont, it was not until 1869 that the Canadian hierarchy finally permitted eight priests to join permanently the Canadian émigrés in New England.[5] Fall River then waited five more years before receiving its first French-Canadian priest, whose presence would assume significance both during his lifetime and even in his death, which marked the opening round of a classic struggle against the assimilating tendencies of the Irish hierarchy. Until very recently, the defense of ethnic parochialism by French Canadians in Fall River as well as other New England locales, though forming an important chapter in American Catholic history, has not received the attention it warrants because of the historical focus on German-American Catholic nationalism and its resistance to Irish domination of the Catholic Church in the United States.[6]

Trickling into Fall River during the Civil War years, a small colony of these immigrants from the north were clustered together by 1865 in a "Petit Canada" tenement area controlled by one of the mills located near the city's center.[7] By 1870 the number of Canadians in the city had surpassed the 1,000 mark. These newcomers worshiped at the Church of St. Mary of the Assumption, a Gothic structure built with Fall River granite to replace a wooden chapel that had catered to Irish residents since the 1830's. The pastor of St. Mary's was the Reverend Edward Murphy, the "Grand Old Man" among the city's

[5] Mason Wade, "French and French Canadians in the United States," *New Catholic Encyclopedia* (15 vols.; New York, 1967), VI, 146.

[6] Mason Wade provides an excellent exception to this generalization in his study of "The French Parish and *Survivance* in Nineteenth Century New England," *Catholic Historical Review*, XXXVI (July, 1950), 163-189. Three doctoral dissertations have also provided correctives to prior historiographical deficiencies regarding the religious perspective of French Canadians, particularly the work of Richard S. Sorrell, "The Sentinelle Affaire (1924-1929) and Militant *Survivance*: The Franco-American Experience in Woonsocket, Rhode Island" (unpublished Ph.D. dissertation, State University of New York at Buffalo, 1975). See also Michael J. Guignard, "Ethnic Survival in a New England Mill Town: The Franco-Americans of Biddeford, Maine" (unpublished Ph.D. dissertation, Syracuse University, 1976), and Peter Haebler, "Habitants in Holyoke: The Development of the French-Canadian Community in a Massachusetts City, 1865-1910" (unpublished Ph.D. dissertation, University of New Hampshire, 1976).

[7] *Le Guide Canadien-Français de Fall River*, p. 123.

Roman Catholic clergy of the nineteenth century.[8]

In response to an obvious need, Father Murphy permitted three missionaries from France to serve under him for short intervals during the late 1860's. This pastoral service for the French Canadians finally assumed a permanent character with the arrival in the summer of 1869 of the Abbé Paul Romain-Louis-Adrien de Montaubricq, a descendant from a long line of nobility, and an honorary canon of Bordeaux.[9]

By January, 1870, ground was being broken for the first church that would accommodate French-Canadian Catholics exclusively. Because of both encouragement by Archbishop Williams and discouragement over a lack of sympathy (toward himself and the Canadians) shown by Father Murphy and some of the Irish Catholics, Montaubricq had worked feverishly to complete this new religious edifice. His rush to achieve independence led to catastrophe when a temporary floor buckled under the weight of those attending a March opening of the church. More than thirty of those worshipers who were cast into the church basement required medical treatment. Despite this tragic accident, St. Anne's Church was again readied and officially dedicated during November by Archbishop Williams in an accident-free ceremony.[10]

In 1872 St. Anne's and Fall River's other parishes became part of the newly created Diocese of Providence, which had a jurisdiction encompassing Rhode Island and crossing into Massachusetts, where it included Bristol and several other counties. The first bishop of Providence was Irish-born Thomas F. Hendricken. Now that the sympathetic Williams of Boston was no longer their immediate spiritual leader, Fall River's Canadians anxiously waited to learn of Hendricken's attitute toward them.

Within two years of assuming office, Bishop Hendricken had approved construction of a second church for Fall River's French Cath-

[8] In the wake of missionary work among the Penobscot Indians of Maine, Murphy had begun in 1840 the first of what became forty-seven consecutive years of service as rector of St. Mary's. Robert H. Lord, John E. Sexton, and Edward T. Harrington, *History of the Archdiocese of Boston in the Various Stages of Its Development, 1604 to 1943* (New York, 1944), II, 164, 282-283, 502.

[9] Hugo A. Dubuque, *Les Canadiens Français de Fall River, Mass.*, ed. H. Boisseau (Fall River, 1883), p. 4; "Les Dominicains à Fall River," *Le Rosaire*, LXXIV (June-August, 1969), 15.

[10] "Les Dominicains à Fall River," p. 17; *Fall River Daily Evening News*, March 21, 26, November 5, 1870.

olics located in proximity to the Flint mill[11] in the city's burgeoning eastern section. Impediments of distance and poor roads, combined with St. Anne's inadequate sanctuary accommodations, were the reasons that inspired more than 600 French living in the Flint to petition the bishop for permission to establish a church in their area staffed by a French-Canadian pastor.

Bishop Hendricken responded by appointing Father Charles Dauray of Woonsocket, Rhode Island, to embark upon a mission to locate a fellow French-Canadian priest for these people. While on his way to Canada, Dauray's journey was unexpectedly shortened. Stopping at Worcester, Massachusetts, he was introduced to Pierre Jean Baptiste Bedard. In the course of conversation Bedard inquired whether he could apply for the pastorate. This thirty-two-year-old priest viewed this as his God-sent opportunity, for he had been vicar of several rural Canadian churches which had taken on ghostly qualities because of a mass exodus to the United States. On a former occasion, after sadly driving fifty of his parishioners bound for the United States to a railroad depot, Bedard had prayed that he might one day be assigned to a United States manufacturing center, because he feared the émigrés' loss of "faith and patriotism."[12]

Upon returning to Providence, Dauray presented Bedard to the bishop, whose first comment, spoken in a heavy Irish brogue, was, "Where did you pick up that big fat fellow?"[13] Hendricken was nevertheless satisfied, and Bedard offered the first Mass at Flint village before a crude altar constructed of planks and lime barrels at the site of a house being built for an Irishman, Henry McGee. A subscription list was then taken, and within six weeks a wooden chapel housed the city's east-end Catholic worshipers. This Flint parish of Notre Dame de Lourdes represented an inversion from the situation at St. Mary's in the late 1860's, for Bedard began as spiritual guide for from 250 to 300 Canadian families, while his Irish-American curate cared for a minority of some forty Irish families.[14]

[11] John D. Flint moved from Vermont to Fall River in 1847, and by 1855 owned a tin peddling business. He profited by real estate sales in 1871 of his two farms which covered the land area of the city's east side. Both this section and the mill that he built in 1872 were named after him. Biographical sketch, Fall River Drawer, Fall River Public Library.

[12] P. U. Vaillant, *Notes Biographiques sur Messire P. J. Bédard* (Fall River, 1886), pp. 10-11; D. M. A. Magnon, *Notre Dame de Lourdes de Fall River, Massachusetts* (Quebec, 1925), pp. 34-36, 42-43.

[13] Magnon, *op. cit.*, p. 37.

[14] *Ibid.*, pp. 33, 47-48; *Le Guide Français de Fall River, Mass.* (Fall River, 1909), p. 119.

During most of the remainder of the 1870's the ministry of the zealous French priest won the admiration of his entire congregation.[15] The English-speaking parish minority were estranged, however, when Bedard became the "knobstick" or scab priest during an 1879 strike. Ignoring a reprimand from the bishop, Bedard actively recruited Canadian strikebreakers and exhorted his people to continue at work and replace Irish and English operatives who had walked off their jobs in protest against a wage reduction. Undeterred at this time by threats on his life and vandalism of church records, Bedard continued to co-operate with management during 1882 by recruiting more potential strikebreakers from Canada. This was more than the Irish Catholics of Flint village could bear; the bishop permitted them to separate from Notre Dame and to construct Immaculate Conception Church.[16]

Bedard's actions created an underlying economic friction which fanned the flames of ethnic hatred when a volatile crisis over the question of religious authority engulfed Notre Dame in 1884. In the six years prior to the "Flint affair," however, most of the danger signals pointing to a degree of French-Irish disharmony had surfaced in a series of incidents at St. Anne's Parish centering around an Irish priest, Thomas Briscoe, who had been appointed in 1878 as Montaubricq's successor by Hendricken. The new pastor's national origins, combined with his indifference toward their budding political aspirations, provoked certain Canadian parishioners to such an extent that they appealed to Rome for a French-Canadian pastor.[17] Nevertheless, this initial ethnocentrism was of an extremely mild variety, for most of his congregation rallied to Briscoe's support.[18] Friction had apparently been muted somewhat because many of those French Canadians most concerned with ethnic identity had removed themselves from Briscoe's and even from Montaubricq's ecclesiastical

[15] *Daily Evening News*, August 24, November 13, 1875, April 19, 1877; *Fall River Daily Herald*, August 18, September 20, November 7, 1877.

[16] *Le Guide Français de Fall River, Mass.*, p. 22; Vaillant, *op. cit.*, pp. 14-20; *Weekly Visitor* (Providence, Rhode Island), July 20, 1879; *New York Times*, March 26, 1882; *Daily Herald*, May 29, 1882. Hendricken explained to Rome that Bedard's "impudence" had driven Irish Catholics from Notre Dame. Hendricken to Giovanni Cardinal Simeoni, Prefect of the Sacred Congregation de Propaganda Fide, September 25, 1880, Archives of the Diocese of Fall River.

[17] *Le Guide Français de Fall River, Mass.*, p. 32; *Daily Evening News*, February 8, 1879; *Daily Herald*, November 13, 20-21, December 11, 17, 1882; Simeoni to Hendricken, April 3, 1879, Archives of the Diocese of Fall River.

[18] *Daily Evening News*, April 19, 1879; *Daily Herald*, December 16-17, 1882.

jurisdiction by transferring to the familiar and comfortable confines of Notre Dame, which more perfectly mirrored Canadian parish life.[19]

But even the meekest of these St. Anne's ethnics was jolted during 1883. The bishop initially consented to a subdivision of St. Anne's during that year. Father Montaubricq, now residing in the southern or Globe section of Fall River, promised to underwrite all construction expenses for a church that would more conveniently service the Canadians of the Globe and its adjacent area, North Tiverton, Rhode Island. Upon learning of this potential loss of parishioners together with the financial support they provided, Briscoe appealed and Hendricken consented to reverse his decision. A broken-hearted Montaubricq sailed for France, never to return.[20] The apparent injustice associated with these developments rankled French Canadians for decades to come; at the time it seemed to confirm their suspicion that Hendricken was callously indifferent to the feelings of Catholics who did not happen to be Irish.[21]

By 1884 a wounded French-Canadian pride looked to Father Bedard of Notre Dame for healing power. To Fall River's Canadians he was already a living legend, a ubiquitous father figure to be trusted in temporal as well as spiritual affairs. It was common practice for family heads recently arrived at Flint village to seek out this priest, who would arrange for living quarters and act as an intermediary securing mill employment for their children. Bedard could also be counted upon to help his people pay debts by lending them money, and his was the binding arbitral word settling numerous domestic quarrels. Whether it was in organizing a religious festival excursion to Montreal, speaking at a French banquet, dealing with musical bands, serving as a director of a co-operative shoe store, or challenging native Americans to substantiate anti-Canadian criticisms,[22] Bedard

[19] Pressured by Rome, Hendricken had acceded reluctantly to Bedard's request to add about 120 families to Notre Dame. The bishop implored Cardinal Simeoni to support his authority which an irreverent Bedard was undermining by inciting the Notre Dame French into making "totally absurd" demands. If these demands were treated with sympathy by Rome, the bishop insisted that he would not be able to govern. Hendricken to Simeoni, September 25, 1880, Archives of the Diocese of Fall River.

[20] *Daily Evening News*, August 20, 1883; *Daily Herald*, August 17, September 20, 1883.

[21] *Le Guide Canadian-Français de Fall River*, p. 141; *Le Guide Français de Fall River, Mass.*, p. 31.

[22] Vaillant, *op. cit.*, p. 13; *Weekly Visitor*, September 6, 1884; *Daily Evening News*, May 27, November 2, 1876, June 23, 1877, June 19, 1880; *Daily Herald*, September 6, 1877, May 25, 1883.

was the omnipresent figure within his ethnic community.[23]

Unfortunately for his dependent parishioners, this priest's huge physique, booming voice, and dynamism masked an ailing body. Though apparently in the prime of life, Bedard's health began to fail, a condition aggravated by work resulting from his obdurate unwillingness to accept any more Irish curates after the formation of Immaculate Conception.[24] The bishop had retaliated on several occasions by refusing to grant French-Canadian priests passing through Fall River the power to assist the overtaxed pastor. The end came on August 24, 1884, with the cause of death officially listed as apoplexy.[25]

The French-Canadian community was stunned. Mills in the eastern section of the city were forced to close their gates on the day of the funeral. The doors of Notre Dame were also shut during the funeral Mass to protect the capacity throng of mourners from the crush of hundreds on the outside trying to squeeze into the church.[26] These bereaved parishioners knew that one of their beloved pastor's last wishes had been for a French-Canadian successor.[27] This became the battlecry of the French Canadians living in Flint village.

By way of material improvements alone, P. J. B. Bedard had contributed greatly to his parish during his ten-year pastorate. Shortly after arriving in the Flint he had purchased the land upon which Our

[23] He was not, however, always omnipotent. Despite their love for the pastor and their own reputation for complete submission to priests, even his most ardent Canadian loyalists recognized that the fiery-tempered Bedard had faults, including a dictatorial nature which they sometimes challenged. Vaillant, *op. cit.*, p. 48; *Daily Evening News*, October 5, 1881; *Daily Herald*, October 25, 1881; *Daily Sun* (Fall River), November 9, 12, 1881.

[24] Magnon, *op. cit.*, p. 56. According to his contemporary biographer, Bedard's previous Irish assistants worked at cross-purposes with their pastor, acted as spies reporting his actions to Hendricken, and, along with other Irish priests in Fall River, ridiculed the French-Canadian priest at every opportunity. Briscoe even refused him permission to enter St. Anne's Rectory. Vaillant, *op. cit.*, pp. 17-18.

[25] *Daily Herald*, August 25, 1884. About a week before, Bedard had cut himself severely with a razor. His critics pointed to this incident as the ultimate cause of death and contended that it was a suicide attempt. The coroner and two French-Canadian physicians swore that the razor wound had been accidentally inflicted. Vaillant, *op. cit.*, pp. 25, 36-37, 48.

[26] *Daily Evening News*, August 27, 1884; Vaillant, *op. cit.*, p. 42. By 1885 the farmland of 1871 had become the foundation for five hundred houses, plus one merino and five cotton textile mills. *Daily Evening News*, October 29, 1885.

[27] *Le Guide Français de Fall River, Mass.*, p. 32.

Lady of Lourdes was raised, along with some adjoining plots, all in the bishop's name. Receiving an inheritance of a few thousand dollars, Bedard used this windfall to buy large tracts adjacent to the bishop's land. He then subdivided and sold most of this property at a time when real estate values were skyrocketing. A portion of his profit was used for building an orphanage. With his own funds, Bedard also built a parish school and purchased a home which was converted into a rectory.[28]

Unfortunately, this physical development led to friction between Bedard and Hendricken because the Canadian priest managed to circumvent his superior's economic control over Notre Dame. The difficulty emerged after Bedard, who had been paying municipal taxes levied upon his parish's educational and charitable buildings, was told by a city tax assessor that incorporation of the property as a religious and charitable organization would make it tax-exempt according to state law. When this information was verified by a lawyer, Bedard, who had been delivering sermons about preserving French-language religious services and was well aware of Hendricken's assimilation philosophy, reverted to the *syndique* or Canadian church method of parish autonomy in financial affairs. In April, 1883, he became president of Notre Dame Corporation. The following February he relinquished control to a group of nine prominent male parishioners, at the same time generously awarding the corporation his entire personal property, which could be sold as the directors willed.[29]

At a March, 1884, meeting these trustees voted to make legal arrangements to restore all property except religious and educational edifices to their priest, but Bedard did not take the time to draw up a contract granting this return. Subsequent to Bedard's death, then, these men, though without the power to prevent Hendricken from appointing a successor of his choosing, did have the right to keep priests off corporation property.[30]

By the time of Bedard's demise in 1884 the bishop was certainly displeased by the economic independence conferred on Notre Dame

[28] *L'Indépendant* (Fall River), April 10, 1885.

[29] *Ibid.*; Magnon, *op. cit.*, pp. 50-51; Jacques Ducharme, *The Shadows of the Trees: The Story of French-Canadians in New England* (New York, 1943), pp. 76-77. Another primary source lists only five rather than nine trustees—a wholesale liquor dealer, pharmacist, funeral director, produce dealer, and a baker. *Le Guide Canadien-Français de Fall River*, pp. 191, 193.

[30] *L'Indépendant*, April 10, 1885.

Corporation. There was, moreover, an overriding cause for contention involving the opposing theories about the proper organization of the Catholic Church in the United States of the late nineteenth century. As is commonly known, the predominantly Irish hierarchy promoted the territorial and opposed the ethnic parish concept, believed in assimilation, and were trying to eliminate *survivance*, or separate ethnic identity.[31] They were convinced that a one-language (English) church would facilitate administration, help repress ethnic rivalry, and pave the way for native-American acceptance of Catholicism as something more than a "foreign" religion.

Bishop Hendricken, a disciple of this thought pattern, was determined to undo the evil caused by Bedard, whom even French Canadians admitted had perhaps been too hypernationalistic.[32] Nevertheless, despite this resoluteness, the bishop permitted a lull to exist before the storm. Until October the Notre Dame Corporation was satisfied with the ministry of Bedard's interim successor Edouard E. Nobert, another French-Canadian priest, who sympathized with his parishioners. Unfortunately for all concerned, Nobert, overburdened by the demands of this large parish, and in poor health, requested and was given another assignment.[33]

The powderkeg of distrust exploded when Hendricken announced the appointment of the Reverend Samuel Patrick McGee as pastor of Notre Dame effective October 11, 1884. McGee, Canadian-born but of Irish parentage,[34] was a young man of thirty who had been ordained at Montreal and had celebrated his first Mass at Notre Dame Church on Christmas morning, 1880. At that time he had been visiting his brother Henry, the Flint village grocer and conspicuous founding member of Notre Dame parish.[35]

The parish trustees, claiming to represent majority sentiment, delegated responsibility to five members who visited the bishop and attempted to persuade him to reverse his decision and appoint a French-Canadian priest. Hendricken's response was disheartening. Condemning their excessive ethnic pride, he forcefully told these

---

[31] Wade, "French Parish and *Survivance*," p. 163.
[32] Magnon, *op. cit.*, p. 63.
[33] *Daily Evening News*, October 16, 1884.
[34] McGee was an exception in the sense that few of the thousands of Anglo-Canadians emigrating to Massachusetts settled in Fall River. Neither were the missionary priests from France joined by their countrymen. Therefore, the terms Canadian, French, and French Canadian have been used interchangeably in this paper.
[35] *Daily Evening News*, November 5, 1885; *Daily Herald*, December 23, 1880.

supplicants that the appointee, McGee, spoke better French than they could speak![36] Obviously disturbed by this hostile reaction, the Notre Dame directors responded by authorizing a campaign of economic coercion against McGee. Parishioners, now bound together to make life trying for the "Irish priest," agreed not to approach him for baptisms or marriages, both of which were sources of priestly income. On November 2, 1884, the corporation laymen collected and appropriated Mass offerings, unruffled by McGee's threat to obtain arrest warrants and prosecute for larceny. The trustees then implemented their power by issuing to McGee a two weeks' notice to vacate the pastoral residence and, when that time had passed, insisted that the priest respect their demand. McGee complied by moving tc the home of his brother Henry, who by now was indulging in "violent language" against the corporation.[37]

Throughout November the *Fall River Daily Evening News* was filled with letters from parishioners explaining developments at Notre Dame. They were written as correctives to various articles appearing in the *Fall River Daily Herald*,[38] a newspaper that was guilty of irresponsible and biased journalism as it campaigned to defend McGee and raise the level of its readers' ire against the French Canadians. Thus, for example, the *Daily Herald* inaccurately reported that the pastor's residence was paid for by parishioner contributions, that Father Nobert had been "disrespectfully treated," that someone had stood up during church services and yelled at McGee "to go to h-ll," and that the English-speaking people at Notre Dame were joined by the better class of French Canadians in favoring the Irish priest.[39] Even Father Nobert, now residing in Rhode Island, entered the fray by forwarding a written communication in which he not only denied the *Daily Herald*'s statement about his treatment, but further labeled it "an outrageous falsehood, tinctured with prejudice, an insult to the congregation of Notre Dame de Lourdes, the French people of Fall River, and to me as a priest."[40] Another letter dwelt upon the

---

[36] *Daily Herald*, November 4, 1884. According to Bedard's biographer, the bishop also said: " 'What! give you another priest like Father Bedard? . . . Father Bedard was a curse to me, a curse to you and a curse to everybody!' " Vaillant, *op. cit.*, p. 30.

[37] *Daily Herald*, November 4, 6, 1884; *Daily Evening News*, November 5, 1884.

[38] Accuracy tinged with condescension marked the *Daily Evening News* reportage of developments involving Notre Dame. This journal was controlled by Yankee Protestants, while the rival *Daily Herald*'s stockholders were primarily Irish Catholics.

[39] *Daily Herald*, November 5, 17, 1884; *Daily Evening News*, November 12, 1884.

[40] *Daily Evening News*, November 10, 1884.

obvious—that there were no exclusively English-speaking, that is, Irish Catholics left at Notre Dame to support McGee. This missive also defended the trustees' confiscation of the Mass offerings, claiming that a prior notice of intent had been issued, and that the donations would be used only for necessary upkeep of corporation property. It was stated, furthermore, that the trustees felt no personal animus toward McGee, but were "simply taking into our hands the management of the temporal affairs of the parish."[41]

There was one unsavory incident during November. The *Daily Herald* informed its clientele that on the evening of November 15 the McGees were awakened by the sound of breaking glass, and discovered that "half a dozen old whiskey bottles filled with sewage from a privy vault were thrown in through the window . . . stifling the air with the sickening odor of the bottles' contents, which were scattered about the room."[42] Inspired by the *Daily Herald*'s denunciation of this criminal action, which it intimated had been devised by a baker, a body of McGee's indignant supporters marched to Mayor Milton Reed's office and demanded protection for the priest. The mayor, concerned with preserving public order, decided to assign a police guard around Notre Dame every Sunday. Corporation director Joseph L. Audet, a baker by vocation, considered a police cordon insulting, and denied that he or any other Notre Dame parishioner had participated in the window-smashing vandalism. Audet insisted that an outsider had plotted this "ruffianly" action in order to discredit the French Canadians who could then be blamed for an action which was entirely contrary to their "usual politeness and decency."[43]

During December, Father McGee met with annoying harassments on several occasions. The *Daily Herald* reported that about fifty Canadians restrained the priest in a passageway located at the rear of the altar. There was also an attempt to prevent Sunday services by blocking the entrance door, while on Christmas Day a furnace pipe was flattened, resulting in a rather cold celebration. At the end of Masses, as McGee attempted to make announcements, the disaffected began the practice of walking out before he had finished speaking. When he resourcefully changed tactics by reading the announcements during Mass, men in the congregation were suddenly seized by violent coughing and sneezing spells which were just as abruptly stifled

[41] *Ibid.*, November 12, 1884.
[42] *Daily Herald*, November 17, 1884.
[43] *Ibid.*; *Daily Evening News*, November 18, 1884.

as soon as McGee turned to a reading of the Gospel![44] This was so maddening to an Irishman partaking in the service that he arose in his pew and threatened several of the dissidents. Now it was the Canadians' turn to visit the harassed mayor and ask him to instruct the police to disperse the large gatherings of Immaculate Conception Irish now appearing at Notre Dame each Sunday ever since the *Daily Herald*'s publication of a letter stating that the time had passed when Irishmen "could be insulted with impunity in the United States," and calling upon the Irish to unite for the purpose of sustaining and protecting Father McGee.[45]

Despite the overt if sometimes exaggerated opposition to an Irish pastor, the bishop, known as a "rigid disciplinarian," offered no concessions, even after learning that a Notre Dame assemblage was communicating with Rome and had voted to sponsor a delegate to the Vatican who would submit the parish case to the highest ecclesiastical authorities. Hendricken was reluctant to believe that the parishioners would appeal over his head and, even after $750 had been raised for this purpose, insisted that resistance to his authority was not only crumbling but that it had been fomented by a minority segment of the Notre Dame populace.[46] The grim opposition did not think so as 1884 drew to an end.

The new year brought no relief for an exasperated McGee. Notre Dame's militant ethnics wanted the public to believe that this priest deserved no peace of mind. They submitted a lengthy resolution for newspaper publication which censured the Irish pastor and insisted that he had brought troubles onto himself, for he was named as the author of some of the *Daily Herald*'s most savage anti-Notre Dame Corporation articles, and was accused of displaying "contempt for our [French-Canadian] race."[47] When eleven men from the parish responded to this epistle by declaring their support of McGee and the bishop, the Notre Dame trustees acknowledged that parish sentiment was not universal, but also stated that approximately two-thirds, or five hundred, male parishioners had supported the recently published anti-McGee tracts.[48]

Shortly thereafter a confrontation took place between the pro- and

---

[44] *Daily Herald*, January 20, 1885; *Daily Evening News*, December 22, 25, 1884.
[45] *Daily Herald*, November 30, December 22-23, 1884.
[46] *Providence Telegram*, quoted in the *Daily Herald*, January 27, 1885; *Daily Evening News*, December 12, 15-16, 23, 1884.
[47] *Daily Evening News*, January 17, 1885.
[48] *Ibid.*, January 21, 1885; *Daily Herald*, January 20, 1885.

anti-McGee parishioners, and "the Naughty Ones of Notre Dame" were again one step ahead of the vexed pastor. A new choir had finally been assembled by Father McGee after the original chorus had refused to co-operate with him. When these fresh recruits approached the choir loft in preparation for delivering their first performance they discovered that their predecessors had already usurped their seats and locked the entrance door. After his command to leave was ignored, police who were summoned by the pastor made four arrests.[49] In the ensuing court case, defense lawyer Hugo Dubuque sought dismissal of disturbing the peace charges by producing witnesses attesting that the original choir singers had been orderly and quiet. Nevertheless, the presiding judge disagreed with Dubuque's contention that his clients had the right to remain in the church loft, and closed the trial by stating:

> . . . as I understand the authority of a priest, he has entire control of his church; he can put a man in this seat or that seat, and if that view is correct the prisoners had no right there when ordered out, and were trespassers. By their not leaving they prevented the vesper service. This being so, what must be the result? The parties were guilty of interrupting religious service. I, therefore, adjudge them guilty and fine them $1 and costs each.[50]

Glad tidings of McGee's sudden removal by the bishop made this verdict easier to swallow for the Notre Dame nationals. There was only ephemeral joy, however, because he was replaced by another priest of Irish heritage, Owen Clarke, who had been serving under Briscoe at St. Anne's. Challenged by this most recent effrontery, most of the parishioners began boycotting Mass. When about 150 women informed him in no uncertain terms that they supported their husbands, and would not appear in church until a French Canadian was appointed pastor, a despairing Clarke fled to the more sympathetic lodgings of the Irish pastor at Immaculate Conception, and then asked the bishop to relieve him of pastoral respsonsibilities.[51]

The tenuous relationship between Hendricken and the Notre Dame parishioners was totally ruptured. As mid-February approached, the bishop reacted to French-Canadian obduracy by placing the parish under interdict. Father Clarke removed all holy objects from the church, and the interdict became effective. Although the clergy were

[49] *Daily Herald*, January 26-27, 1885.
[50] *Daily Evening News*, February 6, 1885; *NewYork Times*, February 7, 1885.
[51] *Daily Herald*, February 7, 1885; *Daily Evening News*, February 9, 11, 1885; *New York Times*, February 9, 1885.

instructed to care for the sick and administer to those from Notre Dame seeking spiritual nurture at other Fall River churches, the parish leaders were specifically denied this consideration.[52]

These men did not beg for reinstatement, nor did they lose the support of their followers. An insuperable stalemate between two equally determined foes had to somehow be resolved while souls hung, as it were, in the fire. Though the risk might be great, the Notre Dame parishioners embraced their cause enthusiastically. They ignored the *Daily Herald*'s contentions that the disobedient were demoralized and rent by bitter internal factionalism as a result of Hendricken's justifiable action, and that "ghostly manifestations" and a child born with horns and the power of speech, probably to a Notre Dame dissident, were symbolic of a devilish, erroneous resistance to the bishop.[53] Instead they took encouragement from a more objective source; the *Daily Evening News* stated that Pope Leo XIII's secretary had replied to Notre Dame correspondents by requesting that further information be forwarded to the pontiff.[54]

Eleven weeks into the interdict period the French Canadians were buoyed by reports that Archbishop Williams would be instructed by Rome to command Hendricken to reconsider the parishioners' case.[55] Time passed, however, without confirmation of this rumor, which contributed to the fervent greeting bestowed upon trustee Narcisse Rodolphe Martineau when he returned to Note Dame in early June. This wholesale liquor dealer had departed for Rome three months earlier, armed with missives which explained and defended the cause of his fellow nationals. The privilege of two audiences with the pontiff had allowed him to discuss the Fall River situation for nearly two hours. It enabled him to deny reports already circulating in Rome that Irish priests had been severely mistreated, and that Notre Dame had rejected offers of potential French-Canadian pastors. With the funds raised by the parishioners, Martineau had also engaged canon lawyers, who assured him that Notre Dame's position was a strong one, and that upon its presentation the Congregation of the Propaganda would probably render a favorable decision.[56]

Martineau thought that his mission had been totally successful, for

[52] *Daily Herald*, February 13, 1885; *Daily Evening News*, February 13, 1885.
[53] *Daily Herald*, February 17, April 10, 25-26, 1885.
[54] *Daily Evening News*, February 13, 1885.
[55] *Boston Herald*, quoted in *Daily Evening News*, April 30, 1885.
[56] *Boston Herald*, June 4, 1885; *Daily Herald*, June 4, 1885.

he had been led to believe, while still in Rome, that the reopening of Notre Dame was imminent. Having returned home, he could not hide his disappointment at finding the parish still interdicted. Nevertheless, Martineau announced at a parish meeting that he possessed sealed papers which would be delivered to Archbishop Williams and which he suspected contained orders for Hendricken to settle the dispute by appointing a French-Canadian priest.[57]

When the bishop sent two priests on Saturday, June 13, to prepare Notre Dame for Sabbath services on the following day, the impasse seemed broken. However, a crowd gathered at the church was agitated upon discovering that the priest with the primary responsibility for performing this function was an Irishman. Someone tolled the church bell; a larger, jeering mass of parishioners surrounded Notre Dame, and police were called upon to disperse them. After closing the church, the Irish priest reported to the bishop.[58]

Hendricken was not about to lift the interdict; summer passed without any change in the situation. The bishop was reportedly gloating about how, in spite of Martineau's boast of an imminent reopening, the church remained securely locked.[59] By autumn the mood of Fall River's Irish and French Catholics had grown more embittered. An Irish curate at St. Anne's went so far as to refer to the Notre Dame parishioners as "animals" in a sermon.[60]

Under these circumstances, it was unexpected, to say the least, when Hendricken, following a visit from Williams and about three weeks after the Propaganda had convened to consider the dispute, publicly referred to the "dear children of Notre Dame."[61] The bishop then came to Fall River to reopen the Flint village church. Hendricken invited and politely received parish delegates at the Immaculate Conception Rectory, where he informed them that since his only concern was for their spiritual needs he would begin celebrating Masses at Notre Dame, assisted by Father Peter Feron. He assured

[57] *Daily Herald*, June 4, 1885; *L'Indépendant*, June 12, 1885. These were the instructions, at least in a qualified sense. Simeoni advised Williams to entice those Canadians who had "behaved wrongly" into apologizing and asking forgiveness. However, he did state that Notre Dame should be reopened under a French-Canadian rector. Simeoni to Williams, May 16, 1885, Archives of the Archdiocese of Boston, John J. Williams Papers, 1885.
[58] *Daily Evening News*, June 13, 1885.
[59] *Ibid.*, August 22, 1885.
[60] *L'Indépendant*, September 4, 1885.
[61] *Ibid.*, September 18, 1885.

them, moreover, that this Irish priest Feron was not a new pastor, and confirmed the reports that Rome had empowered Archbishop Williams, aided by Bishop Goësbriand, to settle the dispute.[62]

Nevertheless, the struggle did not terminate. More than 1,000 adult parishioners agreed to stand firm by not attending the services. On Sunday, September 14, only 200 to 250 worshipers came to the bishop's Mass, while another 300 to 350 were inside Notre Dame during Feron's celebration. Although Bishop Hendricken expressed satisfaction with this turnout, Fall River's French newspaper, *L'Indépendant*, emphasized that this was only a small minority of the parish total, and asserted that one-half of these churchgoers were not from Notre Dame.[63]

French-Canadian expectations of a complete capitulation by Hendricken were further raised when he reappeared on the following Sunday and read a letter from Archbishop Williams requesting that the parish select delegates to attend a conference in Boston. Premature jubilation followed the September 25 announcement by *L'Indépendant* that for all practical purposes this nationality struggle was won, as only a few formalities remained to be ironed out. Upon returning from Boston, the delegates disclosed that the Propaganda had rendered its judgment, and claimed that Williams had received instructions to grant Notre Dame French-Canadian priests. The French newspaper cautioned its readers to temper generously their happiness by avoiding outward display in keeping with the Canadian position that it had never been the purpose to humiliate anyone, but rather to secure justice.[64]

The "victory" took on a Pyrrhic aspect a week later when it became apparent that there would be further delay. In the interim, at a second meeting, Williams had inquired whether Notre Dame was asking for a French-Canadian pastor as a right or as a favor, and whether they would apologize for $ny past injustices suffered by Irish clerics. After a parish meeting, more than 600 signatures graced a document calling for a French-Canadian priest as a right and denying that the parish had been in any way responsible for the misguided actions of a

[62] *Daily Evening News*, September 12, 14, 26, 1885. Simeoni may have been more unnerved by the delay than the French Canadians. Complaining that their incessant letters "weary me without end," he prayed that Williams would resolve the controversy and relieve him "of any further fatigue and annoyance." Simeoni to Williams, August 29, 1885, Archives of the Archdiocese of Boston, John J. Williams Papers, 1885.

[63] *Daily Evening News*, September 14, 1885; *L'Indépendant*, September 18, 1885.

[64] *Daily Evening News*, September 21, 1885; *L'Indépendant*, September 25, 1885.

few individuals.[65]

October was marked by an air of uncertainty, with the Notre Dame parishioners fearful that near-success was turning into defeat. A maze of communications was complicating the settlement. Canadian nationalists of the day believed that the bishops of New England were now intervening and pleading with the Propaganda to reverse its decision and instructions to Williams, arguing that otherwise episcopal authority throughout the six states would be undermined by French Canadians demanding the same rights as their Notre Dame brethren.[66] The timing of the bishops' meddling also disturbed the French Canadians, for they were convinced that it was part of a conspiratorial strategy initiated in the hope that Notre Dame would weary of the struggle.[67]

The parish nearly did so, as its corporation leaders became more cantankerous. Their prime target was the *Daily Herald*, which they condemned for its relentless, malicious attacks that were "the greatest obstacle in the way of a friendly adjustment." They were as equally annoyed when Archbishop Williams questioned whether they would ever support a French-Canadian pastor with sufficient financial contributions. An angered male parishioner responded that the "time has passed when we will go on all fours" before ecclesiastical authorities.[68] The frustration of the wait also took its internal toll in the form of a rancorous exchange between Martineau and those parishioners who were doubting his claim that he had received a letter from the Propaganda assuring Notre Dame of a French-Canadian pastor. Finally, during the latter part of October, there was reversion to vandalism, as the church door was locked, the bellows valve on the organ removed, and the bell rope knotted, preventing Father Feron from signaling a benediction service. The corporation directors, fearing the detrimental effect that this incident could have on their cause, offered to assist in apprehending the culprits.[69]

Although the church remained open during October and November, attendance at services was meager, indicating that the

[65] *Daily Evening News*, September 30, 1885.

[66] This ethnic demand was not confined to Fall River. Canadians from Central Falls, Rhode Island, had previously asked Rome for a French-Canadian pastor. Simeoni to Hendricken, September 7, 1880, Archives of the Diocese of Fall River.

[67] *Daily Evening News*, October 10, 1885; *L'Indépendant*, October 16, 1885, February 26, 1886; *Fall River Daily Globe*, October 20, 1885.

[68] *Daily Globe*, October 20-21, 1885.

[69] *Providence Journal*, quoted in *Daily Evening News*, October 20, 1885; *L'Indépendant*, October 23, 1885; *Daily Evening News*, October 26, 1885.

parishioners would resist until their demand was granted.[70] This adamancy was jolted on November 20 when Hendricken published a letter, sent to him by Williams, which revealed a compromise change by Rome. The Bishop of Providence was authorized to assign a pastor of his own choosing, provided that this appointee was complemented by a Canadian assistant, "until such time as you deem it convenient to appoint a French-Canadian rector."[71] When Feron was subsequently named as pastor, the shocked parish remonstrants termed this a "usurpation of power" by Hendricken because his action was at variance with the communication they had received from Rome. Furthermore, they had not been contacted by the Propaganda about any reversal of its previously favorable decision. Feron's verification of his appointment resulted in a dramatic encounter. The Notre Dame trustees informed him that since September they had watched over his personal safety. But now that the parishioners' patience was worn thin they would be unable to act as a protective buffer. Feron tersely replied that he was "ready to die" for his bishop.[72]

This ultimate sacrifice was not required of him. The parishioners were satisfied to learn that the Reverend Joseph M. Laflamme, pastor of a prospering Quebec church for the past dozen years, would be Feron's curate. Why should this priest accept a position as a subordinate to Feron, a younger man who had never before been a pastor? Their interpretation was that Rome had decided to handle the bishop gently by providing for a face-saving, albeit transparently temporary, Irish pastorate.[73]

The parishioners quietly bided their time. During mid-March, 1886, Martineau received word that a change was imminent. On March 21 a capacity congregation was drawn to Notre Dame by

[70] *Daily Globe*, October 20, 1885; *Fall River Weekly News*, December 17, 1885.
[71] *Daily Evening News*, November 21, 1885.
[72] *Ibid.*, December 10-11, 1885.
[73] *Ibid.*, December 14, 1885; *L'Indépendant*, December 18, 1885. This assessment was uncannily accurate. Though he was by now convinced that the Notre Dame parishioners' request was justified and best for their spiritual needs, Simeoni's newest tactical suggestion was much more acceptable to Hendricken than outright appointment of a French-Canadian pastor. Install an Irish rector, bring in a Canadian assistant, and then transfer the Irishman. "Thus," wrote Simeoni, "little by little and quietly, the wishes of the Canadian faithful will be satisfied, their needs provided for, without creating a precedent which the faithful of other nationalities could stand on to demand a Pastor of their own nationality." Simeoni to Williams, October 23, 1885, Archives of the Archdiocese of Boston, John J. Williams Papers, 1885.

rumor of Feron's impending removal. During a sermon that brought tears of joy to the eyes of his people, Father Laflamme confirmed that he had been promoted to pastor. All ecclesiastical penalties were nullified, and *L'Indépendant* was pleased to accede to Laflamme's request that it refrain from any further discussion of the "Flint affair." During the month of May the pastor announced that he would be given a French-Canadian assistant, and *L'Indépendant* reported that no people could be more attached to their religion than the satisfied communicants of Notre Dame de Lourdes.[74]

Those Notre Dame parishioners who stood in opposition to Bishop Thomas Hendricken from 1884 to 1886 secured the permanent institution of ethnic churches within this immigrant city. The long-range effect has been a present-day plethora of churches brought about by population decline, geographical and social mobility, and weakening nationality ties. Its more immediate effect was that the "new" immigrant Catholics from southern and eastern Europe who began arriving in large numbers during the 1890's were assured of the familiarity of their own churches, priests, and language services. For good or bad, Hendricken's Americanization drive was laid to rest when the bishop died shortly after termination of the "Flint affair."

Hendricken's position had been forcefully stated during the early days of the Notre Dame crisis when he told the church delegates that their strivings for French-Canadian priests were a waste of energy, because in ten years English would be the sole language of the Catholic Church in the United States [other than Latin].[75] Such an assertion struck at the very roots of the French-Canadian religion. To the Notre Dame "rebels" the efforts of Hendricken and priests like Briscoe at "making us Irish in the shortest amount of time" were as much an onslaught against true religion as were insults from nonbelievers.[76] Custom and language were essential ingredients in the make-up of their religion. Even more fundamentally, the French-Canadian mentality equated religion with nationality, and it was nationality above all else that had to be safeguarded from the hostility of the Irish hierarchy. As stated by *Le Castor*:[77] "Faith and nationality form the

[74] *Daily Evening News*, March 18, 1886; *L'Indépendant*, March 26, April 2, May 14, 1886.
[75] *L'Indépendant*, August 28, 1885.
[76] *Le Castor* (Fall River), March 13, 1885.
[77] This French newspaper, first published during 1882 in conjunction with the aforementioned nationality clash between Briscoe and a minority of St. Anne's

noblest marriage of Christian times. Do not separate what God has joined."[78]

It must have been perplexing for Hendricken when weeks of resistance turned into months of stubbornness, despite his interdict. He was defending his authority and was seemingly as determined to rule or ruin as were those Fall River manufacturers who opposed trade union influence in mill operations. While the bishop spoke about not releasing the reins and about the "really sensible Catholics" who recognized their "folly,"[79] the overwhelming majority at Notre Dame remained unbridled. Here was a docile people, obedient to the religious authority of a Bedard, willing to jeopardize their eternal salvation by opposing Hendricken. The bishop could have received a clue to this siege mentality by reading a position statement in *Le Castor*, which mentioned that the French-Canadian fly could be caught with honey, not vinegar, and that religious authority would not be followed when it trampled upon the rights and consciences of Canadian Catholics. Arbitrariness was man's invention, not God's.[80] Their creator would understand the French-Canadian cause.

Throughout the course of the "Flint affair" the Notre Dame parishioners emphatically denied Hendricken's contention that they had become rebellious. They were bolstered by possession of a letter written by the bishop to Bedard, shortly before the death of the "priest-patriot," which referred to Notre Dame as a model parish.[81] What explained the sudden change in the bishop's estimation of them? They insisted that the bishop, having forced the issue because of ethnic bias, could blame only himself. Besides, the Canadians' method of defense was quite proper—appeal to the highest authority. When an Irish priest stationed in Fall River denounced them for adopting this procedure, the Canadians questioned this clergyman's

---

parishioners, passed under new management shortly after the interdict had been imposed. Since defense of the Notre Dame cause was of primary concern, the more appropriate title of *L'Indépendant* was used beginning with the March 27, 1885, edition. *Le Guide Français de Fall River, Mass.*, p. 321.

[78] *Le Castor*, March 13, 1885. In defending their own ethnicity, they denied that they were guilty of racism against priests of Irish heritage. If Germans, Spaniards, or clergymen of any other nationality had been controlling the diocese and attempting to melt down their heritage, the Canadians' stance would have been similar. *Daily Herald*, December 2, 1884.

[79] *Daily Evening News*, August 22, 1885.
[80] *Le Castor*, March 13, 1885.
[81] *L'Indépendant*, November 6, 1885.

allegiance to the pope by wondering whether he considered recourse to Rome a sin.[82]

Finally, the Notre Dame people had examples at hand which they believed substantiated their cause. During Father McGee's tenure, Hendricken had contended that he could not procure a French-Canadian pastor readily. The response was that the Irish pastor's curate, a French Canadian, could be promoted. If this individual was unacceptable, then the bishop could choose from several French-Canadian priests who, after being contacted, had expressed willingness to come to Notre Dame as pastor. Besides, the parishioners declared that they were requesting no more than equal treatment. In Canada, although only a minority, Irish Catholics had their own churches headed by priests of their nationality. The French Canadians could point out that Hendricken had granted the same to the Irish of Notre Dame by approving the establishment of Immaculate Conception Church.[83] Perhaps the most effective argument in the Canadians' quest for understanding came in the form of a pertinent inquiry (with response supplied!) addressed to large numbers of Fall River's Irish Catholics: how would the St. Mary's parishioners like it if a French Canadian was named as their pastor? "Merely to ask the question is to answer it."[84]

[82] *Ibid.*, September 4, 1885.
[83] *Daily Herald*, November 25, 1884, January 27, 1885; *Daily Evening News*, January 29, 1885.
[84] *Daily Evening News*, January 29, 1885.

"IRISH ALL THE TIME:" ETHNIC CONSCIOUSNESS AMONG THE IRISH IN WORCESTER, MASSACHUSETTS, 1880-1905

In 1898 Thomas Kiely became the editor of an Irish-American weekly in Worcester, Massachusetts called the *Messenger*. In his first editorial, he duly, if dispassionately, noted his respect for the United States, the "Yankee Nation." It was not America, however, that roused his fervor. It was Ireland which remained the focus of his devotion. "Ireland free we're sure to see," he closed, "we're Irish all the time."[1]

For Kiely's predecessor as editor at the *Messenger*, Joshua O'Leary, such a conception of loyalties seemed "inexpedient," "sentimental," even "absurd." Committed to the assimilation of his own Irish American people and other ethnic Americans, O'Leary had curtly declared in 1895 that "our foreign Catholic populations...must bring up their children to be Americans in sentiment and aspiration as well as fact."[2]

Kiely was an immigrant, a native of Ireland who came to America when he was in his late teens; O'Leary, whom Kiely repeatedly excoriated as an "anti-Irish Irishman," was born in rural New Hampshire of Irish immigrant parents.[3] Though their argument sometimes seemed to verge on a personal vendetta, it actually reflected a more fundamental divergence in experience and perspective between immigrants and second generation ethnics which has appeared as a critical fissure in almost every American ethnic community or group.

These generational differences have absorbed the attention of students of American ethnicity since the advent of modern study of American immigration. Initially historians and sociologists emphasized the dramatic differences between the perspectives of the immigrants and the first American born generation. According to these early scholars, the foreign born, their attitudes rooted in the concrete experiences of the lost homeland, remained stubbornly loyal to their native land, its cultures and traditions, and the ethnic identity which grew out of them. The second generation on the other hand rejected that burdensome baggage. In Marcus Lee Hansen's words, the American born "wanted to forget everything...lose every evidence of foreign origin." Upwardly mobile and eager for acceptance from native born Americans they, in Hansen's phrase, tried to "out yankee the yankees." According to Robert Park most members of the new generation were remarkably successful in this attempt, becoming almost indistinguishable from native stock Americans. Even today some sociologists find the differences in attitudes and behavior between first and second generation ethnics dramatic proof of the "overwhelming power" of the "American acculturating process."[4]

As early as the 1930's and 1940's, however, certain sociologists and historians found this depiction of the second generation to be vastly oversimplified. "Marginal Man" theorists suggested that even if members of the upwardly mobile American born generation wished to flee their past, they were not always able to do so. Prejudice and discrimination blocked their entry into the American mainstream and thrust them back into their own group. Some, embittered by this rejection, actually became more militantly ethnic than most immigrants. Further studies of ethnic communities in America and Australia have discovered a substantial proportion of the second generation who never sought escape from their past but sincerely and strongly identified with their ethnic group and its traditions. More recently, in the wake of the "ethnic revival" of the 1960's and 1970's, some scholars have argued that ethnic identification is a response to a "primordial" need for a sense of belonging. Ethnic consciousness may submerge under the assault of Americanization but it never really disappears.[5]

Such hypotheses, whether pointing to change or continuity in the transition between the generations, emphasize the relation of ethnic consciousness to the internal life of the group. There is, however, another viewpoint, one which stresses the importance of the environment in determining the intensity of ethnic identification. According to this perspective, it is the political, social, and economic environment that group members confront, as much as their generation or social status which determines the strength of their ethnic loyalty. Donald Horowitz, for example, has found remarkable the stunning "alacrity" with which groups "adjust their identity downwards," into ethnocentric isolation, or "upwards," towards assimilation and incorporation into the mainstream, as "changing contexts dictate."[6]

Few eras in the history of an American ethnic group provide as clear an opportunity for testing these different hypotheses about the impact of generational change and environmental conditions on ethnic consciousness than the history of Irish Americans in Kiely's and O'Leary's own period of the turn of the century. The peak of Irish immigration to the United States had long since passed by that time; the Famine flood of Irish migrants shrinking to a steady stream even before the Civil War. On the other hand, a new generation, the first American born generation was rapidly growing to maturity. They and some members of the immigrant generation had also begun to achieve some prosperity, usually modest but prosperity nonetheless. Thus, for the first time an Irish middle class of substantial proportions began to emerge in most American cities (the term "lace curtain" first came into common parlance in the 1890's). Yet despite this evidence of change, Irish Americans had not yet outgrown their immigrant legacy. Most Irish workers in 1880 or even 1900 earned their livings with their hands as blue collar workers, not with their heads as white collar clerks, professionals, or businessmen.[7] Further, the flow of immigration from Ireland had slowed but not stopped, and the constant infusion of newcomers combined with the longevity of older immigrants contributed to a continual if gradual rise in America's Irish born population up to 1890.[8]

Perhaps as important as these changes within the Irish American population itself was the transformation of the environment outside it. Ireland, Catholicism — the international religion of Irish Americans — and America were all shaken by dramatic upheavals at the turn of the century. Ireland experienced a succession of nationalist revivals, both political and cultural, as it moved toward independence. Catholicism was locked in continual controversy over how to adjust its ancient traditions to a modern world. Meanwhile in America, the immigration of new ethnic groups, the transition of the economy from agriculture to industry, and the shift of population from country to city were all turning the United States into a modern, ethnically plural nation. This American transformation was not painless; indeed, for nearly its entire duration from 1870 to 1910, the United States suffered from severe labor strife, bitter political conflict, and rising ethnic tension.[9]

Thomas Kiely's and Joshua O'Leary's Irish community in Worcester, Massachusetts was no less affected by these tumultuous changes than Irish communities in other parts of the United States. In Worcester, as elsewhere in America, the number of American born Irish men and women was steadily increasing as was the size of the city's lace curtain Irish middle class. Nevertheless, the immigrant Irish still made up a substantial proportion of Worcester's Irish population as late as 1900, and the majority of Worcester's Irishmen remained blue collar workers into the twentieth century. Outside their community Irishmen in Worcester confronted a turbulent world. They followed with passionate interest Parnell's meteoric rise and fall in Ireland as well as the ascent and decline of Liberal Catholicism in the Vatican and in America. More importantly in their own city, politics was in a constant state of flux, immigrants from new nations were pouring in by the thousands and the local economy fluctuated wildly in cycles of boom and bust.

In the midst of this turmoil both within and without their community, Worcester's Irish struggled to sort out their loyalties and define their place in the larger society. In the last two decades of the nineteenth century their conceptions of those loyalties and that place shifted dramatically from an optimistic eagerness to prove themselves good Americans and reconcile their differences with their native stock Protestant Yankee neighbors to sullen and billigerent ethnocentric isolation. This radical shift suggests the volatility of Irish attitudes in Worcester reflecting the effects of dramatic changes both within their community and in their environment. Yet perhaps as important, the chronology of the shift is curious. Both immigrant and American born Irish in Worcester acknowledged that the Irish born seemed far more intensely loyal to their ethnic group than the second generation. These differences in ethnic consciousness seemed to be reinforced by the varying economic statuses and aspirations of the two generations. Nevertheless, the spirit of optimistic accommodation and reconciliation nurtured by Joshua O'Leary and others prevailed in the 1880's and early 1890's when the immigrants far outnumbered the American born Irish in Worcester, and the Irish middle class in the city was still small. On the other hand, Thomas Kiely's brand of ethnic militancy became popular in the late 1890's when the proportion of second generation Irish nearly equalled that of the immigrants in Worcester's Irish foreign stock population, and the "lace curtain" population was significantly larger. This chronology suggests that environmental conditions were far more important than generation or class differences in explaining variations in the intensity of Irish ethnic consciousness in Worcester. Such a conclusion is only partially correct, however. Environmental conditions were important, but they affected different segments of the Irish population in different ways: rousing the hopes of the American born for an accommodation with their Yankee neighbors while at the same time stifling immigrant militancy in the 1880's; and conversely, inspiring a renewal of ethnic militancy among immigrants while rendering the second generation, whose dreams of reconciliation with the Yankees had been dashed, embittered or listless in the 1890's.

Irish immigrants first arrived in Worcester in 1826, but as in many other cities, Worcester's Irish-American community did not reach substantial size until the Famine migration of the 1840's and 1850's. In five short years between 1845 and 1850, Worcester's Irish population increased tenfold, from approximately 500 to over 5,000 people, raising the Irish proportion of the city's population from less than 5% to over 20%. In succeeding years, immigrants from Ireland continued to pour into Worcester, raising the numbers of Irish immigrants to over 10,000 by 1880. Thereafter, the rate of immigration was only high enough to offset the deaths of older immigrants and the Irish foreign born population stabilized at about 10 or 11,000.[10]

By that time, of course, a new American born Irish generation had already begun to appear in the city. Indeed, according to published census statistics, the American born children of Irish immigrants were more numerous than the immigrants themselves by 1885, and by 1900, the second generation Irish population was nearly double the size of the first generation population.[11] Yet such statistics are misleading for they fail to account for the ages of the second generation Irish. Samples from the manuscript schedules of the 1880 Census reveal that among adults, men and women above the age of 18, Irish immigrants still outnumbered the American born Irish by about three to one. By 1900, according to samples from the census schedules of that year, the rapid maturing of the second generation had substantially closed the gap, as the number of American born men and women over the age of 18 nearly equalled that of the immigrants.[12]

Nevertheless, even as early as the 1880's, it seemed clear to many Worcester Irishmen that the emergence of the American born Irish introduced a new conception of ethnic allegiances into their community. The very terminology employed by members of the community to describe the two generations reflected the differences between the American born and Irish born Celts. In the early 1880's, for example, it seemed common parlance among the Worcester Irish to describe Irish immigrants as simply "Irishmen," never "Americans," a term reserved for native stock Yankees, nor even "Irish Americans," a description applied almost exclusively to members of the new Irish generation.[13] Further, Irish immigrants frequently referred to themselves and were described by second generation Irishmen as "exiles" from their true homeland: Ireland.[14] This theme, one quite commonly expressed throughout Irish America as Kirby Miller and others have pointed out, became particularly popular on special occasions such as St. Patrick's Day.[15] On those days, Irish immigrants like Thomas Kiely or Richard O'Flynn lyricized rhapsodically the green fields, white-washed chapels, or simple villages of their youth.[16] The American born Irish, on the other hand, knew little of Ireland except what they had learned from stories around the kitchen table, or nationalist orators.[17] Writers like James Mellen of the *Worcester Daily Times*, himself an American born Irishman, argued that members of his generation not only did not know about their ancestral homeland but had "an aversion to all things Irish."[18] Mellen lamented that the patriotism of his generation seemed to be "essentially American."[19] Such statements, while exaggerated, had some substance. The rhetoric of second generation Irish spokesmen frequently rang with paeans to their own home, their native America. In the early 1890's, for example, Rev. Thomas J. Conaty claimed the founders of the Republic as his true ancestors, and Major John Byrne urged young Irish Catholics "to resolve to stake our better manhood in the patriotic defense of this *our own, our native land*."[20]

There were more tangible differences between the generations as well, differences in economic and social status which perhaps also affected their varying perspectives on ethnic allegiances. In the last two decades of the nineteenth century, nearly one third to two fifths of the Irish immigrant men in Worcester were unskilled workers. Only about 5% to 10% wore white collars and only about one fifth were skilled blue collar workers. For Irish immigrants, this low status may have reinforced their attachments to their ethnic group.[21] Mired at the bottom of the economic hierarchy, with limited possibilities for individual advancement, their hopes for individual progress may have rested largely in the advancement of their entire group.[22] The group's solidarity and power also offered these, its most vulnerable members, a source of protection. Members of the new generation, on the other hand, were more successful. One quarter of the second generation men in 1900 were white collar workers and another third were skilled blue collar workers in that year.[23] Since Yankee Protestants dominated Worcester's economy, it may have been in the new generation's interest to minimize distinctions between Yankees and Irishmen rather than accentuate them.[24]

Despite these differences between the generations, it is important not to overestimate the new American born generation's rejection of their ethnic tradition. The often fulsome spread eagle rhetoric of the new generation hid their retention of many cultural values and customs inherited from the old country. They married late, for example, as the Irish in Ireland did. Second generation Irishmen in Worcester married, on the average, at age 31 in 1900; American born Irish women at age 29 in the same year. Once married, second generation Irish women were more likely to have children, and to have more children than native stock Yankees and indeed seemed to have them at the same rate as Irish immigrant wives.[25] Further, though the American born made significant economic advances, their occupational choices seemed to reflect the biases of their cultural inheritance as well. As spokesmen for their community noted often, the most successful American born seemed to have little interest in business but rather flooded the professions, notably law.[26] Finally, and perhaps most importantly, the vast majority, very nearly all, of the members of the second generation seemed fiercely devoted to their ancestral Catholic religion.

Not only culture but concrete interests also tied many of the American born Irish to their ethnic group. In Worcester unlike many other larger cities, the process of suburbanization took place very slowly. Thus, most of the second generation Irish in Worcester, even many of the economically successful, still lived in, or on the border of, the oldest Irish neighborhoods of the city until the twentieth century.[27] Further, if some members of the American born generation might suffer in their quest for higher status from their group's belligerent assertions, others profited from Irish solidarity and power. For many of the ambitious second generation in Worcester, not just professional politicians, but lawyers, construction bosses, and saloonkeepers, such solidarity and power could pay off handsomely with prized patronage posts, building contracts and operating licenses. Even many American born Irish doctors participated actively in politics, no doubt at least in part for the advantages of prestige and notoriety it afforded them in building up their practices. In all, over 40% of the Irish Catholics (the vast majority of them American born) listed among the city's elite in 1919 had held a political or governmental post at some point in their careers.[28] Even in America, then, practical considerations as well as habits inherited from the old country continued to nurture the Irish ethnic loyalties of many members of the new generation.

Nevertheless, in the 1880's at least, second generation Irishmen in Worcester, and indeed the city's entire Irish community, seemed intent on underplaying their ethnic allegiances and the ethnic differences between themselves and their native stock Yankee neighbors. Evidence of this desire can be seen in the efforts of Irish clergymen and prominent laymen to cooperate with the Yankees such as Irish support of public education, the rise of the Irish temperance movement, and even curiously, the Irish nationalist crusade in the 1880's.

Through the 1880's and early 1890's, a number of Irish Catholic leaders in Worcester sought to encourage more amicable relations between their people and the Yankee Protestants. Clergymen like Rev. John J. Power socialized frequently with members of the Yankee elite, while Power's colleague, Rev. Thomas J. Conaty, spoke often to Protestant religious groups and collaborated with Protestant ministers and lay leaders in civic efforts such as the establishment of a Charity Organization Society in 1889.[29] Laymen like Joshua O'Leary, the editor of Worcester's only Irish newspaper in the late 1880's and early 1890's, also consistently promoted Catholic overtures to their Protestant neighbors. O'Leary's campaign to improve relations between the two groups included praise of Protestant organizations, even the YMCA, which in 1893 he called "an institution of which much can be justly said in praise...a power for good in the community," as well as warnings to his own people to curb their criminal behavior lest they provoke unwarranted anti-Catholic prejudice.[30] There was more tangible evidence of this Irish eagerness to bridge the gaps which separated them from their Yankee neighbors. St. Vincent's Hospital, founded by a Catholic priest in 1893, for example, became a monument to the good will between Irish Catholics and Yankees in Worcester, as both Yankees and Irishmen served together on its board of directors and on its staff and contributed generously to its construction.[31]

The willingness of the Irish to accommodate their native stock neighbors, as well as their desire to absorb American culture, were perhaps more clearly revealed in what the Irish did not build than in what they did construct. Specifically, despite the mandate of the Baltimore Council in 1884 requiring every Catholic parish in America to build its own school, only one of the seven Irish Catholic parishes did so before 1895. (By contrast, all three of the French Canadian parishes in the city erected parochial schools).[32] Though the reasons for this failure were numerous, one of the most important was the high regard Worcester's Irish had for public education. Rev. John J. Power, for example, praised the "necessity of our public schools and their ennobling influence" and O'Leary enthused often about the "grand privileges of our public schools."[33] Even supporters of parochial education in Worcester dismissed as "ridiculous" insinuations that attendance in public schools threatened the faith of Catholic youngsters.[34] By contrast, widespread evidence from this period reveals that not only Irish Catholic leaders but much of the Irish Catholic population was skeptical about the usefulness of parochial education.[35] Particularly subject to criticism by the Irish Catholics of Worcester were the schools maintained by French Canadians and other foreign language ethnic groups. Such institutions could not match the standards set by public education; they, along with national parishes, merely served to perpetuate "sentimental foreignisms."[36] Echoing Archbishop John Ireland, O'Leary proclaimed in 1895 that the best way to "Catholicize America is to Americanize Catholicism."[37]

Yet many Irish Catholics in Worcester felt that not only other Catholic ethnics but their own people, too, had to jettison customs which were incompatible with the norms of their new home. Perhaps the most visible of these old world customs was drinking. During the 1880's, Irishmen in Worcester revealed an acute awareness of the characterization of their people as a "set of inebriates" by native stock Yankees.[38] Many Irishmen in that decade even accepted that characterization, bemoaning the "curse" of their race and admitting, as Rev. Thomas J. Conaty did in 1886, that "intemperance was the one charge that could be fairly lodged against the modern Irishmen."[39]

Such spokesmen, including most of the Irish Catholic clergy, thus became strong advocates of temperance and total abstinence.[40] Though clergymen had preached the virtues of temperance as early as the mid-1870's, it wasn't until the following decade, the 1880's, that they began to receive an enthusiastic response.[41] Suddenly in the early 1880's, the Irish temperance movement in Worcester caught on, and by the end of the decade Irish temperance associations had become the most popular clubs in Worcester's Irish community. Between 1881 and 1889 the number of Irish temperance societies multiplied from one to nine, and the combined memberships of the societies rose from about 200 to over 1,200 in the same period.[42]

Ireland, of course, had a temperance tradition of its own and Worcester's Irish teetotallers had direct links to that tradition.[43] Rev. Theobald Matthew, the great Irish temperance crusader, had himself inspired the organization of Worcester's first permanent Irish temperance society when he visited the city in 1849.[44] Further, Irish temperance societies in Worcester hewed closely to their Church's teaching on the liquor question, strictly avoiding association with Yankee backed Prohibition efforts.[45]

Nevertheless, the American influence on the Irish temperance men in Worcester was quite apparent. As speakers at one Irish temperance meeting proclaimed in 1886, the Celtic total abstainers of Worcester were eager to prove that they had "left" their "bad" traits in Ireland and now had the potential to become better Americans than the Americans themselves.[46] Their self-education programs, including night classes, lectures, concerts, recitals, debates, and declamation contests, and their passionate devotion to baseball and other American amusements reflected their commitment to that goal.[47] Thus, though they were devoted to their church, the Irish teetotallers were more ambivalent about publicly affirming an Irish ethnic identity.[48] Worcester's temperance societies usually voted against holding St. Patrick's Day parades in the city, for example, prompting their critics to upbraid the temperance men for being too "Americanized," lacking the "spirit of their sires" or "ashamed to call themselves Irishmen."[49]

The apparent weakness of ethnic consciousness or ethnic feeling among the temperance men did not mean that they or their community had lost interest in Ireland. Indeed, Irish nationalism thrived in Worcester during the 1880's. From efforts to relieve Ireland's agricultural crisis in 1879, to the downfall of Parnell in 1890, thousands of Worcester Irishmen packed protest meetings, enrolled in local branches of nationalist societies, and contributed hard earned dollars to the nationalist cause.[50] Yet in many ways, the Irish nationalist of the 1880's was but another reflection of the spirit of reconciliation and enthusiasm for American culture which pervaded Worcester's Irish community during that decade. It was generally a conservative agitation. Except for a brief interlude during the Irish land wars of 1882, it did not sway from alignment with the conservative faction of the American nationalist movement led by Patrick Collins, John Boyle O'Reilly, and Worcester's own Rev. Thomas J. Conaty.[51] Further, Worcester's Irish Nationalists welcomed and received considerable financial support from local Yankee businessmen. Indeed, to one local Irish observer in 1880, the "Americans" seemed far more "conscientious" in their commitment to the Irish cause than the Irish themselves.[52] This Yankee involvement stemmed in part from their approval of "the conservative and eminently proper methods" of the agitation. Yet it also reflected the successful efforts of local Irishmen to harmonize Ireland's Home Rule crusade with American ideals and traditions through frequent invocations of analogies to America's own struggle for independence in 1776.[53]

Why was the spirit of accommodation so popular when the local Irish population was so overwhelmingly immigrant and lower class in composition? The answer lies chiefly in the influences of their environment upon the Irish people of Worcester. Yet not all the Irish in Worcester responded to these influences in the same way. Specifically, these influences seemed to inspire the second generation Irish and perhaps lift them to a prominence within the Irish community which their numbers alone did not warrant. Conversely, these environmental conditions seemed to render the immigrants strangely mute and inactive.

Some of the most important influences on the Worcester Irish in the 1880's actually originated outside the city. The rise of Parnell in Ireland was one such significant influence. The almost slavish devotion Parnell inspired in Worcester severely hindered the efforts of more radical nationalists to ignite a more militant nationalist agitation in the city.[54] More important, perhaps, was the rise of Catholic Liberalism in America. Issac Hecker's frequent lectures in Worcester shortly after the Civil War helped prepare the ground for this movement's later growth in the city.[55] By the 1880's and early 1890's Archbishop John Ireland, Bishop John Keane, and even Rev. Edward McGlynn had become heroes to the Worcester Irish.[56] The support of these liberal leaders for temperance and their questioning of parochial education thus both inspired and justified similar movements and sentiments among the Worcester Celts.[57]

As significant as these national or international movements were, their impact on the Worcester Irish might have been blunted if local conditions had not favored them. Circumstances within the city during the 1880's, however, created a nourishing climate for the ideals of Catholic Liberalism and Parnell's moderate nationalism. Memories of Irish sacrifice and Yankee-Irish cooperation in the Civil War still lingered, for example, for that conflict had ended but fifteen years before.[58] Worcester's economy had also rebounded well from the Great Depression of the 1870's producing optimism among the city's Irish workers in the early 1880's.[59] Later in the decade Worcester also largely escaped the labor conflict which inspired nativist revivals in many other parts of the country.[60]

The most important influence on Irish attitudes in the 1880's, however, was the nature of local politics. Irishmen were a powerful political force in Worcester in the 1880's, but their numbers were too small to permit their Democratic party to rule the city.[61] The Republican party, however, was severely fragmented, particularly in municipal politics.[62] Indeed, in some years in the early 1880's, it hardly seemed to function at all on the local level, as local journals of both parties agreed that city politics was in a sense almost nonpartisan.[63] Irishmen thus easily hammered out alliances with liberal Yankee Republicans which insured those independent Yankees the top spots in municipal administrations and also provided a steady flow of appointments to the police force and staffs of the public schools for Irish office seekers, as well as contracts for Irish construction companies.[64]

The effects of these political arrangements on ethnic relations and Irish ethnic consciousness in Worcester were powerful. Specifically, the large number of Irish teachers in the public schools bolstered Irish confidence in public education.[65] More generally, Irish and Yankee politicians both seemed wary of permitting ethnocentric outbursts on either side which might disrupt the city's delicate political balance. Irish politicians thus were instrumental in steering the nationalist movement along a conservative course.[66] Similarly, few Yankee politicians sought to encourage nativist crusades, which might provoke a revival of Irish militancy.[67]

Yet if conditions were favorable to the rising spirit of accommodation among the Worcester Irish in the 1880's, the prominence of the new generation and of prosperous Irishmen in the various movements which reflected that spirit should not be overlooked. Irish Catholic priests, three quarters of them American born in 1880, played particularly critical roles in the efforts to achieve reconciliation with the Yankees, the temperance crusade, and the nationalist agitation.[68] Indeed, the priests, particularly the second generation Irish, Conaty and Rev. John J. McCoy, organized most of the new temperance societies, and along with local Irish politicians dominated the nationalist agitation.[69] American born laymen like the editor, Joshua O'Leary, also contributed mightily to the spirit of accommodation in the 1880's.[70] Further, it appeared that the American born and skilled blue collar or white collar Irish were disproportionately strong among the rank and file of the temperance crusade, and though there is little evidence of the generational composition of the nationalist agitation in this era, skilled blue collar and white collar Irishmen seemed to dominate that movement too.[71] By contrast, societies like the Ancient Order of Hibernians (A.O.H.) which promoted ethnic militancy and drew their members largely from the immigrant and lower class segments of the Irish community floundered in the 1880's.[72] Radical factions of the nationalist movement which also seemed to attract support from lower class Irishmen suffered in the conciliatory atmosphere of the 1880's as well.[73]

That atmosphere would soon pass, however, for the conditions which nourished it proved to be only temporary. In 1890, Parnell fell and by 1893 his home rule dream also seemed dead.[74] Liberal Catholicism came under increasing fire from the Vatican which step by step imposed restrictions on Liberalism's suspected excesses until the Pope finally, if vaguely, condemned it in an 1899 encyclical.[75]

Locally the Irish in Worcester found themselves increasingly isolated in the 1890's. New groups such as the Swedes and French Canadians had begun to flood the city in the late 1880's.[76] These groups invaded Irish neighborhoods and competed with Irish workers for blue collar jobs.[77] Indeed, the Irish charged that Yankee manufacturers had deliberately encouraged the Swedish migration to Worcester in order to oust the Celts from their major source of employment in Worcester's wire mills.[78] Thus the Irish were at loggerheads with the Protestant Swedes almost from the time the Scandinavians arrived in Worcester.[79] Irish relations with their co-religionists, the French Canadians, also soured by the end of the 1890's as the rivalry between the two groups within the Church and in local politics grew increasingly heated.[80]

More important than the rising tension between the Irish and the new immigrants was the steady deterioration of their relations with native stock Yankees. Hints of the rising anger of middle class Yankee Protestants against the old political alliance between Republican independents and Irish Democrats began to surface as early as 1888.[81] This sentiment did not fully crystalize until the 1893 Depression, however. That economic catastrophe prompted the renaissance of organized nativism in Worcester in the form of the American Protective Association (A.P.A.).[82] That organization, drawing largely on working and middle class Yankee support, managed to seize control of the city's school committee and oust an allegedly pro-Catholic school superintendent.[83] Though the A.P.A. quickly declined, its sympathizers remained a powerful force in the Republican Party discouraging G.O.P. independents from seeking new alliances with Irish Democrats.[84] By the late 1890's, Republican independents may have thought twice about entering such coalitions anyway. Their own party's triumphant success in 1896 and the concurrent transformation of the state and national Democratic party into an apparently radical party made such overtures less appealing or necessary.[85] By 1897, then, the Irish were politically isolated. No Yankee Republicans would seek to ally with them, the Swedes were adamantly antagonistic, and the French Canadians, after a brief flirtation with the Democrats in the early 1890's, had deserted them.[86]

While tensions and hostility rose all about them, critical changes were also taking place among the Irish people of Worcester in the late 1880's and 1890's. One such change was the drastic turnover in Worcester's Irish immigrant population. The number of Worcester's Irish born remained relatively stable in the last two decades of the nineteenth century (actually declining slightly), but nearly half the Irish immigrants in Worcester in 1900 were recent newcomers not only to Worcester but to America. 47.4% of them had not emigrated from Ireland until after 1880, 30% had not left until after 1885, and almost a fifth had not departed their homeland until the 1890's.[87] The significance of these figures lies in the transformation of their native Ireland in the last twenty years of the nineteenth century, a transformation which probably made the new immigrants very different people from the Irish who flooded Worcester in earlier years. Many of them, perhaps most, were participants or first-hand observers of the Irish "Land War" and Home Rule Movement of the 1880's, an experience which Joseph Lee argues washed away their traditional habits of deference and seasoned them in the tactics of mass political agitation. Many, too, especially those who did not leave Ireland until the 1890's, were no doubt also familiar with the first stirrings of their homeland's Gaelic cultural revival, particularly the revival of Gaelic athletics.[88] Most significant, however, though also most difficult to document in terms of its impact on Worcester's Irish population, was the shift in the regional sources of Irish immigration in the late nineteenth century. Throughout the late nineteenth century and into the twentieth century a steadily increasing proportion of Irish immigrants to America were coming from the western parts of Ireland, the Province of Connaught and Counties Kerry and Donegal. These regions were not only the poorest areas in Ireland but also its last bastions of traditional Irish culture, only just beginning to feel the effects of political, economic, and cultural modernization.[89] Though Worcester had seemed to attract an especially high proportion of Western immigrants since the Famine, it is very likely that the city's proportion of Irish born hailing from Western Irish counties dramatically increased in the 1880's and 1890's.[90]

Critical changes were occurring in Worcester's American-born Irish population as well. Most important, they were growing older. By 1900 there were nearly three times as many American born Irish over the age of 18 than there had been in 1880 and nearly five times as many over the age of 25.[91] This maturing process had a number of significant effects. It meant, for example, that the proportion of white collar workers among the second generation grew as its members entered the most fruitful years of their careers. Perhaps most important, however, this growing number of second generation adults meant that their whole ethnic group had become much more politically powerful. Because of an alteration in the city's charter and this new political muscle, they were able to consistently elect a number of their own men to aldermanic or common council offices. The nominations for these seats were always hotly contested largely by second generation Irishmen, for not only had the power of the new generation increased but the political expectations of its members had risen as well.[88] By 1900 these expectations had grown so much that Irish Democrats flatly refused to even consider backing an independent Republican Yankee for the top municipal office: the mayoralty.[89] Instead they nominated one of their own to head a straight Democratic, and largely Irish, ticket.[90] In a major upset, this second generation Irishman, Philip O'Connell, won the mayor's office. This did not satiate the hunger for office among his fellow Irish, it merely inflated their expectations. Never again would they seek an alliance with Republican independents. Indeed, the Democratic party would nominate only Irish Catholics for mayor in the next twenty years.[91] As the Irish press in Worcester bellowed in the years following O'Connell's election, their people would never be satisfied until they had gained every bit of political recognition that their political power warranted.[92]

The effects of these many events and trends on Worcester's Irish community in the 1890's were revolutionary. The temperance societies collapsed, albeit temporarily, and moderate nationalist associations disappeared.[93] There was no more talk of improving relations with Yankee Protestants. When Joshua O'Leary, the Liberal Catholic, founded a paper for that purpose in 1898, it attracted no readers and quickly folded.[94] By the early twentieth century, the term Liberal Catholic had become an epithet in Worcester, a phrase used to describe people who denied their faith in order to gain social acceptance from Protestants.[95] By that time, ethnocentric appeals and suspicions of Protestants also laced Irish rhetoric, justifying the building of their new institutions as well.[96]

Perhaps the most important result of the rising ethnic tensions of the 1880's, however, was the revival of organizations which promoted a fiery brand of militant ethnocentrism. The largest and most influential of these was the Ancient Order of Hibernians. As the historian of Worcester's A.O.H. noted in 1901, "things had been running slowly" for the order in the 1880's, but in the late 1890's the organization began to expand at a rapid rate.[97] Between 1896 and 1901, the number of A.O.H. divisions in the city multiplied from three to nine and the combined memberships of the divisions shot up from approximately 500 to over 2,500.[98] In the same period the A.O.H. also built their own new meeting hall in Worcester and took control of the city's only Irish newspaper, the *Messenger*.[99] The Clan Na Gael also rebounded impressively in the 1890's. There is no evidence that the Clan even existed in Worcester in the late 1880's, though it may have simply gone underground in an atmosphere which was hostile to its violent revolutionary nationalism. In any event, the Clan emerged or resurfaced in 1893 about the same time as the defeat of Gladstone's Home Rule Bill and soon became one of Worcester's most popular Irish clubs.[100] Other smaller associations with outlooks similar to the A.O.H. and the Clan also spouted up in the late 1890's, including societies representing natives or descendants of specific counties in Ireland.[101] The rebirth of the latter is startling, for county organizations had not been seen in Worcester since at least the 1870's.

IRISH ALL THE TIME

For the A.O.H. and its allies the old dreams of rapprochement with the Yankees had clearly died by the late 1890's; their own approach to the threatening and hostile groups which surrounded them was a sustained belligerency resting on growing Irish power. In 1898, for example, the A.O.H. led a campaign to prevent British immigrants in Worcester from constructing a Jubilee Memorial to Queen Victoria in a downtown park. Judging the proposed fountain to be a deliberate "insult" to the Irish, the A.O.H. warned city councillors that they risked losing thousands of Irish votes if they approved the proposal. To back up its claims, the A.O.H. flooded the council with petitions opposing the project.[102] Later, in the years after 1900, the A.O.H. backed paper, the *Messenger*, led major drives to increase Irish representation in city government departments and include Irish subjects in the public school curriculum, again invoking threats of Irish political retaliation if their demands were not met.[103] The paper aptly summed up the philosophy of its sponsor, the A.O.H., in 1903 when it asserted that the times called for "an insistence on full rights and unity of action...this thing of keeping still about race and religion while the other fellow uses it for all its worth is about played out."[104]

The same militancy and aggressiveness characterized the perspective of the A.O.H. and its allies on Irish Nationalist issues. The Clan Na Gael, perhaps still chastened by its experiences in the 1880's, rarely publicly proclaimed its commitment to violent revolution in Ireland. Nevertheless, individual members of the Clan were less cautious. In 1904, for example, one leader of the organization proclaimed that "we do not subscribe to that wretched maxim that the freedom of Ireland is not worth the shedding of a drop of blood...emancipation awaits those who dare to achieve it by their intrepidity."[105] The A.O.H., though reluctant to commit itself formally to radical measures or goals, frequently celebrated past revolutionary heroes such as the "Manchester Martyrs" or even O'Donovan Rossa.[106] Further, one of the newly formed divisions of the Order publicly called for a new invasion of Canada in 1898.[107] Finally, while the Order proclaimed its neutrality in the conflict between moderate and militant nationalists, local Yankee newspapers and the moderate Irish nationalists themselves suspected that the A.O.H. worked hard though secretly to undermine moderate nationalist societies.[108]

So intense was the commitment of the A.O.H. and its sympathizers to Ireland and its revolutionary tradition, that it even influenced their perceptions of America's interests. Naturally enough the Hibernians and the Clan Na Gael hoped to foster American hostility towards Britain or at the very least prevent a rapprochement between the two world powers. Not all Irishmen in the city agreed with those aims. Most notably, Joshua O'Leary, the prominent Liberal Catholic of the 1880's, argued that an Anglo-American alliance would be beneficial to the United States.[109] As might be expected, A.O.H. spokesmen condemned O'Leary, but interestingly, they did not even address the question of how well such an alliance would serve American interests. They simply dismissed as "inconceivable" the idea that an Irish American could support such a policy so fraught with dangers to Ireland's fate.[110] The Clan or A.O.H.'s fervent identification with Irish history even colored their opinions of American foreign policy issues which were irrelevant to Ireland's interests. In 1902, for example, the local Clan Na Gael camp condemned American imperialism in the Philippines stating: "we who are banded together in the fight for Irish freedom unqualifiably condemn any movement which has for its object the subjugation of a people or the attempt to deprive them of their God given rights whether in Ireland or the Philippines."[111] Because of their reverence for Irish tradition or because they focused their attention so strictly on current Irish interests, the Hibernians and their allies seemed detached and almost alienated from the wave of fervent American nationalism which swept the United States in the late 1890's and early 1900's. To these Worcester Irishmen, the outburst of American nationalism seemed shallow, "emotional," and smacked of mere "jingoism."[112]

The same passionate loyalty to Ireland and veneration of its traditions had a profound effect on the cultural activities as well as the politics of the Hibernian, the Clan, and their allies. In these activities, the A.O.H., the Clan and others also seemed to draw inspiration from the Gaelic cultural revival which sprouted in Ireland after Parnell's fall. Thus in 1898, for example, the Clan and the Hibernians organized a branch of the Gaelic League in Worcester in order to resuscitate interest in the Gaelic language in the city.[113] A few years earlier they had also promoted Gaelic football clubs in Worcester. These clubs multiplied so rapidly in the mid-1890's that one observer seriously predicted that Irish football would soon replace "brutish" American football as an American national pastime.[114] In addition, the A.O.H., the Clan and other societies like the county clubs also staged numerous concerts on Irish music and Irish dances for their members, and organized affiliated juvenile associations to encourage interest in Irish culture among Irish American youngsters.[115] Perhaps the most ambitious effort made by the A.O.H. and its sympathizers in behalf of Irish culture, however, was the campaign to add Irish history to the curricula of Worcester's public and parochial schools. Though this crusade ended in failure, the energy expended by the A.O.H. and other Irish societies in this cause, the barrage of resolutions, the protest meetings, the blizzard of newspaper articles, further testified to their interest in reviving or preserving Irish culture.[116]

In the turbulence of the 1890's and early 1900's, this cultural and political ethnocentrism preached by the A.O.H. and likeminded societies won broad acceptance, even gaining strong support from some of the American born and upwardly mobile Irish. In 1900, the A.O.H. declared the interest of the new generation in their order "gratifying."[117] Earlier in the 1890's, the Clan Na Gael had also boasted about the support it received from all "classes" of Irishmen in Worcester, including a number of prominent American born doctors and lawyers.[118] That some members of the second generation should find the ethnocentrism of these organizations appealing in the 1890's is understandable. The rise of the A.P.A. and the general increase in ethnic conflict in that decade had snapped the new generation's confidence in proving their acceptability as Americans and blasted their dreams of achieving a reconciliation with their Protestant neighbors. As one second generation Irishmen explained later, after the A.P.A.'s brief ascendancy, members of his American born and bred generation felt "branded," "suspected," "not to be trusted where my country or neighbor's life was concerned" because they were of the "old faith" and "liberty loving Irish blood."[119] Moreover, heightened ethnic consciousness would seem a natural accompaniment, perhaps even a necessity, for the Irish drive for political recognition which the second generation led in the 1890's. Not surprisingly, then, many of the second generation Irishmen running for political life in the late 1890's were members of the A.O.H. or the Clan Na Gael.[120]

The turmoil of the 1890's had an even more profound effect on immigrant and lower class Irishmen in Worcester, however, for it appears that those segments of the city's Irish population supplied the bulk of the new members for the revived A.O.H. and other militantly ethnic Irish associations. Immigrants and lower class Irishmen were perhaps naturally receptive to appeals for Irish solidarity and the preservation of Irish culture. Recent immigrants, in particular veterans of the "Land War" in Ireland or the Gaelic Cultural revival there in the 1890's, were no doubt especially sympathetic to such appeals.[121] Yet, it was events and trends in Worcester which roused them to respond to such appeals, for the rising climate of ethnic tensions affected them even more than the second generation and prosperous Irish, and the mobilization of their people in the drive for political recognition in those years promised them, as well as the American born, new opportunities. It was Irish immigrants, for example, who suffered most from competition with new foreign born groups like the Swedes in Worcester's factories.[122] Further, if the Irish drive for political power aided the American born in achieving the top spots in municipal administration, such power would have also proved beneficial for their Irish born fellow ethnics who sought jobs in the lower ranks of the city government.[123] Little wonder, then, that every surviving list of A.O.H. officers or members reveals the immigrant dominance of the organization.[124] Particularly notable is the overwhelming strength of the Irish born in one of the newly formed A.O.H. divisions, Division 36, organized in 1896.[125] Not surprisingly, too, most of the Irish born on such lists of members or officers were recent arrivals in America (as were, according to the newspapers, most of the best players on the Gaelic football clubs) having left Ireland after 1880, the majority after 1886.[126] Finally, though the officers of A.O.H. tended to include a large proportion of white collar or skilled blue collar workers, the memberships of the order's branches and even the rosters of Hibernian or Clan delegates to conventions of local Irish societies reflected the heavy lower class influence in those associations.[127]

Worcester's Irish ethnocentric revival of the 1890's was shortlived. Like the efforts at reconciliation which preceeded it, it could not survive when changing political and social circumstances altered the conditions which had inspired it in the first place. No sooner had the Irish achieved political supremacy than they realized that they could not maintain their power without allies. Having abandoned their arrangements with Yankee Republicans, they sought those allies in the Catholic immigrants who in the early twentieth century were beginning to flood Worcester.[128] By patching up their differences with the city's French Canadians, and reaching out to these new groups, they hoped to create a new powerful coalition of Catholic ethnics. American born and prosperous Irishmen took the lead in forging this coalition, for their commitment to the revival of a narrow ethnocentrism, particularly to attempts to revive Irish culture, had been shallow at best.[129] The new coalition they sought to lead would be organized around a merger of the two loyalties they seemed to find most congenial: American patriotism, and a devotion to Catholicism.[130]

Yet the emergence of this new conception of identity among the Worcester Irish, the third abrupt shift in their definition of loyalties in little more than three decades, underscores once again the difficulties they experienced in trying to determine who they were and what role they should play in the larger society of their city. Those difficulties were not theirs alone, however. According to William Shannon, Irishmen all across America were wrestling with the same questions. By the 1880's and 1890's most Irish Americans were no longer bewildered peasants cast by a Famine disaster across the sea into an alien American culture and society. Nevertheless, few of them had shed all traces of their Irish inheritance by then, or had gained full acceptance from native stock Americans. They were caught, then, as Shannon says in an "ambiguous indeterminate state" which precipitated an "identity crisis" among them unparalleled in their history.[131]

The solutions the Worcester Irish chose to resolve this crisis were not unique to them either. The Liberal Catholicism and conservative Irish Nationalism which flourished in Worcester during the 1880's were also popular in many other Irish American communities during that decade.[132] These were, of course, not the only Irish responses to their dilemma of identity in the 1880's. Church conservatives remained powerful throughout the country but particularly in New York, while on the other end of the ideological spectrum, radical Irish Nationalists like Patrick Ford won strong support especially in small mill towns and mining communities.[133] It is far more difficult to determine whether the Irish ethnocentric revival which erupted in Worcester in the 1890's also emerged elsewhere, because historians have virtually ignored that decade in Irish American history. There is evidence indicating a renewal of Irish ethnic militancy in cities as different as Boston and San Francisco in the 1890's.[134] On the other hand, there is also evidence which suggests that some Irish communities may have passed over the stage of ethnocentric isolation in the 1890's, and moved directly into a phase of militantly Catholic and patriotically American identification, an identification which did not become popular in Worcester until the 1910's.[135]

As important perhaps as whether the trends occurring among the Irish in Worcester in the late nineteenth century were typical of Irish America as a whole, is the question of whether the different Irish generations and social classes played the same role in those movements in the nation at large, as they did in Worcester. Unfortunately, analyses of the generational composition of such movements are either non-existent or imprecise, and class breakdowns of their supporters are little better. Nevertheless, the evidence such as it is tends to confirm the same pattern of involvement by different generations and social classes which appeared in Worcester. Thomas N. Brown, for example, has contended that the conservative Home Rule agitation of the 1880's seemed particularly appealing to "Horatio Alger types" and the second generation just as it did in Worcester.[136] By contrast, Eric Foner and Victor Walsh have demonstrated that working class Irishmen, especially those from Southern and Western Ireland, seemed uninterested in this moderate and respectable Irish Nationalism during the 1880's. As Foner and Walsh point out these Irishmen seemed to prefer Patrick Ford's economically radical Irish nationalist agitation.[137] Historians of American Catholicism have also noted that the appearance of a new generation of church leaders, particularly second generation Irish bishops coincided with the rise of Liberal Catholicism in America, though these historians have been careful to point out that debates over Liberal church policies did not always divide along generational lines.[138] Focusing almost exclusively on the Church hierarchy, such historians have virtually ignored grassroots local and particularly lay participation in the Liberal Catholic movement, though Robert Cross and Thomas McAvoy have briefly hinted that Catholic economic progress and the maturing of new Catholic generations in the post Civil period contributed to the rise of Liberal Catholicism in the United States.[139]

As suggested earlier, there are only hints in the historical literature of the existence of Irish ethnocentric revivals outside Worcester in the 1890's, and thus almost no evidence of the roles different Irish generations or social classes may have played in them. From the evidence offered by Foner and Walsh on the radicalism or militancy of the Irish workers and immigrants in the 1880's, and Kirby Miller's general analysis of the Irish immigrants' sense of alienation in late nineteenth century America, however, it is not surprising that Worcester's lower class and immigrant Irish supplied the bulk of the support for the city's Irish ethnocentric revival in the 1890's.[140] Nevertheless, William Shannon, analyzing a revival of ethnic militancy among the Boston Irish at the turn of the century, suggests a different interpretation. Shannon contends that the source of Boston's renewed Irish militancy lay in the heightened expectations of an emerging American born generation. He states:

> It is the first generation that meekly obeys the foreman, defers to the teacher, respects the corner cop. It is later generations that rebel...as the (nineteenth) century closed these younger Irish came roaring out of the slums propelled by a hard aggressive urge to strike out at their world...(and) master and punish their enemies...no longer (bearing) the pathetic hopes of tangible tokens of acceptance.[141]

Shannon offers no detailed evidence to support his contention, but his argument, whether true or not, raises a number of larger questions about the role different generations or social classes play in ethnic social or cultural movements or more generally in shifts in ethnic consciousness among ethnic groups. Shannon argues that the new generation of Irishmen did not simply participate in the renewal of Irish ethnic militancy in Boston, but that their growth to maturity or their "emergence" *caused* that ethnocentric revival. The critical question then is determining precisely when a new generation emerges: When and how does it achieve sufficient influence to make its perspective on ethnic identity stand for its entire group or community? Shannon's point rases further questions as well. If he finds a second generation contentious and brawling, spoiling for a fight with their Yankee neighbors, many others have found an American born generation obsessed with respectability and almost painfully eager to accommodate native stock Americans. These divergent interpretations may not be as contradictory as they seem. In Worcester, for example, the second generation Irish appeared to be highly ambivalent about their ethnic identity and capable of both types of responses. Yet for members of such a confused and ambivalent generation what then determines whether they will fight or accommodate their native stock neighbors?

Analysis of demographic and economic trends within Worcester's Irish population and indeed the Irish throughout the United States in the late nineteenth century suggests some caution in trying to explain shifts in ethnic consciousness solely in terms of changes within an ethnic group or ethnic community. Though the American born Irish in Worcester and perhaps throughout the country seemed to play a particularly important role in the various Irish efforts to accommodate their people to American culture and society in the 1880's, the new generation hardly seems to have emerged in that decade. In Worcester, in 1880, only one quarter of the Irish foreign stock adults were second generation, and the vast majority of the new generation were infants or schoolboys. Less precise national data suggest similar immigrant proportionate strength among Irish foreign stock adults until well into the late nineteenth century.[142] Upwardly mobile Irishmen also seemed strong supporters of accommodation efforts in the 1880's, and in Western or even Middle Atlantic Irish American communities the Irish lace curtain class was expanding at a far more rapid rate than in Worcester.[143] Yet, since the trend towards accommodation also flourished in Worcester where less than 10% of the city's Irish foreign stock adults had broken into white collar work by 1880, it is difficult to tie the advent of Catholic Liberalism or conservative nationalism in the 1880's directly to the emergence of an Irish middle class. Further, if in the next two decades the number of American born Irish adults and white collar Irishmen grew enormously, it would seem that the trend toward accommodation should have gained momentum in Worcester and throughout the nation. Yet, in the Massachusetts city, and, it appears, in other parts of the United States, it did not. The American born Irish may, as Shannon suggests, have become increasingly militant as their numbers and thus their political power and expectations grew. In Worcester, however, if the second generation Irish led the political charge in the city's ethnocentric revival in the 1890's, it was the immigrants who supplied the troops for revitalized Irish militant associations such as the AOH and the Clan Na Gael. This immigrant revolt occurred in a decade when the number of Irish immigrants in Worcester and throughout the United States was actually in decline.[144] There were, of course, changes occurring within the immigrant populations in Worcester and elsewhere, most notably the immigration of new Irish exiles whose Irish experience differed substantially from their immigrant predecessors.[145] Nevertheless, in Worcester at least all of these new immigrants accounted for but one fourth of the city's Irish foreign stock population in 1900, and the vast majority of them lay mired at the very bottom of Worcester's occupational hierarchy.

Clearly the maturing of the second generation Irish and the expansion of the Irish middle class in the turn of the century era had a significant effect on the struggle by Irish Americans to sort out their loyalties and define their role in the larger American society. Indeed, these internal trends seemed to precipitate the identity crisis which afflicted Irish America in that period, as they carried Irish Americans into a new transitional era in their history, an era when identities and roles defined earlier in the nineteenth century for a very different Irish people no longer seemed applicable. By introducing experiences and interests which fundamentally differed from those of older lower class Irish immigrants, the new generation, the upwardly mobile Irish and perhaps to a lesser extent, the new Irish immigrants of the late nineteenth century, also broadened the range of potential Irish reactions to this dilemma of identity. Yet if these internal changes sharpened or even posed that dilemma, and increased the variety of potential Irish responses to it, those changes did not by themselves define the nature of the Irish response nor determine when the Irish would respond as they did.

The history of the Worcester Irish in the late nineteenth century suggests that to answer those questions it is necessary to look outside ethnic communities as well as examine their internal transformations. In Worcester in the 1890's, for example, lingering memories of the Civil War, economic prosperity, the rise of Parnell in Ireland and perhaps most important, the emergence of a complicated politics binding Irishmen and Yankees together through mutual interest boosted the second generation's influence beyond their numbers and gave credence to their hopes of peacefully accommodating their people to American society and culture. In the following decade, confusion in Ireland, reaction in the Vatican, economic depression, heightened ethnic tension and political turbulence dashed those hopes. The second generation now seemed confused and uncertain, while the immigrant and lower class Irish, so listless in the 1880's, mobilized ethusiastically behind an Irish ethnocentric revival in the 1890's.

Some of these trends and events affected all or nearly all Irish communities in late nineteenth century America. Virtually all Irish American communities felt some impact from Parnell's rise and fall, the Vatican's shift from tolerance to crackdown on Liberal Catholicism, and the immigration of new immigrants from a host of new countries.[146]

Nevertheless, though there are almost no histories of Irish communities extending beyond 1880, sketchy evidence patched from a number of sources reveals striking variations in the environmental conditions of individual Irish communities and thus significant differences in their responses to those conditions. Some of these variations were regional. In the Western United States economies were more dynamic than in the East, native stock Americans less well entrenched, and nativism perhaps more feeble. These conditions not only permitted the Irish lace curtain class to expand more quickly than in the East, but perhaps encouraged Western Irishmen to embrace American culture more readily, and feel more confident about gaining full entry into the mainstream of their local societies.[147] Yet even these regional generalizations may be too broad. The spirit of accommodation did not flourish only in the West. Efforts at accommodation appeared not only among the Irish in Worcester in the 1880's, but among the Celts in Boston as well. In Boston the Church studiously avoided a confrontation with native stock Protestants, and conservative Irish Nationalism thrived, just as in Worcester.[148] Again, as in Worcester, a political environment which linked Boston's Irishmen and Yankees in a complicated mutual dependence may have nourished these attempts at accommodation in the 1880's and, just as in Worcester, when that mutual dependence dissolved into ethnic war in the 1890's, Irish ethnic militancy became much more popular.[149] In Philadelphia, Irishmen confronted different circumstances than the Massachusetts Gaels, but their response at least in the 1880's seemed similar. Irishmen in Phihladelphia concluded a "Victorian compromise" with the rest of their city in the late nineteenth century, adapting to the power of a well entrenched native stock Republican machine, building a church which if rigidly separated from Protestant society nonetheless inculcated aspirations for respectability and admiration for

American values into its faithful, and finally forging a nationalist movement which was conservative in both goals and methods.[150] Chicago and New York are less easily categorized. In the former city, partisan rivalry was intense, but factionalism wreaked havoc in both parties.[151] The Irish dominated church in Chicago seemed to reflect traces of Liberal optimism, while steadfastly building its own school system and refusing to hasten the process of assimilation among non Irish Catholics.[152] In dramatic contrast to Boston and Worcester, Chicago's militant Irish nationalists organized in the Clan Na Gael dominated the city's nationalist movement in the 1880's.[153] In New York City, chaos appeared to reign, revealing no clear pattern. Factionalism flourished in the Democratic majority, in the Church and in the Nationalist movement.[154] Without further study of these and other Irish communities in the turn of the century era, the impact of local conditions on how Irishmen defined themselves or their roles in the larger societies of their cities remains shadowy. Nevertheless, this brief survey suggests the critical importance of local conditions in influencing the timing and nature of those definitions.

More important, the differences among Irish communities at the turn of the century reinforces the central lesson derived from the history of the Irish in Worcester during that period: that shifts in ethnic consciousness in an ethnic group or community are not caused by internal changes alone but in the interaction of such changes with trends and events taking place in the environment outside those groups or communities. This lesson is relevant not only to the history of the Irish in turn of the century America, but to the study of other ethnic groups in other periods as well. German Americans, for example, were in a state of transition in the 1910's similar to that experienced by Irish Americans a decade or two earlier. A new American-born German generation was reaching maturity while the German American middle class expanded rapidly. In the midst of this transition the United States entered World War I against Germany inciting an outbreak of vicious anti-German nativism and precipitating a crisis of loyalties among German Americans perhaps unprecedented in the history of a major American ethnic group.[155] It would seem difficult to explain the virtual evaporation of German ethnic identification which followed the war without taking into account both these internal changes *and* the war crisis. A more recent example of the effects of interaction between internal and external influences was the white ethnic revival of the late 1960's and early 1970's. Some observers have attributed this revival of white ethnic militancy to the emergence of a new generation of ethnics, a third generation less insecure about their place in American society than their second generation parents and thus psychologically freer to express interest in their ethnic ancestry.[156] Yet the "law" of the third generation's "return" to their ethnic past has also been used to explain the religious revival of the 1950's.[157] Again, it does not appear that internal changes, specifically the emergence of the third generation, can fully explain these two very different revivals. When the third generation reacted, and more important, how it did, seemed heavily influenced in both cases by environmental conditions, first the trend to respectable conformity in the placid 1950's and then to ethnic militance in the turbulence and polarization of the 1960's.[158]

The effects of interaction between internal and external changes on group consciousness can be seen not only in the history of white ethnics in America, but in the history of groups as well, such as Blacks and women. In the histories of these groups the generational schema is more difficult to apply. Blacks even by the late nineteenth century were very distant from their African origins, and there is no original generation like the immigrants to use as a starting point for women. Nevertheless, historians of American Blacks have often noted the roles of new age cohorts as well as external influences in the rise and fall of Afro-American radical consciousness over the last seventy years.[159] Similarly, historians of American women like Peter Filene have suggested the significance of new female generations as well as environmental trends and events in causing the ebb and flow of feminist consciousness in the United States.[160]

The lesson of the Irish in turn of the century Worcester is an important one. It has significant implications beyond the history of their community, their group or their period. With the explosion of self conscious groups in modern American society, and the revitalization of ethnic consciousness that lesson may even be more relevant today than ever before. Those trends in fact have sparked a new debate over the whole concept of group identification. This debate, as Philip Gleason notes, has split social scientists into conflicting camps over the importance of internal versus external or "circumstantial" influences on ethnic and other forms of group consciousness.[161] Analysis of the experience of the Irish in Thomas Kiely's and Joshua O'Leary's Worcester suggests no such strict dichotomy, but rather the effects of a complicated interactive process of internal and external changes.

Archives, Archdiocese of Boston Timothy J. Meagher
Boston, MA 02135

FOOTNOTES

1. *Messenger*, March 26, 1898.

2. *Messenger*, September 14, 1895.

3. *Worcester Evening Gazette*, Dec. 1, 1924; July 16, 1941.

4. Rudolf Vecoli, "Ethnicity: A Neglected Dimension of American History," in Herbert Bass ed. *State of American History* (Chicago, 1970), pp. 70-88; Vecoli, "European Americans: From Immigrants to Ethnics," *International Migration Review* (1972): 403-434; Vladimir Nahirny and Joshua Fishman, "American Immigrant Groups: Ethnic Identification and the Problem of Generations," *Sociological Review* XIII (1965): 311-326; For Hansen, see Marcus Lee Hansen, "The Third Generation," in Oscar Handlin ed. *The Children of the Uprooted* (New York, 1966), p. 258; for Park, see Vecoli, "Ethnicity: A Neglected Dimension," p. 75, and for recent views of acculturating process, see Milton M. Gordon, *Assimilation in American Life* (New York, 1964), p. 78.

5. For Marginal Man, see Everett E. Stonequist, *The Marginal Man: A Study in Personality and Culture Conflict* (New York, 1937). For studies in America and Australia, see Irwin L. Child, *Italian or American? The Second Generation in Conflict* (New Haven, 1943) and Ruth Johnston, *The Assimilation Myth: A Study of Second Generation Polish Immigrants in Western Australia* (The Hague, 1969), and Bernard Lazerwitz, "Contrasting the Effects of Generation, Class, Sex and Age on Group Identification in the Jewish and Protestant Communities," *Social Forces* 49, pp. 50-59; For recent views of primordial ethnicity, see Philip Gleason, "Identifying Identity: A Semantic History," *Journal of American History*, 69 (1983); 910-931.

6. Donald Horowitz, "Ethnic Identity," in Nathan Glazer and Daniel P. Moynihan, eds. *Ethnicity: Theory and Experience* (Cambridge, 1975), p. 135. See also, Horowitz, "Cultural Movements and Ethnic Change," *Annals of the American Association of Political and Social Science* 483 (1977), and perhaps for a more extreme view of the effects of the environment, William Yancey, Eugene P. Erickson and Richard Juliani, "Emergent Ethnicity," *American Sociological Review* 41, 3 (1976): 397. For discussions of internal and external factors in shaping ethnic identity, see Abner Cohen ed., *Urban Ethnicity* (London, 1974), and Gleason, "Identifying Identity," pp. 910-931.

7. William Shannon, *The American Irish: A Political and Social Portrait* (New York, 1970), pp. 131-145.

8. *Reports of the U.S. Immigration Commission*, "Distribution of Immigrants: 1850-1900," Vol. III, pp. 416-417.

9. George Dangerfield, *The Damnable Question: A Study in Anglo Irish Relations* (Boston, 1976); Robert Cross, *The Emergence of Liberal Catholicism in America* (Cambridge, Mass., 1967); Thomas T. McAvoy, *The Americanist Heresy in Roman Catholicism 1895-1900* (Notre Dame, 1963); Robert Wiebe, *The Search for Order 1877-1920* (New York, 1967); Samuel P. Hays, *The Response to Industrialism: 1895-1914* (Chicago, 1957).

10. Vincent Powers, "Invisible Immigrants: The Pioneer Irish of Worcester, Massachusetts, 1826-1860," Clark University, Ph.D. Dissertation, 1976, pp. 94-124, pp. 150-205, pp. 240-286; U.S. Census Office, *Statistics of the Population of the United States at the Tenth Census, June 1, 1880*, "Population," (Washington, 1872), p. 677; *Twelfth Census of the United States Taken in the Year, 1900*, Vol. I, "Population," (Washington, 1901), p. 802.

11. *Census of the Commonwealth of Massachusetts, 1885*, Vol. I, Part I, "Population and Social Statistics," (Boston, 1887), pp. 664-665; George F. Hoar, "Heart of the Commonwealth," *Donahoes Magazine*, Dec., 1884, p. 547; *Twelfth Census of the United States*, Vol. I, "Population," p. 802, p. 881.

12. Only 3,749 second generation Irish were over the age of 18 in 1880 compared to 10,132 immigrants over age 18 and 1,342 were over age 25 in 1880 compared to 9,119 of the immigrants over age 25 in that year. By 1900 the number of American born over age 18 had risen to 9,564, and of these 6,590 were over the age of 25. The number of immigrants over age 18 in 1900 was still larger but only slightly at 10,952, and the number over 25 was 9,617. Based on samples of 966 immigrant men and women over age 18 (one of every nine) and 671 second generation Irish over age 18 (one of every eight taken from the Manuscript Schedules of the 1880 U.S. Census and samples of 1218 Irish immigrant men and women over 18 (one of every 9) and 797 second generation Irish over 18 (one of every 12) taken from the Manuscript Schedules of the 1900 U.S. Census.

13. O'Flynn Mss., Folio I, p. 624a, Holy Cross College Treasure Room.

14. *Messenger*, Mar. 18, 1904; *Worcester Daily Times*, Mar. 17, 1882, Nov. 26, 1881; *Irish World*, Apr. 23, 1881; Clipping, no citation, Mar. 1, 1898, "Records of the Convention of United Irish Societies," Volume III, p. 204, O'Flynn Mss., Holy Cross College Treasure Room.

15. *Messenger*, Mar. 18, 1904; *Worcester Daily Times*, Mar. 17, 1882; "Records of the Convention of United Irish Societies," Volume II, p. 206, O'Flynn Mss., Holy Cross College Treasure Room. Kirby Miller with Bruce Boling and David N. Doyle, "Emigrants and Exiles: Irish Culture and Irish Emigration to North America, 1790-1922," *Irish Historical Studies* XXII (1980): 97-125. See also, Thomas N. Brown, *Irish American Nationalism 1870-1890* (Philadelphia, 1966), p. 21.

16. *Messenger*, Mar. 18, 1904; O'Flynn Mss., "Records of the Conventions," Volume II, p. 206, Holy Cross College.

17. *Worcester Daily Times*, Nov. 26, 1881; *Catholic Messenger*, Mar. 25, 1926.

18. *Worcester Daily Times*, Nov. 26, 1881.

19. *Ibid*.

20. Rev. T.J. Conaty, "The Ideal American," *The Catholic Home and School Magazine*, Apr., 1885, p. 56; Major John Byrne, "Talks to Catholic Young Men," *Catholic School and Home Magazine*, July, 1892, p. 190.

21. Immigrant Sample, 1800 U.S. Census Manuscript Schedules; Immigrant Sample, 1900 U.S. Census Manuscript Schedules.

22. Only 6.3% of the Irish immigrant men who came to America between 1881 and 1885 had become white collar workers by 1900, and only another 17.5% had become blue collar workers. Nearly half were still unskilled workers fifteen to nineteen years after they came to America. Immigrant Sample, 1900 U.S. Census Manuscript Schedules. Such slow individual progress may have reinforced communal attitudes brought from Ireland. See Miller, Boling and Doyle "Emmigrants and Exiles," pp. 105-120. For discussions of similar attitudes of communal solidarity reinforced in America, see John Bodnar, "Immigration and Modernization: The Case of Slavic Peasants in Industrial America," *Journal of Social History* 11, (1976): 44-67, and Herbert Gans, *The Urban Villagers: Group and Class in the Life of Italian Americans* (New York, 1962), pp. 218-225. For discussions in a wider context, see Cohen ed., *Urban Ethnicity*.

23. Second generation sample, 1800 U.S. Census Manuscript Schedules.

24. Sentiments were frequently expressed in the Worcester Irish community condemning Irish Catholics who minimized their faith or hid their ethnic background in order to move up in society. The wealthy and ambitious Irish were frequently attacked for such pandering to native stock Protestants. Rev. John J. McCoy, *History of the Diocese of Springfield* (Boston, Mass., 1900), p. 32; *Messenger*, Sept. 20, 1902; Dedication Souvenir of A.O.H. Hall, p. 69; Byrne, "Advice to Catholic Young Men," *Catholic School and Home Magazine*, July 1892, p. 38. Such sentiments were not confined to the Irish in Worcester, but were significant themes in the Catholic literature of the period. Paul Messbarger, *Fiction with a Parochial Purpose: Social Uses of American Catholic Literature: 1884-1900* (Boston, 1971) pp. 80-85.

25. Marriage Ages based on Irish men and women ever married over age 45. In 1900 40.0% of the second generation Irish males and 39.4% of the second generation Irish females aged 30-34 were unmarried. Fertility information of women aged 45 and over and married 10 to 20 years in 1900:

	Rhode Island Native Stock	Worcester Irish Immigrants	Worcester Second Generation
no children	20%	8.3%	7.0%
over 3 children	41.5%	83.4%	80.7%
		n = 96	n = 57

Data for native stock Rhode Island women taken from *Reports of the Immigration Commission: 61st Congress, Document No. 282* vol. 28 part 1, p. 757. Data for Worcester Irish marriage age and fertility taken from Second Generation Irish Samples: 1900 U.S. Census Manuscript Schedules.

26. Of the Irish elite listed in Nutt's History of Worcester in 1919, only 7.2% owned their own manufacturing firms but 36% were lawyers or doctors. 104 Irishmen were listed. Charles Nutt *History of Worcester and Its People* (New York, 1919), Volumes II and III; *Catholic Messenger*, July 25, 1913, *Alumna*, June, 1886, p. 2; Joseph Lee, *The Modernization of Irish Society* (Dublin: 1973), pp. 9-20.

27. In 1900 65.9% of second generation Irish household heads lived in the oldest Irish neighborhoods or adjacent tenement districts. Second Generation Sample, 1900 U.S. Manuscript Schedules. For the slow pace of suburbanization in the city, see Roger A. Roberge, *The Three Decker Structural Correlate of Worcester's Industrial Revolution* (M.A. Thesis, Clark University, 1965).

28. Of the Irish elite listed in Nutt's *History of Worcester* in 1919, 42.3% held government or political party posts at some point in their lifetime. Nutt, *History of Worcester*, Volumes III and IV, for doctors, see Nutt, *History of Worcester*, Vol. I, p. 398.

29. John J. McGratty, *The Life of Very Rev. John J. Power*, pp. 10-11, pp. 21-26; Miriam Witherspoon, *Forty Years of Family Service: The Story of the Associated Charities in Worcester between 1889 and 1929* (Worcester, 1936), p. 15; Donna Merwick, *Boston Priests: A Study of Social and Intellectual Change* (Cambridge, Mass., 1973), p. 156.

30. *Messenger*, Jan. 28, 1893, Sept. 14, 1893, Sept. 28, 1895, Apr. 6, 1895. On the YMCA, see *Messenger*, Jan. 28, 1893.

31. *Messenger*, Sept. 23, 1893, June 9, 1894; *Worcester Evening Spy*, Sept. 10, 1895; *Catholic Messenger*, Apr. 12, 1914; *First Annual Report of the Sisters of Providence Hospital for the year ending December 31, 1894*.

32. Thomas T. McAvoy, *A History of the Catholic Church in the United States* (Notre Dame, 1969), p. 260; Pamphlet of Clippings, "A Quarter Century of St. John's High School," Worcester Historical Museum Pamphlet File; Catholic Free Press, Apr. 17, 1970; Alexandre Belisle, *Livre D'Or Des Franco-Americaines de Worcester* (Worcester, 1920), pp. 19-52; City Documents, No. 65, p. 1042.

33. Power also served on the Worcester School Committee, McGratty, *Life of Very Rev. John J. Power*, p. 72, pp. 72-81, p. 104, pp. 34-36.

34. *Alumna*, May 1886, p. 4.

35. *Alumna*, May 1886, p. 4, Jan. 1887, p. 2; *Messenger*, July 7, 1894.

36. *Messenger*, Nov. 21, 1891, July 25, 1891, Jan. 11, 1890, Feb. 1, 1890, May 25, 1895.

37. *Messenger*, Sept. 14, 1895.

38. *Worcester Daily Times*, Mar. 18, 1880, Oct. 11, 1880, Mar. 13, 1882, Apr. 20, 1883; Monsignor Griffin Diary and Sermon book, entry Mar. 13, 1876, St. John's Parish Archives; O'Flynn Mss., "Records of the Conventions," Vol. II, p. 21, p. 205, Holy Cross College; Stephen Littleton, "Diaries," Volume II, entry Dec. 11, 1889, American Antiquarian Society.

39. O'Flynn Mss., "Records of the Conventions," Vol. II, no citation, Mar. 18, 1886, p. 71, Holy Cross College.

40. "Harvest Festival Souvenir," St. Stephen's Parish May 1900, St. Stephen's Parish Archives; O'Flynn Mss., Vol. I, "Program Coffee Party: St. Anne's TA Society," Holy Cross College; Littleton, "Diaries," Volume I, entry Dec. 11, 1889; St. Paul's Temperance and Literary Lyceum, "Tenth Anniversary Program," Nov. 22, 1899, American Antiquarian Society.

41. Monsignor Griffin Diary and Sermon Book entries, Mar. 31, 1878, Sept. 29, 1878, Mar. 1, 1876; O'Flynn Mss., Folio 2, p. 286, Holy Cross College.

42. Roy Rosenzweig, *Eight Hours For What We Will: Workers and Leisure in an Industrial City, 1870-1920* (New York, 1983), p. 104; *Messenger*, July 7, 1888; *Worcester Daily Times*, Jan. 13, 1883.

43. Elizabeth Malcolm, "Catholic Church and Irish Temperance," *Irish Historical Studies* XXIII (1982): 4-9.

44. *Fiftieth Anniversary of Rev. Matthew Total Abstinence Society, Father Matthew Hall Wed. Nov. 15, 1899* (Worcester, 1899).

45. *Messenger*, Apr. 28, 1888; Thomas J. Conaty, "Father Matthew," *Catholic School and Home Magazine*, Oct. 1894, p. 166 and Conaty, "The Temperance Idea in Public Instruction," *Catholic School and Home Magazine*, Mar. 1895, p. 10; Records of the St. John's Temperance and Literary Guild, Vol. II, entry Nov. 10, 1901, St. John's Parish Archives.

46. O'Flynn Mss., "Records of the Conventions," Vol. II, clipping, no citation, Mar. 18, 1886, p. 72, Holy Cross College.

47. St. John's Temperance and Literary Guild Records, Vol. I, entries Apr. 20, 1885, Mar. 6, 1887, Mar. 28, 1887, Apr. 20, 1887; *St. Aloysius Echo*, mar. 17, 1887; Littleton, "Diaries," Volume III entry Feb. 22, 1891, American Antiquarian Society; *Messenger*, July 29, 1893; *Worcester Daily Times*, Feb. 26, 1886; *Worcester Evening Spy*, Apr. 4, 1887, Aug. 28, 1895.

48. St. Paul's Temperance and Literary Lyceum, "Harvest Festival Program May 22, 1894," American Antiquarian Society; St. John's Temperance and Literary Guild Records, Vol. I, entries Jan. 20, 1887, Mar. 6, 1887, Mar. 14, 1887. O'Flynn Mss. Folio I, "Coffee Party Program: St. Anne's TA Society," Holy Cross College.

49. Of 34 recorded votes on the parade between 1885 and 1895 parish temperance societies voted against it 20 times: O'Flynn Mss., "Records of the Conventions," Volumes II and III, Holy Cross College; O'Flynn Mss., "Records of the Conventions," Vol. II, p. 78, p. 133, p. 148; *Worcester Daily Times*, Mar. 4, 1882.

50. Gatherings of 4,000 Nov. 21, 1882, 3,000 Feb. 7, 1881 and 2,000 Jan. 13, 1882 reflect this interest which persisted throughout most of the decade. *Boston Pilot*, Mar. 6, 1880, Jan. 31, 1881, Feb. 25, 1882; Worcester Evening Spy, Mar. 1, 1886, Nov. 23, 1885; *Worcester Daily Times*, Jan. 13, 1882; O'Flynn Mss., Folio I, pp. 618-622, Holy Cross College; *Irish World*, May 17, 1881.

51. *Alumna*, Sept. 1886, p. 3; *Worcester Daily Times*, Feb. 22, 1882, Mar. 14, 1882, mar. 18, 1882, Mar. 20, 1882, Mar. 28, 1882, Apr. 26, 1882; *Messenger*, Feb. 2, 1889; June 22, 1889; July 13, 1889, Dec. 26, 1891, Nov. 26, 1892, Feb. 4, 1893, Mar. 4, 1893.

52. *Worcester Evening Spy*, Feb. 7, 1880; O'Flynn Mss., Folio I, p. 615, Holy Cross College.

53. *Worcester Daily Times*, Oct. 14 and 17, 1881, Jan. 13, 1882; *Worcester Evening Spy*, Mar. 1 and 9, 1886, Nov. 30, 1887. Worcester's Yankees contributed $922 or 39% of the funds collected for the Parnell Parliamentary Fund in 1886 for example. O'Flynn Mss., Folio I, p. 173, Holy Cross College.

54. For Parnell's effect on the people of Worcester, see *Worcester Daily Times*, Feb. 22, 1881, Nov. 26, 1880, May 27, 1882, May 23, 1882, Oct. 9, 1882, June 10, 1882, Nov. 11, 1883; O'Flynn Mss., "Records of the Conventions," Volume II, p. 62, Holy Cross College.

55. O'Flynn Mss., "Records of the Conventions," Vol. III, pp. 1-12.

56. *Messenger*, June 20, 1891, Nov. 7, 1889, Mar. 19, 1892, Sept. 1, 1894.

57. *Messenger*, Feb. 8, 1892, May 14, 1892, Nov. 26, 1892.

58. Chauncey Buel, "The Workers of Worcester: Social Mobility and Ethnicity in a New England City 1850 to 1880," (Ph.D. Dissertation, New York University, 1974), pp. 77-78. A.P. Marvin, History of Worcester in the War of the Rebellion (Worcester, 1870), p. 160, p. 234, pp. 506-507; *Celebration of the 200th Anniversary of the Naming of Worcester October 14 and 15, 1884* (Worcester, 1885), pp. 68-75; *Dedication of the Soldiers' Monument at Worcester July 15, 1874* (Worcester, 1875), pp. 16-17; Nutt; *History of Worcester*, II, p. 645, p. 674.

59. *Worcester Daily Times*, Jan. 17, 1883, Dec. 7, 1882; Rosenzweig, *Eight Hours for What We Will*, pp. 16-26.

60. *Worcester Daily Times*, Dec. 7, 1882.

61. The *Times* estimated Irish voting strength at 3,000 in 1881, out of a total electorate of 10

IRISH ALL THE TIME

or 11,000. *Worcester Daily Times*, Nov. 30, 1881. See also, *Worcester Daily Times*, Nov. 24, 1879, Dec. 11, 1879, Nov. 2, 1883, Sept. 6, 1882; *Worcester Evening Spy*, Dec. 5, 1887.

62. *Worcester Evening Gazette*, Oct. 21, 1876, Dec. 6 and 13, 1876, Dec. 7, 1877, Sept. 16, 1879, Dec. 10, 1879; *Worcester Daily Times*, Nov. 1, 1884, Nov. 26, 1884; *Worcester Evening Spy*, Oct. 28, 1894.

63. *Worcester Evening Gazette*, Dec. 1, 1876, Dec. 7, 1877, Nov. 30, 1878; *Worcester Daily Times*, Nov. 24, 1879, Dec. 13, 1880, Nov. 14, 1883, Oct. 17, 1883; *Worcester Evening Spy*, Nov. 2, 1894, Nov. 27, 1896; *Messenger*, Nov. 21, 1891, Nov. 28, 1891, Dec. 5, 1891, Dec. 12, 1891, Feb. 6, 1892.

64. *Worcester Daily Times*, Dec. 5, 1883, Dec. 22, 1882, Nov. 20, 1882; *Worcester Telegram*, Dec. 25, 1887. Republicans also courted Irishmen in state or national elections. *Worcester Evening Gazette*, Sept. 17, 1879; *Worcester Daily Times*, Dec. 1, 1879, Oct. 14 and 22, 1880, Sept. 25, 1882. The number of Irishmen on the police force for example rose from 9 in 1873 to 38 in 1884. O'Flynn Mss., Folio I, p. 483, Holy Cross College.

65. *Worcester Daily Times*, Nov. 15, 1882; *Worcester Evening Gazette*, Dec. 6, 1877; *Alumna*, May, 1886, p. 4.

66. *Worcester Daily Times*, Apr. 20, 1882, Feb. 18, 1882, Nov. 26, 1880, July 13, 1883, Sept. 16, 1884; *Irish World*, June 25, 1881. The principal leaders of the Central Branch of the Land League in Worcester were an alderman who was nominated by both the Democrats and Republicans and a contractor who profited enormously from city contracts. *Worcester Daily Times*, May 5, 1882.

67. *Worcester Daily Times*, Sept. 15, 1882; *Worcester Evening Spy*, Nov. 2, 1894; Oct. 29, 1894.

68. Census Manuscript Schedules: 1880 United States Census, Enumeration District 899, p. 5; Enumeration District 895, p. 31; Enumeration District 881, p. 4; Enumeration District 887, p. 9; Enumeration District 889, p. 4.

69. *Worcester Daily Times*, Jan. 31, 1881, Oct. 18, 1881, Feb. 9, 1882, July 11, 1883; *Irish World*, June 25, 1881; O'Flynn Mss., "Coffee Party Program: St. Anne's TA Society," Folio 6, Holy Cross College; St. Paul's Temperance and Literary Lyceum, "Tenth Anniversary Harvest Festival Program: November 22, 1899," American Antiquarian Society; St. John's Temperance and Literary Guild "Records," Vol. I, entries Mar. 6 and 14, 1887; St. John's Parish Archives; Catholic Total Abstinance Union of Springfield, *Thirtieth Annual Field Day and Games at Holy Cross College, Worcester, Mass. September 2, 1907* (Boston, 1907), pp. 12-20.

70. *Worcester Evening Gazette*, July 6, 1941.

71. In Temperance movement: 33 of the temperance delegates to the Conventions of United Irish Societies held annually between 1884 and 1895 in Worcester could be traced into the 1880 or 1900 U.S. Census Manuscript Schedules. Of the 33, 26 (79% were born in America of Irish parents: sources, O'Flynn Mss., "Records of the Conventions," Volumes II and III, Holy Cross College; Roy Rosenzweig found that two thirds of the members of the St. John's Temperance and Literary Guild which he traced into the 1880 Census Manuscript Schedules were American born: Rosenzweig, *Eight Hours for What We Will*, p. 259; Of 44 members of the St. John's Temperance and Literary Guild from 1897-1898 traced into the 1900 Census Manuscript Schedules, 39 (88%) were second generation Irish. Opponents of the temperance societies also frequently characterized them as American born: O'Flynn Mss., "Records of the Conventions," Volume II, p. 78, p. 133, p. 148, p. 103, p. 169, Volume III, pp. 201-204, Holy Cross College. Of the temperance delegates traced into Worcester City Directories, the occupational breakdown was as follows:

White collar	42% (48)
Skilled Blue collar	32.4% (37)
Semi and Unskilled Blue Collar	25.3% (29)
Total	(114)

There is no evidence breaking down the nationalist movement by generation though the leadership at least seemed to include immigrants like Andrew Athy and Jeremiah Murphy and second generation Irish such as Francis P. McKeon and John F.H. Mooney. *Worcester Daily Times*, Feb. 11, 1881. The occupational breakdown of contributors to the Parnell Parliamentary Fund in 1886 was as follows:

White collar	41.4% (41)
Skilled Blue Collar	40.4% (40)
Semi and Unskilled Blue Collar	18.2% (18)
Total	(99)

Source: O'Flynn Mss., Folio I, p. 605, Holy Cross College.

72. Of the 20 A.O.H. delegates to the Convention of Irish Societies in the 1880's who could be traced into the Census Manuscript Schedules of the 1880 and 1900 Census, 18 (90%) were immigrants. The occupational breakdown of A.O.H. delegates to the Convention was as follows:

White Collar	24.1%
Skilled Blue Collar	37.0%
Semi or Unskilled Blue Collar	39.4%

73. Lower class and immigrant support for the radical wing of the Irish Nationalist movement can be inferred from letters and contributions sent to the *Irish World*, such as those sent from Worcester wire workers, *Irish World*, Dec. 31, 1881; and from recent immigrants such as thirteen men from Achonry in Sligo, *Irish World*, Mar. 1882; and from Clare or West Kerry men living in Worcester, *Irish World*, Apr. 23, 1881, June 3, 1882; Note that all of these men are from the poorer Western part of Ireland. For discussion of the significance of their regional backgrounds, see Victor Walsh, "The Fanatic Heart: The Cause of Irish American Nationalism in Pittsburgh During the Gilded Age," *Journal of Social History* 15 (1981).

74. For the discouragement and confusion Parnell's fall caused in Worcester, see *Messenger*, Feb. 28, 1891, Mar. 21, 1891, Apr. 2, 1891, Apr. 4, 1891, Mar. 4, 1893, Apr. 14, 1894.

75. Thomas T. McAvoy, *The Americanist Hersy in Roman Catholicism 1895-1900* (Notre Dame, 1963), pp. 227-258. Few in Worcester protested against the Vatican's policies, at least openly, though Joshua O'Leary did plead for Issac Hecker' reputation. *Recorder*, July 15, 1895.

76. The Swedish foreign stock population in Worcester rose from approximately 2,112 (The number of second generation Swedes was too small for the census to list in 1885) to 11,742 between 1885 and 1900, while the French Canadian foreign stock population rose from 5,083 to 10,052 in the same period. *The Census of Massachusetts 1885*, Volume I, "Population and Social Statistics," Part I, pp. 563, pp. 665-666, U.S. Census Office, *Twelfth Census, 1900*, Volume I, "Population," Part I, pp. 876-877.

77. South Worcester, for example, a neighborhood over 50% Irish in 1880, feel to 17.6% Irish in 1900 largely because of French Canadian and Swedish invasions. On Southgate Street in that district, the number of Irish families declined from 60 to 40 between 1890 and 1904 while the number of French rose from 29 to 56. Second Generation and Immigrant Samples. 1880 and 1900 U.S. Census Manuscript Schedules; *Worcester House Directory* (Worcester, 1890), pp.

361-363; *Worcester House Directory* (Worcester, 1904), pp. 411-413. The number of Swedes employed in any occupation in the city in 1880 was 762. By 1888 over 800 were employed in the wire mills alone. By 1900 Swedish and French Canadian workers outnumbered the Irish in manufacturing and mechanical pursuits. *Tenth Census of the United States in 1880*, "Population," p. 908; Charles Washburn, *Industrial Worcester* (Worcester, 1917), p. 146; *Twelfth Census of the United States*, "Special Report: Occupations," pp. 760-763.

78. The proportion of Irish immigrants employed in the wire industry for example fell from 17.7% to 12.1% between 1880 and 1900. Immigrant Samples, 1880 and 1900 U.S. Census Manuscript Schedules.

79. *Worcester Daily Times*, Apr. 29, 1886, June 25, 1886; see also, Rosenzweig, *Eight Hours for What We Will*, p. 29.

80. Robert Rumilly, *Histoire Des Franco Americains* (Montreal, 1958), pp. 106-108, pp. 177-178; *L'Opinion Publique*, Oct. 8, 1900, Oct. 22, 1900.

81. O'Flynn Mss., Folio 12, clipping, no citation, Dec. 6, 1888, Dec. 13, 20 and 31, Jan. 14, 1890, Holy Cross College; *Worcester Telegram*, Nov. 19, 1890.

82. *American*, Aug. 8, 1893, Oct. 24, 1893, Apr. 25, 1893, Dec. 1, 1893; Donald Kinzer, *An Episode in Anti-Catholicism: The American Protective Association* (Seattle, 1963), p. 100, p. 180. By January of 1894, there were 1500 men in Worcester's nativist societies. *American*, Jan. 23, 1894.

83. Kinzer, *An Episode in Anti-Catholicism*, p. 100, p. 180; *Worcester Evening Spy*, Dec. 14, 1893.

84. *Worcester Evening Spy*, Dec. 6, 1896; *Worcester Evening Post*, Nov. 17, 1899; *Worcester Evening Gazette*, Nov. 13 and 16, 1899; *Worcester Telegram*, Nov. 9, 1899; *Messenger*, Dec. 19, 1903.

85. McKinley beat Bryan in Worcester, 10,108 votes to 3,636, about three times the size of Harrison's margin over Cleveland in 1892. *Worcester Evening Spy*, Dec. 6, 1896, Nov. 4, 1896; *Worcester Evening Gazette*, Nov. 13 and 16, 1899; Geoffrey Blodgett, *The Gentle Reformers Massachusetts Democrats in the Cleveland Era* (Cambridge, Mass., 1966), pp. 218-259.

86. *Worcester Evening Gazette*, Nov. 23, 1899; *Worcester Telegram*, Nov. 3 and 4, 1899; *Messenger*, Apr. 1, 1899; *Worcester Evening Post*, Dec. 9, 1899.

87. Sample of Immigrants: 1900 U.S. Census Manuscript Schedules.

88. On the Land War's effect, see Lee, *Modernization of Ireland*. David Doyle, however, wonders in the younger Irish, those most likely to immigrate took part in the Land War. See David Doyle, "Unestablished Irishmen" in Dirk Hoerder ed., *American Labor and Immigration History: Recent European Research* (Urbana, 1983), p. 203. On the Gaelic Revival in Ireland, see Lee *Modernization of Ireland*, pp. 137-140. For evidence of Irish in Worcester who had experience in the G.A.A., see *Messenger*, Oct. 13, 1900.

89. Doyle, "Unestablished Irishmen" in Hoerder ed., *American Labor*, pp. 199-215; David Fitzpatrick, "Irish Immigration in the later Nineteenth Century" *Irish Historical Studies* XXII (1980): 126-193.

90. Powers, "Invisible Immigrants," pp. 286-382.

91. The number of second generation Irish over age 18 rose from 3,749 in 1880 to 9,564 in 1900. The number over age 25 rose from 1,322 to 6,590 in the same period. Samples of Second Generation, 1880 and 1900 U.S. Census Manuscript Schedules.

92. On Irish preference for isolation, see *Worcester Telegram*, Nov. 27-28, 1899 and *Worcester Evening Post*, Dec. 9, 1899; *Worcester Telegram*, Nov. 27, 1900. Between 1877 and 1897 Irish Democrats allied with Yankee Republican factions in citizens coalitions in no less than 14 of the 20 city elections. After 1897 there were no more citizens coalitions, and between 1900 and 1916, in all 16 elections the Democratic nominee for mayor was an Irishman. Nutt, *History of Worcester*, Vol. I, pp. 397-398. On increased Irish expectations in the twentieth century, see *Messenger*, Dec. 12, 1903, Jan. 1 and 8, 1904.

93. Catholic Total Abstinence Union of Springfield, *Thirtieth Annual Field Day and Games at Holy Cross College, Worcester, Mass.* (Boston, 1907), pp. 12-20; *Messenger*, July 7, 1894. After the decline of an Irish National Federation Branch in 1893, moderate nationalist groups did not reappear again until 1901 and even then seemed to find little support.

94. The *Messenger* bought out O'Leary's *Recorder* in September of 1899 about one year after it appeared. *Recorder*, Sept. 17, 1898; *Messenger*, Sept. 19, 1899.

95. *Messenger*, Feb. 9, 1901, Feb. 10, 1905; *Catholic Messenger*, Feb. 10, 1907.

96. *Messenger*, Sept. 3, 1898, Nov. 26, 1898, Dec. 2, 1902.

97. *Messenger*, Aug. 23, 1902, Mar. 18, 1899.

98. *Messenger*, Aug. 23, 1902; *Worcester Evening Spy*, Mar. 16, 1903.

99. *Messenger*, July 15, 1899; May 16, 1903. The new editor of the *Messenger* was Thomas Kiely, an immigrant and a member of both the Clan and the A.O.H. *Worcester Evening Gazette*, Dec. 1, 1924.

100. *Messenger*, June 8, 1895.

101. *Worcester Telegram*, Dec. 11, 1907; *Messenger*, Mar. 1, 1907. County sentiment even revived in ward politics. *Messenger*, Nov. 11, 1899.

102. *Messenger*, Oct. 22, 1898. Nov. 19, 1898.

103. *Messenger*, Jan. 1, 1904, Jan. 8 and 16, 1904, Mar. 2, 1906; *Catholic Messenger*, Mar. 1, 1907.

104. *Messenger*, Jan. 1, 1904.

105. *Messenger*, Mar. 18, 1904.

106. *Messenger*, Mar. 2, 1901, Apr. 13, 1901, Aug. 17, 1901, Aug. 30, 1902, Oct. 11, 1902, May 10, 1902.

107. *Messenger*, Oct. 29, 1898.

108. *Worcester Sunday Telegram*, Oct. 26, 1901.

109. *Recorder*, July 8, 1899, Apr. 1, 1899, July 1 and 15, 1899.

110. *Messenger*, Mar. 4, 1899, July 8, 1899.

111. *Messenger*, Mar. 8, 1902.

112. *Messenger*, Oct. 20, 1900.

113. *Messenger*, Apr. 18, 1899, June 3, 1904.

114. *Messenger,* June 8, 1895, Nov. 30, 1895, May 25, 1895, Nov. 30, 1905, July 27, 1901, June 7, 1902, Jan. 5, 1895.

115. *Worcester Evening Post,* Mar. 16, 1909; *Catholic Messenger,* Mar. 1, 1907; *Messenger,* Oct. 13, 1900, July 27, 1901, Feb. 17, 1900.

116. *Messenger,* Sept. 6, 1902, Mar. 26, 1905, Mar. 21, 1906; *Catholic Messenger,* Mar. 2 and 15, 1907, Feb. 1, 1907.

117. *Messenger,* May 12, 1900.

118. *Messenger,* June 8, 1895.

119. Rev. John J. McCoy, *Catholic Viewpoint of the Present French Crisis: Address Before the Congregational Club* (Worcester, 1907), pp. 1-2.

120. In 1899 three of the five second generation Irish running for aldermen were members of the A.O.H. or the Clan or both and in 1900 two new candidates running for aldermen were members of the A.O.H. and/or the Clan. In 1899 all five of the second generation Irishmen slated for state or county contests were members of the A.O.H. or the Clan and in 1900 Philip O'Connell, the new Irish mayor, was a member of the A.O.H. In that same year the *Worcester Sunday Telegram* accused the A.O.H. and the Clan of being a secret political machine working for O'Connell. *Worcester Telegram,* Nov. 26, 1899, Nov. 27, 1900, Dec. 1, 1900; *Worcester Sunday Telegram,* Oct. 26, 1901.

121. The *Messenger,* for example, claimed in 1900 that most of the "good" football players in the city "are lately arrived from Ireland where they have learned the latest wrinkles of the game." *Messenger,* Oct. 13, 1900. For immigrants in Worcester with land war experience, see *Worcester Daily Times,* Apr. 1, 1882.

122. As noted earlier, the proportion of Irish immigrants working in the wire mills where most Swedes began to work in the 1880's and 1890's dropped from 17.7% to 12.1% between 1880 and 1900. See notes 74, 75, 76. Immigrant Samples: 1880 and 1900 U.S. Census Manuscript Schedules.

123. The Messenger's campaign for Irish political recognition in the early 1900's focused heavily on increasing Irish representation among the city government's blue collar workers. *Messenger,* Jan. 1, 3, 15 and 29, 1904.

124. Of the 32 A.O.H. delegates to the Convention of United Irish Societies in the 1890's traced into the Census Manuscript Schedules in 1880 or 1900 U.S. Censuses, 26 (81%) were born in Ireland. Of the 16 officers of A.O.H. divisions in 1899 traced into the Census Manuscript Schedules, 11 (68%) were Irish born and of the 21 officers in 1902 traced into the Census Manuscript Schedules, 17 (80%) were Irish born. O'Flynn Mss., "Records of the Conventions," Volumes II and III, Holy Cross College; *Messenger,* Mar. 18, 1899; *Official Convention Souvenir, A.O.H. Of Massachusetts Worcester Aug. 25 to 28, 1902* (Worcester, 1902); Census Manuscript Schedules: 1880 and 1900 U.S. Census; *Messenger,* Aug. 23, 1902; Mar. 18, 1899.

125. Of the 31 men who joined A.O.H. Division 36 between 1897 (when the Division was founded) and 1902, and who could be traced into the Census Manuscript Schedules of the 1900 U.S. Census, 22 (70.9%) were immigrants. Dues Books of Division 35 A.O.H., Hibernian Hall, Shrewsbury, Mass.

126. Of the 26 immigrant A.O.H. delegates to the Convention of Irish Societies in the 1890's, 15 (57%) came to the United States after 1880, 9 of them (34%) after 1886. Of the members of Division 35 A.O.H. 19 (86%) came to the United States after 1880 and 13 of them (58.9%) came after 1886. O'Flynn Mss., "Records of the Conventions," Volumes II and III, Holy Cross

College; Dues Books of Division 35 A.O.H., Hibernian Hall, Shrewsbury, Mass.; Census Manuscript Schedules: 1880 and 1900 U.S. Census.

127. Occupational breakdowns of A.O.H. members and delegates:

	A.O.H. Delegates to the Convention in the 1890's	Division 36 A.O.H. 1897-1904 Members	Division 35 A.O.H. 1906 Members
White Collar	28.5% (42)	7.5% (3)	7.7% (4)
Skilled Blue Collar	19.2% (28)	27.5% (11)	43.1% (22)
Semiskilled and Semiskilled Blue Collar	54.3% (81)	65% (26)	49% (25)
	(151)	(40)	(51)

O'Flynn Mss., "Records of the Conventions," Volumes II and III; Dues Book, Division 36 A.O.H.; Minutes and Attendance Roll, Division 35 A.O.H., Hibernian Hall, Shrewsbury, Mass.

128. *Messenger*, Apr. 1, 1899, Jan. 1 and 8, 1904, Sept. 16, 1904; *Catholic Messenger*, Dec. 15, 1911. By 1930, the French Canadian foreign stock in Worcester numbered 17,000 people, while the Italians, Poles and Lithuanians counted almost 10,000 people a piece. Rose Zeller, "Changes in the Ethnic Composition and Character of Worcester's Population," (Ph.D. Dissertation, Clark University, 1940), pp. 82-83.

129. *Worcester Telegram*, Sept. 7, 1912.

130. For examples of the new Catholic militancy and American nationalism among the Worcester Irish in the twentieth century, see *Catholic Messenger*, Sept. 30, 1915, Dec. 2 and 16, 1915, Apr. 19, 1918, Jan. 25, 1918, Apr. 22, 1910, Mar. 5, 1915, Feb. 15, 1907, Mar. 30, 1916. Leding this movement was the Worcester branch of the Knights of Columbus. Of 34 members admitted to the Knights of Columbus in Worcester between 1896 and 1902 who could be traced into the Manuscript Schedules of the 1900 United States Census, 25 were second generation Irishmen. Lists of members drawn from the *Cable*, September, October, November, 1929. This seemed typical of the K of C nationally. See Christopher J. Kauffman, *Faith and Fraternalism: The History of the Knights of Columbus 1882 to 1982* (New York, 1982), p. 47. Of the men who applied to the Knights between 1905 and 1915, the occupational breakdown was as follows:

White collar	62.3% (492)
Skilled blue collar	20.2% (158)
Unskilled and semi-skilled blue collar	16.8% (132)
	(782)

Source: Recorder, Knights of Columbus, Alhambra Council no. 88 meeting minutes Alhambra Council Archives, Worcester, Massachusetts.

131. Shannon, *The American Irish*, pp. 131-132.

132. Brown, *Irish American Nationalism*, p. 130. Robert Cross, *The Emergence of Liberal Catholicism in America* (Cambridge, Mass., 1967), pp. 28-70.

133. Cross, *Emergence*, pp. 25-28. Eric Foner, "Class, Ethnicity and Radicalism in the Gilded Age: The Land League and Irish America," *Marxist Perspectives* I (1978).

134. Shannon, *American Irish*, pp. 199-200; James P. Walsh, *Ethnic Militancy: An Irish Catholic Prototype* (San Francisco, 1977). David Doyle notes in his *Native Rights and National Empires: Structures Divisions and Attitudes of the Catholic Minority in the Decade of Expansion 1890-1901* (New York, 1976) evidence of the same Nationalist skepticism about American Imperialism which appeared in Worcester in the 1890's. In addition, the A.O.H. nationally grew rapidly in the late 1880's and early 1890's. John O'Dea, *HIstory of the Ancient Order of Hibernians and Ladies Auxiliary* (Philadelphia, 1927), p. 1090, p. 1129.

135. For example, the Knights of Columbus, the principal backers of militant Catholic Americanism, grew substantially in many parts of the country during the late 1890's and early 1900's. Christopher Kauffman, *Faith and Fraternalism: The History of the Knights of Columbus, 1882-1982* (New York, 1982), pp. 73-121.

136. Brown, *Irish American Nationalism*, p. 24, p. 42.

137. Foner, "Class, Ethnicity and Radicalism," pp. 21-23. Walsh notes that the poorest Irish immigrants in Pittsburgh from the most backward areas of Western Ireland seemed indifferent to all forms of Irish Nationalism in the 1880's, while other Southerners and Westerners better integrated into working class organizations backed Patrick Ford. Walsh, "The Fanatic Heart," p. 193, p. 190. Dennis Clark notes the importance of class lines in splits between moderate and radical nationalists in Philadelphia. Dennis Clark, *The Irish in Philadelphia: Ten Generations of Urban Experience* (Philadelphia, 19), p. 136. Michael Funchion, however, feels that generational and class conflict did not seem to disrupt community solidarity in Chicago. Michael Funchion, "Irish Chicago: Church Homeland Politics and Class in the Making of an Ethnic Group, 1870-1900," in Melvin Holli and Peter D'O. Jones, eds., *Ethnic Chicago* (Grand Rapids, Mich., 1981), pp. 31-33.

138. Thomas McAvoy, *The United States of America: The Irish Clergyman* Vol. VI in Patrick Corish, ed., *A History of Irish Catholicism* (Dublin, 1970), p. 25; Cross, *Emergence*.

139. Cross, *Emergence*, pp. 28-36. McAvoy, *The Great Crisis in American Catholic History*, pp. 17-26.

140. Foner, "Class, Ethnicity and Radicalism," pp. 21-23; Walsh, "Fanatic Heart," pp. 187-204; Miller, et al, "Emigrants and Exiles," pp. 121-123.

141. Shannon, *American Irish*, p. 199.

142. As late as 1900, for example, when the number of all second generation Irish was nearly double that of Irish immigrants, the number of second generation Irish male workers exceeded Irish immigrant male workers by only about 30%. *Reports of the Immigration Commission, U.S. Senate Documents: 61st Congress 3rd Session, Abstract of Reports*, Vol. I, p. 825; *Distribution of Immigrants*, Vol. III, p. 552.

143. R.A. Burchell, *The San Francisco Irish 1848-1880* (Berkeley, 1981), p. 54, pp. 85-87; David Doyle, "Unestablished Irishmen," p. 195.

144. *Reports of the Immigration Commission, Abstract of Reports*, Vol. I, p. 136.

145. Doyle, "Unestablished Irishmen," in Hoerder, *American Labor*, pp. 199-215; David Fitzpatrick, "Irish Immigration in the later Nineteenth Century," pp. 126-143. The best analysis of how the cultural and political outlooks of the new immigrants from Western Ireland differed from the Eastern Irishmen is Walsh, "The Fanatic Heart."

146. Shannon, *American Irish*, pp. 135-136; Brown, *Irish American Nationalism*, p. 97; p. 154. Cross, *Emergence*, pp. 195-205.

147. Lawrence McCaffrey, *The Irish Diaspora in America* (Bloomington, Inc., 1976), pp. 74-79. Jo Ellen McNergny Vinyard, *The Irish on the Urban Frontier: Nineteenth Century Detroit* (New York, 1976). David N. Doyle, "The Regional Bibliography of Irish America, 1880-1930: A Review and Addendum," *Irish Historical Studies* XXIII (1983): 254-257.

148. Donna Merwick, *Boston Priests 1848-1910: A Study of Social and Intellectual Change* (Cambridge, Mass., 1973), pp. 69-110. Shannon, *American Irish*, p. 197.

149. Geoffrey Blodgett, *The Gentle Reformers: Massachusetts Democrats in the Cleveland Era* (Cambridge, Mass., 1966), p.

150. Clark, *Irish in Philadelphia*, pp. 126-144.

151. Michael Funchion, "Irish Chicago," p. 23; Bessie Lore Pierce, *A History of Chicago: The Rise of the Modern City, 1871-1893*, Vol. III (Chicago), pp. 353-367; John M. Allswang, *A House for All Peoples Ethnic Politics in Chicago* (Lexington, Ky., 1971), pp. 15-36; Howard Chudacoff, *The Evolution of American Urban Society* (Englewood Cliffs, N.J., 1975), p. 129.

152. Funchion, "Irish Chicago," in Holli and Jones, eds., *Ethnic Chicago*, pp. 11-16; Charles Shanabruch, *Chicago's Catholics: The Evolution of an American Identity* (Notre Dame, 1981).

153. Though the brand of nationalism was different in Chicago than in Worcester, Funchion points out that the same kind of intricate interrelationships between nationalism and local politics on the one hand and nationalism and the church on the other existed in Chicago as well as Worcester. In Chicago the attitudes of the church hierarchy and local political conditions seemed to foster the rise of the Clan Na Gael, whereas in Worcester those attitudes and local conditions seemed to nourish a more moderate nationalism. Funchion, "Irish Chicago," in Holli and Jones, eds., *Ethnic Chicago*, pp. 17-23.

154. Martin Shefter, "The Electoral Foundations of the Political Machine: New York City, 1884-1897," in Joel H. Sibley, Alan G. Bogue and William H. Flanigan, eds., *The History of American Electoral Behavior* (Princeton, 1978), pp. 263-298; Cross, *Emergence*, pp. 119-124; Robert E. Curran, Michael Augustine Corrigan, *The Shaping of Conservative Catholicism in America, 1878-1902* (New York, 1978); Brown, *Irish American Nationalism*, pp. 134-151. Douglas V. Shaw has found interaction between internal changes and local politics in his study of the Irish in Jersey City, New Jersey in the 1860's and 1870's though the results were different than in Worcester. In Jersey City a heavily second generation "lace curtain" class attempted to lead an abortive ethnic revolt against native stock political dominance. Douglas V. Shaw, *The Making of an Immigrant City: Ethnic and Cultural Conflict in Jersey City, New Jersey 1850-1877*, pp. 168-198.

155. Frederick C. Luebke, *Bonds of Loyalty: German Americans and World War I* (DeKalb, Ill., 1974), p. 29, p. 270, p. 287, p. 329. Phyllis Keller has carried this interactional analysis to its most basic level in analyzing the responses of three German-American intellectuals to World War I in terms of their psychological development. Phyllis Keller, *States of Belonging: German American Intellectuals and the First World War* (Cambridge, Mass., 1979), pp. 1-3; pp. 257-261. Philip Gleason and David Salveterra, "Ethnicity, Immigration and American Catholic History" *Social Thought* IV (1978), 22.

156. Richard Gambino, *Blood of my Blood: The Dilemma of Italian Americans* (Garden City, 1975), p. 356.

157. Will Herberg, *Protestant Catholic Jew: An Essay in Religious Sociology* (Garden City, 1955), pp. 27-41.

158. Herberg, *Protestant Catholic Jew*, pp. 46-71. Gambino, *Blood of My Blood*, p. 370. Nathan Glazer and Daniel P. Moynihan, Beyond the Melting Pot (Cambridge, Mass., 1971), pp. XXVII-XXXVIII.

159. Kenneth L. Kusmer, *A Ghetto Takes Shape Black Cleveland* 1870-1930 (Urbana, 1978), pp. 235-236; p. 247. Martin Kilson, "Blacks and New Ethnicity in American Life," in Nathan Glazer and Daniel P. Moynihan, eds., *Ethnicity: Theory and Experience* (Cambridge, Mass., 1975), pp. 246-247.

160. Peter Filene, *Him Her Self: Sex Roles in Modern America* (New York: New American Library, 1976), p. XII.

161. Philip Gleason, "Identifying Identity: A Semantic History," *Journal of American History* 69, (1983): 918-919. Gleason's own view stated in another article seems to aptly sum up the lesson of the history of the Worcester Irish in the late nineteenth century: "The History of the group is shaped by a multiplicity of factors that can be classed in two broad categories: those that are internal to the group and those that impinge upon it from the surrounding culture. These factors interact with each other and the biological constant of generational transition." Gleason and Salveterra, "Ethnicity, Immigration and America Catholic History," p. 21.

Polish mother and child in front of their newly built home in the Windlake Avenue area of Milwaukee's South Side, ca. 1885. This photograph, like several others which illustrate the article beginning on the facing page, was loaned to the Society for copying by James J. Borzych of Milwaukee.

Politics, Religion, and Change in Polish Milwaukee, 1900–1930

By Donald Pienkos

PRIOR to the Civil War, not more than a few dozen residents of Milwaukee were of Polish origin, but as a result of the massive emigration that began in the 1870's, the Poles became a sizable, if little understood, factor in both Wisconsin and Milwaukee.[1] In 1906, roughly 68,000 of Milwaukee's 313,000 inhabitants were Polish, either by birth or ancestry. They constituted some 22 per cent of the city's population—second only to the Germans, who accounted for 54 per cent of the total.[2] The Poles of Milwaukee differed in several significant ways from Poles who settled in other American cities. By and large they had come from the German-controlled provinces of Poland, which were politically repressed but industrially more advanced than the regions under Austrian and Russian rule.[3] Few Polish emigrants from these economically more backward sections of the partitioned country settled in Milwaukee. Rather, they went to Chicago, Pittsburgh, and Detroit—cities where unskilled work in the stockyards, steel mills, and automotive assembly plants was more plentiful. Fewer jobs like these were available in Milwaukee, which was well known for its many small precision-toolmaking firms and breweries, though many unskilled Poles did find work in the tanneries, rolling mills, and meatpacking houses. The Polish community in heavily German Milwaukee thus became more tightly knit and more parochial than the more diverse, more cosmopolitan Polish settlements (usually called *Polonia* by the Poles themselves) in other American cities. "America's Poznan," one writer called it, alluding to the

AUTHOR'S NOTE: This essay is a revised version of the Fromkin Memorial Lecture, presented at the University of Wisconsin–Milwaukee in the fall of 1974. I should like to express my appreciation to the Fromkin Research and Lectureship Committee and the University of Wisconsin–Milwaukee Library for funds to support this project, and to Don Temple of the University of Wisconsin–Milwaukee Cartographic Laboratory for the map of Milwaukee.

[1] Thaddeus Borun and John Jakusz-Gostomski, eds., *We, the Milwaukee Poles* (Milwaukee, 1946); Bayrd Still, *Milwaukee: The History of a City* (Madison, 1948); Wenceslaus Kruszka, *Historya Polska w Ameryce* (Milwaukee, 1906), parts 3 and 7; Robert Carroon, "Foundations of Milwaukee's Polish Community," in the *Historical Messenger of the Milwaukee County Historical Society* (September, 1970), 88–95.

[2] Kruszka, *Historya Polska*, part 7, 137. In 1900, the Poles of Wisconsin numbered 31,882 and ranked as the third largest immigrant group in the state, after the Germans (242,777) and the Norwegians (61,575). By 1930, the Poles had advanced to second position with 42,359, following the Germans (128,269 foreign-born) and ranking ahead of the Norwegians (34,359 foreign-born). See *Abstract of the Twelfth Census of the United States, 1900* (Washington, 1902); *Fifteenth Census of the United States, 1930* (Washington, 1932); and Bernard Fuller, "Voting Patterns in Milwaukee, 1896–1920" (master's thesis, University of Wisconsin–Milwaukee, 1973), 41–61.

[3] In 1905, 12,482 (80.5 per cent) of the 15,500 foreign-born Poles of Milwaukee had emigrated from German-ruled territories, compared to 2,479 (16 per cent) from "Russian" Poland and 539 (3.5 per cent) from Austrian "Galicia." *Tabular Statements of the State of Wisconsin Census* (Madison, 1906), 170ff.

179

Iron workers, heavily Polish, at the North Chicago Rolling Mills in Bay View, 1886. Two years later, five persons were killed here when state militia put down a strike in support of the eight-hour workday.

common origins of so many Milwaukee Poles in the German provinces of their partitioned homeland.[4]

Because Polish migration to Milwaukee occurred earlier than the movement of Poles from Austrian and Russian Poland to other

[4] Borun, *We, the Milwaukee Poles*, esp. 242–244; Adolph G. Korman, "A Social History of Industrial Growth and Immigrants: A Study with Particular Reference to Milwaukee, 1880–1920" (doctoral dissertation, University of Wisconsin–Madison, 1959), 113–121. Korman's dissertation was published as *Industrialization, Immigrants, and Americanizers: The View from Milwaukee, 1866–1921* (Madison, 1967). See also Henryk Dzulikowski, *Milwaukee Poznanskie Miasto* (Chicago, 1945).

American cities, the institutional development of *Polonia* in the Cream City was virtually complete by 1910. By then Milwaukee's Polish community possessed a stability and degree of organizational completeness that would endure for many years. In the heavily Polish neighborhoods of the city's South Side stood a number of Roman Catholic parishes, which were historically the centers of life in *Polonia*. These included the oldest parish, St. Stanislaus', erected in 1866, St. Hyacinth's (1882), St. Josaphat's (1888), St. Vincent's (1888), Sts. Cyril and Methodius' (1893), St. John Cantius' (1907), and St. Adalbert's (1908). In the smaller *Polonia* on the city's northeast side were St. Hedwig's (1871), St. Casimir's (1894), and St. Mary of Czestochowa parish (1907). Attached to each parish was an elementary school administered by an order of Polish sisters. In addition, several banks and loan associations and scores of small shops and businesses, real estate firms, and two newspapers run by Poles were by then in operation. A large number of Polish fraternal societies, including one founded in Milwaukee, were active.[5]

Into the early 1900's it was Catholic clerics who provided much of the leadership among Milwaukee's Poles. These early priests, nearly all of whom were well-educated and foreign-born, had come to America's immigrant community imbued with a sense of missionary zeal which is difficult to appreciate fully today. They were "confessors, teachers, counselors, social directors, alms givers, and even political leaders...." They gave voice to Polish hopes and aspirations, and when they spoke on secular as well as religious matters, it was with authority.[6] One such priest—an example among many—was the Reverend (and later Monsignor) Hyacinth Gulski. Pastor of St. Stanislaus' parish between 1876 and 1883, Gulski built St. Hyacinth's church and became its first pastor in 1883. A diocesan consultant to the archbishop—and thus the ranking Polish clergyman in Milwaukee—Gulski championed the creation of additional parishes to serve the burgeoning number of Polish immigrants on the South Side. From 1909 to 1911 he was also pastor of St. Hedwig's parish on the North Side. Chaplain for many local fraternal organizations and well-known throughout the community, he was politically influential, although, as he put it, he was "a Democrat, but not active."[7]

Outside their own neighborhoods, of course, the Poles of Milwaukee were a distinct minority whose dealings with non-Poles were usually with Germans. In a city that was noticeably less ethnically cosmopolitan than, for example, Chicago, it was understandable that Poles tended to be defensive in their dealings with the German majority, and to be responsive toward expressions of anti-German rhetoric in the Polish press and pulpit. The self-containment of the Poles—what was called their "clannish" ways—was a phenomenon upon which outsiders frequently remarked.

The Poles were distinct from their fellow Milwaukeeans in class and status as well. The predominantly Polish wards had a decidedly working-class character and a much higher proportion of factory hands and common laborers than of tradesmen and machinists. According to a state census conducted in 1905, only 15 per cent of the residents in the two Polish wards were engaged in proprietary, professional, or clerical occupations, compared with a citywide figure of 32 per cent. In the city, 34 per cent of the inhabitants were listed as skilled workers and 30 per cent as unskilled; for the Polish wards, 29 per cent were skilled and 54 per cent were unskilled.[8] Among the Poles, clergymen played a far more important

---

[5] Boleslaus Goral, "The Poles in Milwaukee," in Jerome Watrous, *Memoirs of Milwaukee County* (2 volumes, Madison, 1909), 1: 613-631; Still, *Milwaukee*, 268-273; Borun, *We, the Milwaukee Poles*, 3-50, 167-222. A second fraternal society, the Federation of Poles in America (today Federation Life Insurance of America) was established in Milwaukee in 1913. Angela Pienkos, *A Brief History of Federation Life Insurance of America, 1913-1976* (Milwaukee, 1976). In size, the Milwaukee *Polonia* was nearly one-third as large as the Chicago Polish community in 1900, equal in numbers to the one found in Buffalo, and larger than the Polish group living in Detroit. However, the continuing influx of Poles into the other cities left Milwaukee far behind. By 1940, the Milwaukee *Polonia* was only 13 per cent as large as Chicago's, 30 per cent of Detroit, and 74 per cent of Buffalo.

[6] Joseph Wytrwal, *America's Polish Heritage* (Detroit, 1961), 159-167.

[7] Borun, *We, the Milwaukee Poles*, 47-49; Goral, "Poles in Milwaukee," 614-616. Gulski's role is also discussed by Anthony Kuzniewski, "Faith and Fatherland: An Intellectual History of the Polish Immigrant Community in Wisconsin, 1838-1918" (doctoral dissertation, Harvard University, 1973), 162-167. Other leading Milwaukee Polish clergymen included a Franciscan, Felix Baran, and Bronislaus Celichowski. For their biographies, see *Dictionary of Wisconsin Biography* (Madison, 1960), 25, 73.

[8] *Wisconsin Census*, 446-450; Roger Wyman, "Voting Behavior in the Progressive Era: Wisconsin as a Case Study" (doctoral dissertation, University of Wisconsin-Madison, 1970), 719. According to the 1905 state census, over 70 per cent of the Polish heads of households listed their occupations as "laborer" or "unskilled laborer." Another 21 per cent were identified as "artisans" and 9 per cent were either businessmen or professional people. Poles were most commonly employed in the tanneries (11 per cent), as molders (7 per cent), carpenters (5 per cent), ironworkers (5 per cent), butchers, saloonkeepers, machinists, blacksmiths, stonemasons (2 per cent each), firemen, grocers, and

more "progressive" than has been generally acknowledged, in that large numbers of Poles voted for socialist candidates, particularly when the Socialist party was a viable force in city politics or when Polish socialists were nominated; and a sizable contingent of Polish socialists attained prominence and was able to win elections between 1910 and 1932. 2) Most Milwaukee Poles remained outside the organized labor movement before the New Deal, primarily because the Milwaukee Federated Trades Council was a crafts-oriented union which by definition excluded most Polish factory workers; but in fact there were Polish trade-unionists in Milwaukee, a number of whom had close ties with the Socialist party. 3) As early as 1900, some Polish leaders in Milwaukee were attracted to Robert M. La Follette's progressive wing of the Republican party, although it was only during the 1920's, when La Follette's sons carried on the progressive tradition, that the Republican party assumed much significance in Polish politics. 4) Far from remaining a monolithic structure of ethnics who thought and acted as one, *Polonia* was deeply divided over several important issues, including the proper role for Polish clerics within the Catholic hierarchy, and the proper response of Polish voters toward the newly forming socialist and progressive movements which challenged the Democratic party. These conflicts within both the ecclesiastical and secular domains, occurring at practically the same time in history, profoundly altered the character of traditional Polish-American life. Over time, the concerns of the Polish community increasingly mirrored the political, cultural, and economic pluralism to be found within the larger Milwaukee environment, and hence the process of the Poles' assimilation into that environment accelerated.[10]

The Poles first achieved recognition as a factor in Milwaukee politics following the suppression of a Polish workmen's strike at the Bay View rolling mills by the Wisconsin National Guard in May, 1886. Nine persons were killed in the confrontation, which was part of a citywide effort led by the Knights of Labor to achieve the eight-hour workday. The incident produced a crisis within *Polonia*, since a Polish unit of the National Guard had taken part in suppressing the strikers; more important, it also provoked a large Polish voter turnout in support of the People's party whose candidates swept all the county races in the spring election of 1886.[11] In 1890, the Catholic sentiments of the Poles roused them against the Republican party, whose leaders were held responsible for passing the Bennett Law the previous year. The law stipulated that certain subjects in all Wisconsin schools (including Catholic and Lutheran parochial schools) must be taught in English, thus arousing the ire of several ethnic groups. In the next election, Democrats swept the state for the first time in many years. Their victory usually is credited to the Germans, who, despite previous party membership, united to defeat the Republican party which had foisted the Bennett Law upon them. But the Poles, too, enjoyed political advancement in the election. A number of them, including Michael Kruszka (running for a state assembly seat), won office, again demonstrating the Poles' political potency.[12]

Two reasons can be given which explain

---

of the Poles. See also, Wyman, "Voting Behavior," 20–21; Paul Kleppner, *The Cross of Culture* (New York, 1970), 22–67; Victor Greene, *For God and Country: The Rise of Polish and Lithuanian Ethnic Consciousness in America, 1860-1910* (Madison, 1975), chapters IV and VI; Walter Borowiec, "Politics and Buffalo's Polish-Americans," paper presented at the 1976 meeting of the Midwest Slavic Conference, Chicago, pages 2–7.

[11] Thomas Gavett, *The Labor Movement in Milwaukee* (Madison and Milwaukee, 1965), 115ff; Korman, "A Social History," 9–10; Borun, *We, The Milwaukee Poles*, 111; Frederick Olson, "The Milwaukee Socialists, 1897–1941" (doctoral dissertation, Harvard University, 1952), 160–185; Wytrwal, *America's Polish Heritage*, 181ff; Kuzniewski, "Faith and Fatherland," 149–222.

[12] Frank Miller, "The Polanders in Wisconsin," in *Parkman Club Papers* (Milwaukee, 1896), 239–246; Jerry Cooper, "The Wisconsin National Guard in the Milwaukee Riots of 1886," in the *Wisconsin Magazine of History*, 55: 31–48 (Autumn, 1971); and Borun, *We, the Milwaukee Poles*, 123–125. In this last piece, members of Company K recalled that no shots had been fired by Polish guardsmen in their efforts to disperse the rioters. See also Roger D. Simon, "The Bay View Incident and the People's Party in Milwaukee," a paper in the files of the Research Division, State Historical Society of Wisconsin.

[13] Still, *Milwaukee*, 296–297; Roger Wyman, "Wisconsin Ethnic Groups and the Election of 1890," in the *Wisconsin Magazine of History*, 51: 269–293 (Summer, 1968).

Outing of the St. Aloysius Foresters, Milwaukee, 1917.

role as community leaders than they did among non-Poles, who tended to be dominated by lawyers, businessmen, and other professional persons. Religion, like ethnicity, inclined the Milwaukee Polish community toward the Democratic party, which was historically the party of the immigrant and the Roman Catholic.[9]

WHAT follows is intended to describe more precisely the political behavior of the Polish voters of Milwaukee during the progressive era, and to examine their response to progressive and socialist ideas and movements in terms of four general themes. 1) Between 1900 and 1940 the Polish population of Milwaukee was far

---

shoemakers (1 per cent), with 37 per cent classified as "laborers." In 1880, 71 per cent had fallen in that category, underscoring the Poles' upward occupational movement over time. Laura Sutherland, "The Immigrant Family: Milwaukee's Poles: 1880–1905" (master's thesis, University of Wisconsin–Milwaukee, 1974), 52, 88, 89. According to Korman, "Social History," Polish workers enjoyed a reputation nearly as favorable as the Germans or Swedes and were believed to be much more industrious than the Greeks, Italians, and Hungarians (42ff). Nonetheless, they were also often limited to unskilled "dirty" jobs.

[9] My analysis of the biographies of eighty-three prominent Polish-American community leaders in comparison with a randomly sampled group of 121 non-Polish community figures drawn from Watrous' 1909 work showed the following: 15.7 per cent of the Polish leaders were clergymen, to 3.3 per cent of the non-Poles. While 31.4 per cent of the non-Poles were professionally educated, this was true for only 13.3 per cent of the Poles. Among the non-Poles, 19 per cent owned large companies, while 23 per cent of the Poles were proprietors of small businesses. Nearly half the Poles (42 per cent) were foreign-born and three-quarters (75.9 per cent) were under forty years of age; the comparable figures for the non-Poles were 26 and 38 per cent, respectively. Three-fifths of the Poles listing their political orientations were Democrats, to fewer than 30 per cent of the non-Poles. Only 19 per cent of the non-Poles were identified as Catholics, to 93 per cent

Louis Kotecki, comptroller and "Polish mayor" of Milwaukee, 1912 to 1933.

the Poles' recognized significance in local politics. On the one hand, it was widely appreciated that the Poles, when voting as a bloc, were capable of delivering huge pluralities for their favorites. As early as 1892, one Milwaukee newspaper concluded that since the German and native-born voters did not behave as a solid group, the "Poles [already possess] the balance of power that will soon make them by far the most important element" in city politics.[13] The staunch support they gave to David Rose, a five-term Democratic mayor of Milwaukee between 1898 and 1910, served to reinforce this opinion.[14]

Equally important, however, was the Poles' ability to elect "their own" to public office. Wenceslaus Kruszka proudly asserted in his 1906 history of Milwaukee's *Polonia* that "as far back as 1892, we in Milwaukee had Poles in every level of public service, from policeman to state senator.... Nowhere in any other Polish settlement in all America did Poles so frequently achieve so many high offices as in Milwaukee, not in Buffalo, nor Detroit, not even Chicago where the largest number of Poles lived."[15]

August Rudzinski had won a place on the county board of supervisors as early as 1878. His son Theodore became Milwaukee's first Polish alderman in 1882, and later that year Francis Borchardt became the first Pole to represent a Milwaukee district in the Wisconsin Assembly. Between 1890 and 1940, thirty-one Polish-Americans were elected to the lower house from Milwaukee legislative districts. Indeed, the most heavily Polish district of Milwaukee, encompassing the South Side's fourteenth ward, was represented by a Pole for forty-two of those fifty years. Nine Polish-American state senators were elected from Milwaukee County constituencies beginning in 1892.[16] As for the city's common council, a large number of Polish-Americans became aldermen. Between 1908 and 1940, twenty-four Poles won seats. Poles were also able to win as candidates for important citywide administrative positions: between 1890 and 1933, four Polish-Americans created a kind of local tradition by winning the comptroller's office (whose incumbents were jocularly known as "the Polish mayor"). The first Pole to hold this prestigious post was Roman Czerwinski, who served two terms between 1890 and 1894. Peter Pawinski held the office between 1902 and 1906, followed by August Gawin in 1908–1910. Most notable among Milwaukee's so-called "Polish mayors" was the American-born Louis Kotecki, who served as comptroller between 1912 and 1933 and won eight consecutive elections.[17]

---

[13] Quoted in Still, *Milwaukee*, 298n.
[14] *Ibid.*, 271–272, 297–299, 308–309.
[15] Kruszka, *Historya*, part three, 133; Wyman, "Voting Behavior," 732.
[16] Goral, "Poles in Milwaukee," 625; Borun, *We, the Milwaukee Poles*, 77, 154–158, 163. Data for Polish-Americans elected to the state legislature were gathered from biennial volumes of *The Wisconsin Blue Book*.
[17] Elected city comptroller in 1912, Kotecki had previously been identified as a Democrat. He met a tragic end when he committed suicide in 1933 at the age of fifty-three, following his indictment on charges of having failed to audit carefully the accounts of the city treasurer. In the forty-five years since Kotecki's death, only one other Polish-American, John Kalupa, was able to win election to the comptroller's office. *Milwaukee Journal*, July 11, 12, 1933.

Robert Taylor, photographer for the Milwaukee Journal, *recorded this summertime outing around 1910.*

THE affinity of Milwaukee's Poles for the Democratic party has been acknowledged by numerous historians, who have tended to discount the Polish role in socialist and progressive reform movements. Thus, Bayrd Still, in his history of Milwaukee, wrote: "The predominance of workingmen among the Poles inclined the group most consistently to the Democratic Party, their coolness toward the Socialists being motivated by both the attitude of the church and the Socialists' opposition to fighting the battles of Poland in World War I."[18] And David Shannon, in his history of American Socialism, concluded: "The Socialists [in Milwaukee] had tremendous strength among the Germans, substantial influence among the Yankees, and their least power among the Poles."[19]

To a certain extent these generalizations are true. Class, religion, and ethnicity did incline the Poles of Milwaukee toward the Democratic party. But for the years 1900 to 1930 —that is, in an era of tremendous political ferment—even a cursory glance at the election returns from the heavily Polish wards shows that the socialists made major inroads within Milwaukee's most heavily Polish districts. In every presidential election between 1908 and 1924, the socialist standard-bearer ran better in wards with substantial Polish populations than in Milwaukee as a whole. In 1912, Eugene V. Debs received a plurality of the vote in those wards.[20] The socialists demonstrated similar strength in the Polish wards for all

---

[18] Still, *Milwaukee*, 468; Korman, "Social History," 24.
[19] David Shannon, *The Socialist Party of America: A History* (New York, 1955), 23.

[20] In the four-cornered race, Debs took 38 per cent of the vote to 34 per cent for the Democrat, Woodrow Wilson, 21 per cent for the Republican incumbent, William Taft, and 7 per cent for Progressive Republican Theodore Roosevelt. Ward data are from Sarah Ettenheim, *How Milwaukee Voted, 1848–1968* (Milwaukee, 1970), and the *Milwaukee Sentinel*. The "Polish wards" were the twelfth and fourteenth (between 1900 and 1911), the eighth, twelfth, fourteenth, and twenty-fourth wards (from 1912 through 1931), and between 1932 and 1940 the first, thirteenth, twenty-first, eighth, eleventh, twelfth, fourteenth, seventeenth, and twenty-fourth.

Wine room in a Milwaukee dance hall, 1913. The poster bearing Kosciusko's portrait and the Polish colors reads "Honor to the Hero."

sixteen gubernatorial elections between 1900 and 1930. In nine such contests—the elections of 1902, 1904, 1906, 1908, 1910, 1914, 1916, 1926, and 1928—Socialist *and* Democratic party candidates ran better in Polish wards than in the city as a whole. In 1900 and 1918 the Democratic nominees outpolled the Socialist party candidates, but in 1912, 1920, and 1924 the reverse was true in the Polish wards.

These same Polish voters were also more supportive of La Follette progressivism than has generally been recognized. In 1922, for example, Senator Robert M. La Follette carried Milwaukee with an 84 per cent majority —and by an 88 per cent majority in the four Polish wards. In 1924, as a presidential candidate, La Follette's 56 per cent majority in the Polish wards equalled his showing in Milwaukee as a whole. And in 1930 La Follette's son Philip, a gubernatorial candidate, won 59 per cent of the vote in the Polish wards, compared to 53 per cent in the city as a whole. In short, both socialist and progressive Republican candidates enjoyed considerable success in Milwaukee wards having large numbers of Poles.[21] Why, then, do historians continue to describe the Polish voter as conventionally Democratic in politics, and therefore unworthy of detailed analysis?

Research about Milwaukee's Polish community during the progressive era has been deficient because of a general reliance upon English-language sources. Recent studies show little evidence that their authors were familiar with the city's Polish-language dailies, the *Kuryer Polski* and *Nowiny Polskie*. Similarly, few interviews seem to have been conducted with members of the Polish community whose recollections could add immeasurably

[21] Wyman, "Voting Behavior," 393; Fuller, "Voting Patterns," 128, 135, 192.

to what is available in printed sources.[22] And finally, although a number of scholars have begun to perform statistical analyses of voting behavior during the progressive era and have made much use of aggregate data in correlating election results with census information about the ethnic and class composition of the Wisconsin electorate, their work (insofar as it has touched upon Polish political behavior) has as yet yielded little that challenges, much less contradicts, conventional wisdom about the Poles in Milwaukee.[23] Why should this be so?

For one thing, in depending upon census enumerations of foreign-born populations in order to determine the identity, size, and location of ethnic voting groups, scholars have made two false assumptions. The first has to do with the fact that censuses themselves name as members of ethnic groups only those persons born on foreign soil (the "first generation" Americans), and they do not identify the native-born descendants of the immigrants as members of the ethnic groups. Some scholars who have relied on such data have tended to write about the political behavior of the entire ethnic group when they really can only consider the political orientations of the foreign-born. This practice is justified by assuming that the voting behavior of second- and third-generation Americans will resemble the voting behavior of the foreign-born parents or grandparents, the only persons counted as ethnic group members in the census. But this assumption is false, since it is precisely these American-born ethnics who were more likely to be active politically, because they (unlike their immigrant forefathers) were automatically eligible to vote. Hence, the traditional methods of analyzing ethnic voting behavior by relying upon enumeration of the foreign-born must be rejected, unless it can be shown that membership in a given ethnic group was synonymous with foreign birth, and that foreign birth was in fact not a serious impediment to political participation.

A second false assumption which scholars have made is that what was true in Milwaukee's single most heavily Polish ward (the fourteenth on the South Side) was true for all Polish voters throughout the city. But, since Poles were found in substantial numbers elsewhere in Milwaukee, it cannot be assumed that all Poles behaved alike, regardless of where they lived.

In order to identify and isolate Polish voting patterns, I decided to forgo the traditional examination of census returns and election results from Milwaukee's Polish wards and turn instead to the lists of registered voters which have been kept by the city since 1888.[24] These lists hold several advantages over election returns in permitting the researcher to determine the shape and thrust of ethnic voting behavior. For one thing, all Poles actually eligible to vote are included, regardless of their country of birth. In addition, since the lists are for precincts having

---

[22] The *Kuryer Polski* was founded in 1888 and continued to operate until 1963. The *Nowiny Polskie* was established in 1906 as a weekly, became a daily in 1907, and ceased publication in 1949. The entire run of the *Kuryer* can be found on microfilm in the Milwaukee Public Library. Sections of the *Nowiny* are in the Center for Research Libraries (Chicago). The Milwaukee Public Library's run has been lost.

The author conducted interviews of one to two hours each with the following gentlemen in 1974 and 1975: Frank Zeidler, Socialist party activist and mayor of Milwaukee between 1948 and 1960; Szymon Deptula, formerly the chairman of the Slavic Languages Department of the University of Wisconsin–Milwaukee; John Polakowski, a socialist politician and Wisconsin assemblyman (1922-1924); Clemens Michalski, longtime Democratic party politician and government official; Francis X. Swietlik, Polish ethnic leader and former circuit court judge; Alfred Sokolnicki, dean of the Marquette University school of speech; Anthony Szymczak, a reporter for the *Kuryer Polski*; Stanley Budny, a socialist politician in Milwaukee; Edmund Choinski, a former Milwaukee alderman; reserve court judge Thaddeus Pruss; former city comptroller John Kalupa; and Mrs. Janet Dziadulewicz Branden.

Works treating the Milwaukee Poles but relying upon English- or German-language sources include Frederick I. Olson's dissertation; Marvin Wachman, "History of the Social Democratic Party of Wisconsin, 1897-1910" (doctoral dissertation, University of Illinois, 1945). I much appreciated the opportunity to interview Professor Sally Miller and to read the paper she delivered on April 3, 1974, entitled "Milwaukee Retrospective: A Profile of Reform" and sponsored by the Department of History and the Center for Twentieth Century Studies of the University of Wisconsin–Milwaukee.

[23] Particularly the works of Roger Wyman and Paul Kleppner.

[24] My thanks to Bert Hardinger, director of the City of Milwaukee Bureau of Records, for his assistance in my gathering of these data. See also Edward Kantowicz, "The Emergence of the Polish Democratic Vote in Chicago," in *Polish American Studies*, 29: 67-80 (1972).

as few as 200 and rarely more than 800 eligible voters, they enable one to pinpoint the most densely Polish precincts, which are usually far more homogeneous (that is, far more Polish) than so-called "Polish" wards containing 15,000 to 25,000 residents. By carefully checking for Polish surnames on the precinct lists of registered voters for the mayoral elections of 1904, 1914, and 1924, I was able to identify a number of Milwaukee precincts containing at least 50 per cent Polish voters. (See Tables 1, 1a, and 1b, and the map of Milwaukee for 1924.) From this it was possible to determine that in 1904, 1914, and 1924 the vast majority of all the Polish voters in Milwaukee was concentrated into ten, a dozen, and two dozen precincts out of 112, 141, and 242 precincts respectively. In 1904 and again in 1924, nearly four-fifths of all of Milwaukee's Polish voters resided in these few precincts.

My analysis of voter-registration lists at the precinct level raises serious doubts about the validity of studies of ethnic voting behavior derived from census data. When a comparison was made between the ward-based census figures about Milwaukee Poles and the actual number of voters having Polish surnames on precinct registration lists, the unreliability of the census data became evident. (See Table 2.)

While Poles comprised upwards of 20 per cent of Milwaukee's population during the progressive era, the number of actual Polish voters seems not to have exceeded 6 or 7 per cent of the electorate. This disparity is explained partially by the fact that a larger proportion of the Polish population was made up of women and children than was true for the city as a whole.[25] Furthermore, since many Poles originally came to America with no intention of remaining permanently, American citizenship, with its right to the franchise, may have held little appeal initially.[26] But among those Poles who did register to vote, participation at the polls was quite high. In the mayoral election of 1914, for example, a count of the names of actual voters who were systematically ticked off the registration lists throughout the city showed that 86.7 per cent

[25] Sutherland, "The Immigrant Family," 84, 68–69.
[26] See Helena Lopata, *The Polish-Americans: Status Competition in an Ethnic Community* (Englewood Cliffs, New Jersey, 1976), 84.

TABLE 1
SIZE AND LOCATION OF MILWAUKEE PRECINCTS WITH VOTING POPULATIONS AT LEAST 50 PER CENT POLISH, 1904.

1904 Precincts (Total = 112)

Ward	Precinct	Location	Total Voters	Per cent Polish
14	6	South	648	93.2%
12	4	South	505	89.7
14	3	South	465	88.0
14	5	South	576	84.7
14	4	South	602	79.1
14	2	South	863	76.4
14	1	South	579	72.7
17	4	South	383	70.5
18	2	North	712	56.6
13	6	North	592	56.1

Total vote in Milwaukee mayoral election: 59,604.
Total eligible Polish voters: 5,856.
Percentage of Polish voters residing in Polish precincts: 79 per cent.

of the eligible Polish voters cast ballots—slightly higher than for the city as a whole.

ANALYSIS of voter registration lists and election returns at the precinct level confirms what is evident from larger, ward-based aggregate statistics: that Polish voters in significant numbers moved away from the Democratic party during the progressive era. Socialists were the major beneficiaries of this trend; however, the La Follettes and other progressives such as John J. Blaine also won large numbers of Polish voters to their side during the 1920's. For example, Blaine received 37.0 per cent of the vote cast in the city's Polish precincts, a figure nearly equaling his citywide share of 37.4 per cent. In 1930, Philip La Follette carried Milwaukee with 52.7 per cent of the total vote; but in the Polish precincts he did even better, winning 59.9 per cent. Polish support of socialist candidates for state and local office was even more pronounced during this era, but the precinct-level data also point up significant differences between the larger South Side Polish community and the smaller enclave on the North Side.

Polish support for socialist candidates was confined exclusively to the *Polonia* on the

TABLE 1a.
SIZE AND LOCATION OF MILWAUKEE PRECINCTS WITH VOTING POPULATIONS AT LEAST 50 PER CENT POLISH, 1914.

1914 Precincts (Total = 141)

Ward	Precinct	Location	Total Voters	Per cent Polish
14	1	South	616	82.5%
14	2	South	518	82.0
14	3	South	244	80.3
24	4	South	206	78.6
14	4	South	260	65.4
17	4	South	257	64.7
8	5	South	438	63.9
8	6	South	542	58.5
8	4	South	586	58.5
12	4	South	539	57.4
13	1	North	674	53.9
1	5	North	523	51.4

Total vote in Milwaukee mayoral election: 66,795.
Total eligible Polish voters: 5,694.
Percentage of Polish voters residing in Polish precincts: 58 per cent.

TABLE 1b.
SIZE AND LOCATION OF MILWAUKEE PRECINCTS WITH VOTING POPULATIONS AT LEAST 50 PER CENT POLISH, 1924.

1924 Precincts (Total = 242)

Ward	Precinct	Location	Total Voters	Per cent Polish
14	1	South	749	91.5%
14	3	South	687	83.7
8	8	South	540	83.5
14	4	South	899	80.0
24	1	South	493	78.7
24	6	South	609	78.3
14	2	South	705	77.2
1	5	North	661	74.7
14	5	South	795	73.5
17	4	South	551	73.3
14	6	South	301	72.3
12	7	South	675	70.7
8	4	South	564	68.6
13	5	North	681	62.3
12	8	South	650	61.8
8	6	South	628	61.1
13	1	North	660	60.0
8	5	South	795	59.9
8	7	South	750	56.4
21	8	North	727	55.9
12	4	South	515	55.3
13	6	North	537	51.8
24	2	South	547	51.2
1	4	North	660	50.2

Total vote in Milwaukee mayoral election: 131,412.
Total eligible Polish voters: 13,412.
Percentage of Polish voters residing in Polish precincts: 78 per cent.

South Side; the Polish voters of the North Side remained overwhelmingly Democratic in their preferences.[27] For example, in 1914 Emil Seidel, Milwaukee's first socialist mayor, received 55.1 per cent of the vote in the South Side Polish precincts; his opponent carried the North Side precincts by a margin of more than two to one while winning re-election with 55.4 per cent of the total vote. In 1916 Daniel W. Hoan, another socialist, was elected to the first of his seven terms as mayor when he won 51.3 per cent of the total vote. Again, the outcome on the Polish South Side was strongly favorable to the socialist, with Hoan gathering 62.7 per cent of the vote. The North Side, however, was divided exactly between Hoan and the Democratic incumbent. Thereafter, Polish support of socialist candidates tailed off, largely because of the Socialist party's strong opposition to World War I (which Poles interpreted as opposition to Poland's independence), but Polish South Siders continued to provide much stronger support for the socialists than did those on the North Side. In 1924, for example, when the irrepressible David Rose unsuccessfully challenged Hoan, the socialist incumbent still won 39.1 per cent of the South Side precinct vote, but only 22.1 per cent on the North Side. In 1928, Hoan won 44.5 per cent of the votes cast in the South Side precincts, but only 26.2 per cent of those from the North Side, while winning 58.2 per cent of the total vote.[28]

[27] No single explanation for this phenomenon exists. Certainly, in an era before mass automobile transportation and the development of the freeway system, the North Side was quite isolated from the larger *Polonia* to the south. Organizational life was also less intense and extensive in a community with a smaller membership upon which to build. This meant that the Polish clergy's role in North Side affairs was less likely to be challenged by socialist-leaning workers' clubs, which do not seem to have appeared in that district.

[28] The socialists' failure to deal with Polish patriotic

POLISH ELECTORATE, 1924

■ ≥ 50% of registered voters

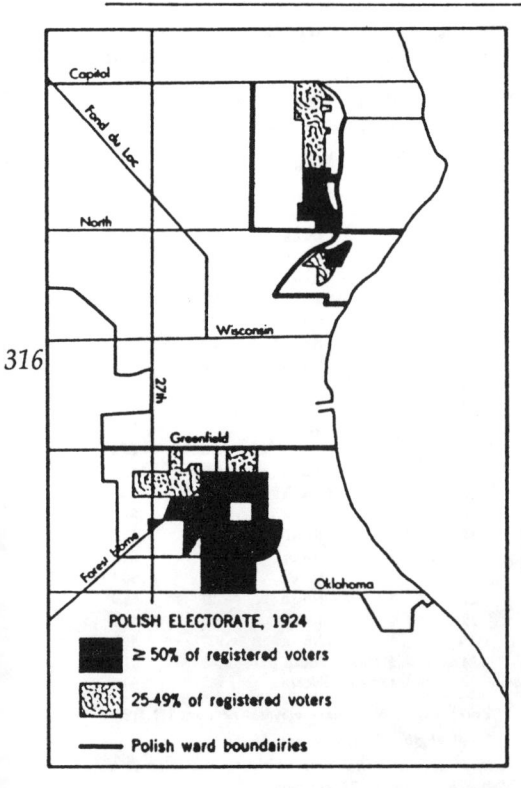

▨ 25-49% of registered voters

— Polish ward boundairies

Map by Don Temple

The impact of residence upon the political preferences of Milwaukee Poles is most evident when one considers elections in which the candidate for comptroller (chief financial officer for the city) was Polish. In the elections of both 1902 and 1904, Peter Pawinski, a Democrat, overwhelmingly carried both the South Side and North Side precincts (even outdistancing the popular Mayor Rose), although he trailed his running-mate in the mayoral race in both elections. In the elections after 1914 for which detailed precinct-level data are available, the victorious Polish candidate for comptroller, Louis Kotecki, was far less successful in the South Side Polish precincts than in the traditionally Democratic stronghold of the North Side. In all these elections, socialist candidates for comptroller captured at least one-third and usually something approaching 40 per cent of the South Side vote, while on the North Side, Kotecki's total generally exceeded 75 per cent of the total. Perhaps the most interesting contest took place in the spring election of 1916, in which the race for city comptroller pitted two Poles against each other: the incumbent Democrat Kotecki and the socialist challenger, alderman Leo Krzycki. In the two North Side precincts, the Democrat destroyed the socialist, winning 72.8 per cent of the 1,030 votes there. But in the two South Side precincts, a great degree of ambivalence as to the relative merits of two "favorite sons" was obvious from the election results. Here, Krzycki received 50.3 per cent of the vote—a majority of twenty-five votes out of 3,949 cast.

From these returns it is possible to detect a significant trend in favor of the socialists on the South Side as early as 1910. (See Tables 3 and 3a.) Indeed, almost from the time that the Milwaukee socialists became a significant factor in the political life of the city, Polish activists were to be found among them. Most were workingmen, up from the ranks, with ties to organized labor. Martin Gorecki, a brewery worker who was elected alderman-at-large in the elections of 1910—the first in which a socialist became mayor—was among the first of many. Gorecki was subsequently elected to the state assembly in 1912, representing the heavily Polish fourteenth and twenty-fourth wards of Milwaukee; and he was involved in the founding of a short-lived Polish-language socialist weekly, *Naprzod* (Forward).[29] Another important early Polish socialist, Casimir Kowalski, had worked as a coal miner in Pennsylvania before settling in Milwaukee in 1906. With his wife, he organized several socialist units among Milwau-

---

feelings is evident from a reading of the resolutions the party convention approved at its 1918 meeting in Milwaukee. There, a resolution condemning American and Japanese intervention against the new Bolshevik regime and calling for immediate U.S. recognition of the Soviet government was approved. There was no mention of Polish independence. See Socialist party archives, Milwaukee County Historical Society.

[29] Olson, "Milwaukee Socialists," 176; *The Wisconsin Blue Book* (Madison, 1913), 675; *Kuryer Polski*, December 20, 1928, p. 10.

TABLE 2.
MILWAUKEE WARDS WITH LARGE POLISH POPULATIONS
(Comparing census findings with precinct-based information on registered Polish voters, 1904–1924)

WARD	LOCATION	FOREIGN-BORN POLES [from Wisconsin census] (1905)	REGISTERED VOTERS WITH POLISH NAMES (1904)
14	South	34%	81.9%
12	South	13	26.9
18	North	10	20.0
11	South	8	15.7
13	North	11	15.3
17	South	8	11.0

WARD	LOCATION	FOREIGN-BORN POLES [from U.S. census] (1920)	REGISTERED VOTERS WITH POLISH NAMES (1914)	(1924)
14	South	24%	70.9%	80.4%
8	South	18	57.8	48.0
12	South	11	29.7	29.5
24	South	16	25.4	25.8
13	North	7	16.0	19.1
1	North	7	15.8	18.7
11	South	14	11.8	21.8
21	North	5	9.0	10.4
17	South	6	6.0	7.5

TABLE 3.
POLISH-AMERICANS ELECTED TO WISCONSIN LEGISLATURE, BY DECADE AND PARTY AFFILIATION, 1891–1940

DECADE	ASSEMBLY			SENATE		
	Democrats	Republicans	Socialists	Democrats	Republicans	Socialists
1891–1900	6	0	0	1	0	0
1901–1910	4	0	0	0	1	0
1911–1920	3	0	3	0	1	0
1921–1930	1	3	4	0	1	1
1931–1940	7	1	1*	3	1	1

*Elected on Progressive party ticket.

TABLE 3a.
TOTAL MAN-YEARS SERVED BY POLISH-AMERICAN LEGISLATORS, BY DECADE AND PARTY AFFILIATION, 1891–1940

DECADE	ASSEMBLY			SENATE		
	Democrats	Republicans	Socialists	Democrats	Republicans	Socialists
1891–1900	10	0	0	4	0	0
1901–1910	10	0	0	0	2	0
1911–1920	10	0	6	0	4	0
1921–1930	2	6	8	0	4	8
1931–1940	24	2	2*	16	4	4

*Elected on Progressive party ticket.

WHi (X3) 34195
Martin Gorecki.

kee's Poles, including a women's branch of the party.[30] An unsuccessful candidate for a number of city and county offices, Kowalski was elected alderman-at-large from 1918 to 1922 and later served as one of Mayor Hoan's secretaries. A third early Polish socialist was Michael Katzban. Born in Illinois, a molder by occupation, and a long-time unionist, he was the first Polish socialist elected to the Wisconsin legislature, where he represented Milwaukee's fourteenth ward between 1911 and 1913. A socialist throughout his long life, Katzban ran unsuccessfully for an assembly seat in 1930 and served for six years

[30] *Milwaukee Leader*, December 28, 1911, p. 4; Olson, "Milwaukee Socialists," 176, 316.

on the Milwaukee Board of Election Commissioners beginning in 1950.[31]

While several other Polish socialists were elected to the state assembly and Milwaukee county board and aldermanic offices after 1910, perhaps the most prominent Polish-American in the entire movement up until the late 1930's was Leo Krzycki. Born in Milwaukee in 1881, Krzycki was active in organized labor throughout his long life, becoming a vice-president of the Lithographic Press Feeders Union at the age of twenty-three and ultimately serving as a national vice-president of the Amalgamated Clothing Workers Union. For a number of years, Krzycki was a Milwaukee County Socialist party secretary and was the party's state secretary at its 1932 convention.[32] A major political figure in the fourteenth ward Socialist party organization, he was that ward's alderman for two terms beginning in 1912, and later was deputy sheriff of Milwaukee County. A serious, forceful, and deliberate thinker, his speeches demonstrated his capacity to discuss American political conditions within a rather sophisticated Marxian framework. For example, in his keynote speech to the Socialist party's state convention in 1934, Krzycki called for an alliance between unorganized Wisconsin farmers and urban laborers under the socialist banner, its purpose being to overthrow the bankrupt capitalist system.[33]

[31] *Milwaukee Journal*, July 3, 1962.
[32] Brief biographies of Krzycki are found in G. M. Fink, ed., *Biographical Dictionary of American Labor Leaders* (Westport, Connecticut, 1974), 194; the *Great Polish Encyclopedia* (13 volumes, Warsaw, 1971, in Polish), 13: 243. See also Eugene Miller, "Leo Krzycki—Polish American Labor Leader," in *Polish American Studies*, 33: 52–64 (Autumn, 1976).
[33] Report of the Wisconsin Socialist Party State Convention, 1934, in the Socialist party archives, Milwaukee County Historical Society. Opinions about Krzycki varied sharply. One interviewee described him as a "brilliant man of the labor movement," another as a "deep thinker and an effective speaker," and a third as "an out and out socialist—maybe even a communist." Two studies that touch on his later activities include Louis Gerson, *The Hyphenate in Recent Politics and Diplomacy* (Lawrence, Kansas, 1964), 164–177; and Edward Kerstein, *Red Star Over Poland* (Appleton, Wisconsin, 1947), 50–63. After World War II, Krzycki was awarded Poland's highest civilian honor, the Cross of Restored Poland, by Communist party leader Boleslaus Bierut. See Bogdan Grzelonski, "Leon Krzycki," *Krajowa Agencja Informacyjna* (Warsaw), June 9–15, 1976, p. 6.

Marine Historical Collection, Milwaukee Public Library
Leo Krzycki.

Most successful of all the Milwaukee Polish socialists in winning elective office was Walter Polakowski. He was born in Buffalo in 1888, but he came to Milwaukee as a boy. Like Krzycki and most other Polish socialists, Polakowski was self-educated. An upholsterer by trade and an energetic unionist, he became one of his union's representatives in the Federated Trades Council at age nineteen. In 1920, he won a seat in the state assembly, representing Milwaukee's eighth ward, and in 1922 was elected to the state senate from the city's third district, which included the heavily Polish eighth, fourteenth, twenty-fourth, and eleventh wards. (In that same election, his younger brother John won a seat in the state assembly, representing the eighth and fourteenth wards.) Walter Polakowski served three consecutive terms in the state senate before a narrow defeat in a four-cornered race in 1934. Physically large and imposing, Polakowski was universally regarded as an effective public speaker, with a booming "lion's roar" oratorical style. A competent legislator, he became known as "the father of Wisconsin's unemployment compensation law," having first proposed this measure as an assemblyman in 1921. The bill became law in 1932. In 1937, he left the Socialist party when it divided over its relationship vis-à-vis Philip La Follette's new Progressive party. He later joined the Democrats and eventually became chairman of their fourteenth ward unit.[34]

Among other notable Polish socialists was a printer, Martin Cyborowski, who unsuccessfully sought public office as early at the 1890's as a populist, later edited a progressive newspaper, *Glos Ludu* (Voice of the People), and worked for Michael Kruszka's liberal daily, the *Kuryer Polski*. Cyborowski fought for the teaching of Polish in Milwaukee's public schools and served as the first president of the Federation of Polish Catholic Laymen, a group which mobilized thousands of Milwaukee Poles in favor of nominating a Polish bishop to serve in the Catholic archdiocese.[35] Other notable figures in the party included Louis Rutkowski, who served one term as county treasurer, the highest county office ever won by a Polish socialist, and Frank Boncel, a twelfth ward alderman between 1932 and 1936 who wrote the so-called Boncel Ordinance, a pro-labor measure which empowered the city to intervene in labor disputes with private businesses to settle strikes—a burning issue in depression-era Milwaukee.[36]

WHAT prompted these Milwaukee Poles to become active in a political movement so much at odds with the views of the traditional secular and religious leaders of *Polonia*? As already noted, many Polish socialists were active in the trade-union movement in an era when very few Polish workers even belonged to labor organizations.

[34] *Milwaukee Journal*, May 31, 1963; *Milwaukee Sentinel*, November 16, 1966. Polakowski's successful 1922 state senate campaign was endorsed by Senator Robert M. La Follette. C. H. Backstrom, "The Progressive Party of Wisconsin, 1934-1946" (doctoral dissertation, University of Wisconsin-Madison, 1957), 324.

[35] See Francis Bolek, ed., *Who's Who in Polish America* (New York, 1943), 228; Angela Pienkos, *Federation Life Insurance*, 1-10.

[36] Cavett, *Labor Movement*, 157-158.

The spirit of trade unionism probably played a larger role in their lives than was the case for other Poles, or for workers in general. John Polakowski recalled that one of his uncles had been active in the Knights of Labor organization in the 1880's. Walter Polakowski was known as "a strong union man, but too radical." Leo Krzycki named his two eldest sons Victor and Eugene, in honor of the socialist labor leader Eugene V. Debs.[37]

Polish socialists in Milwaukee were undoubtedly influenced by working-class German socialists with whom they had considerable contact. Polakowski remembered that "our family was the only Polish one on the block. Everyone else was German." Krzycki's wife's maiden name, Kadau, was German in origin. Stanley Budny recalled that his uncles had belonged to the Socialist party in Prussian Poland. There, Poles and Germans had worked together in opposing the policies of Chancellor Otto von Bismarck.[38] Polish socialists tended to view themselves as "free thinkers" who were intellectually independent of clerical influence. Several old socialists recalled how their fathers continued to subscribe to the *Kuryer Polski* even after the paper was condemned by the archbishop under threat of excommunication. Polakowski recounted how, as a fourteen-year-old at confession, he had disputed his priest's command that he no longer read the newspaper. The priest had quickly retreated from his stand.[39]

The Polish socialists were of course a minority within Milwaukee's *Polonia*, and they were to be found almost exclusively on the city's South Side. Their numbers were kept small by the extremely hostile stand taken against socialism by the Catholic church, a factor which deterred many Polish voters who cast socialist ballots from participating openly in the Socialist party. In 1902, Archbishop Sebastian G. Messmer of Milwaukee had issued an edict forbidding Catholics to join the party or even to vote for socialists under pain of excommunication.[40] This order was reinforced by Polish clergymen, who sometimes expressed their Democratic party preferences publicly. As one declared, "A good Catholic is a good Democrat." Even that stormy petrel of Polish Milwaukee, the Reverend Wenceslaus Kruszka, dismissed socialism's appeals as "the seduction of a serpent."[41]

WHi (X3) 34288
Walter Polakowski.

[37] Conversation with Victor Krzycki, May 2, 1976.
[38] Tadeusz Daniszewski, et al., *Historia Polskiego Ruchu Robotniczego, 1864–1964* (2 volumes, Warsaw, 1967), 1: 30–115; M. K. Dziewanowski, *The Communist Party of Poland: An Outline of History* (Cambridge, Massachusetts, 1959), 18–21.
[39] In later years several old socialists mended fences with the church. For example, Walter Polakowski and Cyborowski were buried with religious services, and a priest spoke at Krzycki's interment. Socialism, however, was not the sole avenue available to freethinkers. One of those interviewed recalled that his family had joined the newly established Polish National Catholic parish in the neighborhood after his father had been ordered in confession to "throw away that rag" (the *Kuryer Polski*) as a condition for absolution. See also Korman, "Social History," 25.
[40] Wyman, "Voting Behavior," 545.
[41] *Ibid.*, 724; *Kuryer Polski*, April 2, 12, 1900; Wenceslaus Kruszka, *Siedm Siedmioleci* [Seven Times Seven] (2 volumes, Poznan, Poland, 1924), 2: 690–692. See also Archbishop John Ireland's "Views on Socialism," in John T. Ellis, ed., *Documents of American Catholic*

Brisbane Hall, the socialist publishers' headquarters in Milwaukee, 1914. Heinrich Bartel, editor of the German-language Vorwaerts, *is descending the stairs; the Polish-language* Naprzod *is hanging on the newsstand wire.*

However, a useful index of the popularity of socialists and socialist ideas among the Polish voters of Milwaukee's South Side is the party affiliation of successful candidates for public office from *Polonia*. From 1890 to about 1910, a Democratic party affiliation seems to have been a prerequisite for election to the state legislature. During the next two decades, however, socialists and progressive Republicans enjoyed far more success than they had earlier; in fact, between 1920 and 1930 only one Democrat of Polish extraction, Mrs. Mary Kryszak, was elected to the Wisconsin Assembly. Of thirty-one Polish politicians who were elected to the assembly between 1890 and 1942, twelve were either socialists or progressive Republicans; of nine state senators elected during the same fifty-two-year span, five were socialists or progressive Republicans.

A similar situation prevailed in the city's common council. Between 1910 and 1940, twenty-three Poles were elected as aldermen, seven of whom were socialists. It was not until the spring election of 1936 that the last Polish socialists were swept from local office, buried in landslides won by five anti-socialist Polish candidates.[42]

This general trend from a traditional Democratic base toward a more liberal outlook—embracing both socialism and La Follette

---

History (Milwaukee, 1962), 485-490; and *Silver Jubilee Album of St. Josaphat's Parish* (Milwaukee, 1913).

[42] In 1932, socialist aldermanic candidates in the five most heavily Polish wards won four of the seats and 52 per cent of the combined vote. Three of the four Poles elected to the common council were pro-socialist. In 1936, however, all five winners were anti-socialist Poles whose combined vote amounted to 62 per cent of the total. John Banachowicz, Kotecki's Polish socialist opponent, narrowly lost the comptroller's contest in winning a majority in the Polish wards and 49.3 per cent of the total vote. In 1936, the Polish socialist candidate Albert Janicki was crushed in the election, receiving only 35 per cent of the vote.

WHi (X3) 34289

Milwaukee assemblywoman Mary Krzyszak, assistant manager and bookkeeper for the Catholic Nowiny Polskie *from 1908 to 1922 before she entered politics in 1929.*

progressivism—reflected broader developments in both municipal and state politics, and indicates that Milwaukee's Poles were increasingly influenced by forces outside the ethnic community. Predictably, when the Democratic party underwent its New Deal renaissance during the Great Depression, both Republican and Socialist party candidates were overwhelmed by a revivified Democratic machine in Polish Milwaukee. Since 1938, for example, not a single Polish-American has been elected to the Wisconsin legislature except as an avowed Democrat. But between 1910 and 1930 the socialists did attain the status of a major party on the South Side. As one Polish-American grudgingly remarked, in a 1946 retrospective on the politics of *Polonia* in Milwaukee: "The Democratic party for many years has been considered the workingman's party, although for a period, some twenty-five years ago, the socialists, with such men as Seidel, Berger, and Hoan pointing the way, made a serious incursion into the Polish-American Democratic ranks with their claims of standing for the rights of the common man."[43]

YET the trend in party politics in favor of socialist and progressive Republican principles could never have become as pronounced within *Polonia* during the period between 1900 and 1930 had it not been for the serious conflict over religious ideas that developed among the community's leaders at the same time. Religion, like politics, underwent a profound change, as many Catholics were called upon to question the traditional leadership of the church hierarchy and to adopt a more critical, intellectually independent attitude toward the Roman Catholic Church. The rise in this new, more critical spirit must be attributed largely to Michael Kruszka, founder, editor, and publisher of the Polish-language daily *Kuryer Polski* from 1888 to his death in 1918. Together with his half-brother, the Catholic priest Wenceslaus Kruszka, Michael Kruszka devoted himself unstintingly to the cause of the Polish immigrant, stimulating a growing self-awareness among his countrymen, questioning the guidance of traditional clerical leaders, supporting ideas which challenged the prevailing values of *Polonia*.[44] The *Kuryer Polski* often took editorial positions which were fiercely nationalistic, somewhat anticlerical, and politically liberal. Predictably, Michael Kruszka's views continually clashed with those of the Reverend Boleslaus Goral, editor of the city's other Polish-language daily, *Nowiny Polskie*, which

[43] Borun, *We, the Milwaukee Poles*, 289.
[44] Biographical data on the Kruszka brothers are in *ibid.*, 50, 54; Edmund Olszyk, *The Polish Press in America* (Milwaukee, 1940), 20ff; *Dictionary of Wisconsin Biography*, 214–215; Bolek, *Who's Who*, 73; *Great Polish Encyclopedia*, 6: 212–213; and the fortieth anniversary issue of the *Kuryer Polski*, June 23, 1928. An invaluable insight into Wenceslaus Kruszka's thinking is found in his 1924 autobiography, which deserves translation. Additional information is provided by Kuzniewski; and by Alexander Syski, "Reverend Waclaw Kruszka: The Nestor of Polish Historians in America," in *Polish American Studies*, 1: 62–70 (1944).

was less nationalistic, more orthodoxly Catholic, and decidedly Democratic in its political leanings. But the ongoing feud between the two newspapers represented more than personal, religious, or party differences; it signified that *Polonia* was not merely heterogeneous in values and priorities, but that profound antagonisms threatened at times to tear the Polish community apart.

The principal agent of change was Michael Kruszka, the immigrant journalist from the town of Slabomierz in German Poland. Energetic and politically ambitious, he had established the *Kuryer Polski* after several earlier unsuccessful ventures into the newspaper business. Financially sound, the *Kuryer Polski* was to become the first long-lived Polish-language daily in America, with its owner claiming as many as 35,000 readers as early as 1893. By 1915, readership was estimated to have reached the more plausible figure of 40,000, making the *Kuryer Polski* one of the most widely circulated Polish newspapers in the country.[45]

Kruszka's *Kuryer* achieved success by catering to immigrant readers' hunger for news about political and economic developments in the German-ruled regions from which most of them had come. Kruszka was also interested in disseminating cultural information broadly. Extensive literary sections could be found in the *Kuryer*, and the work of many popular novelists and essayists was serialized, particularly when it extolled Poland's past greatness and future promise.

In its coverage of domestic affairs, the *Kuryer Polski* was stridently nationalistic. It proclaimed the virtues of Milwaukee's Poles and criticized any real or perceived slight the Poles experienced in dealing with others in the city. Intensely conscious of the low social status of the Milwaukee Poles, Kruszka continually strove to agitate the Polish population to fight for its own betterment. For example, in one editorial, "To Our Women Readers," he urged that women shop at Polish-operated stores whenever possible, rather than at stores run by persons of other nationalities. "And when this is necessary," the editorial went on, "always speak to them in Polish. Otherwise, they will not feel any need to hire Polish-speaking clerks, our people won't be hired and everyone will be worse off!"[46] Another editorial concerned an issue touched off by Kruszka: the teaching of Polish in Milwaukee's public schools. Unceasingly, Kruszka asked why instruction in German was offered in German neighborhoods, while Polish was not available in Polish neighborhood schools. (This struggle was finally won in 1907, when the Milwaukee Board of Education ruled in Kruszka's favor.)[47]

[45] Korman, "Social History," 34n; Wytrwal, *America's Polish Heritage*, 328; Kuzniewski, "Faith and Fatherland," 247. In 1942, the *Kuryer Polski* was recorded as having 26,073 daily and 28,822 Sunday subscriptions: 12,500 daily daily papers went to Milwaukee readers, 6,000 were delivered to persons in the surrounding Milwaukee suburbs, and 1,240 went to others in Wisconsin. A total of 927 subscriptions went to Pennsylvania, the birthplace of the Polish National Church, 825 to Illinois, and 702 to Michigan; 1,240 others were sent to Canadian readers. *Protocols of the Kuryer Polski*, volume 2. See also Still, *Milwaukee*, 270–272.

[46] *Kuryer Polski*, January 18, 1900.

[47] *Ibid.*, June 23, 1918. In a *Kuryer* editorial of March 14, 1912, Polish communities in other cities were urged to follow Milwaukee's example. Kruszka had founded the Polish Educational Society to realize this goal in 1896.

The Reverend Boleslaus Goral, editor of the Polish-language Nowiny Polskie, *in 1899.*

The office of the Kuryer Polski *during the mid-1930's. From left to right: Martin Kedziora, Joe A. Kapmarski, Joseph Karas, and B. J. Adamkiewicz.*

As for local politics, basically Kruszka agreed with the Polish clergymen and their allies that Poles should vote as a bloc in order to win recognition as a serious force in the city. However, he differed with other *Polonia* leaders about the wisdom of a permanent Polish marriage with the Democrats, for he believed that political parties were merely vehicles for gaining appointments and influence, not ends in themselves. Kruszka therefore recommended in his editorials that the Poles support that party which best met their needs. Initially, the *Kuryer* supported the party that promised the Poles the most and nominated Polish candidates for political office over non-Poles. Later, in the 1920's and 1930's, the paper refined its position and supported politically progressive Poles over conservative Polish officeseekers.[48] Kruszka's and the *Kuryer's* independent political position naturally antagonized Democratic party regulars and supporters of the traditional clerical leadership in *Polonia*. Kruszka himself had been a Democrat; but following the 1886 strike at the Bay View rolling mills, he backed the new People's party. Then, as a Democrat, he was elected in 1890 to the assembly and in 1892 to the state senate, but he lost in his try for re-election in 1896 as a self-proclaimed Bryan Democrat. In 1898 Kruszka and the *Kuryer* supported the mayoral candidacy of the Democrat, David Rose, but only on condition that Rose appoint a number of worthy Poles to the city administration—a promise that Rose made, and promptly broke once he was elected.[49] In 1900, Kruszka broke permanently with the Democrats, this time in favor of Robert La Follette's progressive Republican gubernatorial campaign. He justified his action by arguing that the Rose Democrats were

[48] *Ibid.*, March 28, 1900; March 29, September 20, 1912; April 4, 1918; and November 5, 6, 1922, all contain but a few examples of such thinking. See Korman, "Social History," 26–27, for one explanation of this view. One interviewee remembered the words of Chester Dziadulewicz, a successor to Kruszka at the paper commenting about an aldermanic election pitting a Democrat named Smukowski against the socialist Boncel: "I don't care anything whether a candidate's socialist or not, so long as he's Polish."

[49] *Kuryer Polski*, March 29, April 5, 1900.

Courtesy James J. Borzych [WHi (X3) 33111]

St. Josaphat's Basilica, about 1920, facing southwest from Chase Avenue, just south of Lincoln Avenue.

dominated by special interests, a condition not afflicting La Follette's progressives.[60]

Notwithstanding Kruszka's own erratic political position and his newspaper's readiness to criticize church leaders, the *Kuryer Polski* became a popular and commercial success. This achievement, moreover, was not unique. As one early observer of the Polish press in America noted, a number of Polish dailies which promoted liberal and/or anticlerical editorial positions enjoyed more popularity than their conservative competitors. In Buffalo and Detroit, as in Milwaukee, the more liberal paper enjoyed twice the circulation of its conservative rival. Before 1920, the most widely read Polish-language paper in America was the anticlerical and politically radical *Ameryka Echo*, originating in Toledo, Ohio, and claiming a weekly circulation of more than 80,000.[61]

Political disagreements, however, took second place in the intense debate between the Polish clergy and the *Kuryer* over the limits of clerical authority in community as well as parish life. It was Michael Kruszka's position that priests overstepped their bounds when they dictated the political views of their parishioners. His free-thinking orientation led him to criticize the churchmen, sometimes reasonably, often intemperately. Why, he asked, must Polish parishioners pay the heavy expenses of their churches' construction and maintenance when they had no voice in making parish decisions? He was especially critical of the enormous costs incurred by the Reverend William Grutza in building St. Josaphat's church between 1897 and 1901. Kruszka estimated that the project had burdened St. Josaphat's parishioners with a debt of at least $250,000, and he blamed the archdiocese for not exercising greater control over the project.[62]

THE clergy and the archbishop responded to such charges by working against Kruszka's campaign to establish Polish in the Milwaukee public schools. They argued that he was really interested only in undermining the private parish schools, where Polish and the faith were taught, as well as the three R's. They supported the creation of rival newspapers, first the unsuccessful *Slowo*

WHi (X3) 34286
Michael Kruszka, editor and publisher of the Kuryer Polski *from 1888 until his death in 1918.*

(The Word), then in 1899 the *Dziennik Milwaucki* (Milwaukee's Daily). When this paper also went bankrupt, its backers lost over $60,000. Finally, in 1906, they sponsored the *Nowiny Polskie* under the editorship of the Reverend Boleslaus Goral. At first a weekly, the *Nowiny* became a daily competitor of Kruszka in 1907. It remained under its original ownership until 1928, when it was sold to conservative Polish business interests. Never, however, did the *Nowiny* succeed in besting its rival, either in terms of mass circulation or influence within the Polish community.[63]

---

[60] *Ibid.*, March 17, October 13, 1900; Kuzniewski, "Faith and Fatherland," 193–194.
[61] Paul Fox, *The Poles in America* (New York, 1922), 98–99.
[62] Kruszka, *Historya. . .* , part eight, 10ff; Kuzniewski, "Faith and Fatherland," 202–207.
[63] Olszyk, *The Polish Press*, 56ff; Kuzniewski, "Faith and Fatherland," 315–316. Needless to say, Kruszka possessed excellent business instincts. For example, an

Michael Kruszka's attacks gained momentum because they capitalized on a rising nationwide tide of Polish immigrant demands for greater Polish priestly advancement within the hierarchy of the Roman Catholic Church, which was widely believed to be in the tight grasp of the Irish. During the 1890's, breaks between "independent" Polish parishes and the Roman Catholic Church were not uncommon, particularly in Chicago. In 1899, added fuel was poured on when Francis Hodur, a Polish priest working near Scranton, Pennsylvania, was expelled from his pastoral post after a bitter quarrel with his bishop about the extent of episcopal authority over his Polish parishes. Hodur then established his own Polish National Catholic Church, an institution which came to hold several theological positions at odds with the Roman Catholics and also gave great power to a lay board representing the parish community.[54]

Moreover, it was at this time that Michael Kruszka's younger brother, the priest Wenceslaus Kruszka, entered the debate. Working from a relatively obscure parish in Ripon, Wisconsin, from 1895 to 1909, he became a vigorous polemicist. In 1906 he published the first attempt at a historical overview of the Polish people in America, and he took excellent advantage of the opportunity to express

achievement when he served as a state legislator was to win the contract to publish all state documents in Polish for the *Kuryer* company. In 1913, it was Kruszka who convinced the members of the Polish laymen's movement to reorganize into a fraternal insurance society to put it on a sound financial footing. See Angela Pienkos, *Federation Life Insurance*, 13.

[54] Greene, *For God and Country*, chapter VI; Paul Fox, *The Polish National Church in America* (Scranton, n.d.); Hieronym Kubiak, *Polski Narodowy Kosciol Katolicki w Stanach Zjednoczonych, 1897–1965* (Warsaw, 1970). A succinct statement of Michael Kruszka's thinking appeared in a *Kuryer* article of May 13, 1911. In his words, "The most sensitive Polish question in America has for many years concerned the Church, particularly Church finances. . '. . Poles in America have contributed over 200 million dollars for Church property. But this property does not belong to the Poles because ownership has passed into the hands of non-Polish bishops who obtain title under false pretense and who . . . treat the Polish nation with contempt. Therefore, the struggle of the *Kuryer* against foreign bishops is a struggle over the return of 200 million dollars worth of property to the Polish clergy and people. . . . [We, however] do not criticize matters of faith and we respect membership in the Church."

WHi (X3) 34287

The Reverend Wenceslaus Kruszka, spokesman for Polish representation in the Roman Catholic hierarchy.

his thoughts in the family-owned newspaper. In publications and lectures, this charismatic priest mounted powerful arguments for nominating Poles to episcopal posts, and he achieved a certain amount of national attention. Since the Poles represented one-fifth of the Catholic population in America, he argued, they deserved to have their own Polish priests considered for promotion in roughly the same proportion. Wenceslaus Kruszka's outspoken and persuasive arguments in favor of naming a Polish bishop were nowhere more evident than at a 1903 convention of Polish priests in Buffalo. There his position was strongly endorsed, and he was dispatched to Rome to argue its merits before the Pope himself. His thirteen-month European trip had no immediate result, however. Pope Leo XIII was near death and long months passed

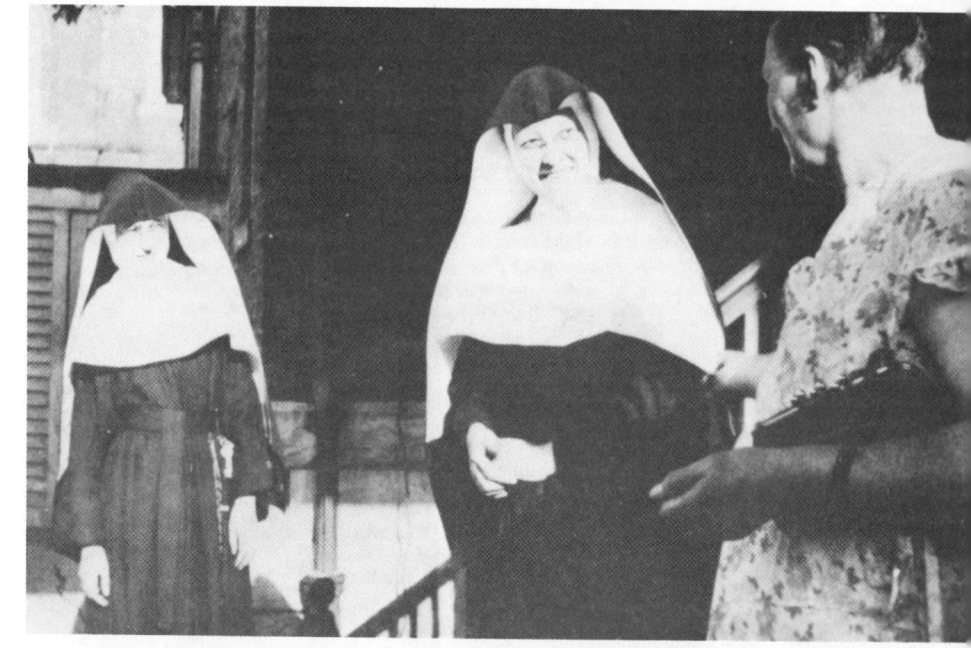

Rear entrance of the sisters' residence at St. Stanislaus Church on Mitchell Street, ca. 1940. The woman seated at the left is unidentified. The others, from the left, are Sister M. Bernadine, Sister M. Moranda (principal of the parish high school), and Mrs. Lily Myszewski.

with no opportunity to discuss the issue with responsible papal representatives. When Kruszka did gain an audience with Leo's successor, Pius X, the new pontiff would make no firm commitment, telling Kruszka, "It will be decided as soon as possible, and it will be made according to your wishes." A Pole, Paul Rhode, was named an auxiliary bishop of Chicago in 1908, to be followed by another, Edward Kozlowski, for Milwaukee in 1914; but this proved to be the sum and substance of the papal response to Kruszka's proposals.[35]

In Milwaukee, Father Kruszka's views tended to be rejected as an expression of "Cahenslyism," that is, the idea that each ethnic group within the Catholic church should have its own representative in the hierarchy. The American church had long perceived this to be at odds with its own self-image as a miniature melting pot, and the idea had been rejected as early as 1884 at its plenary council at Baltimore.[36] Archbishop Sebastian Messmer clearly interpreted the meaning of Kruszka's thinking in these terms, declaring, in a letter he wrote to Archbishop James Gibbons of Baltimore: "The longer I think it over

---

[35] Kuzniewski, "Faith and Fatherland," 211–288; Kruszka, *Siedm....*, 1: 803–806. Greene tends simultaneously to minimize Kruszka's part in the eventual decision to appoint a Polish bishop and to exaggerate the significance of this token action (*For God and Country*, 141–142).

[36] Kuzniewski, "Faith and Fatherland," 61–64, 240ff; Colman Barry, *The Catholic Church and the German Americans* (Milwaukee, 1953); Thomas McAvoy, *A History of the Catholic Church in the United States* (Notre Dame, Indiana, 1969), 245–295; Daniel Buczek, "Polish-Americans and the Roman Catholic Church," in *The Polish Review*, 21: 39–55 (Fall, 1976). Both Kuzniewski and Buczek argue that Kruszka was originally attracted to the Cahensly idea of Polish bishops ministering exclusively to Poles, but modified his view to one arguing for Polish representation in the hierarchy in the face of fierce criticism. See also Greene, *For God and Country*, 132–135; Kruszka, *Historya*, 390ff.

the more it seems to me a dangerous experiment at this stage to give the Polish people a bishop, for the very reason that he would be considered the bishop for all the Poles of the United States. I know it. Wherever a bishop would have any difficulty with a Polish parish, *their bishop* would be appealed to. The Polish are not yet American enough and keep aloof too much from the rest of us."[57]

THAT Messmer—himself a German Swiss and not an Irishman—could make this observation was illuminating, because the Milwaukee diocese was one of the few in the United States that had been headed by German bishops. That achievement itself was due only to a long-running fight by German Catholics over the issue of recognition in a church dominated by an Irish-American hierarchy. In this light, the Poles' quest for recognition clearly demonstrated the plurality of conflicts challenging a Catholic church which incorporated a variety of increasingly restive ethnic groups.[58] Yet, given their anti-German nationalist rhetoric, the Kruszkas were unable to close ranks with German Catholics who might have sympathized with their demand for ethnic recognition.

The conflict between supporters of each side became increasingly heated. Within various *Polonia* organizations, individuals were identified either as Kruszka (and *Kuryer*) or as anti-Kruszka (and *Nowiny*) partisans. Wenceslaus Kruszka, who in 1909 had been named pastor of Milwaukee's St. Adalbert's parish, had already been ordered by Archbishop Messmer not to contribute articles to the *Kuryer Polski*. Though in 1895 Michael Kruszka had helped to found a Milwaukee-based fraternal, the Society of Poles in America, he and his associates in that group's leadership were abruptly ousted from its board of directors by opponents favoring Messmer.[59] In response, Kruszka's supporters created the Federation of Polish Catholic Laymen, which stridently repeated the *Kuryer's* message at parish meetings, particularly its proposals calling for Polish bishops and increased lay involvement in parish decision-making.[60] Then, on February 11, 1912, Messmer, together with seven other bishops, issued an edict forbidding the reading

Archbishop Sebastian Messmer.

WHi (X3) 34285

[57] Thomas Monzell, "The Catholic Church and the Americanization of the Polish Immigrant," in *Polish American Studies*, 26: 4 (1969); Kuzniewski, "Faith and Fatherland," 264; Korman, "Social History," 49–50. According to Greene, Bishop Rhode indeed behaved much as Messmer had predicted. See *For God and Country*, chapter IX; Buczek, "Polish-Americans," 54.

[58] Barry, *The Catholic Church*, 44–50, 128–130, and, for a summary of Messmer's thinking, 165ff. McAvoy asserts that domination by the Irish was one of the two major problems confronting the Roman Catholic Church in its dealings with Protestants. At the Baltimore plenary council, forty-six of seventy-two bishops in attendance were either Irish or of Irish heritage, and some of the latter were militantly "American" in national consciousness. McAvoy, *History of the Catholic Church*, 267, 296.

[59] *Kuryer Polski*, August 10, 12, 13, September 12, 13, 1912.

[60] The Federation's program is to be found in Angela Pienkos, *Federation Life Insurance*, 4.

Patriotic parade, 1917, in the Polish community on Milwaukee's old Fifth Avenue.

of the *Kuryer* and nine other anti-clerical Polish publications. Disobedience of this edict constituted grounds for excommunication.[61]

This final blow, however, did not end the quarrel, which by then was attracting considerable notice among non-Poles. Kruszka's Laymen's Federation organized several mass protests against the edict in Milwaukee, Detroit, and elsewhere. One taking place on June 12, 1912, was termed the "largest demonstration of Poles ever held in Milwaukee" by the sympathetic socialist *Leader*, and consisted of a parade of approximately 25,000 persons culminating in speeches denouncing the bishops' action.[62] Michael Kruszka attempted to sue the bishops who had forbidden parishioners to read the *Kuryer*, arguing that their action abridged freedom of the press. Although his suit ultimately lost, appeals of the decision dragged on for years.[63] In September, 1912, Kruszka organized a new fraternal insurance society to rival the existing organizations which had opposed him. This group, based on the Laymen's Federation, was called the Federation of Poles in America; it remains active to this day as Federation Life Insurance of America, with headquarters in Milwaukee.[64] Ultimately, such divisions with *Polonia* led some Polish parishioners to break away from the church and to establish, in 1914, the first Polish National Catholic parish in Milwaukee. In time, three schismatic national parishes were organized, and land for a Polish cemetery free from diocesan control was also purchased.[65]

[61] The text of the pastoral letter of February 11, 1912, is in Kuzniewski, "Faith and Fatherland," 492–497.
[62] *Milwaukee Leader*, June 8, 10, 1912; *Kuryer Polski*, June 10, 12, 1912. Goral's *Nowiny* estimated that only a thousand persons were in attendance.
[63] Olszyk, *The Polish Press*, 25–27.
[64] At the group's 1912 convention, 50,000 persons were said to have joined, mostly from Wisconsin. In 1913, the Federation claimed 100,000 members. Kuzniewski, "Faith and Fatherland," 382, estimates 10,000–15,000.
[65] Gavett, *Labor Movement*, 115; Borun, *We, the Milwaukee Poles*, 234; Angela Pienkos, *Federation Life Insurance*, 8.

The outbreak of World War I, and the hopes that the war raised for Polish independence, had a marked effect upon the quarrels which had troubled Milwaukee's *Polonia*. For the Poles, optimism that victory over the Central Powers would lead to a restored independent Polish state prompted many young men to join General Jozef Haller's Polish Legion in France early in the war.[66] Woodrow Wilson's support of an independent Poland in his Fourteen Points electrified Polish-Americans and made American entry into the conflict in 1917 a patriotic call on behalf of not one but two fatherlands. More than 108,000 Poles had already volunteered for duty in Haller's army by 1917, and it is estimated that approximately forty thousand of the first hundred thousand Americans to volunteer for American military duty were Poles.[67]

In Milwaukee, a citizens' committee in behalf of Poland was organized, representing a broad cross-section of *Polonia*.[68] In contrast to similar patriotic committees in other cities, the Milwaukee group suffered from few internal divisions brought about by rivalries among competing factions that sought to dominate postwar Poland. Both Kruszka and Goral emphasized Polish patriotic support for the effort and heaped contumely upon the city's socialist administration for its pacifist stand

[66] One interviewee recalled that Milwaukee was the first city where a "Polish legion" of volunteers was organized to fight under General Haller in France; another remembered Wenceslaus Kruszka's speech on the corner of Eighth and Mitchell streets urging support for Haller. A third man told of how "sixty fellows from one block enlisted" when the United States entered the war in 1917. See also Buczek, "Polish-Americans," 55–56; Borun, *We, the Milwaukee Poles*, 213, 205–211.

[67] Eugene Kusielewicz, "Woodrow Wilson and the Rebirth of Poland," in *Polish American Studies*, 12: 1–15 (1955); William Galush, "American Poles and the New Poland," in *Ethnicity*, 1: 209–221 (October, 1974).

[68] *Kuryer Polski*, April 15, 1918.

Polish bond rally, Kosciusko Park, 1920. The first Polish ambassador to the United States was in Milwaukee raising money for war relief in the newborn state of Poland. St. Josaphat's Basilica is in the background.

Courtesy James J. Borzych [WHi (X3) 33112]

on the war issue. The failure of the Milwaukee socialists to recognize the force of nationalistic sentiments among the Polish population in turn weakened the socialists' appeal. Thus, the zenith of Hoan's popularity was to remain his 1916 success in the Polish precincts; never again did he win a majority of the Polish vote from those districts, although in the assembly and in aldermanic contests Polish socialists continued to enjoy increasing success throughout the following decade.

Michael Kruszka's death in 1918 coincided with the end of the war and Poland's rebirth.[69] With these events, the anticlerical era came to an end. Although the *Kuryer Polski* remained steadfast to the goals of promoting greater Polish political representation in gov-

[69] Mayor Hoan ordered the flags of the city flown at half-staff until his funeral. The rival *Nowiny* acknowledged that Kruszka's *Kuryer* had always been "extremely liberal and progressive . . . and at the same time anti-Catholic." *Nowiny Polskie*, December 10, 1918.

ernment, greater Polish clerical visibility in the church, and the promotion of Polish national consciousness, its relationship with its old clerical opponents eased. Too, despite Archbishop Messmer's misgivings about the dangers to Catholic unity posed by a Polish bishop, Msgr. Edward Kozlowski was appointed an auxiliary bishop of the Milwaukee archdiocese in 1914, the second Pole in the United States to be elevated to such a post.

At the parish level, ordinary Polish workmen and housewives could hardly remain unaffected by the debates, although a number of facts indicate that the issues may have been more important to priests, intellectuals, and journalists than they were to the mass of men and women in *Polonia*. Only a relatively few persons actually left the Roman Catholic Church during the height of the controversy, and the circulation of the *Kuryer Polski* actually rose slightly after the announcement of the excommunication edict. Nonetheless, many must have wondered whether the bish-

Work crew of the Wisconsin Tunnel & Construction Company, a Polish-owned firm on Milwaukee's North Side, ca. 1917. The owner, Frank Nakielski, is at center, in vest and tie.

Courtesy Agnes Nakielski Christenson [WHi (X3) 33198]

Courtesy Genevieve Malmarowski Johnson [WHi (X3) 34256]

Polish-owned grocery at 3009 North Pierce on Milwaukee's North Side, around the time of World War II.

ops' interdict was not too extreme, an overreaction to what, at worst, were annoying complaints. As ordinary Poles continued to read the *Kuryer*, they must have asked themselves often what real harm was being done by the local newspaper. At the same time, the evidence that a growing number of Polish voters was willing to cast ballots for the socialist political candidates scorned by their pastors clearly indicates that they were no longer willing to obey the once-unchallenged leaders of *Polonia* in all matters.

DURING the first third of the twentieth century, then, the Poles of Milwaukee had passed through several crises which sent tremors through the traditional pillars of *Polonia*: the Roman Catholic Church and the Democratic party. The *Kuryer Polski*, widely read and presumably influential, had ceaselessly agitated against the clerical hierarchy; and clergymen themselves had in turn agitated for greater Polish representation in the ruling circle of the church. The Democratic party had gone into eclipse at all levels of government (the presidency of Woodrow Wilson being the single exception); and simultaneously there had arisen a broadly based political movement which, under the banners of either socialism or La Follette Republicanism, made substantial inroads among working-class Poles. In short, between the turn of the century and the Great Depression, the very foundations of religion and politics in Polish Milwaukee were shaken by events and ideas from within and without.

Ironically, in spite of this, practically no remnant survives of the progressive era in Milwaukee's Polish enclaves. (The three Polish National churches and a fraternal organization are the rather modest exceptions.) How is one to explain such a phenomenon: a period of social and political ferment whose vestiges are so scanty as to lead one to wonder whether it ever existed?

Politically, of course, the fate of the Polish progressives and socialists depended upon the fortunes of the statewide La Follette movement and the Milwaukee-based Socialist party. Both suffered a severe blow with the election of Franklin Roosevelt in 1932 and the revival of the Wisconsin Democratic party which began about the same time. Among the Poles, the Progressive party of Philip La Follette won very few adherents after 1934. In Milwaukee, the demise of the Polish socialists can be explained in much the same terms as the collapse of the party citywide: lacking a base of mass support, and chronically beset by financial difficulties, the socialists were unable to become an enduring force in local affairs. At its height, prior to World War I, Milwaukee's Socialist party had no more than four to five thousand members; by 1934, countywide membership had fallen to 2,339. The decline in the Socialist party nationally by the late 1920's severely dampened optimism about its possibilities. In Milwaukee as well as in its Polish community, the socialist movement seems to have been a one-generation phenomenon. Few new Bergers, Krzyckis, or Polakowskis arrived on the scene to take over where the early socialists had left off.[70]

A crucial factor explaining the demise of socialism in Polish Milwaukee was the depth of the Poles' commitment to the Roman Catholic Church. Despite their misgivings about many church leaders and about the wisdom of some of their actions, the great majority of Poles remained loyal to their local parishes and priests. To them, Polish nationality and Catholicism were two sides of the same coin. They agreed, after all was said and done, with the solemn admonition of Boleslaus Goral: "Woe to those who would ever dare to conspire against this most sacred heritage of ours."[71] The main institution of *Polonia* continued to be the church, and even the secular fraternal organizations gradually became increasingly dependent on parish members for most of their support, although clergymen no longer monopolized the leadership of *Polonia* as had once been the case.

By the mid-1930's Milwaukee's Poles had overwhelmingly opted to support Roosevelt's New Deal. In 1932, 1936, and 1940, Roosevelt won 67, 78, and 64 per cent of the vote,

---

[70] Miller, "Milwaukee Retrospective...," 7–9. The 1934 membership list is in the Socialist party archives in the Milwaukee Public Library.

[71] Goral, "Poles in Milwaukee," 613. Several of the socialists who were interviewed stressed the impact that unceasing clerical criticism of their party and its program had on the Polish population.

respectively, in Milwaukee as a whole. In the same elections, the nine Polish wards gave him 75, 84, and 76 per cent of their vote.[72] In the four gubernatorial campaigns between 1934 and 1940, the level of voter support in the Polish wards for Progressive party candidates was practically indistinguishable from citywide totals.

Events in Europe also helped to push the experience of the progressive era far back in the consciousness of the Milwaukee Poles. The state of Poland, for whose independence so much had been sacrificed during the First World War, fell under Nazi and then Communist rule, suffering in the process not only the destruction of millions of human lives but also a significant break in its historic ties with Americans of Polish descent.[73]

Yet a strong ethnic consciousness, and a knowledge of how to use their political muscle, had taken root among the Poles of Milwaukee—just as the brothers Kruszka and their rivals had hoped. On the eve of American entry into World War II, five of Milwaukee's twenty-seven aldermen were Poles, a Polish-American from Milwaukee sat in the House of Representatives, and another served on the Milwaukee bench. Symbolic of the new role played by Polish Milwaukee was the way in which the enemies of *Polonia* could be dealt with in election years. In 1900, for example, Michael Kruszka had urged his Polish countrymen to vote against Mayor David Rose, who had appointed only one Polish-American—not the promised fifteen—during his first two-year term. But even without the *Kuryer's* support, Rose had been re-elected with great majorities from the Polish districts of Milwaukee to four additional terms as mayor.

By way of contrast, in 1937 Mayor Hoan replaced a deceased Polish police captain, John Wesolowski, with a non-Pole. This caused a furor, not only in Wesolowski's fourth police district but throughout *Polonia*. A host of Polish organizational leaders asked the mayor to reconsider his decision, but Hoan remained adamant. Letters flooded in. Finally, Hoan produced a detailed list of all appointments he had made during his tenure in office, a list which included a host of Polish names. Hoan then reaffirmed his policy: "All must be treated equally."

Polonia's reaction to the mayor's avowed policy was swift and bluntly phrased. The secretary of the Casimir Pulaski Council (a political-action federation of Polish community organizations formed in 1929), himself a leader in Kruszka's old Laymen's federation, wrote back: "When the proper time arrives, we will know how to deal with matters." Daniel Hoan was ousted at the very next election.[74]

---

[72] In the old socialist stronghold, the fourteenth ward, Roosevelt received 91, 93, and 94 per cent of the vote in 1932, 1936, and 1940, respectively.

[73] Concern for Poland peaked in *Polonia* during the war. A nationwide fund-raising campaign in behalf of Polish victims of the conflict raised $170,000 in Milwaukee alone. See Komitet Ratunkowy Polonii w Milwaukee, *Wisconsin American Relief for Poland* (Milwaukee, 1946), 12. The nature of *Polonia's* concern was defined as early as 1934, when the American delegation to a world congress of *Polonia* groups in Warsaw asserted the limits of their identification with the ancestral homeland. That group, under the leadership of Milwaukee's Francis Swietlik, refused to swear allegiance to Poland and emphasized that Polish-Americans were an "inseparable, harmonious part of the American nation, however tied to Poland by feeling, tradition and culture."

[74] Letter from Leon Kazmierczak, in the Daniel Hoan Papers, Milwaukee County Historical Society. According to Olson, "Milwaukee Socialists," 566, the heavy Polish vote against Hoan was instrumental in causing his 1940 loss to Carl Zeidler. For Hoan's own view, see Edward Kerstein, *Milwaukee's All-American Mayor: A Portrait of Daniel Webster Hoan* (Englewood Cliffs, New Jersey, 1966), 167–185.

A NOTE ON THE ILLUSTRATIONS

When we began searching for pictures to illustrate Professor Pienkos' article, we quickly discovered that the voluminous Iconographic Collection of the State Historical Society of Wisconsin contained little relating to Polish Milwaukee. We are therefore indebted to the following persons and institutions—all of Milwaukee—for their advice, patience, and generosity: James J. Borzych, Agnes Nakielski Christenson, Genevieve Malmarowski Johnson, the Milwaukee County Historical Society, and the Milwaukee Public Library.

—THE EDITORS

The Heritage of American Catholicisim

1. EDWARD R. KANTOWICZ, EDITOR
   MODERN AMERICAN CATHOLICISM, 1900-1965:
   SELECTED HISTORICAL ESSAYS
   New York 1988

2. DOLORES LIPTAK, R.S.M., EDITOR
   A CHURCH OF MANY CULTURES:
   SELECTED HISTORICAL ESSAYS ON ETHNIC AMERICAN CATHOLICISIM
   New York 1988

3. TIMOTHY J. MEAGHER, EDITOR
   URBAN AMERICAN CATHOLICISM:
   THE CULTURE AND IDENTITY OF THE AMERICAN CATHOLIC PEOPLE
   New York 1988

4. BRIAN MITCHELL, EDITOR
   BUILDING THE AMERICAN CATHOLIC CITY:
   PARISHES AND INSTITUTIONS
   New York 1988

5. MICHAEL J. PERKO, S.J., EDITOR
   ENLIGHTENING THE NEXT GENERATION:
   CATHOLICS AND THEIR SCHOOLS, 1830-1980
   New York 1988

6. WILLIAM PORTIER, EDITOR
   THE ENCULTURATION OF AMERICAN CATHOLICISM, 1820-1900:
   SELECTED HISTORICAL ESSAYS
   New York 1988

7. Timothy Walch, editor
   Early American Catholicism, 1634-1820:
   Selected Historical Essays
   New York 1988

8. Joseph M. White, editor
   The American Catholic Religious Life:
   Selected Historical Essays
   New York 1988

9. Robert F. Trisco
   Bishops and Their Priests in the United States, 1789-1918
   New York 1988

10. Joseph Agonito
    The Building of an American Catholic Church:
    The Episcopacy of John Carroll
    New York 1988

11. Robert N. Barger
    John Lancaster Spalding:
    Catholic Educator and Social Emissary
    New York 1988

12. Christine M. Bochen
    The Journey to Rome:
    Conversion Literature by Nineteenth-Century American Catholics
    New York 1988

13. Martin J. Bredeck
    Imperfect Apostles:
    "The Commonweal" and the American Catholic Laity, 1924-1976
    New York 1988

14. Jeffrey M. Burns
    American Catholics and the Family Crisis, 1930-1962:
    The Ideological and Organizational Response
    New York 1988

15. ALFRED J. EDE
   THE LAY CRUSADE FOR A CHRISTIAN AMERICA:
   A STUDY OF THE AMERICAN FEDERATION OF CATHOLIC SOCIETIES, 1900-1919
   New York 1988

16. JO RENEE FORMICOL
   THE AMERICAN CATHOLIC CHURCH AND ITS ROLE IN THE FORMULATION OF UNITED STATES HUMAN RIGHTS FOREIGN POLICY, 1945-1978
   New York 1988

17. THOMAS J. JONAS
   THE DIVIDED MIND:
   AMERICAN CATHOLIC EVANGELSTS IN THE 1890s
   FOREWORD BY MARTIN E. MARTY
   New York 1988

18. MARTIN J. KIRK
   THE SPIRITUALITY OF ISAAC THOMAS HECKER:
   RECONCILING THE AMERICAN CHARACTER AND THE CATHOLIC FAITH
   New York 1988

19. NORLENE M. KUNKEL
   BISHOP BERNARD J. MCQUAID AND CATHOLIC EDUCATION
   New York 1988

20. JAMES M. MCDONNELL
   ORESTES A. BROWNSON AND NINETEENTH-CENTURY CATHOLIC EDUCATION
   New York 1988

21. ELIZABETH MCKEOWN
   WAR AND WELFARE:
   AMERICAN CATHOLICS AND WORLD WAR I
   New York 1988

22. BARBARA MISNER, S. C. S. C.
   "HIGHLY RESPECTABLE AND ACCOMPLISHED LADIES:"
   CATHOLIC WOMEN RELIGIOUS IN AMERICA 1790-1850
   New York 1988

23. BENITA A. MOORE
   ESCAPE INTO A LABYRINTH:
   F. SCOTT FITZGERALD, CATHOLIC SENSIBILITY, AND THE AMERICAN WAY
   New York 1988

24. MARILYN WENZKE NICKELS
   BLACK CATHOLIC PROTEST
   AND THE FEDERATED COLORED CATHOLICS, 1917-1933:
   THREE PERSPECTIVES ON RACIAL JUSTICE
   New York 1988

25. DAVID L. SALVATERRA
   AMERICAN CATHOLICISM AND THE INTELLECTUAL LIFE, 1880-1920
   New York 1988

26. HELENA SANFILIPPO, R. S. M.
   INNER WEALTH AND OUTWARD SPLENDOR:
   NEW ENGLAND TRANSCENDENTALISTS VIEW THE ROMAN CATHOLIC CHURCH
   New York 1988

27. FAYETTE BREAUX VEVERKA
   "FOR GOD AND COUNTRY:"
   CATHOLIC SCHOOLING IN THE 1920s
   New York 1988

28. TIMOTHY WALCH
   THE DIVERSE ORIGINS OF AMERICAN CATHOLIC EDUCATION:
   CHICAGO, MILWAUKEE, AND THE NATION
   New York 1988

THE UNITED STATES AND THE

TREATY LAW OF THE SEA ~~~~~

BY HENRY REIFF

UNIVERSITY OF MINNESOTA PRESS · MINNEAPOLIS

© Copyright 1959 by the University of Minnesota

ALL RIGHTS RESERVED. PRINTED IN THE UNITED STATES OF
AMERICA AT THE NORTH CENTRAL PUBLISHING CO., ST. PAUL

PUBLISHED IN GREAT BRITAIN, INDIA, AND PAKISTAN BY THE OXFORD UNIVERSITY PRESS,
LONDON, BOMBAY, AND KARACHI AND IN CANADA BY THOMAS ALLEN, LTD., TORONTO

The Library of Congress has catalogued this book as follows:

Reiff, Henry, 1899–
    The United States and the treaty law of the sea. Minneapolis, University of Minnesota Press [1959]
    451 p. 24 cm.
    Includes bibliography.

    1. Maritime law.   2. Maritime law—U. S.   I. Title.

JX4411.R43   347.75   58–13747 ‡
Library of Congress

TO MY WIFE, IONE, AND TO
MY SONS, JONATHAN AND
DANIEL, WHO HAVE HEARD
ABOUT THINGS NAUTICAL
AD NAUSEAM

ACKNOWLEDGMENTS

In this centennial year of Charles Darwin's first public announcement of his theory of evolution, decades after his famous voyage around the world in H.M.S. *Beagle*, it should not be inappropriate to cite one of his lesser works, *The Formation of Vegetable Mould through the Action of Worms*, to make a point. The worms, he found, brought up to the surface, enriching the land, as much as 18.12 tons of subsoil per acre per year. This phenomenon has always impressed me as symbolic of what patient, plodding burrowing can achieve, and sometimes I have likened it to the activities of scholars in some untilled field of human knowledge, though on occasion I find myself confusing the scholars with the worms. However that may be, this work at any rate is the product of nearly thirty-five years of grubbing for data, which now at last appear on the surface, hopefully in a form useful to the social scientist.

It is difficult to recollect for acknowledgment here all those who in one way or another, over the past several decades, have contributed to the growth of this work. Judge Manley O. Hudson, Bemis Professor of International Law at the Harvard Law School, will not likely remember the occasion a few years after World War I when he talked to some undergraduates at the Harvard Union about the nature and prospects of international legislation. Yet one freshman in that group took the message to heart and, in time, came to labor in that field. Many of us who profited so much from the teachings of George Grafton Wilson, Professor of International Law at Harvard University, and Jesse S. Reeves, Professor of International Law at the University of Michigan, will remember them with affection and gratitude. And to Everett S. Brown, Professor of Political Science at the University of Michigan, I owe my total loss of fear of government documentation.

Judge Jasper Y. Brinton, formerly President of the Mixed Courts of Egypt, now Nestor of the Egyptian Society of International Law, Herbert W. Briggs, Professor of International Law at Cornell University, and Richard Young of the New York Bar all read the first draft of this work and encouraged me to proceed with it. Mr. Young also read the final draft, rescued me from sundry grievous errors, and still had kind words to say about the bulkier manuscript. Each of these colleagues I thank heartily and caution the reader to lay the remaining faults of this work not against them, but against me for my insistence on some things or my carelessness about others. It would be strange indeed if a few ounces of sand had not gotten mixed up with the tons of mould.

Among my numerous correspondents over the years, all of them courteous and helpful, I am particularly indebted to Dr. G. Bernard Noble, Chief of the Division of Historical Policy Research of the Department of State, for frequent help with archival data, especially those concerning the Whangpoo Conservancy, and to Mr. J. W. P. Chidell, formerly of the United Kingdom Ministry of Fuel and Power and lately Trade Commissioner at New Delhi, for the supply of thitherto elusive information about British undersea mines. To Dr. Karel Naprstek of the Department of Public Information of the United Nations I am especially grateful for his unfailing patience and kindness in supplying me with much needed information and documentation.

To St. Lawrence University and its President, Eugene Garrett Bewkes, I owe much for their consistent encouragement of the faculty in research and creative writing, and to the Dean of the College of Letters and Science, Joseph J. Romoda, I am deeply indebted for unnumbered courtesies over the years in the preparation of this study. Without the wholehearted cooperation of Mr. Andrew K. Peters, University Librarian, and his devoted staff, particularly Mr. Wharton H. Miller, Miss Helen M. Dowd, and Mrs. William D. Mallam, and the successive Reference Librarians, Mrs. Adolph William Mall, Mrs. John J. Carroll, and Mrs. John L. Mentley, I am sure I should still be burrowing. I am especially grateful to Dr. William Reid Willoughby, among my esteemed colleagues in the Department of History and Government, for generous assistance at various points in my preparation of the section on the St. Lawrence Seaway.

And to my wife, many, many, thanks.

HENRY REIFF

St. Lawrence University
Canton, New York
July 1, 1958

TABLE OF CONTENTS

I. FOCUS ON THE SEA.................................... 3

II. USE AND ABUSE OF THE SEA........................... 18
Res Nullius or *Res Communis?* 19. Transportation, 20: BRIDGES, TUNNELS, PIPELINES, POWER CABLES, 21; SEA TRANSPORT, 25; AIR TRANSPORT, 34. Communications, 35: POSTAL COMMUNICATIONS, 35; TELECOMMUNICATIONS, 36. Exploitation of Products, 40: FISHERY RESOURCES, 40; MINERALS, SAND, FRESH WATER, 47; BIRDS, 48; SUBSOIL MINES AND WELLS, 53; ENERGY: ATOMIC, WIND, TIDAL, THERMAL, 57. Disposal of Waste, 59. Recreation, 64: YACHTING, 64; ANGLING, 67; UNDERWATER EXPLORATION, 69; LITERATURE, ART, HOBBIES, 71. Needed: A Social Science of the Sea, 71.

III. FROM INDEPENDENCE TO THE GREAT WAR: UNFOLDING INTEREST IN TREATY LAW FOR THE SEA.................... 73
From Independence to the Civil War, 76. New Nation, New Responsibilities, 77: FREEDOM OF NAVIGATION, 77; ASSISTANCE, SALVAGE, AID TO SEAMEN, 78; FISHERIES, 78; ESTABLISHMENT OF NATIONAL SERVICES, 80. Expanding Nation, Expansion Seaward, 82: SCIENCE AND NAVIGATION, 82; GUANO, PIRATES, AND SLAVES, 85; EXPLORATION, 87; FLAG SIGNAL CODE AND RULES OF THE ROAD, 88; SUMMARY, 89. From the Civil War to the Great War, 91. Safety of Life at Sea, 92: CAPE SPARTEL LIGHTHOUSE, 92; PRIME MERIDIAN, 93; INTERNATIONAL DATE LINE, 96; INTERNATIONAL TIME BUREAU, 98; FIRST INTERNATIONAL CONFERENCE OF AMERICAN STATES, 1889, 99; INTERNATIONAL MARINE CONFERENCE, 1889, 100; WHANGPOO RIVER CONSERVANCY, 101; LOAD LINES, 102; SAFETY OF LIFE AT SEA CONFERENCE, 1914, 104. Communications, 107: POSTAL COMMUNICATIONS, 107; SUBMARINE CABLES, 108; WIRELESS, 109. Health, 110. Exploitation of Products of the Sea, 116; COD FISHERIES, 116; FUR SEALS AND OTTERS, 117; SALMON, HALIBUT, AND STURGEON, 120; FISHERIES EXPOSITIONS, EXHIBITIONS, AND CONGRESSES, 121; OCEANIC BIRDS, 123. Humanitarian Programs, 125: TRAFFIC IN SLAVES, LIQUOR, AND FIREARMS, 125; OPIUM TRAFFIC, 127; TRAFFIC IN WOMEN AND CHILDREN AND OBSCENE LITERATURE, 128. Scientific and Legal Developments, 129: INTERNATIONAL POLAR YEAR, 1882–1883, 129; METEOROLOGY, 130; HYDROGRAPHY, 130; GEODESY, 130; GEOGRAPHY: MAP ON THE MILLIONTH SCALE, 131; INTERNATIONAL MARITIME COMMITTEE, 132; NAVIGATION CONGRESSES, 133; INTERNATIONAL ASSOCIATION FOR LABOUR LEGISLATION, 133. Conclusion, 134.

IV. BETWEEN THE GREAT WARS: PROGRESS IN REGIMES FOR THE SEA...136

Transportation, 138: SAFETY OF LIFE AT SEA, 138; LONDON CONFERENCE, 1929, 138; NORTH ATLANTIC TRACKS, 139; UNITED STATES-MEXICAN RESCUE AGREEMENT, 142; LOAD LINES, 142; BUOYAGE AND LIGHTING OF COASTS, 143; OIL POLLUTION OF NAVIGABLE WATERS, 145; MINE CLEARANCE, 145; LABOR AT SEA, 154; AIR COMMERCE, 156. Communications, 158: PORTS AND WATERWAYS, 158; RADIO, 160. Health, 162: UNIVERSAL REGIME, 164; PAN AMERICAN REGIME, 165. Exploitation of Products of the Sea, 166: CANADIAN-AMERICAN FISHERIES, 167; TUNA FISHERIES, 175; WHALES, 177; FUR SEALS, 182; LEAGUE OF NATIONS EFFORTS, 184; PERMANENT COUNCIL FOR THE EXPLORATION OF THE SEA, 185; PROTECTION OF WILDLIFE, 185. Humanitarian Programs, 186: TRAFFIC IN WOMEN AND CHILDREN AND OBSCENE PUBLICATIONS, 186; TRAFFIC IN SLAVES, LIQUOR, AND FIREARMS, 187; OPIUM TRAFFIC, 187; INTERNATIONAL CRIMINAL POLICE COMMISSION, 189. Legal, Scientific, and Other Developments, 190: INTERNATIONAL MARITIME COMMITTEE, 190; PUBLIC ORGANIZATIONS NOT UNDER TREATY, 190; SPECIALIZED CONFERENCES, 193; PRIVATE ORGANIZATIONS, 195. Summary, 197.

V. EXPANSION IN TREATY LAW FOR THE SEA SINCE WORLD WAR II: TRANSPORTATION AND COMMUNICATIONS.........198

Transportation, 200. International Civil Aviation Organization, 202: CHICAGO CONVENTION, 1944, 202; INTERNATIONAL STANDARDS AND RECOMMENDED PRACTICES, 203; LEGAL COMMITTEE, 204; AIR-NAVIGATION REGIONS, 205; WEATHER-SHIP PROGRAM, 205; JOINT SERVICES IN ICELAND AND DANISH TERRITORY, 209; OTHER JOINT AND COOPERATIVE WEATHER PROGRAMS, 209; COOPERATION WITH PRIVATE AND PUBLIC INTERNATIONAL ORGANIZATIONS, 211. World Meteorological Organization, 213. Intergovernmental Maritime Consultative Organization, 216: MARITIME SAFETY COMMITTEE, 220; COORDINATION OF MARITIME ACTIVITIES, 220; TONNAGE MEASUREMENT, 222; OIL POLLUTION OF NAVIGABLE WATERS, 223. Safety of Life at Sea, 227: COORDINATION OF SAFETY AT SEA AND IN THE AIR, 228; LONDON CONFERENCE OF 1948, 229; NORTH ATLANTIC ICE PATROL, 230; THE ANDREA DORIA-STOCKHOLM COLLISION, 1956, 232; CARRIAGE OF DANGEROUS GOODS, 237. Labor at Sea, 239: NEW CONVENTIONS, 240; WELFARE OF FISHERMEN, 240; FLIGHT FROM HIGH STANDARD FLAGS, 241; UNITED NATIONS FLAG SHIPS, 243; HYGIENE OF SEAFARERS, 245; ILO MARITIME SESSION, 1958, 245; MOVE IN UNITED STATES TO WITHDRAW FROM ILO, 245. Communications, 247. Telecommunications, 247: ATLANTIC CITY REVISION, 1947, 248; SAFETY ON GREAT LAKES, 251; RADIO AMATEUR, 251; CABLES, 253; POSTAL COMMUNICATIONS, 257. United Nations Coordination of Transport and Communications, 258.

VI. EXPANSION IN TREATY LAW FOR THE SEA SINCE WORLD WAR II: HEALTH, RESOURCES, AND OTHER DEVELOPMENTS..261

Health, 261. World Health Organization, 262: INTERNATIONAL SANITARY REGULATIONS, 266; THE UNITED STATES AND THE MIDDLE EAST, 267; U.S. TECH-

Table of Contents

NICAL COOPERATION PROGRAM, 269. Resources of the Sea, 270. Fisheries, 272: NEW U.S. FISHERIES POLICY, 272; NORTHWEST ATLANTIC FISHERIES, 273; NORTH PACIFIC FISHERIES, 278; HALIBUT FISHERIES, 281; PINK OR HUMPBACK SALMON, 283; FUR SEALS, 285; UNITED STATES-CANADA SHELLFISH AGREEMENT, 289; GREAT LAKES FISHERIES, 289; WHALES, 293; TUNA FISHERIES, 297; TECHNICAL ASSISTANCE, 300. *Mare Liberum* or *Mare Clausum*, 300: SEIZURES BY LATIN AMERICAN GOVERNMENTS, 300; REIMBURSEMENT OF FINES ACT OF 1954, 304; LATIN AMERICAN OFFSHORE CLAIMS, 304. The International Law Commission and Resources of the Sea, 315: ROME TECHNICAL CONFERENCE, 1955, 317; INTERNATIONAL LAW COMMISSION FINAL REPORT, 1956, 321. United Nations Conference on the Law of the Sea, 1958, 327. Regional Councils, 334: INDO-PACIFIC FISHERIES COUNCIL, 335; SOUTH PACIFIC COMMISSION, 336; TECHNICAL ASSISTANCE AND COOPERATION AGREEMENTS, 339; CARIBBEAN COMMISSION, 339. Food and Agriculture Organization, 342. Humanitarian, Scientific, and Other Developments, 343. Humanitarian Efforts, 343: SLAVERY AND SLAVE TRAFFIC, 344; TRAFFIC IN NARCOTICS, 346. Scientific Efforts, 348; ECOSOC AND UNESCO, 349; INTERNATIONAL GEOPHYSICAL YEAR, 351. The Great Lakes-St. Lawrence Waterway, 354. Atoms and Missiles, 360: ATOMIC WASTES, 361; NUCLEAR WEAPONS TESTING, 363; GUIDED MISSILES TESTING, 368. Conclusion, 372.

APPENDIX I. PROCLAMATIONS BY PRESIDENT TRUMAN, SEPTEMBER 28, 1945......................................379

APPENDIX II. CHECKLIST OF TREATIES PERFECTED BY THE UNITED STATES CITED HEREIN...........................381

BIBLIOGRAPHY..394

INDEX 427

The United States and the Treaty Law of the Sea

CHAPTER I

FOCUS ON THE SEA

THE interest of the American people in the sea has fluctuated from generation to generation since colonial times.[1] At the moment there is a revival of interest reminiscent of that which flourished almost exactly a century ago, in the decade preceding the outbreak of the Civil War.[2] How has this come about? What does it portend for the future of America? The first question is far easier to answer than the second.

After the Civil War, with the problem of competition between free labor and slave labor in the West settled, America devoted itself to expansion westward. The merchant fleet and the navy declined. So did public interest in affairs maritime. The Spanish War revived interest in the navy, now one of steel. World War I forced the building of a huge merchant marine to offset the losses caused by the German U-boats. But after that war, isolationism and disinterest in the sea set in once again.

The needs of World War II, however, forced the United States to expand its merchant fleet enormously, from 14 per cent of the world's tonnage and second place in rank in 1939, to 51 per cent and first place in 1945. By the middle of 1946, the fleet still comprised almost 50 per cent of the world's tonnage, but if to that were added the lend-lease shipping the percentage would have been 54.[3] Though the total of the world's tonnage has increased since 1946, Lloyd's Register of Shipping in 1955 reported that the United States had about 26 per cent of the world's tonnage and was still in first place among the great maritime nations.

[1] See Samuel W. Bryant, *The Sea and the States: A Maritime History of the American People* (1947), passim.
[2] Charles Lee Lewis, *Matthew Fontaine Maury: The Pathfinder of the Seas* (1927), pp. 80–82.
[3] *Merchant Fleets of the World: September 1, 1939–December 31, 1951*, U.S. Department of Commerce, Maritime Administration (1952), p. 3. In 1957 Lloyd's reported the United States, with 4374 ships of 25,910,855 tons, as the largest shipowner in the world, although about 12,750,000 tons of that shipping is laid up in government reserve fleets. "World Ship Fleet Adds Tonnage," *The New York Times* (hereinafter cited as *N.Y.T.*), Nov. 14, 1957.

The United States and the Treaty Law of the Sea

Far more important in their effects upon public interest than the growth of the merchant fleet were the dramatic exploits of American naval and air forces in World War II on the Seven Seas and over the waters from pole to pole. These have been celebrated in book and verse, on stage and screen, over radio and television, continuously since 1945, and apparently the public has not yet tired of them.

As long, too, as the United States possesses its strategic trusteeship over the former Japanese Mandate in the Marshall, Caroline, and Mariana islands in the Pacific and occupies such hard-won Japanese islands as Okinawa, American thoughts will be directed to vast oceans and tiny faraway islands where so much blood and treasure was spent.

American participation, soon after hostilities ended, in a number of new international organizations directly concerned with the sea — the Provisional Maritime Consultative Council in 1946, the World Meteorological Organization in 1947, the North Atlantic Ocean Weather Stations program and the Northwest Atlantic Fisheries Convention in 1949 — gave unmistakable evidence of the official view that the future of the United States would trend increasingly seaward. The appearance in the *Department of State Bulletin* of over twelve hundred items dealing with sundry aspects of the sea since 1939 supports the same view.

To these historic events must be added the continuing preoccupation with the North Atlantic Treaty Organization; with naval and air bases in the Atlantic, the Caribbean, the Mediterranean, and the Pacific; with guided missiles sped from Florida to Ascension Island, deep in the South Atlantic; with hydrogen-bomb tests at Bikini; with oil beyond Suez in the Middle East. If superpower, or even first-rate power, we wish to remain, we cannot again turn our backs upon the sea. In truth, if we but read the omens correctly, the sea will not let us alone.

At a strategic moment in the affairs of nations, at the close of World War II, President Truman issued his two historic proclamations on September 28, 1945, one declaring "the natural resources of the subsoil and sea bed of the continental shelf beneath the high seas but contiguous to the coasts of the United States as appertaining to the United States, subject to its jurisdiction and control,"[4] the other asserting a national policy with respect to the establishment of conservation zones for the

[4] Proclamation by the President with Respect to the Natural Resources of the Subsoil and Sea Bed of the Continental Shelf, 59 *Stat.* 884–885. See Appendix I for text.

Focus on the Sea

control of fisheries in areas of the high seas contiguous to the coasts of the United States, by means of American legislation or treaty arrangements, as the exploitation of the fisheries might warrant.[5]

Exploitation of oil in the continental shelf off the coasts of California, Texas, and Louisiana was already in process.[6] A great controversy, in the making for several decades, thereupon arose between the states concerned and the federal government, involving claims of right to ownership and control of the subsoil resources. In three important decisions,[7] the Supreme Court repeatedly held that the federal government had full dominion in the resources, and paramount rights in and power over the areas in controversy. The heated issues of public policy involved entered the presidential campaign of 1952. The new Congress promptly adopted two acts. A Submerged Lands Act of May 22, 1953,[8] vested title in the disputed areas in the states up to the three-mile limit or alternatively, as in some cases, to their historic seaward limits, if greater. An Outer Continental Shelf Lands Act of August 7, 1953,[9] retained for the United States all civil and political jurisdiction in the subsoil and sea bed of the continental shelf beyond the seaward boundaries permitted to the states.

The two presidential proclamations of 1945 and the tidelands oil controversy focused the attention of the American people on the new frontiers in the sea. Other nations followed with similar claims to new frontiers or extended old claims. Some governments went far beyond the American claims of jurisdictional rights and asserted sovereignty [10] over extensive areas of the sea, its bed, and the subsoil. International disputes naturally ensued. In the premises, the newly created International

[5] Proclamation by the President with Respect to Coastal Fisheries in Certain Areas of the High Seas, 59 *Stat.* 885–886. See Appendix I for text.

[6] Ernest R. Bartley, *The Tidelands Oil Controversy: A Legal and Historical Analysis* (1953), pp. 56–58; Chs. 5, 6.

[7] United States v. California, 332 U.S. 19 (1947), United States v. Louisiana, 339 U.S. 679 (1950), and United States v. Texas, 339 U.S. 707 (1950).

[8] 67 *Stat.* 29. For the new litigation involving the claim of Louisiana that it is entitled, as Texas and Florida were, to a "historic" boundary up to three leagues, see United States v. Louisiana, 100 *L. Ed.* 1494 (June 11, 1956). For interim agreement between the federal government and Louisiana see *N.Y.T.*, Oct. 13, 1956; and for further proceedings by the federal government against the five claimant states, *N.Y.T.*, Nov. 19, Dec. 10, 1957.

[9] 67 *Stat.* 462.

[10] The distinction is neatly elaborated by Edward W. Allen in "Territorial Waters and Extraterritorial Rights," 47 *American Journal of International Law* (hereinafter cited *A.J.I.L.*), 478–480 (1953).

5

The United States and the Treaty Law of the Sea

Law Commission of the United Nations gave priority at its first session in 1949 to the pressing topic "Regime of the High Seas." The United States has participated wholeheartedly in this work.[11]

The sea has fascinated the American people anew and intensely. Of the thousands of items appearing in the press in recent years, only a few can be cited here as evidence of this phenomenon. Some of the developments are ephemeral. Others suggest a permanent trend.

Thor Heyerdahl's courageous venture on his raft *Kon-Tiki*[12] from Peru to the Marquesas Islands in 1947 won excited acclaim everywhere. Rachel Carson's thoughtful and scholarly work, *The Sea Around Us*, illuminated brilliantly an epoch of writing about the sea already in process in 1951. And since then, there has been no end of works about the sea — historical, dramatic, legal, scientific, military, naval, fictional, anthological, biographic, autobiographic, meditative, poetic. There is a revival of interest in the great classics, such as Herman Melville's *Moby Dick* and the stories of Joseph Conrad. Hollywood has produced screen versions of Jules Verne's *Twenty Thousand Leagues Under the Sea*, Homer's *Odyssey* as *Ulysses*, and *Moby Dick*. J. Donald Adams of *The New York Times* has suggested that one further book needs to be written, "the philosophical book of the sea. . . . It would be a predominantly reflective book which would try to place man in perspective against the sea, to analyze his reactions toward it. It would blend history and psychology, poetry and philosophy."[13] Perhaps that very book is in the presses now.

Americans receive avidly the daily news and broadcasts of floods sweeping away the dikes of Holland or piling up wrecks on the shores of England, of great disasters of ship or plane at sea, of heroic rescues, of archeological discoveries beneath the blue waters of the Mediterranean, of another coelacanth dragged from its primeval solitude off the coasts of Madagascar, of the gift of a new *Mayflower*, of the immersion of a "Christ of the Depths." The International Geophysical Year of 1957–1958 has further fed this apparently insatiable curiosity about the sea with a steady stream of revelations of new wonders of the deep.

For some years in the recent past, the popular craze for things nautical has been reminiscent of the fads following the discovery of the

[11] Discussed below at p. 316.
[12] Thor Heyerdahl, *Kon-Tiki: Across the Pacific by Raft* (1950).
[13] "Speaking of Books," *N.Y.T. Book Review*, Dec. 19, 1954.

Focus on the Sea

tomb of Tutankhamen in the early twenties. Fish, shell, and other sea motifs have entered decorative patterns for dress materials, shirts and ties for men, wallpaper, cutlery, interior furnishings, costume jewelry, and brass fixtures for the household. Seaside "antique" dealers were haunted for relics of the deep. The public craved mementos of the sea. They took to new sea foods or prepared old ones with new recipes. Marine hobbies developed new variations.

Angling, yachting, and tourism have expanded in the past decade to unprecedented dimensions. Of the newer interests the most durable, very likely, will be underwater exploration and sports. This was made possible by the mechanical developments of World War II. One aspect alone, the search for sunken treasure, has induced the Library of Congress to issue a brochure on treasure maps.[14] The new techniques have led to the filming of oceanic life and its presentation upon the screen. A new and beautiful world, a silent world, has been opened up to all mankind.

Educational institutions have not failed to reflect and channelize this amazing interest in the sea. Museums, libraries, and aquariums have expanded their exhibits and offerings. Universities on the Atlantic and Pacific coasts, following in the paths laid down before the war by Harvard University in cooperation with the Woods Hole Oceanographic Institution and by the Scripps Institution at La Jolla, California, have lately added courses in oceanography to their curriculums and, in some instances, have dispatched summer cruises to distant seas. In 1949 Harvard University established a chair of "Oceanic History," the first occupant being the distinguished scholar of maritime affairs, Professor Robert G. Albion.

In recent years, the Marine Historical Association of Mystic, Connecticut, founded in 1929, has been able to re-create Mystic Seaport as it existed a hundred years ago and has established in connection therewith a pre-eminently fine museum of American maritime history.[15] In 1954 the Frank C. Munson Memorial Institute of American Maritime History, a summer graduate school, was added to the unique services rendered at Mystic Seaport.

[14] *Treasure Maps in the Library of Congress: An Annotated List*, compiled by J. Douglas Hill and Richard S. Ladd (1955).

[15] W. Z. Gardner, "The Story of Mystic Seaport and the Marine Historical Association, Inc., Mystic, Connecticut," reprint of an article in *The Ships' Bulletin*, publication of the Esso Shipping Company, New York, Nov.–Dec., 1955.

The United States and the Treaty Law of the Sea

In 1950 the Naval Historical Foundation opened a new Truxton-Decatur Naval Museum in Washington, which will feature related subjects also, such as shipbuilding, exploration, foreign trade, yachting, whaling, and merchant shipping. The world's first library and museum devoted wholly to lore of the submarine was opened in 1955 by the General Dynamics Corporation at Groton, Connecticut. In 1955 and 1956 the expanding Maritime Museum in Aquatic Park, San Francisco, acquired and refurbished the fabulous old windjammer the *Balclutha* (so christened when launched in Glasgow in 1886 but for a time called the *Star of Alaska*), as a "living museum" to recapture some of the magic of yesteryear. These are indeed welcome additions to the other and older museums that are devoted to maritime lore in various parts of the United States.

Increased attention has also been directed in recent years to the training of an adequate supply of officers for the new merchant fleet.[16] Supplementing the training programs at the Naval Academy at Annapolis, established in 1845, and at the Coast Guard Academy at New London, established in 1877, four states had maintained maritime academies for the merchant service under their educational systems: New York at Fort Schuyler,[17] since 1875, Massachusetts at Boston, since 1891, California at Vallejo, since 1929, and Maine at Castine, since 1941. To these was added in 1942 a United States Merchant Marine Academy at Kings Point, New York, at the conflux of Long Island Sound and the East River. In 1956, by special act of Congress,[18] this new national academy was given permanent status, comparable in dignity to the older naval and coast guard academies.

As the lawyers would say, more evidence would be but too plainly cumulative in support of a view already well established that Americans have taken to the sea again, physically, emotionally, and aesthetically. What this portends for the future can be perceived but dimly. Scholars eschew the role of prophets. They feel far safer in recording the past and describing the present. Guardedly they may suggest implications of what they survey, perhaps even courses of action. But no student of present trends needs to turn soothsayer to assert that historians of the

[16] *Merchant Marine Training and Education*, Report of the Committee on Interstate and Foreign Commerce, 84 Cong., 2 Sess., S. Rept. No. 1465 (1956).

[17] One of the national defenses of New York harbor, established in 1856, on Throgs Neck, Bronx, a cape projecting into Long Island Sound.

[18] Act of Feb. 20, 1956, 70 *Stat.* 25.

Focus on the Sea

future having finished their chapter "Westward, America!" will write of these times "Seaward, America!"

Among the myriad aspects of the relation of the United States to the sea and to the other nations using the sea, past and present, are its treaty relations. Of particular value in recognizing and developing a community of interest in the sea are the multipartite or multilateral treaties, agreements among three or more states. These may codify or supplement the customary law of the sea. In most cases they simply create new law of the sea and new international agencies to administer that law or supervise its application by the participating governments. Some of these treaties deal with the conduct of nations and their subjects in time of war; most of them deal with conduct in time of peace. The latter seek to regulate the workaday use of the sea. With them only is this study concerned.

In tracing the record of American participation in these treaties there is considerable emphasis upon the facts — the facts concerning the sea itself, about man's use and abuse of the sea, about the international problems created by use and abuse, and concerning American participation in the efforts of the community to solve those problems. The sea inspires profound respect for the facts. They have a way of obtruding in any discussion of man's relation to the sea. To be durable, solutions of the very practical problems arising out of man's use of the sea must perforce rest firmly upon a realistic appraisal of the material facts. There is little justification for much theorizing at this stage of our knowledge about American participation in the treaty regimes which govern use of the sea. There are, however, many implications arising out of the record which can be of value not only in the formulation of policy for the United States in its relation to the community of the sea but also to the community itself. These will become evident as the discussion proceeds.

A brief summary of the physical aspects of the sea [19] will provide a realistic frame of reference for the subsequent discussion of international

[19] This sketch of the sea was written before the appearance of Rachel Carson's marvelously succinct description in *The Sea Around Us* (1951). For the data about the physical aspects of the sea reliance was therefore chiefly upon H. U. Sverdrup, M. W. Johnson, and R. H. Fleming, *The Oceans: Their Physics, Chemistry, and General Biology* (1946); excellent articles in the standard encyclopedias; D. W. Johnson, *Shore Processes and Shoreline Development* (1919); and U.S. Coast and Geodetic Survey, *Tide and Current Glossary* (1949).

collaboration. It will also indicate the nature of the problems which confront the international community in its efforts to avoid conflict and achieve rational use of the sea, including the exploitation of its resources and those of its bed and subsoil.

In describing the physical aspects of the sea reference will be made to associated phenomena not usually regarded as coming within the scope of oceanography. This arises from the necessity of dealing with the ocean as the center of certain human activities. These activities include not merely use of the surface of the sea, its waters, its bed, its subsoil, and all that they contain but also the air space over the sea for air navigation and the ionosphere beyond for some types of telecommunication. The interdependence of radio communication, air navigation, and surface navigation justify bringing the three physical spheres, hydrosphere, atmosphere, and ionosphere, into a conspectus. Meteorological considerations pertinent to the ocean also embrace all three spheres. The international regimes in operation which deal with transport on and over the ocean assume this interdependence. Finally, in order to visualize correctly some of the problems created in use of the sea, it is necessary to include consideration of the land rim which contains the sea, an area not usually dealt with by the oceanographer. The social scientist may, and to be realistic, must, view the sea in this conspectus.

That portion of the hydrosphere which is called the ocean (the sea) covers about 72 per cent of the surface of the earth. The hydrosphere also includes all the bodies of water lying on and flowing over the land. With these we are not here concerned except as they give access from the sea to a hinterland. One of the principal characteristics of the ocean is its salinity, the degree of which varies under sundry conditions affecting the sea. The ocean lies in several great sheets, called the Atlantic, Pacific, and Indian oceans — all connected one with another. They merge in the south polar region in what is popularly called the Antarctic "Ocean." The Arctic Ocean, sometimes termed an enclosed intercontinental sea, is morphologically distinct. For present purposes the ocean in the physical sense, together with the natural phenomena closely related to it, can be viewed from two points of view: vertically and extensively.

Viewed vertically, the physical phenomena may be grouped in levels or "strata." Upward from the surface of the sea there may be distinguished the atmosphere (consisting of the troposphere and stratosphere, separated by the tropopause), the ionosphere, and the regions beyond.[20] From the surface downward the following may be distinguished: the body of water, lying in various interacting zones, and the bed and subsoil. These latter two strata are part of the lithosphere, the solid part of the earth. Each of the levels has, of course, numerous discrete characteristics which play a part in the creation of problems of concern to the community of nations.

The bottom of the sea is generally divisible into the continental shelf, the continental slope, and the deep sea.

The continental shelf is the gentle slope which extends from the edge of the land to a depth usually about 100 fathoms or 200 metres, though in some cases as much as 300 fathoms or about 600 metres, and is there demarcated by an abrupt increase in the steepness of the slope to ocean depths . . . The continental shelves are those parts of the continental blocks which have been covered by the sea in comparatively recent times, and their surface consequently presents many similarities to that of the land, modified of course by the destructive and constructive work of the waters . . . The continental shelves include not only the oceanic border of the continents but also great areas of the enclosed seas, the origin of which through secular subsidence is often very clearly apparent, as for instance in the North Sea and the tract lying off the mouth of the English Channel.[21]

Some writers appear to detect a series of "shelves" or "terraces" descending to the ocean depths and not merely one shelf.

There is great variation in the width and the degree of slope of the continental shelf off various coasts in the world.

In some cases, as off mountainous coasts, the shelf may be virtually absent, whereas, off glaciated coasts and off the mouths of large rivers and areas with broad lowlands, the shelf may be very wide. For the world as a whole, the shelf width is approximately 30 miles, with a range from zero to over 800 miles. This extremely wide shelf is found in the North Polar Sea along the coast of Siberia.[22]

[20] For an excellent discussion of the accruing new terminology see John C. Hogan, "Legal Terminology for the Upper Regions of the Atmosphere and for the Space Beyond the Atmosphere," 51 A.J.I.L. 362–375 (1957).

[21] *Encyclopaedia Britannica* (1947), Vol. 16, p. 682.

[22] Sverdrup, Johnson, and Fleming, *op. cit.*, pp. 20–21. Reprinted by permission, copyright 1942, by Prentice-Hall, Inc. See chart showing width in the western and eastern hemispheres, facing p. 1 in Martinus Willem Mouton, *The Continental Shelf* (1952).

The United States and the Treaty Law of the Sea

This variation of width from "zero to over 800 miles" has created many difficulties for the United Nations International Law Commission in its task of defining rights of the littoral state in the offshore submarine areas. In its 1956 report the commission used the term "continental shelf" in a special sense wider than the geological sense as "referring to the seabed and subsoil of the submarine areas adjacent to the coast but outside the area of the territorial sea, to a depth of 200 metres (approximately 100 fathoms), or, beyond that limit, to where the depth of the superjacent waters admits of the exploitation of the natural resources of the said areas." [23] It did this to assure justice in the exercise of offshore jurisdiction for those countries which have no continental shelf. The result, however, may be the establishment of two different meanings for the term "continental shelf," one used in treaties or other state papers of the future, the other used by the geologists.

It should be observed at this point, however, that all of the work of the International Law Commission relating to the sea over the past several years was reviewed by the United Nations General Assembly in 1957 and by the great United Nations Conference on the Law of the Sea held in Geneva in the spring of 1958. Those developments and their results, particularly insofar as they deviated from the conclusions of the commission, will be discussed in due course in the final chapter of this work.

Beyond the continental shelf lie the continental slope and the abyss. The bottom of the sea has two types of topographical features — depressions and elevations. Among the depressions are basins, extensions landward which are called embayments; troughs, extensions landward called gullies; trenches, canyons, caldrons, and furrows. The deepest part of a depression is called a deep. Among the elevations are rises, ridges, plateaus, sea-mounts, domes, shoals, reefs, and banks. The highest part of such a feature, if under water, is called a height. Banks, of considerable importance for fisheries purposes, by definition are types of elevations coming nearer the surface of the sea than a hundred fathoms but not so near as six fathoms. Still other features mentioned by the oceanographers are welts, valleys, and mock valleys. Here and there, particularly in the Pacific Ocean, submarine volcanoes erupt, show their cones above the surface long enough to be reported as navigation hazards but not

---

[23] *Report of the International Law Commission* (1956), Article 67, pp. 41–42. This language needed correction to ascribe the "depth" to the superjacent waters, not to the continental shelf itself, but it was adopted without change in the Convention on the Continental Shelf concluded at Geneva in 1958.

Focus on the Sea

long enough to get on the permanent charts, and then silently sink into the sea again.

Viewed extensively, from mid-ocean to margin, the sea reveals numerous features of prime importance in this study of its use. Approaching the rim, there may be distinguished fringing (or partially enclosed) seas and enclosed seas. Among the fringing seas are the North Sea, the Bering Sea, the English Channel and Irish Sea, the Gulf of St. Lawrence, and the Gulf of California. The enclosed seas are of two varieties: intercontinental seas such as the Arctic, Malay, Central American, and Mediterranean seas; and smaller enclosed seas such as the Baltic and Red seas, Hudson Bay, and the Persian Gulf. Subordinate marginal features, such as gulfs and straits, are also classified by the oceanographers.

Gulfs may be classified according to their origin as due to fractures of the crust or overflowing of depressed lands. The former are either the extensions of oceanic depressions, e.g., the Arabian Sea, or such caldron-depressions as the Gulf of Genoa or rift-depressions like the Gulf of Aden. Compound gulfs are formed seawards by fracture and landwards by the overflowing of depressed land, e.g., the Bay of Biscay, Gulf of Alaska, and Gulf of the Lion. Gulfs formed by the overflowing of depressed lands lie upon the continental shelf, e.g., the Gulf of Maine, Bay of Fundy. Straits have been formed (1) by fracture across isthmuses, longitudinally as in the Strait of Bab-el-Mandeb, or transversely as in the Strait of Gibraltar; (2) by erosion, e.g., the Strait of Dover; (3) by overflowing subsided land, as in the Straits of Bering, Torres, and Formosa.[24]

Among connecting waterways such artificial developments as the Suez, Kiel, Corinth, and Panama canals should be mentioned. If the Great Lakes, though consisting entirely of fresh water and not affected by the tides, can be regarded as "inland seas," as commercially they must, then the canals already constructed and those presently under construction in the St. Lawrence Valley qualify as great connecting waterways.

At the rim of the ocean are the coastal waters, sometimes called the marginal sea, lying for the most part over a continental shelf, hence their designation as an epicontinental sea.

The coastal waters present exceedingly complex phenomena, the result in large part of the constant interaction of sea and land dynamics. Change here is endless. Subsidence and upheaval of land and erosion

[24] *Encyclopaedia Britannica* (1947), Vol. 16, p. 681.

by wind and water operate unceasingly to alter the configuration of the coasts. The sea digs tunnels, carves out caves and thunderholes, fashions arches, dividing that it may destroy the too, too solid cliffs. Accretion, alluvion, silting, and sedimentation occur. Beaches are built up and torn away; detritus is deposited. Here and there, over the centuries, coastal cities have sunk beneath the waves. The maw of the sea is indeed insatiable. And elsewhere, once flourishing seaports now lie high and dry as inland towns.

In these coastal waters a great variety of sea and land forms thus exist in mutational relationship. Among the common water forms appearing along coasts are these: basin, bay, bight, channel, cove, creek, estuary, firth, fjord, flow, gulf, gut, haff, harbor or haven, inlet, lagoon, lake, (sea) lough or loch, (salt) marsh, narrows, passage, port, race, road or roadstead, sound, and strait. Shallows and shoals bedevil coasts. For a thousand years the historic Goodwin Sands off the coast of Deal, Kent, England, have engulfed mariners and their vessels, and for centuries the shoals off the North Carolina coast have been a *Graveyard of the Atlantic*.[25] Among the coastal land forms are peninsula, cape, point, head, headland, butt, mull, and isthmus. And off the coasts in tropic seas coral reefs form, the mightiest of them being the Great Barrier Reef, stretching for more than a thousand miles along the eastern seaboard of Queensland, Australia.[26]

This diversity of land and water forms has challenged cartographers from time immemorial to name them aright. Explorers from the fifteenth century to the nineteenth added confusion to difficulty by their casual use of nomenclature. This has resulted in the appearance of conflicting and inconsistent terminology on the maps except where hydrographic and other map services have brought reform. The historic Northeastern Fisheries controversy between the United States and Great Britain, happily settled by arbitration in 1910, involved the meaning of such terms as bays, creeks, harbors, shores, headlands, and coasts as used in treaties and legislation.[27] This is but one example of the serious consequences that can arise out of the inexact use of terminology. Fortunately, both

---

[25] See work so entitled, by David Stick (1952).

[26] See Arthur Charles Clarke, *The Coast of Coral* (1955).

[27] See C. A. Carter and others, *Treaties Affecting the Northeastern Fisheries* (1944), *passim*. There is still no large-scale dictionary of geographic terms in print in English. W. G. Moore's *Dictionary of Geography* (1952), a Penguin Book, is excellent for its planned coverage.

Focus on the Sea

national and international agencies are now at work seeking greater exactness and uniformity in cartography relating to the sea. These efforts will be discussed later.

More closely examined, where sea meets land, there may be rocks, cliffs, marshes, dunes, flats, or some kinds of beach or strand. Artificial works abut upon or project into the water: jetties, causeways, breakwaters, moles, wharves, piers, embankments, quays, ramparts, sea walls or groins, and dikes. Elaborate harbor works exist; basins, marinas, pools, and water airports are constructed; bridge piers rest on the bottom of arms of the sea. Spits reach out from the shore; bars, hooks, and deltas form; and offshore lie rocks, stacks, ledges, reefs, keys, natural and man-made islands. In some parts of the world, the bottom of the sea close to the shore is reclaimed [28] by means of dikes or filled in with the rubbish of civilization to produce land for cultivation, building, or other purposes. Salt marshes are drained and built up to increase the acreage devoted to industry and commerce. A fascinating book could be written of the seaside features of many a port on at least the Atlantic coast of the United States which rest upon the rock ballast brought over by sailing vessels during past centuries and dumped where the harbor masters required it to be dumped.

Lighthouses, cairns, and now structures for drilling into the subsoil for oil stand in the marginal sea, some of the latter dotting the seascape in the Gulf of Mexico 20 to 40 miles off American shores. Artificial islands are also being created for mining purposes. In 1955 a radar tower, part of the DEW system (Distant Early Warning system) for military purposes, was erected in Georges Bank, 110 miles off Cape Cod. Since then, two other towers have been set up in the marginal sea nearby and southward for the same purpose. Buoys, spars, and lightships are moored to the bottom. On or through the bed run cables and pipelines. In the subsoil are tunnels and mines. "Floating islands," great clods of earth bearing forests, grasslands, or bogs, torn from their terrestrial matrix by violent floods in river valleys or deltas, appear sometimes 50 to 100 miles off the mouths of large rivers in America, Asia, and Africa. And within these coastal waters, rendered so complex by nature and man, the tides

[28] In addition to the extensive new projects undertaken recently by the Netherlands, the Japanese are reported to be undertaking the draining of Araike Bay, former navy training base, to create new rice land. *N.Y.T.*, Oct. 12, 1955.

The United States and the Treaty Law of the Sea

roll ceaselessly, flowing and ebbing, leaving their marks upon the dry land, from spring tide to neap tide.

Three other phenomena, intimately related to the sea, should be included under this view of the ocean: the great navigable rivers which give access to the land beyond the rim, the polar regions, and sundry clusters of islands in the sea.

The great river systems of the several continents not only contribute to the hydrological cycle of the sea but are, at the conflux, under tidal conditions, arms of the sea. In their lower reaches "great ships do lie and hover"; by means of their upper reaches, frequently improved by canals and other artificial waterways, there is reciprocal access between hinterland and sea.[29] In many parts of the world the streams that go down to the sea are essential also to the life cycles of anadromous fish like the salmon and catadromous ones like the eel.

From many points of view the polar regions are appurtenances to the sea. In both polar regions ice blends with water. The North Pole is in the North Polar Sea. Access to the Antarctic continent is still over the oceans. Both regions affect the sea profoundly in terms of making weather, influencing currents, and spawning ice and icebergs. Until recently exploration of either region was primarily a sea operation. Exploitation of either area will probably for a long time require use of sea transport.

Finally, among the phenomena which are part of the sea or peculiarly dependent upon it are numerous clusters of islands, such as those in the Caribbean and those in the Pacific, the Japanese archipelago, the Philippines, Micronesia, Indonesia, Melanesia, and Polynesia. The Marianas, Carolines, and Marshalls, for example, constituting the major portion of Micronesia and now administered by the United States as a trust territory under the United Nations, lie in an area which, bounded by the perimeter of the islands, contains nearly three million square miles. Of this only 687 square miles are land. Of the 96 island groups only 64 are inhabited. The total indigenous population of the trust territory is about 52,000. Administration of these islands is thus "essentially a maritime task, a sea job."[30]

[29] Osborne Mance and J. E. Wheeler, *International River and Canal Transport* (1945). The intricate canal system of Europe, particularly, with its complex canal interconnections and connections with the elaborate river systems demands the utmost in international agreement and cooperation in sharing costs of construction and in its maintenance and operation.

[30] Francis B. Sayre, 21 *Department of State Bulletin* (hereinafter cited *DSB*) 133 (1949).

Focus on the Sea

The sea, as visualized for the purposes of this discussion, is yet more intricate. Life in infinite variety teems in its waters, lies at the bottom, or wings its way above the surface. The shores and tidelands as well as countless isles and atolls abound in myriad forms of life in whose ecology the sea is dominant. The waters contain immeasurable chemical and mineral resources, tidal and thermal power, and great mineral deposits are thought to lie in the subsoil of the continental shelves.

The waters themselves, circulating in perpetual rivers, piling up in great masses, disturbed by seismic convulsions from below and responding to cosmic influences from beyond this planet, lie at the bottom of another "ocean," the aerial ocean. In the words of Matthew Fontaine Maury, the "Pathfinder of the Seas,"

The atmosphere is something more than a shoreless ocean, at the bottom of which he (man) creeps along. It is an envelope or covering for the dispersion of light and heat over the surface of the earth; it is a sewer into which, with every breath we draw, we cast vast quantities of dead animal matter; it is a laboratory for purification, in which that matter is recompounded, and wrought again into wholesome and healthful shapes; it is a machine for pumping up all the rivers from the sea, and conveying the waters from their fountains on the ocean to their sources in the mountains; it is an inexhaustible magazine, marvellously adapted for many benign and beneficent purposes . . .[31]

Beyond that aerial ocean lies the ionosphere so essential to radio communication. And among the meteorological phenomena occurring in the interplay of these spheres is weather, whose effects condition all use of sea and land and air.

This is the sea which man has used from time immemorial as a highway, for commerce and communication, as a source of life, wealth, and pleasure. He has found it at times a barrier, at other times made it a rampart. He has struggled for exclusive possession of it; he is learning to share it. Always it has been filled with dangers, and it still is. He has explored it and studied it, revealing new wonders each passing decade, exposing new uses for the community of men.

[31] Lewis, *op. cit.*, pp. 71–72 (used by permission).

CHAPTER II ~~

USE AND ABUSE OF THE SEA

Before proceeding with an examination of the record of participation by the United States in the multipartite agreements which have sought and which seek to regulate use of the sea, it is desirable to take stock of the contemporaneous uses of the sea. Like the physical aspects, they are numerous and diverse.

It is possible, and for present purposes necessary, to distinguish between those uses and activities which have a primary relationship to the sea and those which have an ancillary, or secondary, relationship. The primary relationship involves uses and activities which have fairly direct contact with the sea; the secondary relationship involves activity which depends upon, benefits from, or facilitates the first. Thus, fishing, under this view, including its techniques and the conditions under which it is conducted, is a primary use of the sea; the processing of the products when done on land, the manufacture of by-products, shipyards, ice factories, net factories, marketing, and similar related industries, though intimately if not absolutely dependent upon the act of fishing, are, for present purposes, regarded as having a secondary relationship to the sea.

Obviously no rigid line of demarcation can be drawn between the two types of relationship. The relation of a human activity to the sea is one of degree. For two reasons, however, the distinction is serviceable: as a convenience in limiting the present discussion and because, where international regimes have been established to deal with human relationship to the sea, it has been chiefly with respect to those uses and activities which come into fairly direct contact with the sea. With respect to many of these primary relationships, it may anticipatorily be said, numerous international discussions, both public and private, have been held during the past century and a quarter, and much international collaboration has resulted. The United States has participated substantially in the

Use and Abuse of the Sea

process since the middle of the nineteenth century [1] and is participating very extensively now.

The principal uses and activities group themselves naturally under transportation, communications, exploitation of the products of the sea, its bed, and its subsoil, disposal of waste, and sport and recreation. Each group can be taken to embrace the means and instruments employed; the conditions under which they are employed; the abuses, evils, or malpractices engendered by or associated with the normal or "legitimate" use of the sea; and the problems created for the community of nations in this process of use and abuse.

Res Nullius or Res Communis?

Judgments with respect to what are abuses, evils, or malpractices can be based upon implications from the legal concept *contra bonos mores*, which has a fairly definite content for the international jurist,[2] and upon a consensus of what the several public and private interests involved in the use or activity regard as rational use. The philosophic bent here adopted will therefore be, in a shrinking world, away from the negative concept of the sea as *res nullius* toward the positive concept of it as *res communis*.

This philosophic position does not prejudice the answer to the further question, how the common interest can best be served. Multipartite instruments have been a favorite device for nearly a hundred years. Un-

---

[1] See, for example, *Annuaire de la vie internationale*, Vol. I, 1908/1909, Vol. II, 1910/1911, for the period 1840 to 1911 *ca*. Winifred Gregory (editor), *International Congresses and Conferences 1840–1937* (1938). *International Expositions*, 62 Cong., 2 Sess., S. Doc. No. 917 (1912), relating to the period 1851–1911. *Expositions Which Have Been Aided by Federal Appropriations 1867–1934*, Library of Congress, Legislative Reference Service. *Congresses: Tentative Chronological and Bibliographical Reference List of National and International Meetings of Physicians, Scientists, and Experts*, United States Army Medical Library (1938). *Handbook of International Organizations*, League of Nations (1937). Denys P. Myers, *Handbook of the League of Nations* (1935). Henry Reiff, "The United States and International Administrative Unions: Some Historical Aspects," *International Conciliation* No. 332 (Sept. 1937), and "Participation in International Administration: A Cinderella of American History," 34 *Social Studies* 311–316 (1943). *International Agencies in Which the United States Participates*, Department of State (1946), pp. 2–4. Samuel F. Bemis and Grace G. Griffin, *Guide to the Diplomatic History of the United States, 1775–1921* (1935), Ch. XV and pp. 797, 824.

[2] See discussions in *Memorandum on the Regime of the High Seas*, United Nations International Law Commission (1950), pp. 12–16, 44 (hereinafter cited as UN I.L.C.); Gilbert Gidel, *Le Droit International Public de La Mer*, 3 vols. (1932), Vol. II, pp. 213–224; Herbert W. Briggs, *The Law of Nations* (1952), pp. 328–330.

questionably they will continue to be used and in increasing numbers. Pending the development of adequate international legislative authority, however, other modes can also be used, including the recognition of extensions of national jurisdiction, subject in certain situations, particularly those involving fisheries, to a right of participation in the regulation by other states with demonstrably genuine interests. The United Nations International Law Commission has been working along these lines for several years now. At this stage of emerging community interests and developing international organization, national regulation in some situations, subject to norms laid down by the international community, may very well be in the long-run interest of that community. It may preserve a *res* that might otherwise, under the doctrine of *res nullius*, disappear altogether. Numerous examples of unconscionable damage to community interests under this doctrine will be given in the discussion which follows.

What matters most in this period of changing law relating to use of the sea is acceptance of national self-restraint, a decent regard for the legitimate national interests of other states, and a disposition to share control in the common interest wherever that is feasible or reasonably necessary. Crass national monopolies, unmindful of the legitimate interests of other states or destructive of the *res* involved, would have no status under this view of the common interest. They would but sow the seeds of future wars.

Transportation

In the present context, transportation deals with carriage, for the most part, of goods, mails, and persons, by surface craft or aircraft. It also includes such facilities used in transport as bridges, tunnels, and pipelines, and cables for the transmission of power. Cables for the transmission of intelligence will be considered in connection with communications.

The carriage of persons facilitates travel, for business, pleasure, or health, tourism, "luxury" tours, pilgrimages, immigration, exchange of population, deportations, extradition, and refugee resettlement — all highly significant internationally. The latter can be a large-scale undertaking. Thus, "by June 1949 the International Refugee Organization had the world's largest civilian transportation fleet for migration purposes, operating 36 vessels — including 18 United States army transports — and

Use and Abuse of the Sea

some airplanes, carrying 30,000 DPs monthly."[3] Commerce, trade, and traffic involve the carriage of goods; so do such impressive contemporary large-scale developments as relief from man-made or natural disasters, rehabilitation, and Point Four programs, national and international.

Bridges, Tunnels, Pipelines, Power Cables. Before undertaking discussion of sea transport and transport by air over the sea, we should note briefly some features of the use of bridges, tunnels, pipelines, and cables for the transmission of power, insofar as they impinge upon use of the sea.

With international bridges over inland boundary rivers or lakes we are not immediately concerned. Bridges downstream, over saline waters — the mouths of tidal rivers, estuaries, or bays — if located entirely within the domain of a national state have created no serious international problems as yet. International bridges in coastal waters have likewise apparently created no serious international problems. The need for advance agreement between the states involved with respect to construction, maintenance, and jurisdiction has probably avoided many a controversy. Technical aspects of all three of these classes of bridges come within the purview of the Permanent International Association of Navigation Congresses.[4]

Certain recent developments are of interest in this discussion of bridges. At long last a causeway has been built across the turbulent Gut of Canso between Nova Scotia and Cape Breton Island off the coast of Canada.[5] Consideration has recently been given to the construction of a bridge over the Strait of Messina, between Sicily and Italy, scene of the legendary Scylla and Charybdis.[6] One of the longest suspension bridges in the world is now being built across the Bosporus at Istanbul, Turkey. The Spanish government is currently reported as considering the possibility of a road and railway bridge across the Strait of Gibraltar, "where fabled Hercules tore apart a prehistoric mountain range and created the famous 'pillars' that bear his name."[7] Since the strait is

---

[3] Fred W. Riggs, "The World's Refugee Problem," 26 *Foreign Policy Reports* 194 (1951).

[4] American participation in the organization is discussed below at p. 133.

[5] *N.Y.T.*, Aug. 14, 1955. Because of the ice floes in spring, notion of a bridge had to be abandoned.

[6] Harry Gilroy, "Bridging a Dilemma," *N.Y.T.*, Oct. 11, 1953. The strait was reported as requiring closing in 1955 while electric power cables were being strung across. *N.Y.T.*, June 12, 1955.

[7] *N.Y.T.*, July 16, 30, 1956.

relatively shallow, some engineers have long advocated a tunnel instead. The boldest scheme seriously put forth in recent months comes from Russian scientists. It involves the construction not of a bridge but of a dam across Bering Strait, to carry a railroad linking Alaska and Siberia and to help warm Siberia and Alaska by "creating warm currents resembling the Gulf Stream." The fill for the dam would be produced by small-scale atomic explosions underground.[8] Structures over straits regularly used by international shipping may very well raise questions concerning possible impediments to navigation, though no important controversies appear to have arisen as yet.

Similarly, tunnels have thus far, apparently, not created any serious international problems. Those lying under saline waters appear in every instance to connect territory belonging to the same sovereign. One international tunnel, under the Detroit River, connecting Detroit, Michigan, with Windsor, Ontario, is far removed from the rim of the sea. Very likely there are other tunnels under other boundary rivers in other parts of the world, but they also do not come within the scope of the present discussion.

In 1952 there was a revival of discussion of the old project of a tunnel under the English Channel.[9] In 1875 acts of the British and French parliaments laid the groundwork for construction of such a tunnel, in which the railways were primarily interested. Premature granting of a concession or a "convention" by the French government to a French company was protested by the British government, which desired that there be a basic agreement between the two governments first. Wrangling among the British railways put the matter into politics in England. The War Office became opposed on military grounds and that ended the project. No treaty on the subject was ever concluded between Britain and France. Preliminary tubes on either side of the channel were thereupon abandoned.[10] Marshal Foch expressed the view in 1922 that if the

[8] *N.Y.T.*, May 18, 1956; Harry Schwartz, "Soviet Tunneling by Atom Foreseen," *N.Y.T.*, April 7, 1958. Schwartz also mentions a Soviet scheme for a tunnel under the Caspian Sea.

[9] *N.Y.T.*, Sept. 24, 1952.

[10] The literature on this subject is substantial. See Gidel, *op. cit.*, Vol. I, pp. 510–514; Higgins and Colombos, *The International Law of the Sea* (1950), pp. 59–60; 66 *British and Foreign State Papers* 458–507 (hereinafter cited as *B.&F.S.P.*); 67 *ibid.*, 51–64; 68 *ibid.*, 652–662; *Report of the Channel Tunnel Committee* (1930), Cmd. 3513; and the articles in the standard encyclopedias on "Tunnel" and "Channel Tunnel." See also "Back to the Channel Tunnel," London *Times*, April 6, 1957; *N.Y.T.*, April 8, May 7, June 23, Sept. 15, 25, 1957; and May 4, 1958.

Use and Abuse of the Sea

tunnel had existed in 1914, it would have shortened the Great War by half. Blitzkrieg tactics in 1939, however, would very likely have rendered such a tunnel speedily useless. In 1957, however, with strategic considerations declining and British interest in the European Union increasing, discussion of the project was once more revived, this time with the expectation that the Universal Suez Canal Company and American private capital might participate in it.

Other developments on this subject of tunnels deserve noting. Thus, in 1952 the Library of Congress displayed a report showing that in 1906 the Trans-Alaska-Siberian Company, consisting mostly of Americans, had proposed a scheme for the construction of a fifty-six-mile tunnel under Bering Strait from East Cape, Siberia, to Wales on Seward Peninsula in Alaska.[11] In 1953 there was a rumor that the Russians were working on two submarine tunnels to link Sakhalin Island, north of Japan, with the Siberian mainland.[12] In 1955 it was reported that the West German government was considering the construction of a tunnel under the Kiel Canal near Rendsburg to relieve the traffic over the existing swing drawbridge.[13] In 1956 it was announced that the provincial government of British Columbia was considering the construction of a tunnel under the Fraser River at the delta, south of Vancouver.[14] That river is of crucial importance to both Canada and the United States for its run of salmon, but no tunnel under the river bed could conceivably interfere with the international conservation measures. And in 1957 the Japanese resumed work, started in 1939 but interrupted during World War II, on a vehicular tunnel linking Honshu, their mainland, with Kyushu, the southernmost large island. That tunnel was completed in 1958 and a new railroad tunnel, twenty-two and a half miles long, connecting Honshu with Hokkaido to the north, was begun in the same year.[15]

Pipelines are being used increasingly all over the world for the shipment of water, gas, oil, and other commodities. Most of them are laid overland and within domestic jurisdiction. Where they cross borders on land, prior national permission must be granted or international agreement arranged. Pipelines come within the scope of the present study insofar as they lie in or beneath coastal waters.

[11] *N.Y.T.*, March 24, 1952.
[12] Reuters dispatch, *Egyptian Gazette*, Dec. 4, 1953.
[13] *N.Y.T.*, May 26, 1955.
[14] *Ibid.*, Feb. 5, 1956.
[15] *Ibid.*, Sept. 15, 1957; Jan. 12, March 9, 10, 1958.

The United States and the Treaty Law of the Sea

Probably the most extraordinary undersea pipeline ever devised and put into operation was the flexible one used during World War II to pump gasoline for military purposes under the English Channel from England to the forces in France. Temporarily filled with water to prevent collapsing, it was run from shore to shore by an improvised cable ship. It was manufactured originally in one piece seventy miles long, long enough to reach a beach head in France not yet determined. When ready for use, the Nazis had already been pushed out of northern France. It was thereupon cut into two lengths and so laid.[16]

Pipelines in commercial service are ordinarily rigid. The most extensive use thus far has been by the oil industry. Where the waters are shallow, as in the Persian Gulf, pipelines several miles long are used to load the tankers offshore. Offshore drilling rigs use pipelines to transport the oil to the shore installations. The world's largest undersea pipeline appears to be in the Gulf of Mexico off Louisiana. The forty-eight-mile line connects and serves thirty-two oil and gas wells, some of them twenty miles offshore.[17] Pipelines can be of considerable international concern. They and their pumping stations, if erected in the epicontinental sea, can interfere with fishing and navigation. Leaks and breakages can cause oil pollution affecting other coastal states in that quarter of the sea. In some areas, neighboring states may wish to lay pipelines through the continental shelf appertaining to another state. In consequence, the United Nations International Law Commission has given pipelines consideration in its reports.[18]

Thus far high-voltage cables lying on the sea bed have caused no serious international problems. Most of them probably connect territories under the same sovereign, as in the case of the power cables to San Juan Island in Puget Sound [19] in the state of Washington and from the Swedish mainland to Gotland.[20] Permission to lay them through the coastal waters of an adjoining state may, however, create problems for the jurists in the future. Again, the International Law Commission has given this matter consideration, in connection with the laying of telegraph and telephone cables and pipelines.

[16] *Ibid.*, March 4, 1956.
[17] *Ibid.*, Sept. 26, 1955.
[18] *Op. cit.*, Arts. 61, 64, 70, pp. 38, 39, 43.
[19] *N.Y.T.*, March 23, 1951.
[20] *Ibid.*, June 7, 1953. See also report of British and French plan to exchange electricity by submarine cable, *N.Y.T.*, May 1, Nov. 19, 1957.

Use and Abuse of the Sea

Sea Transport. Amazing as the growth of air transportation has been in recent decades, the bulk of overseas carriage is still performed by surface craft, sea transport, so-called. Its aspects are numerous and complex. Historically, however, international regulation of some of these aspects has set a pattern for regulation of air transport. Hence a double justification for enumerating the principal aspects of sea transport first.

Sea transport involves consideration of the structure and operation of the principal means, vessels; their movement on the high seas and appurtenant waters; their safety; competition among them; their rights and duties in law wherever they go; their relation to the spread of disease; the protection of goods and persons aboard them; and their relation to telecommunications and air navigation. Naturally, there is some abuse, evil, or malpractice associated with each of these aspects.[21] So numerous are the features of each of these aspects that discussion of them can in some instances proceed only by citing sample or symbol.

With few exceptions, merchant vessels (passenger and cargo ships and tankers) are now propelled by mechanical means. It is reliably reported that several hundred sailing vessels still ply a profitable trade over the Seven Seas, but their number is declining steadily. Nevertheless, seventeen nations still use some three dozen square-rigged sailing vessels for merchant marine or naval training purposes. Rotor ships, those "propelled by the pressure and suction of the wind acting on one or more revolving vertical cylinders," have not come into extensive use. For the most part, the larger vessels engaged in international trade use coal- or oil-burning engines or diesel engines. After apparently satisfactory experience with a nuclear-powered submarine, *The Nautilus*, Congress in 1956 authorized the construction of a nuclear-powered merchant ship.

Numerous specialized types of vessels are being developed, in addition to the familiar factory, refrigerator, railroad-car-ferry, ore-carrying, and cable-laying types. Trailer-carrying, so-called roll-on roll-off or lift-on lift-off, ships are coming into common use. Oil tankers are experimenting with carrying loaded trailers on their flat, wide decks, to produce a "pay load" for return trips, which otherwise usually have to be in ballast. Tankers are now used or are being constructed for the carrying in bulk of molasses, orange juice, liquid wood pulp, and wine.

[21] Cf. the grouping of aspects in Osborne Mance and J. E. Wheeler, *International Sea Transport* (1945).

The United States and the Treaty Law of the Sea

A combination tanker-ore carrier is already in service. Specially insulated and heated barges now transport hot molten sulphur. Plans are underway to convert a Liberty-type vessel for the carriage of liquid sulphur and liquefied petroleum gas. Molten steel is now being shipped in so-called thermos bottles by rail; in time it may be carried upon the high seas. An oil tanker of 100,000 tons displacement, or 15 per cent larger than either the *Queen Mary* or the *Queen Elizabeth*, was recently built in Japan for American interests. Others still larger are being planned. Human ingenuity seems to keep pace with human demands.

The construction of modern steel vessels is exceedingly complicated and expensive. It involves proper compartmentalization and subdivision, provision for stability in damaged condition, pumping arrangements, electrical installations, apparatus for fire protection, detection, and extinction, double bottoms, and many other features. International shipping is highly competitive. Cost is a crucial factor. There is always the temptation among some owners and operators to reduce costs of construction, equipment, or operation at the price of safety to produce larger profits for themselves or the stockholders. Crews, the traveling public, shippers of goods, and the underwriters must be protected against this temptation where it exists. If there is to be optimum safety at sea, international agreement on standards of construction, equipment, and operation is essential.

The competency, health, and welfare of officers and crews, historically regarded as part of the "internal economy" of a vessel are now, under present demands for safety, apprehension about contagious and epidemic disease, and considerations affecting labor, matters of international concern. Cost of operation factors and competition for the services of personnel contribute to this international emphasis.

Navigation involves the use of charts; astronomical aids; standardized time; sailing directions; fixed routes or lanes; rules of the road; numerous standardized mechanical aids, instruments, and devices; radio communication ship-to-ship, ship-to-shore, ship-to-plane; visual, audible, and other types of signals; and many other modern necessities, none of which can be utilized most efficiently without some international cooperation.

Within a ship, safety of personnel and passengers must be provided for against fire, flood, accidents, shifting of cargo, explosions, and other hazards. Whatever precautions the flag state may take with respect to its

Use and Abuse of the Sea

own vessels, its nationals also use the shipping of other countries, perchance with inferior standards of safety. Self-interest thus forces another matter of "internal economy" into the field of international concern.

Phenomena external to a vessel expose it to such hazards as collision with other ships, icebergs, ice, wrecks, derelicts, reefs and rocks, coastal and port structures and installations, now radar towers and oil rigs in the epicontinental sea, and naval mines left floating from some recent war at sea; running aground; and capsizing, foundering, or breaking in storms. Close competition for profits invites use of shorter but more dangerous routes, undermanning, inadequate lifeboat and other lifesaving devices, excessive speed under ice and fog conditions, overloading, faulty stowage, and excessive deck cargoes.

Both natural and man-made hazards require the constant attention of national and international agencies. Ripple Rock in the Strait of Georgia between Vancouver Island and the mainland of British Columbia, until it was destroyed in 1958, illustrated vividly one class of natural hazards. The rock, an underwater mountain with two pinnacles reaching up to within nine and twenty feet of low water, lay in Seymour Narrows, a narrow passage within the larger strait. As described in 1955, "Twice daily the tides of the Pacific rush in and out, at the north through the Queen Charlotte Strait, and at the south through the Strait of Juan de Fuca. . . . This massive obstruction in the path of the charging tides causes great turbulence, and whirlpools are so large and powerful that they have upset small craft and diverted large and powerful ships from their course." Since 1875 some 14 large ships had been lost or severely damaged and about 100 smaller vessels had been sunk, with a loss of at least 114 lives. Waiting for the precise slack tide twice daily caused a jamming up of the traffic movement, which in itself added to the hazard.

Two attempts had already been made to blast off the pinnacles by operations from the surface, without success. Then a well-conceived plan was authorized by the Canadian government involving the boring of a shaft down through the rock on Maud Island, which flanks Ripple Rock, then through the bedrock under the separating channel, then up into the two pinnacles. Great quantities of high explosives could then be placed inside the pinnacles to produce one massive explosion. So it transpired. Utilizing 1375 tons of explosives, the detonation on April 5, 1958, lowered the rock to forty-seven feet below low tide surface level.

Such operations, however, are expensive; the decapping of Ripple Rock alone was reported to have cost $3,000,000.[22]

All maritime nations are faced with the necessity of maintaining coast guards and lifesaving systems which serve all, without distinction of nationality, upon the high seas. In addition, ice patrols and weather ships have been established; buoyage, lighting of coasts, and radio beacons have been provided. Obligations of assistance and salvage have been created, and international regulations, based upon either custom or treaty, have been devised with respect to many of these matters relating to safety.

Keen competition exists between shipping interests within most modern states and between the national mercantile fleets of the several maritime powers.[23] To this age-old rivalry is now added the competition of air transportation. Among the most vigorous of national policies will be found the protection and advancement of the national mercantile fleet for purposes of defense, profit, and prestige.[24] Much of the assistance and encouragement to shipping can be justified on economic and security grounds. For centuries, however, governments have sought to give advantages to their own fleets and place at a relative disadvantage those of other countries by means of discriminating tonnage duties, port dues, and fines;[25] building and operational subsidies and bounties;[26] preferential tariffs and charges; unequal canal-transit tolls, drawbacks, and rebates; discriminatory registration requirements; unequally applied hull, cargo, safety, and sanitation inspections; cabotage, and many other devices. For the past half century or more, state-owned and -op-

---

[22] J.-P. Carriere, "Decapping Ripple Rock," 1 *PWDispatch* 1–2 (1955); National Research Council of Canada, *Method of Removing Ripple Rock* (1954). Also *N.Y.T.*, Feb. 19, July 3, 1956; March 7, 1957; March 30, April 6, 1958.

[23] See Daniel Marx, Jr., "International Organization of Shipping," 55 *Yale Law Journal* 1214–1232 (1946), and the excellent recent selective bibliography, *Shipping Policy, Law, and History: Basic Information Sources*, U.S. Department of Commerce (1955); for terminology, Rene de Kerchove, *International Maritime Dictionary* (1948).

[24] J. B. Condliffe, *The Commerce of Nations* (1950), Chs. II, III, IV.

[25] See, e.g., list of 74 different types of dues and charges imposed in ports of Pan America, Inter-American Maritime Conference, Washington, D.C., Nov. 25–Dec. 2, 1940, *Report of the Delegates of the United States* (1941), p. 237; discussion of same, pp. 191–236.

[26] See discussion of practices of 46 countries in Jesse E. Saugstad, *Shipping and Shipbuilding Subsidies* (1932). For the history of the United States policy, Paul M. Zeis, *American Shipping Policy* (1938); Inter-American Maritime Conference, *op. cit.*, pp. 275–320, 458–469. Compilation of U.S. laws, Elmer A. Lewis, *Laws Relating to Shipping and Merchant Marine* (1956).

Use and Abuse of the Sea

erated ships have intensified the competition. Easy registration requirements offered by some governments have invited "flights" of tonnage from high-standard countries. For centuries, bipartite treaties of commerce and navigation have dealt with some of these matters. In recent decades, multipartite conventions have dealt with a few. For the most part, however, competition and discriminatory practices remain unregulated by any intergovernmental body. The Habana Charter of 1948 for an International Trade Organization, which is now probably defunct, broke ground for such regulation.[27] The Intergovernmental Maritime Consultative Organization, discussed later, represents a current approach toward community control.

Since 1875, though, numerous private "conferences" have been established to deal with competition among the liner routes and "trades." They fix freight rates and passenger fares and concern themselves with routes, sailing schedules, and services. They are in effect "regulating bureaus."[28] Sometimes they create "pools" of shipping. Tramp shipping and vessels under charter offer competition from outside the conferences. Only a few governments, the United States included, have sought to exercise some degree of public control over conference agreements.[29] For the United States, the Federal Maritime Board supervises the agreements.

In shipping, as well as in fisheries and air transportation, the competing demands of national policy and of international welfare are vividly focused.

There may be a dearth of intergovernmental regulation of the quantity and competition of shipping but there is a plethora of governmental regulation of flagships on the high seas and of all ships in the marginal or, more strictly speaking, the territorial sea. National civil and criminal law, with exceptions arising out of the superior obligations created by customary maritime law and bipartite or multipartite agreements, ap-

---

[27] *Havana Charter for an International Trade Organization, March 24, 1948, Including a Guide to the Study of the Charter*, Department of State (1948), Ch. IV and Art. 53. See also Clair Wilcox, *A Charter for World Trade* (1949).

[28] Mance and Wheeler, *International Sea Transport*, pp. 26, 95–104. Also, *Inter-American Maritime Conference, op. cit.*, pp. 139–190; Daniel Marx, Jr., *International Shipping Cartels: A Study of Industrial Self-Regulation by Shipping Conferences* (1953); and a brief account in Ervin Hexner and Adelaide Harvey Walters, *International Cartels* (1946), pp. 387–391.

[29] Mance and Wheeler, *International Sea Transport*, p. 98; Marx, *International Shipping Cartels*, Chs. VI, VII.

The United States and the Treaty Law of the Sea

ply to flagships wherever they go, until they enter the territorial sea [30] of some state.

Whether that sea has a width of three nautical miles, the historical limit widely adopted, or a greater width up to twelve miles, as asserted by some states, the law of the littoral sovereign applies, subject to the usual exceptions relating to innocent passage, distress, and the "internal economy" of the vessels, and, of course, any treaty obligations. With respect to the width of the territorial sea, the International Law Commission in 1956 recognized that "international practice was not uniform as regards the traditional limitation of the territorial sea to three miles." It declared, however, that international law did not justify an extension beyond twelve miles. Because of the lack of agreement on the breadth, the commission suggested that an international conference fix it.[31] Historically, the littoral sovereign has exercised jurisdiction in the territorial sea for security purposes, to protect its fiscal, sanitary, and fishery interests, to prevent nuisances, to repress crime, and to assure safety of navigation. That sovereign has also sought to assert maximum control over access to ports and rivers and transit through straits and canals.

Abuses and nuisances plague the littoral sovereign. Outside the marginal sea, valuable fishery grounds are exploited to destruction; runs of anadromous fish are decimated, and seals once were slaughtered. There hover smugglers of illicit goods and persons, liquor, and narcotics; there are anchored gambling ships and brothels. Ships discharge oil wastes, which create fire hazards at sea and in port, destroy fish and aquatic birds, foul surface craft and port installations, and ruin valuable beaches. Now fresh oil escaping from offshore drilling operations threatens to be added to the problem. Inflammable and explosive cargoes, occasionally erupting, make shambles of port cities; great explosions create a potential danger to pipelines in the bed and tunnels in the subsoil beneath harbor waters. Ships drop solid ballast cluttering up channels, discharge disease-laden water ballast polluting the harbor, and damage cables with their anchors at crossings. Their smoke pollutes the air of port cities, creates a health hazard, and damages property, so that many

---

[30] The literature on the territorial sea is, of course, enormous. See, however, Charles Cheney Hyde, *International Law Chiefly as Interpreted and Applied by the United States* (1945), Vol. I, pp. 451–489; Briggs, *op. cit.*, pp. 281–284, 288–290; Philip C. Jessup, *The Law of Territorial Waters and Maritime Jurisdiction* (1927); UN I.L.C., *Bibliography on the Regime of the High Seas* (1950), pp. 17–18, and *Report* (1956), pp. 12–23.

[31] UN I.L.C. *Report* (1956), pp. 12–13.

Use and Abuse of the Sea

American municipalities have in recent years felt obliged to apply their antismoke or air-pollution ordinances to ships in their harbors. And now we are warned by a committee of the National Academy of Sciences "that a serious accident in a nuclear powered merchant ship could contaminate a large harbor with dangerous radioactivity."

Ships carry diseased persons, animals, and plants, agricultural pests and blights, insects which are vectors, and animals, chiefly rats, who are hosts of epidemic disease. Ships introduce obscene literature, pimps, procurers, and prostitutes. Fire is an ever-present threat to ships tied up, their cargoes, the piers, and warehouses. Pilfering takes a steady toll from all sea-borne commerce. In the United States, racketeering has bedeviled the water front. Longshoreman and seafarer strikes paralyze ports. And now sabotage, espionage, subversion, and atomic-weapon threats add burdens to maritime policing. There is no end, apparently, to the infinite variety of assaults made from the seaside upon the safety and well-being of the littoral state. Where one evil is brought under control, another crops up.

Within the ports and territorial sea, however, the littoral state is legally in firm control: it can exercise the powers of a sovereign and take such preventive and remedial measures as it deems necessary, with few impediments arising from its obligations to other states. Beyond the territorial sea, the legal situation is different, jurisdictional claims being frequently opposed by other states in the interest of maintaining freedom of the seas. Nevertheless, states have from time to time and for sundry purposes asserted jurisdiction beyond the territorial sea in areas of the high seas now commonly called contiguous zones.[32] The International Law Commission in its 1956 report reserved that term, however, specifically for the area beyond the territorial sea up to a twelve-mile limit measured outward "from the baseline from which the breadth of the territorial sea is measured," within which additional area the littoral state could exercise control to prevent infringement of its customs, fiscal, or sanitary regulations.[33]

From 1793 to 1958 the United States adhered consistently to the three-mile rule for its territorial sea. At the Geneva Sea Law Conference in 1958, however, it found itself forced to offer a compromise proposal

[32] Jessup, *op. cit.*, Ch. II; S. W. Boggs, "National Claims in Adjacent Seas," 41 *Geographical Review* 185–209 (1951); Briggs, *op. cit.*, pp. 356–385; Mouton, *op. cit.*, pp. 63–109.
[33] Art. 66, pp. 39–40.

The United States and the Treaty Law of the Sea

to extend the limit of territorial waters to six miles, with certain allowable jurisdiction over fisheries in an additional belt of six miles, in an effort to secure reduction of various claims, including full sovereignty, up to twelve miles. The effort failed. The conference was unable to agree upon any new width for the territorial sea. Discussion of this problem will be resumed later in Chapter VI.

The United States has however, at various times in the past asserted jurisdiction, but not sovereignty, over adjacent waters for special limited purposes. Thus, since 1790 it has asserted jurisdiction for customs purposes up to twelve miles from the coast.[34] Under the so-called liquor treaties concluded with Great Britain and a number of other powers during the period of national prohibition, the United States exercises rights of boarding, searching, and seizing suspected vessels within an hour's sailing distance from its shore.[35] After repeal of the Eighteenth Amendment, the United States in 1935[36] adopted an Anti-Smuggling Act which authorizes the President to establish, when needed, so-called customs-enforcement areas up to 50 nautical miles beyond the 12-mile limit and 100 miles in each lateral direction away from the place or the immediate area of the hovering. The enactment of this statute "was not regarded by the United States as authorizing the assertion of any jurisdiction in violation of international law, and the act expressly disclaimed the intention of seizing foreign vessels on the high seas in contravention of any treaty. With the possible exception of one case, the seizure of vessels under the act seems to have been in conformity with international law."[37]

Further extensions of jurisdiction were asserted in two historic presidential proclamations of 1945. In one the United States has asserted a right to establish conservation zones for fisheries in areas of the high seas contiguous to its coasts, either alone "where such activities have been or shall hereafter be developed and maintained by its nationals alone," or in agreement with other states where the development and maintenance of the fisheries has been effected jointly by the respective

---

[34] Act of Aug. 4, 1790, 1 *Stat.* 145, 164; re-enacted by Act of March 2, 1799, 1 *Stat.* 627, 668.

[35] Briggs, *op. cit.*, pp. 374–375.

[36] Act of Aug. 5, 1935, 49 *Stat.* 517. For explanation of operation of statute, see P. C. Jessup, "The Anti-Smuggling Act of 1935," 31 *A.J.I.L.* 101–106 (1937).

[37] Briggs, *op. cit.*, p. 375.

Use and Abuse of the Sea

nationals.[38] Under the other proclamation, the United States has declared "the natural resources of the subsoil and sea bed of the continental shelf beneath the high seas but contiguous to the coasts of the United States as appertaining to the United States, subject to its jurisdiction and control." The Continental Shelf Proclamation further declares "the character as high seas of the waters above the continental shelf and the right to their free and unimpeded navigation are in no way thus affected." [39]

This is not the language of a claim to sovereignty in the areas indicated. It is the careful language of a claim to limited jurisdiction for specific reasonable ends. Even if between the notion of "appertaining" and the concept of ownership inherent in sovereignty there hangs but a thin veil of discreet nomenclature, nevertheless there is no assertion of ownership and control in the overlying waters of the areas concerned or in the superjacent air space. This assertion of limited jurisdiction for specific ends quite reconcilable with the common interest of all states in use of the sea contrasts sharply with the extreme claims put forth by a number of the Latin American states soon after 1945 to "national sovereignty" over offshore areas beyond the territorial sea up to the absurd distance, in the case of Chile, Costa Rica, and Peru, of two hundred miles from the shore. Even allowing for the imprecise use of terminology which characterizes so many of the treaties and state papers of the Latin American states, these solemnly asserted claims have caused great concern to other nations.[40] The United States has from the beginning opposed such extreme claims and the United Nations International Law Commission has consistently refused to recognize them in its work on the law of the sea. The matter will be discussed again later under developments since World War II.

The protection of goods and persons on the high seas, in the police sense, involves not only repression of criminal or tortious acts on board ship but also such matters as piracy, hijacking, scuttling of ships, abuse of distress signals, looting of derelict vessels or vessels in distress, refusal to render assistance, fraud in salvage operations, violence among fishing fleets, criminal negligence in navigation, malicious damage to submarine cables and navigational aids, slave trading, and the traffic in

---

[38] Sept. 28, 1945, 59 *Stat.* 885–886.
[39] Sept. 28, 1945, 59 *Stat.* 884–885.
[40] Richard Young, "Recent Developments with Respect to the Continental Shelf," 42 *A.J.I.L.* 849–857 (1948); Briggs, *op. cit.*, pp. 379–381; discussed more fully below, pp. 304–315.

women and children for immoral purposes. For the most part these offenses are cognizable under national law, which in some cases enforces obligations arising under customary international or maritime law or multipartite agreements. In addition, for centuries aborigines have been debauched by the traffic, chiefly sea-borne, in arms, ammunition, and liquor. National and international efforts beginning in the latter part of the nineteenth century have sought to control these evils with respect to Africa and the islands of the Pacific, at least. Much remains to be done, however, toward making the *res communis* safe for the commerce of nations and denying its use to antisocial conduct.

Air Transport. The relation of ships to radio and aircraft is nowadays exceedingly complex. Much travel and freightage is by combined air-sea journeys. In some countries the laws permit shipping companies to operate air lines. Weather ships on patrol furnish meteorological information essential to overseas flights. They and all surface craft supply search and rescue services to downed aircraft. Both vessels and aircraft constitute mobile stations for commercial radio, and radio communication in various forms from shore-to-ship, ship-to-ship, and aircraft-to-ship is now essential to navigation and safety. A multitude of provisions in the international conventions dealing with safety of life at sea, civil aviation, telecommunications, the weather ships, the World Meteorological Organization, and the Intergovernmental Maritime Consultative Organization attest to this interdependence. The rules of this latter organization put the matter well: its Maritime Safety Committee "shall have the duty of maintaining such close relationship with other intergovernmental bodies concerned with transport and communications as may further the object of the Organization in promoting maritime safety and facilitate the co-ordination of activities in the fields of shipping, aviation, telecommunications and meteorology with respect to safety and rescue.[41]

Much of what has been said about sea transport applies, *mutatis mutandis*, to overseas air transport. Among the principal aspects which have received attention in international organizations and agreements since the close of World War I are these: airworthiness, registration and identification, competence of personnel, proficiency of operation, rules of the air, navigational aids, safety of life and property, rescue at

[41] Art. 29 of the convention concluded at Geneva, March 6, 1948, UN Doc. E/Conf.4/61; entered into force March 17, 1958.

sea, access to airports, routes, transit over national territory, customs, spread of disease, civil liability for damage, competition, discrimination, communications, and meteorological information. In several important respects, however, the development of air transport has differed from that of sea transport. Early advocacy of freedom to navigate in the air space above a nation state, by analogy to the freedom to navigate the high seas, yielded after the experiences of aerial bombardment in World War I to assertions of complete jurisdiction in the air space above its territory and territorial sea by the subjacent state. The impasse arising out of denials of the use of such air space forced relatively speedy international agreement on that use, at Paris in 1919. While insisting on full control over the air space above their domain, objecting vigorously even to the drifting over their territory of weather balloons miles above the terrain, all states possessing any considerable investment in airlines insist on untrammeled freedom in the air over the high seas beyond any territorial seas. The rapid rate of change in the technology of aeronautics has forced the international community to accept more intensive international regulation of technical matters. Although aviation is also an instrument of national policy for purposes of defense, profit, and prestige, competition and discriminatory practices have been brought to a greater degree under some intergovernmental control.[42]

Communications

Postal Communications. Nowadays the postal system and telecommunications are the principal means for transmitting intelligence across the seas. Aircraft increasingly supplement vessels in the carriage of mails. Government postal contracts operate in many cases to subsidize air fleets and the mercantile marine. These subsidies contribute to the problems of competition between airlines and ship lines of the same nationality and between either type of line when of diverse nationality.

"Postal services organized on a national or imperial basis have existed for several thousand years. The great empires of antiquity, the Persian and Roman, had highly developed postal services."[43] By the middle of

[42] See Kenneth W. Colegrove, *International Control of Aviation* (1930); Oliver J. Lissitzyn, *International Air Transport and National Policy* (1942); and Osborne Mance and J. E. Wheeler, *International Air Transport* (1944).

[43] Osborne Mance, *International Road Transport, Postal, Electricity and Miscellaneous Questions* (1947), p. 82. On the background, founding, and development of the Universal Postal Union, see *ibid.*, pp. 79–138, and the excellent bibliography

the nineteenth century the increased international communication by means of mails was in a truly pathetic state. Bewildering variations in "sea postage" and transit charges, depending upon the routes traversed and the national systems of weights and rates imposed, impeded efficient exchange, and the concomitant high costs became intolerable. This finally led to the creation of a General Postal Union in 1874, renamed Universal Postal Union in 1878.

From its beginning the Union has regulated the charges for maritime transit and transportation. Among other numerous matters relating to overseas mails, it has dealt with customs procedures, the posting of correspondence on board ship on the high seas and in port, and articles under restriction, such as explosive or inflammable substances, narcotics, and obscene literature. Provisions relating to sea transportation appear also in the regional agreements, such as that of the Postal Union of the Americas and Spain, and in special agreements such as those dealing with parcel post. Regulation of air transportation of postal matter, begun on a provisional basis at The Hague in 1927, was incorporated in the 1929 universal convention and has continued since.

The Universal Postal Union has avoided political controversies, has devoted itself to its special tasks in peacetime and wartime, and continues an exemplar of efficient international cooperation.

Telecommunications.[44] Overseas telecommunications at the moment employ two means, radio and cable. Among the forms of radio are telegraphy, telephony, television, facsimile, radiolocation, radionavigation, radar, and radio direction-finding. Broadcasting service includes "transmission of sounds" and "transmission by television, facsimile or other means." As indicated in the discussion of sea transport, radio utilizes and serves mobile stations at sea, on the surface, or in the air.

From the very beginning of the development of wireless telegraphy in the late nineteenth century new problems at every stage have plagued the fullest utilization of radio technology and art in the best interests of the world community. The wireless industry started out with dog-eat-dog tactics. Patent cartels were created. Bitter rivalry existed between

---

therein at pp. 135–138; Hubert Krains, *L'Union Postale Universelle: Sa Fondation et Son Developpement* (1924); John F. Sly, "The Genesis of the Universal Postal Union," *International Conciliation* No. 233 (1927).

[44] Osborne Mance and J. E. Wheeler, *International Telecommunications* (1944); G. A. Codding, Jr., *The International Telecommunication Union: An Experiment in International Cooperation* (1952).

the British Marconi group and the German Telefunken group of monopolists. On several occasions, stations on land and sea owned by the Marconi group refused to communicate with stations equipped with apparatus of the rival Telefunken company. If continued, this practice would have destroyed the usefulness of wireless for safety purposes on the high seas. Fortunately, this specific problem was resolved by the obligations created by the first International Wireless Convention in 1906. Some sense of responsibility toward the public was gradually imposed upon the warring systems by treaty engagement and national legislation.

Nevertheless problems continued to arise from the clash of two fundamentally different approaches toward ownership and operation of facilities — the United States insisting on private ownership subject to public regulation, most European states insisting on public ownership and operation, as they had in the case of land telegraphy. That problem continues. Others arose from the necessity of securing use of improved technology, the proper equipping of vessels on the high seas, the connecting of wireless stations with the land telegraph systems, rates, standards of service, and interference.

When radio broadcasting emerged after World War I the air tumbled into chaos. There was a mad scramble to appropriate use of the most extensive wave bands possible by rival private systems and by rival national states. This cutthroat business was also finally brought under control by national legislation, as in the United States by the Federal Radio Act of 1927,[45] and by new international agreements beginning also in 1927.

Problems still arise, continually, from the development of new techniques, such as television; from the need of periodic reallocation of wave bands to various services on land, on sea, in the air; from practices such as monopoly, censorship, jamming, interference, propaganda, incitation — the battling for the minds of men. At least one ship was fitted out recently for the Voice of America "to roam the seas and get close enough to satellite countries to pierce the Soviet jammings of air programs with the American message." It was found too small for such broadcasts.[46] With most of the problems of the radio aspect of telecom-

[45] Feb. 23, 1927, 44 *Stat.* 1162–1174; amended by the Communications Act of 1934, June 19, 1934, 48 *Stat.* 1064–1105.
[46] *N.Y.T.*, Dec. 16, 1951; March 28, 1956.

munications this study is, happily, not concerned. Attention in the forthcoming discussion will be focused on the relation of radio to use of the sea.

Submarine cables have had a century of fascinating history, filled with challenges to ingenuity and drama on the high seas. Their laying and repairing furnish a perpetual source of exciting tales of the sea. The first satisfactory submarine telegraph cable was laid in 1851 between Calais and Dover. Others soon after appeared in European waters. In America, as early as 1853, Cyrus W. Field consulted Matthew Maury on both the electrical and oceanographic problems of a trans-Atlantic cable. Maury laid out a route across a plateau in the North Atlantic for the purpose. Four attempts to lay a cable failed in the years 1857 and 1858. A fifth attempt succeeded in the summer of 1858. Three months later, because of faulty insulation, that cable ceased to operate. The Civil War interrupted further efforts.[47] In 1866 the first successful trans-Atlantic cable was laid. Since then over 400,000 miles of submarine cables have been laid in carefully surveyed and charted paths across the beds of the Seven Seas.

In 1956 the first trans-Atlantic telephone cable (actually two separate cables, one for the eastgoing part of the conversation, the other for the westgoing part), from Clarenville, Newfoundland, to Oban, on the west coast of Scotland, was completed and put into operation.[48] In 1955 it was reported that plans were under way for the laying of another long pair of cables capable of supplying telephone, telegraph, and facsimile types of services from Point Reyes, California, to Koko Head, Oahu, Hawaii.

From the beginning, "cable diplomacy" has dealt with exclusive landing rights, monopolistic concessions and practices, discriminations, and considerations of naval strategy. Strategic landing places, such as Newfoundland, and essential relay islands such as the Azores and Yap, once loomed large in that diplomacy. "The character of relay stations has radically changed with the introduction of new methods of eliminating manual repetition of messages at such stations. . . . The station is just as important as it ever was to the operation of the cables, and there is

[47] Lewis, *op. cit.*, pp. 78–80. See Lissitzyn, *op. cit.*, pp. 30–37; Mance and Wheeler, *International Telecommunications*, pp. 58–66, 78–83; and the excellent articles in the standard encyclopedias under "Submarine Cables" and "Telegraph."

[48] *N.Y.T.*, Dec. 2, 1953; June 9, 1955; Sept. 26, 1956. "Second Phone Tie to Span Atlantic," *N Y.T.*, Oct. 1, 1957.

Use and Abuse of the Sea

nothing in sight now, including the new type of underwater amplifier, which holds any promise of diminishing the necessity for relay stations nor their importance." [49] Since World War I these old rivalries have been complicated further by the competition of radio.

Cables are expensive to construct, lay, and maintain. Men and nature conspire against their integrity. Trawlers near shore pick them up and the fishermen chop off the cable to free their gear. Anchors foul and injure cables. In 1951, China Sea buccaneers tore up and made off with three and a half miles of the Danish Great Northern Telephone Company's cable between Hong Kong and Amoy. That was the third time the Amoy cable had been hijacked. "In 1929, seaquakes snapped twelve trans-Atlantic circuits in twenty-eight spots. The quakes were so powerful that some breaks occurred in 17,000 feet of water 300 miles from the epicenter. Bottom slides — the floor of the ocean caving in — are another cause of failures, and so are floating icebergs." [50] In tropical waters teredos, undersea worms, penetrate the sheathing of cables. Rubbing against coral formations will occasionally wear out a cable. In one strange accident, a huge whale off the coast of Peru got himself tangled in a cable, thrashed about, got further ensnarled, and drowned. In the process, he disrupted the cable.

Despite the increase in the use of radio, cables still carry much of the heavy "freight" of commercial communication, and, when sun spots, cosmic showers, electric storms, the aurora borealis, and other disturbances disrupt radio communication, traffic is diverted over cables. Engineers and oceanographers seek solutions to physical and operating problems. International agreements have sought to protect cables against human damaging acts and have regulated some of the technical aspects and conditions of their use, but many problems relating to competition and practices remain to be solved.

[49] Letter, Western Union Telegraph Company to writer, Jan. 7, 1952, citing a description of the new relay methods by I. S. Coggeshall, "Submarine Telegraphy in the Post-War Decade," in the 1930 *Transactions of the American Institute of Electrical Engineers.* Cf. Lissitzyn, *op. cit.*, p. 35, n. 4, who says: "The importance of relay stations has somewhat declined with the introduction of new methods of eliminating manual repetition of messages at such stations." For accounts of the installation of submerged amplifiers in several trans-Atlantic cables, on the ocean bottom a hundred or more miles offshore, see *N.Y.T.*, June 29, Oct. 25, 1950; Oct. 9, 1951.

[50] Tad Szulc, "Globe-Girdling," *N.Y.T. Magazine*, Aug. 21, 1955. "Cables Are Fouled by Hungry Whales," *N.Y.T.*, May 7, 1958.

Exploitation of Products [51]

The New World was once called into being to redress the balance of the Old. The riches of the sea may yet redress the impoverishment of the land. Scientists confidently predict the availability in the sea of vast quantities of food, petroleum, building and clothing materials, fresh water, power from its tides, and thermal power from its depths. Some predictions verge on the apocalyptic but enough substantial advances have been made to give considerable comfort to the population and other experts who must worry about the implications of the doctrines of the Reverend Thomas Robert Malthus. Apparently man stands at the frontier of another new world, as yet but meagerly explored, whose peaceful development will demand the utmost in international cooperation.

In the present context, the resources of the sea include "the populations of the fishes and other organisms useful to men"; the bird life dependent upon the waters; the minerals in the waters, bed, and subsoil; sand from the bottom; mineral, plant, and animal life from beach, shore, and marsh; power from the tides; thermal power; and soon, perhaps, fresh water in quantity. So great is the variety of the resources of the sea that for present purposes only those which have been impressed with a utilitarian, particularly a commercial, value can be discussed. The range and character of the animal, vegetable, and mineral resources under even this narrowed rubric can be indicated, within present limits, only by way of summary or suggestion.

Fishery Resources.[52] The term "fishery resources," in its broad con-

---

[51] Rachel Carson, *The Sea Around Us* (1951); Frederick G. Walton Smith and Henry Chapin, *The Sun, the Sea, and Tomorrow: Potential Sources of Food, Energy and Minerals from the Sea* (1954); Sverdrup, Johnson, and Fleming, *op. cit.*; *Proceedings of the United Nations Scientific Conference on the Conservation and Utilization of Resources* (1949), 8 vols., especially Vol. I, *Plenary Meetings*, Vol. II, *Mineral Resources*, Vol. III, *Fuel and Energy Resources*, Vol. IV, *Water Resources*, and Vol. VII, *Wildlife and Fish Resources*; Donald K. Tressler and James McW. Lemon, *Marine Products of Commerce*, 2nd ed. (1951); *Background Material on the Scientific and Economic Aspects of the Continental Shelf and Marine Waters*, Inter-American Specialized Conference on "Conservation of Natural Resources: The Continental Shelf and Marine Waters," Pan American Union (1956); Harrison Brown, James Bonner, and John Weir, *The Next Hundred Years: Man's Natural and Technological Resources* (1957); and the usually excellent and detailed articles and bibliographies frequently appended thereto in the standard encyclopedias on each of the terms and topics mentioned in this discussion.

[52] *Fishery Resources of the United States*, S. Doc. 51, 79 Cong., 1 Sess. (1945); *Fishery Statistics of the United States 1953* (1956), which contains also a helpful glossary, pp. 313–319, and pictorial section with notation of mode of gear used in

notation, embraces mammals, fish, crustaceans, mollusks, reptiles, sponges, and algae. To these may be added soon, for commercial purposes, plankton.

Contrary to popular belief, the sea is not "full of fish." Temperature of the sea, depth of water, and currents are the primary limiting factors in the geographical range of fishes and other forms of marine life. Tropical zones are characterized by a greater diversity of species than temperate, polar, or subpolar zones, but each species is present in far less abundance. Temperate zones have fewer species of fish, and the polar and subpolar zones still less, than the tropical zones, but the species are present in far greater numbers. Apart from zonal relationships, the abundance of individual kinds of marine life is definitely related to the continental shelf. . . . Fishes and other marine animals are most abundant on its inner portion, where the fertility of the bottom and the other elements of sunlight and currents are conducive to the production of food organisms and provide favorable conditions for reproduction and growth. The broad expanse of the continental shelf in the North Atlantic Ocean and the North Sea, and the consequent tremendous abundance of a comparatively small number of individual species, have been responsible for the development of large fishery industries.[53]

Among the mammals dwelling in the sea or peculiarly dependent upon it, which have been of commercial value for centuries, are the whale, porpoise, dolphin, fur seal, hair seal, sea lion, sea elephant, walrus, and sea otter. The sea otter, though a land animal, roams the coastal waters of the North Pacific in search of shellfish, and there was nearly exterminated, together with the fur seal, in the days of unrestricted pelagic sealing.

Eschewing any taxonomic approach, the fish with which we are pri-

---

taking, pp. 320–337; Food and Agriculture Organization, *Yearbook of Fishery Statistics 1952–53* (1955), which contains a glossary and also an indication of geographic distribution; FAO, *The State of Food and Agriculture 1955* (1955); UN *Papers Presented at the International Technical Conference on the Conservation of the Living Resources of the Sea, Rome, 18 April to 10 May 1955* (1956); *Five Technical Reports on Food and Agriculture*, UN Interim Commission on Food and Agriculture (1945); John Oliver La Gorce, *The Book of Fishes* (1939); numerous monographic papers on specific species or crafts published by the United States Fish and Wildlife Service now listed in *Fishery Publication Index 1920–1954* (1955); Gustav T. Sundstrom, Illustrator, *Commercial Fishing Vessels and Gear*, Bureau of Commercial Fisheries Circular No. 48, Fish and Wildlife Service (1957); and P. F. Meyer-Waarden, *Electrical Fishing*, FAO Fisheries Study No. 7 (1957).

[53] *Five Technical Reports, op. cit.*, p. 181; see also "Aspects of the Life History of Certain Resources of the Sea in Relation to the Physical Environment," in *Int. Tech. Conf., op. cit.*, pp. 61–80.

marily concerned may be classified thus: *demersal* (bottom-dwelling or "ground fish"), such as the cod, haddock, hake, cusk, halibut, flounder, and pollock; *pelagic* (surface-dwelling), such as sea herring, pilchard, sprat, anchovies, menhaden, tunas, and mackerel. Some species, such as the mullet, are both bottom and surface dwellers. Others roam up and down, depending on their feeding needs or life cycles or other compulsions.

Some species are *anadromous* (dwelling in the sea but spawning upstream), such as the smelt, alewife, shad, striped bass or rockfish, white perch, salmon, and sturgeon; *catadromous* (dwelling in fresh water but spawning at sea), such as the eel, perhaps the mullet, and probably many gobies; or they may have other migrating habits.[54]

"The vast majority of common food fishes live near the shore or at least come near the shore at certain seasons. Many enter harbors, bays, inlets, and estuaries as soon as the weather is warm, and remain only until autumn. These shallow waters are sought because they are good feeding grounds during the warmer seasons. Other fish enter fresh-water streams to spawn, then die or return to the sea. Still others, rarely, if ever, approach the shore, but occupy offshore banks where the water is of a more uniform temperature throughout the year."[55] Some fish, such as the tunas, swordfish, spearfishes, and sailfishes (as well as most cetaceans, that is, whales, porpoises, dolphins) have a world-wide distribution and are believed to migrate over great distances. Sharks also appear to have a wide distribution.

Most species, however, are identified with particular coasts and regions. Obviously, no system of regulation seeking conservation of a fishery resource can be durable which is not based upon careful regard of these and many other biological habits of the species involved.

Crustaceans of commercial value include numerous varieties of crabs, crawfish, lobsters, and shrimp or prawns. Among the mollusks (shellfish) in demand for food and other uses of man are the abalone, several species of clam, conch (particularly the chank), mussel, oyster, periwinkle, scallop, and squid. Each of the fisheries has its distinct characteristics; all of them are confined to coastal waters. The sedentary habits of oysters

---

[54] George S. Myers, "Usage of Anadromous, Catadromous and Allied Terms for Migratory Fishes," *Copeia*, No. 2, June 30, 1949, p. 94; Tressler and Lemon, *op. cit.*, pp. 170–172.

[55] Samuel F. Hildebrand, "Characteristics of Marine Fishes," in Tressler and Lemon, *op. cit.*, p. 176.

Use and Abuse of the Sea

and other mollusks and the limited mobility of the crustaceans encourage farming and sundry cultivating operations from close-by shores. The principal evils affecting these fisheries appear to be overfishing, disease and destruction through effluvia from the land, the roiling of beds by hurricanes and other great disturbances, and impairment of the feeding bottoms. The king crab has been exploited vigorously by the Japanese off the Alaska coasts; the chank fisheries off the southern-most coasts of India have been worked from time immemorial as far as twelve miles out into the Shallow Sea;[56] the pearl fisheries of Ceylon have similarly been worked for twenty miles out into the same sea; and the pearl-shell fisheries have been exploited heavily in various parts of the Pacific, notably along the northwestern coast of Australia for 2000 miles and along the coast of Queensland on the northeast up into and across Torres Strait almost to the shores of New Guinea.

Because of the relatively fixed positions of the fisheries for crustaceans and mollusks, few important international controversies concerning their exploitation have thus far arisen. Assertions of jurisdiction over the sea bed overlying the continental shelf and even beyond are now inviting contests in law.[57] Resolutions of some of these conflicts will depend upon determination of the question whether the marine animal is attached to the sea bed or is free swimming. If the former it comes presumptively under the jurisdiction of the littoral state; if the latter, it comes under the doctrine of the freedom of the seas, except within the territorial sea or such conservation zones beyond as may be set up and acknowledged. The term "sedentary" has been used in the past to describe the attached or relatively immobile animals. The term has no fixed meaning among the lexicographers, the biologists, or the lawyers. The International Law Commission has wrestled with the matter and proposed certain tentative solutions to the problem of jurisdiction. These will be discussed at greater length later.[58]

The aquatic reptiles include the terrapins — which inhabit shallow

---

[56] James Hornell, *The Sacred Chank of India* (1914), is a splendid piece of research, tracing the use of the chank back into antiquity and contemporaneously into multifold cultural avenues.

[57] D. F. O'Connell, "Sedentary Fisheries and the Australian Continental Shelf," 49 *A.J.I.L.* 185–209 (1955), and extensive bibliography cited therein; Mouton, *op. cit.*, pp. 138–161; Gidel, *op. cit.*, pp. 488–501.

[58] Below, p. 322. See the discussion of the I.L.C.'s draft reports at the annual meeting of the American Society of International Law, *Proceedings, 1956*, pp. 116–154, and particularly Richard Young's helpful distinctions at p. 150.

salt- and brackish-water bays, estuaries, and swamps — and the sea turtles. Among the latter, the green turtle and the loggerhead are used for food; the hawksbill is the source of commercial tortoise shell.

Sponges, among the simplest of animals, have a world-wide distribution. They have been harvested from the dawn of history and references to them appear in the literary works of antiquity. They are now found on various kinds of bottoms from tidal flats to abyssal depths. They seem to favor rocky or hard bottom, along the shores and in coral-reef lagoons. Until 1841 the commercial supply for the world came from the Mediterranean. Since then industries have been developed in sundry places, including a limited area in Florida. This American supply has been hit recently by a serious blight.

Sea algae range from microscopic plankton to certain species found along the Pacific coast of North America and in the Antarctic which grow to a length of more than a hundred feet. Among the varieties most valuable commercially are Irish moss, the red alga *Porphyra* of the Orient, and the giant kelp *Macrocystis* from the coast of southern California.

Much fishing is directly for subsistence purposes; some is for sport or amusement; most of it is for commercial purposes. The variety of uses to which marine organisms are put is already amazing, standing as we do upon only the threshold of the technological, particularly the chemical, revolution in relation to them. They range from religious and connubial symbol in chank to potash from kelp for explosives. They include perfume from ambergris; alginates from seaweed for beer, ice cream, and storage batteries; vitamins and hormones from livers and other organs. The products can roughly be divided into edible (for man, beast, and fowl) and nonedible. Fish meal is coming into greater use for livestock. Seaweed flour is being used in Japan for bread. Diminishing supplies of horse meat are driving the mink farmers to use fish, sea-lion, and whale meat. Fisheries all over the world are helping to compensate protein deficiencies.

To the principal use as food can be added such large-scale uses as pharmaceutical products, including the well-known agar-agar from seaweed and now another new drug from seaweed which prevents clotting of the blood, an aid in treating thrombosis; skins for leathers and furs; numerous oils, fats, and acids for industry; fertilizers and glue; isinglass from fish sounds (air bladder or swim bladder); pearls, blister

Use and Abuse of the Sea

pearls, pearl shells, and coral for adornment; conches for cameos; pearl essence from fish scales; mother-of-pearl for buttons and tortoise shell for utensils; sponges for hundreds of uses from the household to the prize ring. Old uses, discovered by primitive man and extended by successive civilizations all over the world, are now being expanded and supplemented by the oceanographer, the marine biologist, the chemist, the nutrition expert, and the technologist.

In recent decades, marine organisms have been used for medical research: sharks and sea cucumbers for cancer, whales for the pituitary gland, Siamese fighting fish for the effects of the new tranquilizing drugs, and now lobsters and whales for heart research. After Dr. Paul Dudley White had seen President Eisenhower safely through his heart attack he departed promptly for the whaling grounds of Baja California, Mexico, to get an electrocardiogram of a living adult gray whale.[59] Very likely there will be expanded use of marine animals for research in other scientific fields also, as porpoises in captivity have been studied for their motion and curvatures as an aid in shipbuilding.

Probably few conservationists would agree with William Schwenck Gilbert that

> There are fish in the sea, no doubt of it,
> As many as ever came out of it.

American experience with fur seals, salmon, both the Atlantic and Pacific variety, halibut, sardines, shad, lobsters, and cod indicate the possibilities of irreparable damage being done to invaluable resources. To this list should be added the sea otter, who barely escaped complete destruction. In the biological cycle, marine fauna and flora are subject to being devoured, one species by another, to disease, to blights, to predatory boring animals, and to parasites. Storms, seismic disturbances, and erosion alter feeding bottoms. Disease or a volcanic explosion is reported recently to have killed two thousand seals in the Weddell Sea region of the Antarctic. Changes in currents and changes in gas content, chemical composition, and temperature of the water can disrupt the life cycles of the organisms. About these natural phenomena there appears little that man can do. Pisciculture of the commercial marine species is apparently still in its infancy.

Added to these hazards to marine organisms, however, are destructive

[59] *N.Y.T.*, Feb. 1, 3, 10, 12, 1956.

agencies well within the control of man: overfishing; fishing in the wrong seasons; destruction of immature fish; use of wrong gear; use of explosives and suction pumps; indiscriminate interception of runs of anadromous fish, such as the salmon and shad; pelagic sealing; pollution of streams and inland waters used by migratory marine species; pollution of coastal waters by industrial and human wastes; oil pollution of coastal waters; improper trawling; dumping rubbish on feeding and breeding bottoms and dredging the same; diking off new areas of the sea, as in the case of Dutch oyster beds.

In the latter part of the nineteenth century, there was great slaughter of the harp and hood herds of hair seals off the Newfoundland coasts, particularly the newborn "whitecoats" of the harps, for the oil distilled from their fat and their skins, which were made into patent leather for the boots of dandies in those days.[60] So great was the annual carnage that it would both the ice floes and

> The multitudinous seas incarnadine,
> Making the Greene, one Red.

Despite the yearly assaults since and the bounties paid for the snouts of harbor seals, because they are regarded as pests by other fisheries, the herds have managed to survive. Lately, however, there is voiced fear of serious depletion. Efforts are being made to get a multilateral agreement to conserve them,[61] as was done ultimately in the case of the Pacific fur seal.

The books are full of examples of other unnecessarily destructive acts or practices. Various species of whales faced extinction until the whaling agreements imposed restraints. Blasting of rocks and rock slides during railroad construction in the narrow gorge of the Fraser River in British Columbia has seriously affected the spawning of the sockeye salmon. Failure to introduce fishways and fish ladders when inland dams are built contributes to depletion of anadromous or catadromous species.[62]

---

[60] Frank Wead, *Gales, Ice and Men: A Biography of the Steam Barkentine Bear* (1937), pp. 19–23. See also "Bear, Famed Polar Vessel, Looks to a New Career Tracking Seals," *N.Y.T.*, Dec. 15, 1957; and *N.Y.T.*, March 11, 1958.

[61] *N.Y.T.*, July 14, Sept. 8, 1955. For current sealing operations for harps and hoods, see Bruce Woodland, "Canada's Atlantic Fishery," *Trade News*, Vol. 10, No. 8, Feb. 1958, pp. 3–6, and G. J. Gillespie, "Halifax Now Main Centre," *ibid.*, pp. 7–8. Norwegian sealers also participate in the fishery.

[62] For federal legislation on fishways since 1888, see *Water Resources Law*, Vol. 3 of the Report of the President's Water Resources Policy Commission (1950), pp. 327–328.

Use and Abuse of the Sea

Factory ships and mechanical devices for the taking of fish and whales increase the dangers of overfishing. Modern refrigeration and freezing avoids waste from spoilage; it can also encourage overfishing by concentration on fish which command high-market prices. Waste occurs in seasonal glutting of markets, in selective utilization of specific small parts, such as roe or scales, and in the discarding of carcasses after pelt, skin, blubber, or viscera are taken. It also occurs in fishing for sport and through religious taboos or excessively narrow food tastes. And now there is contention about the destructive effects of hydrogen-bomb tests in the Pacific.[63]

No single nation has a monopoly of these evils. So far as the United States is concerned, however, it could be said in 1945, "from a conservation viewpoint, the fisheries are perhaps the most poorly managed of all our national resources."[64] Fortunately, within a few years, by 1948, a new enlightened and scientific policy was adopted.[65] A prudent policy would include at least two desiderata: conservation of existing resources and development of new ones. So far as domestic measures can be adequate, such policy requires cooperation of local, state, and national authorities and of the economic and sporting interests involved. On the high seas and for proper protection of the territorial waters international efforts are essential to the success of such policy. As in the case of disease, insect pests, and agricultural blights, political boundaries mean little. Marine organisms have their own ecological zones. The pattern of those zones runs across all historically established maritime frontiers, however measured from the shore. To meet some evils, efforts can be devoted to securing acquiescence in justifiable extensions of littoral state jurisdiction into the high seas for genuine nondiscriminatory conservation purposes. Collective regulation of exploiting practices on the high seas, collaboration in scientific inquiry, and cooperation in eliminating oil pollution in the marginal seas demand continuous international effort.

Minerals, Sand, Fresh Water. Certain other commercial products of

---

[63] See the debate: Emanuel Margolis, "The Hydrogen Bomb Experiments and International Law," Myres S. McDougal and Norbert A. Schlei, "The Hydrogen Bomb Tests in Perspective: Lawful Measures for Security," 64 *Yale Law Journal* 629–647, 648–710, respectively (1955). On balance, Messrs. McDougal and Schlei, who favor the tests, appear to make a good defense for them.

[64] *Fishery Resources of the United States, op. cit.,* p. 131.

[65] Wilbert McLeod Chapman, "United States Policy on High Seas Fisheries," 20 *DSB* 67–71, 80 (1949); William C. Herrington, "U.S. Policy on Fisheries and Territorial Waters," 26 *DSB* 1021–1023 (1952).

the sea must be mentioned: minerals, sand, and fresh water. From time immemorial salt has been derived from the sea by solar evaporation and other methods. Extensive industrial enterprises over the world derive iodine and potash from seaweed. Magnesium is now produced in quantity from sea water. Scientific inquiry is being directed to the utilization of numerous other chemicals and minerals in the water. Sand for landfills and beach and road making is dredged or sucked up from the sea bottom. Amber, a fossilized form of resin, mineralogically known as succinite, has long been gathered from shores and dug out of coastal mines in various parts of the world, particularly along the Baltic littoral.[66] (Despite its name, meerschaum is not a product of the sea. Though sometimes found floating on the Black Sea, it is a mineral mined chiefly in Asia Minor but also in other parts of the world, including the United States.) Coral is used for building blocks in sundry areas of the world. And the day may come when our new shortages of fresh water may be relieved by large-scale conversions of sea water. The United States is already the leading experimenter in this field.[67] Thus far no international conflicts with regard to these products appear to have arisen. The development of this incalculable wealth of the seas presents, however, a dramatic challenge to international scientific collaboration.

Birds.[68] Works on marine resources do not usually include oceanic

[66] A. MacCallum Scott, *Beyond the Baltic* (1926), Ch. 22, "The Amber Coast."

[67] *Production of Fresh Water from Sea Water, Hearings* before Subcommittee on Irrigation and Reclamation, Committee on Interior and Insular Affairs, H. of R., 82 Cong., 2 Sess. (1952); Act authorizing federal research and development, July 3, 1952, 66 Stat. 328–329; and the following works produced by the Department of Interior: *Demineralization of Saline Waters* (1952); *An Investigation of Multiple-Effect Evaporation of Saline Waters from Solar Radiation* (1953); *Results of Selected Laboratory Tests of an Ionic Demineralizer* (1954); *Saline Water Conversion Report for 1956* (1957); *Saline Water Conversion Report for 1957* (1958). See "Ionics and Cart Bring Pure Aqua to Bahrein," N.Y.T., Aug. 3, 1957.

[68] See Robert Cushman Murphy, *Oceanic Birds of South America*, 2 vols. (1936). Though dealing primarily with the littoral and offshore areas from the Caribbean to the Antarctic Continent, Mr. Murphy's excellent survey deals also with avifauna phenomena as far east as St. Helena and west as far as many of the Pacific isles, thus covering most of a quarter of the earth's surface. The economic aspects are dealt with under each species, *passim*. The index on p. 1219 is, however, an excellent guide to the numerous data. For brief descriptions of oceanic birds in other parts of the world, see W. B. Alexander, *Birds of the Ocean: A Handbook for Voyagers Containing Descriptions of All the Sea-Birds of the World* (1928); Junius Henderson, *The Practical Value of Birds* (1934); and the numerous authoritative articles in the standard encyclopedias under the names of species and such titles as "Economic Ornithology" and "Protection of Birds." Numerous works on the polar regions include descriptions of birds, e.g., R. N. R. Brown, *The Polar Regions* (1927). For shore and

Use and Abuse of the Sea

birds. Yet their ecology is absolutely dependent upon the seas. They participate in the life cycle of sundry organisms of the seas; they act as scavengers in many waters; they have in all recorded history given sustenance to seafaring folk; and access to them for commercial purposes is primarily by sea or along shore.

They aid mariners in finding their way. Thus the United States *Sailing Directions for Antarctica*,[69] for example, says:

Navigators should observe the bird life encountered in Antarctic waters, for deductions often may be drawn from the presence of certain species. Shags are sedentary in their habits, rarely going more than half a mile from their rocks. When sighting shags during fog or reduced visibility, it is a sure sign of the close proximity of land. The Black-browed Albatross and the Gray-headed Albatross usually leave the wake of vessels when nearing the belt of pack ice. Departure of these birds is an indication that pack ice is not far distant. The Light-mantled sooty Albatross usually remains northward of the pack but sometimes enters the Ross Sea as far southward as 78° S. It is a good indication of open water in that region.

And so the *Directions* continue, throughout several pages of description of Antarctic avifauna.

As destroyers of insects, many species make substantial contributions to agriculture. The dramatic aid by the Salt Lake sea gulls to the early Mormon settlement, when they destroyed a plague of crickets, is now commemorated by a bronze monument in Salt Lake City. Occasionally sea gulls become agricultural pests and are shot indiscriminately in some parts of the world but in the United States gulls may be shot only with official permission.

For present purposes, birds in relation to the sea may be grouped thus: land birds which must pass over the sea in their seasonal migrations; marsh, swamp, and shore birds in whose ecology salt water and its organisms are important; distinctively oceanic birds who "are bound as peons to their own specific types of surface water."[70]

---

marsh birds, see Alexander Wetmore, *Our Migrant Shorebirds in Southern South America*, U.S. Dept. of Agriculture (1927), a discussion of certain North American species that migrate to points south of the Equator; W. L. McAtee, *Wildlife of the Atlantic Coast Salt Marshes*, ibid. (1939). See also Austin L. Rand, *American Water and Game Birds* (1956); about half of the descriptive matter is devoted to true oceanic species.

[69] *Including the Off-Lying Islands South of Latitude 60°* (1943), pp. 56–62.

[70] Murphy, *op. cit.*, p. 59. See grouping of oceanic birds from the ecological point of view, at p. 326, as (1) Littoral, (2) Inshore, (3) Offshore, and (4) Pelagic.

Important as are the first two groups, attention here is focused upon the lesser-known third. Of these, Robert Cushman Murphy says:

Life zones governing the distribution of birds at sea are ultimately determined by physical properties of the surface waters. The well-nigh inexorable control of certain special types of oceanic environments upon birds has not yet been generally realized by either zoologists or oceanographers. The distributional boundaries and barriers of animals inhabiting land areas, such as mountain walls, deserts, broad rivers, lines of abrupt change in temperature or rainfall, etc., are accepted as a commonplace. Naturalists recognize, moreover, that the ranges of fishes and of innumerable marine invertebrates can be readily correlated with the temperature and chemical content of sea water. But oceanic birds seem, in the main to have been regarded somewhat naively as aerial rather than aquatic animals notwithstanding that their relationship to sea and land, as concerned with feeding and breeding, respectively, are precisely the same as those of the seals among the mammals or the sea turtles among reptiles. Members of none of these groups have escaped the necessity of using the land as a cradle, but their true medium, and the source of their being, is, nevertheless, the sea.[71]

As in the case of many other natural phenomena, sea fowl have been subjected to justifiable economic uses and many abuses. The eggs and flesh of many species are edible; in some cases the chicks are greatly valued as delicacies. Both eggs and meat are consumed locally, marketed commercially, and were once extensively used to replenish ships' stores. In the Arctic the Eskimos supplement their winter food supplies with dovekies gathered in the nesting season. "The usual meal for one Eskimo consists of about eight of these small birds."[72] Eggs are also gathered for their albumen, which is used in industry, particularly for clarification of wines.

Oil rendered out of the blubber of penguins was once used in the tanning industry. The stomach oil of sundry species of petrels is used as food and has some of the medicinal qualities of cod-liver oil. Feathers apparently are used variously; the down harvested from the nests of the eider duck is a staple article of commerce. The more striking plumage is valued by aborigines and was, until restrictive legislation discouraged it, an important item in the civilized millinery trade.[73] The skins of some

---

[71] *Ibid.*, p. 59.

[72] Letter to writer, U.S. Fish and Wildlife Service, May 3, 1951.

[73] For a brief account of the devastating practice which also affected sea birds, see Henderson, *op. cit.*, pp. 103–107.

Use and Abuse of the Sea

species are tanned, and those of the penguins in some cases are used as "fur."

One of the most valuable by-products of sea birds is guano, the best deposits being found on the islands off the Peruvian coast. The rush for guano in the middle nineteenth century, productive of saturnalia reminiscent of the California gold rush, also turned up deposits of smaller quantities in Patagonia, the Caribbean Sea, and "on islets off the arid western coast of southern Africa."[74]

When the wealth accumulated over thousands of years on the islands off Peru had been exhausted, by the end of the past century, the government adopted conservation measures and a rational system of exploitation, including necessary protection for the species producing the guano, chiefly certain cormorants. Lately, this effort to protect the guano deposits has been used to support, in part, the Peruvian claim to a two-hundred-mile territorial sea. Under a "biological complex," or "bioma," theory there is asserted an anchovy-cormorant-guano relationship. Depletion of anchovy by overfishing leads to depletion of bird flocks, and hence to a decrease of guano deposits.[75] Assuming the facts of the relationship and depletion to be accurate, there could be little quarrel with a reasonable effort to conserve the biological chain. The United States insists, however, that such specific needs for conservation measures do not justify what it regards as an excessive claim to territorial waters.[76] Discussion of these claims will be resumed later in dealing with post-World War II developments.

Many hazards, natural and man-made, confront sea birds. Thus, skuas, cannibalistic with respect to their own young and species, also eat the young of penguins; sea leopards eat any penguins; land animals, such as rats, possums, and mongooses prey upon the eggs and young of many species; mysterious water movements may spread disaster, as does the dreaded El Nino, an equatorial countercurrent which periodically brings warm water down the western coast of South America, killing small fish and through them causing disease and death to many colonies of sea

[74] For the dramatic story, vividly told, see Murphy, *op. cit.*, pp. 286–295.

[75] See Enrique Garcia Sayan, *Notas sobre Soberania Maritima del Peru: Defensa de las 200 millas de mar peruano ante las recientes transgressiones* (1955); Aulio Vivaldi Quierolo, "La resurreccion de 'Mare Clausum,'" 23 *Revista de Derecho* (University of Concepcion) 3–57 (1955); *Santiago Negotiations on Fishery Conservation Problems*, Dept. of State (1955), *passim*.

[76] *Santiago Negotiations*, *op. cit.*, *passim*, discussed more fully below, p. 307.

birds. Works such as Murphy's are filled with dramatic accounts of such untimely ends for birds.

We are here concerned, however, chiefly with the man-made hazards. Since many species, when on land can easily be herded or dug out of their burrows, destruction by the tens of thousands is a relatively simple, if tedious, matter. Many colonies in and off South America have been decimated; some species, once abundant, are now rare. The Great Auk or Garefowl, originally called the Penguin, once plentiful in the North Atlantic, "was killed in great numbers in the seventeenth and eighteenth centuries by sealers and fishermen for food and bait, and for its feathers and oil," so that by 1800 it had become scarce and by 1844 extinct. Meanwhile its name had been transferred to the similarly flightless Antarctic bird.[77] The Arctic curlew [78] has now gone the way of its land companion, the passenger pigeon.[79] No doubt, for many an oceanic species an epitaph could be inscribed, as one has been for the last Wisconsin passenger pigeon: "This species became extinct through the avarice and thoughtlessness of man."

Overcollecting of eggs has reduced many colonies or species. Drainage or filling-in of coastal swamps and marshes reduces the available breeding places for some species of oceanic fowl. On the Peruvian isles, "guano contractors in the old time" slaughtered thousands of young pelicans, "purely for the sake of getting them out of the way of the diggers." [80] In some countries, sea fowl are shot for sport, as one shoots clay disks. Some species have been overharvested for their flesh, body oil, fat, stomach oil, or feathers. Added to these depredations is the damage done by collision with light houses, tall buildings with beacons, and airfield lights. The Empire State Building in New York has begun to turn off its beacon during the fall migrating period, and the United States has introduced non-bird-confusing ultraviolet light into its airfield ceilometers to avoid unnecessary attrition. Conversely, large oceanic birds, such as the alba-

---

[77] Alexander, *op. cit.*, pp. 235–236.

[78] Fred Bodsworth, *Last of the Curlews* (1955).

[79] A. W. Schorger, *The Passenger Pigeon: Its Natural History and Extinction* (1955); and review of same by Thomas Foster, *N.Y.T. Book Review*, Feb. 27, 1955. See also Paul Hofmann, "Bird Slaughter in Italy Draws Protests From Northern Europe," *N.Y.T.*, April 14, 1958. Gourmets can find tinned thrushes and larks imported from southern France on sale in a New York department store! Jane Nickerson, "News of Food," *N.Y.T.*, Jan. 27, 1953.

[80] Murphy, *op. cit.*, p. 822.

Use and Abuse of the Sea

tross, can cause damage to aircraft, particularly at low levels near airfields.[81]

An extensive and persistent evil has been oil pollution of sea waters. At the end of voyages, oil-burning vessels flush out their empty tanks, depositing in the waters "a viscous black slime, a sort of emulsion." This oil film ruins beaches and has caused serious harbor fires, such as the one at Belfast in 1922.

Lastly the results to marine life are serious. Floating plankton are killed outright. The interposition of an impassable film between air and water prevents oxygenation of the water, weakening and to a degree actually suffocating the fish and shellfish in the affected area. It is even said that typhoid then more readily attacks the oyster beds, with all the consequent danger to human health — a serious matter to the United States where the oyster industry alone is worth fourteen millions annually. This poisoning works a depletion of the food supply and thus does indirect damage to marine birds, but there is a direct damage as well. Birds alighting on the oil become smeared with it, often so badly that flight is impossible; literally bogged down, they can escape neither from storms nor from animal enemies. Some apparently are drowned in their efforts to rid themselves of the encumbering material, or becoming exhausted by their struggling meet death in some other way. Moreover, the clotting of the feathers spoils their insulating power, body heat escapes and chill water gets through, inducing pneumonia.[82]

National and international efforts to control this evil have been in progress since World War I. They will be discussed later in this work. But to this type of pollution, very likely, there will be added in the future the nuisance of oil escaping from offshore drilling operations.

During the past half century, many governments have adopted protective legislation for migratory land birds and for sea birds. A beginning has been made with treaty protection. Much remains to be done, nationally and internationally, if not for aesthetic or scientific reasons then at least for prudent agricultural, navigational, and commercial ends.

Subsoil Mines and Wells. Two further resources of the sea, embraced

[81] E.g., Dept. of the Interior press release, Feb. 13, 1955, "Stubborn Gooney Birds Baffle Biologists," describing efforts to reduce and remove interfering colonies of albatrosses on Midway Island; also "U.S. To Curb Birds Periling Aircraft," *N.Y.T.*, April 23, 1958.

[82] Sherman Strong Hayden, *The International Protection of Wild Life: An Examination of Treaties and Other Agreements for the Preservation of Birds and Mammals* (1942), pp. 106–107; *Pollution of the Sea by Oil: Results of an Inquiry Made by The United Nations Secretariat* (1956).

within the generous context earlier postulated, remain to be mentioned — the products of mines and wells in the subsoil of offshore areas and power either from the tides or from heat differences in the various layers of ocean water.

With the exception of Antarctica, which has its own continental shelf separated by "hundreds of miles of oceanic depths" from the other continents, "all the other continents lie within the confines of a single encircling belt of shallow water which is essentially continuous — the continental shelf.... The aggregate area of the continental shelves is roughly eleven million square miles. Of this total area about one million square miles is contiguous to the coasts of the United States, including Alaska." [83]

Thus far, the mineral resources which lie in the submerged land areas have been but sparsely exploited, and that chiefly by penetrations from dry-land side. Examples of such operations extending under the sea include the mining of tin in Cornwall [84] and Sumatra; [85] coal in Great Britain,[86] Nova Scotia,[87] Vancouver Island,[88] Australia,[89] Spain,[90] Chile,[91] and Japan; [92] iron ore in Great Britain,[93] Newfoundland,[94] and

---

[83] Wallace E. Pratt, "Petroleum on Continental Shelves," 31 *Bulletin of the American Association of Petroleum Geologists* 657–672 at 657–658 (1947); see J. B. Carsey, "Geology of Gulf Coastal Area and Continental Shelf," 34 *ibid.*, 361–385 (1950).

[84] Clement Reid and J. S. Flett, *The Geology of the Land's End District* (1907), pp. 86, 87, 93, 95, 102, 103, 106, 108, 113, 114, 115, 118, describing separate mines.

[85] *Memorandum on the Regime of the High Seas, op. cit.*, p. 51.

[86] G. M. Bailes, *Modern Mining Practice*, 5 vols. (1906), Vol. 4, pp. 86–89, citing *Reports of the Royal Commission on Coal Supplies*, Cd. 1725 (1903), Cd. 1991 (1904), and Cd. 2362 (1905). Among the coal fields having undersea workings are ones located in Cumberland, Durham, Scotland, and South Wales. See also H. G. A. Hickling, "Undersea Coalfield Extension: Prospects in the North-East," 180 *Colliery Guardian* 267–271 (1950); R. S. McLaren, "Undersea Mining Off the North-East Durham Coast," 165 *Iron and Coal Trades Review* 301–309 (1952); "Mining under the Ocean," *Financial Times* (London), July 3, 1953.

[87] Francis W. Gray and R. Heath Gray, "The Sydney Coalfield," 44 *Transactions of the Canadian Institute of Mining Engineers* 289–330 (1941), and Gidel, *op. cit.*, Vol. I, pp. 510–511, who cites F. W. Gray, "Mining Coal under the Sea in Nova Scotia with Notes on Comparable Undersea Coal Mining Operations Elsewhere," *Proceedings of the Second Empire Mining and Metallurgical Congress*, Canada (1927), Vol. 2, pp. 1–191.

[88] J. Dickins, "Submarine Coal Mining, Nanaino, Vancouver Island, British Columbia," 38 *Transactions of the Canadian Institute of Mining and Metallurgy* 465–472 (1935).

[89] Gidel, *op. cit.*, Vol. I, pp. 510–511.

[90] *Ibid.*

[91] A. L. Toenges, *et al.*, *Coals of Chile*, U.S. Dept. of Interior (1948), pp. 5, 15, and 23; Octavio Astorquiza and Oscar Galleguillos V., *Cien Años Del Carbon De*

54

Use and Abuse of the Sea

France;[95] copper in Eire;[96] and gold in Alaska.[97] Among the other ores found at various times in the Cornish tin mines were copper, cobalt, uranium, zinc, lead, and arsenic.[98] Continental United States apparently has no undersea mines.[99]

Not many problems of international legal significance are likely to arise from such undersea mining operations conducted from the terrain of the littoral state. There are possible conflicts, however, for example, if the borings from England under the Channel should link with the coalfields of the Pas de Calais on the French side, or if borings along the same coast should go beyond the seaward extensions of the land boundaries. Thus far, no mining operations from the surface of the sea appear to have been conducted anywhere, except for the dredging for tin along the coasts of Siam and the Dutch East Indies [100] and sulphur mining by means of shafts driven down from barges through the marshes of Louisiana.[101]

Exploratory drilling for undersea coal deposits has already begun in

---

Lota 1852–1952 (1952), p. 119, describing the Lota undersea workings, pp. 147–149, and two disasters in them in 1927 and 1936; Mouton, *op. cit.*, p. 290.

[92] Gidel, *op. cit.*, Vol. I, pp. 510–511; *N.Y.T.*, Nov. 1, 1950, and May 9, 1958, reporting disasters in undersea coal mines.

[93] N. G. Gedye, "Coast Protection and Land Reclamation," *Encyclopaedia Britannica* (1947), Vol. 5, p. 922, referring to operations at Hodbarrow in Cumberland.

[94] C. M. Anson, "Wabana Iron Ore," paper at annual meeting, Canadian Institute of Mining and Metallurgy (1951), courtesy of Dominion Iron and Steel, Ltd., Sydney, N.S.

[95] *Memorandum on the Regime of the High Seas*, p. 51.

[96] *N.Y.T.*, May 20, 1956. Letter, Embassy of Ireland to writer, Aug. 3, 1956, describes several old undersea copper mines worked in nineteenth century.

[97] W. Lindgren, *Mineral Deposits*, 3rd ed. (1928), p. 757. "In 1917, an invasion of sea water filled most of the mines."

[98] Reid and Flett, *op. cit.*, passim.

[99] Letters to writer, U.S. Geological Survey, Feb. 11, 1952; Bureau of Mines, Feb. 15, 1952. The difficulties encountered in locating materials in this field of undersea mining suggest the desirability of the preparation of a bibliography by some professional library service.

[100] Letter, Bureau of Mines, Feb. 15, 1952. A judgment of the High Court of South-West Africa, rendered on Dec. 10, 1957, rejected the claim of Consolidated Diamond Mines to mine for diamonds in the inter-tidal strip running north from the mouth of the Orange River and sustained the right of a rival company to mine for diamonds from the high water mark out into the ocean for 800 yards from the low water mark. London *Daily Telegraph and Morning Post*, Nov. 8, 1957; London *Times*, Dec. 11, 1957.

[101] Z. W. Bartlett, C. O. Lee, and R. H. Feierabend, "Development and Operation of Sulphur Deposits in the Louisiana Marshes," 4 *Mining Engineering* 803–806 (1952). See *N.Y.T.*, Sept. 21, 1956, for announcement of projected exploitation of "Rich Deposit of Sulphur Found 6 Miles Off Louisiana."

the Firth of Forth, Scotland. The equipment, unlike that used to exploit oil, is moved about and thus presents only temporary obstruction to navigation and fisheries. If, however, as suggested in some of the discussions of British undersea coal mines, which reach in some instances several miles out from the shore, it becomes feasible to install ventilating towers in the offshore waters, similar to those used for long underwater vehicular tunnels in the United States, then legal problems may arise and require adjustment. Similarly if subsidence of the sea bed should occur as a result of mining, causing damage to cables or pipelines, conceivably litigable controversy may arise. These can be safely left for solution to the future because analogies and principles from developed municipal law can be applied.

The principal product now derived from the subsoil of the continental shelf is, of course, oil.[102] Direction drilling from the shore seaward is now extensively supplemented by drilling from "Texas Towers" set up in the offshore areas. But even this method is not, apparently, the only possible approach to this submarine wealth. Wallace E. Pratt suggests:

If we were able to see clearly through the maze of derricks to which we have conditioned our normal vision, we might discover that the most practical approach to great stores of petroleum in the sediments of the continental shelves, once we have proved their existence, is not through the waters of the turbulent sea above them, but along the sea floor beneath those waters; not through a multitude of wells drilled through ocean waters (if wells can be drilled through waters), but through a few galleries constructed upon or excavated into the ocean floor from the adjacent land. Into these galleries, hundreds of miles in aggregate length, perhaps, oil would drain from a score of natural reservoirs distributed along their course, through wells drilled downward and outward in appropriate directions; and through suitable pipelines, traversing these galleries, the oil would then flow landward.[103]

Pratt further is of the opinion "on the basis of our past discoveries in the United States . . . the region of the continental shelves of the earth should contain more than 1,000 billion barrels of oil or approximately 500 times the world's present annual consumption." [104]

[102] Gas, also, is coming into production. See "Natural Gas for Northeastern Cities to Originate in Mexican Gulf," *N.Y.T.*, Aug. 7, 1957. In general, see *Oil and Gas Journal*, published weekly from Tulsa, Oklahoma, since 1902, for world-wide news of the whole integrated industry of oil and gas, including current developments on the continental shelf.

[103] *Op. cit.*, pp. 671–672.

[104] *Ibid.*, p. 669.

Use and Abuse of the Sea

The drilling of wells into the continental shelf from the shore is not likely to raise serious international jurisdictional problems for the immediate future except where they may penetrate the subsoil properly appurtenant to a neighboring coastal state or where such wells may interfere with vehicular or other tunnels sought to be constructed through the subsoil by neighboring states. More pressing are the jurisdictional problems raised by operations from the surface of the epicontinental sea when undertaken beyond the present acknowledged limits of the territorial sea.[105] Aside from possible interference with structures like tunnels in the subsoil, which is not a pressing probability, there may be interference with cables and pipelines already laid or the future laying of them, navigation, fishing from the surface for swimming or sedentary marine organisms, and fishing by means of devices affixed to the sea bed. The United Nations International Law Commission has earnestly studied these problems for several years.[106] Its proposals, which seek to resolve conflicts of national claims to jurisdiction and conflicts of national claims with the principle of the freedom of the seas, were incorporated in the Convention on the Continental Shelf adopted by the United Nations Conference on the Law of the Sea in Geneva in 1958.

Energy: Atomic, Wind, Tidal, Thermal. In the quest for new sources of energy, particularly those capable of commercial use, attention is being focused on the sun and the sea. The development of solar energy is already commanding practical and official interest all over the world.[107] Thought and exploration is also being devoted to utilizing atomic power, the winds, the tides, and the thermal power of the sea. The Economic and Social Council of the United Nations has, in recent years, given considerable impetus to study of these developments.[108]

---

[105] See the important precedental agreement between Great Britain and Venezuela fixing a boundary in the Gulf of Paria, between Trinidad and Venezuela, in relation to submarine areas outside territorial waters, signed at Caracas, Feb. 26, 1942, *British Treaty Series* No. 10 (1942) Cmd. 6400.

[106] *Report* (1956), pp. 38–45; discussed further below, p. 322.

[107] "Symposium in New Delhi: Solar Energy and Wind Power," 121 *Science* 121–122 (1955); "Foreign Scientists to Study U.S. Solar Energy Projects," 33 *DSB* 836 (1955); Guy Benveniste and Merritt L. Kastens, "World Symposium on Applied Solar Energy," 123 *Science* 826–831 (1956); Eugene Ayres and Charles A. Scarlott, *Energy Sources — The Wealth of the World* (1952), Ch. 14; Frederick G. Walton Smith and Henry Chapin, *The Sun, the Sea and Tomorrow: Potential Sources of Food, Energy and Minerals from the Sea* (1954), Ch. 7.

[108] See the marvelous new report by the United Nations Department of Economic and Social Affairs, *New Sources of Energy and Economic Development: Solar En-*

The United States and the Treaty Law of the Sea

There is discussion of harnessing fusion energy derived from the limitless waters of the sea.[109] A program is already under way in Great Britain to use wind power in specially designed aero generators to produce electrical energy. Sites in the Orkney Islands and along the windy coasts of western Scotland, Wales, and Northern Ireland, and at the tip of Cornwall are being considered for the venture.[110] The United States also is interested in the possibility of developing wind turbines for the production of electrical energy.

Tidal power may yet come into extensive practical use. The technical literature contains references to the construction of small tidal mills for mechanical power as early as the eleventh century. Slade's mill at Chelsea, Massachusetts, built in 1734, used the tide. Others appeared in New England and several exist in England. "What was claimed to be the first tidal electric plant was placed in operation" in 1924 at East Saugus, Massachusetts. Since at least 1919 various large-scale projects for the production of tidal power have been promoted in Canada, England, France, the Argentine, and at the Maine-New Brunswick maritime frontier involving use of Cobscook Bay (in the state of Maine) and Passamaquoddy Bay in which the international boundary lies, both bays being arms of the Bay of Fundy. Much exploratory engineering work has been done by both private enterprisers and governments. Hope is entertained that the two-pool device (upper and lower pool) will solve the problem of continuous operation of the plant.[111]

Where the arm of the sea contemplated for use in a tidal power scheme lies wholly within the territorial jurisdiction of the littoral state, no important international problem seems to be created. Where, however, an international boundary runs through one or another of the pools involved or where the construction or operation of the plant affects adversely some fishery resource in the area in which another country claims an interest, as it was thought the Passamaquoddy project would affect the local herring (sardine) crop, problems for international solution arise. Despite this possible interference with a local fishery pri-

---

ergy, Wind Energy, Tidal Energy, Geothermic Energy and Thermal Energy of the Seas, E/2997/ST/ECA/47, May 1957, which contains a selected bibliography of 480 works at pp. 119–150.

[109] Ralph E. Lapp, *Atoms and People* (1956).

[110] Ayres and Scarlott, *op. cit.*, pp. 255–263; *N.Y.T.*, Jan. 31, 1953, July 11, 1955.

[111] *Report to International Joint Commission on Scope and Cost of an Investigation of Passamaquoddy Tidal Power Project*, International Passamaquoddy Engineering Board (1950); Ayres and Scarlott, *op. cit.*, pp. 263–270.

Use and Abuse of the Sea

marily of concern to Canada, both Canada and the United States in 1956 jointly requested the International Joint Commission to conduct investigations and submit a report respecting the Passamaquoddy Tidal Power Project.[112] After the report is made the two governments will determine whether to proceed with the construction of the works.

And, finally, there is being built at Abidjan on the Ivory Coast of French West Africa a sea-thermal engine. This device utilizes the difference of 40° in temperature between the warm surface and cold bottom water in the tropical sea.[113] If successful, it, like the solar energy devices, may contribute to a transformation of many an energy-deficient area of the world.

Disposal of Waste

Both nature and man keep dumping things into the ocean. With the natural processes this study cannot be concerned, except as they affect man's use of the sea. In passing, however, it can be noted that ceaselessly over the geologic ages the elements have deposited debris in the sea. Flowing rivers carry down silt. Over the world millions of tons are deposited on the continental shelf daily. For example, "the Mississippi is building its delta across the shelf at the rate of one mile in 16 to 17 years and is now within 12–15 miles of the edge of the shelf." [114] Rivers carry down "floating islands." Up and down the shores from the Amazon estuary lie "miles of giant forest trees, uprooted and scattered like matches." [115] Glaciers grind off the surface of the dry land; volcanoes spew lava, rock, and dust; offshore winds carry sand and organic matter; waves and currents, where they are not depositing detritus upon the shore, are eating out the shore; and, annually, a million tons of cosmic dust reaches the earth, most of it falling into the abysses. This, together with precipitation from birds and marine organisms, contributes to the great process of sedimentation, so beautifully described by Rachel Carson under the rubric "The Long Snowfall." [116]

Of the many intimately and intricately related shore processes, those

---

[112] "International Passamaquoddy Tidal Power Project," 23 *DSB* 1021–1022 (1950); Act of Jan. 31, 1956, 70 *Stat.* 9; "Passamaquoddy Reference Submitted to IJC," 35 *DSB* 322–323 (1956).

[113] Ayres and Scarlott, *op. cit.*, p. 277; Smith and Chapin, *op. cit.*, pp. 164–169; N.Y.T., Dec. 28, 1953.

[114] Carsey, *op. cit.*, p. 382.

[115] Murphy, *op. cit.*, p. 134, showing pictures of same.

[116] *Op. cit.*, Ch. 6.

are of particular concern here which result in destruction of beaches and other water-front properties, erosion of agricultural and other valuable real estate, the silting up and sand-barring of rivers and harbors, the formation of hooks, the alteration of navigational channels, the flooding of valleys behind the coasts, and the creation of coastal marshes. Coastal communities all over the world have increasingly found it necessary "to take arms against a sea of troubles." National coastal engineering services, to assist local efforts, have been established to devise defenses against the corrosive sea.[117] Annually, much of the "wealth of nations" is being devoured by the sea. It has been estimated that except for such areas as deltas, the coastline of the United States is receding at the rate of a foot a year.

In his seventeenth Meditation, John Donne wrote:

No man is an island entire of itself; every man is a piece of the continent, a part of the main. If a clod be washed away by the sea, Europe is the less, as well as if a promontory were, as well as if a manor of thy friend's or of thine own were.

No doubt the good Dean of St. Paul's was not thinking of our larger problem of erosion, but he chose with uncanny insight a metaphor containing a truth of enduring validity for the community of the sea. Here uniquely is an area in which maximum international cooperation among scientists, engineers, and governmental services ought to be encouraged.

What finds its way into the ocean through the agency of man beggars description. From time immemorial the sea has received into its depths vessels, goods, and human beings, through misadventure and design. Surrendered navies have been sunk, en masse, as at Scapa Flow. Live naval mines, when swept up from their moorings, are sunk by riflefire. Derelicts and floating debris are sunk by gunfire. Hulks are towed out to sea and buried. And now, unhappily, aircraft in discouraging numbers also disappear beneath the waves.

Few tales of the sea are more fascinating than those which deal with the search for sunken treasure. The literature is voluminous. To this are now added accounts of the salvaging of modern vessels, merchant and combat, many millions of tons of which lie strewn over the ocean bottom,

---

[117] *Bulletin of the Beach Erosion Board*, Dept. of the Army, Corps of Engineers, Vol. 10, No. 1 (1956); *Information Circular on Cooperative Studies of Beach Erosion, ibid.* (1956); and *ibid.*, bibliography of *Technical Memorandums*. A graphic example of the problem of erosion occurs along the southern coast of Long Island, New York. See *N.Y.T.*, April 1, 14, 15, 17, 20, 1958.

a considerable number, apparently, in positions from which they may feasibly be recovered.[118]

Into the waters go wastes from surface craft and aircraft, factory ships and whaling ships. Solid ballast was once dumped into harbors and roadsteads. Water ballast, sometimes disease-laden, is discharged into harbors. Oily ballast water from both tankers and dry-cargo ships is discharged into the sea. So is oil sludge when cargo or fuel tanks are cleaned. Flotsam and jetsam are strewn upon the waters until they sink or are cast up on beach or shore. Rubbish and garbage are towed out to sea, though enterprising cities, with valuable beach and shore-front properties, now dispose of them by incineration or use them for land fill. Alert coastal municipalities have spent staggering sums for plants to treat sewage, reducing it to sludge, which, with the grit, is then dumped at sea. Gambling apparatus, firearms, and other implements of crime are ceremoniously consigned to the deeps by the police. Winds offshore steadily deposit in the ocean countless tons of soot, cinders, and dirt. Shore canneries and mills contribute their waste.

From earliest times, the rivers and streams have brought down human and animal wastes, and since the industrial revolution, increasingly enormous quantities of effluents from factory, mill, and municipality.[119] Inexorably the calculus of use and resources has reached the point where great municipalities, faced with shortages of fresh water, may have to reclaim such water from their sewage [120] or consider the possibility of converting sea water to fresh water. For some decades now the pollution of streams and lakes in the United States has reached such dangerous proportions as to require national action.[121]

---

[118] Pierre de Latil and Jean Rivoire, *Man and the Underwater World* (1956), Ch. XV. James Dugan, *Man Under the Sea* (1956), Ch. 10. *N.Y.T.*, Aug. 16, 1948; June 27, Nov. 11, 1950; Dec. 9, 1951; July 5, 1952. *Treasure Maps in the Library of Congress, op. cit.*

[119] See *Publications on Industrial Wastes Relating to Fish and Oysters: A Selected Bibliography*, U.S. Dept. of Health, Education, and Welfare (1953).

[120] *Sewage Treatment in New York City* (pamphlet), City of New York, Department of Public Works (1950); *Bibliography on Sewage Treatment in New York City 1929–1949, ibid.*, citing notably Nathan I. Kass, "Sludge Disposal at Sea," 88 *Water Works and Sewerage* 385–390 (1941), and Henry Liebman, "The Sea-Going Sludge Fleet of New York City," 88 *Water Works and Sewerage* 391 (1941).

[121] *Environment and Health*, Federal Security Agency, Public Health Service (1951), Ch. 3; *Water Pollution in the United States* (1951); *Water Resources Law, Report of the President's Water Resources Policy Commission* (1950), Vol. 3, pp. 118–119; Water Pollution Control Act Amendments of 1956, July 9, 1956, 70 *Stat.* 498–507.

Then there is the strange case of the containers of mustard gas dumped into the sea off Port Elizabeth, Union of South Africa, at the end of World War II. The government of the Union engaged private contractors to take the gas out to a prescribed area and there dump it. That was in April 1946. Subsequently it was discovered that the contractors had dumped a considerable quantity outside and inshore of the prescribed area. When certain trawl fishermen brought up some of the containers in their nets and were injured, the government, in July 1946, prohibited trawling operations forty miles seaward from a considerable distance along shore. Disgruntled fishing companies protested the ban in 1947, 1948, and again in 1952. There is no certainty that a survey of the bottom could locate all the containers. As matters stood in 1952, the ban was being continued but consideration was being given to the possibility of permitting trawlers to operate in the danger area provided the companies furnish the government with suitable indemnities to compensate injured fishermen.[122]

Another oddity arising out of World War II deserves mention. At the end of the war, a large supply of surplus United States naval ammunition was dumped into the Mediterranean about a half mile off Famagusta, Cyprus, in what was believed to be deep water. Actually the water was only forty feet deep. Cypriote fishermen found the cache, retrieved shells from time to time, and used the explosive contents to make bombs wherewith to fish, supplementing their customary dynamiting method. When the recent terrorism broke out in Cyprus, it was believed that the old dump was a source of the explosives used in bombing the British. Efforts were under way in 1956 to destroy the underwater cache or move it out into deeper water.[123]

Now, also since the war, atomic waste is being dumped by some governments into the sea, though the United States is reported to be burying most of its waste on land. In 1956 it was reported that the United States Navy had tested a new atomic antisubmarine depth weapon called the "Lulu." The atomic- and hydrogen-bomb tests in the Pacific have been attended by radioactive pollution of the water and marine life in the immediate vicinity and by radioactive fallout over a larger area. The

[122] *N.Y.T.*, April 29, 1952; letter, Embassy of Union of South Africa to writer, Aug. 6, 1952. Also see U.S. Military Sea Transportation Service announcement of its plan to scuttle a hulk loaded with mustard gas and lewisite in the Pacific Ocean 150 miles off San Francisco. *N.Y.T.*, March 14, 1958.
[123] *N.Y.T.*, June 10, 1956.

Use and Abuse of the Sea

United Nations has given serious attention to these dangers and to the old persistent problem of oil pollution of sea water. These problems will be examined later in the discussion of post-World War II developments.

For the most part no harm appears to be done by this use of the sea for the disposal of waste. It is the great cleanser for all the earth. Everywhere sea birds, marine fauna, bacteria, and gases attack organic matter and restore it, in greater part, to the biological cycle. Chemicals corrode metallic objects; the teredo worm and other organisms destroy other materials. Sediment builds up, measurable in geologic ages. The abysses in many places are miles deep: they can receive much. There, possibly, as well as on the continental shelf, a fallen ship can damage a submarine cable, whether it is plowed in or not. Pipelines can also be injured by falling objects. Floating hulks or debris, until sunk in sufficiently deep water, can endanger shipping. Submarines have been known to strike sunken hulks. Otherwise such dangers as have become evident from deposit of waste in the ocean appear to be confined to the continental shelves, and there primarily to the inner margins.

In bays and harbors, flotsam endangers seaplane areas. Drift jeopardizes pleasure boating and commercial shipping. Ships like the *Driftmaster* in New York Harbor have been specially designed to pick up this floating debris. Sewage pollutes beaches and ruins fisheries, sedentary and migratory. Many a run of anadromous or catadromous fish has been ruined by polluted bays and streams. For several years now, the oyster men of Great South Bay, Long Island, have been in bitter controversy with the duck-farm men on shore, because the runoff waste from the ducks causes disease among the oysters.[124] Tar from road surfaces washed into streams jeopardizes migratory fish. Industrial effluvia, including lethal acids, destroy both plant and animal life in coastal waters. Oil sludge and seepage from shore tanks kill birds, plankton, and fish. Deposits of rubbish can interfere with demersal feeding species. With the new interest in products of the sea and recreation through the sea, all these effects of discharge of waste become increasingly important.

Where extensive reaches of coastal waters are under the control of a single littoral state, much can be done by means of national legislation. Where the coastal waters, in the form of bays, estuaries, and similar indentations, contain the seaward extensions of land boundaries of na-

[124] *N.Y.T.*, April 5, 1951; March 24, 1952; July 17, 1956.

tional states, misuse of those waters immediately creates international problems. Beyond the three-mile limit, misuse of the sea can affect adversely shipping, fisheries, and recreation interests pursued there as well as other interests of the adjacent shore. National states, solicitous of their maritime frontiers, will therefore very likely increasingly seek international solutions for these pressing modern problems.

Recreation

Someday, perhaps, some enterprising scholar will be able to demonstrate a nexus between the rise of the common man, the diffusion of wealth, the new education for health, the increase of leisure, and the mass utilization of the sea for recreational purposes. The comprehensive work on the contemporary relation of the sea to recreation also, apparently, remains to be written.

Incalculable wealth, private and public, local and national, in America and abroad, has in recent generations been invested in seaside cottages, estates, hotels, resorts, amusement parks, wild-life refuges, historic and scenic spots, harbors, infracoastal channels, coastal scenic highways, and beaches. The Mediterranean, the Baltic, the North Sea, the Caribbean and the Gulf of Mexico, the Atlantic and Pacific coast waters of the Americas, and the islands of the Pacific in particular have increasingly been developed with respect to the one phenomenon they all have in common — the protean forms of the sea. The sea gives these numerous developments meaning and has enabled man to create new types of wealth devoted to health, recreation, and aesthetics. Tourism, much of it directed to these littoral areas, has become one of the great staple industries of the modern state, promoted by private national organizations, regulated and subsidized by governmental agencies, and encouraged through several nongovernmental and governmental international organizations.

Among the numerous fascinating uses of the sea for recreational purposes, only four can be selected for comment here: yachting, angling, underwater exploration, and hobbies.

Yachting. Modern yachting, or "pleasure sailing" as distinguished from sailing for commerce or fishing, is thought to be traceable to the prototype pleasure boat which the Dutch East Indies Company presented to Charles II in 1661. Cruising and racing, until the present century the sport of the wealthy or well-to-do, has now, like many of the other sports,

Use and Abuse of the Sea

become available to increasingly large numbers with moderate means. The number of yacht clubs, basins or marinas (nautical hostels), unions, associations, races, regattas, and marine parades have proliferated, embracing both power and sail boats, large and small.[125] Fuel companies now give charts of coastal waters to yachtsmen as they long have given road maps to motorists. Great industries, annual shows, and many popular publications are devoted to supplying the needs of modern yachting.

For a long time, extending well into the nineteenth century, yachting in England was closely related to naval needs, the small vessels being constructed to carry arms in case of need. Thus yachts, maintained at first by wealthy persons, constituted a minor volunteer fleet; they also aided the development of naval architecture. And they still do, many experimental principles and designs being first used in small craft and later transferred, if successful, to larger craft. As the numbers of yachts increased they could contribute substantial services in times of crisis or disaster. Dunkirk in World War II will stand forever as a tribute to the small boat.

In America, for decades, motor-driven yachts have been organized into Power Squadrons, since 1940 as a Coast Guard auxiliary.[126] They render notable service, educating for piloting, navigation, and safety of life and property at sea, conducting search and rescue work, assisting in defense in time of war. Youth recreation is related to yachting not merely through the clubs and associations but also systematically through organizations such as the Girl Scout Mariners and Sea Scout Explorers of the Boy Scouts.

Yacht racing in Europe dates from the early nineteenth century, in America from about 1840. European, American, and international yachting associations or unions now govern periodic regattas and races across the Atlantic or over great distances in the Atlantic and Pacific. Recently the North American Yacht Racing Union, consisting of 23 associations composed of 572 constituent yacht clubs, became a member of the In-

[125] See, annually, *Lloyd's Register of American Yachts: A List of the Power and Sailing Yachts, Yacht Clubs, and Yachtsmen of the United States, the Dominion of Canada, and the West Indies;* and the *American Yachting Trade Directory* (New York); and "Recreational Boating Survey Reveals Staggering Figures," *N.Y.T.*, Dec. 22, 1957.
[126] *The Coast Guard at War, Auxiliary XIX,* U. S. Coast Guard (1948). In 1957 there were 232 branch units of the United States Power Squadrons. See Clarence E. Lovejoy, "Pleasure Boating's Czar," (Charles F. Chapman), *N.Y.T.*, Nov. 8, 1957, and "Executives Guiding Power Squadrons," *N.Y.T.*, Nov. 10, 1957.

The United States and the Treaty Law of the Sea

ternational Yacht Racing Union, which has its seat in England, but with "the complete understanding of autonomy for its affairs in its own area." The codes of racing rules are still separate but in time may be unified.[127] The holding of races or regattas necessitates considerable cooperation from national maritime police, coast guard, and lifesaving services, and navy patrols to safeguard life and property, to maintain order, and to avoid undue interference with commercial shipping.[128]

Some yachtsmen are not gregarious or highly imbued with a competitive spirit: they love to sail the seas alone or with only one or two companions.[129] Annually the press carries accounts of such voyages across the Atlantic or over great distances in other seas. If rafts may be regarded as yachts, then of late a new class of adventurers must be accorded praise for their bold crossing of oceans.

As in the case of other uses of the sea, yachting has its abuses too, the most pressing at the moment arising from small power boats not yet required under the law in the United States to be registered. With twenty-eight million Americans now going afloat per year, many of them in inboard and outboard motor boats on inland and coastal waters, the number of accidents and fatalities has increased enormously in recent years. Unjustifiable hazards are created by immature, reckless, untrained, or irresponsible boat operators. Both the state of New York and the federal government have launched investigations as an aid to legislative remedying.[130]

In sum, yachting, involving numerous supporting industries, a considerable gross investment of wealth, a growing broad base of popular participation, national defense considerations, the new emphasis on

---

[127] *Report of the Annual General Meeting of the N.A.Y.R.U.* (1953). For 1956, the *N.Y.T.*, Dec. 9, 1956, recorded the following: Lloyd's register listed 807 yacht clubs; 820 clubs were affiliated with the North American Yacht Racing Union; 300 motor-boat racing organizations affiliated with the American Power Boat Association; and 10,000 marinas and waterfront docking and launching facilities in operation.

[128] E.g., *U.S. Code of Federal Regulations* (1949), Title 33, Subchapter G [Revised], Part 100, prescribing duties for the Coast Guard in connection with "Marine Regattas or Marine Parades."

[129] Jean Merrien, *Lonely Voyagers* (1954); Ann Davison, *My Ship Is So Small* (1956); and others.

[130] *State of New York: Reports of the Joint Legislative Committee on Motor Boats* (1956–1957); *Study of Recreational Boating Safety*, Hearings before the Committee on Merchant Marine and Fisheries, House of Representatives, 84 Cong., 2 Sess., 1956, and hearings in 1957, under Chairman Herbert C. Bonner; *Study of Recreational Boating Safety*, 85 Cong., 1 Sess., H. Rept. No. 378 (1957); *Small Boat Safety*, 85 Cong., 2 Sess., H. Rept. No. 1603 (1958).

recreative use of leisure, and widespread use of coastal waters and the high seas,[131] must be regarded as a highly important modern use of the sea.

Angling. As in yachting, so in angling, the sea now looms large. Angling is the art of taking fish with a hook and line, with or without a rod, in contradistinction to other methods, as with net, weir, spear, arrow, gaff, or harpoon. Commercial fishermen also use hooks, but the term angling appears to be confined to the particular method when used for sport or recreation.

Much has been written about fresh-water angling since Dame Juliana Berners' *A Treatyse of Fysshynge Wyth an Angle,* 1496, and Izaak Walton's *The Compleat Angler, or the Contemplative Man's Recreation,* 1653. Salt-water angling appears now to be in its infancy. The relation of fresh- to salt-water angling goes beyond mere transference of equipment, technique, and enthusiasms. Pressure of an increasing population of sportsmen upon a limited number of streams, sometimes upon a decreasing supply of fish, and the rise of clubs with control over streams and lakes operated, in England at least, to turn many anglers seaward. Rapid and cheap transportation over land to the shore and reliable, speedy power boats for inshore and offshore fishing have in recent decades unquestionably facilitated this trend to the sea. A new "Brotherhood of the Angle" is in the making.

Fishing for pleasure in salt water utilizes, of course, many different methods and seeks a variety of marine organisms, but for present purposes attention will be focused upon angling. Some migratory fish, anadromous such as the salmon, sea trout, and shad, catadromous such as the eel, are taken in fresh-water streams running to the sea. Otherwise the salt-water denizens are taken inshore — from surf, rocks, piers, jetties, small boats, barges — or offshore, sometimes far out to sea usually from larger boats. Party boats accommodate the public at large, favorite fishing ports supporting dozens or hundreds of them; charter boats carry small parties and frequently are designed to venture far out into deep water for big-game fish.

[131] As an indication of the increased official cognizance given to yachting, see arrangement with Sweden exempting pleasure yachts from all navigation dues, exchange of notes, Stockholm, Oct. 22 and 29, 1930, 47 *Stat.* 2655, *Executive Agreement Series* 21 (hereinafter cited *EAS*), and a similar one with Cuba, Dec. 12 and 17, 1951, 3 *United States Treaties and Other International Agreements* 52 (hereinafter cited *UST*), *Treaties and Other International Acts Series* 2391 (hereinafter cited *TIAS*).

The range of species taken is, of course, enormous, depending on the technique and the locale. The angler can also classify his quarry in terms of nongame and game, small game and big game. "The Contemplative Man" may ruminate while fishing for cod, pollock, or flounder. The piscatorial sportsman seeking bonito, albacore, tuna, broadbill, or marlin, swordfish, tarpon, sailfish, shark, barracuda, amberjack, or squid prepares himself for possibly an exhausting battle. The Waltons of salt-water angling must write not only of philosophy but of drama as well.[132] Though the ancient one in *The Old Man and the Sea* fished for a living and not for pleasure, only a sportsman of the insight and sensitivity of Ernest Hemingway could have dramatized so profoundly man's struggle with great creatures of the deep — noble creatures whom he respects but must nevertheless slay that he may live.

International big-game fishing tournaments, rivaling in excitement the international golf, tennis, and polo matches, have come into vogue beginning with the first tuna-angling matches held at Wedgeport, Nova Scotia, in 1937. Now universities have angling teams representing them in fresh- and salt-water matches. In 1956 the First Intercollegiate Fishing Clinic was held at Wedgeport, with Yale University and St. Francis Xavier University of Antigonish, Nova Scotia, participating. The clinic, sponsored by the Yale Oceanographic Laboratory and the province of Nova Scotia, was rounded off with a tuna match between the two university teams.[133] Numerous local contests, "rodeos," and "salmon derbies" have proliferated, particularly in America.

Fortunately, there was established in 1940 an International Game Fish Association, with headquarters in the American Museum of Natural History and national member clubs throughout the world. At a recent date the I.G.F.A. represented through its International Committee 250 member clubs in over 60 nations and territorial units, and 13 member scientific institutions.[134] It seeks to set standards for the sport, encourage conservation, advance the interests of science, and render informational service to governments and private industry.

Salt-water fishing for sport suggests certain considerations of special

---

[132] See the fascinating accounts in S. Kip Farrington, Jr.'s, two comprehensive works, *Pacific Game Fishing* (1942) and *Fishing the Atlantic, Offshore and On* (1949).

[133] *N.Y.T.*, July 1, 1956.

[134] *The International Game Fish Association Yearbook 1952*, pp. 4–6; letter from Francesca La Monte, secretary, to writer, May 21, 1952. The 1958 "Officials List" shows a growth of numbers in each category.

Use and Abuse of the Sea

importance for the present study, among them the prevention of pollution of streams and coastal waters, the possible effects of mounting annual takes upon the favorite species of marine life, and the need of providing for the safety of the increasing numbers of sportsmen inshore and offshore. Too many disasters, like that of the *Pelican,* off Montauk Point, Long Island, in 1952, with a loss of forty-six out of sixty-five anglers aboard, have occurred in recent decades. Occasionally commercial fishermen protest what they regard as encroachment upon their domains, though usually they cooperate with genuine sportsmen. Conservation schemes must now put into the balance the frequently conflicting demands of fishing for a livelihood and fishing for fun.

Extensive fishing for recreation is here to stay for the foreseeable future. It must be reckoned with. Whether for game fish or nongame fish, angling has increased in various ways the beneficial uses of the sea. It has produced such a constructive multipurpose institution as the International Game Fish Association. It has led to the establishment of the Michael Lerner Marine Laboratory and Live Fish Pools of the American Museum of Natural History at Bimini, in the Bahamas, where important ichthyological studies are conducted, including research in cancer.[135]

In fishing for sport, as in other matters already noted, the national state is primarily responsible for conditions and conduct within the three-mile limit. Beyond that, if it wishes to secure the desiderata for the maintenance of this expanding beneficial and innocent use of the sea, it will find it convenient, if not necessary, to receive the cooperation of other national states.

Underwater Exploration. From the days of antiquity man has sought to free himself from dependence on the atmosphere so that he might penetrate the mysterious realms of the sea. Diving bells, submarines, diving helmets, diving suits, flexible and rigid, bathyspheres, diving masks, one after another, were invented, improved, and exploited. Free-swimming underwater hunting with ingeniously contrived guns was already a popular sport before World War II. The war, as is the case in so many directions, sped up the development of underwater breathing devices. The demolition squads and commandos, the so-called frogmen, to avoid detection from bubbles, used oxygen masks. That type of gear,

---

[135] Farrington, *Fishing the Atlantic,* pp. 224–230; photographs and further description in Paul A. Zahl, "Man-of-War Fleet Attacks Bimini," 101 *National Geographic Magazine* 185–212, at 197–204 (Feb. 1952).

however, had its serious limitations: it could not be used at great depths and it produced dangerous physiological effects. Finally, during the war, the aqualung, utilizing compressed air, was perfected, chiefly through the efforts of Jacques-Yves Cousteau and Philippe Tailliez, French naval officers. Thereupon a new world dawned for man. Now he was really free to descend as far as three hundred feet into the sea, swim about freely, and stay for long periods, without serious physiological effects. Underwater photography having also been perfected in the meantime, the combination of activities has revealed a marvelously beautiful world to the immeasurable profit of man.

A spate of books [136] and articles describing underwater activities and numerous motion pictures of submarine life and adventure have appeared in the past few years. Hunting clubs have been organized in Europe and America. The aqualung has given new impetus to submarine archeology, geology, and biology. It has aided salvaging operations. In conjunction with the submarine camera it has aided underwater fish culture. It has suggested the possible development of underwater agriculture. It has expanded the fields of interest for the oceanographer, the artist, and the writer. If to the demonstrated uses of the aqualung and the submarine camera are added benefits derivable from other developments — medical science; sonar and other electronic devices; deep helmet dives using mixtures of helium and oxygen or hydrogen and oxygen; the benthosphere, an advanced model of Lucius Beebe's pioneering bathysphere; Auguste Piccard's bathyscaphe, the freely operating depth ship; and underwater television — then, indeed, "the best is yet to be."

Already, however, abuses arising out of widespread use of the aqualung are appearing. In the Mediterranean some species of fish have been hunted nearly to extinction; souvenir hunters have despoiled precious submarine archeological remains; holiday makers have ravaged coral formations and sponge beds. In America, where aqualung and other devices can readily be bought in sporting-goods and department stores, great numbers of sportsmen have taken to underwater hunting and have organized numerous clubs, with what effect on various species of marine

---

[136] Especially, Dugan, *op. cit.*, which contains a valuable chronology of underwater history from 415 B.C. to 1955, pp. 309–318, and an excellent classified bibliography, pp. 319–322; Latil and Rivoire, *op. cit.*; Philippe Tailliez, *To Hidden Depths* (1954); Philippe Diole, *4,000 Years under the Sea* (1954); Folco Quilici, *The Blue Continent* (1954).

life it is not yet determined. Underwater "tourism" is being developed in the warmer waters of southern United States and the Caribbean. It may result in control of spoliation of marine life; it may accelerate it. Obviously, the day will soon come when national legislation in various parts of the world will be required to control underwater hunting and exploration if a valuable development is not to result in unnecessary fatalities and irreparable damage to marine life and archeological or other relics in the sea. And it may come about that national administrators will find it necessary to combine their efforts toward reasonable ends under international agreements and agencies.

Literature, Art, Hobbies. Any survey of the uses of the sea for recreational purposes ought at least to mention the literature, art, and hobbies in which the sea is the *sine qua non*. From Homer's *Odyssey* to last week's "best seller," historical and imaginative literature has enabled man vicariously to enjoy the sea. Sundry forms of art from earliest times have depicted seascapes, men and ships at sea, and denizens of the deep. The cultural interests and hobbies centered upon the sea now extant defy mere enumeration. It is sufficient for present purposes to indicate the increasing interest from expert and amateur in the seashore between tides, in weather, in shore and marsh birds, in shell and gem collecting, in bird watching, in photography and painting, in sea chanteys, local history, and regional folklore. The comprehensive guide to these spreading interests and hobbies apparently remains to be written. It would, however, be difficult to find another realm of pleasure so universally shared; in a world of baffling parochialisms the sea in truth remains for countless millions the lingua franca.

Needed: A Social Science of the Sea

Of Matthew Maury's *The Physical Geography of the Sea*, published in 1855, now recognized as the first textbook of modern oceanography, it has been said: "The sea, for the first time, was here viewed as the subject matter of a distinct branch of science with problems of its own." [137] In the century since, oceanography and the score or more other sciences which must deal with the sea have opened up vistas into our oceanic environment which beggar description and defy even cataloguing. Man's use of the sea, of the superjacent airspace, of the bottom and

[137] H. A. Marmer, "Matthew F. Maury," *Dictionary of American Biography*, Vol. 12, pp. 428–431.

the subsoil has, in the same period, expanded *pari passu*. Indeed, ironically, while man is encroaching on the sea, its riches, and its denizens, subjecting them to his will, the sea is encroaching upon the habitat of man. With the geological race this study is not concerned. With man's race against insecurity, disorder, and mutual destruction within his measurable future, it is concerned.

It would be difficult to find any subject, except perhaps religion, about which more has been written than the sea. Voyages and discoveries, as well as the exploitation of products of the sea, have been described from the earliest times. Much has been written about naval warfare and sea power, about commerce, trade, and economic rivalries involving use of the sea. Law governing man's activities relating to the sea has existed from the dawn of history, and it grows apace, stemming continuously from custom, national enactments, and international agreement. International agencies devoted to securing rational use of the sea have arisen in great numbers since the middle of the last century. Individuals, groups, nation-states are now experiencing what appears to be a historic trend toward increased dependence on the sea. There is evident a deepening, world-wide "sense of community" [138] in and about the sea. In these premises it would seem that the time is ripe for a social science of the sea as indeed it was ripe in Maury's time for a physical science of the sea.

The data for the beginnings of such a social science now exist in manageable form: scientific knowledge; the history of man's relation to the oceans; analyses of military, political, and economic forces involving the sea; the records of expanding national services devoted to maritime affairs; a growing international customary and treaty law taking special cognizance of maritime problems; the transactions of numerous international institutions, public and private; the records of an increasing number of international agencies charged with some responsibility concerning use of the sea; vast accumulations of international administrative rules and regulations. Focused on the sea, such a social science would assess the relation of men, groups, nation-states, and international agencies to the central phenomena and seek to discover what the interaction portends for a more secure, orderly, and cooperative world.

[138] For an excellent discussion of the "sense of community" and of "Expanding Community" as a research focus, without, however, any reference to the sea, see Richard W. Van Wagenen, *Research in the International Organization Field: Some Notes on a Possible Focus* (1952).

CHAPTER III

FROM INDEPENDENCE TO THE GREAT WAR: UNFOLDING INTEREST IN TREATY LAW FOR THE SEA

PERHAPS, one day some forward-looking foundation will sponsor the preparation of a comprehensive history and appraisal of the relation of the United States to the sea, as from time to time other monumental works of scholarship have been sponsored, such as the preparation of the papers of Franklin, Jefferson, the Adams family, and Madison. More nearly analogous would be the preparation of the comprehensive history of the Supreme Court made possible by the bequest of the late Justice Oliver Wendell Holmes to the United States. Such a survey of the relation of the United States to the sea would reveal much in perspective and furnish data for the formulation of policy running far into the future. Meanwhile, however, scholars are busy examining specific areas of that relationship. The present study deals with one of those specific areas, the participation of the United States in the formulation and implementation of part of the law of the sea, namely, that part which is embraced in multipartite treaties. That treaty law does not operate *in vacuo*: it arises out of dire necessity to do something intelligible about the facts of the sea and man's relation to those facts.

Some of the law relating to the sea, particularly that governing the rights and duties of shippers, masters, and crews, had its beginnings in the Mediterranean in the pre-Christian era. Through the centuries it has been modified and expanded by custom, by national decrees and legislation, and lately by multipartite treaties.[1] In this process of adjustment and adaptation, private conferences of vessel owners and shippers have

[1] William McFee, *The Law of the Sea* (1950), and Frederic Rockwell Sanborn, *Origins of Early English Maritime and Commercial Law* (1930).

made notable contributions.[2] National and international associations of maritime lawyers, particularly the International Maritime Committee, founded in 1897, have since the late nineteenth century labored to extend the prescriptions of law.

As in many other areas of government, functions once performed by private bodies, such as fire protection and the supply of water, have become public responsibilities. Thus, "life-saving in the country was first conducted on a volunteer basis and at private expense. The beginning was the organization of the Massachusetts Humane Society in 1785 upon the model of the Royal Humane Society of England, which dates from 1774."[3] To this very day, the Trinity Brethren, originally a religious house, incorporated as a guild in 1514 by Henry VIII, are responsible for the maintenance of coastwise lights in England.[4] Nowadays, with governments generally performing the needful safety functions, private organizations primarily perform educative functions and act as pressure groups. Having assumed the responsibilities, governments everywhere during the past century and a half have sought to assure greater safety of life and property offshore and at sea.

Beginning at least with the historic voyages of Captain James Cook in the latter part of the eighteenth century[5] systematic scientific study of the sea has gathered momentum, so that now the number of disciplines and organizations concerned with one or another aspect of the sea is truly staggering. Progressively during the past century and a half, national controversies over fisheries have been subjected to treaty regulation, at first bipartite, now increasingly multipartite. In sum, recent

---

[2] Mance and Wheeler, *International Sea Transport*, Chs. 1–3; see Marx, *International Shipping Cartels*, pp. 176–181 for list of principal conferences and *passim* for description of their activities.

[3] Darrell Hevenor Smith and Fred Wilbur Powell, *The Coast Guard* (1929), p. 23. This is Service Monograph of the United States Government No. 51, of the Institute of Government Research, published by the Johns Hopkins Press, in the 1920s. These monographs (hereinafter cited S.M.), 56 in number, are invaluable to the student of the development of the administrative services of the national government. See also Jeannette Edwards Rattray, *Ship Ashore! A Record of Maritime Disasters off Montauk and Eastern Long Island, 1640–1955* (1955) for additional details of the early lifesaving services; Ch. VI for an interesting account of the New York official called the Wreck Master or Vendue Master, who safeguarded the owners' and insurers' interests or those of the state in wrecked property.

[4] Higgins and Colombos, *The International Law of the Sea*, 2d rev. ed. by C. John Colombos (1951), pp. 233–234.

[5] John Michael Gwyther, *Captain Cook and the South Pacific: The Voyage of the "Endeavour" 1768–1771* (1954); E. W. Hunter Christie, *The Antarctic Problem* (1951), Ch. III.

generations have witnessed a remarkable and unprecedented outpouring of effort to utilize and understand the sea and to regulate human conduct in relation thereto.

It would be possible to describe historically and comprehensively this outpouring of effort; the data exist, but the task would be enormous. For present purposes it is sufficient to slice off a vertical section of this historical development and examine it at least in outline. That section consists of the international official cooperation manifested primarily in multipartite agreements relating to the sea. Our attention will be focused particularly upon those in which the United States has participated. Significantly, one of the earliest multipartite agreements, the Cape Spartel Light Convention, concluded at Tangier, May 31, 1865,[6] was also the first multipartite treaty of any description to which the United States became a party.[7] Since then the technique of using the multipartite agreement for the regulation of matters of common international concern has expanded enormously and the participation by the United States has grown *pro tanto*.

The selection of the multipartite agreements in which the United States has participated as a mode of indicating American official participation in the international regulative process has, in addition to providing a clear historical thread through a labyrinthian development, certain other advantages. These agreements, together with many of the resolutions adopted by intergovernmental bodies, are forms of international legislation. Like domestic legislation, they constitute frequently an end product as well as the beginning of a new process. Any given multipartite agreement, particularly if it deals with an economic, humanitarian, or scientific subject, is likely to be the result of a conflux of efforts exerted by individuals, private national and international groups, and governments.

Since the establishment of the Pan American organization in 1890 and

[6] 14 *Stat.* 679, *Treaty Series* 245 (hereinafter cited *TS*). Also significantly for this study of the sea is the second instrument listed by Manley O. Hudson in his "Introduction" to *International Legislation* (1931 and years following), Vol. 1, p. xix (hereinafter cited Hudson, *I.L.*), the Convention on the Establishment of a Telegraph Line between Europe and America, and Protocol, signed at Paris, May 16, 1864. The United States was not a party to this agreement.

[7] For a classified list of all multipartite agreements of a nonpolitical and nonmilitary character to which the United States was a party in the period 1865–1935, see Reiff, "The United States and International Administrative Unions," *op. cit.*, pp. 629–631.

the League of Nations in 1919, international organizations themselves have contributed significantly to this conflux of efforts. The records of the conferences [8] which produce the multipartite agreements usually contain a summation of the private and public efforts resulting in the conference. These are invaluable data for the student of social processes. The records kept by the international agencies usually established under such treaties then provide a continuing record of development, equally valuable to the social scientist. In brief, multipartite agreements and many of the resolutions of the great international organizations constitute definitive, formal commitments, in writing, supported usually by elaborate and authentic documentation. The social scientist can begin with them and proceed backward or forward. They signalize the end of one process and the beginning of another. In the parlance of the geodetic surveyor, they constitute control points or bench marks from which, by a process of triangulation or traverse, order, at least conceptually, can be brought into sectors of international relations.

As is the case with so much of modern history, the particular developments relating to the sea under present scrutiny fall into three great periods: from the American Revolution to World War I; the interwar period, 1919 to 1939; and the period since then. The first period is characterized by an unfolding interest by the United States, as well as other maritime nations, in international efforts to solve common problems dealing with the sea; the second, by numerous conferences, the extensive use of international legislation, the setting up of many international organizations, among them the League of Nations, itself the progenitor of other organizations; and the third, by the establishment of the United Nations, the revamping of old and creation of new institutions, and the bringing of many international organizations into formal relationship to the United Nations, as specialized agencies, or as other intergovernmental organizations, or as nongovernmental organizations.

FROM INDEPENDENCE TO THE CIVIL WAR

For the purposes of the present discussion, the first period — from the Revolutionary War to World War I — falls naturally into two eras, before

[8] Winifred Gregory, *International Congresses and Conferences 1840–1937* (1938); Hans Aufricht, *Guide to League of Nations Publications: A Bibliographical Survey of the Work of the League 1920–1947* (1951); Ruth D. Masters, *Handbook of International Organizations in the Americas* (1945); and the extensive headnotes to each

From Independence to the Great War

and after the Cape Spartel Light Agreement of 1865. Though no multipartite treaty was signed by the United States in the first era, certain developments should be noted for their influence upon subsequent events. These developments can be summarized briefly under a few heads: freedom of navigation, assistance and salvage, protection of seamen, fisheries, the establishment of national services, advancement of safe navigation, suppression of piracy and the slave trade, and scientific exploration. Each of these topics has its voluminous literature. Certain of the significances can, however, be briefly noted.

New Nation, New Responsibilities

Freedom of Navigation. As a maritime nation, the American people, from earliest colonial times have been interested, with some notable lapses, in building and operating their own merchant marine. They have also, rather uniformly, insisted on freedom of navigation for that marine in rivers and lakes bordering upon the United States, on the high seas, and in waters under the jurisdiction of foreign states. With the merchant marine policy, important as it is, this study cannot be here concerned.[9] With respect to freedom of navigation, the United States, beginning with its first international compact as a political entity, the Treaty of Amity and Commerce with France, signed at Paris, February 6, 1778,[10] regularly sought in its treaties on commerce assurances of free navigation in the coastal waters and harbors of foreign powers.[11]

Traditionally the United States has also insisted on freedom of passage through straits, exemplified in the Danish Sound Dues dispute which was settled in 1857, and on access to international rivers.[12] Not until 1934, however, when it perfected the 1919 convention relating to waters in

---

of the instruments reproduced in Hudson's monumental *International Legislation*. For the period since World War II, *Ten Years of United Nations Publications 1945 to 1955: A Complete Catalog* (1955) and other sources cited below.

[9] See J. G. B. Hutchins, "One Hundred and Fifty Years of American Navigation Policy," 53 *Quarterly Journal of Economics* 238–260 (1939); and works by Saugstad and Bryant, *op. cit.*

[10] 8 Stat. 12, TS 83.

[11] See *Subject Index of the Treaty Series and Executive Agreement Series* (1931), pp. 154–155 (hereinafter cited *Subject Index*). For the best historical notes on the negotiation of each treaty up to the Civil War, see Hunter Miller, *Treaties and Other International Acts of the United States of America* [1776–1863], 8 vols. (1931–1948).

[12] Charles Cheney Hyde, *International Law*, pp. 519–565; Robert Renbert Wilson, *The International Law Standard in Treaties of the United States* (1953), pp. 105–120.

Africa, did the United States become a party to any multipartite agreement on the subject of freedom of navigation in peacetime.[13]

Assistance, Salvage, Aid to Seamen. From the beginning, by means of the existing customary methods, that is, bipartite treaties and diplomacy, the United States also sought assurances of assistance and salvage for vessels in distress and protection of shipwrecked seamen. Thus, Article 18 of the Treaty of Amity and Commerce of 1778 with France promised the following:

> If any Ship belonging to either of the Parties their People or Subjects, shall, within the Coasts or Dominions of the other, stick upon the Sands or be wrecked or suffer any other Damage, all friendly Assistance and Relief shall be given to the Persons shipwrecked or such as shall be in danger thereof; and Letters of safe Conduct shall likewise be given to them for their free and quiet Passage from thence, and the return of every one to his own Country.

The same treaty obligated France to help protect Americans and their vessels against the Barbary powers (Art. 8) and provided for refuge from "stress of weather, pursuit of pirates or enemies, or other urgent necessity" (Art. 19). An agreement of 1840 with Hanover provided that "the ancient and barbarous right to wrecks of the sea shall be entirely abolished with respect to the property belonging to the citizens or subjects of the contracting parties."[14] Similar provisions creating mutual obligations to aid ships and mariners appeared in some fifty treaties with nearly as many seafaring powers up to the Civil War.[15]

Fisheries. Strange as it may seem, the United States concluded very few treaties directly concerned with fishing up to the twentieth century. There were, of course, from the beginning numerous treaty provisions dealing with the importation of fish products and with refuge for fishing vessels. In the decade before the Civil War agreements with the Hawaiian Islands and Peru accorded refitting and trading privileges to whalers. In the last decade of the century there were eight agreements with Great Britain and one with Russia concerning the fur-seal fisheries

---

[13] Convention on Revision of the General Act of Berlin of Feb. 26, 1885, and the General Act and Declaration of Brussels of July 2, 1890, signed at Saint-Germain-en-Laye, Sept. 10, 1919, proclaimed as effective for the United States, Nov. 3, 1934; 49 *Stat.* 3027, TS 877. Generally, in this work short titles for treaties will be used; a checklist of perfected treaties which are cited appears in Appendix II.

[14] Art. 8, Treaty of Commerce and Navigation, concluded May 20, 1840, 8 *Stat.* 552, TS 153.

[15] See *Subject Index,* "Protection of Persons," "Salvage," "Seamen," and "Wrecks."

in the North Pacific, which led up to the settlement of that controversy by means of a multipartite agreement in 1911.

Otherwise stipulations in treaties in the period before 1914 appear chiefly in treaties with France, Russia, and Great Britain. Thus, in the 1778 treaty with France there is a reciprocal obligation to "abstain and forbear to fish" within the possessions of the two parties, respectively (Art. 9), and an obligation upon the United States not to interfere with French fishing on the banks of Newfoundland (Art. 10). In a new treaty in 1800 the two governments repeated these obligations and added: "But the whale and seal fisheries shall be free to both in every quarter of the world." [16]

The treaty of 1824 with Russia reads like a tale from never-never land. It was agreed (Art. 1) that

in any part of the Great Ocean, commonly called the Pacific Ocean or South Sea, the respective citizens or subjects of the high contracting powers shall be neither disturbed nor restrained, either in navigation, or in fishing, or in the power of resorting to the coasts, upon points which may not already have been occupied, for the purpose of trading with the natives,

provided that there be no illicit trading at established posts and no trade in liquor or firearms with the natives.[17]

The principal agreements relating to fishing were with Great Britain and concerned American participation in the fisheries off the Newfoundland coast. The Provisional Articles of Peace in 1782 (Art. 3) granted to the United States a right to continue in the fisheries which the American colonists had shared in common with other British colonists before the separation.[18] Thereupon ensued differences concerning the nature and extent of the right which took thirteen subsequent agreements, an arbitration at The Hague in 1910, and three additional agreements finally to settle.

In sum, then, except for difficulties encountered off the Newfoundland coasts, American fishermen, sealers, and whalers freely roamed the high seas in the Atlantic and the Pacific from the Arctic to the Antarctic for

---

[16] Art. 27, Convention of Peace, Commerce, and Navigation, concluded Sept. 30, 1800, 8 *Stat.* 178, TS 85.

[17] Convention on Navigation, Fishing, Trading, and the Northwest Coast of America, concluded April 17, 1824, 8 *Stat.* 302, TS 298.

[18] Concluded Nov. 30, 1782, 8 *Stat.* 54, TS 102; also Charles A. Carter, *Treaties Affecting the Northeastern Fisheries* (1944).

the century and a half up to the conclusion of sundry conservation treaties in the twentieth century.

Establishment of National Services. As in the case of many other struggles of man against nature, governments have only relatively lately assisted the individual against the sea. The United States, sometimes in imitation, sometimes in advance of other nations, but generally *pari passu* with them established one by one, the governmental services now regarded as indispensable to prudent use of the sea. A few of the more important services established before 1865 can be briefly noted.

"One of the first official acts of President Washington was to write a letter to the keeper of Sandy Hook Light, directing him to keep the light burning until Congress should provide for its maintenance."[19] A Lighthouse Service established by the ninth act of the first Congress in 1789 then took over the lighthouses set up by the colonies and states, supplementing them in time with additional lighthouses, lightships, beacons, and buoys.[20] In 1790 Congress provided for a number of revenue cutters.[21] At first constituting primarily a floating police assisting in the enforcement of payment of customs and tonnage dues it gradually was charged with numerous other maritime duties including defense, assistance and salvage, lifesaving, relief in disasters, and suppression of slave trade and piracy. In 1915 a then separate Life-Saving Service and the Revenue-Cutter Service were consolidated under the name of the Coast Guard.[22] In 1939, the Lighthouse Service was transferred to the Coast Guard.

In the midst of recurring epidemics of yellow fever in New York City and Philadelphia,[23] Congress in 1796 authorized the President to direct revenue officers, officers commanding forts, and the revenue cutters to aid the states in the execution of their quarantine laws.[24] Two years later

[19] George Weiss, *The Lighthouse Service*, S.M. No. 40 (1926), p. 2.
[20] *Ibid.*, pp. 2–3.
[21] Smith and Powell, *The Coast Guard*, p. 3.
[22] *Ibid.*, p. 37. See Stephen H. Evans, *The United States Coast Guard 1790–1915: A Definitive History* (1949); Glen Perry, *Watchmen of the Sea* (1938); and *U.S. Coast Guard: Bibliography* (1950).
[23] J. H. Powell, *Bring Out Your Dead: The Great Plague of Yellow Fever in Philadelphia in 1793* (1949). " 'Bring Out Your Dead!' is the cry tradition assigns to the carters in the great plague in London, 1664/5," and to the Philadelphia visitation as well. P. 290.
[24] Ralph Chester Williams, *The United States Public Health Service 1798–1950* (1951), p. 68. This is one of the most fascinating and heartening accounts of a governmental service within the ken of the present writer.

From Independence to the Great War

Congress provided for the establishment of marine hospitals for sick and disabled seamen of the American merchant service.[25] Subsequent acts, including measures in 1878 and 1893 [26] nationalizing the quarantine systems, contributed to the development of a Public Health Service for the United States which is probably without a peer throughout the world.

On Jefferson's recommendation in 1806, Congress authorized a survey of the coasts within twenty leagues of the shore. Sundry difficulties, including the absence of the necessary instruments and the impediment of the War of 1812, delayed commencement of the work until 1816. By 1843, the Coast Survey also conducted a geodetic survey on land and studied the hydrography of the adjacent coastal waters. Magnetic surveys were begun soon afterward.[27]

In 1830 a depot of charts and instruments was established and in 1842 it became possible for the navy department to set up an astronomical observatory. In passing, the relation of astronomy to the sea should be emphasized. Without accurate time (and chronometers) it is difficult to fix longitude precisely. Precise longitude is essential to safe navigation, charting, and geodetic surveying generally. Under Maury, presently to be noted, the above agencies engaged in extensive astronomical, hydrographical, meteorological, and magnetic work.[28]

Two other fairly separate services which contributed to safety at sea can be mentioned at this point. Supplementing the existing private lifesaving services, Congress for the first time, in 1837, provided for seasonal cruises by the Revenue Cutter Service along the coast for the relief of distressed mariners. By 1847 provision was made for federal shore stations. Subsequent acts, including the organic act of 1878, expanded the service.[29] An act of 1838 provided for the inspection of "vessels propelled

---

[25] *Ibid.*, p. 29.

[26] *Ibid.*, pp. 82–84. See also, Laurence F. Schmeckebier, *The Public Health Service*, S.M. No. 10 (1923), Ch. 1.

[27] Gustavus A. Weber, *The Coast and Geodetic Survey*, S.M. No. 16 (1923), pp. 1–5. See also by the Coast and Geodetic Survey, *Journal of the Coast and Geodetic Survey: Sesquicentennial Number, October 1957*, No. 7 (1957), and A. Joseph Wraight and Elliott B. Roberts, *Coast and Geodetic Survey 1807–1957: 150 Years of History* (1957); and *150 Years of Service 1807–1957, Sesquicentennial Celebration* (1957).

[28] G. A. Weber, *The Naval Observatory*, S.M. No. 39 (1926), pp. 1–17, and *The Hydrographic Office*, S.M. No. 42 (1926), pp. 17–26.

[29] Smith and Powell, *The Coast Guard, op. cit.*, pp. 23–33.

in whole or in part by steam" to detect the causes of explosions in their boilers, and in 1852 a "Steamboat Act" laid the foundations of the present extensive steamboat-inspection service.[30]

In the same period, of course, numerous other statutes imposed multifarious duties upon these agencies and particularly upon the Customs Service,[31] in response, sometimes belatedly, to the demands of individuals and groups and to the needs created by changing technologies related to the sea, notably the change from sail power to steam power. A Bureau of Navigation, charged with a large share of administrative supervision over merchant ship affairs, was created in 1872.[32] Under successive reorganization schemes in the years 1936 to 1946, both the Steamboat Inspection Service and the Bureau of Navigation were transferred to the Coast Guard.

Expanding Nation, Expansion Seaward

Science and Navigation. Three American geniuses contributed to use and understanding of the sea during this period before the Civil War: Benjamin Franklin (1706–1790), Nathaniel Bowditch (1773–1838), and Matthew Fontaine Maury (1806–1873).

Not much attention has been given to Franklin's interest in things maritime, yet the practical and scientific knowledge of the sea received considerable impetus from his ceaseless probings beyond the margin of the accepted. Thus, as postmaster for the colonies, he was consulted in 1769 or 1770 in relation to the differentials in time for the east and westbound packets sailing between England and New York, the westbound voyages taking as much as a fortnight longer. On investigation he found that the packets, under the British masters, sailed in and against the Gulf Stream. American whalers out of Nantucket had long been acquainted with the location and characteristics of the Gulf Stream and used it or avoided it for their purposes, up and down the coast, from New England to the Bahamas. Franklin got a Nantucket mariner to chart the Gulf Stream and provide sailing directions for both east and westbound voyages, to utilize and avoid the Gulf Stream respectively,

---

[30] Lloyd M. Short, *Steamboat-Inspection Service*, S.M. No. 8 (1922), pp. 2–3.

[31] Laurence F. Schmeckebier, *The Customs Service*, S.M. No. 33 (1924), *passim.*

[32] Lloyd M. Short, *The Bureau of Navigation*, S.M. No. 15 (1923), *passim.* For the present comprehensive functions of the Coast Guard in these several fields, see *United States Government Organization Manual 1957–1958*, pp. 122–125, 621.

From Independence to the Great War

and presented a copy to the appropriate British authorities. As he records, quaintly, the British captains "slighted it however." [33]

Franklin's letters teem with observations and suggestions about seafaring matters; among the topics are these: compartmentalization, construction and design of ships and sails, dehydrating of vegetables for sailors' fare, a suggestion of the principle of the screw propeller, the salinity of sea water and its distillation to potability, tides, the double vessel principle, fire and collision prevention, prevention of anchor hawser parting, the use of the thermometer for detecting currents, the steamship, and sundry other ideas, many of which are now in routine use.[34]

Nathaniel Bowditch, a boy when Franklin was an old man, achieved considerable notoriety as a youthful mathematician in his native village of Salem, Massachusetts. There, in recognition of his precocity, he was given access to the philosophical and mathematical library of Dr. Richard Kirwan, of Cloughballymore, Ireland, which then reposed in the Salem Atheneum. An American privateer roaming in British waters had captured the collection on its way to London and had brought it to Beverly. From there it had found its way to Salem — a rare naval prize indeed. Bowditch devoured the works. Later, at sea in his early twenties, he corrected and revised the current navigation handbook of the Englishman, John Hamilton Moore. By 1801 he had finished *The New American Practical Navigator*. "The revision was so thorough that the American product was in effect a different book, although still faintly resembling the original. Bowditch published his *Practical Navigator* in 1802, under his own name, and since it was an unrivaled aid to navigators few vessels, British or American, went to sea without a copy." The Russians, Swedes, and French then adopted it and the fame thereof soon spread throughout all the maritime nations of Europe.[35]

It was Franklin's good fortune to be highly esteemed, while he could

---

[33] Letter No. 1597 to David Le Roy on "Maritime Observations," Aug. 1785, reprinted from the *Transactions of the American Philosophical Society*, Vol. II, 1786, p. 294, in Albert Henry Smyth, *The Writings of Benjamin Franklin*, 10 vols. (1907), Vol. IX, pp. 372–413. A chart and tables of observations of the Gulf Stream accompany this letter. See also letter No. 513 to Anthony Todd, Oct. 29, 1769, in which Franklin relates how he got Captain Folger of Nantucket to take observations of the Gulf Stream, Vol. V, pp. 232–233.

[34] *Writings, op. cit.*, Vols. I, p. 80; V, pp. 232–233; IX, pp. 147–149.

[35] S. W. Bryant, *The Sea and the States*, pp. 144–145; also, *Dictionary of American Biography*, Vol. II, pp. 496–498 (hereinafter cited *D.A.B.*).

still enjoy it, in both Europe and America. It was not so for Lieutenant Matthew Fontaine Maury: he was appreciated in his lifetime only in Europe. One of the tragic ironies of history is the strange oblivion in which Americans have, until recently, kept the "Pathfinder of the Seas," towering figure in the expanding scientific efforts related to the sea in this pre-Civil War period.

Before he took charge of the Depot of Charts and Instruments of the Navy on July 1, 1843, he had already amassed a distinguished record. In 1836 he had published *A New Theoretical and Practical Treatise on Navigation*, which for a time took the place of Nathaniel Bowditch's historic *Practical Navigation* as a textbook for junior officers in the navy. He had advocated great circle navigation, reform in the navy, and a naval academy.

Among his numerous achievements during nearly twenty years as superintendent of the depot, with which the Naval Observatory was for a time combined, were the following: pioneering internationally recognized astronomical work; *Wind and Current Chart of the North Atlantic* (1847); and *Abstract Log for the Use of American Navigators* (1848), later issued as *Explanations and Sailing Directions to Accompany the Wind and Current Charts* (1851), forerunner of the present *Pilot Charts* or *Sailing Directions* of the Hydrographic Office.

As a result of Maury's initiative an international congress was held at Brussels in 1853 at which was adopted a uniform system of recording oceanographic data for the naval vessels and merchant marine of the whole world. He gave advice to Cyrus W. Field on the laying of the first trans-Atlantic cable in 1853. In 1855 he published *The Physical Geography of the Sea*, now recognized as the first textbook of modern oceanography. In the same year he prescribed the North Atlantic shipping lanes or tracks which, unfortunately, came into general use only toward the end of the century.[36] In his amazingly full life he made numerous other contributions to the sciences of astronomy, navigation, hydrography, and meteorology. Maury combined uniquely an insatiable scientific curiosity about the sea with an unquenchable zest to subject it more practically to the use of man.[37]

[36] See appreciative article by Clarence S. Kempff, "Ship Lanes of the North Atlantic," *Encyclopaedia Britannica* (1947), Vol. 20, pp. 539–540.

[37] See Charles Lee Lewis, *Matthew Fontaine Maury: The Pathfinder of the Seas* (1927), a pre-eminently fine biography; *D.A.B.*, Vol. XII, pp. 428–431; for a few intimate glimpses of him on his mission to England, see James Morris Morgan,

From Independence to the Great War

Born in Virginia of a family rooted deep in its traditions, Maury chose the South at the outbreak of the Civil War. He served the cause of the Confederacy ardently. At home he experimented with submarine mines and advocated vigorous naval policies. Critical of the political leaders of the Confederacy, he was soon sent to England as one of the agents to procure blockade runners from British shipyards. After the war he held for a short time a post to encourage immigration under Maximilian's government in Mexico. Returning to the United States from England in 1868, he accepted the chair of meteorology at the Virginia Military Institute, where he remained until his death in 1873. But a strange darkness descended upon his memory and his contributions to the sciences of the sea. A recent monumental work on oceanography does not mention Maury once in its 1087 pages.[38] Happily, Rachel Carson renders him fine tribute in *The Sea Around Us* and calls him the "founder of the science of oceanography."[39] In 1930, Maury was admitted to the Hall of Fame at New York University.

And now that the portrait of General Robert E. Lee has been hung in the halls of West Point and upon the walls of the White House, it may be time to restore Matthew Fontaine Maury fully to the roster of the American Great.

Preoccupation with Maury should not obscure his colleague, John Mercer Brooke, who invented a sounding device which revolutionized oceanographic work.[40]

Guano, Pirates, and Slaves. It would indeed be appropriate to conclude this outline of developments in the pre-Civil War period with the monumental work of Maury. Other events and developments, however, must be noted. Thus, in the feverish scramble for guano deposits in the 1850s, Congress enacted a statute in 1856 declaring that whenever any citizen of the United States discovered a deposit of guano on any island,

---

Recollections of a Rebel Reefer (1917), pp. 96, 100, 102–107, 114; for his rivalry with Charles Wilkes, see Daniel MacIntyre Henderson, *The Hidden Coasts: A Biography of Charles Wilkes* (1953), pp. 32–33, 38, 228.

[38] Sverdrup, Johnson, and Fleming, *The Oceans* (1946). Ch. 1 summarizes the contributions of great oceanographers. Maury is not mentioned, nor is he cited anywhere in the work.

[39] Pp. 214–215, 226.

[40] *D.A.B.*, Vol. III, pp. 69–70. See also appreciative appraisal of both Maury and Brooke in John Scott Douglas, *The Story of the Oceans* (1952), pp. 6–8; and of Maury in N. L. Canfield, "Ships' Weather Observations: Part 1, Developments up to the 20th Century," 1 *Mariners Weather Log* 157–160 (1957).

rock, or key, not within the lawful jurisdiction of any other government, not occupied by the citizens of any other government, and took peaceable possession of it and occupied it, the island, rock, or key could, "at the discretion of the president, be considered as appertaining to the United States." In the following quarter century some seventy islands were registered in the department of state under this act. Consistently with the prevailing attitudes toward wildlife, Congress made no provision for conservation of the wealth-creating oceanic birds.[41]

Piracy, or robbery at sea, appears to be as old as man's use of the sea.[42] It survives now only notably off the China coast, where, as already noted, sea robbers are bold enough to make off with submarine cables and are led on occasion, so it is reported, by female buccaneers. The first treaties concluded by the United States provided for assistance against and refuge from pirates.[43] Congress immediately (1790) passed legislation in pursuance of its constitutional mandate "to define and punish piracies and felonies committed on the high seas."[44] Numerous expeditions were sent out during the first half of the nineteenth century against pirates in the Mediterranean, Caribbean, and Pacific. Congress and the state department were much occupied in the same period with complaints about piratical depredations in the Gulf of Mexico and the waters surrounding the West Indies.[45] Since any national state may take jurisdiction over piracy directly under customary international law, it was thought until recently that no multipartite treaty was necessary on the subject. The International Law Commission in its 1956 report,[46] however, deemed it desirable to enjoin cooperation in the repression of piracy, to define the act to include piracy by aircraft, and to set forth the repressive measures

---

[41] Act of Aug. 18, 1856, 11 *Stat.* 119; John Bassett Moore, *A Digest of International Law*, 8 vols. (1906), Vol. I, pp. 556–580 (hereinafter cited Moore, *Digest*). The act of 1856 seems also to have permitted assumptions of title by the United States, supported by force if necessary, without much consideration of the rights of other states. See Jones v. U.S., 137 U.S. 202 (1890). Green H. Hackworth, *Digest of International Law*, 8 vols. (1940–1944), Vol. I, pp. 502–524 (hereinafter cited Hackworth, *Digest*). See Jenks Cameron, *The Bureau of Biological Survey*, S.M. No. 54 (1929), on history of conservation of wildlife, pp. 1–21, and Appendix 4 on laws.

[42] McFee, *op. cit.*, Ch. VIII.

[43] *Subject Index*, p. 167.

[44] "Piracy Laws of Various Countries," 26 *A.J.I.L. Supp.* 893–902 (1932); Hyde, *op. cit.*, pp. 767–773.

[45] Bryant, *op. cit.*, pp. 136–143, 211–212, 231–234; and Adelaide R. Hasse, *Index to United States Documents Relating to Foreign Affairs 1828–1861*, 3 vols. (1914–1921), Vol. II, pp. 1289–1290.

[46] *Op. cit.*, pp. 27–29.

From Independence to the Great War

that may justifiably be taken. The United Nations Conference on the Law of the Sea in Geneva in 1958 accordingly incorporated these adjustments of the law to modern times in its Convention on the High Seas.

Congress similarly enacted legislation immediately (1794) to discourage slave trading, including a prohibition of the use of American ports to fit out vessels for the slave trade.[47] Nine other acts on the subject were passed up to 1862. Although the United States entered into several agreements with Great Britain, starting in 1814, relating to the ocean-borne slave traffic,[48] it participated in none of the multilateral efforts until the General Act for the Repression of African Slave Trade was adopted at Brussels in 1890. This will be discussed later.

Exploration. Among the more dramatic developments in the two decades immediately preceding the Civil War, besides the designing and exploitation of the clipper ship,[49] were the voyages of exploration sponsored by the United States government. Private sealers, whalers, and traders had since at least the latter part of the eighteenth century ventured boldly into the Far East and Far North and South. An American sealer, Captain Nathaniel B. Palmer, of Stonington, Connecticut, is credited with the first sighting in 1820 of the Antarctic mainland, now named Palmer Peninsula. It was not, however, until 1840, as a result of the expedition under Lieutenant Charles Wilkes, that the existence of Antarctica as a continent became known.[50]

Joining the procession of official exploring and surveying expeditions already commenced by Great Britain, Russia, and France,[51] the United States, beginning with a survey of Georges Shoal and Bank off the Massachusetts coast [52] by Wilkes in 1837, entered upon a vigorous program

---

[47] Act of March 22, 1794, 1 *Stat.* 347.

[48] *Subject Index*, p. 196. For the controversies relating to visit and search connected with the slave traffic, see Hyde, *op. cit.*, pp. 765–767, and Wilson, *op. cit.*, pp. 120–134.

[49] Bryant, *op. cit.*, pp. 236–238, 267–274.

[50] *Sailing Directions for Antarctica*, Hydrographic Office No. 138 (1943), p. 9. Lieutenant Wilkes' own account of the voyage is thrilling, *Narrative of United States Exploring Expedition 1838–1842*, 5 vols. (1845), particularly Vol. II, Chs IX–XI. Also, Henderson, *op. cit.*, Ch. 7.

[51] *Sailing Directions, op. cit.*, pp. 9–13; more extensively, Christie, *The Antarctic Problem*, Chs. 3–9.

[52] For the continuing contemporary importance of Georges Bank, which lies due east off Cape Cod, see Howard A. Schuck, *Offshore Grounds Important to the United States Haddock Fishery*, U.S. Fish and Wildlife Service Research Report No. 32 (1952). Several diagrammatic maps are on pp. 4–16.

of hydrographic surveys and explorations.[53] Among the most important in the period under discussion were these: the United States Exploring Expedition, 1838–1842, under Commander Charles Wilkes, which operated in the Antarctic area and the Pacific; the Expedition to Japan, 1852–1854, under Commodore Matthew Calbraith Perry, which in addition to performing its diplomatic mission gathered great quantities of oceanographic data; the North Pacific Surveying Expedition, 1853–1859, under Commander Cadwallader Ringgold, who, on his illness, was succeeded by Lieutenant John Rodgers; and two expeditions in search of Sir John Franklin in the Arctic, one by Lt. Edward J. De Haven, 1850–1851, and another by Dr. Elisha P. Kane, 1853.[54]

These expeditions, in addition to the numerous routine missions of the hydrographic service in North and South American waters, contributed enormously to the expanding scientific fields of oceanography, hydrography, meteorology, geology, biology, botany, magnetism, geodesy, astronomy, navigation, ethnography, and geography, to mention only the larger categories of disciplines.

Flag Signal Code and Rules of the Road. The United States did not participate in the adoption of the first International Flag Signal Code drafted in 1855 under the direction of the British Board of Trade. Americans continued to use for a time codes devised by private enterprise,

---

[53] For a full detailed list of the hundreds of surveys from 1837 up to 1924, see *Report of the Hydrographic Office*, Oct. 3, 1924, in the *Annual Report of the Navy Department for the Fiscal Year 1924*, at pp. 216–235; lists are also in Weber, *The Hydrographic Office*, pp. 31–33, and *Information on Hydrographic Office Charts and Publications*, H.O. Circular No. 3 (1956).

[54] The bibliography of the Arctic and Antarctic regions is, of course, enormous. For excellent selective lists, see *Sailing Directions, op. cit.*, pp. ix–xi; the "Arctic book list" by V. Stefansson, in M. C. Shelesnyak, *Across the Top of the World*, Office of Naval Research (1947), at pp. 50–71; and the list in Edward H. Smith, *The Marion Expedition to Davis Strait and Baffin Bay Under Direction of the U.S. Coast Guard, Scientific Results, Part 3*, Bulletin No. 19 (1931), pp. 205–216. Students of the subject of polar exploration rejoice to know that Dr. Vilhjalmur Stefansson has in preparation an *Encyclopedia Arctica* (which may run into twenty volumes) and has made available for scholars his extensive collection of Arctic and Antarctic materials at the Dartmouth Library (*N.Y.T.*, Dec. 10, 1951). The massive, long-awaited *Arctic Bibliography, Prepared for and in Cooperation with the Department of Defense, Under the Direction of the Arctic Institute of North America*, edited by Marie Tremaine, has appeared since 1953 in six volumes up to 1956. For an excellent brief "Bibliographical Index" to both polar regions, with helpful critical comment, see R. N. R. Brown, *The Polar Regions: A Physical and Economic Geography of the Arctic and Antarctic* (1927), pp. 225–236. Also, J. D. M. Blyth, "The Polar Regions in Literature," 174 *British Book News* 789–793 (1955).

From Independence to the Great War

chiefly that published by Henry J. Rogers in Baltimore in 1854.[55] In due course, however, American shipping came to use the international code. The advent of radio and other means of communication has not eliminated the need for flag or other visual signals, which remain useful, even essential, on numerous occasions. Anticipatorily it may be noted that in pursuance of a recommendation of the Washington Radiotelegraph Conference of 1927, an international standing committee was set up under the British Board of Trade for the purpose of keeping the flag signal code up to date.[56]

Congress did, however, speedily enact legislation adopting the new rules of the road for navigating on the high seas proposed by Great Britain in 1863.[57] The advent of steam navigation in the first half of the century had necessitated revision of the old rules, which had developed with the slower sailing vessels. Great Britain on this occasion, as on numerous other occasions, until the conference and multipartite treaty methods became routine, was acting on behalf of the maritime community, giving it leadership and furnishing it with a clearinghouse. Subsequent changes in the rules were made at the International Marine Conference in Washington in 1889 and are now regularly made at the conferences devoted to safety of life and property at sea.

Summary. Before proceeding with the post-Civil War era, certain features of the earlier era can be summarized. A few inferences of continuing validity can also be drawn from the record. Immediately upon assertion of national independence, the United States included in its bipartite treaties provisions dealing with the work-a-day use of the sea. That method of securing international cooperation in dealing with common problems arising from use of the sea continues to the present day, supplemented since 1865 by increasing participation in multipartite agreements. In the period before the adoption of the Constitution, the

[55] *International Code of Signals* (American Edition), H.O. No. 37 (1931), Vol. I, Visual, "Preface." For the history, see C. E. Persinger, "Internationalism in the 60's," 20 *Historical Outlook* 324–327 (1929); diplomatic correspondence, *General Index to the Published Volumes of the Diplomatic Correspondence and Foreign Relations of the United States 1861–1899*, for the years 1866–1879, at p. 730; Gidel, *op. cit.*, Vol. I, p. 365.

[56] 5 Hudson, *I.L.* 792. The United States did not become a party to the Agreement Concerning Maritime Signals, opened for signature at Lisbon, Oct. 23, 1930, *ibid.*, pp. 792–800.

[57] Act of April 29, 1864, 13 *Stat.* 58; *The Scotia*, 14 Wall. 170 (1871); E. P. Wheeler, "The International Regulation of Ocean Travel," *Proceedings, American Society of International Law, 1912*, pp. 36–44.

states enacted some legislation and set up sundry governmental agencies relating to maritime affairs.[58] Immediately upon adoption of the Constitution, the federal government enacted legislation and established agencies, one by one, to serve the needs of the seafaring community. In some fields, as in quarantine, state activities were only gradually displaced by national activity.[59]

Jurisdiction over such matters as pilotage, police and sanitation in harbors and coastal waters, erosion, wharfage, safety, and exploitation of the fisheries and other resources of the marginal sea is still variously shared by the federal government with the states. Any international agreement impinging upon the littoral area of the United States must therefore have regard for the vested legal and economic interests of the states. This is part of the enduring problem of federalism. It receives recurring emphasis in such controversies as those relating to jurisdiction over the oil in the continental shelf and fisheries in the Great Lakes. In its most acute form it leads to such misguided movements as that seeking curtailment of the treaty-making power of the United States, concretized in the so-called Bricker Amendment. Because these problems recur repeatedly in history they will be mentioned repeatedly in this discussion.

The national administrative services devoted to matters maritime have been multiplied enormously during the past century and a half, in continuing response to the needs of the people, and have been unified and divided, redistributed and reallocated, repeatedly in accord with the demands for administrative reform, so that for any given decade it may be difficult to ascertain which agency had charge of which function. At any given moment, however, there is now available a vast accumulation of legislation, judicial decision, and administrative regulation and practice, which can be devoted to the enforcement of any new treaty obligation assumed by the United States, frequently with little need for new legislation.[60]

---

[58] See the Service Monographs cited above.
[59] Williams, *op. cit.*, pp. 79–80; Schmeckebier, *op. cit.*, pp. 8–22.
[60] Discussed at length in H. Reiff, "The Enforcement of Multipartite Administrative Treaties in the United States," 34 *A.J.I.L.* 661–680 (1940). That article was written before the outbreak of World War II. In the conclusion is the following passage: "It is evident from the foregoing that improvement of the enforcing process is necessary and desirable. The simplest and most direct reform would consist in an amendment to Article VI of the Constitution preserving the supremacy of a treaty over acts of the states, but eliminating automatic status of a treaty as 'law of the land' and requiring Congress to adopt a comprehensive enforcing statute before the

From Independence to the Great War

As in the field of domestic legislation, so with respect to multipartite agreement, administrators play an important role. Charged with day-by-day rendering of services to individuals and groups, they perforce seek practical solutions to their problems. One of the most efficient of such solutions, in the legal and operational senses, is the multipartite agreement. It achieves optimum collaboration of independent national states with a minimum of negotiation. The reports of American administrators, therefore, since Maury's day, increasingly suggest and recommend the use of conferences and general international agreements for the solution of work-a-day problems which involve the interests of the United States.[61]

FROM THE CIVIL WAR TO THE GREAT WAR

In the period from the close of the Civil War to the peace settlement at Paris in 1919, the United States became a party to twenty-three multi-

---

agreement becomes operative infraterritorially." This suggestion obviously was designed to give *fuller* effect to treaty obligations and to avoid lacunae in statutory authority to proceed with the enforcement of treaties. The suggestion does not imply any restriction of the *scope* of the treaty-making process. The postwar Bricker Amendment advocates, on the other hand, desire to *restrict* the scope of the treaty-making process variously. From time to time they have offered variant texts seeking the same general end. One of the earliest proposals was that "a treaty shall become effective as internal law in the United States only through legislation which would be valid in the absence of treaty." Such an amendment would, of course, negative the doctrine in the Migratory Bird Treaty Case, Missouri v. Holland, 252 U.S. 416 (1920), referred to below at p. 124, and would be destructive of much of the multipartite agreement process. In view of the possibility that an amendment intended to facilitate enforcement might be construed by the courts or Congress to *restrict* either enforcement or the scope of the treaty-making power and in view, further, of the declared purpose of the Bricker Amendment advocates to restrict the scope of the treaty-making power, it now seems wiser to leave Article VI unamended altogether and leave to the political processes the function of controlling the treaty-making power where or if necessary. See John B. Whitton and J. Edward Fowler, "Bricker Amendment—Fallacies and Dangers," 48 *A.J.I.L.* 23–56 (1954); George A. Finch, "The Need to Restrain the Treaty-Making Power of the United States within Constitutional Limits," *ibid.*, pp. 57–82; the debate on the subject in *Proceedings, American Society of International Law, 1954*, pp. 128–163; and Lawrence Preuss, "On Amending the Treaty-Making Power: A Comparative Study of the Problem of Self-Executing Treaties," 51 *Michigan Law Review* 1117–1142 (1953). For clarifying construction of the treaty-making power see language of Mr. Justice Black in Reid v. Covert, 354 U.S. 1 (1957).

[61] Records cited in H. Reiff, *The United States and Multipartite Administrative Treaties* (1934), thesis on deposit at Harvard University; further discussed by the writer in "Participation in International Administration: A Cinderella of American History," 34 *Social Studies* 311–346 (1943). Many a doctoral dissertation could be written on the contributions of administrators to the initiation of multipartite agreements and the genesis of international agencies.

The United States and the Treaty Law of the Sea

partite treaties concerned wholly or in part with peacetime use of the sea. It settled by arbitration the ancient controversy relating to the North Atlantic fisheries. It concluded a first, bipartite, agreement on migratory birds, and became a member of or encouraged official participation in several international organizations not under treaty devoted to improved use of the sea. During the same period, the United States participated in several international conferences devoted to various aspects of the sea aside from those conferences which produced treaties.

In a number of instances, notably those dealing with postal matters, a prime meridian, safety of life at sea, cables, and the opium traffic, the United States took a commendable initiative. Having achieved national political unity, unhappily by war, and launched upon an expanding industrialism, it presently verged upon becoming a first-class naval power and entered the stream of imperialism. Accompanying these basic developments came this increased participation in the international process of dealing with common maritime problems by means of conferences and multipartite agreements.

One by one, insistent problems of real concern to an expanding America were examined with other nations and solutions of them were advanced. They fall into natural patterns and can best be appreciated in that form. They group themselves under these topics: safety of life and property at sea; communications; health; exploitation of the products of the sea; scientific and professional advancement; and humanitarian programs. In the process of securing action on these topics by the community of nations much of the old customary law of the sea was amended and supplemented by means of concurrent national legislation or multipartite agreements, as will appear.

Safety of Life at Sea

The theme of safety of life at sea can be traced through discussion of the Cape Spartel Lighthouse, the Prime Meridian Conference, the International Marine Conference and Inter-American Conference of 1889 in Washington, the Whangpoo River Conservancy, participation in the newly forming scientific and professional international organizations, load lines, radio, and the epochal Safety of Life at Sea Conference in London in 1913–1914.

Cape Spartel Lighthouse. As early as 1849, the American consul at

From Independence to the Great War

Tangier warned his government about the numerous wrecks which were occurring on that dangerous coast and suggested that a war vessel be authorized to cruise along the coast every month or two to pick up shipwrecked crews and to assist stranded merchant vessels.[62] Nothing appears to have been done in response to that suggestion. Wrecks continued. Finally, in pursuance of a commercial treaty between Spain and Morocco, in 1861, the sultan agreed to build a lighthouse. Fear of possible abuse of the light in time of war and other considerations arising out of the rivalry of the great powers led to neutralization, maintenance, and supervision of the lighthouse under the multipartite convention of May 31, 1865.[63] Thus it remained for nearly a century.[64] As a consequence of the recent termination of the international regime of the Tangier Zone and its reintegration into the Sherifian Empire of Morocco, a protocol terminating the convention of May 31, 1865, and transferring the control, operation, and administration of the lighthouse to the government of Morocco was signed at Tangier on March 31, 1958, by the United States and nine other governments.[65] It entered into force the same day.

Prime Meridian. For safe navigation on the high seas it is essential to have accurate latitude and longitude. Methods of determining latitude were known even to the ancient world, so that by the eighteenth century, the determination of latitude was a routine matter. Not so for longitude. Various cumbersome methods were used with varying degrees of inaccuracy. Determination at sea was more difficult than on land. The principal impediment was the lack of an accurate, portable, and dependable clock or chronometer to measure time from some starting place. The search for a reliable method for determining longitude preoccupied scientists as profoundly in the eighteenth century as the search for a cure for cancer preoccupies them today. After many disastrous wrecks involving considerable loss of life, the British Parliament in 1714 offered

---

[62] Graham H. Stuart, *The International City of Tangier*, 2d ed. (1955), p. 27.

[63] 14 Stat. 679, TS 245.

[64] Stuart, *op. cit.*, pp. 26–34; *International Organizations in Which the United States Participates, 1949* (Dept. of State Pub. No. 3655, hereinafter cited *U.S. Int. Org. 1949*), pp. 277–279; and L. F. Schmeckebier, *International Organizations in Which the United States Participates* (1935) (hereinafter cited Schmeckebier, *Int. Org.*), pp. 26–30, for valuable governmental documentation.

[65] "International Conference on the Status of Tangier," 35 *DSB* 841–844 (1956); Richard Young, "The End of American Consular Jurisdiction in Morocco," 51 *A.J.I.L.* 402–406 (1957); protocol announced, 38 *DSB* 749 (1958).

a huge reward to anyone devising a reliable method for determining longitude. By 1761, John Harrison, carpenter and horologist, devised a successful chronometer for use aboard ship. He won the reward and made a major contribution to safety at sea.[66] One further problem, however, remained for the cartographers and chart makers, the acceptance of a single prime meridian for all charts and some agreement on a universal day.

American navigators had, apparently, simply continued to use the British system based on the Greenwich meridian, brought into general use in the early eighteenth century. "Hassler, the first Superintendent of the Coast Survey, observed a solar eclipse on Long Island as early as 1834 to establish longitude datum, relative to Greenwich, for geodetic work. The earliest charts of the Coast and Geodetic survey carry meridians referred to Greenwich."[67] Thus unofficially and officially, the Greenwich meridian was early in wide use in the United States.

Other nations, however, used as their prime meridian for nautical and other purposes one running through their national domain, as through Amsterdam, Berlin, Cadiz, Christiania, Copenhagen, Ferro, Lisbon, Milan, Naples, Paris, Pulkova, Rio de Janeiro, San Fernando, St. Petersburg, Stockholm, Teneriffe, and Turin — cities which usually contained the national astronomical observatories.

As early as 1810 there had been agitation in the United States for an "American" prime meridian. The agitation apparently continued, for as late as in 1849, an important group of American scientists and government officials, including Lt. Charles Henry Davis, superintendent of the Nautical Almanac, and Lt. Matthew Maury, superintendent of the National Observatory, debated the desirability of establishing a prime meridian for certain American purposes running through New Orleans, or, as Maury advocated, further west to clear the Gulf of Mexico.

The Committee on Naval Affairs, "to whom were referred sundry memorials protesting against the establishment of an American prime meridian, in the preparation of the American Nautical Almanac," in accord, apparently, with the prevailing spirit of political compromise reported in favor of using *two* prime meridians: "But it is believed that all controversy may be avoided, and all parties satisfied, by adopting the American meridian for astronomical and geographical purposes, and

[66] Lloyd A. Brown, *The Story of Maps* (1950), Ch. VIII on "The Longitude."
[67] Letter to writer from U.S. Coast and Geodetic Survey, Jan. 11, 1957.

calculating that portion of the Nautical Almanac designed for the exclusive use of navigators, for the meridian of Greenwich."[68] Accordingly, Congress in 1850 ordered that "hereafter the meridian of the observatory at Washington shall be adopted and used as the American meridian for all astronomic purposes and . . . Greenwich for all nautical purposes."[69] This American meridian, however, was used only "as a basis of some of the astronomic boundary surveys of western states, such as Colorado. It was never used as a permanent basis for geodetic surveys in this country."[70]

By 1884, 72 per cent of the world's floating commerce was using the Greenwich meridian for navigational purposes, the remainder being divided among some ten different initial meridians. It was thus propitious, by 1884, to secure agreement to the use of the Greenwich meridian as zero for the world for longitude determination and other purposes.

In the meantime, the International Geographical Congress at its third meeting in Venice in 1881 adopted resolutions calling for international action to fix a universal prime meridian and a uniform standard of time for the world. The United States, because of its width of nearly four thousand miles at the northern border, was particularly plagued by great diversity in local time standards and zones across the country. "Many a railroad station was graced with three or four clocks, each set according to a different zone, and in some cases, when more than one road used the same terminal, it was not uncommon to find clocks set according to the dictates of three or more corporations as well as the location of the sun at different cities."[71]

In the circumstances, Congress welcomed the opportunity to authorize by act of August 3, 1882[72] the holding of an International Meridian Conference in Washington. As a result of the resolutions adopted by the conference in 1884, the Greenwich meridian was accepted as zero and a universal day was finally established.[73]

[68] Report to the House of Representatives on *American Prime Meridian*, 31 Cong., 1 Sess., H. Rept. No. 286, May 2, 1850, Serial 584.
[69] Act of Sept. 28, 1850, 9 *Stat.* 515.
[70] Letter, above, n. 67.
[71] L. A. Brown, *op. cit.*, p. 296, also pp. 294–299 for an excellent account of the problem of prime meridian and universal day.
[72] 22 *Stat.* 217. Report in support of the resolution, 47 Cong., 1 Sess., S. Rept. No. 840, July 18, 1882; p. 2 lists a few of the initial meridians then in use.
[73] *Proceedings of the Prime Meridian Conference*, 48 Cong., 2 Sess., H. Ex. Doc. No. 14, Dec. 4, 1884, at p. 7 of which Admiral Rodgers says that the United States had no desire to urge that the prime meridian be located in the United States.

The plan for establishing twenty-four world time zones of 15° each was ultimately accepted by almost every nation except Holland. Beginning with the meridian of Greenwich (zero longitude) as the center of the first zone, the world was divided into twenty-four time belts, each one hour or 15° apart, and numbered east and west of Greenwich from one to twelve. Thus Greenwich time would be uniformly used with a belt of 7½ degrees of longitude east and west of the prime meridian, while the 12th zone, centered on the 180th meridian, would include the area 7½ degrees on either side of it, and have a time difference of twelve whole hours. For the sake of convenience, certain exceptions have since been made in laying down the meridian boundaries of the time zones.[74]

The universal day was thus to begin at mean midnight at the Greenwich meridian and reckoned thence east and west in accordance with the time zones.

At this point a legislative mystery intervenes. Although the Senate in 1885 passed a measure adopting the resolutions of the Meridian Conference, the House of Representatives, in spite of a repeated request by the President as late as 1888, failed to concur.[75] Nevertheless, the United States conformed to the resolutions of the conference, the administrators of the national services concerned proceeding apparently under their accumulated prior authority and in accordance with their custom. As late as 1918, Congress enacted a law to "save daylight and to provide standard time for the United States," which was based upon the Greenwich meridian.[76] Congress thus statutorily approved what had already been firmly in use for several decades. Other nations also conformed to the schemes adopted at the 1884 conference, some of them only gradually.

International Date Line. Meanwhile, however, the United States made another contribution to the settling of some of these troublesome time problems. From the earliest days of exploration in the Pacific, at points nearly halfway round the world from Europe, there was confusion as to which day was which, reckoning either east or west from any of the prime meridians used in Europe.

[74] L. A. Brown, *op. cit.*, p. 298.
[75] Report of the Senate Foreign Relations Committee in support of measure to adopt the resolutions of the conference for the United States, 48 Cong., 2 Sess., S. Rept. No. 1188, Feb. 7, 1885. Message from President calling for adoption of resolution of 1885 by the House, 50 Cong., 1 Sess., H. Ex. Doc. No. 61, Jan. 9, 1888, S. 2557.
[76] Act of March 19, 1918, 40 *Stat.* 450.

From Independence to the Great War

Serious disputes could arise, as in the rival claims of Charles Wilkes and Dumont d'Urville, the French explorer, for the honor of first sighting the mainland of the Antarctic continent in 1840, on January "19." The Frenchman "claimed that he made his discovery in advance of Wilkes by a few hours, but it afterwards developed that he had forgotten the international date line [sic], and had failed to add a day to his log when he crossed the 180th meridian; this made him later in the sighting of land by about ten hours."[77] If announcement by radio had been possible, such a controversy concerning priority would probably not have arisen and Wilkes might have been spared the charge of falsifying the log in his subsequent court-martialing.

This problem of agreeing on the calendar change in the crucial area persisted until the latter part of the nineteenth century. Reference works generally assert that there was some international treaty or other agreement on the subject fixing an international date line. The facts are, however, otherwise as published by the United States Hydrographic Office in 1938:

There is no International Date Line that has formally been adopted by the various nations of the World, and on the charts of the Hydrographic Office the line delineating the change from American to Asiatic time is designated simply as "Date Line."

The question of a date line in the Pacific had its inception from the time when the early explorers, English, French, Spanish, and Dutch, began to establish colonies in those waters. The Spanish having sailed westward and the others coming from the eastward, the dates as preserved by the colonies they founded differed by a day. Thus it was that the Spanish colony of Luzon, although in practically the same longitude as the Dutch colony of Celebes, kept a time that was 24 hours later than that of the Celebes.

By a decree of the Governor-General of the Philippines, in 1844, it was ordered that Tuesday, December 31, should be reckoned as Wednesday, January 1, 1845, thus bringing the date into accord with those countries east of the Cape of Good Hope.

Russia, in October 1867, sold Alaska to the United States, at which

[77] Henderson, *op. cit.*, pp. 102–103, 211, quoting William Herbert Hobbs. The assumption that there was an agreed "international date line" appears to be in error. Both navigators may have been acting altogether in good faith. This episode suggests also the necessity for scholars to be cautious when dealing with dates in the period of change from the Julian calendar to the Gregorian calendar 1582 to about 1800, particularly around the year 1752, when the Gregorian calendar was adopted in Great Britain and the English colonies in America.

time that territory adopted American time, and on July 4, 1892, Samoa also adopted the same time for the whole of the Samoan group.

In 1884 there was held in Washington, D.C., the International Meridian Conference, which established as a prime meridian from which time was to be reckoned, the meridian passing through Greenwich, England. Thus, theoretically, the 180th meridian became the international date line. However, this meridian bisected certain land areas which made necessary slight deviations from the meridian.

Based on the investigations of Prof. George Davidson of the University of California, who conducted an investigation to determine the date used by the various islands in the North Pacific, the Hydrographic Office published on the Pilot Chart of the North Pacific Ocean for September 1899, a chartlet showing the date line. This line adhered closely to the 180th meridian, and did not change the date of any of the islands concerned, but merely showed how the islands had settled the date question for themselves. The date line shown on the latest Time Zone Chart published by the Hydrographic Office (H.O. Chart No. 5192) is substantially in accord with the original chartlet, except that a zigzag in the vicinity of Morell Island has been eliminated, as that island has been found to be nonexistent, and the line has been extended slightly to the eastward in the southern hemisphere to include the islands mandated to Australia.[78]

International Time Bureau. One further development with respect to the problem of time involves the effort by means of a draft convention and draft statutes, adopted at the International Time Conference held in Paris in 1912 and 1913, to set up an International Time Association and an International Time Bureau. The United States signed the convention and bylaws at Paris, October 25, 1913, and the Senate gave its consent to ratification of the instruments.[79] But the war intervened. Neither the United States nor other governments perfected the agreements and the association was therefore never brought into being. When, however, "the International Research Council and the International Astronomic Union

---

[78] *Hydrographic Bulletin,* No. 2553, for Aug. 10, 1938, a single large sheet issued weekly, no pagination.

[79] *Convention for Creation of an International Time Association and By-laws to Govern the Association,* both signed at Paris, Oct. 25, 1913. Department of State. Confidential, S. Ex. Doc., 63 Cong., 2 Sess. Injunction of secrecy removed June 5, 1914. Report of the Senate Foreign Relations Committee, submitting resolution advising and consenting to ratification of the convention, May 27, 1914, S. Ex. Rept., 63 Cong., 2 Sess. Injunction of secrecy removed June 5, 1914. Neither of these documents is in the congressional set. See also *List of Treaties Submitted to the Senate 1789–1931 Which Have Not Gone Into Effect,* Dept. of State Pub. (hereinafter cited D.S. Pub.) No. 382 (1932), pp. 2, 13. Not listed in 1 Hudson, *I.L.* p. xxxv.

were created in July 1919, the Time Bureau, the expenses of which had chiefly been met by France, where it had continued to work during the war, was placed under the control of the Thirty-first Commission of the International Astronomic Union and made international." [80] The United States, of course, became a member of the International Astronomical Union and has participated in the work of the bureau, which receives time signals from other observatories for intercomparison. Thus, the Washington Bureau of Standards sends the international bureau signals on three wave lengths simultaneously throughout the twenty-four hours.[81]

In addition, nowadays, the time signals sent out by radio from the United States Naval Observatory, accurate on 122 kilocycles to the one-hundredth of a second, are employed generally by navigators at sea in checking their chronometers.[82] This amounts to a universal service performed for the maritime community by the United States.

First International Conference of American States, 1889. In the fall of 1889 two important conferences, called on the initiative of the United States, assembled in Washington: the First International Conference of American States [83] and the International Marine Conference.[84] Both were seminal. To the former may be traced the present elaborate Organization of the American States. Part of its vast program from the beginning has dealt with many maritime matters of particular concern to the western hemisphere, including the undertaking of the erection of a

[80] *Handbook of International Organisations*, League of Nations (1938), pp. 170–171.

[81] *U.S. Int. Org. 1949*, pp. 122–127; *Directory of International Scientific Organizations*, 2d ed., UNESCO (1953), pp. 61–62.

[82] *The Naval Observatory Time Service*, U.S.N.O. Circular No. 14 (1950). For the complexities, see Sir Harold Spencer Jones, "The Determination of Precise Time," Smithsonian *Report 1949*, pp. 189–202, Pub. No. 4000.

[83] James Brown Scott, *The International Conferences of American States 1889–1928* (1931), pp. 1–47 (hereinafter cited Scott, *I.C.A.S. 1889–1928*); *ibid.*, *The International Conferences of American States, First Supplement, 1933–1940* (1940), indexes under "Communications," "Maritime," "Port formalities," and so forth (hereinafter cited Scott, *I.C.A.S. 1933–1940*); *U.S. Int. Org. 1949*, pp. 19–32; and the comprehensive *Report of the Delegates of the United States to the Inter-American Maritime Conference, Washington, D.C., 1940* (1941).

[84] *Protocols of Proceedings of the International Marine Conference, Washington, Oct. 16 to Dec. 31, 1889*, 2 vols., 51 Cong., 1 Sess., Pts. 1 and 2, S. Ex. Doc. No. 53 (1890), S. 2683 and S. 2684. These *Proceedings* constitute a veritable encyclopedia on the subject of safety at sea. See also *Reports of Committees and Report of the United States Delegates to the Secretary of State*, included as Pt. 3 in S. Ex. Doc. No. 53, S. 2684.

Columbus Memorial Lighthouse at Ciudad Trujillo, Dominican Republic, since World War I. In recent years, controversies concerning fisheries and the extension of jurisdiction over the continental shelf and epicontinental sea have involved various members of the organization. These controversies will be discussed in due course.

International Marine Conference, 1889. This conference gave rise in time to the great conferences on safety of life at sea in 1914, 1929, and 1948, and, at long last, to the Intergovernmental Maritime Consultative Organization in 1948.

The Marine Conference of 1889 discussed comprehensively safety of life and property at sea. It adopted no multipartite treaty but instead a series of resolutions, to be put into effect by concurrent national legislation, revising the rules for the prevention of collisions and the rules of the road, and prescribing uniform regulations regarding the designating and marking of vessels, the duties of responsible persons in case of collision, and qualifications for officers and seamen. Unable to agree on definitive rules with regard to other matters discussed by it, the conference adopted resolutions recommending to maritime powers certain methods and standards with respect to the determination of the seaworthiness of vessels; saving life and property from shipwreck; lanes for steamers on frequented routes; night signals; storm warnings; reporting, marking, and removing dangerous wrecks or obstructions to navigation; notice of dangers to navigators; and a uniform system of buoys and beacons. On three matters of great importance the conference took no affirmative action: load lines; ice and derelict patrol; and the setting up of an international agency for the coordinating of national action.[85]

Great Britain continued its historic function of acting as a clearinghouse in the process of adopting the rules and regulations. The Safety of Life at Sea conventions of 1914 and 1929, as well as the Load Line Convention of 1930, continued to entrust to Great Britain these secretarial functions. The 1948 Safety of Life at Sea Convention contemplated, and the Convention of the Intergovernmental Maritime Consultative Organization in 1948 provided for, the establishment of an international secretariat for these functions to be located in London.

[85] *Final Act, Protocols,* pp. 1363–1392; for comment thereon, see Everett P. Wheeler, "The International Regulation of Ocean Travel," *Proceedings, A.S.I.L., 1912,* pp. 36–44.

From Independence to the Great War

In the years immediately following the Marine Conference of 1889 the United States renewed its efforts to secure adequate protection for shipping against derelicts, wrecks, and other menaces to navigation in the North Atlantic. Congress authorized the President to enter into an agreement to that end.[86] The British government, whose cooperation would be necessary for the success of any such regime, and which probably would have to contribute a large share of the expenses, rejected the proposal on the ground that the number of casualties from collisions with derelicts was very small in so large an area of the sea.[87] It was, in sad irony, a British vessel, the *Titanic*, which struck floating ice in that area in 1912, carrying down with it a large number of Americans. Thereupon, the United States immediately instituted an ice patrol at its own expense[88] until, in pursuance of the 1914 Convention on Safety of Life at Sea, the expenses were shared with other powers.

Whangpoo River Conservancy. Meanwhile the United States had become involved in the international efforts to rectify and improve the Whangpoo River from its outlet into the southern branch of the Yangtse River up past the great port of Shanghai to the Kiang-nan Arsenal, a distance of some fifteen miles. The harbor of Shanghai is nine sea miles in length. Unfortunately, the bar at the outlet of the Whangpoo and the shoals in the channel require constant dredging. Other characteristics of the stream required training and restraining of the river. The story of these international efforts is long and complicated. They represent, however, a striking example of international collaboration to assure safety of ocean shipping in a coastal water giving access to a great port, under circumstances indicating reluctance on the part of the littoral state to undertake the measures deemed desirable in the interest of the international community. Briefly, the syllabus is as follows.

As part of the Boxer settlement in 1901, an international Conservancy (or conservation) Board, composed of representatives of the Chinese government and the extraterritorial powers, was set up with operating, regulating, and policing functions for the river. Sundry difficulties, including financing the works, led to several reorganizations of the board

---

[86] J. Res., Oct. 31, 1893, 20 *Stat.* 13.

[87] *Report of Commissioner of Navigation* (1895), p. 94. The story of American efforts in relation to the whole subject of safety of life at sea can be traced in these excellent annual reports from 1884 forward.

[88] *Report of Delegation of the United States to International Conference on Safety of Life at Sea, London, 1929*, D.S. Pub. No. 14, pp. 79–80.

The United States and the Treaty Law of the Sea

and to new agreements in 1905, 1910, and 1912. This last agreement set up a Chinese board advised by foreigners. To avoid return to this subject later, the rest of the saga is as follows. "The work of the Board was carried on until 1941 when contact between foreign advisers of the Board and the Japanese occupation officials was cut off by Japan's entry into World War II. With the abandonment or loss of extraterritorial rights by the principal signatories of the Boxer Protocol, the Board, as reconstituted in October, 1945, was made a semi-autonomous organization under the Chinese Ministry of Finance. In May, 1949, when the Chinese Nationalist officials withdrew to Taiwan, the Board went out of existence. Its work has been continued, however, by a Whangpoo Conservancy Commission set up by the Communist regime."[89] Thus ended a most interesting experiment in internationally sponsored river and harbor development.

Load Lines. Overloaded vessels at sea are difficult to handle, whatever their motive power. In high seas or storms this unmanageability

[89] Letter from G. Bernard Noble, Chief, Division of Historical Policy Research, Department of State, to writer, Sept. 29, 1952. Since there is a dearth of documentation on this subject in the treatises, it is desirable to record here various sources and also valuable data furnished by the Department of State. For the fluvial and engineering aspects: "The Huangpu Conservancy," article from the *North China Daily News*, Aug. 27, 1906, reprinted in 1909 *Foreign Relations* 73–76; "Shanghai," *Encyclopaedia Britannica* (1952), Vol. 20, pp. 445, 456. Negotiations: "Report of William W. Rockhill, Late Commissioner to China, with Accompanying Documents," in *Appendix* to 1901 *Foreign Relations* at pp. 333–337; 1904, pp. 186–200; 1905, pp. 117–124; 1909, pp. 70–92; 1910, pp. 353–360. Agreements: Final Protocol, Boxer Troubles, Peking, Sept. 7, 1901, *TS* 397, *Treaties, Conventions, International Acts, Protocols and Agreements, 1776–1909*, 61 Cong., 2 Sess., S. Doc. No. 357, 2 vols., edited by William M. Malloy, Vol. 2, p. 2006 (hereinafter cited Malloy); Agreement, Peking, Sept. 27, 1905, *TS* 448, 2 Malloy 2013; Agreement, Peking, April 9, 1912, with Supplementary Article (No. 12) adopted Jan. 19, 1916, in the third volume of the "Malloy" series, being *Treaties etc.*, 67 Cong., 4 Sess., S. Doc. No. 348, edited by C. F. Redmond, at p. 3043 (hereinafter cited 3 Redmond). Getting at the records of the several Whangpoo regimes is, however, another matter. The writer is indebted to the Department of State for the following information: "A list of the publications of the Whangpoo Conservancy Board and its predecessors up to the year 1934 may be found on pages i–ii of *The Port of Shanghai* (8th revised edition, 1934), published by Kelly and Walsh, Limited, Shanghai, as Report No. 8 in the Board's General Series. These publications contain information on the work accomplished by the Board during the many years of its operation. The availability of these publications appears to be limited." The unpublished records of the Whangpoo Conservancy Board were not taken out of Shanghai before the fall of that city into the hands of the Chinese Communists. With reference to publications of the board after 1934, "the Board subsequently published a 9th edition of *The Port of Shanghai* in 1936 (a 10th edition was published in 1943 by the Japanese); *A Work Report of the Whangpoo Conservancy Board* for the period from September 1945 to August 1946; and a similar report from September 1946 to December 1947."

From Independence to the Great War

may cause foundering or wrecking. The temptation to overload arises out of the desire to increase the pay-load for that particular voyage. This type of competition has existed from very ancient times, as is evidenced by the archeological remains of probably overloaded wine vessels now being found in the Mediterranean. National law is not fully adequate to the solution of the international problem, at whose root lies the competition between the national marines. Hence some type of international agreement to apply uniform standards of safety is necessary. The Marine Conference in Washington in 1889 took no action on this subject.

In 1876 the British government had, however, adopted the so-called Plimsoll (Load Line) Act, named after the vigorous social reformer, Samuel Plimsoll, who had advocated for years in and out of Parliament the outlawry of "coffinships," unseaworthy, overloaded, and frequently heavily insured vessels, that could go to the bottom with no loss to the owners, only the loss of life to the crew. The Plimsoll Act was therefore designed to prevent the dangerous overloading of cargo carriers, and it applied to all vessels which frequented British ports.[90]

For some years the United States protested application of the statute to American vessels.[91] The American merchant marine at the time consisted chiefly of passenger steamers, tugs and towing steamers, and wooden sail vessels, which, it was argued, did not need load lines.[92] The United States nevertheless for a few years, 1891–1897, required American shipowners to place what they deemed to be safe load lines on their vessels.[93] Thereafter, unrestricted by national legislation, American vessels were also exempted from the application of local law on the subject in foreign ports out of "courtesy" and under a "gentleman's agreement." [94] When, however, the United States itself had acquired a huge cargo-carrying fleet as a result of World War I and faced the competition of unscrupulous foreign shipping, it enacted a compulsory load line statute in 1929 applicable to all domestic and foreign-owned vessels, sailing from American ports for an overseas voyage.[95] Now the United States was

[90] McFee, *op. cit.*, pp. 77, 151, 287; *Reports, Com. of Navig.*, beginning in 1887.
[91] 1 Moore, *Digest* 282–283; correspondence of 1877, 1886.
[92] *Report, Com. of Navig.*, 1904, p. 22.
[93] Act of Feb. 21, 1891, 26 *Stat.* 765, 766; repealed by Act of Jan. 20, 1897, 29 *Stat.* 491, 492.
[94] *Report, Com. of Navig.*, 1918, p. 34; 1920, pp. 951–952, and following years.
[95] Act of March 2, 1929, 45 *Stat.* 1493.

The United States and the Treaty Law of the Sea

ready to participate in international legislation on the subject. This it did by becoming a party to the International Load Line Convention of 1930, which will be discussed later.

Safety of Life at Sea Conference, 1914. As already indicated, there was much unfinished business of crucial character left over from the epochal Marine Conference in 1889. Sometimes, it seems, if enough people die, particularly in some dramatic way, societal reform is speeded up. So, at least it was with respect to the *Titanic* disaster on April 15, 1912.

The International Wireless Telegraph Convention of 1906 gave absolute priority to calls of distress from ships (Art. 9). The United States had signed that agreement in 1906 but it did not perfect its relation to it until after the disaster, on May 25, 1912.[96] Meanwhile, however, an act of Congress in 1910 required the installation of radio apparatus on all ocean passenger ships using American ports.[97] Immediately after the disaster, Congress further provided by act of July 23, 1912, for a continuous wireless watch on board such ships.[98] The principles of both these acts were incorporated later in the 1914 Convention on Safety of Life at Sea.

The loss of the "unsinkable" *Titanic* on its maiden voyage across the North Atlantic after it struck floating ice was probably the most dramatic of all disasters at sea.[99] It was also a great social and legal catalyst. It speeded up reform for the whole maritime community. Within virtually hours after the sinking, the United States dispatched two scout cruisers to the area to give warning of drifting ice. Five days after the disaster, on April 20, 1912, the Senate requested the President to enter into treaties

[96] Proclaimed, May 25, 1912, 37 *Stat.* 1565, *TS* 568.
[97] Act of June 24, 1910, 36 *Stat.* 629.
[98] 37 *Stat.* 199. The complicated history of the relation of American legislation to the wireless conventions at this time is clearly set forth in Short, *The Bureau of Navigation,* pp. 17–18, 54–62.
[99] *Loss of the Steamship "Titanic," Report of a Formal Investigation into the Circumstances Attending the Foundering on April 15, 1912 etc.,* 62 Cong., 2 Sess., S. Doc. No. 933, 1912, S. 6179. Still the finest brief account of this great tragedy is Hanson W. Baldwin's "R.M.S. *Titanic*—1912," originally appearing in *Harper's Magazine,* now a chapter in his *Sea Fights and Shipwrecks: True Tales of the Seven Seas* (1956). For additional dramatic details, see Walter Lord, *A Night to Remember* (1955). For further detail on the human failure in use of the radio, see Codding, *op. cit.,* pp. 97–98. See McFee, *op. cit.,* for accounts of other great sea disasters which also forced reforms which he describes.

From Independence to the Great War

with the other maritime powers to assure increased safety at sea.[100] The British government, however, assumed the burden of holding the conference,[101] which met in London, November 12, 1913.

The resulting convention of January 20, 1914, was the first on the subject in modern maritime history. It picked up the loose ends as they had been left by the Washington conference of 1889 and provided for a new clear-cut regime of safety on the high seas. Provision was made for an internationally supported ice patrol in the North Atlantic, to be operated by the United States; new obligatory rules for masters when meeting derelicts or ice; elaborate rules on the construction of vessels; radiotelegraphy for all merchant vessels; meteorological information; lifesaving appliances and fire protection; safety certificates; and other pertinent matters.[102]

The 1914 convention, however, never went into effect completely as an international instrument. The ensuing war and other causes prevented perfection of the convention by all the signatories. The International Seamen's Union of America, led by the doughty Andrew Furuseth, who had been a member of the American delegation to the conference and who objected to various provisions of the convention on the ground that they set inadequate standards for the safety of the seafarers, opposed ratification of the treaty.[103]

The growing importance of organized seamen at that time — its full strength evidenced nowadays by the extensive program of international legislation adopted by the International Labor Organization — deserves special noting. In 1892 the National Seamen's Union of America was formed out of three scattered and independent unions dating back to 1878. In 1895 the name was changed to International Seamen's Union of America and again in 1937 to the Seafarers' International Union. For many years Andrew Furuseth was the head of that union. He was

---

[100] Senate Res. No. 284, April 20, 1912, 48 *Cong. Rec.* 5036, 5037, 62 Cong., 2 Sess. Congress as a whole passed an authorizing resolution, J. Res. No. 28, June 28, 1912, 37 *Stat.* 637–638.

[101] International Conference on Safety of Life at Sea, 63 Cong., 2 Sess., S. Doc. No. 463, 1914, S. 6594, *Report* of the American Commissioners therein, p. 107.

[102] Text of convention in S. Doc. No. 463, *op. cit.*, and explanation in *Report* of the Commissioners.

[103] Separate report to the President submitted by Furuseth after his resignation from the delegation, S. Doc. No. 463, *op. cit.*, pp. 131–142. The *Memorial of American Seamen*, 63 Cong., 2 Sess., S. Doc. 452, is reprinted in the above document at pp. 111–130. Cf. McFee, *op. cit.*, pp. 180–181.

The United States and the Treaty Law of the Sea

one of the most colorful, fearless, outspoken, and personally disinterested and respected, of all American labour leaders. Furuseth, a Norwegian by birth, was in many respects a reincarnation of his viking ancestors. A thoroughgoing individualist, he was possessed of a passionate desire for freedom, a fierce rebellion against restraint and regimentation, a flaming hatred of injustice, and a fanatical zeal for the interests of seamen. Undoubtedly the character and personality of this man were of the utmost importance in shaping the course of the seamen's movement. . . . Furuseth died in Washington on 22 January 1938, at the age of 84. The last years of his life were marred by a growing incapacity and by the disintegration of the organization which he had built up; but his interest in maritime affairs never flagged. His body was allowed to lie in state in the Department of Labor, an honour never before accorded to any American labour leader. On 12 March 1938, at Savannah (Georgia), his ashes were entrusted to the master and crew of the merchant vessel *Schoharie*; and several days later, when in mid-Atlantic, the *Schoharie* hove to and consigned his remains to the waves.[104]

The Senate, however, did give consent to ratification with a declaration reserving to the United States the right to impose upon foreign vessels using American ports such higher standards of safety and health as the United States exacted from its own vessels.[105] Various governments proceeded to put into effect sundry portions of the 1914 convention, among them the United States. Having already met the radio requirements, it assigned the permanent ice and derelict service to the Coast Guard[106] and adopted the so-called La Follette Seamen's Act of March 4, 1915,[107] a section of which followed almost verbatim the regu-

---

[104] Elmo Paul Hohman, "Maritime Labour in the United States: I: The Seamen's Act and its Historical Background," 38 *International Labour Review* 190–218 (1938), at p. 200. This excellent brief history of the seamen's labor movement in the United States is continued by Professor Hohman in "Maritime Labour . . . II: Since the Seamen's Act," 38 *ibid.*, 376–403 (1938), and "Merchant Seamen in the United States, 1937–1952," 47 *ibid.*, 1–43 (1953). These articles, fortunately, have been reprinted and published in book form, together with some additional material and a bibliography, under the title *History of American Merchant Seamen* (1956). See also Hohman's *Seamen Ashore* (1952).

[105] Senate Resolution, Dec. 16, 1914, quoted in Fred K. Nielsen, "The Lack of Uniformity in the Law and Practice of States in Regard to Merchant Vessels," 13 *A.J.I.L.* 1–21 (1919).

[106] Smith and Powell, *The Coast Guard*, pp. 17–18, 44–47; Evans, *op. cit.*, pp. 193–197; for an example of the work, see *International Ice Observation and Ice Patrol Service in the North Atlantic, Season of 1934*, Coast Guard Bulletin No. 24 (1935); and for thrilling accounts of rescue work, see Frank Wead, *Gales, Ice, and Men* (1937).

[107] 38 *Stat.* 1164, section 14 following Articles 27 to 51 of the *Regulations*.

From Independence to the Great War

lations annexed to the convention dealing with lifesaving appliances and fire protection.

Thus ends the outline of efforts relating to safety at sea in the period preceding World War I.

Communications

The oceanic communications in the period before 1919 which were subjected to international legislation were the mails, cables, and wireless.

Postal Communications. By the middle of the nineteenth century, mail packets were being superseded by subsidized merchant-ship carriage.[108] However routed, overseas postal communications were amazingly complicated and excessively expensive. In the midst of the Civil War, John A. Kasson, first assistant postmaster general, suggested in 1862 to the postmaster general, Montgomery Blair, the formation of an international regime to unsnarl the postal practices.[109] On the initiative of the United States a conference was held in Paris in 1863, which adopted thirty-one general principles to guide existing practice and for incorporation in new bipartite agreements.[110]

In 1874 a "general" union was established at Berne, Article I of the convention declaring that the countries which were party to it formed a single postal territory for the reciprocal exchange of correspondence between their postoffices.[111] In 1878 at Paris the name was changed to Universal Postal Union.[112] The 1874 convention provided for the separate establishment among interested governments of specialized unions and regional unions all subordinate to the general regime. In 1920 the United States joined the Spanish American Postal Union,[113] later renamed the Postal Union of the Americas and Spain.[114] Since so much postal communication is overseas, frequently requiring transshipment over several steamship lines, and since the several postal unions are highly instrumental in repression of the international traffic in narcotics,

---

[108] "Post and Postal Services," *Encyclopaedia Britannica* (1952), Vol. 18, pp. 303–318.

[109] *Report of the Postmaster General*, 1863, p. 10

[110] U.S. circular invitation, 1862 *Foreign Relations* 391–392; Krains, *L'Union Postale Universelle*, p. 13; Sly, *op. cit.*

[111] Oct. 9, 1874; "treaty" in 19 *Stat.* 577.

[112] Convention of June 1, 1878, 20 *Stat.* 734.

[113] Convention of Nov. 13, 1920, 42 *Stat.* 2141.

[114] By convention of Nov. 10, 1931, Madrid, 47 *Stat.* 1924.

The United States and the Treaty Law of the Sea

obscene literature, and other noxious matters by sea, the contribution of the unions to the orderly use of the sea can hardly be overvalued.[115]

Submarine Cables. From 1851 to 1853 several short cables were laid under the English Channel. In 1866 Cyrus W. Field completed his second, successful, trans-Atlantic cable. Meanwhile a scramble for landing rights and monopolized routes was precipitated.[116] A convention of 1864 (nullified in 1872), among several European states and Brazil and Haiti, contemplated a cable from Europe to America.[117] Fearful of abuses, the United States in 1869 invited the leading maritime powers to a conference to provide for protection to cables, prohibition of exclusive concessions, and noncensorship of messages.[118] Nothing definite immediately came of these efforts.

Damage to cables from anchors and trawling, however, continued. Successive international telegraphic conferences studied the subject.[119] A series of conferences called by the French government finally produced in 1884 the Convention on the Protection of Submarine Cables, applicable outside territorial waters, to which the United States became a party.[120] The convention provided for prosecution of willful injuries to cables and indemnities for the loss of gear to avoid injury. It also established rules to be observed by fishermen and cable-laying ships when cables are laid on the high seas.

Injuries to cables continued, however, caused chiefly by fishermen and in European waters primarily. This led the British government to hold another conference in 1913, at which supplemental measures were adopted.[121] The United States, not much bothered by breakages off its shores, did not attend that conference. Since then the method of "plowing in" cables in furrows in areas frequented by trawlers with their

---

[115] *U.S. Int. Org. 1949*, pp. 296–300, 302–307; for the texts of all multipartite postal conventions and bibliographical notes on each for the period 1919–1945, see Hudson, *I.L.*

[116] Mance and Wheeler, *International Telecommunications*, pp. 58–60, 63–65; Lissitzyn, *op. cit.*, pp. 31–35.

[117] 1 Hudson, *I.L.*, xix.

[118] Nov. 23, 1869, 2 Moore, *Digest* 475–476. For the constitutional question relating to the power of the President to grant landing licenses, see Edward S. Corwin, *The President: Office and Powers 1787–1948*, 3rd ed. (1948), p. 239.

[119] *Annuaire de la Vie Internationale*, 1908/1909, p. 283.

[120] Signed at Paris, March 14, 1884, 24 *Stat.* 989; 25 *Stat.* 1424, 1425, *TS* 380, 380-1, 380-2, 380-3.

[121] *Preliminary Conference in London on the Further Protection of Submarine Telegraph Cables, Procès-Verbaux and Annexes*, June 5–10, 1913, Cd. 7079 (1913).

From Independence to the Great War

bottom-dragging gear has been devised. However, other more serious problems, concerning the establishment of routes, landing rights, connections with shore telegraphic systems, and competition with radio, have continued and have not yet, in considerable part, been satisfactorily solved.[122]

Wireless. As in the case of cables, the invention and commercial exploitation of wireless speedily precipitated bitter international controversies, involving, among other things, claims of rival technical systems, concessions, monopolies, and conflicting governmental and private interests.[123] The sea immediately occupied a central position in the exploitation of the new art, as it still does. In its early stages, transoceanic communication depended on the relaying of messages by ships at sea — provided they used the same wireless system. Many a story is told of the refusal of one system to handle messages originating in another system. Thus Prince Henry of Prussia, brother of Kaiser Wilhelm II, on his memorable state visit to President Theodore Roosevelt in 1903, was plagued, both in coming and returning, with interference and the refusal of ship or shore stations to handle his messages. Even the Nantucket Shoals Lightship, which employed the Marconi system, refused to relay the Prince's farewell message to President Roosevelt from aboard the *Deutschland*, which used the German Slaby-Arco system. The Prince and the Kaiser were reported to be wroth, and so, probably, was the President.[124]

With high stakes in the peaceful development of the new invention, the German government called and the United States participated in conferences in 1903 [125] and 1906.[126] In 1912,[127] the United States became

---

[122] See 8 Hackworth, *Digest* 39–41, index to "Cables."

[123] Federal Trade Commission, *Report on Radio Industry, Dec. 1, 1923* (1924), pp. 1–12. *Letter from Secretary of the Navy Recommending Government Control of Wireless Telegraphy*, Feb. 13, 1908, S. Doc. No. 256, 60 Cong., 1 Sess., S. 5264. See G. A. Codding, Jr., *The International Telecommunications Union* (1952), for the early conflicts and rivalries, pp. 81–84; for the start of broadcasting, pp. 111–113; for contributions by amateurs, p. 115. For some of the present-day international problems, see Mance and Wheeler, *International Telecommunications, passim,* and particularly, Francis Colt De Wolf, "The International Control of Radiocommunications," 12 *DSB* 133–136 (1945), and "Telecommunications Tomorrow," *ibid.*, pp. 250–252; Harvey Otterman, "International Regulation of Radio," *ibid.*, pp. 256–259; and Codding, *op. cit., passim*, the finest comprehensive work on the subject.

[124] De Wolf, *op. cit.*, pp. 133–134.

[125] *Report, Chief of Radio Division, Dept. of Commerce, 1927*, p. 6.

[126] 1906 *For. Rel.* 1513–1528.

[127] For an account of the delay, see L. M. Short, *The Bureau of Navigation*, pp.

a party to the first multipartite wireless convention concluded at Berlin, November 3, 1906.[128] Meanwhile, progress in the art and industry forced a revision of the first agreement in a new one of July 5, 1912, concluded at London,[129] which the United States promptly ratified. No further general revision occurred until after World War I, in 1927, at Washington.

The 1912 revision expanded the regulations governing shipboard stations and the certification of operators and provided for the transmission of meteorological [130] radiograms and time signals.[131] Successive revisions of the general convention since then have borne witness, through the number and complexity of the added regulations, to the increasingly intricate relation of the radio regime to modern use of the sea as well as to the other treaty regimes governing that use.

Health

Epidemic and endemic disease has from earliest recorded history played a lethal role in the affairs of nations.[132] Christian pilgrimages and crusades to the Holy Land and Mohammedan pilgrimages to Mecca and Jerusalem have for centuries contributed dangers to the spread of epidemic disease. Increased commerce in the nineteenth century with the Far East and South America and in the Mediterranean, particularly after the opening of the Suez Canal in 1869, created enlarged risks of infection. The replacement of sailing vessels with large steamships and the waves of European immigrants to the Western Hemisphere compounded the risks for America.

From the Middle Ages forward the peoples of Europe relied upon national regulations for protection from the recurring epidemics. These regulations employed chiefly quarantine, isolation, and fumigation methods. They had several important shortcomings. The regulations of

---

17–18, 54–62; *Action of War, Navy, and Commerce and Labor Departments on Wireless Telegraph Convention, April 25, 1908*, S. Doc. No. 452, 60 Cong., 1 Sess., 1908, S. 5265.

[128] Ratification advised by the Senate, April 3, 1912; proclaimed May 25, 1912, 37 *Stat.* 1565, *TS* 568.

[129] Proclaimed July 8, 1913, 38 *Stat.* 1707, *TS* 581.

[130] For the relation of present day meteorological services to the radio regime, see Mance and Wheeler, *International Telecommunications*, pp. 41–44.

[131] *Ibid.*, p. 41.

[132] Hans Zinsser, *Rats, Lice, and History* (1935).

the many large and small principalities of Europe varied enormously; they were based upon an inadequate knowledge of diseases until the emergence of the germ theory in the middle of the nineteenth century; they could be used discriminatively against trade rivals; they caused excessive restrictions upon trade and unnecessary delays; and, finally, they did not get at the principal sources of the infection, namely, areas in the Ottoman Empire, the Far East, and Africa.

During the nineteenth century, Europe was divided by two prevailing theories of sanitary control. Most governments used the old quarantine methods. Men, goods, and ships coming from diseased areas were simply halted and isolated at frontiers and in ports until the health officers were satisfied that they bore no disease. Sometimes the period of detention ran to twenty days, long enough to cover the periods of incubation of dreaded diseases, such as cholera and plague. Unfortunately, this method impeded trade and commerce and could cause cargoes of perishable goods to spoil. Worse still, contraband persons and goods were smuggled through the *cordon sanitaire*. The quarantine method also depended for its effectiveness on adequate advance warnings from the infected areas. Lacking these, national health officers could not take timely defense measures.

Great Britain, interested in the greatest possible scope for trade and commerce, abandoned its old quarantine system after its failure to prevent the cholera epidemic from entering England in 1832, and "gradually adopted a system which became a national policy," and was later adopted in general internationally.

This consisted in inspection of suspected ships, the provision of hospitals at ports and the removal to them of all diseased persons, the disinfection of infected ships, and the improvement of public sanitation in the country. The essence of the system was to detect the presence of the disease and to deal at once with all cases of disease by isolation in properly equipped hospitals, but in this process to subject the movement of men and goods to as little restriction and inconvenience as possible. Accordingly, only persons actually infected were detained; suspected persons were allowed to enter the country freely, provided only that they could furnish an address in order that the medical authorities could keep in touch with them.[133]

[133] L. S. Woolf, *International Government* (Copyright, 1916, by Brentano's; permission to reprint granted by Coward-McCann, Inc.), pp. 221–242, at pp. 228–229.

Even this improved British system, however, depended for maximum effectiveness on advance notice of infected areas abroad from which shipping might come to Great Britain.

If the British system were to be generalized in the interest of reducing restrictions on trade and commerce, international cooperation would have to be secured to assure proper and bona fide advance notice of infected areas, to adopt uniform scientific methods of a maximum and minimum character to replace the old crude methods of quarantine, and to establish some control over the spread of disease from the chief endemic areas and crossroads of commerce outside Europe. To the resolution of these problems most of the remainder of the nineteenth century was devoted. National diplomatic rivalries and the lack of agreement on the causes of the diseases or the mode of their spread impeded agreement. Meanwhile, however, beginning with the establishment of a council at Constantinople in 1838, international sanitary councils were set up by permission of the local sovereigns at Alexandria, Tangier, and Teheran to supervise sanitary control measures in those ports and the Persian Gulf, respectively.

Beginning with one in Paris in 1851, at least ten international conferences on sanitary subjects were held during the second half of the nineteenth century, nine in Europe and one in Washington, in 1881.[134] The first conference "was preceded by the action of the French Government in 1847, in appointing medical sanitary agents in the Near and Middle East. These agents stationed in Constantinople, Smyrna, Beirut, Alexandria, Cairo, and Damascus gathered information on sanitary conditions in the East which formed the basis for the calling of the First Sanitary Conference."[135] The United States was not represented at the first four conferences — Paris in 1851 and 1859, Constantinople in 1866, and Vienna in 1874.[136]

The chief epidemic disease at the time in America was yellow fever, its cause unknown until the end of the century. Thus, in 1895 Surgeon General Wyman pointed out that in the period from 1800 to 1894, "there had been only seven years in which yellow fever had not visited the

---

[134] *Annuaire de la vie Internationale*, 1908/1909, pp. 119–121; Brock C. Hampton, "International Health Organizations," U.S.P.H.S., *Public Health Reports*, Vol. 40, No. 34, Aug. 21, 1925, pp. 1719–1732; Williams, *The United States Public Health Service, 1798–1950*, Ch. VII.

[135] Williams, *op. cit.*, p. 436.

[136] *Ibid.*, p. 438.

United States."[137] From time to time, however, there were also outbreaks of cholera, a water-borne disease, and typhus, a body louse-borne disease.

An interesting example of the dead hand of the past reaching into the present was reported in 1956 from the diggings for the St. Lawrence Seaway. Project workers near Massena found many unmarked and unidentified graves in one area. Local historians suggested that among them were the graves of victims of cholera which on three occasions had been brought by ship up the St. Lawrence to northern New York. "In one such epidemic seven lockmen at the east end of the Cornwall canal died in a single night while there were 30 or 40 cases of the disease in Cornwall, Ontario, alone. As late as the summer of 1847 typhus broke out in a shipload of Irish immigrants and a quarantine station was established by the Canadian government at Grosse Isle, below Quebec. A hospital established at Cornwall on Pette Pointe Maligne was located south of the canal and below the city." Of 234 patients admitted that summer, 52 died.[138]

In these circumstances, Congress by resolution of May 14, 1880,[139] authorized the convening of an international sanitary conference in Washington. An impressive conference was held in 1881, devoted primarily to the problems of yellow fever and cholera. Several resolutions were adopted, but no convention.[140] Thereafter, the United States pursued two policies, one toward Europe and the rest of the world, and one toward the American states, upon the basis of separable problems, yellow fever being the chief epidemic disease of the Western Hemisphere. Both policies, however, matured into treaty commitments for the United States only after the turn of the century.

The United States participated in the universal conferences at Rome in 1885[141] and Paris in 1894 and 1903. It did not attend the conference in Venice in 1892 at which a scheme of control was set up for Suez Canal traffic or the one at Dresden in 1893 at which a convention was adopted making international notification of the outbreak of cholera obligatory.

[137] *Ibid.*, p. 441; cf. J. H. Powell, *Bring Out Your Dead* (1950).
[138] *Watertown* (N.Y.) *Daily Times*, Nov. 15, 1956.
[139] J. Res. No. 33, 21 *Stat.* 306.
[140] *Proceedings of the International Sanitary Conference*, Washington, Jan. 5–March 1, 1881, 47 Cong., Spec. Sess., S. Ex. Doc. No. 1, S. 1985.
[141] *Report of the Superintending Surgeon General of the Marine-Hospital Service*, 1886, p. 279. The efforts of the United States in relation to these international regimes can be traced in detail in these annual reports of the surgeon general.

The conference at Paris in 1894 adopted a convention dealing with the sanitary protection of pilgrimages to Mecca and establishing an inspection system in the Persian Gulf. The United States did not become a party to this agreement and did not attend the conference at Venice in 1897 which developed a convention designed to give protection against bubonic plague, a rat- and flea-borne disease, which had broken out recently in Bombay and Hong Kong.[142] The United States did, however, attend the next conference at Paris in 1903 and became a party to the convention [143] there elaborated, the first of the modern comprehensive multipartite agreements on the subject of control of epidemic disease. An arrangement of 1907 provided for the establishment of an international office of public health in Paris.[144] The treaty of the universal regime was revised once in the period before World War I, at Paris, in 1912.[145]

Meanwhile, in the two decades following the 1881 Washington conference, efforts were directed toward the establishment of an exclusively Pan American sanitary regime. Four South American states bordering on the Atlantic having concluded a sanitary convention at Rio de Janeiro in 1887 [146] and four on the Pacific having drawn up a draft agreement at Lima in 1888,[147] the First International Conference of American States, in 1889, recommended to the remaining American states the general adoption of either.[148]

Verification by the end of the century of Dr. Carlos Finlay's theory of the transmission of yellow fever through the bite of an infected mosquito, which was announced at the 1881 conference, advanced the feasibility of the adoption of international regulations.[149] Hence, in response to a resolution of the Second International Conference of American States at Mexico City in 1902,[150] a sanitary bureau was established

[142] For citations to treaties to which the United States did not become a party, see 1 Hudson, *I.L.* xix.
[143] International Sanitary Convention, Paris, Dec. 3, 1903, 35 *Stat.* 1770, TS 466.
[144] Arrangement concluded at Rome, Dec. 9, 1907, 35 *Stat.* 2061, TS 511.
[145] Sanitary Convention, Jan. 17, 1912, 42 *Stat.* 1823, TS 649.
[146] Signed, Nov. 25, 1887, 1 Hudson, *I.L.* xxvi.
[147] Signed, March 12, 1888; text in 51 Cong., 1 Sess., S. Doc. No. 176, pp. 8–13.
[148] Scott, *op. cit., 1889–1928*, pp. 13–14.
[149] B. J. Lloyd, "Pan American Cooperation in Public Health Work," 66 *Bulletin, Pan American Union* 248 (1932).
[150] Scott, *I.C.A.S., 1889–1928*, pp. 94–96; note on sanitary conferences up to 1932 on p. 94; see also, Warren Kelchner, *Inter-American Conferences 1826–1933*, Dept. of State Pub. No. 499.

From Independence to the Great War

at Washington and a specialized sanitary conference met late in 1902, also in Washington.[151] A second sanitary conference in 1905 in Washington produced the first general convention on the subject for the American States.[152] It embraced the principles of the 1903 Paris convention with regard to bubonic plague and cholera and included special provisions with regard to yellow fever. Numerous resolutions of successive general conferences of American states and of the series of specialized Pan American sanitary conferences have furthered the work of the bureau and the regime.[153] In 1924 a Pan American Sanitary Code, adopted at Havana,[154] superseded the Washington Convention of 1905 and covered a much wider field.

The sanitary conventions of both the universal and the Pan American regimes provided for an elaborate program of maritime defense against disease, including notification of infected areas, measures to be taken at land frontiers, in port and aboard ship, and control of rats. The universal conventions of 1903 and 1912 contained special provisions applicable to the Suez Canal, the Red Sea, the Persian Gulf, pilgrimages, and pilgrim ships. They required the notification of the outbreak of plague, cholera, and yellow fever.

It may be noted here that the United States in 1921 denounced the 1903 agreement, remaining bound by the 1912 revision, on the grounds that sundry of the parties to the 1903 convention, but not yet parties to the 1912 convention, had failed to give the proper notification of the outbreak of disease as required under the agreement, the worst offenders being Great Britain and Italy, the latter having failed to notify the United States of the outbreak of a severe epidemic of cholera in Italy in 1911.[155] Termination thus lawfully of the obligations of the United States toward these two governments under the 1903 agreement enabled the United States to take purely national health defensive measures against shipping arriving from those two countries until they became parties to the 1912 agreement, which prescribed more exacting rules.

In the period after 1919, typhus, smallpox, and dengue fever were

[151] *Report of the Surgeon General, 1903*, pp. 318–320; also Williams, *op. cit.*, pp. 443–447.
[152] Oct. 14, 1905, International Sanitary Convention, 35 *Stat.* 2094, TS 518.
[153] Schmeckebier, *Int. Org.*, pp. 167–173; *U.S. Int. Org. 1949*, pp. 245–249.
[154] Nov. 14, 1924, 44 *Stat.* 2031, TS 714; amended at Lima, Oct. 29, 1927, 45 *Stat.* 2613, TS 763.
[155] 3 Redmond 2877–2879; *Report of the Surgeon General, 1911*, pp. 119–120.

added to the list of notifiable diseases. In general, the emphasis of the health movement in the pre-1919 period was largely on defense against invasion by sea or by land; in the post-1919 period defense against invasion by air was added, but increasingly the emphasis has been toward affirmative establishment of healthful conditions throughout the world as the best long-run insurance against irruptions of epidemic and endemic diseases.

Exploitation of Products of the Sea

In the period before the conclusion of World War I, the United States participated in a few international efforts relating to the exploitation of the products of the sea. These dealt with the North Atlantic cod fisheries, the North Pacific fur seals and sea otter, the Pacific halibut and sockeye salmon, participation in the international fishery congresses, and protection of oceanic birds.

Cod Fisheries. The cod fisheries on the banks off the coasts of Nova Scotia, Newfoundland, and Labrador were exploited by Europeans "years before the establishment of permanent settlements in North America," probably before and increasingly after John Cabot's voyage of 1497. Long and tortuous controversies between France and Great Britain and then Great Britain and the United States ensued.[156]

The terms of the treaty of 1818 between the United States and Great Britain, which still basically governs American participation in the fisheries, gave rise to numerous disputes of interpretation, among them the extent of territorial waters, including the definition and measurement of bays, creeks, straits, and other configurations of the coasts; use of the shore by American fishermen; hiring of local fishermen to serve on American vessels; supply and trading privileges; purchase of bait; payment of light, harbor, and other dues; and the right of the local governments to apply conservation measures to American fishermen. For over a century these technical questions of the construction of a treaty were regularly intermixed with economic and political matters, the most persistent of which appears to have been tariffs, particularly the tariff on Canadian fish products.

[156] C. A. Carter, *Treaties Affecting the Northeastern Fisheries* (1944); Harold A. Innis, *The Cod Fisheries, The History of an International Economy* (1940), Chs. 1, 2. The best compact summation of the controversies is by Carter in 162 pages, prefaced by a Summary of the essentials. See the excellent bibliography at pp. 163–167. See also L. Larry Leonard, *International Regulation of Fisheries* (1944), pp. 17–27.

From Independence to the Great War

At long last, the treaty dispute was submitted to arbitration at The Hague in 1910.[157] Following the award, the United States and Great Britain entered into an agreement of July 10, 1912,[158] implementing the decisions of the tribunal relating to local regulations and the delimitation of the territorial waters. Permanent mixed fishery commissions for Canada and Newfoundland, respectively, were established to consider any objections the United States might have to the reasonableness of the conservation and other regulations applied by those governments to fisheries within their territorial waters. "The conduct of United States fisheries along the treaty coasts since the Hague award and the agreement of 1912 has been on the whole satisfactory both to American fishermen and to the Canadian and Newfoundland authorities. . . . The laws and regulations adopted by the Canadian and Newfoundland authorities under the sanction of the first point of the award have been generally considered reasonable by the American fishermen. There has been little if any occasion for appeal as to their reasonableness to the Permanent Mixed Fishery Commission. . . ."[159]

Fur Seals and Otters. The rapacity of man, particularly toward the alleged inexhaustible bounty of nature, has been at times truly amazing. The extermination of the American passenger pigeon, the Arctic penguin, the South Atlantic fur seals, and other species mentioned from time to time in the discussion thus far, bear mute testimony to this lust for gain. After a decimating attack on the South Atlantic fur seals in the early part of the nineteenth century, in which American sealers very profitably participated, "a second revival of fur sealing occurred in the first decade of the twentieth century, and resulted in the complete extinction of the Southern species everywhere except in the Falkland Islands, where they were protected."[160] The North Pacific fur-seal herds might have gone the same way had not adequate international restraints been applied in time.

The story is well known.[161] When the United States acquired Alaska and the Pribilof Islands from Russia in 1867, the number of fur seals

---

[157] Carter, *op. cit.*, Ch. 11, with records cited.
[158] Agreement Adopting the Rules and Method of Procedure Recommended in the Award of Sept. 7, 1910, signed at Washington, July 20, 1912, 37 *Stat.* 1734, *TS* 572.
[159] Carter, *op. cit.*, p. xxiii.
[160] E. W. Hunter Christie, *The Antarctic Problem* (1951), Ch. VI, and p. 124. Also, Thomas R. Henry, *The White Continent: The Story of Antarctica* (1950), p. 213.
[161] Hayden, *op. cit.*, pp. 114–137. Leonard, *op. cit.*, pp. 55–95.

frequenting the rookeries on the islands was estimated at 4,700,000. By 1890, at the end of the first twenty-year lease of operations to the Alaska Commercial Company, the herd had been reduced to about 1,000,000; [162] by 1910, after the second lease to the North American Commercial Company, to about 125,000.[163] Meanwhile, the United States had become involved in bitter controversy with both Great Britain, on behalf of Canada, and Russia. The imbroglio included destructive sealing methods by the concessionaires; pelagic (high seas) sealing by Americans, Russians, Japanese, and Canadians; poaching on the islands by Japanese; congressional prohibition of pelagic sealing by Americans; an attempt by the United States to declare a large part of the North Pacific a mare clausum to foreign sealing; seizure of American vessels by Russia for sealing in the vicinity of the Commander Islands, off Kamchatka, and Robben Island, off lower Sakhalin Island;[164] and seizure of Canadian vessels by the United States for North Pacific sealing.

In 1887–1888 the United States attempted to secure a multipartite arrangement with several of the European powers, particularly Great Britain and Russia for the better protection of the fur-seal fisheries in Bering Sea. Arbitrations then followed with Great Britain and Russia over wrongful seizures by the United States and Russia, respectively. Indemnities were paid by the United States to Great Britain and by Russia to the United States. In pursuance of the arbitral award of 1892, the United States and Great Britain then engaged in an inadequate effort to establish a sixty-mile zone around the Pribilof Islands and closed seasons. Meanwhile, the United States instituted additional special investigations at and on the Pribilof Islands, to determine exactly the causes of the decimation, bringing the total of such inquiries for the period 1872–1913 up to ten.[165]

Once the scientific facts about the breeding habits of the seals were

---

[162] *Fur Seal Industry of Alaska*, H. Rept. No. 500, 63 Cong., 2 Sess., 1914. S. 6659.

[163] Statement by Ward T. Bower, Chief, Division of Alaska Fisheries, Dept. of Commerce, 75 *Cong. Rec.* 1931–1932, 72 Cong., 1 Sess., April 6, 1932.

[164] In 1875 Japan ceded Sakhalin Island to Russia; at the Peace of Portsmouth in 1905, Russia ceded the lower half of the island, with its seal-island appendage, back to Japan; at the end of World War II, Japan ceded the lower half of Sakhalin back to Russia. See Treaty of Peace with Japan, signed at San Francisco, Sept. 8, 1951, 3 *UST* 3169, *TIAS* 2490, Ch. II, Art. 2.

[165] For the legal aspects, see 1 Moore, *Digest* 890–929; 8 Hackworth, *Digest* 270 for citations. For the list of investigations, see *The Fur Seals and Other Life of the Pribilof Islands, Alaska, in 1914*, 63 Cong., 3 Sess., S. Doc. No. 980; also as Doc. No. 820 of the Bureau of Fisheries, issued June 19, 1915, p. 23.

From Independence to the Great War

established, solution of the problem was relatively easy. The fur-seal controversy is in many ways a classic of the triumph of science over anger, of prudence over cupidity. The investigations finally established that all female seals over two years old are annually pregnant. After bearing their pups upon the rocky shores, they become pregnant again immediately. Each pup is dependent upon its own cow-mother entirely and alone during the summer months. If the cow dies, the pup dies. Hence, if an adult female seal is killed during the summer months, at least two lives, the adult and the potential offspring, are lost to the herd. If a pup has already been born, then the death of the cow causes the loss of a third life. The males and females are not readily distinguishable on the high seas, except for the mane-covered bulls, whose pelts are not desired by the fur industry anyway.

Hence, pelagic (high seas) sealing can quickly reduce a herd. On land, the situation is different. There the bulls fight for and maintain harems of twenty to a hundred cows. The defeated bachelors go off by themselves. They are not necessary to the maintenance of the herd. On their own hauling grounds they can be herded and slaughtered for their pelts in selective fashion. (Lately, surplus females are also so taken.) The principles of good animal husbandry can thus be applied on land but not at sea. The solution to the problem was, therefore, to prohibit the taking of any seals whatever at sea and to compensate in some equitable fashion the countries which cooperated by forbidding pelagic sealing to their own citizens.

The fur-seals agreement of 1911 [166] between the United States, Great Britain, Russia, and Japan did precisely that. In brief the convention provided for a prohibition of pelagic sealing at all times by nationals of the respective parties in a prescribed North Pacific area (which prohibition was also generally observed, so far as the records disclose, by nationals of nonsignatory states); the taking of skins on dry land within the jurisdiction of the respective parties, in an authorized fashion; a sharing, in accordance with stipulated percentages, of the annual take or the money equivalent thereof; and a liberty for aborigines in the North Pacific (Indians, Aleuts, Ainos, and others) to continue to take seals freely in

---

[166] Convention for the Preservation and Protection of Fur Seals, signed at Washington, July 7, 1911, 37 *Stat.* 1542, TS 564. In accordance with Article XV, this agreement superseded the agreement of Feb. 7, 1911, concluded between the United States and Great Britain, on the same subject matter, 37 *Stat.* 1539, TS 563.

their accustomed way for their own use. Under this regime, within twenty years, the Pribilof herd alone increased to a million and a quarter, although in the same period, 1910–1931, nearly a half million skins were taken and marketed by the United States government.[167]

The same treaty of 1911, Article V, prohibited the taking of sea otters by nationals of the respective parties on the high seas beyond territorial waters in the delimited area. This provision closed the loophole in national legislation which sought to protect, within territorial limits, these valuable seagoing fur-bearing land animals.[168] Once in jeopardy of being exterminated, and rare as late as 1940, the sea otter is now resuming its place in the biological cycle. "It appears to be coming back in gratifying numbers in the Aleutian Islands, where it is rigidly protected by the Fish and Wildlife Service, and on the coast of California, where it is protected by that state."[169] It is interesting to recall that it was pursuit of the sea otter which brought the Russians into the Aleutians and Alaska in the eighteenth century and down into the California region in the nineteenth.[170] In 1940, the United States listed the sea otter among the mammals it was giving special protection in the Annex to the Pan American Convention on Nature Protection and Wildlife Preservation in the Western Hemisphere. This agreement will be discussed later.

Salmon, Halibut, and Sturgeon. Two other developments in this period involving fishery interests common to the United States and Canada should be noted, as forerunners of later successful undertakings. In 1908 Great Britain and the United States entered into an agreement[171] to set up an International Fisheries Commission to prepare a system of regulations, which were to be adopted by concurrent legislation in Canada and the United States, for the governance of fisheries in waters contiguous to those two countries, from the territorial waters of Passa-

---

[167] Statement by Ward T. Bower, above. For an excellent brief account of the present-day industry, see *Alaska Fishing and Fur-Seal Industries, 1954*, Statistical Digest No. 37, Fish and Wildlife Service, Department of the Interior (1956), pp. 53–70.

[168] See enforcing act of Aug. 24, 1912, 37 *Stat.* 499–500; *U.S. Code 1952 Ed.*, Tit. 16, Sec. 631 a–q.

[169] Letter to writer from Fish and Wildlife Service, Dec. 8, 1950. By 1957, the Interior Department estimated the population to be as high as 20,000. *N.Y.T.*, Aug. 28, 1957.

[170] See the dramatic story as told by Harold McCracken in *Hunters of the Stormy Sea* (1957). The author does not mention the 1911 convention.

[171] Treaty Concerning Fisheries in United States and Canadian Waters, concluded April 11, 1908, Washington, 35 *Stat.* 2000, TS 498.

From Independence to the Great War

maquoddy Bay westward to Puget Sound. The commission was duly set up; it framed regulations in 1909; the Canadian Parliament adopted them *in toto*; the American Congress failed to enact them. Thereupon the commission went into disuse and Canada gave notice in 1914 of resumption of liberty to regulate fisheries in Canadian waters contiguous to the international boundary in its own way.[172]

In 1918 an American-Canadian Fisheries Conference in Washington discussed pending questions concerning fisheries on both the Atlantic and Pacific coasts. Its final report recommended, *inter alia*, a treaty relating to the sockeye salmon of the Fraser River system; reciprocal legislation on the halibut; prohibition of lobster well-smack fishing just outside the territorial waters off the coast of Nova Scotia; and adoption of legislation by pertinent American states to accord with Canadian legislation relating to the sturgeon in Lake Erie.[173] Thus were laid the foundations for the subsequent agreements on the preservation of the halibut and the salmon fisheries.

Fisheries Expositions, Exhibitions, and Congresses. Some day some enterprising historian or sociologist will explore the subtle influences upon national cultures and the creation of international regimes emanating from international fairs, exhibitions, expositions, and so-called congresses devoted to trade, commerce, and sundry technologies in the nineteenth century. The history of the rise of multipartite treaty regimes demonstrates repeatedly that ideas for international regulation or agencies were first broached at meetings held in connection with such gatherings, particularly before the establishment of the League of Nations. Proposals were made in papers there read or resolutions there adopted. Thus, the setting up of the Metric Union in 1875 may be traced to the Committee on Weights, Measures, and Coins at the Universal Exposition in Paris in 1867.[174] Similarly the beginnings of the Industrial Property Union, established in 1883, can be traced directly to the Vienna Exposition of 1873 and the Paris Exposition of 1878.[175]

The sophisticated scholar will recognize that frequently the real source of some important international development is informal or pri-

---

[172] 1 Hackworth, *Digest* 798–799.

[173] *Ibid.*, p. 799.

[174] *Message of the President Communicating Information in Respect to the Universal Exhibition at Paris, 1867*, 39 Cong., 2 Sess., S. Ex. Doc. No. 5 (1867).

[175] Stephen P. Ladas, *The International Protection of Industrial Property* (1930), pp. 74–75.

vate action and not the formal proposal of a government. Often individuals make an original or a major contribution to the formation of an international agency. Thus, John A. Kasson pressed for the formation of both a postal union and a metric union.[176] David Lubin alone peddled his idea of an international agricultural organization until 1904 when he found in King Victor Emmanuel III of Italy a willing official sponsor.[177] The full story remains to be written of those unsung men and women who in the past century and a half pursued their ideals of international cooperation on economic and social problems into reality.

Among the numerous exhibitions and expositions officially attended by the United States or held in the United States in the post-Civil War period [178] were many devoted to fisheries. Thus, among the earlier ones, Congress authorized participation in the fishery exhibitions at Berlin in 1880,[179] London in 1883,[180] and Bergen in 1898.[181] A World's Fisheries Congress was held in Chicago in 1893.[182] The United States was then regularly represented in the periodic meetings of the International Congress of Aquiculture and Fisheries beginning with the so-called first one in Paris in 1900.[183] The others in the prewar period were held as follows: the second at St. Petersburg in 1902;[184] third at Vienna in 1905;[185] fourth at Washington in 1908;[186] fifth at Rome in 1911;[187] and

---

[176] T. C. Mendenhall, "Legislation Relating to Standards," 4 *Science* 1–8 (1896); resolution of July 16, 1866, sponsored by Kasson, then in the House of Representatives, H. Journal, 39 Cong., 1 Sess. (1865–1866), p. 1021; reply of the Secretary of State, July 17, 1866, 39 Cong., 1 Sess., H. Doc. No. 148.

[177] Lloyd C. Griscom, *Diplomatically Speaking* (1940), p. 297; Asher Hobson, *The International Institute of Agriculture* (1931), p. 6; and Olivia Rossetti Agresti, *David Lubin, A Study of Practical Idealism*, 2nd ed. (1941).

[178] "List of Expositions Which Have Been Aided by Federal Appropriations," Library of Congress Legislative Reference Service, Expositions T 391, 320860; *International Expositions*, 62 Cong., 2 Sess., S. Doc. No. 917 (1912).

[179] J. Res. of Feb. 16, 1880, 21 *Stat.* 301.

[180] J. Res. of July 18, 1882, 22 *Stat.* 388, Sec. 5.

[181] J. Res. of Feb. 17, 1898, 30 *Stat.* 734, No. 8.

[182] U.S., Fish Commission, *Bulletin*, vol. 13, *cit.*, *Document Catalog, 1893–1895*, p. 94.

[183] Data supplied in letter, U.S. Fish and Wildlife Service to writer, Jan. 12, 1953. See comment on the series of congresses by P. C. Jessup in *L'Exploitation des Richesses de la Mer*, Lectures Academie de Droit International, The Hague, 1929 (1929), pp. 25–26.

[184] Data in letter *cit.*, n. 183.

[185] *Report of Commissioner of Fisheries for the Fiscal Year 1905*, 59 Cong., 1 Sess., H. Doc. 717 (1906), S. 4989, p. 42.

[186] *Report, Fiscal Year 1909*, Dec. 6, 1909, pp. 33–34; *Proceedings*, 60 Cong., 2 Sess., H. Doc. 1571, S. 5493, 2 vols.

[187] *Report, Fiscal Year 1911* (1913), p. 527.

From Independence to the Great War

sixth at Ostend in 1913.[188] (A seventh reunion occurred after the war in Paris in 1931.[189]) And from 1912 to 1916 the United States was a member [190] of the International Council for the Exploration of the Sea, founded in 1899 at Stockholm.

Oceanic Birds. As in so many conservation matters, the United States gave protection to oceanic birds late. Despite the efforts of a few states to protect wildlife, nongame birds had been hunted up and down the Atlantic and Pacific coasts for their plumage for decades. In 1883, for example, "forty thousand terns are said to have been killed around Cape Cod. On the New Jersey Coast in the same season, terns were practically exterminated." [191] "Large scale gathering of the eggs of such birds as gulls, terns, herons, murres, etc., for use as food had been going on at various points on the Atlantic and Pacific coasts, as well as on certain Pacific islands and in Alaska for many years." [192]

The episode of the "Great Duck Egg Fake" of the late nineties symbolizes some of the public outcry against the unconscionable commercialized egging. On top of all the other perfectly authentic accounts of professional excessive egging on the Pacific coast and in Alaska, "the country was horrified and enraged to learn that the great summer nesting grounds of the migratory wild fowl in Alaska and the far north of Canada were being systematically ransacked by organized greed year after year to procure raw material for lollypops. It was alleged and believed, that enormous numbers of eggs taken from nests were shipped east . . . for manufacture into egg albumen, a substance indispensable to the confectioner. Somebody apparently was becoming a millionaire by exterminating wild fowl at the source." It was a good story but it was exposed as "without a shred of truth." Nevertheless, the "Great Duck Egg Fake" contributed to the passage by Congress of an act in 1900, "forbidding the destruction, possession, or export of the eggs of cranes, ducks, brant, or geese in Alaska." [193]

---

[188] No data available on American participation.

[189] 75 *Cong. Rec.* 11868–11871 at p. 11871: "U.S. participation without benefit of special appropriation."

[190] Acceptance of invitation to join is "strongly advocated" by the commissioner of fisheries. *Report, Fiscal Year 1911,* Doc. No. 753, May 4, 1912, pp. 526–527. See below, p. 185.

[191] Jenks Cameron, *The Bureau of Biological Survey,* S.M. No. 54 (1929), p. 77.

[192] *Ibid.,* p. 84.

[193] Act of June 6, 1900, 31 *Stat.* 332. For details of the various measures and citations to the acts for the period, see Cameron, *op. cit.,* pp. 73–101; for the "Fake" story, *ibid.,* pp. 84–85.

The United States and the Treaty Law of the Sea

Within the two decades 1894–1913, sundry steps were taken to correct these numerous evils. In addition to the act already mentioned, Congress discouraged interstate traffic in plumage in 1900 and prohibited the importation of plumage in 1913. States and the federal government established wildlife refuges. And finally, in 1913, Congress enacted its first Migratory Bird Act.[194] Doubts having been expressed concerning the constitutionality of this act, efforts were immediately directed toward securing a treaty with Great Britain, as the treaty-making power for Canada then, on the subject.[195] By the time the first act was lost in the courts in 1919,[196] the treaty had been concluded, and the second, treaty-implementing, act had been passed.[197] Both the treaty and the enforcing act were sustained in 1920.[198]

Though designed primarily to protect migratory game birds and birds useful to forestry and agriculture, the treaty also protects, in a more inclusive sense, "such migratory birds as are either useful to man or are harmless" (Preamble). Accordingly Article I of the treaty lists many species of "Migratory Game Birds," "Migratory Insectivorous Birds," and the following species of "Other Migratory Nongame Birds": auks, auklets, bitterns, fulmars, gannets, grebes, guillemots, gulls, herons, jaegers, loons, murres, petrels, puffins, shearwaters, and terns — all of them to a greater or less extent dependent upon the sea, some of them being truly oceanic.[199] The close season for these species is the year round, "except that Eskimos and Indians may take at any season auks, auklets, guillemots, murres, and puffins, and their eggs for food and their skins for clothing, but the birds and eggs so taken shall not be sold or offered for sale" (Art. II). The eider duck receives "special protection" (Art. IV) and the taking of nests or eggs of any of the listed species is prohibited,

---

[194] It was part of the Agricultural Appropriation Act of March 4, 1913, 37 *Stat.* 828, 846, 847, 848.

[195] Cameron, *op. cit.*, p. 99.

[196] United States v. Shauver, 214 Fed. 154 (1914); "the government's appeal from the decision of the Arkansas district court was dismissed on motion of the Attorney General on Jan. 6, 1919." Cameron, *op. cit.*, p. 101.

[197] Convention for the Protection of Migratory Birds, signed at Washington, Aug. 16, 1916, 39 *Stat.* 1702, TS 628. Enforcing act, July 3, 1918, 40 *Stat.* 755.

[198] Missouri v. Holland, 252 U.S. 416. For confirmation of the view of the Supreme Court in this epochal decision see Mr. Justice Black's language in Reid v. Covert, 354 U.S. 1 (1957).

[199] "About 220 species of migratory birds are excluded from the terms of the treaty because they are not specifically named, or because they do not feed chiefly or entirely on insects." Cameron, *op. cit.*, p. 102, n. 14. Among the species so excluded is the cormorant, a distinctly oceanic bird.

From Independence to the Great War

except for scientific and propagative purposes (Art. V). The international traffic in any illicit birds or eggs is interdicted (Art. VI).

Humanitarian Programs

The conscience of puritanic America ran strong in the nineteenth century despite the record of barbaric and inhuman acts perpetrated at times at home by Americans upon fellow Americans and others within their control or abroad upon native peoples in sundry quarters of the globe. This strong humanitarian trend found expression, early, in efforts to repress the traffic in slaves, liquor, firearms, and opium, and later, the traffic in white slavery and obscene publications. In each of these cases use of the sea is essential to the consummation of a major portion of the evil.

Traffic in Slaves, Liquor, and Firearms. Before the United States abolished slavery as a domestic institution by the Thirteenth Amendment in 1865 it already had, as indicated above, extensive legislation on the books repressing the slave trade by persons or vessels under American jurisdiction. It had refused to participate in the Quintuple Treaty of 1841 aimed at the repression of slave trading,[200] had agreed in the Webster-Ashburton Treaty of 1842 [201] to maintain a squadron off the coast of Africa to restrict American slavers, and had concluded a comprehensive treaty on the subject with Great Britain in 1862 providing for mutual visit and search in wide areas of the sea off the Atlantic and Indian Ocean coasts of Africa, in extensive zones around Cuba, and later, around Madagascar, Puerto Rico, and San Domingo.[202] Legislatively and diplomatically the United States after 1865 was prepared to enter into a wider arrangement on slavery.

In the meantime, Americans in the western Indian country, Alaska, the Pacific, and Africa had contributed to the debauchment of natives and aborigines by strong drink and firearms. Congress sought to mitigate

---

[200] 2 Moore, *Digest* 914, 928–930.

[201] Convention as to Boundaries, Suppression of Slave Trade, and Extradition, concluded at Washington, Aug. 9, 1842, 8 *Stat.* 572, *TS* 119; Arts VIII and IX.

[202] Treaty for the Suppression of African Slave Trade, concluded at Washington, April 7, 1862, 12 *Stat.* 1225, *TS* 126; Additional Articles to the Treaty for the Suppression of Slave Trade, concluded at Washington, Feb. 17, 1863, 13 *Stat.* 645, *TS* 127, extending the policing to the sea around Madagascar, Puerto Rico, and San Domingo; and a Convention for the Suppression of Slave Trade, concluded at Washington, June 3, 1870, 16 *Stat.* 777, *TS* 131, abolishing the mixed courts set up in the 1862 convention.

these evils in a series of acts, beginning in 1832,[203] penalizing the traffic in liquor and arms among the Indians, and after 1868,[204] among the natives of Alaska. Missionary and other groups pressed for correction of the evils in the Pacific.[205]

By 1890, therefore, the United States could and did enter the Brussels General Act for the Repression of African Slave Trade,[206] which included measures to restrict the traffic in spirituous liquors in Africa also. Extensive maritime zones in the Atlantic and Indian oceans were set up to achieve the objects of the regime. The tariffs on liquor were revised in several subsequent agreements, the United States participating in those of 1899 [207] and 1906.[208] Beginning in 1889 the United States supported its cooperation in the repression of the slave traffic by including the offense of slave trading in its extradition treaties.[209]

The United States declined to participate in British proposals of 1884 and 1892 looking toward a multipartite arrangement to restrict the traffic in spirituous liquors, firearms, and ammunition in the western Pacific.[210] Instead, it adopted an act of 1902 [211] penalizing persons subject to American jurisdiction who engaged in this traffic and also in the opium traffic among the natives of practically all the Pacific islands, with the exception of those of Hawaii (which by then had become annexed to the United States). Since the turn of the century the United States has displayed a continuing lively interest in these international ef-

[203] Act of July 9, 1832, 4 *Stat.* 564, Sec. 4. See *R.S.* 1878, Sec. 2139; and Act of Feb. 14, 1873, 17 *Stat.* 457, *R.S.* 1878, Sec. 2136.

[204] Act of July 27, 1868, 15 *Stat.* 241, Sec. 4; *R.S.* 1878, Sec. 1955.

[205] E.g., Memorial of Aug. 14, 1893, relating to the traffic in firearms and intoxicants with the natives of New Hebrides by Europeans and Americans, S. Rept. No. 410, 53 Cong., 2 Sess., May 17, 1894, in *Compilation of Reports of Committee on Foreign Relations, U.S. Senate, 1789–1901,* 56 Cong., 2 Sess., S. Doc. No. 231, Part 4. See also *Cong. Rec.,* 57 Cong., 1 Sess., p. 1202, Feb. 1, 1902.

[206] General Act for the Repression of African Slave Trade, signed at Brussels, July 2, 1890, 27 *Stat.* 886, TS 383.

[207] Convention on Regulation of Importation of Spirituous Liquors into Certain Regions of Africa, concluded at Brussels, June 8, 1899, 31 *Stat.* 1915, TS 389.

[208] Convention Revising Duties Imposed by the Brussels Convention of June 8, 1899, concluded at Brussels, Nov. 3, 1906, 35 *Stat.* 1912, TS 467.

[209] The first one appears to have been with Great Britain, concluded July 12, 1889, 26 *Stat.* 1508, TS 139. By the middle 1930s, over two dozen of the extradition treaties included slave trading among the extraditable offenses.

[210] 1892 *For. Rel.* 320.

[211] Act of Feb. 14, 1902, 32 *Stat.* 33. The zone, extending from 20° north latitude to 20° south and from 120° east longitude to 120° west, included the Polynesian group, part of the Dutch East Indies, most of Australia and New Zealand, and most of the Philippine Islands, but not the Hawaiian Islands.

From Independence to the Great War

forts to protect and advance the welfare of native and dependent peoples generally throughout the world.

Opium Traffic. During the 1830s and 1840s American vessels and personnel engaged conspicuously in opium running in the Far East — the "opium clippers" achieving a type of fame therein. From time to time American naval vessels sought to repress the traffic.[212] In the period 1833 to 1903, the United States entered into nine treaties [213] with four Asiatic countries — Siam, beginning with one in 1833, China, beginning with one in 1844, Japan, beginning with one in 1858, and Korea in 1882 — prohibiting or restricting trade in opium by Americans. An act of 1899 prohibited the use of opium for habit-forming purposes in Alaska.[214] The act of 1902, noted above,[215] prohibited the sale of opium to islanders of the Pacific.

On acquisition of the Philippines, however, the United States inherited an opium evil of really first magnitude, which, in addition to the serious increase of opium smoking among non-Chinese in the United States since 1860,[216] forced the United States into greater activity. From the beginning it was recognized that transport by sea, licit or illicit, in addition to production, processing or manufacture, and internal traffic was an essential element in the problem.[217] Hence, when the Hague opium convention was finally adopted in 1912,[218] largely as the result of American initiative, numerous provisions sought to suppress unlawful importation or exportation of raw materials or processed drugs, by land or sea.

The aid of the Universal Postal Union was also invoked by the 1912 conference. Thus, Article 19 of the 1912 Hague Convention obligated the parties to prevent misuse of their postal systems to evade the stipulations of the agreement, and the final protocol of the first conference drew to the attention of the Universal Postal Union the need for regulat-

---

[212] Bryant, *op. cit.*, pp. 236–240.

[213] *Subject Index*, all listed at p. 158.

[214] Act of March 3, 1899, 30 *Stat.* 1253, Secs. 145–149.

[215] Act of Feb. 14, 1902, 32 *Stat.* 33.

[216] Hamilton Wright, *Report on the International Opium Commission and on the Opium Problem as Seen Within the United States and Its Possessions*, 61 Cong., 2 Sess., S. Doc. No. 377 (1910), pp. 34–51.

[217] *Report of the Committee Appointed by the Philippine Commission to Investigate the Use of Opium and the Traffic Therein*, Bureau of Insular Affairs, War Department (1905). See conclusions as stated by Wright, *Report, op. cit.*, p. 27.

[218] Convention and Final Protocol for the Suppression of the Abuse of Opium and Other Drugs, signed at The Hague, Jan. 13, 1912, and July 9, 1913, 38 *Stat.* 1912, TS 612.

ing the transmission by post of raw opium and certain derivatives. As soon as possible, after World War I, the Universal Postal Union, in its general convention concluded at Madrid in 1920, included appropriate restrictive provisions applicable to all members of the union whether participants in the opium arrangements or not.[219] The practice has continued regularly since. Successive multipartite agreements on narcotic drugs since 1912, as well as the postal agreements since 1920, have recognized the maritime aspect of the evil and have sought to control it by appropriate stipulations.

Traffic in Women and Children and Obscene Literature. Two other social evils in which transport by sea plays an important part are white slavery, or, more accurately, the traffic in women and children for immoral purposes, and the circulation of obscene publications. The experience of American administrators, state and federal, had demonstrated, and League of Nations investigations later confirmed,[220] the nexus between the three evils — use of drugs, the seductive influence of pornographic literature, and prostitution. In modern times, at least, the sea also is essential to the propagation of much of the three evils.

Though restricted by the doctrine of the reserved powers of states,[221]

---

[219] Agreement of Nov. 30, 1920, 42 *Stat.* 1971, 1993, Art. 18, par. 2 (e) and par 5.

[220] Resolution, L.o.N. Council, June 7, 1926, 1926 *O.J.* 858; *Report of the Special Body of Experts on the Traffic in Women and Children*, Pts. I and II, C.52.1927.IV, Feb. 1927, pp. 17–18, on the relation of obscene photographs to prostitution.

[221] See the annual reports of the superintendent of immigration, later the commissioner general of immigration, beginning in 1891, and particularly the monumental *Reports of the Immigration Commission* (1907–1910), 41 vols., 61 Cong., 2 and 3 Sess. A general index, intended as Vol. 42, was never published. But see *Abstracts of Reports of the Immigration Commission*, 61 Cong., 3 Sess., S. Doc. No. 747, particularly *Steerage Conditions: Importation and Harboring of Women for Immoral Purposes*, Vol. 37 of *Reports*, 61 Cong., 3 Sess., S. Doc. No. 753. There is very little on the present subject in D. H. Smith and H. G. Herring, *The Bureau of Immigration*, S.M. No. 30 (1924). Since the states are primarily responsible for public morals and since both the maintenance of prostitution and production and circulation of obscene literature are chiefly local (see, e.g., Agnes M. Brown, *Digest of Laws Enacted in the Various States relating to the Possession, Circulation, and Sale of Obscene Literature*, 71 Cong., 2 Sess., S. Doc. No. 54, Oct. 30, 1929), the federal government is restricted to the interstate and foreign commerce aspects of the problem. The Mann White Slave Act of June 25, 1910, 36 *Stat.* 825, 826, an outgrowth of the vast investigation of 1907–1910, gave extensive powers to deal with the international aspects to the commissioner general of immigration (Sec. 6). During the later League discussions of the two problems, the federal government repeatedly asserted it lacked power to deal with the local aspects, particularly the prescription of crimes, though after the *Migratory Bird* case (1920) the reluctance to enter into treaty commitments relating to those aspects could more accurately be attributed to policy rather than want of power. (See U. P. Hubbard, "The Cooper-

the United States nevertheless participated in two of the first fumbling efforts of the international community to deal with white slavery and the circulation of obscene literature.[222] It adhered in 1908 to the administrative Arrangement for the Suppression of the White Slave Traffic which was signed by other powers at Paris on May 18, 1904,[223] and it became an original signatory of the Arrangement Relative to the Repression of the Circulation of Obscene Publications at Paris, May 4, 1910.[224] Subsequently, during the League of Nations period, the United States participated earnestly in its work related to these troublesome social problems.

Scientific and Legal Developments

The United States early displayed interest in international movements and organizations of a scientific or professional character devoted to securing international collaboration toward more rational use of the sea or better understanding of its phenomena.

International Polar Year, 1882–1883. In 1881–1884, the United States participated in the movement to establish circumpolar international stations, which grew out of the deliberations of the several international polar conferences, beginning with that of Hamburg in 1879.[225] Eleven nations cooperated in this scientific work, embracing many fields, such as terrestrial magnetism, astronomy, meteorology, climatology, ice formation, tides, ocean currents, and oceanography. Fourteen stations were set up, three of them in the Southern Hemisphere. The United States set up stations at Lady Franklin Bay (between Greenland and Ellesmere

---

ation of the United States with the League of Nations, 1931–1936," *Int. Con.* No. 329, April 1937, p. 426; Geneva Research Center, "The U.S. and World Organization during 1937," *Int. Con.* No. 341, June 1938, p. 259.) It did not hesitate, for example, to assume extended authority over the manufacture and local distribution of narcotic drugs when the national regulation of those local aspects became essential to an effective international regime.

[222] The United States did not become a party to another, more extensive agreement, the Convention for the Suppression of the White Slave Traffic, and Protocol, signed by other powers at Paris, May 4, 1910 (103 *B.&F.S.P.* 244), which replaced a *projet de convention* elaborated at Paris in a conference in 1902. A draft convention on the criminal aspects of the circulation of obscene publications, elaborated at the same conference in Paris in 1910 which produced the administrative arrangement signed by the United States, never went into effect (103 *B.&F.S.P.* 250).

[223] 35 *Stat.* 1979, *TS* 496.
[224] 37 *Stat.* 1511, *TS* 559.
[225] 1880 *For. Rel.* 940; *International Polar Congress,* 46 Cong., 2 Sess., H. Ex. Doc. No. 41 (1880).

Island)[226] and at Point Barrow in Alaska.[227] This was the first of the so-called International Polar Years, the second being held in 1932–1933. One of their principal features is the simultaneous observation by pre-arrangement of selected phenomena on which scientific data are desired. The third of these tremendous undertakings, designed to serve both the old and the newer sciences, is the International Geophysical Year of 1957–1958.

The polar regions have, apparently, from at least the late eighteenth century, fascinated adventurous souls in Europe and America. Hardly a decade has passed since Wilkes' famous exploring expedition of 1838–1842 which has not witnessed some notable public or private American scientific expedition into one or the other polar region. These expeditions unite in themselves peculiarly a complex of the great sciences essential to understanding of the sea.

Meteorology. Beginning with the First International Congress of Meteorologists held in Vienna in 1873, American officials regularly participated in the work of the congresses and of the organization established at Utrecht in 1878.[228] In 1947 a convention established a superseding World Meteorological Organization, which will be discussed later.

Hydrography. Though Matthew Maury had secured considerable international collaboration in his hydrographic and meteorological work, hydrographic work in the next several generations continued for the most part along individual national lines. In 1884, E. R. Knorr, on retirement from the Hydrographic Office, urged in a pamphlet the establishment of an international board for the performance of certain coordinative functions.[229] His hope did not materialize until the First International Hydrographic Conference in London in 1919 decided to establish a bureau,[230] which in 1921 was set up at Monte Carlo, Monaco.

Geodesy. As early as 1883, American officials participated in European

---

[226] Adolphus W. Greeley, *International Polar Expedition. Report of the Proceedings of the U.S. Expedition to Lady Franklin Bay, Grinnell Land*, 49 Cong., 1 Sess., H. Misc. Doc. No. 393, 2 vols. (1888), Vol. I, p. 1.

[227] F. H. Ray, *Report of the International Polar Expedition to Point Barrow, Alaska*, 48 Cong., 2 Sess., H. Ex. Doc. No. 44 (1885).

[228] *U.S. Int. Org. 1949*, pp. 131–136; G. A. Weber, *The Weather Bureau*, S.M. No. 9 (1922), p. 13.

[229] Schmeckebier, *Int. Org.*, p. 283.

[230] *U.S. Int. Org. 1949*, pp. 127–131; G. A. Weber, *The Hydrographic Office*, S.M. No. 42 (1926), pp. 37–39. For a fascinating account of contemporary hydrographic work, see Commander L. S. Hubbard, "Increasing the Safety of the World's Shipping: The Sixth International Hydrographic Conference," 27 *DSB* 68–70 (1952); and

From Independence to the Great War

conferences devoted to securing international cooperation in the field of geodesy.[231] In 1889, the United States, on invitation of the German government, became a member of the Geodetic Association,[232] which after World War I, in 1919, was superseded by the International Union of Geodesy and Geophysics, a constituent member of the newly created International Council of Scientific Unions and Associated Unions.[233]

Geography: Map on the Millionth Scale. Since the latter part of the nineteenth century Americans, officials and private persons, have participated regularly in the periodic international geographical congresses. Dr. Albrecht Penck, famous geographer of Berlin, suggested to the fifth congress at Bern in 1891 "the idea of publishing a series of maps on a uniform scale to cover the entire world." At the 1908 meeting in Geneva, after successive congresses had discussed the project, the United States delegates "proposed that an international map on the scale 1:1,000,000 should be definitely standardized." In pursuance of a resolution to that effect then adopted and further decisions made at the First International Conference on the International Map held in London in 1909, the actual work of planning and producing such a map was begun.

The International Map, better known as the 1/M Map (1 inch = 15.78 miles) was designed to be the ultimate in accuracy and practicality, shorn of embellishment and nonsense. It was to be a map that could be "read" by any contributing nation or in any nation possessing the key to its system. It was to be a basic map in every sense of the word, a topographic picture on which any amount of specialized information, geographical, geological, political or economic, could be superimposed merely by overprinting. The base map itself would show such elementary features as streams and larger water bodies, towns and cities, railroads and highways, political boundaries and topography. . . . The map was to be a hypsometric map, that is, the successive altitudes would be indicated by a system of color tints; consequently a color chart was necessary for every contributing nation.[234]

William G. Watt, "International Cooperation in the Science of Hydrography: Seventh International Hydrographic Conference, Monte Carlo, Monaco, May 7–17, 1957," 37 *DSB* 361–363 (1957).

[231] W. D. Lambert, "Geodesy," *Encyclopaedia Britannica* (1952), Vol. 10, pp. 127–134.

[232] Act of Feb. 5, 1889, 25 *Stat.* 1019; G. A. Weber, *Coast and Geodetic Survey*, S.M. No. 16 (1923), pp. 13–14.

[233] *U.S. Int. Org. 1949*, pp. 122–127; Lambert, *op. cit.*, p. 134.

[234] Lloyd A. Brown, *The Story of Maps*, pp. 302–303. This work gives the best brief account of the whole project, pp. 299–307. See Schmeckebier, *Int. Org.*, pp. 321–330, for additional documentation.

The United States and the Treaty Law of the Sea

The work of preparing the maps according to the uniform standards and nomenclature decided upon was parcelled out to the various contributing nations. The second conference in Paris in 1913 authorized the establishment of a Central Bureau at the Ordnance Survey Office at Southampton, England. With only eight sheets of the map published by the time of the outbreak of the Great War, the bureau was closed down for the "duration." The third conference, held in Paris in 1919, provided for the revival and reorganization of the Central Bureau and prodded the cooperating national cartographic services into resuming their work on their sections of the map. By 1949, about 40 per cent of the land area had been mapped in accordance with the IMW specifications.[235]

International Maritime Committee. The 1889 Washington Marine Conference had attempted a comprehensive discussion of various aspects of the law relating to ocean travel and commerce. After 1889, specialization in topics came into practice. Division of effort resulted in a series of conferences on safety at sea, already mentioned, and a series on maritime law. At the center of this latter series was the unofficial International Maritime Committee, founded in 1897, with headquarters at Antwerp, and composed of national associations of maritime law. American officials, admiralty judges, and lawyers participated early in the work of the committee. The committee, in a series of conferences, elaborated various draft conventions. Diplomatic conferences called by the Belgian government, at Brussels, then reviewed them and opened them for signature. The conventions so adopted up to World War II sought to produce uniform law with respect to collisions at sea, salvage and assistance, limitation of shipowners' liability, maritime mortgages and liens, immunity of state-owned ships, arrest of ships, civil and penal jurisdiction in collision cases, and bills of lading.[236]

---

[235] *U.S. Int. Org. 1949*, pp. 109–111; *International Agencies in Which the United States Participates*, D.S. Pub. No. 2699 (1946), pp. 101–104 (hereinafter cited *U.S. Int. Agencies 1946*). After World War II the bureau was moved to Chessington, Surrey, England. In 1953, the functions of the bureau were transferred to the United Nations. Discussed below, p. 349.

[236] *Handbook of International Organizations*, League of Nations (1938), pp. 246–247. For texts and bibliographies on all the agreements signed at the diplomatic conferences from 1919 to 1939, see Hudson, *I.L.* For a discussion of all nine conventions, see Erastus Cornelius Benedict, *The Law of American Admiralty*, 6th ed. by Arnold Whitman Knauth (1940), Vol. 4, pp. 258–269, 273–277. For a summary of the work of the conference held in Brussels in 1957, see *N.Y.T.*, Oct. 11, 28, 1957, and "Maritime Conventions Signed at Brussels Conference," 37 *DSB* 759–764 (1957); the latter includes the texts of the two conventions there adopted, one on the Limitation of the Liability of Owners of Seagoing Ships, the other on Stowaways. Signature of

From Independence to the Great War

The United States became a party to those on Assistance and Salvage, 1910,[237] and on Bills of Lading, 1924.[238] "The Salvage Convention won approval in the United States without undue trouble largely because it enacted existing American principles, but the Collisions Convention has been the target of bitter opposition. Although the American delegates to the 1909 conference subscribed to the draft, subject to certain reservations, it has never been ratified by this country. A favorable report by a Senate subcommittee in 1939 represented the convention's high-water mark. America's failure to ratify has left its law of collision liability unique among the maritime nations of the Western World." [239]

Navigation Congresses. The two series of international congresses on navigation, one on inland navigation, initiated at Brussels in 1885, and one on maritime navigation begun at Paris in 1889, were combined at The Hague in 1894 into a single International Navigation Congress, the first of which new series was held in 1898 at Brussels. American representatives helped form the new organization and the United States has contributed to the expenses of the Permanent Association of Navigation Congresses since 1902. "The Congress deals with the improvement and maintenance of harbors and waterways and their accessories but not with ships and the actual navigation thereof." [240]

International Association for Labour Legislation. Finally, among these proliferating organizations of the pre-1914 period must be mentioned the International Association for Labour Legislation, founded in 1900, which performed in the field of international legislation on labor matters a function similar to that of the International Maritime Committee. Americans participated in the work of the association early and governmental subventions to it began in 1902.[241] The International Labor Organiza-

---

either convention by the United States awaits the result of further consultations within the United States. See also Department of State Press Release No. 577 (Oct. 15, 1957).

[237] Signed at Brussels, Sept. 23, 1910, 37 *Stat.* (2) 1658, *TS* 576.

[238] Signed at Brussels, Aug. 25, 1924, 51 *Stat.* (2) 233, *TS* 931.

[239] Anonymous, "The Difficult Quest for a Uniform Maritime Law: Failure of the Brussels Conventions to Achieve International Agreement on Collision Liability, Liens, and Mortgages," 64 *Yale Law Journal* 878–905 (1955). For the 1939 subcommittee report, see 76 Cong., 1 Sess., S. Rept. Ex. No. 4 (1939). For the text of the convention on collisions, 103 *B.&F.S.P.* 434.

[240] Act of June 28, 1902, 32 *Stat.* 485; *U.S. Int. Org. 1949*, pp. 292–296.

[241] Act of April 28, 1902, 32 *Stat.* 120, 168. See *U.S. Labor Bureau Bulletins*, No. 54 (1904), pp. 1080–1086, and No. 86 (1910), pp. 169–184, for administrative reports on the work of the association.

tion took over the work of the association in 1919; the United States joined the organization in 1934.[242] Since 1934 the United States has participated vigorously in this organization and has ratified a number of its conventions dealing with seamen and other matters relating to service aboard ships.

Conclusion

The Great War interrupted this work of dealing collectively with these common problems arising out of use of the sea but did not terminate it. In a sense, the Great War was the first world-wide "civil" war, for once the political problems and power struggles were ended (albeit only temporarily), the international community with respect to its problems on land and its problems at sea had to resume with the integrative process where it left off in August 1914. The accumulated multipartite agreements dealing with day-to-day routine administrative matters of enduring concern to governments, whether applicable to affairs on land or at sea, were applied by the parties to them during the war itself except insofar as military operations or the requirements of the first "total" war rendered application impossible. And when peace was restored, the treaties of Versailles, St. Germain, and Trianon,[243] not only kept in force the extant multipartite agreements on such administrative matters, but required the vanquished in some cases, and both the victors and vanquished in the case of The Hague Opium Convention of 1912, to participate in stipulated multipartite agreements if perchance they had not previously. Thus part of the legal fabric of the pre-1914 community of nations was reknit.

With the coming of peace and the creation of the League of Nations the method of using multipartite agreements to deal with many-faceted problems of common interest to several states received renewed and systematic emphasis from the League and its organs. Where once problems remained unattended to because no single nation would wish to assume the initiative in circularizing governments and inviting them to a conference, now under the League a simple resolution of one of the organs could start the process of international legislation. The initiative

---

[242] Effective Aug. 20, 1934, 40 *Stat.* (2) 2712, *TS* 874.

[243] Texts of these treaties may conveniently be found in 3 Redmond, Appendix 1. The pertinent provisions are these: for Austria, Arts. 234–247; for Germany, Arts. 282–295; for Hungary, Arts. 217–230. The authoritative work on the effect of war and other events on multipartite agreements is still Harold J. Tobin, *The Termination of Multipartite Treaties* (1933).

From Independence to the Great War

taken by such international agencies also had the great advantage of allaying the multitudinous petty rivalries and jealousies between chancellories which impeded on occasion salutary group action, as was conspicuously the case in getting the first multipartite agreement on health in the nineteenth century. The post-1919 period, then, is distinguished by the ready acceptance of the multipartite instrument as a convenient mode of dealing with numerous problems requiring discrete disposition and by the central role which the League of Nations played in the process generally, though not as greatly with respect to affairs at sea as with respect to affairs on land.

CHAPTER IV

BETWEEN THE GREAT WARS: PROGRESS IN REGIMES FOR THE SEA

It is evident from the preceding discussion of the period 1776–1919 that the groundwork had been laid in the United States for an expanding participation in international regimes relating to the sea — in terms of administrative organization, national legislation, scientific interest, a developing merchant marine, sentiment for conservation, alert private pressure groups,[1] and an official disposition to assume commitments of a multipartite character. In that period the United States had taken the initiative in the establishment of several important international agencies under treaty and under other types of constituent instruments. It had assumed commendable leadership in several organizations. By 1919 it had become, indeed, a veteran, if not an inveterate, joiner of "leagues of nations," though only one of them, the Organization of the American States, had any political significance. Furthermore, where it did join even a highly technical administrative union, the record reveals careful consideration of the national interest in so doing.[2]

For present purposes, the period 1919–1946 is distinguished by the emergence of air commerce and radio broadcasting, public concern for the welfare of seamen, and the setting up of the League of Nations and the International Labor Organization. Eschewing at first even routine correspondence with the League, the United States gradually and increasingly participated in its nonpolitical work.[3] When it was too late,

---

[1] See excellent discussion of the phenomenon by Joseph P. Chamberlain, "International Organization," in *International Conciliation*, No. 385, Dec. 1942, pp. 459–523 (hereinafter cited *Int. Con.*).

[2] Reiff, "The United States and International Administrative Unions," *Int. Con.*, No. 332, Sept. 1937, pp. 650–651.

[3] For virtually a continuous story see the several numbers of *Int. Con.*, thus: Ursula P. Hubbard, "The Cooperation of the United States with the League of Nations and with the International Labour Organization" (1919–1931), No. 274, Nov. 1931; *ibid.*, "The Cooperation of the United States with the League of Nations 1931–1936," No. 329, April 1937; and the reprints of the studies by the Geneva Research Center,

the United States displayed some interest in League efforts to maintain the peace, but that is not within the purview of the present discussion.[4] In 1934 the United States joined the International Labor Organization and thereafter played a notable role in its deliberations. The economic and social forces generated in the United States in the pre-1919 era with respect to its relation to those matters which concerned the sea, as well as the administrative techniques then developed and policy attitudes then formulated, for the most part simply continued into the interwar period. World War I (and, for that matter, World War II) interrupted but did not terminate the basic trends previously established. The sea, the problems arising out of its use by man, and the necessity of solving them, endured.

It would be possible to summarize the participation of the United States in international efforts relating to the sea in the period 1919–1946 in terms of institutions, describing programs undertaken outside of the League of Nations, under the League, in the International Labor Organization, and within the Pan American system. It would be more realistic, however, to keep the sea in the foreground, outlining group effort in relation thereto, whatever the auspices of the collaboration. It will appear, toward the end of the interwar period, that the international regimes increasingly overlapped in dealing with some common maritime problems and that established international agencies found it increasingly necessary to act conjointly with others in devising solutions for such problems. The unity of the sea thus imposed a degree of unification of effort and organization. If the United Nations, with its tremendous scope of subject matter and its coordination of specialized agencies and other bodies devoted to international ends, may be regarded as a logical response to the basic drives toward unity implicit in the modern world, then conspicuously among those drives must be reckoned the compulsions arising out of the sea.

The growing interrelations of the regimes in the interwar period make

---

entitled "The United States and World Organization During 1936," No. 331, June 1937; for 1937, No. 341, June 1938; for 1938, No. 352, Sept. 1939; for 1939, No. 361, June 1940. All these articles have the great merit of citing the appropriate League documentation. Now Hans Aufricht's definitive *Guide to League of Nations Publications: A Bibliographical Survey of the Work of the League, 1920–1947* (1951) facilitates use of that documentation. Still the best brief handbook of League work, with citation of League documentation, is Denys P. Myers, *Handbook of the League of Nations* (1935).

[4] See Francis Paul Walters, *A History of the League of Nations*, 2 Vols. (1952).

it difficult to follow closely the categories established for the 1865–1919 era, namely, safety of life and property at sea, communications, health, exploitation of the products of the sea, humanitarian programs, and scientific and legal developments. Some deviation from the pattern already established may therefore be expected. The growing treaty interrelations simply reflect the blending of factual developments. As these become more complex the number of treaties increases and so does their length. Nevertheless, it is still possible to group the activities related to the sea under a few heads and so deal with them in some orderly fashion. If perchance some topic is presented at disproportionate length, it will probably involve data not readily accessible to the researcher in this field or perhaps some subject matter too briefly discussed in the standard treatises.

Transportation

Safety of Life at Sea. The most important developments in this period relating to safety of life and property at sea were the conclusion of the first fully implemented convention of safety at sea, in 1929, and the convention on load lines, in 1930. Extended conference under the League sought greater uniformity of practice in buoyage and lighting of coasts. An oil-pollution conference at Washington in 1926 sought, among other things, to reduce the hazards of fire at sea and in harbors occasioned by that abuse. Seamen and masters found new protection and solicitude for their welfare in the safety-at-sea, load-lines, and radio treaties, as well as in specific conventions produced by the I.L.O. Provisions in the Paris (1919) and Habana (1928) conventions on aerial navigation invoked the law of the sea in the salvage of aircraft. Elaborate provisions in the 1927 Telecommunications Convention provided for extensive use of radio in maritime matters and systematic meteorological services.

London Conference, 1929. The conference on safety of life at sea, held on invitation of the British government in London, April 16–May 31, 1929, revised and amended the 1914 convention.[5] It prescribed the con-

[5] Convention on Safety of Life at Sea, signed at London, May 31, 1929, 50 *Stat.* 1121, TS 910, ratified subject to three understandings laid down by the Senate. Annex I contains the detailed regulations; Annex II contains the rules for preventing collisions at sea. The amendments to the rules on collision, as customary, were to be adopted by concurrent national legislation. An inadvertent omission of a regulation from Annex I in 1929 necessitated an amendment, circulated by the British government, in 1930, effective Jan. 17, 1933, 51 *Stat.* 13, TS 921.

Between the Great Wars

struction of passenger ships (defined as ships carrying twelve or more passengers), and with respect to varying categories of passenger and cargo ships on international voyages, it dealt with lifesaving appliances, radiotelegraphy, safety of navigation, continuation of the ice patrol and derelict-destroying service (by the United States), and the issuance of safety, radiotelegraph, and various kinds of exemption certificates. It provided for sundry types of signals and prescribed rules of the road. Neither the unratified 1914 convention nor this new one applied to commerce on the Great Lakes.[6]

North Atlantic Tracks. One provision of the 1929 agreement, dealing with the North Atlantic tracks or lanes for steamships, takes us back to Matthew Maury. As a result of the sinking, with heavy loss of life, of the United States mail steamer *Arctic* in October 1854 by collision with the French steamer *Vesta*, in thick fog on the route from Liverpool to New York, Matthew Maury included in his *Sailing Directions* (1855) a section on "Steam Lanes Across the Atlantic." These were put into effect by British lines beginning in 1889. Meanwhile, the United States Hydrographic Office in 1891 urged the principal steamship companies to meet and discuss steamer lanes.[7] As a result of these pressures, the principal British and continental passenger shipping companies, under the leadership of the Cunard Steamship Company, formed in 1898 a North Atlantic Track Association and put into effect an agreement among themselves stipulating the various routes to be used in the North Atlantic to and from United States and Canadian ports in the different seasons.

Briefly, the scheme prescribes separate lanes, up to twenty to twenty-five miles wide, widest where most fog is expected, for eastbound and westbound traffic. The routes from Fastnet (the lighthouse off the southwest coast of County Cork, Eire) or Bishop Rock (the lighthouse in the Scilly Isles off Land's End, Cornwall, England) to Boston or New York, and return, are classified as Track A (Extra Southern), Track B (Southern), and Track C (Northern), to be used in accordance with a prescribed scheme that takes into consideration ice conditions. The routes from Fastnet, Inistrahull (the lighthouse off the northernmost

---

[6] *Report*, 1914, 63 Cong., 2 Sess., S. Doc. No. 463, p. 78; Convention, 1929, *Regulations*, Ch. I, Reg. 3 (b): "Notwithstanding any provisions of the present regulations, nothing herein shall apply to ships solely navigating the Great Lakes of North America and their connecting and tributary waters as far east as the lower exit of the Lachine Canal at Montreal in the Province of Quebec, Canada."

[7] J. B. Cochran, *United States Navy Hydrographic Office: 125th Anniversary* (1955), p. 12.

extremity of County Donegal, Eire), or Bishop Rock to Halifax or the Gulf of St. Lawrence and return are classified under Tracks D to G.

The 1914 London Conference on Safety at Sea decided to leave the selection of the routes with the steamship companies concerned. "The designation of such routes by the Governments specially concerned was thoroughly discussed, but it was concluded that such a designation might enable the master of a vessel in collision with another vessel to set up the claim that he was following a route fixed for him by Government, and that the diminution of the master's sense of responsibility would offset the advantages of Government routes or lanes."[8] Hence the convention (Art. 13) provided merely that the contracting parties require their companies to give public notice of the regular routes "which they propose their vessels should follow, and of any changes which they make in them," and, further, that the governments use their influence to induce owners of all vessels crossing the Atlantic to follow the routes adopted by the principal companies.

The 1929 convention (Art. 39) repeated substantially the same provisions but added that the governments should use their influence to induce the owners of all vessels crossing the Atlantic to and from ports of the United States to avoid the fishing banks of Newfoundland during the fishing season and "to pass outside regions known or believed to be endangered by ice." And further, it set up the United States as the "monitor" for the system by requesting it, as the administration managing the ice patrol, to report to the flag state "any ship which is observed not to be on any regular, recognized or advertised route, or which crosses the . . . fishing banks during the fishing season, or which, when proceeding to or from ports of the United States, passes through regions known or believed to be endangered by ice." The flag state could then take disciplinary action, if necessary, toward the master of the vessel so reported. The 1948 convention continued the same arrangement, merely extending it to include Canadian ports.[9]

[8] Comment of U.S. Delegation, *Report*, 63 Cong., 2 Sess., S. Doc. No. 463, p. 81.
[9] Safety of Life at Sea Convention, London, June 10, 1948, 3 *UST* 3450, *TIAS* 2495, *Regulations*, Ch. V, Reg. 8. Bibliographical Note: The *Treaty Series* numbers assigned to treaties from 1776 forward, ended with No. 994, in 1945. All of these treaties, with few exceptions, are also published in *Statutes at Large*. The *Executive Agreement Series*, cited *EAS*, begun with No. 1 in 1929, ran to No. 506 in 1945 and were regularly also published in *Statutes at Large*. Executive agreements concluded in the period before 1929 are difficult to locate. They may in some cases be found in the "Malloy" series of treaties or in *Foreign Relations*. In 1945, the combined numbers of the *Treaty Series* and the *Executive Agreement Series*, having reached 1500,

Between the Great Wars

The few American trans-Atlantic passenger ships operating in 1914 belonged to principal companies which fixed the routes. The present North Atlantic Lane Routes Agreement, participated in currently by American lines, has been in effect since 1923 and is revised periodically.[10] One of the most shocking sea disasters in maritime history, the loss of the Italian liner *Andrea Doria* after collision with the Swedish liner *Stockholm* off Nantucket Lightship on July 25, 1956, involved the charge, among others, that either or both vessels were not keeping to their proper tracks.

Finally, the growing pattern of interrelationships between treaty regimes is exemplified by the 1929 convention. It included, by reference, certain of the regulations annexed to the Radiotelegraph Convention of 1927 relating to the communication of meteorological information and an injunction to conform to the recommendations of the International Meteorological Organization (Art. 35). The Final Act,[11] *inter alia*, made certain recommendations for inclusion in the next radiotelegraph convention and requested the British government to head a study of the problem of collision of vessels and surfaced aircraft at sea.

---

a new series, entitled *Treaties and Other International Acts Series*, which included both types of agreements, was begun, starting with the number 1501. This series is cited *TIAS* and continues to the present. The agreements in this series were also regularly published in *Statutes at Large*. In 1950, however, beginning with *TIAS* 2010, publication of any and all agreements in *Statutes at Large* ceased, but publication in a new separate series of annual volumes called *United States Treaties and Other International Agreements* was begun. These annual volumes are cited *UST*. Agreements since January 1, 1950, are therefore regularly cited both *TIAS*, the pamphlet form, and *UST*, the final form. Treaties and executive agreements before January 1, 1950, are cited from *Statutes at Large*, if there appearing, and in their respective series. Postal agreements until recently appeared in separate prints issued by the post office department and were never included in *TS*. They were, however, regularly printed in *Statutes at Large*. Since 1945 they have regularly appeared in *TIAS* and then in *Statutes at Large* and *UST* as indicated above. See 64 Stat. (3) B1107–B1182 for a check list of all treaties and agreements which have been printed in *Statutes at Large* from the beginning.

[10] Specimen supplied to writer by Cunard Steamship Company, Liverpool, Secretaries to the N.A.L.R.A., under date March 2, 1953. The intriguing story of the origin and operation of the lanes can be traced through Lewis's biography of Maury, *op. cit.*; Everett P. Wheeler, "The International Regulation of Ocean Travel," *Proc. of the A.S.I.L. 1912*, pp. 36, 38–39; Clarence Selby Kempff, "Ship Lanes of the North Atlantic," *Encyclopaedia Britannica* (1952), Vol. 20, pp. 539–540; Kerchove, *op. cit.*, p. 493; Report of the Hydrographic Office, Oct. 3, 1924 in *Annual Reports of the Navy Department 1924*, at p. 198; and Mance and Wheeler, *International Sea Transport*, p. 40.

[11] The Final Act does not appear in the *TS* or in 4 Hudson, *I.L.* 2724, but may be found in the *Report* of the American delegation, 71 Cong., 2 Sess., S. Ex. B, pp. 107–123.

The United States and the Treaty Law of the Sea

United States-Mexican Rescue Agreement. In 1935 the United States and Mexico concluded an interesting agreement authorizing vessels and rescue apparatus, public or private, of either party to go to the assistance of vessels and aircraft of their own nationality on the shores or within the territorial waters of the other state within a radius of 720 nautical miles of the Pacific terminus of the boundary or 200 nautical miles of the Gulf terminus.[12] The agreement is important not only for its relaxation of the customary jealously guarded rule of exclusive jurisdiction over the shore and territorial waters of a sovereign but also because it probably set the pattern for the rule of the International Civil Aviation Convention, adopted in 1944, allowing the owners of the aircraft or the authorities of the state in which it is registered to assist the authorities of the foreign state in their search for, or assistance to, the aircraft in distress.[13]

Load Lines. The Safety of Life at Sea Convention provided for subdivision load lines (Art. 5) but left the principal subject to be regulated by a separate conference and a separate convention. This was done by the International Load Line Convention signed at London, September 30, 1930.[14] It applies to all ships engaged in international voyages, registered under the contracting governments, with certain exceptions, among them ships of war, fishing vessels, pleasure yachts, ships not carrying cargo or passengers, and ships of less than 150 tons gross (Art. 2). The same article permitted the exception also of ships engaged in international voyages of a "sheltered" nature. In pursuance of this clause, the United States and Canada entered into an agreement in 1933, exempting vessels of the United States and Canada "operating solely on certain sheltered waters of the west coast of North America" from the load-line requirements of the London Convention.[15]

Although the Final Protocol of the 1930 convention regarded "ships engaged solely on voyages on the Great Lakes of North America and ships engaged in other inland waters" as outside the scope of the convention, the United States and Canada in due course, 1938–1940, concluded an agreement relating to reciprocal recognition of load-line

---

[12] Treaty Providing for Assistance to and Salvage of Vessels in Territorial Waters, signed at Mexico City, June 13, 1935, 49 *Stat.* 3359, *TS* 905.

[13] Signed at Chicago, Dec. 7, 1944, 61 *Stat.* 1180, *TIAS* 1591, Art. 25.

[14] 47 *Stat.* 2228, *TS* 858. An amendment to the convention was declared effective Aug. 23, 1938, 53 *Stat.* (3) 1787, *TS* 942.

[15] Load Lines Convention, signed at Washington, Dec. 9, 1933, 49 *Stat.* 2685, *TS* 869.

regulations for vessels engaged in international voyages on the Great Lakes.[16] Since the buoyancy of saline water is greater than fresh water, the computations for determining the load lines to be affixed to the sides of Great Lakes steamers will, of course, be different from those for vessels using the high seas.

The affixing of the load lines is done under national law in accordance with the standards laid down in the convention. Pending the coming into force of the London Convention for both countries, the United States concluded a number of temporary executive agreements providing for the reciprocal recognition of load-line certificates with several European countries and Japan in 1931 and 1932.[17] Thus began the concerted effort of the international community to end unfair competition which also jeopardized the safety of human beings. The exigencies of the late war caused the temporary suspension of the convention with respect to most of the parties, including the United States, for the years 1941 to 1945.[18]

Buoyage and Lighting of Coasts. Two of three topics discussed for many years in the League Communications and Transit Organization, buoyage and lighting of coasts and oil pollution, relate closely to safety at sea; the third, tonnage measurements, relates primarily to economic discrimination under national laws, particularly treatment in ports, though principles derived from the elaborate League report of 1928 on the subject were incorporated in the load-line convention of 1930.[19]

Beginning in 1927 the United States actively participated in the work dealing with buoyage and lighting. Successive conferences and meetings since the epochal International Marine Conference in 1889 had dealt with the subject, each reversing the recommendations of its predecessor.

Thus, taking only one feature of the complicated systems of buoyage, the 1889 conference recommended that, for the mariner entering from seaward, the buoys indicating the starboard limits of the channel should

[16] By exchange of notes at Ottawa, from April 29, 1938, to March 4, 1940, 54 *Stat.* 2300, *EAS* 172.

[17] All in *EAS*: Japan, No. 25; Irish Free State, No. 27; Denmark, No. 29; Iceland, No. 30; Germany, No. 31; Sweden, No. 35; Italy, No. 36; Belgium, No. 40; all in 47 *Stat.*; and Netherlands, No. 42, 48 *Stat.* 1757. See Load Line Act, March 2, 1929, 45 *Stat.* 1493, Sec. 5, and Coastwise Load Line Act, Aug. 27, 1935, 49 *Stat.* 888, Sec. 5.

[18] Proclamation of the President, Aug. 9, 1941, 5 *DSB* 114–115 (1941); proclamation revoking suspension, Dec. 21, 1945, 14 *DSB* 132 (1946).

[19] Myers, *Handbook of the League of Nations*, p. 204.

be painted red, those on the port side black. The 1912 St. Petersburg Marine Conference reversed these colors, to accord, apparently with some systems in use in Europe. The Genoa Technical Committee of the League in 1929 endorsed the 1889 system. At the Lisbon Conference in 1930 the British, who had not participated in the work of the Technical Committee, submitted proposals diametrically opposite to the coloring system proposed by that committee. Further conferences followed in London and elsewhere. The upshot was an Agreement for a Uniform System of Maritime Buoyage, finally opened for signature at Geneva, May 13, 1936,[20] which reversed the proposals of the Technical Committee, thus completing an unbroken series of reversals since 1889.

The system proposed in 1936 was almost diametrically opposed to those used on the American continent and along the West Pacific. Furthermore, not one of these "conferences or meetings was able to agree on the superiority of either the lateral or the cardinal system of buoyage over the other, and the cardinal system was adopted at each meeting as an alternative to the lateral system." In brief, adoption of the system proposed in 1936 "would have necessitated reversing approximately 80 per cent of the world's buoyage," without commensurate advantage. The United States could not approve such a change.

The propitious time for international agreement and adaptation to a uniform system of buoyage and lighting was directly after the 1889 conference and in pursuance of its recommendations. "On that occasion buoys were not in extensive use; no one system prevailed, and yet sufficient experience had been obtained to approach the problem objectively. Further, the cost of introducing the scheme would have been comparatively small."[21] Since then, buoyage systems have become extensive, elaborate, established, and expensive. This complicates enormously the problem of securing uniformity.

So the matter stands. Recommendation No. 21 of the 1948 Conference

[20] 7 Hudson, *I.L.* 308.
[21] The writer is indebted to a most helpful long letter from the Coast Guard, Sept. 11, 1952, from which the several quotations are taken, and which alone enabled him to follow the complicated technical negotiations. For a summary of the United States position, see *Report of Small Committee*, Organization for Communications and Transit, C.128.M.67.VIII. March 26, 1936. For a brief account of the negotiations in the League, see *Int. Con.* No. 274, pp. 687–688; No. 329, pp. 302–303. For a glimpse at the complexity of the systems of buoyage and lighting, see the Rules annexed to the convention of 1936, *op. cit.* Also, cf. Gidel, *op. cit.*, Vol. I, p. 11, and Weber, *The Hydrographic Office*, p. 56.

Between the Great Wars

on Safety of Life at Sea, in London, however, urged "Governments to unify, so far as may be practicable, the systems of buoyage employed in the various waters open to international navigation" and recommended "that a further study of this matter be undertaken by the Maritime Safety Committee" of the Intergovernmental Maritime Consultative Organization "as soon as may be possible." [22]

Nor did the United States become a party to the Agreement Concerning Maritime Signals or the Agreement Concerning Manned Lightships not on their Stations, both opened for signature at the Lisbon Conference, October 23, 1930.[23]

Oil Pollution of Navigable Waters. In 1922, Congress requested the President to call a conference of maritime powers to adopt measures to end the nuisance of oil pollution of navigable waters,[24] and by statute in 1924 prohibited the nuisance in waters under American jurisdiction.[25] There remained the necessity of securing international cooperation to control the evil on the high seas and in the waters directly outside the three-mile limit. In preparation for the conference, an Interdepartmental Committee prepared a comprehensive and illuminating report on the subject.[26] A preliminary conference at Washington in 1926 elaborated a draft convention and, in the Final Act, adopted certain recommendations designed to combat the nuisance.[27] Subsequently, in 1934, Great Britain called the matter to the attention of the League, and in the ensuing discussions the United States took an active part.[28] There the matter stood at the outbreak of World War II. Since then discussion and negotiation has been resumed. The recent developments under the United Nations will be noted later.

Mine Clearance. Thus far in the discussion of the efforts to achieve safety at sea, the hazards encountered have been chiefly natural. The hazards created by mines left over from some recent war are, however, distinctly man made. Despite the tremendous and heroic efforts put

---

[22] International Convention for the Safety of Life at Sea, 1948, 81 Cong., 1 Sess., S. Doc. Ex. B, p. 146.

[23] 5 Hudson, *I.L.* 792 and 801, respectively. See p. 792 for the note on the International Code of Signals.

[24] July 1, 1922, 42 *Stat.* 821–822.

[25] June 7, 1924, 43 *Stat.* 604.

[26] *Oil Pollution of Navigable Waters*, Report to the Secretary of State by the Interdepartmental Committee, March 13, 1926 (1926).

[27] *Preliminary Conference on Oil Pollution of Navigable Waters, Washington, June 8–16, 1926* (1926). Final Act, *ibid.*, pp. 430–448; also TS 736-A.

[28] *Int. Con.*, No. 329, p. 302.

The United States and the Treaty Law of the Sea

forth after each recent war to clear the sea of mines, peace-time shipping has sustained serious losses of life and property. Thus, in the ten-year period, from May 1945 to March 1955, precisely 400 vessels, not including minesweepers or other warships, were sunk or damaged in European waters alone by means of mines,[29] left over, most of them, from World War II. Among those losses was the Danish passenger ship *Kjoebenhavn* in 1948 with a loss of 140 persons.[30] Up to December 31, 1957, the worldwide losses of nonmilitary vessels from mines, according to the American Cargo War Risk Reinsurance Exchange in New York, reached the total of 446.[31] *Lloyd's Weekly Casualty Reports* still lists losses and the positions of mines reported.[32] At various times, estimates have been made that the sea would be free of these risks by 1957. The events have not supported the prediction. It needs to be remembered that mines from World War I are still encountered.

With the history of the use of mines for naval purposes we are not here primarily concerned. Crude antecedents go back as far at least as 1585. An American, David Bushnell, is regarded as the "pioneer of underwater attack." In 1776 he built a submersible by means of which he could attach a "magazine" to the hull of an enemy ship. He made several unsuccessful attempts against the British fleet in New York harbor. He then turned to devising other types of "machines" for underwater attack. Robert Fulton devised a "crude form of locomotive torpedo" which he offered to the Revolutionary French government in 1797. Since then much thought and ingenuity has gone into the devising of mines and the contriving of countermeasures.[33] Thus, even Matthew Maury experi-

[29] "Sweeping the Seas for Trade," (London) *Financial Times*, March 5, 1955, tabulating figures received from the Admiralty.

[30] *N.Y.T.*, June 12, 1948. Recently a Soviet cruiser was belatedly reported sunk in the Black Sea with heavy loss of life after hitting a mine. *N.Y.T.*, April 25, 1956.

[31] Their annual bulletins, issued as press releases, give the following data: Bulletin No. 1078, Aug. 8, 1952, total casualties from end of hostilities in World War II up to June 30, 1952, 403; Bulletin No. 1087, Feb. 17, 1953, total as of Dec. 31, 1952, 411; Bulletin No. 1094, Nov. 12, 1953, total as of June 30, 1953, 415; Bulletin No. 1097, March 12, 1954, total as of Dec. 31, 1953, 419; Bulletin No. 1109, March 17, 1955, total as of Dec. 31, 1954, 429; press release, May 23, 1956, total as of Dec. 31, 1955, 438; total as of Dec. 31, 1956, 441; and five additional losses in 1957 brought the total as of Dec. 31, 1957, up to 446. Press release, April 9, 1958, and letters to writer, courtesy of Carroll W. Dawson, Assistant Secretary of the Exchange, Jan. 7, 1957, and July 7, 1958.

[32] E.g., Vol. CXLVI, No. 12, for Dec. 24, 1956, p. 422, reports no losses from mines but lists two mines and their positions reported by an Italian motor tanker and a French trawler, respectively.

[33] A. M. Low, *Mine and Countermine* (1940); Captain J. S. Cowie, *Mines, Minelayers and Minelaying* (1949); Dugan, *Man under the Sea* (1956), *passim*; Latil and

mented with sundry types of electrically operated mines during the Civil War for use against the blockading Union fleet.

Nor are we here particularly concerned with the present-day types of mines and the techniques of their use except as some sketch of them facilitates understanding of the peace-time problem of achieving safety at sea. There are at present many types of these lethal weapons: limpet mines, which are manually attached to a hull; mines controlled from shore; and mines not so controlled. This last variety is also called "independent" mines. It is the independent mines which create the hazards for shipping after a war. Many varieties of these have been developed: ground mines, which rest on the seabed; buoyant mines which are moored; and buoyant mines which are drifting, creeping, or oscillating.

Independent mines are further classified in accordance with the method of actuation. Some mines explode on contact. Others explode on being "influenced" by the passing vessels. All ground mines of necessity must be influenced mines. The actuation may be magnetic, acoustic, by pressure, or, as in the case of the antenna mine, by the setting up of a sea-cell "between the hull of a steel ship and a copper element in the mine, the surrounding salt water acting as the electrolyte." Various timing devices also are used. One of them, the "clicker," introduced by the Germans, postpones the explosion until after the mine has been actuated a preset number of times, ranging from one up to sixteen.[34] This latter type of mine, which rests on the sea bed and which cannot always be found by clearance operations, can be dangerous for a long time because the last fatal actuation may not occur until the unlucky numbered ship passes over it, perhaps many years later in peace time.

The method of laying the mines also affects the subsequent problem of safety. Those laid by surface craft or submarines can be carefully plotted on the charts; those laid by airplanes cannot be so accurately plotted. The latter, therefore, can more readily be missed in clearance operations.

With the international law of war which relates to the laying of mines

Rivoire, *Man and the Underwater World* (1956), *passim*; and "Mines (Naval), Minelaying and Minesweeping," *Encyclopaedia Britannica* (1952), Vol. 15, pp. 533–538.

[34] Cowie, *op. cit.*, Ch. 1 for classification and *passim* for detailed descriptions. This is the best work in nontechnical language on the subject.

we are also not here primarily concerned. Mines were first used extensively in the Russo-Japanese War in 1904. The Hague Convention of 1907 relative to the laying of automatic submarine contact mines (No. VIII) sought to control that method of warfare. The contracting powers undertook in Article 5 to do their utmost at the close of the war "to remove the mines which they had laid, each Power removing its own mines." The same article obligated each power which had laid automatic contact mines off the coasts of another power to notify that power of the position of those mines and further obligated each power to clear the mines in its own waters with the least possible delay.[35]

Much has been written since 1907 about the international law relating to the use of submarine mines.[36] Excellent works also exist which describe the laying and sweeping of mines.[37] But there is a singular dearth of information about the international efforts after each of the Great Wars to clear the seas of mines. Hundreds, perhaps thousands, of books deal with one phase or another of naval combat since 1907; a few scant and scattered paragraphs deal with international cooperation in clearing out the mines since 1907. It would be useful then, to describe at some respectable length these efforts to render the seas safe once more for innocent use.

The problem arising from mines after a war is simply this: moored mines can be swept up by specially equipped ships. Cut from their anchorings and floating on the surface they can then be destroyed and sunk at a distance by rifle fire.[38] This is a considerable task in itself since it has been estimated that over 3,000,000 mines were sown by the various belligerents in World War II. But many mines with their anchors are torn from their plotted places by storms, rough weather, currents, tides, and ice, and reanchor themselves in some unplotted place. Sometimes mooring cables give way, leaving the mines bobbing about on the seas,

[35] Concluded Oct. 18, 1907, 36 *Stat.* 2332, TS 541.

[36] See Amos S. Hershey, *The Essentials of International Public Law and Organization* (1927), pp. 642–644 and the voluminous literature there cited; 7 Moore, *Digest* 364–368; 6 Hackworth, *Digest* 503–512; *Rights and Duties of Neutral States in Naval Warfare*, Harvard Research in International Law, 33 A.J.I.L. No. 3 Supp. 750–756 (1939); Hyde, *op. cit.*, pp. 1936–1948, obligations to sweep mines, pp. 1946–1947.

[37] Works by Low and Cowie, *cit.* above, n. 33.

[38] Minesweeping techniques described in Low, *op. cit.; The Northern Barrage: Taking up the Mines*, Navy Department, Office of Naval Records and Library, Historical Section, Pub. No. 4 (1920); and *His Majesty's Minesweepers*, Ministry of Information (1943).

to be carried hither and yon by tides and currents. The appearance of a reanchored or a floating mine in some unplotted area is thus unpredictable. In 1955 a floating mine appeared in the Blue Grotto on the Isle of Capri off the coast of Italy.

"By international law all moored mines are fitted with a mechanism which renders them harmless when they break away from their moorings. Due to long immersion in the sea, however, mines become encrusted with barnacles and marine growth, and this may prevent the safety mechanism from operating in all cases. It is therefore impossible to state categorically that all floating mines are safe. At the same time it is most unlikely that a ship underway would strike a floating mine, as the bow wave washes it away from the ship's side." [39] Nevertheless, numerous casualties have occurred, as the data cited above for the post-World War II period indicated.

The international efforts to clear the seas after each of the Great Wars are briefly these. In World War I the Allies laid extensive mine fields in the English Channel, off the German coast, across the North Sea, in the Adriatic, and off the Turkish Asia Minor shores. The Central Powers had also mined extensive areas in the North Sea and the Mediterranean. Before even the end of hostilities, the Allied Naval Conference discussed the removal of the mines, at Malta, August 6-9, 1918; at Paris, September 13-14; and in London, Oct. 31, November 1, 4, and 5. Article 4 of the Naval Clauses of the Armistice of November 3 with Austria-Hungary and Articles 24 and 25 of the Armistice of November 11 with Germany [40] required those two governments to hand over the plans relating to the mine fields they had laid during the war.

As a result of the London Conference, the Allied Naval Council recommended "that Great Britain undertake to collate from the allied, associate, and central powers and distribute to the maritime countries of the world, intelligence regarding progress of mine clearance operations. . . . A committee of British naval officers with offices at the Admiralty in London, known as the International Mine Clearance Committee," was "convened to collate this information and in accordance with a further recommendation of the Allied Naval Council mine clearance intelligence officers were appointed by the allied and associated powers

---

[39] Press release, British Admiralty, No. 9, June 29, 1949; courtesy of British Information Services, New York.
[40] 3 Redmond 3147, 3311.

The United States and the Treaty Law of the Sea

to cooperate with this committee."[41] Thereupon, in accord with the Hague convention, the several allied navies, including the United States, which had cooperated in laying down the North Sea barrage from Norway to Scotland,[42] proceeded to sweep the mine fields they had sown.

The International Mine Clearance Committee then did two things: it received information concerning the progress in mine clearance from the cooperating navies, communicating it to the national intelligence officers attached to it for transmission to their various governments, and it issued route warnings and mine warnings to mariners with respect to eight dangerous areas. These areas comprised the Arctic; North Atlantic and English Channel; west coast of United Kingdom; North Sea; Baltic; east coast of France, Spain, and Portugal; Mediterranean; and South Atlantic, Indian Ocean, Red Sea, and Pacific. Up to 1920, the International Committee had issued 245 mine warnings. "In connection with these mine warnings to mariners, there were published a series of charts showing the mine areas and safe channels. These were republished by the United States Hydrographic Office for the information of all mariners, in some cases being published as a supplement to the United States Pilot Chart."[43] This pilot chart is available to all navigators of all nationalities on all oceans. Thus in time the seas were made safe again, until World War II required that they be made unsafe again.

At the end of World War II, an agreement was entered into by the Soviet Union, the United Kingdom, France, and the United States, on November 22, 1945 — Captain R. Pryce signing for the United States — which set up an International Organization for the Clearance of Mines in European Waters.[44] The organization was devised "with a view to

---

[41] *The Northern Barrage and other Mining Activities*, Navy Department, Office of Naval Records and Library, Historical Section, Pub. No. 2 (1920), pp. 139–141. Two charts in rear pockets show mine fields.

[42] *The Northern Barrage: Taking up the Mines*, Navy Department, Office of Naval Records and Library, Historical Section, Pub. No. 4 (1920), pp. 5, 70, and *passim*. Chart relating to sweeping operations in the North Sea Barrage is in rear pocket.

[43] *The Northern Barrage*, Pub. No. 2, *op. cit.*, p. 141; and G. A. Weber, *The Hydrographic Office*, p. 88.

[44] There appears to be no copy of the text of this agreement in any of the series of official publications of the United States now available. Text in UN Security Council, *Official Records*, Second Year, Supplement No. 6, Annex to the record of the 107th Meeting, Feb. 18, 1947, Exhibit III; also in International Court of Justice, *Pleadings, Oral Arguments, Documents, 1949, the Corfu Channel Case*, Vol. I, pp. 54–59. The Security Council was dealing with the dispute between the United Kingdom and Albania concerning the latter's mining of the Corfu Channel. The

meeting the needs of all interested maritime Powers by providing an international machinery for the direction of policy and general control of mine clearance operations."

The European waters were divided into four zones: (1) East Atlantic; (2) Mediterranean; (3) Barents, Baltic, and Black Seas; and (4) Kattegat, Baltic Straits, and their approaches. These zones were further subdivided into areas and subareas, the clearance of which was to "be allocated to the interested littoral and other naval powers under the direction of Boards set up in accordance" with other provisions of the agreement. The limits of each zone were carefully described in an appendix to the agreement.

An International Central Mine Clearance Board was set up, with headquarters in London, consisting of representatives of the four signatory powers and under the presidency of a British naval officer. This board had general direction of the whole program of clearance in European waters and maintained liaison with the several Allied highest-echelon naval, military, and control authorities. Within each zone a Zone Mine Clearance Board was set up consisting of representatives of one or more of the signatory powers and of other United Nations with specific naval interests in the zone concerned. The presidency of the East Atlantic and Mediterranean zone boards was assigned to a British naval officer; that of the Barents, Baltic, and Black Seas zone board to a Soviet naval officer; and the one for the Kattegat and Baltic straits board was to be held for alternate periods by a British and Soviet naval officer. Observers from others of the United Nations and from neutrals with maritime interests in the area were "invited" to attend meetings of the zonal boards. Representatives of the defeated powers in the pertinent areas were "summoned" to attend meetings of the zonal boards. The United States, in addition to its membership on the Central Board, was a member of only the Mediterranean Zone Board, and held no presidency.

A Central International Intelligence Office for the evaluation and promulgation of mine clearance intelligence was established in London. This office consisted of an executive committee, composed of representa-

---

agreement was cited by the United Kingdom before the International Court of Justice in support of its mine-clearance operations in the channel. The court held the agreement not applicable in the special circumstances and gave judgment for the United Kingdom on other grounds. *International Court of Justice Reports*, 1949, pp. 4, 26, as reprinted in Briggs, *op. cit.*, pp. 291–298, at p. 296.

The United States and the Treaty Law of the Sea

tives of the members of the Central Board, and of an administrative section, staffed by the British Admiralty. The information sent up from the zone boards was to be processed and reviewed by the office and then promulgated by the administrative section in accordance with the executive committee's decisions.

As in the case of the methods adopted after World War I, maritime powers were invited to appoint representatives from among their diplomatic or other missions residing in England to maintain liaison with the Intelligence Office and to receive from it "Mine Warnings to Mariners" for transmission to their respective home governments.

The clearance of mines from European waters was carried out by the navies of thirteen nations whose activities were coordinated and directed by the Central Board in London. The United States did not participate in any of these sweeping operations.[45] By the end of June 1949, the British Admiralty could announce that the sweeping for moored mines was then almost completed.[46] In 1950 an International Routeing and Reporting Authority replaced the Central Board.[47] Unfortunately, there is not a single publication available to the public which gives an account of the operations of the International Central Mine Clearance Board.[48] All the information appears to be locked up in official reports.

Despite the concerted sweeping operations in the European theater and the sanguine announcement of the Admiralty in 1949, danger and casualties from mines continued. As late as February 1955, "the Danish Naval Command reported that of an estimated 6,000 to 7,000 mines laid in Danish waters during the last war, 2,000 may still be 'live' and dangerous to shipping. The Danish Navy is actively engaged in clearing traffic lanes of these mines, and will take no responsibility for ships sailing outside the approved lanes." [49] Mines are reported on occasion in the Caribbean and off the eastern coasts of the United States. Current casualties can most probably be attributed to floating mines, mines which have

[45] Yet later, in Oct. 1955, "a United States flotilla of minesweepers was assigned to clear the harbor of Luebeck, Germany, and to broaden the swept corridors in the western Baltic Sea." Exchange Press Release, May 23, 1956, *op. cit.*
[46] Press Release No. 9, June 29, 1949, *op. cit.*
[47] *Financial Times*, March 5, 1955, *op. cit.*
[48] The writer has had to piece together this description from the few works cited and two helpful letters, one dated Oct. 16, 1956, from the Office of Information of the Department of the Navy, and another, dated July 12, 1956, from the Office of the Chief of Naval Operations, Department of the Navy.
[49] Exchange Press Release, May 23, 1956, *op. cit.*

Between the Great Wars

left their fields, remoored themselves and escaped sweeping, and mines, originally resting upon or attached to the ocean floor, which some storm has tossed up into circulation. On being reported, these mines are rendered innocuous, one by one. Hopefully, the last of them may be destroyed by the end of this century.

In the Pacific section, after World War II, the major task of clearance in Empire waters fell to the United States. That task was accomplished by 1946. In addition, Netherlands forces "swept the Dutch East Indies and British Commonwealth navies swept in their areas of responsibility, such as Hong Kong, Singapore, Amoy, and so forth, as well as assisting in the Formosa Strait sweep." The United States resumed sweeping "on a small scale in 1947 in the Trust Territory Islands and eventually in the home waters of the Japanese Islands. The Japanese also swept their home waters, but United States check sweeping was required before the channels could be declared open for foreign merchant ships. United States check sweeping in Japan continued until the advent of the Korean War and played a significant part in re-opening the Japanese industrial ports, and thus rehabilitating the Japanese economy." [50]

Unfortunately, additional mines were sown during the Korean War. "In October 1954, the United States Navy Hydrographic Office issued a new loose-leaf publication called 'DAPAC' (Danger Areas in the Pacific) listing extensive danger areas in Far East waters. It was explained that while at the end of World War II it was believed that mine hazards would be eliminated in a short time, 'such was not the case . . . many areas still remain dangerous.'" [51] And in 1955 "the Chinese Nationalist Government notified all diplomatic representatives in Formosa that it had mined the territorial waters of all Chinese coastal islands controlled by the Nationalists. The mining was aimed not only at possible Communist attacking forces but also at neutral shipping trading into Communist-held ports in China." [52]

Finally, in addition to reports received and disseminated by *Lloyd's Weekly Casualty Reports* and the British and other maritime authorities, information concerning floating mines, torpedoes, depth charges, aerial bombs, and other hazards is issued currently by the United States Navy Hydrographic Office. "Reports of sightings of dangers to navigation are

[50] Letter from Office of Chief of Naval Operations, *op. cit.*
[51] Exchange Press Release, May 23, 1956, *op. cit.*
[52] *Ibid.*

made to this Office by a corps of voluntary cooperating observers consisting of ships' officers the world over. After evaluation, this Office issues appropriate warnings to all ocean shipping. Urgency governing, the warnings may be issued by radio, *Daily Memorandum* or weekly *Notice to Mariners*." This service for the western Atlantic Ocean is provided by the Washington office; for the Pacific Ocean by the United States Navy Branch Hydrographic Office at Honolulu.[53] Thus, in a very commendable fashion, the American Navy Hydrographic Office performs what is substantially an international service for the whole maritime community.

Labor at Sea. As already related in the previous chapter,[54] Andrew Furuseth, President of the International Seamen's Union, helped negotiate the 1914 Safety of Life at Sea Convention but resigned from the delegation in protest against some of its provisions. Furuseth and the Union then opposed ratification of the convention as inadequately protecting the American merchant marine. Since then, the lot of labor at sea has considerably improved. Congress in 1915 passed the epochal La Follette Seamen's Act,[55] a Magna Carta for American seamen, which also profoundly influenced the employment practices in the merchant marines of other countries. At the Senate hearing on the 1929 convention in 1932, Furuseth contended that "if the treaty [of 1914] had been ratified, the seamen's act [of 1915] could never have been passed." [56]

Beginning with its second session in Genoa, in 1920, the International Labor Organization has regularly elaborated conventions and recommendations dealing with sundry aspects of the safety and welfare of seafarers and other persons engaged in the maritime industry. The subject matter of a few of the conventions will indicate the range of attention: minimum age (at sea); unemployment indemnity (ship-

[53] Letter to the writer from the U.S. Navy Hydrographic Office, Jan. 8, 1957; see also *125th Anniversary* brochure, *op. cit.*, pp. 12–14.
[54] At p. 105.
[55] Act of March 4, 1915, 38 *Stat.* 1164. See McFee, *op. cit.*, Ch. XII, "Wards of the Legislature" and the articles by Hohman, cited above at p. 106.
[56] *Hearing* before a Subcommittee of the Committee on Foreign Relations, 72 Cong., 1 Sess., June 28, 1932, p. 3. Furuseth said: ". . . The Senate refused to ratify the treaty, and passed the seamen's act. If the treaty had been ratified, the seamen's act could never have been passed." On the procedure, Furuseth is not quite accurate. The Senate did give its consent to ratification, subject to a reservation, but President Wilson withheld his ratification of the instrument. See *List of Treaties Submitted to the Senate 1789–1931 Which Have Not Gone into Force*, D.S. Pub. No. 382 (1932), No. 181, pp. 13, 2.

Between the Great Wars

wreck); placing of seamen; minimum age for trimmers and stokers; medical examination of young persons (at sea); seamen's articles of agreement; repatriation of seamen; marking of weight (packages transported by vessels); protection against accident (for dockers); officers competency certificates; holidays with pay (sea); shipowners' liability (sick and injured seamen); sickness insurance; and hours of work and manning.[57] Special sessions of the I.L.O. from time to time were devoted to maritime questions.[58]

The United States, having become a member of the International Labor Organization in 1934,[59] ratified promptly five of the conventions dealing with maritime affairs adopted at Geneva on October 24, 1936, namely, those relating to minimum requirement of professional capacity for masters and officers on board merchant ships;[60] liability of shipowners in case of sickness, injury, or death of seamen;[61] minimum age for the admission of children to employment at sea;[62] annual holidays with pay for seamen;[63] and hours of work on board ship and manning.[64] Only the first three listed have, at a recent date,[65] received the necessary number of ratifications to become effective for the United States. After

---

[57] *Lasting Peace the I.L.O. Way: The Story of the International Labour Organization* (1951), Appendix IV. This excellent official handbook includes a most valuable selected bibliography, Appendix VIII. See also *U.S. Int. Agencies 1946*, pp. 225–232; *U.S. Int. Org. 1949*, pp. 227–236. Texts of all conventions for the period are in Hudson, *I.L.*

[58] For an excellent succinct account of the 1936 Maritime Session, see *Int. Con.* No. 331, pp. 599–601. Up to and including the 32d session at Geneva in 1949, 25 conventions and 10 recommendations had been adopted at 7 different sessions of the conference. Of the 7 sessions, 6 were maritime sessions proper: Second, Genoa, 1920; Ninth, Geneva, 1926; Thirteenth, Geneva, 1929; Twenty-first, Geneva, 1936; Twenty-second, Geneva, 1936; and Twenty-eighth, Seattle, 1946. The Third, Geneva, 1921, and the Thirty-second, Geneva, 1949, were not maritime sessions proper, but conventions on maritime subjects were adopted at both of them. No conventions were adopted by the thirteenth (maritime) session of the conference. Data supplied by the I.L.O., Sept. 19, 1952. See also *Catalog of Publications in English of the International Labour Office 1919–1950*, I.L.O. Library, Bibliographical Contributions No. 5, Geneva (1951).

[59] By executive agreement in pursuance of a joint resolution of Congress approved June 19, 1934, 48 *Stat.* 1182; membership effective as of Aug. 20, 1934, 49 *Stat.* 2712, TS 874.

[60] Entered into force for the United States, Oct. 29, 1939, 54 *Stat.* 1683, TS 950.

[61] Entered into force for the United States, Oct. 29, 1939, 54 *Stat.* 1693, TS 951.

[62] Entered into force for the United States, Oct. 29, 1939, 54 *Stat.* 1705, TS 952.

[63] Ratification of the United States deposited Oct. 29, 1938. *Treaties Submitted to the Senate 1935–1944*, D.S. Pub. No. 2311 (1945), p. 14.

[64] Ratification of the United States deposited Oct. 29, 1938. *Ibid.*

[65] *Treaties in Force, January 1, 1958*, D.S. Pub. No. 6626, p. 212.

The United States and the Treaty Law of the Sea

World War II, the I.L.O. at a notable maritime session in Seattle in 1946 carried the international legislative work substantially forward.

Air Commerce. Three regimes devoted to civil air navigation, a regime designed to be universal and two regional ones, grew up in the interwar period, under the so-called Paris, Madrid, and Habana agreements respectively.

The United States signed but did not ratify the Convention on Regulation of Aerial Navigation, opened for signature at Paris, October 13, 1919.[66] Instead, beginning with executive agreements with Colombia and Canada, it concluded a large number of bipartite agreements on sundry aspects of aviation with separate governments.[67] It did not participate in the Ibero-American Arrangement concluded at Madrid in 1926[68] but it did, after some delay, ratify the Pan American Convention on Commercial Aviation, signed at Habana, February 20, 1928.[69]

Each of these conventions applied the principles of maritime law to the salvage of aircraft wrecked at sea, and provided for the use of radio and meteorological services.[70] The Paris Convention also provided for the collection and communication of information relating to "medical science which may be of interest to air navigation" (Art. 34). The Habana agreement uniquely declared that "the commander of an aircraft shall have rights and duties analogous to those of the captain of a merchant steamer according to the respective laws of each state" (Art. 25).

As in the case of other technological developments, separable aspects of air commerce were subjected to international regulation when they became ripe for such treatment. Among the several multipartite conventions concluded in the period under examination which involved use of the sea by aircraft, the United States became a party to the Sanitary

[66] Text, 1 Hudson, *I.L.* 359–390, including the protocols of amendments of 1929. For American reservations to the 1919 convention, see 3 Redmond 3768–3769. For a résumé of treaty developments to 1930, see M. O. Hudson, "Aviation and International Law," 24 *A.J.I.L.* 228–240 (1930); for a "List of International Agreements Concerning Aviation Prior to January 1930," *ibid.*, Supplement, pp. 161–168. For American attitudes in the interwar period, see Lissitzyn, *op. cit.*

[67] List in *Treaties in Force, December 31, 1941,* D.S. Pub. No. 2103 (1944), pp. 128–134. One of Oct. 22, 1929, with Canada, not listed, and apparently superseded, was *EAS* 2. A list of the bipartite agreements in force for other nations in the period up to 1930 is given by Hudson in "List," *op. cit.*, pp. 161–163.

[68] Nov. 1, 1926, 3 Hudson, *I.L.* 2019.

[69] Ratification deposited July 17, 1931, 47 *Stat.* 1911, *TS* 840.

[70] Paris agreement, Arts. 23, 34, 35; Madrid, Arts. 23, 34, 35; Habana, Arts. 26, 31.

Between the Great Wars

Convention for Aerial Navigation, signed at The Hague, April 12, 1933.[71] It participated in the Hague conference on aerial postal matters in 1927 [72] but did not become a party to the temporary agreements there adopted. The Universal Postal conventions since 1929 [73] and those of the Postal Union of the Americas and Spain since 1931 [74] have regularly provided for the regulation of the transport of mails by air, much of it, of course, going overseas.

After 1932, the United States regularly participated in the work of the International Technical Committee of Aerial Legal Experts (or the CITEJA, according to the French title), established in 1926 and devoted to the codification of private air law.[75] Of the several conventions resulting from the work of this body, the United States has become a party to the Convention for the Unification of Certain Rules Relating to International Transportation by Air, concluded at Warsaw, October 12, 1929.[76] It signed but did not ratify the Convention for the Unification of Certain Rules Relating to Assistance and Salvage of Aircraft or by Aircraft at Sea, concluded at Brussels, September 29, 1938.[77]

In the course of its collaboration with the League's Organization for Communications and Transit, which from time to time discussed measures "aimed at facilitating the rapidly growing international air services," the United States participated in a London conference in 1939 which dealt with exemption from taxation of liquid fuel and lubricants used in air traffic and signed but did not ratify the convention [78] dealing with

---

[71] 49 *Stat.* 3279, *TS* 901.

[72] *Documents de Conference sur la Poste Aeriénne*, Berne (1927), p. 99; 3 Hudson, *I.L.* 2117.

[73] Convention signed at London, June 28, 1929, 46 *Stat.* 2523; 4 Hudson, *I.L.* 2869. The regulations appear in "Provisions" appended to the convention.

[74] Convention signed at Madrid, Nov. 10, 1931, 47 *Stat.* 1924; 5 Hudson, *I.L.* 1104. The regulations appear in "Provisions" appended to the convention.

[75] *U.S. Int. Agencies 1946*, pp. 258–264. The Third Commission of this committee in 1936 discussed "Aviation salvage at sea," *American Delegations to International Conferences, Congresses, and Expositions, 1936*, D.S. Pub. No. 1014, p. 61 (hereinafter cited *Am. Del.*).

[76] The United States did not sign this convention but declared adherence to it, June 27, 1934, 49 *Stat.* 3000, *TS* 876.

[77] 8 Hudson, *I.L.* 135. The United States also signed but did not ratify the Convention for the Unification of Certain Rules Relating to Damages Caused by Aircraft to Third Parties on the Surface, concluded at Rome, May 29, 1933, 6 Hudson, *I.L.* 334; and the Additional Protocol to the same, concluded at Brussels, Sept. 29, 1938, 8 Hudson, *I.L.*, 137. See also Stephen Latchford, "Pending Projects of the International Technical Committee of Aerial Legal Experts," 40 *A.J.I.L.* 280–302 (1946).

[78] Convention opened to signature at London, March 1, 1939, 8 Hudson, *I.L.* 269.

The United States and the Treaty Law of the Sea

the subject. It urged at that conference that the scope of the convention be extended to include, *inter alia*, beaching gear and meteorological and other aids to navigation.[79]

In the fullness of time, when men and events were so disposed, a new comprehensive universal regime for civil aviation was created, under the convention concluded at Chicago, December 7, 1944, which expressly superseded the Paris and Habana regimes.[80] The new regime rivals in complexity the older regimes on postal matters, health, and radio and is appropriately integrated with the law, national and international, relating to the sea.

Communications

Ports and Waterways. Part of the great problem confronting the victorious powers in 1918 was the reknitting of the social fabric of the world. Great rents had been torn in it during four long years of hostilities. The repairing was done partly by means of extensive stipulations on concrete subject matters in the peace treaties themselves, by providing for the setting up of new agencies to deal with certain problems continuously, such as the League of Nations and the International Labor Organization, and by the adoption at the peace conference, or by providing for the adoption subsequently, of certain large pieces of international legislation such as the conventions relating to Africa and the Paris agreement on aerial navigation.

The peace treaties of 1919 with Germany,[81] Austria,[82] and Hungary[83] contained in Part XII, in each case, elaborate provisions dealing with ports, waterways, and railways, of great importance to the international maritime community. On failing to ratify these treaties, the United States reserved to itself, in its separate treaties restoring friendly rela-

---

[79] *Int. Con.* No. 361, June 1940, pp. 228–229; also *Am. Del. 1939*, D.S. Pub. No. 1453, pp. 64–65.

[80] Convention on International Civil Aviation, opened for signature at Chicago, Dec. 7, 1944, 61 *Stat.* 1180, *TIAS* 1591. Article 80 of the convention calls for the denunciation of the Paris and Habana conventions by the signatories of the Chicago agreement. The Madrid Convention, apparently, was regarded as defunct. See note in 3 Hudson, *I.L.* 2019.

[81] Treaty of Peace between the Allied and Associated Powers and Germany, signed at Versailles, June 28, 1919, 3 Redmond 3329.

[82] Treaty of Peace between the Allied and Associated Powers and Austria, signed at Saint-Germain-en-Laye, Sept. 10, 1919, 3 Redmond 3149.

[83] Treaty of Peace between the Allied and Associated Powers and Hungary, signed at Trianon, June 4, 1919, 3 Redmond 3539.

Between the Great Wars

tions with Germany,[84] Austria,[85] and Hungary,[86] respectively, the rights and advantages stipulated in, *inter alia*, Part XII of the correlative 1919 treaties.

This study cannot here deal with the history of that peace settlement,[87] but it can be noted that Part XII in each case contemplated the establishment under the League of Nations of a regime relating to waterways having an international character. That was done at Barcelona in 1921, but the United States did not become a party to the convention and its annexed statute.[88]

In pursuance of Article 23e of the League Covenant and in accord with the expectations of the 1919 Peace Conference, an Organization for Communications and Transit was established by a conference at Barcelona in 1921.[89] The United States was invited to that conference but refused the invitation. Unofficial cooperation with this body began in 1923 and continuous official participation in its work started in 1927. Some mention of the cooperation has already been made above in connection with the discussion on buoyage and lighting, oil pollution, and tonnage measurements. Among the numerous important matters dealt with by the organization, of special significance for the present study, was the whole question of the railways and waterways of the Rhine and Danube river systems,[90] subjects in which the United States continues to display lively interest. The United States did not, however, become a party to any of the multipartite treaties produced by the organization, the most important of which were the Barcelona Convention on the

---

[84] Treaty Restoring Friendly Relations, signed at Berlin, Aug. 25, 1921, 42 *Stat.* 1939, TS 658, Art. II.

[85] Treaty Establishing Friendly Relations, signed at Vienna, Aug. 24, 1921, 42 *Stat.* 1946, TS 659, Art. III.

[86] Treaty Establishing Friendly Relations, signed at Budapest, Aug. 29, 1921, 42 *Stat.* 1951, TS 660, Art. II.

[87] See the annotations to the Treaty of Versailles prepared by Denys P. Myers constituting Vol. XIII of *The Paris Peace Conference 1919* series in *Foreign Relations of the United States* (1947). See also Mance and Wheeler, *International River and Canal Transport* (1945), and Louis B. Wehle, "International Administration of European Inland Waterways," 40 *A.J.I.L.* 100–120 (1946).

[88] Convention on the Regime of Navigable Waterways of International Concern, opened for signature at Barcelona, April 20, 1921, 1 Hudson, *I.L.* 638.

[89] Rules for the Organization of General Conferences on Communications and Transit and of the Advisory and Technical Committee, adopted at Barcelona, April 6, 1921, 1 Hudson, *I.L.* 617; Walters, *op. cit.*, Vol. I, pp. 178–180. Excellent brief description of the work of the organization in Myers, *Handbook*, pp. 194–211 and of American participation in *International Conciliation* pamphlets, *op. cit.*, above, n. 3.

[90] *Int. Con.* No. 274, p. 20, citing League documents.

The United States and the Treaty Law of the Sea

Regime of Navigable Waterways of International Concern, noted above, and that on the International Regime of Maritime Ports, opened for signature at Geneva, December 9, 1923.[91] Both of these conventions were ratified in due course by an impressive number of League states.

Radio. In the refashioning of the radio regime after World War I, however, the United States speedily assumed a dominant role. That regime as well as the new health agreements in the interwar period applied increasingly to maritime activities.

The periodic meeting of the radio regime was to have taken place in Washington five years after the 1912 meeting at London. The war, of course, prevented that. Since the field of radio communication had expanded enormously during those years, the Allied and Associated Powers adopted a temporary set of revised regulations in a Radio Protocol of August 25, 1919. In pursuance of a resolution adopted at Paris by the five Principal Powers, a preliminary conference representing them convened in Washington in 1920 and drew up a draft convention and regulations for a universal electrical communications union embracing all international aspects of land telegraphs, cables, and radio. Subsequent discussions indicated, however, that it was still desirable to have two separate regimes, one for telegraphs and one for radio. Accordingly the telegraph conference was held in Paris in 1925 and the first full-scale postwar revisory conference for radio regulation was held in Washington in 1927.[92]

The convention produced at the Washington conference ushered in a new epoch in radio regulation. It revised the old wireless rules to apply to broadcasting, radiotelephony, and aircraft, all of which had come into extensive commercial use since World War I. Provision was made for radio compass and radio beacon services. The meteorological service was extended to aircraft. Repeatedly the regulations incorporated by reference the "radiotelegraph part of the Regulations for the Safety of Life at Sea" and "the special provisions regulating the aerial navigation radio service." Revised rules governed the priority and status of distress, automatic alarm, urgent, and safety signals for ship, aircraft, or other

[91] 2 Hudson, *I.L.* 1156.
[92] Radiotelegraph Convention, signed Nov. 25, 1927, 45 *Stat.* 2760, *TS* 767. For an excellent summary of the complicated situation which existed in these early post-World War I years and expert analysis of the 1927 conference, see Irvin Stewart, "The International Radiotelegraph Conference of Washington," 22 *A.J.I.L.* 28–49 (1928).

mobile station, which "is threatened by grave and imminent danger, and requests immediate assistance."

Notices to navigators, hours of services, other time indexes, such as the time of filing of radiotelegrams, and time signals were explicitly based by the convention on the Greenwich Meridian and Greenwich Mean Time. As already indicated in the previous discussion, the United States renders important service in the giving of time signals.

Time signals are radiated for checking chronometers especially for navigation purposes; for scientific work such as the determination of longitude; for survey work and seismology; for the public to learn the time; and for the regulation of clocks and watches by commercial, manufacturing, transport and other interests. . . . The International Astronomic Congress at Paris in 1935, considered that the U.S.A. Naval Observatory had the best method of determining, dividing, registering and broadcasting time, with an accuracy to within one thousandth of a second and the Washington signals were used for preference in many countries throughout the world.[93]

Article 17 of the convention provided for the establishment of an International Technical Consulting Committee of Radio Communication, with members representing administrations and private enterprises in the signatory countries. The committee was authorized to study technical questions submitted to it by participating administrations and private enterprises and to transmit its advice in relation thereto through the International Bureau of the Telegraph Union at Berne.

A recommendation of the conference [94] provided for the revision of the International Code of Signals by an editorial committee in London and the setting up of an international standing committee under the British Board of Trade for the purpose of keeping the code, which now includes flag, Morse, flashing light, sound, and semaphore signals, up to date.[95]

In due course, and of necessity, the 1927 universal radio rules were revised at Madrid in 1932[96] and at Cairo in 1938.[97] As in the case of

[93] Mance and Wheeler, *International Telecommunications*, p. 41. See *U.S. Naval Observatory Circular No. 14* (1950) for description of the services rendered and the achievement of the high degree of accuracy to which Mance and Wheeler refer.
[94] Note, 5 Hudson, *I.L.* 792.
[95] *International Code of Signals* (American Edition), *op. cit.*; Mance and Wheeler, *International Telecommunications*, pp. 56–57.
[96] International Telecommunications Convention, Regulations and Protocols Annexed Thereto, signed at Madrid, Dec. 9, 1932, 49 *Stat.* 2391, *TS* 867.
[97] Regulations and Protocols as Revised at Cairo, April 4 and 8, 1938, 54 *Stat.*

other world-wide conventions, regional agreements were authorized, and in pursuance thereof, the United States entered into a number of multipartite arrangements governing radio relations in various areas of the western hemisphere.[98]

A few further developments with regard to radio in this pre-World War II period can be noted. The United States took an active part in the work of the Technical Consulting Committee, whose agenda frequently contained questions involving use of the sea.[99] As a leading radio "power," the United States had to be represented at numerous specialized and regional conferences devoted to one or another aspect of radio communication, among them the Third World Conference of Radiotelegraph Experts for Aeronautics, at Paris in 1938, which met for part of the time in joint session with the European Conference of Meteorological Experts,[100] and the Regional Conference Concerning the Use of Radiotelephone in the North and Baltic Seas at The Hague, also in 1938.[101]

Meanwhile, the League of Nations in its health work was utilizing radio warnings, so that by 1939, Surgeon-General Thomas Parran of the United States Public Health Service was able to say:

The League's Bureau at Singapore is the center of a world disease-alarm system, for it receives from all parts of the East immediate cables concerning the occurrence of plague, cholera, smallpox, typhus, and other fevers, and broadcasts this information through ten radio stations, so that it may be picked up by port health officers, ships at sea, and planes in flight.[102]

Health

Political scientists will testify that if there is one area in which progressive governments will stand no nonsense, it is public health. The price

---

1417, *TS* 948. For a discussion of some of the problems involved in use of radio by ships in distress, see *Report to the Secretary of State by the Chairman of the American Delegation* to the Cairo Conference, D.S. Pub. No. 1286 (1939), p. 42.

[98] List for period 1929–1940, *Treaties in Force December 31, 1941*, pp. 231–233. List of bilateral agreements in pursuance of the major multipartite agreements, including arrangements, in 1925, with Canada, Great Britain, and Newfoundland for prevention of interference with radio broadcasting by ships off their coasts, *ibid.*, pp. 234–237.

[99] Irvin Stewart, "The International Technical Consulting Committee on Radio Communication," 25 *A.J.I.L.* 684–693 (1931), list of opinions, pp. 692–693; and, for example, Third Meeting of the I.T.C.C.R.C., Monte Estoril, Portugal, 1934, *Am. Del. 1935*, D.S. Pub. No. 854, pp. 15–17.

[100] *Am. Del. 1939*, pp. 49–50.

[101] *Ibid.*, p. 50.

[102] *Int. Con.*, No. 361, p. 230.

of leniency or carelessness is high; it is death — for somebody. This attitude is exemplified by the American denunciation of the 1903 Sanitary Convention in 1921 because certain of the parties to it failed to observe its obligations.[103] Article 54 of the 1926 Sanitary Convention [104] puts the matter tersely: "Ships unwilling to comply with obligations imposed by the port authority, in virtue of the provisions of this Convention, shall be at liberty to put out to sea."

Many of the developments under examination in the interwar period reflect this demand for stringency, as well as the need for education and cooperation in the avoidance of epidemic disease. The principal contractual and institutional developments in the period, which involved or affected the United States, include the following: the setting up of the League Health Committee and Health Section of the Secretariat in 1921 and in 1923 a League Health Organization [105] designed to embrace and enlarge the functions of the Office of Public Health established at Paris under the 1907 sanitary convention; revision of the 1912 universal convention in 1926 [106] and of the Pan American convention of 1905 in 1924;[107] cooperation between the Universal regime and the United States with the League efforts; adoption of a sanitary convention for aerial navigation in 1933; [108] and transfer of the functions of the international Sanitary, Maritime, and Quarantine Board of Egypt to the government of Egypt in 1938.[109] Then came disruption of the work of the International Office of Public Health in Paris during the Nazi occupation–Vichy government difficulties; [110] temporary entrustment of the operation of the functions of the office in 1944 to UNRRA; [111] and final

---

[103] Above, at p. 115.
[104] Convention Revising the International Sanitary Convention of Jan. 17, 1912, signed at Paris, June 21, 1926, 45 *Stat.* 2492, TS 762.
[105] Walters, *op. cit.*, Vol. I, pp. 180–183; Myers, *op. cit.*, p. 211.
[106] *Cit.* above, n. 104.
[107] Pan American Sanitary Code, Signed at Habana, Nov. 14, 1924, 44 *Stat.* 2031, TS 714.
[108] Opened for signature at The Hague, April 22, 1933, 49 *Stat.* 3279, TS 901.
[109] Convention Amending the International Sanitary Convention of June 21, 1926, opened to signature at Paris, Oct. 31, 1938, 8 Hudson, *I.L.* 189. The United States signed but did not ratify this agreement. "It modified only certain administrative provisions of the 1926 convention and did not replace the substantive health provisions of that convention." "International Health Security in the Modern World: The Sanitary Conventions and the World Health Organization," 17 *DSB* 953, 956 (1947).
[110] *U.S. Int. Agencies 1946*, pp. 225, 230–231.
[111] *Ibid.*, p. 231, and *U.S. Int. Org. 1949*, pp. 254–255. Sanitary Maritime Navigation: Convention Modifying the Convention of June 21, 1926, opened for signature,

The United States and the Treaty Law of the Sea

transfer of League, Paris, and UNRRA functions to the new World Health Organization in the period 1946 to 1948.[112]

Universal Regime. Before the 1912 Maritime Sanitary Convention went into effect in 1920, its provisions already lagged behind the advances made by medical science in the previous eight years. Hence the Permanent Committee of the Public Health Office in Paris immediately discussed a revision thereof.[113] Among the desiderata of the United States were these: inclusion of typhus among the reportable diseases; freedom for the parties to take defensive measures without waiting for official notice of infected areas and to apply special measures in the case of rat-infested ships; maintenance of the separation of the I.O.P.H. at Paris from the League of Nations; and enlargement of the discretion of the authorities of the port of call in granting pratique.[114]

The United States was successful in achieving all these ends. Typhus and also smallpox (clothes-borne disease) were added to the notifiable diseases. In the Protocol of Signature of the 1926 Convention the United States continued to reserve "to itself the right to decide whether from the standpoint of the measures to be applied a foreign district is to be considered as infected and to decide what measures shall be applied to arrival in its own ports under special circumstances." "The American position was untenable but it prevailed."[115] Because of the opposition in some quarters in America to the assumption of any contractual relations to the League, the United States, with the support of Great Britain and France, was able to keep the Paris office institutionally separate from the League Health Organization,[116] but the new convention pro-

---

Washington, Dec. 15, 1944, 59 *Stat.* 955, *TS* 991; Protocol Extending the Convention of Dec. 15, 1944, relating to Sanitary Maritime Navigation, opened for signature, Washington, April 23, 1946, 61 *Stat.* 1115, *TIAS* 1551; and Sanitary Aerial Navigation: Convention Modifying the Convention of April 12, 1933, opened for signature, Washington, Dec. 15, 1944, 59 *Stat.* 991, *TS* 992; Protocol Extending the Convention of Dec. 15, 1944, relating to Sanitary Aerial Navigation, opened for signature, Washington, April 23, 1946, 61 *Stat.* 1122, *TIAS* 1552.

[112] *U.S. Int. Org. 1949*, pp. 254–256; Williams, *op. cit.*, pp. 454–456; World Health Organization: Establishment of an Interim Commission, Arrangement signed at New York, July 22, 1946, 61 *Stat.* 2349, *TIAS* 1561; International Office of Public Health, Protocol transferring duties and functions to the Interim Commission, signed at New York, July 22, 1946, 62 *Stat.* 1604, *TIAS* 1754; and World Health Organization: Constitution, opened for signature, New York, July 22, 1946, 62 *Stat.* 2679, *TIAS* 1808.

[113] *Report of the Surgeon General*, 1922, pp. 139–141.
[114] *Ibid.*, pp. 140–141.
[115] Williams, *op. cit.*, p. 453.
[116] *Report of the S. G.*, 1927, p. 7.

vided (Art. 7) for cooperation with, *inter alia*, the League Health Committee, its epidemiological service, and its Eastern Bureau at Singapore. The convention also assured (Art. 3) priority for notification of outbreak of disease under Article V of the International Telegraphic Convention of 1875.

Meanwhile, the United States participated in numerous separate conferences on health matters, some of them, such as those on the rat [117] and malaria,[118] highly germane to maritime health.

Pan American Regime. With great enthusiasm, the United States also pressed toward a comprehensive health regime for Pan America. The revised code adopted at Habana in 1924 [119] not only imposed most stringent rules for maritime sanitation but also applied them (Art. 61) to aircraft, the landing places for aircraft to "have the same status as quarantine anchorages." The general sanitary conferences of the American states, begun in 1902, were regularly continued; [120] to them were added conferences on specialized topics; [121] and in 1929 the Gorgas Memorial Laboratory, for research in tropical diseases, was established in Panama.[122]

Although the 1924 Pan American Sanitary Code contained no express provision, correlative to Article 7 of the 1926 Paris convention, authorizing cooperation with other international bodies, substantive collaboration between the Paris office, the League Health Organization, and the Pan American Sanitary Bureau in Washington nevertheless ensued, by means of interlocking office holding, mutual acceptance of representatives, and otherwise.[123] Ironically, one of the most dynamic leaders in all three organizations was the United States.

After the 1926 Paris conference the prior largely unofficial coopera-

---

[117] Second International Conference on the Rat, Paris, Oct. 7–12, 1931, *Am. Del. 1932*, D.S. Pub. No. 425, p. 18.

[118] Third Joint International Congress on Tropical Medicine and Malaria, Amsterdam and Rotterdam, Sept. 24–Oct. 1, 1938, *Am. Del. 1939*, pp. 36–37.

[119] *Cit.* above, n. 107. An amendment called an "Addition to the Pan American Sanitary Code," providing for date of effectiveness and duration, was adopted at Lima, Oct. 19, 1927, 45 *Stat.* 2613, *TS* 763. For evaluation of the code, see Williams, *op. cit.*, p. 447.

[120] For list, brief summation of work, and bibliography, see Scott, *I.C.A.S., 1933–1940*, pp. 438–443.

[121] E.g., of National Directors of Public Health, *ibid.*, pp. 436–438; medical, etc., *ibid.*, Table of Contents.

[122] *Am. Del. 1940*, D.S. Pub. No. 1587, p. 128.

[123] See the reviews by U. P. Hubbard, *Int. Con.* No. 274, pp. 722–725, and the summaries of the Pan American Sanitary conferences, *cit.* above, n. 120.

tion of the United States in the League health work became increasingly official and wholehearted. "The United States, after one brief but damaging moment of opposition, changed its attitude to one of unstinted support."[124] Among the League ventures of maritime significance were the extensive epidemiological service, the Singapore Bureau, the training of Chinese health officers in port health work, and ship fumigation.

Though the United States had experienced some dengue fever in Hawaii, from time to time, that mosquito-borne disease had been brought under control there.[125] The United States did not participate in the Convention for Mutual Protection against Dengue Fever, concluded subsequently at Athens, in 1934.[126]

By the end of World War II, then, conditions were ripe, in terms of multilateral regimes, the existence of international agencies, intergovernmental and interagency cooperation, national policy, and the support of professional groups, for the establishment of a comprehensive World Health Organization with provision for the continuance of regional organizations such as the highly successful one of the American states. Thus, what began in 1851 at Paris as a desperate effort to provide a maritime defense against epidemic disease, particularly that endemic to the Near East, developed within a century into one of the most penetrating of all international administrative organizations.

Exploitation of Products of the Sea

The interwar period witnessed a remarkable expansion of American treaty commitments in relation to fisheries.[127] Bipartite agreements dealing with the North Pacific halibut, the sockeye salmon, and the Great Lakes fisheries were concluded with Canada and one dealing with various fisheries problems with Mexico. The United States participated in the multipartite whaling agreement initiated by the League of Nations. The

---

[124] Walters, *op. cit.*, Vol. I, p. 182. See the excellent summaries for the period 1920–1936 by U. P. Hubbard, *Int. Con.* No. 274, pp. 722–725; *ibid.*, No. 329, pp. 332–339; after 1936, the annual reviews *cit.* above, n. 3. For stirring accounts of international health work, see Hans Zinsser, *As I Remember Him: The Biography of R. S.* (1940), and Victor George Heiser, *An American Doctor's Odyssey: Adventures in Forty-Five Countries* (1936).

[125] Williams, *op. cit.*, pp. 655–657.

[126] Signed July 25, 1934, 6 Hudson, *I.L.* 930.

[127] For an excellent discussion of the historic problem of regulation of fisheries by means of treaties, see A. P. Daggett, "The Regulation of Maritime Fisheries by Treaty," 28 *A.J.I.L.* 693–717 (1934).

Between the Great Wars

groundwork was laid for a multipartite convention relating to the fisheries of the Northwest Atlantic. Toward the end of the period, in 1940, Japan denounced the four power fur-seals agreement of 1911, whereupon the United States and Canada in 1942 entered into a Provisional Agreement relating to fur seals.

Canadian-American Fisheries. With the exception of fur sealing in the Antarctic region and whaling in the Atlantic and Pacific oceans, North and South, in the first half of the nineteenth century, American fishing efforts, until recently, have primarily been devoted to waters adjacent to, or as in the case of the Newfoundland Banks at no great distance from, territory subject to American jurisdiction. Among the fisheries problems which became pressing during the early decades of the present century were those involving the Pacific halibut and the sockeye salmon, both of which were the victims of, *inter alia*, overfishing.[128] Accordingly, among the eight main subjects considered by the American-Canadian Fisheries Conference of 1918, mentioned above, were halibut and the sockeye salmon. With respect to the former, the commission recommended reciprocal legislation to provide for a close season and a joint scientific investigation.[129] With respect to the salmon, it recommended a treaty.[130] The report suggested that the commission, provided for under their proposed salmon treaty, supervise the close season for halibut and make the desired investigation concerning the halibut. In 1919, however, the two governments concluded treaties relating to both the halibut and the salmon. The history of the two sets of treaties can now be outlined separately.

Halibut. From 1919 to 1945, Canada and the United States negotiated four separate agreements dealing with the halibut. The first, a draft instrument dated October 24, 1919, dealt with reciprocal port privileges for both Canadian and American fishermen on both the Atlantic and Pacific coasts; control of the lobster fishery; a close season and scientific investigation of the halibut; and reciprocal freedom from duty for im-

---

[128] For a thorough discussion of the problems and citation of voluminous documentary materials, see Leonard, *op. cit.*, pp. 110–114, and H. E. Gregory and K. Barnes, *North Pacific Fisheries: With Special Reference to Alaska Salmon*, American Council, Institute of Pacific Relations (1939), Chs. IV and XIII.

[129] *Report of the American-Canadian Fisheries Conference, 1918*, 1918, *For. Rel.* 439–480, at pp. 472–473.

[130] *Ibid.*, at p. 464; text of draft treaty at pp. 476–479.

ports of fresh and fresh-frozen fish.[131] Strong opposition in the Senate arose to features other than the provision on halibut.[132] Thus Senator Wesley L. Jones thought the provision on the halibut "would be a good thing as a separate treaty. Why is it not made such — It should not be tied up with these other provisions in order to get them through."[133] The president therefore never even submitted the treaty to the Senate.[134]

A new convention, dealing with halibut alone, signed March 2, 1923, encountered a Senate reservation aimed at preventing participation in the fishery by subjects of other parts of the British Empire except in accord with the treaty provisions. When the Canadian Parliament passed legislation closing Canadian ports to vessels engaged in the fishery unless they conformed to the treaty requirements, the Senate approved the treaty without the reservation.[135] So it went into effect.[136] This agreement provided for a closed season for the nationals and inhabitants of the respective countries applicable to both territorial waters and the high seas and the establishment of a joint International Fisheries Commission to investigate the halibut fishery and recommend further regulation.

A revised convention of May 9, 1930,[137] *inter alia*, conferred affirmative power on the commission to regulate the halibut fishery in detail, subject to approval of the president and the governor general of Canada (Art. III). Another treaty, revising the agreement of 1930 and extending the regulative authority of the commission, was concluded January 29, 1937.[138]

The experience of the two countries under this joint regulation of the halibut fishery is significant for two reasons: first, it has brought back the harvest to the earlier optimum levels. "When the Commission began

[131] Text in 1919 *For. Rel.* 258–263. Schmeckebier, *Int. Org.*, at p. 306, found no official text available at the time he wrote. The volume on *Foreign Relations* probably came out later.

[132] Schmeckebier, *Int. Org.*, p. 306; also for excellent outline and documentation on subject of the halibut up to 1932, pp. 304–313.

[133] 1919 *For. Rel.* 266–268, at 267.

[134] *List of Treaties Submitted to the Senate 1789–1934*, D.S. Pub. No. 765, p. 48.

[135] *Ibid.*, note on tentative No. 728, p. 92; see Schmeckebier, *op. cit.*, pp. 306–307.

[136] Convention for the Preservation of the Halibut Fishery of the Northern Pacific Ocean including the Bering Sea, signed at Washington, March 2, 1923, 43 *Stat.* 1841, TS 701. See Ruth D. Masters, *Handbook of International Organizations in the Americas* (1945), pp. 216–222.

[137] Convention on Preservation of Halibut Fishery of Northern Pacific Ocean and Bering Sea, signed at Ottawa, May 9, 1930, 47 *Stat.* 1872, TS 837.

[138] Convention Revising the Convention of May 9, 1930, signed at Ottawa, 50 *Stat.* 1351, TS 917.

Between the Great Wars

managing the halibut fishery the fishermen of both countries together, fishing nine months of the year (all that the weather would permit), could take about 44 million pounds of halibut from the North Pacific. The populations of halibut on the banks have been so carefully managed and built up that now [1949] those fishermen can take 56 million pounds each year in less than two months of fishing."[139] And second, the halibut agreement and the sockeye-salmon agreement, presently to be discussed, were prototypes [140] for the new multipartite convention relating to the Northwest Atlantic fisheries concluded in 1949.

Salmon. With respect to the fisheries devoted to the several species of Pacific salmon, there are in substance two sets of problems of international significance, one concerned with the fishery in Alaskan waters, particularly in Bering Sea and its southeasternmost arm, Bristol Bay; the other concerned with the Puget Sound–Fraser River sockeye species.

Since 1906 the Fish and Wildlife Service of the Department of the Interior has been in charge of the regulation and conservation of the Alaskan salmon fisheries.[141] The principal international problem in connection therewith arose out of the "invasion" of the Bristol Bay fishing grounds, outside territorial waters, by Japanese fishing and cannery vessels in 1937.[142] Diplomatic representations followed, and legislation was proposed to safeguard the national conservation program in offshore waters beyond the customary three-mile limit.[143] In pursuance of Article 9 of the Treaty of Peace of September 8, 1951, which provided that "Japan will enter promptly into negotiations with the Allied Powers so desiring for the conclusion of bilateral and multilateral agreements providing for the regulation or limitation of fishing and the conservation and development of fisheries on the high seas,"[144] a fishing treaty between

---

[139] Wilbert M. Chapman, "United States Policy on High Seas Fisheries," 20 *DSB* 67, 69 (1949); *Hearing before a Subcommittee of the Committee on Foreign Relations of the United States Senate on the Fisheries Conventions*, July 14, 1949, 81 Cong., 1 Sess., p. 40; Leonard, *op. cit.*, pp. 110–113.

[140] *Hearing, op. cit.*, pp. 39–40.

[141] For excellent accounts of the whole history of the Alaska salmon fisheries, see Leonard, *op. cit.*, Ch. III, and Gregory and Barnes, *op. cit.*, several chapters.

[142] Leonard, *op. cit.*, pp. 127–132.

[143] *Ibid.*, pp. 127–132 and pp. 133–136. See also *Hearing before a Subcommittee of the Committee on Commerce, United States Senate, January 20, 1944*, 78 Cong., 2 Sess., on S. 930, "A Bill to Assure Conservation of and to Permit the Fullest Utilization of the Fisheries of Alaska," and the S. Rept. No. 733 on the same bill; both documents review the whole problem and controversy.

[144] Signed at San Francisco, 3 *UST* 3169, *TIAS* 2490.

Japan, the United States, and Canada dealing with the whole area of the North Pacific was concluded in 1952.[145] This will be discussed later when the post-World War II fisheries developments are under consideration.

The sockeye-salmon fishery is another matter: it presents distinct problems of its own. Five species of salmon — the sockeye, the chinook or spring, the coho or silver, the pink or humpback, and the chum or dog, together with the steelhead, which is not of the same genus but is commercially regarded as a salmon — all use the international boundary waters of Juan de Fuca Strait, Washington Sound, and Georgia Strait to reach the Fraser River system in British Columbia for the purpose of spawning.[146] "While salmon of all five species spawn in the Fraser River basin and in streams of Washington, Vancouver Island, and the mainland of British Columbia, the sockeye resorts almost exclusively to the Fraser for spawning purposes." After spawning, the adults die; the young within a few months go down stream to sea and, after reaching maturity in four years, return to, it is believed, "the identical stream or tributary of a stream in which they were born." "Thus each watershed and possibly each stream presents its own problem." For commercial catches, the fish are intercepted, in their periodic runs to their spawning grounds, off the coast, in the straits and the sound, and in the Fraser River itself.

Two special features distinguish this problem of the sockeye. One is that the great majority of fish returning from the sea pass through that portion of Washington Sound which lies within United States jurisdiction. Hence, up to 1918, usually 66 per cent or more of the total catch was taken in the state of Washington. The cooperation of that state and of the United States is therefore essential to the success of any pisciculture efforts of the Canadian government in the Fraser River itself. The other

[145] Signed at Tokyo, May 9, 1952, 4 *UST* 380, *TIAS* 2786. For discussion of the situation as it stood prior to the conclusion of this treaty, see statement of John Foster Dulles, *Hearings before the Committee on Foreign Relations, United States Senate, January 21, 22, 23, and 25, 1952, on Japanese Peace Treaty and other Treaties Relating to Security in the Pacific*, 82 Cong., 2 Sess., at p. 19; William W. Bishop, Jr., "Need for a Japanese Fisheries Agreement," 45 *A.J.I.L.* 712–719 (1951); Edward W. Allen, "A New Concept for Fishery Treaties," 46 *ibid.* 319–323; and Charles B. Selak, Jr., "The Proposed International Convention for the High Seas Fisheries of the North Pacific Ocean," 46 *ibid.* 323–330 (1952).

[146] See the two fine large maps annexed to Sockeye Salmon Fisheries Convention, signed at Washington, May 26, 1930, 50 *Stat.* 1355, *TS* 918.

feature is the phenomenon of periodic unequal runs of the sockeye — three lean or "off years" and the fourth a "big year."

This phenomenon is attributable, according to one theory, to a rock slide in the Fraser River at Hell's Gate Canyon or vicinity sometime preceding the earliest records which date from 1806. (This canyon, which is located in British Columbia, should not be confused with Hells Canyon on the Snake River, which is a tributary of the Columbia River and part of the boundary between Oregon and Idaho. The salmon have their troubles going up the Columbia River and its tributaries, too, though all the dams are required by law to have fish ladders. However, since the Columbia River lies for the most part in American territory and enters the Pacific between Washington and Oregon, the salmon in it have not been the subject of controversy between Canada and the United States.) The slide in the Fraser River, then, is thought to have prevented great numbers of returning adults from proceeding to their spawning grounds; they died without spawning. The adults which reached their natal grounds in the lower reaches of the river spawned. The net yield for one such year would therefore be small. It took, it is thought, three years for the headwaters of the river to cut an adequate channel through the debris, thus permitting in the fourth year spawning by all adults returning to the river. As the demographist would say, three of the years are "hollow classes"; the fourth is normal again. The cycle has persisted to this day, inviting excessive fishing during the "big year" runs, which further complicates normal conservation efforts.

Then, to aggravate the situation, blasting for a railroad above Hell's Gate Canyon in 1913 caused rock slides into a "resting place" used by the fish going up stream, forcing countless thousands back down the canyon into exhaustion and death before reproduction. A drop of nearly 80 per cent in the yield for the next "big year," 1917, bore mute testimony to the catastrophe of 1913.[147] The removal of obstructions and the facilitation otherwise of upstream journeys of adult sockeye in the Fraser River system thus became a matter of prime importance to American fishing interests.

Though the sockeye-salmon fishery had been declining steadily for

---

[147] Data and quotations from *Report of the American-Canadian Fisheries Conference, 1918, op. cit.*, pp. 457–461. See also William F. Thompson, *Effect of the Obstruction at Hell's Gate on the Sockeye Salmon of the Fraser River*, Bulletin 1, International Pacific Salmon Fisheries Commission (1945), pp. 84–96.

decades, so that by 1930 it was described in the treaty of that date (Article VII) as "a fishery that is now largely nonexistent," efforts to secure international regulation had been made beginning at least in 1892.[148] A joint commission appointed in that year and reporting in 1896 endorsed the application of the more stringent type of Canadian regulation to American fishing of the Fraser River runs.[149] In the early 1900s improved regulations were adopted by the state of Washington and by Canada, but they proved inadequate. The fate of the new recommendations and regulations submitted in 1910 by the International Fisheries Commission set up under the convention of April 11, 1908, has already been discussed above.[150] David Starr Jordan, on behalf of the commission, submitted "A System of Uniform and Common International Regulations for the Protection and Preservation of the Food Fishes in International Boundary Waters of the United States and Canada," which was transmitted to Congress in 1910, but Congress failed to enact them.[151]

Another commission in 1918 prepared a draft convention providing for a regulatory joint commission, scientific investigation, and regulations to protect the sockeye salmon.[152] President Wilson submitted this convention, dated September 2, 1919, to the Senate, but criticism arose in that body with respect to certain of the provisions relating to criminal prosecution,[153] and the treaty was withdrawn.[154] An amended treaty, redated May 25, 1920, and stipulating in greater detail the criminal procedure, was then resubmitted to the Senate.[155] This was subsequently also withdrawn, probably in response to the opposition of local American fishery interests. Thus the matter stood while the fisheries worsened. After an exchange of several new drafts early in 1929, another convention, signed at Washington, March 27, 1929, was submitted to the Senate.

[148] See Gregory and Barnes, *op. cit.*, pp. 72–76.

[149] *Report of Joint Commissioners, Relative to the Preservation of Fisheries in Waters Contiguous to the United States and Canada, December 31, 1896*, submitted to Congress, Feb. 24, 1897, 54 Cong., 2 Sess., H. Doc. No. 315, S. 3534, pp. 176–177.

[150] At pp. 120–121.

[151] Transmitted, Feb. 2, 1910, 61 Cong., 2 Sess., H. Doc. No. 638, S. 5834.

[152] *Report* in 1918 *For. Rel.* 439–476; draft treaty in Appendix A at pp. 476–480. Treaty text and portions of the report dealing with the sockeye-salmon problem reprinted in message from President to the Senate on *Sockeye Salmon Fishery Convention*, 66 Cong., 1 Sess., S. Doc. No. 116 (1919), S. 7610.

[153] 1919 *For. Rel.* 236–239; 1920 *For. Rel.* I, 387–390.

[154] *List of Treaties Submitted to the Senate 1789–1934*, listed as No. 684 at p. 48. Also 1919 *For. Rel.* 239. Withdrawn on Jan. 15, 1920.

[155] *List of Treaties*, No. 697, at p. 49. Date of withdrawal not given.

Between the Great Wars

On December 13, 1929, this instrument was ordered by the Senate to be returned to the President.[156] Then finally on May 26, 1930, the first successful sockeye-salmon treaty was concluded.[157]

The Senate, however, delayed giving its consent to ratification of the 1930 treaty until 1936, and then only subject to three understandings, one of which prohibited the promulgation or enforcement of any regulations by the International Pacific Salmon Fisheries Commission "until the scientific investigations provided for in the convention have been made, covering two cycles of Sockeye Salmon runs or eight years."[158] Since ratifications were not exchanged until July 28, 1937, effective regulation could not begin until 1945. Meanwhile, in pursuance of Article III of the convention, which empowered the commission "to improve spawning grounds, construct, and maintain hatcheries, rearing ponds and other such facilities" for the propagation of sockeye salmon and "to recommend removing or otherwise overcoming obstructions to the ascent of sockeye salmon," the cost of all work in pursuance of this program to "be borne equally by the two Governments," the commission recommended, and the two governments agreed in 1944 upon, the construction of fish ladders in Hell's Gate Canyon, and the overcoming of other obstructions, at a total cost of $2,000,000.[159]

Thus ends a record of astonishingly myopic self-destructive acquisitiveness in favor of one of the most forward-looking enterprises ever undertaken jointly by two governments in relation to a common resource of the sea. The story of the joint efforts in relation to the salmon will be resumed in the discussion of post-World War II developments.

Great Lakes Fisheries. Although the Great Lakes fisheries are fresh water phenomena and concern only the two contiguous countries, Canada and the United States, some mention of the international conservation efforts relating to them is desirable for several reasons. The fisheries are an important part of the total world effort to increase aquatic food supplies. Numerous difficulties have been encountered in devising a treaty which would be satisfactory to the American states concerned,

---

[156] 1929 *For. Rel.* II, 55–60, including the text of the convention; *List of Treaties*, No. 861, at p. 93.

[157] Sockeye Salmon Fisheries Convention, signed at Washington, May 26, 1930, proclaimed by the President, Aug. 4, 1937; 50 *Stat.* 1355, TS 918. See Masters, *op. cit.*, pp. 238–245.

[158] In President's Proclamation accompanying treaty text, *op. cit.*

[159] Sockeye Salmon Fisheries, Agreement effected by exchange of notes, signed at Washington, July 21 and Aug. 5, 1944, 59 *Stat.* 1614, EAS 479.

The United States and the Treaty Law of the Sea

thus posing a tough problem in federal-state relationships. Furthermore, various elements in Congress have been opposed to loss of legislative prerogative in such matters through use or extension of the treaty-making process. And finally, the techniques evolved in and under a bipartite treaty, for the handling of some international conservation problem, can usually be adapted and utilized in a multipartite arrangement toward similar ends.

Briefly, the problem of progressive depletion of the Great Lakes fisheries, caused chiefly by destructive gear and overfishing, is complicated by the fouling of the water with mill refuse, fish offal, ashes, industrial effluents and similar foreign substances; extensive use for game fishing involving some discard and waste; and the inability of the several American states bordering upon the lakes to agree upon uniform regulations and conservation programs.[160]

Uniform fishery laws were urged upon the Great Lakes states as early as 1875. At least twenty-seven international and interstate conferences were held in the period 1883–1943 for the purpose of securing coordinated action. The great Canadian-American fisheries commissions of 1892 and 1908 examined the lakes problems in detail and recommended specific action by the respective national governments. Thus the 1892 Commission recommended the establishment of a "permanent joint commission . . . which shall be charged with the direct supervision of these fisheries . . ."[161] The 1908 Commission submitted a draft set of regulations for the lakes fisheries, among others in boundary waters, and recommended concurrent enforcing legislation and, for the United States, a federal patrol system.[162] But the 1918 Commission merely recommended that the states of New York, Pennsylvania, and Ohio enact legislation similar to that of Canada relating to the conservation of the sturgeon in Lake Erie.[163]

In 1940, in response to efforts of such groups as the Council of State Governments, the Izaak Walton League of America, the American Fisheries Society, and the Wildlife Federation, the governments of Canada

---

[160] The problem is described briefly in Leonard, *op. cit.*, pp. 115–120, and fully in *International Board of Inquiry for Great Lakes Fisheries: Report and Supplement* (1943). See also Durand Smith, "The Great Lakes Fisheries Convention," 16 *DSB* 643–644, 675 (1947).

[161] *Report*, p. 15, *cit*: above, n. 149.

[162] *Report*, pp. 16–18, *cit.* above, n. 151.

[163] *Report*, p. 475, *cit.* above, n. 152.

Between the Great Wars

and the United States set up still another commission, called a Board of Inquiry for the Great Lakes Fisheries, to study the problem and to make recommendations.[164] That board reported in 1943.[165] After exploring the possible device of an interstate compact (which would have to include the province of Ontario) and "any attempt to transfer jurisdiction from the eight Great Lakes states to the Federal Government," it firmly recommended an international treaty along the lines of the Migratory Bird Treaty of 1916, rather than one simulating the halibut or salmon conventions. The regulations under these latter conventions are adopted by the respective international commissions, subject in the case of the halibut convention to the approval of the President and Governor General.

The device of a commission for the Great Lakes fisheries would raise, *inter alia*, exceedingly difficult problems of representation for the lakes states concerned. Under a convention of the Bird Treaty type, enabling legislation could for the United States simply vest enforcement in a national agency, the Fish and Wildlife Service. It could further permit states to adopt legislation not inconsistent with the treaty requirements and provide "for reciprocal enforcement of any regulations with the state conservation departments cooperating."[166] Thus might come the beginning of the end of another serious international problem of conservation.

In due course, after World War II, in 1946, the President did negotiate a treaty along these lines, but, meeting with opposition in the Senate, the agreement was withdrawn by the President and replaced by another along less ambitious lines in 1954. These latest efforts to produce an intelligible regime for the Great Lakes fisheries will be discussed in connection with post-World War II developments.

Tuna Fisheries. In the interwar period, the groundwork for the postwar (1949) tuna conventions with Mexico and Costa Rica was also laid. Fishing by Americans off the coasts of California, Lower California, and Mexico proper expanded enormously in the years immediately following World War I, particularly for the several species of tuna and tunalike fish. Although most of the fish off the Mexican coast were caught outside

---

[164] Establishment of Board of Inquiry for the Great Lakes Fisheries, Agreement Effected by Exchange of Notes, signed at Washington, Feb. 29, 1940, 54 *Stat.* 2409, *EAS* 182.

[165] *Cit.* above, n. 160.

[166] *Report*, pp. 38–42, *cit.* above, n. 160.

the three-mile limit, it was necessary for American vessels to enter Mexican waters for shelter and to take sardines and similar small varieties for live-bait operations. The safest and shortest route home happened also to be through Mexican territorial waters. In the circumstances it became necessary for American fishermen "to take out Mexican fishing permits, and pay the export fees on dutiable fish in observance of that country's regulations." "Difficulties arose . . . unfortunate practices crept in, and general dissatisfaction with existing conditions increased." [167]

In the course of correspondence relating to a proposed convention between the United States and Mexico dealing with smuggling, the traffic in narcotics, and other pending difficulties, the Mexican government suggested the addition of "the question of clandestine fishing in territorial waters" to the agenda.[168] Thus, a convention concluded at Washington, December 23, 1925,[169] contained, among a variety of other unrelated subjects, a section on fisheries. The treaty provided (Section III) for the setting up of a joint international commission to study problems and make recommendations with respect to certain purposes, namely, "the conservation and development of marine life resources in the ocean waters off certain coasts of each nation," the prevention of smuggling of all kinds of marine products, and the collection of revenue from fish and other marine products. There was also provision for possible joint regulations to be approved by the two governments (Article XII). Thereupon, "a program of scientific investigations was drafted and preliminary investigations were begun" concerning the yellowfin tuna, skipjack, yellowtail, bonito, spiny lobster, black sea bass, white sea bass, and barracuda, the principal species taken by Americans off the Mexican coasts.[170]

Then, suddenly, the United States gave notice of the termination of the convention, March 21, 1927, effective, in accordance with the terms of the treaty, thirty days later.[171] The United States cited in this connec-

---

[167] Report of the Commissioner of Fisheries in *15th Annual Report of the Secretary of Commerce, June 30, 1927*, pp. 173–174. For data on the early claim of jurisdiction by Mexico over the high seas for fiscal and fishery purposes in a marginal belt twenty kilometers wide, see Stefan A. Riesenfeld, *Protection of Coastal Fisheries under International Law* (1942), pp. 234–239.

[168] 1925 *For. Rel.* II, p. 510n.

[169] Convention for the Prevention of Smuggling and for Certain Other Objects, 44 Stat. 2358, TS 732.

[170] *Report*, p. 173, *cit.* above, n. 167.

[171] 1927 *For. Rel.* III, p. 230.

tion the absence of a commercial treaty with Mexico as making difficult performance under the convention. Other reasons apparently contributed to the decision to denounce the agreement: the fishery "commission failed, among other reasons, because of conflicts among the State of California, the Federal Government, and the affected industry." [172] The problems and the attempts to resolve the conflicts continued over the years until two conventions providing for the investigation of the tuna alone were successfully concluded with Mexico and Costa Rica in 1949. These will be referred to again.

The experience of the United States with the draft Halibut Treaty of October 24, 1919, and this short-lived fisheries agreement of 1925 with Mexico would suggest the desirability wherever possible of dealing with fishery problems in separate treaties, on the one hand, to avoid rejection of them by the Senate because of opposition to some other wholly unrelated provision of the instrument and, on the other hand, to avoid denunciation of them for reasons unrelated to the fisheries clauses. The practice of devoting the whole instrument to the solution of a particular fisheries problem has happily been followed since the 1930s, and, further, where two species with distinct characteristics and problems resort to the same area of the ocean, it may be necessary, in addition, to set up two separate agencies to deal with them, as was done in the case of the Pacific halibut and the sockeye salmon.[173]

Whales. The American-Canadian Fisheries Conference of 1918, charged with an inquiry into the whaling situation among other subjects referred to above, reported that while a bilateral agreement between the two countries for the protection of whales frequenting waters off their coasts would be of some advantage, it would be more effective, in view of the migrations of the whales and the widespread participation in the industry by interests on other continents, to seek world-wide action after the war (that is, the war of 1914–1918).[174]

---

[172] Statement of W. M. Chapman, Special Assistant for Fisheries and Wildlife to the Under Secretary of State, in *Hearing*, p. 61, *cit.* above, n. 139.

[173] Thus the new North Pacific Fisheries Convention, between the United States, Canada, and Japan, signed at Tokyo, May 9, 1952, 4 *UST* 380, *TIAS* 2786, merely supplements but does not replace the prior Canadian-American agreements on halibut and sockeye salmon.

[174] *Report of the Conference,* 1918 *For. Rel.* 439, 475–476. The problem of modern whaling and much of the history of the international effort to bring it under rational control up to 1944 are well told in Leonard, *op. cit.*, pp. 95–109. For an exciting first-hand account of a modern Antarctic whaling expedition by the senior medical

The United States and the Treaty Law of the Sea

Accordingly, both Canada and the United States cooperated heartily in the ensuing efforts of the League of Nations to secure multipartite commitment to a program of conservation.[175] Though the United States was once a great whaling nation, few American vessels participated in the fishery after World War I. Thus in 1935–1936, there were two American shore stations, two floating factories, and fifteen catchers; in 1936–1937, two, three, and twenty-two, respectively; in 1937–1938, one, two, and twenty, respectively. By 1949, the United States had no "important economic interest in whaling operations" as such. It had, however, an important and continuous interest in the economic products of whaling and a "potentially important interest in future whaling operations."[176] The United States was therefore from the beginning of these efforts at conservation intensely interested in their success. Since 1931 it has, accordingly, participated in every multipartite agreement on the subject, and since the end of World War II, it has furnished commendable leadership in the final establishment of effective control measures.

The whaling situation in the decades immediately following World War I was indeed discouraging. Whole species, such as those included under the general term of "right whales," were facing extinction. Numerous abuses emanating from land stations and factories at sea flourished. All seas and seasons were open; all species, males, females, calves, sucklings, mature whales and immature whales, large ones and small ones, were fair game. Unnecessarily cruel methods were used to capture and kill. No nation could regulate its own vessels without giving the field of "free enterprise" over to the unregulated nationals of other states. Moby Dick stood a sporting chance for his life against sailing vessels and row boats; he was doomed in his contest with power-driven vessels and explosives. Shortly, some species would be extinct and others reduced to such paltry remnants as would make whaling no longer a profitable com-

---

officer to one of the largest whaling expeditions of the 1950–1951 season, see R. B. Robertson, *Of Whales and Men* (1954).

[175] For the United States: *Int. Con.* No. 274, pp. 715, 796; *ibid.*, No. 331, p. 551; *ibid.*, No. 352, p. 394. A brief account of the work of the League, up to 1932, is in Gidel, *op. cit.*, Vol. 1, pp. 464–478. See also Phillip C. Jessup, *L'Exploitation des Richesses de la Mer* (1929), pp. 81–104.

[176] *Survey of Activities of the Committee on Foreign Affairs*, H. of R., 81 Cong., 1 Sess., Committee Print (1949), p. 45. By 1956, however, some American whaling on the Pacific coast had been resumed, 145 whales being captured that year. For 1957 the department of interior reported the taking of 237 whales by three vessels, mostly in the vicinity of the Farallon Islands off San Francisco. *N.Y.T.*, March 28, 1958.

Between the Great Wars

mercial enterprise. Thus, abuse of the doctrine of "freedom of the seas" and the concept of *res nullius* would leave both nature and man the poorer.

A beginning for international control was made in the establishment of the International Bureau for Whaling Statistics at Oslo, at the request of the International Council for the Exploration of the Products of the Sea, in 1930. With the facts in hand perhaps some progress could be made. The first multipartite agreement, concluded under the auspices of the League of Nations in 1931 [177] at Geneva, reflected the prevailing reluctance of governments to assume obligations limiting the activities of their nationals. The obligations created were modest enough. Confined to baleens or whalebone whales only (not the numerous species of toothed whales), the convention prohibited the taking of certain species of right whales, the taking or killing of calves or suckling whales, immature whales, and female whales accompanied by calves or suckling whales. It required that gunners and crews be engaged with their pay geared not to the mere number of whales taken but to their size, species, and value for products. It required the fullest use to be made of the carcasses of whales and the licensing of whaling vessels by the participating governments. It obligated each government to secure from its whalers complete biological data concerning each whale taken and from all factories under their jurisdiction full reports of their operations. Article 12 obligated the parties to communicate prescribed "statistical information regarding all whaling operations under their jurisdiction to the International Bureau for Whaling Statistics at Oslo" (later located at Sandefjord). The convention did not, however, fix any limit upon the harvesting of any species or all species.

The process of international regulation having been begun, two tendencies in the treaty making developed which are reminiscent of the history of much municipal regulation. The successive agreements [178] sought to regulate more aspects of the subject matter and gradually to substitute administrative control for mere "statutory" control. This was

---

[177] Concluded Sept. 24, 1931; signed on the part of the United States, March 31, 1932; proclaimed Jan. 16, 1935, 49 *Stat.* 3079, *TS* 880. It was signed by 26 states; some did not ratify. By Dec. 15, 1935, 24 states had ratified or adhered. The United States promptly adopted enforcing legislation, Whaling Treaty Act, May 1, 1936, 49 *Stat.* 1246.

[178] All cited in the bibliographical notes accompanying the texts of the agreements given in 5 Hudson, *I.L.* 1081; 7 *ibid.*, 754, 762, 765; 9 *ibid.*, 111, 114, 117.

The United States and the Treaty Law of the Sea

uphill work, as the treaties themselves and the final acts of the conferences attached to them reveal. Great whaling powers, such as Japan and the Soviet Union, never assumed any obligations under the interwar agreements. Others were willing to assume the moderate obligations under the 1931 convention but not the more extensive ones under the 1937 supplementary convention.

The 1937 agreement,[179] concluded at London, in addition to prohibiting the taking of "Grey Whales and/or Right Whales" and elaborating many of the prior rules, introduced certain new principles. Thus, it required each contracting government to maintain at least one inspector, appointed and paid by the government, on each factory ship under its flag. It established certain closed areas for the taking of baleen whales in the Atlantic, Pacific, and Indian oceans. It set the open season for taking baleen whales in the area south of 40° south latitude from December 8 to March 7. It fixed a maximum of six months use per year for any land station or whale catcher attached thereto and it prescribed minimum lengths for the take of certain species. The Final Act of the conference, however, made many recommendations, urged governments to adopt measures more stringent than those obligated by the convention, and expressed alarm concerning operations conducted under governments not party to the 1937 agreement. Among the recommendations was one directed against the flight of whalers from flag states which had assumed treaty obligations to other states which were not so bound. It suggested, to stop this practice, that such transfers be allowed only under license of the government.

In accord with the desire of the 1937 conference, a review conference was held in London the following year, 1938. A discouraging picture of excessive whaling was presented to it. The conference adopted a certificate extending the agreement of 1937 and a protocol[180] amending certain of its provisions in the interest of better control of operations. The Final Act recommended numerous measures necessary to save the rem-

---

[179] Agreement on Regulation of Whaling, signed June 8, 1937, by 9 governments, 52 *Stat.* 1460, TS 933. See Report of the Delegates of the United States in Message from the President to the Senate, *International Agreement for the Regulation of Whaling*, 75 Cong., 1 Sess., S. Ex. U, July 31, 1937.

[180] Protocol Amending the Agreement of 1937, London, June 24, 1938, 53 *Stat.* 1794, TS 944. Ten states, including Germany, signed this protocol. See Report of the Delegates of the United States in Message from the President to the Senate, *Protocol Amending the International Agreement for the Regulation of Whaling*, 76 Cong., 1 Sess., S. Ex. C, Feb. 9, 1939.

Between the Great Wars

nants of the whale resources. So dire was the situation that the Final Act even posed the question whether, in view of the noncooperation of so many governments, it might not be better to drop all regulations and permit indiscriminate whaling until the stocks of whales had been reduced to the "level at which whaling ceases to be remunerative." Thus the thankless tasks of a dozen earnest governments could be ended — by ending the whales.

One further conference on whaling was held in the period before World War II, at London, in July 1939.[181] It was distinctive for its utilization of the experience of the government inspectors who had seen service on whaling ships or in stations. The inspectors met concurrently with the conference and reported the results of their deliberations to the conference. The conference adopted certain recommendations, including one on the marking of whales, but no amendments to the convention of 1937.

Whaling operations in the areas to which the 1937 agreement applied were, of course, interrupted by the hostilities of World War II. Looking forward, however, to the resumption of whaling at the close of hostilities, a majority of the parties to the 1937 agreement, excepting, of course, Germany, met in London in 1944 and adopted a protocol [182] amending the 1937 instrument. The protocol made certain necessary changes in the open season and introduced a new saving principle. It fixed a total of 16,000 blue-whale units as the maximum to be taken in the area south of 40° south latitude for the open season. A blue-whale unit was defined as "one blue whale equals 2 fin whales or 2½ humpback whales or 6 sei whales." Thus for the first time a top limit was placed on the take permitted in the principal whaling waters. Great Britain was authorized to consult the participating governments "in order to arrange by cooperation and agreement the measures necessary to ensure that the total number of baleen whales caught during the first season" would not exceed the number fixed in the protocol.

Unable to secure the accession of Ireland to the 1944 protocol, a new

[181] 1 *DSB* 37 (1939); *Am. Del. 1940*, pp. 7–8.

[182] Signed Feb. 7, 1944. Text, 10 *DSB* 592–593 (1944). Though ratified by the President, this instrument, as such, never went into effect. Its substance was repeated in the protocol signed at London, Oct. 5, 1945. See Report of the Delegates of the United States in Message from the President to the Senate, *International Agreement for the Regulation of Whaling*, 78 Cong., 2 Sess., S. Ex. D, May 10, 1944.

The United States and the Treaty Law of the Sea

protocol was concluded at London, October 5, 1945,[183] bringing the substance of the 1944 protocol into effect for the governments then ready to proceed with the business in hand.

In addition, certain other instruments had to be adopted to extend the prewar regime to the postwar situation. Thus, a protocol of November 26, 1945,[184] further amended the 1937 agreement and the 1938 protocol, making certain provisions of previous instruments applicable for the 1946–1947 season. A protocol of March 15, 1946,[185] gave permission to certain factory ships to continue whaling operations after March 24, 1946. A protocol of December 2, 1946,[186] concluded at Washington, extended the effectiveness of the protocol of November 26, 1945, and to meet the recalcitrance of Mexico and the Netherlands, a supplementary protocol, bringing into force in entirety the protocol of November 26, 1945, was signed at London, March 3, 1947.[187] Thus ended the efforts to conserve whaling under the interwar convention of 1937. In the meanwhile, however, with the United States taking the leadership, an important whaling conference was held in Washington in the fall of 1946 and a new regime was devised consonant with the bolder views of conservation regulation which had emerged out of World War II. Discussion of the 1946 regime will be resumed in connection with the postwar developments.

Fur Seals. During the interwar period the Japanese government found itself increasingly in controversy with the other governments in relation to conservation efforts devoted to the Pacific salmon,[188] whales,[189] and the North Pacific fur seals.[190] On October 23, 1940, the Japanese govern-

---

[183] *Certified Copy of Supplementary Protocol Concerning Whaling Signed at London, October 5, 1945.* Sen. Ex. J, 79 Cong., 1 Sess., Nov. 23, 1945. It was subsequently withdrawn from the Senate. *Treaty Developments,* D.S. Pub. No. 2851 (1947) for June 1949.

[184] Proclaimed Feb. 10, 1947, 61 *Stat.* (2) 1213, *TIAS* 1597. For the thread through these tangled postwar negotiations, see notes in 9 Hudson, *I.L.* 111–112, 114.

[185] Signed but not in force for the United States. *Treaty Developments* for June 1949. Text in *British Treaty Series* No. 44 (1946) Cmd. 6941.

[186] Entered into force for the United States, Feb 5, 1948, 62 *Stat.* (2) 1577, *TIAS* 1708.

[187] Entered into force with respect to the United States, Aug. 1, 1947, 61 *Stat.* (2) 1240, *TIAS* 1634.

[188] See Leonard, *op. cit.,* pp. 121–132; Gregory and Barnes, *op. cit.,* pp. 285–302.

[189] See Leonard, *op. cit.,* pp. 105–107; Hayden, *op. cit.,* pp. 137–172 *passim.*

[190] Hayden, *op. cit.,* pp. 131–136 *passim;* Leonard, *op. cit.,* pp. 92–93.

ment gave notice,[191] in accordance with Article XVI of the 1911 Fur Seals Agreement,[192] of its denunciation of that agreement, indicating to the government of the United States at the same time that "both direct and indirect damage" had allegedly "been inflicted on the Japanese fishing industry by the increase of fur seals." [193] In accord with Article XVI, the treaty terminated for all four participating governments on October 23, 1941.

Thereupon, the United States and Canada entered into a provisional agreement,[194] effected by exchange of notes, December 8 and 19, 1942, in which the principal features of the 1911 regime were continued insofar as these two governments were concerned. Among the slight changes made by the bipartite agreement were the following: The share of the Pribilof take assigned to Canada was increased temporarily from 15 per cent to 20 per cent. New clauses were included providing for controlled pelagic sealing "in the event of emergency circumstances." This cryptic phrase, in its context of December 1942, suggests the possible fear that the Japanese might conceivably capture the Pribilof Islands and so prevent the customary sealing operations there. Other clauses provided for the taking of seals for scientific purposes, the exchange of research information, and consultation with regard to "the level of population at which the seal herd is to be maintained," among other management matters.

The new arrangement did not, however, carry forward the provision in the 1911 treaty, Article V, relating to the protection of the sea otter. That objective was substantially achieved by new American legislation. "The 1943 amendment of the Alaska Game Law specifically extended protection to the sea otter by including it under the definition of fur animals." An act of 1944 prohibited the taking of sea otters and also implemented the Fur Seal Agreement of 1942.[195]

A subsequent agreement of December 26, 1947,[196] amended that of 1942 to permit its termination on the entry into force "of a new agreement for the preservation and protection of fur seals to which the United

[191] 3 *DSB* 412–413 (1940).
[192] 37 *Stat.* 1542, *TS* 564.
[193] 5 *DSB* 336–337 (1941).
[194] 58 *Stat.* 1379, *EAS* 415.
[195] Act of July 1, 1943, 57 *Stat.* 301. Letter of Fish and Wildlife Service to writer, October 23, 1952.
[196] 62 *Stat.* 1821, *TIAS* 1686.

The United States and the Treaty Law of the Sea

States . . . and Canada, and possibly other interested countries, shall be parties." An agreement of 1952 between the United States, Canada, and Japan [197] providing for cooperative research into the distribution, migration, and feeding habits of the fur seals in the North Pacific Ocean paved the way to resumption of negotiations in 1955 toward a quadripartite treaty to replace that of 1911.

League of Nations Efforts. Two further important developments in the interwar period relating to the exploitation of the products of the sea remain to be noted. Both stem from the efforts of the League of Nations to encourage the codification of international law. The history of those efforts is tortuous,[198] culminating, temporarily, in the First Codification Conference held at The Hague, March 13–April 12, 1930, with 47 states represented, including the United States,[199] and in the work of the Economic Committee of the League which resulted in the first whaling agreement in 1931. Though the Codification Conference produced no convention on territorial waters, the numerous studies which had been made over several years in preparation for the conference included important reports relating to the exploitation of marine products in territorial waters, over the continental shelf, and on the remoter high seas.[200] Up to 1930, distinguished Americans in their private capacities participated in these League efforts; after 1930 the United States, having lost some of its pristine hostility to the organization, participated officially.[201]

---

[197] Fur Seals, Research Programs in the North Pacific Ocean, effected by exchange of notes, signed at Tokyo, Jan. 31 and Feb. 8, 1952, and at Ottawa, Feb. 7 and March 1, 1952, 3 *UST* 3896, *TIAS* 2521.

[198] Briefly summarized, with citation of the pertinent League documents, in Myers, *op. cit.*, pp. 167, 264–267; also, P. C. Jessup, *op. cit.*, pp. 12–16. For further data on the records, see Aufricht, *op. cit.*

[199] For documentation, see Aufricht, *op. cit.*

[200] E.g., "Report of the Sub-Committee of the Committee of Experts for the Progressive Codification of International Law on Territorial Waters," Jan. 29, 1926, reprinted in 20 *A.J.I.L. Special Number*, July 1926, pp. 62–147, Section XIII, "Riches of the Sea," at pp. 107–109; "Report on the Exploitation of the Products of the Sea," by M. José León Suárez to the Committee of Experts, dated Dec. 8, 1925, *ibid.*, at pp. 231–241; "Report to the Council of the League of Nations on the Procedure to be Followed in Regard to the Question of the Exploitation of the Products of the Sea," April 2, 1927, 22 *A.J.I.L. Special Supplement*, Jan. 1928, pp. 44–45.

[201] *Int. Con.* No. 274, p. 106. See also the monumental "Research in International Law," centered at the Harvard Law School, under the direction of Dr. Manley O. Hudson, with its group of distinguished American cooperating scholars; particularly in the present connection, the Draft Convention on Territorial Waters, text, comment, and appendixes, 23 *A.J.I.L. Special Number*, April 1929, pp. 243–380; all of the research was designed to aid the forthcoming conference at The Hague in 1930.

Between the Great Wars

Permanent Council for the Exploration of the Sea. For a few years, 1912–1916, the United States was a member of the scientific organization called the Permanent International Council for the Exploration of the Sea, founded in 1899 at Stockholm, removed in 1902 to Copenhagen, and thereafter called the Copenhagen Council. During the League days it was supported by fourteen European states.[202] The League solicited and received the cooperation of the council in its efforts to produce a whaling convention.[203] The United States maintained contacts during the interwar period with the council through the North American Council on Fishery Investigations, created in 1920 and consisting of twelve fisheries experts, assigned to it by the United States, Canada, Newfoundland, and France.[204]

Protection of Wildlife. With respect to oceanic birds, no new international commitment was assumed by the United States in the period 1919–1945. American delegates, however, attended several international conferences on wildlife in those decades, one of which, the Eighth International Ornithological Congress at Oxford in 1934, urged measures to terminate the oil pollution of navigable waters.[205] Two treaties concluded by the United States, one with Mexico in 1936 dealing with the "Protection of Migratory Birds and Game Animals"[206] and another, a Pan American convention of 1940 on "Nature Protection and Wildlife Preservation in the Western Hemisphere,"[207] do not include protection

---

[202] League of Nations *Handbook of International Organizations* (1938), pp. 164–165; Leonard, *op. cit.*, p. 96; particularly, P. C. Jessup, *L'Exploitation des Richesses de la Mer*, pp. 28–36, and Thomas Wayland Vaughan, *et al.*, *International Aspects of Oceanography*, National Academy of Sciences, Washington (1937), pp. 92–95.

[203] Leonard, *op. cit.*, pp. 97–98; Hayden, *op. cit.*, pp. 149–154; Jessup, *op. cit.*, pp. 81–104.

[204] Masters, *op. cit.*, pp. 284–286. This council also maintained contacts with the International Union of Geodesy and Geophysics. Vaughan, *op. cit.*, pp. 102–103.

[205] *Am. Del. 1935*, pp. 2–3. Brief accounts of the other conferences are these: International Congress for the Protection of Nature, Paris, June 30–July 4, 1931, *Am. Del. 1932*, p. 4; International Conference for the Protection of Flora and Fauna in Africa, London, Oct. 31–Nov. 8, 1933, *Am. Del. 1934*, D.S. Pub. No. 690, pp. 14–15, the United States being invited to accede to the convention adopted at this conference, which, however, it did not do; meeting of the International Hunting Council, Brussels, June 11–12, 1935, which dealt with, *inter alia*, the subject of "Protection of birds, not only against oil residues ejected by ships, but also against oil residues in streams through industrial practices," *Am. Del. 1935*, pp. 59–60; North American Wildlife Conference, Washington, Feb. 3–7, 1936, *Am. Del. 1936*, pp. 58–59; Ninth International Ornithological Congress, Rouen, France, May 8–13, 1938, *Am. Del. 1938*, D.S. Pub. No. 1300, pp. 73–74.

[206] Signed at Mexico City, Feb. 7, 1936, 50 *Stat.* 1311, TS 912.

[207] Signed for United States at Pan American Union, Oct. 12, 1940, 56 *Stat.* 1354,

The United States and the Treaty Law of the Sea

of sea birds. In the annex to this latter treaty, however, the United States listed the sea otter among the mammals it was giving special protection.

Humanitarian Programs

With the tremendous growth of treaties in the interwar period serving "humanitarian" purposes this study cannot be here concerned except to the extent that the United States became a party to any of them and except as these involved use of the sea. The United States continued its interest in international efforts to control the traffic in African slavery, liquor among the aborigines in Africa, arms, opium, white slavery, and obscene publications. With respect to each of these subject matters, import, export, or transport by sea are essential to consummation of part of the evil. In the period 1919–1945 the United States entered into new agreements on the first four topics but not the last two.

Traffic in Women and Children and Obscene Publications. The United States, though sympathetic to the objects, did not sign the 1921 [208] or the 1933 [209] agreements designed to tighten up the regime on the traffic in women and children for immoral purposes. Each of these agreements involved considerable obligation relating to changes in domestic criminal law, which under the American federal system still remains largely within the jurisdiction of the several states. It did not sign the Convention on the Suppression of the Circulation of and Traffic in Obscene Publications, opened for signature at Geneva, September 12, 1923,[210] but the President did submit it to the Senate for advice and consent to adherence.[211] That was never given.

TS 981. For the preparatory work relating to this agreement, see Resolution XXXVIII of the Eighth International Conference of American States, Final Act, Lima, Dec. 27, 1938, Scott, *I.C.A.S., 1933–1940*, p. 262; work of the Inter-American Committee of Experts on Nature Protection and Wildlife Preservation, *Am. Del. 1940*, pp. 112–113; *ibid., 1941*, D.S. Pub. No. 1718, pp. 60–61. For an excellent note on all of the international legislation pertaining to the subject of wildlife, see 8 Hudson, *I.L.* 573–574. For a discussion of the Pan American Convention, see Hayden, *op. cit.*, pp. 62–66.

[208] Convention on the Suppression of Traffic in Women and Children, Opened for signature at Geneva, Sept. 30, 1921, 1 Hudson, *I.L.* 726.

[209] Convention for the Suppression of the Traffic in Women of Full Age, Opened for signature at Geneva, Oct. 11, 1933, 6 Hudson, *I.L.* 469.

[210] Convention on the Suppression of the Circulation of and Traffic in Obscene Publications, Opened for signature at Geneva, Sept. 12, 1923, 2 Hudson, *I.L.* 1051.

[211] Submitted Feb. 10, 1925, *Treaties Submitted to the Senate 1935–1944*, D.S. Pub. No. 2311, p. 12.

Between the Great Wars

Traffic in Slaves, Liquor, and Firearms. Three of the humanitarian treaties were focused on Africa. The Convention to Suppress the Slave Trade and Slavery, concluded at Geneva on September 25, 1926, to which the United States adhered,[212] was designed to implement the affirmation of intention on the subject contained in Article 11 of the Convention of Saint-Germain-en-Laye, of 1919, relating to commerce and navigation in Africa, which the United States perfected in 1934.[213] The United States signed both the liquor [214] and the arms [215] traffic conventions at St. Germain-en-Laye in 1919, but, after some delay, perfected only the liquor convention. Later, with considerable enthusiasm, the United States signed and ratified the revised and extended agreement of 1925 on the arms traffic,[216] which was applicable to Africa, African coastal waters, and the waters bounding the Arabian Peninsula. Because of the failure, however, of certain other powers to ratify, the convention never went into effect.[217]

Opium Traffic. With respect to the treaties regulating the traffic in opium and other narcotic drugs, the record of the United States is not free of diplomatic vagaries, but American legislative and administrative control of the international traffic has been singularly consistent and effective, indeed providing models for some of the international measures.

The 1912 Hague opium treaty, discussed in connection with pre-World War I developments,[218] became effective for numerous additional parties on January 10, 1920, as a result of Article 295 of the Treaty of Ver-

---

[212] Proclaimed March 23, 1929, 46 *Stat.* 2183, TS 778.

[213] Convention on the Revision of the General Act of Berlin of Feb. 26, 1885, and of the General Act and Declaration of Brussels of July 2, 1890, signed at Saint-Germain-en-Laye, Sept. 10, 1919, proclaimed Nov. 3, 1934, 49 *Stat.* 3027, TS 877.

[214] Convention on the Liquor Traffic in Africa, signed Sept. 10, 1919, proclaimed March 26, 1929, 46 *Stat.* 2199, TS 779.

[215] Convention on the Control of Trade in Arms and Ammunition, signed Sept. 10, 1919, 1 Hudson, *I.L.* 323. This agreement applied also to the waters bounding the Arabian Peninsula. Apparently it was never even submitted to the Senate, *List of Treaties Submitted to the Senate 1789–1934*, pp. 47–48. It went into effect for certain ratifying or adhering powers March 30, 1921, 1 Hudson, *I.L.* 323.

[216] Convention on Supervision of International Trade in Arms and Ammunition and in Implements of War, Opened for signature at Geneva, June 17, 1925, 3 Hudson, *I.L.* 1634.

[217] *Treaties Submitted to the Senate 1935–1944*, p. 10; 3 Hudson, *I.L.* 1634. See Leonard H. Pomeroy, "The International Trade and Traffic in Arms: Its Supervision and Control," 22 *DSB* 187–194, 357–364, 381, 507–515, 520 (1950).

[218] Above, p. 127.

sailles of June 28, 1919, and correlative provisions in the other peace treaties.[219]

Under the auspices of the League of Nations two opium conferences were held at Geneva in 1924–1925, the first dealing primarily with smoking opium,[220] the second with the traffic in opium and drugs. The United States attended the second conference, but when it refused to provide for limitation of production of raw materials, the American delegation, in pursuance of strict instructions by Congress, left the conference. Thus the United States did not become a party to the 1925 Convention on Traffic in Opium and Drugs.[221] It did participate, however, in the Convention for Limiting the Manufacture and Regulating the Distribution of Narcotic Drugs, concluded at Geneva, July 13, 1931,[222] but not in the subsequent supplementary convention of 1936 which obligated the parties to take certain criminal measures against the traffic in dangerous drugs.[223]

Few subject matters of international significance have been subjected to such extensive and intricate international control as narcotic drugs.[224] It would be difficult to find any government which has participated more vigorously in this process of control than the United States.[225] Probably no government surpasses the United States in the thoroughness with

[219] Convention and Final Protocol for the Suppression of the Abuse of Opium and Other Drugs, signed at The Hague, Jan. 13, 1912 and July 9, 1913, 38 *Stat.* 1912, TS 612. Effective for the United States, the Netherlands, and China, Feb. 11, 1915 (1915 *For. Rel.* 1101–1102). Effective for three other powers before Jan. 10, 1920; for an additional twenty-five powers on Jan. 10, 1920 (3 Redmond 3025, n. 2).

[220] Agreement Concerning the Suppression of the Manufacture of, Internal Trade in, and Use of Prepared Opium, signed at Geneva, Feb. 11, 1925; in force for other powers, July 28, 1926. 3 Hudson, *I.L.* 1580.

[221] Convention on Traffic in Opium and Drugs, Opened for signature at Geneva, Feb. 19, 1925; in force for other powers, Sept. 25, 1928. 3 Hudson, *I.L.* 1589. See extensive bibliography on the subject, *ibid.*, p. 1580, including accounts of the American position. See also references in n. 224 below.

[222] 48 *Stat.* 1543, TS 863.

[223] Convention for the Suppression of the Illicit Traffic in Dangerous Drugs, Opened for signature at Geneva, June 26, 1936; in force for other powers, Oct. 26, 1936. 7 Hudson, *I.L.* 359.

[224] See Bertil A. Renborg, *International Drug Control: A Study of International Organization By and Through the League of Nations* (1947); "Narcotic Drug Control: Development of International Action and the Establishment of Supervision Under the United Nations," with introduction by Herbert L. May, *Int. Con.* No. 441 (1948).

[225] See the several numbers of *International Conciliation* which deal with American cooperation with the League of Nations: No. 274, pp. 729–738; No. 329, pp. 363–372; No. 331, pp. 583–586; No. 341, pp. 255–258; No. 352, pp. 396–399; No. 361, pp. 234–237.

Between the Great Wars

which it polices the maritime aspects of the drug traffic. Thus, in the years 1928 to 1931, the United States concluded a series of twenty-two arrangements with as many governments providing for "the direct exchange of certain information regarding the traffic in narcotic drugs," by letter or cable, and "mutual cooperation in detective and investigating work."[226] In 1937 it "put forward, and the League distributed by special circular, detailed proposals for preventing the use of ocean-going steamers for illicit traffic, and providing for supervision in the larger seaports through cooperation between governments, shipowners, and labor unions."[227] The annual report of the Bureau of Narcotics on *Traffic in Opium and Other Dangerous Drugs*, prepared and distributed in pursuance of treaty obligations, regularly contains in exemplary detail accounts of the numerous seizures in the maritime areas subject to American jurisdiction, many of the seizures involving keen detective work and even thrilling adventure.[228] Indeed, these reports, prepared for several decades now under the direction of the commissioner of narcotics, Harry J. Anslinger, contain the makings of an American "best seller" if ever they were discovered by a writer capable of converting document into drama.

International Criminal Police Commission. Since 1924 American po-

[226] List in *Treaty Information Bulletin,* Supplement to *Bulletin* No. 39, Dec. 1932, D.S. Pub. No. 436, pp. 80–83. Though some of the agreements listed are noted "To be printed in the Executive Agreement Series," they never did so appear. See *Foreign Relations of the United States,* Price List 65, 25th ed. (1944) for list of EAS 1–391. See also 1928 *For. Rel.* Vol. I, p. 444; *Bulletin of Treaty Information,* No. 5, July 1929, second supplement (mimeographed edition, preceding series of *Treaty Information Bulletin,* which started Oct. 31, 1929); and 1929 *For. Rel.* Vol. I, pp. 389–393.

[227] *Int. Con.* No. 341, pp. 257–258. Smugglers of drugs also use high-speed fishing trawlers in various parts of the world. See, e.g., *N.Y.T.*, Nov. 5, 1952, item relating to dispute between Turkey and Greece about fishing in Aegean Sea. Peddlers of local wares in the "bum-boats" that visit alongside passenger vessels anchored at Gibraltar and other places are also reputed to pass up narcotics under cover of innocent trade. For a map of the "Principal Sea Routes for the Illicit Traffic in Opium," see "Narcotic Drug Control," *Int. Con.*, No. 485 (1952), pp. 513–514. See also documents cited below under discussion of post-World War II developments.

[228] Publication of this report was begun in 1926. Previously the data required under the convention of 1912 was simply transmitted to the Dutch government. The United States continued to route its annual report through the Dutch government, even after the League assumed responsibility for the coordinating work in 1920, until it became a party to the 1931 treaty. Thereafter it reported directly to the League, and, since 1946, it has reported to the United Nations agencies. See recent annual reports, e.g., for the year ended Dec. 31, 1951, pp. 12–26; 1952, pp. 10–22; 1953, pp. 13–27; 1954, pp. 8–28; 1955, pp. 14–31.

lice systems have participated in the International Police congresses, and since 1938 the United States has maintained membership, through the department of justice, in the International Criminal Police Commission (INTERPOL) which organizes the periodic congresses. Through this organization the United States cooperates in the suppression not only of narcotic-drug abuses but also the traffic in women and children.[229] The continued cooperation of the commission in these matters will be noted again in the discussion dealing with post-World War II developments.

Legal, Scientific, and Other Developments

International Maritime Committee. Of the several draft conventions produced by the International Maritime Committee and submitted for adoption at official conferences in the period 1919–1939, the United States signed and ratified the Convention for Unification of Certain Rules Relating to Bills of Lading for the Carriage of Goods by Sea, opened for signature at Brussels, August 25, 1924.[230] It did not, however, participate in the Convention for the Unification of Certain Rules Relating to the Immunity of State-owned Vessels, signed at Brussels, April 10, 1926.[231] With the increase of government-owned and -operated merchant vessels, this matter of immunity from legal process remains an unsolved and vexatious problem.[232]

Public Organizations not under Treaty. Finally, in this survey of activities relating to the sea in the generation before the establishment of the United Nations, it is important to note American participation in agencies or organizations whose existence did not depend upon multipartite treaties. Many of these international organizations were completely public, or intergovernmental; others were predominantly private, composed of unofficial individuals or nonofficial professional, scientific, economic, or social groups; and some were mixed in composi-

---

[229] *U.S. Int. Agencies 1946*, pp. 211–215; *U.S. Int. Org. 1949*, pp. 224–226. See also *Am. Del. 1936*, for 12th meeting at Belgrade, 1936, and *ibid.*, *1937*, D.S. Pub. No. 1163, pp. 82–83, for 13th meeting at London, at both of which the suppression of the traffic was discussed. The commission is known popularly, after its cable address, as INTERPOL.

[230] Proclaimed Nov. 6, 1937, 51 *Stat.* (2) 233, *TS* 931.

[231] 3 Hudson, *I.L.* 1837.

[232] See the excellent comprehensive note in Briggs, *op. cit.*, pp. 447–449, and the American legislation and diplomatic correspondence on the subject in 2 Hackworth, *Digest* 423–465; see also "Changed Policy Concerning the Granting of Sovereign Immunity to Foreign Governments," 26 *DSB* 984–985 (1952).

Between the Great Wars

tion of membership. No useful purpose would be served, in the present context, by pausing to classify these bodies with respect to their composition.[233] A similar observation could be made concerning American participation in many periodic and *ad hoc* conferences, of a public, private, or mixed character held during the interwar period.[234]

Suffice it for present purposes that with respect to each of the organizations or conferences mentioned below, the sea or some aspect thereof plays an important role in its work or deliberations, and further that each has made some contribution to understanding or utilization of the sea or has dealt with some problem of human conduct in relation to the sea. International legislation, like so much domestic legislation, is the end product of a conflux of public and private, individual and group, initiative, demands, and pressures. These demands and pressures will very likely continue, in one form or another, as long as human beings use, are inquisitive about, or are affected seriously by the sea. Given a continuation of the nation-state for the foreseeable future and freedom to form international groupings, it may be expected that these public, private, and mixed international organizations will continue to make their valuable contributions to the adoption of international legislation concerning the sea.

Mention has been made in the text thus far of the following organizations in whose work the United States participated in the period under discussion without a treaty obligation to do so: the Bureau of the International Map of the World on the Millionth Scale; the International Hydrographic Bureau; the Permanent International Association of Navigation Congresses; the International Technical Committee of Aerial Legal Experts (CITEJA); the North American Council on Fishery Investigations (and through it, the Permanent Council for the Exploration of the Sea); the Gorgas Memorial Library; the International Criminal

---

[233] That has been done by Joseph P. Chamberlain in his excellent article, "International Organization," *Int. Con.* No. 385 (1942), and by Lyman White in his two works, *The Structure of Private International Organizations* (1933) and, with M. R. Zocca, *International Non-Governmental Organizations* (1951). Very helpful data for this period can be gleaned from *A Directory of International Organizations in the Field of Public Administration 1936*, Joint Committee on Planning and Cooperation of the International Institute of Administrative Sciences and the International Union of Local Authorities (1936), and the *Directory of International Scientific Organizations*, UNESCO (1950), 2d ed. (1953).

[234] For the multifarious ways in which a government like that of the United States could "participate" in or "encourage" such conferences, see Reiff, "Participation in International Administration," 34 *Social Studies* 311–316 (1943).

Police Commission; the International Maritime Committee; the International Meteorological Organization; and the International Council of Scientific Unions.[235]

The last two organizations listed were highly complex in structure, each of the component units holding periodic meetings of its own. Among the commissions within the Meteorological Organization of importance to the present study were those dealing with aerology, climatology, the Polar Year 1932–1933, clouds, aeronautical meteorology, maritime meteorology, terrestrial magnetism and atmospheric electricity, projections for meteorological charts, polar meteorology, radio-electric meteorology, solar radiation, and synoptic weather information.[236] After World War II this organization was transmuted into the clearly intergovernmental World Meteorological Organization, which will be discussed later.

Among the associations and commissions which are part of the Council of Scientific Unions and of importance to the present study are those dealing with the following: geodesy and geophysics; magnetism (geomagnetism) and electricity; scientific radio; oceanography;[237] geography; hydrology; seismology; vulcanology; continental and oceanic

---

[235] See the excellent brief history for the period by Esther C. Brunauer, "International Council of Scientific Unions: Brussels and Cambridge," 13 *DSB* 371–376 (1945).

[236] *U.S. Int. Agencies 1946*, p. 307; *U.S. Int. Org. 1949*, pp. 131–136. Congress, troubled by the depression, appropriated only $30,000 for United States participation in the Second Polar Year Program, Aug. 1, 1932, to Aug. 31, 1933, the American work being done at College near Fairbanks, Alaska. J. R., March 18, 1932, 47 *Stat.* 68. The documentation, all under the title *Second Polar Year Program*, is: 71 Cong., 3 Sess., S. Doc. No. 270, Feb. 10, 1931, H. Rept. No. 2700, Feb. 17, 1931, S. Rept. No. 1774, Feb. 25, 1931; 72 Cong., 1 Sess., S. Doc. No. 16, Dec. 10, 1931, S. Rept. No. 162, Feb. 3, 1932, H. Rept. No. 371, Feb. 5, 1932, and H. Doc. No. 282, March 19, 1932. For a splendid account of the history and work of the two polar years and the role of geomagnetism in the IGY of 1957–1958, together with an extensive bibliography, see David G. Knapp, *Arctic Aspects of Geomagnetism*, Technical Assistant to Chief of Naval Operations for Polar Projects, OPNAV PO3-10 (Washington, 1956).

[237] For further detail on international activities in this field, see Sverdrup, *et al., The Oceans*, p. 7. Among the works cited by Sverdrup, Henry B. Bigelow, *Oceanography: Its Scope, Problems, and Economic Importance*, Report to the National Academy of Sciences (1931), is a most helpful survey of the whole field, especially valuable to the layman; and Thomas Wayland Vaughan, *International Aspects of Oceanography: Oceanographic Data and Provisions for Oceanographic Research* (1937), includes at pp. 71–255 a descriptive directory of all national and international institutions devoted to study of one or another aspect of oceanography up to 1937. *Research Reviews*, a monthly periodical launched in 1953 by the Office of Naval Research, Department of the Navy, regularly includes excellent articles on technical progress in oceanographic research by navy laboratories and contractors.

Between the Great Wars

structure; snow and glaciers; subterranean waters; biology; and astronomy.[238] Through the International Astronomical Union, founded in 1919, the United States cooperates in the determination and distribution of time and, as indicated in the previous chapter, helps maintain the *Bureau International de l'Heure* at Paris, which "studies and makes detailed reports on the work of the various national observatories," including the American Naval Observatory.[239]

Information which the U.S. Naval Observatory receives from the I.A.U. is organized and made available through three publications, *American Ephemeris*, the *American Nautical Almanac*, and the *American Air Almanac* (for aircraft navigation). The value of these publications is evidenced by the fact that every American ship on the ocean and every American plane on international flight carries [1952] one or both of the latter publications which are basic for celestial navigation. The *American Ephemeris* is a basic reference for astronomers and is essential in the accurate determination of time, which in turn is of extreme importance in civil navigation (including loran), and defense fields. In addition, accurate astronomical data are essential to the U.S. Coast and Geodetic Survey in the construction of charts and maps.[240]

Specialized Conferences. Reference has also been made in the text thus far to attendance by American delegations at conferences aside from those provided for by multipartite agreements, namely: a World Conference of Radiotelegraph Experts for Aeronautics, a European Conference of Meteorological Experts, a Regional Conference Concerning the Use of Radiotelephone in the North Sea, conferences on the rat and malaria, ornithological congresses, a meeting of the International Hunting Council, a North American Wildlife Conference, and others on the protection of nature and on flora and fauna in Africa.

To these must be added other conferences and organizations in which the United States participated between the two Great Wars,[241] all of

---

[238] *U.S. Int. Agencies 1946*, p. 307; *U.S. Int. Org. 1949*, pp. 122–127.

[239] Letter to writer from U.S. Naval Observatory, Aug. 22, 1950; also League of Nations *Handbook of International Organizations*, pp. 170–171.

[240] "International Astronomical Union," 27 *DSB* 462 (1952).

[241] Until the department of state began its *Treaty Information Bulletin* in 1929 and its *American Delegations* series in 1932, it was extremely difficult to compile accurate data about such participation. For the period before 1919, much research is necessary; see above, Ch. II, n. 1. For the period between 1919 and 1929/1932, see Warren Kelchner, *Inter-American Conferences, 1826–1933: Chronological and Classified Lists*, D.S. Pub. No. 499 (1933), and 75 *Cong. Rec.* 11868–11871, 72 Cong., 1 Sess., June 2, 1932. See also, *Document Catalogue* and *Foreign Relations*, in their respective series, for the period since 1861.

them with significant relations to the sea. The mere listing of a conference may not be highly informative, but taken together as a group phenomenon in the interwar period they have considerable significance. American participation in them reveals an expansion of the interest in the sea which was already unfolding in the pre-1914 period. The participation constitutes evidence of a deep-running current of public and private interest in the thousand and one facets of the sea. That interest probably cannot be frustrated and ought not, except at peril to what was indicated at the beginning of this study — the long-range trend of America to the sea. And out of such interest arises ultimately new international legislation and new administrative tasks for international agencies to perform.

To the conferences already listed must therefore be added a number in the Pan American system and a larger number of universal import.

Within the inter-American system [242] the United States took part in meetings or conferences devoted to commercial matters, including tourist facilities (1935); technical aviation (1937); travel (1939); science, including geology, geography, and cartography (1940); regional affairs of the Caribbean, including tourism (1940–1941); maritime problems, including those relating to tourists (1940); resources (1940); development, including fisheries (1940); and financial and economic matters, including maritime affairs (1939). Among the most important of the permanent inter-American agencies of concern here is the Pan American Institute of Geography and History (1924 and the years following), which is the official agency in the Americas for the International Union of Geodesy and Geophysics.[243]

Outside the Pan American system, the United States participated, in the period 1919–1945, in an international congress on oceanography, marine hydrography, and continental hydrology (1929); one on life-saving (1929); a League conference on the health and welfare of merchant seamen (1929); a congress of aerial safety (1930); one on agriculture and fisheries (1931); a Canadian-American investigation of fisheries in Passamaquoddy and Cobscook Bays (1931–1932); the International Society for the Exploration of the Arctic by means of Aircraft

[242] In addition to the works cited in the previous note, see Masters, *Handbook of International Organizations in the Americas* (1945) for data unobtainable elsewhere.

[243] Masters, *op. cit.*, pp. 307–310; *U.S. Int. Agencies 1946*, pp. 130–135; *U.S. Int. Org. 1949*, pp. 136–140.

Between the Great Wars

(1924–1932);[244] a meeting on radio in aviation (1932); the Pacific Science Congress (1933); an aeronautic exposition (1935); an Ibero-American oceanographic conference (1935); meetings of the Far Eastern Association of Tropical Medicine (1935, 1939); a League conference of experts on tourist traffic (1936); and a congress on lifesaving and first aid to the injured (1939).

Though the United States did not participate in any respect in any of the meetings or work of the European International Congress of Official Tourist Propaganda Associations, developed at The Hague in 1935, it did participate, immediately on cessation of World War II in the First International Conference of Official Travel Organizations held in London in 1946 and helped in 1947 to form a new world-wide International Union of Official Travel Organizations, which superseded the old Union.[245]

Private Organizations. Among the more important of the predominantly private organizations [246] devoted in whole or in part to consideration of some aspect of the sea there should be mentioned at this point the Institute of Pacific Relations, whose studies of phenomena dependent on the ecology of the Pacific basin have been of tremendous value to scholars.[247]

There remain to be mentioned the numerous international associations, "conferences," and unions composed of representatives of private economic interests which utilize the sea. Their number is legion.[248] They

---

[244] Schmeckebier, *Int. Org.*, p. 8.

[245] *U.S. Int. Org. 1949*, pp. 286–289; also letter to writer from department of commerce, Nov. 3, 1952. See Masters, *op. cit.*, p. 148, for American private participation in the Inter-American Hotel Association launched in 1939 as a result of the First Inter-American Travel Congress at San Francisco, Calif. Also see H. H. Kelly, "Development of International Travel in the Western Hemisphere: Meeting of Permanent Executive Committee, Inter-American Travel Congress, Washington, May 10–15, 1957," 37 *DSB* 212–213 (1957), and UN, ECOSOC, Transport and Communications Commission, *Report of the Eighth Session*, pp. 8–9, E/2948, E/CN.2/187 (1957).

[246] Various American interests, associations, and organizations are recorded as members of international organizations listed and described in the League of Nations *Handbook of International Organizations* (1938). It would be possible to compile a list of several dozen such organizations meeting the criterion of relation to the sea employed in the present discussion.

[247] Masters, *op. cit.*, pp. 80–84.

[248] Mance and Wheeler, *International Sea Transport*, Ch. 1 and pp. 95–104, on the "conference system" for rate making and pools; Marx, *International Shipping Cartels*. See, e.g., *Inter-American Maritime Conference, 1940, op. cit.*, "Directory of Freight Conferences in the Trades between the United States and Other American Re-

seek to advance the interests, represent the point of view, and in some instances regulate substantively the conduct of their component national elements. They appear notably in such fields as shipping, air transport, radio communications, commerce, and marine insurance.

Private American enterprise is represented in many of these organizations. Among the more important ones are the Transatlantic Track Association;[249] the International Chamber of Commerce;[250] the International Union of Marine Insurance;[251] and the International Shipping Conference, founded in 1921, which, for example, "has dealt with a wide variety of subjects on the regulatory side of shipping, including trade barriers, flag discrimination, safety of life at sea, maritime law, shipping documents, international sanitary regulations, load line, radio, tonnage measurements, passenger insurance and helm orders."[252] David Lubin, peregrinating proponent of an international agricultural organization in the years before World War I, also "believed that shipping conferences enjoyed a monopoly power which they exercised to the detriment of world commerce" and "that shipowners had sufficient advance knowledge of ocean freight rate changes to profit by operating on the grain exchanges. As a result, he pressed before the Congress of the United States a bill to create an International Commerce Commission to regulate ocean rates and to rationalize the movement of cargoes and ships."[253] Nothing immediately came from his advocacy. World War I, however, forced upon the Allies complete centralized control of all shipping for the duration of the conflict.[254] Since then, the fixing of ocean rates and agreement upon practices have remained, as they were before, within the purview of the numerous shipping conferences or cartels, subject to national scrutiny here and there, as in the United States.[255]

---

publics," pp. 50–52, and discussion of problem by Lloyd Tibbott, at pp. 404–411. See also League of Nations *Handbook of International Organizations, passim,* and Mance and Wheeler, *International Telecommunications, passim.*

[249] Mance and Wheeler, *International Sea Transport,* p. 40.

[250] Which, for example, in 1921 "passed a resolution recommending the universal application of a uniform system for determining the net tonnage of ships." Mance and Wheeler, *ibid.,* p. 44; League of Nations *Handbook,* pp. 337–338.

[251] Mance and Wheeler, *International Sea Transport,* p. 59.

[252] *Ibid.,* pp. 4–5; League of Nations *Handbook,* pp. 391–392; Marx, *op. cit.,* p. 269.

[253] Marx, *op. cit.,* p. 272.

[254] J. A. Salter, *Allied Shipping Control* (1921).

[255] E.g., *Annual Report of the Federal Maritime Board and Maritime Administration 1956,* pp. 36–37.

Between the Great Wars

Many of these private organizations maintain liaison for very practical purposes between the fields of shipping, aviation, radio, and meteorology. They participate in the making of international legislation at various stages of the process. Thus, for example, private interests have for decades participated in the consultative committees and administrative conferences of the Telecommunications Union. "In addition to the delegates of governments and representatives of private telecommunication administrations . . . certain international organizations representing amateurs, aviation, broadcasting, meteorology, marine radio and shipping interests, are admitted to the administrative conferences in a consultative capacity . . ."[256] The very existence of these private organizations and their number attests to the amazing range and intricacy of human relations to the sea. They help bring order in the use of the sea.

Summary

Viewing in retrospect this long process of international organizing and international legislating during the nineteenth century and into the twentieth up to World War II, it could fairly be said, by way of summary, that the process suggests movement and patternization, creating almost an illusion of organic growth. The flow of events indicates trends and suggests a certain determinism toward self-shaping ends arising out of the factual situation. They bear witness also to the interplay of human will and inventiveness with this determinism. The social scientist can, at least with respect to many of the phenomena, isolate processes of emergence, development, individuation, proliferation, interrelation, collaboration, coordination, and integration. It would have been surprising, indeed, if the crucible of World War II had not precipitated new crystallizations of forms and new combinations of organizational elements. To these new forms and combinations we can now turn.

[256] Mance and Wheeler, *International Telecommunications*, pp. 2–3.

CHAPTER V~~

EXPANSION IN TREATY LAW FOR THE SEA SINCE WORLD WAR II: TRANSPORTATION AND COMMUNICATIONS

NEVER before in history in any comparable period have so many conferences on such a variety of subjects been held and so many multipartite agreements concluded or international institutions established as in the few brief years since the conclusion of World War II. Indeed, the war had hardly begun in 1939, when the United States and other great powers were already planning the reconstruction of international society, insofar as the formulation of national policy, exploratory international "conversations," and the devising of new organizations could contribute to that end.[1] Before the hostilities had ended, great new or rebuilt organizations had already been set up — a United Nations Interim Commission on Food and Agriculture at Hot Springs in June 1943, the Bank and the Fund at Bretton Woods in July 1944, a Provisional International Civil Aviation Organization at Chicago in December 1944, the United Nations in San Francisco in June 1945. Since then the number of conferences and agreements have multiplied amazingly and American participation in them proportionately.

For the most part this conferring, agreeing, organizing, and reorganizing is in response to genuinely felt needs. Underlying the needs, in most cases, is a substratum of hard facts. These facts may be nature made or man made. So far at least as the facts relate to the sea and man's use of the sea, they have a tough abiding quality. It should be no surprise, then, that as soon as preoccupations permitted, men and nations should resume, with increased knowledge and determination, the task of im-

[1] Harley A. Notter, *Postwar Foreign Policy Preparation 1939–1945* (1949), D.S. Pub. No. 3580, Ch. XVII, "Remaining Economic and Social Preparation and Conferences."

proving, perforce cooperatively, their relation to the sea. They had, fortunately, a century of experience in collaboration to draw upon.

If it were possible to summarize the developments since World War II, insofar as they deal with the sea, they would reveal systematic revision of old regimes, the devising of new ones, with increased reliance upon regional agencies, elaborate correlation of efforts between regimes, as in communications and transport, and some over-all coordination through the United Nations, particularly through the Economic and Social Council. Many of these developments have already been foreshadowed in the discussion of the periods preceding World War II. It remains now to delineate the pattern of efforts and relations in this recent period. It will appear that for the most part that pattern is a result of the projection into contemporary life of forces and trends which have gathered momentum over the past century, since at least the days of Matthew Maury.

The written record of these recent developments is voluminous, almost overwhelming. Whereas for some of the data in the pre-1914 era the social scientist must turn antiquarian, for the period since 1945 he must utilize, if he is to remain efficient, the reporting and summarizing services of such publications as *The Department of State Bulletin*,[2] *Participation of the United States Government in International Conferences*,[3] *United States Participation in the United Nations: Report by the President to the Congress*,[4] *The United Nations Review*,[5] *The Yearbook of the United Nations*,[6] *The American Journal of International Law*,[7] *International Organization*,[8] and *International Conciliation*.[9] Each of

[2] Weekly, begun with the issue of July 1, 1939.

[3] Annual (hereinafter cited *U.S. Int. Conf.*) begun with a volume summarizing the record of the war years July 1, 1941, to June 30, 1945, D.S. Pub. No. 2665; superseding the prior annual publications for the period July 1, 1932, to June 30, 1941, entitled *American Delegations to International Conferences, Congresses and Expositions and American Representation on International Institutions and Commissions, With Relevant Data*, cited often in the previous chapter.

[4] Annual, beginning with the report for the calendar year 1946, D.S. Pub. No. 2735.

[5] As *United Nations Bulletin*, weekly, starting Aug. 3, 1946; semimonthly, starting Jan. 1, 1948; as *United Nations Review*, monthly, starting July 1954.

[6] Starting with volume for 1946–1947; converted to calendar year for 1950.

[7] Quarterly since 1907.

[8] Quarterly, starting with issue of Feb. 1947; World Peace Foundation, Boston, Mass.

[9] Monthly, except July and Aug. prior to Sept. 1953; five issues per year since then; Carnegie Endowment for International Peace, New York, N.Y.

these (with the exception of the President's report to Congress) facilitates use of current official documentation by citation or bibliographical listings. Until comprehensive bibliographical tools adapted to ready use are devised to deal with this wealth of postwar documentation,[10] the social scientist will be especially grateful for the bibliographical services rendered by such publications as those mentioned. He already regrets, however, the end, with Volume IX for the years 1942–1945, of Judge Manley O. Hudson's monumental series of *International Legislation*.[11] Nothing has yet appeared which can take its place for studies such as this.

It would be convenient to discuss the developments in relation to the sea in this period, as it would have been in the period beginning with the League of Nations, in terms of the organizations which sponsored the programs. This would produce a fairly neat intellectual pattern. To some extent, however, it would be deceptive, imputing an orderliness in the affairs of the sea which does not yet exist. Therefore, the discussion will continue under the topics previously used, namely, transportation, communications, health, exploitation of the products of the sea, and humanitarian matters. Scientific developments apply to each of these fields. These fields are grounded on enduring, fairly clearly distinguishable, yet intimately interrelated physical and social facts. The facts have a way of surviving, however the organizations which deal with them may change.

In view of the abundance of documentation available for this post-World War II period, it should be sufficient for the compass of this study merely to outline the principal developments, emphasizing American treaty commitment with respect to them. As will be seen, the participation of the United States in each of the major developments deserves a monograph for itself. If the poets gave us license to reverse the laws of nature, we could say that America is riding a flood tide into the sea.

TRANSPORTATION

In the field of transportation on and over the sea, the postwar years witnessed four major advancements by means of international legisla-

[10] A beginning has been made with *Ten Years of United Nations Publications 1945 to 1955: A Complete Catalogue*, United Nations (1955). See Carol Carter Moor and Waldo Chamberlain, *How To Use United Nations Documents* (1952).

[11] *International Legislation: A Collection of the Texts of Multipartite Interna-*

tion: the establishment of the International Civil Aviation Organization in 1944,[12] which superseded the prior Paris and Habana regimes (Art. 80); the establishment of the World Meteorological Organization as an intergovernmental agency in 1947,[13] replacing the old International Meteorological Organization; the creation of an Intergovernmental Maritime Consultative Organization 1948;[14] and the revision of the great code on safety of life at sea in the same year.[15] Each depends for the effectiveness of part of its program upon the radio regime, particularly as revised at Atlantic City in 1947,[16] and all five have intricate relations, one with another.

In transportation, as in telecommunication, two groups of problems persistently demand solution at the international level, those arising from economic competition and the clash of national policies and those arising from technological changes and the need for safety and efficiency in use. With the first set of problems this study cannot be concerned, though it may be pointed out that both ICAO[17] and IMCO[18] seek peaceable

---

tional Instruments of General Interest, Beginning with the Covenant of the League of Nations (1931–1950).

[12] Convention on International Civil Aviation, opened for signature at Chicago, Dec. 7, 1944, effective April 4, 1947, 61 *Stat.* 1180, *TIAS* 1591; also in *International Civil Aviation Conference, 1944, Final Act and Related Documents*, D.S. Pub. No. 2282 (1945). The best exegesis of these documents is *Aspects of United States Participation in International Civil Aviation*, D.S. Pub. No. 3209 (1948), reprint of articles, but without the names of the authors, appearing originally in *DSB*. For convenience, however, citation here will be to the original articles. Thus, see Stephen Latchford "Comparison of the Chicago Aviation Convention with the Paris and Habana Conventions," 12 *DSB* 411–420 (1945). For the setup of ICAO, see *U.S. Int. Org. 1949*, pp. 271–277. For a comprehensive bibliography on the subject of aviation and the relation of the United States and ICAO to it, see *Foreign and International Aviation: Basic Information Sources*, World Trade Information Service, Part 4, No. 55-7, U.S. Department of Commerce, Bureau of Foreign Commerce (1955). In 1954 the constitution of ICAO was amended to eliminate the annual sessions of the assembly and permit such sessions to be held not less than once in three years; 36 *DSB* 289 (1957), 8 *UST* 179, *TIAS* 3756.

[13] Convention and Related Protocol on World Meteorological Organization, opened for signature at Washington, Oct. 11, 1947, entered into force March 23, 1950, 1 *UST* 281, *TIAS* 2052.

[14] Convention opened for signature at Geneva, March 6, 1948; text in 18 *DSB* 499–505 (1948), and *Toward a World Maritime Organization*, D.S. Pub. No. 3196 (1948), pp. 22–28. Also, *TIAS* 4044.

[15] International Convention for the Safety of Life at Sea, signed at London, June 10, 1948, 3 *UST* 3450, *TIAS* 2495.

[16] Telecommunication Convention, Final Protocol, and Radio Regulations, signed at Atlantic City, Oct. 2, 1947, 63 *Stat.* (2) 1399, *TIAS* 1901.

[17] See Art. 44 on objectives. At Chicago on Dec. 7, 1944, the United States signed the Air Services Transit Agreement, which was accepted by the United States on

solutions of some of them, as did the projected International Trade Organization,[19] now probably defunct. Our concern is primarily with the second set of problems, as they relate to the sea. Some of the significant developments embraced in the new agreements mentioned above will therefore be indicated.

International Civil Aviation Organization

The Chicago Conference of 1944 elaborated, among other instruments, an Interim Agreement on International Civil Aviation, providing for a provisional organization, and a full-length convention, providing for a permanent organization, both agreements being opened for signature on December 7, 1944. The Interim Agreement, accepted by the United States as an executive agreement[20] on February 8, 1945, was to come into force when accepted by twenty-six states, members of the United Nations coalition or associated with them or neutrals in the existing war. The proper number of acceptances having been communicated to the United States, the Provisional International Civil Aviation Organization, known as PICAO, was established on June 6, 1945, at Montreal. It immediately went into operation pending the ratification of the convention. The convention came into force on April 4, 1947, and thereupon PICAO was converted into ICAO.

Chicago Convention, 1944. The new comprehensive convention which established ICAO declared that the rules in force over the high seas shall be those established under the convention (Art. 12). Various pro-

---

Feb. 8, 1945, with an understanding, 59 *Stat.* 1693, *EAS* 487; and the agreement on air transport, which was accepted by the United States on Feb. 8, 1945, also with an understanding, 59 *Stat.* 1701, *EAS* 488. The former agreement, which provides for two of the so-called freedoms of the air, has remained in effect for the United States; the latter, providing for all five of the "freedoms" was denounced by the United States on July 25, 1946. This denunciation became effective one year after that date, i.e., July 25, 1947, in accordance with the terms of the agreement. See also *Report of the Representative of the U.S.A. to ICAO, 1945–1948*, D.S. Pub. No. 3131, Ch. IV. Up to 1953 the United States had concluded 46 bilateral air transport agreements. See Henry T. Snowdon, "Aviation Policy and International Relations," 29 *DSB* 41–45 (1953). By Feb. 1957, one or more such agreements had been concluded with approximately 46 governments. "Air Transport Agreement with Iran Signed," 36 *DSB* 198–202 (1957).

[18] Convention on Intergovernmental Maritime Consultative Organization, Arts. 1, 4.

[19] *Havana Charter for an International Trade Organization March 24, 1948*, D.S. Pub. No. 3206, e.g., Arts. 33 and 36.

[20] 59 *Stat.* 1516, *EAS* 469.

Transportation and Communications since World War II

visions dealt with quarantine (Art. 13), prevention of spread of epidemic disease (Art. 14), search for missing aircraft (Art. 25), radio equipment (Art. 30), and arrangements with other international bodies (Art. 65). Chapter VI of the convention provided for the adoption of "codes" of International Standards and Recommended Practices (called "SARPS" at first) by the Council of ICAO set up under Chapter IX.

International Standards and Recommended Practices. Among the numerous provisions appearing in the draft Standards and Recommended Practices annexed to the convention appear the following of special interest to this discussion of the sea: on water airports (Annex A); use of radio and cable (Annex B); seaplanes (Annex G); meteorological protection, in correlation with the International Meteorological Organization (later, the WMO) and the telecommunications regime (Annex I); aeronautical maps and charts (Annex J); search and rescue, investigation of accidents, and salvage (Annex L). In pursuance of Articles 54 and 90 of the convention the council [21] has from time to time rearranged, amended, and renumbered these "codes" and adopted additional ones, so that by 1953, fifteen "codes" were in existence. It is of pressing importance that these standards and recommended practices be kept abreast of new developments such as use of jet aircraft and stratospheric and supersonic flights. The rules incorporate the latest findings on high-altitude meteorological conditions and require readjustments in ground installations to accommodate the newer high-speed craft. Amendments and new annexes go into effect three months after the council has submitted them to the members of the organization, unless a majority of the members disapprove of them.[22] Here, then, is a

---

[21] See the annual reports of the United States representative to ICAO: *First Report,* 1945–1948, D.S. Pub. No. 3131, pp. 5–6; *Second Report,* 1948–1949, D.S. Pub. No. 3629, pp. 3–7; *Third Report,* 1949–1950, D.S. Pub. No. 3915, pp. 4–7; *Fourth Report,* 1950–1951, mss. ed., pp. 4–11; *Fifth Report,* 1951–1952, mss. ed., pp. 4–12; *Sixth Report,* 1952–1953, mss. ed., pp. 2–6. "Beginning with the year 1953–1954, these reports have been submitted to the Department of State solely for internal use, and copies are not available for distribution." Letter, representative to writer, Feb. 4, 1957. For succinctness, clarity, and comprehensiveness these reports are among the finest in existence. See also the summaries of the work of the council in the annual *U.S. Int. Conf., op. cit.*

[22] Illustrative of the trend toward things nautical are the following recent developments: in 1954, independently of any recommendation by ICAO, the U.S. Civil Aeronautics Board adopted rules converting, for civil aviation, speed and distance requirements from miles per hour and statute miles to knots and nautical miles (Civil Air Regulations Draft Release No. 53–30, Nov. 27, 1953); and in the same year, the National Bureau of Standards, in accord with a recommendation of 1929

close approach to genuine international legislation, similar to the practice of the World Health Organization in the adoption of its sanitary regulations.

Among the other features of this rapidly developing regime of special interest in the present context are the absorption of the work of the old CITEJA; the setting up of ten air-navigation regions, each with its own organization and series of meetings; the establishment of a weather-ship system; and the creation of air-navigation services in Iceland and other far-north areas.

Legal Committee. As a result of the termination of the Paris 1919 Air Navigation Convention, the International Commission for Aerial Navigation (ICAN) was liquidated in 1947. In the same transitional period, a standing Legal Committee of ICAO took over the work of CITEJA, in which work the United States had vigorously participated in the prewar years. With a degree of autonomy not at present enjoyed by the other committees of ICAO, the new Legal Committee continues the study and preparation of draft conventions on private international air law.[23] Among these is the 1951 draft Convention on Damage Caused by Foreign Aircraft to Third Parties on the Surface, which is designed to replace the Rome Convention of 1933. For the purposes of this new convention, "a ship or aircraft on the high seas shall be regarded as part of the territory of the State in which it is registered" (Art. 23, par. 2). The United States attended the revision conference in Rome in 1952 but did not sign the finished convention because it contained provisions which departed substantially from United States views and required further consideration by American interests.[24] The United States did,

---

by the International Hydrographic Bureau, adopted the International Nautical Mile, with a value of 1852 meters, in lieu of the U.S. Nautical Mile, which has a value of 1853.248 meters. This move in favor of standardization, it was announced, "would not affect nautical charts, the calibration of navigational instruments, or navigation." At the same time, the secretary of commerce and the secretary of defense agreed to use the International Nautical Mile within their respective departments (N.B.S., *Technical News Bulletin,* Aug. 1954).

[23] See *Reports of the United States Representative, op. cit.,* and the annual *U.S. Int. Conf., op. cit.;* see also Stephen Latchford, "Coordination of CITEJA with the New International Civil Aviation Organization," 12 *DSB* 310–313 (1945); "CITEJA and the Legal Committee of ICAO," 17 *DSB* 487–497 (1947); G. Nathan Calkins, Jr., "First Meeting of the Legal Committee of the International Civil Aviation Organization," 18 *DSB* 506–513, 523 (1948). See also Herman Phleger, "Some Recent Developments in International Law of Interest to the U.S.," 30 *DSB* 196–201 (1954).

[24] "Convention on Aircraft Damage," 28 *DSB* 221–222 (1953); *U.S. Int. Conf. 1952–1953,* D.S. Pub. No. 5534, pp. 64–66.

however, become a party to the Convention on International Recognition of Rights in Aircraft, a product of the Legal Committee, opened for signature by the Second Assembly of ICAO in Geneva on June 19, 1948.[25] And in 1955 the United States participated in a diplomatic conference at The Hague which adopted a protocol amending the Warsaw Convention of 1929.[26]

Air-Navigation Regions. For the purpose of adapting and expediting the adoption of SARPS throughout the world, ICAO devised in 1946 a series of periodic "route service conferences," in ten air-navigation regions. Maps of the regions [27] and their names indicate the important relation of sea areas to air transport: North Atlantic, European-Mediterranean, Caribbean, Middle East, South Pacific, South American, South Atlantic, African-Indian Ocean, North Pacific, and Southeast Asian. Some combining of regions has since occurred. Thus a new Pacific Region is a combination of the old "North Pacific and South Pacific Regions and covers the entire Pacific basin and adjacent coasts." In addition to surveying "the adequacy of the air-navigation facilities and services within these regions," the regional meetings have cooperated with the International Telecommunications Union in drafting "plans for the assignment of frequencies for the aeronautical mobile route services."[28] The meetings also regularly discuss the meteorological and search and rescue facilities in the regions and arrange when necessary for the establishment of additional meteorology offices or weather stations and rescue coordination centers. The United States, as a world air power, participates in all of these conferences,[29] though some governments, of course, participate only in the conferences of the region in which their territory lies or their lines operate.

Weather-Ship Program. A third important feature of the ICAO regime is its weather-ship program, one of the several "joint support" projects adopted in pursuance of Chapter XV of the Chicago Conven-

[25] Entered into force with respect to the United States, Sept. 17, 1953, 4 *UST* 1830, *TIAS* 2847.

[26] *Int. Conf. 1955–1956*, D.S. Pub. No. 6548, pp. 64–65.

[27] Map appended to *Third Report, op. cit.* For First Pacific Regional Air Navigation Meeting of ICAO at Manila in 1955 see *Int. Conf. 1955–1956*, pp. 67–69.

[28] *First Report, op. cit.*, pp. 11–12; *Third Report*, pp. 26–27.

[29] Beginning with "Caribbean Regional Air Navigational Meeting of PICAO," 15 *DSB* 897–900 (1946), the meetings are described and reported regularly in the *Department of State Bulletin*, the *Reports, op. cit.*, and *U.S. Int. Conf.* The scope and detail of their work, including that relating to routes overseas, is truly staggering.

tion. This derived much of its impetus from the experience of World War II, during which, at one time, the United States and Great Britain operated a total of twenty-one ocean weather stations in the North Atlantic. At the end of hostilities the number was reduced to four, all operated by the United States. The increased trans-Atlantic air traffic, however, indicated that there would be continued need for such ocean weather stations.

In pursuance of a recommendation of the PICAO North Atlantic Route Service Conference, held in Dublin in March 1946, which was approved by the Interim Council of PICAO, a conference invited by the British government elaborated an agreement, signed at London, September 25, 1946, providing for the establishment of thirteen North Atlantic ocean weather stations. Of these, the United States undertook to maintain seven alone and an eighth jointly with Canada — the other parties to the agreement undertaking to maintain the remaining five stations. The conference also decided to keep the program under the supervision of PICAO, rejecting a proposal to establish the International Meteorological Organization as the sole agency for the necessary coordination. This agreement never went into effect.[30] Several of the interested governments, however, kept a number of the stations in operation in the ensuing years. Thus, "as of February 17, 1948, only seven ocean weather stations were in operation: two maintained by the United States, two by the United Kingdom, one by France, one by Belgium and The Netherlands jointly, and one maintained part time by Canada."[31]

A second conference held in London in pursuance of Article 7 of the first agreement concluded a second and superseding agreement on May 12, 1949.[32] This agreement reduced the number of stations to ten, apportioned responsibility for the supply of twenty-five vessels to patrol them, the United States operating fourteen of them, and prescribed a scheme of compensatory financing for the operations. As in the first agreement, the vessels were charged with the performance of meteorological services in collaboration with the International Meteorological

---

[30] Text, D.S. Press Release 697; note on the conference, 15 *DSB* 678–679 (1946); J. Paul Barringer, "PICAO Conference on North Atlantic Ocean Weather Observation Stations," 15 *DSB* 901–904 (1946). On the failure to implement, see *Report on the Second Conference on ICAO North Atlantic Ocean Stations*, ICAO Doc. 7040-JS/551, Chapter I.

[31] "The International Civil Aviation Organization," 18 *DSB* 463, 465 (1948).

[32] North Atlantic Ocean Weather Stations, open for signature at London, May 12–June 30, 1949, 1 *UST* 356, TIAS 2053. *Second Report, op. cit.*, pp. 13–15.

Organization; search and rescue services for both air and surface craft in pursuance of both the ICAO Convention and the Convention for the Safety of Life at Sea; radio communication services; radio navigational aids to aircraft; liaison in reports from merchant ships; and the making of oceanographical and other scientific observations. This agreement went into effect on January 13, 1950. The life of the agreement was extended from June 30, 1953, to June 30, 1954, by a protocol adopted on May 28, 1952.[33]

Meanwhile, Canada and the United States agreed in June 1950 to establish and operate a network of stations in the North Pacific Ocean until ICAO provided a broader arrangement — one of the stations to be continued to be operated by the Japanese government.[34] At the outbreak of the Korean War in the summer of 1950, Canada and the United States immediately agreed upon an interim modified program for the duration of the "emergency."[35]

For several years, however, the United States had felt that it was bearing a disproportionately large share of the burden of maintaining the Atlantic weather stations. In arriving at the 1946 agreement, United States aircraft were regarded as making 64 per cent of the crossings; for the 1949 agreement, 56 per cent. By 1953, the percentage had fallen to 41. A new agreement, it was felt, should reflect these changing proportions of derived benefits. Furthermore, both the United States and Canada had urged in the early conferences that "operating and financial responsibilities be assessed partly on the basis of benefits derived by states in fields other than Atlantic flying. These include meteorological observations which are needed for general weather forecasting services in countries surrounding the North Atlantic, observations useful to maritime interests, and guarding of radio distress frequencies for surface

[33] Entered into force May 28, 1952, 3 *UST* 4402, *TIAS* 2589.

[34] Weather Stations: Pacific Ocean Program, exchange of notes, signed at Washington June 8 and 22, 1950, 1 *UST* 569, *TIAS* 2103. Note on "Pacific Weather Stations Program Agreed upon by U.S.–Canada," 23 *DSB* 214 (1950). Another special agreement between these two governments, effected by exchange of notes signed at Washington Jan. 24 and 31, 1949, waived immigration and customs requirements for public aircraft engaged in "Air Search and Rescue Operations" along the common boundary of the two countries, 63 *Stat.* (3) 2328, *TIAS* 1882.

[35] Weather Stations: Pacific Ocean Interim Program, effected by exchange of notes, dated at Washington Sept. 25, 1950, and Feb. 16, 1951, 2 *UST* 720, *TIAS* 2228. A slight change in the location of two of the stations was effected by an agreement amending that of 1951, effected by an exchange of notes dated at Ottawa Jan. 22 and Feb. 22, 1952, 3 *UST* 3062, *TIAS* 2488.

shipping." These two governments also urged that since "weather movements in the North Atlantic are generally from west to east . . . Western Europe . . . receives proportionately greater benefits from the ocean stations network than do North American states." [36]

A third conference at Brighton, England, in July 1953, devoted to financial and administrative matters only, had no authority to make fundamental changes in the program. It recommended, however, a full conference to review the whole problem. Encountering a reluctance to adjust the burdens, the United States informed ICAO in October 1953 that it would not participate in the ocean station program after the expiration of the existing agreement on June 30, 1954.[37] Later, in December of the same year, having apparently received assurance of a changed disposition on the part of European beneficiaries of the program, the United States announced that it was prepared to discuss a "modified program." [38]

Accordingly, a fourth conference at Paris in February 1954 elaborated an agreement providing for the maintenance of 9 stations, employing 21 vessels, the United States furnishing 10 of them. It was also agreed that benefits derived from the stations were approximately 80 per cent aeronautical and 20 per cent nonaeronautical. The ratio of aggregate nonaeronautical benefits was set at 75 per cent for Europe and 25 per cent for North America. Contributions of vessels and cash payments were accordingly rearranged, with greater satisfaction to the United States and Canada.[39] The new agreement, signed at Paris, February 25, 1954,[40] came into force on July 1, 1954, and was designed to run for an initial period of two years and thereafter from year to year unless denounced in accordance with its terms. Annex I to the agreement contains a map of the ocean stations and Annex II a schedule of the services to be performed by the vessels. Thus, at long last, the North Atlantic Ocean Weather Stations program apparently has been placed on a firm basis for the foreseeable future.

By a supplemental agreement of June 4 and 28, 1954, between the

[36] Ernest A. Lister, "The North Atlantic Ocean Stations Agreement," 30 *DSB* 792–795 (1954).
[37] "U.S. To Cease Participation in Ocean Station Program," 29 *DSB* 629 (1953).
[38] "U.S. To Reconsider Ocean Station Participation," 30 *DSB* 23 (1954).
[39] Lister, *op. cit.*, pp. 794–795.
[40] North Atlantic Ocean Stations, Agreement with Annexes, 6 *UST* 515, *TIAS* 3186.

Transportation and Communications since World War II

United States and Canada, the United States continued to assume full operation of Ocean Station B in the Atlantic in consideration of the full operation by Canada of Ocean Station P in the Pacific.[41]

Joint Services in Iceland and Danish Territory. Further in pursuance of the "joint support" projects of ICAO, the United States has, from the beginning, participated with some ten other governments in the support of air-navigation services in Iceland, Greenland, and the Faroes. These services "include meteorological observations, major communications services, an oceanic traffic control center, and three Loran stations of the North Atlantic chain."[42] In September 1956, ICAO held a Joint Financing Conference to Revise the Danish and Icelandic Agreements at Geneva, which the United States, as a major user of the services, attended.[43]

Other Joint and Cooperative Weather Programs. Two other programs in which the United States participates, though not immediately in pursuance of ICAO obligations, are nevertheless part of the meteorological protective system for aviation and in conformity with the prescriptions of the World Meteorological Organization. One program faces north and the other faces south.

The United States and Canada maintain jointly certain weather stations in the Canadian Arctic. The program was initiated in 1947 "to provide meteorological observations required for more accurate short-range forecasting and to accumulate research data necessary for the solution of long-range forecasting problems." The stations in 1950 were at Resolute Bay, Cornwallis Island; Eureka, on the west coast of Ellesmere Island; Isachsen Peninsula, on Ellef Ringnes Island; Alert, on Ellesmere Island; and Mould Bay, on Prince Patrick Island.[44] No formal treaty or agreement provides for the program, the operations being conducted by the American authorities in pursuance of an act of Congress of 1946 [45] and in cooperation with the Canadian authorities under an

---

[41] Pacific Ocean Weather Stations, 5 *UST* 2765, *TIAS* 3132.

[42] *Fifth Report, op. cit.*, pp. 14–15, listing contributors and contributions. See Paul A. Smith, "ICAO Conference on Air Navigation Services in Iceland," held at Geneva, June 8–25, 1948, 20 *DSB* 164–166 (1949).

[43] 35 *DSB* 429 (1956).

[44] "Re-supply Mission to U.S.-Canadian Arctic Weather Stations," 23 *DSB* 550 (1950). For further details see 17 *DSB* 82 (1947); 18 *DSB* 782 (1948); 19 *DSB* 471 (1948); 21 *DSB* 76 (1949); 21 *DSB* 443 (1949); 22 *DSB* 695 (1950); and 23 *DSB* 214 (1950); also *History Arctic Operations Project*, containing maps, mimeo., supplied by U.S. Weather Bureau, Washington, D.C.

[45] Act of Feb. 12, 1946, 60 *Stat.* 4. For an excellent brief description of the Weather

administrative agreement. "Each year representatives of the various departments of the United States and Canadian Governments meet, and the minutes of that meeting constitute a working agreement for the next year."[46]

Beginning in 1942, the United States launched a program to establish a chain of weather stations in the Caribbean and Mexico, with the cooperation of the several governments involved. In 1955 one was also established on Betio Island in the Gilbert and Ellice Islands Colony of Great Britain in mid-Pacific.[47] The first of the agreements was with Mexico in 1942.[48] That agreement has been revised several times [49] and supplemented by one providing for a cooperative program on Guadalupe Island, off the coast of Lower California.[50] In the first agreement with Cuba in 1944 the United States declared that it "has already established a network of radiosonde observation stations in the United States, the West Indies, Mexico, and the Canal Zone, and feels that establishment of a station in Cuba would fill a gap in the network. Radiosonde observations are needed for the protection of military and commercial aircraft operating in this area, and also to provide advance information on destructive hurricanes that threaten civilian and military installations located in the region of the Caribbean Sea and Gulf of Mexico."[51] Radiosonde (radio sounding apparatus), according to the Weather Bureau manual on the subject, is sent aloft in a balloon filled with helium or

---

Bureau's functions and programs, see *United States Government Organization Manual 1957–1958*, pp. 289–292.

[46] Letter, Weather Bureau to writer, Feb. 20, 1957.

[47] Exchange of notes, signed at Washington, Nov. 15, 1955, 6 *UST* 3877, *TIAS* 3389. Station reopened in pursuance of agreement effected by exchange of notes, signed at Washington, Jan. 20, 1958, *TIAS* 3976. By agreement effected by exchange of notes, signed at Canberra, Feb. 19 and 25, 1958, the United States received permission to establish a station on Australia's trust territory of Nauru Island, *TIAS* 4001.

[48] Signed at Mexico, D.F., Oct. 13 and 20, and Nov. 10, 1942, 61 *Stat.* (4) 4281, text repeated in *TIAS* 1989, below. Somehow this agreement never appeared in *EAS*.

[49] Exchange of notes, signed at Mexico, May 18 and June 14, 1943, 61 *Stat.* (4) 4053, *TIAS* 1806; *ibid.*, May 12, June 16, 21, and 28, 1945, 61 *Stat.* (4) 4276, *TIAS* 1989; *ibid.*, March 29 and Aug. 15, 1949, 63 *Stat.* (3) 2750, *TIAS* 1995; *ibid.*, April 7 and Aug. 22, 1952, 3 *UST* 5081, *TIAS* 2695; *ibid.*, June 30, 1953, 4 *UST* 1700, *TIAS* 2837; *ibid.*, Aug. 23 and 29, 1957, *TIAS* 3905.

[50] Exchange of notes, signed at Mexico, Nov. 6, 1945, and April 12, 1946, 61 *Stat.* (4) 4060, *TIAS* 1807.

[51] Exchange of notes, signed at Habana, July 17 and Aug. 2, 1944, 61 *Stat.* (4) 4084, *TIAS* 1842; amended and extended, *ibid.*, Aug. 21, 1947, and Jan. 27, 1948, 62 *Stat.* (3) 3134, *TIAS* 1847; June 30, 1950, 1 *UST* 658, *TIAS* 2125; June 30, 1953, 4 *UST* 1705, *TIAS* 2838.

Transportation and Communications since World War II

hydrogen "to determine the pressure, temperature, and relative humidity from the surface to the point where the balloon bursts." Having done its work, the radiosonde, which consists of meteorological instruments combined with a radio transmitter, floats down to the earth by means of a parachute. When other instruments are added to record the direction and speed of winds aloft, the whole apparatus is called a rawinsonde.

In an agreement with Colombia in 1956 providing for a cooperative program for "the establishment and operation of a rawinsonde observation station on St. Andrews Island" it was declared that "the purpose of such a program would be to provide essential meteorological information for research into the origin, development, structure, and movement of hurricanes and for the preparation of hurricane warnings. The ultimate object is to achieve greater accuracy and timeliness in forecasts of hurricanes and in warnings of accompanying destructive winds, tides, and floods." [52] Similar agreements were concluded in 1956 with France, applicable to Guadeloupe Island in the French West Indies; [53] with The Netherlands, applicable to Curaçao and St. Martin Islands; [54] with the Dominican Republic; [55] and in 1957 with Chile, [56] Peru, [57] and Ecuador. [58]

In addition to these agreements the United States arranged in 1947 to assist the Philippine Islands in the training of personnel and the establishment of meteorological services "to furnish general weather service as well as meeting the economic requirements of domestic and international aviation and maritime commerce. [59]

Cooperation with Private and Public International Organizations. Before leaving the subject of aviation it is important at least to note the

---

[52] Exchange of notes, signed at Bogotá, Feb. 6 and March 14, 1956, 7 *UST* 2095, *TIAS* 3611.

[53] Exchange of notes, signed at Paris, March 23, 1956, 7 *UST* 2545, *TIAS* 3647.

[54] Exchange of notes, signed at The Hague, Aug. 6 and 16, 1956, 7 *UST* 2562, *TIAS* 3650; extended for another year by agreement of July 8 and Aug. 29, 1957, *TIAS* 3896.

[55] Exchange of notes, signed at Ciudad Trujillo, July 25 and Aug. 11, 1956, 7 *UST* 3197, *TIAS* 3699.

[56] Agreement effected by exchange of notes, signed at Santiago, March 1, 1957, 8 *UST* 436, *TIAS* 3795; concluded to facilitate the work of the International Geophysical Year but extensible beyond that period.

[57] Agreement effected by exchange of notes, signed at Lima, April 17, 1957, 8 *UST* 691, *TIAS* 3823, similarly geared to IGY.

[58] Agreement effected by exchange of notes, signed at Quito, April 24, 1957, 8 *UST* 764, *TIAS* 3833, similarly geared to IGY.

[59] Agreement signed at Manila, May 12, 1947, 61 *Stat.* (3) 2858, *TIAS* 1617.

exceedingly important role which observers and representatives from private and other public international organizations play as consultants in the deliberations of ICAO and the formulation of its Standards and Recommended Practices. Among the private organizations regularly participating in this work are the International Air Transport Association, Air Transport Association of America, International Federation of Airline Pilots Association, International Aeronautical Federation, International Federation of Private Air Transport, International Union of Aviation Insurers, Institute for the Unification of Private Law, as well as on occasion the International Law Association, the International Association of Physical Oceanography, and the International Chamber of Commerce. Among the most active of these leading private organizations is the IATA, founded in 1919, representing over thirty air transport companies, most of them European.[60]

Political scientists need hardly be reminded how much better the international unions, from the United Nations down, handle the problem of representation of private economic and social groups than do most nation states. Practically at every turn in the negotiating of multipartite agreements, in the operations of the international agencies established, in the committee and plenary sessions of the deliberative organs established for unions, and in the preparation of rules and regulations, representatives of private groups are not only present but also welcome. It is not too much to say that none of these great specialized agencies operating in this post-World War II period could function effectively without this continuous liaison with the private groups, many of whom, together with the Economic and Social Council of the United Nations, bridge the "separation of powers" existing between the several great agencies. What is said here in connection with ICAO could be repeated, with only a change in the listing of the associations, for the other unions. Suffice it that with respect to ICAO and the International Telecommunication Union the mechanism for group representation and the channeling of "lobbying" is probably most highly and efficiently developed, for central, special, regional, and other activities.

Similarly, each of the great public unions maintains liaison with the other unions in whose work it has an interest or with respect to which there is some overlapping in jurisdiction. In the case of ICAO, the

[60] Lyman Cromwell White and Marie Ragonetti Zocca, *International Non-Governmental Organizations* (1951), pp. 64–69.

interagency liaison with ITU, the Universal Postal Union, the Intergovernmental Maritime Consultative Organization, and the World Meteorological Organization is probably most intimate. Official representatives of each of these great organizations appear regularly at meetings of the other organizations. Sometimes joint committees are set up and with growing frequency joint or combined sessions are held. There appears to be no end to this increasingly complex business of regulating "one world."

World Meteorological Organization

The second great advancement in the field of transportation on and over the sea in the postwar years was the conversion of the International Meteorological Organization into the World Meteorological Organization. The former, founded in 1878, consisted of directors of meteorological services operating under statutes adopted and amended by successive conferences.[61] In a strict legal sense, it was a nongovernmental technical organization. The new world-wide demands for meteorological services — particularly by agriculture, shipping, and aviation — the advantages of a formal intergovernmental organization operating under a treaty, and the necessity of having official status in order to secure acceptance as a specialized agency of the United Nations influenced the decision of IMO to reconstitute itself as the WMO. An intergovernmental agency also could expect better financial support for its activities than a quasi- or nongovernmental organization.

Hence the twelfth sexennial conference of directors of the International Meteorological Organization which met in Washington in 1947 acted in a dual capacity — as technicians proceeding with the work of their organization and as plenipotentiaries drafting a convention providing for the establishment of a new intergovernmental agency to be called the World Meteorological Organization.[62] The convention was opened for signature at Washington on October 11, 1947.[63]

Until the convention was properly ratified by the signatories, the old organization of directors carried on. The next steps in the conversion of IMO to WMO are reminiscent of the transactions of Pooh-Bah, First

[61] *U.S. Int. Agencies 1946*, pp. 122–129; *U.S. Int. Org. 1949*, pp. 131–136.
[62] John M. Cates, "Meeting of International Meteorological Organization: Conference of Directors," 18 *DSB* 43–46 (1948).
[63] Convention on World Meteorological Organization, 1 *UST* 281, *TIAS* 2052.

Lord of the Treasury of the Mikado, with himself as Lord High Auditor. A last Conference of the Directors of the IMO in Paris in March 1951 formally transferred the functions, assets, and liabilities of the IMO to the WMO. A few days later the First Congress of the WMO met in the same place and with substantially the same personnel, allowing for the changes wrought by the new criteria of membership. It accepted the transfer and the IMO was formally dissolved on April 4, 1951.[64] Thus, nearly a century after Matthew Fontaine Maury secured the holding of the first World Congress on Meteorology at Brussels in 1853, his hopes came into full flower. At the opening of the Washington meeting in 1947 Assistant Secretary of State Garrison Norton had already paid fine and appropriate tribute to the "Pathfinder of the Seas."[65]

Much has already been said in the preceding discussion of the intimate relation of meteorology to use of the sea. As in the case of the IMO, the WMO carries on a large share of its activities through standing technical commissions (reduced now from ten to eight) and six regional commissions.[66] Among the technical commissions those on maritime, synoptic, and aeronautical meteorology are of particular importance in the present context.

The WMO obtains weather data for its members in various ways, one of the most important methods being through cooperative observations by ships' captains at sea. Maury advocated this method as early as 1851. The historic meteorological congress at Brussels in 1853, in accord with his views, adopted an "abstract log for the use of the men-of-war of all nations and also one for all merchant men to use in the system of cooperative observations." The method was enthusiastically received and used by many governments at the time.[67]

Now, a century later, the WMO uses a similar cooperative method. "Practically all weather information obtained from the sea is provided

[64] "World Meteorological Organization," 24 *DSB* 475 (1951); *U.S. Int. Conf. 1950–1951*, D.S. Pub. No. 4571, pp. 240–244.

[65] "International Meteorological Organization: Opening Session of Conference of Directors," 17 *DSB* 678–679 (1947). See N. L. Canfield, "Ships' Weather Observations: Part I, Developments up to the 20th Century," 1 *Mariners Weather Log* 157–160 (1957), and subsequent articles in the same series.

[66] For the present setup, see *U.S. Int. Conf. 1950–1951*, p. 243. For an account of the work of one of its commissions, see Helmut E. Landsberg, "International Cooperation in Climatology: Second Session of Commission for Climatology of WMO," 36 *DSB* 612–614 (1957).

[67] Lewis, *op. cit.*, pp. 56–59.

Transportation and Communications since World War II

by volunteer observers on merchant ships. The ships are supplied with instruments by the meteorological services, and report regularly by radio to the nearest coastal station. There are at present about 2500 observing ships on the oceans (as well as thirteen stationary ocean weather ships). The first edition of an international list of the voluntary observing ships recruited from about 30 different countries was issued in 1955; it indicates the call sign, route and instruments used by these ships." [68] Fishing trawlers in Arctic waters and whaling factory ships operating in the Antarctic are particularly valuable transmitters of data because few observations from merchant ships would normally be available from those regions. The factory ships report in cipher to avoid revealing their positions to competing whalers.[69] The United States Weather Bureau, in recognition of the splendid voluntary assistance from the American merchant marine, launched a new publication in January 1957, *The Mariner's Weather Log: A Bimonthly Climatic Review of Ocean and Lake Areas,* to provide information, similar to that in the *Weekly Weather and Crop Bulletin* for agriculture, for the special use of American maritime interests. The very first issue listed selected observations made by several hundred American and foreign vessels in the summer months of 1956.[70] This publication is further splendid evidence of the existing community of interest in the *res communis.*

The relation of WMO to the other great unions dealing with the sea is emphasized by the incorporation by reference of procedures required by WMO in the instruments creating legal obligations for the members of ICAO, ITU, and IMCO, and in the Convention on Safety of Life at Sea. WMO is regularly represented at meetings of these other

---

[68] *Everyman's United Nations 1945–1955* (1956), pp. 403–404.

[69] *The Sea That Unites Us,* mimeo., WMO. See also C. E. N. Frankcom, "Radio Weather Messages from Ships: Their Practical Value," 3 *WMO Bulletin* 80–86 (1954); *ibid.,* "The Merchant Seaman as a Meteorologist," *Marine Observer,* Vol. XIX, No. 143, Jan. 1949; *ibid.,* "Selected Ships," *Meteorological Magazine,* Vol. 82, No. 971, May 1953; and for the mode of recruitment of the volunteers, *U.S. WB Manual,* Issuance 207, Vol. III, Service Operations, pp. 1–19 (1954). As of July 1, 1956, there were 2800 selected ships in the volunteer program. Letter, Weather Bureau to writer, April 9, 1957. See also W. F. McDonald, "International Cooperation in Reporting Weather Observations from the High Seas: Second Session of Commission for Maritime Meteorology of World Meteorological Organization, Hamburg, Germany, October 16–31, 1956," 37 *DSB* 164–166 (1957), and lists of vessels cooperating with the United States Weather Bureau in the North Atlantic, in various issues of *Mariners Weather Log.*

[70] Jan. 1957, Vol. I, No. 1, Washington, D.C.

The United States and the Treaty Law of the Sea

unions whenever matters of concern to it are on the agenda. And since 1947 the practice has been established of holding simultaneous sessions of correlative commissions of ICAO and WMO. Thus, in 1947 and 1950 the Commission on Aeronautical Meteorology of the old IMO met with the Meteorological Division of ICAO to devise "Specifications for Meteorological Services for International Air Navigation," which were incorporated in the appropriate annex of ICAO and in the regulations of IMO. The WMO continued the same arrangement. At the simultaneous meeting in Montreal in 1954, particular attention was devoted to the preparation of manuals by WMO for use in aviation meteorology, to the provisional adoption of the code for reporting of sea ice by aircraft provisionally used by United States aircraft on sea-ice reconnaissance, and to the needs of high-level and high-speed aircraft.[71]

WMO also cooperates in the UN Expanded Program of Technical Assistance and in other programs of the United Nations and its specialized agencies. Thus it "works closely with the International Union for Geodesy and Geophysics in developing plans for a meteorological program" for the International Geophysical Year of 1957–1958. The Second Congress of WMO in 1955, furthermore, approved a technical program for the ensuing quadrennium including "assistance in the water resource development program of the United Nations; collaboration with UNESCO in arid zone and humid tropics research; continuing survey of artificial control of weather processes; preparation of manuals and guides in the fields of climatology, agricultural meteorology, synoptic meteorology, and aeronautical meteorology; preparation of uniform specifications for climatological atlases; provision of bibliographic services; and international comparison of upper-air sounding equipment and methods." [72]

Intergovernmental Maritime Consultative Organization

The 1889 Washington International Marine Conference recommended the establishment of a permanent international maritime commission, for the purpose, *inter alia*, of coordinating efforts directed toward in-

[71] Delbert M. Little, "Meteorological Services for International Air Navigation," 23 *DSB* 236–237 (1950); *ibid.*, "Weather Services for International Civil Aviation," 31 *DSB* 824–827 (1954).

[72] Francis W. Reichelderfer, "International Cooperation in Meteorology: Second Congress of the WMO, Geneva, April 14–May 13," 33 *DSB* 435–437 (1955).

Transportation and Communications since World War II

creased safety of life and property at sea, although the conference admitted that "for the present" the establishment of such a commission was not expedient.[73] In the following decades conferences devoted to this general topic continued on an *ad hoc* basis, such as those on safety of life at sea in 1914, 1929, and 1948 and on load lines in 1930, or in pursuance of programs, particularly those urged by the International Maritime Committee and the League of Nations Organization for Communications and Transit. During the same half century distinguished professional societies such as the International Law Association [74] and eminent jurists such as Gilbert Gidel [75] advocated the creation of a permanent international body with general oversight in technical matters. In the fullness of time, an agreement providing for the establishment of such an agency, the Intergovernmental Maritime Consultative Organization, was concluded at Geneva, on March 6, 1948.[76] Thus appeared the third great advancement in the field of sea transport in the post-World War II years.

Many discouragements and an exceedingly intricate pattern of developments [77] preceded this final simple solution of the problem of organization. At the risk of creating illusions of simplicity, the developments can be summarized thus: During World War I it became necessary ultimately to establish an Allied Maritime Transport Council to control supply and allocation of shipping.[78] During World War II, it also became necessary to create, at first a Combined Shipping Adjustment Board (1942–1945) for the waging of the war and then a United Maritime Authority (1945–1946)[79] for posthostilities needs, including those of UNRRA. These bodies exercised control functions.

[73] *Protocols of Proceedings of the International Marine Conference held in Washington, D.C. . . . October 16 to December 31, 1889*, 2 Vols., Vol. II, p. 1365.

[74] Higgins and Colombos, *The International Law of the Sea*, 2d rev. ed. by C. J. Colombos (1951), p. 296.

[75] *Le Droit International Public de La Mer Le Temps de Paix*, Vol. 1, pp. 18–36.

[76] Texts in 18 *DSB* 499–505 (1948); "Toward a World Maritime Organization," D.S. Pub. No. 3196, pp. 22–28, and TIAS 4044.

[77] Eula McDonald, "Toward a World Maritime Organization," 18 *DSB* 99–107, 115 (1948), and *ibid.*, 131–137 (1948); and John Martin Cates, Jr., "United Nations Maritime Conference," *ibid.*, 495–505, 523; reprinted as D.S. Pub. No. 3196. See Marx, *International Shipping Cartels*, pp. 272–279.

[78] Salter, *op. cit.*, and McDonald, *op. cit.*, p. 100.

[79] Agreement on Shipping: Principles Having Reference to Continuance of Coordinated Control, signed at London, Aug. 5, 1944, 61 *Stat.* (4) 3784, *TIAS* 1722; and McDonald, *op. cit.*, pp. 103–105.

Before proceeding further, however, with the formation of IMCO, it is important to note that contemporary planning under the North Atlantic Treaty Organization, established in pursuance of the treaty concluded on April 4, 1949,[80] borrows from this experience in World Wars I and II. Thus, in May 1950, the North Atlantic Council, in furtherance of Article 9 of the treaty, established a North Atlantic Planning Board for Ocean Shipping to be composed of representatives of the participating countries concerned.[81] This board then produced an outline plan by May 1951 "for the mobilization of ocean-going shipping in a single pool and its allocation on a world-wide basis in time of war or wartime emergency and for the establishment in such circumstances of an international organization of a civilian character to be named the Defense Shipping Authority."[82] From time to time announcements are made of meetings of the board.[83]

To resume with IMCO, it became increasingly evident in the last years of World War II that some agency for continued cooperation and consultation in shipping matters in the postwar days would be needed. The efforts in this direction moved along two parallel lines, one stemming from these wartime bodies and another one stemming from the new United Nations.

Thus, the United Maritime Authority, before its dissolution on March 2, 1946, recommended the establishment of an interim consultative council to succeed itself. Hence a new agreement, entering into force on March 3, 1946, provided for (a) continued coordination under a Contributory Nations Committee of shipping supplied voluntarily for immediate postwar needs, including the needs of UNRRA, and (b) a United Maritime Consultative Council, which was expressly denied any "executive powers."[84] Out of the deliberations of this council came in due course certain recommendations, among them two urging, respectively, the early establishment of an Inter-Governmental Maritime Consultative Organization, to become a specialized agency of the United

[80] North Atlantic Treaty, signed at Washington, 63 *Stat.* (2) 2241, *TIAS* 1964.
[81] 22 *DSB* 830 (1950).
[82] 24 *DSB* 917–918 (1951), *q.v.* for further details.
[83] E.g., 35 *DSB* 588 (1956), announcing the eighth meeting in Washington, beginning Oct. 8, 1956.
[84] Agreement on Shipping: Arrangements and Recommendations of United Maritime Executive Board, dated at London, Feb. 11, 1946, 61 *Stat.* (4) 3791, *TIAS* 1723.

Transportation and Communications since World War II

Nations, as set forth in a draft convention prepared by the council and the immediate setting up of a Provisional Maritime Consultative Council in accord with an annexed agreement also prepared by the council.[85] This latter agreement, dated at Washington October 30, 1946, was speedily accepted by the stipulated minimum number of twelve governments and entered into force on April 23, 1947.[86] It was designed to remain in operation until the constitution for a permanent body had become effective.

While this succession of organizations and deliberations was going on, the "nuclear" or Temporary Transport and Communications Commission of the Economic and Social Council of the United Nations and its successor, the permanent Transport and Communications Commission, both urged the creation of a permanent world-wide intergovernmental shipping organization.[87] Out of the concurrent and interrelated labors of the two sets of organizations emerged a resolution of the Economic and Social Council dated March 28, 1947,[88] in pursuance of which a conference for the establishment of an intergovernmental shipping organization was called to meet in Geneva in 1948.

As finally elaborated at Geneva, the Convention of March 6, 1948, provided for the establishment of a typical postwar specialized agency with "jurisdiction over questions which any member may raise relating to technical matters of all kinds affecting shipping engaged in international trade, including safety; the encouragement of the removal of discriminatory action and unnecessary restrictions by governments; and consideration of matters concerning unfair restrictive practices by shipping concerns." [89] The organization does not exercise control functions relating to supply, limitation, or allocation of shipping.[90] These basic economic and political matters remain in the domain of national policy and "free" competition.

[85] McDonald, *op. cit.*, pp. 106–107, 115.
[86] Agreement on Shipping: Provisional Maritime Consultative Council, dated at Washington, Oct. 30, 1946, 61 *Stat.* (4) 3796, *TIAS* 1724.
[87] McDonald, *op. cit.*, pp. 131–135, citing the UN documentation.
[88] Doc. E/408, and documentation cited in McDonald, *op. cit.*, pp. 107, 137. Also in *United Nations Maritime Conference, Geneva, 19 February to 6 March, 1948, Final Act and Related Documents*, UN Pub. 1948.VIII.2, pp. 7–8.
[89] Cates, *op. cit.*, p. 497.
[90] These were carefully excluded. See Cates, *op. cit., passim.* For these economic problems, see discussions in Higgins and Colombos, *op. cit.*, pp. 270–275, and Daniel Marx, Jr., "International Organization of Shipping," 55 *Yale Law Journal* 1214–1232 (1946).

The United States and the Treaty Law of the Sea

Maritime Safety Committee. In addition to providing machinery for continuous adoption of international legislation relating to sea transport on subjects within the scope of its authority (Art. 3), thus eliminating the need for sporadic *ad hoc* conferences as in the past, the IMCO convention provides for a Maritime Safety Committee of fourteen members with a jurisdiction which, like a concave mirror, gathers to a focus many of the developments of the past century and a half relating to surface craft discussed up to this point. Article 29 (a) reads:

The Maritime Safety Committee shall have the duty of considering any matter within the scope of the Organization and concerned with aids to navigation, construction and equipment of vessels, manning from a safety standpoint, rules for the prevention of collisions, handling of dangerous cargoes, maritime safety procedures and requirements, hydrographic information, log-books and navigational records, marine casualty investigation, salvage and rescue, and any other matters directly affecting maritime safety.

Article 30 further empowered the Safety Committee to submit to the assembly of IMCO proposals for new safety regulations or for amendments to existing ones, which the assembly could then recommend to its members for adoption [Art. 16 (i)].

Coordination of Maritime Activities. The IMCO is also at the center of a web of interagency relationships. Thus at the Geneva Conference in 1948 a typical postwar phenomenon occurred: observers from nine other organizations attended, namely, ICAO, ILO, ITU, WHO, the International Chamber of Commerce, the International Cooperative Alliance, the International Law Association, and the International Transport Workers Federation.[91] Further, Article 29 (c) of the convention imposes on the Maritime Safety Committee "the duty of maintaining such close relationship with other intergovernmental bodies concerned with transport and communications as may further the object of the Organization in promoting maritime safety and facilitate the co-ordination of activities in the fields of shipping, aviation, telecommunications and meteorology with respect to safety and rescue."

Finally, the Geneva Conference had to relate its work to that of the forthcoming conference on safety of life at sea scheduled to meet in London later that year. Accordingly it adopted two resolutions,[92] the

[91] Cates, *op. cit.*, p. 495.
[92] Annexes B and C, respectively, of the Final Act of the UN Maritime Conference, text, 18 *DSB* 505, 523 (1948).

Transportation and Communications since World War II

first recommending to the Safety Conference that it "draft provisions in its final acts which would take into account the duties and functions relating to maritime safety accorded to IMCO"; and the second, directing that the Safety Conference be informed that the chapter of the IMCO convention (Ch. VII), which deals with the Safety Committee, was drafted "in the light of consideration by the Maritime Conference of the Report of the Committee of Experts on the coordination of safety of life at sea and in the air," [93] which report had been prepared at the request of ECOSOC for use at the Safety Conference. That report [94] will presently be noted in connection with the discussion dealing with the London Safety of Life at Sea Conference.

The Geneva 1948 Conference established a Preparatory Committee of twelve members to proceed with the arrangements for launching IMCO.[95] Article 60 of the IMCO convention provides that it shall enter into force on the date "when 21 states of which 7 shall each have a total tonnage of not less than 1,000,000 gross tons of shipping have become parties to the Convention" in accordance with the provisions of Article 57. The United States was among the first to ratify the convention. The Senate gave its approval on June 27, 1950, subject to a "reservation and understanding" designed to safeguard the effectiveness of American antitrust legislation against any possible application of the convention, particularly of Article 4, which deals with the shipping business and their conferences. A *note verbale* accompanying the instrument of ratification when it was deposited at the United Nations on August 16, 1950, spelled out further the intent of the Senate "reservation and understanding." [96] By 1953, only 14 states, but including 7 states with the million-ton qualification, had become parties.

In pursuance of a resolution of ECOSOC, a meeting of these 14 governments was held in London in October 1953 to consider what measures might be taken with a view to bringing the organization into being. The meeting stressed the "log-jam" that awaited clearing by and through

---

[93] Cates, *op. cit.*, p. 499.

[94] *Report of the Preparatory Committee of Experts to Consider the Coordination of Activities in the Fields of Aviation, Shipping and Telecommunications in Regard to Safety at Sea and in the Air* . . . E/CONF.4/8, E/CN.2/20.Add.1, Feb. 19, 1948.

[95] Text, 18 *DSB* 505 (1948).

[96] 96 *Cong. Rec.* 9255–9260, June 27, 1950; *Status of Multilateral Conventions*, ST/LEG/3, pp. xii–6, Sept. 30, 1956.

IMCO — the setting up of the machinery needed to carry out various portions of the 1948 Safety of Life at Sea Convention and solutions of the problems of tonnage measurement, oil pollution, and removal of discriminatory action and unnecessary restrictions by governments affecting shipping engaged in international trade.[97] It was precisely this last objective of IMCO which delayed acceptance of the convention by a number of states, among them Norway, Sweden, and Denmark, who appear to be reluctant to assume obligations which may operate to restrict their freedom to determine their own national shipping practices. Greece, a million-ton state, accepted and then withdrew its acceptance in 1956. At the beginning of 1957, some nineteen states had become parties to the convention. The loss of the *Andrea Doria* refocused attention on the need for getting IMCO into operation. On March 17, 1958, Japan, the necessary twenty-first state, deposited its acceptance and the long awaited convention came into force. Immediately the preparatory committee provided for in Annex A of the Final Act of the 1948 conference proceeded in London with preparing for the convening of the first assembly of IMCO in January 1959.

The headquarters of IMCO, in accord with Article 44 of the convention and consistently with the historic functions performed by Great Britain in these shipping matters, will be established in London. Thus, at long last, a permanent bureau has come into being.

Tonnage Measurement. In anticipation of the assumption by IMCO of its duties under the convention, ECOSOC has already expressed its view that two further problems which have plagued the maritime industry for a long time should be dealt with by IMCO, namely, the securing of uniformity in the admeasurement of ships' tonnage and control of oil pollution of navigable waters.

International uniformity in the tonnage measurement of ships would produce impressive advantages "in terms of safety; of the methods of determining charges for port facilities, harbor dues, and canal tolls; and of efficiency and simplicity in ship design and construction."[98] As possessor of much merchant shipping and operator of one of the two great interoceanic canals, the Panama Canal, the other being the Suez, the United States is intensely interested in securing a satisfactory uniform system of admeasurement. The problem is exceedingly compli-

[97] *U.S. Int. Conf. 1953–1954*, D.S. Pub. No. 5776, pp. 119–120.
[98] "Meeting of Tonnage Measurement Experts," 26 *DSB* 997 (1952).

cated.[99] As early as 1924 the League of Nations studied the matter. Out of these efforts grew the so-called Oslo rules of 1939. These formed the basis of an international convention signed by powers other than the United States at Oslo in 1947. The United States was, however, represented by technical observers at the two Oslo conferences in 1947 and 1948 and at the conference at Stockholm in 1950 and at The Hague in 1952. Meanwhile, the Transport and Communications Commission of ECOSOC, after having considered the matter in several sessions, stated that "in its opinion, the problem of intergovernmental action on the unification of tonnage measurement should be among the first to be considered by IMCO." [100] Pending the adoption of some uniform scheme, the United states continues its system of mutual recognition of admeasurement standards and certificates by means of administrative action or bipartite agreements.[101]

Oil Pollution of Navigable Waters. The Transport and Communications Commission of ECOSOC, after studying for several years the problem of oil pollution of navigable waters, at first came to the conclusion that action with respect to that problem could also await the establishment of IMCO. As the delay in the perfecting of the IMCO convention continued and the problem worsened in European waters the pressures mounted for some kind of international action. The Transport and Communications Commission therefore continued its survey of the situation. In response to a circular inquiry from the Secretary General the United States replied in 1950 that "a recent study of oil pollution along the coast lines of the United States and its territories disclosed no present need for action" (that is, a conference on the subject), but that if a conference were called, the United States would want to be represented.[102] In response to an invitation of the Secretary General, made in pursuance of a resolution of ECOSOC in 1953, to contribute experts to a joint study of the problem and for the purpose of correlating the replies

[99] John W. Mann, "The Conference on Tonnage Measurement of Ships, Stockholm, June 2–10, 1950," 23 *DSB* 471–474 (1950).
[100] *Yearbook of the United Nations, 1951*, p. 441. Also, *ibid., 1948–1949*, p. 487; *1950*, pp. 485–486.
[101] *Treaties in Force on December 31, 1941*, D.S. Pub. No. 2103, p. 211. Examples are the agreements with Panama, effected by exchange of notes, signed Aug. 17, 1937, 50 *Stat.* 1626, *EAS* 106; and with Venezuela, effected by exchange of notes signed at Caracas, Feb. 21, 1957, 8 *UST* 289, *TIAS* 3774.
[102] John W. Mann, "The Problem of Sea Water Pollution," 29 *DSB* 775–780, at p. 778 (1953) citing UN Doc. E/CN.2/100.

of governments for the use of IMCO, the United States declined to participate in the study but was willing to furnish copies of its laws and regulations and information concerning the educational program used in the United States to secure the cooperation of the maritime industry. Furthermore, it was stated on behalf of the United States that enforcement of the law and voluntary cooperation had over the past thirty years brought the nuisance under effective control in American territorial and contiguous waters.[103]

Meanwhile, the British government, confronted with an increasing amount of oil pollution in waters of concern to it and aware of the mounting problem which plagued its European neighbors, authorized an intensive study to be made of the problem by Percy Faulkner, an under secretary of the Ministry of Transport and Civil Aviation. On the basis of that report, published in 1953 and known as the "Faulkner Report," the United Kingdom took the initiative and called, rather hastily, a conference on oil pollution to meet in London, in April 1954.[104]

The control problem was well stated in the first of several resolutions adopted by the conference:

The Conference have noted that the coasts and coastal waters of many countries are seriously affected by oil pollution, the results of which include great damage to coasts and beaches and consequent hindrance to healthful recreation and interference with the tourist industry, the death and destruction of birds and other wild life, and probable adverse effects on fish and marine organisms on which they feed. There is widespread public concern in many countries about the extent and the growth of this problem.

The pollution is caused by persistent oils, that is to say, crude oil, fuel oil, heavy diesel oil and lubricating oil. While there is not conclusive evidence that these oils persist indefinitely on the surface of the sea, they remain for very long periods of time and are capable of being carried very considerable distances by currents, wind and surface drifts and of building up into deposits on the sea-shore. Very large quantities of persistent oils are regularly discharged into the sea by tankers as a result of the washing of their tanks and the disposal of their oily ballast water. Dry-cargo ships which habitually use their fuel tanks for ballast water also discharge oily ballast water into the sea and this also gives rise to

[103] *Ibid.*, pp. 775–776, 779.
[104] Rear Admiral H. C. Shepheard, U.S. Coast Guard, and John W. Mann, "Reducing the Menace of Oil Pollution: International Conference on Pollution of the Seas and Coasts by Oil, London, April 26–May 12, 1954," 31 *DSB* 311–314 (1954). See also summary of the conference in *U.S. Int. Conf. 1953–1954*, pp. 208–211.

pollution. It is practicable for tankers to adopt a procedure whereby their oily residues can be retained on board and discharged into reception facilities at oil loading ports or repair ports. Pollution resulting from the discharge of ballast water from dry-cargo ships can be reduced or prevented by the installation of efficient oily-water separators or other means, such as the provision in ports of adequate reception facilities for oil residues.[105]

The London Conference produced eight resolutions and an International Convention for the Prevention of Pollution of the Sea by Oil, open for signature for three months from May 12, 1954. The United States did not sign the convention. The convention provided for the establishment of zones, varying in width from 20 to 150 miles offshore, in the Adriatic, the North Sea, the North Atlantic off Europe, and in the waters surrounding Australia, wherein the discharge of oil would be prohibited; the keeping of an oil record book by each vessel in the categories affected by the scheme; and permissible inspection of the same in port by any of the contracting governments. Furthermore, any government party to the agreement could report the violation of any rule by the vessel of another state party to the agreement to the government of that state. Thereupon, the government of the offending vessel was obligated to proceed, after proper investigation, with the application of penalties to the offending vessel.

The decision of the United States not to sign the London convention appears to have been grounded upon the following considerations. At the 1926 Washington Conference on oil pollution,[106] the United States took the position that a logical solution required a multipartite agreement prohibiting the discharge of oil at sea at any time or place. A majority of the states represented at that conference did not then support that view. The United States thereupon proceeded to solve its problem in its own way, by strict enforcement of its Oil Pollution Act of 1924 [107] and

---

[105] *Final Act of Conference and Text of the International Convention for the Prevention of Pollution of the Sea by Oil, 1954*, Cmd. 9197, p. 14.

[106] Shepheard and Mann, *op. cit.*, p. 311. Documents cited above at p. 145.

[107] Act of June 7, 1924, 43 *Stat.* 605. Other acts used in repression of the evil were the New York Harbor Act of 1888, 25 *Stat.* 209; the River and Harbor Act of 1899, 30 *Stat.* 1152; and an act of June 23, 1936, 49 *Stat.* 1889, amended by act of Oct. 9, 1940, 54 *Stat.* 1028. See Mann, *op. cit.*, p. 776. In addition, the following rules and regulations exist: "Rules and Regulations for Tank Vessels (USCG-123)," 46 *C.F.R.* 30 to 39 inclusive; Regulations of Corps of Engineers, 33 *C.F.R.* 209.170. There is also *A Manual for the Safe Handling of Inflammable and Combustible Liquids* (USCG-174), containing several pages of instructions to prevent oil pollution by

other acts in waters and harbors of the United States; by securing extensive cooperation from American shipping and petroleum interests in the establishment of disposal facilities in port and the adoption of oil separators by ships; by the setting up of an offshore no-discharge zone by means of a "gentleman's agreement" with shipping entering American waters; and by means of an extensive educational program to induce voluntary compliance by all vessels using American waters. These methods, it was said, brought about substantial abatement of the nuisance within American territorial waters, even though the use of petroleum products in the United States had increased threefold since 1926. Furthermore, during the London Conference, a special bulletin of the American Merchant Marine Institute urged all American vessels in north European waters to follow the instructions in the American Oil Pollution Manual and take all the preventative measures necessary to avoid polluting those waters. This was by way of American shipping exhibiting "clean hands."

In these premises, the United States view appeared to be that the London convention was, for the time being, at any rate, excessive in its requirements. Foreign governments could by national action along the lines of the American methods reduce the evil and perhaps avoid the need for the stringent measures set forth in the convention. The American experience was, however, gratifyingly reflected in several of the measures recommended in the eight resolutions adopted by the conference, among them the following: the encouragement of the development and use aboard ship of oil separators; the provision of facilities to receive oily wastes and ballasts in port and at oil-loading terminals; the preparation of manuals of guidance for the avoidance of pollution; the creation of national committees to continue review of the problem; and the collection and dissemination by an appropriate organ of the United Nations of technical information about oil pollution.[108]

In pursuance of these recommendations, the United States has set up a National Committee for Prevention of Pollution of the Seas by Oil, consisting of representatives of various government departments. This committee maintains contact through the department of commerce with United States shipbuilders, port and harbor authorities, and hotel

---

tank vessels, pp 33–47. Prepared first in 1938, to supplement the tanker regulations, it has been revised several times since.

[108] Final Act, *op. cit.*, pp. 14–20.

Transportation and Communications since World War II

and beach associations. Liaison is maintained with the shipping industry and with maritime labor through the Oil Pollution Panel of the Merchant Marine Council, which reports to the commandant of the Coast Guard.[109]

In accord with Resolution 8 of the London Conference, ECOSOC solicited the desired technical information. Forty-two governments responded, including the United States. The results of the inquiry were published in 1956.[110] Meanwhile, the International Law Commission recommended in Article 48 of its 1956 report that "every State shall draw up regulations to prevent pollution of the seas by the discharge of oil from ships or pipelines or resulting from the exploitation of the seabed and its sub-soil, taking account of existing treaty provisions on the subject." The 1954 London convention came into force July 26, 1958, without participation therein by the United States. IMCO will assume the duties of the bureau established under Article 21 of the convention.

Safety of Life at Sea

The fourth great advancement in the field of transportation on and over the sea achieved in the post-World War II period was the adoption of a revised Convention for Safety of Life at Sea in London on June 10, 1948.[111] As early as 1943, a special shipping committee organized by the department of state recommended the convoking of a conference for the revision of the 1929 convention as soon as possible after the close of hostilities. Conversations with the British government followed; that government issued invitations November 25, 1946; the conference met April 23, 1948. Meanwhile, in America, under the supervision of the commandant of the Coast Guard, the agency with predominant administrative interest in the subject matter, extensive preparations were made by an elaborate series of committees "upon which served 235 representatives of interested Government agencies and of shipbuilders, shipowners, underwriters, and the admiralty bar." [112]

[109] 35 *DSB* 521–522 (1956). For subsequent developments see *Memorandum on Pollution of the Sea by Oil*, United Nations Conference on the Law of the Sea, A/CONF.13/8, Oct. 29, 1957.

[110] *Pollution of the Sea by Oil*, ST/ECA/41. The data furnished by the United States are on pages 22–24, 107–111, 161–162, 193–194, and 212. This last page lists the laws and regulations cited above.

[111] 3 *UST* 3450, *TIAS* 2495. Text also in *International Conference on Safety of Life at Sea, London, April 23–June 10, 1948, Report of the United States Delegation*, D.S. Pub. No. 3282, pp. 49–194.

[112] *Report, op. cit.*, pp. 2–3.

The United States and the Treaty Law of the Sea

While these preparations were going forward in the United States and similar ones in other maritime countries, the Temporary (or Nuclear) Transport and Communications Commission of ECOSOC in 1946 considered "the question of the coordination of activities in the fields of aviation, shipping, and telecommunications, with respect to safety and rescue at sea and in the air . . . as one of the substantive problems requiring early attention." [113]

Coordination of Safety at Sea and in the Air. In pursuance of a recommendation of the Permanent Commission and the resolution of ECOSOC of March 28, 1947,[114] the United Kingdom government, as host of the forthcoming Safety Conference, convened a Preparatory Committee of Experts on Co-Ordination of Safety at Sea and in the Air which consisted of representatives of ICAO, IMO, ITU, and the Provisional Maritime Consultative Council. This committee met in London, January 27 to February 6, 1948, and produced a remarkable report [115] which surveyed existing arrangements, explored the possibilities for further coordination of intergovernmental agency efforts, stressed the utter need for coordination at the *national* level, and offered certain conclusions for interagency cooperation toward the desired end.

Paragraph 15 of the *Report* pointed up some of the difficulty of coordination thus:

Co-ordination of communications presents a difficult problem because marine and aeronautical traditions and techniques are very different. The normal ship communicates with the land only at intervals and, when a casualty has occurred, the ships in the neighborhood decide among themselves which can best effect the rescue. On the other hand, aircraft are normally in constant touch with their base and must communicate with the utmost rapidity with all rescue agencies immediately a distress incident occurs. It has been found in practice that coordination from the shore is the most effective method of marshalling help to aircraft in distress at sea.

This explains the emphasis in the *Annex* to the *Report* on "Extension of Functions of Rescue Coordination Centers to Serve Maritime Distress Incidents." [116] In sum, the report gathered together the essentials of a

[113] McDonald, *op. cit.*, pp. 134–135.
[114] Doc. E/408.
[115] E/Conf.4/8, E/CN.2/20. Add. 1, Feb. 19, 1948.
[116] *Ibid.*, Item 5 (iii). The Baltic and North Sea Telecommunication Meeting on Rescue Cooperation, held at Göteborg, Sweden, Sept. 22–24, 1955, at which the United States was represented by an observer, recommended "that sea rescue organ-

228

sound program for the immediately foreseeable future. The American delegation to the Safety Conference — also undoubtedly other national delegations — the Maritime Conference in Geneva, and the Safety Conference in London, in their respective deliberations, thereupon all took into account the conclusions of this excellent report.

London Conference of 1948. The formation of the American delegation and the composition of the conference illustrate the present-day practice of bringing to bear upon the international legislative process all appropriate private and public bodies of interest in the subject matter. Thus the American delegation contained, in addition to representatives from six different federal administrative services, representatives appointed from the National Federation of American Shipping, Shipbuilder's Council of America, American Bureau of Shipping, Society of Naval Architects and Marine Engineers, American Federation of Labor, and Congress of Industrial Organizations. The conference included, in addition to national delegations from other states similarly composed,[117] observers from the UN, ICAO, ILO, IMO, ITU, WHO, and the International Hydrographic Bureau.

The 1948 Convention on Safety at Sea, which supersedes that of 1929, went into effect November 19, 1952. The convention itself is brief, consisting of fifteen basic articles, among them provisions integrating the regime with the machinery of IMCO. Pending establishment of IMCO certain necessary "clearing-house" functions were to be performed by the government of the United Kingdom (Article XV). The annexed voluminous regulations, applicable to the high seas and not the Great Lakes, constitute a virtual code on construction, lifesaving appliances, radio communication, safety of navigation, and carriage of grain and dangerous cargoes. The report of the American delegation analyzes and evaluates the new regulations in detail.[118]

izations should use coast stations to the greatest extent possible for communication purposes in international sea rescue cooperation." The United States was also represented by an observer at the Baltic and North Sea Radiotelephone Conference, held at the same place, Sept. 1–21, 1955, which "was called for the purpose of making better utilization of the radiotelephone in the Baltic and North Sea area, particularly for distress and safety purposes." *Int. Conf. 1955–1956,* pp. 94–95; A. Henry, "The Baltic and North Sea Radiotelephone Conference," 22 *Telecommunication Journal* 176–181 (1955), and Thomas Övergaard and Arne Råberg, "Baltic and North Sea Telecommunication Meeting on Rescue Co-Operation," *ibid.,* 192–194.

[117] See list of plenipotentiaries, *Report, op. cit.,* pp. 49–53.

[118] *Op. cit.,* pp. 7–45; also excellent brief analyses in Lt. Lawrence D. Bradley,

The United States and the Treaty Law of the Sea

A few features of the regulations can, however, be noted here. With respect to passenger vessels, for example, "provision is made for greater safety by taking into account the stability of the vessel in an assumed condition of damage." In general, the provisions reflect increased emphasis on radio communication and safety appliances, in accord with inventions and technological advances since 1929; attention to dangerous cargoes (stimulated by the enormous disaster at Texas City on April 16, 1947); the gradual employment of radio-direction finders and other radionic equipment; improved storm and danger warnings and meteorological protection. The obligation on a master of a ship at sea to come to the aid of another ship in distress was extended (Ch. V, Reg. 10) to include aid to aircraft or survival craft as well. Another new rule obligated aid in all cases, whatever the source of the distress message.

North Atlantic Ice Patrol. Under Chapter V, Regulation 6 of the convention, the United States agreed "to continue the management of the ice patrol service and the study and observation of ice conditions, including the dissemination of information received therefrom." The same provision provided for a reallocation of expenses, "each contribution to be based, as far as practicable, upon the total gross tonnage of the vessels of each contributing Government passing through the regions of icebergs guarded by the Ice Patrol." Pending the establishment of the Maritime Safety Committee of IMCO, to whom the convention entrusted the task of computing and assigning the new shares, an interim arrangement revising the 1929 shares was circulated by the British government in the fall of 1948 embodying an understanding reached at the conference. This interim agreement went into effect on January 1, 1951.[119] Then when it became evident that the establishment of IMCO might be delayed further, a new agreement was concluded at Washington in 1956, preserving the ratio of use of the ice-guarded area but allowing deductions from the bill for services rendered for tonnage crossing south of the stipulated guarded routes.[120]

Jr., "Progress on International Maritime Safety Measures," 19 *DSB* 119–121 (1948) and *U.S. Int. Conf. 1947–1948*, D.S. Pub. No. 3443, pp. 200–204. On Aug. 30, 1957, the President ratified an amendment to Regulation 30 of Chapter III of the convention, circulated by the United Kingdom, permitting use of inflatable life rafts as an alternative to the other apparatus prescribed by the convention. 37 *DSB* 509 (1957); 85 Cong., 1 Sess., S. Ex. M and S. Ex. Rept. No. 9 (1957).

[119] 3 *UST* 3771, *TIAS* 2507.

[120] Safety of Life at Sea: Financial Support of the North Atlantic Ice Patrol, agreement done at Washington, Jan. 4, 1956, 7 *UST* 1969; *TIAS* 3597.

Transportation and Communications since World War II

Among the instruments included in the Final Act of the conference,[121] the Regulations for Preventing Collisions at Sea and two of the twenty-three recommendations should be specially noted. These regulations or "Rules of the Road," dealt with separately from the convention, are now made applicable to seaplanes. The government of the United Kingdom was invited to circulate the new rules and then, after it had received substantial agreement thereto, to fix a date of effectiveness for them, giving all states at least one year's notice of this date. Agreement was speedily achieved and notice was given that the date of effectiveness would be January 1, 1954.[122] In anticipation of this general acceptance, Congress adopted the revised regulations in a statute of October 11, 1951, and authorized the President to proclaim them when the date of effectiveness became known.[123] This the President did on August 15, 1953.[124]

In order to assure sufficient and efficient manning of all ships subject to the new regime, the conference urged in Recommendation No. 16 that the ILO and the new IMCO, both of which organizations have some jurisdiction in the matter, should "arrange for a joint examination of this problem" in order to achieve clear definition of their respective jurisdictions and to discover whether universal minimum manning standards will be necessary.

Finally, among the several recommendations dealing with electronic navigation aids is one, No. 20, "adopting the specifications for certain characteristics of radar agreed upon at the International Meeting on Marine Radio Aids to Navigation at New York City and New London, Connecticut, in 1947 and urging governments to encourage the development, manufacture, and installation of radar aboard their national vessels." [125]

[121] *Report, op. cit.*, pp. 164–194.
[122] 28 *DSB* 220–221 (1953); text of agreement, 4 *UST* 2956, *TIAS* 2899. An error in the French text was corrected by a special agreement under notice from the United Kingdom, accepted by the United States Sept. 22, 1955, 7 *UST* 1080, *TIAS* 3590.
[123] 65 *Stat.* 406–420; amended to correct typographical errors, act of June 26, 1953, 67 *Stat.* 83.
[124] No. 3030, 18 *Federal Register* 4983, 68 *Stat.* (2) c5–c17.
[125] Bradley, *op. cit.*, p. 120. For a brief account of this meeting of IMMRAN, see *U.S. Int. Conf. 1946–1947*, D.S. Pub. No. 3081, pp. 173–180; for a full account, see *International Meeting on Marine Radio Aids to Navigation: Proceedings and Related Documents*, D.S. Pub. No. 3060. For brief account of a prior meeting on the same subject, in London, in 1946, see *U.S. Int. Conf. 1945–1946*, D.S. Pub. No. 2817,

The United States and the Treaty Law of the Sea

The Andrea Doria-Stockholm Collision, 1956. Tragic heroes, it is said, contribute to their own destruction because of some inner defect in an otherwise noble character. Under the impact of events from without, the defect contributes to disaster from within. So it is with ships. In law they are persons; for seafaring or sealoving people, they are personalities, with individual traits, capable of great deeds and tragic deaths. It was so with the *Titanic,* a noble ship, but defective withal, because of inadequate lifeboats, structural weaknesses, faulty manning, poor communications, and poorer judgment at the bridge. Under the impact of the external ice, it died, and with it some 1500 trusting human beings. Reform speedily followed disaster: the Ice Patrol was established immediately and the epochal Safety of Life at Sea Conference was held soon thereafter.

In spite of the multitudinous rules and requirements of the international regime and of national legislation, staggering disasters still occasionally occur. The increased speed of vessels nowadays, like that of motor cars, increases geometrically the damage in collision with anything. So it was in the case of the collision of the Swedish motor vessel *Stockholm,* en route from New York to Sweden, with the Italian steamship *Andrea Doria,* coming into New York, on July 25, 1956. They collided approximately one mile south of Nantucket Lightship. The Italian vessel sank with a loss of fifty lives. The excellent radio communications and the prompt response of vessels in the immediate vicinity avoided greater loss of life.

Two days later, the House of Representatives authorized an investigation into the disaster by the Committee on Merchant Marine and Fisheries. A distinguished special staff of maritime experts made the study. The report of the experts, filed by the committee on January 3,

---

pp. 47–48. For a description of the aids, written in layman's language, see *Ocean Electronic Navigational Aids,* rev. ed. (1949), U.S. Coast Guard, CG 157-1 (1949). As part of the Atlantic defense system, the United States has from time to time by means of treaties received permission to establish long-range navigational stations in neighboring countries, e.g., with Canada, agreement providing for transfer of Loran stations in Newfoundland to the Canadian government, effected by exchange of notes, signed at Ottawa, June 26 and 30, 1953, 4 *UST* 2174, *TIAS* 2865, and agreement relating to construction and operation of a Loran station on Cape Christian, Baffin Island, effected by exchange of notes, signed at Ottawa, May 1 and 3, 1954, 5 *UST* 1459, *TIAS* 3019; with the Dominican Republic, agreement providing for the establishment of Loran transmitting stations, signed at Washington, March 19, 1957, 8 *UST* 329, *TIAS* 3780.

Transportation and Communications since World War II

1957,[126] offered certain conclusions with respect to compliance by the two vessels with the 1948 convention and certain recommendations with respect to improvements in the safety regime. The experts were assisted by the record then being taken in the pretrial hearings in the Federal District Court for New York [127] and by some plans and pertinent data of the *Andrea Doria*.

Briefly, it was found that the *Andrea Doria* had a valid safety certificate issued by the Italian government. It had been classed by the Italian Classification Society, the American Bureau of Shipping,[128] and Lloyd's Register of Shipping. It had met "the requirements of the American Bureau of Shipping with respect to the sufficiency of the hull structure and the reliability of its machinery." "The American Bureau of Shipping makes no findings regarding stability and compartmentalization as a condition of class, as such features normally are administered by the Government authorities." The Italian society, Registro Italiano Navale, had approved the stability report.

The role of these national classification societies in these safety matters needs a word of explanation. They are "instrumentalities for the self-regulation of the world shipping industry and are particularly concerned with the structural sufficiencies of hulls and the reliability of machinery. Shipbuilders, shipowners, and underwriters are protected by the checks and balances provided in their mutual interest." [129] The successive Safety of Life at Sea conventions since 1914 have permitted the governments

---

[126] *Safety of Life at Sea Study*, 84 Cong., 2 Sess., H. Rept. No. 2969, 13 pp. The special staff consisted of E. L. Cochrane, vice-admiral, USN (retired); H. L. Seward, emeritus professor of mechanical and marine engineering, Yale University; H. C. Shepheard, rear admiral, USCG (retired); and E. M. Webster, commodore, USCG (retired). See also *Safety of Life at Sea*, 85 Cong., 1 Sess., H. Rept. No. 1179 (1957), and *Hearings* by the House Committee on Merchant Marine and Fisheries, on *Safety of Life at Sea [radio telephone bridge-to-bridge and bridge-to-shore communications]*, 85 Cong., 1 Sess., July 31, 1957, 85 Cong., 2 Sess., Jan. 17, 1958; and *Study of Need for Shipboard Automatic Radiotelegraph Call Selectors* etc., 85 Cong., 1 Sess., H. Doc. No. 117 (1957).

[127] To furnish a basis for settling the numerous private suits for damage which were filed against both steamship companies. See "Doria Settlement Reported; Lines Plan Pool for Claims," *N.Y.T.*, Jan. 22, 1957, and "Damage-Suit Deadline Passes for Claims in Doria Collision," *N.Y.T.*, Feb. 16, 1957.

[128] A fine account of the American society appears in *American Bureau of Shipping: Seventy-Fifth Anniversary 1862–1937* (1937). In Feb. 1957, the American society contracted "to survey and inspect during construction the new passenger ship the Italian Line has ordered as a replacement for the *Andrea Doria*." The Italian society and Lloyd's Register of Shipping "will also be asked to survey and class the vessel." *N.Y.T.*, Feb. 26, 1957.

[129] Committee Report, *op. cit.*, p. 6.

party to them to utilize the services of these national associations for the purpose of surveying some aspects of a new ship, the government bureaus reserving to themselves the inspection of other aspects, both operations seeking to assure conformity of the vessel with the standards laid down by national law and the international regime. The conventions regularly add the caveat, however, that "in every case the Government concerned fully guarantees the completeness and efficiency of the inspection and survey." [130]

Nevertheless, analysis of the data available and evidence of the performance of the ship after the collision showed, according to the experts, "that the *Andrea Doria* met the subdivision requirements of the 1948 Safety of Life at Sea Convention by a very narrow margin," and that she was probably not adequately ballasted at the moment of impact.

One observation of the report suggests the desirability of comment on American ship standards. Said the report: "While facts at hand are not sufficient to state categorically that the *Andrea Doria* would not have sunk had she had the stability at the time of the collision required by the 1948 convention, it seems quite certain (although the calculations to prove this have not been made), that had she been in compliance with the United States standards, she would have survived." Traditionally American standards of construction, at least since 1914, have been higher than those prescribed in the international conventions, which perforce seek the optimum acceptable to the great maritime community. These superior standards, demanded by the American traveling public, the seafarers' unions, and Congress, are imposed on American vessels by national law. They help to explain why it is expensive to maintain an American merchant marine in competition with some lower-standard foreign merchant marines.[131] Both Sweden and Italy are, of course, parties to the 1948 convention. Neither, however, was a party to the IMCO convention at the time of the collision. Italy deposited its ratification of the IMCO convention on January 28, 1957.[132]

The report of the experts then discussed the difficulties encountered in using sea-water ballast in empty fuel tanks. Discharge of such water in

---

[130] E.g., 1948 Convention, Regulations, Ch. I, Reg. 6.

[131] See "U.S. Rules Sought for Foreign Ships," *N.Y.T.*, Jan. 5, 1957, and "U.S. Ships Safer, House Unit Hears," *N.Y.T.*, Aug. 4, 1957.

[132] 36 *DSB* 380 (1957). For the status of the convention as of Jan. 1957, see UN ECOSOC, Transport and Communications Commission, *Report of Eighth Session*, p. 4, E/2948, E/CN.2/187 (1957).

the wrong places may lead to prosecution for oil pollution; failure to fill such tanks may produce instability, unless provision is made for carrying solid ballast or tanks are installed which can be filled with sea water as the fuel tanks are emptied. The evidence about the condition of the tanks aboard the *Andrea Doria* lies at the bottom of the sea, but the evidence concerning the behavior of the vessel after impact was such as to create the suspicion in the minds of the experts that the vessel at the crucial moment was not properly ballasted in accordance with the requirements of the 1948 convention.

"Radio communication surrounding the distress case was carried out in accordance with prescribed International Radio Regulations and practice" and the response of vessels in the vicinity was excellent. But "the *Andrea Doria-Stockholm* collision would have been prevented if the information provided by radar had been properly used."

Finally, with respect to sealanes: "neither the Swedish American Line nor the Italian Line is a party to the North Atlantic Track Agreement. If the ships had been following the recommended sealanes in the area east of Ambrose Lightship in the approaches to New York, the collision would not have happened, for the Stockholm was nearly on the westbound track and some twenty miles north of the recommended track for vessels eastbound to Europe." The report paid tribute to the sealanes thus: "The United States Government has recognized the value and importance of these lanes. United States laws and regulations require adherence by United States passenger vessels to the provisions pertaining to sealanes found in the 1948 convention and fines are provided for noncompliance." As "monitor" of the sealanes under the convention, the United States thus endeavors to keep "clean hands."

According to the report of the experts, then, both vessels were at fault in one way or another. In sum, although all the facts on the collision had not been developed and some may possibly never be ascertained, enough were produced "to raise serious questions as to whether the ships were being operated in accordance with the precepts of good seamanship and the provisions of the International Convention for Safety of Life at Sea; and whether these provisions are adequate as to construction standards and also as to the Regulations for Preventing Collision at sea. There is also the question of the observance of sealanes."

Looking toward improvement in the regime for safety, the report made seven recommendations, three for early action and four to be included in any program for a long-range study of safety at sea. For immediate purposes it recommended: "greater observance of the recognized routes across the North Atlantic; reevaluation of the standards of subdivision, damage stability and ballasting, with the view to the development of realistic provisions for international adoption; and adequate training for deck officers, including a requirement for certification of such officers as radar observers." For long-range study the report recommended: "installation of bridge-to-bridge direct radio telephonic communication; a system of continuing and comprehensive studies by Federal agencies of radio communications in distress cases; the establishment of a mechanism for coordination in the study, development, and application of radio and electronic devices and systems; and effective provisions for the application of regulation 20 of Chapter I of the 1948 Convention . . . [which obligates each Government to investigate casualties occurring to ships flying its flag] particularly the principle laid down for the dissemination of lessons from casualties."

That there was not greater loss of life may be attributed to the splendidly coordinated search and rescue service operating out of New York, which admirably met the standards advocated in the Coordination Report of 1948, mentioned above.[133] In the words of the report of the experts:

Regardless of statutes or treaties, it is traditional for sailormen to answer a call of distress at sea. This case was no exception.

Admiration must be had for the very excellent work performed by all assisting vessels, from Government and merchant marine. Without detracting from the performance of any other vessel, their officers or crews, the exploits of the steamship *Cape Ann,* steamship *Ile de France,* and the U.S.N.S. *Private William H. Thomas* were outstanding. Fortunately, they were close by and were large vessels with ample facilities and lifeboats to effect rescue of the hundreds of passengers and crew.

There is presently a national search and rescue plan under which the United States Coast Guard is the coordinator for the area in which the collision occurred, and had the duty of integrating and organizing the available forces, Government and non-Government, in a cooperative search and rescue network.

In the Coast Guard Coordination Center in New York, communication is provided to the various rescue and communication facilities, the reported positions of ships in the North Atlantic are plotted, thus facili-

[133] Above, p. 228.

tating the dispatch of appropriate rescue units by sea and air as required by the nature of the emergency. In this situation, in addition to keeping in touch with the various ships approaching the scene and with shore units, the Coast Guard also dispatched a number of its own vessels and a Coast Guard helicopter. The latter together with an Air Force helicopter, which had also been dispatched, were instrumental in removing seriously injured to shore.

The plan functioned successfully on the night of July 25, 1956.

As a result of the collision and in response to the questions raised in the report of the experts, Congress urged the department of state to press for a revision of the 1948 Safety of Life at Sea Convention in 1959 to secure better international standards and better compliance therewith. After making inquiries of the leading maritime powers, the department reported that the earliest feasible date appeared to be 1960 but that meanwhile, with the IMCO convention having gone into effect in March 1958, the Maritime Safety Committee of that organization could give attention to the problems raised by the collision in the year 1959.[134]

Carriage of Dangerous Goods. The London Conference of 1948 was also concerned about the danger to ships, particularly cargo vessels and their crews, arising from the carriage of explosive, corrosive, inflammable, gaseous, poisonous, and other similarly dangerous goods. Accordingly, Regulation 3 of Chapter VI of the regulations of the convention defined the term "dangerous goods" and prohibited their carriage except in accordance with the regulations. These regulations required, among other things, that there be "special approved safety measures" for explosives, "adequate precautions" against fire and explosions, properly marked packages, and a special list among the ship's papers setting forth the dangerous goods on board.

In Recommendation 22, the conference further recognized that there should be a special international agreement to secure uniformity in the safety precautions applicable to the carriage of such goods. Pressure of time prevented the conference itself from elaborating such an agreement. It therefore recommended that the Maritime Safety Committee of IMCO undertake the task of promoting the adoption of a convention on the subject.[135]

[134] *Safety of Life at Sea Study*, 85 Cong., 2 Sess., H. Rept. No. 1675 (April 30, 1958).
[135] *Report of U.S. Delegation, op. cit.*, p. 194.

The United States and the Treaty Law of the Sea

Pending the establishment of IMCO, the Transport and Communications Commission of ECOSOC has given the problem attention, though in the wider context of transport by any means over land or sea or by air, and including the transport of perishable biological substances, infectious substances, and radioactive substances, particularly radioisotopes. To this end, WHO, UNESCO, UPU, ICAO, and ILO have collaborated with the commission's committee of experts on the several aspects of the problem. One of the problems, for example, is the devising of a small group of universally acceptable symbols to designate different kinds of dangerous stuffs, easily recognizable and understood by workers handling the materials. Among the six or seven symbols being considered are an "O" surmounted by a flame, for oxidizing substances, the St. Andrew's cross "for use with goods presenting a comparatively slight danger," and a "withered hand" for corrosives. Discussions are continuing on this subject of symbols.

Among the national regulations considered for the purpose of devising international norms are those of the United States Interstate Commerce Commission and the United Kingdom Regulations for Sea-borne Transport. Since the greatest danger arising out of transport of explosive and similar goods anywhere by any means is to the workers handling the goods, the ILO's group of experts on dangerous substances has collaborated closely with the committee of experts of the Transport and Communications Commission. Furthermore, since most of the transport of dangerous goods takes place by sea, it is essential that proper correlation of efforts be maintained between the Safety of Life at Sea regime and the committee. To this end, the United Kingdom, as the government charged with the performance of clearinghouse functions under the 1948 convention, maintains liaison with the committee until the permanent bureau under IMCO is established. The UN committee recommended in 1956 that, pending the conclusion of an international agreement on the transport of dangerous goods by any means, a small committee of experts be set up in the Secretariat of the United Nations to keep up to date the lists of dangerous substances and to seek coordination of effort by various international agencies in safeguarding the transport of them.[136]

[136] *UN Yearbook, 1951,* pp. 440–441; *Report on its Second Session, Submitted by the Committee of Experts on the Transport of Dangerous Goods,* Oct. 17, 1956, E/CN.2/165, E/CN.2/CONF.4/1. See also UN ECOSOC, Transport and Communications Commission, *Report of Eighth Session, op. cit.,* pp. 10–12.

Labor at Sea

At every turn, then, in dealing with safety at sea, one encounters the officers and crews who are essential to the safety of passengers and cargo and who, themselves, must be assured of optimum safety and welfare. Both the International Labor Organization and the International Telecommunications Union contribute to these desiderata.

The intimate relation of the International Labor Organization to commercial use of the high seas has already been indicated for the interwar period. As in the case of others of the great regimes, World War II restricted and impeded but did not terminate the work of the organization. In anticipation of the end of hostilities and the formation of a new universal general organization to succeed the League of Nations, steps were taken during and soon after the war to extend the scope of the ILO, to sever its relation to the League of Nations, and to bring it into relation to the United Nations as a specialized agency. The twenty-sixth session of the International Labor Conference in Philadelphia in the spring of 1944 adopted a "Declaration" emphasizing social in addition to economic objectives for the organization.[137] At the twenty-ninth session of the conference, in Montreal in 1946, two instruments were adopted to which the United States became a party — one, an amended constitution for the organization,[138] and the other, a convention dealing with the final articles of prior labor conventions, substituting the United Nations for the League of Nations in various relations.[139]

Four matters of particular concern for this study of the sea, which fall within the competence of the ILO, can be indicated for this post-World War II period: the adoption of a new group of maritime labor conventions; extension of interest to the lot of fishermen; inquiry into the practices associated with the Panamanian registration of merchant vessels; and cooperation with the World Health Organization.

---

[137] "The Twenty-Sixth Session of the International Labor Conference, Philadelphia, April to May 1944," reprinted from *International Labour Review*, Vol. L, No. 1, July 1944, ILO (1945); *U.S. Int. Conf. 1941–1945*, D.S. Pub. No. 2665, pp. 105–108. Text of Declaration, *Lasting Peace the I.L.O. Way*, ILO (1951), pp. 103–105.

[138] Adopted Oct. 9, 1946, 62 *Stat.* (3) 3485, *TIAS* 1868. The proceedings of the several meetings of the various organs of ILO which dealt with this expansion and transition process can be traced in summary process in *U.S. Int. Conf. 1941–1945, passim; ibid., 1945–1946*, D.S. Pub. No. 2817, *passim; ibid., 1946–1947, passim*. The constitution was amended at Geneva, June 25, 1953, to increase the number of members of the governing body from 32 to 40 and the constituent groups pro rata. 7 *UST* 245, *TIAS* 3500.

[139] Adopted Oct. 9, 1946, 62 *Stat.* (2) 1672, *TIAS* 1810.

New Conventions. The twenty-eighth session of the conference, in Seattle in 1946, was devoted entirely to matters maritime. It produced nine new conventions, four recommendations, and nine resolutions. The conventions dealt with (1) food and catering (ships' crews); (2) certification of ships' cooks; (3) social security; (4) seafarers' pensions; (5) paid vacations (seafarers); (6) medical examination (seafarers); (7) certification of able seamen; (8) accommodation of crews; and (9) wages, hours of work and manning (sea).[140]

In compliance with the obligation in Article 19 (5) of the ILO Constitution, President Truman transmitted all of the instruments to Congress and requested advice and consent of the Senate to ratification of eight of the conventions. He pointed out that while "many of the provisions of the . . . Conventions and Recommendations fall short of standards already in effect in the American merchant marine," general acceptance of them would "result in definite progress being made where that progress is most needed." Any such progress would "benefit the competitive position of American seafarers and shipowners."[141] The Senate approved four of the conventions,[142] but by 1958 only one of them, that dealing with the certification of able seamen, had come into force for the United States.[143]

Welfare of Fishermen. During the interwar period, the ILO had "devoted but limited attention to the interests of fishermen." Hence a resolution (No. 8) of the Seattle Conference requested that the necessary studies and preparations be made "with a view to considering the possibility of the adoption of an International Fisherman's Charter setting out, on the lines of the International Seafarers' Charter, minimum standards of wages and working conditions, continuity of employment, social legislation, etc., for the industry."[144] A remarkable survey

---

[140] *Twenty-Eighth (Maritime) Session of the International Labor Conference, Seattle, Washington, June 6 to June 29, 1946, Report of the United States Government Delegate,* D.S. Pub. No. 2854 (1947); *U.S. Int. Conf. 1945–1946,* pp. 124–128; and *International Labour Conference, Twenty-Eighth Session, Seattle, 1946, Record of Proceedings,* ILO (1946).

[141] President's Message, June 23, 1947, 17 *DSB* 32–33 (1947). See also message of April 8, 1947, 16 *DSB* 726–727 (1947), withdrawing a number of obsolete multilateral conventions from consideration of the Senate, among them several dealing with the sea, including a number of old ILO conventions, and a message of April 22, 1958, to a similar effect, 38 *DSB* 841 (1958).

[142] 27 *DSB* 589 (1952).

[143] Entered into force with respect to the United States, April 9, 1954, 5 *UST* 605, TIAS 2949.

[144] *Proceedings, op. cit.,* p. 331.

Transportation and Communications since World War II

of the fishing industry has, accordingly, since been prepared, in which valuable data supplied by the United States may be found.[145] In 1955 the governing body of the International Labor Office approved the conclusions of a Committee of Experts on Conditions of Work in the Fishing Industry, which had met in Geneva the previous year, and authorized the International Labor Office to continue the study of various aspects of the subject.[146] No doubt these efforts will result one day in the adoption for the first time of a universal code devoted to the welfare of the men who catch the fish for others.

Flight from High Standard Flags.[147] During the interwar period, the International Transport Workers' Federation complained about the "transfer of ships from the flag of one country to the flag of another country with lower standards" of seafarers' employment. In 1948 the "I.T.W.F. decided to threaten a boycott of certain ships which had been transferred to the flag of Panama. The I.T.W.F. alleged that many of the ships thus transferred were obsolete, and that the motive for such transfers was to evade taxation, currency regulations, safety standards and social and labour standards." [148] Subsequently, the new flags so acquired were called "flags of convenience."

Rejecting the allegation, the Panama government requested the ILO to investigate the charges. This was done by a committee of enquiry in 1949. Eschewing any "attempt to establish the motives for which ships are transferred to the Panama flag," the committee detailed the many respects in which the legislation and administrative practices of Panama fell below adequate and accepted standards.[149] The governing body of the ILO issued a statement in 1950, in effect urging the government of Panama to reform its laws and practices in accord with the criticisms made by the committee of enquiry.[150] On August 5, 1957, an arrangement was effected between Panama and the United States permitting "Panamanian nautical inspectors to board vessels of Panamanian registry while

---

[145] *Conditions of Work in the Fishing Industry*, ILO (1952). The American data are found *passim*.

[146] *U.S. Int. Conf. 1954–1955*, D.S. Pub. No. 6335, p. 171.

[147] On the general subject of the nationality of vessels, see the excellent monograph by Robert Rienow, *The Test of the Nationality of a Merchant Vessel* (1937); Briggs, *op. cit.*, pp. 330–333; *Laws Concerning the Nationality of Ships*, ST/LEG/SER.B/5, UN (1955); *Reference Guide to the Report of the International Law Commission*, A/C.6/L.378 Oct. 25, 1956, pp. 96–104.

[148] *Conditions in Ships Flying the Panama Flag*, ILO (1950), p. 1.

[149] *Ibid.*, pp. 37–40.

[150] *Ibid.*, pp. 86–87.

such vessels are within Canal Zone waters for the purpose of ascertaining whether there has been compliance with Panamanian maritime and labor laws applicable to such vessels." The inspection functions are restricted to thirteen stipulated categories of legal obligations of the vessels, including their possession of the several types of certificates required under the Safety of Life at Sea and the Load Line conventions. This *modus operandi* is subject to review at the end of one year.[151]

The situation is very serious, generally deleterious, and still unsolved. Other minuscule states, historically disassociated with any extensive merchant marine, such as Liberia, Honduras, and Costa Rica, have joined the parade of inviting the registration of foreign shipping on easy terms and to the almost painless expansion of their national exchequers. In 1955, Panama, with 3,923,000 gross tons registered under its flag, was exceeded in tonnage only by the United States, Great Britain, and Norway. In 1956, Panama yielded fourth place to Liberia, which since World War II, starting with practically no merchant marine of its own, had registered under its flag 3,997,000 gross tons. "The popularity of the Liberian flag is attributable to the fact that registration fees and the annual tonnage tax not only are low but are guaranteed against any increase for a period of twenty years from the date of initial registration. The only fees imposed by the Government are $1.20 on each net ton of a vessel, representing initial and administrative fees, and an annual tax of ten cents per net ton." [152] Such competition with other marines required to meet stiff national exactions is, of course, destructive of national standards, international norms, shipping conference rate schedules, and the welfare of officers and crews. It would be interesting to see whither these vessels would flee in the event of a naval war involving their flag state.

[151] Inspection of Panamanian Vessels in the Canal Zone, effected by exchange of notes, signed at Panama, Aug. 5, 1957. *TIAS* 3893. See also *N.Y.T.*, Aug. 6, 18, 1957.

[152] "Liberian 'Fleet' Growing Rapidly," *N.Y.T.*, April 8, 1956. See also "Ship Flag Changes May Hurt Market," *N.Y.T.*, June 5, 1955; "'Runaway' Ships Targets of Union," *N.Y.T.*, June 24, 1955. For United States policy and practice with respect to transfers of American merchant shipping to foreign registry, see annual reports of the Federal Maritime Board and Maritime Administration and *Review of Vessel Transfer Activities: History and Policies Relating to Transfer of United States Merchant Ships to Foreign Ownership and/or Registry*, Department of Commerce, Maritime Administration (March 1957); see also *N.Y.T.*, Nov. 6, 1956, Aug. 22, 1957, and April 26, 1958. And for a discussion of the complexities in law created by such registrations, see the pioneering opinion of Judge William B. Herlands in Markakis v. Liberian Mparmpa Christos, decided March 27, 1958, in the federal district court, S.D., N.Y., 161 *F. Supp.* 487; *N.Y.T.*, March 28, April 7, 1958.

Transportation and Communications since World War II

The International Law Commission of the United Nations has studied the problem of diversity in registration laws since its inception. Article 29 of its 1956 report reads:

Each State shall fix the conditions for the grant of its nationality to ships, for the registration of ships in its territory, and for the right to fly its flag. Ships have the nationality of the State whose flag they are entitled to fly. Nevertheless, for purposes of recognition of the national character of the ship by other States, there must exist a genuine link between the State and the ship.

In its commentary, the ILC further declared:

Each State lays down the conditions on which ships may fly its flag. Obviously the State enjoys complete liberty in the case of ships owned by it or ships which are the property of a nationalized company. With regard to other ships, the State must accept certain restrictions. As in the case of the grant of nationality to persons, national legislation on the subject must not depart too far from the principles adopted by the majority of States, which may be regarded as forming part of international law. Only on that condition will the freedom granted to States not give rise to abuse and to friction with other States. With regard to the national element required for permission to fly the flag, a great many systems are possible, but there must be a minimum national element. . . . The grant of its flag to a ship cannot be a mere administrative formality, with no accompanying guarantee that the ship possess a real link with its new State. The jurisdiction of the State over ships, and the control it should exercise in conformity with article 34 of these articles [which obligates each state to enforce international standards relating to safety at sea], can only be effective where there exists in fact a relationship between the State and the ship other than mere registration or the mere grant of a certificate of registry.[153]

The UN Conference on the Law of the Sea[154] which met in Geneva in the spring of 1958 examined the whole problem of "flags of convenience" and the proposal of the International Law Commission that there be a "genuine link" and a "minimum national element" as a prerequisite for registration. The conclusions of the conference will be discussed later.

United Nations Flag Ships. Though not germane to this problem of "flight from high standards," it is of interest to note that the International Law Commission in its 1956 report expressed an opinion that, since "the legal system of the flag State applies to the ship authorized to fly the

[153] *Report, op. cit.*, pp. 24–26.
[154] "Proposed U.N. Conference on Law of the Sea," with text of the General Assembly resolution, A/C.6/L.398 adopted on Dec. 20, 1956, 36 *DSB* 60–67 (1957).

The United States and the Treaty Law of the Sea

flag," and since the United Nations is not a "state," "the flag of the United Nations or of another international organization cannot be assimilated to the flag of a State." The ILC therefore suggested that consideration be given to the possibility that where it was desirable to have vessels operating under the aegis of the United Nations, a general agreement be concluded among the members which would "recognize a special United Nations registration entitling the ship to fly the United Nations flag and to special protection by the United Nations." The United Nations could then further make a special agreement with one or more member states by which such states "would allow the ships concerned to fly their flag in combination with the United Nations flag," thus assimilating such ships to their own for the purpose of meeting the obligations and securing the protection of the various international agreements relating to navigation.[155] In 1955 a fleet of ten fishing trawlers built with the aid of the United Nations Korean Reconstruction Agency, as part of the program to reconstruct the fishing industry of the Republic of Korea, flew the United Nations flag, in company with the Republic's flag, as a first instance of this possibility.[156]

Further, in passing, it is not generally known that in one of the committees at the San Francisco Conference in 1945 which framed the Charter a suggestion was made to authorize the United Nations to adopt a flag, one of the arguments in support of its being precisely this possibility that the United Nations might wish in the future to have ships of its own. When views were expressed that the report of the committee, which was dealing with privileges and immunities of the United Nations, had already gone into sufficient detail and that inclusion of such a provision might lead to accusations in some quarters that the Charter was creating a superstate, the matter was dropped.[157] Later, however, the exigencies of the Greek border troubles forced the United Nations to convert its emblem of San Francisco days into a flag for itself to identify its missions in the field. In 1947 it adopted a code for the proper use and display of the flag.[158] Thus was the United Nations flag developed.

[155] *Report, op. cit.*, p. 25. See also *The Right of International Organizations to Sail Vessels under their Flags*, by J. P. A. François, Special Rapporteur, A/CN.4/103, May 8, 1956.
[156] "The First Ships to Sail Under the United Nations Flag," *United Nations Review*, Vol. 1, No. 11, May 1955, p. 15.
[157] Reiff, "Work of the United Nations 'Legal Committees,'" 15 *DSB* 3, 6 (1946).
[158] *The United Nations Flag Code and Regulations, As Amended by [the Secretary-General on] November 11, 1952*, UN (1954). Cartographers will be amused to find

Transportation and Communications since World War II

Hygiene of Seafarers. Evidencing once again the increasing interrelation of these postwar specialized agencies, particularly with respect to use of the sea, was the establishment in 1951 of a Joint ILO-WHO Committee on Hygiene of Seafarers. It has considered such important topics as the sending of medical advice to ships at sea (with the cooperation of the International Telecommunication Union and the International Radio-Medical Centre at Rome), the examination of seafarers to detect tuberculosis, recommendations to governments concerning the contents of medical chests on board ship, the maritime aspects of the prevention and treatment of venereal diseases, medical services for foreign seafarers, including hospitalization and medical clinics in ports, and medical records and reporting.[159]

ILO Maritime Session, 1958. Another large-scale maritime session of the ILO General Conference, the first since that held in Seattle in 1946, met in Geneva in the spring of 1958 hard upon the conclusion of the UN Conference on Law of the Sea. A Preparatory Technical Maritime Conference of ILO met in London in the fall of 1956 to prepare texts and documents on the following subjects: "general revision of the ILO convention on wages, hours of work, and manning at sea; engagement of seafarers through regularly established employment offices;[160] flag transfer in relation to social conditions and safety; contents of medicine chests on board ship and medical advice by radio to ships at sea; jurisdiction over the suspension of officers' certificates of competency; and reciprocal national identity cards."[161]

Move in United States to Withdraw from ILO. Certain segments of business in the United States, represented in the United States Chamber

---

in the UN records the efforts to present a projection of the globe in such a way as to show all of the land masses and members, as now represented, instead of the projection used at San Francisco, which cut off part of South America.

[159] *Fifth Report of the International Labour Organization to the United Nations,* ILO (1951), p. 96. 11 *Industry and Labor* 456–459 (1954), and *Joint ILO/WHO Committee on the Hygiene of Seafarers,* 2d Report, WHO Technical Report Series No. 92 (1955).

[160] For the views of American labor, see Joseph Curran, *Merchant Marine Policies, Practices, and Problems of Labor, Management and Government, Statement of CIO Maritime Committee Before Merchant Marine and Fisheries Committee, House of Representatives* (1955), and *This is the NMU: A Picture History of the National Maritime Union* (n.d.), pp. 99–103.

[161] "ILO Preparatory Technical Maritime Conference," 35 *DSB* 526–527 (1956). For an excellent review of the work of the ILO relating to maritime matters in the period 1946–1957 see *Report of the Director-General* for the 41st [Maritime] Session 1958 (1957).

of Commerce and the National Association of Manufacturers, have resented the presence of the Soviet Union and its republics, Byelorussia and the Ukraine, in the ILO since 1954. The Soviets, together with the satellite communist states, it is contended, make a "mockery" of the tripartite arrangement of supposedly independent government, employers, and employees representation. In 1954 and 1955 the employers group in the ILO general conferences of those years refused to seat the "employers" delegates from those states on their committees except as "deputy" delegates without a right to vote.[162] These business groups in the United States also object to what they regard as the tendency toward "statism and socialism" in the organization as well as an alleged interference in the internal affairs of the member states. Other evidence of dissatisfaction with the United States participation in the ILO was expressed in the Senate in 1956 in connection with the Forced Labor Convention which a joint committee of ECOSOC and ILO had elaborated and which was on the agenda for discussion by ILO in 1956.[163] On the other hand, the employer delegation to the 1956 ILO conference, all nominated by the N.A.M. and formally appointed by President Eisenhower, in a unanimous report opposed withdrawal of the United States. Labor generally and other business groups in various parts of the United States also insist on continued participation.

In these circumstances, the Departments of State, Commerce and Labor set up in June 1956 an advisory committee of distinguished public members, headed by Dr. Joseph E. Johnson of the Carnegie Endowment for International Peace, to examine the role of the United States in ILO and make recommendations for increased effectiveness in American participation. That committee reported in January 1957. It made numerous concrete suggestions designed to improve American influence in ILO and to remedy some of the complaints directed at the functioning of ILO.[164] A joint report of the Departments of State, Commerce, and Labor in February 1957 endorsed generally the views and conclusions of the Johnson report.[165] The United States, caught for a while between its

[162] *U.S. Int. Conf. 1953–1954*, pp. 167–168; *ibid., 1954–1955*, pp. 177–178.
[163] 102 *Congressional Record* 6335–6346, April 16, 1956, and *ibid.*, 6629–6645, April 19, 1956; *US Participation in UN, Report by the President to Congress for the year 1954*, D.S. Pub. No. 5769, pp. 134–137.
[164] Text, courtesy of Carnegie Endowment for International Peace; summary, *N.Y.T.*, Jan. 17, 1957.
[165] *Measures to be Taken by the Departments of State, Commerce, and Labor to Improve U.S. Participation in the ILO*, mimeo., Feb. 28, 1957.

Transportation and Communications since World War II

historic policy of opposition to the use of forced labor and the demands of domestic groups opposed to the ILO, then abandoned the ambiguous position it had taken in the 1956 ILO meetings with respect to the adoption of the Forced Labor Convention and resumed its position of forthright leadership in support of the convention in the meetings of the following year.[166]

COMMUNICATIONS

It is apparent from the discussion thus far that whithersoever one turns in use of the sea, its contents, and containers, or of the space above it, there one finds use of radio communication and radionic devices. The interrelation is vast, complex, and now inextricable. Much of that interrelation has already been indicated in discussing other aspects of the sea. It remains, however, to outline the principal features of the organizational development of the radio regime in the post-World War II period as part of the picture of the development of maritime communications generally, which includes, of course, cable and postal communication.

Telecommunications

As in the case of aviation and maritime safety, planning to meet the demands of the postwar era proceeded in the United States as early as 1943.[167] The old wireless (or since 1912, radio) regime and the regimes relating to telephone and telegraph had been conjoined into a single International Telecommunication Union at Madrid in 1932. Separate sets of regulations dealing with radio, telegraph, and telephone, respectively, annexed to the convention could be subscribed to separately. The United States, because of its continental detachment from Europe and the private ownership of its telegraph and telephone systems, did not, until recently, in 1949,[168] subscribe to any but the radio regulations. The

---

[166] E. W. Kenworthy, "I.L.O. is Gaining Prestige as a Diplomatic Weapon," *N.Y.T.*, June 2, 1957. See also *N.Y.T.*, May 13, June 8, 22, 1957.

[167] See the marvellously fine articles by Francis Colt DeWolf, "The International Control of Radiocommunications," 12 *DSB* 133–136 (1945), and "Telecommunications Tomorrow," *ibid.*, 250–252; and Harvey Otterman, "International Regulation of Radio," *ibid.*, 256–259.

[168] International Telegraph and Telephone Conference, Paris, May 18–Aug. 5, 1949, *U.S. Int. Conf. 1948–1949*, D.S. Pub. No. 3853, pp. 164–170, at pp. 166–167. Telecommunications: Telegraph Regulations (Paris Revision, 1949), with Final Protocol, Paris, Aug. 5, 1949, 2 *UST* 17, *TIAS* 2175. See discussion below relating to cables.

last prewar revision of the several sets of regulations took place at Cairo in 1938.[169]

Atlantic City Revision, 1947. The framework and guiding principles for the postwar reorganization of the telecommunication union were elaborated at Atlantic City in the summer and fall of 1947.[170] The task was of staggering proportions. It necessitated several preliminary conferences by way of preparation for the major meeting and necessitated, over several years, a series of subordinate conferences and meetings to implement the arrangements devised at Atlantic City.[171] Since many of the results of these conferences and meetings are recorded in resolutions, recommendations, *avis,* and instructions to still more specialized committees and study groups to proceed further with the tasks in hand, relatively few formally signed multipartite agreements have emanated from this process. Among the subjects assigned to study groups of particular interest in this view of the sea were tropospheric propagation, ionospheric propagation, radio time signals, and general technical questions with respect to maritime matters. The relation of sunspots and the eleven-year solar cycle to the assignment of high-frequency broadcasting channel hours to various countries were discussed in a special conference at Florence and Rapallo in 1950.[172]

The 1947 basic convention provided for clear-cut organizational and functional improvements in the union. Thus eight principal organs were carefully delineated (Arts. 4–11): (1) a plenipotentiary conference meeting normally every five years; (2) separate administrative conferences, one for each set of regulations, meeting *regularly* every five years at the same place and date as the plenipotentiary conferences and

---

[169] Telecommunication; General Radio Regulations, etc., signed at Cairo, April 8, 1938, 54 *Stat.* 1417, *TS* 948. For summation of developments up to 1947, see *U.S. Int. Agencies 1946,* pp. 264–270, *U.S. Int. Org. 1949,* pp. 279–286.

[170] Telecommunication Convention, Final Protocol, and Radio Regulations, Atlantic City, Oct. 2, 1947, 63 *Stat.* (2) 1399, *TIAS* 1901. See excellent summary by Francis Colt DeWolf, "The Atlantic City Telecommunications Conference," 17 *DSB* 1033–1034, 1040–1041 (1947).

[171] Exclusive of the three conferences held in part simultaneously at Atlantic City, over thirty separate conferences on one or another aspect of radio were held in the period July 1, 1945, to June 30, 1951. Each is summarized in the volumes of *U.S. Int. Conf.* for the years concerned. Other numerous meetings and conferences have, of course, been held since. Annual summaries, *ibid.*

[172] *U.S. Int. Conf. 1949–1950,* D.S. Pub. No. 4216, pp. 156–159. For further succinct statements of international radio developments and the relation of the United States thereto, see the annual reports of the Federal Communications Commission since 1946.

extraordinary administrative conferences meeting when and if necessary; (3) an Administrative Council for the whole union, composed of eighteen members, meeting every year and as often additionally as necessary; (4) an enlarged General Secretariat; (5) a new International Frequency Registration Board consisting of experts in their individual capacity; and (6) the customary three consultative committees, one each for the fields of telegraph, telephone, and radio. In addition, as in other unions, provision is made (Art. 40) for special nonconflicting arrangements between members and (Art. 41) for regional conferences, agreements, and organizations.[173]

Article 13 of the convention makes all of the sets of regulations binding upon all the members and associate members, but the Final Protocol of Signature affords the delegations an opportunity to exempt themselves from commitment to apply one or another set. The United States, in accordance with its custom, did not in 1947 accept any obligation with respect to the telegraph, telephone, or additional radio regulations.[174] That declaration left it bound only by the convention and the general radio regulations.

As indicated above, a remarkable number of conferences dealing with one or another of the many technical, and sometimes contentious, aspects of radio regulation followed in the next few years. In several instances, long drawn-out meetings had to adjourn to the next year to afford opportunity to reconcile frustrating differences. The limitations imposed by the radio spectrum, the demands of competing countries and services, and the new increased pressures from every direction on radio as a means of communication contribute to this phenomenon of multitudinous international meetings. Fortunately, for the student of international organization, Codding has provided a remarkably clear and comprehensive exposition of these devious developments in his monograph on the International Telecommunication Union up to 1952.[175]

---

[173] E.g., Telecommunications: Agreement between the United States of America and Other American Republics, Replacing Inter-American Agreement of Jan. 26, 1940, signed at Washington, July 9, 1949, 3 *UST* 3064, *TIAS* 2489. A handy list of all telecommunication agreements to which the United States is a party is appended regularly to the annual reports of the Federal Communications Commission. They can also be checked off in the periodic editions of *Treaties in Force*, e.g., edition as of Jan. 1, 1958, D.S. Pub. No. 6626.

[174] See Final Protocol of Signature of the convention, *op. cit.*, and the President's proclamation of the convention accompanying the texts.

[175] G. A. Codding, *The International Telecommunication Union: An Experiment in International Cooperation* (1952).

The United States and the Treaty Law of the Sea

Within this larger picture of world-wide use of radio, the sea relentlessly sets up its demands. The aeronautical mobile, aeronautical radio-navigational, and the maritime mobile services compete for frequencies with the broadcasting, amateur, police, meteorological, press, governmental, public correspondence, geophysical, and other services. The United States, for example, grants licenses to oil companies and geophysical-exploration companies.[176] "Many geological stations operate in the tidelands along the Gulf of Mexico, often miles offshore." [177]

Special provision also has to be made for reports of ice conditions and other navigational hazards; for pratique, epidemiological, and weather reports; for distress, alarm, urgency, and safety signals; for time signals and notices to mariners. And further, provision must be made for intercommunication between ship-and-ship, plane-and-plane, ship-and-plane, and either ship or plane with the shore, for numerous purposes, not the least being search and rescue on the high seas. Whatever the developments on land, it may safely be hazarded that for a long time into the foreseeable future the sea will make specialized burdensome demands upon the radio regime, particularly if man's exploitation of the polar regions progresses at the accelerated pace of recent years.

Of all the unions thus far examined, the Telecommunication Union has probably the most difficult task of correlating its activities with those of other unions. Likely this is because it has control over a means of communication which is essential to the conduct of affairs of each of the other great unions. Hence the practice has arisen for the private national organizations and the private economic and scientific international organizations to seek representation in the deliberations of the several organs of the radio union as well as in those of other unions which deal with their particular subject matters. The international public unions and now the United Nations are regularly and reciprocally represented at each other's meetings. Perhaps in time, procedures can be worked out through ECOSOC to improve the effectiveness and the efficiency of this interorganizational representation. It suggests that possibly some day, in desperation to solve the various problems of interrelation occasioned by use of the sea, some "Council of the Sea" may become necessary — Pelion on Olympus, Ossa on Pelion.

Before turning to the complex problem of cables, it would be desirable

[176] *Federal Communications Commission: Twelfth Annual Report 1946*, p. 50.
[177] *Ibid.*, 13th *Report 1947*, p. 44.

Transportation and Communications since World War II

to note a few other developments in the radio regime of concern here. In accordance with the terms of the Atlantic City convention, the principal convention or constitution of the union was revised five years later, in 1952, at Buenos Aires.[178] In all important matters, the new convention is identical to the Atlantic City convention, "and the revisions contained therein principally concern administrative matters." [179] At the request of the World Health Organization, the highest priority was given to epidemiological telecommunications. Article 36 now reads: "The international telegraph and telephone services must accord absolute priority to telecommunications concerning safety of life at sea, on land, or in the air, and to epidemiological telecommunications of the World Health Organization." It will be noted that when it comes to administering the international health regulations, the underlying theory still seems to be "no impediments" and "no nonsense."

Safety on Great Lakes. In 1952, for the first time, an agreement between the United States and Canada extended to maritime traffic on the Great Lakes the appropriate requirements dealing with the use of radio for safety purposes which are found in the two great universal regimes of safety at sea and telecommunications.[180] The agreement supplements existing American law on the subject going back to 1912.[181]

Radio Amateur. Finally, it is fitting to note the role of the radio amateur, affectionately called radio "ham," in relation to the sea. From the beginning of the use of wireless, the amateur has contributed to the development of its technology and has rendered invaluable service in disasters on land and sea. Thus, the development of the use of short waves for long-distance communication is credited to the amateur.[182] It was amateurs who in 1923 first used the 100-meter wave length to talk

---

[178] Telecommunications Convention and Final Protocol, signed at Buenos Aires, Dec. 22, 1952, 6 *UST* 1213, *TIAS* 3266.

[179] J. Paul Barringer, "Revisions in International Telecommunication Convention," 32 *DSB* 442–443 (1955). See also Richard T. Black, "Telecommunications Policy and the Department of State," 30 *DSB* 83–87 (1954).

[180] Telecommunications: Promotion of Safety on the Great Lakes by Means of Radio, Agreement signed at Ottawa, Feb. 21, 1952, 3 *UST* 4926, *TIAS* 2666.

[181] *Report*, Committee on Interstate and Foreign Commerce, 83 Cong., 2 Sess., S. Rept. No. 1747, July 7, 1954.

[182] Codding, *op. cit.*, p. 115, citing Clinton B. De Soto, *Two Hundred Meters and Down: The Story of Amateur Radio* (1938), and Hiram Percy Maxim, "The Amateur in Radio," 142 *Annals of the American Academy of Political and Social Science*, Supplement 32–35 (1929); Peter B. Schroeder, "The Radio Amateur in International Legislation and Administration," 48 *A.J.I.L.* 421–433 (1954).

across the Atlantic. Amateurs, with their short-wave apparatus which works at times and under conditions when high-powered long-wave sets are ineffective, have accompanied expeditions into the Arctic and Antarctic. They have maintained contact from America with expeditions in far places when other communication has failed. In storms, floods, tidal waves, hurricanes, and under other disastrous circumstances, "hams" somehow get their messages through. They established extraordinary contacts on land and sea, from pole to pole. At times, the *Kon-Tiki* maintained contact with the rest of the world only through an amateur operator in California. On Christmas Eve of 1956 a sixteen-year-old radio "ham" of New Jersey arranged a two-way radio-telephone conversation between an American naval radioman stationed at the South Pole and his family in Massachusetts, the first such phone call from the South Pole to the United States.[183] Amateurs have a record of doing the unexpected, the valiant, sometimes, the heroic.

The first wireless conventions left the regulation of experimental and private stations largely to the national states concerned. The United States in its Radio Act of 1912 restricted amateur operators to wave lengths under 200 meters, which were then considered useless for commercial purposes. Within the next decade, however, the "hams" demonstrated how the short waves could be used for intercontinental communication. The 1927 Radio Convention (Art. 6), seeking to protect the commercial services, restricted amateur communications to messages "for which, by reason of their unimportance, recourse to the public telegraph service might not be warranted," if such communication was acceptable to the governments concerned. The Radio Regulations adopted at Madrid in 1932 (Art. 8) repeated the same rules but added a strict prohibition of the transmitting of messages emanating from third parties, unless authorized "by special arrangements between the interested countries." The United States thereupon promptly entered into three special arrangements in 1934 permitting radio communications between amateur stations on behalf of third parties, with Canada, Peru, and Chile.[184] Amateur communication with South America had always been easy and communication with amateurs in Canada was most natural. Subsequent radio regulations of the Telecommunications Union

[183] *N.Y.T.*, Dec. 25, 1956.
[184] With Canada, effective May 4, 1934, 48 *Stat.* (2) 1876, *EAS* 62; Peru, May 23, 1934, 49 *Stat.* (2) 3555, *EAS* 66; Chile, Aug. 17, 1934, 49 *Stat.* (2) 3667, *EAS* 72.

have continued the same prohibition with the same exception. The United States has accordingly since 1950 concluded additional special arrangements, similar to the earlier ones, with Costa Rica, Cuba, Ecuador, Liberia, Nicaragua, and Panama.[185]

Cables. International control of the use of cables is still peripheral. National economic and political rivalries with respect to routes, landing rights, and monopolies are, however, moderating. "Until the outbreak of the war of 1914–1918 major commercial and diplomatic disputes in what is now known as telecommunications were virtually confined to cables. . . . Soon after the restoration of peace [1919] the different cable interests were disturbed by the appearance of an enemy common to them all — wireless" and during the interwar period telecommunications battles were "fought rather between cable and wireless interests, or between rival wireless interests, than between rival cable interests."[186] In a roundabout way, then, technological progress in one form of telecommunications, radio, has forced national governments to accept international regulation with respect to another competing form, cables, which can be illustrated from the experience of the United States in the past half century or so.

After the United States became a party to the 1884 convention for the protection of submarine cables,[187] it adopted implementing legislation, applicable, as the treaty was, to the high seas.[188] This convention dealt only with the protection of cables as physical properties and protection of cable-laying operations on the high seas. In the United States, in the absence of any congressional act on the subject, the President continued to exercise authority to license the landing of cables within American jurisdiction and to condition their use.[189] That gave the agencies in charge of the conduct of foreign relations, particularly the Department of State, a tremendous weapon in the waging of the early international "telecommunications battle." In 1910 control over rates and services of cable companies operating from the United States was vested by act of

[185] With Liberia, entered into force, Jan. 11, 1951, 2 *UST* 683, *TIAS* 2223; Ecuador, March 17, 1950, 3 *UST* 2672, *TIAS* 2433; Cuba, Feb. 27, 1952, 3 *UST* 3892, *TIAS* 2520; Panama, Sept. 1, 1956, 7 *UST* 2179, *TIAS* 3617; Costa Rica, Oct. 19, 1956, 7 *UST* 2839, *TIAS* 3665; Nicaragua, Oct. 16, 1956, 7 *UST* 3159, *TIAS* 3694.
[186] Mance and Wheeler, *International Telecommunications*, p. 58.
[187] Paris, March 14, 1884, 24 *Stat.* 989; 25 *Stat.* 1424, 1425, *TS* 380, 380-1, 380-2, 380-3.
[188] Act of Feb. 29, 1888, 25 *Stat.* 41.
[189] 4 Hackworth, *Digest* 247–251; Corwin, *op. cit.*, note 118.

Congress in the Interstate Commerce Commission.[190] Otherwise American telegraph and cable companies were free to negotiate with foreign interests and administrations, sometimes with the assistance of the American diplomatic agencies, with respect to securing landing concessions and determining rates, services, and operating conditions at the other end. In practice, the American cable companies operated in accord with provisions of the St. Petersburg 1875 Telegraph Convention and its revisions. The American companies had, of course, to accept the foreign tariffs, if imposed, at the other end.[191]

World War I, resulting in the surrender of enemy-owned cables, introduced many perturbing elements into the international situation. The story is long and complicated. For present purposes it is sufficient to note that the former German cables were distributed among the victorious powers [192] and a special agreement between the United States and Japan in 1922 settled the dispute with respect to American cable interests on the Island of Yap.[193] Meanwhile, the Preliminary International Conference on Electrical Communications held in Washington in 1920 adopted certain principles relating to international cable and wireless rivalries, among them the principle "that permits for the landing of cables or the erection of wireless stations should not confer monopolies or exclusive rights of any kind." [194]

At the same conference, "an agreement between Great Britain, Italy, and the United States was also drawn up . . . to regulate cable landing facilities for relay purposes 'on islands and other points,' but, largely owing to strategic considerations, it was not implemented." [195] Out of

[190] Act of June 18, 1910, 36 *Stat.* 539–545, telegraph, telephone, and cable companies being then designated "common carriers."
[191] Keith Clark, *International Communications: The American Attitude* (1931), pp. 118–119.
[192] 4 Hackworth, *Digest* 270–274.
[193] Treaty Regarding Rights of the Two Governments and Their Respective Nationals in Former German Islands in the Pacific Ocean North of the Equator, and in Particular the Island of Yap, signed at Washington, Feb. 11, 1922, 42 *Stat.* 2149, TS 664.
[194] Mance and Wheeler, *op. cit.*, p. 59. Text in "Report of Subcommittee on International Cable and Radio Law and on Cable Landing Rights," 1920 *F.R.* Vol. 1, pp. 159–161 at 159. See the Bermuda Protocol, 1945, below, in which the United States and Great Britain pledged their efforts toward ending such exclusive concessions in radio-telegraph circuits as they might be able to influence.
[195] Mance and Wheeler, *op. cit.*, p. 59. Text of agreement in 1920 *F.R.* Vol. 1, pp. 161–162. Correspondence on failure to secure ratification, 1922 *F.R.* Vol. 1, pp. 538–542. It should be pointed out that the proceedings of the International Conference on Electrical Communications were never published in the usual form. Copies

these post-World War I negotiations emerged, finally, the Telecommunication Union established at Madrid in 1932, but so far as the record discloses, no multilateral agreement providing for international control of the establishment and use of cables was put into effect in the interwar period.

In 1921, however, Congress finally adopted a statute defining the powers of the President to license the landing and operating of cables in the United States, saving the prior allocated authority to the Interstate Commerce Commission to supervise the transmission of messages.[196] In 1934, domestic jurisdiction over rates and services of cable companies was transferred from the ICC to the new Federal Communications Commission.[197] Thereupon the President by executive order conferred upon the FCC also the task of receiving all applications for the landing of cables and of advising him with respect to the issuance of licenses therefor.[198] So matters stood up to World War II — the cable companies, subject to some supervision by the FCC, continuing, apparently for the most part on their own initiative, to arrange their own affairs with foreign interests and administrations.[199]

The first multipartite agreement on rates and services in cable circuits arose out of the difficulty experienced by the private companies in negotiating with interests within the British Empire. Thus, after World War II the principal American international radiotelegraph and cable carriers were able to establish satisfactory reduced ceiling rates with more than eighty foreign countries outside of the British Empire.[200] To secure them within the Empire it became necessary, however, for the

---

of specific documents may be borrowed from the International Library Loan Section of the Department of State. Most of the important documents and reports of the conference, together with the extensive diplomatic correspondence preceding and following the conference can, however, be found in the volumes of *Foreign Relations* for the years 1920, 1921, and 1922.

[196] Act of May 27, 1921, 42 *Stat.* (1) 8.
[197] Act of June 19, 1934, 48 *Stat.* (1) 1064.
[198] 4 Hackworth, *Digest* 252.
[199] For current scope of supervision by FCC, see their annual reports. The *18th Annual Report, 1952*, pp. 58–59, for example, gives an account of the discontinuance of service over certain Pacific cables by Commercial Pacific Cable Company. For some contemporary aspects of American cable companies, see *Telecommunications: A Program for Progress, A Report by the President's Communications Policy Board* (1951), pp. 129–130, 157–158.
[200] FCC, *12th Annual Report 1946*, p. 31.

The United States and the Treaty Law of the Sea

government of the United States to negotiate a treaty. This was done at the conference in Bermuda in late 1945.[201]

In addition to disposing of certain matters relating to radiotelegraph circuits and establishing telegraph ceiling rates with the participating members of the British Commonwealth, the agreement of December 4, 1945,[202] in Article IV, provided that "in view of the important strategic role which cables as well as radio play in a coordinated telecommunications system, research and development work in both cable and radio communication shall be fostered and promoted. The use of improvements such as submarine repeaters and multi-channel operation shall wherever possible be encouraged." And further it provided: "Inasmuch as the trans-Atlantic cables form an integral part of a world telecommunication system, uniform procedures and techniques shall be adopted in their operation. The present arrangements for mutual consultation and co-operative action with respect to the trans-Atlantic cables shall be continued." In a separate protocol annexed to the multilateral agreement, the United States and the United Kingdom committed themselves to a policy of promoting the relaxation, reciprocally in favor of their national companies, of exclusive privileges which any of their national companies might enjoy or get in third countries.

Thus the United States concluded its first multipartite agreement on the maintenance and operation of submarine cables. Within a few years, however, it became necessary to readjust cable rates. This was done, with respect to the British Commonwealth in a revision of the Bermuda agreement, at London, in 1949,[203] and again in 1952.[204]

The next important development involving cables related to the International Telegraph Regulations. These "constitute basic tariff and operating rules under which nearly all international telegraph communications are carried on."[205] After World War II American telecommunications operations had reached an ambit which indicated the necessity of considering participation, for the first time, in the telegraph regulations customarily annexed to the Telecommunications Convention

---

[201] Helen G. Kelly, "The Bermuda Telecommunications Conference," 14 *DSB* 59–61 (1946); *U.S. Int. Conf. 1945–1946*, pp. 41–44.
[202] 60 *Stat.* 1636, TIAS 1518 .
[203] Signed Aug. 12, 1949, 3 *UST* 2686, TIAS 2435.
[204] Agreement Amending Agreement of Aug. 12, 1949, signed at London, Oct. 1, 1952, 3 *UST* 5140, TIAS 2705.
[205] FCC, *13th Annual Report* 1947, p. 69.

and regularly not subscribed to by the United States. Repeatedly disavowing any participation in the revision of or any subscription to the Telephone Regulations, the United States at the International Telegraph and Telephone Conference in Paris in 1949 nevertheless helped revise and then signed the Telegraph Regulations, August 5, 1949.[206] A few days later, in London, the revision of the Bermuda Convention was brought into accord with these new Telegraph Regulations.[207] After further study, the regulations were ratified and became effective for the United States September 26, 1950.[208] "The changes in regulations and traffic classifications, as well as the principles of rate unification provided for in these revised regulations, were reflected in the tariffs filed by United States cable and radio-telegraph carriers effective July 1, 1950." [209] Thus technology and economic necessity had at last conquered continental disparateness and forced subjection of contentious problems to international regulation.

Postal Communications. With respect to the remaining principal means of overseas communication, namely postal communications, no extraordinary developments have appeared since the interwar period, when air transport supplemented land and maritime transport. Like the telecommunications regime, however, the postal regime is, and has been for nearly eighty years, closely related to use of the sea. It operates so smoothly that seldom is it the subject of controversy either in the American Congress or in international conferences. As in the case of the United Nations and the other specialized agencies, however, it has experienced in this post-World War II period bitter internal contention with respect to the representation of communist China and the split countries of Korea and Germany.[210]

Many of the features of the relation of the UPU to the sea have already

---

[206] *U.S. Int. Conf. 1948–1949*, pp. 164–170. The United States signed with numerous qualifying reservations and declarations, which are repeated in the President's proclamation of the instrument when perfected.

[207] *U.S. Int. Conf. 1949–1950*, D.S. Pub. No. 4216, pp. 146–149.

[208] 2 *UST* 17, *TIAS* 2175. It may be noted that although the agreement entered into force for the United States on Sept. 26, 1950, it was not proclaimed until Nov. 20, 1950. On the general problem of the relation of date of proclamation to date of effectiveness, see Reiff, "The Proclaiming of Treaties in the United States," 30 *A.J.I.L.* 63–79 (1936), and 44 *A.J.I.L.* 572–576 (1950).

[209] FCC, *17th Annual Report 1951*, p. 62.

[210] See declaration made by the U.S.S.R., at the moment of signing the final protocol of the convention concluded at Brussels, July 11, 1952, 4 *UST* 1118, *TIAS* 2800; *U.S. Int. Conf. 1951–1952*, pp. 189–193.

been mentioned.[211] A few others of special interest can be added. An International Transfer Office was established at Panama in 1926 under the Postal Union of the Americas and Spain, in which Canada now also participates.[212] The 1952 Brussels Convention [213] of the UPU, which revised the 1947 Paris Convention,[214] continues to prohibit the sending through the mails of opium, morphine, cocaine, and other narcotics; explosives, inflammable, or dangerous substances; and obscene or immoral articles (Art. 59)— all in accord and in cooperation with regimes on those subjects already discussed. It also continues provisions dealing with mailings aboard merchant ships at sea (Art. 53); maritime transit charges (Art. 78); services to warships (Reg. Art. 168); special warehousing charges at Aden (Final Prot. Art. XIII); special charges for transhipment at Lisbon (Final Prot. Art. XIV); and the obligation to furnish continuously to the central office at Berne detailed information on steamships carrying mail (Reg. Art. 107).

As in the case of other specialized agencies of the United Nations, the UPU is regularly represented at all pertinent meetings of the UN and at meetings of all other intergovernmental organizations in whose operations the UPU has an interest. This relationship is, of course, reciprocal. Especially close relations have, however, been established with ICAO, which has studied for the UPU the complicated problem of rates, priority, routes, and other aspects of air transport of mails.[215]

United Nations Coordination of Transport and Communications

Article 63 (2) of the Charter of the United Nations authorizes the Economic and Social Council to "coordinate the activities of the specialized agencies through consultation with and recommendations to the General Assembly and to the Members of the United Nations." As

---

[211] Above, pp. 35–36, 107. Excellent brief descriptions of contemporary operations of the UPU and of the Postal Union of the Americas and Spain appear in *U.S. Int. Agencies 1945*, pp. 297–303 and 287–292, respectively; and *U.S. Int. Org. 1949*, pp. 302–307 and 296–300, respectively.

[212] Convention signed at Mexico, Nov. 9, 1926, 45 *Stat.* 2409, Art. 15. The post-World War II conventions were concluded at Madrid, Nov. 9, 1950, 2 *UST* 1323, *TIAS* 2286, and at Bogotá, Nov. 9, 1955, 7 *UST* 2599, *TIAS* 3653.

[213] *Op. cit.*

[214] Concluded, July 5, 1947, 62 *Stat.* (3) 3157, *TIAS* 1850.

[215] See *Reports of the Representative of the United States on the Council of ICAO*, sections in each on air mail.

Transportation and Communications since World War II

one of its first acts in 1946, ECOSOC set up a Transport and Communications Commission to help discharge its task.[216] In order that the commission may be informed of current developments in the assigned field, the secretary general renders it each year a "note" on developments. This note, if need be, points out "any situation where there is overlapping, duplication, or conflict" among the specialized agencies and other bodies dealing with transport and communications. The specialized agencies, whose mutual cooperation and interrelations are commented upon in these notes from the Secretariat to the commission, are precisely those which we have had to discuss (or will discuss) because of the relation of part, or, as in the case of IMCO, all, of their jurisdiction to the sea, namely, ICAO, WMO, IMCO, ILO, ITU, UPU, WHO, and UNESCO.

Fortunately for the student of these affairs, the secretary general was able in his note of January 7, 1957,[217] to give all these specialized agencies a "clean bill of health." Reviewing the activities of these specialized agencies over the ten years of existence of the Transport and Communications Commission, the secretary general could report:

In all this time it has never been necessary for the Commission or the Council to take any formal action with respect to improving the coordination of the activities of the specialized agencies as regards transport and communications matters. Their cooperation with the United Nations and with each other has been so smooth and effective that whatever few small differences of opinion or frictions may have arisen have easily been handled without any intervention by the Council.

The secretary general's report notes numerous instances of interagency cooperation and collaboration in recent years. A few of these instances can be gleaned to supplement the examples already given. Thus, "ICAO made a valuable contribution to the WHO Committee on International Quarantine" in 1954 "when the yellow fever provisions of the International Sanitary Regulations were revised." The amended regulations were adopted by the World Health Assembly in May 1955. "WHO and ICAO collaborated in preparing a guide on the hygiene and sanitation of airports." "At the request of the Economic and Social Council, UPU

---

[216] For a brief authoritative account of the setup and work of the Economic and Social Council and its Transport and Communications Commission, see *Everyman's United Nations 1945–1955* (1956), pp. 26–32, 183–188.

[217] *Coordination of the Activities of Specialized Agencies in the Field of Transport and Communications, Note by the Secretary General*, E/CN.2/178, Nov. 10, 1956, considered by the Transport and Communications Commission at its eighth session, Jan. 7, 1957.

distributed to Administrations of Governments the list of narcotic drugs prepared by the United Nations. Proposals will be submitted to the Ottawa Postal Congress in 1957 to change the acts of UPU so as to comply with decisions of the United Nations Commission on Narcotic Drugs and the Economic and Social Council." WMO submitted "reports to ITU's International Telecommunication Consultative Committee (CCIT) on the characteristics of facsimile apparatus used for the transmission of weather charts." Finally, among many other concrete instances of interagency collaboration, appears the following:

Although IMCO was not in operation, there was considerable work done by WMO's Commission for Maritime Meteorology on such matters as an international ice nomenclature, a code for reporting sea ice, a scheme for collecting and transmitting weather reports from whaling ships, exchange of weather information by fishing fleets, rainfall measurement at sea, and methods of observing sea surface temperature. The consideration of these matters could of course be facilitated by the cooperation of IMCO.

If interagency cooperation of this sort can be continued, then it may not become necessary for some time to pile Ossa on Pelion or even Pelion on Olympus.

CHAPTER VI

EXPANSION IN TREATY LAW FOR THE SEA SINCE WORLD WAR II: HEALTH, RESOURCES, AND OTHER DEVELOPMENTS

HEALTH

IN THE discussion of international administration thus far, it should have been apparent how often domestic difficulties have led to solutions at the international level and, conversely, how often international legislative and administrative activities have necessitated changes internal to a national state in order to assure success for the desired international program. Both of these propositions are demonstrated vividly in the field of health.

It was found in the decades immediately preceding World War II that "older methods of quarantine were rapidly become obsolescent with the increasing rapidity of travel and that eradication of disease by attacking it at its source must be the long-range objective in the control of the international spread of disease." Toward this end of "controlling the international spread of disease in the air age" it would become imperative to strengthen, as the "only satisfactory means," "the national health services in all states, by giving technical advice upon request." Such strengthened services would also constitute the "principal means" of achieving the general humanitarian objective of a new World Health Organization, namely, "the attainment by all peoples of the highest possible level of health."[1] In a very profound sense, then, sea and air commerce have contributed to important national domestic results.

In another direction, sea and air commerce have accelerated a trend previously perceivable in international legislation. The traditional method of adopting sanitation rules by means of multipartite conven-

[1] H. Van Zile Hyde, "The International Health Conference," 15 *DSB* 453–454, 459, at p. 454 (1946).

tions created dangerous lags in the application of developing public health methods and produced undesirable "strata" of obligations under several successive unterminated agreements on both maritime and air sanitation.[2] Various unions have suffered from the same phenomena.[3] The "founding fathers" of the World Health Organization accordingly decided to confer upon the new institution a restricted rule-making power exercisable with respect to certain enumerated technical fields previously dealt with by means of multipartite conventions.

World Health Organization

The diplomatic efforts at the close of World War II which resulted in the establishment of the new World Health Organization were complicated because of the number of extant multipartite agreements involved and the number of international bodies then existing which were charged with responsibility in health matters. Part of the story of transition has been told above.[4] The remaining syllabus is as follows.

The United Nations Conference on International Organization at San Francisco in 1945 considered and wrote into the charter certain provisions concerning health. Thus, Article 55 provided that "with a view to the creation of conditions of stability and well-being which are necessary for peaceful and friendly relations among nations based on respect for the principle of equal rights and self-determination of peoples," the United Nations should promote *inter alia* "solutions of international economic, social, health, and related problems . . ." And Article 57 directed that "the various specialized agencies, established by intergovernmental agreement and having wide international responsibilities, as defined in their basic instruments," in various fields, including that of health, should be brought into relationship with the United Nations in accordance with the provisions of Article 63. This article prescribed the making of a special agreement between the two organizations and other pertinent arrangements for coordination with and a degree of supervision by the United Nations. Very promptly after the principal

[2] *Ibid.*, and article cited n. 13 below.

[3] E.g., the Industrial Property Union. See Ladas, *op. cit.*, p. 132. Other unions, e.g., the Universal Postal Union, set a date for the effectiveness of the new convention, on which date the prior applicable convention ceases to have force. See 1952 Convention, *op. cit.*, Art. 23.

[4] In Ch. IV at pp. 163–164. See also the clear and succinct account in Williams, *op. cit.*, pp. 453–470.

organs of the United Nations had been set up in London in the succeeding months, the Economic and Social Council by resolution of February 15, 1946, provided for an International Health Conference to meet in June 1946 and for a Technical Preparatory Committee to prepare basic documents for the conference.[5]

The conference [6] met in New York, June 19th, and adopted on July 22d, besides the Final Act, three multipartite instruments: a Constitution for the World Health Organization; [7] an Arrangement establishing an Interim Commission to perform the necessary international health functions until WHO should be placed in operation; [8] and a Protocol transferring to WHO definitively and to the Interim Commission temporarily the functions previously exercised by the International Office of Public Health in Paris under some fifteen prior separate multilateral agreements.[9] The list included an agreement concluded at Brussels in 1924 concerning Facilities to be given to Merchant Seamen for the Treatment of Venereal Disease,[10] but the United States was not a party to that. The health functions previously performed by the League of Nations,[11] and those then currently being performed by UNRRA,[12] were also transferred by operation of the arrangement and other instruments to the Interim Commission. All this was an exceedingly complex procedure, but in due course it was neatly performed without interruption of the vital international services. When the transition was completed, a

[5] Doc. E/9/Rev. 1. For details of the discussion in ECOSOC, see "World Health Organization," 1 *International Organization* 134–136 (1947).

[6] *International Health Conference, New York, N.Y., June 19 to July 22, 1946, Report of the United States Delegation*, D.S. Pub. No. 2703.

[7] 62 *Stat.* (3) 2679, TIAS 1808, entered into force April 7, 1948; with respect to the United States, June 21, 1948.

[8] 61 *Stat.* (3) 2349, TIAS 1561, signed and effective July 22, 1946.

[9] 62 *Stat.* (2) 1604, TIAS 1754; entered into force Oct. 20, 1947; proclaimed May 19, 1948. The United States was a party to only certain of the agreements listed in Annex I. For tabulation of the parties, see "International Health Security in the Modern World: The Sanitary Conventions and the World Health Organization," 17 *DSB* 953–958 (1947).

[10] Dated Dec. 1, 1924. Text in 2 Hudson, *I.L.* 1540.

[11] On the transfer process, generally, see Reiff, "Transition from League of Nations to United Nations," 14 *DSB* 691–698, 739–748 (1946), and Denys P. Myers, "Liquidation of League of Nations Functions," 42 *A.J.I.L.* 320–354 (1948).

[12] Two conventions opened for signature at Washington, Dec. 15, 1944, on Sanitary Maritime Navigation, 59 *Stat.* 955, TS 991, and on Sanitary Aerial Navigation, 59 *Stat.* 991, TS 992; and two protocols on maritime and aerial navigation, respectively, opened for signature at Washington, April 23, 1946, 61 *Stat.* (2) 1115, TIAS 1551 and 61 *Stat.* 1122, TIAS 1552.

"going concern" was handed over to the first World Health Assembly, which met in Geneva, the headquarters of the new organization, June 24, 1948.[13]

Despite the vigorous and enlightened leadership which the United States had displayed in nearly a half century of world efforts to combat epidemic disease, Congress delayed nearly two years in authorizing the President to accept membership in WHO on behalf of the United States. When it finally did so by Joint Resolution of June 14, 1948,[14] it imposed several conditions upon the President and upon American participation in the organization. Thus, Article 24 of the WHO constitution, which provided for an eighteen-member executive board, stipulated that each of the governments entitled to name the persons "should appoint to the Board a person technically qualified in the field of health." Congress spelled this out for the President, stipulating further that "such representative must be a graduate of a recognized medical school and have spent not less than three years in active practice as a physician or surgeon," the appointment being also subject to confirmation by the Senate. The New York Conference which drew up the constitution, following in the footsteps of the San Francisco Conference, omitted any clause from the instrument permitting withdrawal of a member state. It was generally understood at San Francisco, however, that, with respect to the United Nations, "each member retains the power to withdraw at will."[15] Congress took no chances: it stipulated that, in the absence of any provision in the WHO constitution for withdrawal from the organization, "the United States reserves its right to withdraw from the Organization on a one-year notice," provided, of course, that the United States had met its current financial obligations in the union.

This reservation caused the United States delegation to the first as-

[13] H. Van Zile Hyde, "Challenges and Opportunities in World Health: The First World Health Assembly," 19 *DSB* 391–398 (1948). The 10th Anniversary Commemorative Session of WHO and the 11th World Health Assembly were appropriately held in the United States, in Minneapolis, in 1958. This was the first meeting of WHO in the United States since its organization meeting in New York in 1948. 38 *DSB* 933–934 (1958). See "The First Ten Years of the World Health Organization," Remarks by Assistant Secretary of State Francis O. Wilcox and Address by Dr. Milton Eisenhower at the commemorative session, 38 *DSB* 987–992 (1958).

[14] 62 *Stat.* 441–442.

[15] For comment on the charter omission, see Leland M. Goodrich and Edvard Hambro, *Charter of the United Nations: Commentary and Documents*, 2d ed. (1949), p. 145; discussion at pp. 20–21, 24, 142–145.

sembly in 1948 considerable embarrassment.[16] The United States had deposited its instrument of acceptance with the Secretary General on June 21, 1948. Uncertain whether to accept the instrument, because of this reservation, the Secretary General awaited the decision of the assembly.[17] After a special plenary session devoted to the legal problem raised by the reservation — during which the Soviet Union put in a kind word for the United States — the United States was unanimously admitted as the forty-sixth member on July 2d retroactive to June 21st. And finally, *ex maior cautela*, Congress recorded in its joint resolution its understanding that nothing in the WHO constitution "in any manner commits the United States to enact any specific legislative program regarding any matters referred to in said Constitution."

Practically all public unions, under modern conditions, have ample rule-making power with respect to the governance of their staffs and their subordinate agencies or creations. With regard to control of the conduct of the member nation-states and their subjects, however, rule-making power, where it exists, is relatively modest. The constitution of WMO, for example, empowers the congress of the organization [Art. 7(d)] "to adopt technical regulations covering meteorological practices and procedures." Most of the unions have power only to *recommend* regulations, adoption of the rules as binding obligations being subject to some further manifestation of consent by the member states. Thus, the convention establishing IMCO authorizes its assembly [Art. 16(i)] "to recommend to members for adoption regulations concerning maritime safety, or amendments to such regulations, which have been referred to it by the Maritime Safety Committee." The International Civil Aviation Organization goes further, as explained previously, in permitting adoption of standards and recommended practices by a two-thirds vote of the council, subject to rejection by a majority of the member states (Art. 90). Though the details vary from union to union, there is a general trend toward the practice of adoption by the central organs of rules and regulations which can become obligatory upon the member states under prescribed conditions. This practice relieves some of the increasing burdens upon the multipartite agreement-making

---

[16] Hyde, *op. cit.*, 19 *DSB* 398.

[17] Discussed in Oscar Schachter, "The Development of International Law through the Legal Opinions of the United Nations Secretariat," 25 *British Year Book of International Law* 91–132 (1948), at pp. 122–127.

process and avoids to a considerable extent the delays inherent in the necessity for securing ratification or acceptance [18] of the multipartite instrument.

The World Health Organization makes a considerable advance in this trend. Under Articles 2(k), 21(a), and 22 of the constitution, the World Health Assembly has authority to adopt regulations in certain stipulated fields, concerning, *inter alia*, "sanitary and quarantine requirements and other procedures designed to prevent the international spread of disease." Such regulations are to "come into force for all Members after due notice has been given of their adoption by the Health Assembly except for such Members as may notify the Director-General of rejection or reservation within the period stated in the notice."

International Sanitary Regulations. At its very first meeting in 1948, and in pursuance of this authority, the Assembly adopted a set of regulations, denominated Regulations No. 1,[19] dealing with an old subject matter previously embraced in a multipartite agreement,[20] namely, "nomenclature (including the compilation and publication of statistics) with respect to diseases and causes of death." On May 25, 1951, the Assembly adopted a much more elaborate set of regulations, a revised, composite set of International Sanitary Regulations. These were denominated WHO Regulations No. 2.[21] Thus the process of international legislation came into full fruition.[22] Fortunately, from the point of view of meeting the critics of the process, it is in a field in which a great corpus of practice and regulation had been developed by exceedingly exacting public officials over the past half century. It may be possible, if WHO is successful with the method, to extend it in the decades to

---

[18] See Briggs, *op. cit.*, pp. 852–858, and the numerous works there cited, especially, Yuen-li Liang, "The Use of the Term 'Acceptance' in United Nations Treaty Procedure," 44 *A.J.I.L.* 342–349 (1950).

[19] Adopted at Geneva, July 24, 1948; entered into force for the United States, Jan. 1, 1950, 7 *UST* 79, *TIAS* 3482. Supplementary regulations to Regulations No. 1 were adopted at Rome, June 30, 1949, 7 *UST* 79, *TIAS* 3482.

[20] Agreement on Statistics of Causes of Death, signed at London, June 19, 1934, 49 *Stat.* 3787, *EAS* 80; Protocol Revising the Agreement of 1934, 54 *Stat.* 2308, *EAS* 173.

[21] Entered into force for the United States, Oct. 1, 1952, 7 *UST* 2255, *TIAS* 3625.

[22] See the excellent critique of the method by Herbert W. Briggs, "New Dimensions in International Law," 46 *American Political Science Review* 677–698 (1952), at pp. 692–693.

Health and Resources since World War II

come to other specialized agencies in which a corpus has similarly been developed.

The revised regulations follow in general the pattern in the several conventions on the subject. They are, however, simplified and modernized. Relapsing fever is added to the prior five quarantinable diseases — plague, cholera, yellow fever, smallpox, and typhus. "Ports" and "airports" are systematically subjected to the same rules. The new regulations replace part of the Pan American Sanitary Code signed at Habana, November 14, 1924.[23] Many rules continue to deal with pilgrim traffic by land, sea, or air, to and from the Hedjaz and impose standards of hygiene on pilgrim ships and on aircraft carrying pilgrims, including the disposal of the dead at sea (Annex B 23).

Since 1952, when the code of sanitary regulations was adopted, some ninety governments have accepted it. The actual quarantine work is done, of course, "by the central and local authorities and the sea and airport authorities of each country under governmental regulations which must conform to the international codes, conventions or regulations to which the country is signatory." In sum, the World Health Organization, as its principal task,

is charged with the double job of drawing up, interpreting, administering and, when necessary, amending the International Sanitary Regulations and with receiving, collating and distributing information on the occurrence of pestilential diseases. The national health administrations of 170 countries and territories send in some 7,000 health reports each year. This information is broadcast daily in English and French from Radio Nations in Geneva and the other WHO centres in Singapore, Alexandria, and Washington. By arrangement with other stations, the messages are rebroadcast over a wide area. Broadcasting is supplemented by telegrams and by the *Weekly Epidemiological Record*, a printed bulletin. A monthly report gives information on the occurrence and trends of infectious diseases, including poliomyelitis, influenza, diphtheria, and scarlet fever.[24]

The United States and the Middle East. Few stranger things can be encountered in American history than the connection of the United States, through the international sanitary regime, with the Hegira of Mohammed from Mecca in A.D. 622. The regime started a century ago in

[23] 44 *Stat.* 2031, *TS* 714.
[24] "International Travel and Disease Control," 3 *United Nations Review* (March 1957) 53–55, at p. 54, a splendid summation of the relation of WHO to epidemics.

267

an effort to protect Europe from the recurring epidemics emanating in considerable part from the Near East. Pilgrimages from the larger Middle East and even from the Moslem Far East had contributed for centuries to the foci of infection in the Near East. The successive sanitary conventions and agencies established under them at various ports and land stations gradually brought the epidemics under control. The World Health Organization not only continues the control but more fundamentally by various devices and programs seeks to prevent the emergence of disease in large parts of the world, including the Middle and Far East. In this work the United States cooperates wholeheartedly both as a form of self-defense and as a manifestation of the traditional humanitarian urges characteristic of the American people since the early nineteenth century.

A dramatic instance of involvement in the pilgrimages to Mecca, only peripherally related to the health regime, but definitely related to these humanitarian urges, occurred in August 1952. Some 4000 Moslem pilgrims from Turkey, Syria, Iraq, North Africa, and Iran were stranded at Beirut, Lebanon. Certain Middle Eastern airlines, which had contracted to take them from Beirut to Mecca, had oversold their services. The deadline for the hadj, or great pilgrimage, fixed by the Saudi Arabian government in accord with the religious calendar, loomed a few days ahead. For these pilgrims, the hopes and perhaps savings of a lifetime appeared lost. In the circumstances the Lebanese government appealed to the American ambassador for aid. Literally within hours, planes from the American Military Air Transport Service at Tripoli were dispatched to Beirut. Round-the-clock flights for several days up to within two hours of an extended deadline sped all the stranded pilgrims to the Kaaba and that much nearer Heaven.[25] Such a gracious gesture will long be remembered by those to whom it mattered much. It was not "butter" but it was better than "guns." In 1956, in less dramatic circumstances, the United States International Cooperation Administration, at the request of the Afghanistan government contracted with Pan American World Airways to send a huge plane to Afghanistan to supplement the Afghan airline in its transport of Afghan Moslems to Mecca for the hadj of that year.[26]

[25] Actually, only to the Jidda Airport, since the non-Moslem crews could not enter the Mecca area. "The Mecca Airlift," 27 *DSB* 406 (1952); *Life*, Sept. 8, 1952.
[26] "U.S. Will Help Transport Afghan Pilgrims to Mecca," 35 *DSB* 25 (1956).

Health and Resources since World War II

U.S. Technical Cooperation Program. Under its Technical Cooperation Program, the United States has entered into a number of bipartite agreements with Middle Eastern as well as other states to assist them variously, including the improvement of services in public health and disease control. One project agreement of 1953 [27] with Saudi Arabia, pursuant to a master agreement of 1952 on public health and disease control,[28] provides for aid and cooperation in the functioning of a new quarantine station at Jidda, the port on the Red Sea through which the sea-borne pilgrims must come on their way to nearby Mecca and the slightly more remote Medina, another sacred city, which contains the tomb of Mohammed. In the past, because of inadequate public health services at the port, "each country sending pilgrims furnished medical teams to cooperate with the Saudi Arabian Ministry of Health in caring for the pilgrims." With equipment furnished by the United States and the assistance of technicians from WHO and the United States, the program envisages adequate care for the annual pilgrim traffic and utilization of the center for health services in Saudi Arabia throughout the year. A training program at the station is included for Saudi Arabian health workers. And, finally, provision is made to send a limited number of Saudi Arabian "employees of the Quarantine Service to the United States to work with the United States Quarantine Service for a period of a few months, and to attend some of the field training courses given by the Communicable Disease Center of the U.S. Public Health Service."

Another recent agreement, important in this context of improving health in the Middle East, is that of the United States with Egypt in 1953,[29] providing for technical cooperation in a public health program. Care is exercised in the agreement (Art. VIII) that the projects undertaken by the United States and Egypt will be properly coordinated with those undertaken by Egypt and the World Health Organization. Aside from this program, the United States has maintained in Cairo, under

[27] Project Agreement No. 1 under Technical Cooperation Program in Public Health and Disease Control to Strengthen the Quarantine Services and to Enhance the Public Health Program of the Ministry of Health of Saudi Arabia, signed at Jidda, June 29, 1953, 4 *UST* 1781, *TIAS* 2845.

[28] Signed at Jidda, Dec. 15, 1952, 3 *UST* 5306, *TIAS* 2733.

[29] Signed at Cairo, June 18, 1953, 4 *UST* 1928, *TIAS* 2852, in pursuance of the General Agreement for Technical Cooperation, signed at Cairo, May 5, 1951, 3 *UST* 2960, *TIAS* 2479.

agreement and in cooperation with the Egyptian government, a naval medical research unit. This unit, called NAMRU, uses for the most part war-surplus plant and equipment. One of its principal preoccupations has been the study of cholera.[30]

It is almost a Sisyphean task to summarize the responsibilities and activities of the World Health Organization in relation to use of the sea. Enough has been indicated to suggest its extensive responsibilities in the control of disease, moving by one means or another overseas, and in the improvement of health among those who labor upon the high seas. At numerous points it cooperates with the other great regimes which deal in one way or another with use of the sea — ICAO, WMO, safety at sea (IMCO), the carriage of dangerous and infectious goods, ILO, ITU, UPU, UNESCO. It will appear further that it shares numerous tasks with the Food and Agriculture Organization in the fisheries programs, with the narcotics administration under the United Nations, with the new commissions for cooperation among island possessions, and with various agencies in dealing with atomic radiation.

RESOURCES OF THE SEA

The most significant developments in the post-World War II period concerning transportation, communications, and health in relation to the sea have now been outlined. There remain to be considered the more important postwar developments concerning the exploitation of products of the sea, humanitarian efforts, and scientific matters.

World-wide shortages of food [31] and new pressures on petroleum resources have produced important postwar activities relating to fisheries

[30] *Report, United States Naval Medical Research Unit No. 3, Cairo, Egypt* (1950). A similar Navy Medical Research Unit, No. 2, was established in Taipei, Taiwan, in 1955 "for the purpose of conducting study and research on a long range basis in the field of diseases endemic and epidemic in the Far East." Agreement with China effected by exchange of notes dated at Taipei, March 30, April 26, and Oct. 14, 1955, 7 *UST* 173, *TIAS* 3493; amended by agreement of Dec. 27, 1956, 7 *UST* 3453, *TIAS* 3720. The Cairo agreement, apparently negotiated by the Navy authorities and not formalized at the diplomatic level, does not appear in the *TIAS* series. The primary papers relating thereto appear still to be in the Navy Department. Letter, Dept. of State to writer, Nov. 22, 1957.

[31] P. Lamartine Yates, "Food Resources and Human Needs," 55 *Yale Law Journal* 1233–1241 (1946); Frank L. McDougall, "Food and Population," *International Conciliation* No. 486, Dec. 1952; *Proceedings of the UN Scientific Conference on the Conservation and Utilization of Resources, 1949*, Vol. VII, *Wildlife and Fish Resources* (1951).

and the exploitation of offshore oil deposits. In a strict sense, of course, petroleum is not a marine product,[32] but for convenience its exploitation may be grouped here with other activities which are directed from the surface of the sea. Little appears to have been done with respect to oceanic birds, except to the extent that they may benefit from an amendment to the Tariff Act of 1930 which seeks to halt the illicit diversion of wild-bird feathers to the millinery trade [33] and from the adoption of measures designed to control oil pollution of the seas, which have already been discussed at some length.

In accord with a new carefully formulated policy,[34] the United States has by means of presidential proclamations asserted jurisdiction and control over the natural resources of the subsoil and sea bed of the continental shelf adjacent to the United States [35] and asserted the right "to establish conservation zones in those areas of the high seas contiguous to the coasts of the United States wherein fishing activities have been or in the future may be developed and maintained on a substantial scale," with due regard for the interests of nationals of other states.[36]

By means of multipartite treaties the United States is participating in the development of fisheries in far areas of the sea: the Northwest Atlantic, the North Pacific, the Pacific off the coasts of Mexico and Costa Rica, the Indo-Pacific, the South Pacific, the Caribbean. It continues to display lively interest in the whaling arrangement and has concluded a number of additional agreements with Canada relating to mutual fishery interests.

Through its own Point Four Program and the United Nations program of technical assistance for the economic development of underdeveloped countries it aids the local development of fisheries in sundry parts of the world. It may be noted, in passing, that the United States technical assistance program has dealt with many other matters of concern to this study of the relation of the United States to the sea. Thus,

[32] But in the geologic sense it appears possible that it may be. See R. Carson, *The Sea Around Us*, pp. 197–201.

[33] See *Importation of Wild-Bird Feathers*, S. Rept. No. 1832, 82 Cong., 2 Sess., June 26, 1952; Act of July 17, 1952, 66 *Stat.* 755.

[34] Wilbert McLeod Chapman, "United States Policy on High Seas Fisheries," 20 *DSB* 67–71, 80 (1949); William C. Herrington, "U.S. Policy on Fisheries and Territorial Waters," 26 *DSB* 1021–1023 (1952).

[35] Proclamation, Sept. 28, 1945, 59 *Stat.* 884–885; text in Appendix I.

[36] Proclamation, Sept. 28, 1945, 59 *Stat.* 885–886; text in Appendix I.

"cooperative weather investigations have been undertaken in some countries, and a number of tide stations have been established so that predictions are now made of tides in these ports, and data exist for charting and engineering use. Likewise, magnetic and seismological observations are made under one of the programs of the Interdepartmental Committee. Technical assistance is provided in the development, conservation, and management of fishery resources, and surveys are being made of migratory-bird resources."[37] Withal, as a leading member of the Food and Agriculture Organization,[38] it participates continuously in the efforts of that agency to enhance the fishery resources of the world.

Fisheries

New U.S. Fisheries Policy. The current United States fisheries policy, as enunciated by the responsible administrators, can be stated succinctly. It is firmly rooted in the sciences of the sea. "For any particular population of fish there is an optimum point of fishing intensity which, if sustained, will yield the maximum crop of fish year after year. Less fishing is wasteful, for the surplus of fish dies from natural causes [among them, relative decline of food for the fish and loss to natural predators] without benefit to mankind; more fishing is wasteful because it depletes the population and so results actually in a smaller crop."[39] The essence of United States policy is, then, "'to secure a mechanism which will provide for each high-seas fishery of American concern the possibility of management, to the end that the population of fish upon which the fishery works will be kept at that level at which a maximum crop can be harvested year after year, *ad infinitum.*' Carrying out such a policy involves international agreements, international bodies, legislation, scientific investigation, and regulations."[40]

A new Fish and Wildlife Act of 1956[41] is part of the contemplated legislation. After an investigation into the depressed conditions of the

[37] Ruth S. Donahue, "'Point 4' and Its Relation to Existing Technical Assistance Programs," 20 *DSB* 211–214, 213 (1949).
[38] Constitution, signed at Quebec, Oct. 16, 1945, 60 *Stat.* 1886, *TIAS* 1554.
[39] Chapman, *op. cit.*, p. 68.
[40] *Survey of Activities of the Committee on Foreign Affairs*, House of Representatives, 81 Cong., 1 Sess. (1949), Committee Print, p. 44; see also Edward W. Allen, "Fish Can Be International," 82 *U.S. Naval Institute Proceedings* 1066–1071 (1956).
[41] Approved Aug. 8, 1956, 70 *Stat.* 1119.

California tuna industry and the Alaska salmon fisheries in 1955,[42] Congress adopted in its act of 1956 a comprehensive declaration of policy with respect to the fish, shellfish, and wildlife resources of the United States; reorganized and transferred various separate services into one service under the Department of Interior; authorized loans for fisheries purposes; and, among other things, increased the opportunities for domestic fishery interests to secure through the tariff mechanism the reduction of imports of competing products or their exclusion.

The congressional "declaration of policy" is virtually an essay on the relation of fisheries to the national economy, to the "health, recreation, and well-being of our citizens," to employment, to a trained seafaring citizenry, and to the national defense. Congress further put itself on record in favor of "freedom of enterprise"; "protection of opportunity" against competing products and "protection of opportunity to fish on the high seas in accordance with international law"; and affirmative governmental assistance to the fishery interests similar to that long provided for industry generally. To effectuate the purposes of the act, the pertinent administrative services up to that time distributed in the Departments of Agriculture, Commerce, and Interior were all gathered together into two new bureaus, a Bureau of Commercial Fisheries and a Bureau of Sport Fisheries and Wildlife, in one new service in the Department of Interior, headed by an Assistant Secretary for Fish and Wildlife. The Secretary of State was obligated (Sec. 8) to include the Assistant Secretary for Fish and Wildlife, or his deputy, in all international negotiations dealing with fish and wildlife. For the most part, then, the act of 1956 represents a coming of age within the federal administrative setup of the very interests and trends we have been tracing over the past century and a half.

A survey of recent agreements indicates how this new administrative and congressional policy has thus far been implemented.

Northwest Atlantic Fisheries. On July 3, 1950, the Northwest Atlantic Fisheries Convention went into effect.[43] Prior to this agreement, the

---

[42] *Pacific Coast and Alaska Fisheries*, Report of the Committee on Interstate and Foreign Commerce, U.S. Senate, 84 Cong., 2 Sess., S. Rept. No. 2801 (1956); *Fisheries Act of 1956*, 84 Cong., 2 Sess. S. Rept. No. 2017 (1956).

[43] Dated at Washington, Feb. 8, 1949, 1 *UST* 477, *TIAS* 2089. It was signed by Canada, Denmark, France, Iceland, Italy, Newfoundland, Norway, Portugal, Spain, United Kingdom, and the United States. By Article XV the convention is open to adherence by any other interested governments. Enforcement act: Northwest

United States had entered into a number of bipartite agreements, beginning in 1778, with France and Great Britain (later Canada), dealing "with accessory rights on shore and in adjacent waters" appurtenant to territorial possessions along the western rim of the North Atlantic.[44] This new multipartite agreement deals, for the first time, with formal international cooperation in the development and regulation of fisheries in the offshore and high-seas areas. It declares expressly (Art. 1, par. 2) that nothing in the convention "shall be deemed to affect adversely (prejudice) the claims of any Contracting Government in regard to the limits of territorial waters or to the jurisdiction of a coastal state over fisheries."

The decline in commercially important species of fish in the North Atlantic in the decades after World War I led the British government to call a conference on the subject in 1937. The conference adopted a convention for the regulation of meshes of fishing nets and the size limits of fish.[45] This convention was intended to apply to "the Atlantic Ocean north of the Equator, so much of the Arctic Ocean as lies between 80° west longitude and 80° east longitude, and their dependent seas" (Art. 4 and Annex I). The west longitude line runs along the east coast of Florida. The east longitude line embraces the Arctic well over Siberia. The United States did not participate in the conference or the agreement. Since the convention failed to be perfected by the signatories, the British government held two further conferences, in 1943 and 1946, on the same subject. The United States was represented by observers at these meetings.[46]

Meanwhile it became clear that the fisheries problems of the eastern North Atlantic and the western North Atlantic were severable. Thereupon the 1946 London conference confined the application of the con-

---

Atlantic Fisheries Act of 1950, Sept. 27, 1950, 64 *Stat.* 1067. See Erik M. Poulsen, "Conservation Problems in the Northwestern Atlantic," *Papers Presented at the International Technical Conference on the Conservation of the Living Resources of the Sea, Rome, 1955*, A/CONF.10/7, Jan. 1956, pp. 183–193 (hereinafter cited *Papers*, Rome 1955 Conference).

[44] "Conservation of Fishery Resources in Northwest Atlantic to be Discussed," 19 DSB 669–670 (1948); and Carter, *Treaties Affecting the Northeastern Fisheries*, p. 6 and *passim.*

[45] Convention on the Regulation of Meshes of Fishing Nets and Size Limits of Fish, signed at London, March 23, 1937, by ten western European governments. 7 Hudson, *I.L.* 642–650.

[46] "Conservation of Fishery Resources in Northwest Atlantic etc.," *op. cit.*, p. 670; also "Northwest Atlantic Fisheries," 24 DSB 595–596 (1951).

vention which it adopted to the area east of 42° west longitude.[47] That line, running down the eastern side of the lower tip of Greenland, divided the North Atlantic into two approximately equal areas, one eastern and the other western. The southernmost limit for the eastern area was fixed at 48° north latitude.

The United States, in due course, held a conference[48] in Washington in 1949 to which were invited the governments with fishery interests in the area west of that line, namely, Canada, Denmark, France, Iceland, Italy, Newfoundland, Norway, Portugal, Spain, and the United Kingdom. The FAO and the International (Copenhagen) Council for the Exploration of the Sea were also represented by observers. The United States was particularly interested in securing the restoration of the populations of bottom-dwelling species such as haddock, cod, halibut, and rosefish, upon which the New England ottertrawl fishery chiefly depends. It is of interest to note in passing that the rosefish (or redfish) has only recently been brought into considerable commercial production.[49] It also has a remarkable characteristic for a fish: "The eggs are supposed to hatch within the body of the female which then brings forth living young."[50]

The Northwest Atlantic Fisheries Convention contains some of the most ingenious devices yet invented for international control of a vast, contention-loaded fishery. It applies to a fixed "convention area" which lies generally north of 39° north latitude and west of 42° west longitude (Art. I). This area is divided into five subareas (Art. I, 3), covering waters outside territorial waters off (1) the west coast of Greenland, (2) Labrador, (3) Newfoundland, (4) Nova Scotia, and (5) New England, so numbered in the annex, which also delimits each area. The Truman proclamation with respect to the development of offshore fisheries exploited primarily by one nation-state is safeguarded, presumably, by the stipulation in Article I (2): "Nothing in this Convention shall be deemed to affect adversely (prejudice) the claims of any

---

[47] Art. 1; Final Act and Convention of the International Overfishing Conference, London, 25th March–5th April, 1946, Cmd. 6791, Misc. No. 7 (1946); see also *Final Report of the Standing Advisory Committee to the International Overfishing Conference, London 16th–19th April, 1947*, Cmd. 7387.

[48] *U.S. Int. Conf. 1948–1949*, pp. 110–115; and "Northwest Atlantic Fisheries Convention Signed," 20 *DSB* 319 (1949).

[49] Tressler and Lemon, *op. cit.*, p. 223.

[50] C. M. Breder, Jr., *Field Book of Marine Fishes of the Atlantic Coast from Labrador to Texas* (1948), p. 239.

Contracting Government in regard to the limits of territorial waters or to the jurisdiction of a coastal state over fisheries."

For the whole convention area a commission is set up on which each of the parties to the convention is represented with one vote, decisions of an operational character being made by a two-thirds vote (Art. II). For each of the subareas a panel is set up (Art. IV). On each panel the government or governments with coastlines adjacent to the waters involved are automatically members of that panel. Other governments are assigned to the panels in accordance with their special interests in the subareas concerned. The Annex assigned the United States to the panels for subareas (4) and (5). Subsequently, it was added to the panel for subarea (3) which includes the Grand Banks. The boundaries of the subareas and the representation on each panel are subject to change by the full commission. Representation on each panel is determined "on the basis of current substantial exploitation in the subarea concerned of fishes of the cod group (gadiformes), of flatfishes (Pleuronectiformes), and of rosefish (genus Sebastes), except that each contracting government with coastline adjacent to a subarea shall have the right of representation on the Panel for the subarea" (Art. IV).[51]

The securing of the cooperation of the economic interests concerned with the actual exploitation of the fisheries in any area is facilitated by Article V, which authorizes each contracting government to "set up an Advisory Committee composed of persons, including fishermen, vessel owners and others, well informed concerning the problems of the fisheries of the Northwest Atlantic Ocean." The convention, furthermore, permits representatives of such advisory committees to attend, with the assent of their governments, the nonexecutive meetings of the panels in which their governments participate. This is accruing evidence of the recognition which is steadily being given in recent decades to the private groups and interests whose affairs the treaty regimes are regulating. The same article provided that the commissioners of each contracting government could "hold public hearings within the territories they represent" and that the commission itself (Art. VI) could hold or

[51] For maps of the subareas, see *Hearing on The Fisheries Conventions* before a Subcommittee of the Committee on Foreign Relations of the U.S. Senate, 81 Cong., 1 Sess., July 14, 1949, at p. 57, and S. Ex. Rept. No. 10, 81 Cong., 1 Sess., July 25, 1949, entitled *International Convention for the Northwest Atlantic Fisheries*, at p. 6. Also colored map in British text of the agreement, Treaty Series No. 62 (1950), Cmd. 8071.

arrange such hearings as it deemed helpful to secure factual information to carry out the provisions of the convention. The agreement did not, however, spell out the circumstances and conditions under which such commission hearings could be held. This is an interesting device, however, and, from the point of view of the traditional reticence of a sovereign with respect to the exercise of any functions by any international body in national territory, a bold one. And finally, the financing of the whole organization set up by the treaty is geared to the number of panels on which a party is represented.

The mechanism is designed to provide continuous scientific and other study of the entire area and of each subarea and to provide a procedure for the adoption of "proposals" for the regulation of fisheries in the entire area or in any subarea. Any panel by a two-thirds vote may recommend to the commission a proposal relating to its subarea. After review by the commission, the proposal may be adopted for the subarea by consent of all the governments represented on the panel for that area. It then becomes binding upon *all* parties to the convention. In effect, the governments on each panel may "legislate" for that subarea and, cumulatively, all the governments on the commission by unanimous consent may "legislate" for the entire convention area. Thus, if obstruction is encountered with respect to a regulation for the entire area, one or more panels can proceed to regulate their particular subareas. This arrangement at least nicks the Gordian knot of unanimous consent of the contracting states without loss of protection for the parties with the greatest interest in a particular area. It is indeed one of the most heartening advances in modern international legislation.

Provision is also made for liaison with FAO and the International Council for the Exploration of the Sea as well as possible status as a specialized agency of the United Nations (Art. X). At its meeting in 1952 the commission decided that for the time being it would not seek the status of a specialized agency. The first meeting of the commission was held in Washington in 1951. By 1953 all ten signatories of the convention had perfected the instrument. Halifax was chosen as the headquarters of the organization. It was speedily perceived, however, that it would be convenient and useful to hold annual meetings of the commission on occasion in the territories of its European participants. Since the convention stipulated that both the annual meetings should be held and the headquarters located in North America, an amendment to the convention became necessary. An amendatory protocol signed at Washington, June 25, 1956, authorized the holding of annual meetings outside North America.[52]

By 1955 the machinery authorized to be set up by the convention was in full swing, making investigations,[53] adopting regulations, and cooperating with the organizations already named. In addition to observers from them, others have attended meetings of the commission and panels from the International North Pacific Fisheries Commission, the International Pacific Halibut Commission, the Permanent Commission established by the Overfishing Convention of 1946, and the Special Committee of the International Geophysical year.[54] American fishermen's organizations and seafood producers' and fisheries associations have regularly been represented in the advisory committee attached to the United States commissioners.

North Pacific Fisheries. The second important fisheries convention of the post-World War II period is that relating to the North Pacific.[55] Tensions arising out of the expanding Japanese fishing activities in that sector unquestionably contributed to the deterioration of peaceful relations with Canada and the United States in the pre-1939 period.[56] Accordingly, in pursuance of Article 9 of the Treaty of Peace with Japan of September 8, 1951,[57] a comprehensive convention designed to reduce

[52] 36 *DSB* 506 (1957).

[53] See the illuminating report by William M. Terry, "The North Atlantic Marine Research Program: Meeting of the International Commission for the Northwest Atlantic Fisheries at New Haven, Conn., May 25–30, 1953," 29 *DSB* 19–21 (1953).

[54] See notes in 24 *DSB* 595–596 (1951); 26 *DSB* 398 (1952); Edward Castleman, "International Commission for Northwest Atlantic Fisheries: Report on the First Meeting," 24 *DSB* 954–955 (1951); *U.S. Int. Conf. 1950–1951*, pp. 119–120; *ibid., 1951–1952*, pp. 155–157; *1952–1953*, pp. 83–85; *1953–1954*, pp. 110–111, and especially for *1954–1955*, pp. 118–120.

[55] Signed at Tokyo, May 9, 1952, 4 *UST* 380, *TIAS* 2786. See Hearing on S. 3713, before a Subcommittee of the Senate Committee on Interstate and Foreign Commerce, to give effect to the convention, July 12, 1954; Report on S. 3713, 83 Cong., 2 Sess., S. Rept. No. 1806, July 14, 1954; Hearing on H. R. 9786, before the House Committee on Merchant Marine and Fisheries, to give effect to the convention, July 13, 1954; Report on H. R. 9786, 83 Cong., 2 Sess., H. Rept. 2360, July 21, 1954. Enforcement Act: North Pacific Fisheries Act of 1954, Aug. 12, 1954, 68 *Stat.* 698, which incorporates by reference (Sec. 12) certain sections of the Northwest Atlantic Fisheries Act of 1950, *op. cit.*, amended to expand the area of authorization southward from 54° 40′ N.L. to 48° 30′ N.L. by act of July 24, 1957, 71 *Stat.* 310.

[56] See discussion above at pp. 169, 183.

[57] 3 *UST* 3169, *TIAS* 2490.

tension and lay the foundations for rational use and development of fisheries in the North Pacific was elaborated at a tripartite fisheries conference at Tokyo in the fall of 1951 and signed by the participants, the United States, Canada, and Japan, on May 9, 1952.[58]

In the effort to implement the new American conservation of fisheries policy, the convention had to include certain boldly imaginative principles and devices. For one thing, it introduced "a new principle in international conservation practice on the high seas. Under it special treatment is accorded to fisheries already fully utilized and fully conserved. Each signatory agrees to abstain from exploitation of specified fish stocks which are already exploited to the maximum by one or both of the other parties provided the latter are carrying out programs for the conservation of the stocks and agree to continue to carry out such programs. . . . The convention recognizes three stocks, salmon, halibut, and herring, off the coasts of North America as meeting these conditions. Accordingly, by the terms of the convention, Japan agrees to abstain from fishing salmon, halibut, and herring in specified waters off the coasts of North America, and Canada agrees to abstain from fishing salmon in the Bering Sea east of 175 degrees west longitude." [59] This latter area includes the contention-producing Bristol Bay, in which now Canada as well as Japan will abstain from fishing for the salmon resorting to Alaskan waters. Americans and Canadians will, however, under their existing sockeye-salmon and halibut treaties continue to share those fisheries off their Pacific coasts, but Japan will abstain.

Throughout the convention "provision was made for a high degree of flexibility to enable the Commission to handle both bilateral and trilateral problems and thus eliminate the necessity of negotiating additional fishery treaties among the three nations as new problems devel-

[58] "North Pacific Fisheries," 25 *DSB* 789 (1951); W. C. Herrington, "Problems Affecting North Pacific Fisheries: Tripartite Fisheries Conference at Tokyo, November 4–December 14, 1951," 26 *DSB* 340–346 (1952); "Fisheries Convention Signed by U.S., Canada, Japan," 26 *DSB* 830 (1952); and W. C. Herrington, "U.S. Policy on Fisheries and Territorial Waters," 26 *DSB* 1021–1023, at 1022 (1952). Summary of the conference, *U.S. Int. Conf. 1951–1952*, pp. 146–148; minutes of the *Tripartite Fisheries Conference, Canada-Japan-United States*, November 5–December 14, 1951, published by the Ministry of Foreign Affairs, Japan (1951). See also Edward V. Allen, "A New Concept for Fishery Treaties," 46 *A.J.I.L.* 319–323 (1952) and Charles B. Selak, Jr., "The Proposed International Convention for the High Seas Fisheries of the North Pacific Ocean," *ibid.*, pp. 323–330.

[59] "Fisheries Convention . . ." 26 *DSB* 830 (1952).

oped." [60] Students of the conservation of fisheries will marvel for years to come how boldly the principle of "abstention" has been introduced into treaty regulation and how neatly national and bipartite agreement conservation programs have been geared into a multipartite agreement.

An elaborate mechanism is set up under the new agreement for continuous study and regulation of other stocks of fish by an international commission on which each of the governments is represented by four delegates but with each section having only one vote. Participation in certain decisions and recommendations, for example, to adopt joint conservation measures or to relax the same, is restricted to the national sections of the commission whose countries are engaged in "substantial exploitation" of the stock of fish in question. Detailed provisions (Art. X) establish a procedure for arrest, detention, surveillance, and surrender for trial of nationals of any of the parties apprehended by officers of other parties for violating any of the regulations adopted in pursuance of the treaty. In a protocol annexed to the convention the parties agree that the line of meridian 175° west longitude as the boundary line for conservation measures relating to salmon of Asiatic origin and salmon of North American origin should be considered provisional, subject to rectification after further study of the stocks involved. Like the Northwest Atlantic agreement, this convention stipulated (Art. I) that nothing in the convention should "be deemed to affect adversely (prejudice) the claims of any Contracting Party in regard to the limits of territorial waters or to the jurisdiction of a coastal state over fisheries." That, presumably, again safeguards the American position with regard to offshore fisheries proclaimed by President Truman in 1945.

Like the Northwest Atlantic agreement, the North Pacific Convention provides (Art. II) for advisory committees to be established for each national section on the commission but for attendance of the whole committee at all sessions of the commission "except those which the Commission decides to be *in camera*." The commission is authorized to hold public hearings, but where or how is again not spelled out. Each national section may hold public hearings in its own country. Unlike the

[60] Herrington, *op. cit.*, 26 *DSB* 341. Early in 1953, before the treaty went into effect, Alaskans renewed their complaints that Japanese were not restricted in their exploitation of king crab, cod, mackerel, and shrimp off the Alaskan coasts. "Alaska and Japan Renew Old Feud," *N.Y.T.*, March 15, 1953.

Atlantic agreement, the Pacific Convention permits its commission to meet and establish its headquarters where it pleases.

The convention entered into force June 12, 1953. The first, organizing, meeting of the commission was held in Washington on February 1, 1954. Observers were present representing FAO, the International Pacific Halibut Commission, the International Pacific Salmon Fisheries Commission, the Inter-American Tropical Tuna Commission, and the International Commission for the Northwest Atlantic Fisheries. A group of American businessmen and scientists were also present by invitation. The commission chose the University of British Columbia in Vancouver, B.C., for its temporary headquarters, Vancouver for its first annual meeting in October 1954, and Tokyo for its second annual meeting in October 1955. The Advisory Committee attached to the American section at the Vancouver meeting included, as the treaty contemplated, an impressive list of representatives of the Alaskan territorial government, of the governments of several of the Pacific states, of fishermen's unions, and of cannery interests. Among the numerous topics discussed at the Vancouver meeting was the king crab, long a favorite object of exploitation by the Japanese.[61]

Thus, at long last, the regime got under way to resolve some of the fisheries problems which had for decades embittered the relations of the United States and Japan and which no doubt had made their contribution to the armed conflict begun at Pearl Harbor. In addition to agreeing finally to the principle of abstention, the governments involved agreed "jointly to undertake scientific research in high seas fisheries where needed and jointly to undertake fishing-control measures when science shows them to be desirable." [62] That should bring a little peace and quiet to the North Pacific for some time to come.

Halibut Fisheries. As already indicated, the North Pacific Fisheries Convention of 1952 left the halibut and various salmon fisheries, as well as the fur-seal fisheries, to be dealt with by separate arrangements.

Before examining the 1953 revision of the 1937 halibut convention, it

[61] See "Fisheries Commission Meeting," 30 *DSB* 165 (1954); "Fisheries Commission Selects Headquarters," 30 *DSB* 327 (1954); First Meeting, Washington, Feb. 1–12, 1954, *U.S. Int. Conf. 1953–1954*, pp. 106–109; First Annual Meeting, Vancouver, Oct. 25–29, 1954, *U.S. Int. Conf. 1954–1955*, pp. 115–118; Meeting of U.S. Section at Juneau, Alaska, Sept. 6–7, 1955, 33 *DSB* 357 (1955).

[62] Walter S. Robertson, Assistant Secretary for Far Eastern Affairs, "International Cooperation in Fisheries Conservation," 30 *DSB* 297 (1954).

The United States and the Treaty Law of the Sea

should be noted that an agreement between Canada and the United States, signed at Ottawa, March 24, 1950,[63] extended to the American and Canadian vessels engaged in the halibut fishery certain port privileges, very valuable for vessels often far from home ports. Thus American vessels were given the right to land their catches of halibut and sablefish in Canadian Pacific ports without payment of duties; to sell them locally on payment of the applicable customs duty; to transship them in bond under customs supervision to any port of the United States or sell them in bond for export; and to obtain supplies, repairs, and equipment. Canadian vessels were given the reciprocal privileges in ports of entry of the United States. These privileges had been accorded to American fishermen for fifty years previously on a year-to-year basis, but to Canadian fishermen only for two short war periods.[64] The convention of 1950 placed the privileges upon an assured continuing basis.

In accord with the new post-World War II fisheries conservation policy, namely, "to develop the stocks of halibut in the [designated] waters to those levels which will permit the maximum sustained yield and to maintain the stocks at those levels," a new convention signed at Ottawa, March 2, 1953,[65] replaced the agreement of January 29, 1937, discussed previously for the interwar period.

Among the most important changes made are these. No closed season is mentioned in the new convention: the commission, retained under the agreement, is empowered to establish all the necessary open and closed seasons for any one year. The possibility of having "more than one open season is expected to increase the yield from some halibut stocks which may be under-utilized at present." Regulatory authority is given "respecting halibut caught incidentally to fishing for other species of fish during the open season. The 1937 Convention had provided for this type of regulation only during the closed season."[66] Finally, the commission is enlarged to include three members from each government,

[63] 1 *UST* 536, *TIAS* 2096.
[64] *Legislative History of Committee on Foreign Relations, U.S. Senate, 81 Cong.,* 81 Cong., 2 Sess., S. Doc. No. 247, p. 43.
[65] Preservation of Halibut Fishery of Northern Pacific Ocean and Bering Sea, 5 *UST* 5, *TIAS* 2900. An act of Aug. 8, 1953, 67 *Stat.* 494, made the slight changes necessary in the old act of June 28, 1937, 50 *Stat.* 325, to bring the American legislation into conformity with the new convention. See Henry A. Dunlop, "Management of the Halibut Fishery of the North-Eastern Pacific Ocean and Bering Sea," in *Papers*, Rome 1955 Conference, *op. cit.*, pp. 222–242.
[66] "Halibut Convention with Canada," 29 *DSB* 723–724 (1953).

instead of the prior two, with decisions to be taken by concurrent vote of at least two members from each side (Art. III). This increase of membership was designed to give broader representation of areas and interests on the commission.[67] Thus, as a result, the members of the commission in 1957 included, for the American section, a representative from the Seattle halibut fleet, a resident of Alaska, and an employee of the United States Fish and Wildlife Service; for the Canadian section, an active halibut fisherman, a member of the British Columbia fishing industry, and a representative of the Canadian national Department of Fisheries. The American members are appointed by the President and serve at his pleasure for an indefinite term. Canadian members are appointed for specific terms.[68] This is indeed a most interesting step in the direction of functional representation.

As a result of the new convention and "subsequent changes in the management of the halibut fishing," the Secretary of the Interior could report in 1955 that "the catch in the summer of 1954 broke all records, producing approximately 71 million pounds of fish, a gain of 11 million pounds or 18 per cent over the preceding year's catch."[69]

Pink or Humpback Salmon. It will be recalled from the discussion of the efforts in the interwar period to regulate the salmon fisheries dependent upon the Fraser River system that only one of the five species using that river, namely, the sockeye salmon, was placed under international regulation by the agreement of May 26, 1930.[70] It will also be recalled that in 1944 the United States and Canada entered into an agreement to remove the obstructions in Hell's Gate Canyon in British Columbia which interfered with the spawning of the sockeye salmon.[71] The efforts to rehabilitate this fishery appear to be coming into their reward, for the Secretary of the Interior was able to report in 1955 that the International Pacific Salmon Fisheries Commission "produced striking results. The 1954 catch from the sockeye salmon runs of the Fraser River

---

[67] Message of the President, transmitting the convention to the Senate, 83 Cong., 1 Sess., S. Ex. P, July 1, 1953. See also 83 Cong., 1 Sess., S. Ex. Rept. 7, accompanying the same.

[68] Letter, International Pacific Halibut Commission to writer, March 21, 1957. The headquarters of the commission is at Fisheries Hall No. 2, University of Washington, Seattle 5, Washington.

[69] *1955 Annual Report of the Secretary of the Interior*, p. 328.

[70] 50 *Stat.* 1355, *TS* 918, discussed above at p. 173. The office and laboratory of the commission is in the Dominion Building, New Westminster, B.C.

[71] 59 *Stat.* 1614, *EAS* 479.

system exceeded by far any runs since the organization of the Commission." [72]

On December 28, 1956, the United States and Canada signed a protocol [73] amending the convention of 1930 to place the pink or humpback salmon fishery under regulation by the International Pacific Salmon Fisheries Commission, which, it will be recalled, was set up in 1937 when the 1930 convention went into effect.

The Commission will now have the same powers of research and regulation over pink salmon as it has over sockeye salmon. It is charged with so regulating the pink-salmon fisheries as to achieve maximum sustainable productivity of the pink-salmon stocks. At the same time it must, as far as is possible, divide the catch equally between the United States and Canadian fishermen. The convention area remains unchanged. It covers Juan de Fuca Strait, part of Georgia Strait, the Fraser River System, and an area of the high seas of the Pacific Ocean. The Fraser River pink salmon, which make their spawning runs every 2 years through the straits, account for much of the $10 million pink-salmon catch made every other year by the fishermen of Washington and British Columbia. Other modifications made by the protocol in the convention include . . . a greater flexibility in the Commission's power to issue regulations in certain areas. The protocol also provides for intensive investigation by the Commission and by research agencies on both sides of the border of all pink-salmon stocks which enter convention waters. The protocol calls for a United States-Canadian Government meeting in its seventh year of operation for a review of research findings and a consideration of further arrangements for pink-salmon conservation.[74]

Article V of the protocol makes an additional noteworthy change in the 1930 arrangement. The text of the 1930 convention did not contain any provision for any advisory committee representing the private groups interested in the sockeye salmon regime. At the time of the exchange of the ratifications of the convention, in Washington, on July 28, 1937, however, a protocol [75] was signed containing three understandings, one stipulatiing that the commission should have "no power to authorize

[72] *1955 Report, op. cit.*, p. 328. See Loyd A. Royal, "International Pacific Salmon Fisheries Commission," *Papers*, Rome 1955 Conference, *op. cit.*, pp. 243–255.

[73] "United States and Canada Sign Salmon Conservation Agreement," 36 *DSB* 76–77 (1957), which includes the text of the protocol; see also report on enabling act to implement the agreement, 85 Cong., 1 Sess., S. Rept. No. 302 (1957). Text of protocol also in 8 *UST* 1057, *TIAS* 3867.

[74] 36 *DSB* 76 (1957).

[75] Provisions repeated in President's proclamation containing text of the convention, 50 *Stat.* 1355, *TS* 918.

any type of fishing gear contrary to the laws of the State of Washington or the Dominion of Canada"; a second stipulating that the commission should make no regulations until scientific investigations had been made covering two complete cycles of sockeye-salmon runs or eight years; and a third providing that the commission should set up an advisory committee composed of five persons from each country representing the several branches of the industry, that is, purse seine, gill net, troll, sport fishing, and "one other." This advisory committee was to be invited to attend all nonexecutive meetings of the commission, with full opportunity to present their views and examine all proposed orders, regulations, and recommendations of the commission. The 1956 protocol alters this third understanding by increasing the number of members for each country to six, "who shall be representatives of the various branches of the industry including, but not limited to, purse seine, gill net, troll, sport fishing, and processing." The functions of the advisory committee remain the same.

Fur Seals. The arrangements concerning one further fishery in the North Pacific remained to be revised after World War II, those dealing with the fur seals. The Tripartite Fisheries Conference at Tokyo in 1951 did not discuss fur seals. The regulation of their exploitation remained under the United States-Canadian bipartite agreement of 1942 [76] until a new multipartite convention could be concluded. Looking forward to the formulation of such a new convention, the United States, Japan, and Canada entered into an agreement early in 1952 [77] which provided for joint research programs to expand the existing factual information concerning the distribution, migration, and feeding habits of the fur seals. Preliminary investigations had been conducted in the waters off the coasts of Japan in 1949 and 1950 by the Fisheries Agency of the Japanese government with the cooperation of the Fish and Wildlife Service of the United States and under the auspices of the Supreme Commander for the Allied Powers then still in authority in Japan. The results of the preliminary studies indicated the desirability of a wider study during the months of February to June 1952. Hence the agreement of 1952.

[76] Provisional Fur Seal Agreement, Dec. 8 and 19, 1942, 58 *Stat.* 1379, EAS 415, as amended by the agreement of Dec. 26, 1947, 62 *Stat.* (2) 1821, TIAS 1686.

[77] Effected by exchange of notes signed at Tokyo, Jan. 31 and Feb. 8, 1952, and at Ottawa, Feb. 7 and March 1, 1952. Entered into force with respect to the United States and Japan, Feb. 8, 1952 and with respect to Canada, March 1, 1952, 3 *UST* 3896–3904, *TIAS* 2521.

The Soviet Union was invited to participate but it did not enter into the agreement of 1952.

Since the Japanese government had complained in the years before World War II about the excessive inroads made by the fur seals, particularly those from the largest herd, that is, those frequenting the Pribilof Islands, upon fish stocks essential to Japanese economy, the research program concentrated upon securing data concerning the following matters: "the number of Pribilof fur seals which inhabit coastal waters of Canada, Japan, and the United States of America and the approximate length of time spent in such waters; the feeding habits of the fur seals while inhabiting coastal waters of Canada and of Japan, with special reference to the species of fish, and quantities of each species, consumed by the fur seals during their sojourn in such waters; [and] the commercial value to the several countries of the fish so consumed by fur seals." The agreement allowed approximately 3000 fur seals to be taken pelagically (that is, on the surface) in coastal waters of Japan and approximately 2000 in the same way in the coastal waters of North America for the scientific purposes embraced in the research programs.

Following these investigations, the United States, Canada, Japan, and the Soviet Union entered into negotiations and concluded a new Interim Convention on the Conservation of North Pacific Fur Seals, signed at Washington, February 9, 1957.[78] The new convention is intended to continue in effect for at least an initial period of six years and thereafter indefinitely unless superseded by a revised convention or denounced in accordance with its terms (Art. XIII). When ratified, the convention is deemed to have been operative as from June 1, 1956, provided the parties shall have prohibited the acts proscribed by the convention as of the date of signing.

The new convention has two principal objectives: the maintenance of a research program and control of the harvesting. The provisions relating to control of the taking of skins follow generally along the lines of the old convention concluded in 1911 [79] and terminated, after denunciation by Japan, on October 23, 1941. Thus, the new convention applies to the same three commercially valuable herds, namely, those frequenting the Pribilof Islands in the Bering Sea, under American jurisdiction

[78] Text, 36 *DSB* 376–380 (1957); entered into force Oct. 14, 1957; 8 *UST* 2283, *TIAS* 3948.
[79] Signed at Washington, July 7, 1911, 37 *Stat.* 1542, *TS* 564.

since 1867; the Commander Islands, off the coast of Kamchatka, historically a possession of Russia; and Robben Island,[80] off the coast of the southern part of Sakhalin Island, a Japanese possession in 1911 and up to World War II but since then under Soviet jurisdiction. It prohibits pelagic sealing by unauthorized persons and provides for a mutual right of visit and search and arrest of offenders (the flag state being responsible for the prosecution of the offenders); the taking of pelts for commercial purposes by the governments concerned on dry land; and a sharing of the harvest in accordance with an adjusted system of percentages and quotas. The basic arrangement is that Canada and Japan will receive each year from the Soviet Union and the United States 15 per cent of the sealskins taken on the islands by the latter two governments.

Several new features, however, reflect the progress made over the past half century in conservation theory and also a desire to prevent excessive damage by the seals to other commercial fisheries. It also contains the now usual reservation concerning national jurisdiction over offshore fisheries. The new conservation policy, as stated in the preamble, is geared to the special problem created by the eating habits of the seals: the parties desire "to take effective measures towards achieving the maximum sustainable productivity of the fur seals resources of the North Pacific Ocean so that the fur seal populations can be brought to and maintained at the levels which will provide the greatest harvest year after year, with due regard to their relation to the productivity of other living marine resources of the area." No doubt this task of balancing several highly fluctuating populations of marine life will in time produce a new species of mathematician, the ichthyological calculus expert.

At any rate, the goals are clear. To achieve them, a newly devised North Pacific Fur Seal Commission is set up, with one member from each party. Each member is entitled to one vote and decisions and recommendations are to be made by unanimous vote. This commission has the duties, among others, of directing the elaborate, continuing, and cooperative research program required by the convention (Art. II) and

[80] The word "robben" means "seal" in Dutch. Atlases show a Robben Island off Cape Province, Union of South Africa, but not the one off Sakhalin. However, see Charles O. Paullin, *Atlas of the Historical Geography of the United States* (1932), Plate 166, for the one off Sakhalin.

of recommending, on the basis of the scientific findings, appropriate measures to the parties, "including measures regarding the size and the sex and age composition of the seasonal commercial kill from a herd" (Art. V).

A few other new features of the convention merit noting. Thus, an extensive system of tagging black pups is instituted, 50,000 per year for four years by the United States on the Pribilof Islands and 25 per cent of the black pups annually on the Commander Islands and Robben Island, by the Soviet government. The term "black pups" as used in the agreement refers to pups of the year of both sexes. All pups at birth are jet black in color. Before they leave the islands in the fall or early winter they change to the grayish brown of the older animals. Hence the term is used to differentiate clearly between the newly born pups and yearling seals. The pups are tagged by attaching a Monel metal tag to the thinner margin of one of the flippers. "For further identification, a notch is usually cut in the margin of a second flipper."[81] This procedure facilitates tracing the seals for the purposes of scientific study and proper management of the herds.

Article VIII obligates the parties to prohibit the importation and delivery into and the traffic within its territories of skins taken in contravention of the agreement. Article X (7) obligates each party to contribute to the joint expenses of the commission, in addition to the equal contributions otherwise established, "an amount equivalent to the value of the sealskins it confiscates" under the criminal prosecution process required by Article VI. And, finally, among the data to be ascertained by means of the continuing investigations is the amount of "damage fur seals inflict on fishing gear." This refers to the damage allegedly caused to gill nets by seals feeding on fish caught in their meshes. The Japanese in particular complained about this before World War II. The extent of the damage that can accurately be charged to fur seals has, however, never been ascertained. The new convention now requires the commission to find the facts. Then perhaps something can be done about it.

Having disposed of the current efforts relating to fisheries in the North Pacific it would be most convenient simply to stay in the Pacific and

[81] Letter from the Fish and Wildlife Service to the writer, March 28, 1957. See for further details of this fascinating conservation process Victor B. Scheffer, *Experiments in the Marking of Seals and Sea-Lions, Special Scientific Report: Wildlife No. 4* (1950); Karl W. Kenyon and Victor B. Scheffer, *A Population Study of the Alaska Fur Seal Herd, Special Scientific Report: Wildlife No. 12* (1954).

examine the difficulties created by the tuna fisheries in the south central waters. But various difficulties associated with the tuna fisheries can be traced pretty directly to acts, claims, and policies emanating from sundry Latin American states which assert a considerable national interest in the fisheries. Since the United Nations International Law Commission in its 1956 report dealt with some of these matters, it will be more expedient to postpone discussion of the tuna fisheries until the commission's report can be considered also. This procedure makes it possible first to dispose of two other fisheries topics, the agreements with Canada relating to shellfish and the Great Lakes fisheries and the post-World War II regime on whaling.

United States-Canada Shellfish Agreement. An agreement of March 4 and April 30, 1948, remarkable for its display of mutual confidence in the public administration of the two governments, provided that "whatever manual of recommended practice for sanitary control of the shellfish industry is approved by both the United States Public Health Service and the Canadian Department of National Health and Welfare, will be regarded as setting forth the sanitary principles that will govern the certification of shellfish shippers." The agreement further provided for reciprocal reports of compliance and the facilitation of reciprocal inspection of shellfish handling facilities or of shellfish growing areas.[82]

Great Lakes Fisheries. Though a comprehensive agreement regulating the Great Lakes fisheries remains to be concluded, a modest beginning has been made in the Great Lakes Fisheries Convention signed at Washington, September 10, 1954.[83] The convention area embraces the Great Lakes, their connecting waters, the St. Lawrence River up to the forty-fifth parallel, which is the northern boundary of New York state, and the tributaries of each of these waters to the extent necessary to achieve the objectives of the agreement. The objectives of the convention are threefold: "to formulate and coordinate research programs to determine the type of measures, if any, required to make possible the maximum sustained productivity of any stock of Great Lakes fish which is of common concern to the United States and Canada; to recommend

---

[82] Shellfish: Sanitary Certification of Shippers. Agreement effected by exchange of notes, signed at Washington, March 4 and April 30, 1948, 62 *Stat.* (2) 1898, *TIAS* No. 1747.

[83] Entered into force, Oct. 11, 1955, 6 *UST* 2836, *TIAS* 3326. See Charles B. Selak, Jr., "The United States-Canadian Great Lakes Fisheries Convention," 50 *A.J.I.L.* 122–129 (1956).

appropriate measures to the parties on the basis of the findings of such research programs; and to formulate and implement a comprehensive program to abate the sea lamprey populations in the lakes."[84]

Unlike the 1946 convention,[85] which was never acted upon by the Senate, the 1954 agreement confers no regulatory powers upon the commission set up under it. The commission can only recommend action to the two federal governments. In the case of the United States, a recommendation relating to the regulation of fishing operations would have to be transmitted by the federal government to the eight lake states for such action as the states might see fit to take.[86] Verily it seems sometimes easier to get eight nation-states in the alleged "anarchy" of the international community to agree upon some common course of action than to get eight states in this "more perfect union" to do the same[87] or to yield to national regulation.

As in several other conventions concluded in the post-World War II period, the commission established by the present agreement consists of two national sections composed of three members each. The device of three members to a side permits, as in the case of the halibut and other conservation agreements, the inclusion of commissioners representing areas and interests embraced within the treaty scheme. The United States enforcing statute (Sec. 3) stipulates that one of the American commissioners shall be a federal official and the other two residents of the Great Lakes states, "duly qualified by reason of knowledge of the fisheries of the Great Lakes, of whom one shall be an official of a Great

[84] *Giving Effect to the Convention on Great Lakes Fisheries*, 84 Cong., 2 Sess., H. Rept. No. 2154, May 14, 1956, p. 7. See also: 84 Cong., 2 Sess., S. Rept. No. 1858, April 25, 1956; *Hearing on Great Lakes Fishery Act of 1956 before the Subcommittee on Fisheries and Wildlife Conservation of the Committee on Merchant Marine and Fisheries, House of Representatives*, 84 Cong., 2 Sess., May 3, 1956.

[85] Discussed above, p. 175.

[86] *Great Lakes Fisheries Convention*, 84 Cong., 1 Sess., S. Ex. Rept. No. 7, May 23, 1955, p. 4. For analysis of this convention as well as others already discussed, see "Organization and Operation of International Fishery Commissions" in *Hearing on Great Lakes Fisheries Convention before a Subcommittee of the Committee on Foreign Relations, United States Senate*, 84 Cong., 1 Sess., April 27, 1955, pp. 26–32.

[87] Nevertheless the states have on occasion entered into interstate fisheries compacts serving limited administrative objectives under authorization of Congress: a Columbia River Fish Compact between Oregon and Washington in 1918; an Atlantic Marine Fisheries Compact, 1942; and similar compacts for the Pacific States and the Gulf States in 1947. Full citations in *Interstate Compacts 1783–1956*, Council of State Governments (1956), mimeo. See also note on these compacts on "Regional Education: A New Use of the Interstate Compact?" 34 *Virginia Law Review* 64–76 (1948), at p. 72.

Lakes State."[88] Each section, however, has but one vote under the agreement. Furthermore, the convention does not prescribe any mode for determining how that vote is to be cast. A decision or recommendation of the commission may be made only with the approval of both sections.

The commission may pick a headquarters site, but it must be in the Great Lakes area. Because of the great complexity of interests and jurisdictions in the convention area, the advisory committee device is elaborated somewhat. Each of the parties to the agreement may establish an advisory committee, attached to its section, for each of the Great Lakes. The American enforcing act (Sec. 4) spells this provision out thus: each lake state is entitled to four members. In making the selection from a list proposed by the governor of each state concerned, the United States section must give "due consideration to the interests of state agencies having jurisdiction over fisheries, the commercial fishing industry of the lake, the sports fishing of the lake, and the public at large." The convention provides that each of the advisory committees may attend all the sessions of the commission except those held *in camera* (Art. II).

The commission has wide discretion, in the performance of its duties, to make use of the official agencies of the two governments and of their provinces or states and private or other public organizations, including international organizations, or any person. To achieve its purposes, the commission is authorized to conduct investigations and also to hold hearings in both the United States and Canada.

The convention is intended to serve a long-range objective, the sustaining of the maximum productivity of desirable fish in the Great Lakes, and a hopefully short-range objective, the eradication of the sea lamprey pest.

The parasitic sea lamprey . . . an eel-like creature about 18 inches long, is predatory upon the food fish of the upper lakes. It attacks most readily the more valuable species such as lake trout and white fish. It attaches itself to the fish by the suctionlike cup of its mouth and subsists by draining off the blood and body fluids of its host. . . . The lamprey has lived in Lake Ontario since prehistoric times, but the barrier of Niagara Falls kept it from spreading to the other Great Lakes until the opening of the Welland Canal provided a means of bypassing Niagara.

[88] Act of June 4, 1956, 70 *Stat.* 242.

The lamprey finds the environment of Lake Erie inhospitable, and has never established itself there, but it did pass through Erie and appeared in Lake Huron in the early 1930's and in Lake Michigan shortly thereafter. As a result, the trout catch by American fishermen in Lake Huron declined from 1.7 million pounds in 1935 to less than 50 pounds in 1951. In Lake Michigan the catch dropped from 6,800,000 pounds in 1943 to 3,000 pounds in 1952.

The lamprey spawns in streams of a certain gradient and with certain types of beds. It remains in the beds of these streams for approximately 4½ years, at the end of which time it floats down stream and enters the lake. . . . Once in the lake, the lamprey begins its parasitic life and within 10 months attains an average length of 14.6 inches and a weight of 2.8 ounces. . . . It destroys 94 ounces of fish for each ounce that it grows itself. The annual destruction of fish by 100,000 lampreys would be approximately 1,860,000 pounds. Many streams flowing into the Great Lakes have runs in excess of 20,000 lampreys. . . . After approximately 2 years in the lake, the lamprey goes upstream, spawns, and dies. It is a highly prolific creature. The average number of eggs deposited by each female is 61,000.[89]

Up to the conclusion of the convention the United States Fish and Wildlife Service had developed and used on 71 out of the 230 streams on the American side suitable for spawning certain electrical and mechanical devices which intercept the adult on its way upstream. "Thus prevented from reaching its spawning grounds, the lamprey will die without spawning." The lamprey control devices do not interfere with the movements of other fish. The convention provides for the extension of the system of control on the American side and secures the cooperation of the Canadian government in the establishment of a similar system on the Canadian side. The convention authorizes the commission "to formulate and implement a comprehensive program for the purpose of eradicating or minimizing the sea lamprey populations in the Convention area" (Art. IV). The costs of the joint program are to be shared by Canada and the United States in proportion to the annual take of lake trout and whitefish from Lakes Huron, Michigan, and Superior during the ten years preceding the measureable onset of the sea lamprey.[90] The convention is effective for an initial period of ten years and

[89] Quotations pieced together from H. Rept. No. 2154, p. 6, and S. Ex. Rept. No. 7, pp. 3–4, *op. cit.*

[90] Message of the President transmitting the convention to the Senate, 84 Cong., 1 Sess., S. Ex. B, Jan. 26, 1955, p. 3. For experiments with selective chemical larvicides, see *N.Y.T.*, Aug. 3, 1958.

indefinitely thereafter unless denounced on two years notice by either party.

Thus, finally, a belated beginning has been made to rescue the remaining choice fish from the predatory lamprey; to conduct cooperatively — nation with nation, nation with states, nation with provinces, states with provinces — the research programs upon which may be based measures to achieve maximum sustained productivity of the selected fish stocks; and to secure the cooperation under federal leadership of the jealous rivalry-riven American lake states. Whoever devised the Great Lakes Fisheries Convention and the American statute enforcing the same could have spared Solomon many an anxious moment as he proceeded to judgment upon babies and other equally indivisible entities.

Whales. The post-World War II revision of the 1931 and 1937 agreements on the regulation of whaling, concluded at Washington on December 2, 1946,[91] made a bold attack on the problem in the spirit of the new conservation policy. Briefly, the arrangement set up an international commission with administrative and subordinate rule-making powers; separated the accumulated, revised regulations into a code called a "Schedule," which was attached to the convention and made an integral part thereof; empowered the commission to amend the code of regulations without the necessity of calling a formal conference as in the interwar period; and authorized the commission to make recommendations to any and all the contracting governments to effectuate the purposes of the new arrangement.

After ten years' experience in administering the provisions of the 1946 convention, the commission recommended and secured the adoption in Washington on November 19, 1956, of a protocol amending the principal convention.[92] These amendments make it possible for the

[91] Convention, entered into force Nov. 10, 1948, 62 *Stat.* (2) 1716, *TIAS* 1849. See Report of the Acting Secretary of State in Message from the President to the Senate, S. Ex. L, 80 Cong., 1 Sess., April 8, 1947, reprinted in 16 *DSB* 772–774 (1947); *Hearing* on S. 2080, Subcommittee of the Senate Committee on Interstate and Foreign Commerce, 81 Cong., 1 Sess., July 20, 1949; *Regulation of Whaling,* 81 Cong., 1 Sess., S. Rept. No. 814, Aug. 1, 1949; Whaling Convention Act of 1949, approved Aug. 9, 1950, 64 *Stat.* (1) 421–425. Also see Remington Kellogg, "The International Whaling Commission," *Papers,* Rome 1955 Conference, pp. 256–261.

[92] See Message of the President transmitting the Protocol to the Senate, Feb. 14, 1957, 85 Cong., 1 Sess., S. Ex. E. It may be noted that since the original whaling convention of 1946 had received the advice and consent of the Senate to its ratification by the President, this amendment of its text also must receive such advice and consent to be ratified. The case of the amendments to the Schedule, adopted by the

commission to regulate the use of helicopters and other aircraft in the taking of whales; to reduce the number of government inspectors for refrigerated ships, since these do not engage in taking whales; and to appoint observers responsible to and paid by the commission to supervise the government inspectors provided for in the revised convention of 1946.

The commission, modeled after the other fisheries commissions already discussed, is composed of one member for each contracting government. Each member has one vote. Ordinary decisions are taken by a simple majority of those members voting; changes in the Schedule or code of regulations require a three-fourths majority of those members voting. The commission can meet where and when necessary. It has extensive authority to organize studies and gather data concerning whales and whaling. It can publish reports by itself or in collaboration with the Bureau for Whaling Statistics at Sandefjord or with other public and private agencies.

The heart of the new dispensation is the rule-making power of the commission. Article V of the convention authorizes the commission to amend "the Schedule by adopting regulations with respect to the conservation and utilization of whale resources, fixing protected and unprotected species; open and closed seasons; open and closed waters, including the designation of sanctuary areas; size limits for each species; time, methods, and intensity of whaling (including the maximum catch of whales to be taken in any one season); types and specifications of gear and appliances which may be used; methods of measurements; and catch returns and other statistical and biological records." Although the commission can fix the maximum catch for all operations for any one year, it cannot restrict "the number or nationality of factory ships or land stations, nor allocate specific quotas to any factory ship or land station" or any group of the same. Each such amendment becomes effective for all the contracting governments ninety days following notification to the governments. Opportunity is given to object to any amendment and to "opt out" of its application under certain conditions. In addition to this extensive power to make rules which are legally binding, the commission can make recommendations

---

commission, is different. The protocols into which they are put become effective for the United States as executive agreements, in pursuance of the authority conferred in the original convention.

directed to any specific (possibly laggard) government or to all participating governments.

The convention itself prohibits the payment of any bonus to any gunners or crews of whale catchers with respect to the taking of forbidden whales. A new provision obligates governments to report their prosecutions of illicit acts.

Among the numerous refinements incorporated in the new Schedule is one requiring governments to maintain two government appointed and paid inspectors on each factory ship in order to maintain twenty-four hour inspection. Governments are also required to maintain adequate government inspection at all land stations under their jurisdiction.

The most important refinement, however, solved the problem of enforcement of the maximum gross take provision. Article 4 of the London 1945 protocol had made a beginning in the solution. The scheme adopted by the new Schedule, as further worked out in amendments since then, is briefly this: at its annual meeting during the summer, the commission, utilizing the accumulated data furnished it by the bureau at Sandefjord, prescribes the dates for the forthcoming open season in the principal whaling waters, which are south of 40° south latitude, and fixes a maximum for the gross catch of the pelagic operations. For the 1956/1957 season, for example, a total of 14,500 blue whale units was fixed. Then, during the open season each factory ship which is subject to the treaty regime must report by radio to the bureau at Sandefjord within two days after each calendar week the number of blue whale units caught by its whale catchers. The bureau tabulates the returns. When the mounting total reaches a prefixed "alerting" number, 13,000 for 1956/1957, the bureau so informs the whaling fleets. Thereafter, each factory ship must report its catch daily. When the prefixed grand total for the season is approached, the bureau determines the probable date on which the total will be reached and sends out a warning at least four days in advance. When the date falls, pelagic whaling for that area for that season ends. The inspectors on each vessel are responsible to their governments for securing compliance with all the rules and the governments in turn are responsible to the commission for faithful performance of the treaty obligations. Separate elaborate rules govern land stations and their operations.

The United States and the Treaty Law of the Sea

A new encouraging chapter in conservation of resources of the sea is being opened up by the 1946 agreement and the continuous fact-finding, rule-making, and recommendation-making functions of the commission. Nineteen governments were represented at the Washington conference; fifteen signed the agreement, including the Soviet Union. When the commission met for its first session, in London in June 1949, eleven governments had ratified or adhered. Japan had been permitted to resume whaling operations in 1947.[93] It was represented at this first session by an observer appointed by the Supreme Commander for the Allied Powers, then still in occupation of Japan. By October 31, 1956, seventeen governments, including Japan and all of the principal states with whaling interests except Argentina, Chile, Italy, and Portugal, had become parties to the 1946 convention.

The headquarters of the commission was established at the British Fisheries Department in London but the meetings of the Commission are held in the territories of various contracting governments.[94] Thus since the first meeting in London in 1949, annual meetings have been held as follows: Second, 1950, Oslo; Third, 1951, Cape Town; Fourth, 1952, London; Fifth, 1953, London; Sixth, 1954, Tokyo; Seventh, 1955, Moscow; Eighth, 1956, London; and Ninth, 1957, London. Amendments to the Schedule have been adopted thus far at each meeting. They become treaty commitments for each of the parties to the 1946 convention.[95] They deal with one or another of all species of whales in all seas and for various seasons, prescribing limits for different species, closed seas, sanctuaries, and closed seasons for selected species up to five years duration, as in one case for the humpback whale and the blue whale in the North Atlantic and the North Pacific. The advantages of the flexible administrative method, made possible by means of a permanent commis-

---

[93] 17 *DSB* 48 (1947).

[94] See First meeting, *U.S. Int. Conf. 1948–1949*, pp. 122–123; Second, *ibid.*, *1950–1951*, pp. 127–129; Third and Fourth, *ibid.*, *1951–1952*, pp. 165–170; Fifth, *ibid.*, *1952–1953*, pp. 89–91; Sixth, *ibid.*, *1954–1955*, pp. 134–136.

[95] Amendments adopted at the First Meeting, London, May 30–June 7, 1949, 1 *UST* 506, *TIAS* 2092; Second Meeting, Oslo, July 1950, 2 *UST* 11, *TIAS* 2173; Third Meeting, Cape Town, July 1951, 3 *UST* 2999, *TIAS* 2486; Fourth Meeting, London, June 1952, 3 *UST* 5094, *TIAS* 2699; Fifth Meeting, London, June 1953, 4 *UST* 2179, *TIAS* 2866; Sixth Meeting, Tokyo, July 19–23, 1954, 6 *UST* 645–654, *TIAS* 3198; Seventh Meeting, Moscow, July 18–23, 1955, 7 *UST* 657, *TIAS* 3548; Eighth Meeting, London, July 16–20, 1956, 8 *UST* 69, *TIAS* 3739; Ninth Meeting, London, June 24–28, 1957, 8 *UST* 2203, *TIAS* 3944.

sion, over the "statutory" method used in the interwar period is thus readily perceivable.

The commission uses committees and subcommittees for various purposes, the most important one thus far being the Scientific Committee. It adopts as many as sixteen recommendations in one meeting (1950), to correct abuses and to achieve the purposes of the regime. Several have dealt with the tagging of whales for scientific study and one, in 1950, dealt with "the regular transmission of meteorological reports from the Antarctic by wireless from whaling ships," for the use of the World Meteorological Organization, thus using a source of observation in an area not often traversed by merchant vessels. Studies have been made of the heavy assaults upon the humpback whale in all the seas and of the recently introduced use of helicopters in the killing of whales. As in the case of the commissions established under other recent fisheries conventions, the FAO is regularly represented at the meetings by observers, as are usually also the International Council for the Exploration of the Sea, the International Union for the Protection of Nature, and the Association of Whaling Companies.

When the history of these efforts to curb the rapacity of man and the cupidity of nations in the interest of preserving a valuable resource of the sea is written up, the name of one man, who has labored against overwhelming odds for over two decades and who recently was elected chairman of the Whaling Commission for a term of three years, will stand forth pre-eminently, the Director of the United States National Museum, Dr. A. Remington Kellogg.

Tuna Fisheries.[96] Between 1926 and 1948 the catch of the American tuna fleet, operating out of San Diego and San Pedro, California, and to a lesser extent out of Washington and Oregon ports, increased sevenfold, some 326,000,000 pounds being landed in California in 1948. The wholesale value of the tuna canned in the United States in 1948 was in excess of $125,000,000. These are large stakes in the national economy, which the government of the United States seeks to preserve.

"The principal fishing grounds lie in the high seas off the coast of Central and South America, from Mexico to northern Peru. As much as

[96] See excellent new bibliography by Wilvan G. Van Campen and Earl E. Hoven, *Tunas and Tuna Fisheries of the World: An Annotated Bibliography, 1930–1953*, Fishery Bulletin 111, U.S. Fish and Wildlife Service (1956); also Milner B. Schaefer, "Scientific Investigation of the Tropical Tuna Resources of the Eastern Pacific," *Papers*, Rome 1955 Conference, pp. 194–221.

90 percent of the tuna landed by the American fleet is taken in these waters, which lie south of San Diego and the extension westward of the northern Mexican Border. The American catch accounts for 95 percent of the total tuna harvested by all countries in this area. . . . As the United States tuna fisheries pushed farther south a considerable fishery arose off Costa Rica, and in increasing numbers the American fleet frequented Costa Rican territorial waters for the purpose of securing bait." By 1948, in spite of the sevenfold increase, there were already signs of diminishing returns, measured by catch per vessel. Bait depletion had begun in previously prolific grounds, especially in Costa Rican waters. The coastal shelves and territorial waters of Mexico and other Latin-American republics also furnish the live bait essential to the tuna fleet.[97]

In these circumstances, it was desirable to revive the scheme of a joint fisheries commission with Mexico. There had been provision for one in the short-lived convention of December 23, 1925, denounced within two years by the United States.[98] Accordingly, on January 25, 1949, at Mexico City, the United States and Mexico entered into an agreement to establish a bipartite International Commission for the Scientific Investigation of Tuna.[99] Soon thereafter, the Costa Rican government suggested a convention patterned after the one with Mexico. A convention concluded at Washington on May 31, 1949,[100] between the United States and Costa Rica, provided for the establishment of an Inter-American Tropical Tuna Commission, open to participation by other American states. On September 21, 1953, Panama adhered to this convention. At the same time, the commission having definitely established the disappearance from the Gulf of Puntarenas, Costa Rica, "for reasons not yet known, of the most important bait species, the anchovetta," the Republic of Panama donated two boat loads of anchovetta from the Gulf of Panama to be transplanted in the Gulf of Nicoya, off Costa Rica, in an effort to re-establish the species there.[101]

[97] *Two Tuna Conventions between the United States and Mexico and Costa Rica*, 81 Cong., 1 Sess., S. Ex. Rept. No. 11, July 25, 1949, pp. 2, 4.
[98] Discussed above, pp. 176–177.
[99] 1 *UST* 513, *TIAS* 2094.
[100] 1 *UST* 230, *TIAS* 2044; also in Message from President to the Senate, 81 Cong., 1 Sess., S. Ex. P, June 22, 1949. Comment on convention, 20 *DSB* 766 (1949).
[101] "Panama Joins Inter-American Tropical Tuna Commission," 29 *DSB* 489 (1953).

Health and Resources since World War II

The two conventions are substantially similar and can be discussed together. The preamble to the Mexican agreement cites the mutual desire to facilitate the maintaining of the populations of the fishes covered by the convention "at a level which will permit the maximum reasonable utilization without depletion year after year"; the Costa Rican uses the more familiar formula of maintaining the populations "at a level which will permit maximum sustained catches year after year." Each convention establishes a Joint Commission composed of two national sections, the one with Mexico stipulating four members each, the one with Costa Rica, one to four. Each section has one vote. Decisions require unanimity. The Mexican convention covers "the waters of the Pacific Ocean off the coasts of both countries and elsewhere as may be required," and extends to tuna and tuna-like fishes (that is, yellowfin, bluefin, and albacore tunas, bonitos, yellowtails, and skipjacks) and "the kinds of fishes commonly used as bait in tuna fishing" (Art. II). All these fisheries are of primary concern only to the United States and Mexico. The Costa Rican agreement applies to the yellowfin and skipjack tuna "in the waters of the eastern Pacific Ocean fished by the nationals" of the contracting governments, and "the kinds of fishes used as bait in the tuna fisheries, especially the anchovetta, and of other kinds of fish taken by tuna fishing vessels" (Art. II). These fisheries are in tropical waters and concern other governments besides the United States and Costa Rica. Hence the provision in the agreement permitting other governments to participate in the work of the commission if they wish.

"The functions of the Commissions are substantially the same. They are to gather scientific information. Each is authorized to conduct scientific studies, collect and analyze statistics, and engage in similar fact-finding activities. Each is also authorized to make recommendations to 'the High Contracting Parties' and to publish or otherwise disseminate reports of its findings or other appropriate reports. Neither, however, is authorized to promulgate regulations for the purpose of controlling fishing operations." [102] Each commission has a permanent staff headed by a Director of Investigations.

As in the case of other post-World War II fisheries arrangements, each section of the commission may have an advisory committee attached to

[102] S. Rept. No. 11, *op. cit.*, p. 3.

it with the right of attendance at sessions of the commission. The Inter-American Commission is authorized to hold public hearings, and the sections under both conventions may hold public hearings in their respective countries. The Mexican agreement was designed to run for an initial period of four years, the Costa Rican agreement for ten years, and thereafter indefinitely until denounced, with the usual requirement of a year's notice.

Up to the spring of 1957, the United States-Mexican Tuna Commission, had not been "activated."[103] The Inter-American Tropical Tuna Commission was, however, promptly established in 1951, with headquarters at the Scripps Institution of Oceanography at La Jolla, California.[104]

Technical Assistance. Consistent with this manifestation of a disposition on the part of the United States to solve fisheries problems in a cooperative spirit were certain agreements with Mexico and El Salvador to supply them with technical assistance. Thus in 1942, the United States agreed to furnish experts to study the shrimp and other marine fisheries of Mexico in the Gulf of California and to survey and help develop the fresh-water fish in the streams and lakes of Mexico.[105] These agreements were renewed from time to time up to 1950.[106] Similarly, for the period 1951 to 1955, the United States furnished El Salvador with the services of an expert to guide and advise that government in developing a fisheries industry.[107]

Mare Liberum or Mare Clausum

Seizures by Latin American Governments. While these tranquil transactions were in process, all was not otherwise quiet south of the Rio

[103] Letter from Fish and Wildlife Service to writer, April 8, 1957.

[104] See *Report of the Inter-American Tropical Tuna Commission for the Year 1955* (1956), covering the fifth year of its operations. The commission also publishes the results of its scientific investigations in a bulletin series.

[105] Fisheries Mission, agreement effected by exchanges of communications dated at Mexico, April 17, May 22, July 22 and 27, and Oct. 24, 1942, 58 *Stat.* 1554, *EAS* 443.

[106] Exchange of notes dated Sept. 7 and Oct. 18, 1944, amending and extending agreement of 1942, 58 *Stat.* 1562, *EAS* 443; further amended and extended by agreements entering into force Oct. 22, 1946, 61 *Stat.* (3) 2903, *TIAS* 1624; Oct. 6, 1948, 62 *Stat.* (3) 3575, *TIAS* 1869.

[107] Fisheries Mission, agreements entering into force July 19, 1951, 2 *UST* 2116, *TIAS* 2337; April 18, 1952, 3 *UST* 5200, *TIAS* 2717; Aug. 28, 1953, 4 *UST* 25, *TIAS* 2763; July 25, 1955, 6 *UST* 4111, *TIAS* 3423.

Grande. Many of the Latin American states either revived or formulated new claims to extensive national jurisdiction over resources in the coastal waters, in some cases, up to 200 miles offshore. Numerous American and other fishing vessels were seized and fined for violating these extraordinary decrees. Meanwhile, the United Nations International Law Commission was laboring to bring into some reasonable conspectus the various new national claims and practices related to use of the sea, balancing the new dependence on the sea with the community's need for the widest possible free sea.

The interrelations of these three developments are exceedingly complex. They have already perplexed the best of the jurists and tried the patience of the most peaceably disposed foreign offices for over a decade. It would be too sanguine to assume that they will be resolved in another decade. For the present discussion, therefore, those interrelations can only be outlined and summarized. Attention will be focused on the Latin American claims, though other extreme claims are also being made in other parts of the world, as by South Korea, the Soviet Union for areas off Siberia, Australia, Indonesia, and Iceland. Much has already been written about this controversy and no doubt many a tome will yet appear examining the details and merits of this revival in new guise of many of the issues involved in the old contest between *mare clausum* and *mare liberum*.

Starting with the Gulf of Mexico, various American and other shrimp boats were seized by Mexican officials in 1953 for violation of Mexican law.[108] Until a verified account of such incidents emanates from the Department of State it is difficult to judge the merits of the contending claims. Nevertheless, the official American view is that the shrimp fishery has from time to time "created complications between the people and Governments of the United States and Mexico. It is hoped that some understanding may be developed which will take into account the rights and interests of nationals of the two countries."[109]

---

[108] See: "Mexico Tightens Shrimp Boat Curb," *N.Y.T.*, Feb. 12, 1953; "Mexicans Suggest Shrimp Boat Pact," *N.Y.T.*, Feb. 18, 1953; "U.S. Shrimp Boats Seized by Mexico," *N.Y.T.*, Feb. 22, 1953; "Mexican Sentry Shoots Shrimper," *N.Y.T.*, March 12, 1953. Other incidents reported, *N.Y.T.*, Nov. 14–22, 1956. See also *Rights of Vessels of the United States on the High Seas and in the Territorial Waters of Foreign Countries*, 85 Cong., 1 Sess., S. Rept. No. 837 (1957), for further details of seizures by Mexico, allegedly 55 vessels up to Aug. 7, 1957.

[109] William C. Herrington, "U.S. Policy on Fisheries and Territorial Waters," 26 *DSB* 1021, 1022 (1952).

The United States and the Treaty Law of the Sea

In 1953, the American tuna clipper *Star Crest* was confiscated by a captain of the port in Panama for alleged violations of customs regulations but soon thereafter returned to its owner after appeal to the superior Administrator General of Customs.[110]

Seizure of four American, presumably tuna, fishing vessels by Ecuador led to a conference between the two governments at Quito in the spring of 1953. The conference agreed that it was not "within its competence to resolve differences in legal dispositions and juridical concepts of the United States and Ecuador regarding territorial waters and innocent passage, the principles of which in any event are not susceptible of bilateral determination since these principles are matters for determination only by general agreement of maritime States." Among the recommendations of an interim and long range character adopted, however, was one urging the Ecuadorian government to consider the advantages which might accrue to Ecuador through adherence to the Inter-American Tropical Tuna Convention.[111]

Subsequently, "on March 27, 1955, Ecuador seized two American flag fishing vessels, the *Arctic Maid* and *Santa Ana*, some 14 to 25 miles west of the Island of Santa Clara off the Ecuadorian coast. In the course of the seizure, an American seaman was seriously wounded by gunfire from an Ecuadorian patrol vessel. Although the United States made a strong protest against these illegal acts, fines of more than $49,000 were imposed on the two vessels."[112]

On the other hand, in spite of the fact that Peru is one of the most vigorous contenders for a vast territorial sea, the American tuna industry has "explored and brought into productivity extensive tuna fisheries lying within 30 to 100 miles of the Peruvian coast, well within the 200-mile limit that is now a part of Peruvian domestic law. This development has been undertaken with the full and detailed knowledge of the efficient Peruvian Navy. Not only has there been no hint of friction between the tuna fleet and the Peruvian Navy, but there has developed a degree of friendliness and camaraderie between the fishermen and the naval

[110] "Confiscated U.S. Ship Returned by Panama," *N.Y.T.*, July 5, 1953.
[111] "Conference on U.S.-Ecuadorian Fishery Relations," 28 *DSB* 759–761 (1953). See the illuminating comment on the conference by Charles B. Selak, Jr., "Fishing Vessels and the Principle of Innocent Passage," 48 *A.J.I.L.* 627–635 (1954).
[112] Herman Phleger, Legal Adviser of the Department of State, "Recent Developments Affecting the Regime of the High Seas," 32 *DSB* 934, 937 (1955).

personnel which would be considered somewhat extraordinary under even more normal conditions."[113]

If these were Victorian or Edwardian days of diplomacy, however, Peru would probably have found itself thoroughly at war for the following seizure, which did not involve American vessels. In November 1954, Peruvian war vessels and aircraft seized five whaling vessels flying the Panamanian flag and owned by A. S. Onassis, originally a Greek but at the crucial time an Argentinian citizen. "According to information furnished by Panama to the Organization of American States, two of the vessels were captured approximately 160 miles off the Peruvian coast; two others were attacked with bombs and machine gun fire by Peruvian naval and air units while 300 miles off the coast; and later the factory vessel was attacked by a Peruvian plane 364 miles offshore. These vessels were taken into a Peruvian port and detained until fines of $3 million were paid. Insurance against this hazard was held by Lloyd's (90 per cent) and by insurers in the United States (10 per cent). Panama, the United Kingdom, and the United States protested to Peru concerning the incident."[114]

In accordance with the present-day practice of diplomacy, these tortious acts are protested by the governments concerned and recorded against a grand reckoning to be made some day before a tribunal with either authority to find the law or power to apply the law as ascertained by some other authoritative body or as formulated in some agreement. It will be recalled that that was done with the accumulated claims arising out of the fur-seals controversy and the Northeastern Fisheries disputes. In the meantime, however, while this spirit of "continental solidarity" was thus expressing itself, contrary to the rational norms ascertained by the International Law Commission, some measure had to be taken by the United States to secure the speedy release of American vessels presumptively wrongfully seized and to reimburse them for the fines paid for alleged, or actual, violations of national laws solemnly opposed by the United States as infractions of the international law relating to jurisdiction in marginal seas.

[113] Wilbert M. Chapman, Director of Research, American Tunaboat Association, San Diego, California, ichthyologist and former Special Assistant to the Under Secretary of State (1948–1951), testifying at *Hearing To Protect Rights of United States Vessels on High Seas*, before Committee on Merchant Marine and Fisheries, H. of R., 83 Cong., 2 Sess. on H. R. 9584, July 2, 1954, p. 18.

[114] Phleger, *op. cit.*, p. 937.

The United States and the Treaty Law of the Sea

Reimbursement of Fines Act of 1954. In 1954, therefore, the United States adopted a statute, the like of which has probably not appeared on the books since the days of appropriations to pay the ransoms for American seamen captured by the Barbary Coast pirates. The act of August 27, 1954, provides that "in any case where a vessel of the United States is seized by a foreign country on the basis of rights or claims in territorial waters or the high seas which are not recognized by the United States; and there is no dispute of material facts with respect to the location or activity of such vessel at the time of such seizure, the Secretary of State shall as soon as practicable take such action as he deems appropriate to attend to the welfare of such vessel and its crew while it is held by such country and to secure the release of such vessel and crew." The Secretary of the Treasury is authorized to reimburse the vessel for the fine, if any, paid by it. The act does not apply to seizures by a country at war with the United States or made in accordance with the provisions of any fishery convention or treaty to which the United States is a party. The Secretary of State is, finally, directed to make and collect the appropriate claims against the seizing government.[115]

Latin American Offshore Claims. The claims to jurisdiction which furnished a basis for the seizures just described are, for the most part a perversion of the Truman proclamations of 1945 relating to the continental shelf and offshore fisheries. In part, in some cases, they are based on a new "bioma" theory of the interrelations of coastal communities with the sea.

The doctrinal controversy is devious and detailed.[116] At the risk of

---

[115] 68 *Stat.* 883. See also the *Hearings* on the bill, H. R. 9584, *op. cit.*, which contains a long valuable statement by Dr. Chapman, appended to which are copies of the principal documents involved in this dispute over jurisdiction in the coastal waters; and *Protecting the Rights of Vessels of the United States on the High Seas and in Territorial Waters of Foreign Countries*, 83 Cong., 2 Sess., H. Rept. No. 2449, July 22, 1954, and *ibid.*, S. Rept. No. 2214. An attempt was made in 1957 (S. 1483 and H. R. 5526) to amend the act to authorize reimbursement to owners and members of the crews of such vessels for all expenses resulting from such seizures. See *Protecting Rights of United States Vessels on the High Seas*, 85 Cong., 1 Sess., H. Rept. No. 1177, and *ibid.*, S. Rept. No. 837 (1957).

[116] Well analyzed and summarized in Josef L. Kunz, "Continental Shelf and International Law: Confusion and Abuse," 50 *A.J.I.L.* 828–853 (1956), and Richard Young, "Pan American Discussions on Offshore Claims," 50 *A.J.I.L.* 909–916 (1956), upon which much reliance was placed in writing the text. See also Stojan A. Bayitch, *Interamerican Law of Fisheries* (1957); and particularly Brunson MacChesney, *International Law Situation and Documents 1956: Situation, Documents and Commentary on Recent Developments in the International Law of the Sea*, Naval War

misrepresentation through oversimplification, the principal features of the controversy can be summarized thus. The Truman Continental Shelf Proclamation, concerned primarily with the exploitation of the oil in the subsoil beneath the ocean, simply declared that the United States "regards the natural resources of the subsoil and sea bed of the continental shelf beneath the high seas but contiguous to the coasts of the United States as appertaining to the United States, subject to its jurisdiction and control." Then it expressly stated: "The character as high seas of the waters above the continental shelf and the right to their free and unimpeded navigation are in no way thus affected." [117] Here is no claim to ownership or control over the superjacent waters or the free swimming denizens thereof or over the airspace above the continental shelf. There is not even a claim to sovereignty over the subsoil or sea bed, though, as previously suggested, the line between "appertaining to" and sovereign ownership may be thin.

The Truman Fisheries Proclamation is similarly carefully and restrictively phrased. "The United States regards it as proper to establish conservation zones in those areas of the high seas contiguous to the coasts of the United States wherein fishing activities have been or in the future may be developed and maintained on a substantial scale. Where such activities have been or shall hereafter be developed and maintained by its nationals alone, the United States regards it as proper to establish explicitly bounded conservation zones in which fishing activities shall be subject to the regulation and control of the United States. Where such activities have been or shall hereafter be legitimately developed and maintained jointly by nationals of the United States and nationals of other States, explicitly bounded conservation zones may be established under agreements between the United States and such other States; and all fishing activities in such zones shall be subject to regulation and control as provided in such agreements." The right of any state to establish similar zones off its shores is conceded, "provided that corresponding recognition is given to any fishing interests of nationals

---

College, Newport, Rhode Island, NAVPERS 15031, Vol. LI (1957), pp. 237-294. This latter compilation of official documentation, with its valuable historical and bibliographical notes, appeared when the present work was already in the press. So excellent is its coverage, especially of instruments not readily available, that it could serve as a most helpful documentary companion to much of the discussion in this final chapter.

[117] Sept. 28, 1945, 59 *Stat.* 884-885.

The United States and the Treaty Law of the Sea

of the United States which may exist in such areas." Again the proclamation stipulates: "The character as high seas of the areas in which such conservation zones are established and the right to their free and unimpeded navigation are in no way thus affected." [118]

This is language closely confined to a claim to establish fishery conservation zones, alone where the fishery has been developed by United States nationals alone, and in conjunction with other governments, where their nationals have participated in the development of the fishery. Presumably, if foreign nationals entered fisheries previously developed by American nationals alone and refused to accept the conservation measures imposed by American law upon American nationals and, further, if such refusal operated to jeopardize the conservation scheme set up, the United States would find it necessary to negotiate a conservation treaty with the government or governments of the foreign nationals concerned. This implication appears to have been recognized in the official pronouncements of the United States.[119] It was put into express language by the United States in the Final Act of the Ciudad Trujillo conference of 1956 thus: "The United States maintains that in accordance with international law, fishery regulations adopted by one state cannot be imposed on nationals of other states on the high seas except by agreement of the governments concerned." [120] Nowhere, however, in the proclamation is there any language expressly or impliedly asserting any right to exclude foreign nationals from any of the zones. Nor is there any claim to sovereignty in the waters or its denizens or in the airspace above the waters.

Both proclamations, then, are narrowly confined to specific, legally justifiable objectives. Aside from the measures necessary to achieve these objectives, the high seas retain their character as free and open to all customary uses.

The claims of certain of the Latin American states are in sharp contrast. Thus, Argentina in 1946 declared the Argentine Epicontinental Sea and Continental Shelf as "Subject to the sovereign power of the Nation." In effect, it asserted all the waters lying over the "submarine platform," in some places extending 500 miles from shore, to be of the

---

[118] Sept. 28, 1945, 59 *Stat.* 885–886. See the excellent discussion by Charles B. Selak, Jr., "Recent Developments in High Seas Fisheries Jurisdiction under the Presidential Proclamation of 1945," 44 *A.J.I.L.* 670–681 (1950).

[119] Phleger, *op. cit.*, at pp. 936–937.

[120] 34 *DSB* 897 (1956).

nature of territorial waters, over which it claimed complete sovereignty, subject only to the right of innocent passage. In the same year Panama claimed sovereignty over its continental shelf, the airspace above it, and, for fisheries purposes, the water between. In 1947, Chile, with no appreciable continental shelf, simply laid claim to the sea bottom, the waters above it, and the airspace above them, for a distance of 200 miles from shore. Peru in 1947 and Ecuador, Costa Rica, El Salvador, and Honduras (for the Atlantic only) later made similar claims to sovereign control over a 200-mile offshore belt. Mexico claimed exclusive rights to the offshore fisheries but only within the limits of the continental shelf. Brazil in 1950 claimed jurisdiction over its continental shelf but reserved its position with respect to fishing rights.

At the other end of this claim spectrum, the United States insisted on the historic limit of three miles for the territorial sea and the restricted special-purpose jurisdictions set forth in the Truman Proclamations. This position left the widest possible freedom, consistent with conservation of fisheries objectives, to surface navigation, air navigation, and the free development of new fisheries. Cuba, the Dominican Republic, Guatemala, Nicaragua, and Venezuela, in general, shared the American view.

The principal 200-mile claimants, Chile, Ecuador, and Peru (CEP group), supported their unilateral assertions with a new theory of the relation of man and earth to the sea, the "bioma" theory.

Modern biologists and ecologists have called the sum of non-biotic factors, mainly climatological and hydrological, which are capable of creating a particular situation, that will permit an aggregate of vegetable and animal beings to live within it, an "eco-system."

Within an "eco-system" many living communities, including man, may co-exist in a perfect chain, or succession, constituting a whole which is called a "bioma." Therefore the term "bioma" designates the whole of the complex of living communities of a region, which under the influence of the climate and in the course of centuries, becomes constantly more homogeneous, until, in its final phase, it becomes a definite type.

An "eco-system" may sustain one or more "biomas," but each one of these will maintain its unity within the system, except in the areas of contact where there may be an intermixing. . . . All the complexes that may form a "bioma" are in a state of dynamic equilibrium which is subject to the laws of Nature. . . .

[Thus] a perfect unity and inter-dependence exists between the communities that live in the sea, which supports their life, and the coastal population which requires both to survive.

This is, in short, the concept of biological unity from which is derived, in the scientific field, the preferential right of coastal countries. According to this concept, the human population of the coast forms part of the biological chain which originates in the adjoining sea, and which extends from the microscopic vegetable and animal life (fitoplankton and zooplankton) to the higher mammals, among which we count man.

These "bioma" are proper to each region . . . and it is, therefore, a prime duty of every coastal State to insure that they are not destroyed in the only way that this is possible, which is by the depredations of man.[121]

The United States contested this "bioma" theory when it was put into the record at the Santiago Conference in 1955. "The relationship of coastal communities to the sea is, aside from the limited number of people who depend for sustenance on the sea food they catch, one of economic rather than biological character." The products enter into trade and are for the most part consumed elsewhere. Furthermore, the "eco-systems and biomas" are essentially localized manifestations of major world-wide meteorological and oceanographic forces, such as the Humboldt Current, the several Equatorial Currents, and the California Current. The stocks of fish, such as the tuna, roam wide over the oceans: they do not respect the limits of the "biomas." "The United States, in common with other countries, after long study and experience in varied fisheries has adopted the principle that conservation programs must be based upon the study of the stock of fish to be conserved, its environment, and exploitation, throughout its range, and formulation for the entire stock of measures which those studies indicate to be wise. This was the fundamental approach to the problem of fishery conservation adopted by the Conference on the Conservation of the Living Resources of the Sea, made up of representatives of 45 countries,"[122] and held at Rome in 1955.[123]

---

[121] *Santiago Negotiations on Fishery Conservation Problems, 1955*, Dept. of State, pp. 31–32.

[122] *Ibid.*, pp. 37–38.

[123] *Report of the International Technical Conference on the Conservation of the Living Resources of the Sea, 18 April to 10 May, 1955, Rome*, A/CONF.10/6, "Objectives of Fishery Conservation," p. 2. See also the marvellous *Papers Presented* at the Conference, A/CONF.10/7, several of which have already been cited above.

Health and Resources since World War II

Whatever promise the "bioma" theory may have for science of the future and however plausible it may be as a basis for national governmental policy, it has not persuaded other governments that these claims to 200-mile wide territorial seas are not designed simply to create monopolies of fishing rights for nationals of the claiming states or to establish unilateral revenue-producing licensing and control systems for the benefit of countries possessing inadequate economic ability and exploitative technique to enable them to compete on favorable terms with foreign fishing interests in the offshore waters beyond the three-mile limit. While the United States is not unsympathetic to the desire of the coastal states to derive as much national wealth as possible from their favorable environment and to add to the food resources of a growing population, it insists that the setting up of exclusive areas for national exploitation contrary to the historic international law on the subject is not the acceptable way to achieve these ends. "States still adhering to the 3-mile rule represent about 80 percent of the merchant shipping tonnage of the world and most of its naval power."[124] The United States and other large-scale shipping and fishing countries have therefore protested each new claim to extended territorial waters as illegal restrictions upon the freedom of the seas.

The next gambit in this struggle to set up exclusive areas was to secure, if possible, general recognition of these claims within the orbit of Pan America. Perhaps a *fait accompli* could be achieved, before action could be taken by the United Nations upon the forthcoming final report of the International Law Commission dealing with the Regime of the High Seas. Chronologically, the developments were as follows.

On July 30, 1952, the Inter-American Juridical Committee, consisting of nine member states selected by the periodic Inter-American Conference,[125] and constituting a permanent body subordinate to the Inter-American Council of Jurists,[126] on which all twenty-one members of the Organization of American States are represented, adopted at Rio de Janeiro, by a vote of four to three, the draft text of a convention. That

[124] Phleger, *op. cit.*, p. 935.
[125] Charter of the Organization of American States, signed at Bogotá, April 30, 1948, entered into force, Dec. 13, 1951, 2 *UST* 2394, *TIAS* 2361, Arts. 67–72. See description of the new set-up, *The Organization of American States and The United Nations*, 3rd. ed. by Manuel Canyes, Pan American Union (1955).
[126] *Ibid.*, and for accounts of their work see: First Meeting, Rio de Janeiro, 1950, *U.S. Int. Conf. 1949–1950*, pp. 29–32; Second Meeting, Buenos Aires, 1953, *ibid.*, *1952–1953*, pp. 26–28.

draft recognized the "exclusive sovereignty" of the coastal state "over the soil, subsoil, and waters of its continental shelf, and the air space and stratosphere above it" without any "requirement of real or virtual occupation" (Art. 1) and, further the right "to establish an area of protection, control, and economic exploitation, to a distance of two hundred nautical miles from the low-water mark along its coasts and those of its island possessions (Art. 2)." The dissenting opinion of the delegates of Brazil, Colombia, and the United States attacked the majority text and report as *ultra vires* (going beyond the mandate received from the Inter-American Council of Jurists) and as being ill-founded in law.[127]

In August 1952, the CEP powers held a conference among themselves at Santiago de Chile, to "consolidate" their policies and claims. Apparently the meeting "had been kept strictly secret by the governments involved."[128] The three governments, in a "Declaration on Maritime Zone," dated August 17, 1952, proclaimed "as a rule of their international maritime policy, the exclusive sovereignty and jurisdiction corresponding to each of them over the ocean adjacent to the coasts of their respective countries up to a minimum distance of 200 marine miles from said coasts," subject to the right of "innocent and inoffensive passage through the zone specified for the ships of all nations."[129] They also provided for the establishment of a Permanent Commission for the Exploitation and Conservation of the Maritime Resources of the South Pacific (which was apparently set up in 1954). Its purposes are to "unify fishing and whaling regulations of the three countries; promote scientific investigations; compile statistics and exchange information with other agencies; and co-ordinate the work of the three countries in all matters pertaining to the conservation of the living resources of the sea."[130]

Support for coastal state control over the waters above the continental shelf, or in the case of states without a continental shelf, control over a belt 200 miles wide, came the next year, 1953, from the Hispanic-Luso-American Institute of International Law at São Paulo, Brazil.[131]

[127] Texts in *Hearing* on H. R. 9584, *op. cit.*, Appendix 14, pp. 39–44. Text of the mandate of the Council of Jurists, dated May 8, 1952, is in Appendix 15, pp. 44–45.
[128] Chapman statement in *Hearing* on H. R. 9584, *op. cit.*, at p. 20.
[129] Text of the Treaty, signed Aug. 18, 1952, in Appendix 10, *Hearing* on H. R. 9584, *op. cit.*, at pp. 33–34. See Kunz, *op. cit.*, pp. 835–836.
[130] *Report of the International Technical Conference, op. cit.*, p. 5.
[131] Kunz, *op. cit.*, p. 836.

Health and Resources since World War II

Immediately after the seizure of the Onassis whalers by Peru, the CEP Permanent Commission met, in October 1954, at Santiago and called for a second conference. At this conference, held at Lima, Peru, in December 1954, the CEP powers in a spirit of "solidarity," reaffirmed their extensive claims, pledged themselves to the "juridical defense" of the 200-mile principle, promised each other support in the event any of them became involved in international litigation over their acts or claims, and adopted other measures indicative of the establishment of a permanent regional organization.[132]

In the spring of 1954 the Tenth Inter-American Conference met at Caracas. It authorized the Council of the Organization of American States to convoke a specialized conference for the purpose of studying the whole matter of "Conservation of Natural Resources: The Continental Shelf and Marine Waters" (Resolution LXXXIV).[133] "Pursuant to this decision, the Council . . . convened the Specialized Conference for March 15, 1956, at Ciudad Trujillo. In preparation for the Conference, it requested the Inter-American Council of Jurists . . . to make a preparatory study of the legal aspects of the matters to be considered at Ciudad Trujillo. It was made clear that the purpose of this study was to furnish the Specialized Conference with pertinent background information and that any conclusions or decisions were to be reserved to the Conference." [134] The Council of Jurists in turn requested the permanent Juridical Committee to prepare a working document on the subject for its use. This the Juridical Committee declined to do. Very likely the deep schism revealed in 1952 would prevent agreement on any preparatory work which the Council would find useful. Thus, unprepared, the Council of Jurists approached its meeting at Mexico City, scheduled to begin two months before the crucial conference at Ciudad Trujillo.

United States and the CEP Group. Meanwhile, the United States came into a complete impasse with the CEP powers. On May 13, 1955, the United States proposed to them that the issue of the 200-mile claim be

---
[132] *Ibid.*, pp. 835–836.

[133] Resolutions, *Final Act*, Pan American Union (1954), pp. 84–86; selected resolutions reprinted in 48 *A.J.I.L. Supp.* 123–132, Resol. LXXXIV at pp. 128–130. For summaries of the Tenth Inter-American Conference, March 1–28, 1954, and the meetings of the Council of the OAS before and after the Caracas conference, see *U.S. Int. Conf. 1953–1954*, pp. 22–31 and 31–34, respectively.

[134] "Territorial Waters and Related Matters: Action Taken by the Third Meeting of the Inter-American Council of Jurists, Mexico City, January 17–February 4, 1956," 34 *DSB* 296–299 (1956), at p. 296.

submitted to the International Court of Justice for adjudication and that the four governments undertake negotiations toward the conclusion of a conservation agreement for the eastern Pacific. The CEP governments declined the first proposal but accepted the second. The United States then agreed to proceed with negotiations in conformity with the conclusions of the United Nations International Conference on the Conservation of the Living Resources of the Sea, held in Rome the previous April and May. The United States also stipulated that any agreement produced would have to be drafted "without reference to the claims of any of the four Governments with respect to territorial waters or other forms of special jurisdiction over the seas adjacent to their coasts." Thereupon, a conference was held at Santiago, Chile, September 14 to October 5, 1955.

The United States proposed the setting up of a commission along the lines of the Inter-American Tropical Tuna Commission but with more extensive powers to recommend regulations for unanimous adoption. During the negotiations it became evident that the CEP countries would agree to no convention which did not "in effect recognize their claims to exclusive jurisdiction over large areas of the high seas off their coasts." Upon this rock the conference foundered, though the CEP powers were equally adamant with respect to other positions they took, such as in relation to the "bioma" theory and the procedure for handling infractions of the fishery regulations by nationals of the contracting parties.[135] The United States returned empty handed from this conference to face most extraordinary proceedings at the third meeting of the Council of Jurists in Mexico City the following January.

Mexico City Meeting of Council of Jurists, 1956. After a general debate on the topic assigned to the council, a draft resolution sponsored by eight countries (Argentina, Chile, Ecuador, El Salvador, Guatemala, Mexico, Peru, and Uruguay, later joined by Costa Rica) was introduced in one of the committees. The proposal incorporated the most extreme claims previously put forth by the sponsoring governments. In brief, it rejected the three-mile limit as a rule of international law; declared each state competent to establish the width of its territorial waters, within

[135] "Santiago Negotiations on Fishery Conservation Problems Among Chile, Ecuador, Peru, and the United States: Santiago, Chile, September 14–October 5, 1955," 33 *DSB* 1025–1030 (1955); *Santiago Negotiations on Fishery Conservation Problems*, Dept. of State (1955).

reasonable limits, in accord with its view of its needs; and asserted that the coastal state had "the right of exclusive exploitation of species related to the coast, the life of the country, or the needs of the coastal population." The resolution was not debated. The proponents declined to answer objections raised against its provisions. The committee refused to allow more time for consideration of the proposal and adopted the resolution by a vote of 15 in favor, 1 against (United States), and 5 abstentions (Bolivia, Colombia, Cuba, the Dominican Republic, and Nicaragua). The same vote was repeated in the plenary session of the council.

The United States, of course, objected to this highhanded procedure at every stage of the proceedings and repeated and summarized its objections in the Final Act of the meeting. It objected to the substance of the resolution as inconsistent with the developed international law on the subject and as unsupported by scientific and economic evidence relating to the same. It also took exception to the mode of rushing the resolution through the meeting. Ten other delegations entered reservations to the so-called Principles of Mexico, including the five that had abstained in the voting and five others that had voted for the resolution. This was hardly a manifestation of the much vaunted "continental solidarity." On motion of the Cuban delegation and a vote of 11 to 9, the controversial resolution was "demoted" from the status of a "declaration" to that of a "preparatory study" and so passed on to the Specialized Conference.[136]

Ciudad Trujillo Conference 1956. The Specialized Conference on Conservation of Natural Resources: Continental Shelf and Marine Waters, which met at Ciudad Trujillo, Dominican Republic, March 15–18, 1956, took a more statesmanlike view of its tasks. It had the advantage of devoting all its attention to the one subject matter assigned to it in contrast with the Council of Jurists, which had had numerous items to consider in addition to the territorial-waters problem. It also had the benefit of the presence of numerous technical and scientific experts assigned to it and some forty technical papers prepared by

[136] "Territorial Waters and Related Matters: Action Taken by the Third Meeting of the Inter-American Council of Jurists, Mexico City, January 17–February 4, 1956," including texts of the resolution and the "Declaration and Reservation of the United States," 34 *DSB* 296–299 (1956). Discussed in detail by Kunz, *op. cit.*, pp. 847–848, and Young, *op. cit.*, pp. 911–913.

various national and international scientific bodies.[137] Its conclusions, naturally, were sounder.

The United States took occasion in a statement in the Final Act to call attention "to the fact that broader consideration having been given at this Conference than at any previous inter-American meeting to the various aspects of the subjects on its agenda, the present Resolution of Ciudad Trujillo constitutes the latest and most authoritative expression of the Organization of American States on the subjects discussed therein." This declaration obviously was designed to "demote" further the "preparatory study" which had been dignified with the label "Principles of Mexico."

The conference proceeded upon the basis of certain carefully prepared proposals introduced by the United States delegation. In its brief resolution on the juridical and economic aspects of the problem submitted to it, the conference agreed that the sea bed and subsoil of the continental shelf out to the two hundred-meter depth line, or beyond that line if exploitable, appertained exclusively to the coastal state. It recorded lack of agreement with respect to the juridical regime applicable to the waters superjacent to this submarine area and with respect to the problem of which benthonic species go with the sea bottom and which with the superjacent waters. It urged the need of cooperation to achieve the "optimum sustainable yield of the living resources of the high seas" and declared that the most effective method of achieving this end was through agreements "among the states directly interested in such resources." It acknowledged that a coastal state has "a special interest in the continued productivity of the living resources of the high seas adjacent to its territorial sea." It recorded disagreement concerning the nature and scope of this special interest and how they should be weighted in conservation programs. It simply recorded, finally, that there was disagreement with respect to the breadth of the territorial sea. In another resolution, the conference urged continuation of studies looking

[137] *Inter-American Specialized Conference on "Conservation of Natural Resources: The Continental Shelf and Marine Waters," Ciudad Trujillo, March 15–28, 1956, Final Act,* Pan American Union (1956), list of papers at pp. 31–39. See also *Background Material on the Juridical Aspects of the Continental Shelf and Marine Waters,* prepared by the Department of International Law of the Pan American Union, Conf. Doc. No. 2, and *Background Material on the Scientific and Economic Aspects of the Continental Shelf and Marine Waters,* prepared by the Working Party on Oceanography of the Pan American Institute of Geography and History for use of the Conference, Conf. Doc. No. 3, Pan American Union (1956).

toward the establishment of an Inter-American Oceanographic Institute, as visualized in resolution LXXXIV of the Caracas conference in 1954.[138]

Thus ended a more successful conference. The conferees had the good judgment to proceed to agreement on what they could agree upon and simply to record for future solution, if possible, what they could not agree upon. In such fashion some progress was made, avoiding a real threat to the continued usefulness of the Inter-American system.

The final word in these controversial matters, however, remained to be said in the conference or conferences of a universal character which would deal with the 1956 report of the United Nations International Law Commission.

The International Law Commission and Resources of the Sea

In the interwar period the United States had participated, at first unofficially and then officially, in the efforts of the League of Nations to codify various segments of the law of nations. That collaboration has already been described.[139] The United Nations has continued and expanded the work of the League in this respect. In pursuance of Article 13 of the charter, the General Assembly in 1947 established a permanent International Law Commission for the purpose.[140] As a member of the United Nations, the United States, now, of course, cooperates fully in this work. An eminent American jurist, Dr. Manley O. Hudson, formerly a judge of the Permanent Court of International Justice, was until 1953 one of the fifteen members of the commission. Douglas L. Edmonds, another distinguished American jurist, was elected by the commission in 1954 to succeed Judge Hudson.[141]

---

[138] "Problems Relating to the Economic and Legal Regime of the High Seas: Inter-American Specialized Conference on Conservation of Natural Resources: Continental Shelf and Marine Waters, Ciudad Trujillo, March 15–28 [1956]," 34 *DSB* 894–897 (1956); discussed by Kunz, *op. cit.*, pp. 848–849, and Young, *op. cit.*, pp. 913–916.

[139] Above at p. 184. See also the unexcelled brief history and analysis of the "codification" and "development" process, by Dr. Yuen-Li Liang, "Documents on the Development and Codification of International Law," 41 *A.J.I.L. Supp.* 29–147 (1947).

[140] Leland M. Goodrich and Edvard Hambro, *Charter of the United Nations: Commentary and Documents*, rev. ed. (1949), pp. 174–177. Text of Statute of the International Law Commission, Doc. A/504, Nov. 20, 1947, reprinted in 42 *A.J.I.L. Supp.* 1–8 (1948). For brief summation of the work of the ILC, see *Everyman's United Nations 1945–1955*, pp. 313–326.

[141] When in 1953 Judge Hudson because of ill health was unable to continue on the commission, the General Assembly elected as the American member, John Johnston

In accordance with its statute the commission at its first session in 1949 drew up a provisional list of fourteen topics selected for codification, among them two of central importance for the present study: "(5) Regime of the high seas; (6) Regime of territorial waters." Then the commission gave priority to three of the fourteen, the third being the "Regime of the high seas." [142] In accord with a recommendation of the General Assembly in 1949, the topic of "Regime of territorial waters" was added by the commission as its fourth "priority" item.[143] Aided by a series of remarkably fine studies produced by the Secretariat and the Commission's Rapporteur on the subjects, J. P. A. François of the Netherlands,[144] the commission was able to submit in 1951, for comment by governments, a set of "Draft Articles on the Continental Shelf and Related Subjects" [145] and to elaborate, for further study, a "Draft Regulation" concerning the "Regime of the Territorial Sea." [146] From here on the work of the Commission crystallized to produce the remarkably fine report of 1956, which dealt with both the regime of territorial waters and the regime of the high seas in one comprehensive set of seventy-three articles.

For present purposes it is not necessary to trace in detail the painstaking studies and deliberations of the commission which resulted in the 1956 report. The commission in its deliberations was assisted not only by memoranda submitted by its members and those prepared by the Secretariat, the reports of its distinguished rapporteur, the information supplied by governments and the comments by them upon its draft

---

Parker. On his resignation in 1954, the commission, in conformity with Article 11 of its statute, elected Douglas L. Edmonds as the member for the United States.

[142] "Report of the International Law Commission, Covering its First Session, April 12–June 9, 1949," UN, GA, Official Records, 4th Sess., Supp. No. 10 (A/925), June 24, 1949. The annual reports of the ILC have been reprinted regularly in the *A.J.I.L.* thus: *Supplements*, Vol. 44 (1950), pp. 1, 105 (1st and 2nd Sess.); Vol. 45 (1951), p. 103 (3rd. Sess.); Vol. 47 (1953), p. 1 (4th Sess.); Vol. 48 (1954), p. 1 (5th Sess.); Vol. 49 (1955), p. 1 (6th Sess.); and *Official Documents*, Vol. 50 (1956), p. 190 (7th Sess.); Vol. 51 (1957), p. 154 (8th Sess.).

[143] Yuen-Li Liang, "The First Session of the International Law Commission: Review of Its Work by the General Assembly," 44 *A.J.I.L.* 527–542 (1950) at p. 533. See also Dr. Liang's subsequent similarly invaluable accounts of the annual review of the work of the commission by the General Assembly: 45 *A.J.I.L.* 509–525 (1951); 46 *A.J.I.L.* 483–503 (1952); 48 *A.J.I.L.* 579–591 (1954).

[144] Works cited in *Report* of the *Second Session* (1950), 44 *A.J.I.L.* Supp. 105, at pp. 107, 145.

[145] *Report* of the *Third Session* (1951), 45 *A.J.I.L.* Supp. 103, at pp. 139–147.

[146] *Report* of the *Fourth Session* (1952), 47 *A.J.I.L.* Supp. 1, at p. 25.

articles,[147] a special Legislative Series of national laws compiled by the Secretariat,[148] the discussion of its annual reports in the General Assembly, and the comments in learned journals,[149] but also, uniquely, by an *ad hoc* International Technical Conference on the Conservation of the Living Resources of the Sea, held at Rome in 1955. Probably never since the days of Selden and Grotius has the law of the sea been subjected to such intense, expert, and comprehensive scrutiny as by the commission and its numerous collaborators.

Rome Technical Conference, 1955. While the International Law Commission was engaged in its task of producing draft articles on the international regulation of fisheries, the General Assembly, recognizing that the problems relating to the high seas, territorial waters, contiguous zones, the continental shelf, and the superjacent waters were "closely linked together juridically as well as physically," adopted a resolution on December 14, 1954, requesting the Secretary-General, in cooperation with the Food and Agriculture Organization, to convene at Rome, the headquarters of FAO, a specialized conference devoted to only the scientific and technical aspects of the contention loaded subject.[150] The resolution specifically instructed the conference "not to prejudge the related problems awaiting consideration by the General Assembly."

[147] See detailed summation with full citations in Herbert W. Briggs, "Official Interest in the Work of the International Law Commission: Replies of Governments to Requests for Information or Comment," 48 *A.J.I.L.* 603–612 (1954).

[148] *Laws and Regulations on the Regime of the High Seas,* Vol. I, dealing with 1. Continental Shelf, 2. Contiguous Zones, 3. Supervision of Foreign Vessels on the High Seas, ST/LEG/SER. B/1, 11 Jan. 1951 (1951); *ibid.*, Vol. II, dealing with Laws relating to Jurisdiction over Crimes Committed Abroad or on the High Seas, ST/LEG/SER. B/2, 14 December, 1951 (1952); *Laws Concerning the Nationality of Ships,* ST/LEG/SER. B/5, Nov. 1955 (1956); and *Laws and Regulations on the Regime of the Territorial Sea,* ST/LEG/SER. B/6, Dec. 1956 (1957).

[149] E.g., Richard Young, "The International Law Commission and the Continental Shelf," 46 *A.J.I.L.* 123–128 (1952); Philip C. Jessup, "The International Law Commission's 1954 Report on the Regime of the Territorial Sea," 49 *A.J.I.L.* 221–229 (1955), William W. Bishop, Jr., "International Law Commission Draft Articles on Fisheries," 50 *A.J.I.L.* 627–636 (1956); Kunz, *op. cit.*; the discussions at the 1956 annual meeting of the American Society of International Law (*Proceedings, 1956,* pp. 116–154); Myres S. McDougal and William T. Burke, "Crisis in the Law of the Sea: Community Perspectives Versus National Egoism," 67 *Yale Law Journal* 539–589 (1958); and other works cited in this study *passim.*

[150] G.A. Resolution 900 (IX). For background, see "Requests for Inclusion of Items on Assembly Agenda," 31 *DSB* 422–425 (1954); "Law Commission Asked to Submit Final Report on High Seas Problem," 32 *DSB* 62–64; "U.N. to Convene Conference on Fishery Conservation," 32 *DSB* 64–66; and "U.S. Position on Conservation of Fisheries Resources," 32 *DSB* 696–700 (1955).

The United States and the Treaty Law of the Sea

The Conference was accordingly held the following April 18th to May 10th. Forty-five governments were represented by delegations which included, as the General Assembly requested, "individual experts competent in the field of fishery conservation and regulation." The roster of delegations reveals faithful compliance with this stipulation. In addition, six states sent observers, as did FAO, UNESCO, and eleven inter-governmental (treaty) fishery organizations. Twenty-five technical papers were presented, "of which six had been prepared by individual experts or organizations on subjects suggested by the Secretary-General, acting on the advice of a group of experts who assisted him in preparations for the Conference." [151]

As might have been expected from a conference so prepared and so composed, the conclusions of the conference were squarely in accord with the general policies and methods adopted since the end of World War II by the governments with extensive fishing interests. Thus, the conference endorsed the aim of seeking maximum sustainable yields, the necessity of basing all regulatory schemes upon sound scientific information, and the need for continuous "tailor-made" investigations into stocks selected for conservation.

The conference reviewed the work of the councils and conventions dealing with high-seas fisheries, eleven of them being now active and involving the cooperation of forty-two states. Among the arrangements examined are the following, in which the United States has participated or participates now: the International Council for the Exploration of the Sea;[152] the North American Council on Fishery Investigations, active from 1920 to 1938;[153] the Northwest Atlantic Fisheries Convention; the Indo-Pacific Fisheries Council (to be discussed presently); the Fur Seal Treaty of 1911 (the superseding convention of 1957 not having been concluded at the time of the Conference); the Pacific Halibut Convention; the Sockeye Salmon Convention; the North Pacific Fisheries Convention; the Inter-American Tropical Tuna Convention; and the Whaling Convention. Four other arrangements were examined in which

---

[151] *Papers Presented at the International Technical Conference on the Conservation of the Living Resources of the Sea, Rome, 18 April to 10 May 1955*, A/CONF.10/7 (1956), p. iv; and *Report* of Conference, A/CONF.10/6 (1955). Since the text of the report covers only ten pages, citations to pages will be omitted.

[152] The United States participated in its work for a brief period, 1912–1916. Discussed above, pp. 123, 185.

[153] Discussed above, p. 185.

the United States does not participate: the 1946 Convention for the Regulation of the Meshes of Fishing Nets;[154] the Commission for the Scientific Exploration of the Mediterranean;[155] the General Fisheries Council for the Mediterranean (sponsored by the FAO);[156] and the Commission for the South Pacific (the CEP organization). Americans can justly be proud of this impressive record of United States leadership and activity in the efforts to conserve the resources of the sea by means of international legislation and organization.

The conference noted "with satisfaction conservation measures already carried out in certain regions and for certain species at the national and international level" (Par. 74). Its summation of the principles of international conservation organizations (Par. 43) read like a syllabus for much of the description already given of the fisheries arrangements in which the United States has participated. Briefly, a good treaty conservation scheme includes the following: a sufficiently large geographic area; the encompassing of the whole range of the population of fish concerned; cooperation by all the interested nations, "both the fishing nations and the adjacent coastal states"; adequate prior scientific research; continuing scientific investigations; flexible regulatory power; conventions readily adjustable and revisable; clear rules on rights and duties; and continuing advice from public interest groups.

In its general conclusions, the conference in effect endorsed the multipartite approach which is already so well under way with respect to various species and pointed out the need for additional arrangements for a dozen other species, among them anchovies, herring, sardine, and shrimp. It discussed the "problems created by new entrants into a fishery under conservation management." In the case of fisheries with a long background of joint efforts to regulate, as in the North Pacific, the conference endorsed the principle of "abstention," as exemplified in the convention relating to that area (Pars. 61–62). In the case of a new entrant into a fishery which a coastal state is regulating on bona fide scientific grounds, "the new entrant should declare itself ready to observe the conservation regulations in force and undertake to cooperate with the

[154] Above, pp. 274–275.
[155] See *Directory of International Scientific Organizations*, 2d ed., p. 38.
[156] See Gove Hambidge, *The Story of FAO* (1955), p. 219; *The Work of FAO 1954–1955: Report of the Director-General* (1955), pp. 79–80.

other states concerned in carrying out the relevant program of research and management (Pars. 63–64).[157]

As was expected, sharp controversy arose over the claims of coastal states to control offshore fisheries. These claims ranged from moderate assertions of "special interest" to extreme assertions of control over the whole ecological system in a given maritime zone (Par. 45). Faithful to the terms of reference laid down by the General Assembly, "it was the consensus of the Conference that it was not competent to express any opinion as to the appropriate extent of the territorial sea, the extent of the jurisdiction of the coastal state over fisheries, or the legal status of the superjacent waters of the continental shelf" (Par. 81). With respect to "the question of the special interests, rights, duties, and responsibilities of coastal states," and with respect to the basic question whether the conference was competent to consider them, the conference "was more or less evenly divided" (Art. 82). Nevertheless, it did adopt, by a vote of 18 against 17, with 8 abstentions, the moderate view that "when formulating conservation programs, account should be taken of the special interests of the coastal state in maintaining the productivity of the resources of the high seas near its coast" (Par. 18).

The United States delegate voted against adoption of this view by the Conference as being *ultra vires,* but with the explanation that the vote "did not mean that his delegation believed the coastal States to have no special interests."[158] In fact, the United States had on other occasions declared that it was "entirely ready to recognize that the legitimate interest of coastal states must be given weight in establishing a system of law with reference to fisheries conservation which will resolve the inherent conflict of interests" of coastal states with freedom of fishing on the high seas.[159] This moderate view is recognized in the Northwest Atlantic Fisheries Convention by its provision for representation of each contracting party with a coastline adjacent to a subarea on the panel for that subarea, whether or not it fishes in that subarea. Considering the

[157] For penetrating discussion of this problem of what we can undiplomatically call the "interloper," see William W. Bishop, Jr., "International Law Commission Draft Articles on Fisheries," 50 A.J.I.L. 627–636 (1956), who, however, does not use that term.

[158] Summary Record of the Nineteenth Meeting, May 5, 1955, A/CONF.10/SR.19, p. 6.

[159] "U.S. Position on Conservation of Fisheries Resources," 32 DSB 696, 698 (1955).

Health and Resources since World War II

whole trend of the report, however, it is not surprising that the CEP powers filed reservations against various sections of it.

International Law Commission Final Report, 1956. With the results of the Technical Conference of Rome in hand, the International Law Commission proceeded to revise its draft articles on resources. In due course the revised articles appeared in the 1956 report.[160] It is not within the scope of the present discussion to comment on the full report. That was done voluminously by governments, international organizations, learned societies, and all manner of jurists, in anticipation of the United Nations Conference on Law of the Sea, which was scheduled to be held in Geneva in March 1958. Frequent reference to the report has already been made, however, in one connection or another, as in the discussions on the territorial sea, the continental shelf, flag states, safety of navigation, aerial piracy, and oil pollution of the high seas. There remains the need to indicate the position of the commission on the regulation of fisheries and related juridical problems.

Thus, with respect to the breadth of the territorial sea, the commission noted that many states have fixed a breadth greater than three miles but that many states did not recognize such a breadth when that of their own territorial sea was less. Although international practice in this respect is not uniform, "international law does not permit an extension of the territorial sea beyond twelve miles" (Art. 3). The commission was unable to agree upon a limit between three and twelve miles. It therefore considered that the breadth should be fixed by an international conference. If the conference were not to go beyond the twelve miles, that would help dispose of some of the extravagant claims we have encountered.

"The term 'high seas' means all parts of the sea that are not included in the territorial sea . . . or in the internal waters of a State" (Art. 26). "The high seas being open to all nations, no State may validly purport

[160] *Report of the International Law Commission Covering the Work of its Eighth Session 23 April–4 July 1956*, G.A., Official Records, 11th Session, Supplement No. 9 (A/3159). See also the extraordinarily valuable *Reference Guide to the Articles concerning the Law of the Sea adopted by the International Law Commission at its Eighth Session*, Mimeo., Prepared by the Secretariat, A/C.6/L.378, Oct. 25, 1956, and *Yearbook of the International Law Commission 1956, Vol. I, Summary Records of the Eighth Session, 23 April–4 July 1956*, Sales No. 1956. V. 3, Vol. I; and Vol. II, containing documents of the Eighth Session, A/CN.4/SER.A/1956/Add.1 (Nov. 1956). The report of the commission covering the work of its ninth session in 1957 contains nothing on the subject of the sea (A/3623).

to subject any part of them to its sovereignty. Freedom of the high seas comprises, *inter alia*: (1) freedom of navigation; (2) freedom of fishing; (3) freedom to lay submarine cables and pipelines; (4) freedom to fly over the high seas" (Art. 27).

For the purposes of the commission's draft, "the term 'continental shelf' is used as referring to the seabed and subsoil of the submarine areas adjacent to the coast but outside the area of the territorial sea, to a depth of 200 metres (approximately 100 fathoms), or, beyond that limit, to where the depth of the superjacent waters admits of the exploitation of the natural resources of the said areas" (Art. 67). Over these areas the coastal state has "sovereign rights for the purpose of exploring and exploiting its natural resources" (Art. 68), but those rights "do not affect the legal status of the superjacent waters as high seas, or that of the airspace above those waters" (Art. 69), nor do they permit any impeding of "the laying or maintenance of submarine cables on the continental shelf" (Art. 70). In principle the same rule should apply to the laying of pipelines, but in view of the necessity of accompanying the laying of pipelines by the erection of pumping stations and the probable reluctance of the coastal state to permit such a hindrance to the exploitation of the continental shelf, the commission omitted bracketing pipelines with submarine cables in Article 70. The question, in the judgment of the commission, did not yet seem to be of practical importance. Use of the continental shelf by the coastal sovereign "must not result in any unjustifiable interference with navigation, fishing or the conservation of the living resources of the sea." The sovereign is entitled to construct and maintain installations on the shelf for "exploration and exploitation of its natural resources" and to establish safety zones around the installations, but these installations do not possess the status of islands and, of course, have no territorial sea of their own (Art. 71).

The distinguished jurists on the commission had as much difficulty with so-called sedentary fisheries as the biology experts have had. After various preliminary attempts to devise principles for the resolution of conflicts of jurisdiction, the commission in its final report in 1956 cut the Gordian knot by distinguishing two different uses for the term "sedentary." Fisheries are described as sedentary either by reason of the species caught or by reason of the equipment used. The first case concerns products attached to the bed of the sea; in the second case the 'sedentary' character of the fishery is determined by the fact that the fishing is conducted by means of equipment embedded in the bed of the sea. The Commission decided to keep the term 'sedentary fisheries' for the first type of activity only" (Art. 60 Commentary). In accord with this decision, the commission drew up two different articles, dealing separately with the two different phenomena of bottom-dwelling flora and fauna.

Thus, Article 68 recognizes a sovereign right in the coastal state to explore and exploit the natural resources of the continental shelf. The term "natural" is wide enough to embrace both the mineral resources in the shelf and the living resources "attached" to the surface of the shelf. The term "attached" is deliberately left unqualified. The Commission was urged to restrict it to "permanently attached." It was also urged to expand it to include marine fauna and flora living "in constant physical and biological relationship with the seabed and the continental shelf." The commission refused to do either, preferring that "examination of the scientific aspects of that question should be left to the experts." One thing, however, it made quite clear: the rights of the continental shelf sovereign "do not cover so-called bottom-fish and other fish which, although living in the sea, occasionally have their habitat at the bottom of the sea or are bred there" (Art. 68 Com.). These fish, frequently called demersal, are therefore denizens of the superjacent waters, and if appearing outside the territorial sea, they are subject to the regime of the high seas. On one other interesting point relating to the sea bottom, the commission was also quite explicit: it is clearly understood that the rights of the continental shelf sovereign "do not cover objects such as wrecked ships and their cargoes (including bullion) lying on the seabed or covered by the sand of the subsoil" (Art. 68 Com.).

With respect to the second type of activity on the sea bottom, which employs equipment embedded in the floor of the sea, the commission adopted the following special provision: "The regulation of fisheries conducted by means of equipment embedded in the floor of the sea in areas of the high seas adjacent to the territorial sea of a State, may be undertaken by that State where such fisheries have long been maintained and conducted by its nationals, provided that non-nationals are permitted to participate in such activities on an equal footing with nationals. Such regulations will not, however, affect the general status of the areas as high seas" (Art. 60). This rule, then, became necessary to take care of species that are mobile and are not "attached" to the sea bottom. The "attached" species are covered by Article 68. It remained to be seen which species the experts would put in which verbal category — attached to the bottom, mobile over the bottom, or free-swimming.[161]

Finally, the International Law Commission dealt with jurisdiction over offshore fisheries, that is, beyond territorial waters, whatever their breadth, if twelve miles or less. "All States have the right for their nationals to engage in fishing on the high seas," subject to the treaty obligations of those states and the provisions in the commission's draft (Art. 49). The criterion of "optimum sustainable yield" for conservation measures is adopted in Article 50. Article 51 confirms the right of a state, and imposes a duty on the state, to adopt, when necessary, conservation measures for its nationals when engaged in fishing on the high seas in places where the nationals of other states are not fishing. This may extend even to the coasts of another state, provided that that state has not adopted regulations as permitted under Article 54.

Where the nationals of two or more states fish for the same stock in the same area of the high seas, the two governments are obligated, at the request of either, to enter into a conservation agreement (Art. 52). If the states concerned do not reach agreement within a reasonable period of time, any of the states may invoke the compulsory arbitration procedure contemplated by Article 57. Where newcomers enter the areas and exploit the same stocks regulated in pursuance of Articles 51 or 52, they are subject to the regulations so established (Art. 53). If the governments of the newcomers object to the regulations so adopted and no agreement can be reached within a reasonable period of time, then these governments can invoke the compulsory arbitration procedure. Pending the arbitral decision the adopted regulations remain in force. In connection with this article, the commission noted the "principle of abstention" but, confessing a lack of "the necessary competence in the scientific and economic domains to study" it and other exceptional situations, it simply refrained from making any concrete proposal with respect thereto.

In the articles dealing specifically with coastal states, the commission recognized that "the coastal state, by the mere fact of being coastal,

---

[161] See D. P. O'Connell, "Sedentary Fisheries and the Australian Continental Shelf," 49 *A.J.I.L.* 185–209 (1955), at pp. 206–207, and remarks by Richard Young, *Proceedings of American Society of International Law, 1956*, p. 150.

possesses a special interest in maintaining the productivity of the living resources in a part of the area adjacent to its coasts," and said as much in the first paragraph of Article 54. But, in its general commentary on conservation (Par. 14), the commission made it clear that "the 'special' character of the interest of the coastal State should be interpreted in the sense that the interest exists by reason of the sole fact of the geographical situation," not, presumably, because of some special ecological or biological theory entertained by the coastal state. Furthermore, "the Commission did not wish to imply that the 'special' interest of the coastal State would take precedence *per se* over the interests of the other States concerned." Hence, a coastal state was entitled to participate "on an equal footing in any system of research and regulation in that area, even though its nationals do not carry on fishing there" (Art. 54, Par. 2). In the event of lack of agreement among the states concerned, appeal would lie to the compulsory arbitration procedure.

If negotiations with the states concerned have not led to an agreement within a reasonable period of time, a coastal state may unilaterally adopt regulations for offshore conservation purposes, provided that scientific evidence exists showing "an urgent need for the measures, that the measures adopted are based on appropriate scientific findings," and that the "measures do not discriminate against foreign fishermen" (Art. 55). It is clear from the commentary that this is a limited, nonexclusory, and temporary right, valid as against other states, but subject immediately to appeal to the arbitral process. A special right accorded to the arbitral commission in Article 58, Par. 2, to suspend application of the unilateral regulations pending its award seems, in the judgment of the commission, "an adequate safeguard against abuse."

Article 56 sets up an unusual and salutary right: where a state has a special interest in the conservation of the living resources of an area of the high seas, not adjacent to its coasts and in which its nationals do not fish, but because "exhaustion of the resources of the sea in the area would affect the results of fishing in another area where the nationals of the State concerned do engage in fishing," it may request the state whose nationals are fishing in the unregulated area to adopt the necessary conservation measures. If no agreement is reached within a reasonable time, resort may be had to the arbitral procedure. In effect, this provision introduces the notion that one state may request another state to prevent its nationals from committing a nuisance injurious to the requesting state on the high seas. That is a form of progress.

In its 1953 report, the International Law Commission proposed the establishment within the United Nations framework of an international authority to prescribe regulations for conservation purposes on the high seas.[162] This proposal was not adopted. The commission then considered the possibility of the establishment under the United Nations of a permanent international body, with the status of a specialized agency, "to be responsible not only for making technical and scientific studies of problems concerning the protection and use of living resources of the sea, but also for settling disputes between States on this subject." The commission finally decided, however, that in view of the diversity of interests that might be involved in fisheries disputes, the idea of *ad hoc* arbitral commissions would have a better chance of being carried into practice in the near future than that of a central judicial authority (Gen. Com. Par. 19). Thus it came to the proposing of the compulsory arbitration system provided for in Articles 57 and 58.

Article 57 provides that any disagreement which arises between states under Articles 52 to 56 "shall, at the request of any of the parties, be submitted for settlement to an arbitral commission of seven members, unless the parties agree to seek a solution by another method of peaceful settlement." Two members are selected by each side, the remaining three by agreement between the sides. Failing agreement, the three may be nominated by the Secretary-General after consultation with the President of the International Court of Justice and the Director-General of the Food and Agriculture Organization, from nationals of countries not parties to the dispute. Additional rules provide for sundry contingencies. The arbitral commission must be set up within three months of the date of the original request and render its award within the next five months unless it decides, in case of necessity, to extend that time limit. Pending the rendering of an award, the disputed measures remain in force, except that in the case of the unilateral measures adopted by a coastal state under Article 55, Par. 2, the arbitral commission may decide that, pending its award, those measures shall not remain in force.

So, with respect to the regime of the territorial sea and the regime of

[162] *Report of the International Law Commission Covering the Work of its Fifth Session, 1 June–14 August 1953*, G.A., Official Records: Eighth Session, Supplement No. 9 (A/2456), Article 3, p. 17.

Health and Resources since World War II

the high seas, the International Law Commission has, after eight years of intensive efforts, discharged its task. It will be noted, however, how closely the final report in 1956 accords with the two Truman proclamations and the policy and practice of the United States developed since the end of World War II. The scientific approach and the formula of optimum sustainable yield are adopted. The process of regulation is to be decentralized and multilateral, retaining flexibility and adjustability. Grandiose theories and extravagant claims of jurisdiction over the marginal sea are rejected, diplomatically, to be sure, but firmly, nevertheless. The genuine interests of a coastal state, whether it does or does not, whether it can or cannot, exploit the adjacent sea, are recognized for representation in any regulatory scheme and as justifying the adoption of temporary conservation measures if supported by scientifically valid evidence. Even the possibility of frivolous or harassing suits is guarded against in the arbitral process. Appropriate weight is given to the states with the foresight to institute conservation programs and the scientific skill to make them effective. The high seas are kept wide open for rational, responsible use. The great fishing powers can check each other in practice and the smaller powers can check the greater ones through the mechanism of compulsory arbitration. It remained to be seen what the conference in Geneva in 1958 would do with this neatly articulated scheme proposed in the 1956 report of the International Law Commission. Whatever the fate of the report, however, seldom would a great conference have had *travaux preparatoires* produced by more earnest, competent, high-minded servants of the international community.

United Nations Conference on the Law of the Sea, 1958

After a thorough discussion of the 1956 report of the International Law Commission by the Sixth Committee (Legal Questions) of the General Assembly in November and December, 1956,[163] the General Assembly on February 21, 1957 authorized the convening of a conference on the law of the sea early in March 1958.[164] Accordingly, some

[163] Agenda Item 53, discussed from Nov. 28 to Dec. 20, 1956, summary records A/C.6/SR. 485–505. The verbatim record of the debate was mimeographed in two volumes for use of the conference, A/CONF.13/19, Dec. 3, 1957.

[164] G.A., O.R., 11th Sess., Plenary Meeting 658th, Feb. 21, 1957, Res. 1105 (XI). The Sixth Committee had recommended that the conference be held at Rome; the Fifth Committee (Administrative and Budgetary) in the interest of economy,

The United States and the Treaty Law of the Sea

700 delegates from 87 countries (reduced by one with the merger of Egypt and Syria into the United Arab Republic) met at Geneva from February 24 to April 27, 1958.[165] Seven specialized agencies (FAO, ICAO, ILO, ITU, UNESCO, WHO, and WMO) and nine intergovernmental organizations, among them five devoted to fisheries, were represented by observers. The conference, assisted by elaborate preparatory work [166] in addition to that produced by the International Law Commission over several years, scrutinized, debated, and adopted with few changes the conclusions of the commission as set forth in its 1956 report.

The Final Act, signed on April 29, 1958,[167] recorded the preparation

---

recommended Geneva. The General Assembly left the choice of site to the Secretary General. It was therefore held at the European Office of the United Nations in the Palais des Nations, Geneva.

[165] A preliminary Conference on Land-locked States met in Geneva Feb. 10 to 14 and presented a memorandum to the plenary conference.

[166] Twenty-four mimeographed documents, prepared by the Secretariat of the United Nations, under the direction of Dr. Yuen-li Liang, Director of the Codification Division of the Legal Office of the United Nations, *Initial List of Documents*, A/CONF.13/33, Feb. 4, 1958. Among these uniformly excellent compilations and studies, the following may be noted: *Memorandum Concerning Historic Bays*, A/CONF. 13/1, Sept. 20, 1957; *Scientific Considerations Relating to the Continental Shelf*, Memorandum by UNESCO, A/CONF.13/2, Sept. 30, 1957; *The Economic and Scientific Basis of the Principle of Abstention*, by Richard van Cleve, A/CONF.-13/3, Oct. 4, 1957; *Examination of Living Resources Associated with the Sea Bed of the Continental Shelf with Regard to the Nature and Degree of their Physical and Biological Association with Such Sea Bed*, Memorandum by FAO, A/CONF.-13/13, Nov. 6, 1957; *Technical Particulars Concerning the Methods of Fishing Conducted by Means of Equipment Embedded in the Floor of the Sea*, Memorandum by FAO, A/CONF. 13/12, Nov. 6, 1957; *A Brief Geographical and Hydrographical Study of Bays and Estuaries, the Coasts of Which Belong to Different States*, by R. H. Kennedy, A/CONF.13/15, Nov. 13, 1957; *Bibliographical Guide on the Law of the Sea*, A/CONF.13/17, Nov. 21, 1957; *Certain Legal Aspects Concerning the Delimitation of the Territorial Waters of Archipelagos*, by Jens Evensen, A/CONF.13/18, Nov. 29, 1957; *Guide to the Decisions of International Tribunals Relating to the Law of the Sea*, A/CONF.13/22, Dec. 17, 1957; *List in Chronological Order of International Agreements Relating to Fisheries and Other Questions Affecting the Utilization and Conservation of the Resources of the Sea*, A/CONF.13/23, Dec. 17, 1957; *Information Submitted by Governments Regarding Laws, Decrees and Regulations for the Prevention of Pollution of the Seas* [supplement to *Pollution of the Sea by Oil*, ST/ECA/41, Aug. 1956], A/CONF.13/24, Dec. 18, 1957; *Recent Developments in the Technology of Exploiting the Mineral Resources of the Continental Shelf*, by M. W. Mouton, A/CONF.13/25, Jan. 3, 1958; *Memorandum Concerning the Question of Free Access to the Sea of Land-Locked Countries*, A/CONF.13/29, Jan. 14, 1958, and Add. 1, March 3, 1958.

[167] A/CONF.13/L.58, April 30, 1958. See also, *Roundup of the Conference on the Law of the Sea*, Information Service, European Office of the United Nations, Geneva, Press Release No. L/303; U.S. delegation, 38 DSB 404–405, "U.S. and Canada Advocate Principle of Abstention in Fishing," 38 DSB 708–709, and Loftus Becker, "Some Political Problems of the Legal Adviser," 38 DSB 832–836 (1958).

and opening for signature of four conventions — on the territorial sea and the contiguous zone,[168] on the high seas,[169] on fishing and conservation of the living resources of the High Seas,[170] and on the Continental Shelf [171]; the adoption of one optional protocol concerning the compulsory settlement of disputes [172]; and the adoption of nine resolutions,[173] eight of them dealing with matters of continuing importance.

The conference was unable to resolve the contentious issue of the width of the territorial sea. A majority of states favored a width greater than the traditional three-mile belt — four, six, or twelve miles. After several weeks of debate, compromises were offered successively by Canada, the United Kingdom, and the United States. Canada at first proposed retention of the three-mile limit for all purposes but exclusive control over fisheries up to twelve miles from the base line. This would preserve freedom of navigation in the air space and on the high seas in the additional nine-mile area. Subsequently, when it appeared that some extension of the territorial sea might become necessary, Canada proposed a six-mile limit for the territorial sea and exclusive control over fisheries up to twelve miles from the base line. The United Kingdom proposed an extension of sovereignty to six miles but with the exception of freedom for air navigation in the additional three-mile area. The United States, at first opposed to any extension of the three-mile belt for any purposes,[174] finally proposed a territorial sea of six miles with additional exclusive jurisdiction over fisheries up

---

Customarily the full proceedings of a conference do not appear until several months after the event. The press coverage was unduly scanty. The texts of the four conventions, the protocol, and the resolutions are reprinted in "U.N. Conference on the Law of the Sea," 38 *DSB* 1110–1125 (1958). The United States signed the four conventions and the protocol at the United Nations in New York on Sept. 15, 1958. *N.Y.T.*, Sept. 16, 1958.

[168] A/CONF.13/L.52, April 28, 1958. The official date for each convention is April 29, 1958.

[169] A/CONF.13/L.53, April 28, 1958.

[170] A/CONF.13/L.54, April 28, 1958.

[171] A/CONF.13/L.55, April 28, 1958.

[172] A/CONF.13/L.57, April 30, 1958.

[173] A/CONF.13/L.56, April 30, 1958.

[174] Arthur H. Dean, "The Law of the Sea," statement at the conference, 38 *DSB* 574–581 (1958). See also his closing statement on April 28 in which he reaffirmed American adherence to the 3-mile rule as "established international law" and asserted that there was "no obligation on the part of states adhering to the 3-mile rule to recognize claims on the part of other states to a greater breadth of territorial sea," but pledged American cooperation to the securing of international agreement on the breadth of the territorial sea and on fishing rights. 38 *DSB* 1110–1111 (1958).

to twelve miles but with an exception in favor of foreign fisheries already conducted in the six-to-twelve-mile area over the past five years. No proposal on this subject received the necessary two-thirds vote. The American proposal, however, received the largest number of votes (45 for, 33 against, 7 abstentions, Yemen absent), a good augury for future possible disposal of the issue. The conference therefore proceeded to conclude the convention on the territorial sea without stipulating its width. In a resolution it requested the thirteenth (1958) General Assembly to study the advisability of holding a second conference for the purpose of resolving this issue and to deal with other unfinished business.

The Convention on the Territorial Sea and the Contiguous Zone authorized the use of the base-line system, defined internal waters, including therein bays less than twenty-four miles wide, assimilated essential roadsteads to territorial waters, and prescribed extensively (Arts. 14–23) the rules for innocent passage. Saudi Arabia opposed vigorously, as tailor-made to dispose of the Gulf of Aqaba issue, paragraph 4 of Article 16 which forbids the suspension of the innocent passage of foreign ships through straits used for international navigation between one part of the high seas and another or the territorial sea of a state. Article 24 deals with the contiguous zone, the area between the three-mile limit and 12 miles, in which "the coastal state may exercise the control necessary to prevent infringement of its customs, fiscal, immigration, or sanitary regulations." If ultimately the territorial sea is extended any distance up to 12 miles, then the applicability of this provision would be reduced *pro tanto*.

Neither the International Law Commission nor the conference were able to prescribe a regime for historic waters, including so-called historic bays. The conference therefore requested the General Assembly to arrange for further study of this problem.

The Convention on the High Seas follows very closely the draft articles of the commission, stressing the four freedoms of navigation, fishing, laying submarine cables and pipelines, and flying over the high seas. In addition to modernizing old rules relating to safety, collisions, piracy, and hot pursuit, it provides for access to the sea by land-locked states (Arts. 3–4), assimilates government owned vessels in commercial service to private vessels on the high seas (Art. 9), imposes a new obligation on all coastal states to provide adequate search and rescue services (Art. 12), and extends the right of boarding slave-traders to all warships in all areas (Art. 22), disregarding the maritime zones established by the old multipartite agreements on the subject. In connection with clarification of the use of identifying national flags (Art. 6), the convention leaves open the question of ships employed by and flying the flag of an intergovernmental organization (Art. 7). Articles 24 and 25 create obligations to prevent pollution of the sea by oil or radioactive wastes and pollution of the sea or air space above "by activities with radioactive materials or other harmful agents."

For several weeks the conference debated the commission's proposal that "for purposes of recognition of the national character of the ship by other states, there must exist a genuine link between the state and the ship." The United States vigorously opposed adoption of this concept, on various grounds, but primarily because an estimated 9,000,000 tons of American shipping, chiefly tankers, now fly "flags of convenience." In the end the conference struck out the "recognition" clause to reduce the opportunities for discrimination against such vessels and added a clause designed to increase the responsibilities of the flag state beyond the formal act of granting registry. Article 5 of the convention therefore now reads: "Each state shall fix the conditions for the grant of its nationality to ships, for the registration of ships in its territory, and for the right to fly its flag. Ships have the nationality of the state whose flag they are entitled to fly. There must exist a genuine link between the state and the ship; in particular, the state must effectively exercise its jurisdiction and control in administrative, technical and social matters over ships flying its flag." Needless to say, many European merchant fleets which must compete with the foreign-owned marines of Panama, Liberia, Honduras, and Costa Rica, as well as much of the American flag fleet, labor organizations in the United States and abroad, and the ILO are not likely to be content with this modest approach to a solution of a vexing problem.

The Convention on Fishing and Conservation of the Living Resources of the High Seas incorporates the principles endorsed by the Rome Technical Conference of 1955 and the International Law Commission. In brief, the convention adopts the criterion of "optimum sustainable yield" for conservation measures, giving priority to the supplying of "food for human consumption" (Art. 2); imposes upon the states whose nationals fish on the high seas the responsibility of adopting unilaterally or where necessary jointly non-discriminatory regulations for their nationals (Arts. 3–4); and requires the governments of newcomers to such fisheries to apply the regulations already established for those fisheries, subject to a right of appeal through the "arbitral" process set up by the convention (Art. 5). The special interest of the coastal state in the living resources of "the high seas adjacent to its territorial sea" is repeatedly safeguarded (Art. 1) by guaranteeing to it participation "on an equal footing in any system of research and regulation for purposes of conservation . . . in that area, even though its nationals do not carry on fishing there" (Art. 6). The convention nowhere acknowledges the extreme claims of certain of the Latin American states to control of fisheries in extensive areas off their coasts but a resolution adopted by the conference recommends that the states establishing regulations for the offshore fisheries "shall recognize any preferential requirements" of the coastal population where it depends peculiarly for food or livelihood upon those fisheries. With good will on both sides, that injunction should take care of the genuine interests of such coastal areas at no great loss to the large-scale commercial fishing on the high seas.

Articles 9–12 provide for the settlement of disputes by special *ad hoc* commissions of five members. The procedure follows in the main that suggested by the commission, but the term "arbitral" is studiously avoided. Article 11 adds appeal to the Security Council under Article 94 of the Charter in the event there is noncompliance with the decisions of the special commissions. Article 13 leaves the regulation of high seas sedentary fisheries by means of fixed equipment unilaterally to the coastal state on a nonexclusory basis "except in areas where such fisheries have by long usage been exclusively enjoyed by the nationals" of such coastal state. On the whole, if given a chance, the convention should produce substantially fair results and contribute to the maintenance of *mare liberum*.

The fourth convention elaborated by the conference, on the continental shelf, is the first multipartite agreement on the subject. Like the other agreements, it follows very substantially the proposals of the International Law Commission. It adopts the commission's definition of the term (including its grammatical awkwardness) as "referring to the seabed and subsoil of the submarine areas adjacent to the coast but outside the area of the territorial sea, to a depth of 200 meters or, beyond that limit, to where the depth of the superjacent waters admits of the exploitation of the natural resources of the said areas" and, additionally, "to the seabed and subsoil of similar submarine areas adjacent to the coasts of islands" (Art. 1). In this area the coastal state exercises sovereign rights for the purpose of exploring it and exploiting its natural resources (Art. 2). The rights vest automatically, without "any express proclamation." The legal status of the superjacent waters and air space remains unaffected (Art. 3). If the coastal state does not exploit the shelf, no one else may without the consent of that state (Art. 2).

A few of the other striking provisions may be noted. The natural resources, living and mineral, in and under the bed, which the coastal state may exclusively exploit include "sedentary species," which, at long last, are defined as "organisms which, at the harvestable stage, either are immobile on or under the sea-bed or are unable to move except in constant physical contact with the sea-bed or the subsoil" (Art. 2).

The coastal state may not interfere with the laying or maintenance of submarine cables or pipelines (Art. 4), navigation, fishing, conservation measures, or *bona fide* scientific research in the convention area (Art. 5). It may establish safety zones surrounding installations to a distance of 500 meters, which all shipping must respect, and it is responsible for the removal of abandoned or disused installations. The installations and safety zones must not interfere with recognized international sea lanes (Art. 5). The coastal state is entitled to exploit the subsoil by means of tunnels (from the land side) without regard to the criterion of the 200 meter depth of water (Art. 7). Thus man's newest venture into the sea is brought under adequate international control.

All four of the conventions were opened to signature up to October 31, 1958, and to accession thereafter, by states members of the United Nations or of any of the specialized agencies and by any other state invited by the General Assembly to become a party. Only a few members of the conference signed the instruments on April 29, 1958, the date of adoption of the final act. None of the leading maritime powers did so. All of the conventions require a minimum of 22 ratifications or accessions to enter into force. At the end of five years of effectiveness, any party to a convention may request its revision. The General Assembly is authorized to decide then what steps, if any, should be taken with respect to such request. The conventions on fishing and conservation of the living resources of the high seas and on the continental shelf provide for reservations but the other two do not.

In addition to the resolutions already noted, the conference adopted six others. It left to the General Assembly "for appropriate action" the important problem of nuclear explosions at sea. It urged the International Atomic Energy Agency to deal with the problem of the disposal of radioactive wastes in the sea, suggesting the promulgation of standards and the drawing up of "internationally acceptable regulations" to prevent pollution. It recommended the utilization of the types of fishery conservation organizations endorsed by the Rome 1955 Technical Conference for the implementation of the pertinent provisions in the new conservation convention. Again taking note of the conclusions of the Rome Conference, it urged coastal states to cooperate with such organizations as may be devised to conserve stocks of fish or other living marine resources which inhabit areas comprising both high seas and waters under the jurisdiction of the coastal state. The conference further requested all states "to prescribe, by all means available to them, those methods for the capture and killing of marine life, especially of whales and seals, which will spare them suffering to the greatest extent possible." And finally the conference paid "a tribute of gratitude, respect, and admiration to the International Law Commission" for its contributions to this process of codifying international law. In the words of the president of the conference, Prince Wan Waithayakon of Siam, the work of the commission had been truly "monumental," the results of the conference itself, "fruitful" and "successful."

So ended the largest and most significant conference in maritime history. The community of nations has once more made a substantial contribution to the community of the sea.

Regional Councils

One of the significant developments in the post-World War II period is the increased use of regional councils, not only for defense as in NATO and Western Europe, but also for relatively routine administrative purposes such as the development of fisheries and other activities related to the sea conducted from widely separated territorial units under separate sovereignties in a particular sector of the oceans. It may be that any federalism of the world, should it arise in the future, will be based in part upon functional units such as these and bodies such as an Atomic Energy Commission supplementing the sovereign national territorial

Health and Resources since World War II

units.[175] Be that as it may, councils have come into considerable vogue where the sea is the dominant ecological factor.

Thus one of the first acts of the new Food and Agriculture Organization [176] was to recommend, at its second meeting, in Copenhagen 1946, the establishment of several councils for fisheries patterned on the old Copenhagen Council for the Exploration of the Sea.[177] A resolution of the third conference at Geneva in 1947 visualized the establishment of such councils for seven oceanic regions: North Western Atlantic; South Western Pacific and Indian Ocean; Mediterranean Sea and contiguous waters; North Eastern Pacific; South Eastern Pacific; Western South Atlantic; and Eastern South Atlantic and Indian Ocean.[178] The first of the councils directly in pursuance of this initiative was promptly established by means of an agreement elaborated at a meeting in Baguio, the Philippines, and signed February 26, 1948.[179]

Indo-Pacific Fisheries Council. At a recent date sixteen countries bordering upon or with possessions (in the case of the United States, a trust territory) bordering upon the Indo-Pacific were parties to the agreement: Australia, Burma, Cambodia, Ceylon, France, India, Indonesia, Japan, Korea, Netherlands, Pakistan, Philippines, Thailand, the United Kingdom, the United States, and Vietnam. China, an original member, ceased to be one on its withdrawal from FAO in 1952. "The principal functions of the Council are: to formulate the oceanographical, biological, and other technical aspects of the problems of development and proper utilization of the living aquatic resources of the Indo-Pacific area; to encourage and coordinate research and the application of improved methods in everyday practices; and to assemble, publish, or

---

[175] See Francis H. Russell, "Toward a Stronger World Organization," 23 *DSB* 220–224 (1950); Willard N. Hogan, "Alternative to Atlantic Union," 38 *Bulletin of the American Association of University Professors* 304–311 (1952); and for a most penetrating analysis of the role of functionalism, Inis L. Claude, Jr., *Swords Into Plowshares: the Problems and Progress of International Organization* (1956).

[176] Constitution adopted at Quebec, Oct. 16, 1945, 60 *Stat.* 1886, TIAS 1554.

[177] Andrew W. Anderson, "The Indo-Pacific Fisheries Council," 19 *DSB* 12–13 (1948); *U.S. Int. Conf. 1946–1947*, pp. 68–72.

[178] Anderson, *op. cit.*; *U.S. Int. Conf. 1947–1948*, pp. 79–84; *The Work of FAO 1950/1951, Report of the Director General* (1951), pp. 22–23.

[179] Establishment of the Indo-Pacific Fisheries Council, 62 *Stat.* (3) 3711, TIAS 1895; revised to improve organization and operation by agreement concluded at Sixth Session of the Council, Tokyo, Sept. 30–Oct. 14, 1955, 7 *UST* 2927, TIAS 3674. For a brief description of the set-up see *Directory of International Scientific Organizations*, 2d ed., pp. 295–297.

otherwise disseminate oceanographical, biological, and other technical information relating to living aquatic resources." [180]

Thus far the research and development functions of the council have operated through two committees, one on hydrology and biology, the other on technology. The breakdown of the specific problems studied by these two committees constitute a veritable synopsis of the aquatic biosphere and its utilization for man.[181] In many respects the council is conducting a laboratory of incalculable value for the social scientist of the future. The council has proposed the establishment of an Indo-Pacific Oceanographic Institute. Headquarters for the organization were early established at Bangkok, but the council has met annually in different places in the area under study. Significantly, in addition to liaison with UNESCO [182] and FAO, there is collaboration with the International Commission for Zoological Nomenclature,[183] the General Fisheries Council for the Mediterranean, the Pacific Science Congress,[184] and the South Pacific Commission.

South Pacific Commission. The South Pacific Commission was established by an agreement concluded by the governments of Australia, France, the Netherlands, New Zealand, the United Kingdom, and the United States at Canberra, February 6, 1947.[185] The agreement applies to the nonself-governing territories in the Pacific Ocean which are administered by the participating governments and which lie wholly or in part south of the equator and east from and including Netherlands New Guinea. In this area lie American Samoa and certain other small islands possessed by the United States. The scheme of the agreement utilizes the experience derived from the Caribbean Commission and is in accord with, though not in pursuance of, a resolution of the General

[180] Art. III of the agreement and "Indo-Pacific Fisheries," 24 *DSB* 234 (1951).

[181] Summarized in the annual volumes of *U.S. Int. Conf. 1946–1947* and *1947–1948, loc. cit.*, and *1948–1949*, pp. 70–72; *1949–1950*, pp. 88–90; *1950–1951*, pp. 80–82; *1952–1953*, pp. 37–39; *1953–1954*, pp. 51–54.

[182] Constitution of the United Nations Educational Scientific and Cultural Organization, concluded at London, Nov. 16, 1945, 61 *Stat.* (3) 2495, *TIAS* 1580.

[183] See *Directory of International Scientific Organizations*, 2d ed., pp. 38–39.

[184] *Ibid.*, pp. 300–302; a semi-governmental organization; founded at Hawaii in 1920; secretariat at Honolulu. Also, see *Science and Foreign Relations*, Dept. of State Pub. No. 3860 (1950), p. 41. This latter publication is an invaluable aid to tracing the interrelations of the numerous scientific organizations with UNESCO and other international bodies mentioned from time to time in this work.

[185] Entered into force July 29, 1948, 2 *UST* 1787, *TIAS* 2317. An amendment signed at Canberra, April 5, 1954, provided for greater flexibility in the frequency of sessions, 5 *UST* 639, *TIAS* 2952.

Health and Resources since World War II

Assembly, December 14, 1946, which sought to implement Chapter XI of the charter, which deals with nonself-governing territories.[186] Article XV of the agreement makes it clear that the commission has no organic connection with the United Nations but will cooperate as fully as possible with that body and the appropriate specialized agencies.[187]

Dedicated to the encouragement and strengthening of international cooperation in the promotion of the economic and social welfare and advancement of the peoples of the territories involved, the agreement provides for a commission consisting of two representatives from each of the governments concerned, a research council, a periodic conference of the several peoples inhabiting the islands and the usual secretariat. Headquarters were established at Nouméa, New Caledonia.[188] The agreement deliberately eschews political and defense functions for the area,[189] but enumerates (Art. IV) a large number of economic and social objectives, including the development of communications, transport, and fisheries. Among the thirty or more projects under study by the Research Council are the following of particular pertinence to the present discussion: epidemiological intelligence, standardization of quarantine regulations, atoll and low island economy, "fishery methods in their many indigenous and commercial aspects," vulcanology, and seismology. There is naturally collaboration with the Indo-Pacific Fisheries Council and the Pacific Science Congress.[190] In 1952, in fulfillment of desires expressed at the South Seas Conference in 1947, the commission held a special conference on fisheries at Nouméa.[191]

When the agreement setting up the South Pacific Commission was concluded in 1947, the Security Council had not as yet agreed to the trusteeship of the Pacific Islands for the United States. Since the social

---

[186] *UN Journal*, No. 63/A, p. 708; *UN Weekly Bulletin*, Vol. 1, No. 21, 27–29 (1946); 1 *International Organization* 68–69 (1947).

[187] For the debate on this matter of jurisdiction see *ibid.*, and Emil J. Sady, "Report on the South Seas Conference, With Analysis of the Agreement Establishing the South Pacific Commission," 16 *DSB* 459–465, at p. 465 (1947).

[188] Felix M. Keesing, "The South Pacific Commission Makes Progress," 21 *DSB* 839–843 (1949).

[189] Sady, *op. cit.*, pp. 461–462.

[190] Keesing, *op. cit., passim*; and "South Pacific Commission Research Program 1949–1950," 21 *DSB* 259–261 (1949). The work of the commission, the Research Council, and the conferences can be traced in further commendable detail in *U.S. Int. Org. 1949*, pp. 197–201; and in the annual volumes of *U.S. Int. Conf.* beginning with that for 1946–1947. See also Felix M. Keesing, "The South Pacific Commission: The First Ten Years," 37 *DSB* 422–430 (1957).

[191] *U.S. Int. Conf. 1951–1952*, pp. 151–152.

and economic problems of the islands in the trust territory and of the United States territory of Guam (in the Marianas) are common to those of the South Pacific, the United States, after receiving the trusteeship, sought their inclusion within the scope of application of the agreement of February 6, 1947, in pursuance of Article II thereof, which permits the territorial scope to be altered by agreement of all the participating governments. This was done by a new agreement signed at Nouméa, November 7, 1951.[192] Thus the efforts of the United States to develop the fisheries, notably of the tuna, of the Pacific Island Trust Territory,[193] among other programs designed for the advancement of the peoples inhabiting the Marianas, the Carolines, and the Marshalls, were brought into relation with the comprehensive program of the South Pacific Commission.

The administration of the Trust Territory of the Pacific by the United States deserves more than passing reference, but unfortunately extensive discussion of what is essentially a "sea job" is not feasible here. Suffice it that the United States has devoted commendably serious efforts to the execution of a "policy of carefully measured evolution" for the peoples and institutions of the islands.[194] The Trusteeship Council and its visiting missions have repeatedly bestowed encomiums upon American administration of the islands.[195] The annual reports of the United States to the United Nations pursuant to Article 88 of the Charter are a model of comprehensiveness, clarity, and candor.[196] Even its use of some of the

---

[192] 3 UST 2851, TIAS 2458.

[193] "Policy on Commercial Fishing in Pacific Island Trust Territory," 19 DSB 468–469 (1948).

[194] "Blending New with Old in Pacific Trust Islands," 1 UN Review (Oct. 1954) 47–54. See also John Wesley Coulter, The Pacific Dependencies of the United States (1957).

[195] E.g., Report of the Trusteeship Council to the Security Council on the Trust Territory of the Pacific Islands Covering the Period from 23 July 1955 to 14 August 1956. S/3636, Aug. 15, 1956. Mimeo.

[196] Published by the Department of the Navy, 1948 to 1951; the Department of the Interior, 1952–1953; the Department of State, beginning with the Seventh Annual Report, for the period July 1, 1953, to June 30, 1954, Dept. of State Pub. No. 5735 (1955); for 1955, Pub. No. 6243 (1956); for 1956, Pub. No. 6457 (1957). In addition, the DSB has regularly carried articles concerning the Trust Territory and has reprinted the oral statements of American representatives in the Trusteeship Council, e.g., Frank E. Midkiff, High Commissioner of the Trust Territory, "U.S. Administration of the Trust Territory of the Pacific Islands," 31 DSB 96–109, and "Problems of the Pacific Trust Territory," 31 DSB 141–145 (1954); and Delmas H. Nucker, "A Year of Progress in the Trust Territory of the Pacific Islands," 35 DSB 35–41 (1956), and "The Trust Territory of the Pacific Islands," 37 DSB 248–258 (1957).

atolls and sea areas within the trust territory for atomic testing, to be adverted to later, has not qualified the consistent approval of American administration voiced in the Trusteeship Council since the trusteeship agreement was entered into in 1947.[197]

Technical Assistance and Cooperation Agreements. Before leaving the Pacific, it would be desirable to note certain bipartite agreements recently concluded by the United States, each of which involves some important aspect of that ocean. Thus, by an agreement of March 14, 1947,[198] the United States undertook to cooperate with the Philippine government in a three-year program to develop fisheries in those islands. Three other agreements with that government, signed at Manila May 12, 1947, provided for similar extensive cooperation in the development of coast and geodetic,[199] air navigation,[200] and meteorological[201] programs, the air navigation agreement having been noted in the discussion above. An unusual agreement with France, signed at Paris, November 27, 1948,[202] provided for the aerial mapping by the United States of New Caledonia, its dependencies, and numerous other French island possessions in the South Pacific.

Caribbean Commission. The last of the regional councils to be considered here but the first in point of origin is the Caribbean Commission. It arose out of the submarine threat to communications in the "American Mediterranean" in 1942. At first the joint efforts of the United States and Great Britain were devoted to preventing dire famine in the area. After that danger was overcome, those efforts were devoted to positive programs designed to improve the whole mode of life on the numerous islands which are subject to their respective jurisdictions. The story of the development from bipartite to multipartite collaboration is now well known.[203] In 1945 France and the Netherlands

[197] Resolution of the Security Council, April 2, 1947, UN Doc. S/318 and *UN Yearbook 1946–1947*, pp. 398–400; approved by Act of Congress, July 18, 1947, 61 *Stat.* (1) 397; text 61 *Stat.* (3) 3301, *TIAS* 1665.
[198] 61 *Stat.* (3) 2834, *TIAS* 1611.
[199] 61 *Stat.* (3) 2852, *TIAS* 1616.
[200] 61 *Stat.* (3) 2864, *TIAS* 1618.
[201] 61 *Stat.* (3) 2858, *TIAS* 1617.
[202] Aerial Mapping: Pacific Area Project, 3 *UST* 491, *TIAS* 2407.
[203] "Anglo-American Caribbean Commission," 6 *DSB* 229–230 (1942); Charles W. Taussig, "The Anglo-American Caribbean Commission," 11 *DSB* 377–379 (1944); *ibid.*, "Regionalism in the Caribbean: Six Years of Progress," 18 *DSB* 691–693 (1948); and numerous other articles on current developments in the *DSB* since 1942. The work of the Anglo-American Commission, the enlarged commission, and

accepted invitations to participate as full members of the commission. Thereupon the name was informally changed from Anglo-American Caribbean Commission to Caribbean Commission. By October 30, 1946, it was possible to conclude an agreement formalizing the existing arrangements between the four governments concerned.[204]

Confined to the advancement of the economic and social well-being of the peoples in the territories possessed by the participants in the Caribbean, the agreement provides for a consultative and advisory commission, consisting of four representatives from each party, meeting at least twice a year; a Caribbean Research Council of not less than seven nor more than fifteen members appointed by the commission, meeting whenever necessary; a West Indian Conference consisting of two delegates from each territorial government for consultative purposes and with a power to make recommendations to the commission, meeting biennially; and a Central Secretariat.

Article IV of the 1946 agreement empowers the commission to study, formulate, and recommend measures, programs, and policies with respect to social and economic problems of the area, particularly those arising out of agriculture, communications, education, fisheries, health, housing, industry, labor, social welfare, and trade. Under Article XVIII, the commission and its auxiliary bodies, "while having no present connection with the United Nations," [205] are required nevertheless to "cooperate as fully as possible with the United Nations and with appropriate specialized agencies on matters of mutual concern within the terms of reference of the Commission." Cooperation with other governments of the Caribbean area, not members of the commission, is also enjoined (Art. XVII).

---

the successive conferences of the inhabitants of the islands can be traced in *U.S. Int. Org. 1949*, pp. 192–197, which includes bibliographical notes, and the successive issues of *U.S. Int. Conf.* beginning with that for *1945–1946* at pp. 225–236. Also, see a summation up to 1949 by James A. Bough, "The Caribbean Commission," 3 *Int. Org.* 643–655 (1949), and an extensive survey of the whole Caribbean problem, by Bernard L. Poole, *The Caribbean Commission: Background of Cooperation in the West Indies* (1951). This latter work contains a valuable bibliography on the Caribbean Commission up to 1950, pp. 277–288.

[204] Opened for signature at Washington, Oct. 30, 1946; entered into force Aug. 6, 1948, 62 *Stat.*(3) 2618, *TIAS* 1799. The Central Secretariat of the commission was established at Kent House, Port-of-Spain, Trinidad, B.W.I.

[205] For the controversy arising out of efforts of some members of the United Nations to subject nonself-governing territories to supervision by ECOSOC, see the works cited above, n. 186.

Health and Resources since World War II

The range of subject matters of concern to the commission is, of course, enormous, creating problems of selection, emphasis, and priority. From the beginning, however, the development of fisheries has had high priority. Thus, extensive surveys of the fisheries in various groups of islands were conducted in 1943 [206] and 1944.[207] In 1943, the governments of the United States and the Bahamas reached an agreement "for commercial exploitation of the tuna-run passing through the eastern edge of the Gulf Stream." Under the Research Council, one research committee is specially charged with investigations relating to agriculture, fish, wildlife, and forestry. It has produced a series of studies on fisheries.[208] In addition to the discussions on the subject conducted by the commission itself and the biennial conferences, special conferences have been devoted to cooperatives,[209] some of them concerned with fisheries; trade statistics,[210] one of the recommendations dealing with fish landed from the original fishing vessel; and a comprehensive examination of Caribbean fisheries.[211]

In addition to fisheries, the Caribbean Commission has naturally had to deal with many other problems in which the sea plays a dominant role and which have been discussed in the present work, among them maritime communications and transport, epidemiological control and quarantines, meteorology, especially with respect to hurricanes, and oceanographic research. The tendency of the commission has been to invite the attention and cooperation of the appropriate specialized agencies to the problems, particularly ITU, WHO, IMCO, WMO, ICAO, UNESCO, and, of course, FAO. Under a reorganization of the Pan American Sanitary Organization effected after World War II, representatives of France, the Netherlands, and the United Kingdom, on behalf of their territories in the Western Hemisphere, now participate

---

[206] Poole, *op. cit.*, p. 205.

[207] Richard T. Whiteleather and Herbert H. Brown, *An Experimental Fishery Survey in Trinidad, Tobago, and British Guiana: With Recommended Improvements in Methods and Gear*, Anglo-American Caribbean Commission (1945).

[208] Poole, *op. cit.*, pp. 280–281, and the *Year Book of Caribbean Research* (1949) listing 800 projects and investigations under way, including many on fisheries, 21 *DSB* 159 (1949). See also, "Scientific and Economic Development in the Caribbean," 19 *DSB* 19–20 (1948). The commission has also issued a *Guide to Commercial Shark Fishing in the Caribbean Area* (1945).

[209] *U.S. Int. Conf. 1950–1951*, pp. 77–80; 24 *DSB* 191 (1951); 34 *DSB* 224–225 (1956).

[210] *U.S. Int. Conf. 1950–1951*, pp. 9–12.

[211] At Port-of-Spain, Trinidad, March 24–28, 1952, 26 *DSB* 593–594 (1952).

in the work of the Directing Council of PASO.[212] Much effort has been devoted to building up tourism as a permanent industry for the area.[213]

In passing, it should be pointed out that the Caribbean Commission is confronted not only with the task of promoting the viability of the area but also with the demands of sundry Latin American states, voiced in the OAS, that various of the dependencies be annexed to neighboring republics or be given independence.[214] Thus an interesting race is in process between the possibilities of federation for the area and the possibilities of liquidation for the remnants of empire. The establishment of the West Indies Federation, a union of several of the British island possessions in the area, in 1958, may be the forerunner of a larger federation in the decades to come, which may include possessions of the other powers.

Food and Agriculture Organization

As a direct result of its relation to the Food and Agriculture Organization the United States has thus far participated in only one multipartite fisheries agreement sponsored by that body, the one establishing the Indo-Pacific Fisheries Commission discussed above. Another agreement, however, providing for the establishment of a Latin American Fisheries Council, has been elaborated. In 1950 the Second Latin American Regional Meeting on Food and Agricultural Programs and Outlook, held at Montevideo, requested the Director General of FAO to invite FAO members in Latin America to meet for the purpose of formulating a draft agreement for the establishment of such a council.[215] Accordingly, the meeting was held in Lima, Peru, in 1951.[216] Delegates from France, the Netherlands, and the United Kingdom, representing the interests of those governments in their American possessions, appropriately attended. The draft agreement there adopted provides for the establishment of a council with nonregulatory functions devoted to scientific, technical, and publication activities. Although only five acceptances are necessary to bring the agreement into force, this goal had

[212] "Directing Council, Pan American Sanitary Organization," 35 *DSB* 496–497 (1956).
[213] Poole, *op. cit.*, pp. 225–229.
[214] *Final Act, Tenth Inter-American Conference, Caracas, Venezuela, March 1–28, 1954,* Resols. XCVI and XCVII.
[215] *U.S. Int. Conf. 1950–1951,* pp. 72–75.
[216] Latin American Fisheries Meeting of the FAO, Lima, Peru, Sept. 17–22, 1951, *U.S. Int. Conf. 1951–1952,* pp. 77–79.

Health and Resources since World War II

not been achieved by the spring of 1957, doubtless because of the preoccupation of the United States and several of the Latin American states with the controversy over offshore claims.

In addition to cooperating in all the work undertaken by the FAO devoted to enhancing the marine sources of food,[217] the United States has participated in several separate conferences sponsored by the FAO concerned entirely with fisheries, that is, on herring and allied species, at The Hague, 1949;[218] on herring technology, at Bergen, Norway, 1950;[219] of fisheries technologists, at Bergen, 1950;[220] and on fisheries statistics, at Copenhagen, 1952.[221]

HUMANITARIAN, SCIENTIFIC, AND OTHER DEVELOPMENTS
Humanitarian Efforts

Fortunately, most of the humanitarian efforts relating to the sea are now being directed, in one way or another, through the Economic and Social Council of the United Nations. Thus by means of four special protocols the functions thitherto performed by the League of Nations and certain host governments with respect to the traffic in women and children,[222] the circulation of obscene publications,[223] the control of various aspects of narcotic drugs,[224] and the traffic in slaves[225] were

---

[217] The work can be traced in admirable outline in *U.S. Int. Org. 1949*, pp. 36–44, which includes a good bibliographical start, and in the annual volumes of *U.S. Int. Conf.*, beginning with the one for the period July 1, 1941–June 30, 1945, pp. 58–67. Also, see the special articles and quarterly chronological development in *International Organization* since 1947. Among the numerous publications of FAO relating to fisheries, some of which have been cited in this work *passim*, is *Fishery Research and Educational Institutions in North and South America*, Prepared by Gerald V. Howard and Eileen R. Godfrey, FAO (1950).

[218] *U.S. Int. Conf. 1949–1950*, pp. 68–70; 21 *DSB* 294 (1949).

[219] *U.S. Int. Conf. 1950–1951*, pp. 59–60; 23 *DSB* 514 (1950).

[220] *U.S. Int. Conf. 1950–1951*, pp. 60–61.

[221] *U.S. Int. Conf. 1951–1952*, pp. 152–154.

[222] Suppression of White Slave Traffic, Protocol with Annex, Amending Agreement of May 18, 1904, and Convention of May 4, 1910, opened for signature at Lake Success, May 4, 1949, entered into force for the United States Aug. 14, 1950, annex June 21, 1951, 2 *UST* 1997, *TIAS* 2332. For the developments under the United Nations, see *UN Yearbook* since 1946.

[223] Suppression of the Circulation of Obscene Publications, Protocol with Annex, Amending Agreement of May 4, 1910, opened for signature at Lake Success, May 4, 1949, 1 *UST* 849, *TIAS* 2164. For developments since 1946 see *UN Yearbook*.

[224] Narcotic Drugs, Protocol with Annex, Amending the Agreements, Conventions, and Protocols of Jan. 23, 1912, Feb. 11, 1925, Feb. 19, 1925, July 13, 1931, Nov. 27, 1931, and June 26, 1936, opened for signature at Lake Success, Dec. 11, 1946, 61 *Stat.* (2) 2230, *TIAS* 1671; and Narcotic Drugs, Entry into Force of Amendments Set Forth in the Annex to the Protocol of Dec. 11, 1946, Proclamation

The United States and the Treaty Law of the Sea

transferred to the United Nations. The United States became a party to each of these acts of transfer. No extraordinary developments in relation to the first two regimes have occurred in recent years requiring special note.[226] It is possible, therefore, to proceed directly to consideration of the developments relating to slavery and narcotics.

Slavery and Slave Traffic. The ancient institutions of slavery, in its many and disguised forms, and of the traffic in slaves naturally will die hard. Despite all the efforts of the international community [227] since the Peace of Vienna in 1815, where the first generalized antislavery commitments were entered into, the two institutions still persist in areas of the world, such as the Middle East, parts of Africa and Asia, and certain of the Pacific islands, where many human beings exist marginally. Concerned with this persistence ECOSOC undertook the preparation of a Supplementary Convention on the Abolition of Slavery, the Slave Trade, and Institutions and Practices Similar to Slavery, which was opened to signature on September 4, 1956, at a special conference in Geneva.[228] The United States attended the conference but did not sign the conven-

---

by the President of the United States of America at Washington, March 30, 1948, 62 *Stat.* (2) 1796, *TIAS* 1859. Pending the elaboration of a single convention to replace these and other agreements to which the United States is not a party, a United Nations Opium Conference, meeting in New York in 1953, adopted another protocol of an interim character for Limiting and Regulating the Cultivation of the Poppy Plant, the Production of, International and Wholesale Trade in, and Use of Opium, opened for signature June 23, 1953. The Senate approved this agreement Aug. 20, 1954. Only 16 of the required 25 states had at a recent date ratified it. *U.S. Int. Conf. 1952–1953*, pp. 203–205; *Laws Controlling Illicit Narcotics Traffic*, 84 Cong., 2 Sess., S. Doc. No. 120 (1956), pp. 83–84; *Control of Narcotics*, 84 Cong., 2 Sess., S. Rept. No. 2483 (1956), pp. 4–6; *Report of Commission on Narcotics*, E/2891, E/CN.7/315, 8 June 1956, par. 32.

[225] Slavery Convention, signed at Geneva, Sept. 25, 1926, 46 *Stat.* 2183, *TS* 778; Protocol amending same, done at New York, Dec. 7, 1953, entered into force for the United States, March 7, 1956, 7 *UST* 479, *TIAS* 3532.

[226] For the work of the ECOSOC in relation to them see *UN Yearbook* since 1946, and, in general, for a comprehensive account of United Nations Welfare programs, Robert E. Asher, Walter M. Kotschnig, *et al., The United Nations and Promotion of the General Welfare* (1957).

[227] See the memoranda prepared by the Secretariat to assist the ECOSOC *ad hoc* Committee on Slavery, *The Suppression of Slavery*, ST/SOA/4,1951.XIV.2,EF; a subsequent report of the Secretary General, 11 February 1954, Doc. E/2540, ECOSOC, *Official Records*, 17th Session (1954), Agenda Item 15; and the splendid survey of replies from governments by Rapporteur Hans Engen, dated 9 Feb., 1955, Doc. E/2673, *ibid.*, 19th Session (1955), Agenda Item 8.

[228] "Preparation of the Convention," E/CONF. 24/3, 8 June 1956; Text in *Final Act* of the Conference, E/CONF. 24/23; summary of conference, "Thirty Three Nations Sign Anti-Slavery Convention," 3 *UN Review* (Oct. 1956) 6–7.

tion and furthermore expressed its intention not to sign or ratify the instrument.[229] Thereby hangs a tale.

When the Bricker Amendment, seeking to restrict the treaty-making power of the United States, was being considered by the Senate in the spring of 1953, Secretary Dulles appeared before the Judiciary Committee, opposed adoption of the resolution, and announced as the policy of the new administration that it intended "to encourage the promotion everywhere of human rights and individual freedoms, but to favor methods of persuasion, education, and example rather than formal undertakings which commit one part of the world to impose its particular social and moral standards upon another part of the world community, which has different standards." He then announced that the administration did "not intend to sign the Convention on Political Rights of Women," and declared that the "same principles will guide our action in other fields which have been suggested by some as fields for multilateral treaties."[230]

In line with this policy, therefore, Mrs. Oswald B. Lord, American representative on the ECOSOC Commission on Human Rights, announced to the commission at its spring meeting in 1953 that the United States did not intend to sign or ratify the Draft Covenants on Human Rights, but proposed instead a new action program stressing annual reports, studies on specific aspects of human rights, and advisory services along the lines of those already being provided in other fields, as a substitute for multilateral treaty undertakings.[231]

Most of the provisions of the supplementary convention of 1956 aim to secure the abolition or abandonment of practices and institutions similar to slavery, such as debt bondage, serfdom, forced transfers of women in marriage and inheritance, and exploitation of children. The slave-trade provisions obligate the parties to take measures with respect to use of ships, aircraft, ports, airfields, and coastlines for the more effective repression of the traffic. One clause, in Article 4, is noteworthy:

[229] "U.S. Position on Proposed Slavery Convention," statement by Walter Kotschnig, 35 *DSB* 561–562 (1956).
[230] "The Making of Treaties and Executive Agreements," statement by Secretary Dulles, April 6, 1953, 28 *DSB* 591–595 (1953).
[231] Mrs. Oswald B. Lord, "New U.S. Action Program for Human Rights," 29 *DSB* 215–222 (1953). See also "U.S. Policy on Human Rights," 28 *DSB* 579–582 (1953), and Report by the President to the Congress for the Year 1953, *US Participation in the UN*, D.S. Pub. No. 5459, pp. 155–158.

"Any slave who takes refuge on board any vessel of a State Party to this Convention shall *ipso facto* be free."[232]

The United States representative at the Geneva Conference suggested that it might be more fruitful to secure additional ratifications of the 1926 convention, already long on the books, and declared that since many of the provisions of the new convention dealt with matters "generally considered to be in the area of domestic jurisdiction," it would be better to proceed along the lines of the "action program" proposed by the United States with respect to human rights generally.[233] So the matter stands.

Traffic in Narcotics. With the vast system of international control of the production, manufacture, and distribution of narcotics,[234] important as it is, we cannot be here concerned. With the illicit traffic in narcotics we must be concerned because so much of it occurs by sea, by air, and through the postal system.

Despite the persistent efforts of the League of Nations and the United Nations, "the total quantities of drugs actually discovered and confiscated in the illicit traffic are estimated not to exceed ten per cent of the total quantities of drugs in the world illicit markets."[235] Traditionally the traffic has been by sea and overland, in recent years by air. The special Committee on Illicit Traffic, recently established by the ECOSOC Commission on Narcotics, reported in 1956 that "the use of aircraft by traffickers appeared to be increasing, particularly in the Far East." It was careful, however, to absolve the air crews on the principal lines from complicity because of the high standards applied in recruitment. Otherwise and in general, however, passengers and ground crews were

---

[232] Article 37 of the 1956 Report of the International Law Commission proposes the extension of the obligation to "any ship, whatever its colours."

[233] Kotschnig, statement, *op. cit.*

[234] Bertil A. Renborg, "International Control of Narcotics," 22 *Law and Contemporary Problems* 86–112 (1957); on the illicit traffic, pp. 95, 101–103. See also the excellent summaries in "Narcotic Drug Control," Introduction by Herbert L. May, *Int. Con.* No. 441 (1948) and in *Everyman's United Nations 1945–1955*, pp. 251–256.

[235] "The Illicit Traffic in Narcotics Throughout the World," 3 *Bulletin on Narcotics* 1–14, at p. 2 (1951), which contains a map of the principal sea routes. See also *Narcotic Drugs: Summary of Illicit Transactions and Seizures*, E/NS 1954/Summary 1, 15 March 1954; and *Report of the Committee on Illicit Traffic*, UN Commission on Narcotic Drugs, E/CN.7/L.129/Add.1, 2 May 1956, for "Indications of Origins of Drugs Seized in 1955," "Regional World Totals of Drugs Seized, 1950–1955," and "World Totals of Seizures of Drugs Selected for Certain Years from 1931 to 1955."

involved, as well as perhaps at times air crews of smaller, less circumspect companies.[236]

In addition to passenger traffickers, the crews of merchant vessels have always been involved in the illicit business. In 1953 the Narcotics Commission "agreed that smuggling by seamen is the largest source of illegal drugs." [237] This is borne out by the lists of seizures of contraband and arrests of personnel regularly appearing in the reports of the United States and the United Nations. The web of routes of the clandestine traffic is heaviest in the Western Pacific from Japan down around Australia, in the Indian Ocean, in the waters around the Arabian Peninsula, in the Mediterranean, and around Northern Europe. Ports vary with respect to being foci of direct and indirect traffic, Singapore being one of the worst of the foci.

The principal ports of entry for illicit drugs in the United States appear to be, on the Pacific Coast, Seattle and San Francisco; on the Atlantic, Norfolk, Baltimore, Philadelphia, New York, and Boston, for the traffic from Capetown, the Mediterranean, and Europe; on the Gulf, Galveston, for the traffic from northern Europe via Curaçao in the Dutch West Indies. Small wonder that the United States in 1950 submitted to the Narcotics Commission a resolution calling for, *inter alia*, the imposition of severe penalties upon officers and seamen engaged in the traffic.[238] No doubt the single convention now being elaborated by the commission to replace the existing eight conventions dealing with the international control system, will include new and more stringent rules for the repression of the traffc by sea and by air.

In addition to the hearty cooperation which the United Nations has received from the Universal Postal Union in repressing the illicit traffic,[239] the United Nations has increasingly relied upon the efficient work of the International Criminal Police Commission for detection and apprehension of traffickers. Founded in 1923 at the instance of Dr. Schober, police president of Vienna, the organization, with headquarters now in Paris, furnishes a practical basis for direct cooperation between the

---

[236] *Report of the Committee on Illicit Traffic*, E/CN.7/L.129, 28 April 1956, par. 74.

[237] Report by the President to the Congress, 1953, *US Participation in the UN*, D.S. Pub. No. 5459, p. 142; see *Report of the Commission on Narcotic Drugs* to ECOSOC, E/2891, E/CN.7/315, 8 June 1956, pars. 168–172.

[238] E/1889/Rev.1, E/CN.7/216/Rev. 1, 29 Dec. 1950, pp. 5, 7.

[239] *Report of the Commission, op. cit.*, pars. 66–70, 173.

national police authorities of over thirty countries, in the suppression of international criminals. The United States has been a member of the ICPC since 1938. Among the fields of endeavour to which the commission devotes itself, of particular concern in this study of the sea, are the suppression of narcotic-drug abuses, suppression of the traffic in women and children, and suppression of publications and films dangerous to public morals. Frequently, when it tracks down counterfeiters or other miscreants within its purview, it uncovers at the same time illicit traffic in drugs.[240] The League of Nations valued its cooperation highly. In the United Nations, the ICPC is represented regularly at the meetings of the Narcotics Commission. So effective has its cooperation become, that the United Nations "no longer functions as clearing house for uncovering and pursuing the illicit narcotic drug traffic," but leaves the task largely to the ICPC.[241] Indeed, the day may well come when no trafficker in illicit drugs, whithersoever he may flee, to darkest dive or uttermost parts of the sea, will be safe from the long arm of the International Criminal Police Commission.

Scientific Efforts

As is evident from the discussion throughout this work, scientific research and other similar activities relating to the sea are at present widely dispersed. They are conducted by numerous national private and governmental organizations, international private and intergovernmental organizations. Some agencies, particularly those concerned with fisheries, are under treaties, some operate under nontreaty constitutions, some have been gathered together under the International Council of Scientific Unions.[242] Most of the great operational specialized agencies, such as ICAO, ITU, WHO, FAO, WMO, and IMCO, foster and promote scientific activities as essential to progress in their respective technologies. For the first time in history, however, the possibility exists of correlating and coordinating, where desirable and feasible, these dispersed efforts, in the interest of wider dissemination of the accruing

---

[240] Paul Marabuto, "The International Criminal Police Commission and the Illicit Traffic of Narcotics," 3 *Bulletin on Narcotics* 3–15 (1951); *U.S. Int. Agencies 1946*, pp. 211–215; *U.S. Int. Org. 1949*, pp. 224–226.

[241] Renborg, *op. cit.*, pp. 102–103. See also *Memorandum by the International Criminal Police Commission for 1954 on Illicit Traffic*, Commission on Narcotic Drugs, E/CN.7/293, 17 March 1955.

[242] Discussed above at p. 192.

knowledge and its better application to the uses of man. That possibility is represented by the two new international agencies, the United Nations Educational, Scientific and Cultural Organization [243] and the Economic and Social Council of the United Nations. As the record of these two agencies discloses, research relating to the sea is part of the total intellectual assault upon man's environment.

ECOSOC and UNESCO. For present purposes it should be sufficient to note only a few of the developments under ECOSOC and UNESCO which illustrate the trend of affairs.

Thus ECOSOC, on proposals from the United States, France, and Denmark, the latter forwarding a communication from the International Council for the Exploration of the Sea,[244] in 1948 commenced the correlation of efforts in the field of cartography. Three heartening developments resulted. By 1950, a Cartographic Office had been established in the Secretariat of the United Nations, with the usual consultative, coordinative, and publication functions, including the launching of a new annual publication, *World Cartography*, the first number of which appeared in 1951.[245] On July 23, 1953, a protocol was concluded at London between the Central Bureau of the International Map of the World[246] and ECOSOC, providing for the transfer of the functions of the Bureau to the Cartographic Office of the United Nations.[247] In 1955 the first of a projected series of regional cartographic conferences, this one for Asia and the Far East, was held at Mussoorie, India. The conference sought the improvement of the cartographic work pertaining to the area and the obtaining of the "basic cartographic data required by those countries which were engaged in the preparation of programs of economic and social development." Among the score of resolutions adopted were several dealing directly with the sea — the desirability of having the Special Committee for the International Geophysical Year include

[243] Constitution concluded at London, Nov. 16, 1945, effective for the United States, Nov. 4, 1946, 61 *Stat.* (3) 2495, *TIAS* 1580; amended to provide for a right of withdrawal and for other purposes of an organizational character at Montevideo, Nov. 22 and Dec. 8, 1954, 6 *UST* 6157, *TIAS* 3469.

[244] *UN Yearbook 1947–1948*, p. 653.

[245] ST/SOA/SER.L/1, 20 June 1951.

[246] Discussed above, pp. 131–132.

[247] Text of protocol in 4 *World Cartography* 2–3 (1954). This number is devoted to a most illuminating "First Progress Report on the International Map of the World on the Millionth Scale (1954)," prepared by the Secretariat. At p. 30 is a map of the world showing the coverage by sheets already published.

in its program provision for making magnetic observations in the Indian Ocean, the Bay of Bengal, and the Arabian Sea; the furthering of gravity measurements at sea; the desirability of establishing national hydrographic services; the completion of various aeronautical maps and charts needed to meet the requirements of civil aviation.[248] The United States, represented primarily by the Coast and Geodetic Survey, has, of course, been intensely interested in these several developments.[249] As part of its mutual aid program, the United States has in recent years furnished a number of governments with American mapping service. Thus by agreements with Thailand in 1952[250] and Cambodia in 1957[251] the United States pledged the cooperation of the Army Map Service in projects planned by those governments.

UNESCO has also made notable contributions to study and use of the sea. Thus, in producing its *Directory of International Scientific Organizations*,[252] it has in effect taken an inventory of what is in process, including the advancement of knowledge concerning the sea. It annually has given subventions[253] to the International Council of Scientific Unions to aid the work of several of its constituent bodies.[254] It has provided technical missions to give advice on shipbuilding problems and harbor improvements.[255] It has set up an International Advisory Committee on Marine Science to coordinate research on sea resources.[256]

In response to a request from ECOSOC, UNESCO has explored the

[248] *UN Yearbook 1955*, p. 247, with documentation cited; *United Nations Regional Cartographic Conference for Asia and the Far East*, Vol. 1, Report of the Conference, E/CONF.18/6 (1955); *U.S. Int. Conf. 1954–1955*, pp. 205–206; "Maps and their Role in World Development," 1 *UN Review* (Oct. 1954) 26–29; *International Cooperation in Cartography*, Report of the Secretary General, E/2823, 2 Feb. 1956.

[249] Charles Pierce, *Geodetic Operations in the United States and in Other Areas Through International Cooperation 1954–1956*, Coast and Geodetic Survey Publication 60-1 (1957), a report to the International Association of Geodesy of the International Union of Geodesy and Geophysics, International Council of Scientific Unions. This report details the assistance rendered to the Survey by the Army Map Service and the Air Force.

[250] Agreement effected by exchange of notes, signed at Bangkok, Nov. 8 and Dec. 3, 1952, 3 *UST* 5893, *TIAS* 2759.

[251] Agreement signed at Phnom Penh, Oct. 17, 1957, 8 *UST* 1761, *TIAS* 3929.

[252] First edition, Paris, 1950, second, Paris, 1953.

[253] Beginning 1947–1948, *UN Yearbook 1947–1948*, p. 852.

[254] *Directory*, 1953, *op. cit.*, pp. 45–48; see also excellent description of interrelations of UNESCO and ICSU by Bart J. Bok, "Science in International Cooperation," 121 *Science* 843–847 (1955).

[255] "A Chart for all the Oceans," 2 *UN Review* (March 1956) 28–35; (April 1956), 29–35.

[256] *UN Yearbook 1955*, p. 396.

Health and Resources since World War II

possibility of the establishment of sundry international laboratories,[257] several of them dealing directly with the sea or its associated phenomena. Thus, among the seventeen subjects of first priority were one or more institutes of oceanography and fisheries in Asia; "an Antarctic Research Institute, including a Meteorological Institute for the Southern Hemisphere if sufficient support is forthcoming from ICAO"; an Astronomical Observatory in the Southern Hemisphere; and an Arctic Research Institute. Among the other specific proposals were astronomical, meteorological, and geophysical observatories; floating laboratories; a marine biological station; and a cartographic center. Questions pertinent to the sea suggested for study at international laboratories included oceanography, seismology; vulcanology; solar and terrestrial relationship; cosmic rays; and the Arctic regions.[258] Finally, in its promotion of cooperation in the social sciences,[259] UNESCO may find it expedient one day to encourage the development of a social science of the sea.

And now, through an impressive chain of relationships — through ECOSOC, a principal organ of the United Nations, to UNESCO, a specialized agency reporting to ECOSOC, to the International Council of Scientific Unions, a nontreaty organization subsidized in part by UNESCO — we are led to the Comité spéciale de l'année géophysique internationale (CSAGI), set up by the ICSU for the purpose of organizing a marvelous demonstration of international cooperation, the International Geophysical Year of 1957–1958.

International Geophysical Year. As already related, the United States participated in the International Polar Years of 1882–1883[260] and 1932–1933.[261] According to the theory behind these original schemes of concentrated international scientific cooperation devoted to learning more about the earth, the sea around us, and the firmament above, the periods of simultaneous inquiry and observation should come at intervals of fifty years.

[257] *Report of UNESCO*, UNESCO/Nat. Sci. 24/1947, reproduced in Report of the Secretary General to ECOSOC, Aug. 1948, E/620 (mimeo.), pp. 49–145; also included in UN Department of Social Affairs, *The Question of Establishing United Nations Research Laboratories*, Sales No.:1949.IV.1. Admirably discussed in 164 *Nature* 1120–1121 (1949).
[258] *UN Yearbook 1947–1948*, pp. 648–650; *ibid., 1948–1949*, pp. 664–665; *ibid., 1950*, pp. 637–639; *ibid., 1951*, pp. 576–577.
[259] *UN Yearbook 1950*, p. 916; *ibid., 1951*, p. 887.
[260] Discussed above at pp. 129–130.
[261] Above at p. 192.

Early in 1950, however, a small group of scientists,[262] meeting informally in Washington, D.C., took the view that the scientists of the world could not afford to wait until 1982 "to replenish their warehouse of scientific data on man's physical environment." They noted, too, that a "period of intense solar activity was predicted for 1957–1958," an excellent occasion to observe geophysical phenomena in the earth's atmosphere. Accordingly, they proposed that the Third Polar Year follow the Second at an interval of twenty-five years. They brought this proposal to the attention of several international scientific organizations. The result was that in 1951 the Executive Committee of the ICSU appointed a special committee to draw up preliminary plans for the undertaking. The general assembly of the ICSU in 1952 expanded the scope of the "Year" to include "not only the north polar region (as in the First and Second Polar Years) but the entire earth."

Under the chairmanship of Sydney Chapman, distinguished British scientist, the membership of the Comité spécial de l'année géophysique internationale was drawn from the four international scientific unions concerned with geophysical and related sciences and from the World Meteorological Organization. "All countries were invited by ICSU to establish national committees of scientists to prepare national programs which their countries would carry out as part of an overall program to be coordinated by CSAGI. In February 1953 the United States National Committee for the IGY was formed by the National Academy of Sciences, which adheres to ICSU on behalf of the United States."[263]

Much has already appeared in print about the programs and activities of the sixty-four countries participating in one way or another in the IGY, July 1, 1957, to December 31, 1958.[264] For present purposes it

---

[262] Among them, Lloyd V. Berkner, whose survey of the role of the Department of State in science has been cited above, n. 184. See his excellent description of the IGY in layman's language, "Assault on the Secrets of the Earth," *N.Y.T. Magazine*, Jan. 27, 1957.

[263] Wallace W. Atwood, Jr., "The International Geophysical Year: A Twentieth-Century Achievement in International Cooperation," 35 *DSB* 880–886 (1956).

[264] See excellent descriptions in Atwood, *op. cit.*; Walter M. Rudolph, "Geophysical Science and Foreign Relations," 33 *DSB* 989–991 (1955); Hugh Odishaw, "The Satellite Program for the International Geophysical Year," 35 *DSB* 280–285 (1956); *International Geophysical Year, A Special Report by the National Academy of Sciences*, 84 Cong., 2 Sess., S. Doc. No. 124 (1956); progress "Report on International Geophysical Year" by the National Science Foundation in *Hearings* before the Subcommittee of the Committee on Appropriations, House of Representatives, 85 Cong., 1 Sess. (1957), which contains most valuable memoranda on the program of IGY; International Geophysical Year: The Arctic, Antarctica, 85 Cong., 2 Sess.,

Health and Resources since World War II

should be sufficient merely to summarize the scope of the undertaking, emphasizing those aspects which especially involve the sea.

In the effort to learn more about the earth and its environment through physics, coordinated and in some cases simultaneous studies will be made of phenomena which are the subjects of interrelated disciplines — solar activity, longitude and latitude determinations, glaciology, oceanography, meteorology, geomagnetism, gravity, aurora and airglow, seismology, ionospheric physics, cosmic rays, and the upper atmosphere. Some 2000 IGY stations have been planned, including five meridianal pole-to-pole chains of stations. Other networks of stations have been created in the Arctic, Antarctic, and Equatorial regions.

About a thousand weather stations will dot the globe, and many other types of observation posts will be set up. Plane and ship pilots, including whalers, will report on weather conditions, especially off main lanes. Cameras and telescopes, satellites and rockets, seismographs and spectographs, radar and multifrequency auroral noise receivers will search the secrets of land, sea, and air. Air reconnaissance, deep-sea soundings, glacier studies, high altitude balloons, and other devices for measuring man's environment will be used.[265]

Among the most dramatic of the undertakings will be the work in the Antarctic and the launching of the research satellites, by the United States and the Soviet Union.[266] Twelve nations will man approximately fifty-six stations in the Antarctic region in 1957–1958. The United States, pledged to establish seven of them, began its program in 1954 with the dispatch of the ice-breaker U.S.S. *Atka* to the Antarctic to study sea-ice conditions and to establish a site for an IGY station in Little America. In 1955, Operation Deep Freeze I set up additional stations and prepared for future IGY operations. By 1957–1958, the total population of Antarctica is expected to number six hundred scientists and supporting personnel.

Nearly every phase of these mammoth undertakings of the IGY will

---

H. Rept. No. 1348 (Feb. 17, 1958); "World Meteorological Organization: The International Geophysical Year," 3 *UN Review* (Feb. 1957) 35–39; Walter Sullivan, "As International Geophysical Year Opens — The Over-All Picture," *N.Y.T.*, June 30, 1957, Sec. 4, pp. 6–7; Elliot B. Roberts and David G. Knapp, "Geomagnetism in the International Geophysical Year," *The Journal*, Coast and Geodetic Survey, Aug. 1955, No. 6, pp. 4–10, which also gives an excellent summary of the work in the prior Polar Years; and Hugh Odishaw, "International Geophysical Year: A Report on the United States Program," 127 *Science* 115–128 (Jan. 17, 1958).

[265] "WMO: The IGY," *op. cit.*, p. 36.
[266] Atwood, *op. cit.*, p. 882.

contribute to man's knowledge and use of the sea — to advances in radio and other electronic communications, to knowledge about weather, winds, tides, storms, earthquakes and seaquakes, the movement of waters in the depths of the sea, and the replenishment of life therein. We may discover whether it is safe to dispose of atomic wastes in the abysses or whether the deep currents spread the risks of lethal pollution. We may learn more about energy and power potentials in the sea. The charting of coasts and islands should become more precise. Air and sea navigation should become safer. We may even learn how soon, if at all, our coasts will be inundated by a sea receiving the waters of melting polar icecaps. Some of the knowledge derived from the IGY may make us neither free nor happy, but it cannot fail to challenge us to new adventure, on land and sea and in the air.

It would be eminently fitting to conclude this study of United States participation in international cooperative efforts relating to the sea with this marvel of the twentieth century, the IGY. But two other topics should at least be noted to round out the picture of American relationships — the Great Lakes-St. Lawrence Waterway and the use of the sea for atomic weapons and missile testing.

The Great Lakes-St. Lawrence Waterway. The Great Lakes "possess all the general characteristics of open seas, except in the freshness of their waters, and in the absence of the ebb and flow of the tide. In other respects they are inland seas." [267] For some purposes under American law they are regarded as "high seas." [268] We have given them peripheral attention thus far in the discussions relating to fisheries,[269] radio,[270] safety of life at sea,[271] and load lines.[272] Though discussion of connecting waterways has, in the interest of limiting the scope of the present work, been regularly omitted, the historic importance of the lakes to the United States and their impending greater importance to world shipping warrant some brief summary of the development of the Great Lakes-St. Lawrence Waterway. Before World War II, the total traffic carried on

[267] Mr. Justice Field in Illinois Central Railroad Co. v. Illinois, 146 U.S. 387 (1892).
[268] U.S. v. Rodgers, 150 U.S. 249 (1893). See criticism in Harry E. Hunt, "How the Great Lakes Became 'High Seas' and Their Status Viewed from the Standpoint of International Law," 4 *A.J.I.L.* 285 (1910), but *cf.* 1 Moore, *Digest* 670, 1 Hackworth, *Digest* 616, and 2 *ibid.* 652.
[269] Above, pp. 120–121, 173–175.
[270] Above, p. 251.
[271] Above, pp. 139, 229.
[272] Above, pp. 142–143.

the lakes annually exceeded the combined traffic of the Kiel, Panama, and Suez Canals.[273] This traffic has, however, been chiefly domestic or between the United States and Canada. When the works now under way in the lakes and St. Lawrence River are completed in 1959, it is expected that an increased portion of regular ocean-going shipping will be added. For practical purposes, then, the lakes will be an arm of the Atlantic, an eighth sea added to the seven.

The Great Lakes and the St. Lawrence River lie in a drainage basin serving approximately 303,000 square miles, of which 95,000 square miles are water surface. The lakes and the river provide a natural waterway 1500 miles in length from Duluth at the head of Lake Superior to the head of the tidal estuary of the Gulf of St. Lawrence at the port of Quebec. Thence to the Atlantic Ocean through the Gulf of St. Lawrence and the Straits of Belle Isle (between Newfoundland and Labrador) is another 843 miles. When fully developed, therefore, the waterway will provide a safe route to a considerable portion of the world's ocean-going marine from the high seas to the inland seas.

Aside from the opposition of powerful economic and political pressure groups and sections in the United States and Canada, but chiefly in the United States, at least two great sets of factors have impeded the simple straightforward development of the waterway over the years — jurisdictional problems and geological features.

For part of its full length from Lake Ontario northeastward into the Gulf of St. Lawrence, the St. Lawrence River serves as a boundary water between the United States and Canada, separating the State of New York from the Province of Ontario. This part of the river, called the International Section, is 114 miles long. In it, the international boundary line zigzags from the outlet of Lake Ontario to St. Regis, New York. Below (north of) St. Regis, the river lies wholly within Canadian jurisdiction, passing the ports of Montreal and Quebec on its way to the sea. The 114-mile stretch of the International Section is generally divided further into two smaller fluvial areas, a Thousand Islands Section, 68 miles long, from Lake Ontario to Ogdensburg, New York, and an International Rapids Section, 46 miles long, from Ogdensburg to St. Regis. The jurisdictional problems arising from this division of ownership and authority in a part of the river were, of course, utilized by opposition

[273] Mance and Wheeler, *International River and Canal Transport* (1945), pp. 82–85.

groups over the years to frustrate development of the waterway and to impede the undertaking of electrical power programs.

Certain durable geological characteristics of the waterway from Duluth to Quebec create engineering problems. From Duluth to sea level in the gulf is a drop of 602 feet. That drop occurs most precipitously at three great natural barriers — in the St. Mary's River between Lakes Superior and Huron, in the Niagara River, between Lakes Erie and Ontario, and in the St. Lawrence River, between the Thousand Islands and Montreal, most pronouncedly in the International Rapids Section. These characteristics have made it necessary, from the earliest days of colonization to construct artificial waterways to circumvent the barriers. Within the past three quarters of a century they have also made possible the development of great quantities of electrical power.

The saga [274] of the development of the navigation works necessary to give continuous transport from one part of the waterway to another starts with an unsuccessful effort of the Sulpician monks in 1700 to build a canal around the Lachine Rapids near Montreal. Thenceforward, particularly after 1783, and little by little, numerous successful canals were constructed, together with the necessary dams and locks, culminating in the present great works at Sault Ste. Marie, the fourth Welland Canal paralleling the Niagara River, and the intricate system of canals flanking the north shore of the St. Lawrence in the rapids section. With the notable exception of the works at Sault Ste. Marie, the canals are entirely within Canadian jurisdiction. Beginning with the Webster Ashburton Treaty of 1842, however, a series of agreements between the United States and Great Britain assured freedom of navigation to both countries in the St. Lawrence from the sea to the Great Lakes.[275] In 1909, a Boundary Waters Convention dealt with the uses of the boundary waters and provided for the establishment of an international joint commission with jurisdiction over all cases involving the use, obstruction, or diversion of such waters.[276]

The story of the development of the waterway and the deriving of

[274] See the helpful *Chronology* in Appendix A, at pp. 175–200 in *St. Lawrence Seaway Manual: A Compilation of Documents on the Great Lakes Seaway Project and Correlated Power Development*, 83 Cong., 2 Sess., S. Doc. No. 165 (1955).

[275] Signed at Washington, Aug. 9, 1842, 8 *Stat.* 572, TS 119; for subsequent developments see 1 Moore, *Digest* 676–683.

[276] Signed at Washington, Jan. 11, 1909, 36 *Stat.* 2448, TS 548. For prior and subsequent developments see 1 Hackworth, *Digest* 755–763, 6 *ibid.* 4–5.

Health and Resources since World War II

power from it is one of the most intricate in the annals of diplomacy and politics.[277] Suffice it for present purposes that as new needs for commerce arose and the possibilities of the development of so-called All-American waterways through the Erie Canal or down the Mississippi were discussed, the Great Lakes and St. Lawrence canals and their locks were repeatedly widened and deepened. For optimum use of ocean-going shipping, however, a channel throughout the length of the waterway twenty-seven-feet deep became a necessity. The channels in the waterway upwards from the International Rapids, that is, in the Thousand Islands and Great Lakes sections, could be readily enlarged, but new canals in the International Rapids section and beyond in the Canadian section of the river would become essential. Either the United States alone or Canada alone could build the necessary facilities on their side of the boundary line in the International Rapids Section. The construction of facilities in the river downstream from St. Regis, however, would devolve upon Canada solely, since it had complete jurisdiction over that section of the river. Thus, for the United States, to avoid the building of unnecessarily duplicative facilities in the International Rapids Section and to assure the building of adequate facilities in the section of the river downstream beyond the northern boundary of the United States, some type of understanding with Canada became necessary.

Meanwhile, the increased needs for electrical power on both sides of the border from the turn of the present century set up additional pressures to develop the vast potential of the International Rapids Section. Other sections of the watercourse up from the Rapids Section to Lake Superior were already well exploited and could reasonably be somewhat further exploited. The section at the international rapids, however, remained largely unexploited. The most effective utilization of the potential there, moreover, required that a dam be built *across* the boundary in the section from American territory (Barnhart Island) to the Canadian shore on the north. That very definitely would require some type of international agreement. The development of a deep waterway and the development of the power potential in the St. Lawrence River were thus linked together in politics and diplomacy.

[277] See the forthcoming full length study of the subject entitled *The Politics and Diplomacy of the St. Lawrence Waterway* by Dr. William Reid Willoughby of St. Lawrence University, to whom the present writer is already deeply indebted for assistance in preparing this discussion of the waterway topic. See also his "Power Along the St. Lawrence," 34 *Current History* 283–290 (1958).

The United States and the Treaty Law of the Sea

For nearly fifty years the two governments sought some type of cooperative development of the seaway and the power. A Great Lakes-St. Lawrence Deep Waterway Treaty, designed to meet both these objectives, was finally concluded in 1932 but was rejected by the American Senate in 1934.[278] Attempts to revise the treaty to make it acceptable to groups opposed to it in the United States then followed and also failed. In 1941 an executive agreement was concluded which provided not only for the development of St. Lawrence navigation and power but also for the redevelopment of Niagara Falls and the planned development of the entire Great Lakes-St. Lawrence Basin.[279] This failed to receive the necessary approval of Congress.

Then by 1952 another arrangement was worked out contemplating the building of the dam and development of the power by Ontario and New York jointly and the building of the facilities necessary to provide a twenty-seven-foot channel from Lake Erie to the Port of Montreal by Canada within its own jurisdiction and at its own expense.[280] This plan, though approved by President Truman and the St. Laurent government and by the authorities of both Ontario and New York, failed nevertheless to receive the approval of Congress. Instead, Congress by act approved May 13, 1954,[281] created a federal agency called the St. Lawrence Seaway Development Corporation and authorized it to construct, on a self-liquidating basis, twenty-seven-foot navigation works on the United States side of the international section of the St. Lawrence River. A similar entity called The St. Lawrence Seaway Authority had already been established by Canada in 1951 for the purpose of constructing the canal facilities that might be built by Canada alone or in conjunction with works undertaken by the United States.[282]

Meanwhile, in 1952, the United States and Canada both filed concurrent and complementary applications with the International Joint Commission for approval of plans for the power development in the In-

---

[278] Treaty signed July 18, 1932; rejected by the Senate March 14, 1934. Text in *Great Lakes–St. Lawrence Deep Waterway Treaty* (1932), D.S. Pub. No. 347. See also 1 Hackworth, *Digest* 605–606.

[279] Agreement signed at Ottawa, March 19, 1941; see *Text of Agreement between United States and Canada Pertaining to St. Lawrence River*, 77 Cong., 1 Sess., H. Doc. No. 153 (1941), S. 10598.

[280] Texts of notes signed at Washington, June 30, 1952, in 5 UST 1784, TIAS 3053.

[281] 68 *Stat.* 92.

[282] Assented to 21 Dec. 1951, 15–16 George VI, Chap. 24; text in *Manual, op. cit.*, pp. 11–16.

ternational Rapids Section of the St. Lawrence River. The Joint Commission approved both applications in 1952 and indicated the Canadian entity to be the Hydro-Electric Power Commission of Ontario. In the United States, however, controversy continued with respect to whether private enterprisers, the federal government, or the state of New York should develop the power project in conjunction with the Ontario Hydro-Electric Commission. Finally, in 1953, the Power Authority of the state of New York was authorized by the government of the United States to proceed with the power project.[283]

After Congress passed the Wiley-Dondero Act of May 13, 1954, a modification of the agreement of 1952 with Canada became necessary. This was accomplished by an exchange of notes signed at Ottawa August 17, 1954.[284] In brief, the 1954 agreement acknowledged the desire of the United States to participate in the Seaway Project by constructing certain navigation works on United States territory but recorded the intention of Canada to proceed with the construction of the canal and lock at Iroquois, on the Canadian side of the International Rapids Section, upstream from the American locks near Massena. The Canadian government, furthermore, declared its intention in the agreement to complete twenty-seven-foot navigation works on the Canadian side of the International Rapids Section if and when it considered that parallel facilities were required to accommodate existing or potential traffic.

So, at long last, both the seaway and the power projects are under way.[285] The Power Authority of the State of New York and the Hydro-Electric Power Commission of the Province of Ontario are jointly building the power project across the boundary at Barnhart Island and will share equally in the resulting electrical power. The American entity, the St. Lawrence Seaway Development Corporation, is building the Grass River and Robinson Bay locks on the American side near Massena, and the Canadian entity, the St. Lawrence Seaway Authority, is building

---

[283] *Manual, op. cit.*, pp. 30–31.

[284] 5 *UST* 1784; *TIAS* 3053. See "The St. Lawrence Seaway and Power Project," 6 *External Affairs* 332–346 (1954). Also the tart exchange of notes in Saint Lawrence Seaway, Deep-Water Dredging in Cornwall Island Channels, signed at Ottawa, Nov. 7 and Dec. 4, 1956, 7 *UST* 3271, *TIAS* 3708.

[285] See the excellent, clear summary of the present situation in "The Saint Lawrence Seaway: Report to the President on the Status and Progress of the Saint Lawrence Seaway for the Fiscal Year Ended June 30, 1955," 34 *DSB* 215–219 (1956), and the 22 page summation of the history, engineering, industrial, and other aspects of the project, "The St. Lawrence Seaway," *N.Y.T.*, June 29, 1958.

the lock at Iroquois in the International Rapids Section as well as four more locks in that portion of the river downstream which lies entirely within Canadian jurisdiction.[286]

Other agreements [287] have become necessary to achieve the general plans for full utilization of the Great Lakes-St. Lawrence Waterway such as one of 1950 dealing with uses of the waters of the Niagara River [288] and another of 1954 providing for the construction of remedial works at Niagara Falls.[289] The two governments have also reached agreement [290] with respect to the deepening and widening of the channels upstream from the International Rapids Section to the head of the lakes, the United States undertaking most of the work. By 1959, then, a new chapter will open up for maritime transport from the high seas to the docks at Duluth.

Atoms and Missiles

There remain to be discussed those aspects of the development of atomic energy and guided missiles which relate to peace-time use of the sea.

Nuclear powered submarines are already here; similarly powered surface craft are on the way and nuclear powered aircraft may be in the offing. There is discussion of the possibility of deriving atomic power

---

[286] See the maps in *Manual, op. cit.*, at p. 16.

[287] E.g., on Establishment of Saint Lawrence River Joint Board of Engineers, effected by exchange of notes, signed at Washington, Nov. 12, 1953, 5 *UST* 2538, *TIAS* 3116, and on Relocation of Roosevelt Bridge, effected by exchange of notes, signed at Washington, Oct. 24, 1956, 7 *UST* 2865, *TIAS* 3668.

[288] Convention on Uses of the Waters of the Niagara River, signed at Washington, Feb. 27, 1950, 1 *UST* 694, *TIAS* 2130.

[289] Effected by exchange of notes, signed at Ottawa, Sept. 13, 1954, 5 *UST* 1979, *TIAS* 3064. See also: "U.S. and Canada Inaugurate Niagara Falls Remedial Project," 30 *DSB* 954–958 (1954), and *Niagara Redevelopment Act of 1956*, 84 Cong., 2 Sess., S. Rept. No. 1408 (1956). In 1956, an effort by several of the lake states to secure congressional approval of a "Great Lakes Basin Compact" for "comprehensive development, use, and conservation of the water resources of the Great Lakes Basin," to which the provinces of Ontario and Quebec were to be invited to become parties, was opposed by the Department of State. *Hearings before a Subcommittee of the Committee on Foreign Relations of the United States Senate on The Great Lakes Basin*, 84 Cong., 2 Sess. (1956), pp. 13–21; reprinted in 35 *DSB* 421–424 (1956).

[290] Saint Lawrence Seaway: Navigation Improvements of the Great Lakes Connecting Channels, Arrangement effected by exchange of notes, dated at Ottawa July 23 and Oct. 26, 1956, and Feb. 26, 1957, 8 *UST* 279, *TIAS* 3772; *ibid.*, Agreement effected by exchange of notes, dated at Ottawa Nov. 30, 1956 and April 8 and 9, 1957, 8 *UST* 637, *TIAS* 3814; and *Report, op. cit.*, pp. 215, 219.

Health and Resources since World War II

from the waters of the sea. Radioactive materials can be used in studying oceanic mixing processes and circulation, including the tracing of food chains through the various levels of water by means of isotopes. Other uses of such materials will help solve problems involving "the dynamics of marine populations, including the mass of living material in the given volume of water, the flux of organic substances from one organism to the other and between the organism and the sea water, and the interrelations of animal and plant communities." [291]

At the moment, however, two pressing problems have been created by the advent of atomic energy — disposal of atomic wastes and weapon testing at sea.

Atomic Wastes. Land installations in the United States now dispose of atomic wastes, depending on their character, by storage in underground tanks or pits, by discharge into rivers, and by dumping them encased in concrete into the sea. In England radioactive wastes from an atomic installation are being piped into the Irish Sea. There is always the possibility of accidental escapage of wastes into rivers which find their way into the sea. The problem of safe disposal will increase as power reactors and fuel-processing plants reach their expected development. If they are established in the large communities along the seacoast, there is always the possible danger of inadvertent contamination of coastal waters. Countries fronting the sea, but with small land areas, will find it virtually mandatory to dispose of their atomic wastes at sea. Permanent storage in geological structures such as salt domes is being studied. By and large, however, the most practical solution for the present appears to be disposal at sea.

But where in the sea is it safe to deposit atomic waste? The answer seems to depend upon a large number of factors at present unknown or with respect to which insufficient data exist. Among the factors are the decay time of the radioactive substances and the rate of vertical interchange of waters in the sea, that is, "the time required for most of the deep water to move near the surface and be replaced with new water mixing downward." In the deepest parts of the Black Sea, for example, the "flushing time" is estimated to take 2500 years. In the deeps of the Atlantic and Pacific the replacement process takes only a few hundred

---

[291] *The Biological Effects of Atomic Radiation: Summary Reports From a Study by the National Academy of Sciences* (1956), pp. 80–81; *Radioisotope Uptake in Marine Organisms*, U.S. Atomic Energy Commission (1955).

years, in other areas a hundred years or less. The IGY is expected to make important contributions to scientific knowledge of this sector of sea dynamics.

Meanwhile, however, investigations into the problem of disposal are under way. On the initiative of the United States, the General Assembly of the United Nations in 1955 set up a Scientific Committee on the Effects of Atomic Radiation, consisting of representatives from fifteen states. Among the aspects under its consideration is the disposal of radioactive wastes in the seas and oceans.[292] The National Academy of Sciences of the United States has recently made a study of the biological effects of atomic radiation. The Committee on Oceanography and Fisheries, contributing one of the reports in the study, posed the problem of disposal thus: "Remembering the importance both of isolation (to allow time for radioactive decay) and dispersal (to reduce the amount of radioactivity per unit volume) the problem is to find places in the ocean where the rate of transfer of radioactive materials to the surface waters would be slow, or where great dilution would occur before radioactive materials came in contact with marine food products or human beings, and preferably where both conditions would prevail." Much research is still necessary to find these conditions. The committee therefore recommended in 1956 that a national scientific committee be set up on a continuing basis to study the problem; that international scientific collaboration on the subject be intensified on an urgent basis; and "that cognizant international agencies formulate as soon as possible conventions for the safe disposal of atomic wastes at sea, based on existing scientific knowledge." "The pollution problems of the past and present, though serious, are not irremediable. The atomic waste problem, if allowed to get out of hand, might result in a profound, irrecoverable loss."[293]

---

[292] *U.S. Participation in the UN 1955*, D.S. Pub. No. 6318, pp. 41–44. Data on Atomic Radiation Transmitted to U.N. Committee," 35 *DSB* 687–688 (1956); *First Yearly Progress Report* of the committee to the General Assembly, A/3365, 17 Nov. 1956; *Second Yearly Progress Report*, A/3659, 31 Oct. 1957. The committee finished its final report, for submission to the 13th General Assembly, in June 1958, *N.Y.T.*, June 14, 1958; text, A/3838 (1958).

[293] *Op. cit.*, pp. 73, 82–83. See also its full report, *The Effects of Atomic Radiation on Oceanography and Fisheries*, Pub. No. 551 (1957), and the report of the Committee on Disposal and Dispersal of Radioactive Wastes in the *Summary Reports, op. cit.*, pp. 101–108; *Handling Radioactive Wastes in the Atomic Energy Program*, U.S. Atomic Energy Commission (1949); and *Twenty-first Semiannual Report of the Atomic Energy Commission* (1957), pp. 151–161.

Health and Resources since World War II

The Convention on the High Seas, concluded at Geneva in 1958, adopting the proposal of the International Law Commission, prescribed in Article 25 (1): "Every state shall take measures to prevent pollution of the seas from the dumping of radioactive waste, taking into account any standards and regulations which may be formulated by the competent international organizations."

Nuclear Weapons Testing. The testing of nuclear weapons at sea poses a different assortment of problems. The testing may be a short-range problem, depending upon progress in disarmament negotiations. The problem of disposal of wastes from atomic installations on land (or, for that matter, aboard ship) is long-range and will increase in the decades to come with the mounting development of nuclear uses. Nevertheless, the testing has already produced accidental injury, legal controversy, and international protests.

In the course of the series of testings conducted by the United States at Eniwetok and Bikini in the Marshall Islands since 1946,[294] some Japanese fishermen suffered personal and property damage in 1954. By agreement in 1955 the United States paid Japan two million dollars to compensate the injured parties.[295] In 1954 also the Marshallese people complained to the Trusteeship Council that certain of their number on Rongelab and Uterik atolls had been injured by drinking water polluted by radioactive debris and that, as one or another of their islands were being rendered unsafe for habitation, some of them were losing their homes. The petition requested cessation of the testing in the area or, if that were not possible, that adequate precautions be taken and compensation be paid where removal became necessary.[296] After full debate, the Trusteeship Council adopted a mollifying resolution (with the U.S.S.R., India, and Syria in opposition) which noted that compensation and other remedial measures had already been undertaken by the

---

[294] "U.S. Policies and Actions in the Development and Testing of Nuclear Weapons," 35 *DSB* 704–715 (1956).

[295] Settlement of Japanese Claims for Personal and Property Damages Resulting from Nuclear Tests in Marshall Islands in 1954, effected by exchange of notes signed at Tokyo, Jan. 4, 1955, 6 *UST* 1, *TIAS* 3160.

[296] "Thermonuclear Tests in Pacific Trust Territory," 30 *DSB* 886–888 (1954), including text of petition. See the two medical studies of the situation since published by the U.S. Atomic Energy Commission: *Some Effects of Ionizing Radiation on Human Beings: A Report on the Marshallese and Americans Accidentally Exposed to Radiation from Fallout and a Discussion of Radiation Injury in the Human Being* (1956), and *Radioactive Contamination of Certain Areas in the Pacific Ocean from Nuclear Tests* (1957).

United States and which recommended that if the administering authority considered it necessary to make further tests, the indicated precautions should be taken.[297] The United States has accordingly taken all the necessary measures.[298]

Aside from these inadvertent injuries, the tests have caused concern because of their meteorological effects,[299] the pollution of sea water and marine life by underwater explosions or fall-out [300] and the interference with fishing and navigation of the sea and air in the areas involved.

Since the United Nations Scientific Committee on the Effects of Atomic Radiation was studying the first two of these concerns when the International Law Commission was preparing its 1956 report, the commission contented itself with proposing in Article 48 (3) that "all states shall cooperate in drawing up regulations" to prevent pollution of the sea or the airspace above arising from these causes. The Geneva Convention on the High Seas in Article 25 (2) requires all states to "cooperate with the competent international organizations in taking measures" to the same end.

Margolis, McDougal, and Schlei have discussed in great detail the international legal problems involved in the nuclear tests at sea, including that concerned with the setting up of areas closed temporarily to normal uses of navigation and fishing.[301]

It should be sufficient for present purposes to comment briefly on only this last point of warning or danger areas. At various times since 1946 the United States has warned mariners and fishermen to avoid delimited

---

[297] "Marshall Islanders' Petition to Trusteeship Council," 31 *DSB* 137–140 (1954), including text of resolution; "Islanders Appeal to United Nations on Bomb Tests in Pacific Trust Area," 1 *UN Review* (Sept. 1954) 14–16.

[298] "People of Eniwetok and Bikini Compensated for Leaving Homes," 36 *DSB* 101 (1957).

[299] Report of Committee on Meteorology in *The Biological Effects of Atomic Radiation, op. cit.*, at pp. 47–70.

[300] See entries of papers in Robert J. List, Weather Bureau, *Annotated Bibliography on the Transport and Deposition of Atomic Debris*, Atomic Energy Commission (1956).

[301] Emanuel Margolis, "The Hydrogen Bomb Experiments and International Law," 64 *Yale Law Journal* 629–647 (1955), and Myres S. McDougal and Norbert A. Schlei, "The Hydrogen Bomb Tests in Perspective: Lawful Measures for Security," 64 *Yale Law Journal* 648–710. The writer is deeply indebted for most of his data on this topic to the wealth of materials brought together by Messrs. McDougal and Schlei in their pioneering study. See also M. S. McDougal, "The Hydrogen Bomb Tests and the International Law of the Sea," 49 *A.J.I.L.* 356–361 (1955). See also "U.S. Replies to Japan on Atom and Hydrogen Bomb Tests," 36 *DSB* 901–904 (1957).

Health and Resources since World War II

areas of the high seas surrounding Eniwetok and Bikini during certain periods when tests were planned. At times of actual danger, air and surface patrols ensured that no ships or aircraft entered the areas inadvertently. At various times the areas contained 180,000 or 20,000 or 30,000 or 50,000 square miles. After the miscalculation of March 1, 1954, which caused the damage to the Japanese fishermen and the Marshallese referred to above, an area of 400,000 square miles was set up. No regular steamship track lies through any of the areas. Only one airline route had to be shifted slightly to avoid the areas. Other governments have set up similar testing areas which include high seas. Thus Australia created a prohibited area of 6000 square miles surrounding one of the Monte Bello Islands in Western Australia, where the United Kingdom has done some of its weapons testing. For the British hydrogen-bomb tests in May 1957, an area extending 900 miles north and south and 780 miles east and west of Christmas Island, an atoll 1200 miles south of the Hawaiian Islands, was declared a danger zone for shipping from March 1 to August 1.[302] Obviously, if more governments indulge in more testing at sea, a problem of first magnitude will arise. Since the Soviet government apparently does its testing within its land area, the only sea areas affected thus far have been those used by the American, British, and Australian governments.

The legal situation is not without precedent. From time immemorial, extensive fleet anchorages have been maintained offshore, and naval exercises, parades, and maneuvers have been held at sea. Target practice is held at sea and from coasts outward. Various types of "proving grounds" are established. Since 1950 the United States has maintained Air Defense Identification Zones (ADIZ), reaching 250 miles seaward on the Atlantic side and 300 miles seaward on the Pacific side, in which aircraft bound for the United States must identify themselves. Canada has a similar system. In addition, all governments with maritime interests establish warning, danger, restricted or prohibited areas for numerous purposes, large areas and small, areas temporarily established and others permanently. They deal with various hazards to navigation. They are regularly marked on hydrographic charts or otherwise through the

---

[302] "British Detonate a Hydrogen Bomb over Mid-Pacific," *N.Y.T.*, May 16, 1957; "2d British H-Bomb is Fired in Pacific," *N.Y.T.*, June 1, 1957; third test announced by radio, June 19, 1957; another on Nov. 2, 1957; see *N.Y.T.*, Nov. 9, 11, 1957. The press early in April 1958 reported the intention of the French government to launch tests soon, place unspecified.

customary channels brought to the attention of mariners and fisher-folk. At a recent date the United States had "established a total of 447 such warning and/or danger areas." The United States as early as 1947 had advised the United Nations of the establishment of the warning area surrounding Eniwetok and Bikini, "and appropriate notices were carried then and subsequently in marine and aircraft navigational manuals." [303]

Several events in the spring of 1958 helped to focus attention further on the nuclear testing in the Pacific. On May 1 and June 4, 1958, a Coast Guard cutter seized the ketch *Golden Rule* and its crew of four American pacifists at sea out of Honolulu on their way to the Eniwetok proving grounds. They had twice sailed in defiance of injunctions issued by a federal court in support of an order promulgated by the Atomic Energy Commission on April 12, 1958. That order prohibited American citizens and all others subject to the jurisdiction of the United States from entering or attempting to enter the warning area previously established for the HARDTACK nuclear test series. The crew were promptly tried and jailed.[304]

Far more important, however, were the developments in the summer of 1958. Despite increased protests, appeals, and criticism from various quarters, and an announcement by the Soviet Union that it would unilaterally cease conducting any further nuclear tests, the United States proceeded to hold its tests in the Eniwetok area as scheduled. The United Kingdom also continued its tests. In the spring the United States had invited the fourteen other governments represented on the United Nations Scientific Committee on the Effects of Atomic Radiation, which included members of the Soviet bloc, to send observers to a demonstration shot of a weapon with reduced fallout in the HARDTACK series.

[303] Lewis L. Strauss, "Hydrogen Bomb Tests in the Pacific," 30 *DSB* 548–549 (1954). For documentation on American and Canadian Air Defense Identification Zones see MacChesney, *op. cit.*, pp. 577–600; for the 1956 notices relating to the testing areas, *ibid.*, pp. 627–628.

[304] Warning of test area, Feb. 14, published in *Notice to Mariners*, March 1, effective April 5; A.E.C. order published, 23 *Federal Register* 2401, April 12; *N.Y.T.*, Feb. 15, May 2, 7, 8, 24, June 7, 1958. In another proceeding, on April 4, a number of eminent persons brought suit in the District of Columbia District Court to enjoin the Atomic Energy Commission and others from conducting any more tests of nuclear weapons, *N.Y.T.*, April 5, 1958; suits dismissed, *N.Y.T.*, Aug. 1, 1958. A second American protesting ketch, the *Phoenix*, arrested within the test area, *N.Y.T.*, July 9, 1958. See also: "U.S. Cancels Demonstration of Reduced Fallout," 39 *DSB* 237 (1958); "Text of Geneva Experts' Conclusions on Policing Suspension of Atom Tests," *N.Y.T.*, Aug. 31, 1958; "U.S. Offers to Negotiate Nuclear Test Suspension," 39 *DSB* 378–379 (1958).

Health and Resources since World War II

When it appeared that the demonstration could not be held until late August and that it would interfere with the attendance of the observers at the Second International Conference on the Peaceful Uses of Atomic Energy, scheduled to meet at Geneva on September 1, the United States cancelled the demonstration.

Meanwhile, the United Nations Scientific Committee on the Effects of Atomic Radiation released its final report, which included its conclusions on fallout from nuclear testing. Meanwhile, also, after considerable exchange of correspondence, the United States and its allies secured agreement from the Soviet Union to a special conference of technicians for the purpose of studying methods of detecting nuclear tests. That conference, meeting in the Palais des Nations in Geneva, submitted toward the end of August their agreed conclusions on the policing of a possible suspension of nuclear tests. The scheme would include a number of "monitoring" ships at sea.

Thereupon the United States immediately announced, on August 22, that it was "prepared to proceed promptly to negotiate an agreement, with other nations which have tested nuclear weapons, for the suspension of nuclear tests and the actual establishment of an international control system on the basis of the experts' report. If this is accepted in principle by the other nations which have tested nuclear weapons, then in order to facilitate the detailed negotiations the United States is prepared, unless testing is resumed by the Soviet Union, to withhold further testing on its part of atomic and hydrogen weapons for a period of one year from the beginning of the negotiations. As part of the agreement to be negotiated, and on a basis of reciprocity, the United States would be further prepared to suspend the testing of nuclear weapons on a year-by-year basis subject to a determination at the beginning of each year that: (A) the agreed inspection system is installed and working effectively; and (B) satisfactory progress is being made in reaching agreement on and implementing major and substantial arms control measures such as the United States has long sought." In a note delivered to the Soviet government the same day, the United States proposed that negotiations begin in New York on October 31, 1958, and that the progress and results of the negotiations be reported to the United Nations General Assembly and Security Council. Thus the matter stood on the eve of the convening of the Thirteenth General Assembly of the United Nations.

Control of nuclear weapons testing is, however, only part of the larger problem of disarmament. With respect to that problem the position of the United States has been, and appears still to be, that the proper agency for the achievement of this objective is the United Nations and that no limitation in arms can be effective without a foolproof inspection system. The Soviet views have been opposed to this position at various points. At bottom is the need for mutual confidence. If suspension of nuclear weapons testing is achieved under a foolproof detection system, then real progress will have been made toward solution of the larger problem of the reduction of armaments.

In a very profound sense, however, the United States and the United Kingdom are acting as "trustees" for that share of the armed potential of the world which the United Nations could reliably call upon to defend the basic objectives of the Charter. Seen in this light, nuclear weapons testing and the problem of warning or danger areas recede into more realistic perspective.

Guided Missiles Testing. Some phases of the testing of long-range missiles (guided missiles, rockets, drones, and pilotless aircraft) require use of extensive areas at sea, thus also affecting adversely normal maritime activities on the surface and in the air. In 1950, to facilitate execution of its long-range missiles program, the United States concluded an agreement with the United Kingdom which established a proving ground in the Bahama Islands for guided missiles launched from Patrick Air Force Base on the east coast of Florida near Cape Canaveral. Within the territory of the Bahama Islands and their territorial waters the United States was accorded the right "to launch, fly and land guided missiles; to establish, maintain and use an instrumentation and communications system including radar, radio, land lines and submarine cables for operational purposes in connection with the Flight Testing Range; and to operate such vessels and aircraft as may be necessary for purposes connected directly with the operation of the Flight Testing Range." The flight testing range, running southeast through the Bahamas and the open sea adjacent thereto, was delimited in an accompanying map. The agreement accorded to the United Kingdom a joint right to share in the range program.[305]

As the range of the guided missiles increased, the United States found

[305] Agreement by exchange of notes, signed at Washington, July 21, 1950, 1 *UST* 545, *TIAS* 2099; announcement, 23 *DSB* 191 (1950).

Health and Resources since World War II

it necessary to conclude additional agreements to extend the testing range and to establish facilities on land for tracking, control, reporting, and warning purposes. Thus, by a series of agreements with the Dominican Republic in 1951,[306] with Haiti in 1952,[307] with the United Kingdom in 1952,[308] 1953,[309] 1955,[310] 1956,[311] and 1957,[312] supplemental facilities

[306] Agreement Extending the Long Range Proving Ground for the Testing of Guided Missiles, signed at Ciudad Trujillo, Nov. 26, 1951, 3 *UST* 2569, *TIAS* 2425.

[307] Short-Range-Aid-to-Navigation Ground Station in Haiti, temporary agreement effected by exchange of notes signed at Port-au-Prince, Aug. 22 and 29, 1952, 3 *UST* 5102, *TIAS* 2701.

[308] Extension of the Bahamas Long Range Proving Ground, agreement and exchange of notes, signed at Washington, Jan. 15, 1952, 3 *UST* 2594, *TIAS* 2426 (through Caicos and Turks Islands in West Indies), accompanied by map.

[309] Bahamas Long Range Proving Ground: Establishment of High Altitude Interceptor Range, agreement effected by exchange of notes, signed at Washington, Feb. 24 and March 2, 1953, 4 *UST* 429, *TIAS* 2789, accompanied by map.

[310] Bahamas Long Range Proving Ground: Use of Certain Facilities by Civil Aircraft, agreement effected by exchange of notes, signed at Washington, July 11 and 22, 1955, 6 *UST* 3783, *TIAS* 3379.

[311] Bahamas Long Range Proving Ground: Establishment of Additional Sites in Saint Lucia, agreement signed at Washington, June 25, 1956, 7 *UST* 1939, *TIAS* 3595; Bahamas Long Range Proving Ground: Establishment of Additional Sites in Ascension Island, agreement signed at Washington, June 25, 1956, 7 *UST* 1999, *TIAS* 3603.

[312] Bahamas Long Range Proving Ground: Civil Air Services within the Bahamas, Turks, and Caicos Islands and Jamaica, agreement effected by exchange of notes, signed at Washington, Dec. 6, 1956 and Jan. 4, 1957, 8 *UST* 1, *TIAS* 3727; and Bahamas Long Range Proving Ground: Extension of Flight Testing Range, agreement effected by exchange of notes, signed at Washington, April 1, 1957, 8 *UST* 493, *TIAS* 3803. A tracking station is reported, *N.Y.T.*, Aug. 11, 1957, in process of erection on the American naval base at Chaguaramas, Trinidad. This base is one of those leased to the United States by Great Britain for a term of ninety-nine years under the arrangement effected by exchange of notes signed at Washington Sept. 2, 1940, 54 *Stat.*(2) 2405, *EAS* 181. See also "Naval and Air Bases," 3 *DSB* 199–207 (1940). For the controversy arising out of the desire of the new West Indies Federation to use the site of the base for a capital see *N.Y.T.*, March 30, 1958, and the report of the Technical Joint Commission recommending retention of the present site for the U.S. base, 38 *DSB* 961 (1958). To these several agreements dealing with the testing range should be added the following devoted to "a joint naval program of oceanographic research" not made explicit in the agreements: Establishment of an Oceanographic Research Station in Barbados, agreement signed at Washington, Nov. 1, 1956, 7 *UST* 2901, *TIAS* 3672, and Establishment of an Oceanographic Research Station in the Turks and Caicos Islands, agreement signed at Washington, Nov. 27, 1956, 7 *UST* 3169, *TIAS* 3696. The efforts of the two navies during World War II in combatting the enemy submarine menace indicated the need for continuing research in water conditions in the area. "Agreement on Grand Turk Ocean Research Station," 35 *DSB* 922 (1956). An agreement supplementing the agreement of Nov. 1, 1956, relating to the Barbados station, was effected by exchange of notes at Washington, Oct. 30, 1957, 8 *UST* 1737, *TIAS* 3926. An agreement for the establishment of a third station, in the Bahama Islands, was signed at Washington, Nov. 1, 1957, 8 *UST* 1741, *TIAS* 3927.

were acquired to carry the range through the West Indies and past the bulge of Brazil to Ascension Island in the mid-South Atlantic, off the African coast, 4400 miles from the launching base on Cape Canaveral. In addition, by agreement with Brazil in 1957 [313] a tracking station was established on the Island of Fernando de Noronha, off the coast of Natal.

On the whole, the testing of guided missiles as presently conducted by the United States creates far fewer hazards for users of the sea and the airspace above it than the testing of atomic weapons. None of the missiles used in the American program carry warheads, atomic or otherwise; they are loaded with concrete blocks instead. A missile weighing many tons can, however, do considerable damage on mere impact. Even the pieces of a missile destroyed in flight for safety purposes could cause damage below. Guided missiles are designed to remain under control throughout flight; ballistic missiles can be controlled or guided only during the first, or powered, stage of their flight.[314] Each guided missile has at least three methods of self-destruction built into it: automatic explosion if it receives no command through the radio instrumentation; self-destruction on radio command; and by a built-in chain reaction of failures if any one part should fail. Nevertheless accidents can occur, as in the case of the errant flight of a Snark into the wilds of Brazil in December 1956, which was attributed to a failure in the guidance system, since corrected.[315]

Elaborate safety precautions are taken throughout the testing range. Various types of warnings are issued to sea and air traffic. Scout planes warn fishing vessels away from danger areas. Safety officers at each tracking station can, if necessary, cause an errant missile to destroy itself. The policy with respect to range clearance is that "no missile will be launched when it is ascertained that the total probability of hitting a ship within the range area is greater than one in 100,000 and the hit probability for any particular ship is greater than one in 1,000,000." [316]

[313] Defense: Establishment of Guided Missile Station on Island of Fernando de Noronha, agreement effected by exchange of notes, signed at Rio de Janeiro, Jan. 21, 1957, 8 *UST* 87, *TIAS* 3744.

[314] Hanson W. Baldwin, "Ballistic Missiles: What the New Weapons Are and How They Work," *N.Y.T.*, April 29, 1956.

[315] Jack Raymond, "Little Peril Seen in Missiles Tests," *N.Y.T.*, March 25, 1957; *N.Y.T.*, "Lost Missile Crashed in Brazil, U.S. Says," *N.Y.T.*, Dec. 8, 1956.

[316] *Research and Development: Range Safety Policy for Missiles*, Headquarters Air Force Missile Test Center, AFMTC Regulation No. 80–9, Sept. 13, 1956, p. 2; see also the elaborate rules in the *General Range Safety Plan*, March 5, 1957, pub-

To these extensive and carefully evaluated safety precautions is added the desire to maintain satisfactory relations with the governments which have accorded the treaty rights to the United States.

Thus far no official complaints from other governments, comparable to those voiced in and out of the United Nations with respect to the nuclear weapons testing, have apparently been made to the government of the United States. None of the agreements entered into by the United States can reasonably be construed as setting up any "closed sea." All of them, insofar as they affect the interests of nonparticipants in the agreements, assume merely reasonable response to appropriate warnings in specific areas when testing is in process. On the other hand, the Soviet Union in July 1957 declared Peter the Great Bay to be "internal waters," within a line 115 miles long running from Cape Povorotny in Siberia to the estuary of the River Tyumen-Ula, at the boundary between Siberia and North Korea. Foreign ships and aircraft were required to obtain permission from the Soviet authorities to enter Peter the Great Bay. Japanese investigators reported that the Russians had installed guided missile facilities at two points overlooking Vladivostok. Great Britain, Japan, and the United States promptly protested this unilateral attempt to annex a portion of the high seas.[317] If more missile-testing ranges of any considerable extent are set up by the United States or by others,[318] following the American pattern, in other areas of the world, or if more areas of the high seas are closed off by the Soviet government or by other governments in imitation of them, then indeed will a problem of first magnitude have arisen. The solution of that problem would again involve the power potential of the free world. For the purposes of the present study it must remain unfinished business.

---

lished by Headquarters, courtesy of Col. Robert L. Johnson, USAF, Deputy Director, Research and Development.

[317] *N.Y.T.*, Aug. 18, 1957; "U.S. Protests to U.S.S.R. on Closing of Peter the Great Bay," 37 *DSB* 388 (1957); Soviet reply of Jan. 7, 1958, and United States repeated protest of March 6, 1958, 38 *DSB* 461–462 (1958); text of British note, London *Times*, Sept. 19, 1957; reference to third Japanese protest, *N.Y.T.*, Jan. 19, 1958.

[318] See "Japanese Plans for Missile-Testing Site on Isolated Island Opposed by Teachers," *N.Y.T.*, Nov. 25, 1957. On Jan. 29, 1958, the Defense Department announced its intention to establish a missile range on the Pacific Coast, the launching site to be at Point Mugu, Calif., thirty-three miles northwest of Los Angeles. *N.Y.T.*, Jan. 30, 1958. The amazing voyages of the American atomic powered submarines, the *Nautilus* and the *Skate*, under the north polar ice, in August 1958, aside from their significance in the strategy of missiles warfare, open up vast possibilities in new uses of the sea.

CONCLUSION

One important difference between summarizing a discussion and bringing it to a conclusion is that the former takes considerable industry, the latter, mere resolution.

In conclusion, then, it may be said that there is a community of the sea which preceded the nation-state and which will most probably survive the transmutation of the state system into something else. Meanwhile, nation-states and other social groups have devised rules to govern their own activities and those of individuals in relation to the sea. The rules are found in customary law, treaty law, the regulations of international agencies, and the prescriptions of private groups. The record reveals substantial contributions by the United States to the growth of these rules. Like the sea itself, the rules take Protean forms. Where they have status as law, they are intermixed with international law and national law; they are, in brief, a species of transnational law.[319] Though many lacunae exist, the pattern of rules is growing, *pari passu* with man's augmented dependence upon the sea. If ever the sea was completely *res nullius*, the portents now are that in a shrinking world it will become increasingly *res communis*.

The community depending upon the *res communis* will, however, find it necessary to organize better the governance of its use. At the moment, as we have seen, there is a great multiplicity of public and private agencies asserting some control over one or another aspect of use of the sea. The United Nations is fully aware of this proliferating and overlapping multiplicity. One of the first tasks to which the General Assembly devoted its attention in 1946 was the promotion, through ECOSOC, of the coordination, combination, liquidation, or transfer to the United Nations or to one of the great specialized agencies of functions thitherto performed by numerous international bodies, public and private, many of them concerned with the sea.[320] We have seen how the Transport and Communication Commission of ECOSOC seeks to coordinate the activ-

---

[319] Philip C. Jessup, *Transnational Law*, pp. 111–113 (1956).

[320] Res. 50(I), Dec. 14, 1946, *UN Yearbook 1947–1948*, pp. 109–118, 676–685. See also: *UN Yearbook 1948–1949*, pp. 674–714; for Brazilian resolution on "proliferation and overlapping," pp. 691–693; for relations with intergovernmental organizations, recommendations concerning 72 organizations, pp. 702–704; for report on nongovernmental organizations, pp. 711–714. Copy of resolution on intergovernmental organizations, 21 *DSB* 456–458 (1949). For further developments, see *UN Yearbook, 1950*, pp. 639–667; *1951*, pp. 578–602; *1952*, pp. 537–538; *1953*, pp. 494–495; *1955*, pp. 469–470.

Health and Resources since World War II

ities and programs of the specialized agencies in its field [321] and how the functions of the bureau of the Map of the World on the Millionth Scale were transferred to the United Nations. ECOSOC has also made a number of recommendations urging the combination of other agencies dealing with the sea.

There are, however, at present, limits of a budgetary and administrative character which impede fuller organizational consolidation. In addition, some problems still require attention by separate expert bodies, as in the case of fisheries. We have seen how the International Law Commission, on second thought, declined to recommend the setting up of a "central authority with legislative powers" or even a specialized agency to make technical and scientific studies for fisheries purposes.[322] The United Nations Conference on the Law of the Sea in Geneva in 1958 agreed with the Commission and recommended merely the setting up of separate organizations to deal with distinct fisheries problems. We have also seen how reluctant some states are to subject their shipping practices to scrutiny by such an organization as IMCO.[323] If for a time the most prudent and efficient way to deal with specific problems of use of the sea will be to set up independent international agencies, the day may nevertheless come when jurisdictional difficulties will force the creation of some type of coordinating body, some kind of Council of the Sea.

A few remaining possibilities and proposals, focused on the sea, should be mentioned. In providing for sanctions, both the League of Nations, in Article 16 of the Covenant,[324] and the United Nations, in Article 41 of the Charter, visualized interruption of access to the sea and use of it by the recalcitrant state. If present trends of reliance upon the sea continue, and if the sanctioning measures were effectively applied, it would be a rare state in the future that could not be brought speedily into line. We rejoice in our new conquests of the sea, but the sea is making hostages of us all.

Admiral Richard Evelyn Byrd once expressed the hope that Antarctica would forever remain accessible to the scientists of all nations for the benefit of all mankind. National claims to portions of the icy mass

[321] Above, pp. 258–260.
[322] Above, p. 326.
[323] Above, p. 222.
[324] For comment, see Mance and Wheeler, *International Sea Transport*, p. 160.

continued to pile up, however, threatening both the advancement of science and the peace of the world. In these circumstances, the United States in 1948 proposed to seven other states with territorial claims in the continent that the area should be internationalized.[325] Nothing immediately came of this proposal. The British Parliamentary Group for World Government, under the presidency of Lord Boyd Orr, in 1955 proposed that title to both Antarctica and the sea bed outside territorial waters be vested in the United Nations and that the world organization be given jurisdiction over the high seas.[326] Other groups additionally suggested the possibility of utilizing Antarctica and the sea as sources of revenue for the United Nations.[327] In 1956 India introduced, but subsequently withdrew, a resolution in the General Assembly seeking "The Peaceful Utilization of Antarctica" by all nations.[328] Then came the unprecedented cooperative effort of twelve nations in the Antarctic under the International Geophysical Year of 1957–1958. Out of this cooperation for purely scientific purposes came a least expected result, diplomatic developments which may yet provide a solution for the political rivalries in Antarctica.

These developments have a dramatic quality. On its return from a visit to the American stations in the Arctic and Antarctic engaged in IGY work, a subcommittee of the House Committee on Interstate and Foreign Commerce, in a letter to the President on January 17, 1958, recommended a re-evaluation of the United States position with respect to territorial claims in Antarctica.[329] On May 13, 1958, the United States announced it had proposed to the eleven other countries participating in the IGY activities in Antarctica that a conference be held to conclude a treaty to assure continuation of scientific cooperation in the Antarctic after the end of IGY, to guarantee "freedom of scientific investigation

[325] "Discussions Asked on Territorial Problems," 19 *DSB* 301 (1948).

[326] Mimeo., Ref. PG 55318.35.C and PG 55321.40.C. The part of the scheme relating to the sea was called NEPTUNO. Headquarters for the Group is House of Commons, London; secretary, Patrick Armstrong.

[327] E.g., Arthur N. Holcombe, *Strengthening the United Nations: Commission to Study the Organization of Peace* (1957), pp. 208–209, 216, 260, 262.

[328] A/3118, 21 Feb. 1956; A/3118/Add.1, 13 Sept. 1956; A/3118/Add.2, 17 Oct. 1956; withdrawn, Eleventh Session; discussed in "Issues before the Eleventh General Assembly," *Int. Con.* No. 510 (Nov. 1956), pp. 135–140.

[329] *International Geophysical Year: The Arctic, Antarctica*, 85 Cong., 2 Sess., H. Rept. No. 1348 (1958), p. 46. For the U.S. position see 1 Hackworth *Digest* 449–465; for an illuminating analysis of recent developments see discussion by Robert D. Hayton, Oscar Svarlien, John Hanessian, and others, *Proceedings of the American Society of International Law 1958*.

Health and Resources since World War II

throughout Antarctica by citizens, organizations, and governments of all countries," and to freeze the legal *status quo* of all claims in Antarctica for the duration of the treaty.[330] The arrangement would provide for cooperation with the United Nations and its specialized agencies but place responsibility for the administration of affairs on the continent in the treaty organization of the twelve states most directly concerned. On June 4, 1958, the state department announced the acceptance of the proposal by all eleven nations, including the U.S.S.R.[331] If successful, such a scheme would not only tend to solve one of the most perplexing political problems of modern times but also constitute a fitting acknowledgement of the efforts over a century and a half of men who braved many hazards and who, in some cases, gave their lives, to unlock for the benefit of all peoples the secrets of the White Continent.[332]

Whatever becomes of any of these possibilities and proposals, it is not premature to consider the sea as an important complex, directly involving individuals, groups, and nation-states, in which exist all the elements essential to "the process by which sense of community, integration, and hence security-communities are attained." [333] By its steady and increasing participation in the treaty law we have described, the United States has not only advanced its own considerable interests in the sea but has made important contributions to the welfare of the community of the sea — "The Sea That Unites Us." [334]

[330] "United States Proposes Conference on Antarctica," 38 *DSB* 910–912 (1958). Meanwhile the United Kingdom exchanged views with New Zealand and Australia on the same subject. *N.Y.T.*, Feb. 13, 1958.

[331] *N.Y.T.*, June 5, 1958.

[332] See *Antarctica: The Last Frontier. The Annual Report of the Officer in Charge United States Antarctic Programs Fiscal Year 1956* (1957), whose foreword contains a fine tribute to Admiral Byrd. The report also contains a large colored map of the territorial claims in Antarctica.

[333] Van Wagenen, *op. cit.*, p. 14.

[334] Title of mimeo. circular on weather reporting ships, WMO.

Appendixes, Bibliography, and Index

APPENDIX I ~~ PROCLAMATIONS BY PRESIDENT TRUMAN, SEPTEMBER 28, 1945

A. With Respect to the Natural Resources of the Subsoil and Sea Bed of the Continental Shelf *

WHEREAS the Government of the United States of America, aware of the long range world-wide need for new sources of petroleum and other minerals, holds the view that efforts to discover and make available new supplies of these resources should be encouraged; and

WHEREAS its competent experts are of the opinion that such resources underlie many parts of the continental shelf off the coasts of the United States of America, and that with modern technological progress their utilization is already practicable or will become so at an early date; and

WHEREAS recognized jurisdiction over these resources is required in the interest of their conservation and prudent utilization when and as development is undertaken; and

WHEREAS it is the view of the Government of the United States that the exercise of jurisdiction over the natural resources of the subsoil and sea bed of the continental shelf by the contiguous nation is reasonable and just, since the effectiveness of measures to utilize or conserve these resources would be contingent upon cooperation and protection from the shore, since the continental shelf may be regarded as an extension of the land-mass of the coastal nation and thus naturally appurtenant to it, since these resources frequently form a seaward extension of a pool or deposit lying within the territory, and since self-protection compels the coastal nation to keep close watch over activities off its shores which are of the nature necessary for utilization of these resources;

Now, therefore, I, HARRY S. TRUMAN, President of the United States of America, do hereby proclaim the following policy of the United States of America with respect to the natural resources of the subsoil and sea bed of the continental shelf.

Having concern for the urgency of conserving and prudently utilizing its natural resources, the Government of the United States regards the natural resources of the subsoil and sea bed of the continental shelf beneath the high seas but contiguous to the coasts of the United States as appertaining to the United States, subject to its jurisdiction and control. In cases where the continental shelf extends to the shores of another State, or is shared with an adjacent State, the boundary shall be determined by the United States and the State concerned in accordance with equitable principles. The character as high seas of the waters above the continental shelf and the right to their free and unimpeded navigation are in no way thus affected.

In witness whereof, I have hereunto set my hand and caused the seal of the United States of America to be affixed.

Done at the City of Washington this twenty-eighth day of September, in the year of our Lord nineteen hundred and forty-five, and of the Independence of the United States of America the one hundred and seventieth.

[SEAL]

HARRY S. TRUMAN

By the President:
Dean Acheson
Acting Secretary of State

---

* 59 Stat. 884–885.

The United States and the Treaty Law of the Sea

B. With Respect to Coastal Fisheries in Certain Areas of the High Seas *

WHEREAS for some years the Government of the United States of America has viewed with concern the inadequacy of present arrangements for the protection and perpetuation of the fishery resources contiguous to its coasts, and in view of the potentially disturbing effect of this situation, has carefully studied the possibility of improving the jurisdictional basis for conservation measures and international coöperation in this field; and

WHEREAS such fishery resources have a special importance to coastal communities as a source of livelihood and to the nation as a food and industrial resource; and

WHEREAS the progressive development of new methods and techniques contributes to intensified fishing over wide sea areas and in certain cases seriously threatens fisheries with depletion; and

WHEREAS there is an urgent need to protect coastal fishery resources from destructive exploitation, having due regard to conditions peculiar to each region and situation and to the special rights and equities of the coastal State and of any other State which may have established a legitimate interest therein;

Now, therefore, I, HARRY S. TRUMAN, President of the United States of America, do hereby proclaim the following policy of the United States of America with respect to coastal fisheries in certain areas of the high seas:

In view of the pressing need for conservation and protection of fishery resources, the Government of the United States regards it as proper to establish conservation zones in those areas of the high seas contiguous to the coasts of the United States wherein fishing activities have been or in the future may be developed and maintained on a substantial scale. Where such activities have been or shall hereafter be developed and maintained by its nationals alone, the United States regards it as proper to establish explicitly bounded conservation zones in which fishing activities shall be subject to the regulation and control of the United States. Where such activities have been or shall hereafter be legitimately developed and maintained jointly by nationals of the United States and nationals of other States, explicitly bounded conservation zones may be established under agreements between the United States and such other States; and all fishing activities in such zones shall be subject to regulation and control as provided in such agreements. The right of any State to establish conservation zones off its shores in accordance with the above principles is conceded, provided that corresponding recognition is given to any fishing interests of nationals of the United States which may exist in such areas. The character as high seas of the areas in which such conservation zones are established and the right to their free and unimpeded navigation are in no way thus affected.

In witness whereof, I have hereunto set my hand and caused the seal of the United States of America to be affixed.

Done at the City of Washington this twenty-eighth day of September, in the year of our Lord nineteen hundred and forty-five, and of the Independence of the United States of America the one hundred and seventieth.

[SEAL]

HARRY S. TRUMAN

By the President:
Dean Acheson
 Acting Secretary of State

---

* 59 Stat. 885–886.

APPENDIX II ~~ CHECKLIST OF TREATIES PERFECTED BY THE UNITED STATES CITED HEREIN

NOTE: Classification in general follows *Treaties in Force 1956*. The following abbreviations are used. *TS*: *Treaty Series*. *EAS*: *Executive Agreement Series*. *Stat.*: *Statutes at Large*. *TIAS*: *Treaties and Other International Acts Series*. *UST*: *United States Treaties and Other International Agreements*. *LNTS*: League of Nations *Treaty Series*. *UNTS*: United Nations *Treaty Series*.

Agriculture

TIAS 1554; 60 *Stat.* 1886. Food and Agriculture Organization of the United Nations, Constitution, Quebec, October 16, 1945.

Aviation

TS 840; 47 *Stat.* 1901. Commercial Aviation, Pan American, Habana, February 20, 1928, 129 *LNTS* 223.
TS 876; 49 *Stat.* 3000. Air Transportation, Warsaw, October 12, 1929, 137 *LNTS* 11.
EAS 2; 47 *Stat.* 2575. Canada, Civil Aircraft, Exchange of Notes at Washington, August 29 and October 22, 1929.
TIAS 1591; 61 *Stat.* 1180. International Civil Aviation, Chicago, December 7, 1944, 15 *UNTS* 295.
EAS 469; 59 *Stat.* 1516. International Civil Aviation: Provisional Organization, Chicago, December 7, 1944.
EAS 487; 59 *Stat.* 1693. Air Services Transit Agreement, Chicago, December 7, 1944, 84 *UNTS* 389.
EAS 488; 59 *Stat.* 1701. Air Transport Agreement, Chicago, December 7, 1944.
TIAS 1618; 61 *Stat.* 2864. Republic of the Philippines, Air Navigation Program in the Philippines, Manila, May 12, 1947, 16 *UNTS* 137.
TIAS 1882; 63 *Stat.* 2328. Canada, Air Search and Rescue Operations, Exchange of Notes at Washington, January 24 and 31, 1949, 43 *UNTS* 119.
TIAS 2847; 4 *UST* 1830. International Recognition of Rights in Aircraft, Geneva, June 19, 1948.
TIAS 3756; 8 *UST* 179. International Civil Aviation, Amending Convention of December 7, 1944, Montreal, June 14, 1954.

Bahamas Long Range Proving Ground

TIAS 2099; 1 *UST* 545. United Kingdom, Long-Range Proving Ground for Guided Missiles to be Known as "The Bahamas Long Range Proving Ground," Washington, July 21, 1950, 97 *UNTS* 193.
TIAS 2425; 3 *UST* 2569. Dominican Republic, Extending the Long Range Proving Ground for the Testing of Guided Missiles, Ciudad Trujillo, November 26, 1951, 150 *UNTS* 227.
TIAS 2426; 3 *UST* 2594. United Kingdom, Extension of the Bahamas Long Range

Proving Ground, Agreement and Exchanges of Notes at Washington, January 15, 1952, 127 *UNTS* 3.

TIAS 2701; 3 *UST* 5102. Haiti, Short-Range-Aid-To-Navigation: Ground Station in Haiti, Exchange of Notes, at Port-au-Prince, August 22 and 29, 1952.

TIAS 2789; 4 *UST* 429. United Kingdom, Bahamas Long Range Proving Ground: Establishment of High Altitude Interceptor Range, Exchange of Notes at Washington February 24 and March 2, 1953, 172 *UNTS* 257.

TIAS 3379; 6 *UST* 3783. United Kingdom, Bahamas Long Range Proving Ground: Use of Certain Facilities by Civil Aircraft, Exchange of Notes, Washington, July 11 and 22, 1955.

TIAS 3595; 7 *UST* 1939. United Kingdom, Bahamas Long Range Proving Ground: Establishment of Additional Sites in Saint Lucia, Washington, June 25, 1956.

TIAS 3603; 7 *UST* 1999. United Kingdom, Establishment of Additional Sites in Ascension Island, Washington, June 25, 1956.

TIAS 3727; 8 *UST* 1. United Kingdom, Bahamas Long Range Proving Ground: Civil Air Services Within the Bahamas, Turks, and Caicos Islands and Jamaica, Exchange of Notes at Washington, December 6, 1956, and January 4, 1957.

TIAS 3744; 8 *UST* 87. Brazil, Defense: Establishment of Guided Missile Station on Island of Fernando de Noronha, Exchange of Notes, Rio de Janeiro, January 21, 1957.

TIAS 3803; 8 *UST* 493. United Kingdom, Bahamas Long Range Proving Ground: Extension of Flight Testing Range, Exchange of Notes at Washington, April 1, 1957.

Caribbean Commission

TIAS 1799; 62 *Stat.* 2618. Caribbean Commission, Washington, October 30, 1946, 27 *UNTS* 77.

Conservation (Birds)

TS 628; 39 *Stat.* 1702. Great Britain (Canada), Migratory Birds, Washington, August 16, 1916.

TS 912; 50 *Stat.* 1311. Mexico, Migratory Birds and Game Animals, Mexico City, February 7, 1936, 178 *LNTS* 309.

TS 981; 56 *Stat.* 1354. Nature Protection and Wildlife Preservation in the Western Hemisphere, Washington, October 12, 1940.

Cultural Relations

TIAS 1580; 61 *Stat.* 2495. United Nations Educational, Scientific and Cultural Organization, Constitution, London, November 16, 1945, 4 *UNTS* 275.

TIAS 3469; 6 *UST* 6157. United Nations Educational, Scientific and Cultural Organization, Amendment to Constitution, Montevideo, November 22 and December 8, 1954.

TIAS 3889; 8 *UST* 1395. United Nations Educational, Scientific and Cultural Organization, Amendments to Constitution, New Delhi, November 10, 1956.

Extradition

TS 139; 26 *Stat.* 1508. Great Britain, Extradition, Washington, July 12, 1889.

Fisheries

TS 498; 35 *Stat.* 2000. Great Britain (Canada) Fisheries, Washington, April 11, 1908.

Appendixes

TS 572; 37 *Stat.* 1634. Great Britain (Canada), North Atlantic Coast Fisheries, Washington, July 20, 1912.

TS 701; 43 *Stat.* 1841. Canada, Halibut, Washington, March 2, 1923.

TS 837; 47 *Stat.* 1872. Canada, Halibut Fishery of Northern Pacific Ocean and Bering Sea, Ottawa, May 9, 1930.

TS 917; 50 *Stat.* 1351. Canada, Halibut Fishery of Northern Pacific Ocean and Bering Sea, Ottawa, January 29, 1937, 181 *LNTS* 209.

TS 918; 50 *Stat.* 1355. Canada, Sockeye Salmon Fisheries, Washington, May 26, 1930, 184 *LNTS* 305.

EAS 182; 54 *Stat.* 2409. Canada, Board of Inquiry for Great Lakes Fisheries, Exchange of Notes at Washington, February 29, 1940.

EAS 443; 58 *Stat.* 1554. Mexico, Fisheries Mission, Exchanges of Notes at Mexico, April 17, May 22, July 22 and 27, and October 24, 1942, and Exchange of Notes, Amending and Extending the Agreement, at Mexico, September 7 and October 18, 1944, 21 *UNTS* 189.

EAS 479; 59 *Stat.* 1614. Canada, Sockeye Salmon Fisheries, Exchange of Notes at Washington July 21 and August 5, 1944, 121 *UNTS* 299.

TIAS 1611; 61 *Stat.* 2834. Republic of the Philippines, Fishery Program in the Philippines, Manila, March 14, 1947, 16 *UNTS* 31.

TIAS 1624; 61 *Stat.* 2903. Mexico, Fisheries Mission, Amending and Extending the Agreement Effected by Exchanges of Communications Dated April 17, May 22, July 22 and 27, and October 24, 1942, Exchange of Notes at Mexico, D.F., September 23 and October 22, 1946, 21 *UNTS* 13.

TIAS 1747; 62 *Stat.* 1898. Canada, Shellfish: Sanitary Certification of Shippers, Exchange of Notes at Washington, March 4 and April 30, 1948, 77 *UNTS* 191.

TIAS 1869; 62 *Stat.* 3575. Mexico, Fisheries Mission, Further Extending the Agreement Effected by Exchanges of Communications Dated April 17, May 22, July 22 and 27, and October 24, 1942, Exchange of Notes at Washington, September 15 and October 6, 1948, 80 *UNTS* 306.

TIAS 1895; 62 *Stat.* 3711. Establishment of the Indo-Pacific Fisheries Council, Baguio, February 26, 1948, 120 *UNTS* 59.

TIAS 2044; 1 *UST* 230. Costa Rica, Fisheries: Establishment of an Inter-American Tropical Tuna Commission, Washington, May 31, 1949, 80 *UNTS* 3.

TIAS 2089; 1 *UST* 477. Northwest Atlantic Fisheries, Washington, February 8, 1949, 157 *UNTS* 157.

TIAS 2094; 1 *UST* 513. Mexico, Fisheries: Establishment of an International Commission for the Scientific Investigation of Tuna, Mexico, January 25, 1949, 99 *UNTS* 3.

TIAS 2096; 1 *UST* 536. Canada, Halibut Fishing Vessels, Port Privileges on the Pacific Coasts of the United States of America and Canada, Ottawa, March 24, 1950.

TIAS 2337; 2 *UST* 2116. El Salvador, Fisheries Mission to El Salvador, Exchange of Notes at San Salvador, July 19, 1951.

TIAS 2717; 3 *UST* 5200. El Salvador, Fisheries Mission to El Salvador, Extending Agreement of July 19, 1951, Exchange of Notes, at San Salvador, September 23 and November 20, 1952.

TIAS 2763; 4 *UST* 25. El Salvador, Fisheries Mission to El Salvador, Extending Agreement of July 19, 1951, as Extended, Exchange of Notes at San Salvador, August 18 and 28, 1953.

TIAS 2786; 4 *UST* 380. High Seas Fisheries of the North Pacific Ocean, Tokyo, May 9, 1952.

TIAS 2900; 5 *UST* 5. Canada, Halibut Fishery of Northern Pacific Ocean and Bering Sea, Ottawa, March 2, 1953.

TIAS 3326; 6 *UST* 2836. Canada, Great Lakes Fisheries, Washington, September 10, 1954.

TIAS 3423; 6 *UST* 4111. El Salvador, Fisheries Mission to El Salvador, Extending Agreement of July 19, 1951, as Extended, Exchange of Notes at San Salvador, September 13, 1954, and July 25, 1955.
TIAS 3674; 7 *UST* 2927. Indo-Pacific Fisheries Council, Tokyo, September 30–October 14, 1955.
TIAS 3867; 8 *UST* 1057. Canada, Sockeye and Pink Salmon Fisheries, Protocol Amending Convention of May 26, 1930, Ottawa, December 28, 1956.

Health

TS 466; 35 *Stat.* 1770. Sanitary Convention, Paris, December 3, 1903.
TS 518; 35 *Stat.* 2094. Sanitary Convention, Pan American, Washington, October 14, 1905.
TS 511; 35 *Stat.* 2061. International Office of Public Health, Rome, December 9, 1907.
TS 649; 42 *Stat.* 1823. Sanitary Convention, Paris, January 17, 1912, 4 *LNTS* 281.
TS 714; 44 *Stat.* 2031. Sanitary Convention, Pan American, Habana, November 14, 1924, 86 *LNTS* 43.
TS 762; 45 *Stat.* 2492. Sanitary Convention, Paris, June 21, 1926, 78 *LNTS* 229.
TS 763; 45 *Stat.* 2613. Sanitary Convention, Pan American, Lima, October 19, 1927, 87 *LNTS* 453.
TS 901; 49 *Stat.* 3279. Sanitary, Aerial Navigation, The Hague, April 12, 1933, 161 *LNTS* 65.
EAS 80; 49 *Stat.* 3785. Statistics of Causes of Death, London, June 19, 1934, 154 *LNTS* 381.
EAS 173; 54 *Stat.* 2308. Statistics of Causes of Death, Revision, Paris, October 6, 1938, 200 *LNTS* 520.
TS 991; 59 *Stat.* 955. Sanitary Maritime Navigation, Washington, December 15, 1944, 17 *UNTS* 305.
TS 992; 59 *Stat.* 991. Sanitary Aerial Navigation, Washington, December 15, 1944, 16 *UNTS* 247.
TIAS 1551; 61 *Stat.* 1115. Sanitary Maritime Navigation, Washington, April 23, 1946, 17 *UNTS* 3.
TIAS 1552; 61 *Stat.* 1122. Sanitary Aerial Navigation, Washington, April 23, 1946, 16 *UNTS* 179.
TIAS 1561; 61 *Stat.* 2349. World Health Organization: Interim Commission, New York, July 22, 1946.
TIAS 1754; 62 *Stat.* 1604. International Office of Public Health, New York, July 22, 1946, 9 *UNTS* 66.
TIAS 1808; 62 *Stat.* 2679. World Health Organization, Constitution, New York, July 22, 1946, 14 *UNTS* 185.
TIAS 2733; 3 *UST* 5306. Saudi Arabia, Technical Cooperation: Public Health and Disease Control Program, Jidda, December 15, 1952.
TIAS 2845; 4 *UST* 1781. Saudi Arabia, Technical Cooperation: Public Health and Disease Control Program, Quarantine Services for Pilgrims, Jidda, June 29, 1953.
TIAS 2852; 4 *UST* 1928. Egypt, Technical Cooperation, Public Health Program, Cairo, June 18, 1953.
TIAS 3482; 7 *UST* 79. World Health Organization, Regulations No. 1 Regarding Nomenclature with Respect to Diseases and Causes of Death, Geneva, July 24, 1948, and Supplement to same, Rome, June 30, 1949, 66 *UNTS* 25, 38.
TIAS 3493; 7 *UST* 173. China, Establishment of U.S. Navy Medical Research Center at Taipei, Taiwan, Exchanges of Notes at Taipei, March 30, April 26, and Oct. 14, 1955.
TIAS 3625; 7 *UST* 2255. Sanitary, World Health Organization Regulations No. 2, Geneva, May 25, 1951, 175 *UNTS* 215.

Appendixes

TIAS 3720; 7 *UST* 3453. China, U.S. Navy Medical Research Center at Taipei, Taiwan, Amending Agreement of October 14, 1955, Exchange of Notes at Taipei, December 27, 1956.

Labor

TS 874; 49 *Stat.* 2712. International Labor Organization, Membership of the U.S., Effective August 20, 1934, 158 *LNTS* 45.
TS 950; 54 *Stat.* 1683. ILO Officers' Competency Certificates, Geneva, October 24, 1936, 40 *UNTS* 153.
TS 951; 54 *Stat.* 1693. ILO Shipowners' Liability (Sick and Injured Seamen), Geneva, October 24, 1936, 40 *UNTS* 169.
TS 952; 54 *Stat.* 1705. ILO Minimum Age (Sea) (Revised), Geneva, October 24, 1936, 38 *UNTS* 109, 40 *UNTS* 205.
TIAS 1810; 62 *Stat.* 1672. International Labor Organization, Final Articles Revision Convention, 1946, Montreal, October 9, 1946, 38 *UNTS* 3.
TIAS 1868; 62 *Stat.* 3485. International Labor Organization: Amendment of Constitution, Montreal, October 9, 1946, 15 *UNTS* 35.
TIAS 2949; 5 *UST* 605. International Labor Organization: Certification of Able Seamen, Seattle, June 29, 1946, 94 *UNTS* 11.
TIAS 3500; 7 *UST* 245. International Labor Organization: Amendment of the Constitution, 1953, Geneva, June 25, 1953.

Liquor Traffic

TS 389; 31 *Stat.* 915. Liquor Traffic in Africa, Brussels, June 8, 1899.
TS 467; 35 *Stat.* 1912. Liquor Traffic in Africa, Brussels, November 3, 1906.
TS 779; 46 *Stat.* 2199. Liquor Traffic in Africa, St. Germain-en-Laye, September 10, 1919, 8 *LNTS* 11.

Maritime Matters

TS 245; 14 *Stat.* 679, 18(2) *Stat.* 525. Cape Spartel Lighthouse, Tangier, May 31, 1865.
TS 576; 37 *Stat.* 1658. Assistance and Salvage at Sea, Brussels, September 23, 1910.
TS 736-A. Oil Pollution of Navigable Waters, Washington, June 16, 1926.
TS 910; 50 *Stat.* 1121. Safety of Life at Sea, London, May 31, 1929, 136 *LNTS* 81.
TS 858; 47 *Stat.* 2228. Load-line Convention, London, July 5, 1930, 135 *LNTS* 301.
EAS 21; 47 *Stat.* 2655. Sweden, Pleasure Yachts, Exchange of Notes at Stockholm, October 22 and 29, 1930, 109 *LNTS* 181.
EAS 25; 47 *Stat.* 2678. Japan, Load-line Certificates, Exchange of Notes at Tokyo, February 13, March 19 and 30, August 25, and September 7, 1931.
EAS 27; 47 *Stat.* 2685. Irish Free State, Load-line Certificates, Exchange of Notes at Dublin, September 21 and November 18, 1931.
EAS 29; 47 *Stat.* 2690. Denmark, Load-line Certificates, Exchange of Notes at Washington, January 16, 1932.
EAS 30; 47 *Stat.* 2693. Iceland, Load-line Certificates, Exchange of Notes at Washington, January 16, 1932.
EAS 31; 47 *Stat.* 2695. Germany, Load-line Certificates, Exchange of Notes at Berlin, September 11 and December 16, 1931.
EAS 35; 47 *Stat.* 2707. Sweden, Load-line Certificates, Exchange of Notes at Stockholm, January 27 and June 1, 1932.
EAS 36; 47 *Stat.* 2711. Italy, Load-line Certificates, Exchange of Notes at Rome, September 8, 1931, and June 1, 1932.
EAS 40; 47 *Stat.* 2736. Belgium, Load-line Certificates, Exchange of Notes at Brussels, October 7, 1931, February 4, and April 19, 1932.

EAS 42; 48 *Stat.* 1757. The Netherlands, Load-line Certificates, Exchange of Notes at Washington, August 26 and November 16, 1931, March 18, April 22, June 29, and September 30, 1932.
TS 869; 49 *Stat.* 2685. Canada, Load Lines, Washington, December 9, 1933, 152 *LNTS* 39.
TS 905; 49 *Stat.* 3359. Mexico, Salvage of Vessels, Mexico City, June 13, 1935, 168 *LNTS* 135.
TS 921; 51 *Stat.* 13. Safety of Life at Sea, Amendment, London, December 31, 1930.
TS 931; 51 *Stat.* 233. Bills of Lading, Brussels, August 25, 1924, 120 *LNTS* 155.
TS 942; 53 *Stat.* 1787. Load Lines, Amendment, London, October 22, 1936, 193 *LNTS* 271.
EAS 106; 50 *Stat.* 1626. Panama, Ship Measurement Certificates, Exchange of Notes at Washington, August 17, 1937, 182 *LNTS* 159.
EAS 172; 54 *Stat.* 2300. Canada, Load-line Certificates, Great Lakes, Exchanges of Notes at Ottawa, April 29, August 24, and October 22, 1938, September 2, and October 18, 1939, January 10, and March 4, 1940, 202 *LNTS* 429.
TIAS 1616; 61 *Stat.* 2852. Republic of the Philippines, Coast and Geodetic Program in the Philippines, Manila, May 12, 1947, 16 *UNTS* 109.
TIAS 1722; 61 *Stat.* 3784. Shipping: Principles Having Reference to Continuance of Co-ordinated Control, London, August 5, 1944.
TIAS 1723; 61 *Stat.* 3791. Shipping: Arrangements and Recommendations of United Maritime Executive Board, London, February 11, 1946.
TIAS 1724; 61 *Stat.* 3796. Shipping: Provisional Maritime Consultative Council, Washington, October 30, 1946, 11 *UNTS* 107.
TIAS 2391; 3 *UST* 52. Cuba, Pleasure Yachts, Reciprocal Exemption from Navigation Dues, Exchange of Notes at Washington, December 12, and 17, 1951, 152 *UNTS* 87.
TIAS 2495; 3 *UST* 3450. Safety of Life at Sea, London, June 10, 1948, 164 *UNTS* 113.
TIAS 2507; 3 *UST* 3771. Safety at Sea: North Atlantic Ice Patrol, Interim Arrangement Revising the Scale of Contributions Under Article 37 of the International Convention on Safety of Life at Sea Signed at London, May 31, 1929. Entered into Force, January 1, 1951.
TIAS 2865; 4 *UST* 2174. Canada, Navigation: Transfer of Loran Stations in Newfoundland to the Canadian Government, Exchange of Notes at Ottawa, June 26 and 30, 1953.
TIAS 2899; 4 *UST* 2956. International Regulations for Preventing Collisions at Sea, 1948, Proclaimed by the President, August 15, 1953.
TIAS 3019; 5 *UST* 1459. Canada, Navigation: Loran Station on Cape Christian, Baffin Island, Exchange of Notes at Ottawa, May 1 and 3, 1954.
TIAS 3590; 7 *UST* 1080. Safety of Life at Sea: Correction of Error in the Regulations annexed to the Convention of June 10, 1948, Notifications by the United Kingdom, June 5, 1953 and August 25, 1955.
TIAS 3597; 7 *UST* 1969. Safety of Life at Sea: Financial Support of the North Atlantic Ice Patrol, Washington, January 4, 1956.
TIAS 3774; 8 *UST* 289. Venezuela, Exemption of Merchant Vessels from Admeasurement Requirements, Exchange of Notes at Caracas, February 21, 1957.
TIAS 3780; 8 *UST* 329. Dominican Republic, Navigation: Establishment of Loran Transmitting Stations, Washington, March 19, 1957.
TIAS 3893; 8 *UST* 1413. Panama, Inspection of Panamanian Vessels in the Canal Zone, Exchange of Notes at Panama, August 5, 1957.
TIAS 4029. Cape Spartel Light: Transfer of Management to Morocco, Termination of Convention of May 31, 1865. Protocol, Tangier, March 31, 1958.
TIAS 4044. Convention of the Intergovernmental Maritime Consultative Organization, Geneva, March 6, 1948.

Appendixes
Meteorology and Weather Stations

61 *Stat.* 4281. Mexico, Weather Stations, Exchange of Notes at Mexico, D.F., October 13 and 20 and November 10, 1942. Text also in *TIAS* 1989, 66 *UNTS* 307.

TIAS 1617; 61 *Stat.* 2858. Republic of the Philippines, Meteorological Program in the Philippines, Manila, May 12, 1947, 16 *UNTS* 123.

TIAS 1806; 61 *Stat.* 4053. Mexico, Weather Stations, Cooperative Program in Mexico, Exchange of Notes at Mexico, D.F., May 18 and June 14, 1943, 66 *UNTS* 331.

TIAS 1807; 61 *Stat.* 4060. Mexico, Weather Stations, Cooperative Program on Guadalupe Island, Exchange of Notes at Mexico, D.F., November 6, 1945, and April 12, 1946, 66 *UNTS* 293.

TIAS 1842; 61 *Stat.* 4084. Cuba, Weather Stations, Cooperative Program in Cuba, Exchange of Notes at Habana, July 17 and August 2, 1944, 67 *UNTS* 221.

TIAS 1847; 62 *Stat.* 3134. Cuba, Weather Stations, Cooperative Program in Cuba, Amending and Extending Agreement of July 17 and August 2, 1944, Exchange of Notes at Habana, August 21, 1947 and January 27, 1948, 67 *UNTS* 3.

TIAS 1989; 61 *Stat.* 4276. Mexico, Weather Stations, Cooperative Program in Mexico, Amending and Extending Agreement of October 13 and 20 and November 10, 1942, Exchanges of Notes at Mexico, D.F., May 12, June 16, 21 and 28, 1945; and Agreement, Exchanges of Notes at Mexico, D.F., October 13 and 20 and November 10, 1942, 66 *UNTS* 313.

TIAS 1995; 63 *Stat.* 2750. Mexico, Weather Stations, Cooperative Program in Mexico, Exchange of Notes at Mexico, D.F., March 29 and August 15, 1949, 66 *UNTS* 13.

TIAS 2052; 1 *UST* 281. World Meteorological Organization, Washington, October 11, 1947, 77 *UNTS* 143.

TIAS 2053; 1 *UST* 356. North Atlantic Ocean Weather Stations, London, May 12–June 30, 1949.

TIAS 2103; 1 *UST* 569. Canada, Weather Stations, Pacific Ocean Program, Exchange of Notes at Washington, June 8 and 22, 1950, 70 *UNTS* 115.

TIAS 2125; 1 *UST* 658. Cuba, Weather Stations, Cooperative Program in Cuba, Exchange of Notes at Habana, June 30, 1950, 89 *UNTS* 378.

TIAS 2228; 2 *UST* 720. Canada, Weather Stations, Pacific Ocean Interim Program, Exchange of Notes at Washington, September 25, 1950, and February 16, 1951, 87 *UNTS* 390.

TIAS 2488; 3 *UST* 3062. Canada, Weather Stations, Pacific Ocean Interim Program, Amending Agreement of February 16, 1951, Exchange of Notes at Ottawa, January 22 and February 22, 1952.

TIAS 2589; 3 *UST* 4402. North Atlantic Ocean Weather Stations, Extending Agreement of May 12, 1949, Montreal, May 28, 1952.

TIAS 2695; 3 *UST* 5081. Mexico, Weather Stations, Cooperative Program in Mexico, Extending Agreement of March 29 and August 15, 1949, Exchange of Notes at Mexico, D.F., April 7 and August 22, 1952.

TIAS 2837; 4 *UST* 1700. Mexico, Weather Stations, Cooperative Program in Mexico, Extending Agreement of March 29 and August 15, 1949, as Extended, Exchange of Notes at Mexico, D.F., June 30, 1953.

TIAS 2838; 4 *UST* 1705. Cuba, Weather Stations, Cooperative Program in Cuba, Exchange of Notes at Habana, June 30, 1953.

TIAS 3132; 5 *UST* 2765. Canada, Pacific Ocean Weather Stations, Exchange of Notes at Ottawa, June 4 and 28, 1954.

TIAS 3186; 6 *UST* 515. North Atlantic Ocean Stations, Paris, February 25, 1954.

TIAS 3389; 6 *UST* 3877. United Kingdom, Weather Stations, Betio Island, Exchange of Notes at Washington, November 15, 1955.

TIAS 3611; 7 UST 2095. Colombia, Weather Stations, Cooperative Program on St. Andrews Island, Exchange of Notes at Bogotá, February 6 and March 14, 1956, and Amending Agreement, Exchange of Notes at Bogotá, June 7, 13, and 20, 1956.

TIAS 3647; 7 UST 2545. France, Weather Stations, Cooperative Program on Guadeloupe Island, Exchange of Notes at Paris, March 23, 1956.

TIAS 3650; 7 UST 2562. The Netherlands, Weather Stations, Cooperative Program on Curaçao and St. Martin Islands, Exchange of Notes at The Hague, August 6 and 16, 1956.

TIAS 3699; 7 UST 3197. Dominican Republic, Weather Stations, Cooperative Program in the Dominican Republic, Exchange of Notes at Ciudad Trujillo, July 25 and August 11, 1956.

TIAS 3795; 8 UST 436. Chile, Weather Stations, Cooperative Program at Antofagasta, Quintero and Puerto Montt, Exchange of Notes at Santiago, March 1, 1957.

TIAS 3823; 8 UST 691. Peru, Weather Stations, Cooperative Program at Lima, Exchange of Notes at Lima, April 17, 1957.

TIAS 3833; 8 UST 764. Ecuador, Weather Stations, Cooperative Program at Guayaquil, Exchange of Notes at Quito, April 24, 1957.

TIAS 3896; 8 UST 1425. The Netherlands, Weather Stations, Cooperative Program on Curaçao and St. Martin Islands, Extending Agreement of August 6 and 16, 1956, Exchange of Notes at The Hague, July 8 and August 29, 1957.

TIAS 3905; 8 UST 1541. Mexico, Weather Program, Cooperative Program in Mexico, Relating to Agreement of June 30, 1953, Exchange of Notes at Mexico, August 23 and 29, 1957.

TIAS 3976. United Kingdom, Weather Stations, Betio Island, Exchange of Notes at Washington, January 20, 1958.

TIAS 4001. Australia, Weather Stations, Nauru Island, Exchange of Notes at Canberra, February 19 and 25, 1958.

Mines (Naval)

TS 541; 36 Stat. 2332. Automatic Submarine Contact Mines, The Hague, October 18, 1907.

Agreement Constituting the International Organization for the Clearance of Mines in European Waters, Signed by Representatives of the United States, France, Great Britain, and the U.S.S.R., November 22, 1945, UN Security Council, *Official Records*, Second Year, Supplement No. 6, Annex to the record of the 107th Meeting, February 18, 1947, Exhibit III; also in International Court of Justice, *Pleadings, Oral Arguments, Documents, 1949*, the *Corfu Channel Case*, Vol. I, pp. 54–59.

Miscellaneous

TS 664; 42 Stat. 2149. Japan, Rights in Former German Islands in Pacific Ocean, Washington, February 11, 1922, 12 LNTS 201.

TS 732; 44 Stat. 2358. Mexico, Smuggling, Washington, December 23, 1925.

TS 877; 49 Stat. 3027. Revision of Act of Berlin and Act and Declaration of Brussels, St. Germain-en-Laye, September 10, 1919, 8 LNTS 27.

EAS 181; 54 Stat. 2405. Great Britain, Naval and Air Bases, Exchange of Notes at Washington, September 2, 1940, 203 LNTS 201.

TIAS 1665; 61 Stat. 3301. Trusteeship for Former Japanese Mandated Islands: Agreement approved by the Security Council of the United Nations April 2, 1947; approved by the President of the United States of America July 18, 1947, 8 UNTS 189.

Appendixes

TIAS 1964; 63 *Stat.* 2241. North Atlantic Treaty, Washington, April 4, 1949, 34 *UNTS* 243.

TIAS 2407; 3 *UST* 491. France, Mapping of Certain French Territories in the Pacific, Exchange of Notes at Paris, November 27, 1948, 168 *UNTS* 119.

TIAS 2479; 3 *UST* 2960. Egypt, General Agreement for Technical Cooperation, Cairo, May 5, 1951.

TIAS 2759; 3 *UST* 5893. Thailand, Aerial Mapping, Exchange of Notes at Bangkok, November 8 and December 3, 1952.

TIAS 3160; 6 *UST* 1. Japan, Settlement of Japanese Claims for Personal and Property Damages Resulting From Nuclear Tests in Marshall Islands in 1954, Exchange of Notes at Tokyo, January 4, 1955.

TIAS 3929; 8 *UST* 1761. Cambodia, Aerial Mapping, Phnom Penh, October 17, 1957.

Narcotic Drugs

TS 612; 38 *Stat.* 1912. Opium and Other Drugs, The Hague, January 23, 1912, and July 9, 1913, 8 *LNTS* 187.

TS 863; 48 *Stat.* 1543. Narcotic Drugs, Geneva, July 13, 1931, 139 *LNTS* 301.

TIAS 1671; 61 *Stat.* 2230. Narcotic Drugs, Lake Success, December 11, 1946, 12 *UNTS* 179.

TIAS 1859; 62 *Stat.* 1796. Narcotic Drugs, Entry Into Force of Amendments Set Forth in the Annex to the Protocol of December 11, 1946, Proclamation by the President, Washington, March 30, 1948, 12 *UNTS* 179.

Oceanographic Research Stations

TIAS 3672; 7 *UST* 2901. United Kingdom, Establishment of an Oceanographic Research Station in Barbados, Washington, November 1, 1956.

TIAS 3696; 7 *UST* 3169. United Kingdom, Establishment of an Oceanographic Research Station in the Turks and Caicos Islands, Washington, November 27, 1956.

TIAS 3926; 8 *UST* 1737. United Kingdom, Establishment of an Oceanographic Research Station in Barbados, Exchange of Notes at Washington, October 30, 1957.

TIAS 3927; 8 *UST* 1741. United Kingdom, Establishment of Oceanographic Research Stations in the Bahama Islands, Washington, November 1, 1957.

Organization of American States

TIAS 2361; 2 *UST* 2394. Charter of the Organization of American States, Bogotá, April 30, 1948, 119 *UNTS* 3.

Peace Treaties

TS 102; 8 *Stat.* 54; 18(2) *Stat.* 261. Great Britain, Preliminary, Articles of Peace, Paris, November 30, 1782.

TS 658; 42 *Stat.* 1939. Germany, Restoring Friendly Relations, Berlin, August 25, 1921, 12 *LNTS* 192.

TS 659; 42 *Stat.* 1946. Austria, Establishing Friendly Relations, Vienna, August 24, 1921, 7 *LNTS* 156.

TS 660; 42 *Stat.* 1951. Hungary, Establishing Friendly Relations, Budapest, August 29, 1921, 48 *LNTS* 191.

TIAS 2490; 3 *UST* 3169. Treaty of Peace with Japan, San Francisco, September 8, 1951, 136 *UNTS* 45.

Postal Arrangements

19 *Stat.* 577. General Postal Union Convention, Berne, October 9, 1874.
20 *Stat.* 734. Universal Postal Union Convention, Paris, June 1, 1878.
42 *Stat.* 2141. Spanish-American Postal Union Convention, Madrid, November 13, 1920.
42 *Stat.* 1971. Universal Postal Union Convention, Madrid, November 30, 1920.
45 *Stat.* 2409. Pan American Postal Union Convention, Mexico City, November 9, 1926.
46 *Stat.* 2523. Universal Postal Union Convention, London, June 28, 1929, 102 *LNTS* 245.
47 *Stat.* 1924. Postal Union of the Americas and Spain, Convention, Madrid, November 10, 1931, 131 *LNTS* 327.
TIAS 1850; 62 *Stat.* 3157. Universal Postal Union, Paris, July 5, 1947.
TIAS 2286; 2 *UST* 1323. Postal Union of the Americas and Spain, Madrid, November 9, 1950.
TIAS 2800; 4 *UST* 1118. Universal Postal Union, Brussels, July 11, 1952, 169 *UNTS* 3.
TIAS 3653; 7 *UST* 2599. Postal Union of the Americas and Spain, Bogotá, November 9, 1955.

Publications (Obscene)

TS 559; 37 *Stat.* 1511. Obscene Publications, Paris, May 4, 1910, 11 *LNTS* 438.
TIAS 2164; 1 *UST* 849. Suppression of the Circulation of Obscene Publications, Lake Success, May 4, 1949, 30 *UNTS* 3.

Saint Lawrence Seaway

TS 548; 36 *Stat.* 2448. Great Britain (Canada), Boundary Waters, Washington, January 11, 1909.
TIAS 2130; 1 *UST* 694. Canada, Uses of the Waters of the Niagara River, Washington, February 27, 1950, 132 *UNTS* 223.
TIAS 3053; 5 *UST* 1784. Canada, Saint Lawrence Seaway, Exchanges of Notes at Ottawa, August 17, 1954, and at Washington, June 30, 1952.
TIAS 3064; 5 *UST* 1979. Canada, Construction of Remedial Works at Niagara Falls, Exchange of Notes at Ottawa, September 13, 1954.
TIAS 3116; 5 *UST* 2538. Canada, Saint Lawrence Waterway, Establishment of Saint Lawrence River Joint Board of Engineers, Exchange of Notes at Washington, November 12, 1953.
TIAS 3668; 7 *UST* 2865. Canada, Relocation of Roosevelt Bridge, Exchange of Notes at Washington, October 24, 1956.
TIAS 3708; 7 *UST* 3271. Canada, Saint Lawrence Seaway, Deep-Water Dredging in Cornwall Island Channels, Exchange of Notes at Ottawa, November 7 and December 4, 1956.
TIAS 3772; 8 *UST* 279. Canada, Saint Lawrence Seaway, Navigation Improvements of the Great Lakes Connecting Channels, Exchange of Notes at Ottawa, July 23 and October 26, 1956, and February 26, 1957.
TIAS 3814; 8 *UST* 637. Canada, Saint Lawrence Seaway, Navigation Improvement of the Great Lakes Channels, Exchange of Notes at Ottawa, November 30, 1956, and April 8 and 9, 1957.

Seals (Fur)

TS 563; 37 *Stat.* 1538. Great Britain (Canada), Fur Seals, Washington, February 7, 1911.

Appendixes

TS 564; 37 *Stat.* 1542. Fur Seals, Washington, July 7, 1911.
EAS 415; 58 *Stat.* 1379. Canada, Fur Seals, Exchange of Notes at Washington, December 8 and December 19, 1942, 26 *UNTS* 363.
TIAS 1686; 62 *Stat.* 1821. Canada, Fur Seals, Amending the Provisional Agreement of December 8 and 19, 1942, Exchange of Notes at Washington, December 26, 1947, 27 *UNTS* 29.
TIAS 2521; 3 *UST* 3896. Fur Seals: Research Programs in the North Pacific Ocean, Exchanges of Notes at Tokyo, January 31 and February 8, 1952, and at Ottawa, February 7 and March 1, 1952, 168 *UNTS* 9.
TIAS 3948; 8 *UST* 2283. North Pacific Fur Seals: Interim Convention, Washington, February 9, 1957.

Slave Trade

TS 119; 8 *Stat.* 572; 18(2) *Stat.* 315. Great Britain, Boundaries, Slave Trade, Extradition, Washington, August 9, 1842.
TS 126; 12 *Stat.* 1225; 18(2) *Stat.* 334. Great Britain, Slave Trade, Washington, April 7, 1862.
TS 127; 13 *Stat.* 645; 18(2) *Stat.* 345. Great Britain, Slave Trade, Washington, February 17, 1863.
TS 131; 16 *Stat.* 777; 18(2) *Stat.* 350. Great Britain, Slave Trade, Washington, June 3, 1870.
TS 383; 27 *Stat.* 886. Slave Trade, Brussels, July 2, 1890.
TS 778; 46 *Stat.* 2183. Slavery, Geneva, September 25, 1926, 60 *LNTS* 253.
TIAS 3532; 7 *UST* 479. Slavery, Amendments to Convention Signed at Geneva, September 25, 1926, New York, December 7, 1953.

South Pacific Commission

TIAS 2317; 2 *UST* 1787. South Pacific Commission, Canberra, February 6, 1947, 97 *UNTS* 227.
TIAS 2458; 3 *UST* 2851. South Pacific Commission, Extending Territorial Scope to Include Guam and the Trust Territory of the Pacific Islands, Canberra, November 7, 1951.
TIAS 2952; 5 *UST* 639. South Pacific Commission, Frequency of Sessions, Canberra, April 5, 1954.

Telecommunications

TS 380, 380-1, 380-2, 380-3; 24 *Stat.* 989; 25 *Stat.* 1424, 1425. Submarine Cables, Paris, March 14, 1884, December 1, 1886, and July 7, 1887.
TS 568; 37 *Stat.* 1565. Wireless Telegraphy Convention, Berlin, November 3, 1906.
TS 581; 37 *Stat.* 1672. Radiotelegraph, London, July 5, 1912, 1 *LNTS* 135.
TS 767; 45 *Stat.* 2760. Radiotelegraph Convention and General Regulations, Washington, November 25, 1927, 84 *LNTS* 97.
TS 767-A. Canada, Radio Communications between Private Experimental Stations, Exchanges of Notes at Washington, October 2 and December 29, 1928, and January 12, 1929, 102 *LNTS* 143.
TS 867; 49 *Stat.* 2391. Telecommunications, Madrid, December 9, 1932, 151 *LNTS* 5.
EAS 62; 48 *Stat.* 1876. Canada, Radio Communications Between Private Experimental Stations and Between Amateur Stations, Continuing the Arrangement Effected by Exchange of Notes Signed October 2, 1928, December 29, 1928, and January 12, 1929, Exchange of Notes at Ottawa, April 23 and May 2 and 4, 1934, 147 *LNTS* 338.

EAS 66; 49 *Stat.* 3555. Peru, Radio Communications Between Amateur Stations on Behalf of Third Parties, Exchange of Notes at Lima, February 16 and May 23, 1934.

EAS 72; 49 *Stat.* 3667. Chile, Radio Communications, Exchange of Notes at Santiago, August 2 and 17, 1934, 157 *LNTS* 15.

TS 948; 54 *Stat.* 1417. Telecommunications, Cairo, April 8, 1938.

TIAS 1518; 60 *Stat.* 1636. Telecommunications, Bermuda, December 4, 1945, 9 *UNTS* 101.

TIAS 1901; 63 *Stat.* 1399. Telecommunication Convention, Final Protocol, and Radio Regulations, Atlantic City, October 2, 1947.

TIAS 2175; 2 *UST* 17. Telecommunications: Telegraph Regulations (Paris Revision, 1949) with Final Protocol, Paris, August 5, 1949.

TIAS 2223; 2 *UST* 683. Liberia, Radio Communications between Amateur Stations on Behalf of Third Parties, Exchange of Notes at Monrovia, November 9, 1950, and January 8, 9, and 10, 1951, 132 *UNTS* 255.

TIAS 2433; 3 *UST* 2672. Ecuador, Radio Communications Between Amateur Stations on Behalf of Third Parties, Exchange of Notes at Quito, March 16, and 17, 1950.

TIAS 2435; 3 *UST* 2686. Telecommunications, Replacing Agreement Signed at Bermuda, December 4, 1945, London, August 12, 1949, 87 *UNTS* 131.

TIAS 2489; 3 *UST* 3064. Telecommunications: Replacing Inter-American Radio Agreement of January 26, 1940, Washington, July 9, 1949, 168 *UNTS* 143.

TIAS 2520; 3 *UST* 3892. Cuba, Exchange of Third-Party Messages between Radio Amateurs, Exchange of Notes at Habana, September 17, 1951, and February 27, 1952.

TIAS 2666; 3 *UST* 4926. Canada, Telecommunications: Promotion of Safety on the Great Lakes by Means of Radio, Ottawa, February 21, 1952.

TIAS 2705; 3 *UST* 5140. Telecommunications, Amending Agreement of August 12, 1949, London, October 1, 1952, 151 *UNTS* 378.

TIAS 3266; 6 *UST* 1213. Telecommunication Convention and Final Protocol, Buenos Aires, December 22, 1952.

TIAS 3617; 7 *UST* 2179. Panama, Radio Communications Between Amateur Stations on Behalf of Third Parties, Exchange of Notes at Panama, July 19 and August 1, 1956.

TIAS 3665; 7 *UST* 2839. Costa Rica, Radio Communications Between Amateur Stations on Behalf of Third Parties, Exchange of Notes at Washington, August 13 and October 19, 1956.

TIAS 3694; 7 *UST* 3159. Nicaragua, Radio Communications Between Amateur Stations on Behalf of Third Parties, Exchange of Notes at Managua, October 8 and 16, 1956.

Trade and Commerce

TS 83; 8 *Stat.* 12; 18(2) *Stat.* 203. France, Amity and Commerce, Paris, February 6, 1778.

TS 85; 8 *Stat.* 178; 18(2) *Stat.* 224. France, Commerce and Navigation, Paris, September 30, 1800.

TS 153; 8 *Stat.* 552; 18(2) *Stat.* 387. Hanover, Commerce and Navigation, Berlin, May 20, 1840.

TS 298; 8 *Stat.* 302; 18(2) *Stat.* 664. Russia, Navigation, Fishing, Trading, St. Petersburg, April 17, 1824.

Traffic in Women and Children

TS 496; 35 *Stat.* 1979. Traffic in Women and Children, Paris, May 18, 1904, 1 *LNTS* 83.

Appendixes

TIAS 2332; 2 *UST* 1997. Suppression of White Slave Traffic, Lake Success, May 4, 1949, 92 *UNTS* 19.

United Nations

TS 993; 59 *Stat.* 1031. United Nations: Charter and Statute of ICJ, San Francisco, June 26, 1945.

Whaling

TS 880; 49 *Stat.* 3079. Whaling, Geneva, September 24, 1931, 155 *LNTS* 349.
TS 933; 52 *Stat.* 1460. Whaling, London, June 8, 1937, 190 *LNTS* 79.
TS 944; 53 *Stat.* 1794. Whaling, London, June 24, 1938, 196 *LNTS* 131.
TIAS 1597; 61 *Stat.* 1213. Whaling, Protocol, London, November 26, 1945, 11 *UNTS* 43.
TIAS 1634; 61 *Stat.* 1240. Whaling, Supplementary Protocol, London, March 3, 1947, 11 *UNTS* 52.
TIAS 1708; 62 *Stat.* 1577. Whaling, Protocol, Washington, December 2, 1946.
TIAS 1849; 62 *Stat.* 1716. Whaling, Washington, December 2, 1946, 161 *UNTS* 72.
TIAS 2092; 1 *UST* 506. Whaling, Amendments to the Schedule, London, May 30–June 7, 1949.
TIAS 2173; 2 *UST* 11. Whaling, Amendments to the Schedule, Oslo, July 21, 1950.
TIAS 2486; 3 *UST* 2999. Whaling, Amendments to the Schedule, Cape Town, July 27, 1951.
TIAS 2699; 3 *UST* 5094. Whaling, Amendments to the Schedule, London, June 6, 1952.
TIAS 2866; 4 *UST* 2179. Whaling, Amendments to the Schedule, London, June 26, 1953.
TIAS 3198; 6 *UST* 645. Whaling, Amendments to the Schedule, Tokyo, July 19–23, 1954.
TIAS 3548; 7 *UST* 657. Whaling, Amendments to the Schedule, Moscow, July 18–23, 1955.
TIAS 3739; 8 *UST* 69. Whaling, Amendments to the Schedule, London, July 16–20, 1956.
TIAS 3944; 8 *UST* 2203. Whaling, Amendments to the Schedule, London, June 24–28, 1957.

Whangpu Conservancy

TS 397. China and Other Powers: Boxer Protocol, Peking, September 7, 1901, 2 Malloy 2006.
TS 448. China and Other Powers: Whangpu Conservancy, Peking, September 27, 1905, 2 Malloy 2013.
China and Other Powers: Whangpu Conservancy Agreement (with Supplementary Article of 1915), Peking, April 9, 1912, 3 Redmond 3043.

BIBLIOGRAPHY

NOTE: Because of the large number of United Nations and United States documents cited, it has been deemed advisable to list separately, by subject matter, those documents of the United Nations and the United States which cannot readily be attributed to individual authors. Otherwise all publications are listed alphabetically by author or issuing agency under Books, Articles, Newspapers, and Other Sources.

United Nations Documents

GENERAL

United Nations Bulletin, 1946–1954.
The Yearbook of the United Nations, 1946–
United Nations Review, 1954–
The United Nations Flag Code and Regulations, As Amended by [the Secretary-General on] November 11, 1952 (1954).
Ten Years of United Nations Publications 1945 to 1955: A Complete Catalogue. Sales No.: 1955.I.8. New York: United Nations, 1955.
Everyman's United Nations 1945–1955. 5th ed. New York: 1956.

ATOMIC RADIATION

General Assembly. *First Yearly Progress Report of the Scientific Committee on the Effects of Atomic Radiation.* A/3365, 17 Nov. 1956. Second Report, A/3659, 31 Oct. 1957. Final Report, A/3838, 1958.

CARTOGRAPHY

ECOSOC. *United Nations Regional Cartographic Conference for Asia and the Far East, 15–25 February 1955, Mussoorie, India. Vol. 1, Report of the Conference.* E/CONF.18/6 (1955).
———. Report of the Secretary General, *International Cooperation in Cartography.* E/2823, 2 Feb. 1956.

LAW OF THE SEA

General Assembly. *Official Records, Eleventh Session, Sixth Committee, Legal Questions, Summary Records, 12 November to 21 December, 1956.* A/C.6/SR.-478–506.
International Law Commission. *Reports,* 1949–. Session I, 1949, A/925; II, 1950, A/1316; III, 1951, A/1358; IV, 1952, A/2163; V, 1953, A/2456; VI, 1954, A/2693; VII, 1955, A/2934; VIII, 1956, A/3159; IX, 1957, A/3623. (Also reprinted regularly in *A.J.I.L.*)
———. *Bibliography on the Regime of the High Seas.* A/CN.4/26, 25 April 1950.
———. *Memorandum on the Regime of the High Seas.* A/CN.4/32, 14 July 1950.
———. *Laws and Regulations on the Regime of the High Seas.* 2 vols. ST/LEG/-SER.B/1 (1951), B/2 (1952).
———. *Laws Concerning the Nationality of Ships.* ST/LEG/SER.B/5 (1956).

Bibliography

———. *Reference Guide to the Articles Concerning the Law of the Sea Adopted by the International Law Commission at its Eighth Session.* (mimeo.) A/C.6/L.378 (1956).

———. *The Right of International Organizations to Sail Vessels under Their Flag.* J. P. A. François, Special Rapporteur. A/CN.4/103 (1956).

———. *Yearbook of the International Law Commission 1956,* Vol. I, *Summary Records of the Eighth Session, 23 April–4 July 1956* (Sales No. 1956.V.3, Vol. I). Vol. II, *Documents of the Eighth Session including Report of the Commission to the General Assembly* (A/CN.4/SER.A/1956/Add.1. Nov. 1956).

———. *Laws and Regulations on the Regime of the Territorial Waters.* ST/LEG/SER.B/6 (1957).

United Nations Conference on the Law of the Sea. *Memorandum Concerning Historic Bays.* A/CONF.13/1, Sept. 20, 1957.

———. *Scientific Considerations Relating to the Continental Shelf.* A/CONF. 13/2, Sept. 30, 1957.

———. *The Economic and Scientific Basis of the Principle of Abstention,* by Richard van Cleve. A/CONF.13/3, Oct. 4, 1957.

———. *Memorandum on Pollution of the Sea by Oil.* A/CONF.13/8, Oct. 29, 1957.

———. *Technical Particulars Concerning the Methods of Fishing Conducted by Means of Equipment Embedded in the Floor of the Sea,* prepared by FAO. A/CONF.13/12, Nov. 6, 1957.

———. *Examination of Living Resources Associated with the Sea Bed of the Continental Shelf with Regard to the Nature and Degree of their Physical and Biological Association with Such Sea Bed,* prepared by FAO. A/CONF.13/13, Nov. 6, 1957.

———. *A Brief Geographical and Hydrological Study of Bays and Estuaries, the Coasts of Which Belong to Different States,* prepared by Commander R. H. Kennedy. A/CONF.13/15, Nov. 13, 1957.

———. *Bibliographical Guide to the Law of the Sea.* A/CONF.13/17, Nov. 21, 1957.

———. *Certain Legal Aspects Concerning the Delimitation of the Territorial Waters of Archipelagos,* by Jens Evensen. A/CONF.13/18, Nov. 29, 1957.

———. *Verbatim Record of the Debate in the Sixth Committee of the General Assembly, at its Eleventh Session, Relating to Item 53(a).* 2 vols. A/CONF.13/19, Dec. 3, 1957.

———. *Guide to Decisions of International Tribunals Relating to the Law of the Sea.* A/CONF.13/22, Dec. 17, 1957.

———. *List in Chronological Order of International Agreements Relating to Fisheries and other Questions Affecting the Utilization and Conservation of the Resources of the Sea.* A/CONF.13/23, Dec. 17, 1957.

———. *Information Submitted by Governments regarding Laws, Decrees and Regulations for the Prevention of Pollution of the Seas.* A/CONF.13/24, Dec. 18, 1957.

———. *Recent Developments in the Technology of Exploiting the Mineral Resources of the Continental Shelf,* prepared by Dr. M. W. Mouton. A/CONF.13/25, Jan. 3, 1958.

———. *Memorandum Concerning the Question of Free Access to the Sea of Land-Locked Countries.* A/CONF.13/29, Jan. 14, 1958. Addendum 1 to same, A/CONF.13/29/Add. 1, March 3, 1958.

———. *Initial List of Documents for the United Nations Conference on the Law of the Sea.* A/CONF.13/33, Feb. 4, 1958.

———. *Roundup of the Conference on the Law of the Sea,* February 24–April 28, 1958. Information Service, European Office of the United Nations, Geneva, Press Release No. L/303.

———. *Convention on the Territorial Sea and the Contiguous Zone.* A/CONF.13/L.52, April 28, 1958; also 38 *DSB* 1111–1115 (1958).

———. *Convention on the High Seas.* A/CONF.13/L.53, April 29, 1958; also 38 *DSB* 1115–1118 (1958).
———. *Convention on Fishing and Conservation of the Living Resources of the High Seas.* A/CONF.13/L.54, April 28, 1958; also 38 *DSB* 1118–1121 (1958).
———. *Convention on the Continental Shelf.* A/CONF.13/L.55, April 28, 1958; also 38 *DSB* 1121–1123 (1958).
———. *Resolutions Adopted by the United Nations Conference on the Law of the Sea.* A/CONF.13/L.56, April 30, 1958; also 38 *DSB* 1124–1125 (1958).
———. *Optional Protocol of Signature Concerning the Compulsory Settlement of Disputes.* A/CONF.13/L.57, April 30, 1958; also 38 *DSB* 1123 (1958).
———. *Final Act of the United Nations Conference on the Law of the Sea* (Geneva, 24 February–27 April 1958). A/CONF.13/L.58, April 30, 1958.

MARITIME MATTERS

ECOSOC. *Report of the Preparatory Committee of Experts to Consider the Coordination of Activities in the Fields of Aviation, Shipping and Telecommunications in Regard to Safety of Life at Sea and in the Air.* E/CONF.4/8, E/CN.2/20. Add. 1, Feb. 19, 1948.
———. *Pollution of the Sea by Oil.* ST/ECA/41 (1956).
———. Transport and Communications Commission. *Coordination of the Activities of Specialized Agencies in the Field of Transport and Communications, Note by the Secretary General.* E/CN.2/178 (1956).
———. Transport and Communications Commission. *Report on its Second Session, Submitted by the Committee of Experts on the Transport of Dangerous Goods.* E/CN.2/165, E/CN.2/CONF.4/1. Oct. 17, 1956.
———. Transport and Communications Commission. *Report of the Eighth Session, 7–16 January 1957.* E/2948, E/CN.2/187 (1957).
Secretariat. *Pollution of the Sea by Oil: Results of an Inquiry made by the United Nations Secretariat.* ST/ECA/41. New York: 1956.
United Nations Maritime Conference, Geneva, 19 February to 6 March, 1948, *Convention of the Intergovernmental Maritime Consultative Organization.* Doc. E/CONF.4/61, March 6, 1948. *Final Act and Related Documents.* UN Pub. 1948.VIII.2.

MINES (NAVAL)

International Court of Justice. *Pleadings, Oral Arguments, Documents, 1949, the Corfu Channel Case.* Vol. I, pp. 54–59.
Security Council. *Official Records.* Second Year, Supplement No. 6, Annex to the record of the 107th Meeting, Feb. 18, 1947, Exhibit III.

NARCOTIC DRUGS

ECOSOC Commission on Narcotic Drugs. *Report of the Fifth Session* (1–15 December 1950). Supplement No. 2 E/1889/Rev.1. E/CN.7/216/Rev.1. 29 Dec. 1950.
———. *Summary of Illicit Transactions and Seizures.* Vol. IX, No. 1, E/NS 1954/Summary 1 (1954); Vol. IX, No. 2, E/NS 1954/Summary 2 (1954).
———. *Memorandum by the International Criminal Police Commission for 1954 on Illicit Traffic.* E/CN.7/293, 17 March 1955.
———. *Report of the Committee on Illicit Traffic.* E/CN.7/L.129, 28 April 1956, and Add.1, 2 May 1956.
———. *Report.* E/2891, E/CN.7/315, 8 June 1956.

RESOURCES

Department of Economics and Social Affairs. *New Sources of Energy and Economic*

Bibliography

Development: Solar Energy, Wind Energy, Tidal Energy, Geothermic Energy and Thermal Energy of the Seas. E/2997/ST/ECA/47, May 1957.
International Technical Conference on the Conservation of the Living Resources of the Sea, Rome, 18 April to 10 May, 1955, Rome, Report. A/CONF.10/6 (1955). Papers Presented at the Conference, A/CONF.10/7 (1956).
United Nations Scientific Conference on the Conservation and Utilization of Resources, 1949, Proceedings, 8 vols. Vol. VII, *Wildlife and Fish Resources* (1951). 1950.II.B.8.E.

SLAVERY

ECOSOC. *The Suppression of Slavery.* ST/SOA/4, 1951.XIV.2, EF. (1951).
———. *Official Records, 17th Session, 30 March–30 April 1954, Annexes, Agenda Item 15, Slavery.* Doc. E/2540 (1954).
———. *Official Records, 19th Session, 29 March–7 April 1955, and 16–27 May 1955, Annexes, Agenda Item 8, Slavery, Report of Rapporteur* [Hans Engen]. Doc. E/2673 (1955).
———. *United Nations Conference of Plenipotentiaries on a Supplementary Convention on the Abolition of Slavery, the Slave Trade, and Institutions and Practices Similar to Slavery.* E/CONF.24/3 (1956).
———. *United Nations Conference of Plenipotentiaries on a Supplementary Convention on the Abolition of Slavery, the Slave Trade, and Institutions and Practices Similar to Slavery Held at Geneva, Switzerland, from 13 August to 4 September 1956: Final Act and Supplementary Convention.* E/CONF.24/23 (1957).

TRUST TERRITORIES

Trusteeship Council. *Report to the Security Council on the Trust Territory of the Pacific Islands Covering the Period from 23 July 1955 to 14 August 1956.* S/3636 (1956) (Mimeo.).

United States Documents

GENERAL

Coast Guard. *The Coast Guard at War: Auxiliary XIX.* Washington: 1948.
———. Public Information Division. *Coast Guard Bibliography,* CG-230. Washington: 1950.
Commerce Department. Coast and Geodetic Survey. *Tide and Current Glossary.* Special Publication No. 228, rev. (1949) ed. Washington: 1949.
———. Coast and Geodetic Survey. *150 Years of Service 1807–1957.* Washington: 1957.
———. *The Journal of the Coast and Geodetic Survey: Sesquicentennial Number,* October 1957, No. 7. Washington: 1957.
Congressional Record. 1873–
Federal Register Division. *Code of Federal Regulations* (1949 ed. revised as of Jan. 1, 1957).
———. *United States Government Organization Manual 1957–1958.* Washington: 1957.
Government Printing Office. *Document Catalog, 1893–1940; Monthly Catalog,* 1895–
———. *Foreign Relations of the United States.* Price List 65, 25th ed. (1944).
House of Representatives. *Survey of Activities of the Committee on Foreign Affairs.* 81 Cong. 1 Sess. 81 Cong., 1 Sess. Committee Print (1949).
Interior Department. *Annual Reports.* 1849–
Navy Department. *Annual Reports.* 1823–
———. *Research Reviews.* Washington: 1953–

The United States and the Treaty Law of the Sea

Senate. *Legislative History of Committee on Foreign Relations, 81 Cong.* 81 Cong., 2 Sess., S. Doc. No. 247 (1950).

———. Committee on Foreign Relations. *Hearings on Japanese Peace Treaty and Other Treaties Relating to Security in the Pacific.* 82 Cong., 2 Sess. (1952).

State Department. *Treaty Series.* 1776–1945, Nos. 1–994.

———. *Foreign Relations.* 1861–

———. *General Index to the Published Volumes of the Diplomatic Correspondence and Foreign Relations of the United States 1861–1899.* Washington: 1902.

———. *Treaty Information Bulletin.* 1929–1939.

———. *Executive Agreement Series.* 1929–1945, Nos. 1–506.

———. *Subject Index of the Treaty Series and Executive Agreement Series, July 1, 1931.* Pub. No. 291. Washington: 1932.

———. *A List of Treaties and Other International Acts of the United States of America in Force December 31, 1932.* In Bulletin of Treaty Information (mimeo.) 1929. Republished as Supplement to *Treaty Information Bulletin* No. 39 (1932).

———. *List of Treaties Submitted to the Senate 1789–1931 Which Have Not Gone Into Effect.* Pub. No. 382. Washington: 1932.

———. *American Delegations to International Conferences, Congresses and Expositions and American Representation on International Institutions and Commissions, With Relevant Data.* Washington: 1932–1941.

———. *List of Treaties Submitted to the Senate 1789–1934.* Pub. No. 765. Washington: 1935.

———. *Department of State Bulletin.* Washington: 1939–

———. *Treaties in Force on December 31, 1941.* Pub. No. 2103. Washington: 1944.

———. *Participation of the United States Government in International Conferences.* Washington: 1945–

———. *Treaties and Other International Acts Series.* 1945–, Nos. 1501–

———. *Treaties Submitted to the Senate 1935–1944.* Pub. No. 2311. Washington: 1945.

———. *International Agencies in which the United States Participates.* Pub. No. 2699. Washington: 1946.

———. *United States Participation in the United Nations: Report by the President to the Congress.* Washington: 1946–

———. *Treaty Developments* (loose-leaf). Pub. No. 2851 (Dec. 1947).

———. *Havana Charter for an International Trade Organization, March 24, 1948, Including a Guide to the Study of the Charter.* Pub. No. 3206. Washington: 1948.

———. *International Organizations in which the United States Participates 1949.* Pub. No. 3655. Washington: 1950.

———. *Science and Foreign Relations.* Pub. No. 3860. Washington: 1950.

———. *United States Treaties and Other International Agreements.* Vol. 1 (1950), beginning with TIAS 2010.

———. *Treaties in Force* (as of) *October 31, 1956.* Pub. No. 6427. Washington: n.d.; (as of) *January 1, 1958.* Pub. No. 6626. Washington: n.d.

Statutes at Large. 1789–

Supreme Court Reports. 1789–

United States Code. 1952 ed.

ARMS AND LIQUOR TRAFFIC

Senate. *Memorial in Regard to the Traffic in Firearms and Intoxicants with Natives of New Hebrides.* 53 Cong., 2 Sess., S. Rept. No. 410 (1894). Also in *Compilation of Reports of Committee on Foreign Relations. U.S. Senate, 1789–1901.* 56 Cong., 2 Sess., S. Doc. No. 231, Part 4, pp. 533–535.

Bibliography

ATOMIC ENERGY

Atomic Energy Commission. *Handling Radioactive Wastes in the Atomic Energy Program.* Washington: 1949.
——. *Radioisotope Uptake in Marine Organisms.* Washington: 1955.
——. *Annotated Bibliography on the Transport and Deposition of Atomic Debris.* By Robert J. List, Weather Bureau, Department of Commerce. TID-3061. Washington: 1956.
——. *Some Effects of Ionizing Radiation on Human Beings, A Report on the Marshallese and Americans Accidentally Exposed to Radiation from Fallout and a Discussion of Radiation Injury in the Human Being.* Washington: 1956.
——. *Semiannual Reports.* 21st., Jan. 1957. Washington: 1957.
——. *Radioactive Contamination of Certain Areas in the Pacific Ocean from Nuclear Tests.* Edited by Gordon M. Dunning. Washington: 1957.

AVIATION

Commerce Department. Bureau of Foreign Commerce. *Foreign and International Aviation: Basic Information Sources.* World Trade Information Service, Part 4, No. 55–7. Washington: 1955.
State Department. *International Civil Aviation Conference, 1944, Final Act and Related Documents.* Pub. No. 2282. Washington: 1945.
——. *Aspects of United States Participation in International Civil Aviation.* Pub. No. 3209. Washington: 1948.
——. *International Civil Aviation.* Reports of the Representative of the United States of America to the International Civil Aviation Organization, 1945–1950. Pub. Nos. 3131, 3629, 3915. Washington: 1948–1950.

BIRDS

Senate. *Importation of Wild-Bird Feathers.* 82 Cong., 2 Sess., S. Rept. No. 1832 (1952).

DEFENSE

Air Force Missile Test Center, Headquarters, Patrick Air Force Base, Florida. *Research and Development: Range Safety Policy for Missiles.* AFMTC Regulation No. 80–9, 13 September 1956 (Mimeo.).
——. *General Range Safety Plan,* January 1957 (Mimeo.).

EROSION

Army Department Corps of Engineers. *Information Circular on Cooperative Studies of Beach Erosion and Federal Participation in Construction of Protective Works.* Washington: 1950.
——. *Beach Erosion Board Publications: Technical Memorandums* (Typewritten, 1955).
——. *Bulletin of the Beach Erosion Board.* Vol. 10, No. 1. Washington: 1956.

EXHIBITIONS AND EXPOSITIONS

Library of Congress Legislative Reference Service. *Expositions Which Have Been Aided by Federal Appropriations 1867–1934.* Expositions T 391, 320860.
——. *Appropriations of the Federal Government for Expositions and Celebrations January 1922 to March 15, 1936.* Expositions T 391, 421079.
Senate. *Message of the President Communicating Information in Respect to the Universal Exhibition at Paris, 1867.* 39 Cong., 2 Sess., S. Ex. Doc. No. 5 (1867).
——. *International Expositions.* 62 Cong., 2 Sess., S. Doc. No. 917 (1912).

The United States and the Treaty Law of the Sea

FISHERIES

Commissioner of Fisheries. *Annual Reports.* 1904–

Fish Commission. *Bulletins.* 1881–

Health, Education, and Welfare Department. Public Health Service. *Selected Bibliography of Publications on Industrial Wastes Relating to Fish and Oysters.* P. H. Bibliography Series No. 10. Washington: 1953.

House of Representatives. *Report of Joint Commissioners, Relative to the Preservation of Fisheries in Waters Contiguous to the United States and Canada, December 31, 1896.* 54 Cong., 2 Sess., H. Doc. No. 315. S.3534.

———. *Report of Commissioner of Fisheries for the Fiscal Year 1905.* 59 Cong., 1 Sess., H. Doc. No. 717 (1906), S. 4989.

———. *Proceedings of the 4th International Congress of [Aquiculture and] Fisheries,* Washington, Sept. 22–26, 1908. 2 vols. 60 Cong., 2 Sess., H. Doc. No. 1571, S.5493. Also in *Fisheries Bureau Bulletin,* 1908, vol. 28, 2 pts.

———. *Message from the President, Protection and Preservation of Food Fishes in International Boundary Waters of the United States and Canada.* 61 Cong., 2 Sess., H. Doc. No. 638 (1910) S.5834.

———. Committee on Merchant Marine and Fisheries. *Hearing on H.R. 9584 to Protect Rights of United States Vessels on the High Seas.* 83 Cong., 2 Sess. (1954).

———. Committee on Merchant Marine and Fisheries. *Hearing on H.R. 9786 to give effect to the International Convention for the High Seas Fisheries of the North Pacific Ocean.* 83 Cong., 2 Sess. (1954).

———. *Report to Accompany H.R. 9786 Giving Effect to the International Convention for the High Seas Fisheries of the North Pacific Ocean.* 83 Cong., 2 Sess. H. Rept. No. 2360 (1954).

———. *Protecting the Rights of Vessels of the United States on the High Seas and in Territorial Waters of Foreign Countries.* 83 Cong., 2 Sess. H. Rept. No. 2449 (1954).

———. Committee on Merchant Marine and Fisheries, Subcommittee on Fisheries and Wildlife Conservation. *Hearing on H.R. 9951 to give Effect to the Convention on Great Lakes Fisheries.* 84 Cong., 2 Sess. (1956).

———. *Giving Effect to the Convention on Great Lakes Fisheries.* 84 Cong., 2 Sess. H. Rept. No. 2154 (1956).

———. *Protecting Rights of United States Vessels on the High Seas.* 85 Cong., 1 Sess., H. Rept. No. 1177 (1957).

Interior Department Fish and Wildlife Service. Research Report No. 32. *Offshore Grounds Important to the United States Haddock Fishery,* by Howard A. Schuck. Washington: 1952.

———. Circular 36. *Fishery Publication Index 1920–1954.* Washington: 1955.

———. Statistical Digest 36. *Fishery Statistics of the United States 1953,* compiled by A. W. Anderson and E. A. Power. Washington: 1956.

———. *Alaska Fishing and Fur-Seal Industries, 1954.* Statistical Digest No. 37 (1956).

Senate. *Message from the President, Sockeye Salmon Fishery Convention.* 66 Cong., 1 Sess., S. Doc. No. 116 (1919). S.7610.

———. Subcommittee of the Committee on Commerce. *Hearing on S. 930, Alaska Fishery Act.* 78 Cong., 2 Sess. (1944).

———. *Assuring Conservation of and to Permit the Fullest Utilization of the Fisheries of Alaska.* 78 Cong., 2 Sess. S. Rept. No. 733 (1944).

———. *Fishery Resources of the United States.* 79 Cong., 1 Sess., S. Doc. No. 51 (1945).

———. *Message from the President. Inter-American Tropical Tuna Commission.* 81 Cong., 1 Sess., S. Ex. P (1949).

———. Subcommittee of the Committee on Foreign Relations. *Hearing on the Fisheries Conventions.* 81 Cong., 1 Sess. (1949).

Bibliography

———. *International Convention for the Northwest Atlantic Fisheries.* 81 Cong., 1 Sess., S. Ex. Rept. No. 10 (1949).
———. *Two Tuna Conventions between the United States and Mexico and Costa Rica.* 81 Cong., 1 Sess., S. Ex. Rept. No. 11 (1949).
———. *Message from the President transmitting the Convention with Canada for Preservation of the Halibut Fishery of the Northern Pacific Ocean and Bering Sea.* 83 Cong., 1 Sess., S. Ex. P (1953).
———. *Convention for the Preservation of the Halibut Fishery of the Northern Pacific Ocean and the Bering Sea.* 83 Cong., 1 Sess., S. Ex. Rept. No. 7 (1953).
———. Subcommittee on Interstate and Foreign Commerce. *Hearing on S. 3713 . . . to give effect to the International Convention for the High Seas Fisheries of the North Pacific Ocean.* 83 Cong., 2 Sess. (1954).
———. *Implementation of the International Convention for the High Seas Fisheries of the North Pacific Ocean.* Report to accompany S.3713. 83 Cong., 2 Sess., S. Rept. No. 1806 (1954).
———. *Protecting the Rights of Vessels of the United States on the High Seas and in Territorial Waters of Foreign Countries.* 83 Cong., 2 Sess., S. Rept. No. 2214 (1954).
———. *Message from the President transmitting A Convention on Great Lakes Fisheries between the United States and Canada.* 84 Cong., 1 Sess. S. Ex. B (1955).
———. Subcommittee of the Committee on Foreign Relations. *Hearing on Great Lakes Fisheries Convention.* 84 Cong., 1 Sess. (1955).
———. *Great Lakes Fisheries Convention.* 84 Cong., 1 Sess., S. Ex. Rept. No. 7 (1955).
———. *Great Lakes Fishery Act of 1956.* 84 Cong., 2 Sess., S. Rept. No. 1858 (1956).
———. *Fisheries Act of 1956.* 84 Cong., 2 Sess., S. Rept. No. 2017 (1956).
———. Committee on Interstate and Foreign Commerce. *Pacific Coast and Alaska Fisheries.* 84 Cong., 2 Sess., S. Rept. No. 2801 (1956).
———. *Enabling Act to Provide for the Implementation of the Pink Salmon Treaty between United States and Canada.* 85 Cong., 1 Sess., S. Rept. No. 302 (1957).
———. *Rights of Vessels of the United States on the High Seas and in the Territorial Waters of Foreign Countries.* 85 Cong., 1 Sess., S. Rept. No. 837 (1957).
State Department. *Santiago Negotiations on Fishery Conservation Problems 1955.* Washington: 1955.
Tariff Commission. *Treaties Affecting the Northeastern Fisheries*, by Charles A. Carter and others. Report No. 152, Second Series. Washington: 1944.

HEALTH

Army Medical Library. *Congresses: Tentative Chronological and Bibliographical Reference List of National and International Meetings of Physicians, Scientists, and Experts.* Washington: 1930.
Naval Medical Research Unit No. 3, Cairo, Egypt, *Report.* Cairo: U.S. Offices of Information and Educational Exchange, 1950.
Senate. *Proceedings of the International Sanitary Conference*, Washington, Jan. 5–March 1, 1881. 47 Cong., 1 Sess., S. Ex. Doc. No. 1 (1881). S.1985.
State Department. *International Health Conference, New York, New York, June 19 to July 22, 1946, Report of the United States Delegation.* Pub. No. 2703.
Surgeon General. *Annual Reports of the Superintending Surgeon General of the Marine Hospital Service.* 1872–

HYDROGRAPHY

Hydrographic Office. Annual *Report*, fiscal year 1924 (1924). Also in Navy Dept. *Reports*, 1924 (1925), pp. 177–235.

―――. *International Code of Signals* (American Edition). H.O. No. 37, 1931 ed. reprinted with changes 1952. Vol. 1, *Visual and Sound Signalling.* Washington: 1952.
―――. *Hydrographic Bulletin.* No. 2553, Aug. 10, 1938.
―――. *Sailing Directions for Antarctica: Including the Off-Lying Islands South of Latitude 60°.* H.O. No. 138. Washington: 1943.
―――. *Information on Hydrographic Office Charts and Publications.* Circular No. 3. Washington: 1956.

LABOR

Labor Bureau. *Bulletins.* 1885–
State Department. *Twenty-Eighth (Maritime) Session of the International Labor Conference, Seattle, Washington, June 6 to June 29, 1946, Report of the United States Government Delegate.* Pub. No. 2854. Washington: 1947.
State, Commerce, and Labor Departments. *Measures to be taken by the Departments of State, Commerce, and Labor to Improve U.S. Participation in the ILO.* (Mimeo.) Feb. 28, 1957.

MARITIME MATTERS

Coast Guard. *The Marion Expedition to Davis Strait and Baffin Bay under Direction of the U.S. Coast Guard.* Bulletin No. 19. *Scientific Results, Part 3,* by Edward H. Smith. Washington: 1931.
―――. *International Ice Observation and Ice Patrol Service in the North Atlantic, Season of 1934.* Bulletin No. 24 (1935).
―――. *Ocean Electronic Navigational Aids.* Revised edition (1949), CG 157. Washington: 1949.
―――. *A Manual for the Safe Handling of Inflammable and Combustible Liquids,* (USCG-174).
Commerce Department. Federal Maritime Board and Maritime Administration. *Annual Reports.* 1950–
―――. Maritime Administration. *Merchant Fleets of the World: September 1, 1939–December 31, 1951.* Washington: 1952.
―――. Bureau of Foreign Commerce. *Shipping Policy, Law, and History: Basic Information Sources.* World Trade Information Service, Part 4, No. 55-11. Washington: 1955.
―――. Maritime Administration. *Review of Vessel Transfer Activities: History and Policies Relating to Transfer of United States Merchant Ships to Foreign Ownership and/or Registry.* Washington: 1957.
House of Representatives. Committee on Merchant Marine and Fisheries. *Hearings on Study of Recreational Boating Safety.* 84 Cong., 2 Sess., Parts 1, 2, 3, June 2–Dec. 7, 1956. Washington: 1956–1957.
―――. *Study of Recreational Boating Safety.* 85 Cong., 1 Sess., H. Rept. No. 378 (1957).
―――. Merchant Marine and Fisheries Committee. *Hearing on Safety of Life at Sea; [Radio Telephone, Bridge-to-Bridge and Bridge-to-Shore Communications].* 85 Cong., 1 Sess., July 31, 1957. Part 2, 85 Cong. 2 Sess., Jan. 17, 1958.
―――. *Safety of Life at Sea.* 85 Cong., 1 Sess., H. Rept. No. 1179 (1957).
―――. *Safety of Life at Sea Study.* 84 Cong., 2 Sess., H. Rept. No. 2969 (1957); and 85 Cong., 2 Sess., H. Rept. No. 1675 (1958).
―――. *Study of Need for Shipboard Automatic Radiotelegraph Call Selectors and Other Such Safety Devices and the Feasibility Thereof.* 85 Cong., 1 Sess., H. Doc. No. 117 (1957).
―――. Committee on Merchant Marine and Fisheries. *Small Boat Safety.* 85 Cong. 2 Sess., H. Rept. No. 1603 (1958).
Inter-American Maritime Conference, Washington, D.C., November 25, 1940, to December 2, 1940, Report of Delegates of United States. Washington: 1941.

Bibliography

Laws Relating to Shipping and Merchant Marine, compiled by Elmer A. Lewis. Washington: 1956.

Naval War College. *International Law Situation and Documents 1956: Situation, Documents and Commentary on Recent Developments in the International Law of the Sea,* by Brunson MacChesney. NAVPERS 15031, Vol. LI. Washington: 1957.

Navigation Bureau. *Reports of the Commissioner of Navigation.* Washington: 1884–

Navy Department Office of Naval Records and Library. Historical Section. Pub. No. 2. *The Northern Barrage and other Mining Activities.* Washington: 1920.

———. Historical Section. Pub. No. 4. *The Northern Barrage: Taking up the Mines.* Washington: 1920.

Senate. *International Marine Conference, Washington, October 16 to December 31, 1889.* 51 Cong., 1 Sess., S. Ex. Doc. No. 53 (1890). Pts. 1, 2, *Protocols of Proceedings,* S.2683 and S.2684. Pt. 3, *Reports of Committees and Report of the United States Delegates to the Secretary of State,* S.2684.

———. *Loss of the Steamship "Titanic": Report of a Formal Investigation into the Circumstances Attending the Foundering on April 15, 1912.* 62 Cong., 2 Sess., S. Doc. No. 933 (1912). S.6179.

———. *Memorial of American Seamen.* 63 Cong., 2 Sess., S. Doc. 452 (1914).

———. *International Conference on Safety of Life at Sea.* 63 Cong., 2 Sess., S. Doc. No. 463 (1914). S.6594.

———. Subcommittee of the Committee on Foreign Relations. *Hearing on Convention for Promoting Safety of Life at Sea.* 72 Cong., 1 Sess. (1932).

———. *Rules to Govern Liability of Vessels when Collisions Occur Between Them. International Convention for Unification, etc., and Protocol.* Signed at Brussels, Sept. 23, 1910. State Department. 75 Cong., 1 Sess., S. Ex. K. (April 29, 1937).

———. Foreign Relations Committee. *International Convention for Unification of Rules to Govern Liability of Vessels in Collision.* 76 Cong., 1 Sess., S. Ex. Rept. No. 4 (June 15, 1939).

———. *Message from the President transmitting a Certified Copy of the International Convention for Safety of Life at Sea, 1948.* 81 Cong., 1 Sess., S. Ex. B (1949).

———. Committee on Interstate and Foreign Commerce. *Implementation of Agreement for Promotion of Safety on Great Lakes by Means of Radio.* 83 Cong., 2 Sess., S. Rept. No. 1747 (1954).

———. Committee on Interstate and Foreign Commerce. *Merchant Marine Training and Education.* 84 Cong., 2 Sess., S. Rept. No. 1465 (1956).

———. *Amendment Recommended to the International Convention for the Safety of Life at Sea.* 85 Cong., 1 Sess., S. Ex. M, and S. Ex. Rept. No. 9 (1957).

State Department. *Oil Pollution of Navigable Waters.* Report to the Secretary of State by the Interdepartmental Committee, March 13, 1926. Washington: 1926.

———. *Preliminary Conference on Oil Pollution of Navigable Waters, Washington, June 8–16, 1926.* Washington: 1926.

———. *Report of Delegation of the United States to International Conference on Safety of Life at Sea, London, 1929.* Pub. No. 14. Washington: 1929.

———. *International Meeting on Marine Radio Aids to Navigation: Proceedings and Related Documents.* Pub. No. 3060. Washington: 1948.

———. *Toward a World Maritime Organization.* Pub. No. 3196. Washington: 1948.

———. *International Conference on Safety of Life at Sea, London, April 23–June 10, 1948, Report of the United States Delegation.* Pub. No. 3282. Washington: 1948.

METEOROLOGY

Weather Bureau. *WB Manual.* Issuance 207, Vol. III, Service Operations. Washington: Oct. 11, 1954.

NARCOTICS

Senate. *Control of Narcotics.* 84 Cong., 2 Sess., S. Rept. No. 2483 (1956).

———. *Laws Controlling Illicit Narcotics Traffic.* 84 Cong., 2 Sess., S. Doc. No. 120 (1956).

War Department. Bureau of Insular Affairs. *Report of the Committee Appointed by the Philippine Commission to Investigate the Use of Opium and the Traffic Therein,* Washington: 1905.

POLAR AFFAIRS, INTERNATIONAL GEOPHYSICAL YEAR

Defense Department. *Arctic Bibliography: Prepared for and in Cooperation with the Department of Defense Under the Direction of the Arctic Institute of North America,* Marie Tremaine, Director and Editor. 6 vols. Washington: 1953–1956.

House of Representatives. *International Polar Congress,* Message from the President, February 16, 1880. 46 Cong., 2 Sess., H. Ex. Doc. No. 41 (1880). S.1922.

———. *Second Polar Year.* 71 Cong., 3 Sess., H. Rept. No. 2700 (1931), S.9327; 72 Cong., 1 Sess., H. Rept. No. 371 (1932), S.9491; H. Doc. No. 282 (1932), S.9549.

———. Committee on Appropriations, Subcommittee on Independent Offices. *Hearings on Report on International Geophysical Year by National Science Foundation.* 85 Cong., 1 Sess. (1957).

———. *International Geophysical Year: The Arctic, Antarctica.* 85 Cong., 2 Sess., H. Rept. No. 1348 (1958).

Navy Department. Office of Naval Research. *Across the Top of the World,* by M. C. Shelesnyak. Washington: 1947.

———. *Antarctica: The Last Frontier, The Annual Report of the Officer in Charge United States Antarctic Programs Fiscal Year 1956.* Washington: 1957.

Senate. *Second Polar Year.* 71 Cong., 3 Sess., S. Doc. No. 270 (1931), S.9347; S. Rept. No. 1774 (1931), S.9323; 72 Cong., 1 Sess., S. Doc. No. 16 (1931), S.9520; S. Rept. No. 162 (1932), S.9487.

———. *International Geophysical Year: A Special Report prepared by the National Academy of Sciences for the Committee on Appropriations of the United States Senate.* 84 Cong., 2 Sess., S. Doc. No. 124 (1956).

POSTAL MATTERS

Postmaster General. Annual *Reports.* 1823–

PRIME MERIDIAN

House of Representatives. *American Prime Meridian.* 31 Cong., 1 Sess., H. Rept. No. 286 (1850), S.584.

———. *Proceedings of the Prime Meridian Conference.* 48 Cong., 2 Sess., H. Ex. Doc. No. 14 (1884), S.2296.

———. *Message from the President urging adoption of resolutions of Prime Meridian Conference.* 50 Cong., 1 Sess., H. Ex. Doc. No. 61 (1888), S.2557.

Senate. *Report* to accompanying H. Res. 209 authorizing calling of *Prime Meridian Conference.* 47 Cong., 1 Sess., S. Rept. No. 840 (1882), S.2007.

———. *Report* to accompany concurrent resolution of Feb. 7, 1885, adopting resolutions of the *Prime Meridian Conference.* 48 Cong., 2 Sess., S. Rept. No. 1188 (1885).

Bibliography

RESOURCES

Federal Security Agency Public Health Service. *Water Pollution in the United States.* Water Pollution Series No. 1, P. H. S. Pub. No. 64. Washington: 1951.
——. *Environment and Health.* P. H. S. Pub. No. 84. Washington: 1951.
House of Representatives. Committee on Interior and Insular Affairs, Subcommittee on Irrigation and Reclamation. *Hearings on Production of Fresh Water from Sea Water.* 82 Cong., 2 Sess., June 19, 20, 22, 1951, and March 11, 1952. Washington: 1952.
Interior Department. Bureau of Mines, Bulletin No. 474, *Coals of Chile,* by A. L. Toenges and others. Washington: 1948.
——. *Demineralization of Saline Waters.* Washington: 1952.
——. Saline Water Conversion Program. Research and Development Progress Report No. 2. *An Investigation of Multiple-Effect Evaporation of Saline Waters from Solar Radiation.* Washington: 1953.
——. Saline Water Conversion Program. Research and Development Report No. 1. *Results of Selected Laboratory Tests of an Ionics Demineralizer.* Washington: 1954.
——. *Saline Water Conversion Report for 1956.* Washington: 1957. *Saline Water . . . for 1957.* Washington: 1958.
President. *Water Resources Law, Report of the President's Water Resources Policy Commission.* 3 vols. Washington: 1950.

ST. LAWRENCE SEAWAY

House of Representatives. *Text of Agreement between United States and Canada Pertaining to St. Lawrence River.* 77 Cong., 1 Sess., H. Doc. No. 153 (1941), S.10598.
Senate. *St. Lawrence Seaway Manual: A Compilation of Documents on the Great Lakes Seaway Project and Correlated Power Development.* 83 Cong., 2 Sess., S. Doc. No. 165 (1955).
——. *Niagara Redevelopment Act of 1956.* 84 Cong., 2 Sess., S. Rept. No. 1408 (1956).
——. Subcommittee of the Committee on Foreign Relations. *Hearings on The Great Lakes Basin.* 84 Cong., 2 Sess. (1956). Statement by Willard B. Cowles, Deputy Legal Adviser of the Department of State, reprinted in 35 *DSB* 421–424 (1956).
State Department. *Great Lakes-St. Lawrence Deep Waterway Treaty.* Pub. No. 347 (1932).

SEALS (FUR)

House of Representatives. *Fur Seal Industry of Alaska.* 63 Cong., 2 Sess., H. Rept. No. 500 (1914), S.6659.
Senate. *The Fur Seals and Other Life of the Pribilof Islands, Alaska, in 1914.* 63 Cong., 3 Sess., S. Doc. No. 980 (1915), S.6774; also as Doc. No. 820 of the Bureau of Fisheries, June 19, 1915.

TELECOMMUNICATIONS

Commerce Department. Radio Division, Annual *Report* of Director, to Secretary of Commerce 1927–1932. (Division transferred to Federal Radio Commission, July 20, 1932).
Federal Communications Commission. *Annual Reports.* 1935–
Federal Radio Commission. Annual *Reports.* 1927–1934.
Federal Trade Commission. *Report on Radio Industry, December 1, 1923.* Washington: 1924.

The United States and the Treaty Law of the Sea

President's Communications Policy Board. Report on *Telecommunications: A Program for Progress.* Washington: 1951.

Senate. *Letter from Secretary of the Navy Recommending Government Control of Wireless Telegraphy, February 13, 1908.* 60 Cong., 1 Sess., S. Doc. No. 256 (1908). S.5264.

———. *Action of War, Navy, and Commerce and Labor Departments on Wireless Telegraph Convention, April 25, 1908.* 60 Cong., 1 Sess., S. Doc. No. 452 (1908). S.5265.

State Department. *International Telecommunications Conferences, Cairo 1938: Report to the Secretary of State by the Chairman of the American Delegation, With Appended Documents.* Pub. No. 1286. Washington: 1939.

TIME

Naval Observatory. *The Naval Observatory Time Service.* Circular No. 14 (1950).

Senate. *Convention for Creation of an International Time Association and By-laws to Govern the Association, Signed at Paris, October 25, 1913.* Department of State. Confidential. 63 Cong., 2 Sess., S. Ex. D (1914).

———. *International Time Association.* 63 Cong., 2 Sess., S. Ex. Rept. to accompany S. Ex. D (1914).

TRAFFIC IN WOMEN AND CHILDREN

Commissioner General of Immigration. Annual *Reports.* 1892–

Senate. *Steerage Conditions: Importation and Harboring of Women for Immoral Purposes.* Vol. 37 of *Reports of the Immigration Commission.* 61 Cong., 3 Sess., S. Doc. No. 753 (1910).

TRUST TERRITORY

State Department. *Report on the Administration of the Territory of the Pacific Islands.* Seventh Annual Report, 1953–1954, Pub. No. 5735 (1955); Eighth, 1954–1955, Pub. No. 6243 (1956); Ninth, 1955–1956, Pub. No. 6457 (1957). By the Department of the Navy 1948 to 1951; by the Department of the Interior 1952 and 1953.

WHALING

Senate. *Message from the President transmitting an International Agreement for the Regulation of Whaling Signed at London on June 8, 1937.* 75 Cong., 1 Sess., S. Ex. U (1937).

———. *Message from the President transmitting Protocol Amending the International Agreement for the Regulation of Whaling.* 76 Cong., 1 Sess., S. Ex. C (1939).

———. *Message from the President transmitting International Agreement for the Regulation of Whaling* (Protocol of Feb. 7, 1944). 78 Cong., 2 Sess., S. Ex. D (1944).

———. *Message from the President transmitting the International Convention for the Regulation of Whaling.* 80 Cong., 1 Sess., S. Ex. L (1947). Reprinted in 16 DSB 772–774 (1947).

———. Subcommittee of the Committee on Interstate and Foreign Commerce. *Hearing on S.2080 to Authorize the Regulation of Whaling and to Give Effect to the International Convention for the Regulation of Whaling.* 81 Cong., 1 Sess., (1949).

———. *Regulation of Whaling.* 81 Cong., 1 Sess., S. Rept. No. 814 (1949).

———. *Message of the President transmitting the Protocol to the International Convention for the Regulation of Whaling.* 85 Cong., 1 Sess., S. Ex. E (1957).

Bibliography

Books, Articles, Newspapers, and Other Sources

"Adoption of International Nautical Mile." *Technical News Bulletin*. Aug. 1954. National Bureau of Standards. Washington: 1954.

"Agreement on Grand Turk Ocean Research Station." 35 *DSB* 922 (1956).

Agresti, Olivia Rossetti. *David Lubin, A Study of Practical Idealism*. 2d ed. Berkeley and Los Angeles: University of California Press, 1941.

Alexander, W. B. *Birds of the Ocean: A Handbook for Voyagers Containing Descriptions of All the Sea-Birds of the World*. New York, London: G. P. Putnam's Sons, The Knickerbocker Press, 1928.

Allen, Edward W. "A New Concept for Fishery Treaties." 46 *A.J.I.L.* 319–323 (1952).

———. "Fish Can Be International." 82 *U.S. Naval Institute Proceedings* 1066–1071 (1956).

American Bureau of Shipping: Seventy-fifth Anniversary, 1862–1937. New York: 1937.

American Cargo War Risk Reinsurance Exchange. Annual *Bulletin* (New York).

American Journal of International Law. Washington: 1907–

American Society of International Law. *Proceedings*. Washington: 1907–

Anderson, Andrew W. "The Indo-Pacific Fisheries Council." 19 *DSB* 12–13 (1948).

"Anglo-American Caribbean Commission." 6 *DSB* 229–230 (1942).

Annals of the American Academy of Political and Social Sciences. 1890–

Annuaire de la vie internationale. 2. series, v. 1–2, 1908/09–1910/11. Bruxelles: Office central des institutions internationales, 1909–1912.

Anson, C. M. "Wabana Iron Ore." Annual Meeting, Canadian Institute of Mining and Metallurgy (1951).

Asher, Robert E., Walter M. Kotschnig, et al. *The United Nations and Promotion of the General Welfare*. The Brookings Institution: Washington, 1957.

Astorquiza, Octavio, and Oscar Galleguillos V. *Cien Años Del Carbon De Lota 1852–1952*. Santiago de Chile: 1952.

Atwood, Wallace W., Jr. "The International Geophysical Year: A Twentieth-Century Achievement in International Cooperation." 35 *DSB* 880–886 (1956).

Aufricht, Hans, *Guide to League of Nations Publications: A Bibliographical Survey of the Work of the League 1920–1947*. New York: Columbia University Press, 1951.

Ayres, Eugene, and Charles A. Scarlott. *Energy Sources — The Wealth of the World*. New York: McGraw-Hill Book Company, Inc., 1952.

Bailes, George Mitcheson. *Modern Mining Practice*. 5 vols. Sheffield, Yorkshire: J. H. Bennett and Co., 1906.

Baldwin, Hanson W. *Sea Fights and Shipwrecks: True Tales of the Seven Seas*. Garden City, N.Y.: Hanover House, 1956.

———. "Ballistic Missiles: What the New Weapons Are and How They Work." *N.Y.T.* (April 29, 1956).

Barringer, J. Paul. "PICAO Conference on North Atlantic Ocean Weather Observation Stations." 15 *DSB* 901–904 (1946).

———. "Revisions in International Telecommunication Convention." 32 *DSB* 442–443 (1955).

Bartlett, Z. W., C. O. Lee, and R. H. Feierabend. "Development and Operation of Sulphur Deposits in the Louisiana Marshes." 4 *Mining Engineering* 803–806 (1952).

Bartley, Ernest R. *The Tidelands Oil Controversy: A Legal and Historical Analysis*. Austin: University of Texas Press, 1953.

Bayitch, Stojan A. *Interamerican Law of Fisheries*. New York: Oceana Publications, 1957.

Becker, Loftus. "Some Political Problems of the Legal Adviser." 38 *DSB* 832–836 (1958).
Benedict, Erastus Cornelius. *The Law of American Admiralty*, 6th ed. by Arnold Whitman Knauth. 7 vols. New York and Albany: M. Bender & Company; New York: Baker Voorhis & Company, 1940–
Benveniste, Guy, and Merritt L. Kastens. "World Symposium on Applied Solar Energy." 123 *Science* 826–831 (1956).
Bemis, Samuel F., and Grace G. Griffin. *Guide to the Diplomatic History of the United States, 1775–1921*. Library of Congress, Washington: 1935.
Berkner, Lloyd V. "Assault on the Secrets of the Earth." *N.Y.T. Magazine* (Jan. 27, 1957).
Bigelow, Henry B. *Oceanography: Its Scope, Problems, and Economic Importance*, Report to the National Academy of Sciences. Boston and New York: Houghton Mifflin Co., 1931.
Bishop, William W., Jr. "Need for a Japanese Fisheries Agreement." 45 *A.J.I.L.* 712–719 (1951).
———. "International Law Commission Draft Articles on Fisheries." 50 *A.J.I.L.* 627–636 (1956).
Black, Richard T. "Telecommunications Policy and the Department of State." 30 *DSB* 83–87 (1954).
"Blending New with Old in Pacific Trust Islands." 1 *United Nations Review* (Oct. 1954) 47–54.
Blyth, J. D. M. "The Polar Regions in Literature." 174 *British Book News* 789–793 (1955).
Bodsworth, Fred. *Last of the Curlews*. New York: Dodd, Mead & Co., 1955.
Boggs, S. W. "National Claims in Adjacent Seas." 41 *Geographical Review* 185–209 (1951).
Bok, Bart J. "Science in International Cooperation." 121 *Science* 843–847 (1955).
Bough, James A. "The Caribbean Commission." 3 *International Organization* 643–655 (1949).
Bradley, Lawrence D., Jr. "Progress on International Safety Measures." 19 *DSB* 119–121 (1948).
Breder, C. M., Jr. *Field Book of Marine Fishes of the Atlantic Coast from Labrador to Texas*. Rev. ed. New York and London: G. P. Putnam's Sons, 1948.
Briggs, Herbert W. *The Law of Nations*. 2nd ed. New York: Appleton-Century-Crofts, 1952.
———. "New Dimensions in International Law." 46 *American Political Science Review* 677–698 (1952).
———. "Official Interest in the Work of the International Law Commission: Replies of Governments to Requests for Information or Comment." 48 *A.J.I.L.* 603–612 (1954).
British Year Book of International Law. 1920/21–
Brown, Agnes M. *Digest of Laws Enacted in the Various States relating to the Possession, Circulation, and Sale of Obscene Literature*. 71 Cong., 2 Sess., S. Doc. No. 54 (1929).
Brown, Harrison, James Bonner, and John Weir. *The Next Hundred Years: Man's Natural and Technological Resources*. New York: The Viking Press, 1957.
Brown, Lloyd Arnold. *The Story of Maps*. Boston: Little, Brown and Company, 1950.
Brown, R. N. Rudmose. *The Polar Regions: A Physical and Economic Geography of the Arctic and Antarctic*. New York: E. P. Dutton and Company, 1927.
Brunauer, Esther C. "International Council of Scientific Unions: Brussels and Cambridge." 13 *DSB* 371–376 (1945).

Bibliography

Bryant, Samuel W. *The Sea and the States: A Maritime History of the American People.* New York: Crowell, 1947.

Burke, William T., and Myres S. McDougal. "Crisis in the Law of the Sea: Community Perspectives Versus National Egoism." 67 *Yale Law Journal* 539–589 (1958).

Cameron, Jenks. *The Bureau of Biological Survey.* Service Monograph No. 54. Baltimore: Johns Hopkins Press, 1929.

Calkins, G. Nathan, Jr. "First Meeting of the Legal Committee of the International Civil Aviation Organization." 18 *DSB* 506–513, 523 (1948).

Canada. *External Affairs.* Monthly Bulletin, 1949–

———, National Research Council. *Method of Removing Ripple Rock.* Prepared by Associate Committee for Navigation Facilities on the West Coast. Ottawa: 31 Aug. 1954.

Canfield, N. L. "Ships Weather Observations: Part 1, Developments up to the 20th Century." 1 *Mariners Weather Log* 157–160 (1957).

Caribbean Commission. *Guide to Commercial Shark Fishing in the Caribbean Area.* Washington: Kaufman Press, Inc., 1945.

———. Central Secretariat, Research Branch. *Year Book of Caribbean Research.* Gainesville, Fla.: University of Florida Press, 1948–

"Caribbean Regional Air Navigational Meeting of PICAO." 15 *DSB* 897–900 (1946).

Carriere, J.-P. "Decapping Ripple Rock." 1 *PW Dispatch* 1–2 (1955).

Carsey, J. B. "Geology of Gulf Coastal Area and Continental Shelf." 34 *Bulletin of the American Association of Geologists* 361–385 (1950).

Carson, Rachel L. *The Sea Around Us.* New York: Oxford University Press, 1951.

Carter, Charles A., and others. *Treaties Affecting the Northeastern Fisheries.* U.S. Tariff Commission, Report No. 152, Second Series. Washington: 1944.

Castleman, Edward. "International Commission for Northwest Atlantic Fisheries: Report on the First Meeting." 24 *DSB* 954–955 (1951).

Cates, John Martin, Jr. "Meeting of International Meteorological Organization: Conference of Directors." 18 *DSB* 43–46 (1948).

———. "United Nations Maritime Conference." 18 *DSB* 495–505, 523 (1948).

Chamberlain, Joseph P. "International Organization." *International Conciliation*, No. 385, December 1942.

"Changed Policy Concerning the Granting of Sovereign Immunity to Foreign Governments." 26 DSB 984–985 (1952).

Chapman, Wilbert McLeod. "United States Policy on High Seas Fisheries." 20 *DSB* 67–71, 80 (1949).

"Chart for all the Oceans." 2 *United Nations Review* (March 1956) 28–35, and (April 1956) 29–35.

Christie, E. W. Hunter. *The Antarctic Problem.* London: Allen & Unwin, 1951.

Clark, Keith. *International Communications: The American Attitude.* New York: Columbia University Press, 1931.

Clarke, Arthur Charles. *The Coast of Coral.* New York: Harper and Brothers, 1955.

Claude, Inis L., Jr. *Swords Into Plowshares: The Problems and Progress of International Organization.* New York: Random House, 1956.

Cochran, J. B. *United States Navy Hydrographic Office: 125th Anniversary.* U.S. Navy Hydrographic Office. Washington: 1955.

Codding, G. A., Jr. *The International Telecommunication Union: An Experiment in International Cooperation.* Leiden: E. J. Brill, 1952.

Coggeshall, I. S. "Submarine Telegraphy in the Post-War Decade." *Transactions of the American Institute of Electrical Engineers* (1930).

Colegrove, Kenneth W. *International Control of Aviation.* Boston: World Peace Foundation, 1930.

Condliffe, J. B., *The Commerce of Nations.* New York: W. W. Norton and Company, 1950.
"Conference on U.S.–Ecuadorian Fishery Relations." 28 *DSB* 759–761 (1953).
"Conservation of Fishery Resources in Northwest Atlantic to be Discussed." 19 *DSB* 669–670 (1948).
"Convention on Aircraft Damage." 28 *DSB* 221–222 (1953).
Corwin, Edward S. *The President: Office and Powers 1787–1948.* 3d. ed. New York: New York University Press, 1948.
Coulter, John Wesley. *The Pacific Dependencies of the United States.* New York: Macmillan Company, 1957.
Council of State Governments. *Interstate Compacts 1783–1956.* (Mimeo.) Chicago: 1956.
Cowie, J. S. *Mines, Minelayers and Minelaying.* London, New York: Oxford University Press, 1949.
Curran, Joseph. *Merchant Marine Policies, Practices, and Problems of Labor, Management and Government. Statement of CIO Maritime Committee before Merchant Marine and Fisheries Committee, House of Representatives.* Washington: July 13, 1955.
Daggett, A. P. "The Regulation of Maritime Fisheries by Treaty." 28 *A.J.I.L.* 693–717 (1934).
"Data on Atomic Radiation Transmitted to U.N. Committee." 35 *DSB* 687–688 (1956).
Davison, Ann. *My Ship Is So Small.* New York: William Sloane Associates, 1956.
Dean, Arthur H. "The Law of the Sea." Statement at the United Nations Conference on the Law of the Sea. 38 *DSB* 574–581 (1958).
———. "U.N. Conference on the Law of the Sea." Closing Statement, April 28. 38 *DSB* 1110–1111 (1958).
De Wolf, Francis Colt. "The International Control of Radiocommunications." 12 *DSB* 133–136 (1945).
———. "Telecommunications Tomorrow." 12 *DSB* 250–252 (1945).
———. "The Atlantic City Telecommunications Conference." 17 *DSB* 1033–1034, 1040–1041 (1947).
De Soto, Clinton B. *Two Hundred Meters and Down: The Story of Amateur Radio.* West Hartford, Conn.: The American Radio Relay League, Inc., 1936.
Dickins, J. "Submarine Coal Mining, Nanaino, Vancouver Island, British Columbia." 38 *Transactions of the Canadian Institute of Mining and Metallurgy* 465–472 (1935).
Dictionary of American Biography. American Council of Learned Societies. 20 vols. New York: C. Scribner's Sons, 1928–1936.
"Difficult Quest for a Uniform Maritime Law: Failure of the Brussels Conventions to Achieve International Agreement on Collision Liability, Liens, and Mortgages." 64 *Yale Law Journal* 878–905 (1955).
Diole, Philippe. *4,000 Years Under the Sea.* New York: J. Messner, 1954.
"Directing Council, Pan American Sanitary Organization." 35 *DSB* 496–497 (1956).
Directory of International Organizations in the Field of Public Administration 1936. Joint Committee on Planning and Cooperation of the International Institute of Administrative Sciences and the International Union of Local Authorities. Brussels: 1936.
"Discussions Asked on Territorial Problems." 19 *DSB* 301 (1948).
Donahue, Ruth S. "'Point 4' and Its Relation to Existing Technical Assistance Programs." 20 *DSB* 211–214 (1949).
Douglas, John Scott. *The Story of the Oceans.* New York: Dodd Mead and Co., 1952.
Dugan, James. *Man Under the Sea.* New York: Harper, 1956.

Bibliography

Dulles, John Foster. "The Making of Treaties and Executive Agreements." 28 *DSB* 591–595 (1953).

Dunlop, Henry A. "Management of the Halibut Fishery of the North-Eastern Pacific Ocean and Bering Sea." *Papers Presented at the International Technical Conference on the Conservation of the Living Resources of the Sea.* Rome, 1955. A/CONF.10/7 (1956), pp. 222–242.

Egyptian Gazette, Cairo.

Eisenhower, Milton. "The First Ten Years of the World Health Organization." Address, 38 *DSB* 987–992 (1958).

Encyclopaedia Britannica. Editions 1947, 1952. Chicago: University of Chicago.

Evans, Stephen H. *The United States Coast Guard 1790–1915: A Definitive History.* Annapolis: United States Naval Institute, 1949.

Farrington, S. Kip, Jr. *Pacific Game Fishing.* New York: Coward-McCann, Inc., 1942.

———. *Fishing the Atlantic, Offshore and On.* New York: Coward-McCann, Inc., 1949.

Financial Times (London).

Finch, George A. "The Need to Restrain the Treaty-Making Power of the United States within Constitutional Limits." 48 *A.J.I.L.* 57–82 (1954).

"First Progress Report on the International Map of the World on the Millionth Scale (1954)." 4 *World Cartography* 1–59 (1956) ST/SOA/SER.L/4.

"Fisheries Commission Meeting." 30 *DSB* 165 (1954).

"Fisheries Commission Selects Headquarters." 30 *DSB* 327 (1954).

"Fisheries Convention Signed by U.S., Canada, Japan." 26 *DSB* 830 (1952).

Food and Agriculture Organization. Interim Commission. *Five Technical Reports on Food and Agriculture.* Washington: 1945.

———. *Report of the Director-General, The Work of FAO 1950–1951.* Rome: 1951. *Report . . . 1954–1955.* Rome: 1955.

———. *The State of Food and Agriculture 1955: Review of a Decade and Outlook.* Rome: 1955.

———. *Yearbook of Fishery Statistics 1952–1953.* Vol. IV, Part 1, *Production and Craft.* Rome: 1955.

———. *Electrical Fishing,* by P. F. Meyer-Waarden. FAO Fisheries Study No. 7. Rome: 1957.

"Foreign Scientists to Study U.S. Solar Energy Projects." 33 *DSB* 836 (1955).

Frankcom, C. E. N. "The Merchant Seaman as a Meteorologist." *Marine Observer*, Vol. xix, No. 143 (Jan. 1949).

———. "Selected Ships." *Meteorological Magazine*, Vol. 82, No. 971 (May 1953).

———. "Radio Weather Messages from Ships: Their Practical Value." 3 *WMO Bulletin* 80–86 (1954).

Garcia Sayan, Enrique. *Notas sobre Soberania Maritime de Peru: Defensa de las 200 millas de mar peruano ante las recientes transgressions.* Lima, 1955.

Gardner, W. Z. "The Story of Mystic Seaport and the Marine Historical Association, Inc., Mystic, Connecticut." New York: *The Ships' Bulletin*, Nov.–Dec., 1955.

Gedye, N. G. "Coast Protection and Land Reclamation." *Encyclopaedia Britannica* (1947), Vol. 5, pp. 922–928.

Geneva Research Center. "The United States and World Organization During 1936." *International Conciliation* No. 331 (1937); for 1937, No. 341 (1938); for 1938, No. 352 (1939); for 1939, No. 361 (1940).

Gidel, Gilbert. *Le Droit International Public de La Mer.* 3 vols. Chateauroux: Mellottée, 1932–1934.

Gillespie, G. J. "Canada's Atlantic Sealfishery: Halifax Now Main Centre." *Trade News* (Department of Fisheries of Canada), Vol. 10, No. 8, pp. 7–8, Feb. 1958.

Goodrich, Leland M., and Edvard Hambro. *Charter of the United Nations: Commentary and Documents.* 2d ed. Boston: World Peace Foundation, 1949.

Gray, Francis W., and R. Heath Gray. "The Sydney Coalfield." 44 *Transactions of the Canadian Institute of Mining Engineers* 289–330 (1941).

Greeley, Adolphus W. *International Polar Expedition. Report of the Proceedings of the U.S. Expedition to Lady Franklin Bay, Grinnell Land.* 49 Cong., 1 Sess., H. Misc. Doc. No. 393, 2 vols. Washington: 1888.

Gregory, H. E., and K. Barnes. *North Pacific Fisheries: With Special Reference to Alaska Salmon.* San Francisco, New York, Honolulu: American Council, Institute of Pacific Relations, 1939.

Gregory, Winifred, ed. *International Congresses and Conferences 1840–1937.* New York: The H. W. Wilson Company, 1938.

Griscom, Lloyd C. *Diplomatically Speaking.* New York: The Literary Guild of America, Inc., 1940.

Gwyther, John Michael. *Captain Cook and the South Pacific: The Voyage of the "Endeavour" 1768–1771.* Boston: Houghton Mifflin, 1955.

Hackworth, Green H. *A Digest of International Law,* 8 vols. Washington: G.P.O., 1940–1944.

Hambidge, Gove. *The Story of FAO.* New York: Van Nostrand, 1955.

Hampton, Brock C. "International Health Organizations." U.S.P.H.S., *Public Health Reports,* Vol. 40, No. 34, Aug. 21, 1925, pp. 1719–1732.

Harvard Research in International Law. *Rights and Duties of Neutral States in Naval Warfare.* 33 A.J.I.L. No. 3 Supp. 750–756 (1939).

Hasse, Adelaide R. *Index to United States Documents Relating to Foreign Affairs 1828–1861.* 3 vols. Washington: Carnegie Institution of Washington, 1914–1921.

Hayden, Sherman Strong. *The International Protection of Wild Life: An Examination of Treaties and other Agreements for the Preservation of Birds and Mammals.* New York: Columbia University Press, 1942.

Heiser, Victor George. *An American Doctor's Odyssey: Adventures in Forty-Five Countries.* New York: W. W. Norton and Company, Inc., 1936.

Henderson, Daniel MacIntyre. *The Hidden Coasts: A Biography of Charles Wilkes.* New York: Sloane, 1953.

Henderson, Junius, *The Practical Value of Birds.* New York: Macmillan Company, 1934.

Henry, Thomas R. *The White Continent: The Story of Antarctica.* New York: Wm. Sloane Associates, 1950.

Herrington, William C. "Problems Affecting North Pacific Fisheries: Tripartite Fisheries Conference at Tokyo, Nov. 4–December 14, 1951." 26 *DSB* 340–346 (1952).

———. "U.S. Policy on Fisheries and Territorial Waters." 26 *DSB* 1021–1023 (1952).

Hershey, Amos S. *The Essentials of International Public Law and Organization.* Rev. ed. New York: Macmillan Company, 1927.

Hexner, Ervin and Adelaide Harvey Walters. *International Cartels.* Chapel Hill: University of North Carolina Press, 1945.

Heyerdahl, Thor. *Kon-Tiki: Across the Pacific by Raft.* Chicago, New York, San Francisco: Rand McNally and Company, 1950.

Hickling, H. G. A. "Undersea Coalfield Extension: Prospects in the North-East." 180 *Colliery Guardian* 267–271 (1950).

Higgins and Colombos. *The International Law of the Sea.* 2d rev. ed., by C. John Colombos. London, N.Y., Toronto: Longmans, Green and Co., 1951.

Hill, J. Douglas, and Richard S. Ladd. *Treasure Maps in the Library of Congress: An Annotated List.* Library of Congress. Washington: 1955.

Hobson, Asher. *The International Institute of Agriculture.* Berkeley, Calif.: University of California Press, 1931.

Bibliography

Hogan, John C. "The Legal Terminology for the Upper Regions of the Atmosphere and for the Space Beyond the Atmosphere." 51 *A.J.I.L.* 362–375 (1957).

Hogan, Willard N. "Alternative to Atlantic Union." 38 *Bulletin of the American Association of University Professors* 304–311 (1952).

Hohman, Elmo Paul. "Maritime Labour in the United States: I: The Seamen's Act and its Historical Background." 38 *International Labour Review* 190–218 (1938).

———. ". . . II: Since the Seamen's Act". 38 *International Labour Review* 376–403 (1938).

———. *Seamen Ashore*. New Haven, Conn.: Yale University Press, 1952.

———. "Merchant Seamen in the United States, 1937–1952." 47 *International Labour Review* 1–43 (1953).

———. *History of American Seamen*. Hamden, Conn.: Shoe String Press, 1956.

Holcombe, Arthur N. *Strengthening the United Nations: Commission to Study the Organization of Peace*. New York: Harper & Bros., 1957.

Hornell, James. *The Sacred Chank of India*. Madras: Printed by the Superintendent, Government Press, 1914.

Howard, Gerald V., and Eileen R. Godfrey. *Fishery Research and Educational Institutions in North and South America*. Food and Agriculture Organization. Washington: 1950.

Hubbard, L. S. "Increasing the Safety of the World's Shipping: The Sixth International Hydrographic Conference." 27 *DSB* 68–70 (1952).

Hubbard, Ursula P. "The Cooperation of the United States with the League of Nations and with the International Labour Organization." *International Conciliation*, No. 274 (1931).

———. "The Cooperation of the United States with the League of Nations, 1931–1936." *International Conciliation*, No. 329 (1937).

Hudson, Manley O. "Aviation and International Law." 24 *A.J.I.L.* 228–240 (1930).

———. *International Legislation: A Collection of the Texts of Multipartite International Instruments of General Interest, Beginning with the Covenant of the League of Nations*. 9 vols. (Vols. VIII and IX with the collaboration of Louis B. Sohn.) Washington: Carnegie Endowment for International Peace, 1931–1950.

Hunt, Harry E. "How the Great Lakes Became 'High Seas' and Their Status Viewed from the Standpoint of International Law." 4 *A.J.I.L.* 285–313 (1910).

Hutchins, J. G. B. "One Hundred and Fifty Years of American Navigation Policy." 53 *Quarterly Journal of Economics* 238–260 (1939).

Hyde, Charles Cheney. *International Law Chiefly as Interpreted and Applied by the United States*. 3 vols. 2 rev. ed. Boston: Little, Brown, 1945.

Hyde, H. Van Zile. "The International Health Conference." 15 *DSB* 453–454, 459 (1946).

———. "Challenges and Opportunities in World Health: The First World Health Assembly." 19 *DSB* 391–398 (1948).

"Illicit Traffic in Narcotics Throughout the World." 3 [United Nations] *Bulletin on Narcotics* 1–14 (1951).

"Indo-Pacific Fisheries." 24 *DSB* 234 (1951).

Industry and Labour. I.L.O., Geneva, 1949–

Innis, Harold A. *The Cod Fisheries: The History of an International Economy*. New Haven: Yale University Press, 1940.

Inter-American Specialized Conference. "Conservation of Natural Resources: The Continental Shelf and Marine Waters." *Background Material on the Scientific and Economic Aspects of the Continental Shelf and Marine Waters*. Washington: Pan American Union, 1956.

Inter-American Tropical Tuna Commission, Report for the Year 1955. La Jolla, California: 1956.

"International Astronomical Union." 27 *DSB* 462 (1952).

International Board of Inquiry for the Great Lakes Fisheries: Report and Supplement (June 1942). Washington: G.P.O., 1943.
"International Civil Aviation Organization." 18 DSB 463, 465 (1948).
International Civil Aviation Organization. *Report on the Second Conference on ICAO North Atlantic Ocean Stations*, Doc. 7040JS/551. Montreal: 1949.
International Conciliation. New York: 1907–
"International Conference on the Status of Tangier." 35 DSB 841–844 (1956).
International Game Fish Association: Yearbook 1952. New York: 1952.
"International Health Security in the Modern World: The Sanitary Conventions and the World Health Organization." 17 DSB 953–958 (1947).
International Labor Organization. "The Twenty-Sixth Session of the International Labor Conference, Philadelphia, April to May 1944." Reprinted from *International Labour Review*, Vol. L, No. 1, July 1944.
———. *International Labour Conference, Twenty-Eighth Session, Seattle, 1946, Record of Proceedings.* Geneva: 1947.
———. *Conditions in Ships Flying the Panama Flag.* Geneva: 1950.
———. Library, Bibliographical Contributions No. 5, *Catalog of Publications in English of the International Labour Office 1919–1950*. Geneva: 1951.
———. *Lasting Peace the I.L.O. Way: The Story of the International Labour Organization.* Geneva: 1951.
———. *Fifth Report of the International Labour Organization to the United Nations.* Geneva: 1951.
———. *Conditions of Work in the Fishing Industry.* Geneva: 1952.
———. *Report of the Director-General.* International Labor Conference, 41st [Maritime] Session, 1958. Geneva: 1957.
"International Meteorological Organization: Opening Session of Conference of Directors." 17 DSB 678–679 (1947).
International Organization. Boston: 1947–
International Passamaquoddy Engineering Board. *Report to International Joint Commission on Scope and Cost of an Investigation of Passamaquoddy Tidal Power Project.* Ottawa, Ontario, Washington: March 1950.
"International Passamaquoddy Tidal Power Project." 23 DSB 1021–1022 (1950).
"International Travel and Disease Control." 3 *United Nations Review* (March 1957) 53–55.
"Islanders Appeal to United Nations on Bomb Tests in Pacific Trust Area," 1 *United Nations Review* (Sept. 1954) 14–16.
"Issues before the Eleventh General Assembly." *Int. Con.* No. 510 (1956).
Japan, Ministry of Foreign Affairs. (Minutes of the) *Tripartite Fisheries Conference, Canada-Japan-United States, November 5–December 14, 1951.* Tokyo: 1951.
Jessup, Philip C. *The Law of Territorial Waters and Maritime Jurisdiction.* New York: G. A. Jennings Company, Inc., 1927.
———. *L'Exploitation des Richesses de la Mer.* Academie de Droit International, The Hague, 1929.
———. "The Anti-Smuggling Act of 1935." 31 *A.J.I.L.* 101–106 (1937).
———. "The International Law Commission's 1954 Report on the Regime of the Territorial Sea." 49 *A.J.I.L.* 221–229 (1955).
———. *Transnational Law.* New Haven: Yale University Press, 1956.
Johnson, Douglas Wilson. *Shore Processes and Shoreline Development.* 1st ed. New York: John Wiley and Sons, 1919.
Jones, Sir Harold Spencer. "The Determination of Precise Time." *Smithsonian Report 1949*, pp. 189–202, Pub. No. 4000.
Keesing, Felix M. "The South Pacific Commission Makes Progress." 21 DSB 839–843 (1949).

Bibliography

———. "The South Pacific Commission: The First Ten Years." 37 *DSB* 422–430 (1957).

Kelchner, Warren. *Inter-American Conferences 1826–1933: Chronological and Classified Lists.* Department of State Pub. No. 499 (1933).

Kellogg, Remington. "The International Whaling Commission." *Papers Presented at the International Technical Conference on the Conservation of the Living Resources of the Sea.* Rome, 1955, A/CONF.10/7 (1956), pp. 256–261.

Kelly, Helen G. "The Bermuda Telecommunications Conference." 14 *DSB* 59–61 (1946).

Kempff, Clarence S. "Ship Lanes of the North Atlantic." *Encyclopaedia Britannica*, Vol. 20, pp. 539–540 (1947).

Kenyon, Karl W., Victor B. Scheffer, and Douglas G. Chapman. *A Population Study of the Alaska Fur-Seal Herd.* Special Scientific Report Wildlife No. 12, Department of the Interior. Washington: 1954.

Kerchove, René de. *International Maritime Dictionary.* Toronto, New York, London: D. Van Nostrand Company, Inc., 1948.

Knapp, David G. *Arctic Aspects of Geomagnetism.* U.S. Navy, OPNAV PO3-10. Washington: 1956.

Kotschnig, Walter. "U.S. Position on Proposed Slavery Convention." 35 *DSB* 561–562 (1956).

Krains, Hubert. *L'Union Postale Universelle: Sa Fondation et Son Developpement.* Einsiedeln, Suisse, Publié par le bureau international, 1924.

Kunz, Josef L. "Continental Shelf and International Law: Confusion and Abuse." 50 *A.J.I.L.* 828–853 (1956).

Ladas, Stephen P. *The International Protection of Industrial Property.* Cambridge, Mass.: Harvard University Press, 1930.

La Gorce, John Oliver. *The Book of Fishes.* Rev. and enlarged ed. Washington: National Geographic Society, 1939.

Lambert, W. D. "Geodesy." *Encyclopaedia Britannica* (1952), Vol. 10, pp. 127–134.

Landsberg, Helmut E. "International Cooperation in Climatology: Second Session of Commission for Climatology of WMO." 36 *DSB* 612–614 (1957).

Lapp, Ralph E. *Atoms and People.* New York: Harper and Brothers, 1956.

Latchford, Stephen. "Coordination of CITEJA with the New International Civil Aviation Organization." 12 *DSB* 310–313 (1945).

———. "Comparison of the Chicago Aviation Convention with the Paris and Habana Conventions." 12 *DSB* 411–420 (1945).

———. "Pending Projects of the International Technical Committee of Aerial Legal Experts." 40 *A.J.I.L.* 280–302 (1946).

———. "CITEJA and the Legal Committee of ICAO." 17 *DSB* 487–497 (1947).

Latil, Pierre de, and Jean Rivoire. *Man and the Underwater World.* New York: Putnam, 1956.

"Law Commission Asked to Submit Final Report on High Seas Problem." 32 *DSB* 62–64 (1955).

League of Nations. "Report on the Exploitation of the Products of the Sea," by M. José León Suárez to the Committee of Experts, Dec. 8, 1925. 20 *A.J.I.L. Special Number*, July 1926, pp. 231–241.

———. "Report of the Sub-Committee of the Committee of Experts for the Progressive Codification of International Law on Territorial Waters," Jan. 29, 1926. 20 *A.J.I.L. Special Number*, July 1926, pp. 62–147.

———. *Report of the Special Body of Experts on the Traffic in Women and Children.* Pts. I and II, C.52.1927.IV, Feb. 1927.

———. Committee of Experts for the Progressive Codification of International Law. "Report to the Council of the League of Nations on the Procedure to be followed in Regard to the Question of the Exploitation of the Products of the Sea," April 2, 1927. 22 *A.J.I.L. Spec. Supp.*, Jan. 1948, pp. 44–45.

———. Organization for Communications and Transit. *Report of Small Committee.* C.128.M.67.VIII. March 26, 1936.

———. *Handbook of International Organizations.* Geneva: 1938.

Leonard, L. Larry. *International Regulation of Fisheries.* Washington: Carnegie Endowment for International Peace, 1944.

Lewis, Charles Lee. *Matthew Fontaine Maury: The Pathfinder of the Seas.* Annapolis: United States Naval Institute, 1927.

Lewis, Elmer A. *Laws Relating to Shipping and Merchant Marine.* Washington: 1956.

Liang, Yuen-li. "Documents on the Development and Codification of International Law." 41 *A.J.I.L.* Supp. 29–147 (1947).

———. "The Use of the Term 'Acceptance' in United Nations Treaty Procedure." 44 *A.J.I.L.* 342–349 (1950).

———. "The First Session of the International Law Commission: Review of Its Work by the General Assembly." 44 *A.J.I.L.* 527–542 (1950); Second Session, 45 *A.J.I.L.* 509–525 (1951); Third Session, 46 *A.J.I.L.* 483–503 (1952); Fifth Session, 48 *A.J.I.L.* 579–591 (1954).

Lindgren, Waldemar. *Mineral Deposits.* 3d ed. New York: McGraw-Hill Book Company, Inc., 1928.

Lissitzyn, Oliver J. *International Air Transport and National Policy.* New York: Council on Foreign Relations, 1942.

Lister, Ernest A. "The North Atlantic Ocean Stations Agreement." 30 *DSB* 792–795 (1954).

Little, Delbert M. "Meteorological Services for International Air Navigation." 23 *DSB* 236–237 (1950).

———. "Weather Services for International Civil Aviation." 31 *DSB* 824–827 (1954).

Lloyd, B. J. "Pan American Cooperation in Public Health Work." 66 *Bulletin, Pan American Union* 248 (1932).

Lloyd's Register of American Yachts: A List of the Power and Sailing Yachts, Yacht Clubs, and Yachtsmen of the United States, the Dominion of Canada, and the West Indies; and the American Yachting Trade Directory. New York: Lloyd's Register of Shipping, 1952.

Lloyd's Weekly Casualty Reports. Vol. CXLVI, No. 12, Dec. 24, 1956 (London).

Lord, Mrs. Oswald B. "New U.S. Action Program for Human Rights." 29 *DSB* 215–222 (1953).

Lord, Walter. *A Night to Remember.* New York: Henry Holt and Company, 1955.

Low, A. M. *Mine and Countermine.* New York: Sheridan House, 1940.

McAtee, Waldo Lee. *Wildlife of the Atlantic Coast Salt Marshes.* Department of Agriculture, Circular No. 520. Washington: 1939.

MacChesney, Brunson. *International Law Situation and Documents 1956: Situation, Documents and Commentary on Recent Developments in the International Law of the Sea.* U.S. Naval War College, NAVPERS 15031, Vol. LI. Washington: 1957.

McCracken, Harold. *Hunters of the Stormy Sea.* New York: Doubleday and Company, 1957.

McDonald, Eula. "Toward a World Maritime Organization." 18 *DSB* 99–107, 115, 131–137 (1948).

McDonald, W. F. "International Cooperation in Reporting Weather Observations from the High Seas: Second Session of Commission for Maritime Meteorology of World Meteorological Organization, Hamburg, Germany, Oct. 16–31, 1956." 37 *DSB* 164–166 (1957).

Bibliography

McDougall, Frank L. "Food and Population." *International Conciliation*, No. 486 (Dec. 1952).

McDougal, Myres S. "The Hydrogen Bomb Tests and the International Law of the Sea." 49 *A.J.I.L.* 356–361 (1955).

———, and William T. Burke. "Crisis in the Law of the Sea: Community Perspectives Versus National Egoism." 67 *Yale Law Journal* 539–589 (1958).

———, and Norbert A. Schlei. "The Hydrogen Bomb Tests in Perspective: Lawful Measures for Security." 64 *Yale Law Journal* 648–710 (1955).

McFee, William. *The Law of the Sea*. New York: J. B. Lippincott Co., 1950.

McLaren, R. S. "Undersea Mining off the North-East Durham Coast." 165 *Iron and Coal Trades Review* 301–309 (1952).

Malloy, William M. *Treaties, Conventions, International Acts, Protocols and Agreements Between the United States of America and Other Powers, 1776–1909*. 2 vols., 61 Cong., 2 Sess., S. Doc. No. 357 (1910).

Mance, Osborne. *International Road Transport, Postal, Electricity and Miscellaneous Questions*. London, New York, Toronto: Oxford University Press, 1947.

———, and J. E. Wheeler. *International Air Transport*. London, New York, Toronto: Oxford University Press, 1943.

———. *International Telecommunications*. London, New York, Toronto: Oxford University Press, 1944.

———. *International River and Canal Transport*. London, New York, Toronto: Oxford University Press, 1945.

———. *International Sea Transport*. London, New York, Toronto: Oxford University Press, 1945.

Mann, John W. "The Conference on Tonnage Measurement of Ships, Stockholm, June 2–10, 1950." 23 *DSB* 471–474 (1950).

———. "The Problem of Sea Water Pollution." 29 *DSB* 775–780 (1953).

"Maps and their Role in World Development." 1 *United Nations Review* (Oct. 1954) 26–29.

Marabuto, Paul. "The International Criminal Police Commission and the Illicit Traffic of Narcotics," 3 [United Nations] *Bulletin on Narcotics* 3–15 (1951).

Margolis, Emanuel. "The Hydrogen Bomb Experiments and International Law." 64 *Yale Law Journal* 629–647 (1955).

"Maritime Conventions Signed at Brussels Conference." 37 *DSB* 759–764 (1957).

Marmer, H. A. "Matthew F. Maury." *Dictionary of American Biography*, Vol. 12, pp. 428–431.

"Marshall Islanders' Petition to Trusteeship Council." 31 *DSB* 137–140 (1954).

Marx, Daniel, Jr. "International Organization of Shipping." 55 *Yale Law Journal* 1214–1232 (1946).

———. *International Shipping Cartels: A Study of Industrial Self-Regulation by Shipping Conferences*. Princeton, New Jersey: Princeton University Press, 1953.

Masters, Ruth D. *Handbook of International Organizations in the Americas*. Washington: Carnegie Endowment for International Peace, 1945.

Maxim, Hiram Percy. "The Amateur in Radio." 142 *Annals of the American Academy of Political and Social Sciences, Supplement* 32–35 (1929).

"Mecca Airlift." 27 *DSB* 406 (1952).

"Meeting of Tonnage Measurement Experts." 26 *DSB* 997 (1952).

Mendenhall, T. C. "Legislation Relating to Standards." 4 *Science* 1–8 (1896).

Merrien, Jean. *Lonely Voyagers*. New York: G. P. Putnam's Sons, 1954.

Midkiff, Frank E. "U.S. Administration of the Trust Territory of the Pacific Islands." 31 *DSB* 96–109 (1954).

———. "Problems of the Pacific Trust Territory," 31 *DSB* 141–145 (1954).

Miller, Hunter. *Treaties and Other International Acts of the United States of America, 1776–1863*. 8 vols. Washington: G. P. O., 1931–1948.

"Mines (Naval), Minelaying and Minesweeping." *Encyclopaedia Britannica* (1952), Vol. 15, pp. 533–538.

"Mining Under the Ocean." *Financial Times* (London), July 3, 1953.

Moor, Carol Carter, and Waldo Chamberlain. *How To Use United Nations Documents.* New York: New York University Press, 1952.

Moore, John Bassett. *A Digest of International Law.* 8 vols. Washington: G. P. O., 1906.

Moore, W. G. *Dictionary of Geography.* Harmondsworth, Middlesex: Penguin Books, 1952.

Morgan, James Morris. *Recollections of a Rebel Reefer.* Boston and New York: Houghton Mifflin Company, 1917.

Mouton, Martinus Willem. *The Continental Shelf.* The Hague: Martinus Nijhoff, 1952.

Murphy, Robert Cushman. *Oceanic Birds of South America.* 2 vols. New York: Macmillan Company, American Museum of Natural History, 1936.

Myers, Denys P. *Handbook of the League of Nations.* Boston: World Peace Foundation, 1935.

———. *The Paris Peace Conference 1919.* Vol. XIII, being annotations to the Treaty of Versailles, *Foreign Relations of the United States.* Washington: 1947.

———. "Liquidation of League of Nations Functions." 42 *A.J.I.L.* 320–354 (1948).

Myers, George S. "Usage of Anadromous, Catadromous, and Allied Terms for Migratory Fishes." *Copeia,* No. 2, June 30, 1949.

"Narcotic Drug Control: Development of International Action and the Establishment of Supervision under the United Nations." Introduction by Herbert L. May. *International Conciliation,* No. 441 (1948).

"Narcotic Drug Control." *International Conciliation,* No. 485 (1952).

National Academy of Sciences. National Research Council. *The Biological Effects of Atomic Radiation: A Report to the Public.* Washington: 1956.

———. *The Biological Effects of Atomic Radiation: Summary Reports.* Washington: 1956.

———. *The Effects of Atomic Radiation on Oceanography and Fisheries.* Pub. No. 551. Washington: 1957.

National Maritime Union. *This is the NMU: A Picture History of the National Maritime Union.* Produced by the William P. Gottlieb Co., New York, ca. 1955.

Nature (London). 1869–

"Naval and Air Bases." 3 *DSB* 199–207 (1940).

New York City, Department of Public Works, Division of Sewage Disposal. *Bibliography on Sewage Disposal in New York City* 1929–May 1, 1949 (Mimeo., 1949).

———. *Sewage Treatment in New York City* (Leaflet, 1950).

New York, State of. *Report of the Joint Legislative Committee on Motor Boats.* Legislative Document (1956) No. 17; *Report* . . . (1957), No. 16 (Albany, New York).

New York Times.

Nielson, Fred K. "The Lack of Uniformity in the Law and Practice of States in Regard to Merchant Vessels." 13 *A.J.I.L.* 1–21 (1919).

North American Yacht Racing Union. *Report of the Annual General Meeting 1953.* Bulletin No. 69. New York: 1953.

"North Pacific Fisheries." 25 *DSB* 789 (1951).

"Northwest Atlantic Fisheries." 24 *DSB* 595–596 (1951).

"Northwest Atlantic Fisheries Convention Signed." 20 *DSB* 319 (1949).

Notter, Harley A. *Postwar Foreign Policy Preparation 1939–1945.* Dept. of State Pub. No. 3580. Washington: 1949.

Bibliography

Nucker, Delmas H. "A Year of Progress in the Trust Territory of the Pacific Islands." 35 *DSB* 35–41 (1956).

———. "The Trust Territory of the Pacific Islands." 37 *DSB* 248–258 (1957).

O'Connell, D. F. "Sedentary Fisheries and the Australian Continental Shelf." 49 *A.J.I.L.* 185–209 (1955).

Odishaw, Hugh. "The Satellite Program for the International Geophysical Year." 35 *DSB* 280–285 (1956).

———. "International Geophysical Year: A Report on the United States Program." 127 *Science* 115–128 (1958).

Oil and Gas Journal. Tulsa, Oklahoma: 1902–

Otterman, Harvey. "International Regulation of Radio." 12 *DSB* 256–259 (1945).

"Pacific Weather Stations Program Agreed Upon By U.S.–Canada." 23 *DSB* 214 (1950).

"Panama Joins Inter-American Tropical Tuna Commission." 29 *DSB* 489 (1953).

Pan American Union. *Tenth Inter-American Conference, Caracas, Venezuela, March 1–28, 1954, Final Act*. Washington: 1954.

———. *The Organization of American States and the United Nations*. 3rd. ed. by Manuel Canyes. Washington: 1955.

———. *Inter-American Specialized Conference on "Conservation of Natural Resources: The Continental Shelf and Marine Waters," Ciudad Trujillo, March 15–28, 1956. Final Act*. Washington: 1956.

———. *Background Material on the Juridical Aspects of the Continental Shelf and Marine Waters*. Prepared by the Department of International Law of the Pan American Union. Ciudad Trujillo Conference, Doc. No. 2. Washington: 1956.

———. *Background Material on the Scientific and Economic Aspects of the Continental Shelf and Marine Waters*. Prepared by the Working Party on Oceanography of the Pan American Institute of Geography and History. Ciudad Trujillo Conference, Doc. No. 3. Washington: 1956.

Parliamentary Group for World Government. *Neptuno*, PG.55318.35.C and PG.-55321.40.C (mimeo.). London: 1955.

"Passamaquoddy Reference Submitted to IJC." 35 *DSB* 322–323 (1956).

Paullin, Charles O., and John K. Wright. *Atlas of the Historical Geography of the United States*. Published Jointly by Carnegie Institution of Washington and the American Geographical Society of New York, 1932.

"People of Eniwetok and Bikini Compensated for Leaving Homes." 36 *DSB* 101 (1957).

Perry, Glen. *Watchmen of the Sea*. London: C. Scribner's Sons, Ltd., 1938.

Persinger, C. E. "Internationalism in the 60's." 20 *Historical Outlook* 324–327 (1929).

Phelger, Herman. "Some Recent Developments in International Law of Interest to the U.S." 30 *DSB* 196–201 (1954).

———. "Recent Developments Affecting the Regime of the High Seas." 32 *DSB* 934–940 (1955).

Pierce, Charles. *Geodetic Operations in the United States and in Other Areas Through International Cooperation 1954–1956*. Coast and Geodetic Survey Pub. 60-1. Washington: 1957.

"Policy on Commercial Fishing in Pacific Island Trust Territory." 19 *DSB* 468–469 (1948).

Pomeroy, Leonard H. "The International Trade and Traffic in Arms: Its Supervision and Control." 22 *DSB* 187–194, 357–364, 381, 507–515, 520 (1950).

Poole, Bernard L. *The Caribbean Commission: Background of Cooperation in the West Indies*. Columbia, S.C.: University of South Carolina Press, 1951.

"Post and Postal Services." *Encyclopaedia Britannica* (1952), Vol. 18, pp. 303–318.

Poulsen, Erik M. "Conservation Problems in the Northwestern Atlantic." *Papers*

Presented at the International Technical Conference on the Conservation of the Living Resources of the Sea, Rome, 1955. A/CONF.10/7 (1956), pp. 183–193.

Powell, J. H. *Bring Out Your Dead: The Great Plague of Yellow Fever in Philadelphia in 1793.* Philadelphia: University of Pennsylvania Press, 1949.

Pratt, Wallace E. "Petroleum on Continental Shelves." 31 *Bulletin of the American Association of Petroleum Geologists* 657–672 (1947).

Preuss, Lawrence. "On Amending the Treaty-Making Power: A Comparative Study of the Problem of Self-Executing Treaties." 51 *Michigan Law Review* 1117–1142 (1953).

"Problems Relating to the Economic and Legal Regime of the High Seas: Inter-American Specialized Conference on Conservation of Natural Resources: Continental Shelf and Marine Waters, Ciudad Trujillo, March 15–28 [1956]." 34 *DSB* 894–897 (1956).

Quierolo, Aulio Vivaldi. "La resurrection de 'Mare Clausum.'" 23 *Revista de Derecho* (University of Concepcion) 3–57 (1955).

Quilici, Folco. *The Blue Continent.* New York: Rinehart, 1954.

Rand, Austin L. *American Water and Game Birds.* New York: E. P. Dutton and Co., 1956.

Rattray, Jeannette Edwards. *Ship Ashore! A Record of Maritime Disasters off Montauk and Eastern Long Island, 1640–1955.* New York: Coward-McCann, Inc., 1955.

Ray, F. H. *Report of the International Polar Expedition to Point Barrow, Alaska.* 48 Cong., 2 Sess., H. Ex. Doc. No. 44. Washington: 1885.

Raymond, Jack. "Lost Missile Crashed in Brazil, U.S. Says." *N.Y.T.*, Dec. 8, 1956.

———. "Little Peril Seen in Missiles Tests." *N.Y.T.*, March 25, 1957.

Redmond, C. F. *Treaties, Conventions, International Acts, Protocols, and Agreements Between the United States of America and Other Powers, 1910–1923.* 67 Cong., 4 Sess., S. Doc. No. 348 (1923). (Vol. III of the "Malloy" Series.)

"Regional Education: A New Use of the Interstate Compact?" 34 *Virginia Law Review* 64–76 (1948).

Reichelderfer, Francis W. "International Cooperation in Meteorology: Second Congress of the WMO, Geneva, April 14–May 13." 33 *DSB* 435–437 (1955).

Reid, Clement, and J. S. Flett. *The Geology of the Land's End District.* London: Printed for H. M. Stationery Office by Wyman and Sons, Ltd., 1907.

Reiff, Henry. *The United States and Multipartite Administrative Treaties.* Unpublished thesis in Widener Library, Harvard University, 1934.

———. "The United States and International Administrative Unions: Some Historical Aspects." *International Conciliation*, No. 332 (Sept. 1937).

———. "The Enforcement of Multipartite Administrative Treaties in the United States." 34 *A.J.I.L.* 661–680 (1940).

———. "Participation in International Administration: A Cinderella of American History." 34 *Social Studies* 311–316 (1943).

———. "Transition from League of Nations to United Nations." 14 *DSB* 691–698, 739–748 (1946).

———. "Work of the United Nations 'Legal Committees,'" 15 *DSB* 3–15, 302–312, 343–351 (1946).

———. "The Proclaiming of Treaties in the United States." 30 *A.J.I.L.* 63–79 (1936) and 44 *A.J.I.L.* 572–576 (1950).

Renborg, Bertil A. *International Drug Control: A Study of International Organization by and through the League of Nations.* Washington: Carnegie Endowment for International Peace, 1947.

———. "International Control of Narcotics." 22 *Law and Contemporary Problems* 86–112 (1957).

"Requests for Inclusion of Items on Assembly Agenda." 31 *DSB* 422–425 (1954).

Bibliography

"Re-supply Mission to U.S.–Canadian Arctic Weather Stations." 23 *DSB* 550 (1950).
Rienow, Robert. *The Test of the Nationality of a Merchant Vessel.* New York: Columbia University Press, 1937.
Riesenfeld, Stefan A. *Protection of Coastal Fisheries Under International Law.* Washington: Carnegie Endowment for International Peace, 1942.
Riggs, Fred W. "The World's Refugee Problem." 26 *Foreign Policy Reports* 194 (1951).
Roberts, Elliot B., and David G. Knapp. "Geomagnetism in the International Geophysical Year." *The Journal*, Coast and Geodetic Survey, Aug. 1955, No. 6, pp. 4–10.
Robertson, R. B. *Of Whales and Men.* New York: Alfred A. Knopf, 1954.
Robertson, Walter S. "International Cooperation in Fisheries Conservation." 30 *DSB* 297 (1954).
Royal, Loyd A. "International Pacific Salmon Fisheries Commission." *Papers Presented at the International Technical Conference on the Conservation of the Living Resources of the Sea*, Rome, 1955. A/CONF.10/7 (1956), pp. 243–255.
Rudolph, Walter M. "Geophysical Science and Foreign Relations." 33 *DSB* 989–991 (1955).
Russell, Francis H. "Toward a Stronger World Organization." 23 *DSB* 220–224 (1950).
Sady, Emil J. "Report on the South Sea Conference, With Analysis of the Agreement Establishing the South Pacific Commission." 16 *DSB* 459–465 (1947).
"St. Lawrence Seaway and Power Project." 6 *External Affairs* 332–346 (1954).
"Saint Lawrence Seaway: Report to the President on the Status and Progress of the Saint Lawrence Seaway for the Fiscal Year Ended June 30, 1955." 34 *DSB* 215–219 (1956).
"St. Lawrence Seaway." *N.Y.T.*, Section 11 (June 29, 1958), 22 pp.
Salter, Sir Arthur. *Allied Shipping Control: An Experiment in International Administration.* New York: Oxford University Press, 1921.
Sanborn, Frederic Rockwell. *Origins of Early English Maritime and Commercial Law.* New York, London: Century Co., 1930.
"Santiago Negotiations on Fishery Conservation Problems Among Chile, Ecuador, Peru, and the United States: Santiago, Chile, September 14–October 5, 1955." 33 *DSB* 1025–1030 (1955).
Saugstad, Jesse E. *Shipping and Shipbuilding Subsidies.* U.S. Department of Commerce, Bureau of Foreign and Domestic Commerce, Trade Promotion Series No. 129. Washington: 1932.
Sayre, Francis B. "U.S. Report on Trust Territory of the Pacific Islands." 21 *DSB* 133–141 (1949).
Schacter, Oscar. "The Development of International Law through the Legal Opinions of the United Nations Secretariat." 25 *British Year Book of International Law* 91–132 (1948).
Schaefer, Milner B. "Scientific Investigation of the Tropical Tuna Resources of the Eastern Pacific." *Papers Presented at the International Technical Conference on the Conservation of the Living Resources of the Sea.* Rome, 1955. A/CONF.10/7 (1956), pp. 194–211.
Scheffer, Victor B. *Experiments in the Marking of Seals and Sea-Lions.* Special Scientific Report Wildlife No. 4, Department of the Interior. Washington: 1950.
Schmeckebier, Laurence F. *The Public Health Service.* Service Monograph No. 10. Baltimore: Johns Hopkins Press, 1923.
———. *The Customs Service.* Service Monograph No. 33. Baltimore: Johns Hopkins Press, 1924.

──────. *International Organizations in which the United States Participates.* Washington: Brookings Institution, 1935.
Schorger, A. W. *The Passenger Pigeon: Its Natural History and Extinction.* Madison, Wis.: University of Wisconsin Press, 1955.
Schroeder, Peter B. "The Radio Amateur in International Legislation and Administration." 48 *A.J.I.L.* 421–433 (1954).
Schuck, Howard A. *Offshore Grounds Important to the United States Haddock Fishery.* U.S. Fish and Wildlife Service Research Report No. 32. Washington: 1952.
Science, 1880–
"Scientific and Economic Development in the Caribbean." 19 *DSB* 19–20 (1948).
Scott, A. MacCallum. *Beyond the Baltic.* New York: George H. Doran Company, 1926.
Scott, James Brown. *The International Conferences of American States 1889–1928.* New York: Oxford University Press, 1931.
──────. *The International Conferences of American States, First Supplement, 1933–1940.* Washington: Carnegie Endowment for International Peace, 1940.
Selak, Charles B., Jr. "Recent Developments in High Seas Fisheries Jurisdiction under the Presidential Proclamation of 1945." 44 *A.J.I.L.* 670–681 (1950).
──────. "The Proposed International Convention for the High Seas Fisheries of the North Pacific Ocean." 46 *A.J.I.L.* 323–330 (1952).
──────. "Fishing Vessels and the Principle of Innocent Passage." 48 *A.J.I.L.* 627–635 (1954).
──────. "The United States–Canadian Great Lakes Fisheries Convention." 50 *A.J.I.L.* 122–129 (1956).
"Shanghai." *Encyclopaedia Britannica* (1952). Vol. 20, pp. 455–458.
Shelesnyak, M. C. *Across the Top of the World.* Office of Naval Research. Washington: 1947.
Shepheard, H. C., and John W. Mann. "Reducing the Menace of Oil Pollution: International Conference on Pollution of the Seas and Coasts by Oil, London, April 26–May 12, 1954." 31 *DSB* 311–314 (1954).
Short, Lloyd M. *Steamboat-Inspection Service.* Service Monograph No. 8. New York, London: D. Appleton and Company, 1922.
──────. *The Bureau of Navigation.* Service Monograph No. 15. Baltimore: Johns Hopkins Press, 1923.
Sly, John F. "The Genesis of the Universal Postal Union." *International Conciliation,* No. 233 (1927).
Smith, D. H., and H. G. Herring. *The Bureau of Immigration.* Service Monograph No. 30. Baltimore: Johns Hopkins Press, 1924.
Smith, Darrell Hevenor, and Fred Wilbur Powell. *The Coast Guard.* Service Monograph No. 51. Washington: Brookings Institution, 1929.
Smith, Durand. "The Great Lakes Fisheries Convention." 16 *DSB* 643–644, 675 (1947).
Smith, Edward H. *The Marion Expedition to Davis Strait and Baffin Bay under Direction of the U.S. Coast Guard, Scientific Results, Part 3.* Bulletin No. 19. Washington: 1931.
Smith, Frederick G. Walton, and Henry Chapin. *The Sun, the Sea, and Tomorrow: Potential Sources of Food, Energy and Minerals from the Sea.* New York: Scribner, 1954.
Smith, J. L. B. *The Search Beneath the Sea: The Story of the Coelacanth.* New York: Henry Holt, 1956.
Smith, Paul A. "ICAO Conference on Air Navigation Services in Iceland." 20 *DSB* 164–166 (1949).

Bibliography

Smyth, Albert Henry. *The Writings of Benjamin Franklin.* 10 vols. New York: Macmillan Company, 1907.
Snowdon, Henry T. "Aviation Policy and International Relations." 29 *DSB* 41–45 (1953).
"South Pacific Commission Research Program 1949–1950." 21 *DSB* 259–261 (1949).
Stewart, Irvin. "The International Radiotelegraph Conference of Washington." 22 *A.J.I.L.* 28–49 (1928).
———. "The International Technical Consulting Committee on Radio Communication." 25 *A.J.I.L.* 684–693 (1931).
Stick, David. *Graveyard of the Atlantic.* Chapel Hill: University of North Carolina Press, 1952.
Strauss, Lewis L. "Hydrogen Bomb Tests in the Pacific." 30 *DSB* 548–549 (1954).
Stuart, Graham H. *The International City of Tangier.* 2d ed. Stanford, Calif.: Stanford University Press, 1955.
Sullivan, Walter. "As International Geophysical Year Opens — The Over-All Picture." *N.Y.T.*, June 30, 1957, Sec. 4, pp. 6–7.
Sundstrom, Gustaf T., Illustrator. *Commercial Fishing Vessels and Gear.* Bureau of Commercial Fisheries Circular 48, Fish and Wildlife Service, Department of the Interior. Washington: 1957.
Sverdrup, H. U., M. W. Johnson, and R. H. Fleming. *The Oceans: Their Physics, Chemistry, and General Biology.* New York: Prentice-Hall, Inc., 1946.
"Symposium in New Delhi: Solar Energy and Wind Power." 121 *Science* 121–122 (1955).
Szulc, Tad. "Globe-Girdling." *N.Y.T. Magazine*, August 21, 1955.
Tailliez, Philippe. *To Hidden Depths.* New York: Dutton, 1954.
Taussig, Charles W. "The Anglo-American Caribbean Commission." 11 *DSB* 377–379 (1944).
———. "Regionalism in the Caribbean: Six Years of Progress." 18 *DSB* 691–693 (1948).
Telecommunication Journal. Geneva, 1934–
"Territorial Waters and Related Matters: Action Taken by the Third Meeting of the Inter-American Council of Jurists, Mexico City, January 17–February 4, 1956." 34 *DSB* 296–299 (1956).
Terry, William M. "The North Atlantic Marine Research Program: Meeting of the International Commission for the Northwest Atlantic Fisheries at New Haven, Conn., May 25–30, 1953." 29 *DSB* 19–21 (1953).
"Thermonuclear Tests in Pacific Trust Territory." 30 *DSB* 886–888 (1954).
"Thirty Three Nations Sign Anti-Slavery Convention." 3 *United Nations Review* (Oct. 1956) 6–7.
Thompson, William F. *Effect of the Obstruction at Hell's Gate on the Sockeye Salmon of the Fraser River.* Bulletin 1, International Pacific Salmon Fisheries Commission (1945).
Tobin, Harold J. *The Termination of Multipartite Treaties.* New York: Columbia University Press, 1933.
Toenges, A. L., and others. *Coals of Chile.* U.S. Department of the Interior, Bureau of Mines, Bulletin No. 474. Washington: 1948.
Trenwith, Edward J. *Treaties, Conventions, International Acts, Protocols, and Agreements Between the United States and Other Powers, 1923–1937.* 75 Cong., 3 Sess., S. Doc. No. 134 (1938). (Vol. IV of the "Malloy" Series.)
Tressler, Donald K., and James McW. Lemon. *Marine Products of Commerce.* 2nd ed. New York: Rheinhold Publishing Co., 1951.
United Kingdom. *British and Foreign State Papers.*
———. *Preliminary Conference in London on the Further Protection of Submarine*

Telegraph Cables, Procès-Verbaux and Annexes, June 5–10, 1913. Cd. 7079 (1913).

———. *Report of the Channel Tunnel Committee.* Cmd. 3513 (1930).

———. *Treaty Relating to the Submarine Areas of the Gulf of Paria.* Great Britain and Venezuela. Signed at Caracas, Feb. 26, 1942. *British Treaty Series,* No. 10 (1942), Cmd. 6400.

———, Ministry of Information. *His Majesty's Minesweepers.* London: 1943.

———. *Final Report of the Standing Advisory Committee to the International Overfishing Conference, London, 16th–19th April, 1947.* Cmd. 7387.

———. *Final Act of Conference and Text of the International Convention for the Prevention of Pollution of the Sea by Oil, 1954.* Cmd. 9197.

United Nations Educational, Scientific and Cultural Organization. *Report on the Question of United Nations Research Laboratories and Observatories.* UNESCO/-Nat.Sci.24/1947, reproduced in Report of Secretary General to ECOSOC, Aug. 1948, E/620, (Mimeo.), pp. 49–145; also in United Nations, Department of Social Affairs. *The Question of Establishing United Nations Research Laboratories.* Sales No.: 1949.IV.1, pp. 37–111.

———. *Directory of International Scientific Organizations,* 1st ed. Paris: 1950; 2nd ed. Paris: 1953.

"U.N. Conference on the Law of the Sea," 38 *DSB* 1110–1125 (1958).

"U.N. to Convene Conference on Fishery Conservation." 32 *DSB* 64–66 (1955).

"United Nations Research Laboratories." 164 *Nature* 1120–1121 (1949).

"U.S. and Canada Inaugurate Niagara Falls Remedial Project." 30 *DSB* 954–958 (1954).

"United States and Canada Sign Salmon Conservation Agreement." 36 *DSB* 76–77 (1957).

"U.S. Cancels Demonstration of Reduced Fallout," 39 *DSB* 237 (1958).

"U.S. Offers to Negotiate Nuclear Test Suspension," 39 *DSB* 378–379 (1958).

"U.S. Policies and Actions in the Development and Testing of Nuclear Weapons." 35 *DSB* 704–715 (1956).

"U.S. Policy on Human Rights." 28 *DSB* 579–582 (1953).

"U.S. Position on Conservation of Fisheries Resources." 32 *DSB* 696–700 (1955).

"United States Proposes Conference on Antarctica." 38 *DSB* 910–912 (1958).

"U.S. Protests to U.S.S.R. on Closing of Peter the Great Bay." 37 *DSB* 388 (1957).

"U.S. Repeats Protest on Closing of Peter the Great Bay." 38 *DSB* 461–462 (1958).

"U.S. Replies to Japan on Atom and Hydrogen Bomb Tests." 36 *DSB* 901–904 (1957).

"U.S. To Cease Participation in Ocean Station Program." 29 *DSB* 629 (1953).

"U.S. To Reconsider Ocean Station Participation." 30 *DSB* 23 (1954).

"U.S. Will Help Transport Afghan Pilgrims to Mecca." 35 *DSB* 25 (1956).

Universal Postal Union. *Documents de Conference sur la Poste Aeriénne.* Berne: 1927.

Van Campen, Wilvan G., and Earl E. Hoven. *Tunas and Tuna Fisheries of the World: An Annotated Bibliography 1930–1953.* Fishery Bulletin 111, United States Fish and Wildlife Service. Washington: 1956.

Van Wagenen, Richard W. *Research in the International Organization Field: Some Notes on a Possible Focus.* Publication No. 1 of the Center for Research on World Political Institutions, Princeton University. Princeton: 1952.

Vaughan, Thomas Wayland, et al. *International Aspects of Oceanography.* National Academy of Sciences. Washington: 1937.

Walters, Francis Paul. *A History of the League of Nations.* 2 vols. London, New York: Oxford University Press, 1952.

Watertown (New York) *Daily Times.*

Watt, William G. "International Cooperation in the Science of Hydrography:

Bibliography

Seventh International Hydrographic Conference, Monte Carlo, Monaco, May 7–17, 1957." 37 *DSB* 361–363 (1957).
Wead, Frank. *Gales, Ice and Men: A Biography of the Steam Barkentine Bear*. New York: Dodd, Mead and Co., 1937.
Weber, Gustavus A. *The Weather Bureau*. Service Monograph No. 9. New York, London: D. Appleton and Company, 1922.
———. *The Coast and Geodetic Survey*. Service Monograph No. 16. Baltimore: Johns Hopkins Press, 1923.
———. *The Naval Observatory*. Service Monograph No. 39. Baltimore: Johns Hopkins Press, 1926.
———. *The Hydrographic Office*. Service Monograph No. 42. Baltimore: Johns Hopkins Press, 1926.
Wehle, Louis B. "International Administration of European Inland Waterways." 40 *A.J.I.L.* 100–120 (1946).
Weiss, George. *The Lighthouse Service*. Service Monograph No. 40. Baltimore: Johns Hopkins Press, 1926.
Wetmore, Alexander. *Our Migrant Shorebirds in Southern South America*. Department of Agriculture Technical Bulletin No. 26. Washington: 1927.
Wheeler, E. P. "The International Regulation of Ocean Travel." *Proceedings, A.S.I.L., 1912*, pp. 36–44.
White, Lyman. *The Structure of Private International Organizations*. Philadelphia: George S. Ferguson Company, 1933.
White, Lyman Cromwell, and Marie Ragonetti Zocca. *International Non-Governmental Organizations*. New Brunswick: Rutgers University Press, 1951.
Whiteleather, Richard T., and Herbert H. Brown. *An Experimental Fishery Survey in Trinidad, Tobago, and British Guiana: With Recommended Improvements in Methods and Gear*. Anglo-American Caribbean Commission. Washington: G. P. O., 1945.
Whitton, John B., and J. Edward Fowler. "Bricker Amendment — Fallacies and Dangers." 48 *A.J.I.L.* 23–56 (1954).
Wilcox, Clair. *A Charter for World Trade*. New York: Macmillan Company, 1949.
Wilcox, Francis O. "The First Ten Years of the World Health Organization." Remarks. 38 *DSB* 987–992 (1958).
Wilkes, Charles. *Narrative of United States Exploring Expedition 1838–1842*. 5 vols. Philadelphia: Lea and Blanchard, 1845.
Williams, Ralph Chester. *The United States Public Health Service 1798–1950*. Washington: Commissioned Officers Association of the United States Public Health Service, 1951.
Willoughby, William R. "Power Along the St. Lawrence." 34 *Current History* 283–290 (1958).
Wilson, Robert Renbert. *The International Law Standard in Treaties of the United States*. Cambridge, Mass.: Harvard University Press, 1953.
Woodland, Bruce. "Canada's Atlantic Sealfishery." *Trade News* (Department of Fisheries of Canada), Vol. 10, No. 8, pp. 3–6, Feb. 1958.
Woolf, L. S. *International Government*. New York: Brentano's, 1916.
"World Health Organization." 1 *International Organization* 134–136 (1947).
World Health Organization. *Joint ILO/WHO Committee on the Hygiene of Seafarers, Second Report*. Technical Report Series No. 92. Geneva: 1955.
"World Meteorological Organization." 24 *DSB* 475 (1951).
"World Meteorological Organization: The International Geophysical Year." 3 *United Nations Review* (Feb. 1957) 35–39.
World Meteorological Organization. "The Sea That Unites Us." Mimeo. Geneva: n.d.
Wraight, A. Joseph, and Elliott B. Roberts. *Coast and Geodetic Survey 1807–1957:*

150 Years of History. U.S. Department of Commerce, Coast and Geodetic Survey. Washington: 1957.

Wright, Hamilton. *Report on the International Opium Commission and on the Opium Problem as Seen Within the United States and its Possessions.* 61 Cong., 2 Sess., S. Doc. No. 377 (1910).

Yates, Lamartine. "Food Resources and Human Needs." 55 *Yale Law Journal* 1233–1241 (1946).

Young, Richard. "Recent Developments with Respect to the Continental Shelf." 42 *A.J.I.L.* 849–857 (1948).

———. "The International Law Commission and the Continental Shelf." 46 *A.J.I.L.* 123–128 (1952).

———. "Pan American Discussions on Offshore Claims." 50 *A.J.I.L.* 909–916 (1956).

———. "The End of American Consular Jurisdiction in Morocco." 51 *A.J.I.L.* 402–406 (1957).

Zahl, Paul A. "Man-of-War Fleet Attacks Bimini." 101 *National Geographic Magazine* 185–212 (Feb. 1952).

Zeis, Paul M. *American Shipping Policy.* Princeton: Princeton University Press, 1938.

Zinsser, Hans. *As I Remember Him: The Biography of R. S.* Boston: Little, Brown and Company, 1940.

———. *Rats, Lice, and History.* Boston: Printed for Atlantic Monthly Press by Little, Brown, and Company, 1935.

INDEX

Aborigines: of Africa, 34, 125; of the Pacific, 34, 125, 126; of Alaska, 79, 125; and British treaty proposals, 126
Abstention, principle of, 279–281, 319, 324
Adams, J. Donald, 6
ADIZ, 365
Admeasurements, 223n
Administration, international, 261–262, 296–297. *See also* International legislation; International organization
Aerial navigation, conventions on: Paris *1919*, 35, 138, 156, 158, 201, 204; Ibero-American, Madrid *1926*, 156, 158n; Pan American, Habana *1928*, 138, 156, 158, 201; sanitary convention *1933*, 156–157, 263, 266–267; with Philippines *1947*, 339. *See also* Aviation; International Civil Aviation Organization; Navigation
Africa, 34, 78, 125, 187
Agencies, *see* Specialized agencies
Air Defense Identification Zones (ADIZ), 365
Air Services Transit Agreement *1944*, 201n–202n
Air Transport Association of America, 212
Airspace, terminology, 10–11
Albion, Robert G., 7
Algae, 41, 44
Allied Maritime Transport Council, 217
American Air Almanac, 193
American Bureau of Shipping, 229, 233
American Cargo War Risk Reinsurance Exchange, 146
American Ephemeris, 193

American Federation of Labor, 229
American Fisheries Society, 174
American Merchant Marine Institute, 226
American Museum of Natural History, 68, 69
American Nautical Almanac, 94, 193
Ammunition dumping, 62
Anchovetta, 298–299
Andrea Doria-Stockholm collision, 141, 222, 232–237
Angling, 67–69
Anglo-American Caribbean Commission, 340
Anslinger, Harry J., 189
Antarctica: discovery of, 87, 97; IGY relation to, 353; U.S. proposal of international regime for, 373–375
Archipelagos, 16
Arctic, The, 139
Arctic: exploration by aircraft, 194; weather stations, 209–210
Arctic Maid, The, 302
Armistice agreements: with Germany *1918*, 149; with Austria-Hungary *1918*, 149
Arms traffic, 34, 125–127, 187; *1919* and *1925* conventions on, 187
Armstrong, Patrick, 374n
Arrest of ships, *1937* convention on, 132
Art, and the sea, 71
Assistance and salvage, 78; *1910* convention on, 132–133; *1935* U.S.-Mexican agreement on, 142; *1938* convention on, 157
Association of Whaling Companies, 297
Astronomy, 81; Prime Meridian Conference, 92–96; International Astronomical Union, 98–99, 193
Atka, The, 353

Atomic energy, 57, 334, 360–361, 366, 367; wastes, 62–63, 331, 334, 354, 361–363
Australia, *1958* agreement on weather station with, 210n
Austria: *1919* treaty of peace with, 134, 158, 159, 188; *1921* treaty with, 159
Austria-Hungary, *1918* armistice agreement with, 149
Aviation: for transport, 34–35, 157, 202n, 205, 212; collisions, 141; bipartite agreements on, 156; in interwar period, 156–158; taxation of fuel, 157; assistance and salvage, 157; and radiotelegraph, 162; since World War II, 202–213; and nautical mile for, 203n–204n; convention on damage to third parties on the surface, 157n, 204; air navigation regions for, 205; convention on recognition of rights in aircraft, 205; and telecommunications, 205; joint support programs for, 205–211; and private and public international organizations, 211–212; coordination of safety at sea and in the air, 221, 228–229. *See also* Aerial navigation; Health; International Civil Aviation Organization; United Nations, Transport and Communications Commission

Bahamas Long Range Proving Ground, agreements relating to, 368–369
Balclutha, The, 8
Baltic and North Sea, telecommunication meetings, 228n, 229n
Barcelona conventions, on waterways and maritime ports, 159–160
Bear, The, 46n
Beebe, Lucius, 70
Belgium, *1932* agreement on load lines with, 143n
Bering Strait, 22, 23
Berkner, Lloyd V., 352n
Bermuda, *1945* agreement on telecommunications, 256–257
Berners, Dame Juliana, 67
Bikini, 4, 363, 366
Bills of Lading, *1924* convention on, 132–133, 190

Bioma theory, 51, 307–309, 312
Birds, 48–53, 86, 186, 224, 271; and oil pollution, 53, 224; migratory, 91n, 124–125, 128n, 185; *1916* treaty with Great Britain on, 124–125; ornithological congresses, 185. *See also* Bioma theory; Eco-systems, CEP; Guano
Blair, Montgomery, 107
Bowditch, Nathaniel, 82–83, 84
Boxer settlement, 101, 102
Boyd Orr, Lord, 374
Brazil, and *1957* agreement relating to Bahamas Long Range Proving Ground, 370
Bricker Amendment, 90–91, 345
Bridges, 21–22
Briggs, Herbert W., 32
Bristol Bay, 169–170, 279
British Commonwealth, *1945* agreement on telecommunications at Bermuda, 256–257. *See also* Great Britain; United Kingdom
British Parliamentary Group for World Government, 374
Brooke, John Mercer, 85
Brown, L. A., 95, 96
Brussels, General Act and Declaration of, 78
Bryant, Samuel W., 83
Bubonic plague, 111, 114, 115, 267
Buoyage: and lighting of coasts, 143–145; agreement for a uniform system *1936*, 144
Bureau International de l'Heure, 98–99, 193
Bushnell, David, 146
Byrd, Admiral Richard Evelyn, 373, 375n

"Cable diplomacy," 38–39
Cables, *see* Submarine cables
Caicos Islands, 369n
Calendar changes, 97
Cambodia, *1957* agreement on mapping service with, 350
Canada: *1908* agreement on fisheries commission, 120; agreements on load lines, 142–143; agreements on aviation, 156; agreements on radio, 162n, 251, 252; and weather stations, 206–210; agreements on weather ships, 207–209; *1949*

Index

agreement on air search and rescue operations, 207n; agreements on long-range navigational stations, 232n; *1950* agreement on port privileges, 282; *1948* shellfish agreement, 289; agreements on Great Lakes-St. Lawrence Waterway, 354–360; and air defense identification system, 365, 366n. *See also* Canadian-American fisheries; Halibut fishery; Salmon fisheries; Seals, fur

Canadian-American Board of Inquiry for Great Lakes Fisheries, 175

Canadian-American fisheries, 120–121, 167–175, 177–178, 289–293; *1918* conference, 121, 167. *See also* Cod fisheries; Great Lakes fisheries; Halibut fishery; North Pacific fisheries; Northeastern fisheries; Northwest Atlantic fisheries; Salmon fisheries; Seals, fur

Canals, 13

Cape Ann, The, 236

Cape Spartel Light: *1865* convention, 75, 77, 92–93; *1958* transfer of management to Morocco, 93

Caribbean Commission, 336, 339–342

Carnegie Endowment for International Peace, 246

Carsey, J. B., 59

Carson, Rachel, 6, 9n, 59, 85

Cartels, 29, 195–196. *See also* Shipping

Carter, Charles A., 117

Cartography, 14, 94, 349; International Map on the Millionth Scale, 131–132, 191, 349, 373; mapping services 339, 350

CEP (Chile, Ecuador, Peru), 307–15, 319, 321. *See also* Latin American offshore claims

Certification, of seamen, 240

Chaguaramas, Trinidad, 369n

Chamber of Commerce, 196, 212, 220, 245–246

Chank fisheries, 43

Chapman, Sydney, 352

Chapman, Wilbert M., 177n, 304n

Children, traffic in, 31, 128; agreements on, 129, 186, 343

Chile: *1957* agreement on weather station with, 211; *1934* agreement on amateur radio with, 252; and bioma theory, 307–309

China: Whangpoo River agreements with, 92, 101–102; Boxer settlement with, 101–102; treaties on opium traffic with, 127; agreements on health with, 270n

Cholera, 111, 113, 115, 267, 270. *See also* Diseases; Health; Sanitary conventions; World Health Organization

CITEJA, 157, 191, 204

Ciudad Trujillo Conference *1956*, 306, 311, 313–315

Civil aviation, *see* International Civil Aviation Organization

Classification societies, 233–234

Coast and geodetic program, *1947* agreement with Philippine Islands on, 339

Coast Guard, 8, 28, 80, 82, 106, 227, 236–337

Coastal waters, 13–14, 30–31. *See also* International Law Commission; Territorial sea

Cochrane, E. L., 233n

Cod fisheries, 42, 45, 116–117, 276. *See also* Northeastern fisheries; Northwest Atlantic fisheries

Codding, G. A., 249

Codification, of international law, 184, 315–317

"Coffinships," 103

Collisions, 27, 100, 132, 133, 141, 231, 330; *1910* convention on, 132, 133; *1948* convention on, 231, 235. *See also* Rules of the Road, Safety of Life at Sea

Colombia: *1929* agreement on aviation with, 156; *1956* agreement on weather station with, 211

Columbus Memorial Lighthouse, 100

Combined Shipping Adjustment Board, 217

Comité spécial de l'année géophysique internationale (CSAGI), 351–352

Commander Islands, 287, 288

Commercial Pacific Cable Company, 255n

Commission for the Scientific Exploration of the Mediterranean, 319

Communications: types and problems of, 35–39; before World War I,

107–110; in the inter-war period, 158–162; coordination with transport, 228, 258–260; since World War II, 247–260. *See also* Postal communications; Radio; Submarine cables; Telecommunications; Wireless
Congress of Industrial Organizations, 229
Conservation, 319; *1958* UN convention on fishing and, 329, 331–332
Contiguous zones, 5, 31, 32, 329, 330; *1958* UN convention on the territorial sea and, 329, 330. *See also* International Law Commission; Territorial sea
Continental shelf: Truman proclamation on, 4; U.S. interest in, 4–6; International Law Commission on, 5, 12, 57, 322–324, 332; characteristics of, 11–12; area of, 54; estimates of oil in, 56; jurisdictional problems relating to, 57; League of Nations on, 184; Latin American claims relating to, 304–315; *1958* UN convention on, 329, 332–333. *See also* United Nations Conference on Law of the Sea 1958
Contra bonos mores, 19
Cook, Captain James, 74
Copenhagen Council for the Exploration of the Sea, *see* International Council for the Exploration of the Sea
Corfu Channel dispute, 150n–151n
Costa Rica: and flags of convenience, 241–242; *1956* agreement on amateur radio with, 253
Council of the Sea, 250, 373
Council of State Governments, 174
Cousteau, Jacques-Yves, 70
Crews, *see* Seamen
Crustaceans, 41, 42–43. *See also* Fish
CSAGI, 351–352
Cuba: *1951* agreement on pleasure yachts, 67n; *1944* to *1953* agreements on weather stations, 210; *1952* amateur radio agreement, 253
Cunard Steamship Company, 141n
Customs, U.S., 32, 82

Dangerous goods, carriage of, 30, 237–238

Danish Sound Dues dispute, 77
DAPAC (Danger Areas in the Pacific), 153
Dartmouth Library Arctic and Antarctic collection, 88n
Date Line, 96–98
Davidson, George, 98
Davis, Charles Henry, 94
Dean, Arthur H., 329n
Declaration on Maritime Zone, CEP *1952*, 310
Defense Shipping Authority, 218
De Haven, Lt. Edward J., 88
Dengue fever, 115, 166. *See also* Health
Denmark, *1932* agreement on load lines with, 143n
Derelict patrol, 100–101
Deutschland, The, 109
DEW (Distant Early Warning) system, 15
Diseases: quarantinable and infectious, 267; endemic and epidemic, 110, 116. *See also* Health
Dominican Republic: *1957* agreement on weather station with, 211; *1957* agreement on long-range navigational station with, 232n; *1951* agreement relating to Bahamas Long Range Proving Ground with, 269
Donne, John, 60
Driftmaster, The, 63
Duck, eider, 50, 124
Dulles, John Foster, 345

ECOSOC, *see* UN Economic and Social Council
Eco-systems, CEP, 307–308
Ecuador: *1957* agreement on weather station with, 211; *1950* agreement on amateur radio with, 253; and bioma theory, 307–309
Edmonds, Douglas L., 315
Egypt: *1953* health agreement with, 269; U.S. technical assistance agreement with 269–270; U.S. naval medical research unit agreement with, 270
Electrical communications, *1920* convention on, 160. *See also* Radiotelegraph conventions; Telecommunications, Conventions; Wireless

Index

El Salvador, agreements on fisheries mission *1951–1955*, 300
Energy: solar, 57; from the sea, 57–59; UN report on, 57n
Eniwetok, 363, 366. *See also* Nuclear weapons testing
Erosion, 60
European International Congress of Official Tourist Propaganda Associations, 195
Exhibitions, 121–123
Exploration: underwater, 69–71; in 19th century, 87–88
Expositions, 121–123
Extradition, treaties on slave traffic, 126

Fairs, 121–123
FAO, *see* Food and Agriculture Organization
Far Eastern Association of Tropical Medicine, 195
Faulkner, Percy, on oil pollution, 224
FCC, 255
Federalism: problem of, 90; in relation to traffic in women and children, 128–129; in relation to Great Lakes fisheries, 173–175; world federalism, 334–335
Field, Cyrus W., 38, 84, 108
Finlay, Dr. Carlos, 114
Firearms traffic, 34, 125–127, 187
Fish: abundance and distribution of, 41–42; pelagic, 42; anadromous, 42; catadromous, 42; demersal, 42; classifications of, 42–44; sedentary, 42–43, 322–323, 332–333; king crab, 43, 280n, 281; commercial uses of, 44–45; medical and scientific uses of, 45, 69; hazards and abuses affecting, 45–47, 70; fishways and fish ladders, 46, 171; fishing for recreation, 67–69; flatfish, 276. *See also* Angling; Cod fisheries; Fisheries; Halibut fishery; Resources; Salmon fisheries; Tuna fisheries
Fish and Wildlife Act of *1956*, 272–273
Fisheries: Truman proclamation on offshore, 4–5, 305–306; scope of, 40–47; hazards confronting, 45–47; U.S. policy on, 47, 272–273; treaty relations before Civil War, 78–80; *1818* treaty with Great Britain, 116; treaty relations from Civil War to World War I, 116–121; *1908* agreement with Canada, 120; exhibitions, expositions, and congresses, 121–123; inter-war developments relating to, 166–184; interstate compacts, 175, 290n; and League of Nations, 179, 184–185; welfare of fishermen, 240–241; and post-World War II developments, 272–327; *1937* regulation on fishing nets and size limits, 274; public hearings, 276–277, 280, 291, 300; Latin American claims relating to, 300–315, 332; International Law Commission on, 315–327; *1955* Rome Technical Conference on, 317–321; Mediterranean council, 319, 336; *1958* UN convention on conservation, 329, 331–332; *1958* UN Conference on the Law of the Sea on, 331–333; *1947* agreement with the Philippines, 339; conferences on statistics and technologists, 343. *See also* Bioma theory; Canadian-American fisheries; Cod fisheries; Ecosystems, CEP; Food and Agriculture Organization; Great Lakes fisheries; Halibut fishery; International Council for the Exploration of the Sea; North Pacific fisheries; Northeastern fisheries dispute; Northwest Atlantic fisheries; Overfishing; Regional councils; Resources; Salmon fisheries; Technical assistance; Tuna fisheries
Flag Signal Code: adoption of, 88–89; and *1927* radiotelegraph convention, 89
Flags: flight from high standard flags, 180, 241–243, 331; for UN ships, 243–244
Flora and fauna, *1933* convention on preservation in Africa, 185n
Folger, Captain, 83n
Food and Agriculture Organization, 272, 317, 318, 335, 336, 342–343; *1943* convention on interim commission, 198; *1945* constitution of, 335

Food and catering, *1946* ILO convention on, 240
France: *1778* treaty of Amity and Commerce with, 77, 78, 79, 274; *1800* treaty on Peace, Commerce, and Navigation with, 79; *1956* agreement on weather station with, 211; *1948* agreement on aerial mapping with, 339
François, J. P. A., 316
Frank C. Munson Memorial Institute of American Maritime History, 7
Franklin, Benjamin, 82–83
Franklin, Sir John, 88
Fraser River, 170–172
Fresh water, experiments with, 48
Fulton, Robert, 146
Fumigation, 110, 166. See also Health; Sanitary conventions; World Health Organization
Fur seals, see Seals, fur
Furuseth, Andrew, 105, 106, 154

Gas, undersea, 56n
General Act and Declaration of Brussels *1890*, *1919* revision of, 78
General Act of Berlin, on navigation in Africa *1885*, 78
General Dynamics Corporation submarine museum, 8
General Fisheries Council for the Mediterranean, 319, 336
General Postal Union, 36, 107. See also Universal Postal Union
Geodesy, 131; International Union of Geodesy and Geophysics, 131, 194, 216, 350n; U.S. Coast and Geodetic Survey, 81, 94, 95, 193, 350
Geodetic Association, 131, 194, 216, 350n
Geography, 14–15, 131–132; mapping, 13, 94, 339, 349, 350; geographical congresses, 95, 131–132
Georges Shoal and Bank, 15, 87
Germany: *1919* treaty of peace with, 134, 158, 159, 187–188; *1931* agreement on load lines with, 143n; *1918* armistice agreement with, 149; *1921* treaty restoring friendly relations with, 159
Gidel, Gilbert, 217
Gilbert, William Schwenck, 45
Golden Rule, The, 366

Gorgas Memorial Laboratory, 165, 191
Graveyard of the Atlantic, 14
Great Britain: *1942* agreement with Venezuela, 57n; fur seal agreements with, 78, 119–120, 167, 183, 184, 286, 318; *1818* convention on fisheries with, 79, 116; *1782* provisional treaty of peace with, 79, 274; agreements and treaties on slavery, 87, 124–125; and rules of the road, 89; as a clearing house for maritime matters, 89, 100, 238; early sanitation measures of, 111–112; *1912* agreement on North Atlantic fisheries, 117; *1908* agreement on fisheries commission, 120; *1916* migratory bird treaty with, 124–125; and Pacific aborigines, 126; and code of signals, 161; *1925* agreement on interference with broadcasting, 162n; clearing house for whaling limits, 181; *1940* agreement on naval and air bases, 269n; parliamentary group for world government, 374. See also British Commonwealth; United Kingdom
"Great Duck Egg Fake," 123. See also Birds
Great Lakes: as inland seas, 13, 354; relation of safety of life at sea regimes to, 139, 229; relation of load lines to, 142–143; relation of radio regime to, 251. See also Fisheries; Great Lakes fisheries; Great Lakes–St. Lawrence Waterway
"Great Lakes Basin Compact," 360n
Great Lakes fisheries: before World War I, 120–121; conventions with Canada on, 166, 174–175, 290, 289–293; in inter-war period, 173–175; board of inquiry for, 175; since World War II, 289–293. See also Canadian-American fisheries; Lamprey
Great Lakes–St. Lawrence Waterway, 354–360; *1932* agreement, 358; *1941* agreement, 358; *1950* agreement on Niagara River, 360; *1952* agreement, 358, 359; *1953* agreement, 360n; *1954* agreement, 359; *1954* agreement on Niagara Falls, 360; *1956* agreement on Cornwall Island Channels, 359n; *1956* agree-

Index

ment on relocation of Roosevelt Bridge, 360n; *1957* agreement on connecting channels, 360n

Greenwich meridian, 94–96, 98, 161

Group representation, with respect to: International Civil Aviation Organization, 212; International Telecommunication Union, 212, 250; Intergovernmental Maritime Consultative Organization, 220; Safety of Life at Sea Conference *1948*, 227, 229; Northwest Atlantic Fisheries Commission, 276, 278; North Pacific Fisheries Commission, 280–281; Pacific Salmon Commission, 284–285; Great Lakes Fisheries Commission, 291; tuna fisheries commissions, 299–300

Guano, 51, 52, 85–86. *See also* Bioma theory; Eco-systems, CEP; Latin American offshore claims

Guided missiles, 4, 368–371

Gulf stream, 82

Gulfs, 13

Hague Arbitral Award in Northeastern fisheries dispute, 117

Hair seals, 46

Haiti, *1952* agreement relating to Bahamas Long Range Proving Ground with, 369

Halibut fishery: before World War I, 120–121; between the wars, 166, 167–169; *1919* draft convention with Canada, 167–168, 177; *1923* and *1930* conventions with Canada, 168; *1937* convention with Canada, 168, 175, 177, 279, 281, 282, 318; since World War II, 281–283; *1950* convention with Canada, 282; *1953* convention with Canada, 282–283, 318. See also Fisheries

Hanover, *1840* agreement with, 78

HARDTACK nuclear test series, 366–367

Harrison, John, 94

Harvard University, 7

Hassler, Ferdinand R., 94

Hawaiian Islands, *1849* agreement on whalers with, 78

Hayden, Sherman Strong, 53

Health: early control measures for, 110–112; conferences before World War I, 112–116; International Office of Public Health, 114; Pan American regime of, 114–115, 165–166, 341–342; ILO conventions on medical examinations, 155, 240; relation of League of Nations to, 163, 166, 263; developments in interwar period relating to, 162–166; radio warnings on, 162, 251, 267; relation of UNRRA to, 163–164, 263; hygiene of seafarers, 245; post-World War II developments relating to, 261–270; establishment of World Health Organization, 262–265; international sanitary regulations, 266–267; in Middle East, 267–270; NAMRU, 269–270; interorganizational cooperation for, 259, 270; agreements with China on, 270n. *See also* Diseases; Sanitary conventions; World Health Organization

Hearings, public, by international fisheries commissions, 276–277, 280, 291, 300

Hell's Gate Canyon, 171, 173

Hemingway, Ernest, 68

Henderson, D. M., 85n, 97n

Henry of Prussia, Prince, 109

Herlands, Judge William B., 242n

Herring, conference on, 343

Heyerdahl, Thor, 6

High seas: International Law Commission report on, 321–322; *1958* UN convention on, 329, 330–331, 363, 364

Hildebrand, S. F., 42

Hispanic-Luso-American Institute of International Law, 310

Hobbies, 6–7, 71

Hobbs, William Herbert, 97n

Hohman, Elmo Paul, 106

Holidays, *1936* ILO convention on, 155

Hornell, James, 43n

Hudson, Manley O., 184n, 200, 315

Humanitarian programs: before World War I, 125–129; in the inter-war period, 186–190; since World War II, 343–348. *See also* Arms traffic; Liquor traffic; Narcotics; Literature, obscene; Slave traffic; Women, traffic in

433

Hungary: *1920* treaty of peace with, 134, 158, 159, 188; *1921* treaty restoring friendly relations with, 159
Hydro-Electric Power Commission of the Province of Ontario, 359
Hydrography, 88, 130
Hydrosphere, 10

IATA, 212
Ibero-American Oceanographic Conference, 195
ICAN, 204
ICAO, *see* International Civil Aviation Organization
ICC, 238, 254, 255
Ice patrol, 100, 101, 104, 105, 230, 232
Iceland, *1932* agreement on load lines with, 143n
ICPC, 189–190, 191, 347–348
ICSU, 131, 192, 348, 350, 351–352
IGY, 6, 130, 192n, 216, 349, 351–354, 362, 374
ILC, *see* International Law Commission
Ile de France, the, 236
Illinois Central Railroad Co. v. Illinois *1892*, 354n
ILO, *see* International Labor Organization
IMCO, *see* Intergovernmental Maritime Consultative Organization
Immunity of state-owned ships, *1926* convention on, 132, 190
IMO, 141, 192, 201, 206, 213–214
Indo-Pacific Fisheries Council, 318, 335–336, 337, 342; *1948* convention on, 335, 342
Industrial Property Union, 121; conventions on, 262n
Institute for the Unification of Private Law, 212
Institute of Pacific Relations, 195
Inter-American conferences: first, at Washington *1889*, 92, 99; specialized, 194; tenth, at Caracas *1954*, 311, 315. *See also* International Conferences of American States; Organization of American States; Pan American Organization
Inter-American Council of Jurists, 309, 311, 312

Inter-American Hotel Association, 195n
Inter-American Juridical Committee, 309, 311
Inter-American Oceanographic Institute, 315
Inter-American Travel Congress, 195n
Inter-American Tropical Tuna Commission, 298–300, 312, 318
Intercollegiate Fishing Clinic, 68
Intergovernmental Maritime Consultative Organization: and community control of shipping, 29, 373; relation to other intergovernmental bodies, 34, 220; secretariat of, 100; *1948* convention on, 34, 100, 201, 202, 217–222, 229, 234, 237, 238, 265; and buoyage, 145; creation of, 201, 216–222; U.S. ratification of convention of, 221; and tonnage measurement, 223; and oil pollution, 227; relation to *1948* Safety of Life at Sea Convention, 229; relation to ice patrol, 230; relation to carriage of dangerous goods, 237–238; relation to UN Transport and Communications Commission, 260. *See also* Collisions; International Marine Conference *1889*; Safety of life at sea
International administration, 261–262; 296–297. *See also* International legislation; Organizations
International Advisory Committee on Marine Science, 350
International Aeronautical Federation, 212
International Air Transport Association, 212
International Association for Labour Legislation, 133–134
International Association of Navigation Congresses, 21, 133, 191
International Association of Physical Oceanography, 212
International Astronomical Union, 98–99, 193
International Atomic Energy Agency, 334
International Bank for Reconstruction and Development, 198
International Bureau for Whaling Statistics, 179, 294

434

Index

International Bureau of the Telegraph Union at Berne, 161
International Central Mine Clearance Board, 151
International Chamber of Commerce, 196, 212, 220
International Civil Aviation Organization: and rescue of aircraft, 142; *1944* convention on civil aviation, 142, 158, 201, 202–205, 207, 265; superseding Paris and Habana regimes, 158; relation to economic competition and national policies, 201; establishment of PICAO, 202; establishment of, 202–205; Standards and Recommended Practices (SARPS) of, 203–204; legal committee of, 204–205; air navigation regions of, 205–206; and weather ship program, 205–209; and joint services in Iceland and Danish territory, 209; relation to other weather programs, 209–211; relation to private and public international organizations, 211–212; relation to World Meteorological Organization, 215–216; coordination of safety at sea and in the air, 221, 228–229. *See also* Aviation; International Technical Committee of Aerial Legal Experts; International Telecommunication Union; United Nations, Transport and Communications Commission; World Health Organization
International Commerce Commission, 196
International Commission for Aerial Navigation (ICAN), 204
International Commission for the Scientific Investigation of Tuna, 298–300
International Commission for Zoological Nomenclature, 336
International Conference for the Protection of Flora and Fauna *1933*, 185n
International Conference of Official Travel Organizations, First, 195
International Conference on Electrical Communications *1920*, 254
International Conference on the Peaceful Uses of Atomic Energy, Second, 367
International Conferences of American States: *1889*, 92, 99–100; *1954*, 311, 315
International Congress for the Protection of Nature *1931*, 185n
International Congress of Meteorologists *1873*, 130
International Cooperative Alliance, 220
International Council for the Exploration of the Sea, 123, 179, 185, 191, 275, 277, 297, 318, 335, 349
International Council of Scientific Unions, 131, 192, 348, 350, 351–352
International Court of Justice, 312, 326; and Corfu Channel Case, 150n–151n
International Criminal Police Commission, 189–190, 191, 347–348
International Date Line, 96–98
International Federation of Airline Pilots Association, 212
International Federation of Private Air Transport, 212
International Fisheries Commission, U.S. and Canada, *1908*, 120–121, 168, 172. *See also* Canadian-American fisheries
International Game Fish Association, 68–69
International Geographical Congress *1881*, 95
International Geophysical Year *1957–1958*, 6, 130, 192n, 216, 349, 351–354, 362, 374
International Hunting Council *1935*, 185n
International Hydrographic Bureau, 191, 204n, 229
International Hydrographic Conference *1919*, 130
International Labor Organization: antecedents of, 133–134; *1934* agreement on U.S. membership in, 134, 155; conventions on labor at sea, 154–155, 240, 245; maritime sessions of, 155–156, 245; and manning of ships, 231; constitution amended, 239; final articles convention *1946*, 239, 240; post-World

435

See also International Law Commission

League of Nations: establishment of, 76, 134–135, 136; on traffic in women and children and obscene literature, 128–129; and multipartite agreement method, 134–135; U.S. relation to, 136–137; Communications and Transit Organization, 143, 157, 159; health functions, 163, 263; and epidemiological service, 166; and whaling, 178, 179, 184; and codification of international law, 184, 315; and territorial waters, 184; on products of the sea, 184; on continental shelf, 184; on control of narcotics, 188–189; and safety of life at sea, 217; on tonnage measurement, 223; and International Criminal Police Commission, 348; and sanctions, 373

Legislation, see International legislation

Lerner, Michael, 69

Liability of Owners of Seagoing Ships, conventions on: *1924*, 132; *1957*, 133n; *1936*, 155

Liang, Dr. Yuen-li, 316n, 328n

Liberia: and flags of convenience, 242; *1951* agreement on amateur radio with, 253

Library of Congress, 7, 23

Liens, 132

Life-saving services, 74

Lighthouses: Cape Spartel, 75, 77, 92–93; Columbus Memorial, 100

Lightships, 145

Liquor traffic: and Great Britain, 32; in Africa and the Pacific, 34; in Alaska, the Pacific, and Africa, 125–127, 187; in inter-war period, 187

Lissitzyn, Oliver, 39n

Literature, obscene, 108, 128–129, 183, 186, 343

Lloyd's Register of Shipping, 3, 3n, 233

Lloyd's Weekly Casualty Reports, 146, 153

Load lines: *1930* convention, 100, 104, 138, 142–143, 242; history of, 102–104; U.S. legislation on, 103–104; *1930* London conference, 142–143;

agreements with Canada, 142–143; certificates, 143

Lobbying, 212

Lobster, 24, 45, 121, 167. See also Fish

LORAN, 232n

Lord, Mrs. Oswald B., 345

Lubin, David, 122, 196

MacChesney, Brunson, 304n

McDougal, Myres S., 47, 364

Malaria, 165. See also Health; World Health Organization

Malthus, T. R., 40

Mance, O., on postal services, 35

Mapping, 14, 94, 131–132, 191, 339, 349, 350, 373

Mare liberum or *mare clausum*, 118, 300–315, 332

Marginal sea, 30–31. See also Contiguous zones; Territorial sea; International Law Commission; United Nations Conference on the Law of the Sea 1958

Margolis, Emanuel, 47, 364

Marine Conference, International *1889*, 89, 100–101, 143, 144, 216–217

Marine Insurance, International Union of, 196

Mariner's Weather Log, 215

Maritime Committee, International, see International Maritime Committee

Maritime law: growth of, 73–74. See also International legislation; International Maritime Committee

Maritime Safety Committee of the Intergovernmental Maritime Consultative Organization, 34, 220. See also Intergovernmental Maritime Consultative Organization

Markakis v. Liberian Mparmpa Christos, *1958*, 242n

Marmer, H. A., 71

Marshall Islanders, 363–365. See also Nuclear weapons testing

Marx, Daniel, Jr., 196

Massachusetts Humane Society, 74

Maury, Matthew Fontaine: on aerial ocean, 17; on submarine cables, 38; and oceanography, 71, 72; scientific contributions of, 81, 82, 84,

Index

130; and International Meteorological Congress at Brussels *1853*, 84, 214; career of, 85; and an "American" prime meridian, 94; on North Atlantic tracks, 139, 141n; and naval mines, 146–147. *See also* Hydrography; Meteorology; Oceanography

Mecca, 267–268. *See also* Pilgrimages

Mediterranean, 319

Merchant marine, 3, 8, 77, 226, 227, 242, 331

Merchant vessels: types, 25–26; construction of, 26; hazards confronting, 27; U.S. standards of construction for, 234

Meteorology: contributions of Maury to, 84; *1853* Brussels congress on, 84; other congresses on, 130; *1938* conference of experts, 162; *1947* agreement with the Philippines, 211, 339; reports by whalers on, 297. *See also* Antarctica; International Civil Aviation Organization; International Geophysical Year; International Meteorological Organization; International Telecommunication Union; Maury, Matthew; Radio; Technical assistance; Weather ships; Weather stations; Wireless; World Meteorological Organization

Metric Union, 121

Mexico: *1935* rescue agreement with, 142; *1925* fisheries agreement with, 166, 176–177; *1925* smuggling convention with, 176–177; *1936* convention on birds and game animals, 185; agreements on weather stations with, 210; *1942* agreement on fisheries missions with, 300; Principles of, 313, 314

Michael Lerner Marine Laboratory, 69

Middle East, U.S. relation to, 267–270. *See also* Health; Sanitary conventions; World Health Organization

Migratory Bird Act *1913*, 124

Migratory Bird Treaty *1916*, 124–125, 175

Migratory Bird Treaty Case *1920*, 91n, 124n, 128n

Migratory Birds and Game Animals, convention on Protection of, with Mexico, *1936*, 185

Minerals, 47–48, 53–57

Mines, naval: casualties from, 145–146; historic development of, 146–147; present day types of, 147; international law concerning, 147–148; *1907* Hague convention, 147–148, 150; hazards created by, 148–149; international committee on clearance, 149–150; clearance of, 149–154; after World War I, 149–150; *1945* agreement on European waters, 150; international organization for clearance of, 150–152; relation of U.S. Hydrographic Office to, 150, 153, 154; after World War II, 150–153; zones and boards, 151; International Routeing and Reporting Authority, 152; after Korean War, 153–154

Mines, undersea: minerals in, 53–57; types of, 54–55; diamond, 55n; sulphur, in Gulf of Mexico, 55; legal problems relating to, 55–56; *1958* continental shelf convention on, 333

Missiles, guided, 368–371

Missouri v. Holland *1920*, 91n, 124n, 128n

Moby Dick, 6, 178

Mollusks, 41, 42–43. *See also* Fish

Monte Carlo, 130

Moore, John Hamilton, 83

Morgan, J. M., 84n

Mortgages and liens, *1924* convention on, 132

Mparmpa Christos, the, 242n

Multipartite or multilateral treaties: functions of, 9; increased use of, 20; relation to law of the sea, 73–76; U.S. participation in, 75n; records of conferences elaborating, 76; relation of Great Britain to, 89; relation of administrators to, 91; enforcement in U.S., 90n–91n; relation of fairs, expositions, exhibitions, and congresses to, 121–123; effect of World War I on, 134; relation of *1919* peace treaties to, 134; relation of League of Nations to, 134; trends in inter-war period,

197; utilization after World War II, 198–199; relation of pressure groups to, 212; *1955* Rome Technical Conference endorsement of, 319; International Law Commission's endorsement of, 326, 373; U.S. reluctance to participate in, 345. *See also* Group representation; International legislation

Munson, Frank C., 7

Murphy, Robert Cushman, 48n, 50, 52, 59

Museums, 7–8, 68, 69, 297

Mustard gas dumping, 62

Mystic, Connecticut, 7

NAMRU, 269–270

Narcotics: smuggling in marginal sea, 30; bipartite agreements on, 127, 189; manufacture and local distribution of, 129n; international control before World War I, 127–128; conventions on, 188, 343, 344n; smuggling by "bum-boats" and trawlers, 189n; international control in inter-war period, 187–189; international control since World War II, 343, 346–348; smuggling by aircraft, 346–347; smuggling by seamen, 347; principal sea routes for illicit traffic in, 347. *See also* International Criminal Police Commission; League of Nations; Opium traffic; United Nations' Commission on Narcotics; Universal Postal Union; World Health Organization

National Academy of Sciences, 31, 352, 361–362

National Association of Manufacturers, 246

National Federation of American Shipping, 229

National Seamen's Union of America, 105, 154

NATO, 4, 218, 334

Nature Protection and Wildlife Preservation, *1940* Pan American Convention on, 120, 185–186

Nautical Almanac, American, 94

Nautilus, the, 25, 371n

Naval and air bases, agreement with Great Britain *1940*, 369n

Naval Historical Foundation, 8

Naval Medical Research Units, U.S. (NAMRU): in Egypt, 269–270; in Taiwan, 270n

Naval Observatory, U.S., 81, 84, 94–95, 99, 193

Navigation: Permanent International Association of Navigation Congresses, 21, 133, 191; instruments for, 26; and birds, 49; freedom of, 77–78; in Africa, 78, 187; *1885* General Act of Berlin, 78, 187; *1890* General Act and Declaration of Brussels, 78, 187; rules of the road, 88–89, 231; radio aids to, 231n–232n, 236; long-range stations, 232n. *See also* Aerial navigation; Collisions; High Seas; International Time Bureau; Maury, Matthew; Prime Meridian Conference; Safety of life at sea

NEPTUNO, 374n

Netherlands: *1932* agreement on load lines with, 143n; *1956* agreement on weather station with, 211

Newfoundland, *1925* agreement on interference by ships with broadcasting, 162n

Niagara Falls and River, *see* Great Lakes-St. Lawrence Waterway

Nicaragua, *1956* agreement on amateur radio with, 253

Noble, Dr. G. Bernard, 102n

North American Council on Fishery Investigations, 185, 191, 318. *See also* Canadian-American fisheries

North American Wildlife Conference *1936*, 185n

North American Yacht Racing Union, 65–66

North Atlantic Ice Patrol, 100, 101, 104, 105, 230, 232; agreements on expenses of, 230

North Atlantic Lane Routes Agreement, 84, 139–141, 196, 235

North Atlantic Planning Board for Shipping, 218

North Atlantic Track Association, 139–140

North Atlantic tracks, 84, 139–141, 196. *See also Andrea Doria-Stockholm* collision; Maury, Matthew; Safety of life at sea

Index

North Atlantic Treaty Organization, 4, 218, 334; *1949* treaty on, 218
North Pacific fisheries, 278–281; *1952* convention on, 170, 177n, 278–281, 318. *See also* Halibut fishery; Japan; Salmon fisheries
North Pacific Fur Seal Commission, 287
Northeastern fisheries, 14, 79, 92, 116–117
Northwest Atlantic fisheries, 4, 273–278, 280, 318, 320. *See also* Canadian-American fisheries; Overfishing convention *1946*
Norton, Garrison, 214
Nuclear weapons testing, 4, 47, 331, 334, 339, 363–368

OAS, 75, 99–100, 303, 309–315, 342
Obscene literature, 108, 128–129, 186, 343
Oceanography, 88, 362; scope of, 10; and Maury, 84, 85; institutions devoted to, 192n; and UNESCO, 350–351; research stations in West Indies, 369n; agreements with United Kingdom, 369n. *See also* International Council of Scientific Unions; International Geophysical Year; International Polar Years; Weather ships
Officers, ILO convention on competency certificates *1936*, 155
Offshore claims, *see* International Law Commission; Latin American offshore claims; United Nations Conference on the Law of the Sea
Oil, 5, 56–57. *See also* Continental shelf, Oil pollution
Oil pollution: from drilling operations, 24, 30, 227, 331; hazards and nuisances from, 30, 63, 224–225; affecting birds, 53, 224; League of Nations on, 143, 145; Washington conference *1926*, 138, 145, 225; U.S. statute *1924*, 145; international acts on, 145, 225, 225–227; U.S. relation to post-World War II developments on, 223–227; "Faulkner Report" on, 224; *1954* London conference on, 225–227; International Law Commission on, 227; Merchant Marine Council panel on, 227; prosecution for, 235; UN Conference on Law of the Sea on, 331
Onassis, A. S., 303
Opium traffic: nineteenth century agreements on, 126, 127–128; pre-World War I legislation relating to, 127; *1912* convention on, 127, 134, 187; *1925* convention on, 188. *See also* Narcotics
Organization of American States, 75, 92, 99–100, 303, 309–315, 342. *See also* Inter-American conferences; Latin American offshore claims; Pan American organization; Pan American conferences
Organizations: 198–199; public international nontreaty, 190–193; private international, 195–197; rulemaking power of, 265–266, 294–295
Oslo rules, on tonnage measurement, 223
Otter, sea, 45, 117, 120, 183, 186
Outer Continental Shelf Lands Act of *1953*, 5
Overfishing convention, *1946*, 275, 278, 319

Pacific Science Congress, 195, 336, 337
Pacific trust territory, *see* Nuclear weapons testing; Trust territory
Palmer, Capt. Nathaniel B., 87
Pan American Convention on Nature Protection and Wildlife Preservation *1940*, 120
Pan American Institute of Geography and History, 194, 314n
Pan American Organization, 75, 99–100, 194. *See also* Inter-American conferences; International Conferences of American States; Latin American offshore claims; Organization of American States
Pan American Sanitary Organization, 114–115, 163, 165–166, 267, 341–342
Panama: *1937* agreement on tonnage measurement with, 223n; ILO inquiry into flags of convenience under, 241–242; and inspection of vessels in Canal Zone, 241–242; *1956* agreement on amateur radio with, 253

441

Paria, Gulf of, 57n
Parker, John Johnston, 316
Parran, Thomas, 162
PASO, 114–115, 341–342
Passamaquoddy Bay: tidal project in, 58–59; fisheries in, 58–59, 194
Peace treaties: with Japan *1951*, 118n, 169, 278; with Austria *1919*, 134, 158, 159; with Germany *1919*, 134, 158, 159; with Hungary *1920*, 134, 158, 159
Pelagic sealing, 118. See also Seals, fur
Pelican disaster, the, 69
Penck, Dr. Albrecht, 131
Permanent Commission for the Exploitation and Conservation of the Maritime Resources of the South Pacific, 310–311, 319
Permanent International Association of Navigation Congresses, 21, 133, 191
Permanent International Council for the Exploration of the Sea, see International Council for the Exploration of the Sea
Permanent Mixed Fishery Commissions, for Canada and Newfoundland, 117
Perry, Commodore Matthew Calbraith, 88
Peru: and bioma theory, 51, 307–309; *1851* agreement on whalers, 78; *1957* agreement on weather station, 211; *1934* agreement on amateur radio, 252
Peter the Great Bay, 371
Philippine Islands: and opium traffic, 127; agreements with, 211, 339
Phoenix, the, 366n
PICAO, 198, 202. See also International Civil Aviation Organization
Piccard, Auguste, 70
Pilgrimages, 110, 114, 115, 267, 268, 269. See also Health; Sanitary conventions; World Health Organization
Pipelines, 23–24, 330, 333. See also Continental shelf; International Law Commission
Piracy: of submarine cables, 39, 86; early treaties on, 85, 86; legislation on, 86; jurisdiction over, 86;

International Law Commission *1956* report on, 86–87; by aircraft, 87, 330; UN *1958* Conference on the Law of the Sea on, 87, 330
Pisciculture, 45
Plague, 111, 114, 115, 267. See also Health; Rats; Sanitary conventions; World Health Organization
Plankton, 41, 44
Plimsoll (Load Line) Act *1876*, 103
Plimsoll, Samuel, 103
Point Four Program, 271–272
Polar years, 129–130, 192, 192n, 351. See also Antarctica; International Geophysical Year
Police protection, on high seas, 33–34
Ports: and waterways, 158–160; privileges for halibut fishing vessels, 282
Postal communications: relation to the sea, 35–36; aerial, 36, 157; in pre-World War I period, 107–108; conferences and congresses, 107, 260; relation to traffic in narcotics, 128, 258, 260; developments since World War II, 257–258. See also General Postal Union; Universal Postal Union
Postal Union of the Americas and Spain, agreements on: *1926*, 258; *1931*, 36, 107, 157; *1950*, 258n; *1955*, 258n
Powell, J. H., 80n
Power Authority of the State of New York, 359
Power boats, 66
Power cables, 21
Power Squadrons, 65
Practical Navigator, 83, 84
Pratique, 164
Pratt, Wallace E., 56
Pressure groups, 136, 197, 212. See also Group representation
Pribilof Islands, 117–120, 285–289. See also Seals, fur
Prime Meridian Conference, 92–96
Principles of Mexico, 313, 314. See also Latin American offshore claims
Private international organizations, 195–197
Private William H. Thomas, the, 236
Protection against accident, *1929* ILO convention on, 155

Index

Provisional International Civil Aviation Organization (PICAO), 198, 202. *See also* International Civil Aviation Organization
Provisional Maritime Consultative Council, 4, 219, 228. *See also* Intergovernmental Maritime Consultative Organization
Pryce, Capt. R., 150
Public health, 114, 163. *See also* Health
Public international organizations, 190–193
Publications, obscene: traffic in, 108, 128–129, 186, 343; *1910* administrative arrangement on, 129n; agreements on, 129, 183, 343

Quarantine, 110–111, 267. *See also* Health; Sanitary conventions; World Health Organization

Radar, 231, 231n–232n, 236
Radio: forms of, 36; early development of, 36–37; and flag signal code, 89; inter-war developments of, 110, 160–162; and safety of life at sea, 141; multipartite agreements on, 162; epidemiological reports by, 162, 251, 267; bilateral agreements on, 162n; agreements on interference by ships, 162n; aids to navigation, 231n–232n; amateur operators, 251–253. *See also* International Telecommunication Union; Telecommunications; Wireless
Radiotelegraph conventions: *1927*, 89, 110, 138, 141, 160–161, 252; *1912*, 110, 247; *1919*, 160. See also Telecommunications, Wireless
Radiotelephone: North Sea and Baltic Sea Conference *1938*, 162; bridge-to-bridge communication, 236
Rats, 31, 115, 164, 165. *See also* Health; Plague; Sanitary conventions; World Health Organization
Rattray, J. E., 74n
Recognition of Rights in Aircraft, *1948* convention on, 205
Recreation, 64–71
Refugee organization, international, 20–21
Regional councils, 334–342

Reid v. Covert *1957*, 91n, 124n. *See also* Bricker Amendment
Reiff, H.: on Bricker Amendment, 90n; on proclaiming of treaties in the United States, 257n
Reimbursement of Fines Act of *1954*, U.S., 304
Reptiles, 41, 43–44
Res communis, 19–20, 372
Res nullius, 19–20, 372
Rescue, 207n; agreement with Mexico *1935*, 142; *1948* report of Committee of Experts on, 228–229; use of telecommunications in, 228n–229n; and rescue coordination centers, 228, 236–237. *See also* International Civil Aviation Organization; International Telecommunication Union; Safety of life at sea; Weather ships
Resources, of the sea: scope of, 40; fishery, 40–45; mineral, 47–48; bird, 48–51; in subsoil mines and wells, 53–57; energy, 57–59; exploitation before World War I, 116–125; exploitation in inter-war period, 166–186; and League of Nations efforts, 184–185; and developments since World War II, 270–272; Latin American claims relating to, 300–315; International Law Commission and, 315–327; *1955* Rome Technical Conference on, 317–321; *1958* UN Conference on Law of the Sea conventions and resolutions on, 329, 331–332. *See also* Angling; Atomic energy; Fisheries; Nuclear weapons testing; Oil pollution; Regional councils; Sea otter; Seals, fur; Seals, hair; Truman proclamations; Exploration; Wastes, disposal of; Whales; Whaling
Ringgold, Commander Cadwallader, 88
Ripple Rock, 27–28
Rivers: relation to sea, 16; international rivers, 77; European, 159
Robben Island: off Sakhalin Island, 118, 287, 288; off Cape Province, Union of South Africa, 287n. *See also* Seals, fur
Rodgers, Admiral Christopher R. P., 95n

443

Rodgers, Lt. John, 88
Rogers, Henry J., 89
Rome Technical Conference on the Conservation of the Living Resources of the Sea *1955*, 308, 311, 317–321, 331, 334
Roosevelt, Theodore, 109
Rosefish (redfish), 275, 276
Royal Humane Society, 74
Rules of the Road, 88–89, 231. *See also* Collisions; Navigation; Safety of life at sea
Russia: *1824* agreement on navigation, fishing, etc. in the Pacific, 79; *1894* agreement on fur seals, 78–79; *1911* quadripartite agreement on fur seals, 119–120, 167, 183, 184, 286, 318. *See also* Soviet Union

Sablefish, 282
Safety of life at sea: hazards to, 26–28; and dangerous goods, 30, 237–238; and telecommunications, 36–37, 104, 141, 160; and birds, 49; boating, 66; and early private services, 74; and Cape Spartel Light, 75, 92–93; and national public services, 89–92; contributions of Maury to, 84–85; and flag signal code, 88–89; and *19th* century changes in rules of the road, 89, 92, 100–101, 103, 104; and prime meridian, 93–96; and time service, 98–99, 161; conference of *1889* on, 89, 100–101, 103, 105; relation of load lines to, 102–104; conference of *1914* on, 92, 104–107; conference of *1929* on, 138–141; buoyage and lighting, 143–145; conference of *1948* on, 220–222; 227–231; and safety in the air, 221, 228–229. *See also Andrea Doria-Stockholm* collision; Collisions; Intergovernmental Maritime Consultative Organization; International Civil Aviation Organization; International Meteorological Organization; International Telecommunication Union; Load Lines; Mines, naval; North Atlantic Ice Patrol; North Atlantic tracks; Oil pollution; Radio; Rescue; Safety of life at sea conventions; *Titanic* disaster; United Nations, Transport and Communications Commission; Weather ships; Wireless; World Meteorological Organization

1914 Safety of Life at Sea Convention, 100, 101, 104, 105, 107, 138–139, 140, 154, 160, 233

1929 Safety of Life at Sea Convention: and Great Britain as clearing house, 100; provisions of, 138–142; revision of, 227, 229–230; and national classification societies, 233; and North Atlantic tracks, 139–141, 235; amendment of *1930*, 138n; and Radiotelegraph Convention of *1927*, 141; and International Meteorological Organization, 141; and load lines, 142

1948 Safety of Life at Sea Convention: and Great Britain as clearing house, 100; and North Atlantic tracks, 140, 235; and buoyage, 145; as revision of *1929* convention, 201; and weather ship program, 207; and World Meteorological Organization, 215; and Intergovernmental Maritime Consultative Organization, 222; elaboration of, 227–231; and North Atlantic Ice Patrol, 230; and *Andrea Doria-Stockholm* collision, 233–238; and carriage of dangerous goods, 237; and flags of convenience, 242

Sailing Directions for Antarctica, 49
St. Francis Xavier University of Antigonish, Nova Scotia, 68
St. Germain, treaty of *1919*, 134
St. Lawrence Seaway, *see* Great Lakes-St. Lawrence Waterway
St. Lawrence Seaway Authority (Canada), 358–359
St. Lawrence Seaway Development Corporation, 358–359
St. Petersburg Telegraph Convention *1875*, 254
Sakhalin Island, 118. *See also* Seals, fur
Salmon fisheries: hazards confronting, 45, 46, 171–172; and developments before end of World War I, 120–121; and developments in the interwar period, 169–173; in Bristol Bay, Alaska, 169–170, 279; species

Index

in, 170; and Fraser River system, 170–172; and Hell's Gate Canyon, 171–172, 173; agreement with Canada on sockeye, 173; regulatory commission for sockeye, 173; and North Pacific fisheries convention, 279; regulation of pink or humpback, 283–285. *See also* Canadian-American fisheries

Agreements with Canada: draft agreement *1919*, 167, 172; amended agreement *1920*, 172; *1929*, 172–173; *1930*, 166, 170n, 172, 173, 175, 177, 279, 283, 284, 318; *1937*, 284; relating to Hell's Gate Canyon *1944*, 173, 283; amending *1930* agreement, 284–285

Salvage and assistance: 78; *1910* convention, 132–133; U.S.-Mexican agreement *1935*, 142; *1938* convention, 157

Sanctions, 373

Sand, 47–48. *See also* Resources

Sanitary conferences: before World War I, 112–116; in inter-war period, 162–166; since World War II, 261–266. *See also* Health; Pan American Sanitary Organization; Sanitary conventions; World Health Organization

Sanitary conventions: universal, 113, 114, 115, 163, 164–165, 263n; Latin American, 114; Pan American, 115, 163, 165, 267; for aerial navigation, 156–157, 163, 164n, 263n. *See also* Health, World Health Organization

Santa Ana, the, 302

Santiago conference, *1955*, 308, 311. *See also* Latin American offshore claims

SARPS, 203–204. *See also* International Civil Aviation Organization

Saudi Arabia, 269

Schlei, Norbert A., 47, 364

Schober, Dr., 347

Scientific developments: before Civil War, 82–85; in pre-World War I period, 129–132; in inter-war period, 190–197; since World War II, 348–354. *See also* Astronomy, Cartography; Geodesy; Hydrography; International Council of Scientific Unions; International Geophysical Year; International Polar Years; Maury; Meteorology; Oceanography; Radio; Telecommunications; United Nations, Economic and Social Council; United Nations, Educational, Scientific and Cultural Organization

Scotia, the, 89n

Scripps Institution, 7

Sea gulls, 49

Sea lamprey, 290–293

Sea otter, 45, 117, 120, 183, 186

Seafarers' International Union, 105. *See also* Furuseth, Andrew; National Seamen's Union of America; International Seamen's Union of America

Seals, fur: decimation of, 45, 46, 117–120; controversies before *1911*, 117–119; breeding habits of, 119; quadripartite agreement of *1911* on, 119–120; developments in inter-war period, 182–184, 285; Japanese complaints about, 183, 285; Japanese denunciation of *1911* agreement on, 183; Canadian-American arrangements during World War II, 183–184, 285; post-World War II arrangements concerning, 285–289; black pups, 288; humane methods of killing, 334; and UN Conference on the Law of the Sea *1958*, 334

Agreements: with Great Britain before *1900*, 78; with Russia *1894*, 78; with Great Britain *1911*, 119n; with Japan, Russia, and Great Britain *1911*, 119–120, 167, 183, 184, 286, 318; with Canada *1942*, 167, 183, 285; with Canada *1947*, 183, 285; with Canada and Japan *1952*, 184, 285; with Canada, Japan, and Soviet Union *1957*, 184, 286–289, 318

Seals, hair, 46

Seamen: pre-Civil War treaties on aid to, 78; Act of *1915*, 106, 154; minimum age of, 154, 155; ILO conventions on, 154, 155, 240; articles of agreement, 155; hours of work and manning, 155; repatriation of, 155; placing of, 155; holiday pay

445

for, 155; accommodation of, 240; pensions for, 240; certification of, 240; paid vacations for, 240; venereal disease of, 263; smuggling of narcotics by, 347

Search and rescue service, 207, 236–237, 330. *See also* Rescue

Seizures, of fishing vessels, 300–303, 304. *See also* Latin American offshore claims

Seward, H. L., 233n

Shellfish, 42–43, 289. *See also* Fish

Shepheard, H. C., 233n

Ship lanes, *see* North Atlantic tracks

Shipbuilder's Council of America, 229

Shipowners' liability, conventions on, 132, 133n, 155

Shipping: competition in, 28–29; conferences, 29, 195–196; national regulation of, 29–30; cartels, 29, 195–196; conferences, 73, 195–196

Shrimp, 280n, 300, 301, 319

Siam, *1833* treaty on opium traffic with, 127. *See also* Thailand

Sickness insurance, *1936* ILO convention on, 155

Signals, *1930* Agreement Concerning Maritime, 145

Signals, International Code of, 88–89

Skate, the, 371n

Slave trade: and policing of high seas, 33–34; early American legislation on, 87, 125; agreements with Great Britain on, 87, 125; *1890* Brussels agreement on, 87, 126; Quintuple treaty of *1841* on, 125; extradition treaties on, 126; League of Nations and, 187; *1926* convention on, 187, 343, 344n; Convention on the High Seas *1958*, 331; *1953* convention on, 343, 344n; UN Economic and Social Council on, 343, 344–346; *1956* convention on, 344–345; International Law Commission on, 346n. *See also* Humanitarian programs

Smallpox, 115, 164, 267. *See also* Health; Sanitary conventions; World Health Organization

Smuggling, *1925* convention with Mexico, 176–177

Social science, of the sea, 71–72, 351

Social security, *1946* ILO convention on, 240

Society of Naval Architects and Marine Engineers, 229

South Pacific Commission, 336–339; *1947* convention on, 336, 338

South Seas Conference *1947*, 337

Soviet Union: and *1957* agreement on fur seals, 184, 286–289, 318; and Peter the Great Bay controversy, 371. *See also* Russia

Spanish American Postal Union, *1920* convention on, 107. *See also* Postal communications; Postal Union of the Americas and Spain

Specialized agencies: and the United Nations, 76; interrelations of, 212–213, 215–216, 220, 228–229; and the UN Transport and Communications Commission, 258–260

Sponges, 41, 44. *See also* Fish

Star Crest, the, 301–302

Stefansson, Dr. Vilhjalmur, 88n

Stick, David, 14

Stockholm, the, 141, 222, 232–237

Stowaways, *1957* convention on, 132n–133n

Sturgeon, 120–121. *See also* Canadian-American fisheries

Submarine cables: for power, 21, 24; early history of, 38–39; relay stations for, 38–39; telephone, 38; cable diplomacy, 38–39; hazards confronting, 39; between Europe and America, 75n, 108; conventions on, 75n, 108, 253, 254, 256–257; damage to, 108; U.S. call for *1869* conference on, 108; conference and convention of *1884* on, 108; London conference of *1913* on, 108; Washington conference of *1920* on, 160; developments since *1919*, 253–257; Bermuda agreements on, 255–257; and International Telegraph Regulations 256–257; International Law Commission on, 322; *1958* Convention on the High Seas and, 330; *1958* Convention on the Continental Shelf and, 333. *See also* International Telecommunication Union; Telecommunications

Submerged Lands Act of *1953*, U.S., 5

Sverdrup, *et al.*, 85n

Sweden: *1930* agreement on pleasure

Index

yachts with, 67n; *1932* agreement on load lines with, 143n
Szulc, Tad, 39

Tailliez, Philippe, 70
Technical assistance agreements: 271–272; on health, 269; with Saudi Arabia, 269; with Egypt, 269; on fisheries, 300, 339; with Mexico, 300; with El Salvador, 300; with Philippine Islands, 339; on coast and geodetic work, 339; on air navigation, 339; on meteorological work, 339; with Philippines, 339; on mapping services, 350; with Thailand, 350; with Cambodia, 350
Telecommunications: developments after World War II, 247–257; Atlantic City conference *1947*, 201, 248–250; and group representation, 250; relation to use of the sea, 228n–229n, 250; International Telecommunication Union, 247–250; and Buenos Aires conference, 251; and epidemiological notices, 162, 251, 267; and safety on the Great Lakes, 251; and the radio amateur, 251–253; and submarine cables, 253–257; international regulations, 256–257. *See also* Radio; Wireless
Conventions: of Madrid *1932*, 161, 247, 252, 255; of Cairo *1938*, 161, 248; Inter-American *1940*, 249n; of Atlantic City *1947*, 201, 235, 248–251; *1949*, 247; *1952*, 251; for Great Lakes *1952*, 251; for amateurs *1934*, 252, 253. *See also* Radiotelegraph conventions
Telegraph Convention of St. Petersburg, *1875*, 254
Telegraph Line between Europe and America, Convention on Establishment of, *1864*, 75n, 108
Territorial sea: national regulation of, 30; abuses in, 31; width of, 31–32, 321, 329–330; League of Nations on, 184; Latin American claims relating to, 300–321; International Law Commission on, 321; *1958* UN Conference on the Law of the Sea and convention on, 329–330
Texas City, 230
"Texas towers," 56

Thailand, *1952* agreement on mapping service with, 350. *See also* Siam
Thermal energy, 59
Tidal power, 58–59
Time: relation to navigation, 93–94; universal standards of, 95–96; universal day, 96; standard in United States, 96; International Bureau, 98–99; U.S. Naval Observatory, 99, 161, 193. *See also* Aviation; International Astronomical Union; International Civil Aviation Organization; International Date Line; International Telecommunication Union; Prime Meridian Conference; Radio; Safety of life at sea; Wireless
Time Association, *1913* convention for creation of, 98
Titanic, the, 101, 104, 232
Tonnage measurement: League discussions of, 143, 223; ECOSOC discussions of, 222–223; Oslo rules of *1939* on, 223; *1947* Oslo convention on, 223; IMCO and, 223; bipartite agreements on, 223n
Tourism, 20, 64, 71, 195, 342
Tracks, North Atlantic, 84, 139–141, 196
Transatlantic Track Association, 196
Transportation: means and facilities, 20–35; inter-war developments in, 138–158; since World War II, 200–247; and communications, 228, 258–260. *See also* Aviation; League of Nations Communications and Transit Organization; Safety of life at sea; Shipping; United Nations, Transport and Communications Commission
Treasure maps, 7
Treaties, *see* Multipartite or multilateral treaties
Tremaine, Marie, 88
Trianon, treaty of *1920*, 134
Trinity Brethren, 74
Truman proclamations: on continental shelf, 4, 33, 271, 304–307, 327, 379; on offshore fisheries, 5, 32–33, 271, 275, 280, 304–307, 327, 380
Trust territory, of the Pacific, 4, 16, 337–339, 363–364

447

Trusteeship Council, UN, 338–339, 363–364
Truxton-Decatur Museum, 8
Tuna fisheries: in inter-war period, 175–177; agreements with Mexico, 175, 176, 177, 298–300; agreements with Costa Rica, 175, 177, 298–300, 318; since World War II, 289, 297–300, 301–302, 341; Inter-American Tropical Tuna Commission, 298–300, 312, 318; agreements with Bahamas, 341. See also Latin American offshore claims
Tunnels, 22–23, 333. See also Mines
Turks Islands, 369n
Typhus, 113, 115, 164, 267. See also Health; Sanitary conventions; World Health Organization

Unemployment indemnity, *1920* ILO convention on, 154
United Kingdom: agreements on weather stations with, 210; as headquarters for IMCO, 222; and *1948* regime on safety of life at sea, 229, 238; on oil pollution, 224–227; agreements relating to Bahamas Long Range Proving Ground with, 368–370; agreements on oceanographic research stations in Caribbean, 369n. See also British Commonwealth, Great Britain
United Maritime Authority, 217, 218
United Maritime Consultative Council, 218
United Nations: and specialized agencies, 76; program of technical assistance, 216; flag of, 244; flag ships, 243–244, 331; charter of, 258, 262, 337, 338, 373; and codification of international law, 315–316; and settlement of disputes, 329; and sanctions, 373

    Atomic Energy Commission, 334
    Commission on Human Rights, 345
    Commission on Narcotics, 346–348
    Economic and Social Council: and pressure groups, 212; and formation of Intergovernmental Maritime Consultative Organization, 218–219; and safety of life at sea, 219–222, 228; and tonnage measurement, 222–223; and oil pollution, 223–227; and interorganizational representation, 250; and coordination of transport and communications, 258–260; and nonself-governing territories, 337, 340n; and slavery, 344–346; and cartography, 349; and science, 349–350, 351; and coordination of work of specialized agencies, 372–373
    Educational, Scientific and Cultural Organization: cooperation with World Meteorological Organization, 216; and carriage of dangerous goods, 238; at Rome Technical Conference, 318; and Indo-Pacific Fisheries Council, 336; and scientific organizations, 336n; constitution of, 349; contributions to study and use of the sea, 349–351; and International Geophysical Year, 351
    General Assembly: and international Law Commission, 12, 315–316, 317; and the *1958* Conference on the Law of the Sea, 327–328, 330, 333; and nuclear tests at sea, 334, 367; and nonself-governing territories, 337; and atomic radiation, 362; and coordination of international organizations, 372
    Interim Commission on Food and Agriculture, 198
    International Law Commission, *see* International Law Commission
    Relief and Rehabilitation Administration: and health, 163–164, 263; and shipping, 217, 218
    Scientific Committee on the Effects of Atomic Radiation, 362, 364, 366, 367
    Security Council, 150n, 332, 337, 339n, 367
    Transport and Communications Commission: and tonnage measurement, 222–223; and oil pollution, 223–224; and carriage of dangerous goods, 237–238; and coordination of specialized agencies, 258–260, 372–373
    Trusteeship Council, 338–339, 363–364

Index

United Nations Conference on International Organization, San Francisco *1945*, 198, 262

United Nations Conference on the Law of the Sea *1958*, 12, 31–32, 57, 243, 321, 327–334, 373; Final Act, 328

United States: Submerged Lands Act of *1953*, 5; Outer Continental Shelf Lands Act of *1953*, 5; Anti-Smuggling Act of *1935*, 32; liquor treaties with Great Britain, 32; Federal Radio Act of *1927*, 37; fisheries policies, 47, 272–273; Power Squadrons, 65; quarantine systems, 80, 81; life saving, 80; maritime services, 80–82; marine hospitals, 81; treaty-making power and Bricker Amendment, 90–91; federal system, 90, 128–129, 173–175; Seamen's Act of *1915* (La Follette Act), 106, 154; Oil Pollution Act of *1924*, 225; and the Middle East, 267–270; Naval Medical Research Units, 269–270; technical cooperation program, 269–270, 271–272, 339; Fish and Wildlife Act of *1956*, 272–273; Reimbursement of Fines Act of *1954*, 304

    Atomic Energy Commission, 366

    Bureau of Commercial Fisheries, 273

    Bureau of Narcotics, 189

    Bureau of Navigation, 82

    Bureau of Sport Fisheries and Wildlife, 273

    Bureau of Standards, 99, 203n

    Civil Aeronautics Board, 203n

    Coast and Geodetic Survey, 81, 94, 95, 193, 350

    Coast Guard, 8, 80, 82, 106, 227, 236

    Customs Service, 32, 82

    Federal Communications Commission, 255

    Federal Maritime Board, 29

    Fish and Wildlife Service, 120

    Hydrographic Office: publications of, 84; and International Date Line, 97–98; and international conferences, 130; on steamer lanes, 139; on naval mine warnings, 150, 153–154

    Interstate Commerce Commission: and carriage of dangerous goods, 238; and cables, 254, 255

    Lighthouse Service, 80

    Merchant Marine, 3, 8, 77, 226, 227, 242, 331

    National Academy of Sciences: on radioactivity in harbors, 31; and International Geophysical Year, 352; on biological effects of atomic radiation, 361–362

    National Committee for International Geophysical Year, 352

    National Committee for Prevention of Pollution of the Seas by Oil, 226–227

    Naval Observatory, 81, 84, 94–95, 99, 193

    Public Health Service, 81, 269

    Revenue Cutter Service, 80, 81

    Steamboat Inspection Service, 82

    Trust Territory of the Pacific: *1947* agreement with Security Council on, 337, 339; administration of, 337–339; and nuclear weapons testing, 363–368

United States Department of State Bulletin, 4, 199

United States Executive Agreement Series, 140n–141n

United States Statutes at Large, 140n–141n

United States Treaties and Other International Acts Series, 140n–141n

United States Treaty Series, 140n–141n

United States v. California *1947*, 5n

United States v. Louisiana *1950*, 5n; *1956*, 5n

United States v. Rodgers *1893*, 354n

United States v. Shauver *1914*, 124n

United States v. Texas *1950*, 5n

Universal Postal Union: creation of, 36, 107; *1878* convention, 36, 107, 157; specialized and regional unions under, 107; and narcotics traffic, 107, 127–128, 258, 260, 347; relation to the sea, 107–108, 257–258; *1920* convention, 128; and air mail, 157, 213, 258; *1952* convention, 257, 258, 262n; *1947* convention, 258; *1957* convention, 260. See also Postal communications

UPU, see Universal Postal Union
d'Urville, Dumont, 97
U.S.S.R., see Soviet Union

Van Wagenen, Richard W., 72, 375
Venereal disease of merchant seamen, *1924* agreement on treatment of, 263
Venezuela, *1942* agreement with Great Britain on Gulf of Paria, 57n; *1957* agreement on tonnage measurement, 223n
Versailles, *1919* treaty of, 134
Vesta, the, 139
Victor Emmanuel III, 122
Voice of America, 37

Wages, *1946* ILO convention on, 240
Walters, Francis P., 166
Walton, Izaak, 67
Wan Waithayakon, Prince, 334
Warning areas, 364–366
Warsaw Convention, 205
Washington, George, 80
Wastes, disposal of: various, 59–64; mustard gas, 62; ammunition, 62; radioactive, 62, 63, 331, 334, 354, 361–363. See also Atomic energy; International Law Commission; Oil pollution; United Nations Conference on the Law of the Sea *1958*
Water pollution, 61
Waterways, *1921* Barcelona convention on, 159
Weather ships, agreements on: 4, 205; *1946*, 206, 207; *1949*, 206; Jan. *1950*, 207; Sept. *1950*, 207; *1951*, 207n; *1952*, 207, 208; Feb. *1954*, 208; June, *1954*, 208–209
Weather stations, agreements on: Mexico *1942* to *1957*, 210; Cuba *1944* to *1953*, 210; Canada *1947*, 209–210; United Kingdom *1955* and *1958*, 210; Colombia *1956*, 211; France *1956*, 211; Netherlands *1956*, 211; Dominican Republic *1956*, 211; Chile *1957*, 211; Peru *1957*, 211; Ecuador *1957*, 211; Australia *1958*, 210n
Webster-Ashburton treaty *1842*: on slavery, 125; on navigation in St. Lawrence, 356
Webster, E. M., 233n

Wells, subsoil, 53, 56–57
West Indies, 336, 339–342
West Indies Federation, 342, 369n
Whales, 45, 46, 177–182, 293–297, 334. See also Whaling
Whaling: and Hawaii and Peru, 78; and Gulf Stream, 82; American interest in, 167, 178, 178n; Canadian-American Fisheries Commission on, 177; developments in inter-war period, 177–182; League of Nations and, 178–179; International Council for the Exploration of the Sea and, 179; and high standard flags, 180; international bureau for statistics on, 179, 294; and weather reports, 215; developments since World War II, 293–297; contributions of Dr. A. Remington Kellogg to, 297; and Peru, 303, 311; and Rome Technical Conference *1955*, 318; and UN Conference on the Law of the Sea *1958*, 334
Agreements: 78; *1931*, 166, 179, 180, 184, 185, 293; *1937*, 180, 181, 182, 293; *1938*, 180, 182; *1939*, 181; *1944*, 181, 182; Oct. *1945*, 182, 295; Nov. *1945*, 182; March *1946*, 182; Dec. *1946*, 182, 293n, 293–297, 318; Mar. *1947*, 182; *1949*, 296n; *1950*, 296n; *1951*, 296n; *1952*, 296n; *1953*, 296n; *1954*, 296n; *1955*, 296n; *1956*, 296n; amendment of *1946* convention, *1956*, 293; *1957*, 296n
Whangpoo River Conservancy, 92; agreements, 101–102
White, Dr. Paul Dudley, 45
White slave traffic, 31, 128, 129, 186, 343
Wildlife, protection of, 120, 174, 185–186
Wiley-Dondero Act *1954*, 359. See also Great Lakes-St. Lawrence Waterway
Wilhelm II, Kaiser, 109–110
Wilkes, Lt. Charles, 85n, 87, 88, 97, 130
Williams, Ralph C., 164
Willoughby, William Reid, 357n
Wind power, 58
Wireless: development of, 36–38; conventions, 37, 104, 110, 160, 247,

Index

252; and *Titanic* disaster, 101, 104; pre-World War I conferences on, 109–110; safety of life at sea, 104–105. *See also* International Telecommunication Union; Radio; Telecommunications

WMO, *see* World Meteorological Organization

Women, traffic in, 31, 128; agreements on, 129, 186, 343

Woods Hole Oceanographic Institution, 7

Woolf, L. S., 111

World Cartography, 349

World government, British parliamentary group for, 374

World Health Organization: conventions on, 164n, 263–267; establishment of, 166, 262–264; and international legislative process, 204, 266–267; and ILO on hygiene of seafarers, 245; United States membership in, 264–265; rule-making, 266; and sanitary regulations, 266–267; and the Middle East, 269; cooperation with other regimes, 270. *See also* Health; International Labor Organization; Labor at sea; Narcotics; Pan American Sanitary Organization; Pilgrimages; Regional councils; Sanitary conferences; Sanitary conventions; Specialized agencies; Technical assistance; United Nations, Economic and Social Council; United Nations, Transport and Communications Commission

World Meteorological Organization: establishment of, 4, 130, 201, 213–216; interrelations with other regimes, 34, 215–216, 258–260, 372–373; *1947* convention on, 130, 201, 213; relation to air navigation, 215–216; and UN Expanded Program of Technical Assistance, 216; and International Geophysical Year, 351–354. *See also* International Meteorological Organization; Meteorology; Radio; Safety of life at sea; Telecommunications; Weather ships; Weather stations; Wireless

Wyman, Surgeon General, 112

Yachting, 64–67

Yale Oceanographic Laboratory, 68

Yap, Island of, 254

Yellow fever, 80, 112–113, 114, 115, 259, 267. *See also* Health; Pan American Sanitary Organization; Sanitary conventions; World Health Organization